June 5–9, 2011
San Jose, CA, USA

Association for
Computing Machinery

Advancing Computing as a Science & Profession

EC 2011

Proceedings of the 12th ACM Conference on
Electronic Commerce

Sponsored by:

ACM SIGecom

Supported by:

Facebook, Google, Microsoft Research, Yahoo! Labs & ebay

Association for
Computing Machinery

Advancing Computing as a Science & Profession

The Association for Computing Machinery
2 Penn Plaza, Suite 701
New York, New York 10121-0701

Notice to Past Authors of ACM-Published Articles
ACM intends to create a complete electronic archive of all articles and/or other material previously published by ACM. If you have written a work that has been previously published by ACM in any journal or conference proceedings prior to 1978, or any SIG Newsletter at any time, and you do NOT want this work to appear in the ACM Digital Library, please inform permissions@acm.org, stating the title of the work, the author(s), and where and when published.

ISBN: 978-1-4503-0261-6 (Digital)

ISBN: 978-1-4503-1384-1 (Print)

Additional copies may be ordered prepaid from:

ACM Order Department
PO Box 30777
New York, NY 10087-0777, USA

Phone: 1-800-342-6626 (USA and Canada)
+1-212-626-0500 (Global)
Fax: +1-212-944-1318
E-mail: acmhelp@acm.org
Hours of Operation: 8:30 am – 4:30 pm ET

Printed in the USA

Foreword

The papers in these proceedings were presented at the 12th ACM Conference on Electronic Commerce — EC'11, held June 5–9, 2011, in San Jose, California, USA. Since its inception in 1999, ACM EC has served as the leading scientific conference on advances in theory, systems, and applications for electronic commerce. The conference is interdisciplinary and addresses a number of facets of electronic commerce, including (1) theory and foundations; (2) architectures and languages; (3) automation, personalization, and targeting; (4) security, privacy, encryption, and digital rights; (5) applications, experimental and empirical studies; and (6) social factors. In addition to the main technical program, EC'11 featured five workshops and six tutorials. EC'11 was also co-located this year with fifteen other computer science conferences as part of the 2011 ACM Federated Computing Research Conference.

The call for papers attracted 189 submissions from authors in academia and industry from all around the world. Each paper was reviewed by at least three program committee members and one senior program committee member on the basis of scientific novelty, technical quality, and importance to the field. After discussion and deliberation among the program committee, senior program committee and program chairs, 49 papers were selected for presentation at the conference. Thirty-eight of these are published in these proceedings. For the remaining eleven, at the authors' request, only abstracts are included along with pointers to full working papers. This option accommodates the practices of fields outside of computer science in which conference publishing can preclude journal publishing. It is expected that many of the papers in these proceedings will appear in a more polished and complete form in scientific journals in the future.

After the review process, an Outstanding Papers committee of Shuchi Chawla, David Reiley and Rahul Sami was established. The committee singled out the following two papers as co-winners of the EC'11 Best Student Paper Award:

• Polynomial-time Computation of Exact Correlated Equilibrium in Compact Games, by Albert Xin Jiang and Kevin Leyton-Brown, University of British Columbia;

• A Truthful Randomized Mechanism for Combinatorial Public Projects via Convex Optimization, by Shaddin Dughmi, Stanford University.

Putting together EC'11 was a team effort. We first thank the authors for providing the content of the program. We are grateful to the program committee and the senior program committee, who worked very hard in reviewing papers and providing feedback to authors. We also thank Workshops Chair Sanmay Das, Tutorials Chair Vahab Mirrokni, Webmaster Ann Marie King, and Lisa Tolles of Sheridan Printing Company. Finally, we thank our sponsor, ACM SIGecom, and our generous corporate supporters, Facebook, Google Research, Microsoft Research, Yahoo! Labs and eBay.

Yan Chen
EC'11 Program Chair
University of Michigan, USA

Tim Roughgarden
EC'11 Program Chair
Stanford University, USA

Yoav Shoham
EC'11 General Chair
Stanford University, USA

Table of Contents

Session 9: Mechanisms with Near-Optimal Equilibria

Session 10: Market-making and Computational Finance

Session 11: Matching

Session 12: Novel Equilibrium Analyses

ACM EC'11 Organization

General Chair: Yoav Shoham *(Stanford University, USA)*

Program Chairs: Yan Chen *(University of Michigan, USA)*
Tim Roughgarden *(Stanford University, USA)*

Workshops Chair: Sanmay Das *(Rensselaer Polytechnic Institute, USA)*

Tutorials Chair: Vahab Mirrokni *(Google Research, USA)*

Webmaster: Ann Marie King *(Harvard University, USA)*

Senior Program Committee: Craig Boutilier *(University of Toronto, Canada)*
Felix Brandt *(University of Munich, Germany)*
Shuchi Chawla *(University of Wisconsin, USA)*
David Easley *(Cornell University, USA)*
Joan Feigenbaum *(Yale University, USA)*
Anindya Ghose *(New York University, USA)*
Jason Hartline *(Northwestern University, USA)*
Ramesh Johari *(Stanford University, USA)*
Robert Kleinberg *(Cornell University, USA)*
Kevin Leyton-Brown *(University of British Columbia, Canada)*
John Morgan *(University of California at Berkeley, USA)*
Rudolf Muller *(Maastricht University, The Netherlands)*
Michael Ostrovsky *(Stanford University, USA)*
Christos Papadimitriou *(University of California at Berkeley, USA)*
David Reiley *(Yahoo! Research, USA)*
Rahul Sami *(University of Michigan, USA)*
Michael Wellman *(University of Michigan, USA)*
Berthold Voecking *(RWTH Aachen University, Germany)*

Program Committee: Gagan Aggarwal *(Google, USA)*
Christina Aperjis *(HP Labs, USA)*
Krzysztof Apt *(CWI, The Netherlands)*
Aaron Archer *(AT&T Research, USA)*
Itai Ashlagi *(MIT, USA)*
Ned Augenblick *(UC Berkeley, USA)*
Moshe Babaioff *(Microsoft Research, USA)*
Maria-Florina Balcan *(Georgia Tech, USA)*
Andreas Blume *(University of Pittsburgh, USA)*
Larry Blume *(Cornell University, USA)*
Liad Blumrosen *(Hebrew University, Israel)*
Aaron Bodoh-Creed *(Cornell University, USA)*
Patrick Briest *(University of Paderborn, Germany)*
Eric Budish *(University of Chicago, USA)*
Yiling Chen *(Harvard University, USA)*
Giorgos Christodoulou *(University of Liverpool, England)*
Vincent Conitzer *(Duke University, USA)*

Program Committee: Constantinos Daskalakis *(MIT, USA)*
Xiaotie Deng *(University of Liverpool, England)*
Nikhil Devanur *(Microsoft Research, USA)*
Shahar Dobzinski *(Cornell University, USA)*
Edith Elkind *(Nanyang Technological University, Singapore)*
Boi Faltings *(EPFL, Switzerland)*
Jon Feldman *(Google, USA)*
Michal Feldman *(Hebrew University, Israel)*
Amos Fiat *(Tel Aviv University, Israel)*
Felix Fischer *(Harvard University, USA)*
Arpita Ghosh *(Yahoo! Research, USA)*
Ashish Goel *(Stanford University, USA)*
Sharad Goel *(Yahoo! Research, USA)*
Paul Goldberg *(University of Liverpool, England)*
Bin Gu *(University of Texas at Austin, USA)*
Sangpil Han *(New York University, USA)*
Tobias Harks *(Technical University of Berlin, Germany)*
Paul Harrenstein *(Technical University of Munich, Germany)*
P. Jean-Jacques Herings *(Maastricht University, The Netherlands)*
Martin Hoefer *(RWTH Aachen University, Germany)*
Samuel Ieong *(Microsoft Research, USA)*
Nicole Immorlica *(Northwestern University, USA)*
Aaron Jaggard *(Rutgers University, USA)*
Jim Jansen *(Pennsylvania State University, USA)*
Lian Jian *(University of Southern California, USA)*
Patrick Jordan *(Yahoo! Research, USA)*
Karthik Kannan *(Purdue University, USA)*
Anna Karlin *(University of Washington, USA)*
Piotr Krysta *(University of Liverpool, England)*
Nicolas Lambert *(Stanford University, USA)*
Jérôme Lang *(Université Paris-Dauphien, France)*
Kate Larson *(University of Waterloo, Canada)*
Ron Lavi *(Technion, Israel)*
Robin Lee *(New York University, USA)*
Katrina Ligett *(Cornell University, USA)*
Mohammad Mahdian *(Yahoo! Research, USA)*
Vangelis Markakis *(Athens University of Economics and Business, Greece)*
Preston McAfee *(Yahoo! Research, USA)*
Aranyak Mehta *(Google, USA)*
Moritz Meyer-ter-Vehn *(UCLA, USA)*
Debasis Mishra *(Indian Statistical Institute, India)*
Herve Moulin *(Rice University, USA)*
Ahuva Mu'alem *(California Institute of Technology, USA)*
Hamid Nazerzadeh *(Microsoft Research, USA)*
Henrik Orzen *(University of Mannheim, Germany)*
Mallesh Pai *(University of Pennsylvania, USA)*
David Parkes *(Harvard University, USA)*
Georgios Piliouras *(Georgia Institute of Technology, USA)*
Maria Polukarov *(University of Southampton, England)*

Program Committee (continued):

Pearl Pu *(EPFL, Switzerland)*
Vijay Ramachandran *(Colgate University, USA)*
Justin Rao *(Yahoo! Research, USA)*
Heiko Röglin *(University of Bonn, Germany)*
Aaron Roth *(Microsoft Research, USA)*
Amin Saberi *(Stanford University, USA)*
Maher Said *(Washington University in St. Louis, USA)*
Tuomas Sandholm *(CMU, USA)*
Guido Schäfer *(CWI, The Netherlands)*
Michael Schapira *(Princeton University, USA)*
Michael Schwarz *(Yahoo! Research, USA)*
Param Singh *(CMU, USA)*
Aleksandrs Slivkins *(Microsoft Research. USA)*
Kunal Talwar *(Microsoft Research, USA)*
Eva Tardos *(Cornell University, USA)*
Olivier Tercieux *(Paris School of Economics, France)*
Timothy Van Zandt *(INSEAD, France)*
Jennifer Wortman Vaughan *(UCLA, USA)*
Milan Vojnovic *(Microsoft Research, USA)*
Yevgeniy Vorobeychik *(Sandia National Laboratories, USA)*
Michael Wooldridge *(University of Liverpool, England)*
Yinyu Ye *(Stanford University, USA)*
Ali Yurukoglu *(Stanford University, USA)*

Additional reviewers:

Ittai Abraham
Pranjal Awasthi
Michael Benisch
Ben Birnbaum
Avrim Blum
Yang Cai
Elisa Celis
Po-An Chen
Florin Constantin
Johannes Dams
Alan Deckelbaum
Paul Duetting
Yuval Filmus
Gianluigi Greco
Mingyu Guo
Chinmay Karande
Thomas Kesselheim
Nitish Korula
David Malec
Tomasz Michalak
Ilya Mironov
Vahab Mirrokni
Victor Naroditskiy
Eddie Nikolova
Joel Oren
Sigal Oren
Abe Othman
Renato Paes Leme
Lev Reyzin
Gil Segev
Jay Sethuraman
Sven Seuken
Balu Sivan
Pingzhong Tang
Vasileios Tzoumas
Jan Vondrak
Lei Wang
Chris Wilkens
Lirong Xia

EC 2011 Sponsor & Supporters

Sponsor: SIGecom

Supporters: facebook

Google

Microsoft Research

Yahoo! Labs

ebay

Network Formation in the Presence of Contagious Risk *

Larry Blume
Dept. of Economics
Cornell University;
IHS Vienna; Santa Fe Inst.

David Easley
Dept. of Economics
Cornell University

Jon Kleinberg
Dept. of Computer Science
Cornell University

Robert Kleinberg
Dept. of Computer Science
Cornell University

Éva Tardos
Dept. of Computer Science
Cornell University

ABSTRACT

There are a number of domains where agents must collectively form a network in the face of the following trade-off: each agent receives benefits from the direct links it forms to others, but these links expose it to the risk of being hit by a cascading failure that might spread over multi-step paths. Financial contagion, epidemic disease, and the exposure of covert organizations to discovery are all settings in which such issues have been articulated.

Here we formulate the problem in terms of strategic network formation, and provide asymptotically tight bounds on the welfare of both optimal and stable networks. We find that socially optimal networks are, in a precise sense, situated just beyond a phase transition in the behavior of the cascading failures, and that stable graphs lie slightly further beyond this phase transition, at a point where most of the available welfare has been lost. Our analysis enables us to explore such issues as the trade-offs between clustered and anonymous market structures, and it exposes a fundamental sense in which very small amounts of "over-linking" in networks with contagious risk can have strong consequences for the welfare of the participants.

Categories and Subject Descriptors

J.4 [**Social and Behavioral Sciences**]: Economics

General Terms

Economics, Theory

Keywords

algorithmic game theory, financial contagion, random graphs, social contagion, strategic network formation

*This research was supported in part by the MacArthur Foundation, a Google Research Grant, a Yahoo! Research Alliance Grant, ONR grant N00014-98-1-0589. NSF grants CCF-0325453, IIS-0910664, CCF-0910940, and CCF-0729006, and WWTF Grant Die Evolution von Normen and Konventionen in der Wirtschaft.

EC'11, June 5–9, 2011, San Jose, California, USA.

1. INTRODUCTION

There are many situations in which self-interested agents form links with one another, producing an underlying network structure. A growing body of work on *strategic network formation* [21] has sought to analyze the structure of networks that develop through such types of interaction: what characteristic properties do they have, and are they approximately as efficient as networks created through central planning and coordination? A common theme running through this literature is the view that links are costly to form, and this cost must be traded off against the benefits of indirect access to other parts of the network through multi-step paths, as measured by distances [12, 13, 18], component sizes [7], or point-to-point connectivity [6].

In a wide range of settings where network formation occurs, however, this trade-off is inverted. Instead of costly links that confer indirect benefits, the agents receive benefits via their direct links, but through these links they risk exposure to negative payoffs from a broader set of nodes reachable on multi-step paths. A canonical example is the problem of financial contagion [2, 3, 11, 16]. In a highly simplified formulation of this problem, two parties A and B engaging in a transaction must balance the benefits arising from the intended successful outcome of their transaction against the underlying *counterparty risk*: the possibility that the other side will fail to complete the transaction. This risk can now spread across the links formed by multiple transactions: if A defaults on its agreement with B, this may mean that B lacks the resources needed to complete a concurrent transaction with C, and so B too defaults. In this way the failure of A has spread via B to affect a transaction involving C, and perhaps further. The fear of such cascading failures, and the behavior of financial institutions in response to this perceived increase in counterparty risk, played an important role in the financial crisis of Fall 2008.

Financial contagion, however, is just one setting in which strategic agents balance the benefits of linking against concerns about contagious risk. Other basic examples include the following.

- During a disease epidemic within a human population, high-risk groups will alter their interaction patterns to reduce the risk of contagion, including focusing more on "in-group" members who belong to similar social circles. In the setting of HIV/AIDS, for example, this has been studied in the context of sexual contacts [19] and needle-sharing among intravenous drug users [8].

- In any type of distributed file-sharing application, the spread of malware from one host to another creates a very similar form of contagious risk, which can be incorporated into decisions about which hosts to download content from.

- In a different setting, participants in a clandestine organization benefit from the links they form to other members for purposes of coordination and mutual assistance, but by forming such links they expose themselves to a form of contagious risk: if certain members are compromised by an adversary, they may in turn reveal the identities and whereabouts of others to whom they are linked, and this process could potentially spread for multiple steps through the organizational network [15].

Formulating a Model

In all these different settings, the precise formulation of the payoffs to the participants will depend on details of the domain — for example, precisely how does a node benefit from the presence of a link, and precisely how does the risk of negative payoff propagate from one node to another? One of the advantages that general models of strategic network formation have offered is the ability to draw qualitative insights about the effects of self-interested behavior on network structure across a range of scenarios, using stylized formulations that capture the basic trade-offs without delving into the idiosyncracies of any one domain.

A natural modeling strategy for studying strategic network formation is to define a non-cooperative game whose outcomes are graphs. The precise networks that will emerge will depend on the precise details of the game. An enumeration of the possibilities is huge, and the likelihood of finding tractable formulations seems low. Network theorists, following [18], have finessed this problem by identifying properties of networks that we could expect to be satisfied by all equilibrium networks of games of conceivable interest.

In this paper, we develop a general model in this spirit to capture the underlying trade-off between the benefit of link formation and the problem of contagious risk, using simple definitions for the payoffs arising from these underlying processes. The model is formulated as follows. To begin with, we have a set V of n players, and players can choose to form bilateral relationships with one another, resulting in an undirected graph $G = (V, E)$. A player receives a payoff of $a > 0$ from each relationship it takes part in. We will generally assume there is an upper bound Δ on the number of links any one node is able to form.

Now, once the network is formed, a random process creates cascading failures as follows. First nodes fail independently with probability q, and then failed nodes have a probability of p of causing their neighbors to fail as well, with the failure potentially continuing to spread from these newly failed nodes. In more detail:

- First, each player randomly experiences a failure, independently with probability $q > 0$. We will refer to these as the *root failures* in the graph.

- Next, we declare each edge of G to be *live* independently with probability p and *blocked* with probability $1 - p$. We think of the live edges as those that transmit failure, and the blocked edges as those that do not transmit failure. Any node that can reach a root failure using a path consisting entirely of live edges is declared to fail also.

If a player fails, it loses any benefit from the links it forms, and instead its payoff is defined to be $(-b) < 0$.

Thus, if d_i denotes the degree of node i in G, and ϕ_i denote the probability that it fails (taken over the random choices of root failures and live edges), then we can write i's expected payoff as

$$\pi_i = ad_i(1 - \phi_i) - b\phi_i = ad_i - (ad_i + b)\phi_i.$$

As noted above, our formulation of the payoffs is intended to capture the basic trade-off in a simple way. Links confer benefits that scale linearly in the degree, and failures spread through direct probabilistic contagion across edges. One can imagine more complex models for both of these aspects of the payoff, with more complex notions of the way in which a node's links increase its payoff, and more complex mechanisms for the spread of failures. These are interesting directions for further analysis. Here we will see that the present model already exhibits rich behavior, and suggests avenues for pursuing such generalizations.

Optimality and Stability.. For most of the discussion, we will measure the "quality" of a graph via its *minimum welfare* (henceforth abbreviated *min-welfare*), which is the minimum payoff of any node in the graph. Unless otherwise specified, a socially optimal graph is one that maximizes this quantity.

In addition to socially optimal graphs, we will also consider graphs that arise under a solution concept representing strategic behavior by the nodes. We say that a graph is *stable* if (i) no node can strictly increase its payoff by deleting all its incident links (hence removing itself from the network), and (ii) there is no pair of nodes (i, j) such that (i, j) is not an edge of G, but both i and j would have higher payoffs, with at least one of them strictly higher, if (i, j) were added to G. This notion of stability is in the spirit of solution concepts for the formation of undirected graphs, capturing the notion that it takes two nodes to agree on the formation of a link, but any node can unilaterally withdraw from its links. Our definition of stability is a relaxation of the notion of *pairwise Nash stability* [17], which modifies (i) to allow a node to drop any subset of its incident links. Thus, any pairwise Nash stable graph is also stable under our definition, and so when we show upper bounds on the welfare of all stable graphs, it applies to all pairwise Nash stable graphs as well.

When we consider the structures of socially optimal and stable graphs, much of the interesting behavior emerges in a natural range of the parameters a, b, p, and q motivated by the following considerations. Suppose we had just two nodes i and j, and suppose that i is deciding whether to link to j. If it forms the link, it receives a benefit of a but there is a probability of pq that j will fail and that this failure will spread to a. We want i to be willing to form the link to j under these conditions, and so we assume $a > bqp$. Otherwise no links will form. On the other hand, suppose that i knew that j were going to fail, so that the only thing protecting i from failure is the transmission probability p. Under these conditions we do not want i to form the link to j, so we assume $a < bp$. Otherwise there will be no strategic component to the analysis. Analogously, suppose that i knew that any failure at j would definitely spread to i, so that the only thing protecting i from failure is the chance $1 - q$ that j does not fail. Under these conditions we also do not want i to form the link to j, so we assume $a < bq$.

In our analysis, we will focus on the range of parameters where the payoff a from a link greatly exceeds the loss bqp caused by direct failure of a neighbor, so nodes will want to form multiple links; and on the other hand, the benefit a is much smaller than either bp or bp, so nodes do not want to form links to others that are too likely to fail. That is, we will consider the case in which p and q are small, and for some sufficiently large constant d, the quantity a exceeds bqp by at least a factor of d, and $\min(bp, bq)$ in turn exceeds a by at least a factor of d. So with $\delta = 1/d$, we have $\delta^{-1}bqp < a < \delta \min(bp, bq)$; we will refer to δ as the key *separation parameter* in our model. Finally, we will consider the case in which the number of nodes n is arbitrarily large compared to these other quantities (and/or their reciprocals).

Our Results

Our main results provide asymptotically tight characterizations of the welfare obtained by both socially optimal and stable graphs, as well as structural insights into the properties of such graphs. In a sense to be made precise below, we find roughly that social optimality occurs just beyond the edge of a phase transition that controls how failures propagate, while stable graphs lie slightly further still past this phase transition, at a point where most of the welfare has already been wiped out. This narrow region where optimality occurs, and the inability of strategic agents to stay within this region, is one of the key qualitative behaviors to emerge from our model.

Social Optimality.. For social optimality, our first main result is that there is a small $\varepsilon > 0$, going to 0 with our separation parameter δ, such that no graph can have min-welfare greater than $(1+\varepsilon)a/p$. We show this by establishing that once each node forms more than $1/p$ links, the live edges — those that transmit failure — form a large connected component with high probability; this causes the probability of node failure to rise abruptly and to correspondingly reduce the welfare. This phenomenon is an analogue of the giant-component phase transition in the traditional random graph model $\mathcal{G}(n,p)$ [10], but since we are dealing with the random choice of live edges in an arbitrary underlying graph defined by the agents, we need to study the random subgraphs of this arbitrary graph; and hence we must adapt the arguments about the emergence of giant components to this setting.

This analysis establishes node degrees of $1/p$ as an important critical point in the behavior of the nodes' payoffs: at a degree of $1/p$, a node is receiving a benefit of a/p, and in order to raise all the nodes' payoffs further, we must push the graph into a region where the propagation of failures via live edges increases dramatically. It is therefore useful to look more carefully at the structure of graphs and their resulting payoffs right at the edge of this region. Accordingly, we say that a family of graphs, with n going to infinity, has *super-critical payoffs* if their min-welfares exceed a/p by a multiplicative constant (necessarily depending on the separation parameter δ) that is strictly greater than 1 — in other words, if they have min-welfare at least $(1+f(\delta))a/p$. Otherwise, we will say that they have *sub-critical payoffs*. It then becomes an interesting question to consider whether there exist families of graphs achieving super-critical payoffs, and what can be said about their structure.

Clustered vs. Anonymous Markets.. We construct a family of graphs with super-critical payoffs, by having the agents form a union of disjoint cliques, where each clique has a size chosen to be very slightly above $1/p$. The analysis of such graphs in fact highlights an interesting qualitative contrast between two kinds of network structures in which the agents can be organized: (i) a union of disjoint cliques each of size $k+1$, or (ii) a random graph formed by linking each node to k other nodes selected uniformly at random. Viewing this contrast in terms of an underlying motivation via economic contagion, we see that the two network structures correspond to two very different kinds of market formations: (i) is a *clustered market* where people engage in mutual dealing within their own community, and thereby insulate themselves from trouble originating in other communities, while (ii) is an *anonymous market* where agents can only specify the *number* of counterparties they would like to deal with, but cannot specify *who* these counterparties will be.

What our analysis shows is that while it is possible for clustered markets to yield super-critical payoffs, anonymous market structures can only produce sub-critical payoffs. In other words, if we connect each agent to k other random agents, then once k reaches $(1+\gamma)/p$ for any positive constant γ (and n sufficiently large), the node payoffs become sub-optimal. This yields potential insights into the different contagion dynamics of the two kinds of structures — when the market institution enables people to separate themselves into protected communities, then it becomes feasible to form a number of links that pushes past the crucial phase transition; but when interactions happen anonymously, it is necessary to stay safely on the low side of the phase transition.

Stable Graphs.. We then consider the class of stable graphs, and here our main result is that there is a small $\varepsilon > 0$ (again going to 0 with the separation parameter δ) such that no stable graph can have min-welfare greater than $\varepsilon a/p$. It is interesting that this gap between welfare at social optimality and at stability arises because of relatively subtle structural differences between the two kinds of graphs; socially optimal graphs are poised at the edge of a dangerous precipice in parameter space, and intuitively, we can think of stable graphs as exhibiting a small amount of additional linking that send them over this precipice.

Our analysis provides a useful way of thinking about how this additional linking occurs. When a node evaluates forming an extra link, its own change in payoff comes from the benefit of this new link offset by the increased risk of failure. However, while only the two endpoints of the new link can experience the benefits of the link, a potentially much larger set of nodes can experience a payoff decrease due to greater risk. This creates a negative externality by which nodes do not account for the full amount of risk they generate in forming links, and since we are in a region of parameter space where small structural changes can yield large payoff changes, this externality is sufficient to eliminate most of the payoff to nodes.

Finally, as part of our analysis, we also provide a proof that stable graphs exist, and in fact that one can build stable graphs from unions of disjoint cliques. This construction requires some amount of care, since the stability condition requires that we produce cliques large enough that nodes will not want to form links into other cliques, but not so large that nodes will want to drop out of their own cliques. Arguing that there exists a clique size achieving both of these conditions involves maintaining control of the payoff functions in the vicinity of the phase transition.

Further Related Work

There have been several papers that deal with problems where one optimizes parameters of a network under the risk of node failure, but these other models have been quite different from ours both in the general questions they consider and in the specifics of their formulations.

Caballero and Simsek consider a model of financial contagion in which the failure of nodes in a network can lead other nodes to engage in a cascade of "fire sales," in which the price of assets plummets [11]. However, in addition to the fact that their cascade mechanism is quite different, they study only the case in which the network structure is simple and given: the nodes are assumed to be connected in a cycle. Goyal and Vigier consider "attack-defense" games on networks, in which a designer must choose a network structure, and then an attacker tries to disrupt it by destroying nodes [14]. Their work assumes that failure spreads deterministically between nodes, and hence leads to very different considerations. Gutfraind [15], motivated by the organization of terrorist cells, considers the question of how to centrally design a network that can optimize a distance-based function in the presence of probabilistic contagion; in his work, the objective function is again very different from ours, and the design of such networks is explored through simulation. Finally, the line of research beginning with Albert, Jeong, and Barabási on the attack-tolerance of random graphs [1] focuses on the increase in average node distances when an adversary deletes nodes from an underlying graph, and it leads to different types of questions as well.

2. AN UPPER BOUND ON THE OPTIMAL MIN-WELFARE

We begin by establishing an upper bound on the min-welfare of any graph. We use the parametrization of the model described in the introduction; recall that we will be making the following assumption (motivated there): for a small constant $\delta > 0$, we have

$$\delta^{-1}bqp < a < \delta \min(bp, bq).$$

For ease of future reference, we will call this *Assumption* $\mathcal{P}(\delta)$. Recall also that we are assuming an upper bound of Δ on the maximum number of edges any one node can form. As discussed above, much of the interesting behavior in this model turns out to take place in graphs where the average degree is close to $1/p$. As a result, we will assume that Δ is larger than $1/p$, but not so large that any single node can dominate the structure of the graph. In particular, we will assume that $\Delta = c^*/p$ for a constant $c^* > 1$.

Our basic plan for the upper bound is as follows. If the min-welfare in a graph G exceeds $\frac{(1+\varepsilon)a}{p}$, then in particular it implies that all node degrees are at least $\frac{(1+\varepsilon)}{p}$. We declare each edge to be *live* independently with probability $p > 0$, and then study the extent to which nodes are able to reach one another along *live-edge paths* — that is, paths consisting entirely of live edges. If there is a node that can reach many others with reasonable probability, this node experiences a large probability of failure, and hence has a sharply reduced payoff, which will ultimately contradict our assumption that G has large min-welfare.

Now, how do we show that some node has a reasonably high chance of reaching many others on live-edge paths? There is a connection to the basic random graph model $\mathcal{G}(n,p)$, in which an edge is inserted between each pair among n nodes independently with probability p. We can think of $\mathcal{G}(n,p)$ equivalently as the model in which one starts with an n-node clique and, declares each edge to be live independently with probability p, and then considers the live-edge subgraph. The challenge in our case is that our graphs G are not necessarily cliques, or even close to being cliques, and relatively little is known about adapting results from $\mathcal{G}(n,p)$ to the case of arbitrary underlying base graphs [4]. Fortunately, however, we are able to prove a result that is strong enough for our purposes, adapting techniques for analyzing connected components in $\mathcal{G}(n,p)$ to the setting of live-edge subgraphs of arbitrary underlying graphs.

We begin with this part of the analysis, as follows.

(2.1.) *For all $\varepsilon > 0$ there exist constants $\alpha, \beta > 0$ such that the following holds. Let H be a graph in which each node has degree at least $r \geq \frac{1+\varepsilon}{p}$. Construct a random subgraph of H by declaring each edge to be "live" with probability p. Then for every node $i \in V$, the number of nodes reachable from i on live-edge paths is at least αr with probability at least β.*

Proof. Let i be any node in H. We now describe a method for exploring the live edges outward from i, based on Karp's analysis of random subgraphs of the bidirected complete graph [20] and Alon and Spencer's analysis of infinite branching processes [5]. We first take all the nodes (if any) that i can reach via live edges and put them in a queue. We then repeatedly delete a node j from the queue and add to the queue all the nodes (if any) that j can reach via live edges, other than the ones already "discovered" (added to the queue) in previous iterations. Notice, crucially, that the outcome of the random live/blocked decision for each edge (j, j') is only examined once in this process, when one of nodes j or j' first comes to the front of the queue. Thus, we can assume that the live/blocked status of (j, j') is first determined at that moment.

For a small constant $\alpha > 0$, we say that this process *succeeds* if at least αr nodes are added to the queue before the queue ever becomes empty. If the process succeeds with probability at least β, for a constant $\beta > 0$, then our result follows.

Let Q_t be the number of nodes in the queue at the end of iteration t, where we define $Q_0 = 1$ to indicate that i starts in the queue. We have

$$Q_t = Q_{t-1} - 1 + X_t,$$

where the "-1" is because we delete a node j_t from the queue in iteration t (with $j_1 = i$), and X_t is a random variable equal to the number of not-yet-discovered nodes that j_t can reach via live edges. (This is where it is useful to assume that the live/blocked status of edges from j_t to not-yet-discovered nodes is only determined when j_t reaches the front of the queue.) Unrolling this recurrence, we have

$$Q_t = \left(\sum_{u=1}^{t} X_u\right) - t.$$

We are interested in showing that the probability of $Q_t > 0$ for all t from 1 until at least αr nodes have been discovered (added to the queue); in this case, the search for nodes using live-edge paths continues successfully for a sufficient number of steps, as required.

The expectation of X_t, prior to the point at which at least αr nodes have been discovered, can be determined as follows. The node j_t has degree at least r in H, and at most αr nodes have been discovered by the process thus far, so there are at least $(1-\alpha)r$ edges emanating from j_t leading to not-yet-discovered nodes. We choose α small enough that $(1-\alpha)r \geq \frac{1+\varepsilon/2}{p}$; since each of these edges is live with probability p, we have $\mathbf{E}[X_t] \geq 1 + \varepsilon/2$. Thus, until αr nodes have been discovered, we can think of the queue length as a random walk on the integers with positive drift; as a result, there is a positive probability that the walk never returns to 0, which is the result we want.

We can briefly verify this in more detail for our particular case as follows. Let $S_t = \sum_{u=1}^{t} X_u$; by the Chernoff Bound, we have

$$\Pr[S_t \leq t] < \Pr[S_t \leq (1-\varepsilon/4)\mathbf{E}[S_t]] < e^{-\frac{1}{2}\frac{\varepsilon^2}{16}t}.$$

Now, the sum $\sum_{t=1}^{\infty} e^{-\frac{1}{2}\frac{\varepsilon^2}{16}t}$ converges; we choose t_0 large enough that $\sum_{t=t_0}^{\infty} e^{-\frac{1}{2}\frac{\varepsilon^2}{16}t} < 1$. For p sufficiently small, there is a positive probability that X_1, the number of nodes i can reach directly via live edges, is at least t_0. It then follows that $S_t > t$ for all $t < t_0$. Finally, for all t we have $\Pr[S_t \leq t \mid X_1 \geq t_0] \leq \Pr[S_t \leq t] < e^{-\frac{1}{2}\frac{\varepsilon^2}{16}t}$; summing over t we obtain

$$\sum_{t=0}^{\infty} \Pr[S_t \leq t \mid X_1 \geq t_0] < 1. \quad ■$$

Next, we simply want to argue that if a node can reach many other nodes via live-edge paths with reasonably large probability, then it has a large probability of failing and hence a negative payoff. To do this, we first state a simple lemma about the union of many independent events, and then we use this to draw the resulting conclusion for a node's payoff.

(2.2.) *Consider a collection of independent events $\mathcal{E}_1, \ldots, \mathcal{E}_n$, each of probability $p > 0$. Then the probability of their union is at least* $\min(\frac{1}{3}, \frac{2}{3}np)$.

Proof. If $p \geq \frac{1}{3}$ then the result follows immediately. Otherwise, if $np \leq \frac{2}{3}$, then we have

$$\begin{aligned}
\Pr\left[\bigcup_{j=1}^{n} \mathcal{E}_j\right] &\geq \sum_{j=1}^{n} \Pr[\mathcal{E}_j] - \sum_{j,j'} \Pr[\mathcal{E}_j \cap \mathcal{E}_{j'}] \\
&= np - \binom{n}{2} p^2 \\
&\geq np - \frac{1}{2}(np)^2 \\
&= np(1 - \frac{1}{2}np) \\
&\geq \frac{2}{3}np.
\end{aligned}$$

Otherwise, we can choose a subset S of $k \leq n$ of the events such that $\frac{2}{3} < kp \leq 1$. We have

$$\begin{aligned}
\Pr\left[\bigcup_{j \in S} \mathcal{E}_j\right] &\geq \sum_{j \in S} \Pr[\mathcal{E}_j] - \sum_{j,j' \in S} \Pr[\mathcal{E}_j \cap \mathcal{E}_{j'}] \\
&= kp - \binom{k}{2} p^2 \\
&\geq kp - \frac{1}{2}(kp)^2 \\
&= kp(1 - \frac{1}{2}kp) \\
&\geq \frac{2}{3} \cdot \frac{1}{2} = \frac{1}{3}.
\end{aligned}$$

■

Now, for a node i, let the set of nodes it can reach on live-edge paths in G be called its *live component*, and let $r_i(G)$ be a random variable denoting the size of i's live component.

(2.3.) *For all $\gamma_0, \gamma_1 > 0$ there exist $\alpha, \delta > 0$ such that when $p, q \leq \alpha$ and Assumption $\mathcal{P}(\delta)$ holds, we have the following. If G is a graph with a node i for which $r_i(G) \geq \frac{\gamma_1}{p}$ with probability at least γ_0, then the payoff of node i satisfies $\pi_i(G) < -bq$. (We note that the right-hand side is the payoff i would receive if it had no links).*

Proof. If i can reach at least $\gamma_1 p^{-1}$ nodes on live-edge paths, then by (2.2), the probability that it fails is at least $\min(\frac{1}{3}, \frac{2}{3}\gamma_1 p^{-1} q)$. Removing the conditioning on this event, the probability it fails is at least $\phi_i \geq \min(\frac{1}{3}\gamma_0, \frac{2}{3}\gamma_0\gamma_1 p^{-1} q)$. We also have $d_i \leq \Delta = c^* p^{-1}$.

If $\phi_i \geq \frac{1}{3}\gamma_0$, then

$$\begin{aligned}
\pi_i &\leq ad_i - b\phi_i \leq ac^* p^{-1} - \frac{1}{3}b\gamma_0 \\
&\leq \delta bc^* - \frac{1}{3}b\gamma_0 = b(\delta c^* - \frac{1}{3}\gamma_0)
\end{aligned}$$

where the last line is less than $-bq$ for δ sufficiently small and $q < \frac{1}{3}\gamma_0$.

If $\phi_i \geq \frac{2}{3}\gamma_0\gamma_1 p^{-1} q$, then defining $\gamma_2 = \frac{2}{3}\gamma_0\gamma_1$, we have

$$\begin{aligned}
\pi_i &\leq ad_i - b\phi_i \\
&\leq ac^* p^{-1} - \gamma_2 bqp^{-1} \\
&= ac^* p^{-1} - (\gamma_2 p^{-1} - 1)bq - bq \\
&< \delta c^* b - (\gamma_2 p^{-1} - 1)bq - bq.
\end{aligned}$$

This last line is less than $-bq$ provided that $1 + \delta c^* - \gamma_2 p^{-1} < 0$, which holds provided that p is sufficiently small relative to δ. ■

Finally, combining (2.1) with (2.3), we get an immediate consequence for the payoffs when all nodes have large degrees. The upper bound on min-welfare follows directly from this.

(2.4.) *For all $\varepsilon > 0$, there exist $\alpha, \delta > 0$ such that when $p, q \leq \alpha$ and Assumption $\mathcal{P}(\delta)$ holds, we have the following. If each node has degree at least $\frac{(1+\varepsilon)}{p}$, then for each node i we have $\pi_i < -bq$.*

Proof. For each node $i \in V$,(2.1)implies that we have $r_i(G) \geq \frac{\gamma_1}{p}$ with probability at least γ_0, It then follows from(2.3)that $\pi_i < -bq$. ■

(2.5.) *For all $\varepsilon > 0$, there exist $\alpha, \delta > 0$ such that when $p, q \leq \alpha$ and Assumption $\mathcal{P}(\delta)$ holds, no graph can have min-welfare greater than $\frac{(1+\varepsilon)a}{p}$.*

Proof. Choose $\alpha, \delta > 0$ as in (2.4), and suppose by way of contradiction that there is a graph with min-welfare greater than $\frac{(1+\varepsilon)a}{p}$. It follows that every node i has degree greater than $\frac{1+\varepsilon}{p}$. But then by (2.4) we have $\pi_i < -bq$, contradicting the assumption that the min-welfare is greater than $\frac{(1+\varepsilon)a}{p}$. ■

3. SUPER-CRITICAL PAYOFFS AND ANONYMOUS MARKETS

We now show that the upper bound in Section 2 can essentially be achieved, in an asymptotic sense, and also consider some of the structural implications of this fact.

To begin with, it is instructive to think about the analysis in Section 2 in terms of the random graph $\mathcal{G}(k, r)$.[1] One of the central facts about $\mathcal{G}(k, r)$ is that in a small window around probability $r = 1/k$, the expected size of the largest connected component jumps from a constant value to a constant fraction of k. This is the basic phase transition for $\mathcal{G}(k, r)$, and (2.1) in Section 2 is a reflection of this phase transition for an arbitrary underlying graph.

In order for a graph to achieve *super-critical payoffs* — those of the form $\frac{(1+\varepsilon)a}{p}$ for some $\varepsilon > 0$ — it must lie on the side of the phase transition where the live components are likely to be large, proportional to $1/p$. For this to be possible, it must cross the phase transition by little enough that these large components

[1]Since n and p are basic parameters in our model, we adopt the different variable names k and r in discussing $\mathcal{G}(k, r)$. Also, in keeping with standard terminology, we will often refer informally to $\mathcal{G}(k, r)$ as "a random graph," as though it is a single graph rather than a distribution over graphs.

do not eliminate the payoff of the nodes. We now show how to do this, constructing a family of graphs built from disjoint cliques that achieve min-welfare of the form $\frac{(1+\varepsilon)a}{p}$.

Some Basic Facts about $\mathcal{G}(k, r)$.. We begin by carefully stating some quantitative results about the phase transition in $\mathcal{G}(k, r)$ in a form that will be useful for the analysis.

(3.1.) *Let C_i denote the component containing node i in $\mathcal{G}(k, r)$. If we fix some other node j and look at the event $j \in C_i$, then we have* $\Pr[j \in C_i] = \frac{1}{k} \cdot \mathbf{E}[|C_i|] - \frac{1}{k}$.

Proof.

$$\begin{aligned} \Pr[j \in C_i] &= \sum_{s=1}^{k} \Pr[|C_i| = s] \cdot \Pr[j \in C_i \mid |C_i| = s] \\ &= \sum_{s=1}^{k} \frac{s-1}{k} \Pr[|C_i| = s] \\ &= \frac{1}{k} \sum_{s=1}^{k} (s-1) \Pr[|C_i| = s] \\ &= \frac{1}{k} \cdot \mathbf{E}[|C_i|] - \frac{1}{k} \end{aligned}$$

■

Thus, looking at the probability a node belongs to i's component is equivalent to looking at the expected size of i's component.

The following pair of standard results describe the contrasting behavior of component sizes on opposite sides of $r = 1/k$.

(3.2.) *Fix $x < 1$, and consider the component of a given node i in $\mathcal{G}(k, r)$, where $kr = x$. Then for k sufficiently large, we have the following:*

- *(i) The probability that i's component exceeds size c decreases exponentially in c.*
- *(ii) Consequently, the expected size of i's component is bounded by a constant $c = c(x)$, independent of k, and the maximum size of any component in the graph is thus $O(\log k)$.*

(3.3.) *There is an increasing function $\theta : [1, \infty] \to [0, 1]$ that is continuously differentiable on $(1, \infty)$ and continuously differentiable from the right at $x = 1$, with $\theta(1) = 0$ and $\theta'(1)$ a positive real number, such that the following holds. Fix $x > 1$ and $\varepsilon > 0$, and consider $\mathcal{G}(k, r)$, where $kr = x$. Then for $k = k(x, \varepsilon)$ sufficiently large, we have the following:*

- *(i) With probability $1 - \exp(-k)$, there is a component of size between $(1-\varepsilon)\theta(x)k$ and $(1+\varepsilon)\theta(x)k$.*
- *(ii) Conditioned on not belonging to the giant component in (i), the probability that a node i belongs to a component of size greater than c decreases exponentially in c.*
- *(iii) Consequently, the expected size of i's component is between $(1-\varepsilon)^2\theta(x)^2 k$ and $(1+\varepsilon)^2\theta(x)^2 k + c$ for a constant $c = c(x)$.*

Point (iii) follows from (i) and (ii) by considering that with probability $(1 \pm \varepsilon)\theta(x)$, node i belongs to a component of size $(1 \pm \varepsilon)\theta(x)k$, and with the remaining probability i belongs to a component of expected size at most c.

A Family of Graphs with Super-Critical Payoffs.. For parameters k and s, let $F_s(k)$ denote the disjoint union of s cliques of size k. We will show that $F_s\left(\frac{1+\gamma}{p}\right)$, for arbitrary $s \geq 1$ and a small constant $\gamma > 0$, achieves super-critical node payoffs.

For our construction, we will focus on the special case $p = q$. A nice feature of this special case is that we can represent the spread of failures in $F_s(k)$ in the following equivalent way. We imagine a single "failure node" i^* associated with each clique, and attached to each real node in the clique, resulting in a clique on $k+1$ nodes. There is a transmission probability p on the edges from i^* to each node in its clique, as there is on all other edges. In this view, a node i fails if it is in the same live-edge component as i^*; in other words, the probability i fails is the probability it belongs to the same component as a given fixed node i^* in $\mathcal{G}(k+1, r)$. By (3.1) we know this is

$$\frac{1}{k+1} \cdot \mathbf{E}[|C_i|] - \frac{1}{k+1},$$

where C_i denotes the live-edge component of i.

With $p = q$, we define σ to be the ratio $a/bp = a/bq$; by assumption $\mathcal{P}(\delta)$, we have $\sigma < \delta$, and we assume as usual that δ and p are sufficiently small. We let the number of nodes k in each clique be $(1+\gamma)/p$ for a small value $\gamma > 0$ that we determine below.

First, (3.3)(iii) implies that the probability ϕ_i that i fails satisfies

$$(1 - \varepsilon_0)\theta(1+\gamma)^2 \lesssim \phi_i \lesssim (1+\varepsilon_0)\theta(1+\gamma)^2$$

for a constant ε_0 that goes to 0 with p. Thus, the payoff to a node i is

$$\begin{aligned} \pi_i &\geq \frac{a(1+\gamma)}{p} - \left(b + \frac{a(1+\gamma)}{p}\right)(1+\varepsilon_0)\theta(1+\gamma)^2 \\ &= \frac{a(1+\gamma)}{p} - b(1+\sigma(1+\gamma))(1+\varepsilon_0)\theta(1+\gamma)^2 \\ &\geq \frac{a(1+\gamma)}{p} - 2b\theta(1+\gamma)^2 \\ &= \frac{\sigma bp(1+\gamma)}{p} - 2b\theta(1+\gamma)^2 \\ &= b(\sigma(1+\gamma) - 2\theta(1+\gamma)^2). \end{aligned}$$

Now, let

$$h_0(x) = \sigma x - 2\theta(x)^2,$$

so that

$$\pi_i \geq b h_0(1+\gamma).$$

We have

$$h_0'(x) = \sigma - 4\theta(x)\theta'(x).$$

Since $\theta(1) = 0$ and $\theta'(1)$ is a positive real number, we have $h_0'(1) = \sigma$, and hence the function $h_0(x)$ is strictly increasing over the interval $x \in [1, w_0]$ for a constant w_0 depending on σ. Since $h_0(1) = \sigma$, we have $h_0(w_0) = \sigma(1+\sigma_0)$ for a constant $\sigma_0 > 0$ depending on σ.

Returning to the lower bound on π_i, we choose $\gamma = w_0 - 1$, and so

$$\pi_i \geq b h_0(w_0) = \frac{a}{\sigma p} \cdot \sigma(1+\sigma_0) = \frac{a(1+\sigma_0)}{p}.$$

Consequently, the payoff to each node exceeds $\frac{a}{p}$ by a multiplicative factor greater than 1 that depends on σ.

Comparison to an Anonymous Structure.. The construction above achieves super-critical payoffs by allowing nodes to cluster into communities of an appropriate size, and thus to insulate themselves from failures originating in other communities. Drawing on a market motivation, it is interesting to ask whether super-critical payoffs can be achieved through structures that are based instead on *anonymous* interaction, where nodes can specify the number of partners they want to connect to, but have no control over who these partners are — the partners are chosen uniformly at random from the population. As we now show, in fact, anonymous interaction structures are not able to yield super-critical payoffs.

To define these anonymous structures precisely, we use the *configuration model* for random graphs [9, 10, 22]. Each of the n nodes is assigned k "half-edges"; these half-edges are then matched up uniformly at random into pairs, with each matching pair of half-edges forming an edge in the resulting random graph. Note that the pairing may cause two edges to go between the same pair of nodes, or for a node to form an edge that loops to itself; we remove these parallel edges and self-loops to obtain the final graph. Failures then propagate in this graph according to our model, spreading from root failures along live-edge paths.

With high probability, the local neighborhood of a node in this random graph will have a particularly simple structure, as follows. For node i, define $B(i,\ell)$ to be the ball of radius ℓ centered at i, i.e. the induced subgraph of G on the set of all nodes reachable from i in ℓ or fewer hops. For fixed integers k, ℓ and any node i, the probability that $B(i,\ell)$ is a tree of depth ℓ and degree k (i.e. one whose internal nodes all have degree k and whose leaves are all at distance ℓ from the root) tends to 1 as $n \to \infty$.

For our analysis, we will therefore connect the propagation of failures in the configuration model to a related, simpler model based on an infinite k-regular tree. In particular, let $\mathcal{B}(k,r)$ denote the distribution over trees obtained by starting with an infinite k-regular tree and including each edge in the random tree with probability r. We now have a pair of results analogous to(3.2)and(3.3).

(3.4.) *Let $x < 1$, and consider a tree generated from $\mathcal{B}(k,r)$ where $kr = x$.*

(i) The probability that the tree's size exceeds size c decreases exponentially in c.

(ii) The expected size of the tree is bounded by a constant $c = c(x)$.

(3.5.) *There is an increasing function $\tau : [1,\infty] \to [0,1]$ that is continuously differentiable on $(1,\infty)$ and continuously differentiable from the right at $x = 1$, with $\tau(1) = 0$ and $\tau'(1)$ a positive real number, such that the following holds. Consider a tree generated from $\mathcal{B}(k,r)$, and let $\psi_r(k)$ be the probability that it has an infinite node set.*

(i) If $kr > 1$, then $\psi_r(k) > \tau(kr)$.

(ii) For all integers $c_0, c_1 > 1$ and $k \geq c_0c_1/r$, we have

$$\psi_r(k) \geq 1 - (1 - \psi_r(c_0/r))^{c_1} > 1 - (1 - \tau(c_0))^{c_1}.$$

(iii) Conditioned on not having an infinite node set, the probability that the tree's size exceeds c decreases exponentially in c. Its expected size is thus bounded by a constant $c = c(x)$.

Proof. Part (iii) of the claim is a standard result; parts (i) and (ii) are formulated in ways that are adaped to our present purposes, and we give proofs of them here.

First we prove (i). The probability that the tree is infinite is the unique solution to $z = 1 - (1 - pz)^k$ in the interval $(0,1)$. Define τ to be the unique solution to $\tau = 1 - e^{-x\tau}$ in the interval $(0,1)$. Writing $f_0(v) = (1 - pv)^k$ and $f_1(v) = e^{-xv}$, we have

$$f_0(v) = (1 - pv)^k = (1 - pv)^{x/p} < e^{-xv} = f_1(v).$$

Thus, the curve $y = 1 - f_0(v)$ lies above the curve $y = 1 - f_1(v)$ on the interval $(0,1)$, and so $y = 1 - f_0(v)$ intersects the line $y = v$ to the right of where $y = 1 - f_1(v)$ intersects it. It follows that $z > \tau$, and hence we can take $\tau = \tau(x)$ as our function.

To prove (ii), consider $k' = \dfrac{c_0c_1}{r}$ subtrees of the root in the complete k-ary tree (before edges are randomly included), and group them into c_1 blocks of $\dfrac{c_0}{r}$ subtrees each. For any block, if we consider just the root and the subtrees in a single block, the probability that the resulting random tree is infinite is at least $\psi_r(c_0/r)$ (since the root has this degree in the restricted tree, and the nodes in the subtrees have degree $k \geq c_0/r$). The tree is infinite if it is infinite in any of the blocks, and so the probability it is infinite is at least

$$1 - (1 - \psi_r(c_0/r))^{c_1} > 1 - (1 - \tau(c_0))^{c_1}$$

where the latter inequality follows directly from (i). ■

We now want to show that when each node forms k links in the anonymous structure, for any $k = \dfrac{1+\beta}{p}$, the node payoffs can be at most a/p as $n \to \infty$. Clearly this is true for $\beta \leq 0$, so we consider the case of an arbitrary $\beta > 0$.

When the random graph G is sampled using the configuration model, for any node i the probability that the ball $B(i,\ell)$ is a tree of degree k and depth ℓ is $1 - o(1)$ as $n \to \infty$. Applying 3.5(i), the probability that i belongs to a live path of length ℓ is at least $\tau(1+\beta) - o(1)$; for n sufficiently large, this probability is at least $\tau(1+\beta/2)$. In the event that i belongs to a live path of length ℓ, it fails with probability at least $1-(1-q)^\ell$. By taking ℓ large enough, we may assume that $\tau(1+\beta/2)(1-(1-q)^\ell) \geq \tau(1+\beta/3)$ and thus node i fails with probability at least $\tau(1+\beta/3)$.

Thus, if n is sufficiently large then we have

$$\begin{aligned}\pi_i &\leq \left(\frac{a(1+\beta)}{p}\right)\left(1 - \tau\left(1+\frac{\beta}{3}\right)\right) - b\tau\left(1+\frac{\beta}{3}\right)\\ &= b\sigma(1+\beta)\left(1 - \tau\left(1+\frac{\beta}{3}\right)\right) - b\tau\left(1+\frac{\beta}{3}\right).\end{aligned}$$

Let

$$h_1(x) = \sigma(1+3x)\left(1 - \tau(1+x)\right) - \tau(1+x),$$

so that $\pi_i \leq bh_1(\beta/3)$. By (3.5)(ii), we know that for $y \geq 4$, we have

$$\tau(y) \geq 1 - (1 - \tau(2))^{\lfloor y/2 \rfloor} \geq 1 - (1 - \tau(2))^{y/4}.$$

We can thus choose $w_1 \geq 4$ such that

$$\tau(y) \geq 1 - \frac{1}{1+y}$$

for all $y \geq w_1$. If $1 + x \geq w_1$, we have

$$h_1(x) \leq \sigma(1+3x)\left(\frac{1}{2+x}\right) - \frac{1+x}{2+x} < 0,$$

provided $\sigma < \dfrac{1}{3}$. Now, if $\sigma \leq \dfrac{1}{3}\sup_{y\in[1,w_1]}\tau'(y)$, then we have the following for all $x \in [0, w_1 - 1]$:

$$\begin{aligned}h_1'(x) &= 3\sigma(1 - \tau(1+x)) - (\sigma + 3\sigma x + 1)\tau'(1+x)\\ &\leq 3\sigma - \tau'(1+x) \leq 0.\end{aligned}$$

Thus, for all $x \in [0, w_1 - 1]$, we have $h_1(x) \leq h_1(0) = \sigma$. Since we also have $h_1(x) < 0$ for $x \geq w_1 - 1$, it follows that $h_1(x) \leq \sigma$ for all $x \geq 0$.

Thus, for any $\beta > 0$, we have $\pi_i \leq b\sigma = \frac{a}{p}$ when each node forms $k = \frac{1+\beta}{p}$ links. Since $\pi_i \leq \frac{a}{p}$ when nodes form at most $k \leq \frac{1}{p}$ links, it follows that for any constant c, if nodes form $\frac{c}{p}$ links then $\pi_i \leq \frac{a}{p}$ provided n is sufficiently large as a function of c.

Clustered vs. Anonymous Markets.. It is instructive to consider why a union of disjoint cliques was able to achieve qualitatively higher payoffs than an anonymous interaction pattern. In particular, the nodes in the cliques we constructed are linking at a degree beyond the phase transition point, whereas attempting to do this in the anonymous structure has negative effects on the payoff.

A quantitative way to think about the contrast is to observe that in the union of cliques, the failure probability of a node i was approximately controlled by a conjunction of two events: i belonging to the giant component of the clique, and the "failure node" i^* also belonging to the giant component of the clique. As a result, the failure probability involves a term of the form $\theta(x)^2$, and this has a derivative of 0 at $x = 1$ — hence, it is safe to increase x a bit past 1 without blowing up the failure probability. On the other hand, in the anonymous structure, once i belongs to the giant component, it fails with overwhelming probability; thus, i's failure probability involves a term of the form $\tau(x)$, which has a strictly positive derivative at $x = 1$, and this makes it unprofitable to increase x even arbitrarily little past 1. This is the fundamental difference between the behavior of the two kinds of structures in the region just past the phase transition.

4. UPPER BOUND ON THE MIN-WELFARE OF ANY STABLE NETWORK

We now show that any stable graph must have small min-welfare. (We defer the proof that stable graphs exist to the next section.) To upper-bound the min-welfare, we proceed as follows. Recall that we assumed that Δ is an upper bound on the number of links any one node is able to form. So nodes of degree Δ cannot form further edges. We first show, in (4.1), that if two nodes i and j are not connected by an edge, and neither is at the maximum degree Δ, then at least one of them must have a large failure probability — this is what dissuades the other from forming the link.

It follows that in a stable network, all low-degree nodes of low failure probability must form a clique, since any unlinked pair of them would have an incentive to connect. If the number of nodes n is sufficiently large, we can then find a node i that is far from this clique. Hence node i, and every node within a large number of steps of i, must have large degrees; we can thus apply an analogue of(2.1) to show i has a large failure probability, and this will conclude the proof.

(4.1.) *Suppose Assumption $\mathcal{P}(\delta)$ holds. Let G be a stable graph, and let i and j be two nodes of G such that (i, j) is not an edge of G, and the degrees of i and j are each strictly less than Δ. Then we have* $\max(\phi_i, \phi_j) \geq \frac{(1-\delta)a}{(1+\delta c^*)bp}$.

Proof. Since the degrees of i and j are each strictly less than Δ, at least one of i or j does not have a strictly higher payoff if the edge (i, j) is included; let us assume it is node i. Thus, if G' denotes the graph G with the edge (i, j) included, then we have $\pi_i(G') \leq \pi_i(G)$.

We imagine evaluating failure in G' by first making all random root failure decisions and all random live/blocked decisions in G, then determining which additional nodes fail, and finally deciding whether the edge (i, j) is live or blocked and determining further failures. Let $\Phi_i(G)$ be the event that i fails in G before (i, j) is examined, and let $\mathcal{F}_{ij}(G)$ be the event that (i, j) is live and j fails in G. Then $\Phi_i(G') = \Phi_i(G) \cup \mathcal{F}_{ij}(G)$, so

$$\Pr[\Phi(G')] \leq \Pr[\Phi_i(G)] + \Pr[\mathcal{F}_{ij}(G)].$$

Since $\Pr[\mathcal{F}_{ij}(G)] = p\phi_j$, we have

$$\phi_i(G') - \phi_i(G) \leq p\phi_j(G).$$

Now,

$$\pi_i(G') = a(d_i + 1) - (ad_i + a + b)\phi_i(G'),$$

so the fact that $\pi_i(G') \leq \pi_i(G)$ implies that

$$a(d_i + 1) - (ad_i + a + b)\phi_i(G') \quad \leq \quad ad_i - (ad_i + b)\phi_i(G)$$

and hence

$$\begin{aligned} a &\leq (ad_i + a + b)(\phi_i(G') - \phi_i(G)) + a\phi_i(G) \\ &\leq (ad_i + a + b)p\phi_j(G) + a\phi_i(G) \\ &\leq (1 + \delta c^*)bp\phi_j(G) + \delta bp\phi_i(G), \end{aligned}$$

where the last line follows from the fact that $a < \delta bp$ and $d_i + 1 \leq c^* p^{-1}$.

Now, if $\phi_i(G) \geq \frac{a}{bp}$, we are done. Otherwise, we have

$$a \leq (1 + \delta c^*)bp\phi_j(G) + \delta a,$$

so

$$(1 - \delta)a \leq (1 + \delta c^*)bp\phi_j(G),$$

and hence

$$\phi_j(G) \geq \frac{(1-\delta)a}{(1+\delta c^*)bp}. \quad \blacksquare$$

Following our informal plan above, we note that a stable graph might have some low-degree nodes, so we require the following direct adaptation of (2.1), which applies to nodes that are far from all low-degree nodes.

(4.2.) *For all $\varepsilon > 0$ there exist constants $\alpha, \beta > 0$ such that the following holds. Let H be a graph, and let A be the set of nodes of degree less than $\frac{1+\varepsilon}{p}$. Let i be a node of distance greater than $\frac{1}{p}$ from A. Construct a random subgraph of H by declaring each edge to be "live" with probability p. Then the number of nodes reachable from i on live-edge paths is at least αp^{-1} with probability at least β.*

Proof. Consider the node-discovery process described in the proof of(2.1) starting from the node i, and recall that we declare it to *succeed* if it adds at least $\frac{\alpha}{p}$ nodes to the queue before it ever becomes empty, for the small constant $\alpha < 1$ used there. The event that the process succeeds depends only on the live/blocked decisions for nodes within distance $\frac{\alpha}{p}$ of i, and all such nodes have degrees at least $\frac{1+\varepsilon}{p}$; hence, for this whole time we can apply the argument used in(2.1) $\blacksquare$

Finally, we conclude the proof strategy outlined at the beginning of the section, resulting in our upper bound.

(4.3.) *Let $n > \Delta^{\Delta+2}$. For all $\varepsilon > 0$ there exist $\alpha, \delta > 0$ such that when $p, q \leq \alpha$ and Assumption $\mathcal{P}(\delta)$ holds, no stable graph can have min-welfare greater than $\frac{\varepsilon a}{p}$.*

Proof. Suppose by way of contradiction that $G = (V, E)$ is a stable graph in which $\pi_i \geq \frac{\varepsilon a}{p}$ for all $i \in V$.

Let $A \subseteq V$ denote the set of all nodes i of G for which $d_i < \Delta$ and $\phi_i < \frac{(1-\delta)a}{(1+\delta c^*)bp}$. Since any node in A is able to form an additional edge, (4.1) implies that there must be an edge between each pair of nodes in A — in other words, A induces a clique in G.

Let $B \subseteq V$ denote the set of all nodes in G of degree equal to Δ. For any $i \in V - (A \cup B)$, we have $\phi_i \geq \frac{(1-\delta)a}{(1+\delta c^*)bp}$. Since $\pi_i \geq \frac{\varepsilon a}{p}$ by assumption, we have

$$\frac{\varepsilon a}{p} \leq ad_i - b\phi_i \leq ad_i - \frac{(1-\delta)a}{(1+\delta c^*)p}$$

and hence

$$d_i \geq \frac{\varepsilon}{p} + \frac{1-\delta}{(1+\delta c^*)p}.$$

For δ sufficiently small, the right-hand side of this inequality is at least $\frac{1+\varepsilon_1}{p}$ for a constant $\varepsilon_1 > 0$ Choosing $\varepsilon_2 = \min(\varepsilon_1, c^* - 1)$, it follows that all nodes $i \in V - A$ have degree at least $\frac{1+\varepsilon_2}{p}$.

Now, for any $j \in A$, there are at most $1+\Delta+\Delta^2+\cdots+\Delta^{\Delta+1} < \Delta^{\Delta+2} < n$ nodes within distance $\Delta + 1$ of j, and hence within distance Δ of some node in A. Hence there is some node $i \in V$ at distance greater than $\Delta > p^{-1}$ from A. For this node i,(4.2)implies that $r_i \geq \frac{\gamma_1}{p}$ with probability at least γ_0, for constants $\gamma_0, \gamma_1 > 0$. By (2.3), it follows that $\pi_i < -bq$, contradicting the assumption that the min-welfare of G is greater than $\frac{\varepsilon a}{p}$. ■

5. EXISTENCE OF STABLE NETWORKS

Finally, we show that there exist arbitrarily large stable networks. As with our constructions in Section 3, we will consider graphs that consist of disjoint cliques — graphs $F_s(k+1)$ with $k = \frac{1+\gamma}{p}$ for an appropriately chosen $\gamma > 0$.

The challenge is to find a k where the union of cliques is stable, and this requires some care for the following reason. Stability requires that no unlinked pair of nodes wants to form an edge — this can be achieved by making k sufficiently large that creating a link between two cliques brings about too large an increase in failure probability to the nodes forming the link. Unfortunately, making k large also raises the failure probability of each node i based simply on its current set of edges — so we must not raise k so high that a node i wants to drop all its existing links. The crux of the problem is thus the following: is there a k that is large enough to discourage the formation of cross-clique links, but not so large that nodes will drop their current links? The main part of our analysis will be to show that such a k exists.

As in Section 3, we will consider the case in which $p = q$; defining σ to be the ratio $a/bp = a/bq$, we have $\sigma < \delta$, and we assume δ and p are sufficiently small.

(5.1.) *Given a, b, p, q as above, there exists $\gamma > 0$ such that with $k = \frac{1+\gamma}{p}$, the union of cliques $F_s(k+1)$ is stable.*

Proof. For the analysis of the construction, we will work with the function $\theta(x)$ defined in (3.3), as well as the related function $\lambda(x) = x(1-\theta(x)^2)$. Observe that $\lambda(1) = 1$, since $\theta(1) = 0$. Taking derivatives, we have

$$\lambda'(x) = (1-\theta(x)^2) - 2x\theta(x)\theta'(x),$$

and hence $\lambda'(1) = 1$. Thus we have

(5.2.) *For some constant $w > 1$, the function $\lambda(x)$ is strictly increasing on the closed interval $[1, w]$.*

As in Section 3, we analyze the failure process by attaching a single "failure node" i^* to each clique. The probability ϕ_i that node i fails is the probability that i belongs to the same live-edge component as i^* in the $(k+2)$-node clique where i^* is added to i's clique. The payoff to node i is

$$\pi_i = ak - (ak+b)\phi_i.$$

If i drops all its edges, it receives a payoff of $-bq < 0$. If i forms an edge to a node j in another clique, it receives an added benefit of a, and incurs an increased expected loss of at least

$$(ak+b)p\phi_i(1-\phi_i).$$

There are four terms here; the second and third represent the chance that j's failure (which is $\phi_j = \phi_i$ by symmetry) spreads to i, and the fourth term represents the fact that this only matters if i had not already failed in its own clique. In more detail: the payoff to node i before the addition of this edge is $ak - (ak+b)\phi_i$, and afterward it is

$$a(k+1) - (ak+a+b)(\phi_i + p\phi_i - p\phi_i^2),$$

so the change in payoff is less than $a - (ak+b)p\phi_i(1-\phi_i)$.

Now, what is ϕ_i? By(3.1)and(3.3), we have

$$(1-\varepsilon_1)^2\theta(p(k+2))^2 \leq \phi_i \leq (1+\varepsilon_1)^2\theta(p(k+2))^2 + c_1 p$$

for a constant ε_1 that goes to zero as p does. By choosing a slightly larger ε_2, and using the fact that $\theta(\cdot)$ has a bounded first derivative, we have

$$(1-\varepsilon_2)\theta(1+\gamma)^2 \leq \phi_i \leq (1+\varepsilon_2)\theta(1+\gamma)^2,$$

with ε_2 going to zero as p does.

In the expression $\phi_i(1-\phi_i)$, provided the upper bound $(1+\varepsilon_2)\theta(1+\gamma)^2 \leq \frac{1}{2}$, we have

$$\begin{aligned}\phi_i(1-\phi_i) &\geq (1-\varepsilon_2)\theta(1+\gamma)^2(1-(1-\varepsilon_2)\theta(1+\gamma)^2) \\ &\geq (1-\varepsilon_2)\theta(1+\gamma)^2(1-\theta(1+\gamma)^2).\end{aligned}$$

Since $a = \sigma bp$ and $k = (1+\gamma)/p$, if we write $\sigma_1 = \sigma(1+\gamma)$, then we have $ak = \sigma(1+\gamma)b = \sigma_1 b$. Now we have

$$\begin{aligned}&(ak+b)pk\phi_i(1-\phi_i) \\ &\quad= b(1+\sigma_1)(1+\gamma)\phi_i(1-\phi_i) \\ &\quad\geq b(1+\sigma_1)(1+\gamma)(1-\varepsilon_2)\theta(1+\gamma)^2(1-\theta(1+\gamma)^2) \\ &\quad= b(1+\sigma_1)(1-\varepsilon_2)\lambda(1+\gamma)\theta(1+\gamma)^2 \\ &\quad\triangleq f_1(\gamma),\end{aligned}$$

where the last line is taken as the definition of $f_1(\gamma)$. Observe that $f_1(0) = 0$, and by (5.2), there is an $x_1 < 1$ such that the function $f_1(x)$ is strictly increasing for x in a closed interval $[0, x_1]$.

We also have

$$\begin{aligned}(ak+b)\phi_i &\leq b(1+\sigma_1)(1+\varepsilon_2)\theta(1+\gamma)^2 \\ &\triangleq f_0(\gamma),\end{aligned}$$

where once again the last line is taken as the definition of $f_0(\gamma)$. We see that $f_0(x)$ is also strictly increasing in $[0, x_1]$ (and beyond this interval as well).

Now, since $\lambda(1) = 1$ and $\lambda(\cdot)$ is monotone increasing on $[0, x_1]$, for any small enough $\varepsilon_2 > 0$, there is a unique $x_0 < x_1$ such that

$$\lambda(1 + x_0) = \frac{1 + \varepsilon_2}{1 - \varepsilon_2}.$$

Moreover, $f_1(x) > f_0(x)$ for all $x \in (x_0, x_1]$, and the value of x_0 goes to 0 as ε_2 goes to 0. Also, we observe that for $\gamma \in (x_0, x_1]$, we have

$$f_1(\gamma) > f_0(\gamma) \geq b\theta(1 + \gamma)^2.$$

Now, we choose σ small enough that $2\sigma < \theta(1 + x_1)^2$. We then choose ε_2 small enough (by choosing p small enough) so that $f_1(x_0) = f_0(x_0) < b\sigma$. Finally, let $g(\gamma) = ak = (1 + \gamma)b\sigma$. Since $b\sigma < g(\gamma) < 2b\sigma$ for all $\gamma \in (x_0, x_1]$, it follows that $f_0(x_0) < g(x_0)$ but $g(x_1) < f_1(x_1)$. Therefore, since $f_0(\cdot)$ and $f_1(\cdot)$ are continuous functions, there exist $\gamma^*, \gamma^{**} \in (x_0, x_1]$ for which $g(\gamma^*) = f_1(\gamma^*)$ and $g(\gamma^{**}) \geq f_0(\gamma^{**})$, with $\gamma^* < \gamma^{**}$.

We choose any $\gamma \in [\gamma^*, \gamma^{**}]$ as the value of γ we use to define k. With this value of k, the payoff i receives from keeping all its edges is

$$\pi_i = ak - (ak + b)\phi_i \geq g(\gamma) - f_0(\gamma) \geq 0,$$

and hence i prefers to keep its edges rather than deleting all of them. The change in payoff i receives from linking to a node j in a different clique is less than

$$\begin{aligned}
&k^{-1}\left(ak - (ak + b)pk\phi_i(1 - \phi_i)\right) \\
&\quad \leq k^{-1}\left(ak - b(1 + \sigma_1)(1 - \varepsilon_2)\lambda(1 + \gamma)\theta(1 + \gamma)^2\right) \\
&\quad = k^{-1}\left(g(\gamma) - f_1(\gamma)\right) \\
&\quad \leq 0,
\end{aligned}$$

and hence i will not form this link. Thus, the graph $F_s(k + 1)$ is stable. ■

A Stable Graph with Unequal Clique Sizes.. We observe that starting with a set of disjoint cliques $F_s(k + 1)$, we can create a different stable graph by adding one additional clique Γ of size $\ell < k+1$ on a disjoint set of nodes. The size ℓ can be chosen in any way such that the payoffs of nodes in the clique Γ each exceed $-bq$. In this way, nodes in Γ will not want to drop their incident edges. Moreover, there is still no edge that can form so as to improve the payoffs of both its endpoints, since any edge involving a node i in Γ must have its other end at a node j in one of the cliques of size $k + 1$, in which case the argument for (5.1) shows that i would not want to form the link.

In particular, this means that we can take ℓ to be a clique yielding the maximum possible node payoff over all clique sizes, as in Section 3; this shows how certain nodes in a stable graph can have higher payoffs than others.

6. REFERENCES

[1] R. Albert, H. Jeong, and A.-L. Barabási. Error and attack tolerance in complex networks. *Nature*, 406:378–382, 2000.

[2] F. Allen and A. Babus. Networks in finance. Technical Report 08-07, Wharton Financial Institutions Center, Aug. 2008.

[3] F. Allen and D. M. Gale. Financial contagion. *Journal of Political Economy*, 108(1):1–33, Feb. 2000.

[4] N. Alon, I. Benjamini, and A. Stacey. Percolation on finite graphs and isoperimetric inequalities. *Annals of Probability*, 32:1727–1745, 2004.

[5] N. Alon and J. Spencer. *The Probabilistic Method.* John Wiley & Sons, second edition, 2000.

[6] E. Anshelevich, A. Dasgupta, É. Tardos, and T. Wexler. Near-optimal network design with selfish agents. In *Proc. 35th ACM Symposium on Theory of Computing*, pages 511–520, 2003.

[7] V. Bala and S. Goyal. A non-cooperative model of network formation. *Econometrica*, 68:1181–1229, Sept. 2000.

[8] M. A. Barnard. Needle sharing in context: Patterns of sharing among men and women injectors and HIV risks. *Addiction*, 88:805–812, 1993.

[9] E. A. Bender and E. R. Canfield. The asymptotic number of labeled graphs with given degree sequences. *Journal of Combinatorial Theory (Series A)*, 24:296–307, 1978.

[10] B. Bollobás. *Random Graphs.* Cambridge University Press, second edition, 2001.

[11] R. J. Caballero and A. Simsek. Fire sales in a model of complexity. Technical Report 15479, National Bureau of Economic Research (NBER), Nov. 2009.

[12] J. Corbo and D. C. Parkes. The price of selfish behavior in bilateral network formation. In *Proc. 24th ACM Symposium on Principles of Distributed Computing*, pages 99–107, 2005.

[13] A. Fabrikant, A. Luthra, E. N. Maneva, C. H. Papadimitriou, and S. Shenker. On a network creation game. In *Proc. 22nd ACM Symposium on Principles of Distributed Computing*, pages 347–351, 2003.

[14] S. Goyal and A. Vigier. Robust networks, Apr. 2010. Working paper, Cambridge University.

[15] A. Gutfraind. Mathematical terrorism, 2010. Ph.D. Thesis, Cornell University.

[16] A. G. Haldane and R. M. May. Systemic risk in banking ecosystems. *Nature*, 469:351–355, 2011.

[17] M. O. Jackson. *Social and Economic Networks.* Princeton University Press, 2008.

[18] M. O. Jackson and A. Wolinsky. A strategic model of social and economic networks. *Journal of Economic Theory*, 71(1):44–74, 1996.

[19] J. A. Jacquez, C. P. Simon, J. Koopman, L. Sattenspiel, and T. Perry. Modeling and analyzing HIV transmission: The effect of contact patterns. *Mathematical Biosciences*, 102(2):119–199, Dec. 1988.

[20] R. M. Karp. The transitive closure of a random digraph. *Random Structure and Algorithms*, 1(1):73–93, 1990.

[21] É. Tardos and T. Wexler. Network formation games and the potential function method. In N. Nisan, T. Roughgarden, É. Tardos, and V. Vazirani, editors, *Algorithmic Game Theory*, pages 487–516. Cambridge University Press, 2007.

[22] N. C. Wormald. *Some problems in the enumeration of labelled graphs.* PhD thesis, Newcastle University, 1978.

Optimal Auctions with Positive Network Externalities

Nima Haghpanah
Northwestern University
Evanston, IL
nima.haghpanah@gmail.com

Nicole Immorlica*
Northwestern University
Evanston, IL
nicimm@gmail.com

Vahab Mirrokni
Google Research
New York, NY
mirrokni@gmail.com

Kamesh Munagala†
Duke University
Durham, NC
kamesh@cs.duke.edu

ABSTRACT

We consider the problem of designing auctions in social networks for goods that exhibit *single-parameter submodular network externalities* in which a bidder's value for an outcome is a fixed private type times a known submodular function of the allocation of his friends. Externalities pose many issues that are hard to address with traditional techniques; our work shows how to resolve these issues in a specific setting of particular interest. We operate in a Bayesian environment and so assume private values are drawn according to known distributions. We prove that the optimal auction is APX-hard. Thus we instead design auctions whose revenue approximates that of the optimal auction. Our main result considers *step-function externalities* in which a bidder's value for an outcome is either zero, or equal to his private type if at least one friend has the good. For these settings, we provide a $\frac{e}{e+1}$-approximation. We also give a 0.25-approximation auction for general single-parameter submodular network externalities, and discuss optimizing over a class of simple pricing strategies.

Categories and Subject Descriptors

H.4 [**Computer Applications**]: Social and Behavioral Sciences—*Economics*

General Terms

Algorithms, Economics

*Supported by Microsoft New Faculty Fellowship, and by NSF grant SMA-1019169.

†Supported by an Alfred P. Sloan Research Fellowship, and by NSF via CAREER award CCF-0745761 and grant CCF-1008065.

Keywords

Auctions, Social Networks, Externalities

1. INTRODUCTION

Many goods have higher value when used in conjunction with others. A classic example of this phenomenon is the telephone, which clearly has positive value for a consumer only if he or she has people to call. Telephones, and other goods with similar stories, are called *networked goods* and said to exhibit *network effects* or *network externalities*. Modern technology has given birth to a new generation of networked goods. Internet services like email, instant messaging, and online social networks are used primarily to connect with friends and, as such, have strong network externalities. But even more significantly, these services, particularly online social networks, provide platforms upon which developers can generate new applications – applications with very strong networking components. It is now possible to play poker in *Texas HoldEm*, visit cafes in *Cafe World*, and even be a virtual farmer in the immensely popular *FarmVille* with friends in online social networks like Facebook. Such applications are more fun when used with friends, and many such applications even explicitly reward players with many friends. The unique feature of such modern networked goods is that the underlying social network is *explicit*. This enables application distributors to use the network structures to market and sell these goods.

In this paper, we leverage explicit network structure to design mechanisms for selling networked goods. We primarily focus on goods, such as applications like *FarmVille* in online social networks, that are available in unlimited supply or, more precisely, can be produced at zero marginal cost. The network externalities of the good are implied by the private valuations of the social network users. In the most general case, users have a private value for each possible allocation of the good to a subset of users. This allows for arbitrary externalities, enabling say John Doe to value the good only if Kim Kardashian owns it despite having no direct relationship to her. While this makes sense for some goods, like fashion, many network goods like telephones or social network applications have value to a user only if users in his or her immediate neighborhood also own the good. The main focus of the paper is on special case of this sort of direct externality, which we call *step function externalities*: that is, we suppose a user's value for the good is zero unless at least one of his or her neighbors or friends in the social network is also allocated the good.

We study *auction mechanisms*, or mechanisms that solicit bids from agents indicating their private value for various allocations, and then determine an allocation and prices in a way that maximizes expected revenue. As is common in economics, we work in a Bayesian setting where, while the realization of the private value is known only to the agent, it is drawn according to a commonly known distribution. Most literature on auction design assumes that agents value allocations solely based on the bundle of goods they receive, i.e., they are indifferent for the allocation of the other players. This is clearly violated in settings with externalities. Unfortunately, externalities significantly complicate auction design for the following reasons:

1. The efficient representation of values is no longer a trivial task, since in the most general case each bidder might need to report a value for each subset of allocated bidders.
2. More dimensions make satisfying incentive constraints harder (multi-parameter mechanism design is not well understood).
3. The space of feasible allocations might be more complex, which can make finding the optimal allocation a computationally hard problem.
4. Furthermore, the complexity of the feasible allocation space can easily cause the setting to violate *downward-closure*, i.e., not every subset of a feasible allocation is necessarily feasible. Thus the few known results for multi-parameter mechanism design can not be adopted generically.

We circumvent the first two issues by assuming a special structure on the players' values, namely that valuations satisfy step function externalities as defined above. Thus our problem is a single-parameter one, and so the representation and incentive constraints straight-forward. Revenue maximization is also well understood for single-parameter settings. The seminal paper by Myerson [15] fully characterizes mechanisms that maximize revenue. By this characterization, the expected revenue of any auction is equal to the expected *virtual value* of the allocated agents, where the virtual value of an agent is a function of the valuation and its distribution and may be negative. In our setting, this characterization converts the optimal allocation problem to a combinatorial optimization problem, which is to maximize the sum of the virtual values over all *feasible* subsets. For step-function externalities, the feasibility constraint requires that all allocated agents have a neighbor who is also allocated. Graph-theoretically, this equates to finding, in a vertex-weighted graph with possibly negative vertex weights, a maximum-weight subset of vertices whose induced subgraph has no singleton components.

Although the optimal auction is easy to define, the third and fourth issues of auction design with externalities remain in our setting. We observe via reduction to set-buying that approximating the optimization problem within even a linear factor on *every* sampling of the values is NP-hard. On the other hand, we only need to find algorithms that perform well *in expectation* rather than in worst case. Even on average, we prove that our problem remains APX-hard. However, we are able to design constant approximations for several versions of the problem.

We first note that there's a simple $(1/2)$-approximation for our problem. The algorithm divides the graph into two subsets of vertices, such that each vertex in each set has a neighbor in the other. This can be done, for example, by constructing a spanning tree of the graph and then taking a bipartite partitioning of it. The allocation strategy is to then pick the set with better expected revenue, extract revenue from that set, and allocate to all users in the other set in order to maintain feasibility. This very simple algorithm does not use the structure of the social network in any deep way, and is therefore unable to give better approximations in even very simple social networks consisting of a single edge. In order to leverage knowledge of the network structure, we construct a linear program (LP) whose variables represent the allocation and whose constraints use the network structure to characterize feasibility. Our main result shows how to use this LP formulation to give a $\frac{e}{e+1} \approx 0.73$-approximation to the optimal revenue for any distribution of values. The interesting observation is that, although the gap of this LP is linear in the number of agents for a particular instantiation of values, we manage to prove a constant approximation through a novel average-case analysis of the rounding technique. We also show that the expected integrality gap of our LP is 0.828, and thereby bound the approximation ratio of any LP-based mechanism. In the full version, we also give a simple greedy-based $\frac{e}{e+1}$-approximation for our problem.

We extend our setting to *single-parameter submodular externalities* in which a bidder's value for an outcome is his private value times a known function of the set of players who receive the item. For such settings we study a class of strategies called *influence and exploit* in which some bidders (the *influencers*) are given the good for free and the remainder (the *exploited*) are offered an optimal price conditioned on the set of influencers. We show that the revenue is a submodular function of the set of influencers and hence can use recent submodular function maximization results [7, 8] to design an influence-and-exploit strategy whose revenue is within a 0.41-factor of the optimal influence and exploit strategy. We also show that a randomization over influence and exploit strategies gives a 0.25-approximation to the optimal expected revenue by further submodularity arguments.

Related Work. Various settings with positive, negative, or mixed externalities have been studied in economics as well as computer science literature. Rohlfs [16] discusses positive externalities in the telephone industry in which a person's value for a telephone increases as more friends use it. A well-studied scenario with negative externalities is the allocation of ad slots in which, a company's valuation for being listed as one of the *sponsored search* results decreases if their competitor is also listed [1, 4, 9, 10, 13, 14]. Finally, the valuation might have mixed externalities, as in the sale of nuclear weapons [12], in which countries prefer their allies rather than their foes to win the auction. Our work can be viewed as another in this line of literature, which addresses the difficulties of externalities in a specific setting of practical import by making application-specific assumptions.

Our work considers *auctions* with externalities. In contrast, some prior work considers instead posted price mechanisms [3, 2, 5, 11]. Particularly relevant to our work is that of Hartline, Mirrokni, and Sundararajan [11]. They consider the problem of finding a revenue-maximizing sequence of prices that are offered sequentially to myopic buyers. They observed that simple influence and exploit strategies have revenue within a constant factor of the revenue of any equilibrium of any pricing sequence. They are reminiscent of our auctions which subsidize certain subsets of agents, and also our influence and exploit strategies for general single-parameter submodular externalities. However, unlike Hartline, Mirrokni, and Sundararajan [11], we provide approximation results with regards to the optimal auction revenue, which can be larger than the upper bound in their paper.

2. PRELIMINARIES

We consider a society of n bidders located on the vertices in a social network $G(V, E)$, where the undirected edges model *friendship*. We assume for ease of exposition that the social network is connected. There is a limited supply k of a homogeneous good. Unless otherwise specified, we assume $k \geq n$ so that the supply is essentially unlimited (equivalently, the good can be reproduced at zero marginal cost).

An outcome $o \in \Omega = \{0,1\}^n$ is a distribution of goods among bidders, where $o_i = 1$ if bidder i receives a copy of the good and 0 otherwise. Bidder i's *type* $v_i : \Omega \to \mathbb{R}^+ \cup \{0\}$ maps outcomes to non-negative real numbers, where $v_i(o)$ represents his value for outcome o and is positive only if he receives a copy of the good (i.e., $o_i = 1$). We study Bayesian mechanism design, in which one assumes that each type $v_i(\cdot)$ is drawn independently from a commonly-known distribution F_i. Let $F = F_1 \times \ldots \times F_n$ be the product distribution of F_i for all i; v be the vector of types, called the *type profile*; v_{-i} be the vector of types of agents other than i, and F_{-i} the distribution of v_{-i}. Throughout the paper, our algorithms assume access to expectations defined with respect to the distribution F. We assume these can be computed to within sufficient accuracy via sampling.

A (direct) mechanism is specified by two functions $\chi : \mathbb{R}^{n2^n} \to \Omega$ and $\rho : \mathbb{R}^{n2^n} \to \mathbb{R}^n$ in which $\rho_i(v)$ is the *payment* of agent i given the reported type profile v. The utility of an agent for outcome o and price p is his value for the outcome minus the price he pays, $v_i(o) - p$. We say that a mechanism (χ, ρ) is Bayesian incentive compatible (BIC) if reporting the true type maximizes any player i's expected utility assuming that other players also report their true types, that is for every agent i and types v_i and v_i',

$$\begin{aligned}\mathbf{E}_{v_{-i}\sim F_{-i}}&[v_i(\chi(v)) - \rho_i(\chi(v))] \\ &\geq \mathbf{E}_{v_{-i}\sim F_{-i}}[v_i(\chi(v_i', v_{-i})) - \rho_i(\chi(v_i', v_{-i}))].\end{aligned}$$

Note that this is an interim notion, i.e., the agent's choose the strategy that gives them the highest expected utility after observing their own private value. Similarly, we assume an interim notion of *individual rationality*, i.e., each agent's expected utility conditioned on their private value should be non-negative.

We consider *single-parameter* settings. In these settings, agents values are a function of just one private parameter, called their *type*. As types are represented by a single parameter, v_i, the Bayesian assumption reduces to assuming that v_i is drawn independently from a distribution F_i over the non-negative reals, henceforth referred to as the type distribution of bidder i. We assume type distributions are *regular* and hence the corresponding *virtual values* are non-decreasing (see Subsection 2.1 for definitions).

In the following subsection, we discuss optimal auction design for single-parameter settings. We encourage the reader familiar with these subjects to skip to Subsection 2.3 where we define the problem studied in this paper.

2.1 Optimal Auction Characterization

In his seminal paper [15], Myerson characterized the revenue of the optimal (i.e., revenue-maximizing) auction in terms of the *virtual values* of the agents. We first define virtual values and then discuss the characterization result.

DEFINITION 1. *Suppose type v_i is drawn independently from a distribution $F_i(v) = \Pr[v_i \leq v]$ and let $f_i(v)$ be the density function of the distribution (note that if the distribution is discrete then $f_i(v)$ is simply $Pr[v_i = v]$). Then the virtual value function $\phi_i(v)$ is $v - \frac{1-F_i(v)}{f_i(v)}$.*

Note that virtual values may be negative. However, they are non-negative in expectation, a fact which enables many of our results.

FACT 1. *For any distribution F and value v, the virtual value $\phi(v)$ is non-negative.*

We will further assume that the distributions we study are *regular*, meaning that the corresponding virtual value function is non-decreasing in the support of F.

For a mechanism (χ, ρ), let $x_i(v) = v_i(\chi(v))/v_i$ if $v_i > 0$, and zero otherwise. In Myerson's characterization, it is the function x that is relevant for determining the revenue of the mechanism, and hence in a slight abuse of terminology we will refer to x as the *allocation function* even though there may be bidders i with $x_i(v) = 0$ that receive copies of the good (however they do not value the copy of the good because of the externalities). Accordingly define $x_i(v_i) = \mathbf{E}_{v_{-i}\sim F_{-i}}[x_i(v_i, v_{-i})]$ to be agent i's expected allocation for type v_i, where the expectation is over the types of other players.

In the single-parameter setting with regular distributions, Myerson showed that for any monotone increasing rule x, there is a unique corresponding payment rule ρ such that the resulting mechanism (χ, ρ) is BIC (where χ is any function that induces allocation function x and is not necessarily unique). The expected revenue of the mechanism is equal to its expected virtual value, $\sum \mathbf{E}_{v_i \sim F_i}[x_i(v_i)\phi_i(v_i)]$. Furthermore, if x is not monotone increasing, then there is no payment rule that makes the corresponding mechanism BIC. Restricting attention to BIC mechanisms is without loss of generality due to the revelation principle, and so to maximize revenue, one simply needs to find a rule χ satisfying all exogenous constraints (e.g., limited supply) whose corresponding feasible allocation function x is monotone and maximizes expected virtual value. We can therefore analyze the revenue of any monotone mechanism without explicitly defining the prices.

2.2 Submodular Externalities

In this setting, we assume that each player i is assigned *local influence function* $g_i : 2^V \to \Re$ which is common knowledge. Following the previous literature on network influence, we assume that this local influence function is submodular for each player, i.e., $g_i(S \cup \{j\}) - g_i(S) \geq g_i(S' \cup \{j\}) - g_i(S)$, for all $S \supseteq S'$, and $j \notin S$. Submodularity models the diminishing return properly and makes sense in this context. Without loss of generality assume g_i is normalized such that $g_i(V) = 1$. Given this function and i's type v_i, define $S(o) = \{j : o_j = 1\}$ to be the set of players that are given the item in an outcome o. Then the value of i for o is defined to be $v_i(o) = v_i \cdot g_i(S(o))$.

Given any mechanism (χ, ρ), define the *allocation function* $x_i(v) = g_i(S(\chi(v)))$. Using this definition we can write $v_i(\chi(v)) = v_i x_i(v)$. Now we can invoke Myerson's characterization and write the expected revenue of the mechanism to be $\sum_i E[x_i(v)\phi_i(v_i)]$.

We consider two special cases of submodular externalities: *concave externalities* and *step-function externalities.* In concave externalities, for each player i and subset S, $g_i(S) = \mathcal{G}(|S \cap N_i|)$ for some concave function $\mathcal{G}(.)$ if $i \in S$. That is, the valuation of each bidder i depends on *the number* of his neighbors who have the good but not their identity, and also the local influence function is the same among all players. Step-function externalities are detailed in the next section.

2.3 Step-Function Externalities

Step-function externalities are a special case of submodular externalities in which the value of the influence function is 0 if the set of neighbors who receive the item is empty, and 1 otherwise. Let $N(i)$ be the neighborhood of i in G, $N(i) = \{j : (i,j) \in E\}$. Formally, bidder i's value for an outcome is:

$$v_i(o) = \begin{cases} v_i & : o_i = 1, |j \in N(i), o_j = 1| \geq 1 \\ 0 & : \text{otherwise} \end{cases}$$

We say that a bidder i is *satisfied* by an allocation if $v_i(o) = v_i$. This models applications, like bridge tournaments, that require just one friend to be of value.

In this setting, for any mechanism (χ, ρ), we have $x_i(v) = 1$ if outcome $\chi(v)$ satisfies bidder i and zero otherwise. Note that χ and x may differ on certain bidders i. In particular, it can be that outcome $o = \chi(v)$ gives a good to bidder i (i.e., $o_i = 1$) and yet does not satisfy the bidder (i.e., $o \notin O_i$) so that $x_i(v) = 0$. As a result, allocation functions x must satisfy the condition that $x_i(v) = 1$ only if for at least one (more generally, s) neighbor $j \in N(i)$ of i, we also have $x_j(v) = 1$. This means that in the subgraph induced by the allocated agents, every vertex must have degree at least 1 (more generally, s). Call such a subset of agents *feasible.* By the Myerson characterization discussed above, the optimal auction is thus specified by an allocation function that, given a type profile, allocates to a feasible subset of agents with maximum sum of virtual values (note this rule is necessarily monotone).

Graph-theoretically, the problem of finding an optimal allocation function equates to finding a subset of vertices of maximum weight whose induced subgraph has no isolated vertices. Unfortunately, we show in Section 3 that this problem is more general than the *set buying* problem, and therefore hard to approximate within a linear factor *on every* sampling of values. We also show that the problem of maximizing the *expected* revenue (over randomness of values), is APX-hard.

As the problem is NP-hard to solve optimally, we instead design a polynomial-time monotone allocation function whose expected revenue (as defined by the sum of virtual values) is close to the optimal expected revenue OPT, where the expectations are over the type distributions. We say an auction is an α*-approximation* if its expected revenue is at least $\alpha \times OPT$.

3. HARDNESS

By Myerson's characterization of optimal allocations, the problem of finding an optimal allocation function equates to finding a subset of vertices of maximum weight whose induced subgraph has no isolated vertices. Unfortunately, since virtual values and hence vertex weights might be negative, this problem is more general than the set buying problem (see, e.g., Feige et. al. [6]). We prove this formally in lemma3. We next show that the problem of maximizing the expected, over the randomness of values, revenue is APX-hard, and therefore does not admit a PTAS unless P=NP, which justifies the search for constant factor approximations to the problem in later sections. The reduction is from a special case of set buying, which we call the *prize collecting set cover problem* (PCSCP).

DEFINITION 2. *A set buying instance is specified by a set of elements U and a collection $\mathcal{F}$ of subsets of U. There is a non-negative cost $c(S)$ associated with each set $S \in \mathcal{F}$, and a non-negative value $v(u)$ associated with each element $u \in U$. The problem to pick some subsets $\mathcal{S} \subseteq \mathcal{F}$ to maximize the value of the elements covered by those sets minus the total cost of those sets, that is $\sum_{u \in Span(\mathcal{S})} v(u) - \sum_{S \in \mathcal{S}} c(S)$, where $Span(\mathcal{S}) = \cup_{S \in \mathcal{S}} S$.*

THEOREM 2 (FEIGE ET AL [6]). *It is NP-hard to approximate the set-buying problem to within a linear factor.*

LEMMA 3. *The optimal auction with step-function externalities is NP-hard to approximate to within a linear factor on every instantiation of values.*

PROOF. For any instance $\mathcal{I} = (U, \mathcal{S})$ of the set-buying problem we construct a bipartite graph $G_{\mathcal{I}} = ((L, R), E)$ with a vertex $l_u \in L$ for each $u \in U$ and a vertex $r_S \in R$ for each $S \in \mathcal{F}$. We introduce an edge $(l_u, r_S) \in E$ for any element u and set S such that $u \in S$.

Consider an instance $\mathcal{I}$ and social network defined by the corresponding bipartite graph $G_{\mathcal{I}}$. Let the type of bidder l_u be $v(u)$ with probability 1 and the type of bidder r_S be $-c(S)$ with probability 1. Note these point mass distributions are in fact regular, and furthermore a subset of bidders with maximum sum of virtual values directly corresponds to an optimal solution to the set-buying instance. The first claim follows from the inapproximability of set buying. □

The PCSCP is a special case of set buying problem in which all set and all elements have equal costs and values, respectively. We first give an approximation preserving reduction from PCSCP to our problem, and then prove that PCSCP is APX-hard, which using the approximation preserving reduction implies the APX-hardness of our problem.

DEFINITION 3. *In the prize collecting set cover problem, there is a collection of n sets $\{S_1, S_2, \ldots, S_n\}$ over a universe U. For a collection C of sets, let $Q_C = \cup_{i \in C} S_i$. The goal is to find a collection C^* that maximizes $\alpha|Q_{C^*}| + n - |C^*|$ for some $\alpha > 0$.*

Note that this is equivalent to maximizing the value of covered elements plus the cost of unused sets. While this is equivalent, in optimality, to maximizing the value of covered elements minus the cost of the used sets, the two problems differ in approximability. The PCSCP is easier to approximate: there is a $e/(e+1)$-approximation for it. On the other hand, set-buying is not approximable to within a linear factor. We will show an approximation-preserving reduction from PCSCP to our problem and then give an $e/(e+1)$-approximation for our problem.

LEMMA 4. *There is an approximation preserving reduction from the prize collecting set cover problem to our problem.*

PROOF. Given an instance of the prize collecting set cover problem, where the sets are denoted $\{S_1, S_2, \ldots, S_n\}$ and the elements are denoted $e_1, e_2, \ldots, e_m$, we construct a graph where there is a vertex for each set and each element, and an edge between S_i and e_j if $e_j \in S_i$. For each element e_j, the value is deterministic α. Let $L \gg mn\alpha$. For each set S_i, the valuation follows distribution Bernoulli$(L, 1/L)$, so that the virtual valuation is -1 w.p. $1 - 1/L$ and $(L-1)$ w.p. $1/L$.

To compute the revenue, we let $L \to \infty$. There are two events:

1. If at least one set has positive virtual valuation (which happens w.p. approximately $n/L \to 0$), the solution chooses all such sets to obtain expected revenue n. The expected revenue from the remaining nodes (sets with negative virtual valuation and elements) is at most $\alpha m/L \ll 1$. Therefore, the optimal solution has contribution n from this event as $L \to \infty$, and this solution is trivial to compute.

2. If no set has positive virtual valuation (which happens w.p. $1-n/L \to 1$), the value of the solution is precisely $\alpha|Q_{C^*}| - |C^*|$, and this is the contribution from this event.

Therefore, the value of the optimal revenue solution is $\alpha|Q_{C^*}| + n - |C^*|$ as $L \to \infty$, and this completes the reduction. □

THEOREM 5. *The prize collecting set cover problem (PCSCP) is* APX*-complete.*

PROOF. We start with a 4-regular graph. On such a graph with $n = 152k$ nodes, for any $\epsilon > 0$, it is NP-HARD to decide if there is an independent set of size at least $(74-\epsilon)k$ or at most $(73+\epsilon)k$.

Given this graph, construct the following prize collecting set cover instance: There is a set for every vertex, and an element for every edge. α is set to $1/3$. It is easy to check that any feasible solution will correspond to choosing an independent set of vertices, and the incident edges. The goal becomes to maximize $\frac{1}{3}(3n+I)$, where I is the size of an independent set. Therefore, the optimal solution has value $(530-\epsilon)k/3$, and it is NP-HARD to find a solution of value $(529+\epsilon)k/3$, so that the approximation ratio is at least $\frac{530}{529} \approx 1.002$. □

COROLLARY 6. *The problem of maximizing the expected revenue is APX-hard.*

4. STEP-FUNCTION EXTERNALITIES

Although the optimal auction is NP-hard to compute and NP-hard to approximate on *every* instantiation of values, it is in fact easy to approximate on average. The following very simple allocation function has expected revenue within a factor $1/2$ of the optimal expected revenue. In Appendix A, we show that this can be generalized to a $(1/4)$-approximation for the limited-supply setting.

> Divide vertices into two sets S_0 and S_1 such that each vertex $i \in S_0$ (respectively S_1) has a neighbor in the opposing set S_1 (respectively S_0). Note that this can be done efficiently, e.g. by computing a spanning tree of G and considering an arbitrary 2-coloring of it. Suppose S_0 has higher expected positive virtual value, that is,
>
> $$\sum_{i \in S_0} E[\max(\phi_i(v_i), 0)] \geq \sum_{i \in S_1} E[\max(\phi_i(v_i), 0)].$$
>
> Let $S_0^+ = \{i \in S : \phi(v_i) \geq 0\}$ be the bidders with positive virtual value in set S_0 for a particular instantiation of values. Then give a copy of the good to every bidder $i \in S_0^+ \cup S_1$.[1]

To see that this is a $(1/2)$-approximation, note that the expected optimum revenue is at most $\sum_i E[\max(\phi_i(v_i), 0)]$ since at best an auction can extract $\phi_i(v_i)$ from all bidders i with positive virtual value. The above strategy gets expected revenue $\sum_{i \in S_0^+} E[\max(\phi_i(v_i), 0)]$ from the bidders in S_0^+, which is at least half the optimum expected revenue by linearity of expectation and our choice of S_0. Although a copy of the good is always given to any $i \in S_1$, i is not always satisfied. In particular, for i to be satisfied it needs to have a neighbor in $S_0^+ \cup S_1$. But note that i's expected allocation is independent of its value, i.e., we have $x_i(v_i) = x_i$ for some constant x_i. As a result, the revenue from i is $E[x_i\phi_i(v_i)] = x_i E[\phi_i(v_i)]$. Thus, since the expected virtual value of any bidder is non-negative (see Fact 1), the expected revenue of bidders in S_1 is non-negative.

Further note that this analysis is tight, as shown by the simple example of a single edge whose endpoints have value 1 with probability p and 0 with probability $1-p$ for some $0 < p < 1$. Then the virtual value is 1 with probability p and $\frac{-p}{1-p}$ with probability $1-p$. Consider the strategy in which we allocate both nodes when at least one of them has positive value. The value that we get is $2p^2 + 2p(1-p)(1 + \frac{-p}{1-p}) = 2p^2 + 2p(1-2p) = 2p - 2p^2$. The $(1/2)$-approximation algorithm described above gets expected value p. The ratio of the algorithm's solution to the given strategy goes to $1/2$ as $p \to 0$.

There are two reasons why this simple algorithm can not guarantee better than a 0.5-approximation of the optimum solution. First, the current upper bound that we are using is quite loose. Second, the current algorithm gives the good to a bidder solely based on that bidders value, without considering the values of its neighbors. We can generalize this algorithm to a broader class of *threshold strategies* in which,

[1]A plausibly more natural strategy would be to select set S_0 based on the instantiation of the virtual values rather than their expectation. Such a strategy is still monotone, but bounding its revenue is more complex since the virtual value of S_1 conditional on the selection is now less than zero.

there exists a threshold assigned to each player and he receives the item when his value passes that threshold. Note that the simple algorithm falls in that class since each player is either assigned the threshold of zero, or $\phi^{-1}(0)$. We show in the full version that no threshold strategy can have better than 0.5 approximation.

In order to improve this approximation ratio, we need to leverage detailed knowledge of the graph structure. In the remainder of this section, we present a linear-programming-based approach that gets a 0.73-approximation for general distributions. In the full version, we also provide a simple greedy-based algorithm that gets this same approximation ratio.

4.1 Linear Program

As discussed above, the main hurdle in the analysis of the simple auction schemes was the loose upper bound on the optimal expected revenue. In this section, we significantly improve the upper bound using linear programs whose constraints characterize the feasible allocation rules. We then use these LPs to bound the expected revenue of an LP-based auction. As a result, we are able to get a better approximation ratio and also generalize the setting to non-identical distributions.

Recall that for each profile of types v with virtual valuation functions $\{\phi_i(\cdot)\}$, the optimal revenue is equal to the maximum sum of virtual values among feasible allocations. In step-function externalities, an allocation $x(\cdot)$ is feasible if each vertex i with $x_i(v) = 1$ had a neighbor j with $x_j(v) = 1$. Hence we can write the following LP relaxation of the optimum revenue:

$$\begin{aligned} \max_x \quad & \textstyle\sum_i x_i(v)\phi_i(v_i) && (1)\\ s.t. \quad & x_i(v) \le \textstyle\sum_{j\in N(i)} x_j(v) && \forall i\\ & 0 \le x_i(v) \le 1 && \forall i. \end{aligned}$$

Each instantiation of types induces one such LP. As discussed in Section 3, given the instantiation of types, our problem is more general than the set-buying problem studied in Feige et. al. [6] whose LP-relaxation is shown to have linear gap. Hence the LP value might seem like a very loose upper bound. However, recall that we only require our auction to have close-to-optimal revenue *on average*. In other words, we need a rounding scheme whose expected value, over the distribution of LPs induced by the type distributions, is close to the expected value of the LPs. Thus we can perform poorly on hard instances so long as we do well on average, and so LPs with linear worst-case integrality gaps might still be useful in designing an LP-based auction with constant approximation ratios.

4.2 Auction Scheme

We present an LP-based auction whose expected value is within a constant factor of the expected LP value. Note the LP gets positive contributions from two types of nodes: those with positive virtual value who also have a neighbor with positive virtual value, and those with positive virtual value whose neighbors all have negative virtual value. Our auction first estimates the relative contributions of these two types and then tailors its strategy accordingly. In the extremes, where one type contributes most of the revenue, a simple deterministic scheme has a good approximation. When the contributions are more-or-less equal, we use a randomized rounding of the LP solution.

To define the auction, we first introduce some notation to capture the LP contribution from the types discussed above. For an instantiation of values v, let $x_i^*(v)$ be the optimum LP value of variable $x_i^*(v)$. Recall that the LP for any instantiation v bounds the optimal revenue for that instantiation and hence the optimal expected revenue is at most $E_v[\max_x \sum_i x_i(v)\phi_i(v_i)] = E_v[\sum_i x_i^*(v)\phi_i(v_i)]$. Fix a player i and define the following events:

- P_i^+ is the event that $\phi_i(v_i) \ge 0$ and there exists $j \in N(i)$ such that $\phi_j(v_j) \ge 0$.
- P_i^- is the event that $\phi_i(v_i) \ge 0$ and all neighbors of i have negative virtual value.
- N_i is the event that $\phi_i(v_i) < 0$.

Observe that the expected revenue of the optimum allocation from agent i can be written as

$$\begin{aligned} E_v[x_i^*(v)\phi_i(v_i)] &= E_v[x_i^*(v)\phi_i(v_i)|P_i^+]Pr(P_i^+)\\ &\quad + E_v[x_i^*(v)\phi_i(v_i)|N_i]Pr(N_i)\\ &\quad + E_v[x_i^*(v)\phi_i(v_i)|P_i^-]Pr(P_i^-) \end{aligned}$$

Define

$$A_i^* = E_v[x_i^*(v)\phi_i(v_i)|P_i^-]Pr(P_i^-),$$

$$B_i^* = E_v[x_i^*(v)\phi_i(v_i)|P_i^+]Pr(P_i^+),$$

and

$$C_i^* = E_v[x_i^*(v)\phi_i(v_i)|N_i]Pr(N_i)$$

(note C_i^* is negative). The auction works as follows.

> **LP-Based Auction.** Compute $A^* = \sum_i A_i^*$, $B^* = \sum_i B_i^*$, and $C^* = \sum_i C_i^*$, where the expectation is computed via sampling, and let $R = (1-1/e)A^* + B^* + C^*$. Solve LP 1 for the instantion of types v and let x^* be an optimal solution. If
>
> - $A^* \ge \max(B^*, R)$, allocate to all the nodes i for which $\phi_i(v_i) \ge 0$ as well as all nodes i for which N_i happens *and* the LP value $x_i^*(v) > 0$,
> - else if $B^* \ge \max(A^*, R)$, allocate to all the nodes for which P_i^+ happens.
>
> Otherwise
>
> 1. For each i with $\phi_i(v_i) < 0$, give i a copy of the good with probability $x_i^*(v)$.
> 2. For each i with $\phi_i(v_i) \ge 0$, give i a copy of the good if it has a neighbor j that either
>   (a) has non-negative virtual value $\phi_j(j) \ge 0$, or
>   (b) has negative virtual value $\phi_j(j) < 0$ and received a copy of the good in step 1.

4.3 Analysis

The proof of the approximation guarantee requires two technical lemmas that appear at the end of this section. The first lemma shows that the contribution of a node i when P_i^+ happens outweighs his contribution when N happens (for reasonable allocation rules). The second lemma provides the key argument for the analysis of the randomized rounding step: the LP constraints corresponding to an agent i with positive virtual value must be tight in an optimal solution $x^*(v)$. Namely, $x_i^*(v) = \min(1, \sum_{j \in N(i)} x_j^*(v))$. Hence to round and get constant contribution from these agents, we can round the nodes with negative virtual value with probability equal to their LP values and then round nodes with positive virtual value to one if some neighbor was rounded to one. To bound the expected allocation of such an agent i in the rounding, we note that in the worst-case all neighbors of i have negative virtual value. However, even in this case, i is allocated so long as at least one $j \in N(i)$ receives the good. This happens with probability x_j^* for neighbor j and so the allocation probability of i from the rounding scheme is at least $1 - \prod_{j \in N(i)}(1 - x_j^*)$. This is within a $(1 - 1/e)$ fraction of x_i^*.

THEOREM 7. *The LP-based auction is a $e/(e+1) \approx 0.73$ approximation.*

PROOF. For an instantiation of values v, let $x_i(v)$ be the expected allocation of i (over the randomization of the auction). Correspondingly, define A_i, B_i, C_i and A, B, C for the auction's allocation function as we did for the LP. There are three cases.

If $B^* \geq \max(A^*, R)$, then $x_i(v) \in \{0, 1\}$ and is 1 only for those i for which P_i^+ happens. In the LP, $x_i^*(v)$ also equals 1 for all such i and hence the revenue of the auction $B = B^*$.

If $A^* \geq \max(B^*, R)$, then $x_i(v) = 1$ for all i for which $\phi_i(v_i) \geq 0$ so $A \geq A^*$. Lemma 8 further shows that $B + C \geq 0$ and so the total revenue of the auction is at least $A \geq A^*$.

Finally, if $R \geq \max(A^*, B^*)$, then Lemma 9 shows $A \geq (1 - 1/e)A^*$. Furthermore, from the construction of x we see that conditioned on P^+ and N, x and x^* are equal so $B + C = B^* + C^*$. Therefore the total revenue of the auction is at least $(1 - 1/e)A^* + B^* + C^*$

The optimal expected revenue is at most $A^* + B^* + C^*$, and so the approximation ratio of the auction is at least

$$\min \frac{\max(A^*, B^*, (1 - 1/e)A^* + B^* + C^*)}{A^* + B^* + C^*}.$$

For computing the above minimum, normalize $A^* = 1$ and suppose $B^* = x$ and $B^* + C^* = rx$ for $0 \leq r \leq 1$ (such r exists since $B^* + C^* \geq 0$ by Lemma 8 and $C^* \leq 0$). Thus we want to compute the minimum of $\max(1, x, 1 - 1/e + xr)/(1 + xr)$ where $0 \leq r \leq 1$. We can do a case analysis on the maximum:

1. $xr \leq 1/e$. Then, we are minimizing $\max(1, x)/(1 + xr)$. We can set $xr = 1/e$, so that the lowest possible value is $e/(e+1)$.

2. $xr \geq 1/e$ and $x(1 - r) \leq 1 - 1/e$. Then we have $(1 - 1/e + xr)/(1 + xr)$. Setting $xr = 1/e$ implies $e/(e+1)$.

3. $x \geq 1$ and $x(1 - r) \geq 1 - 1/e$. Then we have $x/(1 + xr)$. But $xr \leq x + 1/e - 1$, so that we are minimizing $x/(x + 1/e)$ for $x \geq 1$, so that we again have $e/(e+1)$.

Thus the approximation ratio is $e/(e+1) \approx 0.73$. □

LEMMA 8. *For any monotone non-decreasing allocation function x that allocates to nodes i with $\phi_i(v_i) < 0$ only if there is a neighbor j with $\phi_j(v_j) \geq 0$, and corresponding B, C, we have $B - C \geq 0$.*

PROOF. We prove the inequality for each node i separately. Let $N(i)$ be the neighborhood of i and note that:

$$\begin{aligned}
B_i - C_i &= E_{v_i}[x_i(v_i)\phi_i(v_i)|P^+]Pr(P^+) \\
&\quad + E_{v_i}[x_i(v_i)\phi_i(v_i)|N]Pr(N) \\
&= E_{v_i}[x_i(v_i)\phi_i(v_i)|P^+]Pr(P^+) \\
&\quad + (E_{v_i}[x_i(v_i)\phi_i(v_i)|N, \exists j \in N(i), \phi_j(v_j) \geq 0] \\
&\quad \cdot Pr(\exists j \in N(i), \phi_j(v_j) \geq 0)Pr(N) \\
&\quad + E_{v_i}[x_i(v_i)\phi_i(v_i)|N, \forall j \in N(i), \phi_j(v_j) < 0] \\
&\quad \cdot Pr(\forall j \in N(i), \phi_j(v_j) < 0))Pr(N).
\end{aligned}$$

But by assumption conditioned on N and the event $[\forall j \in N(i), \phi_j(v_j) < 0]$, $x_i^*(v_i) = 0$, and therefore, letting E be the event $[\exists j \in N(i), \phi_j(v_j) \geq 0]$, we have

$$\begin{aligned}
B - C &= E_{v_i}[x_i(v_i)\phi_i(v_i)|P^+]Pr(\phi_i(v_i) \geq 0)\Pr(E) \\
&\quad + E_{v_i}[x_i(v_i)\phi_i(v_i)|N, E]\Pr(N)\Pr(E) \\
&= (E_{v_i}[x_i^*(v_i)\phi_i(v_i)|P^+, E]Pr(\phi_i(v_i) \geq 0) \\
&\quad + E_{v_i}[x_i^*(v_i)\phi_i(v_i)|N, E]Pr(N))\Pr(E) \\
&= E_{v_i}[x_i^*(v_i)\phi_i(v_i)|E]\Pr(E) \\
&\geq 0,
\end{aligned}$$

where the second equality follows because the event P_i^+ implies event E and the last inequality follows because $x^*(v_i)$ is a monotone non-decreasing function of v_i as $\phi(\cdot)$ is regular and also that $E_{v_i}[\phi_i(v_i)] = 0$ (see Fact 1). □

LEMMA 9. *If $R \geq \max(A^*, B^*)$, then $A \geq (1 - 1/e)A^*$.*

PROOF. First note that conditioned on event P^-, we have $x_i^*(v) = \min(1, \sum_{j \in N(i)} x_j^*(v))$, and $x_i(v) = 1 - \prod_{j \in N(i)}(1 - x_j^*(v))$. Let $y = \sum_{j \in N(i)} x_j^*(v)$ and $d = |N(i)|$. Fixing the value of $\sum_{j \in N(i)} x_j^*(v)$, the minimum of $1 - \prod_{j \in N(i)}(1 - x_j^*(v))$ happens when all the variables are equal, in which case we have $x_i(v) = 1 - (1 - \frac{y}{d})^d \geq 1 - \frac{1}{e^y}$. Thus when $y \leq 1$, we have $x_i^*(v) = y$ and so $\frac{x_i(v)}{x_i^*(v)}$ is at least $\frac{1 - e^{-y}}{y}$, whose minimum value is equal to $1 - \frac{1}{e}$. When $y \geq 1$, we have $x_i^*(v) = 1$ and so $\frac{x_i(v)}{x_i^*(v)}$ is at least $1 - e^{-y}$, whose minimum value is again $1 - \frac{1}{e}$. Therefore we have

$$\begin{aligned}
A_i &= E_{v_i}[x_i(v_i)\phi_i(v_i)|P^-]Pr(P^-) \\
&\geq (1 - \frac{1}{e})E_{v_i}[x_i^*(v_i)\phi_i(v_i)|P^-]Pr(P^-) \\
&= (1 - \frac{1}{e})B_i^*
\end{aligned}$$

Summing over i yields the result. □

4.4 Integrality Gap

We now prove that the above LP has integrality gap at most 0.828. This means that we can not use the LP solutions as an upper bound in order to get approximation guarantees better than 0.828. We show the gap by proving the gap on the analogous LP for the PCSCP, which using the reduction in lemma 3 implies the gap on the original LP.

THEOREM 10. *The above LP has integrality gap at most 0.828.*

PROOF. We construct an LP gap instance for the prize collecting set cover problem. In our instance, the input is a graph; the sets are vertices and the elements are edges, so that each edge is present in the sets corresponding to its incident vertices. For an n-vertex graph, the goal is to choose a subset X of vertices to maximize $\alpha|E(X)|+n-|X|$, where $E(X)$ is the subset of edges incident to some vertex in X.

The LP has a variable x_e for each edge, which is 1 if the edge is selected in the event that all vertices in the graph have negative virtual valuation. Similarly, y_v is the variable denoting whether vertex v is selected in the same event. The LP can be reformulated as:

$$\text{Maximize} \quad n - \sum_v y_v + \alpha \sum_e x_e$$

$$\begin{array}{rcll} x_e & \leq & y_u + y_v & \forall e = (u,v) \in E \\ x_e, y_u & \in & [0,1] & \forall e \in E, u \in V \end{array}$$

Consider a complete graph on n vertices, for large n. By appropriate scaling, let us rewrite the objective as $|E(X)| + \alpha n(n - |X|)$. Set all $y_v = 1$ and $x_e = 1/2$. For this fractional solution, the objective is approximately $n^2(1+\alpha)/2$. Suppose the optimal integer solution chooses k vertices and all incident edges. Its value is approximately $nk - k^2/2 + \alpha n(n-k)$. Optimizing over k, we obtain $k = n(1-\alpha)$, so that the optimal value is $n^2(1+\alpha^2)/2$. The ratio is therefore $(1+\alpha^2)/(1+\alpha)$, so that $\alpha = \sqrt{2}-1$. This yields a ratio of $2(\sqrt{2}-1) = 0.828$. □

5. SUBMODULAR EXTERNALITIES

In order to design an approximately optimal mechanism for the more general problem with submodular externalities, we identify a set of mechanisms, called *influence-and-exploit* mechanisms. In the following, we first show that a simple random-sapling mechanism which belongs to this category of mechanisms achieves a 0.25-approximate mechanism for this problem. Then, we focus on optimizing over these mechanisms and design improved approximation algorithms for this problem. We start by defining influence and exploit-mechanisms:

DEFINITION 4. *Let S be a set of users, called the influence set. For a fixed price p and any set of players S, define the Influence-and-Exploit Mechanism $IE(S)$ as follows. Give the item to any $i \in V \backslash S$ regardless of its value. Give the item to any $i \in S$ if his value is more than the threshold p.*

5.1 Constant Approximation

First, we observe that a simple IE mechanism gives a 0.25-approximation to the optimal revenue for the setting of single-parameter submodular externalities. Consider the following algorithm:

- Let S be a random subset of bidders where each $i \in S$ is chosen independently with probability $\frac{1}{2}$.
- *Influence:* Give the good to all $i \in V \setminus S$ regardless of the value.
- *Exploit:* Give the good to a bidder $j \in S$ if $v_j \geq p_j(S)$, where $p_j(S) = \phi_j^{-1}(0)$ is the inverse virtual value of zero for the distribution $F_{j,S}$, where $F_{j,S}(p) = Pr_{v_j \in F_j}(v_j g_j(S)) \leq p)$.

In order to prove the approximation guarantee, we make use of the following lemma.

LEMMA 11 ([7]). *For a ground set V, Let $f : 2^V \rightarrow \Re$ be a monotone submodular set function. Form set S by picking elements $i \in V$ independently at random with some fixed probability p. Then*

$$\mathbf{E}[f(S)] \geq p\mathbf{E}[f(V)]$$

Now define the *revenue function* $R_i(S) = \max_p p(1 - F_{i,S}(p))$. We first prove that $\sum_i R_i(V)$ is an upper bound on the revenue of any mechanism.

LEMMA 12. *The expected revenue of any truthful mechanism is at most $\sum_i R_i(V)$.*

PROOF. Recall that we normalized $g_i(V) = 1$. As a result, $F_{i,V}(p) = F_i(p)$. So by definition $R_i(V) = \max_p p(1 - F(p))$. Consider any mechanism with allocation function $x_i(v_i) \leq 1$. By Myerson's characterization, the expected revenue of the mechanism is

$$\begin{aligned} \sum_i E_{v_i}[x_i(v_i)\phi_i(v_i)] &\leq \sum_i E[\max(0, \phi_i(v_i))] \\ &= \int_{\phi^{-1}(0)}^{\infty} \phi_i(x) f(x) dx \\ &= \int_{\phi^{-1}(0)}^{\infty} (x f(x) - (1 - F(x))) dx \\ &= -x(1-F(x))|_{\phi^{-1}(0)}^{\infty} \\ &= p_i(S)(1 - F_{i,S}(p_i(S))) \\ &= R_i(V). \end{aligned}$$

□

LEMMA 13. *If the revenue function is submodular for all agents, then the above mechanism is a 4-approximation of the optimal mechanism.*

PROOF. Consider any agent i. With probability 1/2, it chosen to be in S. Fixing the set S, the expected revenue we get from i is $R_i(S) = p_i(S)(1 - F_{i,S}(p_i(S)))$. Now note that each agent is independently sampled, so over the random choices of the mechanism, and by submodularity of $R_i(S)$, the expected revenue from i (conditioned on being in S) is at least $R_i(V)/2$. Since we get this revenue with probability 1/2, the expected revenue from i is at least $R_i(V)/4$. This gives a 4-approximation. □

Similar to [11], we may simply assume that the revenue function R_i is monotone and submodular for each bidder, and indeed our result holds for any settings that induce monotone submodular revenue functions. Interestingly, for the single-parameter submodular setting, the submodularity of the revenue function follows from the submodularity of the local influence function.

LEMMA 14. *The revenue function is submodular for the single-parameter submodular externality setting and the concave externality setting.*

PROOF. Consider a player i with distribution F_i over v_i. Then

$$\begin{aligned} R_i(S) &= \max_p p(1 - F_{i,S}(p)) \\ &= \max_p p(1 - F_i(p/g(S))) \\ &= g(S) \max_{p'} p'(1 - F(p')) \end{aligned}$$

where $p' = p/g(S)$. Submodularity of $R_i(.)$ then follows directly from submodularity of $g(.)$. $\square$

Applying the above two lemmas, we conclude that the following:

THEOREM 15. *There exists a $\frac{1}{4}$-approximate IE mechanism to the optimum revenue in the single-parameter submodular externality model, and thus in the concave externality model.*

5.2 Optimizing over IE Mechanisms

Now that we proved that IE mechanisms achieve constant-factor approximation to the optimal revenue, it would be interesting to optimize among IE mechanisms. To do so we need to find a set $V \setminus S$ of initial (influential) bidders to get the item regardless of their value, and then exploit the remaining bidders S by setting optimal thresholds as above. Let $x_S(v)$ be the outcome of this strategy, that is, $x_{i,S}(v) = 1$ if the item is given to i for the profile of types v in IE(S). Let $\Phi(S)$ be the expected revenue of IE(S). Our goal is to find a subset S of bidders that maximizes $\Phi(S)$. We do so by arguing that $\Phi(S)$ is a (not necessarily monotone) submodular function and then using submodular function maximization results. We present the results in this section with regard to concave externalities in order to keep notation simple; the results extend easily to the more general submodular externalities. We first characterize the expected revenue of any IE strategy.

LEMMA 16. *Let $X_{i,S}(v) = |\{j \in N(i) : \chi_j(v) = 1\}|$. Then the expected revenue of any IE strategy, IE(S), for each $i \in S$ is equal to $p(1 - F_i(p))E_v[h(X_{i,S}(v))]$ where $h(\cdot)$ is the concave function defining the externality (i.e., $g_i(o) = o_i \cdot h(|\{j \in N(i) : o_j = 1\}|)$).*

PROOF. Consider IE(S) with allocation function x and outcome function χ. By Myerson's characterization, we can write the expected revenue of i in IE(S) as

$$\begin{aligned} E_v[x_i(v)\phi_i(v_i)] &= E_v[g_i(\chi(v))\phi_i(v)] \\ &= E_v[\chi_i(v)h(X_{i,S}(v))\phi_i(v)]. \end{aligned}$$

Note in any IE strategy, $\chi_i(v)$ and $\chi_j(v)$ are independent random variables (when v is drawn from F) for any $i \neq j$. Thus $\chi_i(v)$ is also independent from $X_{i,S}(v)$. So we can write the revenue of i as $E[h(X_{i,S}(v))]E[\chi_i(v)\phi_i(v_i)]$. Since we set $\chi_i(v_i) = 1$ when $\phi(v_i) \geq 0$, $E[\chi_i(v)\phi(v_i)]$ is equal to the optimum revenue from distribution F_i, which is equal to $p(1 - F(p))$. $\square$

We next prove the key structural property of the revenue function $\Phi(S)$ for IE mechanisms, namely that it is submodular.

LEMMA 17. *The set function Φ is a non-negative submodular function of S.*

PROOF. First note that each agent $i \in V \backslash S$ contributes 0 to the revenue, and each $i \in S$ contributes

$$p(1 - F(p))E_v[g(X_{i,S}(v))],$$

where $X_{i,S}(v)$ is a random variable denoting the number of i's neighbors that are given the item to at profile v, that is $X_{i,S}(v) = \sum_{j \in N(i)} x_{i,S}(v)$. For all i, S, let $F_{i,S}$ be the distribution (with density function $f_{i,S}$) of $X_{i,S}(v)$ when v is drawn from the joint distribution of types. We show submodularity of $\Phi(.)$ by proving submodularity of all $\Phi_i(.)$ for all i, that is $\Phi_i(S \cup \{j\}) - \Phi_i(S) \leq \Phi_i(S' \cup \{j\}) - \Phi_i(S')$, for all $S' \subseteq S$ and all i and j. Submodularity of $\Phi(.)$ follows from submodularity of $\Phi_i(.)$'s, since $\Phi(S) = \sum_{i \notin S} \Phi_i(S)$, and First note that if i is not a neighbor of j, then we have $0 = \Phi_i(S \cup \{j\}) - \Phi_i(S) \leq \Phi_i(S' \cup \{j\}) - \Phi_i(S') = 0$. Now assume that i is a neighbor of j. Define $\Phi = \Phi_i(S \cup \{j\}) - \Phi_i(S)$. Now we have

$$\begin{aligned} \Phi &= p(1 - F(p))(E_v[g(X_{i,S\cup\{j\}}(v))] - E_v[g(X_{i,S}(v))]) \\ &= p(1 - F(p))(E_{k \sim F_{i,S\cup\{j\}}}[g(k)] - E_{k \sim F_{i,S}}[g(k)]) \\ &= p(1 - F(p)) \sum_k g(k)(f_{i,S\cup\{j\}}(k) - f_{i,S}(k)) \end{aligned}$$

Note that we can write $f_{i,S\cup\{j\}}(k) = F(p)f_{i,S}(k+1) + (1 - F(p))f_{i,S}(k)$. As a result,

$$\begin{aligned} \Phi &= p(1 - F(p))F(p) \sum_k g(k)(f_{i,S}(k+1) - f_{i,S}(k)) \\ &= p(1 - F(p))F(p) \sum_k f_{i,S}(k)(g(k-1) - g(k)) \end{aligned}$$

Now recall that g is a concave function of k. As a result, $G(k) = g(k-1) - g(k)$ is a non-decreasing function of k. Therefore,

$$\begin{aligned} & \Phi_i(S' \cup \{j\}) - \Phi_i(S') - (\Phi_i(S \cup \{j\}) - \Phi_i(S)) \\ &= p(1 - F(p))F(p) \sum_k G(k)(f_{i,S'}(k) - f_{i,S}(k)) \\ &= p(1 - F(p))F(p) \sum_k G(k)(F_{i,S'}(k) - \\ & \quad F_{i,S'}(k-1) - (F_{i,S}(k) - F_{i,S}(k-1))) \\ &= p(1 - F(p))F(p) \\ & \quad \cdot \sum_k (F_{i,S'}(k) - F_{i,S}(k))(G(k) - G(k+1)) \end{aligned}$$

Note that for $S' \supset S$, $F_{i,S'}(k) \geq F_{i,S}(k)$, and therefore $F_{i,S'}(k) - F_{i,S}(k) \geq 0$ for all k. Also, Since G is a non-decreasing function, $G(k) - G(k+1) \leq 0$.

It only remains to consider the revenue function of j when we add j to sets. If For S such that $j \notin S$, we have

$$\Phi_j(S \cup \{j\}) - \Phi_j(S) = p(1 - F(p))E_v[g(X_{j,S}(v))]$$

Again, note that for $S' \supset S$, $F_{j,S}(k) \leq F_{j,S'}(k)$, therefore

$$\begin{aligned} E_{F_{j,S'}}[g(k)] &- E_{F_{j,S}}[g(k)] \\ &= \sum_k g(k)(f_{j,S'}(k) - f_{j,S}(k)) \\ &= \sum_k (F_{j,S'}(k) - F_{j,S}(k)) \\ & \quad \cdot (g(k) - g(k+1)) \leq 0 \end{aligned}$$

$\square$

Function $\Phi(.)$ as described above is non-negative and submodular, but not necessarily monotone. In order to obtain a constant-factor approximation for maximizing over IE mechanisms, we can simply apply non-monotone submodular maximization algorithms for this problem [7, 8]. For example, the following simple local search algorithm gives a 0.33-approximation to this problem[7]: (i) Let $S = \{v | v = \text{argmax} max_{i \in V}(\Phi(\{i\})\}$, and (ii) at each step either add or remove a bidder i from S if this adding or removing increases the value of $\Phi(S)$ be a $1+\frac{\epsilon}{n}$ factor, (ii) After reaching a local optimal L, output the better of L and $\bar{L}$. The above simple algorithm achieves 0.33-approximation for the problem of maximizing over IE strategies. One can apply a recently-developed randomized local search algorithm [8] to achieve a 0.41-approximation for this problem.

6. REFERENCES

[1] G. Aggarwal, J. Feldman, S. Muthukrishnan, and M. Pál. Sponsored search auctions with markovian users. In *WINE*, pages 621–628, 2008.

[2] H. Akhlaghpour, M. Ghodsi, N. Haghpanah, V. S. Mirrokni, H. Mahini, and A. Nikzad. Optimal iterative pricing over social networks (extended abstract). In *WINE*, pages 415–423, 2010.

[3] N. Anari, S. Ehsani, M. Ghodsi, N. Haghpanah, N. Immorlica, H. Mahini, and V. S. Mirrokni. Equilibrium pricing with positive externalities (extended abstract). In *WINE*, pages 424–431, 2010.

[4] S. Athey and G. Ellison. Position auctions with consumer search. Forthcoming, Quarterly Journal of Economics, 2010.

[5] O. Candogan, K. Bimpikis, and A. E. Ozdaglar. Optimal pricing in the presence of local network effects. In *WINE*, pages 118–132, 2010.

[6] U. Feige, N. Immorlica, V. S. Mirrokni, and H. Nazerzadeh. Pass approximation. In *APPROX-RANDOM*, pages 111–124, 2009.

[7] U. Feige, V. S. Mirrokni, and J. Vondrak. Maximizing non-monotone submodular functions. In *FOCS '07*, pages 461–471, Washington, DC, USA, 2007. IEEE Computer Society.

[8] S. O. Gharan and J. Vondrak. Submodular maximization by simulated annealing. In *SODA*, 2011.

[9] I. Giotis and A. R. Karlin. On the equilibria and efficiency of the gsp mechanism in keyword auctions with externalities. In *WINE*, pages 629–638, 2008.

[10] R. Gomes, N. Immorlica, and V. Markakis. Externalities in keyword auctions: an empirical and theoretical assessment. In *WINE'09*, 2009.

[11] J. D. Hartline, V. S. Mirrokni, and M. Sundararajan. Optimal marketing strategies over social networks. In *WWW*, pages 189–198, 2008.

[12] P. Jehiel, B. Moldovanu, and E. Stacchetti. How (not) to sell nuclear weapons. *American Economic Review*, 86(4):814–829, 1996.

[13] P. Jeziorski and I. Segal. What makes them click: Empirical analysis of consumer demand for internet search advertising. working paper, 2009.

[14] D. Kempe and M. Mahdian. A cascade model for externalities in sponsored search. In *WINE*, pages 585–596, 2008.

[15] R. Myerson. Optimal auction design. *Mathematics of Operations Research*, pages 58–73, 1981.

[16] J. Rohlfs. A theory of interdependent demand for a communications service. *The Bell Journal of Economics and Management Science*, 5(1):16–37, 1974.

APPENDIX

A. LIMITED-SUPPLY SETTING

THEOREM 18. *There is a (1/4)-approximate auction for the limited-supply setting.*

PROOF. Suppose that the auctioneer has k copies of the good. Compute a spanning tree of the social network and color the nodes red and blue such that each red node has a blue neighbor in the spanning tree (and vice versa). Pick a color uniformly at random and name the nodes of this color S_1 and nodes of the other color S_2. Allocate to the $k/2$ highest positive virtual values in S_1, and their neighbors in S_2 to ensure feasibility. We now compute the expected virtual value of this allocation for the red nodes. We condition on the event E that the red nodes were chosen to be set S_1.

$$\begin{aligned}
E_v[\sum_{i \text{ red}} x_i(v)\phi_i(v_i)] &= E_v[\sum_{i \text{ red}} x_i(v)\phi_i(v_i)|E]\Pr[E] \\
&\quad + E_v[\sum_{i \text{ red}} x_i(v)\phi_i(v_i)|\overline{E}]\Pr[\overline{E}] \\
&\geq \left(\frac{1}{2}\right) E_v[\sum_{i \text{ red}} x_i(v)\phi_i(v_i)|E] \\
&= \left(\frac{1}{2}\right) E_v[\max_{S\subseteq \text{ red}:|S|\leq k/2} \sum_{i\in S} \phi_i(v_i)]
\end{aligned}$$

where the second step follows since the expected allocation of any red node i is independent of its value conditioned on $\overline{E}$. Therefore by fact 1 each such vertex contributes a non-negative amount to the revenue. The third step follows since conditioned on E we picked the best set of size at most $k/2$ from the red nodes.

Now to prove the approximation guarantee first define $X = E[\max_{S:|S|\leq k} \sum_{i\in S} \phi(v_i)]$, and note this is an upper bound on the optimum revenue, since in the best case we can allocate the highest (positive) k virtual values. But we know that for any sampling of the values,

$$\begin{aligned}
\max_{S:|S|\leq k} \sum_{i\in S} \phi(v_i) &\leq \max_{S\subseteq \text{ red}:|S|\leq k} \sum_{i\in S} \phi(v_i) \\
&\quad + \max_{S\subseteq \text{ blue}:|S|\leq k} \sum_{i\in S} \phi(v_i) \\
&\leq 2\cdot(\max_{S\subseteq \text{ red}:|S|\leq k/2} \sum_{i\in S} \phi(v_i) \\
&\quad + \max_{S\subseteq \text{blue}:|S|\leq k/2} \sum_{i\in S} \phi(v_i)),
\end{aligned}$$

and therefore,

$$\begin{aligned}
X &= E[\max_{S:|S|\leq k} \sum_{i\in S} \phi(v_i)] \\
&\leq 2(E[\max_{S\subseteq S_1:|S|\leq k/2} \sum_{i\in S} \phi(v_i)] \\
&\quad + E[\max_{S\subseteq S_2:|S|\leq k/2} \sum_{i\in S} \phi(v_i)]),
\end{aligned}$$

by linearity of expectation. Recalling that the expected value of our allocation is at least

$$E[\max_{S\subseteq S_1:|S|\leq k/2} (\sum_{i\in S} \phi_i(v_i))],$$

and noting that we picked each of the two sets with probability 1/2 to be S_1, we conclude that the expected revenue of our allocation, is at least 1/4 of the upper bound. □

Does More Connectivity Help Groups to Solve Social Problems?

Daniel P. Enemark
University of California, San Diego
9500 Gilman Drive
San Diego, California 92093
denemark@ucsd.edu

Mathew D. McCubbins
Marshall School of Business
University of Southern California
Los Angeles, California 90089
mmccubbins@marshall.usc.edu

Ramamohan Paturi
University of California, San Diego
9500 Gilman Drive
San Diego, California 92093
paturi@cs.ucsd.edu

Nicholas Weller
University of Southern California
Los Angeles, California 90089
nweller@college.usc.edu

ABSTRACT
A growing literature on human networks suggests that the way we are connected influences both individual and group outcomes. Recent experimental studies in the social and computer sciences have claimed that higher network connectivity helps individuals solve coordination problems. However, this is not always the case, especially when we consider complex coordination tasks; we demonstrate that networks can have both constraining edges that inhibit collective action and redundant edges that encourage it. We show that the constraints imposed by additional edges can impede coordination even though these edges also increase communication. By contrast, edges that do not impose additional constraints facilitate coordination, as described in previous work. We explain why the negative effect of constraint trumps the positive effect of communication by analyzing coordination games as a special case of widely-studied constraint satisfaction problems. The results help us to understand the importance of problem complexity and network connections, and how different types of connections can influence real-world coordination..

Categories and Subject Descriptors
J.4 [**Social and Behavioral Sciences**]: Economics; E.1 [**Data Structures**]: Graphs and Networks; F.1.3 [**Computation by Abstract Devices**] Complexity Measures and Classes—*machine-independent complexity*

General Terms
Algorithms, Economics, Experimentation, Human Factors, Theory.

Keywords
human-subject experiments, graph coloring, coordination, game theory, social network

1. INTRODUCTION
Networks are a key element of social, economic, and political interaction. Social scientists have argued that connections in a network affect health outcomes [12], social behavior [27], and economic exchange [16, 8]. In medicine and computer science, network structure has been identified as a key determinant of the spread of human and computer viruses [23, 30]. Despite the prevalence of networks in social situations and the vast amount of knowledge that has been accumulated about network structures across a broad spectrum of human endeavors, we still know relatively little about the effects of networks on strategic interaction and group outcomes.

In this paper we study how networks facilitate groups solving coordination problems. We show that network connectivity structure (as given by the adjacency matrix of the underlying graph) affects outcomes when groups are incentivized to solve common tasks. We show that there is an interaction between the connectivity of the network and the complexity of the task under consideration.

How do we build networks that maximize the efficiency with which distributed agents can achieve coordination? Watts [31] noted the problem but could not find a satisfactory answer, considering it "a hard question to answer, requiring as it does a balance between local capacity constraints and global (system-wide) performance." Previous work in this vein concluded that greater network connectivity improves coordination. Kearns et al. [18] explain that adding chords to a cycle "apparently makes the collective problem easier by reducing the number of links coloring conflicts must travel to be resolved." McCubbins et al. [20] conclude that "increasing the density of the network, ceteris paribus, can improve coordination."

Our results show that the coordination-enhancing effect of additional edges is only true under certain narrow conditions. Higher connectivity can impede coordination because the network not only defines the amount of communication; it also constrains the number of solutions to the coordination problem. In particular, we show that adding "constraining edges" that eliminate solutions causes groups to be less successful in solving the coordination game (even though these edges also increase communication), whereas adding "redundant edges" that facilitate communication without affecting the number of solutions causes groups to be more successful. In the Conclusion, we provide a complexity-theoretic explanation for this finding. We hope this work will help unify the disparate game-theoretic and complexity-theoretic network literatures identified by Schweitzer et al [26].

Our distinction between constraining and redundant edges may help to resolve a conflict in the literature on networked coordination. Observational studies have come to differing conclusions about the effect of network structure on coordination and cooperation: while some argue that network connections help foster coordination [24], others argue that more connections hinder efforts at coordination [1, 13]. We show that some edges constrain the number of solutions to the coordination problem, while others merely increase communication without affecting the number of solutions. Further, we show that the former hinders coordination while the latter helps it.

2. GRAPH COLORING, CONNECTIVITY, AND COMPLEXITY

To study experimentally how network structure affects coordination, we use a distributed version of the Graph Coloring Problem (GCP), first adapted for experiments by Kearns et al. [18]. In our experiments, each of 16 human subjects controls the color of one node in a network, and the subjects are asked to choose a color from a choice of three or four, so that no two directly connected nodes share the same color. (A coloring that satisfies this condition is called a *proper coloring* of the graph.) Each subject can change the color of his node costlessly at any time and can only observe the color of their network neighbors, though they also have two pieces of weak global information: the elapsed time and the percentage of edges whose end nodes have different colors. If all the subjects together achieve a proper coloring of the graph within three minutes, they are each paid a dollar. Each experimental session included about 35 trials.

The GCP is a workhorse problem in computer science, operations research, and applied mathematics, with applications to complex allocation problems like air traffic management [5] and radio channel assignment [19]. The GCP is a constraint satisfaction problem that is known to be equivalent (under polynomial-time reductions) to other important combinatorial optimization problems. It is used to model complex phenomena because it is simple to describe but can be difficult to solve, and these qualities make it an ideal experimental task. The distributed GCP is a natural analog to many social settings in which decisions are not centrally coordinated, but rather arise as a byproduct of the interaction of decentralized decision makers. From a game-theoretic perspective, because there are multiple proper colorings, and each proper coloring constitutes a pure-strategy Nash equilibrium, the distributed GCP is a coordination game [22].

Even with pure common incentives and plenty of information, this coordination game is a difficult one. Computer scientists have shown that coordination problems such as the graph coloring problem can be extremely difficult even for a centralized decision-maker. In particular, it is shown that the decision problem whether a graph is k-colorable for $k \geq 3$ is NP-complete [14]. Even if the graph is known to be k-colorable, finding a proper k-coloring is shown to be NP-hard for $k \geq 3$ [17]. There are highly efficient algorithms for checking if a graph is 2-colorable and finding a proper coloring if it is. But until recently, even for 2-colorable graphs it was not clear that distributed human agents could find proper colorings. Pioneering experiments of Kearns et. al. [18] and their subsequent elaboration by McCubbins et. al. [20] have clearly demonstrated that without conflicting incentives, small groups of subjects (up to 38) can solve the distributed 2-coloring problem. Both studies conclude that increased network connectivity leads to faster solution times.

This paper is motivated by the hypothesis that the effect of connectivity on solvability is not always positive. This hypothesis, that some connections impede coordination, can be deduced from computational complexity theory.

A key to understanding the complexity of individual instances of an NP-complete problem is the number of solutions (proper colorings in the case of graph coloring problem). It is well known in the literature on computational complexity that detecting whether a NP-complete problem instance has a unique solution is as hard as detecting whether it has any solution [29, 9]. Furthermore, for the important subclass of NP-complete problems called constraint satisfaction problems—of which graph coloring is a member—there are several centralized algorithms for finding a solution whose speed improves with an increase in the number of solutions [25, 21, 9]. Theoretical evidence shows that the complexity of 3-coloring a 3-colorable graph increases nonlinearly as the number of proper colorings decreases and is highest when the number of proper colorings is small or unique [29].

To understand the effect of adding edges on the solvability and solution time for the graph-coloring problem, one must consider the effect of adding edges on the number of solutions or proper colorings. Starting with an existing graph, we call any additional edge *constraining* if it decreases the number of proper k-colorings. On the other hand, any additional edge whose constraint is implied by the existing edges, we call *redundant*. Redundant edges do not decrease the number of proper colorings.

Guided by complexity considerations, we propose two hypotheses about the effect of increased connectivity on the solvability of the distributed GCP.

H1: *Increasing the number of constraining edges, ceteris paribus, will decrease the probability of human subjects successfully solving the graph-coloring problem.*

H2: *Increasing the number redundant edges, ceteris paribus, will increase the probability of human subjects successfully solving the graph-coloring problem.*

Instance complexity also explains why previous work concluded that higher connectivity is good for collective action. This work focused on 2-colorable graphs, and all such graphs are maximally constrained. Since a minimally connected bipartite graph (a tree) has a unique (up to isomorphism) 2-coloring, every additional edge which maintains 2-colorability is redundant. Our experiments use 3- and 4-colorable graphs, so that we have the opportunity to add constraining edges, edges that actually decrease the number of solutions to the coloring problem.

2.1 An Illustration of Constraining and Redundant Edges in 3-Colorable Graphs

We illustrate the effect of adding edges on the number of proper colorings by considering the simple network in Figure 1A. Figure 1A presents a line with a single added edge—a minimally constrained connected 3-colorable graph. If subjects select colors in order from left to right, and each subject is given three colors from which to choose, then the leftmost node can select any one of the three colors, the next can select either of the two remaining colors, and the third node must pick the one color unused by the first two. The rest of the 13 nodes can choose either one of the two colors not chosen by the preceding node. The number of solutions to the GCP on this network is $3 \times 2 \times 1 \times 2^{13}$, or 49,152.

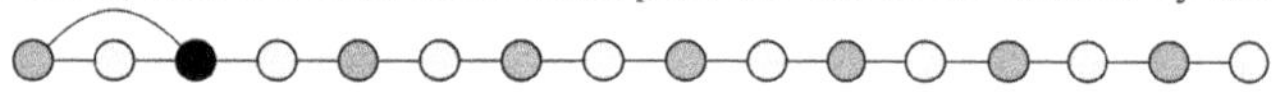

(A) *A minimally constrained connected 3-colorable graph*

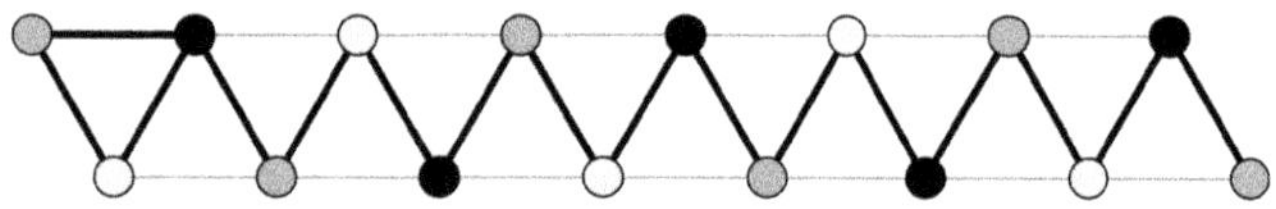

(B) *A maximally constrained, minimally redundant 3-colorable supergraph of A*

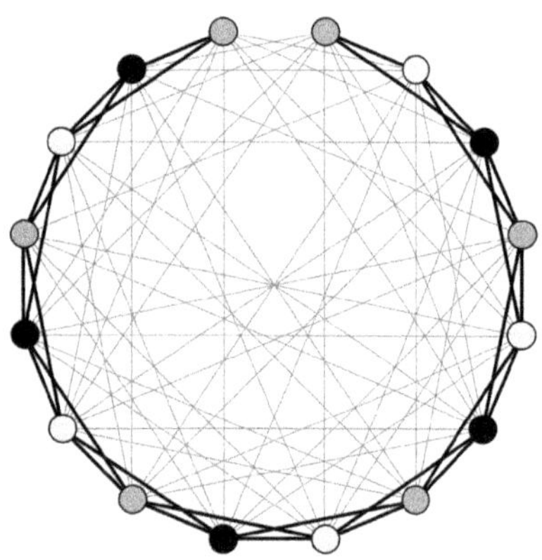

(C) *A maximally constrained, maximally redundant 3-colorable supergraph of B*

Figure 1. Examples of three-colorable graphs with varying degrees of constraint and redundancy. Bold edges in (C) belong to the subgraph in (B), and bold edges in (B) belong to the subgraph in (A).

If we add a constraining edge between the second and fourth nodes of the graph in Figure 1A, the number of choices available to the fourth node decreases from 2 to 1, reducing the number of solutions from 49,152 to 24,576. We can continue adding constraining edges between all pairs of nodes v_i and v_{i+2}, reducing the number of solutions by half with each new edge, until we arrive at the graph in Figure 1B, a line of tessellated triangles, for which there are only six solutions. This is a maximally constrained 3-colorable graph; a 3-colorable network can have no fewer than six solutions because there are six permutations of three colors.

Finally, starting with a maximally constrained network as in Figure 1B we can add redundant edges between any two nodes that must have different colors as implied by the existing constraints, until we create the graph in Figure 1C (in which the original line is curved for the sake of clarity). These edges are redundant, because they do not affect the number of solutions to the graph-coloring problem. These additional edges do, however, provide subjects more information about each other's actions.

3. EXPERIMENTAL RESULTS

Our experiments systematically vary the number of constraining and redundant edges in the graphs our subjects attempt to solve. For k = 3 or 4, we generate a series of k-colorable graphs from minimal constraint to maximal constraint to considerable redundancy: we start with a *k*-colorable graph with minimal number of edges and then add a series of constraining edges while maintaining k-colorability until the number of such edges is maximized. We then add a series of redundant edges while maintaining k-colorability. The order in which we presented these graphs to our subjects was randomized. The networks are all "small-world" networks [32] that are designed to limit leadership or hierarchy, unlike "scale-free" networks in which the degree distribution follows a power law [4]. Because the election of a leader helps autonomous agents to solve coordination problems, and because variance in degree (which is locally observable in our experiments) would facilitate leadership election, we hold the variance in degree close to zero. Examples of 3-colorable graphs used in our experiments are shown in Figure 1.

We conducted experiments with five different groups of 16 subjects (all undergraduates at the University of California, San Diego). We collected data from 179 different trials to solve instances of the GCP. Of those 179 attempts, 75 trials involved 3-colorable graphs and 104 involved 4-colorable graphs. The payment for coordination was $1 per subject and groups had three minutes to achieve coordination. Each experimental trial ends either when the time limit is reached or the group achieves coordination successfully, and all subjects in the experiment know this. Each experimental group completed a large subset of the 3- and 4-colorable graphs to allow us to make within- and between-group comparisons.

The computer interface that subjects use provides them with a view of the other nodes to which they are connected and the degree of each of these nodes. The interface also provides subjects with a bar showing the portion of the network already solved, and a time bar showing the amount of time remaining. Subjects are only paid if the group successfully achieves coordination. All these aspects of the experiment (but not the full structure of the networks) were common knowledge among the subjects.

The experimental results indicate that network structure has enormous effects on a group's ability to solve the coordination problem. In particular, constraining edges clearly hinder coordination, and redundant edges clearly help it, as shown in Figure 2. In fact, successful coordination depends crucially on the number of constraining and redundant edges in the network connecting players. The charts in Figure 2 show that the proportion of trials solved decreases with the number of constraining edges until the graph is fully constrained, at which point the proportion solved increases with the number of redundant edges. At the minimum number of constraining edges, both 3- and 4-colorable graphs were solved in every trial. With the addition of more constraining edges, success rates dropped precipitously, and without redundant edges, subjects were completely unable to solve maximally-constrained graphs of either three or four colors.

Figure 2 clearly shows that adding edges can impede coordination. However, the addition of redundant edges can make an otherwise unsolvable problem tractable. Adding these edges does not change the actions, outcomes, incentives, or solutions to

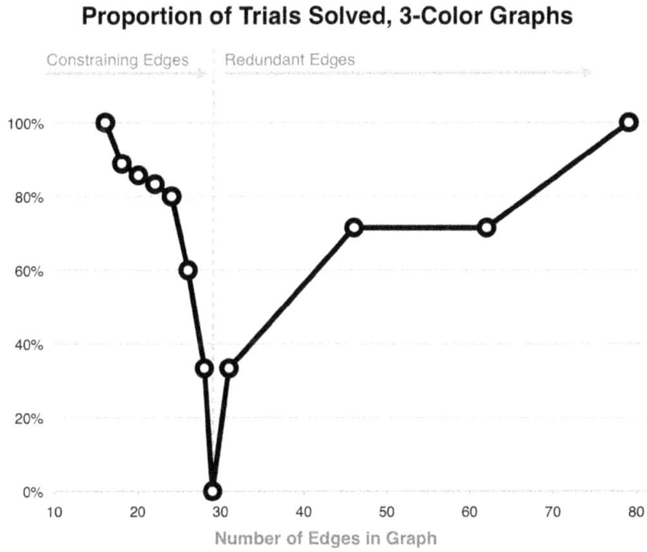

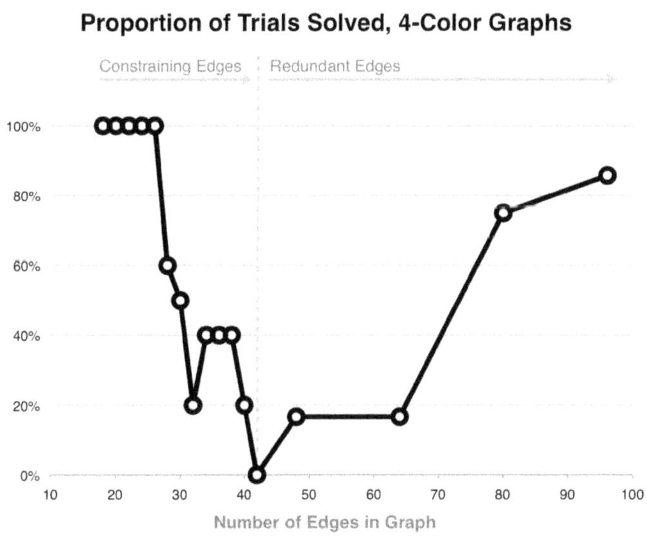

Figure 2: Adding edges first decreases, and then increases a group's ability to solve coordination problems. Starting with the minimally connected graph, increasing connectivity decreases the proportion of trials subjects are able to solve, until the least-connected fully-constrained graph is reached. Once maximum constraint is reached, further increasing connectivity increases the proportion of trials solved.

the game; it simply increases the amount of information available to actors. Nonetheless, the frequency with which subjects solved maximally-constrained graphs rose sharply with the addition of redundant edges. This results shows that redundant edges facilitate coordination even when we start with the most difficult coordination problem possible for a given chromatic number.

While constraining edges inhibit coordination, each constraining edge has both a positive and a negative effect, that is, it allows two nodes to communicate and it reduces the number of solutions. We use a statistical model to estimate the relative strength of the effects of communication and constraint. Specifically, we employ a random-effects logistic regression using the combined data from 3- and 4-colorable graphs. The results are presented in Table 1.

Table 1: Logistic regression showing the effect of constraint and communication on likelihood of success. Constraint is measured by the inverse of (logged) random solution likelihood, and communication is measured by the number of edges. Trial number and a subject group parameter are included to control for any learning or group differences.

Variable	Coefficient (Standard Error)
$\log_2$(Random Solution Likelihood)	0.48** (0.074)
Number of edges	0.084** (0.016)
Trial number	0.017 (0.021)
Random effects parameter: subject group	0.44 (0.31)
Number of trials	179
Number of subject groups	5

Entries are logit coefficients, with standard errors in parentheses. Positive coefficients indicate a higher likelihood of solution.
** $p < 0.05$ and ** $p < 0.001$*

To estimate directly the effect of constraint in our statistical model, we introduce a new measure, Random Solution Likelihood (RSL). RSL is the probability of reaching a proper coloring by chance if every subject simultaneously chooses a color at random, that is, the number of proper colorings divided by the number of possible colorings. RSL is the inverse of constraint, and a negative exponential function of the number of constraining edges. Since we are interested in the effect of the constraint introduced by a single constraining edge, we take the logarithm of RSL in our statistical analysis, as log(RSL) is a linear function of the number of constraining edges.

Measuring constraint directly (rather than by the number of constraining edges) allows us to pool the 3- and 4-color data. In charting the relationship between constraining edges and success rates, graphs of different chromatic number must be analyzed separately, since each constraining edge in a 3-color graph eliminates only one of three available colors, whereas each constraining edge in a 4-color graph eliminates only one of four possible actions. By contrast, when we use log(RSL) we can estimate the effect of additional constraint on success rates independent of chromatic number. Since RSL accounts for the constraint introduced by a constraining edge, any remaining effect of a constraining edge is the effect of communication. We therefore use the total number of edges (rather than the number of redundant edges) as a measure of the amount of communication between subjects, since both constraining and redundant edges enable communication.

Finally, we attempt to control for two unwelcome sources of variation: trial order and group effects. To control for order we simply add a variable for trial number, in case subjects do better or worse later in the session (due to learning or fatigue). To account for potential variation between subject groups, we allow for random effects associated with each group. Our estimated logit model is shown in Table 1.

Table 1 shows that increasing constraint impedes coordination and increasing communication facilitates coordination. Table 1 also shows that trial ordering and subject-group effects are statistically insignificant. The lack of correlation between trial number and success rate suggests that subject performance is not affected by learning or fatigue. The fact that the random effects were statistically insignificant indicates that the subject groups did not vary in their ability to perform the experimental task.

4. CONCLUSIONS

In this paper we argue theoretically and show experimentally that network edges affect coordination through two mechanisms: by spreading information in the network and defining the constraints that determine successful coordination. The ambiguous effect of additional edges mirrors the model of Siegal [27], and comports with the claim of Borgatti et al. [7]: "Perhaps the most fundamental axiom in social network research is that a node's position in a network determines in part the opportunities and constraints that it encounters, and in this way plays an important role in a node's outcomes."

Our experiments show that increased connectivity can impede the ability of groups to solve collective problems, when complex coordination games in the form of k-colorability for $k \geq 3$ are considered. As we add edges to a 3- or 4-colorable graph (while maintaining its 3- or 4-colorability), solvability of the problem by human subjects decreases to zero. The further addition of redundant edges improves the solvability.[1] This is in contrast to the situation in two-colorable graphs where human subjects have always been to solve the problem and moreover they have been able to solve the problem faster with increased connectivity (because the edges that provide this increase are redundant) as reported in Kearns et al. [18] and McCubbins et al [20].

We can provide a complexity-theoretic explanation for this phenomenon: when we consider centralized algorithms, theoretical evidence shows that the complexity of coloring a 3-colorable graph increases nonlinearly as the number of proper colorings decreases and is highest when the number of proper colorings is small or unique [29, 9, 2]. On the other hand, it is well known that the centralized complexity of coloring a 2-colorable graph is linear in the number of edges. It turns out that we can add edges to *constrain* the solutions of a 3-colorable graph until it has a unique (up to symmetry) 3-coloring. Once the network has a unique 3-coloring, we can add edges (maintaining 3-colorability) to increase the local information available to the human subjects without constraining solutions thereby leading to improved solvability. Our motivation is to explore how this aspect of complexity plays out in the case of distributed decision-making over a network (a restricted case of centralized algorithms). Our work provides the first evidence that complexity as well as connectivity is an important factor in determining outcomes in networked context and the interaction between the two factors can be subtle.

This paper shows that the computational complexity of a coordination game has a significant bearing on the ability of *humans* to find solutions. Before we ran our experiments with 3-colorable graphs, based on our general understanding of the complexity of NP-complete problems, we guessed that additional edges would increase the difficulty to a point, after which adding more edges would make the coloring problem easier (assuming that we maintain 3-colorability all the while). However, we do not know of any results that state how the complexity of finding a 3-coloring behaves as a function of density. For a related and well-studied problem of k-SAT, there are algorithms which show that a satisfying assignment can be found quickly for random formulas of high density with a planted solution [3]. Even if similar results were to hold for the 3-coloring problem, it is not clear whether *humans* would be able to solve the problem with similar ease in the presence of a large number of redundant edges in a distributed set-up with only local information. Indeed, there was some reason to wonder wonder whether human performance would mirror that of a well-designed distributed algorithm. For example, Kearns [18] compared their subjects' behavior to that of a simple algorithm they developed, and found the differences "striking, with the order of difficulty within the cycle family exactly reversed…and the preferential attachment networks being relatively easy for the heuristic."

Given that more connections don't always help groups to solve coordination problems, under what circumstances might more connections be a good thing? Our taxonomy of constraining and redundant edges suggests a solution to this outstanding problem. When a particular subgraph is already maximally constrained (that is, when there exists a unique solution to the coordination problem, forcing every member of the subgraph to align with that one solution), then any additional edges are redundant. For example, if there are units within a firm that necessarily require high connectivity (for example, in an assembly line where the success of each individual's task is contingent upon the successful completion of all his predecessors' tasks), then it may be that the addition of redundant edges would help spread information efficiently enough to overcome the complexity of the coordination problem.

We have identified two ways in which network structure affects collective outcomes: by defining the level of constraint and communication. However, our experimental method has two major limitations: the size of our networks is relatively small and the subjects do not create their own networks. It may be that in situations where agents create networks endogenously, they build them to minimize constraining edges and maximize redundant edges by only building connections to agents like themselves, giving rise to the well documented feature of homophily in social networks. If this is true, we may not see many constraining edges in real-world networks. More fundamentally, our analysis deals only with collective outcomes. We have data and simulations designed to shed light on individual strategies, and this work is still in progress. (Chaudhuri et al. [11] have developed a distributed algorithm that converges to solution when agents have at least two more colors than the maximum degree.)

---

[1] We only added redundant edges to the fully-constrained graph, so our results do not directly speak to the effects of redundant edges on networks that are not fully constrained. However, since redundant edges do not reduce the number of solutions but do add information we expect they should improve coordination even if network is not fully constrained.

5. ACKNOWLEDGMENTS

This material is in part based upon work supported by the National Science Foundation under Grant No. 0905645. Any opinions, findings, and conclusions or recommendations expressed in this material are those of the authors and do not necessarily reflect the views of the National Science Foundation.

6. REFERENCES

[1] E. Abrahamson and L. Rosenkopf. Social network effects on the extent of innovation diffusion: A computer simulation. Organization Science, 8(3):289–309, May 1997.

[2] D. Achlioptas and F. Ricci-Tersenghi. On the solution-space geometry of random constrain satisfaction problems. In Symposium on Theory of Computing, pages 130–139, Seattle, Washington, May 2006. Association for Computing Machinery, Association for Computing Machinery.

[3] Amiri, Ehsan, and Skvortsov, Evgeny. Pushing Random Walk Beyond Golden Ratio. In Diekert, Volker, Volkov, Mikhail, and Amiri, Ehsan, editors, Computer Science – Theory and Applications, pages 44-55. Springer Berlin, 2007.

[4] A.-L. Barabási and R. Albert. Emergence of scaling in random networks. Science, 286(5439):509–512, October 1999.

[5] N. Barnier and P. Brisset. Graph coloring for air traffic flow management. Annals of Operations Research, 130:167–178, August 2005.

[6] R. L. Berger. A necessary and sufficient condition for reaching consensus using degroot's method. Journal of the American Statistical Association, 76:415–418, 1981.

[7] S. P. Borgatti, A. Mehra, D. J. Brass, and G. Labianca. Network analysis in the social sciences. Science, 323(5916):892–895, February 2009.

[8] E. Bueno de Mesquita and M. Stephenson. Legal institutions and informal networks. Journal of Theoretical Politics, 18(1):40–67, 2006.

[9] C. Calabro, R. Impagliazzo, and R. Paturi. A duality between clause width and clause density for sat. In CCC '06: Proceedings of the 21st Annual IEEE Conference on Computational Complexity, Washington, DC, 2006. IEEE Computer Society.

[10] A. Calvó-Armengol and J. de Martì. Communication networks: Knowledge and decisions. American Economic Review, 97(2):86–91, May 2007.

[11] K. Chaudhuri, F. Chung, and M.S. Jamall. A network coloring game. In Proceedings of the 4th International Workshop on Internet and Network Economics, pages 552–530, 2008.

[12] N. Christakis and J. Fowler. The spread of obesity in a large social netowrk over 32 years. New England Journal of Medicine, 357:370–379, July 2007.

[13] M. Chwe. Communication and coordination in social networks. Review of Economic Studies, 67:1–16, 2000.

[14] M. R. Garey and D. S. Johnson. The complexity of near-optimal graph coloring. Journal of the Association for Computing Machinery, 23(1):43–49, January 1976.

[15] J. Hagenbach and F. Koessler. Strategic communication networks. February 2009.

[16] M. Jackson. Social and Economic Networks. Princeton University Press, Princeton, New Jersey, 2008.

[17] R. M. Karp. Reducibility among combinatorial problems. In R. E. Miller and J. W. Thatcher, editors, Complexity of Computer Computations: Proceedings of a Symposium on the Complexity of Computer Computations, The IBM Research Symposia Series, pages 85–103, New York, NY, 1972. Plenum Press.

[18] M. Kearns, S. Suri, and N. Montfort. An experimental study of the coloring problem on human subject networks. Science, 313:824–827, August 2006.

[19] S. O. Krumke, M. V. Marathe, and S. Ravi. Models and approximation algorithms for channel assignment in radio networks. Wireless Networks, 7(6):575–584, November 2001.

[20] M. D. McCubbins, R. Paturi, and N. Weller. Connected coordination: Network structure and group coordination. American Politics Research, 37:899–920, September 2009.

[21] R. Paturi, P. Pudlák, M. E. Saks, and F. Zane. An improved exponential-time algorithm for k-sat. Journal of the Association for Computing Machinery, 52(3):337–364, 2005.

[22] E. Rasmusen. Games and Information: An Introduction to Game Theory. Blackwell Publishers, Oxford, England, 4 edition, 2006.

[23] R. B. Rothenberg, J. J. Potterat, D. E. Woodhouse, S. Q. Muth, W. W. Darrow, and A. S. Klovdahl. Social network dynamics and hiv transmission. AIDS, 12:1529–1536, April 1998.

[24] J. T. Scholz, R. Berardo, and B. Kile. Do networks solve collective action problems? credibility, search, and collaboration. Journal of Politics, 70(2):393–406, April 2008.

[25] U. Schöning. A probabilistic algorithm for k-sat and constraint satisfaction problems. In FOCS '99: Proceedings of the 40th Annual Symposium on Foundations of Computer Science, Washington, DC, 1999. IEEE Computer Society.

[26] F. Schweitzer, G. Fagiolo, D. Sornette, F. Vega-Redondo, A. Vespignani, and D. R. White. Economic networks: The new challenges. Science, 325:422–425, July 2009.

[27] D. Siegel. Social networks and collective action. American Journal of Political Science, 53(1):122–138, 2009.

[28] S. H. Strogatz. From kuramoto to crawford: exploring the onset of synchronization in populations of coupled oscillators. Physica D: Nonlinear Phenomena, 143:1–20, 2000.

[29] L. G. Valiant and V. V. Vazirani. Np is as easy as detecting unique solutions. In Proceedings of the Seventeenth Annual ACM Symposium on Theory of Computing, pages 458–463, New York, NY, 1985.

[30] P. Van Mieghem, J. Omic, and R. Kooij. Virus spread in networks. IEEE/ACM Transactions on Networking, 17(1):1–14, February 2009.

[31] D. J. Watts. Six Degrees: The Science of a Connected Age. W.W. Norton & Company, Inc., New York, NY, 2003.

[32] D. J. Watts and S. H. Strogatz. Collective dynamics of 'small-world' networks. Nature, 393:440–442, June 1

Yield Optimization of Display Advertising with Ad Exchange

[Abstract]*

Santiago Balseiro
Columbia Business School
New York, NY
srb2155@columbia.edu

Jon Feldman
Google, Inc.
New York, NY
jonfeld@google.com

Vahab Mirrokni
Google, Inc.
New York, NY
mirrokni@google.com

S. Muthukrishnan
Google, Inc.
New York, NY
muthu@google.com

Categories and Subject Descriptors

F.2.0 [**Analysis of Algorithms and Problem Complexity**]: General; J.4 [**Computer Applications**]: Social and Behavioral Sciences—*Economics*; K.4.4 [**Computers and Society**]: Electronic commerce

General Terms

Algorithms, Economics, Theory

ABSTRACT

In light of the growing market of Ad Exchanges for the real-time sale of advertising slots, publishers face new challenges in choosing between the allocation of contract-based reservation ads and spot market ads. In this setting, the publisher should take into account the tradeoff between short-term revenue from an Ad Exchange and quality of allocating reservation ads. In this paper, we formalize this combined optimization problem as a stochastic control problem and derive an efficient policy for online ad allocation in settings with general joint distribution over placement quality and exchange bids.

Ad Exchanges like RightMedia, AdECN or DoubleClick are an emerging market for the real-time sale of display advertising slots in publishing sites on the Internet. While exchanges differ in their implementations, in a generic Ad Exchange (AdX) [1], publishers post an ad slot with a reservation price, advertisers post bids, and an auction is run; this happens between the time a user visits a page and the ad is displayed.

From the publisher's point of view, the goal is to maximize revenue gained from sale of the ad inventory. In isolation, this problem is similar to optimal auction design, and Myerson [2] shows that the optimal reserve price can be calculated from the bid distribution. However, AdX represents only one possible sales outlet for the publisher. In fact, even in the presence of this efficient real-time market, many web publishers still get a significant portion of their revenue from making individual deals with specific advertisers or agencies. These deals usually take the form of a specific number of ad impressions reserved over a particular time horizon (e.g., one million impressions over a month). A publisher can make many such deals with different advertisers, with potentially sophisticated relationships between the advertisers' targeting criteria. So for a given piece of ad inventory, the publisher must decide—quickly—whether to send the inventory to AdX (and at what price), or to assign it to an advertiser with a reservation.

In this paper, we study the problem faced by the publisher, jointly optimizing over AdX and the reservations. We bring to bear techniques from revenue management and stochastic optimization, and derive an efficient policy for making real-time ad allocation decisions. We prove that our policy is asymptotically optimal in terms of an arbitrary (i.e., publisher-defined) trade-off between quality delivered to reservation ads and revenue from the exchange. Our policy and analysis is quite general, and works for any joint distribution over placement quality and exchange bids, even allowing correlation between advertisers, or between quality and exchange bids. In particular, we provide a rigorous bound on the convergence rate of our policy to the optimal policy. We also give experimental results on data derived from real publisher inventory, showing that our policy lets us achieve any pareto-optimal point on the quality vs. revenue curve.

Finally, we study a parametric training-based algorithm in which instead of learning the dual variables from a sample data (as is done in non-parametric training-based algorithms), we learn the parameters of the distribution and construct those dual variables from the learned parameter values. We compare parametric and non-parametric ways to estimate from data both analytically and experimentally in the special case without the ad exchange, and show that though both methods converge to the optimal policy as the sample size grows, our parametric method converges faster, and thus performs better on smaller samples.

*A working paper version is available at `http://arxiv.org/abs/1102.2551`.

EC'11, June 5–9, 2011, San Jose, California, USA.
ACM 978-1-4503-0261-6/11/06.

1. REFERENCES

[1] S. Muthukrishnan. Ad exchanges: Research issues. In *Internet and Network Economics, Lecture Notes in Computer Science*, pages 1–12, 2009.

[2] R. Myerson. Optimal auction design. *Mathematics of Operations Research*, 6(1):58–73, 1981.

Near Optimal Online Algorithms and Fast Approximation Algorithms for Resource Allocation Problems *

Nikhil R. Devanur
Microsoft Research
Redmond, WA, USA
nikdev@microsoft.com

Kamal Jain
Microsoft Research
Redmond, WA, USA
kamalj@microsoft.com

Balasubramanian Sivan†
Computer Sciences Dept.,
Univ. of Wisconsin-Madison
Madison, WI, USA
balu2901@cs.wisc.edu

Christopher A. Wilkens‡
Computer Science Division,
Univ. of California at Berkeley
Berkeley, CA, USA
cwilkens@cs.berkeley.edu

ABSTRACT

We present algorithms for a class of resource allocation problems both in the online setting with stochastic input and in the offline setting. This class of problems contains many interesting special cases such as the Adwords problem. In the online setting we introduce a new distributional model called the adversarial stochastic input model, which is a generalization of the i.i.d model with unknown distributions, where the distributions can change over time. In this model we give a $1 - O(\epsilon)$ approximation algorithm for the resource allocation problem, with almost the weakest possible assumption: the ratio of the maximum amount of resource consumed by any single request to the total capacity of the resource, and the ratio of the profit contributed by any single request to the optimal profit is at most $\frac{\epsilon^2/\log(1/\epsilon)^2}{\log n + \log(1/\epsilon)}$ where n is the number of resources available. There are instances where this ratio is $\epsilon^2/\log n$ such that no randomized algorithm can have a competitive ratio of $1 - o(\epsilon)$ even in the i.i.d model. The upper bound on ratio that we require improves on the previous upper-bound for the i.i.d case by a factor of n.

Our proof technique also gives a very simple proof that the greedy algorithm has a competitive ratio of $1 - 1/e$ for the Adwords problem in the i.i.d model with unknown distributions, and more generally in the adversarial stochastic input model, when there is no bound on the bid to budget ratio. All the previous proofs assume that either bids are very small compared to budgets or something very similar to this.

In the offline setting we give a fast algorithm to solve very large LPs with both packing and covering constraints. We give algorithms to approximately solve (within a factor of $1 + \epsilon$) the mixed packing-covering problem with $O(\frac{\gamma m \log n}{\epsilon^2})$ oracle calls where the constraint matrix of this LP has dimension $n \times m$, and γ is a parameter which is very similar to the ratio described for the online setting.

We discuss several applications, and how our algorithms improve existing results in some of these applications.

Categories and Subject Descriptors

F.2.0 [**Analysis of Algorithms and Problem Complexity**]: General; J.4 [**Social and Behavioral Sciences**]: Economics

General Terms

Algorithms, Economics, Theory

Keywords

Online algorithms, Stochastic input, Packing-Covering

1. INTRODUCTION

The results in this paper fall into distinct categories of competitive algorithms for online problems and fast approximation algorithms for offline problems. We have two main results in the online framework and one result in the offline setting. However they all share common techniques.

There has been an increasing interest in online algorithms motivated by applications to online advertising. The most well known is the *Adwords* problem introduced by Mehta et. al. [MSVV05], where the algorithm needs to assign keywords arriving online to bidders to maximize profit, subject to budget constraints for the bidders. The problem has been analyzed in the traditional framework for online algorithms: worst-case competitive analysis. As with many online problems, the worst-case competitive analysis is not entirely satisfactory and there has been a drive in the last few years to go beyond the worst-case analysis. The predominant approach has been to assume that the input satisfies some stochastic property. For instance the *random permutation* model (introduced

*A full version of this paper, with all the proofs, is available at `http://arxiv.org`

†Part of this work was done while the author was at Microsoft Research, Redmond

‡Part of this work was done while the author was at Microsoft Research, Redmond

by Goel and Mehta [GM08]) assumes that the adversary picks the set of keywords, but the order in which the keywords arrive is chosen uniformly at random. A closely related model is the *i.i.d* model: assume that the keywords are i.i.d samples from a fixed distribution, which is *unknown* to the algorithm. Stronger assumptions such as i.i.d samples from a *known* distribution have also been considered.

First Result.

A key parameter on which many of the algorithms for Adwords depend is the bid to budget ratio. For instance in Mehta et. al. [MSVV05] and Buchbinder, Jain and Naor [BJN07] the algorithm achieves a worst case competitive ratio that tends to $1 - 1/e$ as the bid to budget ratio (let's call it γ) tends to 0. ($1 - 1/e$ is also the best competitive ratio that any randomized algorithm can achieve in the worst case.) Devanur and Hayes [DH09] showed that in the random permutation model, the competitive ratio tends to 1 as γ tends to 0. This result showed that competitive ratio of algorithms in stochastic models could be much better than that of algorithms in the worst case. The important question since then has been to determine the optimal trade-off between γ and the competitive ratio. [DH09] showed how to get a 1- $O(\epsilon)$ competitive ratio when γ is at most $\frac{\epsilon^3}{n\log(mn/\epsilon)}$ where n is the number of advertisers and m is the number of keywords. Subsequently Agrawal, Wang and Ye [AWY09] improved the bound on γ to $\frac{\epsilon^2}{n\log(mn/\epsilon)}$. The papers of Feldman et. al. [FHK+10] and Agrawal, Wang and Ye [AWY09] have also shown that the technique of [DH09] can be extended to other online problems.

The first main result in this paper is the following 3-fold improvement of previous results: (Theorems 2 - 4)

1. We give an algorithm which improves the bound on γ to $\frac{\epsilon^2/\log(1/\epsilon)^2}{\log(n)+\log(1/\epsilon)}$. This is almost *optimal*; we show a lower bound of $\frac{\epsilon^2}{\log(n)}$.
2. The bound applies to a more general model of stochastic input, called the *adversarial stochastic input* model. This is a generalization of the i.i.d model with unknown distribution, but is incomparable to the random permutation model.
3. It applies to a more general class of online problems that we call the *resource allocation framework*. A formal definition of the framework is presented in Section 2.2 and a discussion of many interesting special cases is presented in Section 7.

Regarding the bound on γ, the removal of the factor of n is significant. Consider for instance the Adwords problem and suppose that the bids are all in [0,1]. The earlier bound implies that the budgets need to be of the order of n/ϵ^2 in order to get a $1 - \epsilon$ competitive algorithm, where n is the number of advertisers. With realistic values for these parameters, it seems unlikely that this condition would be met. While with the improved bounds presented in this paper, we only need the budget to be of the order of $\log n/\epsilon^2$ and this condition is met for reasonable values of the parameters.

We note here that so far, all the algorithms for the i.i.d model (with unknown distribution) were actually designed for the random permutation model. It seems that any algorithm that works for one should also work for the other. However we can only show that our algorithm works in the i.i.d model, so the natural question is if our algorithm works for the random permutation model. It would be very surprising if it didn't.

One drawback of the stochastic models considered so far is that they are time invariant, that is the input distribution does not change over time. The adversarial stochastic input model allows the input distribution to change over time. The model is as follows: in every step the adversary picks a distribution, possibly adaptively depending on what the algorithm has done so far, and the actual keyword in that step is drawn from this distribution. The competitive ratio is defined with respect to the optimum fractional solution for an *offline* instance of the problem, called the *distribution instance*, which is defined by the distribution (see Section 2.2). In Section 2.2, where we define the distribution instance, we also prove that the optimal fractional solution for the distribution instance is at least as good as the commonly used benchmark of expected value of optimal fractional solution, where the expectation is with respect to the distribution. A detailed description of this model, how the adversary is constrained to pick its distributions and how it differs from the worst-case model is presented in Section 2.2.

Second Result.

Another important open problem is to improve the competitive ratio for the Adwords problem when there is no bound on γ. The best competitive ratio known for this problem is $1/2$ in the worst case. Nothing better was known, even in the stochastic models. (For the special case of online bipartite matching, in the case of i.i.d input with a *known* distribution, recent series of results achieve a ratio of better than 1-1/e, for instance by Feldman et. al. [FMMM09] and Bahmani and Kapralov [BK10]. The best ratio so far is .702 by Manshadi, Gharan and Saberi [MGS11].) *The second result in this paper is that for the Adwords problem in the adversarial stochastic input model, with no assumption on γ, the greedy algorithm gets a competitive ratio of $1 - 1/e$ against the optimal fractional solution to the distribution instance (Theorem 5).* The greedy algorithm is particularly interesting since it is a natural algorithm that is used widely for its simplicity. Because of its wide use, previously the performance of the greedy algorithm has been analyzed by Goel and Mehta [GM08] who showed that in the random permutation and the i.i.d models, it has a competitive ratio of $1 - 1/e$ with an assumption which is essentially that γ tends to 0.

Third Result.

Charles et. al. [CCD+10] considered the following (offline) problem: given a lopsided bipartite graph $G = (L, R, E)$, that is a bipartite graph where $m = |L| \gg |R| = n$, does there exist an assignment $M : L \to R$ with $(j, M(j)) \in E$ for all $j \in L$, and such that for every vertex $i \in R$, $|M^{-1}(i)| \geq B_i$ for some given values B_i. Even though this is a classic problem in combinatorial optimization with well known polynomial time algorithms, the instances of interest are too large to use traditional approaches to solve this problem. (The value of m in particular is very large.) The approach used by [CCD+10] was to essentially design an online algorithm in the i.i.d model: choose vertices from L uniformly at random and assign them to vertices in R in an online fashion. The online algorithm is guaranteed to be close to optimal, as long as sufficiently many samples are drawn. Therefore it can be used to solve the original problem (approximately): the online algorithm gets an almost satisfying assignment if and only if the original graph has a satisfying assignment (with high probability).

The third result in this paper is a generalization of this result to get fast approximation algorithms for a wide class of problems in the resource allocation framework (Theorem 6). Problems in the resource allocation framework where the instances are too large to use traditional algorithms occur fairly often, especially in the context of online advertising. Formal statements and a more detailed discussion are presented in Section 2.3.

The underlying idea used for all these results can be summarized at a high level as thus: consider a hypothetical algorithm called

Pure-random that knows the distribution from which the input is drawn and uses an optimal solution w.r.t this distribution. Now suppose that we can analyze the performance of Pure-random by considering a potential function and showing that it decreases by a certain amount in each step. Now we can design an algorithm that does not know the distribution as follows: consider the same potential function, and in every step choose the option that minimizes the potential function. Since the algorithm minimizes the potential in each step, the decrease in the potential for this algorithm is better than that for Pure-random and hence we obtain the same guarantee as that for Pure-random.

For instance, for the case where γ is small, the performance of Pure-random is analyzed using Chernoff bounds. The Chernoff bounds are proven by showing bounds on the expectation of the moment generating function of a random variable. Thus the potential function is the sum of the moment generating functions for all the random variables that we apply the Chernoff bounds to. The proof shows that in each step this potential function decreases by some multiplicative factor. The algorithm is then designed to achieve the same decrease in the potential function. A particularly pleasing aspect about this technique is that we obtain very simple proofs. For instance, the proof of Theorem 5 is extremely simple: the potential function in this case is simply the total amount of unused budgets and we show that this amount (in expectation) decreases by a factor of $1 - 1/m$ in each step where there are m steps in all.

On the surface, this technique and the resulting algorithms[1] bear a close resemblance to the algorithms of Young [You95] for derandomizing randomized rounding and the fast approximation algorithms for solving covering/packing LPs of Plotkin, Shmoys and Tardos [PST91], Garg and Könemann [GK98] and Fleischer [Fle00]. In fact Arora, Hazan and Kale [AHK05] showed that all these algorithms are related to the multiplicative weights update method for solving the *experts* problem and especially highlighted the similarity between the potential function used in the analysis of the multiplicative update method and the moment generating function used in the proof of Chernoff bounds and Young's algorithms. Hence it is no surprise that our algorithm is also a multiplicative update algorithm. It seems that our algorithm is closer in spirit to Young's algorithms than others. It is possible that our algorithm can also be interpreted as an algorithm for the experts problem. In fact Mehta et. al. [MSVV05] asked if there is a $1 - o(1)$ competitive algorithm for Adwords in the i.i.d model with small bid to budget ratio, and in particular if the algorithms for experts could be used. They also conjectured that such an algorithm would iteratively adjust a budget discount factor based on the rate at which the budget is spent. Our algorithms for resource allocation problem when specialized for Adwords look exactly like that and with the connections to the experts framework, we answer the questions in [MSVV05] in the positive.

Organization: The rest of the paper is organized as follows. In Section 2, we define the resource allocation framework, the adversarial stochastic model and state our results formally as theorems. We also discuss one special case of the resource allocation framework — the adwords problem and formally state our results. In Section 3, we consider a simplified "min-max" version of the resource allocation framework and present the proofs for this version. The other results build upon this simple version. In Section 4 we give a fast approximation algorithm for the mixed covering-packing problem (Theorem 6). The $1 - O(\epsilon)$ competitive online algorithm for the resource allocation framework with stochastic input (Theorem 2) is in Section 5. The $1-1/e$ competitive algorithm (Theorem 5) for the Adwords problem is in Section 6. Several special cases of the resource allocation framework are considered in Section 7. Section 8 concludes with some open problems and directions for future research.

[1]For the case of small γ. It is not clear if this discussion applies to the case of large γ, that is to Theorem 5

2. PRELIMINARIES & MAIN RESULTS

2.1 Resource allocation framework

We consider the following framework of optimization problems. There are n resources, with resource i having a capacity of c_i. There are m requests; each request j can be satisfied by a vector $\mathbf{x}_j$ that is constrained to be in a polytope $\mathcal{P}_j$. (We refer to the vector $\mathbf{x}_j$ as an option to satisfy a request, and the polytope $\mathcal{P}_j$ as the set of options.) The vector $\mathbf{x}_j$ consumes $\mathbf{a}_{i,j} \cdot \mathbf{x}_j$ amount of resource i, and gives a profit of $\mathbf{w}_j \cdot \mathbf{x}_j$. Note that $\mathbf{a}_{i,j}$, $\mathbf{w}_j$ and $\mathbf{x}_j$ are all vectors. The objective is to maximize the total profit subject to the capacity constraints on the resources. The following LP describes the problem:

$$\text{maximize} \sum_j \mathbf{w}_j \cdot \mathbf{x}_j \text{ s.t.}$$

$$\forall\, i, \sum_j \mathbf{a}_{i,j} \cdot \mathbf{x}_j \leq c_i$$

$$\forall\, j, \mathbf{x}_j \in \mathcal{P}_j.$$

We assume that we have the following oracle available to us: given a request j and a vector $\mathbf{v}$, the oracle returns the vector $\mathbf{x}_j$ that maximizes $\mathbf{v}.\mathbf{x}_j$ among all vectors in $\mathcal{P}_j$. Let $\gamma = \max(\{\frac{\mathbf{a}_{i,j} \cdot \mathbf{x}_j}{c_i}\}_{i,j} \cup \{\frac{\mathbf{w}_j \cdot \mathbf{x}_j}{W^*}\}_j)$ be the notion corresponding to the bid to budget ratio for Adwords. Here W^* is the optimal offline objective to the distribution instance, defined in Section 2.2.

The canonical case is where each $\mathcal{P}_j$ is a unit simplex in $\mathbf{R}^K$, i.e. $\mathcal{P}_j = \{\mathbf{x}_j \in \mathbf{R}^K : \sum_k x_{j,k} = 1\}$. This captures the case where there are K discrete options, each with a given profit and consumption. This case captures most of the applications we are interested in, which are described in Section 7. All the proofs will be presented for this special case, for ease of exposition. The co-ordinates of the vectors $\mathbf{a}_{i,j}$ and $\mathbf{w}_j$ will be denoted by $a(i,j,k)$ and $w_{j,k}$ respectively, i.e., the kth option consumes $a(i,j,k)$ amount of resource i and gives a profit of $w_{j,k}$. For an example of an application that needs more general polytopes see Section 7.4.

We consider two versions of the above problem. The first is an online version with stochastic input: requests are drawn from an unknown distribution. The second is when the number of requests is much larger than the number of resources, and our goal is to design a fast PTAS for the problem.

2.2 Online Algorithms with Stochastic Input

We now consider an online version of the resource allocation framework. Here requests arrive online. We consider the i.i.d. model, where each request is drawn independently from a given distribution. The distribution is unknown to the algorithm. The algorithm knows m, the total number of requests. The competitive ratios we give for resource allocation problems with bounded γ are with respect to an upper bound on the expected value of fractional optimal solution, namely, the fractional optimal solution of the distribution instance, defined below.

Consider the following *distribution instance* of the problem. It is an offline instance defined for any given distribution over requests and the total number of requests m. The capacities of the resources in this instance are the same as in the original instance. Every request in the support of the distribution is also a request in this instance. Suppose request j occurs with probability p_j. Assume w.l.o.g that $p_j \leq 1/m$. (If $p_j > 1/m$ for some request then repeat that request $\lfloor mp_j \rfloor$ times with probability $1/m$ and one more time with probability $p_j - \lfloor mp_j \rfloor/m$. This "breaking up" of a request j with $mp_j > 1$ is done in order not to increase γ.) The resource consumption of j in the distribution instance is given by $mp_j\mathbf{a}_{i,j}$ for all i and the profit is $mp_j\mathbf{w}_j$. The intuition is that if the requests were drawn from this distribution then the expected number of times request j is seen is mp_j and this is represented in the distribution instance by scaling the consumption and the profit vectors by mp_j. To summarize, the distribution instance is as follows.

$$\text{maximize} \sum_{j \text{ in the support}} mp_j\mathbf{w}_j.\mathbf{x}_j \text{ s.t.}$$

$$\forall\, i, \sum_j mp_j\mathbf{a}_{i,j}.\mathbf{x}_j \leq c_i$$

$$\forall\, j, \mathbf{x}_j \in \mathcal{P}_j.$$

We now prove that the fractional optimal solution to the distribution instance is an upper bound on the expectation of OPT, where OPT is the offline fractional optimum of the actual sequence of requests.

LEMMA 1. *OPT*[Distribution instance] $\geq \mathbf{E}[OPT]$

PROOF. The average of optimal solutions for all possible sequences of requests should give a feasible solution to the distribution instance with a profit equal to $E[\text{OPT}]$. Thus the optimal profit for the distribution instance could only be larger. □

The *competitive ratio* of an algorithm in the i.i.d model is defined as the ratio of the expected profit of the algorithm to the fractional optimal profit for the distribution instance. The main result is that as γ tends to zero, the competitive ratio tends to 1. In fact, we give the almost optimal trade-off.

THEOREM 2. *For any $\epsilon > 0$, we give an algorithm such that if $\gamma = \frac{\epsilon^2/\log(1/\epsilon)^2}{\log(n)+\log(1/\epsilon)}$ then the competitive ratio of the algorithm is $1 - O(\epsilon)$.*

THEOREM 3. *There exist instances with $\gamma = \frac{\epsilon^2}{\log(n)}$ such that no algorithm can get a competitive ratio of $1 - o(\epsilon)$.*[2]

Also, our algorithm works when the polytope $\mathcal{P}_j$ is obtained as an LP relaxation of the actual problem.[3] To be precise, suppose that the set of options that could be used to satisfy a given request corresponds to some set of vectors, say $\mathcal{I}_j$. Let the polytope $\mathcal{P}_j \supseteq \mathcal{I}_j$ be an α *approximate relaxation* of $\mathcal{I}_j$ if for the profit vector $\mathbf{w}_j$ and for all $\mathbf{x}_j \in \mathcal{P}_j$, there is an oracle that returns a $\mathbf{y}_j \in \mathcal{I}_j$ such that $\mathbf{w}_j.\mathbf{y}_j \geq \alpha\mathbf{w}_j.\mathbf{x}_j$. Given such an oracle, our algorithm achieves a competitive ratio of $\alpha - O(\epsilon)$.

THEOREM 4. *Given a resource allocation problem with an α approximate relaxation, and for any $\epsilon > 0$, we give an algorithm such that if $\gamma = \frac{\epsilon^2/\log(1/\epsilon)^2}{\log(n)+\log(1/\epsilon)}$ then the competitive ratio of the algorithm is $\alpha - O(\epsilon)$.*

We prove Theorem 4 in the full version of the paper.

In fact, our results hold for the following more general model, the *adversarial stochastic input* model. In each step, the adversary adaptively chooses a distribution from which the request in that step is drawn. The adversary is constrained to pick the distributions in one of the following two ways. In the first case, we assume that a target objective value OPT_T is given to the algorithm, and that the adversary is constrained to pick distributions such that the fractional optimum solution of *each* of the corresponding distribution instances is at least OPT_T (or at most OPT_T for minimization problems). The competitive ratio is defined with respect to OPT_T. In the second case, we are not given a target, but the adversary is constrained to pick distributions so that the fractional optimum of each of the corresponding distribution instances is the same, which is the benchmark with respect to which the competitive ratio is defined.

Note that while the i.i.d model can be reduced to the random permutation model, these generalizations are incomparable to the random permutation model as they allow the input to vary over time. Also the constraint that each of the distribution instances has a large optimum value distinguishes this from the worst-case model. This constraint in general implies that the distribution must contain sufficiently rich variety of requests in order for the corresponding distribution instance to have a high optimum. To truly simulate the worst-case model, in every step the adversary would chose a "deterministic distribution", that is a distribution supported on a single request. Then the distribution instance will simply have m copies of this single request and hence will not have a high optimum. For instance consider online bipartite b-matching where each resource is a node on one side of a bipartite graph with the capacity c_i denoting the number of nodes it can be matched to and the requests are nodes on the other side of the graph and can be matched to at most one node. A deterministic distribution in this case corresponds to a single online node and if that node is repeated m times then the optimum for that instance is just the weighted (by c_i) degree of that node. If the adversary only picks such deterministic distributions then he is constrained to pick nodes of very high degree thus making it easy for the algorithm to match them.

We refer the reader to Section 7 for a discussion on several problems that are special cases of the resource allocation framework and have been previously considered. Here, we discuss one special case — the adwords problem.

2.2.1 The Adwords problem

In the i.i.d *Adwords* problem, there are n bidders, and each bidder i has a daily budget of B_i dollars. *Keywords* arrive online with keyword j having an (unknown) probability p_j of arriving in any given step. For every keyword j, each bidder submits a bid, b_{ij}, which is the profit obtained by the algorithm on allocating keyword j to bidder i. The objective is to maximize the profit, subject to the constraint that no bidder is charged more than his budget. Here, the resources are the daily budgets of the bidders, the requests are the keywords, and the options are once again the bidders. The amount of resource consumed and the profit are both b_{ij}.

For this problem, with no bounds on γ, we show that the greedy algorithm has a competitive ratio of $1 - 1/e$. For our results for the adwords problem with bounded γ, see Section 7.1

THEOREM 5. *The greedy algorithm achieves a competitive ratio of $1-1/e$ for the Adwords problem in the adversarial stochastic input model with no assumptions on the bid to budget ratio.*

We note here that the competitive ratio of $1 - 1/e$ is tight for the greedy algorithm [GM08]. It is however not known to be tight for an arbitrary algorithm.

2.3 Fast algorithms for very large LPs

Charles et al. [CCD+10] consider the following problem: given a bipartite graph $G = (L, R, E)$ where $m = |L| \gg |R| = n$, does

[2]The proof of this theorem is obtained by a modification of a similar theorem for random permutations presented in [AWY09].

[3]There may be trivial ways of defining $\mathcal{P}_j$ such that its vertices correspond to the actual options. The motivation for allowing nontrivial relaxations is computational: recall that we need to be able to optimize linear functions over $\mathcal{P}_j$.

there exist an assignment $M : L \to R$ with $(j, M(j)) \in E$ for all $j \in L$, and such that for every vertex $i \in R$, $|M^{-1}(i)| \geq B_i$ for some given values B_i. They gave an algorithm that runs in time linear[4] in the number of edges of an induced subgraph obtained by taking a random sample from R of size $O\left(\frac{m \log n}{\min_i\{B_i\}\epsilon^2}\right)$, for a gap-version of the problem with gap ϵ. When $\min_i\{B_i\}$ is reasonably large, such an algorithm is very useful in a variety of applications involving ad assignment for online advertising.

We consider a generalization of the above problem (that corresponds to the resource allocation framework). In fact, we consider the following mixed covering-packing problem. Suppose that there are n_1 packing constraints, one for each $i \in \{1..n_1\}$ of the form $\sum_{j=1}^{m} \mathbf{a}_{i,j}\mathbf{x}_j \leq c_i$ and n_2 covering constraints, one for each $i \in \{1..n_2\}$ of the form $\sum_{j=1}^{m} \mathbf{b}_{i,j}\mathbf{x}_j \geq d_i$. Each $\mathbf{x}_j$ is constrained to be in $\mathcal{P}_j$. Does there exists a feasible solution to this system of constraints? The gap-version of this problem is as follows. Distinguish between the two cases:

YES: There is a feasible solution.

NO: There is no feasible solution even if all of the c_i's are multiplied by $1+\epsilon$ and all of the d_i's is multiplied by $1-\epsilon$.

We note that solving (offline) an optimization problem in the resource allocation framework can be reduced to the above problem through a binary search on the objective function value.

Suppose as in [CCD+10] that m is much larger than n. Assume that solving the following costs unit time: given j and $\mathbf{v}$, find $\mathbf{x}_j \in \mathcal{P}_j$ that maximizes $\mathbf{v}.\mathbf{x}_j$. Let $\gamma = \max\{i \in [n_1], j \in [m] : \frac{\mathbf{a}_{i,j}\cdot\mathbf{x}_j}{c_i}\} \cup \{i \in [n_2], j \in [m] : \frac{\mathbf{b}_{i,j}\cdot\mathbf{x}_j}{d_i}\}$.

THEOREM 6. *There is an algorithm that solves the gap version of the mixed covering-packing problem with a running time of* $O\left(\frac{\gamma m \log n}{\epsilon^2}\right)$.

Applications to online advertising:

The matching problem introduced by [CCD+10] was motivated by the problem of computing the available inventory for display ad allocation (see the original paper for details). In fact, the matching problem was a simplified version of the real problem, which fits into the resource allocation framework. Moreover, such algorithms are used in multiple ways. For instance, although the technique of Devanur and Hayes [DH09] was originally designed to solve the purely online problem, it can be used in the PAC model where the algorithm can make use of a prediction of the future arrival of requests (see for instance Vee, Vassilvitskiiy and Shanmugasundaram [VVS10]). The key technique is to formulate an LP relaxation of the problem and learn the optimal dual variables using the prediction, and these duals can then be used for the allocation online. Even if the prediction is not entirely accurate, we note that such an approach has certain advantages. This motivates the problem of finding the optimal duals. We observe that our algorithm can also be used to compute near optimal duals which can then be used to do the allocation online. Problems such as the Display ad allocation problem (please see full version of the paper for details) can benefit from such an algorithm.

A similar approach was considered by Abrams, Mendelevitch and Tomlin [AMT07] for the following problem motivated by sponsored search auctions: for each *query* j, one can show an advertiser in each of the K slots. Each advertiser i bids a certain amount on each query j, and has a daily budget. However, the cost to an advertiser depends on the entire ordered set of advertisers shown (called a *slate*), based on the rules of the auction. Given the set of queries that arrive in a day (which in practice is an estimate of the queries expected rather than the actual queries), the goal is to schedule a slate of advertisers for each query such that the total cost to each advertiser is within the budget and maximize a given objective such as the total revenue, or the social welfare. This problem is modeled as an LP and a column-generation approach is suggested to solve it. Also, many compromises are made, in terms of limiting the number of queries, etc. due to the difficulties in solving an LP of very large size. We observe that this LP fits in the resource allocation framework and thus can be solved quickly using our algorithm.

[4]In fact, the algorithm makes a single pass through this graph.

3. MIN-MAX VERSION

In this section, we solve a slightly simplified version of the general online resource allocation problem, which we call the min-max version. In this problem, m requests arrive online, and each of them must be served. The objective is to minimize the maximum fraction of any resource consumed. (There is no profit.) The following LP describes it formally.

$$\text{minimize } \lambda \text{ s.t.}$$
$$\forall\, i, \sum_{j,k} a(i,j,k)x_{j,k} \leq \lambda c_i$$
$$\forall\, j, \sum_{k} x_{j,k} = 1,$$
$$\forall\, j,k, x_{j,k} \geq 0.$$

For ease of illustration, we assume that the requests arrive i.i.d (unknown distribution) in the following proof. At the end of this section, we show that the proof holds for the adversarial stochastic input model also.

The algorithm proceeds in steps. Let λ^* denote the fractional optimal objective value of the distribution instance of this problem. Let X_i^t be the random variable indicating the amount of resource i consumed during step t, that is, $X_i^t = a(i,j,k)$ if in step t, request j was chosen and was served using option k. Let $S_i^T = \sum_{t=1}^{T} X_i^t$ be the total amount of resource i consumed in the first T steps. Let $\gamma = \max_{i,j}\{\frac{a(i,j,k)}{c_i}\}$, which implies that for all i, j and k, $a(i,j,k) \leq \gamma c_i$. Let $\phi_i^t = (1+\epsilon)^{S_i^t/(\gamma c_i)}$. For the sake of convenience, we let $S_i^0 = 0$ and $\phi_i^0 = 1$ for all i. The algorithm is as follows.

ALG Min-max.

In step $t+1$, on receiving request j, use option

$$\arg\min_k \left\{ \sum_i \frac{a(i,j,k)\phi_i^t}{c_i} \right\}.$$

LEMMA 7. *The algorithm* ***ALG Min-max*** *described above approximates* λ^* *within a factor of* $(1+\epsilon)$, *with a probability at least* $1-\delta$, *where* $\delta = n \exp\left(\frac{-\epsilon^2\lambda^*}{4\gamma}\right)$

We will prove Lemma 7 through a series of lemmas, namely Lemmas 8, 9 and 10. Before we begin the proof, we give some intuition. Consider a hypothetical algorithm, call it *Pure-random*, that knows the distribution. Let $\mathbf{x}_j^*$ denote the optimal fractional solution to the distribution instance. Pure-random is a non-adaptive algorithm which uses $\mathbf{x}_j^*$ to satisfy request j, i.e., it serves request j using option k with probability x_{jk}. Suppose we wanted to prove a bound on the performance of Pure-random, that is show that with high probability, Pure-random is within $1+O(\epsilon)$ of the optimum, say λ^*. This can be done using Chernoff bounds: for each resource separately bound the probability that the total consumption is more than $\lambda^* c_i(1 + O(\epsilon))$ using Chernoff bounds and take a union bound. Note that the Chernoff bounds are shown by proving an upper bound on the expectation of the moment generating function of the random variables. If we could show the same bound for our algorithm, then we would be done. Let $\phi^t = \sum_i \phi_i^t$. We wish to upper bound the expectation of ϕ^m.

Consider the state of the algorithm after the first t steps. Let $\tilde{X}_i^{t+1}$ denote the amount of resource i consumed in step $t+1$ had we served the request at step $t+1$ using the Pure-random algorithm instead of our algorithm. Then we show that the expectation of ϕ^{t+1} is upper bounded by $\sum_i \phi_i^t \left(1 + \epsilon \frac{\tilde{X}_i^{t+1}}{\gamma c_i}\right)$, and the rest of the proof is along the lines of the Chernoff bound proof.

LEMMA 8. *For all t,*

$$\phi^{t+1} \leq \sum_i \phi_i^t \left(1 + \epsilon \frac{\tilde{X}_i^{t+1}}{\gamma c_i}\right).$$

PROOF.

$$\begin{aligned} \phi^{t+1} &= \sum_i \phi_i^{t+1} = \sum_i \phi_i^t (1+\epsilon)^{\frac{X_i^{t+1}}{\gamma c_i}} \\ &\leq \sum_i \phi_i^t \left(1 + \epsilon \frac{X_i^{t+1}}{\gamma c_i}\right) \leq \sum_i \phi_i^t \left(1 + \epsilon \frac{\tilde{X}_i^{t+1}}{\gamma c_i}\right) \end{aligned}$$

The first inequality is because the convexity of the function $(1+\epsilon)^x$ can be used to upper bound it by $1 + \epsilon x$ for all $x \in [0, 1]$, and $X_i^t \leq \max_{j,k} a(i,j,k) \leq \gamma c_i$. The second inequality follows from the definition of our algorithm as it chooses the option that minimizes $\left\{\sum_i \frac{a(i,j,k)\phi_i^t}{c_i}\right\}$ □

LEMMA 9. *For all T, $\mathbf{E}[\phi^T] \leq n \exp\left(\frac{\epsilon \lambda^* T}{\gamma m}\right)$, where λ^* is the optimal solution to the LP.*

PROOF. From Lemma 8, it follows that

$$\begin{aligned} \mathbf{E}\left[\phi^{t+1} \mid \phi_i^t \text{ for all } i\right] &\leq \mathbf{E}\left[\sum_i \phi_i^t \left(1 + \epsilon \frac{\tilde{X}_i^{t+1}}{\gamma c_i}\right)\right] \\ &\leq \sum_i \phi_i^t \left(1 + \epsilon \frac{\lambda^*}{\gamma m}\right) \\ &= \phi^t \left(1 + \epsilon \frac{\lambda^*}{\gamma m}\right) \\ &\leq \phi^t \exp\left(\frac{\epsilon \lambda^*}{\gamma m}\right) \end{aligned}$$

and hence the lemma follows since $\phi^0 = n$. The second inequality follows from the fact that $\mathbf{E}[\tilde{X}_i^{t+1}] \leq \frac{\lambda^* c_i}{m}$ for all i. This is because requests are drawn i.i.d, and hence the optimal value of the distribution instance is the same for all time steps and is equal to λ^*. □

We prove Lemma 10 in the full version of the paper.

LEMMA 10.

$$\mathbf{Pr}\left[\max_i \left\{\frac{S_i^T}{c_i}\right\} > \frac{T}{m}\lambda^*(1+\epsilon)\right] \leq n \exp\left(\frac{-\epsilon^2 T \lambda^*}{4\gamma m}\right).$$

Substituting $T = m$ in Lemma 10, we get Lemma 7.

Adversarial stochastic input model.

In the above lemmas, we assumed that the requests are drawn i.i.d, i.e., we used the fact that $\mathbf{E}[\tilde{X}_i^t] \leq \lambda^* c_i/m$ for all t. But in an adversarial stochastic model, since the distribution from which a request is drawn changes each step, the optimal objective of the distribution instance also changes every step, i.e., it could be λ_t^* at step t. So, in the proof Lemma 9, where we proved that

$$\mathbf{E}\left[\phi^{t+1} \mid \phi_i^t \text{ for all } i\right] \leq \phi^t \exp\left(\frac{\epsilon \lambda^*}{\gamma m}\right),$$

we would instead have $\mathbf{E}\left[\phi^{t+1} \mid \phi_i^t \text{ for all } i\right] \leq \phi^t \exp\left(\frac{\epsilon \lambda_t^*}{\gamma m}\right)$. But given a target λ^*, we know the adversary is constrained to pick distributions whose distribution instance has an optimum objective *at most* λ^* (recall that this is a minimization problem). Therefore, we can upper bound $\phi^t \exp\left(\frac{\epsilon \lambda_t^*}{\gamma m}\right)$ by $\phi^t \exp\left(\frac{\epsilon \lambda^*}{\gamma m}\right)$. The rest of the steps in the proof remain the same. Thus, the adversary is not constrained to pick requests from the same distribution at every time step. All we require is that, whatever distribution it uses for drawing its request, the corresponding distribution instance has an optimum objective value at most λ^*, which is the target value we aim for.

In the following sections, we illustrate all our proofs in the i.i.d model with unknown distribution and it is easy to convert them to proofs for the adversarial stochastic input model.

4. MIXED COVERING-PACKING AND ONLINE RESOURCE ALLOCATION

4.1 Mixed Covering-Packing

In this section, we consider the mixed packing-covering problem stated in Section 2.3. and prove Theorem 6. We restate the LP for the mixed covering-packing problem here.

$$\begin{aligned} &\forall\, i, \sum_{j,k} a(i,j,k) x_{j,k} \leq c_i \\ &\forall\, i, \sum_{j,k} b(i,j,k) x_{j,k} \geq d_i \\ &\forall\, j, \sum_k x_{j,k} = 1, \\ &\forall\, j,k, x_{j,k} \geq 0. \end{aligned}$$

The goal is to check if there is a feasible solution to this LP. We solve a gap version of this problem. Distinguish between the two cases:

YES: There is a feasible solution.

NO: There is no feasible solution even if all of the c_i's are multiplied by $1+\epsilon$ and all of the d_i's are multiplied by $1-\epsilon$.

For convenience of description, we refer to the quantities indexed by j as requests, those indexed by i as resources and those indexed by k as options.

As before, the algorithm proceeds in steps. In each step, the algorithm samples a request i.i.d from the total of m possible requests. We will prove that if the number of samples $T \geq \Theta(\frac{\gamma m \ln(n/\delta)}{\epsilon^2})$, then the algorithm solves the gap version with probability at least $(1-\delta)$. Since the time taken for serving any given request is one (by taking the time consumed by a single oracle call to be one), this proves that the total run-time is $O(\frac{\gamma m \ln(n/\delta)}{\epsilon^2})$, thus proving Theorem 6, if δ is a constant.

Let $X_i^t, \tilde{X}_i^t, S_i^t$ be as defined in Section 3. Let Y_i^t be the random variable indicating the amount of demand i satisfied during step t, that is, $Y_i^t = b(i,j,k)$ if in step t, request j was chosen and was served using option k. Let $\tilde{Y_i}^t$ denote the amount of demand i satisfied during step t by the optimal algorithm for the distribution instance of this problem. Let $V_i^T = \sum_{t=1}^T Y_i^t$. Let $\phi_i^t = \eta_c(1+\frac{\epsilon}{2})^{\frac{S_i^t}{\gamma c_i}}(1+\frac{\epsilon}{2\gamma m})^{T-t}$, where $\eta_c = (1+\frac{\epsilon}{2})^{-(1+\frac{\epsilon}{2})\frac{T}{\gamma m}}$. Let $\psi_i^t = \eta_d(1-\frac{\epsilon}{2})^{\frac{V_i^t}{\gamma d_i}}(1-\frac{\epsilon}{2\gamma m})^{T-t}$, where $\eta_d = (1-\frac{\epsilon}{2})^{-(1-\frac{\epsilon}{2})\frac{T}{\gamma m}}$. Let $\phi^t = \sum_i \phi_i^t$, let $\psi^t = \sum_i \psi_i^t$ and $\Phi^t = \phi^t + \psi^t$. As before, we let $S_i^0 = 0$ and $V_i^0 = 0$. The algorithm is as follows.

ALG Packing-Covering.

Given request j in step $t+1$, use the option

$$\arg\min_k \left\{ \begin{array}{r} \frac{1}{\left(1+\frac{\epsilon}{2\gamma m}\right)} \sum_i \phi_i^t \frac{a(i,j,k)}{c_i} \\ -\frac{1}{\left(1-\frac{\epsilon}{2\gamma m}\right)} \sum_i \psi_i^t \frac{b(i,j,k)}{d_i} \end{array} \right\}$$

At the end of T steps, the algorithm checks if $\max_i \frac{S_i^T}{c_i} < \frac{T}{m}(1+\frac{\epsilon}{2})$ and if $\min_i \frac{V_i^T}{d_i} > \frac{T}{m}(1-\frac{\epsilon}{2})$. If true, the algorithm answers YES. Else it says NO. We now proceed to prove that, whenever the real answer is YES, the algorithm says YES with a high probability. Lemmas 11 and 12 prove this case. We prove them in the full version of the paper.

LEMMA 11. *For a* YES *instance* $\mathbf{E}\left[\Phi^T\right] \le \Phi^0$.

LEMMA 12. *For a* YES *instance*

$$\mathbf{Pr}\left[\max_i \frac{S_i^T}{c_i} > \frac{T}{m}(1+\frac{\epsilon}{2})\right] + \mathbf{Pr}\left[\min_i \frac{V_i^T}{d_i} < \frac{T}{m}(1-\frac{\epsilon}{2})\right] \le \Phi^0$$

Observe that $\Phi^0 = \eta_c(1+\frac{\epsilon}{2\gamma m})^T + \eta_d(1-\frac{\epsilon}{2\gamma m})^T$, which is upper bounded by $n\exp\left(\frac{-\epsilon^2 T}{16\gamma m}\right) + n\exp\left(\frac{-\epsilon^2 T}{8\gamma m}\right)$. If $T = O(\frac{\gamma m \log(n/\delta)}{\epsilon^2})$, we have the failure probability to be at most δ. Thus Lemma 12 proves that the algorithm **ALG Packing-Covering** says YES with a probability at least $1-\delta$ when the real answer is YES.

We now proceed to prove that when the real answer is NO, our algorithm says NO with a probability at least $1-\delta$, i.e.,

LEMMA 13. *For a* NO *instance, if* $T \ge \Theta(\frac{\gamma m \log(n)}{\epsilon^2})$*, then*

$$\mathbf{Pr}\left[\max_i \frac{S_i^T}{c_i} < \frac{T}{m}(1+\frac{\epsilon}{2}) \ \&\ \min_i \frac{V_i^T}{d_i} > \frac{T}{m}(1-\frac{\epsilon}{2})\right] < \delta.$$

The proof appears in the full version of the paper.

Lemmas 11, 12 and 13 prove that the gap-version of the mixed covering-packing problem can be solved in time $O(\frac{\gamma m \log(n)}{\epsilon^2})$, thus proving Theorem 6.

REMARK 1. *We show that a greedy-type algorithm won't solve the gap version of even just the covering problem. This answers an open question from [CCD+10] regarding whether or not the greedy algorithm solves the gap version. The precise algorithm and why it fails are included in the full version of the paper.*

5. ONLINE ALGORITHMS WITH STOCHASTIC INPUT

In this section, we use the potential function based algorithm to solve the online version of the resource allocation problem introduced in Section 2.2. The following LP describes the resource allocation problem.

$$\begin{aligned} &\text{maximize} \sum_{j,k} w_{j,k} x_{j,k} \text{ s.t.} \\ &\forall\, i, \sum_{j,k} a(i,j,k) x_{j,k} \le c_i \\ &\forall\, j, \sum_k x_{j,k} \le 1, \\ &\forall\, j,k, x_{j,k} \ge 0. \end{aligned} \qquad (1)$$

Similar to the algorithm in [AWY09], our algorithm computes increasingly better estimates of the objective value by computing the optimal solution for the observed requests, and uses it to guide future allocations. Through Lemmas 14 and 15, we show that our algorithm achieves a competitive ratio of $1-O(\epsilon)$ thus proving Theorem 2. We assume that the number of requests m is known in advance. Algorithm 1 describes our algorithm.

Algorithm 1 : Algorithm for stochastic online resource allocation

Initialize $t_0 : t_0 \leftarrow \lceil \epsilon m \rceil$
for $r = 0$ to $l-1$ **do**
  for $t = t_r + 1$ to t_{r+1} **do**
    If the incoming request is j, use the following option k:

$$\arg\min_k \left\{ \begin{array}{r} \frac{\epsilon_c/\gamma}{\left(1+\frac{\epsilon_c}{\gamma m}\right)} \sum_i \phi_i^{t-1} \frac{a(i,j,k)}{c_i} \\ -\frac{\epsilon_o/w_{\max}}{\left(1-\frac{\epsilon_o Z(r)}{w_{\max} m}\right)} \phi_{\text{obj}}^{t-1} w_{j,k} \end{array} \right\}.$$

    if $t = t_r + 1$ **then**
      For all i, $S_i^t(r) = X_i^t$, and $V^t(r) = Y^t$.
    else
      For all i, $S_i^t(r) = S_i^{t-1}(r) + X_i^t$, and, $V^t(r) = V^{t-1}(r) + Y^t$.
    end if
  end for
end for

The first ϵm requests are not served but used just for computational purposes. After these first ϵm requests, the algorithm proceeds in l stages, namely $0, 1, \ldots, l-1$, where l is such that $\epsilon 2^l = 1$ and ϵ is a positive number between 0 and 1 that the algorithm designer gets to choose. In stage r the algorithm serves $t_r = \epsilon m 2^r$ requests. Note that the stage r consists of all steps $t \in (t_r, t_{r+1}]$.

Let W^* denote the optimal solution to the distribution instance of the problem. Let X_i^t be as defined in Section 3. Let Y^t be the amount of profit earned during step t, i.e., $Y^t = w_{j,k}$, if in step t, request j was served using option k. Instead of the usual S_i^t, we now define $S_i^t(r) = \sum_{u=t_r+1}^t X_i^u$, which is the sum of X_i^u's till t for u's belonging to stage r alone, i.e., $u \in (t_r, t_{r+1}]$. Similarly, $V^t(r) = \sum_{u=t_r+1}^t Y^u$. Let $w_{\max} = \max_{j,k} w_{j,k}$.

The potential function for constraint i in step t when $t \in (t_r, t_{r+1}]$

is defined by

$$\phi_i^t = \eta_c(r)(1+\epsilon_c(r))^{\frac{S_i^t(r)}{\gamma c_i}} \left(1+\frac{\epsilon_c(r)}{\gamma m}\right)^{t_{r+1}-t},$$

$$\eta_c(r) = (1+\epsilon_c(r))^{-(1+\epsilon_c(r))\frac{t_r}{\gamma m}},$$

$$\epsilon_c(r) = \sqrt{\frac{4\gamma m \ln((n+1)/\delta)}{t_r}}.$$

Similarly, the potential function for objective at step t is,

$$\phi_{\text{obj}}^t = \eta_{\text{obj}}(r)(1-\epsilon_o(r))^{\frac{V^t(r)}{w_{\max}}} \left(1-\frac{\epsilon_o(r)Z(r)}{w_{\max}m}\right)^{t_{r+1}-t},$$

$$\eta_{\text{obj}}(r) = (1-\epsilon_o(r))^{-(1-\epsilon_o(r))\frac{t_r Z(r)}{m w_{\max}}}.$$

$$\epsilon_o(r) = \sqrt{\frac{2w_{\max}m \ln((n+1)/\delta)}{t_r Z(r)}}.$$

Note that apart from constants, the only difference between $\epsilon_o(r)$ and $\epsilon_c(r)$ is that instead of γ, $\epsilon_o(r)$ has $w_{\max}/Z(r)$. The value $Z(r)$, as we define below, gets progressively updated, but within a single stage r remains the same. After stage r, the algorithm computes the optimal objective value e_r to the following instance $\mathcal{I}_r$: the instance $\mathcal{I}_r$ has the t_r requests of stage-r, and the capacity of resource i is $\frac{t_r c_i(1+\epsilon_c(r))}{m}$, i.e., the capacity of resources are scaled down according to the number of requests, but has a slight extra allowance by a factor of $(1+\epsilon_c(r))$. It uses e_r to compute the value $Z(r+1)$ to be used in the potential function for objective in stage $r+1$.

LEMMA 14. *With probability at least* $1-\delta(2+\frac{1}{\alpha_r})-4\frac{\epsilon_c(r)}{\alpha_r}$,

$$\frac{t_r W^*(1-\epsilon_c(r))}{m} \le e_r \le \frac{t_r W^*(1-\epsilon_c(r))(1+\alpha_r)}{m}.$$

We prove Lemma 14 in the full version of the paper.

Using these e_r's, we define our $Z(r+1)$ as follows:

$$Z(r+1) = \frac{m e_r}{t_r(1-\epsilon_c(r))(1+\alpha_r)}.$$

Using the bounds on e_r in Lemma 14, we note that $Z(r+1) \le W^*$ and that $Z(r+1) \ge \frac{W^*}{1+\alpha_r}$. Thus with probability at least

$$1-\sum_{r=0}^{l-1}\left[\delta(2+\frac{1}{\alpha_r})+4\frac{\epsilon_c(r)}{\alpha_r}\right],$$

$Z(r)$ satisfies these bounds for all r. Given the bounds on $Z(r)$, we use Lemma 12 to see that with a probability at least $(1-\delta)$, the objective value achieved in stage r is at least $\frac{t_r Z(r)}{m}(1-\epsilon_o(r))$, and the amount of resource i consumed in stage r is at most $\frac{t_r c_i}{m}(1+\epsilon_c(r))$. Hence, these bounds are true for all r with probability at least $1-\log(1/\epsilon)\delta$, since the total number of stages $l=\log(1/\epsilon)$.

The total failure probability is the sum of the failure probability during estimation of $Z(r)$ through e_r, given by

$$\sum_{r=0}^{l-1}\left[\delta(2+\frac{1}{\alpha_r})+4\frac{\epsilon_c(r)}{\alpha_r}\right]$$

and the failure probability of our algorithm in all stages together given by $\log(1/\epsilon)\delta$. Thus, the total failure probability is given by

$$\begin{aligned} TFP &= \sum_{r=0}^{l-1}\left[\delta(2+\frac{1}{\alpha_r})+4\frac{\epsilon_c(r)}{\alpha_r}\right]+\log(1/\epsilon)\delta \\ &= 3\log(1/\epsilon)\delta+\sum_{r=0}^{l-1}\left[\frac{\delta}{\alpha_r}+4\frac{\epsilon_c(r)}{\alpha_r}\right] \end{aligned}$$

With a probability of $1-TFP$, the algorithm obtains an objective value of at least

$$\sum_{r=0}^{l-1}\frac{t_r W^*}{m}\left(\frac{1-\epsilon_o(r)}{1+\alpha_r}\right),$$

and for each i, the amount of resource i consumed is at most

$$\sum_{r=0}^{l-1}\frac{t_r c_i}{m}(1+\epsilon_c(r)).$$

On setting $\gamma = O\left(\frac{\epsilon^2/(\log(1/\epsilon))^2}{\log(n)+\log(1/\epsilon)+\log(1/\delta')}\right)$, for some positive constant $\delta' < 1$, and setting $\alpha_r = \frac{\log(1/\epsilon)\epsilon_c(r)}{\delta'}$ and $\delta = \delta'\epsilon$, the above equations can be simplified to yield the following lemma.

LEMMA 15. *With probability higher than* $(1-8\delta')$, *the value of the objective function achieved at the completion of the algorithm is at least* $W^*(1-O(\epsilon/\delta'))$ *and no resource is consumed more than its capacity.*

For a fixed constant δ', we have $\gamma = O\left(\frac{\epsilon^2/(\log(1/\epsilon))^2}{\log(n)+\log(1/\epsilon)}\right)$. Thus Lemma 15 proves that, our algorithm achieves a competitive ratio of $(1-O(\epsilon))$ and hence proves Theorem 2.

6. ADWORDS IN I.I.D SETTING

In this section, we give a simple proof of Theorem 5: greedy algorithm achieves a competitive ratio of $(1-1/e)$ in the adwords problem, where the impressions come from an adversarial stochastic input model. As before, we illustrate our proofs for the i.i.d model with unknown distribution below. We now briefly describe the adwords setting.

Setting.

There are a total of n advertisers, and queries arrive online, from some pool of queries. Let the (unknown) number of queries that arrive be m. The queries that appear each day are drawn i.i.d from some unknown distribution. Advertiser i bids an amount b_{ij} on query j. Advertiser i has a budget B_i denoting the maximum amount of money that can be spent on a given day. The bid amounts b_{ij} are revealed online as the queries arrive. The objective is to maximize the sum of the bid amounts successfully allocated, subject to budget constraints. Whenever a query j arrives, with a bid amount $b_{ij} >$ remaining budget of i, we are still allowed to allot that query to advertiser i, but we only earn a revenue of the remaining budget of i, and not the total value b_{ij}.

Goel and Mehta [GM08] prove that the greedy algorithm gives a $(1-1/e)$ approximation to the adwords problem when the queries arrive in a random permutation or in i.i.d, but under an assumption which almost gets down to bids being much smaller than budgets. We give a much simpler proof for a $(1-1/e)$ approximation by greedy algorithm for the i.i.d unknown distributions case, and our proof works irrespective of the the relation between the size of the bids and the budgets involved.

Let p_j be the probability of query j appearing in any given impression. Let $y_j = mp_j$. Let x_{ij} denote the offline fractional optimal solution for the distribution instance. Let $w_i(t)$ denote the amount of money spent by advertiser i at time step t, i.e., for the t-th query in the greedy algorithm. Let $f_i(0) = \sum_j b_{ij} x_{ij} y_j$. Let $f_i(t) = f_i(0) - \sum_{r=1}^{t} w_i(r)$. Let $f(t) = \sum_{i=1}^{n} f_i(t)$. Note that $f_i(0)$ is the amount spent by i in the offline fractional optimal solution to the distribution instance.

Consider the greedy algorithm which allocates the query j arriving at time t to the advertiser who has the maximum effective bid for that query, i.e., $\underset{i}{\text{argmax}} \min\{b_{ij}, B_i - \sum_{r=1}^{t-1} w_i(r)\}$. We prove that this algorithm obtains a revenue of $(1 - 1/e)\sum_{i,j} b_{ij} x_{ij} y_j$ and thus gives the desired $1 - 1/e$ competitive ratio against the fractional optimal solution to the distribution instance. The proof is similar to the proof we presented in Lemma 8 for the resource allocation problem. Consider a hypothetical algorithm that allocates queries to advertisers according to the x_{ij}'s. We prove that this hypothetical algorithm obtains an expected revenue of $(1 - 1/e)\sum_{i,j} b_{ij} x_{ij} y_j$, and argue that the greedy algorithm only performs better. Let $w_i^h(t)$ and $f_i^h(t)$ denote the quantities analogous to $w_i(t)$ and $f_i(t)$ for the hypothetical algorithm, with the initial value $f_i^h(0) = f_i(0) = \sum_j b_{ij} x_{ij} y_j$. Let $f^h(t) = \sum_{i=1}^{n} f_i^h(t)$.

LEMMA 16. *The hypothetical algorithm satisfies the following:* $\mathbf{E}[f^h(t) | f^h(t-1)] \le f^h(t-1)(1 - 1/m)$

LEMMA 17. $\mathbf{E}[\text{GREEDY}] \ge (1 - 1/e)\sum_{i,j} b_{ij} x_{ij} y_j$

We prove Lemma 16 and 17 in the full version of the paper.

Lemma 17 proves Theorem 5.

7. APPLICATIONS

We now list the problems that are special cases of the resource allocation framework and have been previously considered. See the full version of the paper for more special cases.

7.1 Adwords Problem

While in Section 2.2.1 we noted that we could get a $1 - 1/e$ approximation to the adwords problem with unbounded γ, we note here that γ is small, i.e. $\max_{i,j} \frac{b_{ij}}{B_i} \le \frac{\epsilon^2/\log(1/\epsilon)^2}{\log(n) + \log(1/\epsilon)}$, we get a $1 - O(\epsilon)$ approximation to the maximum profit through the resource allocation framework.

7.2 Network Routing and Load Balancing

Consider a graph (either undirected or directed) with edge capacities. Requests arrive online; a request j consists of a source-sink pair, (s_j, t_j) and a bandwidth ρ_j. In order to satisfy a request, a capacity of ρ_j must be allocated to it on every edge along some path from s_j to t_j in the graph. In the *congestion minimization* version, all requests must be satisfied, and the objective is to minimize the maximum (over all edges) congestion, which is the ratio of the allocated bandwidth to the capacity of the edge. In the *throughput maximization* version, the objective is to maximize the number of satisfied requests while not allocating more bandwidth than the available capacity for each edge. (Different requests could have different values on them, and one could also consider maximizing the total value of the satisfied requests.) Both the congestion minimization version and the throughput maximization version can be solved through our algorithm 1 for resource allocation framework. Kamath, Palmon and Plotkin [KPP96] considered a variant of this problem with the requests arriving according to a stationary Poisson process, and show a competitive ratio that is very similar to ours.

7.3 Combinatorial Auctions

Suppose we have n items for sale, with c_i copies of item i. Bidders arrive online, and bidder j has a utility function $U_j : 2^{[n]} \rightarrow \mathbf{R}$. If we posted prices p_i for each item i, then bidder j buys a bundle S that maximizes $U_j(S) - \sum_{i \in S} p_i$. We assume that bidders can compute such a bundle. The goal is to maximize social welfare, the total utility of all the bidders, subject to the supply constraint that there are only c_i copies of item i. Firstly, incentive constraints aside, this problem can be written as an LP in the resource allocation framework. The items are the resources and agents arriving online are the requests. All the different subsets of items form the set of options. The utility $U_j(S)$ represents the profit $w_{j,S}$ of serving agent j through option S, i.e. subset S. If an item $i \in S$, then $a_{i,j,S} = 1$ for all j and zero otherwise. Incentive constraints aside, our algorithm for resource allocation at step t, will choose the option k (or equivalently the bundle S) as specified in point 4 of algorithm 1, i.e., minimize the potential function. That can be equivalently written as,

$$\arg\max_k \left\{ \begin{array}{c} \frac{\epsilon_o / w_{\max}}{\left(1 - \frac{\epsilon_o Z(r)}{w_{\max} m}\right)} \phi_{\text{obj}}^{t-1} w_{j,k} \\ - \frac{\epsilon_c/\gamma}{\left(1 + \frac{\epsilon_c}{\gamma m}\right)} \sum_i \phi_i^{t-1} \frac{a(i,j,k)}{c_i} \end{array} \right\}$$

Now, maximizing the above expression is the same as picking the k to maximize $w_{j,k} - \sum_i p_i a(i,j,k)$, where

$$p_i = \frac{\frac{\epsilon_c/\gamma}{\left(1+\frac{\epsilon_c}{\gamma m}\right)}}{\frac{\epsilon_o/w_{\max}}{\left(1-\frac{\epsilon_o Z(r)}{w_{\max} m}\right)} \phi_{\text{obj}}^{t-1}} \cdot \frac{\phi_i^{t-1}}{c_i}.$$

Thus, if we post these prices p_i on items, agents will do exactly what the algorithm would have done otherwise. Suppose that the bidders are i.i.d samples from some distribution (or they arrive as in the adversarial stochastic input model). Here $\gamma = 1/\min_i\{c_i\}$ and we can use Theorem 2 to get an incentive compatible posted price auction[5] with a competitive ratio of $1 - O(\epsilon)$ whenever $\min_i\{c_i\} \ge \frac{\log(n) + \log(1/\epsilon)}{\epsilon^2/\log(1/\epsilon)^2}$. Further if an analog of Theorem 2 also holds in the random permutation model then we get a similar result for combinatorial auctions in the offline case: we simply consider the bidders one by one in a random order.

7.4 Selective Call-out

Chakraborty et. al. [CEDG+11] formulated the following problem that arises in the design of an ad-exchange. An exchange gets *ad-requests* online; each ad-request may have multiple slots with different *qualities*. Whenever the exchange gets an ad-request, it calls out to a subset of ad-networks for a bid. Given the bids it then allocates the slots to the highest bidders. The ad-networks have constraints on how frequently they want to be called out. In addition, the following assumptions are made: the ad-requests are i.i.d samples from an unknown distribution, and for every ad-network its values for all ad-requests of a certain type are i.i.d from a distribution that is known to the exchange. They consider various objective functions, such as social welfare, revenue of a particular auction, GSP with reserve, and so on. They state their results in the PAC model, where they use an initial sample of impressions to train their algorithm. They give a bound on the number of samples needed in order to get a $1 - 1/e - \epsilon$ competitive algorithm. We

[5] Here we assume that each agent reveals his true utility function *after* he makes his purchase. This information is necessary to compute the prices to be charged for future agents.

can use our algorithms (with an approximate relaxation, Theorem 4) to improve their results in the following two ways. Either we are given the target objective value, in which case we achieve the same competitive ratio in the online setting without the need for an initial sample. If we are not given the target objective value then we need an initial sample to estimate that value. The number of samples we need is less than what is required by [CEDG+11] by a factor of n. Further, our algorithm would also work in the adversarial stochastic input model.

8. CONCLUSION AND FUTURE WORK

Our work raises the following open questions.

- As mentioned in the introduction, we can show that our algorithm works in the i.i.d model, so the natural question is if our algorithm works for the random permutation model.
- Currently in our algorithm for the online case, we need to estimate the optimum objective function value periodically. For this we need to solve (at least approximately) an offline instance of the problem repeatedly. Is there an algorithm that avoids this?
- Perhaps the holy grail for an online algorithm for say, Adwords, is to get a guarantee of the following form: if the input is i.i.d from some given distribution then get a competitive ratio that is close to 1, while simultaneously getting a competitive ratio of $1-1/e$ if the input is adversarial. Our algorithm for Adwords (or some simple variant) could actually achieves this. At the very least, can we get such a guarantee for online b-matching with different budgets? Note that when all the budgets are the same then our algorithm for the min-max version is equivalent to a simple algorithm called BALANCE that achieves this. (This observation follows from the results in Kalyanasundaram and Pruhs [KP00] and Motwani, Panigrahy and Xu [MP06].)
- A high level goal is to come up with other reasonable definitions that go beyond worst case. The motivation for this is to bridge the gap between the theory and practice of online algorithms.

9. REFERENCES

[AHK05] Sanjeev Arora, Elad Hazan, and Satyen Kale. The multiplicative weights update method: a meta algorithm and applications. Technical report, 2005.

[AMT07] Zoe Abrams, Ofer Mendelevitch, and John Tomlin. Optimal delivery of sponsored search advertisements subject to budget constraints. In *EC '07: Proceedings of the 8th ACM conference on Electronic commerce*, pages 272–278, New York, NY, USA, 2007. ACM.

[AWY09] Shipra Agrawal, Zizhuo Wang, and Yinyu Ye. A dynamic near-optimal algorithm for online linear programming. arXiv:0911.2974v1, 2009.

[BJN07] Niv Buchbinder, Kamal Jain, and Joseph Seffi Naor. Online primal-dual algorithms for maximizing ad-auctions revenue. In *ESA'07: Proceedings of the 15th annual European conference on Algorithms*, pages 253–264, Berlin, Heidelberg, 2007. Springer-Verlag.

[BK10] Bahman Bahmani and Michael Kapralov. Improved bounds for online stochastic matching. In *ESA*, pages 170–181, 2010.

[CCD+10] Denis Charles, Max Chickering, Nikhil R. Devanur, Kamal Jain, and Manan Sanghi. Fast algorithms for finding matchings in lopsided bipartite graphs with applications to display ads. In *EC '10: Proceedings of the 11th ACM conference on Electronic commerce*, pages 121–128, New York, NY, USA, 2010. ACM.

[CEDG+11] Tanmoy Chakraborty, Eyal Even-Dar, Sudipto Guha, Yishay Mansour, and S. Muthukrishnan. Selective call out and real time bidding. In *To appear in WINE*, 2011.

[DH09] Nikhil R. Devanur and Thomas P. Hayes. The adwords problem: online keyword matching with budgeted bidders under random permutations. In John Chuang, Lance Fortnow, and Pearl Pu, editors, *ACM Conference on Electronic Commerce*, pages 71–78. ACM, 2009.

[FHK+10] Jon Feldman, Monika Henzinger, Nitish Korula, Vahab S. Mirrokni, and Clifford Stein. Online stochastic packing applied to display ad allocation. In *ESA*, pages 182–194, 2010.

[Fle00] Lisa K. Fleischer. Approximating fractional multicommodity flow independent of the number of commodities. *SIAM J. Discret. Math.*, 13(4):505–520, 2000.

[FMMM09] Jon Feldman, Aranyak Mehta, Vahab Mirrokni, and S. Muthukrishnan. Online stochastic matching: Beating 1-1/e. In *FOCS '09: Proceedings of the 2009 50th Annual IEEE Symposium on Foundations of Computer Science*, pages 117–126, Washington, DC, USA, 2009. IEEE Computer Society.

[GK98] Naveen Garg and Jochen Koenemann. Faster and simpler algorithms for multicommodity flow and other fractional packing problems. In *FOCS '98: Proceedings of the 39th Annual Symposium on Foundations of Computer Science*, page 300, Washington, DC, USA, 1998. IEEE Computer Society.

[GM08] Gagan Goel and Aranyak Mehta. Online budgeted matching in random input models with applications to adwords. In *SODA '08: Proceedings of the nineteenth annual ACM-SIAM symposium on Discrete algorithms*, pages 982–991, Philadelphia, PA, USA, 2008. Society for Industrial and Applied Mathematics.

[KP00] Bala Kalyanasundaram and Kirk R. Pruhs. An optimal deterministic algorithm for online b-matching. *Theor. Comput. Sci.*, 233(1-2):319–325, 2000.

[KPP96] Anil Kamath, Omri Palmon, and Serge Plotkin. Routing and admission control in general topology networks with poisson arrivals. In *SODA '96: Proceedings of the seventh annual ACM-SIAM symposium on Discrete algorithms*, pages 269–278, Philadelphia, PA, USA, 1996. Society for Industrial and Applied Mathematics.

[MGS11] Vahideh Manshadi, Shayan Gharan, and Amin Saberi. Online stochastic matching: Online actions based on offline statistics. In *To appear in SODA*, 2011.

[MP06] Rajeev Motwani, Rina Panigrahy, and Ying Xu 0002. Fractional matching via balls-and-bins. In *APPROX-RANDOM*, pages 487–498, 2006.

[MSVV05] Aranyak Mehta, Amin Saberi, Umesh Vazirani, and Vijay Vazirani. Adwords and generalized on-line matching. In *In FOCS '05: Proceedings of the 46th Annual IEEE Symposium on Foundations of Computer Science*, pages 264–273. IEEE Computer Society, 2005.

[PST91] Serge A. Plotkin, David B. Shmoys, and Éva Tardos. Fast approximation algorithms for fractional packing and covering problems. In *FOCS '91: Proceedings of the 32nd annual symposium on Foundations of computer science*, pages 495–504, Washington, DC, USA, 1991. IEEE Computer Society.

[VVS10] Erik Vee, Sergei Vassilvitskii, and Jayavel Shanmugasundaram. Optimal online assignment with forecasts. In *EC '10: Proceedings of the 11th ACM conference on Electronic commerce*, pages 109–118, New York, NY, USA, 2010. ACM.

[You95] Neal E. Young. Randomized rounding without solving the linear program. In *SODA '95: Proceedings of the sixth annual ACM-SIAM symposium on Discrete algorithms*, pages 170–178, Philadelphia, PA, USA, 1995. Society for Industrial and Applied Mathematics.

Hiring a Secretary from a Poset

Ravi Kumar
Yahoo! Research
701 First Ave
Sunnyvale, CA 94089.
ravikumar@yahoo-inc.com

Silvio Lattanzi*
Google Inc.
76 Ninth Avenue
New York, NY, 10011.
silviol@google.com

Sergei Vassilvitskii
Yahoo! Research
111 W 40th Street
New York, NY 10018.
sergei@yahoo-inc.com

Andrea Vattani*
UC San Diego
9500 Gilman Drive
La Jolla, CA 92093.
avattani@cs.ucsd.edu

ABSTRACT

The secretary problem lies at the core of mechanism design for online auctions. In this work we study the generalization of the classical secretary problem in a setting where there is only a *partial* order between the elements and the goal of the algorithm is to return one of the maximal elements of the poset. This is equivalent to the auction setting where the seller has a multidimensional objective function with only a partial order among the outcomes. We obtain an algorithm that succeeds with probability at least

$$k^{-k/(k-1)}\left(\left(1+\log k^{1/(k-1)}\right)^k-1\right),$$

where k is the number of maximal elements in the poset and is the only information about the poset that is known to the algorithm; the success probability approaches the classical bound of $1/e$ as $k \to 1$. On the other hand, we prove an almost matching upper bound of $k^{-1/(k-1)}$ on the success probability of any algorithm for this problem; this upper bound holds even if the algorithm knows the complete structure of the poset.

Categories and Subject Descriptors

F.2.2 [**Theory of Computation**]: Analysis of Algorithms and Problem Complexity—*Nonumerical Algorithms and Problems*

General Terms

Algorithms, Theory

*Part of this work was done while the authors were visiting Yahoo! Research.

EC'11, June 5–9, 2011, San Jose, California, USA.

Keywords

Secretary problem, Partial order

1. INTRODUCTION

The secretary problem [7, 8] is a perfect example of online decision-making under uncertainty. The setting is humble: candidates for a secretary position arrive online in a random order and the goal is to choose the best candidate, with the constraint that no past decision can be reverted. The optimal algorithm is to skip the first $1/e$ fraction of the candidates and to choose the next arriving candidate who is the best seen so far; this algorithm yields a success probability of $1/e$. The secretary problem has a rich history dating back at least a century, and is a frequent object of study even to this day. See the survey article by Ferguson [8] for an excellent historical perspective of the secretary problem.

Implicit in the classical setting is the assumption that there is a total order on the candidates, but this assumption rarely holds in real life since candidates often have incomparable attributes. This leads to the natural *poset secretary problem*: if the elements of the permutation (candidates) are only partially ordered, how to maximize the probability of returning a maximal element in the poset? Note that the incomparable elements present the main challenge: many simple modifications of the total order algorithm to handle the incomparable elements can be shown to have vanishing success probabilities.

Secretary problems have recently been shown to lie at the core of online auction and mechanism design problems [4]. For instance, Hajiaghayi, Kleinberg, and Parkes [13] showed how to convert the classic secretary problem into a group strategy-proof mechanism for the online single item auction. The algorithm we present can be adapted in a similar fashion to a setting where the seller has a multidimensional utility function that does not lead to a total ordering on the bidders. The bidders arrive with potentially incomparable bids and the goal is to sell the item at a no-regret price, i.e., to select a bidder who is not dominated by any of the others.

The poset secretary problem was first studied by Preater [19], who proposed an algorithm with a success probability of 1/8. Recently, Georgiou et al. [10] improved this bound to 1/4; they also showed that this bound is tight for Preater's algorithm. These algorithms suffer from two major drawbacks. First, the success probability does not match

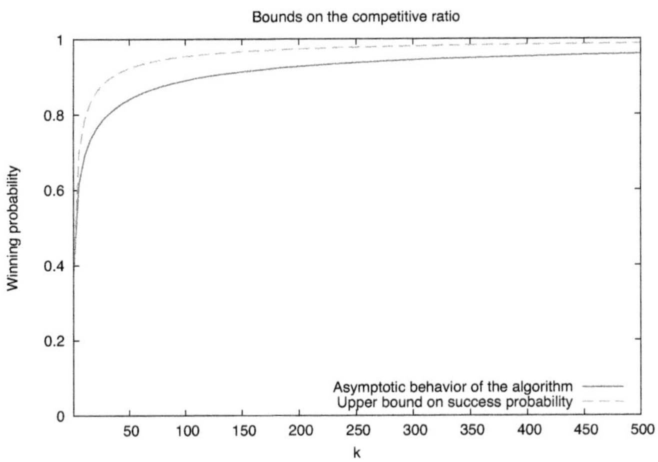

Figure 1: A visualization of the upper and lower bounds for the poset secretary problem as a function of the number of maximal elements in the poset.

the classical bound when the poset is a total order. Second, these bounds do not improve with the number of maximal elements in the poset, which is undesirable since the problem should only become easier as the number of solutions grows.

1.1 Main results

In this paper we study the secretary problem in the partial order setting. We assume that we know k, the number of maximal elements in the poset. Our algorithms take on the standard form with one subtle difference. As before, we examine all of the elements up to a threshold and then consider the first undominated element. We select this element only if the poset at the time has at most k maximal elements. The latter condition may make us pass on a maximal element early in the sequence, but we will never pass on the last maximal element. We show that for a judicious choice of the threshold (that depends on k) our algorithm succeeds with probability roughly $k^{-\frac{k}{k-1}}\left(\left(1+\log k^{1/(k-1)}\right)^k-1\right)$; see Theorem 3 for a precise statement. This quantity recovers the $1/e$ bound in the limit as $k \to 1$, but quickly surpasses it, reaching 0.47 at $k=2$ and 0.52 at $k=3$. We show an almost matching upper bound of $k^{-1/(k-1)}+o(1)$ (Theorem 9), showing that no algorithm succeeds with probability better than 0.5 for $k=2$ and better than 0.57 for $k=3$. Figure 1 shows these bounds. Closing the gap between the two remains an interesting open problem.

On the technical side, we proceed as follows. To analyze the algorithm, we concentrate on the probability of the algorithm reaching the last maximal element. We introduce the concept of a *blocking set* and show that if the blocking set occurs early in a random permutation of elements, then the second condition on accepting an element (requiring that the number of maximal elements in the induced poset be at most k) prevents the algorithm from returning a suboptimal element. We then proceed to construct such permutations by starting from the end and increasing the suffix so as to keep the blocking sets early in the sequence.

For an upper bound on the success probability of any algorithm, we use a linear programming approach introduced in the work of Buchbinder, Jain, and Singh [6]. We use this approach to consider the very specific poset of k disjoint total orders, each on n/k elements, and show that no algorithm has a good competitive ratio on this poset. To that end, we construct a linear program whose value upper bounds the probability of success of any algorithm on this poset. We then present a feasible solution to the corresponding dual, thus establishing a bound on the success probability of any algorithm for this problem. It is worth to note that this bound holds even if the algorithm knows that the poset under consideration consists of k disjoint total orders.

1.2 Related work

Independently and concurrently with our work, Freij and Wästlund [9] recently proposed an algorithm for the partially ordered secretary problem and claimed a bound of $1/e$ on its success probability. Their algorithm works as follows. Assign a score uniformly at random in $[0,1]$ as elements arrive, skip the first $1/e$ fraction of elements, and pick the first element which is the greedy maximum of the poset seen so far including this element. Here, the greedy maximum of a poset with weighted elements is defined inductively: it is the lowest weight element if it is the maximal or it is the greedy maximum of the sub-poset induced by the elements that are bigger than the lowest weight element. Their algorithm has the same downside as that of [10, 19], namely, the competitive ratio does not increase with the number of maximal elements and remains bounded by $1/e$.

The poset secretary problem has been previously considered for specific cases of posets. For example, Morayne [18] and Kubicki et al. [16] present an optimal stopping time for the case of the complete binary tree. Gnedin [11] explored other specific poset structures. Generally, Bruss [5] defined a way (known as the Odds algorithm) to compute optimal stopping rules for any last-success problem, which applies to the classical version of the secretary problem as well as to the case of any known poset with a single maximal element. For poset-oblivious algorithms, very recently, Kozik [15] proposed a dynamic threshold algorithm that selects a maximal element of any poset with probability at least $1/4+\epsilon$ (for some small $\epsilon>0$), therefore beating the 1/4 bound of Georgiou et al. [10].

Other variants of secretary problems have been previously applied to the online auction setting. For example, designing mechanisms to maximize some function of the top k elements [1, 2, 14] or some function on the accepted set of elements, such as online submodular function maximization [12, 17], finding the heaviest weight independent set of a matroid [3, 20], etc. See [4] for a survey of some of these results.

2. PRELIMINARIES

Let U be a universe of n elements. A *poset* $\mathcal{P} \subseteq U^2$ is a binary relation that is reflexive, anti-symmetric, and transitive. We use $a \prec_{\mathcal{P}} b$ to denote $(a,b) \in \mathcal{P}$ and use $a \|_{\mathcal{P}} b$ to denote $(a,b) \notin \mathcal{P} \wedge (b,a) \notin \mathcal{P}$, i.e., a and b are incomparable. A *linear extension* of $\mathcal{P}$ is a permutation π on U such that $a \prec_{\mathcal{P}} b \implies \pi^{-1}(a) < \pi^{-1}(b)$.

An element a is *maximal* (aka a *secretary*) if there is no element b such that $a \prec_{\mathcal{P}} b$. Let $\max \mathcal{P}$ be the set of all secretaries of $\mathcal{P}$ and let $k = |\max \mathcal{P}|$, the number of secretaries.

We denote by $S_i = \bigcup_{j<i}\{\pi(j)\}$ the set of elements preceding i in the permutation.

Given $S \subseteq U$, let $\mathcal{P}|_S = \mathcal{P} \cap S^2$, the poset obtained from $\mathcal{P}$ by using the elements only in S.

DEFINITION 1 (PARETO FRONTIER). *Given a poset $\mathcal{P}$ and a subset $S \subseteq U$, the* Pareto frontier *$\mathcal{F}_{\mathcal{P}}(S)$ is defined to be* $\max \mathcal{P}|_S$.

3. ALGORITHM AND ANALYSIS

Let $\mathcal{P}$ be the given poset. We assume that the algorithm is given $k = |\max \mathcal{P}|$, the number of secretaries. Our algorithm proceeds in a way similar to the algorithm in the total order setting. It examines all of the elements before a threshold τ. An element a arriving after the threshold is returned if two conditions are met. First, the element must be *undominated*, i.e., $a \in \mathcal{F}_{\mathcal{P}}(S)$, where S is the set of all of elements seen thus far; since any dominated element cannot be maximal, this is without loss of generality. Second, the total size of $\mathcal{F}_{\mathcal{P}}(S)$ is at most k. While the second condition may lead the algorithm to pass on a maximal element, it will never pass on the last maximal element in the permutation.

We will denote by π the order in which the elements arrive. To describe the algorithm, let τ_k be the *stopping threshold*:

$$\tau_k = \begin{cases} n/e, & k = 1, \\ n/k^{\frac{1}{k-1}}, & k > 1. \end{cases}$$

Note that $\lim_{k \to 1^+} \tau_k = n/e$.

Algorithm 1 SECRETARY (π, k).

```
S = {π(1), ..., π(τ_k)}
for i = τ_k + 1 ... n do
  a = π(i)
  S ← S ∪ {a}
  if a ∈ F_P(S) ∧ |F_P(S)| ≤ k then
    return a
  end if
end for
```

3.1 Warmup: Analysis for $k = 1$

THEOREM 2. *For any poset $\mathcal{P}$ with $k = 1$, Algorithm 1 succeeds with probability at least $1/e$.*

PROOF. Let $\mathcal{P}_L$ be an arbitrary linear extension of $\mathcal{P}$; by definition, if $a \prec_{\mathcal{P}_L} b$, then either $a \prec_{\mathcal{P}} b$ or $a \|_{\mathcal{P}} b$. Now, we compare the performance of Algorithm 1 on $\mathcal{P}$ and $\mathcal{P}_L$. Consider any permutation π such that the algorithm outputs the secretary when run on $\mathcal{P}_L$. We claim that the algorithm outputs the secretary when run on $\mathcal{P}$ as well. This will complete the proof since Algorithm 1 on a linear order (i.e., $\mathcal{P}_L$) is the optimal algorithm for the classical secretary problem, and therefore succeeds with probability at least $1/e$.

To prove the claim, we only need to show that the algorithm does not output any element before encountering the secretary. Let i^* be the position in π where the secretary occurs and consider any position $i \in (\tau_1, i^*)$. It must be the case that $\pi(j) \succ_{\mathcal{P}_L} \pi(i)$ for some $j < i$, since otherwise the algorithm would have output $\pi(i)$ when run on $\mathcal{P}_L$. Therefore, either $\pi(j) \succ_{\mathcal{P}} \pi(i)$ or $\pi(j) \|_{\mathcal{P}} \pi(i)$. In both cases, the element $\pi(i)$ is not output when the algorithm runs on $\mathcal{P}$: indeed, in the former case, $\pi(i) \notin \mathcal{F}_{\mathcal{P}}(S_i)$ and in the latter $|\mathcal{F}_{\mathcal{P}}(S_i)| \geq 2 > k$, where $S_i = \bigcup_{j \leq i}\{\pi(j)\}$. □

3.2 Analysis for general k

In this section we show that the algorithm succeeds with increasing probability as k increases.

THEOREM 3. *For any poset $\mathcal{P}$ with k maximal elements, Algorithm 1 succeeds with probability at least*

$$\frac{\binom{\tau_k}{k}}{\binom{n}{k}} \cdot \left(\left(1 + \log \frac{n-k}{\tau_k}\right)^k - 1 \right).$$

Before proceeding further, let us briefly interpret the above bound. Let $k = \epsilon n$, and consider a slightly different threshold $\tau'_k = (1-\epsilon)\tau_k = (1-\epsilon)nk^{-\frac{1}{k-1}}$. Note that holding k fixed and letting $n \to \infty$, we have $\epsilon \to 0$.

Then, we can bound $\binom{\tau'_k}{k}/\binom{n}{k}$ as:

$$\frac{\prod_{i=0}^{k}(1-\epsilon)nk^{-\frac{1}{k-1}}}{\prod_{i=0}^{k}(n-i)} > \left(\frac{(1-\epsilon)k^{-\frac{1}{k-1}} - \epsilon}{(1-\epsilon)}\right)^k$$
$$\geq k^{-\frac{k}{k-1}} - O(\epsilon).$$

And,

$$\left(1 + \log \frac{n-k}{\tau'_k}\right)^k = \left(1 + \log \frac{(1-\epsilon)nk^{\frac{1}{k-1}}}{(1-\epsilon)n}\right)^k$$
$$= \left(1 + \frac{1}{k-1}\log k\right)^k \geq k(1 - o_k(1)).$$

Combining the two, we obtain that the probability of winning is at least

$$\left(k^{-\frac{k}{k-1}} - O(\epsilon)\right) k(1 - o_k(1)) = (1 - o_k(1))k^{-\frac{1}{k-1}} - O(\epsilon).$$

As we will show in Section 4, the term $k^{-\frac{1}{k-1}}$ is tight and thus the maximum difference between the lower bound and the upper bound approaches 0 for large k (Figure 1).

3.2.1 Proof of Theorem 3

To prove the theorem, we will describe the set of permutations on which the algorithm is guaranteed to succeed. In particular, we focus on the probability that the algorithm does not return an element before reaching the last secretary in the permutation. Observe that the algorithm will never pass on the last secretary: it will surely be in $\mathcal{F}_{\mathcal{P}}(S)$, and at that point $\mathcal{F}_{\mathcal{P}}(S) = k$. Obviously, the algorithm will fail if all of the secretaries come before the threshold. A harder to analyze failure mode is that of returning a *faux*-secretary: an element that looks like a maximal element before reaching the actual secretary that dominates it. A way to avoid it is to insist that either $\mathcal{F}_{\mathcal{P}}$ is of size at least $k+1$ before the last secretary is reached or that the maximal element comes before any of the potential faux-secretaries (the latter is exactly the analysis in the $k = 1$ case).

We begin by describing the permutations on which Algorithm 1 will succeed. We first give few definitions that we use in the proof.

Let $\tau = \tau_k$. Fix any $k+1$ special positions in the permutation $1 \leq \ell_0 \leq \cdots \leq \ell_k \leq n$, such that for some $0 \leq i^* < k$ we have $\ell_{i^*} = \tau$, and the other positions are all distinct from each other. We define the set $P = P_{\ell_0,\ldots,\ell_k}$ of all permutations such that the positions ℓ_i with $i \neq i^*$ are occupied by the secretaries in any order.

For a suffix t_i of elements from position ℓ_i to n, we define $P(t_i)$ be the set of all permutations in P that have t_i as a suffix. For a set of suffixes T, we let $P(T) = \bigcup_{t \in T} P(t)$.

We will now inductively define a set T_{i^*} of suffixes such that Algorithm 1 returns a maximal element in all permutations in $P(T_{i^*})$. To begin, let T_k be the set of all suffixes from ℓ_k to n; thus we have that $P(T_k)$ contains all the permutations in P. Inductively, define T_i, for $i = k-1, \ldots, i^*$, in the following way. Let the $\mathcal{F}_{\mathcal{P}}(U \setminus t_{i+1})$ be Pareto frontier of the elements that are *not* in t_{i+1}, and define $\mathcal{G}(t_{i+1})$ to be the set of non-secretary elements of $\mathcal{F}_{\mathcal{P}}(U \setminus t_{i+1})$.

Now let $B(t_{i+1})$ be any subset of $\mathcal{G}(t_{i+1})$ of $\min\{k - i, |\mathcal{G}(t_{i+1})|\}$ elements; we call the set $B(t_{i+1})$ a *blocking set.* Note that in a permutation π where all of the elements in $B(t_{i+1})$ come before ℓ_i, Algorithm 1 cannot terminate with any element between ℓ_i and ℓ_{i+1}. In this case, we say that $B(t_{i+1})$ is a *good* blocking set in π. In order to find a lower bound on the number of winning permutation for a fixed position of i^*, we can bound the number of permutations where $B(t_{j+1})$ is a good blocking set for every $i^* \leq j < k$. To this end, let $A(t_{i+1})$ be the set of all suffixes from ℓ_i to n that agree with t_{i+1} and that do not contain elements from $B(t_{i+1})$. Let $T_i = \bigcup_{t_{i+1} \in T_{i+1}} A(t_{i+1})$.

LEMMA 4. *Algorithm 1 returns a maximal element on all permutations in $P(T_{i^*})$.*

PROOF. Suppose not and consider any permutation in $P(T_{i^*})$ where the algorithm fails. Suppose the returned element is in the interval between ℓ_i and ℓ_{i+1} for some $i^* \leq i \leq k-1$. Then, this permutation has to be in $P(T_i)$ (since $P(T_i) \subseteq P(T_{i+1})$). But by definition of T_i, if $\mathcal{G}$ is the Pareto frontier of the elements before ℓ_{i+1}, either all of $\mathcal{G}$ or a subset of at least $k-i$ elements of $\mathcal{G}$ comes before ℓ_i. Either way, in the positions $t_i, \ldots, t_{i+1}$, the Pareto frontier is composed of at least i secretaries and the good blocking set B_{i+1}. Thus the **if** statement in step 5 of Algorithm 1 avoids that an element is returned in the interval between ℓ_i and ℓ_{i+1}. So we have a contradiction. $\square$

Suppose there were j secretaries that came after the threshold. In this case, we can look at the fraction of the permutations whose suffix agrees with T_{k-j}. Let

$$\gamma(j) = \frac{|P(T_{k-j})|}{|P|}.$$

Note that γ is implicitly a function of $\ell_k, \ldots, \ell_{i^*}$. We begin by bounding $\gamma(j)$ from below. Let

$$\gamma'(j) = \prod_{i=k-j}^{k-1} \left(\prod_{w=0}^{k-i-1} \left(\frac{\ell_i - i - w}{\ell_{i+1} - (i+1) - w} \right) \right).$$

LEMMA 5. $\gamma(j) \geq \gamma'(j)$.

PROOF. By definition, $P(T_i) \subseteq P(T_{i+1})$ and hence

$$\begin{aligned} |P(T_i)| &= |P(T_{i+1})| \cdot (\text{fraction of permutation} \\ &\qquad \text{in } P(T_{i+1}) \text{ with good } B_{t_{i+1}}) \\ &\geq |P(T_{i+1})| \cdot (\text{fraction of permutation} \\ &\qquad \text{in } P(T_{i+1}) \text{ with } k \text{ elements of} \\ &\qquad \mathcal{G}(t_{i+1}) \text{ before } k-i-1) \\ &\geq |P(T_{i+1})| \prod_{w=0}^{k-i-1} \left(\frac{\ell_i - i - w}{\ell_{i+1} - (i+1) - w} \right). \end{aligned}$$

Therefore, we can conclude that

$$|P(T_{i^*})| \geq |P| \prod_{i=i^*}^{k-1} \left(\prod_{w=0}^{k-i-1} \left(\frac{\ell_i - i - w}{\ell_{i+1} - (i+1) - w} \right) \right).$$

And,

$$\begin{aligned} \gamma(k-i^*) &= \frac{|P(T_{i^*})|}{|P|} \\ &\geq \prod_{i=i^*}^{k-1} \left(\prod_{w=0}^{k-i-1} \left(\frac{\ell_i - i - w}{\ell_{i+1} - (i+1) - w} \right) \right) \\ &= \gamma'(k-i^*). \quad \square \end{aligned}$$

We first show that $\gamma'(r)$ can be rewritten in a more convenient way; the proof is in Appendix A.

LEMMA 6.

$$\gamma'(r) = \frac{(\ell_{k-r} - (k-r))!}{(\ell_{k-r} - k)!} \prod_{s=0}^{r-1} \frac{1}{\ell_{k-s} - k}.$$

Next, we obtain an analytical bound that will be useful later; the proof is in Appendix B.

LEMMA 7.

$$\sum_{\substack{\ell_k, \ldots, \ell_{k-j+1}: \\ n \geq \ell_k > \cdots > \ell_{k-j} = \tau}} \prod_{s=0}^{j-1} \frac{s+1}{\ell_{k-s} - k} \geq \log^j \frac{n-k}{\ell_{k-j} - (k-j)}.$$

Now we are ready to put all of the pieces together. To count the total number of permutations on which the algorithm succeeds, we begin by conditioning on the number of secretaries that come after the specified threshold, τ. Let E_j be the event such that there are exactly $j \geq 1$ fixed secretaries after the threshold $\ell_{k-j} = \tau$ and let WIN be the event of the algorithm returning a maximal element.

LEMMA 8.

$$\Pr[\text{WIN}|E_j] \geq \frac{(\tau - (k-j))!}{(\tau - k)!} \frac{(n - \tau - j)!}{(n - \tau)!} \log^j \left(\frac{n-k}{\tau - (k-j)} \right).$$

PROOF. We enumerate over all permutations that have j maximal elements after the threshold. Since $\gamma(j)$ depends only on the position and not on the order of these elements, we have:

$$\Pr[\text{WIN}|E_j] = j! \cdot \sum_{\substack{\ell_k, \ldots, \ell_{k-j+1}: \\ n \geq \ell_k > \cdots > \ell_{k-j} = \tau}} \left(\frac{1}{n-\tau} \cdots \frac{1}{n - \tau - (j-1)} \right) \gamma(j).$$

Since $\ell_{k-j} = \tau$, applying Lemma 5, Lemma 6, and Lemma

7 completes the proof.

$$\begin{aligned}
&\Pr[\text{WIN}|E_j] \\
&\geq \frac{(\tau-(k-j))!}{(\tau-k)!}\frac{(n-\tau-j)!}{(n-\tau)!}j! \\
&\quad\cdot \sum_{\substack{\ell_k,\ldots,\ell_{k-j+1}:\\ n\geq\ell_k>\cdots>\ell_{k-j}=\tau}} \prod_{s=0}^{j-1}\frac{1}{\ell_{k-s}-k} \\
&= \frac{(\tau-(k-j))!}{(\tau-k)!}\frac{(n-\tau-j)!}{(n-\tau)!} \\
&\quad\cdot \sum_{\substack{\ell_k,\cdots,\ell_{k-j+1}:\\ n\geq\ell_k>\cdots>\ell_{k-j}=\tau}} \prod_{s=0}^{j-1}\frac{s+1}{\ell_{k-s}-k} \\
&\geq \frac{(\tau-(k-j))!}{(\tau-k)!}\frac{(n-\tau-j)!}{(n-\tau)!} \\
&\quad\cdot \log^j\left(\frac{n-k}{\tau-(k-j)}\right). \quad\square
\end{aligned}$$

PROOF OF THEOREM 3. Finally, we can remove the conditioning in Lemma 8 to prove an overall bound on the success probability of the algorithm.

$$\begin{aligned}
\Pr[E_j] &= \binom{k}{j}\left(\frac{\tau}{n}\cdots\frac{\tau-(k-j-1)}{n-(k-j-1)}\right) \\
&\quad\cdot\left(\frac{n-\tau}{n-(k-j)}\cdots\frac{n-\tau-(j-1)}{n-(k-1)}\right) \\
&= \binom{k}{j}\frac{\tau!}{(\tau-(k-j))!}\cdot\frac{(n-\tau)!}{(n-\tau-j)!}\cdot\frac{(n-k)!}{n!}.
\end{aligned}$$

Now, using Lemma 8, we have that

$$\begin{aligned}
\Pr[\text{WIN}] &= \sum_{j=1}^{k}\Pr[\text{WIN}|E_j]\Pr[E_j] \\
&= \frac{\tau!}{(\tau-k)!}\cdot\frac{(n-k)!}{n!}\cdot\sum_{j=1}^{k}\binom{k}{j}\log^j\frac{n-k}{\tau-(k-j)} \\
&\geq \frac{\tau!}{(\tau-k)!}\cdot\frac{(n-k)!}{n!}\cdot\sum_{j=1}^{k}\binom{k}{j}\log^j\frac{n-k}{\tau} \\
&= \frac{\tau!}{(\tau-k)!}\cdot\frac{(n-k)!}{n!}\cdot\left(\left(1+\log\frac{n-k}{\tau}\right)^k-1\right). \quad\square
\end{aligned}$$

4. UPPER BOUNDS ON SUCCESS

In this section we prove an upper bound on the success probability of any algorithm for the poset secretary problem. For $k=1$, it is well-known that no algorithm can succeed with probability more than $1/e$. Here we explore how the bound grows with k. Our main result is the following:

THEOREM 9. *Let $2\leq k=o(\sqrt{n})$. For any poset $\mathcal{P}$ with k maximal elements, every algorithm has success probability at most $k^{-\frac{1}{k-1}}+o(1)$.*

To prove this result we will analyze the performance of any algorithm on a specific poset $\mathcal{P}_k$. Let $\mathcal{L}$ be a total order on n/k elements; we will call such a poset a *line*. We define $\mathcal{P}_k$ to be the poset consisting of k disjoint lines: $\mathcal{P}_k=\{\mathcal{L}_1,\ldots,\mathcal{L}_k\}$.

Our strategy is to write down a linear program whose value is an upper bound on the success probability of any algorithm. We will then analyze the dual formulation and derive a feasible solution for it, which will serve as the bound in Theorem 9.

We begin by restricting the class of algorithms and the class of permutations we consider. A *τ-threshold* algorithm is one that never returns any of the first τ elements. Recall that $S_i=\cup_{j<i}\{\pi(j)\}$ denotes the set of elements preceding i in the permutation and $\mathcal{F}(S_i)$ denotes the set of maximal elements of S_i. We insist that the algorithms we consider are *sane*, i.e., they never knowingly return a dominated element; formally, if the element at position i is returned by the algorithm, then $\pi(i)\in\mathcal{F}(S_{i+1})$.

We also restrict the permutations under consideration. A permutation π is called *τ-covering* if the following two conditions hold:

1. $\mathcal{F}(S_\tau)\cap\mathcal{F}_\mathcal{P}=\emptyset$, i.e., π has no maximal elements in the first τ positions; and
2. for any $1\leq j\leq k$, $\mathcal{F}(S_\tau)\cap\mathcal{L}_j\neq\emptyset$, i.e., at least one descendant of each maximal element occurs among the first τ elements.

These restrictions on the algorithm and the permutations do not change the success probability substantially.

LEMMA 10. *Consider any algorithm $\mathcal{A}$ that succeeds with probability ρ. Then $\mathcal{A}$ succeeds with probability at least $\rho-o(1)$ on all $(2k\log n)$-covering permutations. Furthermore, when run on $(2k\log n)$-covering permutations, $\mathcal{A}$ is a sane and $(2k\log n)$-threshold algorithm without loss of generality.*

PROOF. To prove the first claim, observe that $(2k\log n)$-covering permutations constitute an

$$O\left(\left(1-\frac{1}{k}\right)^{2k\log n}+\left(1-\frac{2k\log n}{n}\right)^k\right)=o(1)$$

fraction of all of the permutations, when $k=o(\sqrt{n})$. Moreover, on these permutations, any algorithm returning one of the first $2k\log n$ elements is guaranteed to fail, therefore we can assume that the algorithm is a $(2k\log n)$-threshold algorithm without loss of generality. $\square$

For the remainder of the proof we therefore assume that the algorithms under consideration are sane and $(2k\log n)$-threshold. We proceed by writing down a linear program that encodes the success probability of any algorithm on $\mathcal{P}_k$.

LEMMA 11. *Consider any optimal solution of the linear program in Fig. 2 and let v be its value. Then, any sane $(2k\log n)$-threshold algorithm $\mathcal{A}$, has success probability at most v on the poset $\mathcal{P}_k$.*

PROOF. Let $p_i=\Pr[\mathcal{A}\text{ returns }\pi(i)]$ denote the probability that $\mathcal{A}$ returns the ith element of the permutation[1]. Similarly, let $q_i=\Pr[\mathcal{A}\text{ returns }\pi(i)|\pi(i)\in\mathcal{F}(S_{i+1})]$. Note that since $\mathcal{A}$ is sane, $\mathcal{A}$ never returns $\pi(i)$ if $\pi(i)\notin\mathcal{F}(S_{i+1})$. Therefore we can write $p_i=q_i\Pr[\pi(i)\in\mathcal{F}(S_{i+1})]$. Moreover, $\mathcal{A}$ returns an element $\pi(i)$ only if it discards all of the

[1]The probability is over both the permutations and the coins of the algorithm.

$$\max_{q_1,\dots,q_n} \frac{k}{n}\sum_{i=1}^{n} q_i$$

$$q_i + \sum_{j=1}^{i-1}\frac{k}{j}q_j \le 1, \qquad 1 \le i \le n$$

$$q_i \ge 0, \qquad 1 \le i \le n$$

$$\min_{x_1,\dots,x_n} \sum_{i=1}^{n} x_i$$

$$x_i + \frac{k}{i}\sum_{j=i+1}^{n} x_j \ge \frac{k}{n}, \qquad 1 \le i \le n$$

$$x_i \ge 0, \qquad 1 \le i \le n$$

Figure 2: Linear program (left) and its dual (right).

elements in positions $j < i$. Thus we can write:

$$q_i \le 1 - \sum_{j<i} p_j = 1 - \sum_{j<i} f_j q_i, \tag{1}$$

where $f_j = \Pr[\pi(j) \in \mathcal{F}(S_{j+1})]$.

We can express the probability that $\mathcal{A}$ returns a maximal element as

$$\begin{aligned}
&\Pr[\mathcal{A}\text{ wins}]\\
&= \sum_{j=1}^{k}\sum_{i=1}^{n}\Pr[\mathcal{A}\text{ returns }\pi(i)|\pi(i)\in\mathcal{F}(\mathcal{L}_j)]\\
&\quad\cdot\Pr[\pi(i)\in\mathcal{F}(\mathcal{L}_j)]\\
&= \frac{k}{n}\sum_{i-1}^{n}\Pr[\mathcal{A}\text{ returns }\pi(i)|\pi(i)\in\mathcal{F}(S_{i+1})]\\
&= \frac{k}{n}\sum_{i=1}^{n} q_i,
\end{aligned}$$

where the second step follows because the algorithm cannot determine whether a maximal element of the poset induced from the first i elements in π is a maximal element of the whole poset or not, and hence the contributions are equal. More formally, we observe that, for every $1 \le j \le k$, $\Pr[\mathcal{A}$ returns $\pi(i)|\pi(i) \in \mathcal{F}(\mathcal{P}_k) \cap \mathcal{L}_j] = \Pr[\mathcal{A}$ returns $\pi(i)|$ $\pi(i) \in \mathcal{F}(S_{i+1}) \cap \mathcal{L}_j]$. This follows because for any two permutations π, π' identical up to $i-1$, and with $\pi(i) \in \mathcal{F}_\pi(\mathcal{P}_k) \cap \mathcal{L}_j$ and $\pi'(i) \in \mathcal{F}_{\pi'}(S_{i+1}) \cap \mathcal{L}_j$, we have that the poset induced by the first i elements is exactly the same. Hence, the algorithm's behavior is unchanged (here the subscript on $\mathcal{F}$ denotes the permutation of the elements under consideration).

Finally we show that we correctly captured the constraints on q. Assume that $i > 2k\log n$, and denote by S_τ the set of elements appearing before the threshold. Since for all j, $S_\tau \cap \mathcal{L}_j \ne \emptyset$, the size of the Pareto set at i is exactly k. Therefore $f_i = k/i$. For $i > 2k\log n$, inequality (1) implies that $q_i + \sum_{j<i}\frac{k}{j}q_j \le 1$.The same inequality trivially holds when $i \le 2k\log n$ since $q_i = 0$ for these elements. □

Next, we focus on the feasible solution to the dual program.

Lemma 12. *There exists a feasible solution to the dual program in Figure 2 that has value* $k^{-\frac{1}{k-1}} + o(1)$.

Proof. We define the following feasible solution to the dual program in Figure 2: inductively, $x_n = \frac{k}{n}$ and $x_i = \max\{0, \frac{k}{n} - \frac{k}{i}\sum_{j=i+1}^{n} x_j\}$. Note that the value of the objective function for this solution is $\sum_{i=1}^{n} x_i = \sum_{i=T+1}^{n} x_i$, where T is the maximum index such that $x_T = 0$. Consider the sequence a_i inductively defined by $a_n = \frac{k}{n}$ and $a_i = a_{i+1} + \left(\frac{k}{n} - \frac{k}{i}a_{i+1}\right)$. We observe that for any $j \ge T+1$, it holds that $a_j = \sum_{i=j}^{n} x_i$ and that $\frac{k}{n} - \frac{k}{j}a_{T+1} \le 0$. Specifically, either $a_T < a_{T+1}$ and $a_{T+1} > \cdots > a_n$, or $a_{T-1} < a_T = a_{T+1}$ and $a_{T+1} > \cdots > a_n$.

Note that the problem of computing $\sum_{i=1}^{n} x_i$ now reduces to the problem of finding the last local maximum of the sequence $\{a_i\}_{i=1}^{n}$.

We proceed as follows. First, we introduce the function $s(z)$ defined over the real domain $[1, n]$ by

$$s(z) = \frac{k}{n}\sum_{\ell=0}^{n-z}\prod_{t=1}^{\ell}\left(1 - \frac{k}{z+t-1}\right).$$

Note that $s(i) = a_i$ for every $i \in \{1, \dots, n\}$. We study $s(z)$ in $[g(n), n]$ with $g(n) = \omega(1)$ and show that it has only one stationary point (a maximum) in this interval at $z^* = (1 \pm o(1))n/k^{1/(k-1)}$. Finally, since $s(z)$ is continuous, we can conclude that $T + 1 = \max\{\lfloor z^*\rfloor, \lceil z^*\rceil\}$.

We have

$$\begin{aligned}
s(z) &= \frac{k}{n}\sum_{\ell=0}^{n-z}\prod_{t=1}^{\ell}\left(1 - \frac{k}{z+t-1}\right)\\
&= \frac{k}{n}\sum_{\ell=0}^{n-z}\exp\left[\sum_{t=1}^{\ell}\log\left(1 - \frac{k}{z+t-1}\right)\right]\\
&\ge \frac{k}{n}\sum_{\ell=0}^{n-z}\exp\left[\int_{t=1}^{\ell}\log\left(1 - \frac{k}{z+t-1}\right)dt\right]\\
&= \frac{k}{n}\sum_{\ell=0}^{n-z}\exp\Bigg[(z+t-1)\log\left(1 - \frac{k}{z+t-1}\right)\\
&\qquad -k\log(z-1-k+t)\Bigg|_{t=1}^{\ell}\Bigg]\\
&= \frac{k}{n}\sum_{\ell=0}^{n-z}\frac{\left(1-\frac{k}{z+\ell-1}\right)^{z+\ell-1}(z-k)^k}{\left(1-\frac{k}{z}\right)^z(z+\ell-1-k)^k}.
\end{aligned}$$

One can similarly show that

$$s(z) \le \frac{k}{n}\sum_{\ell=0}^{n-z}\frac{\left(1-\frac{k}{z+\ell}\right)^{z+\ell}(z-k)^k}{\left(1-\frac{k}{z}\right)^z(z+\ell-k)^k}.$$

For $z \ge k\log n$, we have that $\left(1 - \frac{k}{z+l-1}\right)^{z+l-1} = (1 - o(1))e^{-k}$ and $\left(1-\frac{k}{z}\right)^z = (1 - o(1))e^{-k}$, where the $o(1)$ term hides factors going to 0 as $n \to \infty$. So we can write $s(z)$ as

$$s(z) \geq (1-o(1))\frac{k}{n}(z-k)^k \sum_{\ell=0}^{n-z} \frac{1}{(z+\ell-1-k)^k}$$
$$\geq (1-o(1))\frac{k}{n}(z-k)^k \int_{\ell=0}^{n-z} \frac{1}{(z+\ell-1-k)^k} d\ell$$
$$= (1-o(1))\frac{k}{n}\frac{1}{k-1}(z-k)^k \left(\frac{1}{(z-k-1)^{k-1}} - \frac{1}{(n-k-1)^{k-1}}\right)$$
$$\geq (1-o(1))\frac{k}{n}\frac{1}{k-1}\left((z-k) - \frac{(z-k)^k}{(n-k-1)^{k-1}}\right).$$

One can similarly show that

$$s(z) \leq (1+o(1))\frac{k}{n}\frac{1}{k-1}\left((z-k) - \frac{(z-k)^k}{(n-k-1)^{k-1}}\right).$$

Taking the derivative and setting it to zero gives a maximum at z^* at $\frac{n}{k^{1/(k-1)}}(1\pm o(1))$. Define $i^* = \max\{\lfloor z^* \rfloor, \lceil z^* \rceil\}$. By definition of a_i and the maximality of i^*, it must be that $\frac{k}{n} - \frac{k}{i^*}a_{i^*+1} \geq 0$, which implies

$$a_{i^*+1} \leq \frac{i^*}{n} \leq k^{-1/(k-1)}(1+o(1)).$$

Finally,

$$\sum_{i=1}^{n} x_i = a_{i^*} \leq a_{i^*+1} + \frac{k}{n} \leq k^{-1/(k-1)} + o(1).$$

This gives a feasible solution to the dual and a bound on its value. □

5. TIGHTNESS OF ALGORITHM 1

In Section 4 we showed that no algorithm can succeed with probability more than $k^{-\frac{1}{k-1}} - o(1)$ on the poset $\mathcal{P}_k$ consisting of k disjoint total orders. In this section we use a different analysis to show that Algorithm 1 achieves this bound on a large family of posets including $\mathcal{P}_k$.

The main idea is to define an event of the algorithm passing on a maximal element after the threshold τ_k and then returning a non-maximal element; call this event PASS. For any $\tau_k < i \leq n$, we define A_i as the event that the first secretary after the threshold occurs at position i and D_i as the event that the algorithm discards the element $\pi(i)$; let $D_{i_1:i_2} = D_{i_1} \wedge \cdots \wedge D_{i_2}$. Now, if WIN denotes the event that the algorithm returns a secretary, then $\text{PASS} = \cup_{i>\tau_k} \text{PASS}_i$, where $\text{PASS}_i = D_{\tau_k+1:i} \wedge A_i \wedge \overline{\text{WIN}}$.

We begin by showing that the disjoint events WIN and PASS together account for the vast majority of the outcomes of the algorithms. We then show how to upper bound the probability of PASS on particular posets, leading to a bound on the success probability of the algorithm.

LEMMA 13. $\Pr[\text{WIN}] + \Pr[\text{PASS}] \geq \frac{k}{n}\sum_{i=\tau_k+1}^{n} \frac{\binom{\tau_k}{k}}{\binom{i-1}{k}}$.

PROOF. Suppose the first secretary after the threshold is at i. Then the algorithm can win by returning $\pi(i)$ or discarding $\pi(i)$ and then winning later on. In the first case, it must be that $\mathcal{F}(S_{i+1}) \leq k$ while in the other, $\mathcal{F}(S_{i+1}) \geq k+1$. Let F_i denote the event that $|\mathcal{F}(S_{i+1})| \geq k+1$. Then, we have

$$\Pr[\text{WIN}] = \sum_{i>\tau_k} \big(\Pr[D_{\tau_k+1:i-1} \wedge A_i \wedge \overline{F_i}] + \Pr[D_{\tau_k:i-1} \wedge A_i \wedge F_i \wedge \text{WIN}]\big).$$

The second term can be rewritten as

$$\Pr[D_{r_k:i-1} \wedge A_i \wedge F_i \wedge \text{WIN}]$$
$$= (1 - \Pr[\overline{\text{WIN}}|D_{r_k:i-1} \wedge A_i \wedge F_i]) \cdot \Pr[D_{r_k:i-1} \wedge A_i \wedge F_i]$$
$$= \Pr[D_{r_k:i-1} \wedge A_i \wedge F_i] - \Pr[\text{PASS}_i].$$

Since the events PASS_i are disjoint, we have that $\Pr[\text{WIN}] + \Pr[\text{PASS}] = \sum_{i=\tau_k+1}^{n} \Pr[D_{\tau_k:i-1} \wedge A_i]$. We proceed to bound $\Pr[D_{\tau_k:i-1} \wedge A_i]$. Note that the probability of $\pi(i)$ being a secretary is k/n. Consider any subset B of $\mathcal{F}(S_i)$ that contains all secretaries in $\mathcal{F}(S_i)$ and is of size $\min\{|\mathcal{F}(S_i)|, k\}$. B is a blocking subset: if all elements in B appear before the threshold, no element between $\tau_k + 1$ and $i-1$ (inclusive) will be accepted. Moreover, this implies that there are no maximal elements between τ_k+1 and $i-1$. The lemma follows observing that the probability of this event is at least $\frac{\binom{\tau_k}{\ell}}{\binom{i-1}{k}}$. □

We can now prove a concrete bound on the winning probability that closely resembles the bound in Section 4.

THEOREM 14. *For any k,*

$$\Pr[\text{WIN}] \geq k^{-\frac{1}{k-1}} - \Pr[\text{PASS}] - O(k/n).$$

PROOF. By Lemma 13,

$$\Pr[\text{WIN}] + \Pr[\text{PASS}]$$
$$\geq \frac{k}{n}\sum_{i=r_k+1}^{n} \frac{\tau_k \cdots (\tau_k - k + 1))}{(i-1)\cdots(i-k)}$$
$$\geq \frac{k}{n}(\tau_k - k + 1)^k \cdot \sum_{i=\tau_k+1}^{n} \frac{1}{(i-k)^k}$$
$$\geq \frac{k}{n}(\tau_k - k + 1)^k \cdot \int_{i=\tau_k+1}^{n+1} \frac{1}{(i-k)^k}$$
$$= \frac{k}{n}(\tau_k - k + 1)^k \frac{1}{k-1} \left(\frac{1}{(\tau_k - k+1)^{k-1}} - \frac{1}{(n-k+1)^{k-1}}\right)$$
$$= \frac{\tau_k - k + 1}{n}\frac{k}{k-1}\left(1 - \left(\frac{\tau_k - k+1}{n-k+1}\right)^{k-1}\right)$$
$$\geq \frac{\tau_k - k + 1}{n}\frac{k}{k-1}\left(1 - \left(\frac{\tau_k}{n}\right)^{k-1}\right).$$

Now, by definition, we have $\tau_k = n/k^{\frac{1}{k-1}}$. Therefore,

$$\Pr[\text{WIN}] + \Pr[\text{PASS}] \geq \frac{\tau_k - k + 1}{n} = k^{-\frac{1}{k-1}} - \frac{k+1}{n},$$

which concludes the proof. □

Note that the only way for the algorithm to discard a secretary $\pi(i)$ with $i > \tau_k$ is if $|\mathcal{F}(S_{i+1})| > k$. This event has zero probability in the poset $\mathcal{P}_k$ consisting of k disjoint total orders.

COROLLARY 15. *Algorithm 1 succeeds with probability at least $k^{-\frac{1}{k-1}} - O(k/n)$ on any poset of width at most k. In particular, this holds true for the poset $\mathcal{P}_k$.*

Acknowledgements

The last author was supported by NSF grant CCF-0905645. Any opinions, findings, and conclusions or recommendations expressed in this material are those of the authors and do not necessarily reflect the views of the National Science Foundation.

6. REFERENCES

[1] M. Ajtai, N. Megiddo, and O. Waarts. Improved algorithms and analysis for secretary problems and generalizations. *SIAM J. Discrete Math.*, 14(1):1–27, 2001.

[2] M. Babaioff, M. Dinitz, A. Gupta, N. Immorlica, and K. Talwar. Secretary problems: Weights and discounts. In *Proc. 20th SODA*, pages 1245–1254, 2009.

[3] M. Babaioff, N. Immorlica, and R. Kleinberg. Matroids, secretary problems, and online mechanisms. In *Proc. 18th SODA*, pages 434–443, 2007.

[4] Moshe Babaioff, Nicole Immorlica, David Kempe, and Robert Kleinberg. Online auctions and generalized secretary problems. *SIGecom Exchanges*, 7(2), 2008.

[5] F. T. Bruss. Sum the odds to one and stop. *Annals of Probability*, 28:1384–1391, 2000.

[6] N. Buchbinder, K. Jain, and M. Singh. Secretary problems via linear programming. In *Proc. 14th IPCO*, pages 163–176, 2010.

[7] E. B. Dynkin. The optimum choice of the instant for stopping a Markov process. *Sov. Math. Dokl.*, 4:627–629, 1963.

[8] T. Ferguson. Who solved the secretary problem. *Statist. Sc.*, 4:282–296, 1989.

[9] R. Freij and J. Wästlund. Partially ordered secretaries. *Electronic Communication in Probability*, 15:504–507, 2010.

[10] N. Georgiou, M. Kuchta, M. Morayne, and J. Niemiec. On a universal best choice algorithm for partially ordered sets. *Random Struct. Algorithms*, 32(3):263–273, 2008.

[11] A. V. Gnedin. Multicriteria extensions of the best choice problem: Sequential selection without linear order. *Contemp. Math*, 125:153–172, 1992.

[12] A. Gupta, A. Roth, G. Schoenebeck, and K. Talwar. Constrained non-monotone submodular maximization: Offline and secretary algorithms. In *Proc. 6th WINE*, pages 246–257, 2010.

[13] M. T. Hajiaghayi, R. Kleinberg, and D. C. Parkes. Adaptive limited-supply online auctions. In *Proc. 5th EC*, pages 71–80, 2004.

[14] R. Kleinberg. A multiple-choice secretary problem with applications to online auctions. In *Proc. 16th SODA*, pages 630–631, 2005.

[15] J. Kozik. Dynamic threshold strategy for universal best choice problem. In *Proc. 21st International Meeting on Probabilistic, Combinatorial, and Asymptotic Methods in the Analysis of Algorithms*, pages 439–452, 2010.

[16] G. Kubicki, J. Lehel, and M. Morayne. A ratio inequality for binary trees and the best secretary. *Combinatorics, Probability, and Computing*, 11:146–161, 2002.

[17] M. Zadimoghaddam M. H. Bateni, M. T. Hajiaghayi. Submodular secretary problem and extensions. In *Proc. 6th WINE*, pages 39–52, 2010.

[18] M. Morayne. Partial-order analogue of the secretary problem; the binary tree case. *Discrete Math*, 184:165–181, 1998.

[19] J. Preater. The best-choice problem for partially ordered objects. *Oper. Res. Lett*, 25:187–190, 1999.

[20] J. A. Soto. Matroid secretary problem in the random assignment model. In *Proc. 22nd SODA*, pages 1275–1284, 2011.

APPENDIX

A. PROOF OF LEMMA 6

PROOF. We prove the statement by induction. By inspection, the equality holds for $r = 1$. Now suppose it holds up to a certain $1 \le r < k$. Then, we have

$$\begin{aligned}
\gamma'(r+1) &= \prod_{i=k-r}^{k-1} \left(\prod_{w=0}^{k-i-1} \left(\frac{\ell_i - i - w}{\ell_{i+1} - (i+1) - w} \right) \right) \\
&= \gamma'(r) \cdot \prod_{w=0}^{r} \left(\frac{\ell_{k-(r+1)} - (k-(r+1)) - w}{\ell_{k-r} - (k-r) - w} \right) \\
&= \frac{(\ell_{k-r} - (k-r))!}{(\ell_{k-r} - k)!} \left(\prod_{s=0}^{r-1} \frac{1}{\ell_{k-s} - k} \right) \\
&\quad \cdot \frac{(\ell_{k-r} - (k-r) - (r+1))!}{(\ell_{k-r} - (k-r))!} \\
&\quad \cdot \frac{(\ell_{k-(r+1)} - (k-(r+1)))!}{(\ell_{k-r+1} - (k-(r+1)) - (r+1))!} \\
&= \frac{(\ell_{k-(r+1)} - (k-(r+1)))!}{(\ell_{k-r+1} - k)!} \cdot \frac{1}{\ell_{k-r} - k} \\
&\quad \cdot \left(\prod_{s=0}^{r-1} \frac{1}{\ell_{k-s} - k} \right),
\end{aligned}$$

which concludes the proof. $\square$

B. PROOF OF LEMMA 7

PROOF. For convenience, define ϕ as $\phi(k+1) = 1$ and for $r \le k$,

$$\phi(r) = \sum_{\ell_r : \ell_r = \ell_{r-1}+1}^{n-(k-r)} \frac{k-r+1}{\ell_r - k} \phi(r+1).$$

It is easy to see that

$$\sum_{\substack{\ell_k, \ldots, \ell_{k-j+1}: \\ n \ge \ell_k > \cdots > \ell_{k-j} = \tau}} \prod_{s=0}^{j-1} \frac{s+1}{\ell_{k-s} - k} = \phi(k - (j-1)).$$

We now provide a lower bound on $\phi(r)$.

$$\phi(r) \ge \log^{k-r+1} \frac{n-k}{\ell_{r-1} - (r-1)}.$$

We proceed by backward induction on r. For $r = k+1$, the claim holds trivially. Suppose the claim holds down to a certain $r+1$. Then,

$$\begin{aligned}
\phi(r) &= \sum_{\ell_r=\ell_{r-1}+1}^{n-(k-r)} \frac{k-r+1}{\ell_r - k}\phi(r+1) \\
&= \sum_{\ell_r=\ell_{r-1}+1}^{n-(k-r)} \frac{k-r+1}{\ell_r - k}\log^{k-r}\frac{n-k}{\ell_r - r} \\
&\geq \sum_{\ell_r=\ell_{r-1}+1}^{n-(k-r)} \frac{k-r+1}{\ell_r - r}\log^{k-r}\frac{n-k}{\ell_r - r} \\
&\geq \int_{\ell_{r-1}+1}^{n-(k-r)} \frac{k-r+1}{x-r}\log^{k-r}\frac{n-k}{x-r} \\
&= -\log^{k-r+1}\frac{n-k}{x-r}\bigg|_{x=\ell_{r-1}+1}^{n-(k-r)} \\
&= \log^{k-r+1}\frac{n-k}{\ell_{r-1}-(r-1)}. \quad \square
\end{aligned}$$

The Effects of Exposure Time on Memory of Display Advertisements

Daniel G. Goldstein
Yahoo! Research
New York, NY, USA
dgg@yahoo-inc.com

R. Preston McAfee
Yahoo! Research
Burbank, CA, USA
mcafee@yahoo-inc.com

Siddharth Suri
Yahoo! Research
New York, NY, USA
suri@yahoo-inc.com

ABSTRACT

Display advertising is a multi-billion dollar industry that has traditionally used a pricing scheme based on the number of impressions delivered. The number of impressions of an ad is simply the number of downloads of that ad. One impression, however, does not differentiate between an ad that is in view for five seconds or five minutes. Since advertisers seek brand recognition and recall, we ask whether a time-based accounting of advertising can better align with advertisers' goals. This work aims to model the basic relationship between ad exposure time and the probability that a viewer will remember an advertisement. We investigate this question via two behavioral experiments, conducted using Amazon Mechanical Turk, in which people viewed Web pages accompanied by ads. The amount of time the ads were in view was either determined endogenously (as a function of reading speed) or exogenously (as a function of a timer and random assignment). Our results suggest that for exposure times of up to one minute, there is a strong, causal influence of exposure time on ad recognition and recall, with the marginal effects diminishing at durations beyond this level. Simple models describing memory response as a function of the logarithm of exposure time provide a good fit. In addition, we find that advertisements that are displayed when the Web page loads attain greater marginal increases in recognition per unit time than do ads that come into view second in a sequence. Nonetheless, for both types of ads, exposure time has a substantial effect. A psychologically-informed accounting system based on ad exposure duration, sequence and onset time may more closely align with advertiser goals than the industry standard of impression-based accounting.

Categories and Subject Descriptors

J.4 [**Social and Behavioral Sciences**]: Economics

General Terms

Economics, Experimentation

Keywords

advertising, memory, display, recall, recognition, time, exposure

1. INTRODUCTION

Internet display advertising is a business that generates over $20 billion in annual revenue [8] from advertisers paying to place graphical ads on publisher's websites. Customarily, advertisers pay for a certain number of impressions, where one impression is one download of the ad. These impressions are typically sold in "guaranteed contracts", which specify a number of impressions and a set of targeting variables, for example 10 million impressions on automobile-related pages sold to women between 30 and 50 years of age, or 7 million impressions targeted to people interested in women's fashion. In addition, display ads are also sold in exchanges like Google's DoubleClick exchange (GDC) or Yahoo!'s Right Media exchange (RMX). In these exchanges, display ads can be individually targeted to a specific user, such that when a targeted user clicks on a page, the exchange sells the right to show an ad to that particular user as that page loads.

Since pricing based on thousands of impressions delivered was familiar to advertisers who bought and sold newspaper ads, Internet display advertising may be sold on an impression basis for reasons that are largely historical. Newspapers and early Web sites were both fairly static, making impression-based pricing straightforward. However, the rapid adoption of AJAX and similar technologies are making the practice of tying impressions to the loading of a page obsolete. For example, popular email programs like Gmail and Yahoo! Mail update page content as new mail comes in, without any action by the user. When a page automatically updates its content in a continuous fashion, without changing its URL, it becomes difficult to define what it means for the page to be replaced and consequently what constitutes an impression.

One alternative to selling display ads based on impressions is to sell them based on time, much like how television and radio ads are traditionally sold. In fact, it has already been shown that increasing the duration of a television ad slightly increases the probability the ad will be remembered in an aided recall task [11]. However, advertising on the web is different than advertising on TV and radio because ads on the web are usually placed alongside the content whereas ads on TV and radio appear instead of the content. As a result, many Internet users claim to ignore ads completely, and studies around the concept of "banner blindness" frequently suggest that they do [1]. It is also possible that just seeing

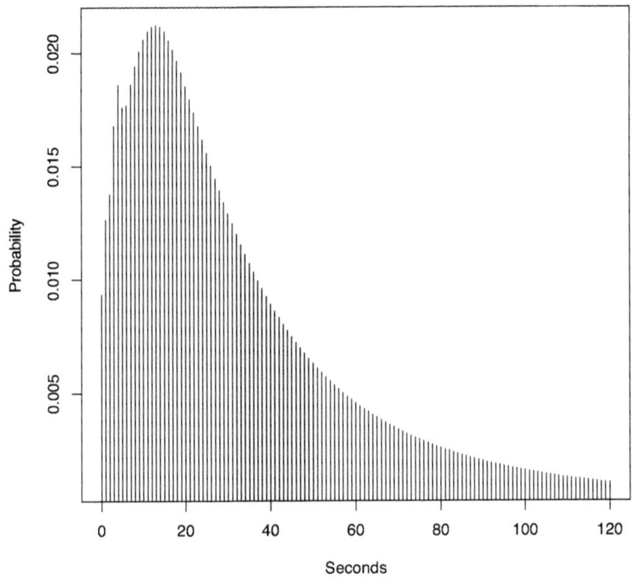

Figure 1: Distribution of time spent on a popular Yahoo! site

an advertisement produces recognition and recall, but that continued exposure does not lead to substantial increases in these measures. Indeed, if users initially scan the page, taking in ads, and then proceeded to focus narrowly on the page content, the duration of exposure would not matter much, beyond the initial few seconds. For these reasons, it is not clear *a priori* that ad exposure time will have an effect on memory, and if it does, what the magnitude of the effect will be.

Measuring the amount of time a user spends on a web page, which is an upper bound on how much time that user is exposed to an ad, is straightforward: simple Javascript code can track the amount of time a page is open, or better still, remains in focus. The result of such measurements is illustrated in Figure 1 for a popular Yahoo! property. Time spent ranges from a couple of seconds to well over two minutes. In practice, one would need to cap the amount of time spent on the page to use it as a measure of ad exposure time. For example, the person who spends 10 hours on a page may not even be twice as likely to recall an ad as the person who spends ten seconds.

Should advertisements be sold by impressions or by ad exposure time? Or more fundamentally, does amount of ad exposure time actually matter? Theoretically, the right metric is the one that most closely approximates advertiser value, because this induces the efficient use of resources [6]. Advertisers primarily judge campaigns by two criteria: ad recall and ad recognition. Thus the central focus of this work is to study if and how exposure time affects memory for advertisements.

2. RELATED WORK

Dreze and Husshern [4] ran a two-part study on the effectiveness of banner advertisements, which are long skinny ads that often appear at the top of a web page. In the first part, they used eye-tracking technology to show that users focus directly on banner ads rather infrequently, and argued that since those who do not directly focus on a banner ad are unlikely to click on it, click-through rate is not a good metric of ad effectiveness. In the second part of their study, users did simple tasks on web pages—such as typing a word into a box—with a banner ads present. Twenty-four hours after the task was completed, the subjects were asked unaided and aided recall questions, as well as various recognition and awareness questions. The authors found, for example, an 11% unaided recall rate, a 30% aided recall rate and a 19% aided recognition rate. As a result, Dreze and Husshern argue that brand awareness measures, such as recall and recognition, are more appropriate than clicks as metrics for display ads. In what follows, we shall use the metrics these authors advocate to measure the effect of display ad exposure time.

Perhaps the work most closely related to ours is a two-part study by Danaher and Mullarkey [3]. In the first part of their study, participants looked at a series of five web pages for 20, 40, or 60 seconds each. Crucially, the participants were not allowed to navigate away from the page before the assigned time expired. Participants were next asked recognition and recall questions. In the second part of the study, the same participants navigated a small, closed set of web pages containing advertisements for a fixed duration (again without the option to end the task when they finished reading), after which they were again asked questions about ad recognition and recall.

While this study found that higher exposure time was correlated with increased recognition and recall, there are a few design issues that would prevent drawing strong conclusions, especially causal ones. In the first part of the study, participants who finished the text quickly had more unoccupied time to look around the page and notice the ads. Because of this, differences in reading speed could account for differences in memory for ads in a way that would not arise during natural Web browsing. Furthermore, this design should disproportionately increase the recall and recognition rate of the longer duration treatments in which more people would have more "dead" time to look at ads.

In addition, Danaher and Mullarkey presented participants with memory questions for ads between the two parts of their study. After having seen questions about ads at the end of the first part of the study, participants would have payed greater attention to the ads in the second party of the study, thereby compromising the second set of tests. Lastly, since subjects could surf among a limited set of pages in the second part of the study, the number of ad impressions delivered was confounded with the time of exposure, leaving open the question of whether impressions or time of exposure matters more for predicting memory. To improve upon past investigations, in what follows we: manipulate the time of ad exposure exogenously, eliminate the confounding effect of reading speed, give no advance warning that memory for ads will be tested, and hold the number of impressions delivered constant.

3. RELATING MEMORY TO EXPOSURE TIME

Both of the experiments described in this paper were conducted on Amazon's Mechanical Turk[1], a crowdsourcing website where requesters can post jobs, called human in-

[1] `http://www.mturk.com`

telligence tasks (HITs), and workers can do those HITs for pay. After a worker submits their work for a HIT, requesters review the work and either accept it or reject it. Mechanical Turk was originally built for humans to do tasks that are hard for machines to do such as extracting data from images, audio transcription and filtering adult content. We used Mechanical Turk by posting our experiment as a HIT and using workers as our experimental participants. (There is a burgeoning literature that shows that the behavior of Mechanical Turk workers is comparable to laboratory studies [10, 7, 12].) Throughout this experiment, we used the Mechanical Turk API to restrict our subject pool to participants who live in the United States and who have a high approval rating (over 90%). By tracking the IDs of the workers who accepted our HITs, we could enforce that participants were only allowed to participate in one of two experiments, and they were only allowed to do that experiment one time. Next, we describe the results of our first experiment, which formed the basis for our second experiment, which exhibits the main results of this paper.

3.1 Experiment One: Time of Exposure Varied Endogenously

The first experiment aimed to establish a correlation between endogenous (self-determined) time spent on a web page and memory for a display ad on that page. Participants were recruited from Mechanical Turk by means of a HIT offering a fixed payment in addition to a smaller payment per question answered (to avoid the possibility of collusion, payment was not based on the correctness of answers). The preview page for the HIT consisted of a consent form and instructions indicating that the task involved reading and answering questions about a Web page.

In order to spread out the distribution of reading times, participants were assigned to conditions in which the article was either short or long. Randomization occurred at the moment the HIT was undertaken, precluding any confound between time of day and condition assignment. In addition to article length, random assignment also governed which of two display ads (for either Netflix or Jeep) and which of two articles (about either schoolteachers or an oil spill) would be shown. Thus, this experiment had a $2 \times 2 \times 2$ design in which there were two treatments each for the subject of the article, the length of the article, and the ad shown next to the article. Manipulation of ad and article was undertaken towards the aim of generalizable results under the methodological principle of representative design [2].

In the task, participants were shown high-resolution screen captures of web pages, as shown in Figure 2. In all conditions, the assigned display ad appeared next to the text. The image of each web page was chosen to be 600 pixels high. This height was chosen because 99% of screens on the Web are able to show at least 600 pixels in height[2] ensuring that the user could see the pages and the display ad, in their entirety without scrolling, and that the display ad was always in view.

After reading the first page of their assigned article, participants clicked a button to continue on to a second page, which featured the same display ad as the first page. In the short condition, the second page contained just one sentence of text, while in the long condition the text extended to the bottom of the second page. After the participants read both pages at their own pace, they proceeded on to the questionnaire and were unable to direct the browser to display the ad or article again.

[2]See `http://www.w3schools.com/browsers/browsers_display.asp` for the distribution of screen sizes on the web.

Figure 2: Screenshot of the first page of the New York public school teachers article with the Netflix ad.

The questionnaire first presented two, five-alternative multiple choice reading comprehension questions to assess to what extent participants paid attention to the text. After that, it contained one unaided recall question: "Which advertisements, if any, did you see on the page during the experiment? Type the name of any advertisers here if you can remember seeing their ads on the last page, or indicate that you are unable to remember any." On the subsequent page, participants were asked "Did you see the following advertisement during this HIT?", accompanied by a picture of the Netflix ad, and were next presented the same question for the Jeep ad. See Appendix A for pictures of the ads. Note that participants were shown only one of these two ads in the experiment, making the other ad a lure which is useful for establishing the false positive recall and recognition rates. After submitting, the task was completed and answers could not be changed.

Before proceeding with the analysis, the initial sample of 479 was reduced to the inner 98% of reading times to eliminate outliers, reducing the sample by 10, after which 16 participants (4.6%) were excluded for answering both reading comprehension questions incorrectly, leaving 453 participants with a mean reading time of 123 seconds. The length manipulation was effective in spreading out reading times as reflected by the per-condition means (143 and 103 in the long and short conditions) and the interquartile ranges: the 75th percentiles were 181 and 125 seconds, and the 25th percentiles were 96 and 72 seconds in the long and short conditions, respectively.

Each participants' questionnaire responses were coded as four binary items. The first two binary items coded whether the unaided recall question mentioned the two advertisements. The latter two binary items coded the answer to the pictorial recognition task.

3.2 Experiment One Results

Figure 3 shows the result of Experiment 1. The false pos-

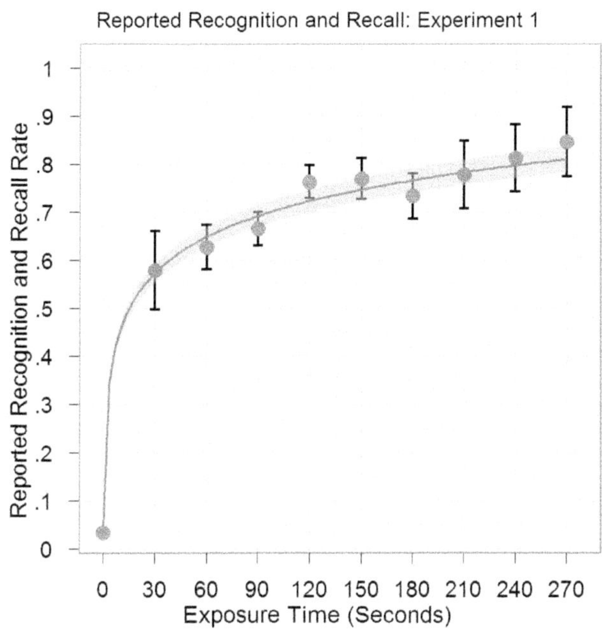

Figure 3: Memory as a function of reading time. Observe the steep increase in the 0–60 second range followed by the slower, but sustained increase after 60 seconds. The points are the mean of the recognition and recall items binned at 30 second intervals with error bars at ± 1 standard error. The blue curve is the best fitting one in its family, with the gray region showing a 95% confidence interval over its parameters.

itive data (claims of remembering the "lure" ad which was not shown) make up the point on the x-axis at 0 seconds of exposure time. The rest of the data contribute to points on the x-axis with an exposure time strictly greater than 0 seconds. Figure 3 also shows the result of fitting a curve of the form $y = a + b\log(x + c)$ to the data along with the 95% confidence interval, where x is the reading time and a, b and c are free parameters. Previous psychological studies on memory have found that memory rates are well described by functions of this form [5]. To indicate the quality of the fit, we also plot the average rate of recognition and recall binned at 30 second intervals. There were 10 responses that took upwards of 270 seconds, which were excluded from the plot owing to sparsity of data within each bin. Note the standard errors are smallest where data are most plentiful, in the region around 120 seconds.

Figures 4(a) and 4(b) are the same type of plots except with the recall and recognition data separated. The same functional form is fit with different parameters. Again, to indicate the quality of the fit, we also plot the mean recognition or recall rate. Since these plot each have half of the data shown in Figure 3 the mean recall and recognition rates are binned in 60 second intervals.

There are a few trends that emerge from examination of Figures 3 and 4. First, if one compares Figure 4(a) to Figure 4(b), one can easily see that unaided recall is harder then recognition yet the unaided recall rate is still reasonably high over a long range of exposure times: roughly 50% or more with 60 seconds or more of exposure. False positive rates are less than 10% for recognition measures and, as would be expected, 0% for the recall measures; this gives some indication that the reported memory rates are reasonably accurate, though false recognition rates always depend on the properties of the ad in question. In the next study we use lures that deliberately resemble the targets to approximate an upper bound on false recognition for the targets. Since the binned means lie so close to the curve that was fit to the data one can easily see that the logarithmic function described above describes the data well. Finally, for both the recall, recognition, and combined measures there is a sharp increase from the false positive rate at 0 seconds to 30 seconds. This suggests that most of an ad's effect on memory is likely to take effect soon after the page loads.

In the experiment described previously the exposure time of the advertisement was determined by the participants' reading time. Figures 3 and 4 show that the more time the participant spent reading, the higher the recall and recognition rates. Because this experimental manipulation of ad exposure depends on a participant's reading speed, one cannot establish a causal link between exposure time and memory. For example, it could be the case that slower readers are more careful individuals who examine the entire page, including the text and the display ad, more closely than faster readers. Or there could be a latent variable that causes both slow reading and good memory in select individuals. Such a variable could create the appearance of a relationship between exposure time and memory across individuals, even though it may not exist within any homogeneous set of individuals. Were this the case, our result would be of little interest to advertisers who wish to target homogeneous segments.

Experiment 2 will address the above concerns by manipulating exposure time exogenously. Because there was a steep rise in the recall and recognition rates in the 0–60 second range we will focus our attention there.

3.3 Experiment Two: Exogenously Varying Time of Ad Exposure

Whereas in the previous study, ad exposure time was roughly equivalent to reading time, this experiment manipulates exposure time exogenously to estimate the causal effect of ad exposure time on memory. This external manipulation was accomplished by using a Javascript timer to display ads for a pre-determined number of seconds while people are reading and then having them disappear from view. To make the scenario as realistic as possible, when the first ad shown disappears, it is immediately replaced with a second ad, as is the case on many Web sites that rotate multiple ads into one slot.

Participants were again drawn from Amazon Mechanical Turk as in Experiment 1. Instructions again indicated that the task involved reading and answering questions about a Web page. Participants were again paid a flat rate for completing the experiment, plus a specified amount per question answered. The article used is depicted in Figure 2. Participants were randomly assigned into one of four treatments which governed how long they were exposed to two display ads (one for Jeep and one for Netflix). Simultaneous with the loading of the article, one ad was displayed, depending on condition, for either 5, 10, 25, or 40 seconds. The 5 and

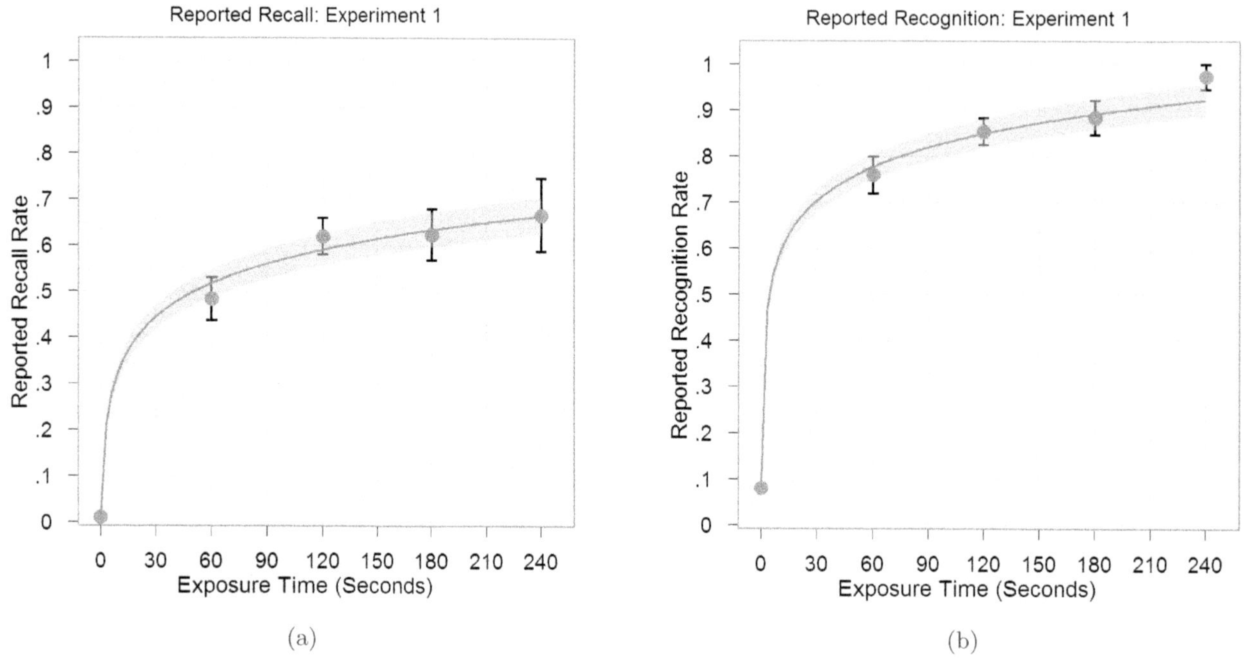

Figure 4: The recall and recognition rates, respectively, as a function of reading time. Both show the steep increase in the 0–60 second range followed by the slower, but sustained increase after 60 seconds. The points are the mean of the recognition and recall items binned at 60 second intervals with error bars at $\pm$ 1 standard error. The blue curve is the best fitting one in its family, with the gray region showing a 95% confidence interval over its parameters.

25, as well as the 10 and 40 second exposure times, were paired in the following manner. If the first ad was shown for 5 seconds, then the second ad was shown for 25 seconds; conversely, if the first ad was shown for 25 seconds, then the second ad was shown for 5 seconds. Similarly, if the first ad was shown for 10 seconds, then the second ad was shown for 40 seconds; conversely, if the first ad was shown for 40 seconds, then the second ad was shown for 10 seconds. After the display time for the second ad expired, it was replaced with a white rectangle, giving the appearance of it disappearing altogether. Data collection proceeded in two waves, one comprising 300 subjects that randomly assigned participants to the 10 and 40 second treatments, and the latter one randomly assigning 250 individuals to the 5 and 25 second treatments. Within the four conditions, participants were randomly assigned to see the Netflix ad before the Jeep ad or *vice versa*, resulting in a 4×2 design (four exposure time sequences by two orderings of the advertisements).

To stabilize forgetting time, which is the amount of time between the first ad disappearing and the questionnaire, the reading task was followed by a buffer task in which participants played a game for a pre-determined, condition-specific amount of time. Tetris, a visual game consisting of primary shapes, was chosen to avoid ad-specific linguistic memory interference. The game was rendered in black and white to reduce visual memory interference with the colors present in the stimuli ads. The duration of this buffer task was calculated to equalize forgetting time for the average participant in each condition and ranged between 20 and 55 seconds. After the buffer task time expired, participants were automatically forwarded to the questionnaire, and were not able to exit the game early.

In the questionnaire phase, the same two, five-alternative multiple choice reading comprehension questions were asked followed by the same unaided recall question as in Experiment 1, which asked: "Which advertisements, if any, did you see on the page during this HIT? Type the name of any advertisers here if you can remember seeing their ads on the last page, or indicate that you are unable to remember any." The subsequent page presented four recognition questions with textual cues of the form "Did you see a __ ad?", with Netflix, Jeep, American Express and Avis being the advertisers filling in the blank. Netflix and Jeep were the "target" advertisers whose ads were indeed shown, while American Express and Avis were "lure" advertisers, whose advertisements were not shown. For pictures of the ads and their respective lures see Appendix A. Inclusion of lures was particularly relevant for the next four questions, which were recognition questions with pictorial cues asking "Did you see this ad?" and showing the actual two ads from the experiment as well as the two lure ads. The lures were chosen for bearing a strong visual resemblance to the targets in order to approximate an upper bound on the false positive rate. The Avis lure is primarily red, much like the Netflix ad, and the American Express lure is primarily black, much like the Jeep ad.

Each participant's data was coded as twelve binary responses. The first four responses coded mentions of the two target ads and lures from the unaided recall question. The next four were the recognition questions with textual cues, and the final four were the recognition items with pictorial cues (the ads themselves).

Before analyzing the effect of exposure on the memory items, 14 participants (2.5%) were excluded for not completing the task, after which 7 (1.3%) were excluded for answering both reading comprehension questions incorrectly. The very small percentages of incomplete or careless responses speak to the quality of data which can be collected via Mechanical Turk.

3.4 Experiment Two Results

Experiment 1 showed a correlation between exposure time and memory for advertisements. Will a similar relationship arise when ad exposure time is manipulated exogenously?

Based on reading time estimates from Experiment 1, we designed this experiment such that about 80% of people would take long enough reading the article that they would be exposed to both ads for the prescribed amounts of time. This estimate turned out to quite accurate as the fastest 20% of readers finished in 51 seconds, and only 50 seconds were needed to see both ads in the longest condition (in which two ads are shown for 10 and 40 seconds). The median reading time was 77 seconds, the 75th percentile was 98 seconds and the 25th percentile was 55 seconds. The purest exogenous analysis would exclude the fastest 20% of readers from all conditions to ensure the sample consists only of those who saw both first and second ads for the intended amount of time. However, since even fast readers were likely exposed to at least one ad for the intended amount of time, and since only three out of 12 questions attributable to a participant are tied to each target ad, one may simply drop the questions (as opposed to the participants) for which full intended treatment was not received and thus retain 96%, as opposed to 80%, of the observations. Doing so may introduce a slight bias, so as a preventive measure, all analyses were run dropping the fastest 20% of individuals, dropping the affected 4% of observations for which the full treatment was not received, or doing neither. The effect of such filters on derived estimates was negligible. For example, in Figure 5 after the application of such filters, the average point estimate moved by less than one percentage point, and no estimate moved by as many as two percentage points. Accordingly, in the analyses which follow, we retain the 96% of items for which the intended level of exposure was received.

As shown in Figure 5, there is a clear increasing trend in the probability of reporting memory of an advertisement as a function of manipulated exposure time. The combined recall and recognition measure increases sharply in the first 10 seconds and then still increases, albeit at a slower rate after that. Thus there are diminishing returns to increased exposure time suggesting that the first seconds of exposure are more valuable to advertisers then later seconds, a topic we will revisit in Section 3.5. Nonetheless, increased exposure time increased the probability that the ad was remembered.

The best fitting curve took on the form $y = -.009 + 0.106 \log(x + 1.681)$, where y is the memory response and x is the time of exposure. The basic shape of this curve, which shows the causal effect of exposure time on memory, can shed light on the results of Experiment 1. Substituting in the mean reading times from Experiment 1's two conditions, 143 and 103 seconds, this curve predicts a difference of 3.4 percentage points, a modest difference, not unlike that realized in this range in Experiment 1. While the relation in

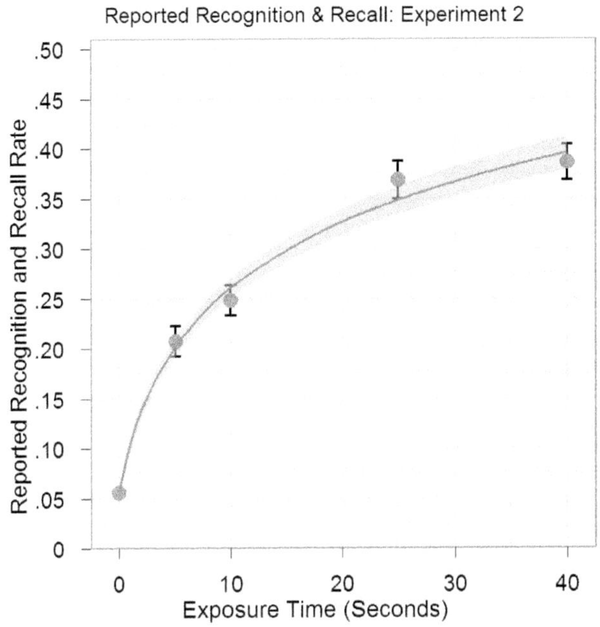

Figure 5: Memory as a function of time of exposure time which was exogenously imposed on the subjects. The points are the mean of the recognition and recall items with error bars at ± 1 standard error. The blue curve is the best fitting one in its family, with the gray region showing a 95% confidence interval over its parameters.

Figure 5 does not make point predictions about Experiment 1—the two curves occupy different ranges, possibly due to the buffer task in Experiment 2 and the two impressions delivered in Experiment 1 versus one impression delivered in Experiment 2—the same basic logarithmic relationship predicts that large relative differences in recall and recognition are difficult to attain beyond exposure times of 100 seconds. For this reason, and for the reason that most Web pages are viewed for less than this long (see again Figure 1), a prudent accounting system may discount or disregard exposure times beyond this threshold.

As in Experiment 1, decomposing the aggregate curve into recall and recognition measures shows relationships of the same basic shape, with recognition, as is most often the case [3], proving to be an easier task than recall. Recall and recognition are shown separately in Figure 6. Despite the lures bearing a strong resemblance to the target ads, false alarm rates were low: 6% on text recognition items, and reaching a maximum of 7.8% for the pictorial recognition items. As expected, the false alarm rate for recall items was 0%. A logistic random effects model, with participants and advertisers as random effects, confirmed that both both time of exposure and presentation order to be strong predictors of what is remembered, as treated in the next section.

3.5 The Effects of an Advertisement Appearing First or Second

Next we discuss the effect of showing an ad first versus second. Recall that users were exposed to an ad for 10 sec-

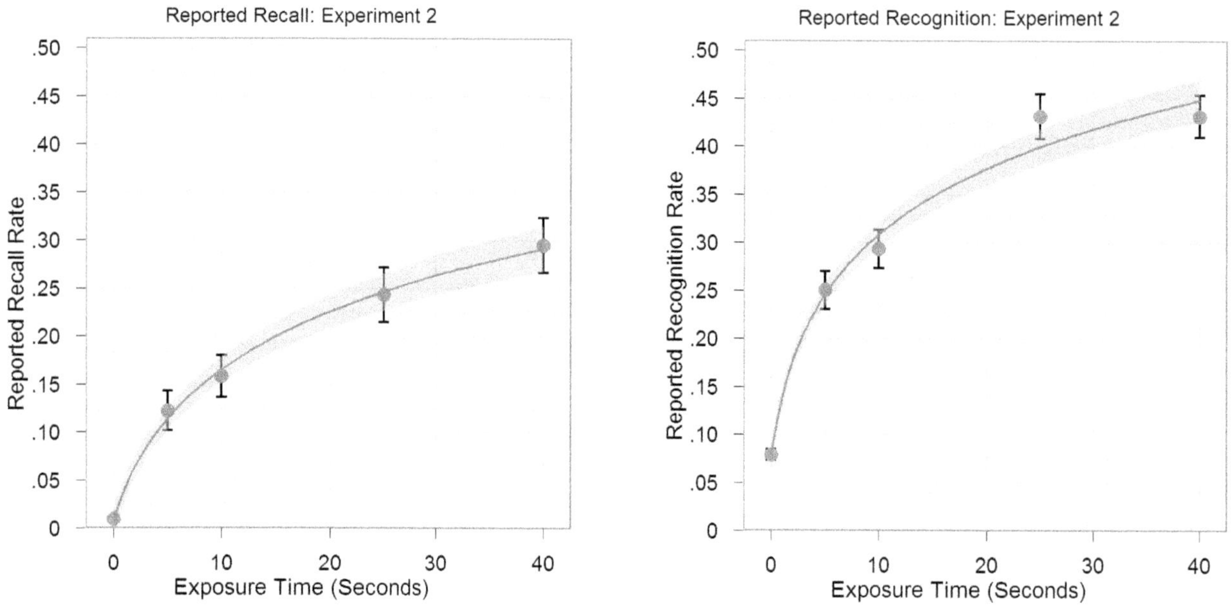

(a) (b)

Figure 6: The recall and recognition rates, respectively, as a function of the exposure time which was exogenously imposed on the subjects. The points are the mean of the recognition and recall items with error bars at ± 1 standard error. The blue curve is the best fitting one in its family, with the gray region showing a 95% confidence interval over its parameters.

onds then another for 40 seconds, or *vice versa*, or they were shown an ad for 5 seconds then another for 25 seconds, or *vice versa*. One might expect that due to their sudden appearance on the page, ads which appear second might have an attentional advantage [9] over ads that load with the rest of the page's content. However, the opposite appears to be the case. Figure 7 shows the result of plotting the combined recall and recognition for the first and second ads. Observe that the recall and recognition rate for the second ad does not have the steep increase at low exposure times as first ads do. Moreover, the combined recognition and recall rate for the second ad displayed for 40 seconds was still 30%.

Figure 7(a) shows that the seconds soon after the page loads cause a higher increase in recall and recognition than do later seconds. Consider a 10 second ad shown second, which appeared 40 seconds after the page loaded. Also consider a 5 second ad shown second, which appeared after 25 seconds. The 5 second ad will be seen during a higher recall period of time than the 10 second ad. Thus, in our design, the recall of the 5 second ad will be slightly inflated relative to that of the 10 second ad. One can make a symmetric argument which shows that the recall and recognition of the 25 second ad will also be slightly inflated relative to a 40 second ad shown second. Despite this observation, Figure 7 shows the first ad has a higher recall and recognition rate then the second. Figure 7 also shows that 5–10 seconds of exposure of the first ad shown is roughly equivalent to 40 seconds of exposure of the second ad shown. From an advertiser's perspective, having an ad shown second is less valuable the being shown first. Nonetheless, in either case, increasing the exposure time adds value.

4. CONCLUSION

The main result of this work is giving evidence for a causal effect of exposure time on the recall and recognition of display advertisements. More specifically, we showed that display ad recognition and recall increase as exposure time increases, with the steepest effect occurring for low values of exposure time. A log-linear function is a good approximation of the psychological response. The secondary result of this work is that only the first ad shown in a sequence benefits from this steep increase of recognition and recall in the first seconds of exposure, but that both the first and second ads shown benefit from more exposure time.

As mentioned in the introduction, display ads are currently sold by the impression. This pricing scheme ignores how long ads are in view. Advertisers value ad recognition and ad recall, and time of exposure causally impacts both. Pricing based on better measures of advertiser value than impressions offers three distinct advantages. First, it permits efficient allocation. When pricing is based on an average, allocating pieces to different buyers is impossible, since the pieces have the same average value. Similarly, with noisy measures of value, more allocation mistakes will be made. Second, pricing based more closely on value mitigates buyer risk, since pricing corresponds more closely to the value actually delivered. Risk matters most in environments with great supply variability like digital advertising. Finally, pricing based on value permits price discrimination—charging advertisers based on the value delivered may let the seller capture a larger fraction of the value generated.

Thus this work provides evidence that publishers should charge based on the amount of time users spend with an ad

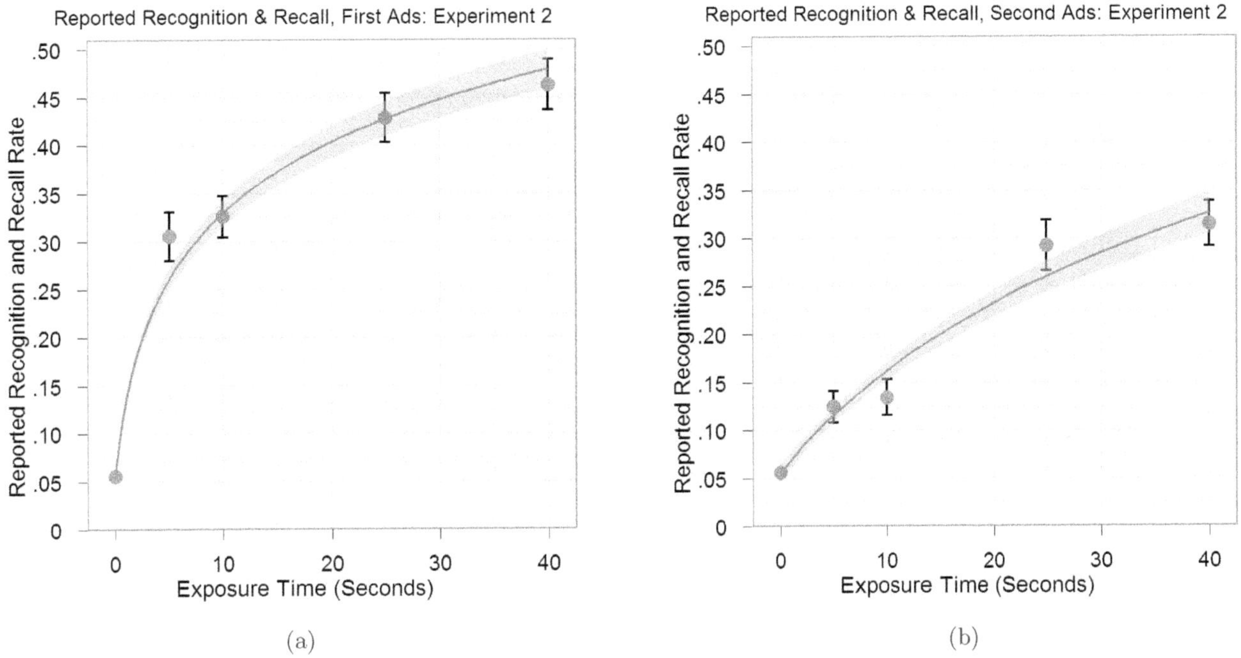

Figure 7: The combined recognition and recall rates for the first and seconds ads shown. Observe that the first ad shown has a steep increase in memory in the first few seconds and the second ad shown does not. Yet both show that increasing exposure time increases memory. The points are the mean of the recognition and recall items with error bars at ± 1 standard error. The blue curve is the best fitting one in its family, with the gray region showing a 95% confidence interval over its parameters.

in view. There are two obvious systems by which publishers could achieve this. First, publishers could simply measure how long a user spends with an ad in view, then charge based on a functional transformation of this. A second method could involve advertisers buying 30-second "spots", for example. In this system, even as the user navigated the site, the ad would stay in view for 30 seconds. Moreover, if a user leaves the site before the 30 seconds has expired, publishers could either serve the ad to the user when he or she returns, or prorate the purchase of that spot for the amount of time the user actually spent with the ad in view. Publishers could differentially price spots of different lengths. A clear direction for future work is to analyze theoretical pricing models of systems that take the time of exposure into account.

Acknowledgments

We would like to thank Randall A. Lewis, David H. Reiley and Duncan J. Watts for many helpful conversations.

5. REFERENCES

[1] Jan P. Benway. Banner blindness: The irony of attention grabbing on the world wide web. In *Proceedings of the Human Factors and Ergonomics Society 42nd Annual Meeting*, volume 1, pages 463–467, October 1998.

[2] Egon Brunswik. *Perception and the representative design of experiments (2nd ed.).* University of California Press, Berkeley, CA, 1956.

[3] Peter J. Danaher and Guy W. Mullarkey. Factors affecting online advertising recall: A study of students. *Journal of Advertising Research*, 43:252–267, 2003.

[4] Xavier Drèze and François-Xavier Hussherr. Internet advertising: Is anybody watching? *Journal of Interactive Marketing*, 17(4), 2003.

[5] Fernand Gobet and Herbert A. Simon. Five seconds or sixty? presentation time in expert memory. *Cognitive Science*, 24(4):651–682, 2000.

[6] Bengt Holmstrom and Paul Milgrom. The firm as an incentive system. *American Economic Review*, 84(4):972–991, September 1994.

[7] John J. Horton, David G. Rand, and Richard J. Zeckhauser. The online laboratory. *Experimental Economics*, 2011. To Appear.

[8] IAB internet advertising revenue report, 2009.

[9] John Jonides and Steve Yantis. Uniqueness of abrupt visual onset in capturing attention. *Perception & Psychophysics*, 43(3):346–354, 1988.

[10] Gabriele Paolacci, Jesse Chandler, and Panagiotis G. Ipeirotis. Running experiments on Amazon Mechanical Turk. *Judgment and Decision Making*, 5:411–419, 2010.

[11] Gordon L. Patzer. Multiple dimensionsof performance for 30-second and 15-second commercials. *Journal of Advertising Research*, 31(4):18–25, 1991.

[12] Siddharth Suri and Duncan J. Watts. Cooperation and contagion in networked public goods experiments. *PLoS ONE*, 2011. To Appear.

APPENDIX

A. ADVERTISEMENTS AND LURES

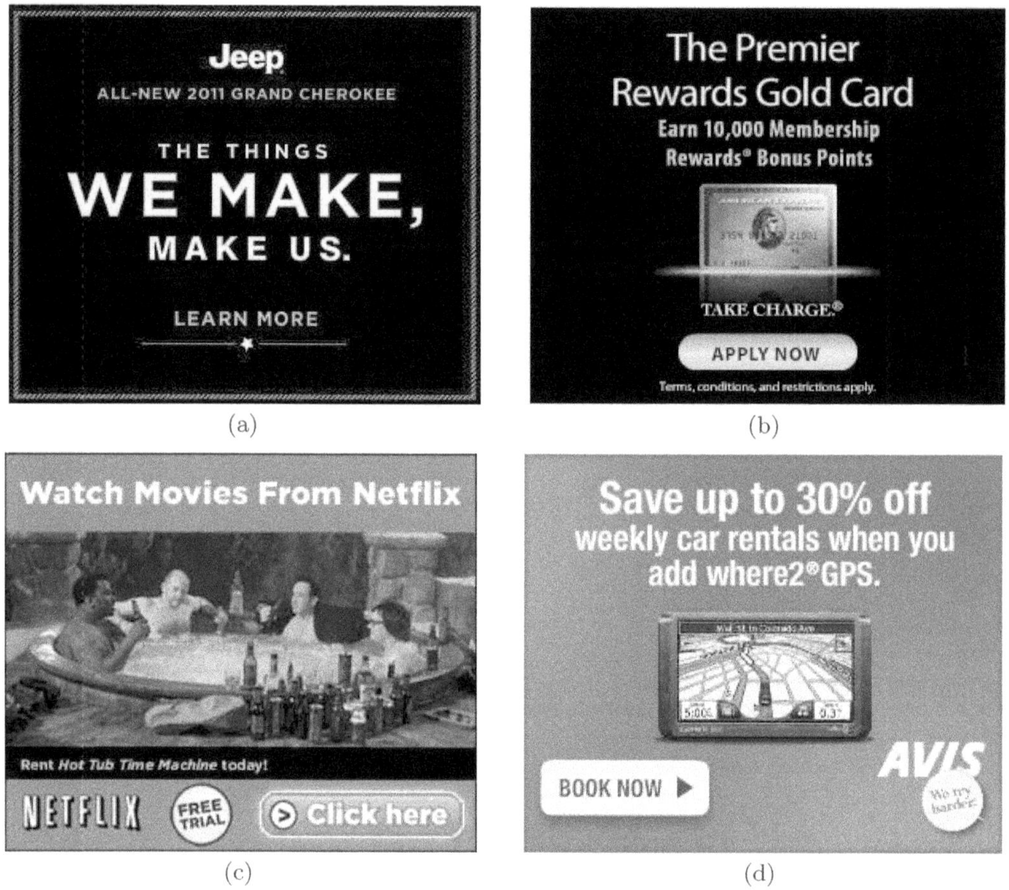

Figure 8: Panels 8(a) and 8(c) are the ads used in the experiment with endogenous exposure time (Experiment 1). Panel 8(b) was the lure for 8(a), and Panel 8(d) was the lure for 8(c) in the experiment with exogenously imposed exposure time (Experiment 2).

Reserve Prices in Internet Advertising Auctions: A Field Experiment*

[Working Paper Abstract]†

Michael Ostrovsky
Stanford University
518 Memorial Way
Stanford, CA 94305
ostrovsky@gsb.stanford.edu

Michael Schwarz
Yahoo! Labs
2397 Shattuck Ave.
Berkeley, CA 94704
mschwarz@yahoo-inc.com

ABSTRACT

We present the results of a large field experiment on setting reserve prices in auctions for online advertisements, guided by the theory of optimal auction design suitably adapted to the sponsored search setting. Consistent with the theory, following the introduction of new reserve prices revenues in these auctions have increased substantially.

Categories and Subject Descriptors

J.4 [**Social and Behavioral Sciences**]: Economics

General Terms

Economics, Experimentation

1. INTRODUCTION

Auctions are used to sell a wide variety of objects, ranging from flowers, paintings, and used cars to electromagnetic spectrum and Internet advertisements. One of the most natural questions about the design of an auction is revenue maximization: How should an auction be designed to generate the highest expected payoff to the seller? This question was answered by Myerson (1981) and Riley and Samuelson (1981) for the setting with one object for sale and independently distributed private bidder values. For the case with symmetric bidders, the answer is particularly elegant: the optimal mechanism can be implemented by a second-price auction with an appropriately chosen reserve price.

In this paper, we study the effects of applying a suitable modification of this theoretical result in practice. Specifically, we present the results of a large-scale field experiment on reserve prices in a particular setting: "sponsored search" auctions conducted by Yahoo! to sell advertisements (Edelman, Ostrovsky, and Schwarz, 2007; Varian, 2007). The scale of the experiment is substantially larger than that in the previous studies of the effects of reserve prices in practice (Reiley, 2006; Walsh et al., 2008; Brown and Morgan, 2009), and there are several other important differences.

In the experiment, reserve prices in the randomly selected "treatment" group were set based on the guidance provided by the theory of optimal auctions, while in the "control" group they were left at the old level of 10 cents per click. The revenues in the treatment group have increased substantially relative to the control group: our conservative estimate is that the impact of reserve prices was equal to additional 2.7% of revenues. This shows that suitably chosen reserve prices in auctions can in fact play an important role in increasing revenues, and that theory provides a useful guide for setting them. We also study the effects of reserve prices on revenues in various subgroups of keywords, and find that the increase is especially pronounced for keywords with relatively high search volumes, for keywords in which the theoretically optimal reserve price is relatively high, and for keywords with a relatively small number of bidders.

*We are especially indebted to the engineers at Yahoo!, too numerous to list here, without whom this project could never have been implemented. We are also grateful to David Reiley and Preston McAfee for many helpful discussions and to Ken Hendricks and Jon Levin for helpful comments and suggestions.

†This working paper is available online at http://faculty-gsb.stanford.edu/ostrovsky/papers/rp.pdf.

EC'11, June 5–9, 2011, San Jose, California, USA.
ACM 978-1-4503-0261-6/11/06.

2. REFERENCES

[1] Brown, J., and J. Morgan (2009), "How Much Is a Dollar Worth? Tipping Versus Equilibrium Coexistence on Competing Online Auction Sites," *Journal of Political Economy,* 117.

[2] Edelman, B., M. Ostrovsky, and M. Schwarz (2007), "Internet Advertising and the Generalized Second Price Auction: Selling Billions of Dollars Worth of Keywords," *American Economic Review*, 97.

[3] Myerson, R. (1981), "Optimal Auction Design," *Mathematics of Operations Research,* 6.

[4] Reiley, D. (2006), "Field Experiments on the Effects of Reserve Prices in Auctions: More Magic on the Internet." *RAND Journal of Economics,* 37.

[5] Riley, J., and W. Samuelson (1981), "Optimal Auctions," *American Economic Review,* 71.

[6] Varian, H. (2007), "Position Auctions," *International Journal of Industrial Organization,* 25.

[7] Walsh, W., D. Parkes, T. Sandholm, and C. Boutillier (2008), "Computing Reserve Prices and Identifying the Value Distribution in Real-World Auctions with Market Disruptions," *Proceedings of the Twenty-Third AAAI Conference on Artificial Intelligence.*

Stochastic Variability in Sponsored Search Auctions: Observations and Models *

Furcy Pin†
École Normale Supérieure
Paris, France
furcy.pin@ens.fr

Peter Key
Microsoft Research
Cambridge, CB3 0FB, UK
peter.key@microsoft.com

ABSTRACT

Sponsored search advertisement slots are currently sold via Generalized Second Price (GSP) auctions. Despite the simplicity of their rules, these auctions are far from being fully understood. Our observations on real ad-auction data show that advertisers usually enter many distinct auctions with different opponents and with varying parameters. We describe some of our findings from these observations and propose a simple probabilistic model taking them into account. This model can be used to predict the number of clicks received by the advertisers and the total price they can expect to pay depending on their bid, or even to estimate the players valuations, all at a very low computational cost.

Categories and Subject Descriptors

J4 [**Social and Behavioral Sciences**]: Economics; K4.4 [**Computers and Society**]: Electronic Commerce

General Terms

Economics, Algorithms, Theory

Keywords

Sponsored search auctions, position auctions, generalized second price auction, game theory, click-through rates

1. INTRODUCTION

Each time someone types a query in a search engine such as Bing or Google, an auction is run and used to determine which sponsored links will appear and what price will be paid by the advertiser if their ad is clicked. The *Generalized Second Price (GSP)* auction is the current mechanism used. Although these auctions are very simple to describe and have been in use since at least 2002, their behavior in practice is far from being fully understood. In this paper we develop a new analytical model for such a position auction, motivated and informed by measurements from actual ad-auctions, which attempts to account for some of the real-world variability in such auctions.

In a simplified version of a GSP, each *advertiser* (or *player*) places a bid for a keyword. The *auctioneer* (namely the ad-platform) then displays the ads with the highest bids, allocating the highest bidder to the best slot, and so on, until all the allowed slots are allocated. Payment is then organized on a Pay-Per-Click (PPC) basis: an advertiser only pays when her ad is clicked, and pays the price equal to the bid of the player just below her.

A prerequisite to improving auction design is the ability to predict accurately the behavior of bidders. In particular, one challenge is to estimate a player's *valuation* knowing her bid, and conversely to predict the bids when the valuations are given.

We describe a new analytical model, which allows us to predict a player's valuation given her bid and her opponents' bids. This model relies on the observation that the players participate with the same bid in a great number of auctions with varying conditions. For instance, we noticed that the number and the identity of the opponents of a given player usually vary across successive auctions. Moreover, the players' bids are in practice multiplied by weights which depend on many criteria, and vary from one auction to another. We also observed that most players do not change their bid often.

For these reasons, the classical model of a single auction repeated an infinite number of times is inappropriate. Because of the stochastic noise in our model, in general players have a unique optimal response to a given opponent's bidding profile, whereas in the classical model where only one single auction is considered (or one auction repeated with the same weights and players), there typically is a complete interval of optimal bids.

Contributions. The main contributions of this paper are first, insights into the inherent randomness of ad-auctions, and a description of the type of randomness encountered, namely high variability in the weights associated with bids, and variability in both the number and identity of players participating in different instances of the same keyword-auction. Second, we describe a model which captures this inherent variability, and which allows us, under additional simplifying assumptions on the distribution of bids, to de-

*The authors wish to thank Anton Schwaighofer and Alexandre Proutiere for their help and comments on this paper.

†Work performed while author was an intern at Microsoft Research Cambridge.

rive closed form expressions for the optimal bid for a given player assuming they know their own valuation. The simplifying assumptions are that the bids an opponent faces in any particular instance of an auction are well approximated by sampling independently a random number of players with a common bid distribution. There are both empirical and theoretical reasons why this is good approximation for heavily contested keywords, and this assumption also allows players to work with observable-in-principle quantities (bids) of other opponents rather than unobservable valuations, offering the potential for advertisers to find their optimal bid easily. Our model produces utility functions that are smooth functions of a player's own value, in contrast to the discontinuous step functions of classical GSP models. Third, for the ad-platform, our model allows fast computation of players' valuations and click-through estimates to be derived from bids by assuming bids are optimal and finding the appropriate value, with the computation being two orders of magnitude faster than an Incremental Cost Per Click (ICC) model [3].

Related Work. GSP auctions have been studied by Varian in [12], and by Edelman, Ostrovsky and Schwarz (EOS) in [6]. Both examine Nash equilibria in a single auction with complete information. Most subsequent papers [1, 2, 7] have followed this simple model of a single auction. Some works [4, 5, 13] have looked at the dynamics of these auctions by considering an auction repeated multiple times with a fixed set of participants and most parameters fixed. Some others [10] even studied the dynamics of ad auctions with incoming and departing participants using tools from queueing theory.

The beneficial effects of noise on bids was emphasized in [4], where the authors noticed that such noise made some low-revenue equilibria unstable, and suggested adding some artificial noise to the bids. However they did not mention that such variability is naturally present in practice.

The other type of variability we observed in real auctions was a randomness in the identity of players participating in the auctions. The results on equilibria obtained for a single auction are hard to generalize to multiple auctions with varying opponents, and there is a lack of research in this area.

One paper which does consider multiple auctions with varying opponents and a random noise on the weights, is Athey and Nekipelov [3]. It is also probably the closest to our work in spirit. The main difference between our model and theirs is that they assume that players still have full information on their opponent's identity in each auction they enter, while in our model players ignore this information, and are given instead the bid distribution of their opponents. The advantage of our model compared to Athey-Nekipelov's is its simplicity, inducing a low computational cost of the estimation. However, our model being asymmetrically focused on a single player, cannot be used to directly manipulate Nash Equilibria, which Athey-Nekipelov's allows.

Gomes and Sweeney[8] consider a Bayes Nash equilibria of a GSP. Using the standard setting of Bayes-Nash, assuming a common prior distribution $F_v(v)$ of players values, they derive an integral equation which a bidding function $\beta(v)$ has to satisfy in an efficient symmetric equilibrium, and provide a way to calculate the solution recursively. They also discuss conditions under which efficient equilibria do not exist. It is possible to connect their main equation to ours in the case of a fixed number of players, by transforming the value distribution $F_v(v)$ into a distribution across bids $F_b(\cdot)$, using the optimal bid function $\beta(v)$. We comment on this more fully in section 6.2.

Organization. In Section 2, we give a quick introduction to the GSP auction mechanism and our model. We then present in Section 3 the results of studies done on real auctions in the Bing database, and show with these observations that the classical model of a single repeated auction is far from reality. We propose in Section 4 our new analytical model which is based on more realistic assumptions inspired from our observations on real data. Section 5 presents the results of estimations made using that model, Section 6 explores in detail similarities and differences between our model and some other works [3, 8], and we conclude in Section 7.

2. NOTATIONS AND ASSUMPTIONS

An overview of sponsored search and some of the technology is given in Jansen and Mullen [9]. In the GSP mechanism currently used, the auctioneer (the ad-platform of a search engine, e.g. Google or Bing) sells to *advertisers* a finite set of *slots* in which ads are displayed. Each time a search query is returned, an auction is run to decide which ad will appear in each slot. The payment is then organized on a *price-per-click (PPC)* basis: an advertiser pays only when someone clicks on her ad.

All slots are sold simultaneously in one single auction, although the slots are not all equivalent. For example, the slots at the top of the result page (called the *mainline*) offer a greater visibility than the ones displayed in the *sidebar*. The *click-through-rate (CTR)* measures the probability of an ad being clicked on. Although CTRs may depend on multiple factors, a classical assumption is that they are *separable* as a product of two independent factors depending respectively on the slot position (*slot-CTR*) and the ad displayed in it (*ad-CTR*).

Notation.

Consider a set of N *players* (or *bidders*) competing for K slots. Each player i has a private *value* (or *valuation*) v_i she attributes to a click. To each player i is attributed a *weight*, which corresponds to the *ad-CTR* of the player's ad, and each slot j has a specific *slot-CTR* s_j, such that when player i is assigned to slot j she receives a CTR equal to $w_i s_j$.

Without loss of generality, we assume the slots to be ordered in decreasing order of slot-CTR: $s_0 \geq s_1 \geq \cdots \geq s_K$, and we assume $K > N$, by adding fictitious undisplayed slots with slot-CTR $s_j = 0$ if needed.

The auctioneer fixes a *reserve price* r corresponding to the lowest price at which it accepts to display ads.

GSP.

The GSP mechanism consists as follows. Each player i submits a bid b_i. The players whose weighted bid is lower than the reserve price r are rejected from the auction. The remaining k players are then ordered in decreasing order of their weighted bids, such that $b_1 w_1 \geq b_2 w_2 \geq \cdots \geq b_k w_k \geq r$, breaking ties randomly. The first player according to that order is then displayed in the first slot, the second player in the second slot, and so on, until all players are placed. Each player then pays per click a price equal to the minimal bid necessary to maintain their position. That is, player $i < k$

must bid at least $b_i \geq b_{i+1}w_{i+1}/w_i$ in order to stay above player $i+1$, and thus she has to pay $p_i(b) = b_{i+1}w_{i+1}/w_i$ per click. Similarly, the last player above the reserve price has to pay $p_k(b) = r/w_k$ per click. The *utility* (or *payoff*) of player i is then given by $U_i(v_i, b) = (v_i - p_i(b))w_i\varphi_i(b)$ where the *allocation function* $\varphi_i(b) \in \{s_0, s_1, \ldots, s_K\}$ denotes the CTR of the slot obtained by player i.

However, this simple description is far from being sufficient for a full understanding of the real GSP auctions used in practice. Indeed, we described here the mechanism of one single auction, while in practice, a player enters many distinct auctions with the same single bid, while the other parameters (opponents, weights) vary from one auction to the other, as we will show in the next section. In addition, the weights attributed to each advertiser are only estimates computed by the ad-platform and are not directly communicated to the advertisers.

3. REAL DATA ANALYSIS

We now present some observations derived from the analysis of full records of one week of auctions run on Microsoft's search engine Bing.

We focused on several aspect of these auctions, such as the evolution of ad qualities or players' behavior during these auctions. In particular, several observations indicate that the classical model of one single auction is inaccurate to describe real auctions, in particular for ads shown frequently.

3.1 Stochastic Variability of the Weights

We study the behavior of two typical and distinct ads chosen from the set of ads that participated in the most auctions during the one week period. We will refer to these two ads as Player A and B. Each one of these two ads was associated with one single keyword, and could only participate in an auction when this keyword matched a user query. The two keywords associated to Player A and B were distinct and unrelated.

One of the most important features in ad auctions is the fact that the weights attributed to players are in practice estimations of their ad-CTR computed by the ad-platform itself, and are thus significantly variable.

Figure 1(a) shows the evolution of Player A's weight. As we can see, it is extremely variable (the standard deviation is 40% of the mean). An explanation for this could be the fact that the estimation of ad-CTR depends on multiple factors. Some of them are specific to the ad, but do not evolve fast enough to explain this variability. Some other factors are specific to the auction entered by the player, like the profile of the user performing the query and his propensity to click on ads. However, such factors are common to all ads entering the auction, and should not affect the weight ratio between two given players. To test this, we selected one of Player's A most frequent opponents and measured the weight ratio between these two players. The evolution of this ratio across time is displayed in Figure 1(b). We see that this ratio is also highly variable (the standard deviation is 9.5% of the mean). This suggests that the weights of the players are subject to some additional noise. We were unable to explain where this noise exactly comes from. We believe that the auction-specific parameters may simply have a non-multiplicative effect on the estimations, and may thus alter the weight ratio of two players even if shared by them.

Additionally, we find diurnal variation in real CTRs, and that real players' weighted bids and allocations can vary dramatically between players. When we look at the bids a particular player "faces", we see even if the opponents' bids are concentrating around a few values (for example, a few round numbers) the relative weighted bid distribution is smoothed by the randomness of the player's weights.

Further observations arising from the data can be found in the full version of this paper [11].

3.2 Insights from our observation

These observations reveal that real ad auctions are far from the classical model of one single auction with known players and complete information. In practice, a player enters many distinct auctions, with distinct opponents, varying weights and reserve prices. For this reason, a player cannot learn her opponents' bids or valuations, since they change from one auction to the other. But she could learn the distribution of the number of opponents and the distribution of their bids, assuming she had access to such information[1].

This inspires the analytical model presented in the next section, where we focus on one single player to whom these distributions would be given.

4. ANALYTICAL MODEL

Our analytical model basically consists in considering a player with known value competing in a GSP auction against a given number of unknown opponents submitting random i.i.d. weighted bids with known probability distributions, and studying the player incentives in that auction.

We first emphasize that the assumptions needed for this model are realistic and fit our previous empirical observations.

4.1 Discussion on the relevance of the model

This model may seem far from reality at first sight, since we would expect the player to learn the bids of her adversaries with time. But there are a few effects that make real-life auctions closer to the model than it seems. In practice the player places a single bid on a keyword, and that bid is used for a great number of auctions with different configurations. We observed in particular that most players did not change their bid very often; unfortunately we cannot give any precise data on this for confidentiality reasons.

First the identity of the opponents can change over time, because the players enter auctions when the user query matches their ad. For instance, if a player places a bid on the keyword "insurance", she may enter an auction for the query "house insurance" and another for "car insurance", facing distinct opponents in the two auctions while submitting the same bid to both. We observed from the data set that frequently appearing ads met a wide range of opponents, unfortunately qualitative results are confidential.

Second, the profile of the user performing the query, such as his age or his geographical location, can change the relevance of ads and thus change the opponents met in an auction.

[1]Of course, in practice players do not have access to the full auction records and they probably never will. We emphasize however that it would be easy for the ad-platforms to provide advertisers with the distribution of the number of opponents and the distribution of their bids, or even with real-time estimates of their total number of clicks received and total price paid depending on their bid, by using our model.

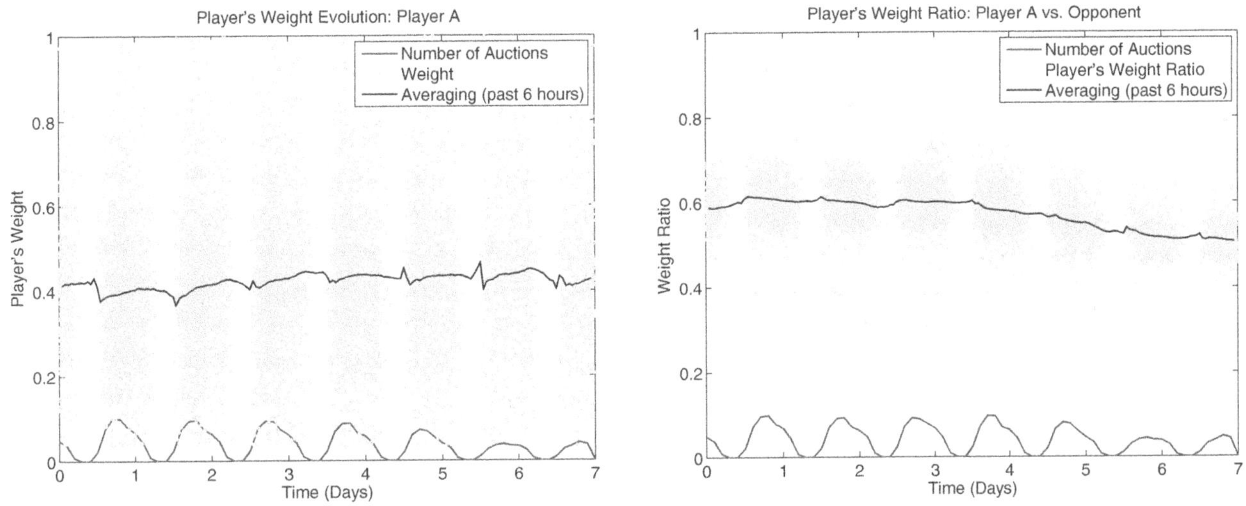

(a) Player A's weight

(b) Weight ratio between Player A and an opponent

Figure 1: Estimated probability of click (weight) of Player A's ad across the week and weight ratio against one of her opponents. Each green dot correspond to an auction in which Player A's participated (we display each 10th auction only). The solid black line indicates the average of these weights for the past 6 hours. The solid blue line at the bottom of each figure indicates the frequency of auctions in which Player A participated depending on the time of the day. The vertical axes have been renormalized to 1 for confidentiality reasons.

Third, bidders have in practice a monthly (or even daily) budget to spend, and when a bidder runs out of budget, she simply stops bidding until next month. This can also change the identity of a player's opponents across time. Lastly, advertisers may have several ads in the same campaign, and the ad-platform performs a rotation among these ads, so that if the same user performs the same query twice, he does not necessarily see the same ads twice.

In addition to the identity of the opponents, their weighted bids change as well across time, for several reasons. First the opponents can change their bid to explore and to optimize their revenue. Second, their weights, as well as the player's weight, change across time since they depend on several non-constant factors like the number of clicks received in the past, the profile of the user, and the keyword-query matching process.

Because of all these effects and others, the adversary bids faced by a player can be quite irregular, and the relative weighted bids are even more irregular. We also observed that the number of opponents faced in one auction was not fixed, but varied from auction to auction. Further details can be found in [11].

We later generalize our model to an uncertain number of opponents.

4.2 Model

We consider the following model: A *player* called Player 0 with known value v_0 and weight w_0 competes in a GSP auction with *reserve price* r against n *opponents*. These opponents submit random i.i.d. weighted bids with a known probability density function (*p.d.f.*) f, and we denote by F the corresponding cumulative distribution function. The slots are numbered from 0 to n, where we add dummy slots with a CTR of zero if necessary.

Without loss of generality, we assume that all players (including Player 0) have the same weights $w_i = 1$, since we can interpret the relative weighted bids $b_i w_i / w_0$ seen by Player 0 as simple bids. Thus the p.d.f. f corresponds to the distribution of opponents' relative weighted bids. We also denote by $\varphi(b)$ the CTR of the slot attributed to Player 0 when she bids b.

Under these assumptions, when Player 0 bids $b > r$ (we only consider Player 0's bids above the reserve price, but opponents may bid under), the probability that Player 0 gets the k-th slot for $k \le n$ is then: $\mathbb{P}(\varphi(b) = s_k) = \binom{n}{k} F(b)^{n-k}(1-F(b))^k$.

When in k-th position, Player 0 has $n-k$ players below her, and the maximum of their bids is a random variable with cumulative distribution $\mathbb{P}(b_1 < t, \ldots, b_{n-k} < t) = \mathbb{P}(b_1 < t)^{n-k} = F(t)^{n-k}$. Therefore, Player 0's expected price per click in that position is:

$$\begin{aligned}
&\mathbb{E}\left[p(b) \mid \varphi(b) = s_k\right] \\
&= \frac{1}{F(b)^{n-k}}\left(rF(r)^{n-k} + \int_r^b t f(t)(n-k)F(t)^{n-k-1}dt\right) \\
&= b - \int_r^b \frac{F(t)^{n-k}}{F(b)^{n-k}}dt \qquad (1)
\end{aligned}$$

by integrating by parts.

Thus, her expected price per click is:

$$\begin{aligned}
\mathbb{E}[p(b)] &= \sum_{k=0}^{n} \mathbb{E}[p(b) \mid \varphi(b) = s_k]\mathbb{P}(\varphi(b) = s_k) \\
&= \sum_{k=0}^{n} \binom{n}{k} F(b)^{n-k}(1-F(b))^k \left(b - \int_r^b \frac{F(t)^{n-k}}{F(b)^{n-k}}dt\right) \\
&= b - \int_r^b (F(t) + (1-F(b)))^n dt \ . \qquad (2)
\end{aligned}$$

It is interesting to notice that the expected price of our player is equal to her bid minus some discount depending on her bid, the reserve price, the number of opponents and the distribution function of their bids. In particular, we see that when the reserve price or the number of opponents increase, this discount becomes smaller and tends toward zero when r tends to b or n tends toward infinity. That is, for a high reserve price or with a high number of players, the GSP mechanism becomes closer to a First Price mechanism (where players pay their bids for each received click).

Using (1), we then see that the player expected utility is:

$$\begin{aligned}&\mathbb{E}[U(v,b)]\\&=\sum_{k=0}^{n}\mathbb{P}(\varphi(b)=s_k)s_k(v-\mathbb{E}[p(b)|\varphi(b)=s_k])\\&=\sum_{k=0}^{n}\binom{n}{k}F(b)^{n-k}(1-F(b))^k s_k\Big(v-b+\int_r^b\frac{F(t)^{n-k}}{F(b)^{n-k}}dt\Big)\end{aligned}$$

which can be rewritten with a more compact notation as:

$$\mathbb{E}[U(v,b)]=\sum_{k=0}^{n}\binom{n}{k}s_k\int_r^v(1-F(b))^kF(t\wedge b)^{n-k}dt \quad (3)$$

where $t\wedge b := \min(t,b)$.

The optimal bid b^{opt} of our player will maximize their expected utility, at which point the partial derivative of the expected utility with respect to the bid is zero. This lead to the following necessary condition, whose proof is given in [11]:

THEOREM 4.1. *The optimal bid b^{opt} of Player 0 (as well as any local extrema of $\mathbb{E}[U(v,b)]$) must satisfy the following equation in b^*:*

$$v=b^*+\frac{\sum_{k=0}^{n-1}\binom{n-1}{k}s_{k+1}(1-F(b^*))^k\int_r^{b^*}F(t)^{n-k-1}dt}{\sum_{k=0}^{n-1}\binom{n-1}{k}(s_k-s_{k+1})(1-F(b^*))^kF(b^*)^{n-k-1}}. \quad (4)$$

Notice that this is a necessary but not sufficient condition: the equation does not characterize entirely the optimal bid which may have several solutions in b^*, namely all the local extrema of $\mathbb{E}[U(v,b)]$. However, we see that this equation determines entirely the value v as a function of b^*, allowing us to retrieve the player's valuation if we know her optimal bid.

It is also immediate that $b^{opt}\leq v$, since the slot-CTRs are decreasing. The player thus never has any incentive to overbid.

4.2.1 Study of the solutions of the equation

We first study the solutions of equation (4) in a simpler special case: A common approximation in the literature [5] consists in assuming that the slot-CTRs are geometrically decreasing. In the circumstances, the previous equation admits a much simpler form, whose proof is straightforward:

COROLLARY 4.2. *Assuming the slot-CTRs are geometrically decreasing, i.e. $s_j=\gamma^j$ for some $\gamma\in(0,1)$, then equation (4) can be reduced to:*

$$v=b^*+\frac{\gamma}{1-\gamma}\int_r^{b^*}\left(\frac{F(t)+\gamma(1-F(b^*))}{F(b^*)+\gamma(1-F(b^*))}\right)^{n-1}. \quad (5)$$

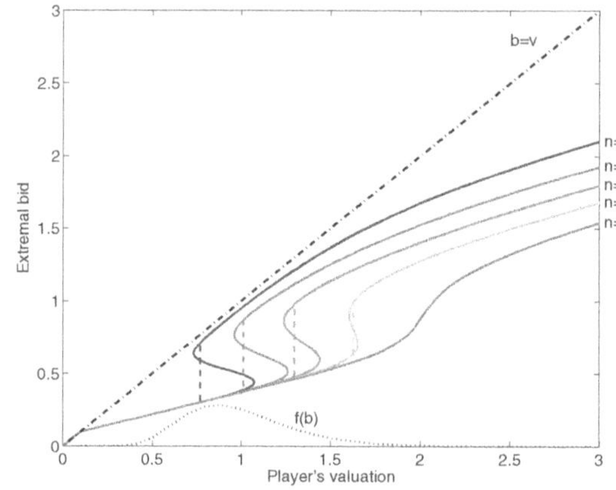

Figure 2: Plot of the solutions of equation (5) for several numbers of opponents ($n = 2, 3, 5, 10, 30$). When the equation has multiple solution, the dashed lines indicate where the optimal bid jumps from one solution to the other. The dash-dotted line indicates the main diagonal and the dotted line gives the opponent's bid distribution f ($\times 0.2$).

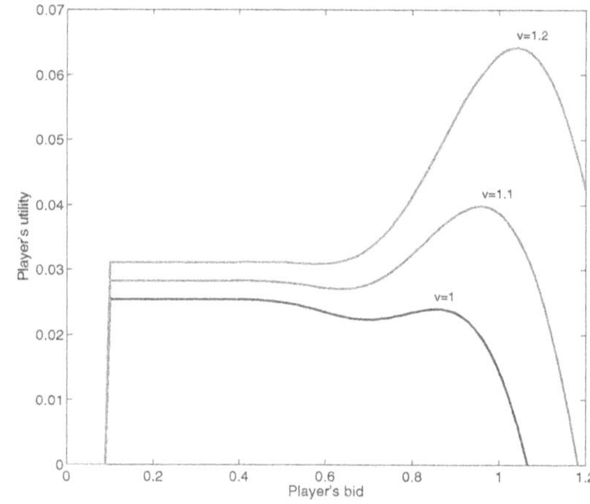

Figure 3: Player 0's expected utility depending of her bid, against $n = 10$ opponents and for several valuations of the player.

Figure 2 shows a plot of the extremal bids which are solutions of Equation (5) depending on the player's valuation v when the number of opponents varies[2]. We notice that for some valuations, there are 3 solutions to Equation (5). These solutions correspond to local extrema of the player's utility, but only one of them corresponds to the optimal bid. The dashed lines show were the optimal bid jumps from a solution to the other.

To better understand that effect, Figure 3 represents the Player's expected utility as a function of her bid when she plays against $n = 10$ opponents and when her value is $v = 1$, 1.1 and 1.2 (values for which Equation (5) has several solutions, according to Figure 2). As we can see in Figure 3, the Player's utility curve has 3 local extrema: 2 local

[2]We used the following parameters for all figures in that paragraph: reserve price $r = 0.1$ and decaying rate $\gamma = 0.7$. The considered opponents' bids distribution was a lognormal distribution with mean 1 and variance 0.1.

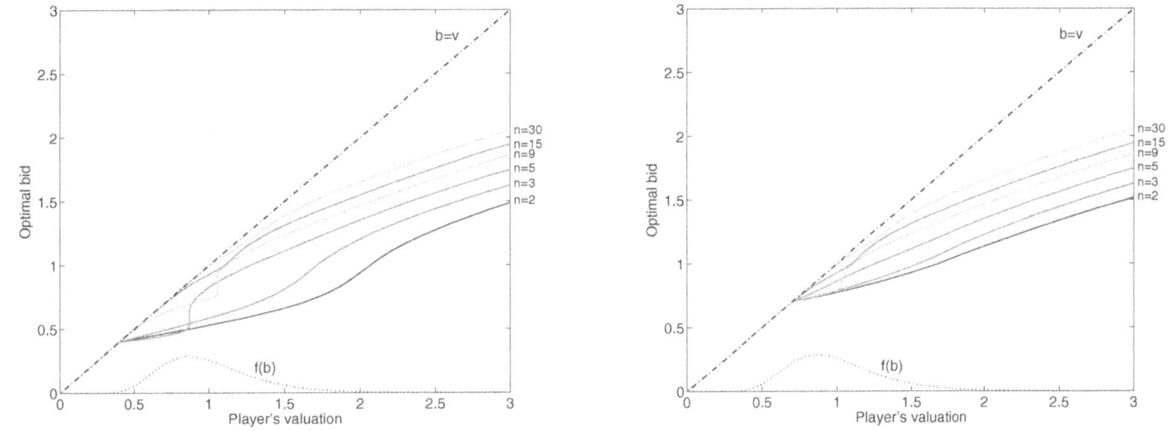

(a) Reserve price $r = 0.4$ (b) Reserve price $r = 0.7$

Figure 4: Optimal bid depending on the player's valuation for several numbers of opponents ($n = 2, 3, 5, 9, 15, 30$) in an auction with reserve price $r = 0.4$ and $r = 0.7$ and 9 allocated slots with slot-CTRs corresponding to those we observed in practice. The bid distribution is a lognormal with mean 1 and variance 0.1.

maxima and 1 local minimum in-between. When the player's value increases, the global maximum suddenly jumps from one local maximum to the other.

When the player's value is low, her utility curve becomes mostly flat, and the maximum given by the analytic solution of (5) becomes less meaningful, since it belongs to a sort of "plateau" (see curve $v = 1$ on Figure 3).

4.2.2 *Results for realistic slot-CTRs*

We now show some results obtained with the general equation (4). In particular we can study the impact of the reserve price and the number of players.

Figure 4 shows the optimal bids against various number of opponents when the reserve price is $r = 0.4$ and $r = 0.7$ and the slots-CTRs s_i are taken similar to those observed in practice[3]. As we can see, we still have a discontinuity in the optimal bid for some values of n, but the general shape is much harder to understand and seems to depend highly on the number of opponents, particularly when this is smaller than the number of available slots. Observe, however, that when the reserve price or the number of players increases, this discontinuity tends to disappear.

Our main observation, from both real observation and synthetic models, is that the utility curve of a player is in general not quasi-concave, which causes a discontinuity in the optimal bid response of our player when her value changes. This highlights the pitfalls of an advertiser trying to find their optimal bid by local search, which may only find a local optimum.

4.3 Generalization to an Uncertain Number of Opponents

In practice, the number of opponents of a considered player may vary from one auction to another. We now enhance our model by considering the number of opponents as a random variable $\mathcal{N}$ in $\{0, \ldots, N\}$, independent of the bids, with $\mathbb{P}(\mathcal{N} = n) = p_n$.

In that case, the Player's expected utility becomes:

$$\mathbb{E}[U(v,b)] = \sum_{n=0}^{N}\sum_{k=0}^{n}\binom{n}{k} p_n s_k \int_r^v (1-F(b))^k F(t \wedge b)^{n-k} dt, \tag{6}$$

and the optimal bid must thus verify the following equation:

$$v = b^* + \frac{\sum_{n=1}^{N}\sum_{k=0}^{n-1}\binom{n-1}{k} n p_n s_{k+1}(1-F(b^*))^k \int_r^{b^*} F(t)^{n-k-1} dt}{\sum_{n=1}^{N}\sum_{k=0}^{n-1}\binom{n-1}{k} n p_n (s_k - s_{k+1})(1-F(b^*))^k F(b^*)^{n-k-1}}. \tag{7}$$

We also have the expected allocation:

$$\mathbb{E}[\varphi(b)] = \sum_{n=0}^{N}\sum_{k=0}^{n}\binom{n}{k} p_n s_k (1-F(b))^k F(b)^{n-k}, \tag{8}$$

and the expected total price paid by the player:

$$\mathbb{E}[p(b)\varphi(b)] = \sum_{n=0}^{N}\sum_{k=0}^{n}\Bigg[\binom{n}{k} p_n s_k (1-F(b))^k F(b)^{n-k} \left(b - \int_r^b \frac{F(t)^{n-k}}{F(b)^{n-k}} dt\right)\Bigg]. \tag{9}$$

4.4 Adding a Mainline Reserve Price

Our model can easily be modified to take into account an additional mainline reserve price R. However, if we consider this reserve price to be fixed, we obtain a discontinuity in the player's utility. To avoid this, we added a random noise on the sidebar and mainline reserve prices, which smooths the utility curve and allows to take its partial derivative according to b. This gives a closed form equation similar to (7). We omit this equation due to lack of space — details are given in [11]. The estimation results of the next section were obtained using this generalized analytical model with a mainline reserve price.

[3]In practice on Bing, the first four slots in the mainline have a high CTR with high discrepancy between slots, while the 5 slots on the sidebar have a much lower CTR, which does not decrease much from one slot to the next.

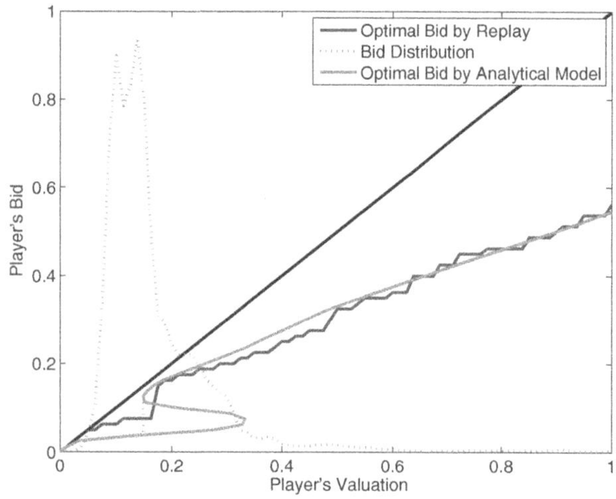

Figure 5: Optimal bid curves computed for an ad from real auction data. The Optimal Bid by analytical model was computed using the optimal bid equation derived from the analytical model, while the Optimal Bid by Replay was computed by replaying all the auctions with all possible bids and selecting the bid with the best utility. The Bid Distribution line represents the distribution of the opponents' relative weighted bid observed by the considered player. Both axes have been arbitrarily renormalized to 1.

4.5 Results

We selected an ad from the auction database, and by looking at all the auctions it participated in we estimated both the distribution of the number of opponents and the distribution of their relative weighted bids. With these distributions, we computed the optimal bid curve of the player using the generalized analytical model with a mainline reserve price, and compared it to the optimal bid curve computed greedily by replaying all the auctions for all possible bids (with a low resolution on bids, since it is a heavy computation) and then choosing the optimal bid.

Figure 5 shows the comparison of the two optimal bid curves. The Optimal Bid Replay curve is not continuous because the bid resolution used to compute it was low. However both curves are quite close and present a similar discontinuity in the optimal bid.

This shows that this discontinuity is not an artifact of our model, and still happens when the parameters are measured from real auctions, or even when we compute explicitly the optimal bid with real auction data.

5. EXPERIMENTS

One of the main benefits of our model is that it provides a simple method, easy to implement and with low computational cost, for estimating the expected number of clicks a player receives, (8), their expected total price (9), and even their valuations via (7). In this section we present the results of click estimation and value inference using generalized versions of these equation which incorporate a mainline reserve price as sketched in Section 4.4.

We used the full records of 132 millions auctions played over a given time period on the Bing ad-platform. We considered a randomly chosen set of 15777 ads, each associated with one specific keyword (or set of keywords) and with one specific bid. More precisely, each triple formed by an ad and its associated keyword and bid were considered as one specific player (Player 0). We then looked at the record of all auctions in which this player participated and estimated from these the distributions of the number of opponents[4] and of their relative weighted bids $b_i w_i / w_0$. Using this information only, we then estimated the expected number of clicks received per auction by each player and inferred their valuations, assuming their bids were chosen optimally.

5.1 Valuation Inference Results

We compared our valuation estimations with the ones obtained from the ICC (Incremental Cost per Click) method[5] designed by Athey and Nekipelov in [3].

Figure 6 shows the comparison of our valuation estimation with the analytical model against the player's bids and against the estimations from Athey-Nekipelov's ICC model. A key parameter for the accuracy of the estimations is the slot-CTR : In real auctions, players receive a click with some probability, which is estimated by the CTR $w_i s_j$ for player i in slot j. When replaying the auctions, each displayed player is assumed to receive a fraction of a click corresponding to this probability. That is, player i in slot j will receive $w_i s_j < 1$ click in that auction. For a fair comparison, the same slot-effect estimations were used in both models.

It is interesting to notice in the figure that under both models, the estimated value is significantly higher for the advertisers who submitted a high bid. This suggest that players with a high valuation have a strong incentive to shade their bids, as already suggested by Figures 4 and 5. Also, since the key assumption for both models to infer valuations is that players are playing optimally, this may also suggest that players with high valuations do not play optimally in practice and do not shade their bids enough, which results in an over-approximation of their values by both models.

5.2 Estimations of the Number of Clicks

Since the real valuations are not known in practice, it is impossible to test directly the accuracy of the valuation estimations. We can however test the accuracy of both models by comparing the estimations of the expected number of clicks received by each player to the real number of clicks they actually received.

Figure 7 shows a summary histogram of the results, while the full plots are given in [11]. It shows the comparisons of the estimations of each model against the realizations (actual number of clicks received), and against each other. To test the predictive power of these estimations, we also com-

[4]Because the maximal number of slots displayed on Bing was 9 at the of this study, we considered only the 9 opponents with the highest weighted bids in each auction, since the other opponents have no impact on the result of the auction. The number of opponents was also taken to be at most 9.

[5]The ICC method consists basically in replaying all the auctions in which a given player placed a given bid and estimating the value as being equal to the incremental cost per click at the bid placed. When the number of auctions is too low to have a smooth cost per click curve, virtual auctions are added by replaying the real one and adding an artificial noise on weights. This method also requires the assumption that advertisers are playing optimally.

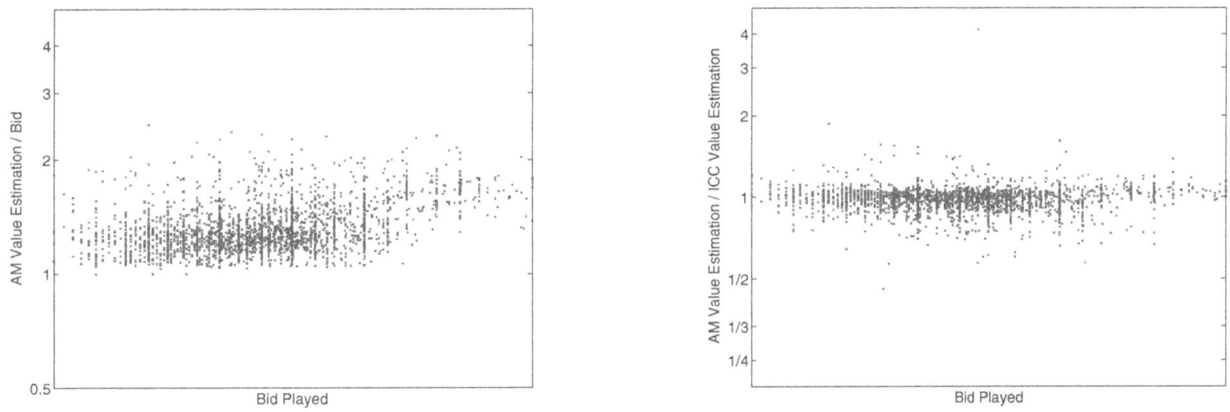

(a) Analytical model estimations

(b) Analytical model against ICC model

Figure 6: Estimations of the valuations from our analytical model compared to the original bids and to the estimations from the ICC model. Each point corresponds to one player. We show here the results for the players who received more than 100 clicks. The horizontal axes use a logarithmic scale; the labels have been removed for confidentiality reasons.

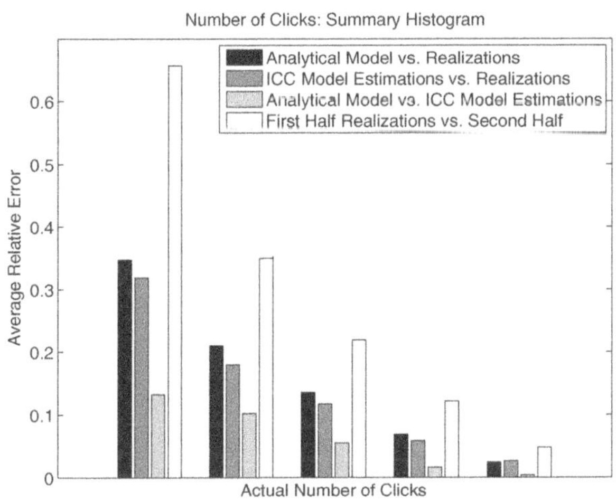

Figure 7: Summary histogram of the click estimations results for various ranges of received click (the number of click increasing exponentially from the left to the right). We show the average relative error of our model against the realizations, of the ICC model against the realizations, of our model against ICC, and of the realizations of the click obtained in the first half of the considered time period against the second half.

pared the actual number of click received per auction in the first half of the considered time period against the second half.

As we can see, the estimations of our model and the replays are much closer than they are from the realizations, and as Figure 7 shows, the realizations are much more volatile than our estimations are inaccurate. This underline the difficulty of obtaining good predictions of the number of clicks received by a given ad, and shows that both models provide satisfactory estimations, particularly for the ads frequently shown.

5.3 Implementation and Performances

While our estimation results confirm that the accuracy of our estimation method is comparable to Athey-Nekipelov's, our analytical model has a significant advantage over their ICC method: its speed.

The analytical model was implemented in F#. Most of the computing time was spent loading the auction data, the processing of these data was done in parallel of the loading. The total time spent loading and processing 132 million auctions was around 1 hour and a half with a single 8-core computer. Once the data processed, estimating the valuations, total number of clicks received and total price paid using the analytical model took less than 15 minutes, which is less than 0.1 second per ad. As a comparison, the replays of auctions and estimations using Athey-Nekipelov's ICC method was implemented in F# as well and took around half a day running on several HPC nodes.

The great advantage of our model over Athey-Nekipelov's is that ours is tractable on a large scale, and could even be implemented to give predictions for all of Bing's or Google's ads. Indeed, it would suffice to keep records for each ad of the distributions of the number of opponents and their relative weighted bids - which can be done online by updating them at each auction - to give in less than a second the prediction of the number of clicks and the total price depending on the chosen bid, while replaying all past auctions would take several minutes.

Using this, it would be possible to give the advertisers a precise feedback on their ad campaign, by providing them estimates of their click and price curves, so that they could chose their bid optimally, and the search engine would know as an extra their valuation using the analytical equation (7).

6. COMPARISON WITH OTHER MODELS

In this section we give theoretical comparisons between our model with Athey and Nekipelov's [3] first, and with Gomes and Sweeney's model [8].

6.1 Comparison with Athey and Nekipelov

Under some assumptions, it is possible to give a theoretical bound on the difference between the expected allocation, price and utility of players predicted by our analytical model and the Athey-Nekipelov model.

Athey and Nekipelov consider a set of $N+1$ players, that we will number from 0 to N, participating in several auctions, with fixed private valuations v_i and submitting public bids b_i. When an auction is run, a random set C of players is chosen to participate, and each player receives a random weight w_i according to a given distribution. All auctions are assumed to be independent from each other. Athey and Nekipelov assume that every player has full knowledge of the distribution of the set C and the weights w_i.

From a player's point of view, say Player 0, the set C^0 of his opponents in a given auction in which she participates is a random variable with known distribution, and thus the set of relative weighted bids to which Player 0's bid will be confronted is a random variable $B^{AN} = (b_i w_i / w_0)_{i \in C^0}$ with known distribution.

In the version of our model generalized to an uncertain number of opponents (Section 4.3), Player 0 is facing a random opponent bid vector with known distribution obtained as $B^{PK} = (b_1, \dots, b_{\mathcal{N}})$ where $\mathcal{N}$ is a random variable with distribution p and $b_1, \dots, b_{\mathcal{N}}$ i.i.d. random variables with c.d.f. F.

Thus, both our analytical model and Athey-Nekipelov's fall under the same general framework, were Player 0 is facing a random vector of opponent bids B taking values in $E = \bigcup_{n=0}^{N} \mathbb{R}^n$, with known probability distribution.

Using this we obtain the following result, whose proof is given in [11]:

PROPOSITION 6.1. *Let us assume that the set C^0 is drawn uniformly across the subsets of $\{1, \dots, N\}$ of size n, and that the weights w_i are drawn independently. We define the bid c.d.f. F as: $\forall b, F(b) = \frac{1}{n} \sum_{i=1}^{N} \mathbb{P}_w(b_i w_i < b_0 w_0)$, and take B^{AN} and B^{PK} as defined previously from these parameters. Let $\mathbb{E}_B(\varphi(b))$ denote the expected utility of player 0 when bidding b against the random vector of bids B. Similarly, let $\mathbb{E}_B(p(b)\varphi(b))$ denote her expected total price and $\mathbb{E}_B(U(v,b)) = \mathbb{E}_B((v-p(b))\varphi(b))$ denote her expected utility. Then,*

$$|\mathbb{E}_{B^{AN}}(\varphi(b)) - \mathbb{E}_{B^{PK}}(\varphi(b))| \leq \frac{n(n-1)}{2N}$$

$$|\mathbb{E}_{B^{AN}}(p(b)\varphi(b)) - \mathbb{E}_{B^{PK}}(p(b)\varphi(b))| \leq \frac{n(n-1)}{2N} b$$

$$|\mathbb{E}_{B^{AN}}(U(v,b)) - \mathbb{E}_{B^{PK}}(U(v,b))| \leq \frac{n(n-1)}{2N} v$$

In particular, when the total number of players N grows to infinity and the number of players per auction n remains bounded, the difference between the estimations of the two models tends to zero.

As we showed previously, the utility curve of a player may not be quasi-concave in her bid (even with realistic parameter choices). The proposition thus implies that the utility curves are not always quasi-concave under Athey-Nekipelov's model either. Therefore their theorem showing existence and uniqueness of a Nash equilibrium under certain conditions (one of them being that the utility curves are quasi-concave) do not apply in general.

6.2 Comparison with Gomes and Sweeney

In [8], Gomes and Sweeney consider a Bayesian model where N players with random i.i.d. valuations with density $f_v(v)$ and corresponding c.d.f. $F_v(v)$ compete in a single GSP auction with no reserve price (we therefore assume $r = 0$ in this section).

They study the existence of symmetric efficient equilibrium where each player chooses her bid according to a strictly increasing optimal bid function $b = \beta(v)$. An equilibrium is said to be *efficient* if a player with a higher valuation than another player always obtains a higher slot than her. This implies that the bid function $\beta(v)$, if it exists, has to be strictly monotone. They show that, when it exists, the optimal bid function $\beta(v)$ must verify a closed form equation.

The following proposition, whose proof is given in [11], states that under such circumstances, their equation can be derived directly from our equation (4):

PROPOSITION 6.2. *If the optimal bid function $\beta(v)$ exists and is continuous and strictly monotone (and thus invertible), then the opponent bid vector for a given player is a vector of $N-1$ i.i.d. bids with c.d.f. $F(b) = F_v(\beta^{-1}(b))$. It must thus verify (4):*

$$v = \beta(v) + \frac{\sum_{k=0}^{N-2} \binom{N-2}{k} s_{k+1} (1 - F(\beta(v)))^k \int_0^{\beta(v)} F(t)^{N-k-2} dt}{\sum_{k=0}^{N-2} \binom{N-2}{k} (s_k - s_{k+1}) (1 - F(\beta(v)))^k F(\beta(v))^{N-k-2}}, \quad (10)$$

which can be turned into:

$$\beta(v) = v - \frac{\sum_{k=2}^{N} \binom{N-2}{k-1} s_{k-1} (1 - F_v(v))^{k-2} \int_0^{v} (v - \beta(x)) F_v(x)^{N-k-1} f_v(x) dx}{\sum_{k=1}^{N-1} \binom{N-2}{k-1} s_{k-1} (1 - F_v(v))^{k-1} F_v(v)^{N-k-1}} \quad (11)$$

which corresponds to equation (1) of [8], up to notations (Gomes and Sweeney number their slots from 1 to $S < N$, while we number ours from 0 to $K > N$, but we can take $s_k = 0$ for $k \geq S$).

Although our equation (4) and Gomes-Sweeney's related equation (10) are close typographically, the two models have many differences, ranging from the assumptions used in them to the nature of the solutions obtained and their interpretation.

Assumptions. First, our model focuses on the incentives of a single player against a fixed randomized profile of opponents, while Gomes and Sweeney consider the behavior of several players in a symmetrical equilibrium. Given the highly dynamic aspect of these auctions and the very important number of advertiser participating in them, it is unclear how such equilibrium could happen in practice, while a best response approach seems more suitable.

Second, randomness does not arise from the same assumptions and do not apply to the same variables in the two models. In Gomes and Sweeney, randomness applies to the valuations and comes from an uncertainty in the players beliefs, while in our model, randomness is applied directly to the weighted bids and arises from the inherent variability of the weights. In particular, the Gomes-Sweeney model does not take into account the weights attributed to each player, and although their model is easy to generalize to fixed weights (a renormalization would allow to take the weights equal to 1), it cannot be generalized to randomized weights.

Solutions of the equations. The two models also differ in the nature of the solutions of their equations. The unknown of equation (11) is the whole function $\beta(v)$, while the unknown of (4) is just a tuple (v, b^*). Therefore, our equation is much simpler to solve, since v is uniquely determined by b^*, while Gomes and Sweeney show that the solutions of their equation can be computed as the limit of an recursively defined sequence of functions $\beta^{(n)}(v)$.

Moreover, when the distributions of the bids or values (depending on the model) are smooth, the solution curve of (11) is a continuous mapping from the values to the bids while the solution curve of (4) is a continuous mapping from the values to the bids. As observed earlier, the optimal bid function $b^{opt}(v)$ may thus present a discontinuity in our model, while it is continuous in the Gomes-Sweeney model.

Interpretations. Because of the different nature of the solutions, each model leads to a different interpretation. While Gomes and Sweeney shows that no symmetric efficient equilibrium is possible if the slot-CTRs are too close to each other, we give several examples where the utility curve of a player is not quasi-concave in her bid, resulting in a discontinuity of the optimal bid curve. Because of this, we believe that even asymmetric and inefficient Nash equilibria may not always exist in practice.

7. CONCLUSION AND FURTHER WORK

We have developed a new analytical model of GSP auctions centered on the behavior of one single player facing multiple unknown opponents who submit random bids. This approach has been inspired by a conclusion drawn from real auction data, which showed that most ads enter many auctions with the same bid, facing multiple opponents whose identities differ from one auction to the other, and with highly irregular weights attributed to the bids.

Using this model, we were able to derive simple, yet very general, closed form expressions for the expected number of clicks, total price and utility of the considered player, using only information on the distribution of the number of opponents and of their relative weighted bids. We also expressed exactly the relation between the optimal bid and the player's valuation, highlighting the fact that in some cases encountered in practice, the optimal bid jumps discontinuously from one value to the other when the valuation increases. However, we noticed that this discontinuity tends to disappear when the number of opponents or the reserve price (i.e. the competition) increases.

The main advantage of this model is its very low computational and memory cost, compared to replaying all auctions. Because of this, it will be practical to give better feedback to advertisers by providing them with personalized estimates of their click and price curves, thus helping them to chose their bids more efficiently.

In our analysis, we have assumed that the weights come from independent stochastic processes. In practice, as we alluded to, the actual CTR and its estimated weight is affected by the "type" of the searcher, and advertisers can take this into account when bidding. A simple example of this is demographic targeting, where certain demographics are valued more highly by certain advertisers, and such advertisers can automatically or manually adjust their bids for search queries coming from favored locations. In addition, keywords associated with the same ad or campaign are not independent. The extension of our model to cater for these interesting and practical scenarios is for future work.

8. REFERENCES

[1] Abrams, Z., and Ghosh, A. Auctions with revenue guarantees for sponsored search. In *Proceedings of the 3rd International Workshop on Internet and Network Economics* (2007), WINE'07.

[2] Aggarwal, G., Goel, A., and Motwani, R. Truthful auctions for pricing search keywords. In *Proceedings of the 7th ACM conference on Electronic Commerce* (2006), EC '06.

[3] Athey, S., and Nekipelov, D. A structural model of sponsored search advertising auctions. In *Sixth Ad Auctions Workshop* (2010), adauctions2010.

[4] Borgs, C., Chayes, J., Immorlica, N., Jain, K., Etesami, O., and Mahdian, M. Dynamics of bid optimization in online advertisement auctions. In *Proceedings of the 16th international conference on World Wide Web* (2007), WWW '07.

[5] Cary, M., Das, A., Edelman, B., Giotis, I., Heimerl, K., Karlin, A. R., Mathieu, C., and Schwarz, M. Greedy bidding strategies for keyword auctions. In *Proceedings of the 8th ACM conference on Electronic commerce* (2007), EC '07.

[6] Edelman, B., Ostrovsky, M., and Schwarz, M. Internet advertising and the generalized second price auction: Selling billions of dollars worth of keywords. *American Economic Review* (2007), 242–259.

[7] Edelman, B., and Schwarz, M. Optimal auction design and equilibrium selection in sponsored search auctions. *American Economic Review* (2010).

[8] Gomes, R. D., and Sweeney, K. S. Bayes-nash equilibria of the generalized second price auction. In *Proceedings of the 10th ACM conference on Electronic Commerce* (New York, NY, USA, 2009), EC '09.

[9] Jansen, B. J., and Mullen, T. Sponsored search: an overview of the concept, history, and technology. *Int. J. Electronic Business 6*, 2 (2008), 114–131.

[10] Menache, I., Ozdaglar, A., Srikant, R., and Acemoglu, D. Dynamic online-advertising auctions as stochastic scheduling. In *Workshop on the Economics of Networks, Systems and Computation* (2009), NetEcon '09.

[11] Pin, F., and Key, P. Stochastic variability in sponsored search auctions: Observations and models. Technical Report MSR-TR-2011-40, Microsoft Research, March 2011.

[12] Varian, H. R. Position auctions. *International Journal of Industrial Organization* (2007), 1163–1178.

[13] Vorobeychik, Y., and Reeves, D. M. Equilibrium analysis of dynamic bidding in sponsored search auctions. In *Proceedings of the 3rd international Workshop on Internet and Network Economics* (2007), WINE'07, Springer-Verlag.

GSP Auctions with Correlated Types

Brendan Lucier*
Dept of Computer Science
University of Toronto
blucier@cs.toronto.edu

Renato Paes Leme†
Dept of Computer Science
Cornell University
renatoppl@cs.cornell.edu

ABSTRACT

The Generalized Second Price (GSP) auction is the primary method by which sponsered search advertisements are sold. We study the performance of this auction in the Bayesian setting for players with correlated types. Correlation arises very naturally in the context of sponsored search auctions, especially as a result of uncertainty inherent in the behaviour of the underlying ad allocation algorithm. We demonstrate that the Bayesian Price of Anarchy of the GSP auction is bounded by 4, even when agents have arbitrarily correlated types. Our proof highlights a connection between the GSP mechanism and the concept of smoothness in games, which may be of independent interest.

For the special case of uncorrelated (i.e. independent) agent types, we improve our bound to $2(1-1/e)^{-1} \approx 3.16$, significantly improving upon previously known bounds. Using our techniques, we obtain the same bound on the performance of GSP at coarse correlated equilibria, which captures (for example) a repeated-auction setting in which agents apply regret-minimizing bidding strategies. Moreoever, our analysis is robust against the presence of irrational bidders and settings of asymmetric information, and our bounds degrade gracefully when agents apply strategies that form only an approximate equilibrium.

Categories and Subject Descriptors

J.4 [**Social and Behavioral Sciences**]: Economics; F.2.2 [**Analysis of Algorithms and Problem Complexity**]: Nonnumerical Algorithms and Problems

General Terms

Algorithms, Economics, Theory

*Part of this work was performed while the author was visiting Microsoft Research, New England.

†Supported in part by NSF grant CCF-0729006. Part of this work was performed while the author was visiting Microsoft Research, New England.

Keywords

Sponsored search auctions, Price of anarchy

1. INTRODUCTION

The sale of advertising space is the primary source of revenue for many providers of online services. This is due, in part, to the fact that providers can tailor advertisements to the preferences of individual users. A search engine, for example, can choose to display ads that synergize well with a query being searched. However, such dynamic provision of content complicates the process of selling ad space to potential advertisers. The now-standard method has advertisers place bids – representing the amount they would be willing to pay per click – which are resolved in an automated auction whenever ads are to be displayed.

By far the most popular bid-resolution method currently in use is the Generalized Second Price auction (GSP), a generalization of the well-known Vickrey auction. In the GSP, there are multiple ad "slots" of varying appeal (i.e. slots at the top of the page are more effective). Advertisers are assigned slots in order of their bids, with the highest bidders receiving the best slots; each advertiser then pays an amount equal to the bid of the next-highest bidder. While simple to understand and use, the GSP has some notable drawbacks: unlike the Vickrey auction it is not truthful, and it does not generally guarantee the most efficient outcome (i.e. the outcome that maximizes social welfare). Nevertheless, the use of GSP has been extremely successful in practice. This begs the question: *are there theoretical properties of the Generalized Second Price auction that would explain its prevalence?*

Since the GSP auction is invoked every time a user queries a keyword of interest, it is best characterized as a repeated auction in which players repeatedly bid for ad slots. However, modeling equilibrium strategies in a repeated game of this nature is notoriously difficult; optimal bidding strategies must account for threatened behaviour in future rounds, optimal exploration of the bidding space, and so on. A common simplification used in the literature is to focus on auctions for a single keyword, and suppose that agents will quickly learn each others' valuations and reach a stationary equilibrium. Under this assumption, the stationary equilibrium would correspond naturally to a Nash equilibrium in the full information, one-shot version of the GSP auction [7]. It has therefore become common practice to study pure, full-information equilibria of the one-shot game, as an approximation to expected behaviour in the more general repeated game [6, 24, 20].

In reality, however, the set and types of players can vary significantly between rounds of a GSP auction. The reason for this is that each query is unique, in the sense that it is defined not only by the set of keywords invoked but also the time the query was performed, the location and history of the user and many other factors. This *context* is taken into account by an underlying *ad allocation algorithm*, which is controled by the search engine. The ad allocation algorithm not only selects which players will participate in an auction instance, but also assigns a *quality factor* to each player: a score that measures how likely that participant's ad will be clicked for that query. These quality factors are then used to scale the bids of the advertisers. The effective bid and effective type of a player are therefore random variables, which can be thought as the original values times some exogenous quality score. Thus, even if agents converge to a stationary bidding pattern, it is not necessarily the case that this implies full certainty about agent types in each round.

The uncertainty about the types of other agents can be modelled in a Bayesian, partial information setting. Bayes-Nash equilibria for GSP have been studied previously [8, 19], but these works require that valuations are drawn from independent distributions. However, the independence assumption fails to capture the source of randomness due to query context and the ad allocation algorithm, which inherently introduces correlations among agent values. Our main contribution is to extend the analysis of quality of outcomes of Bayesian GSP to cases where player values are arbitrarily correlated, thereby capturing sources of uncertainty that occur in practical sponsored search auctions.

Our techniques are general enough to apply even when our model is extended to capture various additional features of agent behaviour. For instance, there are different types of players in the AdMarkets, which may have differing degrees of information about their competitors. Some smaller players (such as individual advertisers) might be clueless about the valuations of the other players and expected behaviour of quality scores, while others (say bidding agencies or large companies with web advertising departments) may have a much better understanding of how individual rounds of the auction will proceed. Even among those, there are various levels of market research one can perform. Our bound on social efficiency in the Bayesian model holds in settings with this natural asymmetry in information.

One of the fundamental assumptions in auction analysis is that all players are perfectly rational, i.e., utility optimizers. However, in reality (and especially in large online settings), it is natural to assume that some fraction of the players participating in an AdAuction might have particularly unsophistcated bidding strategies. In fact, some agents may not even play at equilbrium in the single-shot approximation of the GSP auction, or may only be able to converge to an approximate equilibrium. We discuss the robustness of our bounds to the presence of players bidding with limited (or no) rationality.

We also consider an equilibrium model suited to long-run bidder behaviour in GSP, where it is not required that agents converge to a stable equilibrium. Namely, returning to the repeated-game form of GSP, we consider situations in which agents play in order to minimize *regret*. Such strategies are not necessarily in equilbrium in the repeated game, but capture the intuition that agents attempt to learn beneficial bidding strategies over time. Roughly speaking, such a model assumes that agents observe the bidding patterns of others and modify their own bids in such a way that their long-term performance approaches that of a single optimal strategy chosen in hindsight. It is well-known from learning theory that such regret minimization is easy to achieve via simple bidding techniques [11]. We demonstrate that our techniques apply to this setting and bound the Price of Total Anarchy [2], which is the ratio between the social welfare of the optimal allocation and the average social welfare obtained by GSP when agents minimize regret over a sufficiently long number of rounds.

Results.

Our main result is a bound on the social welfare obtained at Bayes-Nash equilbrium for the GSP auction. Specifically, we show that the Bayesian Price of Anarchy for GSP is at most 4 for correlated valuations. At the heart of this proof lies a structural characterization of the GSP auction that has a flavor similar to the characterization of smooth games introduced by Roughgarden [23], even though it is known that GSP is not a smooth game. Furthermore, if valuations can be assumed to be independent, we can improve this bound to $2(1-1/e)^{-1} \approx 3.164$. This improves upon the previous best-known bounds of 8 for BNE and 4 for (mixed) NE [19].

Perhaps just as important as the improved bounds, however, is the straightforward and robust nature of our analysis. In particular, our results extend to give the same bound for coarse correlated equilibria (see Section 4.2), which implies that the social welfare when agents play repeatedly in order to minimize total regret is within a $2(1-1/e)^{-1}$ factor of the optimal social welfare. Also, we prove that the factor of 4 for agents with correlated distributions continues to hold even if agents have asymmetric access to distributional information, in the form of exogenously provided signals.

Moreover, our results are resilient against the presence of irrational agents, in the following sense. Suppose that, in addition to the rational participants in the auction, there is also some set of agents who apply arbitrary strategies. We can view these as irrational participants who do not understand how to bid strategically. Note that, in such a setting, it is not possible for an auction to guarantee a fraction of the social welfare obtainable from the irrational bidders; after all, a bidder with very large value may decide (irrationally) to bid 0 and effectively not participate in the auction. What we *can* show, however, is that the presence of the irrational bidders does not interfere with the auction's ability to approximate the welfare obtainable from the rational bidders. That is, the ratio of the optimal social welfare *of the rational bidders* to the total social welfare obtained at any BNE is at most $2(1-1/e)^{-1} \approx 3.164$. This result requires an assumption on the play of the irrational bidders, which is that no player bids more than his true value. We feel that this is a reasonable assumption, as overbidding is a dominated strategy that is easily avoided; we therefore view the irrational bidders as novice or uninformed participants who would avoid dominated strategies, rather than truly adversarial agents. Finally, if rational agents are limited in their rationality in that they can be assumed only to reach a δ-approximate equilibrium, our welfare bounds continue to hold with the addition of an extra factor of $(1+\delta)$.

Our results hold for a standard model of separable click-through rates, where the probability that a user clicks on an advertisement j in slot i is of the form $\alpha_i\gamma_j$. That is, it is a product of two separable components: one for the advertiser, and one for the slot. For ease of exposition, we will focus on the special case that $\gamma_j = 1$ for all j. However, we note that our results extend to the more general case of separable click-through rates.

Related work.

In recent years there has been a surge of work on algorithmic mechanism design for sponsored search, beginning with Mehta et al. [17, 16]. See the survey of Lahaie et al [13] for an overview of subsequent developments. The GSP model applied in this manuscript is due to Edelman et al [6] and Varian [24].

The work most closely related to ours is that of Paes Leme and Tardos, who also study equilibria of GSP [19]. They give upper bounds on the Price of Anarchy in pure, mixed, and Bayesian strategies; achieving bounds of 1.618, 4, and 8, respectively. Our main result is a simplification and strengthening of their results for the mixed and Bayesian cases, as well as an extension to different but related solution concepts.

The study of Price of Anarchy for non-truthful auction mechanisms (specially in the Bayesian setting) is a quite successful research line initiated by Christodoulou, Kovács and Schapira [4] and developed in Borodin and Lucier [15], Lucier [14], Paes Leme and Tardos [19] and most recently in the work of Bhawalkar and Roughgarden [1]. To the best of our knowledge, this is the first paper in that research line whose Price of Anarchy bounds hold when player valuation are drawn from a correlated distribution. In the study of optimal truthful mechanism design, correlated valuations have recently been studied by Papadimitriou and Pierrakos [22] and Dobzinski, Fu and Kleinberg [5].

Edelman et al [6] and Varian [24] study Envy-free equilibria of GSP (a special case of Nash equilibrium) in the full information setting. They demonstrate that such equilibria exist, and that all such equilibria are socially optimal. Gomes and Sweeney [8] study the Generalized Second Price Auction in the Bayesian context. They show that, unlike the full information case, there may not exist symmetric or socially optimal equilibria in this model, and obtain sufficient conditions on click-through-rates that guarantee the existence of a symmetric and efficient equilibrium. Lahaie [12] also considers the problem of bounding the social welfare obtained at equilibrium, but restricts attention to the special case that click-through-rate α_i decays exponentially along the slots with a factor of $\frac{1}{\delta}$. Under this assumption, Lahaie proves a price of anarchy of $\min\{\frac{1}{\delta}, 1 - \frac{1}{\delta}\}$.

The study of regret-minimization goes back to the work of Hannan on repeated two-player games [9]. Kalai and Vempala [11] extend the work of Hannan to online optimization problems, and Kakade et al [10] further extend to settings of approximate regret minimization. Blum et al [2] apply regret-minimization to the study of inefficiency in repeated games, coining the phrase "price of total anarchy" for the worst-case ratio between the optimal objective value and the average objective value when agents minimize regret.

Many of the above solution concepts have been tied together by Roughgarden [23], who showed that for a class of *smooth* games the price of anarchy, Bayesian price of anarchy, and price of total anarchy are identical. The smoothness criterion is quite strong, and does not apply in general to the GSP mechanism. However, we note that the methods used to analyze mechanisms at Nash Equilibrium share a common flavour with the results for smooth games. As part of the proof of our main result, we isolate a property related to smoothness that encapsulates many of the insights that drives our bounds.

In an independent work, Caragiannis et al [3] also improve the bounds in [19]. The authors prove a bound of 1.282 for the Full Information setting, almost matching the 1.259 lower bounds, and improve and extend the techniques of Paes Leme and Lucier [21] (a previous arXiv version of the present paper), showing bounds of 2.310 for correlated equilibria in the Full Information setting and 3.037 for Bayes-Nash equilibria with independent types.

2. PRELIMINARIES

We consider an auction with n advertisers and n slots[1]. Each advertiser i has a private type v_i, representing his or her value per click received. The sequence $\mathbf{v} = (v_1, \ldots, v_n)$ is referred to as the *type profile*. We will write $\mathbf{v}_{-i}$ for $\mathbf{v}$ excluding the ith entry, so that $\mathbf{v} = (v_i, \mathbf{v}_{-i})$.

An *outcome* is an assignment of advertisers to slots. An outcome can be viewed as a permutation π with $\pi(k)$ being the player assigned to slot k. When advertiser i is assigned to the k-th slot, he gets $\alpha_k\gamma_i$ clicks, where $\alpha_1 \geq \alpha_2 \geq \ldots \geq \alpha_n$ are called *click-through-rates* and γ_i are called *quality factors*. Without loss of generality and for clarity of exposition, we consider for the rest of the paper $\gamma_i = 1$ for all players.

A mechanism for this auction elicits a bid $b_i \in [0, \infty)$ from each agent i, which is interpreted as a type declaration, and returns an assignment as well as a price p_i per click for each agent. We assume $b_i \leq v_i$, since overbidding is clearly a dominated strategy. If advertiser i is assigned to slot j, his *utility* is $\alpha_j(v_i - p_i)$, which is the number of clicks received times profit per click. The *social welfare* of outcome π is $SW(\pi, \mathbf{v}) = \sum_j \alpha_j v_{\pi(j)}$, the total value of the solution for the participants. The optimal social welfare is $OPT(\mathbf{v}) = \max_\pi SW(\pi, \mathbf{v})$.

We focus on a particular mechanism, the Generalized Second Price auction, which works as follows. Given bid profile $\mathbf{b}$, the auction sets $\pi(k)$ to be the advertiser with the kth highest bid (breaking ties arbitrarily). That is, GSP assigns slots with higher click-through-rate to agents with higher bids. Payments are then set according to $p_i = b_{\pi(\pi^{-1}(i)+1)}$. That is, the payment of the kth highest bidder is precisely the bid of the next-highest bidder (where we take $b_{n+1} = 0$). We will write $u_i(\mathbf{b})$ for the utility derived by agent i from the GSP when agents bid according to $\mathbf{b}$.

For the remainder of the paper, we will write $\pi(\mathbf{b}, j)$ to be the player assigned to slot j by GSP when the agents bid according to $\mathbf{b}$. We will also write $\sigma(\mathbf{b}, i)$ for the slot assigned to bidder i by GSP, again when agents bid according to $\mathbf{b}$. In other words, $\sigma(\mathbf{b}, \cdot) = \pi^{-1}(\mathbf{b}, \cdot)$. We write $\pi^i(\mathbf{b}_{-i}, j)$ to be the player that would be assigned to slot j by GSP if agent i did not participate in the auction. We will write $\nu(\mathbf{v})$ for the optimal assignment of slots to bidders for value profile $\mathbf{v}$, so that $\nu(\mathbf{v}, i)$ is the slot that would be allocated to agent i in the optimal assignment[2].

[1] we handle unequal numbers of slots and advertisers by adding virtual slots with click-through-rate zero or virtual advertisers with zero value per click.

[2] We note that, since GSP makes the optimal assignment for

2.1 Pure and Mixed Nash Equilibrium

A *(pure) strategy* for agent i is a function $b_i : \mathbb{R}_{\geq 0} \to \mathbb{R}_{\geq 0}$ that maps each private value to a declared bid. A *mixed strategy* maps a private value to a distribution over bids, corresponding to a randomized declaration. Given a value profile $\mathbf{v}$, we say that strategy profile $\mathbf{b}$ is a mixed Nash equilibrium if, for all i and all alternative strategies $b'_i(\cdot)$,

$$\mathbb{E}[u_i(b_i(v_i), b_{-i}(v_{-i}))] \geq \mathbb{E}[u_i(b'_i(v_i), b_{-i}(v_{-i}))].$$

That is, each agent i maximizes his utility by bidding according to strategy $b_i(\cdot)$. We say this is a pure Nash equilibrium if, in addition, all strategies are pure. We define the *(mixed) Price of Anarchy* to be the worst-case ratio between social welfare in the optimum and expected social welfare in GSP across all valuation profiles and all mixed Nash equilibria:

$$\sup_{\mathbf{v}, \mathbf{b}(\cdot) NE} \frac{OPT(\mathbf{v})}{\mathbb{E}_b[SW(\pi(\mathbf{b}(\mathbf{v})), \mathbf{v})]}.$$

2.2 Bayesian setting

In a Bayesian setting, we suppose that each agent's type is drawn from a publicly known (possibly correlated) distribution, i.e., $\mathbf{v} \sim \mathbf{F}$. We then say that strategy profile $\mathbf{b}$ is a Bayes-Nash equilibrium for distributions $\mathbf{F}$ if, for all i, all v_i, and all alternative strategies b'_i,

$$\mathbb{E}_{\mathbf{v}_{-i}|v_i}[u_i(b_i(v_i), \mathbf{b}_{-i}(\mathbf{v}_{-i}))] \geq \mathbb{E}_{\mathbf{v}_{-i}|v_i}[u_i(b'_i(v_i), \mathbf{b}_{-i}(\mathbf{v}_{-i}))]$$

That is, each agent maximizes his expected utility by bidding in accordance with strategy $b_i(\cdot)$, where expectation is taken over the distribution of the other agents' types and any randomness in their strategies. We define the *Bayes-Nash Price of Anarchy* to be the worst-case ratio between social welfare in the optimum and social welfare in GSP across all distributions and all Nash equilibria:

$$\max_{\mathbf{F}, \mathbf{b}(\cdot) BNE} \frac{\mathbb{E}_{\mathbf{v} \sim \mathbf{F}}[OPT(\mathbf{v})]}{\mathbb{E}_{\mathbf{v} \sim \mathbf{F}, \mathbf{b}(\mathbf{v})}[SW(\pi(\mathbf{b}(\mathbf{v})), \mathbf{v})]}.$$

2.3 Signals and Information Assymmetry

We define an extension of the setting above, incorporating a Bayesian version of information assymmetry. In this model, each player's type consists of a value v_i and a signal s_i drawn from an arbitrary signal space. The signals can be thought of as privately-gained insight that refines agent i's conditional distribution over the space of other agents' types. It is publicly known that $(\mathbf{v}, \mathbf{s})$ comes from a certain distribution $\mathbf{F}'$, which can be arbitrarly correlated. As a special case, one could choose for the value of a player to be a function of his signal (or even the vector of signals).

The presence of signals captures the notion that some agents might have a better potential to infer the other players valuations than others, or may be endowed with priviledged information. We do note, however, that agents are aware of the bidding strategies $\mathbf{b}(\cdot, \cdot)$ and the distribution $\mathbf{F}'$, so that agents can rationalize about the effects of signals upon the bidding behaviour of their opponents.

In this model, a strategy is a bidding function mapping (v_i, s_i) to a distribution of possible bids. The bid profile is a Bayes-Nash in the assymmetric information model if:

$$\mathbb{E}_{\mathbf{v}_{-i}|v_i,s_i}[u_i(b_i(v_i, s_i), \mathbf{b}_{-i}(\mathbf{v}_{-i}, s_{-i}))] \geq$$
$$\mathbb{E}_{\mathbf{v}_{-i}|v_i,s_i}[u_i(b'_i(v_i, s_i), \mathbf{b}_{-i}(\mathbf{v}_{-i}, s_{-i}))]$$

2.4 Repeated Auctions and Regret Minimization

We now consider the GSP auction in a repeated setting. In this model, the GSP auction is run $T \geq 1$ times with the same slots and agents. The private value profile $\mathbf{v}$ of the agents does not change between rounds, but the agents are free to change their bids. We write b_i^t for the bid of agent i on round t. We refer to $D = (b^1, \ldots, b^T)$ as a *declaration sequence*. We will write $\pi(D)$ for the sequence of permutations generated by GSP on input sequence D. The average social welfare generated by GSP is then $SW(\pi(D), \mathbf{v}) = \frac{1}{T}\sum_t SW(\pi(\mathbf{b}^t), \mathbf{v})$.

The full range of equilibria in such a repeated game is very rich, so we restrict ourselves to a particular non-equilibrium form of play that nevertheless captures the intuition that agents learn appropriate bidding strategies over time, without necessitating convergence to a stationary equilibrium.

We say that declaration sequence $D = (b^1, \ldots, b^T)$ *minimizes external regret* for agent i if, for any fixed declaration b_i,

$$\sum_t u_i(b_i^t, b_{-i}^t) \geq \sum_t u_i(b_i, b_{-i}^t) + o(T).$$

That is, as T grows large, the utility of agent i approaches the utility of the optimal fixed strategy in hindsight. The *Price of Total Anarchy* [2] is the worst-case ratio between social welfare in the optimum and the average social welfare obtained by GSP across all declaration sequences that minimize external regret for all agents. That is, the price of total anarchy is

$$\lim_{T \to \infty} \max_{\mathbf{v}, D} \frac{OPT(\mathbf{v})}{SW(\pi(D), \mathbf{v})}$$

where the maximum is taken over declaration sequences that minimize external regret for all agents.

We note that the above model can be generalized to account for player uncertainty between rounds. For instance, one could assume that there is a large pool Ω of players, and on each round t the ad allocation algorithm (modeled as a randomized exogenous process) selects a subset of players $S_t \subseteq \Omega$ to participate in the auction that round. In this case, each player $i \in \Omega$ has a fixed valuation v_i, but agents are necessarily uncertain of the valuations (i.e. the identities) of their opponents on each round. The notion of regret minimization extends readily to such partial-information settings: if we write $\tau(T, i)$ for the set of rounds $t \leq T$ in which player i is selected, we say that the bid sequence b_i^t minimizes external regret if, for all b'_i,

$$\sum_{t \in \tau(T,i)} u_i(b_i^t, b_{-i}^t) \geq \sum_{t \in \tau(T,i)} u_i(b'_i, b_{-i}^t) + o(|\tau(T, i)|).$$

Such a model more directly captures the fact that an auction participant cannot perfectly predict the set of competitors she will face on any given round. A more thorough discussion of such generalized models appears in the full version of this paper.

a given bid declaration, we actually have that $\nu(\mathbf{v}, i)$ and $\sigma(\mathbf{v}, i)$ are identically equal. We define ν mainly for use when emphasizing the distinction between an optimal assignment for a value profile and the assignment that results from a given bid profile.

3. CORRELATED PRICE OF ANARCHY

Our main result is a bound of 4 on the Bayes-Nash PoA for GSP, which holds even if we allow agent types to be arbitrarily correlated. The same result holds for the Bayesian model of information assymmetry as well - extending the proof to this case is straightforward - but for clarity of exposition, we will give the proof without considering signals.

Theorem 1 *The Correlated Bayesian Price of Anarchy of GSP is at most 4.*

Our proof of Theorem 1 is related to the concept of smoothness due to Roughgarden [23]. Write $SW(s)$ for the social welfare generated by strategy profile s for some (implicitly defined) game. Roughgarden defines a game as (λ, μ)-smooth if, for all pairs of strategy profiles $\mathbf{s}, \mathbf{s}'$, we have

$$\sum_i u_i(s_i', s_{-i}) \geq \lambda SW(s') - \mu SW(s).$$

Roughly speaking, smoothness captures the property that if strategy profile s' results in a significantly larger social welfare than another strategy profile s, then this gap in welfare can be captured by the marginal increases in the individual agents' utilities when unilaterally switching their strategies from s to s'.

Paes Leme and Tardos showed in [18] that GSP auction is not smooth for any choice of parameters. The intuition is that in a mechanism game, welfare is determined not by strategy profiles directly, but through the intermediate space of outcomes. Thus, even if a bidding strategy s' yields an outcome that is much more efficient than s, it may be that the outcome does not change when any single agent deviates from s to s'. Nevertheless, we now note that GSP satisfies a conceptually weaker but related property: there is a *particular* strategy profile s' that maximizes social welfare, and for which a smoothness-like inequality holds for any other strategy profile s.

Definition 2 (Semi-Smooth Games) *We say that a game is (λ, μ)-**semi-smooth** if there exists some $\mathbf{s}'$ maximizing the social welfare such that, for any strategy profile $\mathbf{s}$,*

$$\sum_i u_i(s_i', s_{-i}) \geq \lambda SW(s') - \mu SW(s).$$

As we now demonstrate, the GSP auction corresponds to an semi-smooth game.

Lemma 3 *GSP in the full information setting is $(\frac{1}{2}, 1)$-semi-smooth.*

PROOF. Fix valuation profile $\mathbf{v}$ and agent i. Consider any bid profile $\mathbf{b}$ and define $b_i' = \frac{v_i}{2}$. We claim that

$$u_i\left(\frac{v_i}{2}, \mathbf{b}_{-i}\right) + \alpha_i v_{\pi(\mathbf{b},i)} \geq \frac{1}{2}\alpha_i v_i.$$

Summing the above expression for all i gives us the desired result. To see that the above expression holds, consider two cases:

1. By switching his bid from $b_i(v_i)$ to $v_i/2$, player i wins some slot $j \leq i$. In this case $u_i(\frac{v_i}{2}, \mathbf{b}_{-i}) \geq \frac{1}{2}\alpha_i v_i$.
2. Otherwise, the player who wins slot i under bidding profile $\mathbf{b}$ is bidding more than $v_i/2$. In this case $\alpha_i v_{\pi(i)} \geq \frac{1}{2}\alpha_i v_i$.

■

We now prove Theorem 1 using the semi-smoothness of GSP. Notice that the statement of semi-smoothness doesn't place any restrictions on strategy profile $\mathbf{b}$, and in particular does not require that it be a Nash equilibrium. So, in the Bayesian setting, for any type profile $\mathbf{v}$ and for any $\mathbf{b}(\mathbf{v})$, Lemma 3 implies that

$$\sum_i u_i(b_i'(v_i), \mathbf{b}_{-i}(\mathbf{v}_{-i})) \geq \frac{1}{2}OPT(\mathbf{v}) - SW(\pi(\mathbf{b}(\mathbf{v})), \mathbf{v}).$$

for $b_i'(v_i) = v_i/2$.

A proof of Theorem 1 is now straightforward by taking expectations and using the Bayes-Nash inequality for a given Bayes-Nash equilibrium strategy profile $\mathbf{b}$:

$$\begin{aligned}\mathbb{E}[SW(\pi(\mathbf{b}(\mathbf{v})), \mathbf{v})] &= \sum_i \mathbb{E}_{v_i}\mathbb{E}_{\mathbf{v}_{-i}|v_i}[u_i(b_i(v_i), \mathbf{b}_{-i}(\mathbf{v}_{-i}))] \\ &\geq \sum_i \mathbb{E}_{v_i}\mathbb{E}_{\mathbf{v}_{-i}|v_i}[u_i(b_i'(v_i), \mathbf{b}_{-i}(\mathbf{v}_{-i}))] \\ &\geq \frac{1}{2}\mathbb{E}[OPT(\mathbf{v})] - \mathbb{E}[SW(\pi(\mathbf{b}(\mathbf{v})), \mathbf{v})].\end{aligned}$$

which proves the Price of Anarchy of 4.

4. INDEPENDENT VALUATIONS

We now wish to tighten the bound obtained in Theorem 1 beyond 4, for the special case that player valuations are not correlated. Let us begin by describing the high-level idea, and the way in which it relies on type independence. We can rephrase the main idea of Theorem 1 as follows: at equilibrium, for each bidder i, it must be that the expected outcome for bidder i is no worse than the expected outcome that results from applying any alternative strategy. In particular, this must be true for the strategy that prescribes a bid equal to half of bidder i's true value. This, in turn, implies that the expected bid for slots much better than the expected allocation to agent i must be at least $v_i/2$, as otherwise agent i would have incentive to deviate. However, this suggests that, on average, a bidder with value at least $v_i/2$ will obtain such high-valued slots, which makes up for any loss in social welfare due to those slots not being assigned to agent i.

The key to the above argument was in identifying an alternative strategy for agent i to consider - namely, bidding half of his true value - and using the fact that this alternative strategy either gives player i a high utility or the player currently in slot i is paying a high price. This strategy has the strong property that it does not depend on the expected bids of the other agents; it is in this way that the argument is related to smoothness. However, more generally, we may be able to obtain tighter bounds by reasoning about strategies that are motivated by other agents' behaviour at equilibrium. In particular, it may be that a certain gap in social welfare implies the existence of some agent with some beneficial deviating strategy, but it might not be the case that a single strategy leads to an improvement in utility in every instance.

Indeed, what we will show is that if, for a given fixed valuation profile, the expected winning bid for some slot i is sufficiently low, then there must exist a deviating strategy for agent i that improves his welfare. The precise nature of this strategy will depend on the particular strategies employed by the other agents. Note that this argument does not immediately imply a bound on the expected welfare of GSP, since the existence of a deviating strategy for agent i conditions on agent i's type, whereas the expected social welfare is in expectation over all types. It is here that we use independence to convert conditional bounds into bounds on the overall expected social welfare.

In the remainder of the section we will first formalize the above argument, then demonstrate that the analysis extends to coarse correlated equilibria, outcomes of learning strategies, and the presence of irrational agents.

4.1 Performance at Bayes-Nash Equilibrium

We are now ready to prove the following theorem.

Theorem 4 *The Bayesian Price of Anarchy of GSP is at most $2(1-1/e)^{-1} \approx 3.164$, assuming that agent types are independently distributed.*

The proof of Theorem 4 proceeds in two steps. We first show that a structural property of bidding profiles implies a bound on the social welfare obtained by GSP (Lemma 5). We then show that this structural property holds at all BNE of the GSP (Lemma 6).

Lemma 5 *Suppose that $\mathbf{v} \sim \mathbf{F}$ and agents apply strategy profile $\mathbf{b}(\cdot)$. Suppose further that the following is true:*

$$\mathbb{E}_{\mathbf{v}_{-i}}[\alpha_{\sigma(\mathbf{b}(\mathbf{v}),i)}v_i] + \mathbb{E}_{\mathbf{v}_{-i}}[\alpha_k b_{\pi^i(\mathbf{b}_{-i}(\mathbf{v}_{-i}),k)}] \geq \gamma\alpha_k v_i \quad (1)$$

for all slots k, players i, and values v_i. Then

$$\mathbb{E}_{\mathbf{v}\sim\mathbf{F}}[SW(\pi(\mathbf{b}(\mathbf{v})),\mathbf{v})] \geq \frac{1}{2}\gamma\mathbb{E}_{\mathbf{v}\sim\mathbf{F}}[OPT(\mathbf{v})].$$

.

Lemma 6 *At any BNE of GSP, (1) holds with $\gamma = 1 - \frac{1}{e}$.*

Lemma 5 and Lemma 6 immediately imply Theorem 4. Note that it is in Lemma 5 that we make use of the assumption that agent types are independent.

Proof of Lemma 5 : Fix some value profile $\mathbf{v}$. For notational convenience, let Γ be the induced distribution on bid profiles $\mathbf{b} = \mathbf{b}(\mathbf{v})$ when $\mathbf{v} \sim \mathbf{F}$. Then for any player i, value v_i, and slot k, if we write $b_i = b_i(v_i)$, then we can express (1) as:

$$\mathbb{E}_{\mathbf{b}_{-i}}[\alpha_{\sigma(\mathbf{b},i)}v_i] + \mathbb{E}_{\mathbf{b}_{-i}}[\alpha_k b_{\pi^i(\mathbf{b}_{-i},k)}] \geq \gamma\alpha_k v_i.$$

This inequality essentially states that, under the bidding strategies employed by the other agents, the expected value of the slot obtained by agent i plus the expected bid required to obtain slot k is at least γ times the value agent i would obtain from slot k. Note that $\mathbf{v}_{-i}$ does not appear in this expression; bids $\mathbf{b}_{-i}$ are taken to be drawn from induced distribution Γ_{-i}. Now, recalling that $\nu(\mathbf{v},i)$ is the slot assigned to player i in the optimal assignment for values $\mathbf{v}$, we can take $k = \nu(\mathbf{v},i)$ in the above inequality. We then have

$$\mathbb{E}_{\mathbf{b}_{-i}}[\alpha_{\sigma(\mathbf{b},i)}v_i] + \mathbb{E}_{\mathbf{b}}[\alpha_{\nu(\mathbf{v},i)}b_{\pi^i(\mathbf{b}_{-i},\nu(\mathbf{v},i))}] \geq \gamma\alpha_{\nu(\mathbf{v},i)}v_i$$

for all $\mathbf{v}$ and all i, where we used the fact that strategy $b_i(\cdot)$ does not appear in the second term. Summing over all i and taking expectation over $\mathbf{v}$, we have

$$\mathbb{E}_{\mathbf{v}\sim\mathbf{F}}\left[\sum_i \mathbb{E}_{\mathbf{b}_{-i}}[\alpha_{\sigma(\mathbf{b},i)}v_i]\right] + \mathbb{E}_{\mathbf{v}\sim\mathbf{F}}\left[\sum_i \mathbb{E}_{\mathbf{b}}[\alpha_{\nu(\mathbf{v},i)}b_{\pi^i(\mathbf{b},\nu(\mathbf{v},i))}]\right] \geq \quad (2)$$

$$\geq \gamma\mathbb{E}_{\mathbf{v}\sim\mathbf{F}}\left[\sum_i \alpha_{\nu(\mathbf{v},i)}v_i\right]$$

Consider each of the three expectations in (2). For the third term, we note

$$\mathbb{E}_{\mathbf{v}\sim\mathbf{F}}\left[\sum_i \alpha_{\nu(\mathbf{v},i)}v_i\right] = \mathbb{E}_{\mathbf{v}\sim\mathbf{F}}[OPT(\mathbf{v})].$$

For the first term, linearity of expectation and independence of agent types implies

$$\mathbb{E}_{\mathbf{v}\sim\mathbf{F}}\left[\sum_i \mathbb{E}_{\mathbf{b}_{-i}}[\alpha_{\sigma(\mathbf{b},i)}v_i]\right] = \mathbb{E}_{\mathbf{v}\sim\mathbf{F}}\left[\sum_i \alpha_{\sigma(\mathbf{b}(\mathbf{v}),i)}v_i\right] = \mathbb{E}_{\mathbf{v}\sim\mathbf{F}}[SW(\pi(\mathbf{b}(\mathbf{v})),\mathbf{v})].$$

For the second expectation, notice that (again using type independence):

$$\mathbb{E}_{\mathbf{v}\sim\mathbf{F}}\mathbb{E}_{\mathbf{b}\sim\Gamma}\left[\sum_i \alpha_{\nu(\mathbf{v},i)}b_{\pi^i(\mathbf{b}_{-i},\nu(\mathbf{v},i))}\right] \leq \mathbb{E}_{\mathbf{v}\sim\mathbf{F}}\mathbb{E}_{\mathbf{b}\sim\Gamma}\left[\sum_i \alpha_{\nu(\mathbf{v},i)}b_{\pi(\mathbf{b},\nu(\mathbf{v},i))}\right] = \mathbb{E}_{\mathbf{b}\sim\Gamma}\left[\sum_k \alpha_k b_{\pi(b,k)}\right]$$

which is at most $\mathbb{E}_{\mathbf{v}\sim\mathbf{F}}[SW(\pi(\mathbf{v}),\mathbf{v})]$.

We therefore conclude from (2) that $2\mathbb{E}_{\mathbf{v}\sim\mathbf{F}}[SW(\pi(\mathbf{v}),\mathbf{v})] \geq \gamma\mathbb{E}_{\mathbf{v}\sim\mathbf{F}}[OPT(\mathbf{v})]$, completing the proof. ■

Proof of Lemma 6 : Fix slot k, player i, and value v_i. We wish to show that

$$\mathbb{E}_{\mathbf{v}_{-i}}[\alpha_{\sigma(\mathbf{b}(\mathbf{v}),i)}v_i] + \mathbb{E}_{\mathbf{v}_{-i}}[\alpha_k b_{\pi^i(\mathbf{b}_{-i}(\mathbf{v}_{-i}),k)}] \geq \gamma\alpha_k v_i. \quad (3)$$

The intuition is that if agent i's expected welfare at equilibrium and the expected bid required to obtain slot k are both very low compared to agent i's value for slot k, then agent i should attempt to deviate to a strategy aimed at obtaining slot k. The complicating factor is that the bid needed to win slot k is only known to be low in expectation, so it is not immediately clear how agent i should optimally attempt to win slot k. We must therefore bound the size of a gap in welfare that implies the existence of a single strategy that provides a benefit to player i in expectation.

For notational convenience we write $W = \mathbb{E}_{\mathbf{v}_{-i}}[\alpha_{\sigma(\mathbf{b}(\mathbf{v}),i)}v_i]$ note that W is precisely the expected welfare of agent i given that his type is v_i. First note that if $\alpha_k v_i < W$ then (3) is trivial. So we will consider $\alpha_k \geq W/v_i$. We will prove that

$$W + \mathbb{E}_{\mathbf{v}_{-i}}[\alpha_k b_{\pi^i(\mathbf{b}_{-i}(\mathbf{v}_{-i}),k)}] \geq \geq \alpha_k v_i - W \cdot \log\frac{\alpha_k v_i}{W}$$

and then dividing everything by $\alpha_k v_i$ and using that $\frac{\log(x)}{x} \leq \frac{1}{e}$ we arrive at inequality (3).

Consider any bid b_i' for agent i such that $b_i < b_i' < v_i$. Then for each slot k, since bid b_i is utility-maximizing for agent i, the utility of bidding b_i' satisfies

$$W \geq \mathbb{E}_{\mathbf{v}_{-i}}[u_i(b_i', \mathbf{b}_{-i})].$$

Also, if agent i bids b_i' and moreover it is true that $b_{\pi^i(\mathbf{b}_{-i},k)} < b_i'$, then agent i will win a slot with at least α_k clicks. Thus,

$$\mathbb{E}_{\mathbf{v}_{-i}}[u_i(b_i', \mathbf{b}_{-i})] \geq (v_i - b_i')\alpha_k \mathbb{P}_{\mathbf{v}_{-i}}[b_{\pi^i(\mathbf{b}_{-i}(\mathbf{v}_{-i}),k)} < b_i'].$$

Combining these two inequalities and substituting $z = v_i - b_i'$, we get

$$\mathbb{P}_{\mathbf{v}_{-i}}[v_i - b_{\pi^i(\mathbf{b}_{-i}(\mathbf{v}_{-i}),k)} > z] \leq \frac{W}{z \cdot \alpha_k}.$$

We are now able to estimate the expected value of $v_i - b_{\pi^i(\mathbf{b}_{-i},k)}$. Since $v_i - b_{\pi^i(\mathbf{b}_{-i}(\mathbf{v}_{-i}),k)} \leq v_i$ with probability 1, we have

$$\begin{aligned}\mathbb{E}[v_i - b_{\pi^i(\mathbf{b}_{-i},k)}] &= \int_0^{v_i} \mathbb{P}_{\mathbf{v}_{-i}}[v_i - b_{\pi^i(\mathbf{b}_{-i}(\mathbf{v}_{-i}),k)} > z]dz \\ &\leq \int_0^{W/\alpha_k} 1dz + \int_{W/\alpha_k}^{v_i} \frac{W}{\alpha_k z}dz \\ &\leq \frac{W}{\alpha_k} + \frac{W}{\alpha_k}\left(\log v_i - \log \frac{W}{\alpha_k}\right).\end{aligned}$$

Multiplying both sides by α_k and rearranging gives the required inequality. ■

4.2 Coarsely Correlated bids and Price of Total Anarchy

Notice that the proof of the previous section applies even in cases where agent bids are coarsely correlated. In such a case, we can consider a common source of randomness $\mathcal{R}$ and each bidding function to be a function $b_i(v_i, r)$, where $r \sim \mathcal{R}$. We call a profile of bidding functions a coarse correlated equilibrium if:

$$\begin{aligned}&\mathbb{E}_{\mathbf{v}_{-i}\sim\mathbf{F}_{-i}}[u_i(b_i(v_i,r), \mathbf{b}_{-i}(\mathbf{v}_{-i},r))] \geq \\ &\quad \mathbb{E}_{\mathbf{v}_{-i}\sim\mathbf{F}_{-i}}[u_i(b_i'(v_i,r), \mathbf{b}_{-i}(\mathbf{v}_{-i},r))], \forall i, v_i, r\end{aligned}$$

We still suppose $v_i \sim F_i$ where F_i are independent distributions. In this case, F and $\mathcal{R}$ induce a distribution Γ on the bids.

Adapting Lemma 6 to this context is straightforward. Now, to adapt Lemma 5, we observe that the proof follows as before, except that we must argue that

$$\mathbb{E}_{\mathbf{b}_{-i}\sim\Gamma_{-i}}[\alpha_{\sigma(v,i)} b_{\pi^i(\mathbf{b}_{-i},\sigma(v,i))}] = \mathbb{E}_{\mathbf{b}\sim\Gamma}[\alpha_{\sigma(v,i)} b_{\pi^i(\mathbf{b}_{-i},\sigma(v,i))}].$$

However, this follows because the marginal distribution of $b \sim \Gamma$ restricted to $-i$ is precisely $b_{-i} \sim \Gamma_{-i}$, as the shared randomness from $\mathcal{R}$ is not affected by restriction to a marginal distribution.

We now note that the result from the previous section implies a bound on the price of total anarchy for GSP. This follows because, whenever bidding sequence $D = (\mathbf{b}^1, \ldots, \mathbf{b}^T)$ minimizes regret for all agents, the bidding strategy with shared randomness $b_i(v_i, t) = {b_i}^t(v_i)$ for $t \in [T]$ is a coarse correlated equilibrium. Lemmas 5 and 6 therefore imply that, for all $\mathbf{v}$,

$$\mathbb{E}_{t\in[T]}[SW(\pi(\mathbf{b}^t(\mathbf{v})), \mathbf{v})] \geq \frac{1}{2}(1 - 1/e)OPT(\mathbf{v})$$

which implies that the price of total anarchy is bounded by $2(1-1/e)^{-1}$. Thus, even when agents apply strategies that minimize regret but do not necessarily converge to a stationary equilibrium, we still obtain bounds on the average social welfare obtained by GSP over many rounds.

4.3 Irrational Agents

We now consider a setting in which, in addition to the n advertisers who bid rationally, there are m "irrational" advertisers who cannot be assumed to bid at equilibrium. Write N for the set of rational advertisers, and M for the set of irrational advertisers. Note that we still think of the irrational advertisers as being true players, who still receive value per click. The irrational bidders simply cannot be assumed to apply optimal strategies; for example, they may not have experience with the GSP auction, or not know about historical bidding patterns.

Given an outcome π (which is an assignment of these $n+m$ bidders to $n+m$ slots), the definition of social welfare is unchanged: it is $SW(\pi, \mathbf{v}) = \sum_{i\in N\cup M} v_i \alpha_{\pi(i)}$. We define the social welfare of bidders in N to be precisely that: $SW_N(\pi, \mathbf{v}) = \sum_{i\in N} v_i \alpha_{\pi(i)}$. The optimal social welfare for bidders in N is $OPT_N(\mathbf{v}) = \max_\pi SW_N(\pi, \mathbf{v})$.

We wish to show that the total social welfare obtained by GSP is a good approximation to $OPT_N(\mathbf{v})$ when the players in N play at equilibrium and the players in M play arbitrarily. That is, the addition of irrational players does not degrade the social welfare guarantees of GSP had they not participated. In order to make this claim, we must impose a restriction on the behaviour of the irrational players: that they do not overbid. In other words, we require that $b_i(v_i) \leq v_i$ for all $i \in M$ and all v_i. We feel this is a natural restriction: overbidding is easily seen to be a dominated strategy (i.e. any strategy that bids higher than v_i is dominated by a strategy that lowers such bids to be at most v_i). Moreover, it is arguable that inexperienced bidders would bid conservatively, and not risk a large payment with no gain.[3]

Given that irrational agents do not overbid, we note that our BPoA bounds go through in this setting almost without change. In particular, our structural property (1) continues to hold for all agents in N.

Lemma 7 *Equation* (1) *holds with* $\gamma = 1 - \frac{1}{e}$ *for all* $i \in N$.

PROOF. This proof follows the proof of Lemma 6 without change. Note that in that proof we used only the fact that the bidding strategy of agent i is a best response, so the fact that other agents may not bid at equilibrium does not affect the argument. ■

The corresponding version of Lemma 5 then follows from (1) just as in the setting without irrational agents, with only minor modifications.

Lemma 8 *If* (1) *holds for all* $i \in N$, *then*

$$\mathbb{E}_{\mathbf{v}\sim\mathbf{F}}[SW(\pi(\mathbf{b}(\mathbf{v})), \mathbf{v})] \geq \frac{1}{2}\gamma \mathbb{E}_{\mathbf{v}\sim\mathbf{F}}[OPT_N(\mathbf{v})].$$

[3]This relies on the simplifying assumption that all bidders have knowledge of their own private valuations. Admittedly, this requires a certain level of sophistication and may be difficult to attain in practice. Our argument is thus limited to imperfect strategy choice given perfect knowledge of types. It remains open to extend this analysis to agents who may misunderstand their own valuations.

PROOF. Precisely as in the proof of Lemma 5, we obtain

$$\mathbb{E}_{\mathbf{v}\sim\mathbf{F}}\left[\sum_{i\in N}\mathbb{E}_{\mathbf{b}_{-i}}[\alpha_{\sigma(\mathbf{b},i)}v_i]\right]+$$
$$\mathbb{E}_{\mathbf{v}\sim\mathbf{F}}\left[\sum_{i\in N}\mathbb{E}_{\mathbf{b}}[\alpha_{\nu(\mathbf{v},i)}b_{\pi^i(\mathbf{b},\nu(\mathbf{v},i))}]\right]\geq \quad (4)$$
$$\geq \gamma\mathbb{E}_{\mathbf{v}\sim\mathbf{F}}\left[\sum_{i\in N}\alpha_{\nu(\mathbf{v},i)}v_i\right]$$

where we note that the summations are over agents in N. Then, as in Lemma 5,

$$\mathbb{E}_{\mathbf{v}\sim\mathbf{F}}\left[\sum_{i\in N}\alpha_{\nu(\mathbf{v},i)}v_i\right]=\mathbb{E}_{\mathbf{v}\sim\mathbf{F}}[OPT_N(\mathbf{v})].$$

and

$$\mathbb{E}_{\mathbf{v}\sim\mathbf{F}}\left[\sum_{i\in N}\mathbb{E}_{\mathbf{b}_{-i}}[\alpha_{\sigma(\mathbf{b},i)}v_i]\right]=\mathbb{E}_{\mathbf{v}\sim\mathbf{F}}[SW_N(\pi(\mathbf{b}(\mathbf{v})),\mathbf{v})]$$
$$\leq \mathbb{E}_{\mathbf{v}\sim\mathbf{F}}[SW(\pi(\mathbf{b}(\mathbf{v})),\mathbf{v})].$$

For the second expectation in (4), we require a slight deviation from the previous argument. We notice that

$$\mathbb{E}_{\mathbf{v}\sim\mathbf{F},\mathbf{b}\sim\Gamma}\left[\sum_{i\in N}\alpha_{\nu(\mathbf{v},i)}b_{\pi^i(\mathbf{b}_{-i},\nu(\mathbf{v},i))}\right]$$
$$\leq \mathbb{E}_{\mathbf{v}\sim\mathbf{F}}\mathbb{E}_{\mathbf{b}\sim\Gamma}\left[\sum_{i\in N}\alpha_{\nu(\mathbf{v},i)}b_{\pi(\mathbf{b},\nu(\mathbf{v},i))}\right]$$
$$=\mathbb{E}_{\mathbf{b}\sim\Gamma}\left[\sum_{k:\exists i\in N,\nu(\mathbf{v},i)=k}\alpha_k b_{\pi(\mathbf{b},k)}\right]$$
$$\leq \mathbb{E}_{\mathbf{b}\sim\Gamma}\left[\sum_{k}\alpha_k v_{\pi(\mathbf{b},k)}\right]=\mathbb{E}_{\mathbf{v}\sim\mathbf{F}}[SW(\pi(\mathbf{v}),\mathbf{v})].$$

We therefore conclude from (4) that $2\mathbb{E}_{\mathbf{v}\sim\mathbf{F}}[SW(\pi(\mathbf{v}),\mathbf{v})]\geq \gamma\mathbb{E}_{\mathbf{v}\sim\mathbf{F}}[OPT_N(\mathbf{v})]$, completing the proof. ∎

Together, Lemma 7 and Lemma 8 imply that the Bayesian Price of Anarchy of GSP is at most $2(1-1/e)^{-1}$ even in the presence of irrational bidders. Following the comments in Section 4.2, we can apply the same argument to obtain a matching bound on the Price of Total Anarchy with irrational bidders.

4.4 Approximate Equilibria

It is commonly assumed that rational bidders apply strategies at equilibrium. However, it may be that due to limits on rationality or indifference between small differences in utility, agents converge only on an approximate Bayes-Nash equilibrium. Given type distribution $\mathbf{F}$, we say that strategy profile $\mathbf{b}$ is an ϵ-BNE if, for all agents i and all types v_i,

$$\mathbb{E}_{\mathbf{v}_{-i}}[u_i(b_i(v_i),\mathbf{b}_{-i}(\mathbf{v}_{-i}))]\geq(1-\epsilon)\mathbb{E}_{\mathbf{v}_{-i}}[u_i(b_i{}'(v_i),\mathbf{b}_{-i}(\mathbf{v}_{-i}))].$$

Note that our choice of the multiplicative definition of approximate equilibrium, motivated by the fact that we elected not to scale values to lie in [0, 1].

We now claim that our bound for social welfare at equilibrium depends on the Bayes-Nash equilibrium condition in a continuous way, so that the bound degrades gracefully as we increase the degree to which a bidding strategy only approximates an equilibrium. Specifically, if agents apply strategy profile $\mathbf{b}$ which forms an ϵ-BNE, for $0\leq\epsilon<1-1/e$, then the expected social welfare of GSP is within a factor of $2(1-\epsilon-1/e)^{-1}$.

The proof requires only a minor modification to the proof of Theorem 4. Lemma 5 is not affected by this change. The statement of Lemma 6 is then modified to $\gamma=1-\epsilon-1/e$. To obtain this bound, we need only note that the inequality due to $\mathbf{b}$ being a BNE becomes

$$W\geq(1-\epsilon)\mathbb{E}_{\mathbf{v}_{-i}}[u_i(b_i',\mathbf{b}_{-i})],$$

from which we conclude (in the same way as in the proof of Lemma 6) that

$$(1-\epsilon)\mathbb{E}[v_i-b_{\pi^i(\mathbf{b}_{-i},k)}]\leq\frac{W}{\alpha_k}+\frac{W}{\alpha_k}\left(\log v_i-\log\frac{W}{\alpha_k}\right).$$

Multiplying through by α_k and rearranging yields

$$\mathbb{E}[\alpha_{\sigma(\mathbf{b}(\mathbf{v}),i)}v_i]+\mathbb{E}[\alpha_k b_{\pi^i(\mathbf{b}_{-i},k)}]\leq(1-\epsilon)\alpha_k v_i-W\cdot\log\frac{\alpha_k v_i}{W}$$

which implies the desired result, using that $\frac{log(x)}{x}\leq\frac{1}{e}$.

Acknowledgments: We thank Éva Tardos for the many fruitful discussions. We also thank Silvio Micali and Costis Daskalakis for pointing us to the asymmetric information model.

5. REFERENCES

[1] K. Bhawalkar and T. Roughgarden. Welfare guarantees for combinatorial auctions with item bidding. In *SODA 2011*, 2011.

[2] A. Blum, M. Hajiaghayi, K. Ligett, and A. Roth. Regret minimization and the price of total anarchy. In *STOC08*, 2008.

[3] I. Caragiannis, P. Kanellopoulos, C. Kaklamanis, and M. Kyropoulou. On the efficiency of equilibria in generalized second price auctions. In *EC'11*, 2011.

[4] G. Christodoulou, A. Kovács, and M. Schapira. Bayesian combinatorial auctions. In *ICALP '08: Proceedings of the 35th international colloquium on Automata, Languages and Programming, Part I*, pages 820–832, Berlin, Heidelberg, 2008. Springer-Verlag.

[5] S. Dobzinski, H. Fu, and R. Kleinberg. Optimal auctions with correlated bidders are easy. In *STOC 2011*, 2011.

[6] B. Edelman, M. Ostrovsky, and M. Schwarz. Internet advertising and the generalized second-price auction: Selling billions of dollars worth of keywords. *The American Economic Review*, 97(1):242–259, March 2007.

[7] B. Edelman and M. Schwarz. Optimal auction design and equilibrium selection in sponsored search auctions. In *Working Paper*, 2010.

[8] R. D. Gomes and K. S. Sweeney. Bayes-nash equilibria of the generalized second price auction. In *EC '09: Proceedings of the tenth ACM conference on Electronic commerce*, pages 107–108, New York, NY, USA, 2009. ACM.

[9] J. Hannan. Approximation to bayes risk in repeated plays. In M. Dresher, A. Tucker, and P. Wolfe, editors, *Contributions to the Theory of Games*, volume 4. Princeton University Press, 1957.

[10] S. Kakade, A. Kalai, and K. Ligett. Playing games with approximation algorithms. In *STOC07*, 2007.

[11] A. Kalai and S. Vempala. Efficient algorithms for online decision problems. *J. Comput. Syst. Sci.*, 2005.

[12] S. Lahaie. An analysis of alternative slot auction designs for sponsored search. In *EC '06: Proceedings of the 7th ACM conference on Electronic commerce*, pages 218–227, New York, NY, USA, 2006. ACM.

[13] S. Lahaie, D. Pennock, A. Saberi, and R. Vohra. *Algorithmic Game Theory*, chapter Sponsored search auctions, pages 699–716. Cambridge University Press, 2007.

[14] B. Lucier. Beyond equilibria: Mechanisms for repeated combinatorial auctions. In *ICS10: Innovations in Computer Science 2010*, 2010.

[15] B. Lucier and A. Borodin. Price of anarchy for greedy auctions. In *SODA '10*. ACM, 2010.

[16] A. Mehta, A. Saberi, U. V. Vazirani, and V. V. Vazirani. Adwords and generalized on-line matching. In *FOCS*, pages 264–273, 2005.

[17] A. Mehta, A. Saberi, U. V. Vazirani, and V. V. Vazirani. Adwords and generalized online matching. *J. ACM*, 54(5), 2007.

[18] R. Paes Leme and Éva Tardos. Bayes-nash price of anarchy for gsp. In *AdAuctions Workshop 2010*, 2010.

[19] R. Paes Leme and Éva Tardos. Pure and bayes-nash price of anarchy for generalized second price auctions. In *FOCS10: 51st Annual IEEE Symposium on Foundations of Computer Science*, 2010.

[20] R. Paes Leme and Éva Tardos. Sponsored search equilibria for conservative bidders. In *AdAuctions Workshop 2009*, 2010.

[21] R. Paes Leme and B. Lucier. Improved social welfare bounds for gsp at equilibrium. In *arXiv*, 2011.

[22] C. Papadimitriou and G. Pierrakos. On optimal single-item auctions. In *STOC 2011*, 2011.

[23] T. Roughgarden. Intrinsic robustness of the price of anarchy. In *STOC '09: Proceedings of the 41st annual ACM symposium on Theory of computing*, pages 513–522, New York, NY, USA, 2009. ACM.

[24] H. R. Varian. Position auctions. *International Journal of Industrial Organization*, 2006.

On the Efficiency of Equilibria in Generalized Second Price Auctions

Ioannis Caragiannis　Christos Kaklamanis
Panagiotis Kanellopoulos　Maria Kyropoulou
Department of Computer Engineering and Informatics
University of Patras and RACTI, Greece
{caragian,kakl,kanellop,kyropoul}@ceid.upatras.gr

ABSTRACT

In sponsored search auctions, advertisers compete for a number of available advertisement slots of different quality. The auctioneer decides the allocation of advertisers to slots using bids provided by them. Since the advertisers may act strategically and submit their bids in order to maximize their individual objectives, such an auction naturally defines a strategic game among the advertisers. In order to quantify the efficiency of outcomes in generalized second price auctions, we study the corresponding games and present new bounds on their price of anarchy, improving the recent results of Paes Leme and Tardos [16] and Lucier and Paes Leme [13]. For the full information setting, we prove a surprisingly low upper bound of 1.282 on the price of anarchy over pure Nash equilibria. Given the existing lower bounds, this bound denotes that the number of advertisers has almost no impact on the price of anarchy. The proof exploits the equilibrium conditions developed in [16] and follows by a detailed reasoning about the structure of equilibria and a novel relation of the price of anarchy to the objective value of a compact mathematical program. For more general equilibrium classes (i.e., mixed Nash, correlated, and coarse correlated equilibria), we present an upper bound of 2.310 on the price of anarchy. We also consider the setting where advertisers have incomplete information about their competitors and prove a price of anarchy upper bound of 3.037 over Bayes-Nash equilibria. In order to obtain the last two bounds, we adapt techniques of Lucier and Paes Leme [13] and significantly extend them with new arguments.

Categories and Subject Descriptors

F.2 [**Theory of Computation**]: Analysis of Algorithms and Problem Complexity—*Miscellaneous*; J.4 [**Computer Applications**]: Social and Behavioral Sciences—*Economics*

General Terms

Algorithms, Economics, Theory

Keywords

Auctions, equilibria, generalized second price, price of anarchy

1. INTRODUCTION

Sponsored search auctions [11] have become extremely popular during the last decade as the main tool used by search engines and other information services in order to create income. A number of advertisement slots are available which can be thought of as ranked according to their significance (e.g., according to the number of clicks by viewers an advertisement assigned to a slot is expected to have). A sponsored search auction aims to allocate advertisement slots to advertisers. Advertisers cast their bids for the available slots and the auctioneer uses the bids in order to compute the allocation to slots and the fee each advertiser should pay for this service. The particular rule used in order to compute both the allocation and the payments defines a distinct auction.

We consider generalized second price auctions whose variations are widely used by leaders in the sponsored search industry such as Google and Yahoo! In generalized second price auctions, the advertisers are assigned the slots in decreasing order of their bids (i.e., the advertiser with the highest bid is assigned to the most significant slot, and so on) and each of them is required to pay the next highest bid (i.e., the advertiser assigned to the most significant slot will pay per click an amount equal to the bid of the advertiser assigned to the second significant slot, and so on).

Traditionally, Auction Theory (see [9] for an introduction) has given a central role to the requirement that an auction should impose truthful behavior by the potentially strategically acting participants. This requirement has several implications to the maximization of the social welfare, i.e., the quantity that includes both the auctioneer's revenue and the profit of the participants. Even though generalized second price auctions generalize the famous truthful Vickrey auction [21], they are known neither to be truthful [1] nor to guarantee social welfare maximization [11, 20] and this seems to come in sharp contrast to their recent success. In an attempt to provide a partial justification of this success, following previous work, we consider the following question:

how much can the strategic behavior of the advertisers affect the social welfare?

We address this question by considering the natural strategic games among the advertisers that generalized second price auctions define. Each advertiser (henceforth also called bidder) has her own valuation for each click and her utility from an allocation depends on the total valuation from the clicks on the slot she is assigned to minus her payment to the auctioneer. Hence, acting strategically means that each bidder aims to maximize her utility given the strategies (bids) of the other bidders. Such a behavior naturally leads to an equilibrium, i.e., a set of strategies from which no bidder has an incentive to deviate. We consider both the full information and the more realistic incomplete information (or Bayesian) setting. The corresponding equilibrium concepts of interest are the pure Nash, mixed Nash, correlated, and coarse correlated equilibria in the former and Bayes-Nash equilibria in the latter setting. In both cases, we make the reasonable assumption that bidders always cast conservative bids that do not exceed their valuations. We provide new social welfare guarantees for generalized second price auctions that are expressed as bounds on the price of anarchy of the corresponding games over equilibria of particular classes, improving previous results in the literature. In a nutshell, our results indicate that, despite the strategic behavior of the advertisers, the social welfare is always high.

Related work. The game-theoretic model we adopt in the current paper was proposed by [5] and [20] and was further used in the sequence of papers [6, 10, 13, 16, 19] (see also the surveys [11, 15]). Edelman et al. [5] and Varian [20] prove that Nash equilibria with optimal social welfare always exist for generalized second price auction games in the full information setting. In contrast, this is not the case for games in the Bayesian setting as proved in [6]. Lahaie [10] provides bounds on the social welfare of equilibria under strong assumptions for the click-through rates of the slots. Thompson and Leyton-Brown [19] study the efficiency of equilibria through experimentation.

Our work is closely related to, and improves the recent results of Paes Leme and Tardos [16] and Lucier and Paes Leme [13]. They consider conservative bidders and justify this assumption since bidders' strategies are dominated otherwise. This is a natural assumption that is usually made in similar contexts as well, such as in combinatorial auctions (e.g., see [3, 4, 12]). The authors of [16] consider pure and mixed Nash equilibria in the full-information setting, for which they upper-bound the price of anarchy by 1.618 and 4, respectively. Their result for mixed Nash equilibria is valid for more general equilibrium classes as well. Furthermore, they present a tight (lower and upper) bound of 5/4 for pure Nash equilibria and two bidders. For the incomplete information setting and Bayes-Nash equilibria, they show an upper bound of 8. The authors of [13] improve this last bound to 3.162, while (in the preliminary version of their paper) they present a tight bound of 1.259 on the price of anarchy over pure Nash equilibria for the case of three bidders (the lower bound has also been claimed in [16] without presenting the explicit construction).

Roughgarden [18] presents a sufficient condition for games, termed smoothness, so that the price of anarchy of a smooth game over pure Nash equilibria immediately extends also to mixed Nash, correlated, and coarse correlated equilibria as well. Smoothness arguments have been implicitly or explicitly used (see [18] and the references therein) in order to provide such "robust" bounds on the price of anarchy of several games. As observed in [16], generalized second price auctions do not correspond to smooth games.

Our results. We first consider pure Nash equilibria of generalized second price auction games under the full information setting (Section 3). We warm up by considering the case of three bidders (in Section 3.1), for which we present the upper bound of approximately 1.259 (by providing an alternative proof to the one in the preliminary version of [13]). This upper bound together with the bound of 5/4 for two bidders from [16] serves as the base of the inductive proof of our more general result presented in Section 3.2: an extremely low upper bound of 1.282 on the price of anarchy in games with arbitrarily many bidders. This result implies that the number of bidders involved in the auction has almost no effect on the price of anarchy. The proof elaborates on techniques developed in [16] and follows by a detailed reasoning about the structure of equilibria and a novel relation of the price of anarchy to the objective value of a compact mathematical program.

Then, in Section 4, we consider the broad class of coarse correlated equilibria in the full information setting and prove an upper bound of 2.3102 on the price of anarchy, improving the upper bound of 4 from [16]. Clearly, this bound holds for more restricted equilibria classes, namely correlated and mixed Nash equilibria. In the incomplete information setting, we prove an upper bound of 3.037 on the price of anarchy over Bayes-Nash equilibria (Section 5), improving the bound of 3.162 from [13]. The proofs of these results explicitly take into account the bids of the bidders and bound their utility (in different ways) by considering several possible deviations. In order to obtain our bounds, we adapt techniques from [13] and significantly extend them with new arguments.

All our bounds hold (with appropriate adaptations in the proofs) in the more general model of separable click-through rates [11] in which the click-through rate of a slot depends on the bidder allocated to that slot as well. In order to keep the exposition simple, we do not consider this extension in the current text.

We begin with preliminary definitions in Section 2 and conclude with open problems in Section 6. Due to lack of space, some proofs have been omitted.

2. PRELIMINARIES

Before proceeding with the presentation of our results, we give some formal definitions. Throughout the paper, we consider generalized second price auctions with n bidders and n slots. In such an auction, each bidder i has a *valuation* v_i that denotes how much the bidder values a click on her ad. Each slot i has a non-negative *click-through rate* a_i that denotes the rate by which this slot is clicked by the viewers. Without loss of generality, we assume that bidders and slots are sorted according to their valuations and their click-through rates, so that $v_1 \geq v_2 \geq ... \geq v_n \geq 0$ and $a_1 \geq a_2 \geq ... \geq a_n \geq 0$. Given a vector of bids $\mathbf{b} = (b_1, b_2, ..., b_n)$ with one bid per bidder, the generalized second price auction defines an assignment π according to which the bidder with the j-th highest bid is assigned to slot j (ties are broken arbitrarily). We denote by $\pi(j)$ the bidder assigned to slot j and by $\pi^{-1}(i)$ the slot to which bidder i is allocated. Then, each bidder i is required to pay the bid of the bidder that is assigned to the slot below hers (i.e., slot $\pi^{-1}(i)+1$) if any.

We study the strategic game among the bidders that is induced by such an auction and we refer to it as a *GSP auction game*. In this game, each bidder acts selfishly and aims to maximize her utility given the bids of the other bidders. Given a bid vector $\mathbf{b}$ and the corresponding assignment π it induces, the *utility* of bider i is

$$u_i(\mathbf{b}) = a_{\pi^{-1}(i)}\left(v_i - b_{\pi(\pi^{-1}(i)+1)}\right),$$

assuming that $b_{\pi(n+1)} = 0$. We assume that bidders are conservative, i.e., each bidder selects as her strategy a bid that does not exceed her valuation. A *pure strategy* for bidder i consists of a single bid $b_i \in [0, v_i]$, while a *mixed strategy* is a probability distribution over pure strategies. We say that a bid vector $\mathbf{b}$ is a *mixed Nash equilibrium* for a GSP auction game if no bidder has an incentive to unilaterally deviate from her strategy in order to strictly increase her expected utility. I.e., for each bidder i and each alternative bid $b'_i \in [0, v_i]$, it holds that

$$\mathbb{E}[u_i(\mathbf{b})] \geq \mathbb{E}[u_i(b', \mathbf{b}_{-i})],$$

where $\mathbf{b}_{-i}$ denotes the bids of all bidders apart from i and the expectation is taken according to the randomness of the bids. If all bidders play pure strategies, then $\mathbf{b}$ is a *pure Nash equilibrium*.

Correlated and coarse correlated equilibria can be viewed as generalizations of mixed Nash equilibria, where the bidders have a joint probability distribution instead of independent ones. Informally, in both settings, a mediator draws a bid vector from a publicly known distribution and secretly informs each bidder of her suggested strategy. If no bidder has an incentive to deviate from the suggested strategy, then this is a *correlated equilibrium* [2], while if no bidder has a pure strategy that she can always follow, irrespective of the outcome, and improve her expected utility, then this is a *coarse correlated equilibrium* [14] (see also [22]). More formally, there exists a joint probability distribution that draws the bid vector $\mathbf{b}$ from the universe $\mathcal{B}$ of all bid vectors $(y_1, y_2, ..., y_n)$ with $y_i \in [0, v_i]$. The expected utility of a bidder is then

$$\mathbb{E}[u_i(\mathbf{b})] = \sum_{y \in \mathcal{B}} \Pr[\mathbf{b} = y] \cdot u_i(y).$$

In a coarse correlated equilibrium, for any bidder i, there exists no alternative bid $b' \in [0, v_i]$ such that

$$\mathbb{E}[u_i(\mathbf{b})] < \mathbb{E}[u_i(b', \mathbf{b}_{-i})].$$

A correlated equilibrium is also a coarse correlated one.

The *social welfare* of an assignment π induced by a bid vector $\mathbf{b}$ is then defined as

$$\mathcal{W}(\mathbf{b}) = \mathbb{E}[\sum_i a_i v_{\pi(i)}],$$

where the expectation is taken according to the randomness of the bids. Equivalently, we have

$$\mathcal{W}(\mathbf{b}) = \mathbb{E}[\sum_i a_{\pi^{-1}(i)} v_i] = \mathbb{E}[\sum_i u_i(\mathbf{b})] + \mathbb{E}[\sum_i a_i b_{\pi(i+1)}].$$

The *optimal social welfare* is

$$\mathrm{OPT} = \sum_i a_i v_i.$$

We also consider the Bayesian setting [7] where bidders' valuations are random. In this setting, each bidder has a probability distribution on her valuation and her strategy depends on the actual valuation, i.e., a bid is now a function on the valuation. The optimal social welfare is defined as

$$\mathrm{OPT} = \mathbb{E}[\sum_i a_{o(i)} v_i],$$

where $o(i)$ is the random variable denoting the slot that bidder i occupies in the optimal assignment and the expectation is taken according to the randomness in the bidders' valuations. In a *Bayes-Nash equilibrium*, for any bidder i, any possible value x for her valuation, and any alternative bid $b'_i(x)$, it holds that

$$\mathbb{E}[u_i(b_i(x), \mathbf{b}_{-i}(v_{-i}))|v_i = x] \geq \mathbb{E}[u_i(b'_i(x), \mathbf{b}_{-i}(v_{-i}))|v_i = x].$$

The social welfare is again

$$\mathcal{W}(\mathbf{b}) = \mathbb{E}[\sum_i a_i v_{\pi(i)}],$$

where the expectation is taken according to the randomness in the valuations and the bids.

The *price of anarchy* (introduced in [8]; see also [17]) of a game over a given class of equilibria is defined as the worst ratio of the optimal social welfare over the social welfare of an equilibrium (over all equilibria of the class), i.e., $\max_{\mathbf{b}} \mathrm{OPT}/\mathcal{W}(\mathbf{b})$, where $\mathbf{b}$ is restricted to equilibria. The price of anarchy for a class of games (over equilibria of a particular type) is the worst price of anarchy among the games in the class (over equilibria of the same type).

3. THE PRICE OF ANARCHY OVER PURE NASH EQUILIBRIA

In this section we present our results for pure Nash equilibria. We consider GSP auction games with n bidders with valuations $v_1 \geq ... \geq v_n \geq 0$ and n slots with click-through rates $a_1 \geq ... \geq a_n \geq 0$. We assume that neither all slots have the same click-through rate nor all bidders have the same valuation (in both cases, the price of anarchy is 1). We elaborate on the approach taken in [16] and use the notion of weakly feasible assignments defined therein.

DEFINITION 1. *An assignment π is* weakly feasible *if for each pair of bidders i, j, it holds that $a_{\pi^{-1}(i)} v_i \geq a_{\pi^{-1}(j)}(v_i - v_j)$.*

We refer to the inequalities in this definition as *weak feasibility conditions*. With some abuse of notation, we denote by $\mathcal{W}(\pi) = \sum_i a_i v_{\pi(i)}$ the social welfare of assignment π and use the term *efficiency* of assignment π to refer to the ratio $\mathrm{OPT}/\mathcal{W}(\pi)$. As proved in [16], every pure Nash equilibrium corresponds to a weakly feasible assignment. Hence, the price of anarchy of a GSP auction game over pure Nash equilibria is upper-bounded by the worst-case efficiency among weakly feasible assignments.

DEFINITION 2. *An assignment π is called* proper *if for any two slots $i < j$ with equal click-through rates, it holds $\pi(i) < \pi(j)$.*

Clearly, for any non-proper weakly feasible assignment, we can construct a proper weakly feasible one with equal social welfare. Hence, in order to prove our upper bounds, we essentially upper-bound the worst-case efficiency over proper weakly feasible assignments.

Given an assignment π, consider the directed graph $G(\pi)$ that has one node for each slot, and a directed edge for each bidder i that connects the node corresponding to slot i to the node corresponding to slot $\pi^{-1}(i)$. In general, $G(\pi)$ consists of a set of disjoint cycles and may contain self-loops.

DEFINITION 3. *An assignment π is called* reducible *if its directed graph $G(\pi)$ has more than one cycles. Otherwise, it is called* irreducible.

Given a reducible assignment π such that $G(\pi)$ has $c \geq 2$ cycles, we can construct c GSP auction subgames by considering the slots and the bidders that correspond to the nodes and edges of each cycle. Similarly, for $\ell = 1, ..., c$, the restriction π^ℓ of π to the slots and bidders of the ℓ-th subgame is an assignment for this game. The next fact is implicit in [16].

FACT 4. *If assignment π is weakly feasible for the original GSP auction game, then π^ℓ is weakly feasible for the ℓ-th subgame as well, for $\ell = 1, ..., c$. Then, the efficiency of π is at most the maximum efficiency among the assignments π^ℓ for $\ell = 1, ..., c$.*

When considering irreducible weakly feasible assignments, we further assume that the index of the slot bidder 1 occupies is smaller than the index of the bidder that is assigned to slot 1. This is without loss of generality due to the following argument. Consider an irreducible weakly feasible assignment π for a GSP auction game with n bidders such that $\pi^{-1}(1) > \pi(1)$. We construct a new game with click-through rate $a'_i = v_i$ for slot i and valuation $v'_i = a_i$ for bidder i, for $i = 1, ..., n$ and the assignment $\pi_* = \pi^{-1}$. Observe that $\pi_*^{-1}(1) = \pi(1) < \pi^{-1}(1) = \pi_*(1)$. Clearly, the optimal social welfare is the same in both games while the social welfare of π_* for the new game is $\mathcal{W}(\pi_*) = \sum_i a'_i v'_{\pi_*(i)} = \sum_i v_i a_{\pi_*(i)} = \sum_i a_{\pi^{-1}(i)} v_i = \mathcal{W}(\pi)$. We can also prove the weak feasibility conditions for π_* in the new game for each i, j. In order to do so, consider the weak feasibility condition for π in the original game for bidders $\pi(j), \pi(i)$. It is $a_{\pi^{-1}(\pi(j))} v_{\pi(j)} \geq a_{\pi^{-1}(\pi(i))}(v_{\pi(j)} - v_{\pi(i)})$ and, equivalently, $v_{\pi(i)} a_{\pi^{-1}(\pi(i))} \geq v_{\pi(j)}(a_{\pi^{-1}(\pi(i))} - a_{\pi^{-1}(\pi(j))})$. By the definition of the click-through rates and the valuations in the new game and the definition of π_*, we obtain that $a'_{\pi_*^{-1}(i)} v'_i \geq a'_{\pi_*^{-1}(j)}(v'_i - v'_j)$ as desired.

We furthermore note that when $v_n = 0$, any proper weakly feasible assignment is reducible. This is obviously the case if all bidders with zero valuation use the last slots. Otherwise, consider a bidder i with non-zero valuation that is assigned a slot $\pi^{-1}(i) > \pi^{-1}(j)$ where j is a bidder with zero valuation. Since the assignment is proper, it holds that $a_{\pi^{-1}(i)} < a_{\pi^{-1}(j)}$. Then, we obtain a contradiction by the weak feasibility condition $a_{\pi^{-1}(i)} v_i \geq a_{\pi^{-1}(j)}(v_i - v_j)$ for bidders i, j.

3.1 GSP auction games with three bidders

We are ready to present our first result (Theorem 6). In the proof, we use the following technical lemma.

LEMMA 5. *Let $\zeta = 0.129567$. For any $\lambda \in [0, 1]$, it holds that $\sqrt{\lambda^3 + 1} \geq 1 - \zeta\lambda + \frac{\lambda^2}{2}$.*

PROOF. Since both parts of the inequality are non-negative for $\lambda \in [0, 1]$, it suffices to show that the function $f(\lambda) = (\lambda^3 + 1) - \left(1 - \zeta\lambda + \frac{\lambda^2}{2}\right)^2$ is non-negative for $\lambda \in [0, 1]$. Let $g(\lambda) = -\frac{\lambda^3}{4} + (1 + \zeta)\lambda^2 - (1 + \zeta^2)\lambda + 2\zeta$ and observe that $f(\lambda) = \lambda \cdot g(\lambda)$. The proof will follow by proving that $g(\lambda) \geq 0$ when $\lambda \in [0, 1]$. Observe that the derivative of g is strictly negative for $\lambda = 0$ and strictly positive for $\lambda = 1$. Hence, the minimum of g in $[0, 1]$ is achieved at the point $\lambda^* = \frac{4+4\zeta-2\sqrt{\zeta^2+8\zeta+1}}{3}$ where the derivative of g becomes zero. Straightforward calculations yield that $g(\lambda^*) > 0$ and the lemma follows. □

THEOREM 6. *The price of anarchy over pure Nash equilibria of GSP auction games with three conservative bidders is at most 1.259134.*

PROOF. Consider a GSP auction game with three slots with click-through rates $a_1 \geq a_2 \geq a_3 \geq 0$ and three bidders with valuations $v_1 \geq v_2 \geq v_3 \geq 0$ and a proper weakly feasible assignment π of slots to bidders. We will prove the theorem by upper-bounding the efficiency of π by 1.259134. If π is reducible, then the efficiency is bounded by the efficiency for games with two bidders and the theorem follows by the upper bound of 5/4 proved in [16] for this case. So, in the following, we assume that π is irreducible; by the observation above, this implies that $v_3 > 0$. There are only two such assignments which are in fact symmetric: in the first, slots 1, 2, 3 are allocated to bidders 3, 1, 2, respectively, and in the second, slots 1, 2, 3 are allocated to bidders 2, 3, 1, respectively. Without loss of generality (see the discussion above), we assume that π is the former assignment.

Let β, γ, λ, and μ be such that $a_2 = \beta a_1$, $a_3 = \gamma a_1$, $v_2 = \lambda v_1$, and $v_3 = \mu v_1$. Clearly, it holds that $1 \geq \beta \geq \gamma \geq 0$ and $1 \geq \lambda \geq \mu > 0$. The social welfare of assignment π is $\mathcal{W}(\pi) = a_1 v_1(\mu + \beta + \gamma\lambda)$ whereas the optimal social welfare is $\text{OPT} = a_1 v_1(1 + \beta\lambda + \gamma\mu)$. Furthermore, since π is weakly feasible, the weak feasibility conditions for bidders 1 and 3 and bidders 2 and 3 are $a_2 v_1 \geq a_1(v_1 - v_3)$ and $a_3 v_2 \geq a_1(v_2 - v_3)$, respectively, i.e., $\beta \geq 1 - \mu$ and $\gamma \geq 1 - \frac{\mu}{\lambda}$. We are now ready to bound the efficiency of π. Let $\delta, \epsilon \geq 0$ be such that $\beta = 1 - \mu + \delta$ and $\gamma = 1 - \frac{\mu}{\lambda} + \epsilon$. We have

$$\begin{aligned}
\frac{\text{OPT}}{\mathcal{W}(\pi)} &= \frac{1 + \beta\lambda + \gamma\mu}{\mu + \beta + \gamma\lambda} \\
&= \frac{1 + \lambda - \mu\lambda + \mu - \frac{\mu^2}{\lambda} + \delta\lambda + \epsilon\mu}{1 + \lambda - \mu + \delta + \epsilon\lambda} \\
&\leq \frac{1 + \lambda - \mu\lambda + \mu - \frac{\mu^2}{\lambda}}{1 + \lambda - \mu}.
\end{aligned}$$

The inequality follows since $1 \geq \lambda \geq \mu > 0$ implies that $1 + \lambda - \mu\lambda + \mu - \frac{\mu^2}{\lambda} = 1 + \lambda - \mu + \mu(1 - \lambda) + \mu(1 - \mu/\lambda) \geq 1 + \lambda - \mu \geq 1$ and $\delta + \epsilon\lambda \geq \delta\lambda + \epsilon\mu \geq 0$.

For $\mu \in [0, 1]$, this last expression is maximized for the value of μ that makes its derivative with respect to μ equal to zero, i.e., $\mu = -\sqrt{\lambda^3 + 1} + \lambda + 1$. By substituting μ, we obtain that

$$\begin{aligned}
\frac{\text{OPT}}{\mathcal{W}(\pi)} &\leq \frac{\lambda^2 + \lambda + 2 - 2\sqrt{\lambda^3 + 1}}{\lambda} \\
&\leq 1 + 2\zeta \\
&= 1.259134,
\end{aligned}$$

where $\zeta = 0.129567$ and the second inequality follows by Lemma 5. □

3.2 GSP auction games with many bidders

In this section, we prove our main result for pure Nash equilibria.

THEOREM 7. *The price of anarchy over pure Nash equilibria of GSP auction games with conservative bidders is at most* $\frac{61+7\sqrt{217}}{128} \approx 1.28216$.

In our proof, we will need the following technical lemma.

LEMMA 8. *Let* $r = \frac{61+7\sqrt{217}}{128} \approx 1.28216$ *and* $f(\beta,\gamma,\lambda,\mu) = \mu + \beta\left(1-\frac{\lambda}{r}\right) + \gamma(\lambda-\mu) - \frac{1}{r}$. *Then, the objective value of the mathematical program*

$$\begin{aligned} \textit{minimize} \quad & f(\beta,\gamma,\lambda,\mu) \\ \textit{subject to} \quad & \beta \geq 1-\mu \\ & \gamma \geq 1-\mu/\lambda \\ & 1 \geq \lambda \geq \mu > 0 \\ & 1 \geq \beta,\gamma \geq 0 \end{aligned}$$

is non-negative.

PROOF. Since $\mu \leq \lambda \leq 1$, we have that $f(\beta,\gamma,\lambda,\mu)$ is non-decreasing in β and γ. Using the first two constraints, we have that the objective value of the mathematical program is at least

$$f\left(1-\mu, 1-\frac{\mu}{\lambda}, \lambda, \mu\right) = 1-\frac{1}{r}+\lambda-\frac{\lambda}{r}-\mu\left(2-\frac{\lambda}{r}\right)+\frac{\mu^2}{\lambda},$$

which is minimized for $\mu = \lambda - \frac{\lambda^2}{2r}$ to

$$f\left(1-\lambda+\frac{\lambda^2}{2r}, \frac{\lambda}{2r}, \lambda, \lambda-\frac{\lambda^2}{2r}\right) = 1-\frac{1}{r}-\frac{\lambda}{r}+\frac{\lambda^2}{r}-\frac{\lambda^3}{4r^2}.$$

In order to complete the proof it suffices to show that the function $g(\lambda) = 1-\frac{1}{r}-\frac{\lambda}{r}+\frac{\lambda^2}{r}-\frac{\lambda^3}{4r^2}$ is non-negative for $\lambda \in [0,1]$. Observe that $g(\lambda)$ is a polynomial of degree 3 and, hence, it has at most one local minimum. Also observe that the derivative of $g(\lambda)$ is $-\frac{1}{r}+\frac{2\lambda}{r}-\frac{3\lambda^2}{4r^2}$ which is strictly negative for $\lambda = 0$ and strictly positive for $\lambda = 1$. Hence, its minimum in $[0,1]$ is achieved at the point $\lambda^* = \frac{4r-2\sqrt{4r^2-3r}}{3}$ where the derivative becomes zero. Straightforward calculations yield that $g(\lambda^*) = 0$ and the lemma follows. $\square$

PROOF OF THEOREM 7. In order to prove the theorem, we will prove that the worst-case efficiency among weakly feasible assignments of any GSP auction game is at most $r = \frac{61+7\sqrt{217}}{128} \approx 1.28216$. We use induction. As the base of our induction, we use the fact that GSP auction games with one, two, or three bidders have worst-case efficiency among weakly feasible assignments at most 1.28216. For a single bidder, the claim is trivial. For two bidders, it follows by [16], and for three bidders, it follows by the proof of Theorem 6. Let $n \geq 4$ be an integer. Using the inductive hypothesis that the worst-case efficiency among weakly feasible assignments of any GSP auction game with at most $n-1$ bidders is at most r, we will show that this is also the case for any GSP auction game with n bidders.

Consider a GSP auction game with n bidders with valuations $v_1 \geq v_2 \geq \ldots \geq v_n \geq 0$ and n slots with click-through rates $a_1 \geq a_2 \geq \ldots \geq a_n \geq 0$ and let π be a proper weakly feasible assignment. If π is reducible, the claim follows by Fact 4 and the inductive hypothesis. So, in the following, we assume that π is irreducible; this implies that $v_n > 0$. Let j be the bidder that is assigned slot 1 and i_1 be the slot assigned to bidder 1. Without loss of generality, we assume that $i_1 < j$ since the other case is symmetric; see the discussion at the beginning of Section 3. Also, let i_2 be the slot assigned to bidder i_1. By our assumptions, the integers j, 1, i_1, and i_2 are different.

We will show that

$$\mathcal{W}(\pi) \geq a_1 v_j + a_{i_1}\left(v_1 - \frac{v_{i_1}}{r}\right) + a_{i_2}(v_{i_1} - v_j) - \frac{a_1 v_1}{r} + \frac{\text{OPT}}{r}. \quad (1)$$

Assuming that (1) holds, we apply Lemma 8 with $\beta = a_{i_1}/a_1$, $\gamma = a_{i_2}/a_1$, $\lambda = v_{i_1}/v_1$, and $\mu = v_j/v_1$. Clearly, the last two constraints of the mathematical program in Lemma 8 are satisfied. Also, observe that the weak feasibility conditions for bidders 1 and j and bidders i_1 and j in assignment π are $a_{i_1}v_1 \geq a_1(v_1 - v_j)$ and $a_{i_2}v_{i_1} \geq a_1(v_{i_1} - v_j)$, respectively, i.e., $\beta \geq 1-\mu$ and $\gamma \geq 1-\mu/\lambda$ and the first two constraints of the mathematical program in Lemma 8 are satisfied as well. Now, using inequality (1) and Lemma 8, we have that

$$\mathcal{W}(\pi) \geq f\left(\frac{a_{i_1}}{a_1}, \frac{a_{i_2}}{a_1}, \frac{v_{i_1}}{v_1}, \frac{v_j}{v_1}\right) \cdot a_1 v_1 + \frac{\text{OPT}}{r} \geq \frac{\text{OPT}}{r}$$

and the proof follows.

It remains to prove inequality (1). We distinguish between three cases depending on the relative order of j, i_1, and i_2; in each of these cases, we further distinguish between two subcases.

Case I.1: $1 < i_1 < j < i_2$ **and** $a_j \leq a_{i_2} r$. Consider the restriction of the original game that consists of the bidders different than j, 1, and i_1 and the slots different than 1, i_1, and i_2. Let π' be the restriction of π to the bidders and slots of the new game. Clearly, this assignment is weakly feasible for the new game since the weak feasibility conditions for π' are just a subset of the corresponding conditions for π (for the original game). Also, note that the optimal assignment for the restricted game assigns bidder k to slot k for $k = 2, \ldots, i_1-1, i_1+1, \ldots, j-1, i_2+1, \ldots, n$ and bidder $k+1$ to slot k for $k = j, \ldots, i_2-1$. By the inductive hypothesis, we know that the efficiency of π' is at most r. Hence, we can bound the social welfare of π as

$$\begin{aligned} & \mathcal{W}(\pi) \\ = \; & a_1 v_j + a_{i_1} v_1 + a_{i_2} v_{i_1} + \sum_{k \notin \{1,i_1,i_2\}} a_k v_{\pi(k)} \\ = \; & a_1 v_j + a_{i_1} v_1 + a_{i_2} v_{i_1} + \mathcal{W}(\pi') \\ \geq \; & a_1 v_j + a_{i_1} v_1 + a_{i_2} v_{i_1} + \frac{1}{r}\left(\sum_{k=2}^{i_1-1} a_k v_k \right. \\ & \left. + \sum_{k=i_1+1}^{j-1} a_k v_k + \sum_{k=j}^{i_2-1} a_k v_{k+1} + \sum_{k=i_2+1}^{n} a_k v_k\right) \end{aligned}$$

$$\geq a_1 v_j + a_{i_1} v_1 + a_{i_2} v_{i_1} + \frac{1}{r}\left(\sum_{k=2}^{i_1-1} a_k v_k + \sum_{k=i_1+1}^{j-1} a_k v_k + \sum_{k=j+1}^{i_2} a_k v_k + \sum_{k=i_2+1}^{n} a_k v_k\right)$$

$$= a_1 v_j + a_{i_1} v_1 + a_{i_2} v_{i_1} + \frac{1}{r}\left(\sum_{k=1}^{n} a_k v_k - a_1 v_1 - a_{i_1} v_{i_1} - a_j v_j\right)$$

$$= a_1 v_j + a_{i_1} v_1 + a_{i_2} v_{i_1} - \frac{1}{r}(a_1 v_1 + a_{i_1} v_{i_1} + a_j v_j) + \frac{\mathrm{OPT}}{r}$$

$$\geq a_1 v_j + a_{i_1}(v_1 - \frac{v_{i_1}}{r}) + a_{i_2}(v_{i_1} - v_j) - \frac{a_1 v_1}{r} + \frac{\mathrm{OPT}}{r}$$

and inequality (1) follows. The first inequality follows by the inductive hypothesis and the definition of the optimal assignment for the restricted game. The second inequality follows since $a_k \geq a_{k+1}$ for $k = j, ..., i_2 - 1$. The last inequality follows since $a_j \leq a_{i_2} r$.

Case I.2: $1 < i_1 < j < i_2$ **and** $a_j > a_{i_2} r$**.** Consider the restriction of the original game that consists of the bidders different than j and 1 and the slots different than 1 and i_1. Let π' be the restriction of π to the bidders and slots of the new game. Again, this assignment is weakly feasible for the new game since the weak feasibility conditions for π' are just a subset of the ones for π (for the original game). Also, note that the optimal assignment for the restricted game assigns bidder k to slot k for $k = 2, ..., i_1 - 1, j+1, ..., n$ and bidder $k-1$ to slot k for $k = i_1 + 1, ..., j$. By the inductive hypothesis, we know that the efficiency of π' is at most r. Hence, we can bound the social welfare of π as

$$\mathcal{W}(\pi)$$

$$= a_1 v_j + a_{i_1} v_1 + \sum_{k \notin \{1, i_1\}} a_k v_{\pi(k)}$$

$$= a_1 v_j + a_{i_1} v_1 + \mathcal{W}(\pi')$$

$$\geq a_1 v_j + a_{i_1} v_1 + \frac{1}{r}\left(\sum_{k=2}^{i_1-1} a_k v_k + \sum_{k=i_1+1}^{j} a_k v_{k-1} + \sum_{k=j+1}^{n} a_k v_k\right)$$

$$= a_1 v_j + a_{i_1} v_1 + \frac{1}{r}\left(\sum_{k=1}^{n} a_k v_k - a_1 v_1 - a_{i_1} v_{i_1} + \sum_{k=i_1+1}^{j} a_k (v_{k-1} - v_k)\right)$$

$$\geq a_1 v_j + a_{i_1} v_1 + \frac{1}{r}\left(\sum_{k=1}^{n} a_k v_k - a_1 v_1 - a_{i_1} v_{i_1} + a_j \sum_{k=i_1+1}^{j} (v_{k-1} - v_k)\right)$$

$$= a_1 v_j + a_{i_1} v_1 - \frac{1}{r}(a_1 v_1 + a_{i_1} v_{i_1} + a_j v_j - a_j v_{i_1}) + \frac{\mathrm{OPT}}{r}$$

$$> a_1 v_j + a_{i_1}(v_1 - \frac{v_{i_1}}{r}) + a_{i_2}(v_{i_1} - v_j) - \frac{a_1 v_1}{r} + \frac{\mathrm{OPT}}{r}$$

and inequality (1) follows. The first inequality follows by the inductive hypothesis and the definition of the optimal assignment for the restricted game. The second inequality follows since $a_k \geq a_j$ and $v_{k-1} - v_k \geq 0$ for $k = i_1 + 1, ..., j$. The last inequality follows since $a_j > a_{i_2} r$.

Case II.1: $1 < i_1 < i_2 < j$ **and** $v_{i_2} \leq v_j r$**.** Consider the restriction of the original game that consists of the bidders different than j, 1, and i_1 and the slots different than 1, i_1, and i_2. Let π' be the restriction of π to the bidders and slots of the new game. Clearly, this assignment is weakly feasible for the new game since the weak feasibility conditions for π' are just a subset of the ones for Π (for the original game). Also, note that the optimal assignment for the restricted game assigns bidder k to slot k for $k = 2, ..., i_1 - 1, i_1 + 1, ..., i_2 - 1, j+1, ..., n$ and bidder $k-1$ to slot k for $k = i_2 + 1, ..., j$. By the inductive hypothesis, we know that the efficiency of π' is at most r. Hence, we can bound the social welfare of π as

$$\mathcal{W}(\pi)$$

$$= a_1 v_j + a_{i_1} v_1 + a_{i_2} v_{i_1} + \sum_{k \notin \{1, i_1, i_2\}} a_k v_{\pi(k)}$$

$$= a_1 v_j + a_{i_1} v_1 + a_{i_2} v_{i_1} + \mathcal{W}(\pi')$$

$$\geq a_1 v_j + a_{i_1} v_1 + a_{i_2} v_{i_1} + \frac{1}{r}\left(\sum_{k=2}^{i_1-1} a_k v_k + \sum_{k=i_1+1}^{i_2-1} a_k v_k + \sum_{k=i_2+1}^{j} a_k v_{k-1} + \sum_{k=j+1}^{n} a_k v_k\right)$$

$$\geq a_1 v_j + a_{i_1} v_1 + a_{i_2} v_{i_1} + \frac{1}{r}\left(\sum_{k=2}^{i_1-1} a_k v_k + \sum_{k=i_1+1}^{i_2-1} a_k v_k + \sum_{k=i_2+1}^{j} a_k v_k + \sum_{k=j+1}^{n} a_k v_k\right)$$

$$= a_1 v_j + a_{i_1} v_1 + a_{i_2} v_{i_1} + \frac{1}{r}\left(\sum_{k=1}^{n} a_k v_k - a_1 v_1 - a_{i_1} v_{i_1} - a_{i_2} v_{i_2}\right)$$

$$= a_1 v_j + a_{i_1} v_1 + a_{i_2} v_{i_1} - \frac{1}{r}(a_1 v_1 + a_{i_1} v_{i_1} + a_{i_2} v_{i_2}) + \frac{\mathrm{OPT}}{r}$$

$$\geq a_1 v_j + a_{i_1}(v_1 - \frac{v_{i_1}}{r}) + a_{i_2}(v_{i_1} - v_j) - \frac{a_1 v_1}{r} + \frac{\mathrm{OPT}}{r}$$

and inequality (1) follows. The first inequality follows by the inductive hypothesis and the definition of the optimal assignment for the restricted game. The second inequality follows since $v_{k-1} \geq v_k$ for $k = i_2 + 1, ..., j$. The last inequality follows since $v_{i_2} \leq v_j r$.

Case II.2: $1 < i_1 < i_2 < j$ **and** $v_{i_2} > v_j r$**.** Consider the restriction of the original game that consists of the bidders different than 1 and i_1 and the slots different than i_1 and i_2. Let π' be the restriction of π to the bidders and slots of the new game. Again, this assignment is weakly feasible for the new game since the weak feasibility conditions for π' are just a subset of the ones for π (for the original game). Also, note that the optimal assignment for the restricted game assigns bidder k to slot k for $k = i_2+1, ..., n$, bidder i_1+1 to slot i_1-1, and bidder $k+1$ to slot k for $k = 1, ..., i_1-2, i_1+1, ..., i_2-1$. By the inductive hypothesis, we know that the efficiency of π' is at most r. Hence, we can bound the social welfare of π as

$$\begin{aligned}
&\mathcal{W}(\pi)\\
&= a_{i_1}v_1 + a_{i_2}v_{i_1} + \sum_{k\notin\{i_1,i_2\}} a_k v_{\pi(k)}\\
&= a_{i_1}v_1 + a_{i_2}v_{i_1} + \mathcal{W}(\pi')\\
&\geq a_{i_1}v_1 + a_{i_2}v_{i_1} + \frac{1}{r}\left(\sum_{k=1}^{i_1-2} a_k v_{k+1} + a_{i_1-1}v_{i_1+1}\right.\\
&\quad\left. + \sum_{k=i_1+1}^{i_2-1} a_k v_{k+1} + \sum_{k=i_2+1}^{n} a_k v_k\right)\\
&= a_{i_1}v_1 + a_{i_2}v_{i_1} + \frac{1}{r}\left(\sum_{k=1}^{n} a_k v_k + \sum_{k=1}^{i_1-2}(a_k - a_{k+1})v_{k+1}\right.\\
&\quad + (a_{i_1-1} - a_{i_1+1})v_{i_1+1}\\
&\quad\left. + \sum_{k=i_1+1}^{i_2-1}(a_k - a_{k+1})v_{k+1} - a_1v_1 - a_{i_1}v_{i_1}\right)\\
&\geq a_{i_1}v_1 + a_{i_2}v_{i_1} + \frac{1}{r}\left(\sum_{k=1}^{n} a_k v_k + \sum_{k=1}^{i_1-2}(a_k - a_{k+1})v_{i_2}\right.\\
&\quad + (a_{i_1-1} - a_{i_1+1})v_{i_2}\\
&\quad\left. + \sum_{k=i_1+1}^{i_2-1}(a_k - a_{k+1})v_{i_2} - a_1v_1 - a_{i_1}v_{i_1}\right)\\
&= a_{i_1}v_1 + a_{i_2}v_{i_1} - \frac{1}{r}(a_1v_1 + a_{i_1}v_{i_1} + a_{i_2}v_{i_2} - a_1v_{i_2})\\
&\quad + \frac{\mathrm{OPT}}{r}\\
&> a_1v_j + a_{i_1}(v_1 - \frac{v_{i_1}}{r}) + a_{i_2}(v_{i_1} - v_j) - \frac{a_1v_1}{r} + \frac{\mathrm{OPT}}{r}
\end{aligned}$$

and inequality (1) follows. The first inequality follows by the inductive hypothesis and the definition of the optimal assignment for the restricted game. The second inequality follows since $a_k - a_{k+1} \geq 0$ and $v_{k+1} \geq v_{i_2}$ for $k = 1, ..., i_1 - 2, i_1+1, ..., i_2-1$ and $a_{i_1-1} - a_{i_1+1} \geq 0$ and $v_{i_1+1} \geq v_{i_2}$. The last inequality follows since $v_{i_2} > v_j r$, and $a_1 > a_{i_2}$.

Due to lack of space, the third case where $1 < i_2 < i_1 < j$ is omitted. □

4. COARSE CORRELATED EQUILIBRIA

In this section, we prove our upper bound on the price of anarchy over coarse correlated equilibria. Unlike the proof of previous upper bounds (e.g., in [16]), our proof is based on taking into account the bids in the analysis. We consider a GSP auction game with n slots with click-through rates $a_1 \geq a_2 \geq ... \geq a_n \geq 0$ and n bidders with valuations $v_1 \geq v_2 \geq ... \geq v_n \geq 0$. Let $\mathbf{b}$ denote the random bid vector drawn according to a probability distribution that corresponds to a coarse correlated equilibrium. We denote by π the random assignment induced by $\mathbf{b}$. Also, let $b_{\pi(i)}$ be the random variable denoting the i-th highest bid among all bidders.

We can extend the main argument in the proof of Lemma 6 in [13] (adapted to coarse correlated equilibria) in order to obtain the following lower bound on the expected utility of each bidder at a coarse correlated equilibrium.

LEMMA 9. *Consider a coarse correlated equilibrium and bidder i. For any $\beta > 0$, it holds that*

$$\mathbb{E}[u_i(\mathbf{b})] \geq \beta(1 - e^{-1/\beta})a_i v_i - \beta\mathbb{E}[a_i b_{\pi(i)}].$$

We are now ready to prove the main result of this section. In our proof, we combine the above lemma together with a stronger property concerning the bidder with the highest valuation.

THEOREM 10. *The price of anarchy over coarse correlated equilibria of GSP auction games with conservative bidders is at most* 2.3102.

PROOF. We prove the theorem by lower-bounding the expected utility of each bidder at a coarse correlated equilibrium. Let $\beta \geq 1$ be a parameter to be fixed later. Consider bidder 1 and her deviation to the bid v_1. Then, bidder 1 would always be allocated slot 1 and pay a_1 times the highest bid among the remaining bidders (which is upper bounded by $b_{\pi(1)}$). Hence,

$$\begin{aligned}
\mathbb{E}[u_1(\mathbf{b})] &\geq \mathbb{E}[u_1(v_1, \mathbf{b}_{-1})]\\
&\geq a_1v_1 - \mathbb{E}[a_1b_{\pi(1)}]\\
&\geq \beta(1-e^{-1/\beta})(a_1v_1 - \mathbb{E}[a_1b_{\pi(1)}]), \quad (2)
\end{aligned}$$

where the last inequality follows since $v_1 \geq b_{\pi(1)}$ and since $\beta \geq 1$ implies that $\beta(1 - e^{-1/\beta}) \leq 1$.

Now, we will use the fact that the social welfare is the sum of the expected utilities of the bidders plus the total bids paid. We have

$$\begin{aligned}
\beta\mathcal{W}(\mathbf{b}) &= \mathcal{W}(\mathbf{b}) + (\beta-1)\mathcal{W}(\mathbf{b})\\
&= \mathbb{E}[u_1(\mathbf{b})] + \mathbb{E}[\sum_{i\geq 2} u_i(\mathbf{b})] + \mathbb{E}[\sum_i a_i b_{\pi(i+1)}]\\
&\quad + (\beta-1)\mathbb{E}[\sum_i a_i v_{\pi(i)}]\\
&\geq \beta(1-e^{-1/\beta})a_1v_1 - \beta(1-e^{-1/\beta})\mathbb{E}[a_1b_{\pi(1)}]\\
&\quad + \beta(1-e^{-1/\beta})\sum_{i\geq 2} a_i v_i - \beta\sum_{i\geq 2}\mathbb{E}[a_i b_{\pi(i)}]\\
&\quad + \sum_{i\geq 2}\mathbb{E}[a_i b_{\pi(i)}] + (\beta-1)\mathbb{E}[a_1 v_{\pi(1)}]\\
&\quad + (\beta-1)\sum_{i\geq 2}\mathbb{E}[a_i v_{\pi(i)}]\\
&\geq \beta(1-e^{-1/\beta})\mathrm{OPT} + (\beta e^{-1/\beta} - 1)\mathbb{E}[a_1 b_{\pi(1)}],
\end{aligned}$$

where the first inequality follows by the lower bounds on the bidders' utilities in Lemma 9 and inequality (2) and the fact that $a_i \geq a_{i+1}$ for $i = 1, ..., n-1$, and the second inequality follows by the definition of OPT and since $\beta \geq 1$ and $v_{\pi(i)} \geq b_{\pi(i)}$ for any i.

By setting β such that $\beta e^{-1/\beta} = 1$, we obtain that the price of anarchy $\text{OPT}/\mathcal{W}(\mathbf{b})$ is at most $\beta/(\beta-1)$. This occurs for $\beta \approx 1.76322$, where the ratio becomes 2.3102. □

5. THE BAYESIAN SETTING

In this section, we prove our upper bound on the price of anarchy in the Bayesian setting. In our proof, we consider a GSP auction game with n slots with click-through rates $a_1 \geq a_2 \geq ... \geq a_n \geq 0$ and n bidders with random valuations $v_1, v_2, ..., v_n \geq 0$. Let $\mathbf{b}$ denote the bid functions of the bidders at a Bayes-Nash equilibrium. We denote by π the random assignment induced by $\mathbf{b}$ and by $o(i)$ the random variable that indicates the slot bidder i occupies in the optimal assignment; therefore, $o^{-1}(j)$ stands for the bidder that occupies slot j in the optimal assignment. Also, let $b_{\pi(i)}$ be the random variable denoting the i-th highest bid among all bidders.

We will prove our main result by appropriately combining two lower bounds for the expected utilities of the bidders. In the proof of the first lower bound (Lemma 12), we will need the following technical lemma.

LEMMA 11. *For any ξ and any non-negative X, Y, it holds that*

$$(X-Y)^2 \geq \left(\xi - \frac{\xi^2}{4}\right) X^2 - \xi XY.$$

PROOF. Let $f(X,Y) = (X-Y)^2 - (\xi - \xi^2/4)X^2 + \xi XY$. It suffices to prove that $f(X,Y) \geq 0$ for any ξ. Then, $f(X,Y) = (1-\xi+\xi^2/4)X^2 + Y^2 - (2-\xi)XY = ((1-\xi/2)X - Y)^2 \geq 0$. □

LEMMA 12. *Consider a Bayes-Nash equilibrium. Then, for any γ and δ, it holds that*

$$\begin{aligned}\sum_i \mathbb{E}[u_i(\mathbf{b})] \geq\ & (\gamma/2 - \gamma^2/8)\,\text{OPT} - \gamma/2 \sum_i \mathbb{E}[a_i b_{\pi(i)}] \\ & + \left(\delta - \delta^2/4 - \gamma/2 + \gamma^2/8\right) \mathbb{E}[a_1 v_{o^{-1}(1)}] \\ & - (\delta - \gamma/2)\,\mathbb{E}[a_1 b_{\pi(1)}].\end{aligned}$$

PROOF. By the definition of the Bayes-Nash equilibrium, it holds that any bidder i can not increase her expected utility when her valuation is $v_i = x$, by deviating to any bid $b'_i < x$. We will argue about all possible slots that bidder i can be assigned to, when having valuation x and bidding b'_i. Observe that for any bid $b'_i < x$ such that $b'_i > b_{\pi(1)}$, bidder i is allocated to the first slot when bidding b'_i and pays at most $a_1 b_{\pi(1)}$. Similarly, for any bid $b'_i < x$ such that $b'_i > b_{\pi(j)}$, bidder i is allocated to slot j (or a higher one) and pays at most b'_i per click. Let A_x^{ij} denote the event that $v_i = x$ and $o(i) = j$ and B_x^{ij} denote the event that $o(i) = j$ given that $v_i = x$. Since the bid b_i maximizes the expected utility of bidder i, we have that

$$\begin{aligned}& \mathbb{E}[u_i(\mathbf{b})|v_i = x] \\ \geq\ & \mathbb{E}[u_i(b'_i, \mathbf{b}_{-i})|v_i = x] \\ =\ & \sum_{j=1}^n \mathbb{E}[u_i(b'_i, \mathbf{b}_{-i})|A_x^{ij}] \cdot \Pr[B_x^{ij}]\end{aligned}$$

$$\begin{aligned}\geq\ & a_1 \left(x - \mathbb{E}[b_{\pi(1)}|A_x^{i1}]\right) \cdot \Pr[b_{\pi(1)} < b'_i|A_x^{i1}] \cdot \Pr[B_x^{i1}] \\ & + \sum_{j=2}^n a_j \left(x - b'_i\right) \cdot \Pr[b_{\pi(j)} < b'_i|A_x^{ij}] \cdot \Pr[B_x^{ij}] \\ =\ & a_1 \left(x - \mathbb{E}[b_{\pi(1)}|A_x^{i1}]\right) \cdot \left(1 - \Pr[b_{\pi(1)} \geq b'_i|A_x^{i1}]\right) \\ & \cdot \Pr[B_x^{i1}] \\ & + \sum_{j=2}^n a_j \left(x - b'_i\right) \cdot \left(1 - \Pr[b_{\pi(j)} \geq b'_i|A_x^{ij}]\right) \cdot \Pr[B_x^{ij}].\end{aligned}$$

Using this inequality we have

$$\begin{aligned}& x\mathbb{E}[u_i(\mathbf{b})|v_i = x] \\ =\ & \int_0^x \mathbb{E}[u_i(\mathbf{b})|v_i = x]\,\mathrm{d}b'_i \\ \geq\ & a_1 \int_0^x \left(x - \mathbb{E}[b_{\pi(1)}|A_x^{i1}]\right) \cdot \left(1 - \Pr[b_{\pi(1)} \geq b'_i|A_x^{i1}]\right) \mathrm{d}b'_i \\ & \cdot \Pr[B_x^{i1}] \\ & + \sum_{j=2}^n a_j \int_0^x \left(x - b'_i\right) \cdot \left(1 - \Pr[b_{\pi(j)} \geq b'_i|A_x^{ij}]\right) \mathrm{d}b'_i \\ & \cdot \Pr[B_x^{ij}] \\ =\ & a_1 \left(x^2 - 2x\mathbb{E}[b_{\pi(1)}|A_x^{i1}] + \mathbb{E}^2[b_{\pi(1)}|A_x^{i1}]\right) \cdot \Pr[B_x^{i1}] \\ & + \sum_{j=2}^n a_j \left(\frac{x^2}{2} - x\mathbb{E}[b_{\pi(j)}|A_x^{ij}] + \frac{1}{2}\mathbb{E}[b_{\pi(j)}^2|A_x^{ij}]\right) \cdot \Pr[B_x^{ij}] \\ \geq\ & a_1 \left(x - \mathbb{E}[b_{\pi(1)}|A_x^{i1}]\right)^2 \cdot \Pr[B_x^{i1}] \\ & + \frac{1}{2}\sum_{j=2}^n a_j \left(x - \mathbb{E}[b_{\pi(j)}|A_x^{ij}]\right)^2 \cdot \Pr[B_x^{ij}],\end{aligned}$$

where the second equality holds since A_x^{i1} implies $b_{\pi(1)} \leq x$ and, hence, $\mathbb{E}[b_{\pi(1)}|A_x^{i1}] = \int_0^x \Pr[b_{\pi(1)} \geq b'_i|A_x^{i1}]\,\mathrm{d}b'_i$, and, furthermore, since $\int_0^\infty z \Pr[Z \geq z]\,\mathrm{d}z = \frac{1}{2}\mathbb{E}[Z^2]$, for any random variable Z that takes non-negative values. The second inequality holds since $\mathbb{E}[X^2] \geq \mathbb{E}^2[X]$ for any non-negative random variable X.

We will now use the above inequality and will apply Lemma 11 to its right-hand side (with $X = x$, $Y = \mathbb{E}[b_{\pi(j)}|A_x^{ij}]$ and ξ equal to γ and δ) in order to lower-bound $\mathbb{E}[u_i(\mathbf{b})|v_i = x]$. We will also exploit the fact that $x = \mathbb{E}[v_i|A_x^{ij}]$, for any $j = 1, ..., n$, when $\Pr[B_x^{ij}] > 0$. We have

$$\begin{aligned}& \mathbb{E}[u_i(\mathbf{b})|v_i = x] \\ \geq\ & \left((\delta - \delta^2/4)\,\mathbb{E}[a_1 v_i|A_x^{i1}] - \delta\mathbb{E}[a_1 b_{\pi(1)}|A_x^{i1}]\right) \cdot \Pr[B_x^{i1}] \\ & + \frac{1}{2}\sum_{j=2}^n \left((\gamma - \gamma^2/4)\,\mathbb{E}[a_j v_i|A_x^{ij}] - \gamma\mathbb{E}[a_j b_{\pi(j)}|A_x^{ij}]\right) \\ & \cdot \Pr[B_x^{ij}].\end{aligned}$$

We can now bound the unconditional expected utility of bidder i using this last inequality. We have

$$\begin{aligned}& \mathbb{E}[u_i(\mathbf{b})] \\ =\ & \int_0^\infty \mathbb{E}[u_i(\mathbf{b})|v_i = x] \cdot \Pr[v_i = x]\,\mathrm{d}x\end{aligned}$$

$$
\begin{aligned}
\geq\ & (\delta-\delta^2/4)\int_0^\infty \mathbb{E}[a_1 v_i|A_x^{i1}]\cdot\Pr[B_x^{i1}]\cdot\Pr[v_i=x]\,\mathrm{d}x\\
& -\delta\int_0^\infty \mathbb{E}[a_1 b_{\pi(1)}|A_x^{i1}]\cdot\Pr[B_x^{i1}]\cdot\Pr[v_i=x]\,\mathrm{d}x\\
& +(\gamma/2-\gamma^2/8)\\
& \cdot\sum_{j=2}^{n}\int_0^\infty \mathbb{E}[a_j v_i|A_x^{ij}]\cdot\Pr[B_x^{ij}]\cdot\Pr[v_i=x]\,\mathrm{d}x\\
& -\gamma/2\sum_{j=2}^{n}\int_0^\infty \mathbb{E}[a_j b_{\pi(j)}|A_x^{ij}]\cdot\Pr[B_x^{ij}]\cdot\Pr[v_i=x]\,\mathrm{d}x\\
=\ & (\delta-\delta^2/4)\,\mathbb{E}[a_1 v_i|o(i)=1]\cdot\Pr[o(i)=1]\\
& -\delta\mathbb{E}[a_1 b_{\pi(1)}|o(i)=1]\cdot\Pr[o(i)=1]\\
& +(\gamma/2-\gamma^2/8)\sum_{j=2}^{n}\mathbb{E}[a_j v_i|o(i)=j]\cdot\Pr[o(i)=j]\\
& -\gamma/2\sum_{j=2}^{n}\mathbb{E}[a_j b_{\pi(j)}|o(i)=j]\cdot\Pr[o(i)=j]\\
=\ & (\gamma/2-\gamma^2/8)\,\mathbb{E}[a_{o(i)}v_i]-\gamma/2\cdot\mathbb{E}[a_{o(i)}b_{\pi(o(i))}]\\
& +\left((\delta-\delta^2/4)-(\gamma/2-\gamma^2/8)\right)\\
& \cdot\mathbb{E}[a_1 v_i|o(i)=1]\cdot\Pr[o(i)=1]\\
& -(\delta-\gamma/2)\,\mathbb{E}[a_1 b_{\pi(1)}|o(i)=1]\cdot\Pr[o(i)=1],
\end{aligned}
$$

where the second equality holds since

$$
\begin{aligned}
& \int_0^\infty \mathbb{E}[Z|A_x^{ij}]\cdot\Pr[B_x^{ij}]\cdot\Pr[v_i=x]\,\mathrm{d}x\\
=\ & \mathbb{E}[Z|o(i)=j]\cdot\Pr[o(i)=j],
\end{aligned}
$$

for any non-negative random variable Z.

By summing over all bidders, we have

$$
\begin{aligned}
& \sum_i \mathbb{E}[u_i(\mathbf{b})]\\
\geq\ & (\gamma/2-\gamma^2/8)\sum_i\mathbb{E}[a_{o(i)}v_i]-\gamma/2\sum_i\mathbb{E}[a_{o(i)}b_{\pi(o(i))}]\\
& +\left((\delta-\delta^2/4)-(\gamma/2-\gamma^2/8)\right)\\
& \cdot\sum_i\mathbb{E}[a_1 v_i|o(i)=1]\cdot\Pr[o(i)=1]\\
& -(\delta-\gamma/2)\sum_i\mathbb{E}[a_1 b_{\pi(1)}|o(i)=1]\cdot\Pr[o(i)=1]\\
=\ & (\gamma/2-\gamma^2/8)\,\mathrm{OPT}-\gamma/2\sum_i\mathbb{E}[a_i b_{\pi(i)}]\\
& +(\delta-\delta^2/4-\gamma/2+\gamma^2/8)\,\mathbb{E}[a_1 v_{o^{-1}(1)}]\\
& -(\delta-\gamma/2)\,\mathbb{E}[a_1 b_{\pi(1)}],
\end{aligned}
$$

and the lemma follows. □

The next lemma provides a second lower bound on the sum of expected utilities. Its proof (omitted due to space constraints) extends the arguments in [13]. Besides the use of a technical lemma in order to relate the quantities to parameter β, a subtle (and rather surprising) technical point is that the bound is obtained by ignoring possible gains the bidders may have when allocated to the slot with the highest click-through rate. This point is crucial in order to obtain our improved bound.

LEMMA 13. *Consider a Bayes-Nash equilibrium. Then, for any $\beta>0$, it holds that*

$$
\begin{aligned}
\sum_i \mathbb{E}[u_i(\mathbf{b})]\ \geq\ & \beta(1-e^{-1/\beta})\mathrm{OPT}-\beta\sum_i\mathbb{E}[a_i b_{\pi(i)}]\\
& -\beta(1-e^{-1/\beta})\mathbb{E}[a_1 v_{o^{-1}(1)}]+\beta\mathbb{E}[a_1 b_{\pi(1)}].
\end{aligned}
$$

We are now ready to prove our main result concerning the price of anarchy for Bayes-Nash equilibria. The proof follows by appropriately taking into account the lower bounds on the sum of expected utilities that are proven in Lemmas 12 and 13.

THEOREM 14. *The price of anarchy over Bayes-Nash equilibria of GSP auction games with conservative bidders is at most 3.037.*

PROOF. Consider a Bayes-Nash equilibrium. We will use the fact that the social welfare is the sum of the expected utilities of the bidders plus the total bids paid. Let $\beta>0$, $\mu\in[0,1]$, and non-negative γ,δ and λ be parameters to be fixed later. We have

$$
\begin{aligned}
& (1+\lambda)\mathcal{W}(\mathbf{b})\\
=\ & \mu\mathbb{E}[\sum_i u_i(\mathbf{b})]+(1-\mu)\mathbb{E}[\sum_i u_i(\mathbf{b})]+\mathbb{E}[\sum_i a_i b_{\pi(i+1)}]\\
& +\lambda\mathbb{E}[\sum_i a_i v_{\pi(i)}]\\
\geq\ & \mu\mathbb{E}[\sum_i u_i(\mathbf{b})]+(1-\mu)\mathbb{E}[\sum_i u_i(\mathbf{b})]\\
& +(1+\lambda)\mathbb{E}[\sum_{i\geq 2} a_i b_{\pi(i)}]+\lambda\mathbb{E}[a_1 b_{\pi(1)}]\\
\geq\ & \mu\Bigg(\beta(1-e^{-1/\beta})\mathrm{OPT}-\beta\sum_i\mathbb{E}[a_i b_{\pi(i)}]\\
& -\beta(1-e^{-1/\beta})\mathbb{E}[a_1 v_{o^{-1}(1)}]+\beta\mathbb{E}[a_1 b_{\pi(1)}]\Bigg)\\
& +(1-\mu)\Bigg(\left(\frac{\gamma}{2}-\frac{\gamma^2}{8}\right)\mathrm{OPT}-\frac{\gamma}{2}\sum_i\mathbb{E}[a_i b_{\pi(i)}]\\
& +\left(\delta-\frac{\delta^2}{4}-\frac{\gamma}{2}+\frac{\gamma^2}{8}\right)\mathbb{E}[a_1 v_{o^{-1}(1)}]\\
& -\left(\delta-\frac{\gamma}{2}\right)\mathbb{E}[a_1 b_{\pi(1)}]\Bigg)+(1+\lambda)\mathbb{E}[\sum_{i\geq 2}a_i b_{\pi(i)}]\\
& +\lambda\mathbb{E}[a_1 b_{\pi(1)}]\\
=\ & \left(\mu\beta(1-e^{-1/\beta})+(1-\mu)\left(\frac{\gamma}{2}-\frac{\gamma^2}{8}\right)\right)\mathrm{OPT}\\
& +\left(\lambda+1-\mu\beta-(1-\mu)\frac{\gamma}{2}\right)\sum_{i\geq 2}\mathbb{E}[a_i b_{\pi(i)}]\\
& +\left((1-\mu)\left(\delta-\frac{\delta^2}{4}-\frac{\gamma}{2}+\frac{\gamma^2}{8}\right)-\mu\beta(1-e^{-1/\beta})\right)\\
& \cdot\mathbb{E}[a_1 v_{o^{-1}(1)}]+(\lambda-(1-\mu)\,\delta)\,\mathbb{E}[a_1 b_{\pi(1)}].
\end{aligned}
$$

The first inequality follows since $a_i\geq a_{i+1}$ for $i=1,...,n-1$ and $v_{\pi(i)}\geq b_{\pi(i)}$, and the second one follows by applying Lemmas 12 and 13. By setting $\lambda=0.76$, $\mu=0.2$, $\beta=5.05$, $\gamma=1.86$, and $\delta=0.95$, we have that the second, third and fourth term in the right-hand side of the above inequality are non-negative and the ratio $\mathrm{OPT}/\mathcal{W}(\mathbf{b})$ is then bounded by 3.037 as desired. □

6. OPEN PROBLEMS

Our work leaves several open problems. Still, there is a small gap between the upper and lower bounds on the price of anarchy over pure Nash equilibria. Even though we have found several weakly feasible assignments with efficiency higher than 1.259 in games with more than three bidders, none of them corresponds to a pure Nash equilibrium. So, it is interesting to prove or disprove whether the worst price of anarchy over pure Nash equilibria is obtained in GSP auction games with just three bidders. A proof of such a statement would require an explicit accounting of the bids and should not be based on weakly feasible assignments.

The case of more general equilibria is even more challenging. Here, there is no known lower bound besides the one for pure Nash equilibria. Computing tight bounds for mixed Nash, correlated, or coarse correlated equilibria are challenging open problems. Is the price of anarchy over equilibria in some of these classes worse than the price of anarchy over pure Nash equilibria? The same question applies to the Bayesian setting as well. The fact (observed in [16]) that GSP auction games are not smooth games according to the definition in [18] does not preclude a negative answer. On the positive side, our new upper bound for pure Nash equilibria might make the search for a game with a strictly worse non-pure Nash equilibrium easier.

7. REFERENCES

[1] G. Aggarwal, A. Goel, and R. Motwani. Truthful auctions for pricing search keywords. In *Proceedings of the 7th ACM Conference on Electronic Commerce (EC)*, pages 1–7, 2006.

[2] R. J. Aumann. Subjectivity and correlation in randomized strategies. *Journal of Mathematical Economics*, 1(1):67–96, 1974.

[3] K. Bhawalkar and T. Roughgarden. Welfare guarantees for combinatorial auctions with item bidding. In *Proceedings of the 22nd Annual ACM-SIAM Symposium on Discrete Algorithms (SODA)*, 2011.

[4] G. Christodoulou, A. Kovács, and M. Shapira. Bayesian combinatorial auctions. In *Proceedings of the 35th International Colloquium on Automata, Languages and Programming (ICALP)*, pages 820–832, 2008.

[5] B. Edelman, M. Ostrovsky, and M. Schwarz. Internet advertizing and the generalized second-price auction: selling billions of dollars worth of keywords. *The American Economic Review*, 97(1):242–259, 2007.

[6] R. Gomes and K. Sweeney. Bayes-Nash equilibria of the generalized second price auction. In *Proceedings of the 10th ACM Conference on Electronic Commerce (EC)*, page 107, 2009.

[7] J. C. Harsanyi. Games with incomplete information played by Bayesian players, parts i-iii. *Management Science*, 14:159–182, 330–334, 486–502, 1967-1968.

[8] E. Koutsoupias and C. H. Papadimitriou. Worst-case equilibria. In *Proceedings of the 16th Annual Symposium on Theoretical Aspects of Computer Science (STACS)*, pages 404–413, 1999.

[9] V. Krishna. *Auction Theory*. Elsevier Science, 2002.

[10] S. Lahaie. An analysis of alternative slot auction designs for sponsored search. In *Proceedings of the 7th ACM Conference on Electronic Commerce (EC)*, pages 218–227, 2006.

[11] S. Lahaie, D. Pennock, A. Saberi, and R. Vohra. Sponsored search auctions. In N. Nisan, T. Roughgarden, E. Tardos, and V. V. Vazirani, editors, *Algorithmic Game Theory*, pages 699–716. 2007.

[12] B. Lucier and A. Borodin. Price of anarchy for greedy auctions. In *Proceedings of the 21th Annual ACM-SIAM Symposium on Discrete Algorithms (SODA)*, pages 537–553, 2010.

[13] B. Lucier and R. Paes Leme. GSP auctions with correlated types. In *Proceedings of the 12th Annual ACM Conference on Electronic Commerce (EC)*, 2011. Preliminary version: Improved social welfare bounds for GSP at equilibrium. arXiv:1011.3268, 2010.

[14] H. Moulin and J. P. Vial. Strategically zero-sum games: the class of games whose completely mixed equilibria cannot be improved upon. *International Journal of Game Theory*, 7:201–221, 1978.

[15] S. Muthukrishnan. Internet ad auctions: insights and directions. In *Proceedings of the 35th International Colloquium on Automata, Languages and Programming (ICALP)*, pages 14–23, 2008.

[16] R. Paes Leme and E. Tardos. Pure and Bayes-Nash price of anarchy for generalized second price auctions. In *Proceedings of the 51st Annual IEEE Symposium on Foundations of Computer Science (FOCS)*, pages 735–744, 2010.

[17] C. H. Papadimitriou. Algorithms, games and the Internet. In *Proceedings of the 33rd Annual ACM Symposium on Theory of Computing (STOC)*, pages 749–753, 2001.

[18] T. Roughgarden. Intrinsic robustness of the price of anarchy. In *Proceedings of the 41st Annual ACM Symposium on Theory of Computing (STOC)*, pages 513–522, 2009.

[19] D. R. M. Thompson and K. Leyton-Brown. Computational analysis of perfect-information position auctions. In *Proceedings of the 10th ACM Conference on Electronic Commerce (EC)*, pages 51–60, 2009.

[20] H. Varian. Position auctions. *International Journal of Industrial Organization*, 25:1163–1178, 2007.

[21] W. Vickrey. Counterspeculation, auctions, and competitive sealed tenders. *The Journal of Finance*, 16(1):8–37, 1961.

[22] H. P. Young. *Strategic Learning and its Limits*. Oxford University Press.

Multi-Keyword Sponsored Search

Peerapong Dhangwatnotai*
Department of Computer Science, Stanford University
460 Gates Building, 353 Serra Mall, Stanford, CA
pdh@cs.stanford.edu

ABSTRACT

We investigate search engines' mechanism for allocating impressions generated from different search terms. This mechanism is equivalent to running an independent GSP auction for each search term *only* when the number of search terms is small. In practice, the number of search terms is so large that an advertiser cannot possibly communicate to the search engine all the GSP auctions that he wishes to participate in. For example, a travel agency is interested in all search terms pertaining to flight, including "flight to boston", "ticket to SFO", "cheap airfare", etc. Therefore, the search engine introduces broad match keywords as a bidding language that allows an advertiser to submit a bid for multiple GSP auctions at once. However, with broad match keywords, the GSP auctions are no longer independent, i.e. an advertiser's bid in one auction may depend on his bid in another auction.

We propose the broad match mechanism as a model that captures this aspect of the multi-keyword sponsored search mechanism. We study the performance of this mechanism under the price of anarchy (POA) framework. We identify two properties of broad match keywords, namely expressiveness and homogeneity, that characterize the POA and we prove almost tight bounds on the POA. The bounds allow us to explore trade-offs between the two properties. We introduce the exact-match-only mechanism whose performance, when compared to that of broad match mechanisms, gives us an insight into the net benefit of broad match keywords. The broad match mechanism can also be viewed as a mechanism that copes with severe communication constraint i.e. the valuation of an advertiser is described by many more numbers than the search engine can solicit.

Categories and Subject Descriptors

F.0 [**Theory of Computation**]: General; J.4 [**Computer Applications**]: Social and Behavioral Sciences—*Economics*

*Supported in part by the ONR Young Investigator Award of Tim Roughgarden.

EC'11, June 5–9, 2011, San Jose, California, USA.

General Terms

Economics, Theory

Keywords

Sponsored search, mechanism design, auctions

1. INTRODUCTION

It is important to distinguish *search terms* from *keywords* when we discuss search advertising with multiple search terms. When a user enters a *search term* into a search engine, the search engine has an opportunity to show an ad to the user by putting it alongside the user's search result. This opportunity is called an *impression*. Advertisers want to buy impressions because they are a source of traffic to their websites. Therefore, the commodity that the search engine sells to the advertisers is impression.[1] However, each advertiser values the impressions generated from certain search terms more than others.[2] Therefore, the search engine sells impressions by running a separate auction for each search term. We call the mechanism that allocates impressions generated from *all* different search terms the *multi-keyword sponsored search mechanism* (MKSS), for reasons that will become clear later. The auction that the MKSS mechanism uses to allocate impressions generated from a *specific* search term is called the *GSP auction*. The big problem with this approach is that the number of search terms that an advertiser wants is enormous e.g. every phrase that contains "android". It will take practically forever for an advertiser to communicate all the desired search terms to the search engine.

The search engine introduces keywords to deal with the large number of search terms. A keyword can be associated with multiple search terms. When an advertiser bids using a keyword, he automatically bids on all search terms associated with it. We can think of the keywords as a bidding language that allows an advertiser to bid on many search terms at once. There are two important types of keywords. A *broad match* keyword "b" is associated with all search terms deemed relevant to b by the search engine. For example, broad match keyword "apple" is associated with search

[1]Search engines may sell impressions by clicks. As long as the number of clicks per impression (CTR) for each advertiser is fixed, clicks and impressions are just different units of the same commodity.

[2]For example, Disney values impressions generated from the search term "disney" much more than those generated from "grocery" (because users who search for "disney" are more likely to follow the ad to Disney's website).

terms "apple", "apple cider", "apple iphone", "fruit", etc. In contrast, an *exact match* keyword "b" is associated with the only search term "b". One benefit of a broad match keyword is that it allows advertisers to bid on rare search terms e.g. search terms with more than 3 words. Since there are many of them, the set of such search terms cannot be communicated efficiently without broad match keywords and some would have gone wasted because of the lack of bidders.

Our understanding of the GSP auction does not extend easily to the multi-keyword sponsored search mechanism. A number of papers studied the GSP auction [7, 4, 6, 5, 20, 14, 17, 10]. All of them assume the GSP auction is run in isolation or, in other words, there is only one search term in the world. Without broad match keywords, the sponsored search mechanism is equivalent to multiple of those GSP auctions running independently. With broad match keywords, such equivalence no longer holds.[3] The performance metric that we use to study sponsored search is welfare. In this setting, it corresponds to the sum of each advertiser's value for his allocated impressions.[4] [4] showed that, under some assumptions, the welfare of every equilibrium of every GSP auction is close to the optimal. It would be nice to have an analogous theorem for the multi-keyword sponsored search mechanism.

Broad match keywords play an important role in the performance of the sponsored search mechanism. Broad match keywords can improve welfare because they allow advertisers to obtain impressions that would otherwise be wasted. Broad match keywords also have their drawbacks. For example, if we search for "blackberry preserve" on a popular search engine, we may find an ad from Research in Motion, the company that makes smartphones, at the top position. The welfare would have been greater if the search engine had allocated this impression to a jam company instead (replaced Research in Motion's ad with the jam company's ad).[5] We suspect this phenomenon occurs because Research in Motion places a bid on the broad match keyword "blackberry" which is associated with the search term "blackberry preserve". In short, broad match keywords can cause the mechanism to misallocate an impression, taking away an impression from the advertiser who values it the most and giving it to another advertiser who does not value it at all.

The communication constraint necessitates the use of broad match keywords. Since the GSP auction is not truthful, advertisers may need to continually adjust their bids to respond to others' bids. An advertiser with limited resources may find the task of adjusting one million bids every hour daunting. On the search engine side, hundreds of thousands of advertisers collectively submitting 100000000000 new bids every hour can put too much load on the server. Search engines typically place a limit on the number of keywords per advertiser, which is the same as a limit on the number of bids. We can also view this as an implementation constraint. Here's an excerpt from AdWords' documentation:

> To ensure that accounts do not place unnecessary load on our advertising servers, we ask that you keep the overall number of keywords in your account to a manageable size (typically 50,000 keywords or less).

With this contraint, broad match keywords become necessary for the advertisers and for any model of the multi-keyword sponsored search mechanism.

Our model, called the broad match mechanism, is designed to capture the effects of broad match keywords on advertiser behavior and the performance of the MKSS mechanism. In our model, each advertiser can submit a bid for each predefined keyword but the total number of keyword bids must not exceed κ. Then each advertiser's keyword bids are translated into bids on search terms. A GSP (Vickrey) auction[6] is run for each search term to allocate the corresponding impressions. To better illustrate the effects of broad match keywords, we assume that the GSP auction has only 1 slot and, while keeping the allocation rule the same, the search engine charges payment per impression. We believe these two details are not important for understanding the effects of broad match keywords and can only serve as a distraction.

There is also a theoretical motivation for studying the broad match mechanism. It is an example of a mechanism with severely constrained communication. Each advertiser has a different valuation for each search term. Since it is impossible for advertisers to communicate their valuations for every search term, it is impossible for the mechanism to obtain enough information to maximize welfare. It is also a situation when the revelation principle does not apply. It is a situation where designing the bidding language is as important as designing the mechanism. We attempt to answer the question: What makes good broad match keywords? We identify two properties of broad match keywords that characterize the upper bound on the price of anarchy of the mechanism. The two properties are expressiveness and homogeneity. They are in conflict with each other and thus it is difficult for the mechanism designer to obtain both at the same time. Therefore, the best mechanism needs to strike a balance between the two.

Our Results .

- We propose a model of the multi-keyword sponsored search mechanism, called the broad match mechanism. The model captures the interactions between advertisers in the presence of broad match keywords. It is also an example of a mechanism that copes with severe communication constraint.

- We prove almost-tight worst-case bounds on the welfare of equilibria of broad match mechanisms. We assume that the advertisers have additive valuations. While it is impossible to prove any bound on every equilibrium, even when there is only one search term[7], our bounds apply to "plausible" equilibria. Implausible equilibria are equilibria in which an advertiser

[3]When an advertiser uses a broad match keyword, he is forced to use the same bid for all GSP auctions whose search terms are associated with that keyword.

[4]Welfare also correlates with user experience. Users tend to have good experience when the right impression is matched to the right advertiser.

[5]We have been observing the sponsored search result and notice that indeed jam companies lose some impressions with this search term to Research in Motion.

[6]The GSP auction is equivalent to the Vickrey auction if there is only 1 slot.

[7]Single-item Vickrey auction is a special case of the broad match mechanism. Then consider two bidders with valuations 1 and 0 who bid 0 and 1 respectively.

plays a weakly dominated strategy. An analogy for the Vickrey auction would be when a bidder bids higher than his valuation. We identify a particular set of undominated strategies for each bidder. The bounds are parameterized by expressiveness (α) and homogeneity (c). We prove that the welfare of every pure Nash equilibrium, in which bidders play undominated strategies, in fully-expressive broad match mechanisms is at least $\frac{1}{(c^2+c)}$ times that of the welfare-maximizing allocation. This almost matches our lower bound of $\frac{4}{c^2}$ in the worst case.

- We add a flexibility for the mechanism designer to trade off expressiveness and homogeneity of the broad match mechanism. We prove that the welfare of every pure Nash equilibrium, in which bidders play undominated strategies, in broad match mechanisms with parameters (α, c) is at least $\frac{\alpha}{(c^2+c)}$ times that of the welfare-maximizing allocation.

- To weigh the net benefit of broad match keywords, we introduce the exact-match-only (EMO) mechanism, a mechanism that does not have any broad match keyword. A comparison of the price of anarchy between a broad match mechanism and an EMO mechanism can be used as a quick test to show how much broad match keywords benefit the multi-keyword sponsored search mechanism.

- We extend our bound on the price of anarchy of the EMO mechanism to subadditive valuation. EMO mechanisms corresponds to combinatorial auctions with item-bidding in [3, 15]. However, our mechanisms have an extra constraint on communication complexity. Communication constraint is parameterized by γ, the number of items an advertiser is interested in divided by the number of items that κ keywords can cover. We prove that the upper bound on the price of anarchy of EMO mechanisms degrades gracefully with parameter γ.

Related Work.

Even-Dar et al. studied the algorithmic problem of computing the utility-maximizing bid for a single bidder when there are broad match keywords [12]. Mahdian and Wang observed that after the advertisers commit to a set of keywords (but not bid amounts), the sponsored search mechanism with overlapping broad match keywords may not have an equilibrium [13]. They also gave an algorithm for computing a set of non-overlapping broad match keywords that approximate the welfare of the optimal non-overlapping broad match keywords in a setting where advertisers are not allowed to bid on exact match keywords. The main difference from our work is they assume the algorithm knows the valuations of advertisers. Kumar et al. studied the problem of allocating a large number of distinct items (impressions) to bidders whose valuations are drawn from distributions [18]. The realized valuation is more complex than what the auctioneer can elicit but the distributions are known. Singh et al. studied the setting in which the auctioneer can withhold information on the presence of some search terms [19]. They don't consider any communication restriction as each bidder can submit a different bid for every search term.

Our approach of using the price of anarchy to evaluate mechanisms without dominant strategies is similar to [3, 15, 4]. [3, 15] studied combinatorial auctions (CA) with item-bidding, which run a separate auction for each item and allow bidders to bid in every auction. The mechanism uses less communication than the complexity of bidder valuation which is subadditive in [3]. However, the number of items in our setting is much larger and so large that bidders cannot participate in every auction that they are interested in. Our work also introduces broad match keywords into the bidding language and investigates the problem of designing the mechanism with the best equilibria.

As mentioned earlier, many works focus on single search-term GSP auctions. For example, [4, 7, 16, 20, 14, 2, 17] study the revenue or the efficiency of the equilibria of single search-term GSP auctions. [5, 6] designed truthful auctions for a single search term. It is impossible to have truthful auctions in our setting with many search terms because of the communication constraint. There are models and results for multi-search-term algorithms/mechanisms but they don't consider communication requirements and thus effectively don't have keywords [8, 9, 11]. Ghosh et al. studied the algorithmic problem of bundling search terms to maximize revenue and welfare [1].

2. THE MODEL

Assume all impressions generated from the same search term are identical. We denote the group of impressions generated from the same search term j by *query* j.[8] We consider a one-period model i.e. the search engine has a set M of m queries available for sale in a given period (the number of impressions in each query is known to all parties). The number of queries m is finite but very large. There are n advertisers. Each advertiser i has a *valuation* $v_i : 2^m \rightarrow \mathbb{R}^+$ that describes his value for each subset of the queries.[9] We also define $v_i(j) = v_i(\{j\})$. We assume $v_i(\emptyset) = 0$ and $v_i(S) \leq v_i(T)$ for all $S \subseteq T$. The advertisers' valuations are additive across queries i.e. $v_i(A) = \sum_{j \in A} v_i(j)$. We will point out when our results also apply to subadditive valuations. One can see that this model is a type of combinatorial auction, which may be of independent interest. We will now use "advertiser" and "bidder" interchangeably.

Bidder i's *support* $\mathcal{S}_i$ is defined by $\mathcal{S}_i = \{j | v_i(j) > 0\}$, i.e. the set of queries for which i has positive valuation. One of the main challenges of sponsored search is some $|\mathcal{S}_i|$'s are so large that it is impossible for the bidders to communicate all $v_i(j)$'s in their supports. An allocation $X = \{X_1, X_2, ..., X_n\}$ is an assignment of queries to bidders (X_i to bidder i) such that each query is assigned to at most one bidder, i.e. $X_i \subseteq M$ and $X_i \cap X_j = \emptyset$ for all i, j. The *welfare* $SW(X)$ of an allocation X is defined as $\sum_i v_i(X_i)$. We will examine the welfare of a few mechanisms under reasonable communication requirements (which will be defined later on).

[8]Since we consider a setting with one slot and no budget, an advertiser who wins an auction for search term j will win all impressions with that search term.

[9]If we assume the number of impressions in query j (in the given period) is η, an advertiser whose value-per-click is c and click-through-rate is μ will have valuation $v_i(\{j\}) = \eta\mu c$.

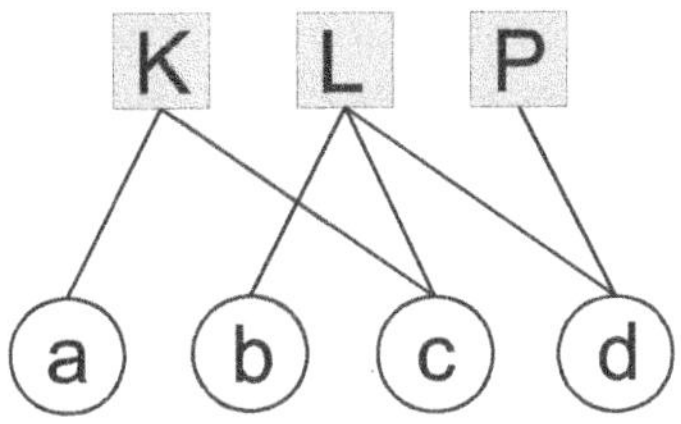

Figure 1: An example of a broad match mechanism. The queries (a,b,c,d) are shown as circles on the bottom and the keywords (K,L,P) are shown as squares. The broad match keywords are K and L. The exact match keyword is P. An advertiser who places a bid of 2 on K and 3 on L automatically bids 2 on queries a and 3 on queries b,c,d.

2.1 The Broad Match Mechanism

We propose a model of the multi-keyword sponsored search mechanism employed by popular search engines. The broad match mechanism deals with the enormous number of queries by defining sets over them. Each set is called a *keyword*. For example, keyword "apple" contains queries "apple", "apple cider", "apple iphone", etc. When an advertiser bids on a keyword, he automatically bids on all queries contained in that keyword (using the same bid amount). There are three types of keywords: exact match, phrase match and broad match. An exact match keyword b contains the only query "b". A phrase match keyword b contains all queries containing b, e.g. "a b c". A broad match keyword b contains all queries deemed relevant to b by the search engine (they can be anything). Since phrase match is just a special case of broad match, we will lump them together and call them broad match from now on. Figure 1 shows an example of a mechanism with multiple keywords.

Using set notation, we denote the set of queries that keyword A contains by A. To control communication complexity, each bidder is allowed to bid on at most κ keywords (all types combined). Let $\mathbf{b} = (b_1, b_2, ..., b_n)$ denote the bid profile where b_i is bidder i's bid vector. Denote bidder i's bid on keyword A by $b_i(A)$ and, overloading the notation, bidder i's bid on query j by $b_i(j)$, interpreting $b_i(A) = 0$ for keywords without a bid. We allow keywords to be overlapping. To resolve the bid on query j for bidder i, $b_i(j) = \max_{A:j\in A} b_i(A)$, the maximum of i's bids over all keywords containing the query j. For each query, the mechanism runs a Vickrey auction i.e. allocates query j to the highest bidder i at a price $p_i(j)$ equal to the second-highest bid $\max_{k\neq i} b_k(j)$ for that query. The following summarizes the broad match mechanism:

1. Each bidder i submits bid b_i on keywords upfront. The number of keywords A such that $b_i(A) > 0$ must be at most κ.
2. Each bidder's bid is translated into bids on queries using the formula $b_i(j) = \max_{A:j\in A} b_i(A)$.
3. For each query j, allocate the query to the bidder with the highest $b_i(j)$ and charge him the price $p_i(j) = \max_{k\neq i} b_k(j)$.

Since this broad match mechanism charges a price $p_i(j)$ for the entire search term, it is called the per-search-term model. One might want to consider a per-impression model that charges payment per impression. We present a per-impression model in section 7 and show that our analysis of this per-search-term model generalizes to the per-impression model.

Denote the queries allocated to bidder i by $X_i(\mathbf{b})$. Each bidder i wants to maximize his *utility*: $u_i(X_i(\mathbf{b}), b_{-i}) = \sum_{j\in X_i(b)} v_i(j) - p_i(j)$.

As mentioned in the introduction, no welfare guarantee is possible if a bidder uses an unreasonable bid. We refine the bidders' strategy spaces using the concept of undominated strategy. We say bidder i's bid vector b_i *weakly dominates* b'_i if for all bid profiles b_{-i} of the other bidders, $u_i(X_i(b_i, b_{-i}), b_{-i}) \geq u_i(X_i(b'_i, b_{-i}), b_{-i})$, where (b'_i, b_{-i}) denotes the bid profile when bidder i bids b'_i and all other bidders bid according to $\mathbf{b}$. For the rest of this paper, we restrict the strategy space of each bidder to a set of undominated strategies. The strategy space D_i of bidder i is the set of bid vectors b_i such that 1) the number of keywords A with $b_i(A) > 0$ is at most κ and 2) for every keyword A, there exists a query $j \in A$ such that $b_i(A) \leq v_i(j)$. The bid vectors outside of D_i are unreasonable in the sense that they overbid on every single query associated with some keyword. Observe that for every bid vector $b'_i \notin D_i$, there exists a bid vector in D_i that weakly dominates it and this transition is polynomial-time computable.

2.2 The Bidding Game

Players generally have no dominant strategies in this mechanism. Therefore, we analyze the performance of this mechanism by looking at its equilibria. Let $\mathbf{v} = \{v_1, v_2, ..., v_n\}$ denote the fixed valuation profile of the bidders. A bid profile $\mathbf{b} = \{b_1, b_2, ..., b_n\}$ is a *pure Nash equilibrium* if $u_i(\mathbf{b}) \geq u_i(b'_i, b_{-i})$ for every player i and b'_i. Note that any Nash equilibrium in which bidders use strategies in $D = \{D_i\}$ is also a Nash equilibrium without any strategy-space restriction.

Let $OPT(\mathbf{v})$ denote the optimal allocation, i.e. $OPT(\mathbf{v}) = argmax_X SW(X)$. The *pure price of anarchy* (POA) is the ratio between the welfare of the optimal allocation and the welfare of the worst pure Nash equilibrium:

$$\text{pure POA} = \max_{\mathbf{b}:\text{ a pure Nash eq.}} \frac{SW(OPT(\mathbf{v}))}{SW(\mathbf{b})}$$

where we define $SW(\mathbf{b}) = SW(X(\mathbf{b}))$.

As is standard in Nash equilibrium analysis, our setting is a full-information setting. That is every bidder knows all the information necessary to compute the payoff matrix, including every bidder's valuation. The search engine (auctioneer) needs not know anything about bidder valuations.

3. HOMOGENEOUS KEYWORDS

We begin by showing that the performance of broad match mechanisms can be parameterized by a property of the keywords, called homogeneity. When a bidder uses broad match keywords, the mechanism loses some information about the bidder's valuation. This loss can be minimized by designing only keywords that, in the bidders' perspectives, group similar queries. We conceptualize this notion in the following definition.

Definition 3.1 (Homogeneity)
A keyword A is *c-homogeneous* if for every bidder i and every two queries $q_1,q_2 \in A$, $v_i(q_1) \le c \cdot v_i(q_2)$.

By definition, exact match keywords are 1-homogeneous. Note that valuations of different bidders for the same query can still differ greatly.

Recall that the number of keyword bids is limited for each bidder. Therefore, in order to provide any welfare guarantee, the keywords must have good coverage of the bidders' valuations.

Definition 3.2 A set K of keywords is said to be *fully expressive* if for every bidder i, it is always possible to simultaneously bid on every query in $\mathcal{S}_i$ using at most κ keywords from K.

Definition 3.3 A broad match mechanism is said to be *fully expressive* if the set of all keywords in the mechanism is fully expressive.

Now we will prove a bound of c^2+c on the price of anarchy for broad match mechanisms. The main technique is to use each bidder's equilibrium condition to bound the optimal welfare by prices, which, in turns, are bounded by the welfare of the equilibrium. The main challenge is that the limited number of keywords requires the bidder to drop one of the current keyword bids before he can bid on a new keyword. This adds to the equilibrium condition a switching cost, which works against our bound. We limit the total switching cost by using only κ equilibrium conditions per bidder. The limited number of equilibrium conditions means we need to carefully choose deviation bids to obtain the desirable bound.

Theorem 3.4 *For every fully-expressive broad match mechanism with c-homogeneous keywords and at least one pure Nash equilibrium, the pure POA is at most c^2+c.*

PROOF. Let $SW(\mathbf{b})$ denote the welfare of a pure Nash equilibrium. Let $OPT(\mathbf{v}) = \{O_1, O_2, ..., O_n\}$ denote the welfare-maximizing allocation. WLOG, we assume that $O_i \subseteq \mathcal{S}_i$. We have that $SW(OPT(\mathbf{v})) = \sum_i \sum_{j\in O_i} v_i(j)$. We will show that $SW(OPT(\mathbf{v})) \le (c^2+c)SW(\mathbf{b})$.

Fix a bidder i. Consider the set of queries $Q = O_i \backslash X_i(\mathbf{b})$. Let $h(q)$ denote the highest bidder other than i for query $q \in Q$, i.e. $b_{h(q)}(q) = p_i(q)$. Let K_i be the set of keywords on which bidder i is currently bidding. Since the mechanism is fully-expressive, there exists a set of at most κ keywords $K'_i = \{A_1, A_2, A_3, ...\}$ such that $Q \subseteq \bigcup_{A\in K'_i} A$ (K'_i covers all queries in Q). Now we assign each query in Q to a keyword in K'_i. Let $A_k(Q)$ denote $Q \cap (A_k \backslash \bigcup_{i=1}^{k-1} A_i)$.

Next we consider a particular deviation for i. Consider a keyword $A \in K'_i$ and the set $A(Q)$, dropping the subscript for succinctness. Order the queries $q_1, q_2, ..., q_l \in A(Q)$ so that $p_i(q_1) \le p_i(q_2) \le ... \le p_i(q_l)$. Let t be the largest integer such that $\frac{1}{c}v_i(q_t) > p_i(q_t)$. Let b_i^A be the bid vector obtained by 1) removing a keyword bid from b_i if b_i has κ keyword bids, and 2) setting the keyword bid $b_i^A(A)$ to $p_i(q_t)$. Observe that b_i^A is in i's undominated strategies. Let $\sigma(A)$ denote the keyword bid that is removed when b_i^A is constructed from b_i ($\sigma(A)$ is a dummy keyword $\emptyset$ if no keyword bid is removed). We choose the removed bids so that $\sigma(A)$ is unique for each A (this is possible because $|K'_i| \le \kappa$). Let $W = X_i(b_i, b_{-i})$. Consider bidder i switching his bid vector from b_i to b_i^A. Let $W' = X_i(b_i^A, b_{-i})$. The equilibrium condition implies $\sum_{j\in W} v_i(j) - p_i(j) \ge \sum_{j\in W'} v_i(j) - p_i(j)$.

Let $U_i^A = \sum_{j\in W\backslash W'} v_i(j) - p_i(j)$ (the switching cost). Since the price that a bidder pays is independent of his bids, $p_i(j)$ remains the same for $j \in W \cap W'$. Canceling out the terms with $j \in W \cap W'$, we have

$$
\begin{aligned}
U_i^A &\ge \sum_{j\in W'\backslash W} v_i(j) - p_i(j) \\
&\ge \sum_{r=1}^{t} v_i(q_r) - p_i(q_r) + \sum_{j\in (W'\backslash W)\backslash Q} v_i(j) - p_i(j) \\
&\ge \sum_{r=1}^{t} v_i(q_r) - p_i(q_r) + \sum_{j\in (W'\backslash W)\backslash Q} \frac{1}{c} v_i(q_t) - p_i(q_t)
\end{aligned}
$$

We obtain the second inequality by separating the terms with queries in Q from the other terms and noting that i wins only queries with $p_i(j) \le p_i(q_t)$. The last inequality comes from the assumption that keywords are homogeneous and the fact that $p_i(j)$ is at most the bid of $p_i(q_t)$. Next we drop the terms $\sum \frac{1}{c}v_i(q_t) - p_i(q_t)$, using the fact that they are positive.

$$U_i^A + \sum_{r=1}^{t} p_i(q_r) \ge \sum_{r=1}^{t} v_i(q_r) \tag{1}$$

$$U_i^A + \sum_{r=1}^{t} p_i(q_r) + \sum_{r=t+1}^{l} p_i(q_r) \ge \sum_{r=1}^{t} v_i(q_r) + \sum_{r=t+1}^{l} \frac{1}{c} v_i(q_r) \tag{2}$$

$$c \cdot U_i^A + c \cdot \sum_{r=1}^{l} p_i(q_r) \ge \sum_{r=1}^{l} v_i(q_r) \tag{3}$$

$$c \cdot U_i^A + c^2 \cdot \sum_{r=1}^{l} v_{h(q_r)}(q_r) \ge \sum_{r=1}^{l} v_i(q_r) \tag{4}$$

$$c \cdot U_i^A + c^2 \sum_{j\in A(Q)} v_{h(j)}(j) \ge \sum_{j\in A(Q)} v_i(j) \tag{5}$$

We obtain (2) using the fact that $\frac{1}{c}v_i(q_r) \le p_i(q_r)$ for all $r > t$. Inequality (4) uses the assumption that $p_i(q_r) = b_{h(q_r)}(q_r)$ is in undominated strategies (of bidder $h(q_r)$), which implies there exists a keyword A and a query $j \in A$ such that $q_r \in A$ and $b_{h(q_r)}(q_r) = b_{h(q_r)}(A) \le v_{h(q_r)}(j)$; then the homogeneity of keyword A implies $v_{h(q_r)}(j) \le c \cdot v_{h(q_r)}(q_r)$.

Now we bound the total switching cost $\sum_{A\in K'_i} U_i^A$ by the total welfare of bidder i. Recall that $U_i^A = \sum_{j\in W\backslash W'} v_i(j) - p_i(j)$ which implies

$$U_i^A \le \sum_{j\in W\backslash W'} v_i(j) = \sum_{j\in X_i(b_i,b_{-i})\backslash X_i(b_i^A,b_{-i})} v_i(j).$$

Summing both sides over $A \in K'_i$, we have

$$\sum_{A\in K_i'} U_i^A \leq \sum_{A\in K_i'} \sum_{j\in X_i(b_i,b_{-i})\setminus X_i(b_i^A,b_{-i})} v_i(j) \qquad (6)$$

Let $\delta(A)$ denote the set of queries that bidder i would lose if he drops his bid on keyword A. The set $X_i(b_i, b_{-i})\setminus X_i(b_i^A, b_{-i})$ is precisely $\delta(\sigma(A))$. Using the fact that $\sigma(A) \in K_i$ and the fact that $\sigma(A)$'s are distinct, we have

$$\sum_{A\in K_i'} U_i^A \leq \sum_{A\in K_i'} \sum_{j\in\delta(\sigma(A))} v_i(j) \qquad (7)$$

$$\leq \sum_{A\in K_i} \sum_{j\in\delta(A)} v_i(j) \qquad (8)$$

Since bidder i can lose a query j only if he drops his bid on the keyword $argmax_{A:j\in A} b_i(A)$, for every two distinct keywords $A, B \in K_i$, the sets $\delta(A)$ and $\delta(B)$ are disjoint. Therefore, $\sum_{A\in K_i}\sum_{j\in\delta(A)} v_i(j) \leq \sum_{j\in X_i(b_i,b_{-i})} v_i(j)$ and thus

$$\sum_{A\in K_i'} U_i^A \leq \sum_{j\in X_i(b_i,b_{-i})} v_i(j) \qquad (9)$$

Summing both sides of inequality (5) over $A \in K_i'$ and applying inequality (9), we have

$$\sum_{j\in Q} v_i(j) \leq c\cdot \sum_{j\in X_i(\mathbf{b})} v_i(j) + c^2 \sum_{j\in Q} v_{h(j)}(j)$$

$$\sum_{j\in O_i\setminus X_i(\mathbf{b})} v_i(j) \leq c\cdot \sum_{j\in X_i(\mathbf{b})} v_i(j) + c^2 \sum_{j\in O_i\setminus X_i(\mathbf{b})} v_{h(j)}(j) \qquad (10)$$

Then summing both sides over i, adding $\sum_i \sum_{j\in O_i\cap X_i(\mathbf{b})} v_i(j)$ to the left and adding $c^2\sum_i \sum_{j\in O_i\cap X_i(\mathbf{b})} v_i(j)$ to the right yields

$$\sum_i \left(\sum_{j\in O_i\setminus X_i(\mathbf{b})} v_i(j) + \sum_{j\in O_i\cap X_i(\mathbf{b})} v_i(j) \right) \leq c\cdot\sum_i \sum_{j\in X_i(\mathbf{b})} v_i(j) + c^2 \sum_i \left(\sum_{j\in O_i\setminus X_i(\mathbf{b})} v_{h(j)}(j) + \sum_{j\in O_i\cap X_i(\mathbf{b})} v_i(j) \right)$$

$$SW(OPT(\mathbf{v})) \leq c\cdot SW(\mathbf{b}) + c^2 \cdot SW(\mathbf{b})$$

Rearranging the terms yields the POA of $c^2 + c$. □

4. THE LOWERBOUND

In this section, we show that the bound given by theorem 3.4 is almost tight. Consider the following broad match setting (see figure 2). There are c bidders, namely $0, 1, ..., c-1$. There are $c-1$ queries, namely $b_1, b_2, ..., b_{c-1}$. The only keyword is $A = \{b_1, b_2, ..., b_{c-1}\}$. $v_0(b_1) = c, v_0(b_j) = 1, \forall j > 1$. For each $i > 0$, $v_i(b_i) = \frac{1}{2}c^2$ and $v_i(b_j) = \frac{1}{2}c$ for all $j \neq i$. There is a pure Nash equilibrium where bidder 0 bids c on keyword A and the other bidders bid nothing. The welfare of this equilibrium is $c+c-2$. The optimal welfare is $\frac{1}{2}c^2(c-1)$, which results from the allocation: $X_0 = \emptyset, X_i = \{b_i\}$. Hence the pure POA is at least $\frac{1}{4}c^2$.

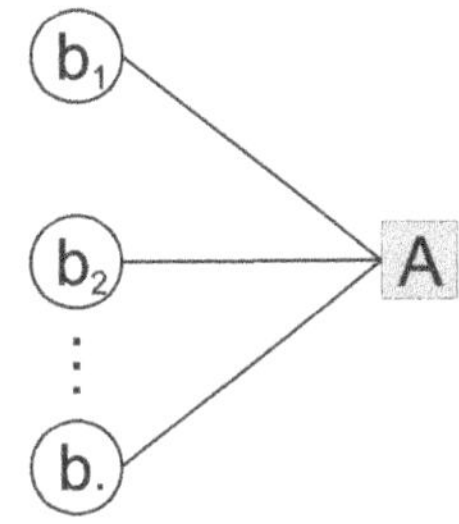

Figure 2: An example with POA at least $\frac{1}{4}c^2$. Queries are $b_1, b_2, ..., b_{c-1}$ and the keyword is A.

Theorem 4.1 *There exists a fully-expressive broad match mechanism with c-homogeneous keywords such that its pure POA is at least* $\frac{1}{4}c^2$.

5. THE EXPRESSIVENESS-HOMOGENEITY TRADE-OFF

In this section, we tackle the mechanism design problem: How to design keywords for a broad match mechanism? As shown in the previous two sections, the designer wants the keywords to be homogeneous and fully-expressive. However, designing such keywords can be difficult or even impossible, given the constraint on κ, the number of keyword bids. Note that it is easy to design keywords that are fully-expressive but not necessarily homogeneous: create 1 keyword that contains all queries in the universe. It is also easy to design keywords that are 1-homogeneous but not necessarily expressive: for every query j, create a keyword $J = \{j\}$. That leads us to explore the trade-off between the two properties. The best mechanism probably lies between those two extremes. First, we define semi-expressiveness.

Definition 5.1 A set L of keywords is *α-expressive* if for every bidder i and every set $Q \subseteq \mathcal{S}_i$ of queries such that $|Q| \leq \lceil\alpha|\mathcal{S}_i|\rceil$, there exists a set $K \subseteq L$ such that $|K| \leq \kappa$ and $Q \subseteq \bigcup_{A\in K} A$.

We say a broad match mechanism is *α-expressive* if the set of all keywords in the mechanism is α-expressive. We can show that the upper bound on the POA of broad match mechanisms is a function of α and c.

Theorem 5.2 *For every α-expressive broad match mechanism with c-homogeneous keywords and at least one pure Nash equilibrium, the pure POA is at most* $\frac{1}{\alpha}(c^2 + c)$.

This bound advises us that when we introduce a set of new broad match keywords that improves expressiveness by a factor of x, the homogeneity constant of the keywords should not increase by more than a factor of $\sqrt{x}$.

Note that the mechanism designer does not need to know bidder valuation in order to design broad match keywords. For homogeneity, the designer only needs to know the relative valuations of a bidder for different queries. For example, it is enough to know that advertisers value "sneakers" and "running shoes" roughly the same to create a keyword for them. For expressiveness, the designer only needs to know the set of queries that each bidder is interested in (queries with positive valuation).

The proof of theorem 5.2 combines the arguments in the proof of theorem 3.4 with the next lemma.

Lemma 5.3 *For every constant $0 \leq \alpha \leq 1$, every additive valuation v and every set T, there exists a set $T' \subseteq T$ of size at most $\lceil \alpha |T| \rceil$ such that $v(T') \geq \alpha v(T)$.*

PROOF. Rename the elements in $T = \{1, 2, ...\}$ so that $v(1) \geq v(2) \geq v(3) \geq ....$ Let $T' = \{1, 2, ..., \lceil \alpha |T| \rceil\}$. If $v(T') \geq \alpha v(T)$, we are done. Suppose not. That means $v(\lceil \alpha |T| \rceil) < \frac{\alpha v(T)}{\lceil \alpha |T| \rceil}$. Let $S = T \backslash T'$. Then $v(S) \leq \frac{\alpha v(T)}{\lceil \alpha |T| \rceil}(|T| - \lceil \alpha |T| \rceil)$. That implies $v(T') + v(S) < \alpha v(T) + \frac{\alpha v(T)}{\lceil \alpha |T| \rceil}(|T| - \lceil \alpha |T| \rceil) = \alpha v(T) \left(\frac{|T|}{\lceil \alpha |T| \rceil} \right) \leq v(T)$. Contradiction to the assumption that v is additive. □

Now we modify the proof of theorem 3.4 to obtain the proof of theorem 5.2.

Proof of Theorem 5.2: Using the same notation, the welfare-maximizing allocation is $\{O_1, O_2, ..., O_n\}$. WLOG, assume $O_i \subseteq S_i$. By lemma 5.3, there exists a set $O'_i \subseteq O_i$ such that $|O'_i| \leq \lceil \alpha |O_i| \rceil$ and $v_i(O'_i) \geq \alpha v_i(O_i)$. Then we redefine Q in the original proof as $Q = O'_i \backslash X_i(\mathbf{b})$. We redefine K'_i using the new definition of expressiveness. By the assumption that the mechanism is α-expressive, there exists a set of keywords K'_i such that $|K'_i| \leq \kappa$ and $Q \subseteq O'_i \subseteq \bigcup_{A \in K'_i} A$. Then we proceed as in the original proof. Inequality (10) becomes

$$\sum_{j \in O'_i \backslash X_i(\mathbf{b})} v_i(j) \leq c \cdot \sum_{j \in X_i(\mathbf{b})} v_i(j) + c^2 \sum_{j \in O'_i \backslash X_i(\mathbf{b})} v_{h(j)}(j)$$

Summing both sides over i, adding $\sum_i \sum_{j \in O'_i \cap X_i(\mathbf{b})} v_i(j)$ to the left and adding $c^2 \sum_i \sum_{j \in O'_i \cap X_i(\mathbf{b})} v_i(j)$ to the right yields

$$\sum_i \left(\sum_{j \in O'_i \backslash X_i(\mathbf{b})} v_i(j) + \sum_{j \in O'_i \cap X_i(\mathbf{b})} v_i(j) \right) \leq c \cdot \sum_i \sum_{j \in X_i(\mathbf{b})} v_i(j)$$

$$+ c^2 \sum_i \left(\sum_{j \in O'_i \backslash X_i(\mathbf{b})} v_{h(j)}(j) + \sum_{j \in O'_i \cap X_i(\mathbf{b})} v_i(j) \right)$$

Combining the terms, we have $\sum_i v_i(O'_i) \leq c \cdot SW(\mathbf{b}) + c^2 \cdot SW(\mathbf{b})$. Using the fact that $v_i(O'_i) \geq \alpha v_i(O_i)$, we obtain $\alpha SW(OPT(\mathbf{v})) \leq c \cdot SW(\mathbf{b}) + c^2 \cdot SW(\mathbf{b})$. Therefore,

$$SW(OPT(\mathbf{v})) \leq \frac{1}{\alpha}(c^2 + c) SW(\mathbf{b}).$$

■

We note one special case, when the mechanism does not have any broad match keyword.

Definition 5.4 (EMO mechanism)

The *exact-match-only* mechanism is a broad match mechanism that has one exact match keyword $J = \{j\}$ for each query j and no other keywords.

All keywords in EMO mechanisms are 1-homogeneous. Let $\rho = max_i |S_i|$ and $\gamma = \rho / \kappa$. By observing that an EMO mechanism is $\frac{1}{\gamma}$-expressive, we have the following corollary.

Corollary 5.5 *For every EMO mechanism that limits the number of keyword bids to κ, the pure POA is at most 2γ.*

For example, if every advertiser has a positive valuation for at most 500,000 queries and the EMO mechanism limits the number of keyword bids to 50,000, the pure POA of this mechanism is at most 20.

6. AN EXTENSION TO SUBADDITIVE VALUATION

In this section, we generalize our bound for EMO mechanisms to cover subadditive valuation. A valuation v is *subadditive* if for all subsets $S_1, S_2, ..., S_k$ of the queries, $v(S_1 \cup S_2 \cup ... \cup S_k) \leq v(S_1) + v(S_2) + ... + v(S_k)$. Define the strategy space D_i of each bidder i to be the set of bid vectors b_i such that 1) the number of keywords A with $b_i(A) > 0$ is at most κ and 2) $\sum_{j \in S} b_i(j) \leq v_i(S)$ for every set S of queries. In short, D_i corresponds to the set of bid vectors that don't overbid on any subset of queries. The next lemma, which is proven by [3], implies that for every bid vector $b'_i \notin D_i$, there exists a bid vector in D_i that weakly dominates it.

Lemma 6.1 *Let O be a set of at most κ queries and $p(j)$ be a price for the query $j \in O$. Let v_i be a subadditive valuation of bidder i. There is a bid vector $b_i \in D_i$ such that $b_i(j) = 0$ for all $j \notin O$ and*

$$v_i(S) - \sum_{j \in S} p(j) \geq v_i(O) - \sum_{j \in O} p(j)$$

where $S = \{j \in O : b_i(j) \geq p(j)\}$.

We can think of $v_i(S) - \sum_{j \in S} p(j)$ as the utility of bidder i from bidding b_i against prices p induced by the bids of other bidders.

Unfortunately, lemma 5.3 does not hold for subadditive valuation but we can show that it holds when the requirements are slightly relaxed.

Lemma 6.2 *For every constant $0 < \alpha \leq 1$, every subadditive valuation v and every set T, there exists a set $T' \subseteq T$ such that*

$$|T'| \leq \lceil \alpha |T| \rceil \quad \textit{and} \quad v(T') \geq \frac{1}{\lceil \frac{1}{\alpha} \rceil} v(T).$$

PROOF. Let $a = \lceil \frac{1}{\alpha} \rceil$. Divide T arbitrarily into a sets of size at most $\lceil \alpha |T| \rceil$ and name them $S_1, ..., S_a$. By the subadditivity of v, $\sum_{i=1}^{a} v(S_i) \geq v(T)$. That implies $\frac{1}{a} \sum_{i=1}^{a} v(S_i) \geq \frac{1}{a} v(T)$. There must be at least one set $S_i \in \{S_1, S_2, ..., S_a\}$ such that $v(S_i) \geq \frac{1}{a} \sum_{i=1}^{a} v(S_i) \geq \frac{1}{a} v(T)$. □

We keep the same definition for ρ and γ.

Theorem 6.3 *For every EMO mechanism that has only bidders with subadditive valuations and a limit of κ on the number of keyword bids, the pure POA is at most $2 \lceil \gamma \rceil$.*

PROOF. Denote the welfare-maximizing allocation by $O = \{O_1, O_2, ..., O_n\}$. WLOG, assume $O_i \subseteq S_i$. Let $\mathbf{b}$ denote an equilibrium bid profile. Let $\alpha = \frac{1}{\gamma}$. Consider bidder i. According to lemma 6.2, there exists a set of queries $Q_i \subseteq O_i$

such that $|Q_i| \leq \lceil \alpha |O_i| \rceil$ and $v_i(Q_i) \geq \frac{1}{\lceil \gamma \rceil} v_i(O_i)$. Observe that $|Q_i| \leq \kappa$. Now we will invoke lemma 6.1, by letting $p(j)$ be the price of query j for bidder i when the other bidders bid b_{-i}. By lemma 6.1, there exists a bid vector $b'_i \in D_i$ such that $b'_i(j) = 0$ for all $j \notin Q_i$ and

$$v_i(X_i(b'_i, b_{-i})) - \sum_{j \in X_i(b'_i, b_{-i})} p_i(j) \geq v_i(Q_i) - \sum_{j \in Q_i} p_i(j).$$

Consider bidder i switching his bid from b_i to b'_i. Denote bidder i's utility in the equilibrium by u_i. The equilibrium condition gives

$$\begin{aligned} u_i &\geq v_i(X_i(b'_i, b_{-i})) - \sum_{j \in X_i(b'_i, b_{-i})} p_i(j) \\ &\geq v_i(Q_i) - \sum_{j \in Q_i} p_i(j) \\ &\geq \frac{1}{\lceil \gamma \rceil} v_i(O_i) - \sum_{j \in Q_i} p_i(j) \end{aligned}$$

Summing both sides over i, we have

$$\begin{aligned} \sum_i u_i &\geq \frac{1}{\lceil \gamma \rceil} \sum_i v_i(O_i) - \sum_i \sum_{j \in Q_i} p_i(j) \\ &\geq \frac{1}{\lceil \gamma \rceil} SW(OPT(\mathbf{v})) - \sum_i \sum_{j \in Q_i} p_i(j) \\ &\geq \frac{1}{\lceil \gamma \rceil} SW(OPT(\mathbf{v})) - \sum_i \sum_{j \in X_i(\mathbf{b})} b_i(j) \\ &\geq \frac{1}{\lceil \gamma \rceil} SW(OPT(\mathbf{v})) - \sum_i v_i(X_i(\mathbf{b})) \end{aligned}$$

The third inequality comes from the fact that the price of an item is at most the bid of the winner. The last inequality uses the assumption that $b_i \in D_i$. Applying the fact that $SW(\mathbf{b}) \geq \sum_i u_i$, $SW(\mathbf{b}) \geq \sum_i v_i(X_i(\mathbf{b}))$, and rearranging the terms, we have

$$SW(\mathbf{b}) \geq \frac{1}{2\lceil \gamma \rceil} SW(OPT(\mathbf{v}))$$

□

7. THE PER-IMPRESSION BROAD MATCH MECHANISM

In this section, we analyze a per-impression variant of the broad match mechanism. The main difference between the model in section 2 and the per-impression model is that in the latter, the number of impressions for each search term is made explicit. As a result, we can explicitly model each bidder's valuation per impression. This leads to a more practical definition of homogeneity, which now operates on value-per-impression (rather than value-per-search-term in section 2). Despite this fundamental difference, their analyses are syntactically very similar and our bound on the POA for the per-impression mechanism mirrors that of the per-search-term mechanism.

7.1 The Per-impression Model

There are n bidders and m search terms. For each search term j, the search engine (auctioneer) has η_j impressions for sale. Bidder i has valuation $v_i(j)$ for each impression of search term j. The bidders' valuations are additive across impressions. An allocation is an assignment of impressions to bidders such that each impression is assigned to at most one bidder. The per-impression broad match mechanism is defined as follows

1. Each bidder i submits bid b_i on keywords upfront. The number of keywords A such that $b_i(A) > 0$ must be at most κ.

2. Each bidder's bid is translated into bids on search terms using the formula $b_i(j) = \max_{A: j \in A} b_i(A)$.

3. For each search term j, for each impression generated from j, allocate the impression to the bidder with the highest $b_i(j)$ and charge him the price $p_i(j) = \max_{k \neq i} b_k(j)$.

Note that this mechanism always allocates all impressions from the same search term to the same bidder. The optimal (welfare-maximizing) allocation assigns each impression from search term j to the bidder i with the highest $v_i(j)$. Therefore, our analysis deals only with allocations that assign all impressions from the same search term to the same bidder. Denote an allocation by $X = \{X_1, X_2, ..., X_n\}$ where X_i is the set of search terms that go to bidder i. Given a set of search terms T, we define $v_i(T) = \sum_{j \in T} \eta_j v_i(j)$. The *welfare* $SW(X)$ of an allocation X is defined as $\sum_i \sum_{j \in X_i} \eta_j v_i(j)$. The utility of bidder i is $\sum_{j \in X_i(b)} \eta_j (v_i(j) - p_i(j))$. We restrict the strategy space of each bidder i to D_i which is defined the same way as before.

One can view the previous per-search-term mechanism as a special case of the per-impression mechanism where $\eta_j = 1$ for all j.

7.2 The Upper Bound on the POA

In this model, we use value-per-impression in the definition of homogeneity.

Definition 7.1 A keyword B is c-homogeneous if for every bidder i and every two search terms $j_1, j_2 \in B$, $v_i(j_1) \leq c \cdot v_i(j_2)$.

The support of a bidder is defined as in section 2 except it is done in terms of search terms instead of queries. The definition of α-expressiveness remains the same. We have a lemma similar to lemma 5.3.

Lemma 7.2 *For every constant $0 \leq \alpha \leq 1$, every additive valuation v and every set T of search terms, there exists a set $T' \subseteq T$ of size at most $\lceil \alpha T \rceil$ such that $v(T') \geq \alpha v(T)$.*

We have an upper bound on the POA similar to theorem 5.2.

Theorem 7.3 *For every α-expressive broad match mechanism with c-homogeneous keywords and at least one pure Nash equilibrium, the pure POA is at most $\frac{1}{\alpha}(c^2 + c)$.*

Since the proof is very similar to the proof of theorem 5.2, we present here a proof sketch.

Proof (sketch): We use the same notations as in the proof of theorem 5.2 except the queries are now search terms. The equilibrium condition implies

$$U_i^A \geq \sum_{j \in W' \setminus W} \eta_j (v_i(j) - p_i(j))$$

Then we proceed as before except we now have η_j in the terms involving $v_i(j)$ and $p_i(j)$. Whenever we use the fact that $\frac{1}{c} v_i(q_t) > p_i(q_t)$, we substitute it with $\frac{1}{c}\eta_j v_i(q_t) > \eta_j p_i(q_t)$. Then we have (compared to inequality (5))

$$c \cdot U_i^A + c^2 \sum_{j \in A(Q)} \eta_j v_{h(j)}(j) \geq \sum_{j \in A(Q)} \eta_j v_i(j)$$

We can bound the total switching cost and combine it with the above inequality as before. Then we have

$$\sum_{j \in O_i' \setminus X_i(\mathbf{b})} \eta_j v_i(j) \leq c \sum_{j \in X_i(\mathbf{b})} \eta_j v_i(j) + c^2 \sum_{j \in O_i' \setminus X_i(\mathbf{b})} \eta_j v_{h(j)}(j)$$

We conclude the proof by summing both sides over i and following similar syntactic manipulations as in the proof of theorem 5.2. ■

8. CONCLUSION

Broad match keywords are a crucial part of search advertising. Our tight bounds on the price of anarchy of broad match mechanisms suggest that the performance of the multi-keyword sponsored search mechanism depends heavily on the design of each broad match keyword (the set of queries it is associated with). Our parameterization of the upper bound on the price of anarchy by expressiveness and homogeneity gives the mechanism designer a flexible design space that ranges from no broad match keyword to a fully-expressive bidding language.

Another useful design choice is to personalize keywords for advertisers. That is to create keywords that are exclusive to each advertiser. We believe that this is happening the in the industry. Our model can be easily modified to allow such keywords by changing the definition of homogeneity to bind only for the advertisers who can bid on them, and our bounds will remain the same.

Our work suggests a number of interesting open questions. First, is it possible to generalize theorem 3.4 to subadditive valuation? Second, broad match keywords are just one way to design the bidding language. What else can we do? Third, since we cannot make the assumption that a GSP auction for a search term is independent from GSP auctions for other search terms, we might as well not use them. What are other alternative mechanisms for allocating impressions for *all* different search terms?

Acknowledgments

We thank Tim Roughgarden and anonymous reviewers for helpful comments.

9. REFERENCES

[1] A. Ghosh, H. Nazerzadeh, and M. Sundararajan. Computing Optimal Bundles for Sponsored Search. In *WINE*, pages 576-583, 2007.

[2] A. Ghosh and A. Sayedi. Expressive auctions for externalities in online advertising. In *WWW*, pages 371-380, 2010.

[3] K. Bhawalkar and T. Roughgarden. Welfare Guarantees for Combinatorial Auctions with Item Bidding. In *SODA*, 2011.

[4] B. Lucier and Renato Paes Leme. Improved Social Welfare Bounds for GSP at Equilibrium. *CoRR abs*, 1011.3268, 2010.

[5] G. Aggarwal, S. Muthukrishnan, D. Pál, and M. Pál. General auction mechanism for search advertising. In *WWW*, pages 241-250, 2009.

[6] G. Aggarwal, A. Goel, and R. Motwani. Truthful auctions for pricing search keywords. *ACM Conference on Electronic Commerce*, pages 1-7, 2006.

[7] B. Edelman, M. Ostrovsky, and M. Schwarz. Internet advertising and the generalized second price auction: Selling billions of dollars worth of keywords. *American Economic Review*, 97(1), pages 242–259, 2007.

[8] G. Goel and A. Mehta: Online budgeted matching in random input models with applications to Adwords. In *SODA*, pages 982-991, 2008.

[9] C. Borgs, J. T. Chayes, N. Immorlica, K. Jain, O. Etesami, and M. Mahdian. Dynamics of bid optimization in online advertisement auctions. In *WWW*, pages 531-540, 2007

[10] D. J. Martin, J. Gehrke, and J. Y. Halpern. Toward Expressive and Scalable Sponsored Search Auctions. In *ICDE*, pages 237-246, 2008.

[11] P. Rusmevichientong and D. P. Williamson: An adaptive algorithm for selecting profitable keywords for search-based advertising services. *ACM Conference on Electronic Commerce*, pages 260-269, 2006.

[12] E. Even-Dar, V. S. Mirrokni, S. Muthukrishnan, Y. Mansour, and U. Nadav. Bid optimization for broad match ad auctions. In *WWW*, 231-240, 2009.

[13] M. Mahdian and G. Wang. Clustering-Based Bidding Languages for Sponsored Search. In *ESA*, pages 167-178, 2009.

[14] I. Giotis and A. R. Karlin: On the Equilibria and Efficiency of the GSP Mechanism in Keyword Auctions with Externalities. In *WINE*, pages 629-638, 2008.

[15] G. Christodoulou, A. Kovács, and M. Schapira: Bayesian Combinatorial Auctions. In *ICALP*, pages 820-832, 2008.

[16] H. Varian, Position Auctions, *International Journal of Industrial Organization*, pages 1163-1178, 2007.

[17] Z. Abrams, A. Ghosh, and E. Vee. Cost of Conciseness in Sponsored Search Auctions. *WINE*, pages 326-334, 2007.

[18] R. Kumar, M. Mahdian, and A. Sayedi. Mechanism Design for Complexity-Constrained Bidders. In *WINE*, pages 513-520, 2009.

[19] S. K. Singh and V. P. Roychowdhury. To Broad-Match or Not to Broad-Match : An Auctioneer's Dilemma ?. *CoRR abs*, 0802.1957, 2008.

[20] S. K. Singh, V. P. Roychowdhury, M. Bradonjic, and B. A. Rezaei. Exploration via design and the cost of uncertainty in keyword auctions. *CoRR abs*, 0707.1053, 2007.

A Revealed Preference Approach to Computational Complexity in Economics

Federico Echenique
Humanities and Social Sciences
California Institute of Tech.
Pasadena, CA 91125
fede@caltech.edu

Daniel Golovin
Center for the Mathematics of Information
California Institute of Tech.
Pasadena, CA 91125
dgolovin@caltech.edu

Adam Wierman
Computer and Mathematical Sciences
California Institute of Tech.
Pasadena, CA 91125
adamw@caltech.edu

ABSTRACT

Recent results in complexity theory suggest that various economic theories require agents to solve computationally intractable problems. However, such results assume the agents are optimizing explicit utility functions, whereas the economic theories merely assume the agents behave *rationally*, where rational behavior is defined via some optimization problem. Might making rational choices be easier than solving the corresponding optimization problem? For at least one major economic theory, the theory of the consumer (which simply postulates that consumers are utility maximizing), we find this is indeed the case. In other words, we prove the possibly surprising result that computational constraints have *no empirical consequences* for consumer choice theory.

Our result motivates a general approach for posing questions about the empirical content of computational constraints: *the revealed preference approach to computational complexity*. This approach complements the conventional worst-case view of computational complexity in important ways, and is methodologically close to mainstream economics.

Categories and Subject Descriptors

F.2.0 [**Analysis of Algorithms and Problem Complexity**]: General

General Terms

Algorithms, Economics, Theory

Keywords

Computational Complexity, Rationalization, Revealed Preference, Theory of the Consumer

1. INTRODUCTION

Questions related to the computational complexity of economic models have been a driving force inspiring research at the intersection of computer science and economics. Over the last decade, many traditional economic models have been examined with the goal of understanding the computational requirements placed on the agents involved. For many models, this question has now been (partially) resolved.

For example computing Nash equilibria is now known to be hard [13, 15] even for 2-player games [11], modulo reasonable complexity-theoretic assumptions[1]. Similarly, computing Walrasian equilibria in instances where agents have utilities that are separable over the goods and concave piecewise linear for each good is also hard [10, 35], specifically, PPAD-complete. On the positive side, it is known how to compute Walrasian equilibria in polynomial time if all agents have *linear* utility functions [20, 36]. Still other results concern the complexity of the problems faced by individual agents within the market, such as a seller seeking profit-maximizing envy-free prices [19], or a seller seeking profit-maximizing prices when facing a collection of customers with known utility functions [3]. Both of those problems are NP-hard. From the buyers' perspective, problems as basic as maximizing utility under a budget constraint are NP-hard [18].

Computer scientists have often cited results such as those mentioned above as strong critiques of the applicability of classic economic models, claiming, for example:

> "If an equilibrium is not efficiently computable, much of its credibility as a prediction of the behavior of rational agents is lost"
>
> – Christos Papadimitriou [25]

> "If your laptop cannot find it, neither can the market"
>
> – quote attributed to Kamal Jain [25]

The critique amounts to a claim that either these computationally-hard models should be rejected, or that some suitable justification must be found for keeping them in spite of their worst-case hardness, e.g., by discovering some additional structure in real-world markets which allows computationally-bounded agents to behave in a manner consistent with them.

Economists have, in general, been slow to accept such critiques of these classic models. We posit that this is *partially* due to a differing view of the purpose of economic models, which leads to a contrasting notion of how computational issues should be incorporated. In particular, to an economist, models provide tools for thinking about reality; that is, about data. Thus, economic models/theories provide

[1]Computing 3-player Nash Equilibria is FIXP-complete [15]; the 2-player case is PPAD-complete [11]. These classes capture the difficulty of computing fixed points for large classes of functions. For additional background, we refer the interested reader to [12] and to [28]; the latter is specifically geared towards economists.

EC'11, June 5–9, 2011, San Jose, California, USA.

'as-if' tools: economists postulate a model, and claim the observable variables behave as if the model were true. More specifically, given data from an observed phenomenon, we want to know if the theory can *explain* the data, i.e., if the data is consistent with an instance of the theory. If it is inconsistent, then the theory is refuted.

This differing view does not eliminate the need to consider computational issues in the model, it simply motivates a different, complementary approach for studying computational complexity. Specifically, the model still loses credibility if the agents must solve computationally hard problems; however, worst-case complexity is no longer the relevant concept. Instead, the question is whether data from an observed phenomenon can always be explained by the theory with the additional constraint that agents not be required to solve computationally hard problems, i.e., whether the data is consistent with an instance of the theory where the agents perform only computationally easy tasks. Note, of course, that this may be true even when the model is computationally hard in a worst-case sense.

This new perspective on computational complexity is strongly motivated by the revealed preference literature in economics [29]. This literature seeks to understand the empirical implications of economic models: given data from an observed phenomenon, the task is to understand how generally a model is applicable (i.e., how large the class of explainable data is) and to determine what instance of the theory is revealed by the data (e.g., to determine the properties of the utility functions that are consistent with the data). Examples of such results include [1, 2, 32, 33, 24, 7, 6, 14, 8, 9]. Hal Varian [34] has an excellent survey of revealed preference theory.

Revealed preference theory, however, traditionally disregards computational issues. Our proposed perspective on complexity changes this by adding to revealed preference theory the constraint that the instance revealed does not require agents to solve any computationally hard problems. Thus, the question becomes: does the addition of computational constraints limit the class of data explainable by the theory? Or, more colloquially, *do computational constraints have empirical consequences for economic models*?

The goal of this paper is to formalize this "revealed preference view" of computational complexity, and to begin to explore whether it leads to different conclusions than the standard "worst-case view." To this end, we study a classic economic model: consumer choice theory.

Consumer choice theory involves ideas that are familiar and important to both the computer science and economics communities: the theory is the basic building block of economics. Its central postulate is that consumers are utility maximizing, and yet the very task of utility maximization can be seen to be NP-hard as an immediate consequence of classical results in computer science. For consumer choice theory, the case made above—that the theory is flawed because it assumes that agents solve hard problems—is very natural, and easy to understand. A recent presentation of this view of consumer choice theory is in [18]; but the case has been presented (albeit informally) many times before, e.g., in [31].[2] In this paper, we shall present a different view, based on the revealed preference approach to consumer choice theory.

The specific model we consider (Section 2) is that of a single consumer who, when presented with a budget and prices for d goods, must decide on a consumption bundle. It is not difficult to see that, in this model, utility-maximizing consumers must solve a generalization of the knapsack problem, and thus, in a worst-case sense, the model requires consumers to solve an NP-hard problem. However, when the model is considered using the "revealed preference view" of computational complexity the conclusion is different. We prove that, given data for the observed behavior of a consumer, the data either corresponds to irrational behavior (it cannot be reconciled with the optimization of any utility function) or it can be explained using *tractable* utility functions, i.e., those that are computationally easy to maximize subject to a budget constraint. *Thus, if there exist utility functions that explain the data, then there exists a tractable utility function that explains the data.* In other words, the constraint that the consumer's utility function is tractable does not alter the range of consumer behavior that may be explained by the theory. So, for this model, computational constraints have no empirical consequences—despite the fact that the underlying problems the agents must solve are NP-hard in the worst-case.

As an application of our results on consumer choice, we study Walrasian (competitive) equilibrium theory (Section 3). The specific model we consider is that of an exchange economy with d goods and m utility-maximizing agents, each having an endowment and a utility function. A simple extension to the results for the consumer choice model described above shows that: given a data set including observations of prices and allocations of goods to agents, either the data corresponds to behavior that is manifestly irrational or the data can be explained using utility functions that are computationally easy to maximize and that explain the market behavior. So, again, for this model, computational constraints have no empirical consequences. We should stress, however, that the results for Walrasian equilibrium do not address the computational complexity of finding an equilibrium. We only focus on the complexity of the agents' maximization problem.

In both economic models considered in this paper, agents must perform computations that are hard in the worst-case sense. An "economist's view," however, of computational complexity shows that computational constraints do not limit the applicability of the economic models any further than the assumption of rationality does already. This provides a stark contrast to the message from the worst-case computational complexity studies of these models.

We emphasize that this paper considers only two basic models, and an important goal for further research is to understand whether similar results hold for other classic economic models such as Nash equilibrium, or for the problem of finding an equilibrium in a competitive market. Toward this end, in Section 4, we present a general formulation of the revealed preference view of computational complexity which provides a framework for approaching the analysis of other economic theories.

2. CONSUMER CHOICE THEORY

The revealed preference approach we propose is widely applicable, but consumer choice theory is a natural starting point since the theory is computationally hard and a basic building block for most of economics. It is the first topic covered in every introductory course in economics, and it remains a very active research field until this day — active in both empirical and theoretical research. Further, the revealed preference approach in economics was first proposed and developed for consumer choice theory.

Before introducing the model formally, we introduce some notation that will be used throughout the remainder of the paper. For integer n, we let $[n] := \{1, 2, \ldots, n\}$. Let $\mathbb{Z}_+$ and $\mathbb{R}_+$ denote the nonnegative integers and real numbers, respectively, and let $\mathbb{Z}_{++}$ and $\mathbb{R}_{++}$ and denote the set of positive integers and real numbers, respectively. For a binary relation R, we let R^* denote its transitive closure. A binary relation R is ***acyclic*** if $x\, R^*\, y$ and $y\, R^*\, x$ implies that $x = y$. All logarithms are base 2 unless otherwise noted. We

[2]Herbert Simon was one of the earliest advocates for incorporating computational constraints in economic models. Simon was aware, however, that the complexity of the procedures involved in decision making would only matter to the extent that they made a difference *empirically;* see [31].

denote a d-dimensional vector with all coordinates equal to c by $\mathbf{c}$ and denote the ith basis vector, which is one at coordinate i and zero at the other $d-1$ coordinates, by $\hat{e}_i$.

We can now define the consumer choice problem as follows. We wish to consider the case of a single consumer and d different goods. However, to model a variable number of goods, we instead consider the case in which there are (countably) infinitely many different goods, of which the consumer only has the opportunity to purchase up to d different types of goods[3], which we relabel as goods $1, 2, \dots, d$. Formally, a d-dimensional ***consumption bundle*** is a vector $x \in \mathbb{R}^d_+$, where x_i indicates the amount of good i consumed, and $\mathcal{X}^d$ is the ***consumption space*** consisting of all valid d-dimensional consumption bundles. We define the *full consumption space* as $\mathcal{X} := \bigcup_{d \geq 0} \mathcal{X}^d$.

We consider two settings for the consumption space: (i) infinitely divisible goods and (ii) indivisible goods. In the case of infinitely divisible goods, each of the goods is available in perfectly divisible quantities, and so $\mathcal{X}^d = \mathbb{R}^d_+$. In the case of indivisible goods, the goods can not be divided, and thus $\mathcal{X}^d = \mathbb{Z}^d_+$. In either case, we denote by $\leq$ the natural partial order on $\mathcal{X}^d$: so $x \leq y$ iff $x_i \leq y_i$ for each coordinate $i \in [d]$. The d goods generate a lattice $(\mathcal{X}^d, \leq)$.

An instance of the consumer choice problem is specified by a price vector $p \in \mathbb{R}^d_{++}$ for some d and a consumer income $b \in \mathbb{R}_+$. Let $B(p,b) := \left\{x : x \in \mathcal{X}^{\dim(p)},\ p \cdot x \leq b\right\}$ denote the budget set under prices p and budget b, where $\dim(p)$ is the dimension of p.

The standard economic theory of the consumer then postulates that the consumer behaves (i.e. chooses x) as if he has a ***utility function*** $u : \mathcal{X} \to \mathbb{R}$ and solves the problem

$$\max\left\{u(x) : x \in B(p,b)\right\} \tag{1}$$

to determine what consumption bundle to select when faced with prices p and budget b.

To incorporate computational considerations, we make the distinction between *tractable* and *intractable* utility functions, using the standard demarcation of polynomial-time computability.

DEFINITION 1 (TRACTABLE UTILITY FUNCTIONS). *A utility function $u : \mathcal{X} \to \mathbb{R}$ is* tractable *if and only if problem (1) can be solved for all p and b in polynomial time*[4]*, by which we mean polynomial in $d = \dim(p)$, $\max_i(\log p_i)$, and $\log b$. Otherwise, u is said to be* intractable.

2.1 Infinitely divisible goods

We first discuss the case of infinitely divisible goods, which serves as a simple motivational example for the idea of a "revealed preference" view of computational complexity.

In the case of divisible goods, the consumption space is $\mathcal{X}^d = \mathbb{R}^d_+$. Thus, the standard economic theory of the consumer postulates that the consumer behaves (i.e. chooses x) as if solving the problem

$$\max\left\{u(x) : x \in \mathbb{R}^d_+ \text{ and } p \cdot x \leq b\right\}. \tag{2}$$

[3]Allowing the number of goods to be variable, rather than constant, can only strengthen the critiques of classic economic models on complexity–theoretic grounds. However, we will show that even in this regime, computational constraints have no empirical consequences for the theory of the consumer.

[4]For continuous optimization problems, we take the notion of "solving in polynomial time" to mean obtaining an additive ϵ-approximation in time polynomial in the natural problem parameters and $\log(1/\epsilon)$. To be completely formal, we may also specify a precise model of computation, e.g., a RAM with word size $\Theta(\log n)$. However we feel that this level of formalism adds little in precision to our results and detracts from the main discussion, and so we avoid it in the remainder of the paper.

when faced with a price vector $p \in \mathbb{R}^d_{++}$ and a budget of $b \in \mathbb{R}_+$.

We examine this model according to a worst-case view of computational complexity and a revealed preference view of computational complexity.

A worst-case view

From a worst-case perspective, it is immediately clear that if the utility function is allowed to be general, the consumer could be required to solve an arbitrary non-convex optimization, which is computationally intractable. (For completeness, we prove this rather basic fact for monotone utilities in Lemma 16 in Appendix B. A similar result is in [18].) Thus, without additional assumptions on the allowable utility functions, a worst-case view of computational complexity leads to a critique of the model as unrealistically assuming that consumers are solving a problem that is not computationally tractable. Taking a revealed preference view of computational complexity will lead to a different conclusion.

A revealed preference view

At its core, our revealed preference view is an empirical approach to computational complexity; thus it starts from data about observed behavior. Specifically, suppose that we have finitely many observations of the purchases made by a consumer at prices p^i and incomes b^i, $i = 0, \dots, n$. That is, we have ***data*** of the form $\left\{(x^i, p^i, b^i)\right\}_{i=0}^n$.

We say that the data is ***rationalizable*** if there is a monotone increasing function $u(\cdot)$ such that x^i is the solution to (2) at prices p^i and income b^i. Then, revealed preference theory provides the following well-known result [1, 32], which says that the data results either from a consumer that is manifestly irrational or from a consumer whose behavior can be explained using a concave utility function:

THEOREM 2. ***(Afriat's Theorem)*** *In the consumer choice problem with infinitely divisible goods, the data $\left\{(x^i, p^i, b^i)\right\}_{i=0}^n$ is rationalizable if and only if it is rationalizable by a monotone increasing, piecewise linear, and concave utility function.*

Though Afriat's Theorem does not explicitly address computational constraints, there exist computationally efficient approaches to solving continuous monotone concave maximization problems with convex feasible sets [5]. Thus, an immediate consequence of Afriat's Theorem is that a data set $\left\{(x^i, p^i, b^i)\right\}_{i=0}^n$ is either manifestly irrational or can be explained using a utility function for which it is computationally efficient to solve (2). So, in the case where goods are infinitely divisible, the constraint that consumers can solve (2) in a computationally efficient manner has no empirical consequences, since it does not impose any additional restriction on the applicability of the model beyond the restrictions imposed by the assumption of rationality. Note that a consumer has no need to find the utility function guaranteed by Afriat's Theorem using the data, since consumers are presumed to know their own preferences. This is in contrast to an empirical economist who is attempting to learn about a consumer's preferences from the data; for the latter, there are efficient algorithms to generate and evaluate the promised utility function, though this is not the focus of our current investigation.

Relating the worst-case and revealed preference views

The simple motivational example of infinitely divisible goods provides an illustration of the contrast between the worst-case and revealed preference views. This example highlights that the two views can lead to fundamentally different conclusions about the role of computation. However, observe that if an economic model is polynomial time computable in a worst-case sense, then it is immediate to see that computational restrictions will have no empirical consequences in the revealed preference view. So, the revealed preference view is weaker than the worst-case view.

The revealed preference view is weaker because the power of an adversary to choose a hard instance is limited. Instead of being able to specify a hard instance precisely (e.g., specify a hard utility function for the consumer), the instance must be specified via a data set. Since this interface is not precise, even if hard instances exist, they may not have empirical consequences in the revealed preference view if a data set specified by a hard instance can always be explained by an easy instance (e.g., all data sets are rationalizable via a monotone, concave utility function).

2.2 Indivisible goods

We now move to the computationally more interesting case of indivisible goods, i.e., $\mathcal{X}^d = \mathbb{Z}^d_+$. It is a realistic case, as many consumption goods are clearly indivisible. The standard economic theory of the consumer postulates that the consumer behaves (i.e., chooses x) as if solving the problem

$$\max\left\{u(x) : x \in \mathbb{Z}^d_+ \text{ and } p \cdot x \leq b\right\} \tag{3}$$

when faced with a price vector $p \in \mathbb{R}^d_{++}$ and a budget of $b \in \mathbb{R}_+$.

The analysis in this setting is significantly more involved than that for infinitely divisible goods. The main result, however, will be the same: that the consumer problem is computationally hard in a worst-case sense, but that computational constraints have no empirical consequences in the revealed preference view.

A worst-case view

As in the case of infinitely divisible goods, it is immediately clear that if the utility function is allowed to be general, the consumer could be required to solve an arbitrary discrete optimization, which is computationally intractable. In fact, optimization over a discrete space is intractable for seemingly simple utility functions: we show in Lemma 16 that solving (3) is NP-hard, even with *linear* utility functions. Thus, without additional assumptions on the allowable utility functions, a worst-case view of computational complexity leads to a critique of the model as unrealistically assuming that consumers are solving a problem that is not computationally tractable.

A revealed preference view

We now switch to a revealed preference view of computational complexity. As in the case of infinitely divisible goods, it provides a very different perspective than the worst-case view.

To define the revealed preference view, we must first define the form of the observed data about consumer behavior. We model the data (input) as a sequence of some number n of consumer choices $\left\{(x^i, p^i, b^i)\right\}_{i=0}^n$ where $x^i \in \mathbb{Z}^d_+$ is the consumer choice observed under prices p^i and budget b^i (i.e., under budget set $B^i := \{x : p^i \cdot x \leq b^i\}$) for each $i \geq 1$. We assume that if $x^i < y$ then $y \notin B^i$; so x^i is maximal in B^i. For technical reasons, we add a fictitious observation (x^0, p^0, b^0) with $x^0 = \mathbf{0}$, $p^0 = \mathbf{1}$, $b^0 = 0$; that is, a consumer with no money chooses the only feasible choice, namely nothing at all.[5]

Adopting the language of revealed preference theory, we let $X = \{x^0, x^1, \ldots, x^n\}$ be the set of bundles purchased at any time in the input and observe that the data induces a revealed preference relation

$$R_0 := \left\{(x^i, x^j) : (x^i, x^j) \in X^2,\ x^i \in B^j\right\}.$$

[5]The assumption is purely technical, and does not interfere with the rationalizability of the data.

As in the case of infinitely divisible goods, we say that the data $\left\{(x^i, p^i, b^i)\right\}_{i=0}^n$ is ***rationalizable*** if there is a monotone increasing function $u(\cdot)$ such that $x^i \in \arg\max\left\{u(x) : x \in B(p^i, b^i)\right\}$ for $i = 0, \ldots, n$.

Now, as in the case of indivisible goods, revealed preference theory provides a characterization of the set of data that is rationalizable. Specifically, the following well-known result (see, for example, [26] or [27]) highlights the relationship between rationalizability and the preference relation R_0:

THEOREM 3. *In the consumer choice problem with indivisible goods, data $\left\{(x^i, p^i, b^i)\right\}_{i=0}^n$ is rationalizable if and only if the binary relation R_0 is acyclic.*

There are results analogous to Theorem 2 for infinitely divisible goods. The following result is due to [8] (and extended by [30]). Of course, concave utility is not appropriate in the indivisible case, but supermodularity and submodularity are useful properties of utility one can potentially exploit.

THEOREM 4. *In the consumer choice problem with indivisible goods, the following statements are equivalent:*

(i) The data $\left\{(x^i, p^i, b^i)\right\}_{i=0}^n$ is rationalizable.

(ii) The data is rationalizable by a supermodular utility function.

(iii) The data is rationalizable by a submodular utility function.

At this point, however, the parallel with the case of infinitely divisible good ends. Unlike in the case of infinitely divisible goods, we can not immediately apply Theorem 4 to arrive at utility functions for which it is computationally efficient for consumers to solve (3). The reason is that solving (3) for either submodular or supermodular utility functions is not computationally efficient. Specifically, submodular maximization subject to a budget constraint is NP-hard, even to approximate to better than a $(1 - 1/e)$ factor [16]. Further, supermodular maximization subject to a budget constraint is likewise NP-hard [21], and extremely inapproximable under reasonable complexity assumptions, as we show in Theorem 17.

The main result of this paper is that, when data is rationalizable, it is possible to rationalize the data using a utility function for which solving (3) is computationally efficient. Specifically:

THEOREM 5. *In the consumer choice problem with indivisible goods, data $\left\{(x^i, p^i, b^i)\right\}_{i=0}^n$ is rationalizable if and only if it is rationalizable via a tractable monotone utility function.*

The message in Theorem 5 is that computational constraints do not impose any further restrictions on the ability of consumer choice theory to explain data than are already imposed by the assumption of rationality. This is in stark contrast to the message suggested by the worst-case view of computational complexity for this model.

In order to prove Theorem 5, we must prove that the data is either not rationalizable, or there is a utility function rationalizing the data such that for any p and b, (3) can be solved in strongly polynomial time. That is, using only computation time polynomial in n, d, and the number of bits required to write down the prices and budgets.

We cannot use Theorem 4 to prove Theorem 5. Instead, we proceed by working with the demand function instead of the utility function. Specifically, to prove the result we construct an efficient algorithm $\mathcal{A} = \mathcal{A}_{\{(x^i,p^i,b^i)\}_{i=0}^n}$ to compute a ***demand function***[6] $\psi : \mathbb{R}^d_{++} \times \mathbb{R}_+ \to \mathbb{Z}^d_+$ such that

[6]That is to say, $\psi(p, b)$ is the choice of the consumer faced with budget set $B(p, b)$.

(i) the demand function explains the data, i.e., $\psi(p^i, b^i) = x^i$ for all $i \in [n]$, and

(ii) there is a monotone increasing utility function $u(\cdot)$ rationalizing the data, and for all $p \in \mathbb{R}^d_{++}$ and $b \in \mathbb{R}_+$ we have

$$\psi(p, b) = \arg\max\{u(x) \ : \ x \in B(p, b)\}.^7$$

We prove this fact as Corollary 15 in Appendix A. Interestingly, the algorithm does not explicitly construct a tractable utility function; rather, a utility function is implicit in the demand function which our algorithm computes.

In the remainder of this section, we explain the algorithm for computing a demand function from the data. It consists of two steps: (i) A preprocessing phase, $\mathcal{A}$.preprocess, in which a ranking r on $X = \{x^0, x^1, \ldots, x^n\}$ is computed. (ii) A core phase, $\mathcal{A}$.evaluate_demand, that uses the ranking in order to evaluate the demand function $\psi(p, b)$. Let lex max S denote the lexicographically maximum element of S. We provide pseudocode below.

```
Algorithm 𝒜

𝒜.preprocess(Data {(x^i, p^i, b^i)}_{i=0}^n)
begin
    Let X := {x^0, x^1, ..., x^n};
    Let E_0 := {(x, y) ∈ X^2 : x ≠ y, x ≤ y} be the transitive
    closure of the lattice poset restricted to elements of X;
    Let E := E_0 ∪ R_0, and define a directed graph
    G := (X, E);
    Perform a topological sort of G to get vertex ordering π;
    Output r : X → Z_{++} defined such that r(x) = i iff x is
    the i^th element according to π;
end

𝒜.evaluate_demand(Prices p, Budget b)
begin
    Obtain the rank function r computed during preprocessing;
    Compute z(p, b) = arg max {r(x) : x ∈ B(p, b) ∩ X}
    by iterating over the elements of X;
    Let ψ(p, b) := lex max {x : x ∈ B(p, b), z(p, b) ≤ x},
    and compute ψ(p, b) as follows.
    Set z_0 := z(p, b);
    for i = 1 to d do
        Compute δ_i := max {δ : z_{i-1} + δ · ê_i ∈ B(p, b)};
        z_i ← z_{i-1} + δ_i · ê_i;
    end
    Output z_d;                          // Note z_d = ψ(p, b)
end
```

A first remark on Algorithm $\mathcal{A}$ is that, if we envision adding data points to a given data set, the algorithm will 'learn' or approximate a limiting demand function, e.g., see [23]. This learning perspective on the algorithm is not the goal of the current work, but is interesting in its own right. See [4] for another example of a learning approach in this context. For the purpose of this paper, we simply note that if one looks at the design of $\mathcal{A}$ from a learning perspective, the use of lex max in $\mathcal{A}$.evaluate_demand is artificial. Many other choices are possible, e.g., one could parameterize the algorithm with prior beliefs about consumer demand to select among them.

[7]Note the divergence from the more classical approach in revealed preference theory; e.g [1, 32, 8]. Most studies of revealed preference construct a rationalizing utility. Here the approach is to construct a demand function, and then show that it is rationalizable.

We defer the proof of the correctness of Algorithm $\mathcal{A}$ to Appendix A and discuss only the running time of the algorithm here. It is immediate to see that phase (ii), $\mathcal{A}$.evaluate_demand, can be implemented in $\mathcal{O}(nd)$ time. Phase (i), $\mathcal{A}$.preprocess, can be implemented in $\mathcal{O}(n^2 d)$ time, since we may iterate over X^2, and test if each element belongs to $E_0 \cup R_0$ in $\mathcal{O}(d)$ time, and topological sort is well–known to have a linear–time implementation, i.e., one taking $\mathcal{O}(|X| + |E|)$ time, which is this case amounts to $\mathcal{O}(n^2)$. The total time is thus $\mathcal{O}(n^2 d)$.

One, possibly surprising, observation about the running time of algorithm $\mathcal{A}$ is that it depends on n, the size of the data set. One may reasonably take n to be a constant when evaluating the running time of the demand function ψ since it is the tractability with respect to p and b that is relevant when the choice function is evaluated for future demands (i.e., the data set is fixed for all future evaluations of the demand function). However, one may also reasonably ask whether the dependence of the running time on n is necessary or if it is an artifact of specific algorithm presented here.

It turns out that there is an unavoidable dependence of any rationalization algorithm on the size of the data in (at least) two ways. First, when determining a demand function to rationalize the data, the algorithm must process every 'distinct' element of the data set, which highlights that the running time must be at least the size of the minimal representation of the data set. Second, the resulting demand function must at least encode each entry of the data set. Thus, the space needed to represent the demand function must also be bounded below by the size of the minimal representation of the data set. More formally, we can prove the following lower bounds on the running time of any algorithm for rationalizing the data set and for the space needed to represent the resulting demand function. The proofs are deferred to Appendix C.

PROPOSITION 6. *Any algorithm that takes as input a data set with n data points, a price vector p, and a budget b and outputs $\psi(p, b)$ for a ψ which rationalizes the data set requires, in the worst case, $\Omega(n)$ running time on a RAM with word size $\Theta(\log n)$, even when there are only two goods.*

PROPOSITION 7. *Any demand function ψ that rationalizes a data set with n data points requires $\Omega(n \log n)$ bits of space to represent, in the worst case, even when there are only two goods.*

These two propositions highlight that the dependence of the running time on the size of the data set is unavoidable. However, observe that the running time of algorithm $\mathcal{A}$ does not match the lower bound above, since it has a quadratic dependence on n. On the other hand, our preprocessing step is space-optimal, since it can be implemented using linear space by performing the topological sort in a lazy manner that generates the adjacently list of each vertex of G on the fly, and hence avoids the need to explicitly construct G. The running time of this lazy implementation is also $\mathcal{O}(n^2 d)$.

3. WALRASIAN EQUILIBRIUM THEORY

The theory of the consumer is an important component in many economic theories. The most important of these is general equilibrium theory, which in turn is the most widely applied model in mainstream micro economics (it underlines most of modern macro economics, international trade and financial economics). In this section, we present the implications of our results on consumer choice theory for general equilibrium theory, specifically the implications for the empirical content of Walrasian equilibrium as formulated by [6].

The basic model of general equilibrium assumes a finite number of goods and agents. Agents have preferences and are endowed with initial quantities of the goods. (We ignore production in our discussion.) The theory predicts which prices will emerge for the different goods, and what the quantities of the goods consumed by the agents will be. Specifically, the theory predicts that the prices and quantities conform to a Walrasian equilibrium: a situation where agents choose quantities optimally given prices, endowments, and the incomes derived from selling their endowments; and where supply equals demand for all goods simultaneously.

We can describe the revealed preference formulation of Walrasian equilibrium as follows [6]. Given data on prices and resources for an economy, we want to know if the data are rationalizable as Walrasian equilibrium outcomes. The rationalization involves specifying utility functions for the agents. We want to study if these utility functions can be chosen so that they are tractable.

Consider the standard model of an exchange economy. Suppose there are d goods and m agents. Each agent i is described by a consumption space $\mathcal{X}_i^d \subseteq \mathbb{R}_+^d$, a monotone increasing utility function $u_i : \mathcal{X}_i^d \to \mathbb{R}$, and an endowment $\omega_i \in \mathcal{X}_i^d$. An economy is therefore described by $(\mathcal{X}_i^d, u_i, \omega_i)_{i=1}^m$. By changing the consumption space $\mathcal{X}_i^d$, we can work with either indivisible or divisible goods. To apply the results in Section 2 we assume that $\mathcal{X}_i^d = \mathbb{Z}_+^d$.

An ***allocation*** is a collection $\mathbf{x} = (x_i)_{i=1}^m$ with $x_i \in \mathcal{X}_i^d$, and such that $\sum_{i=1}^m x_i = \sum_{i=1}^m \omega_i$. A ***Walrasian equilibrium*** is a pair $(\mathbf{x}, p)$, where $\mathbf{x} = (x_i)_{i=1}^m$ is an allocation and $p \in \mathbb{R}_{++}^d$ is a price vector such that, for all i, x_i solves the problem

$$\max \left\{ u_i(x) : x \in \mathcal{X}_i^d,\ p \cdot x \leq p \cdot \omega_i \right\}.$$

We assume that we have data on prices, incomes and resources. Specifically, a ***data set*** is a collection $(p^k, (\omega_i^k)_{i=1}^m)_{k=0}^K$. We follow [6] in assuming that individual consumption vectors are not observable. We say that a data set is ***rationalizable*** if there are utility functions u_i for each agent, and vectors x^k, $k = 1, \ldots, K$, such that (x^k, p^k) is a Walrasian equilibrium of the economy $(\mathcal{X}_i^d, u_i, \omega_i^k)_{i=1}^m$.[8]

Given the above setup, the results in Section 2 imply that in the case of indivisible goods (i.e., when $\mathcal{X}_i^d = \mathbb{Z}_+^d$), a data set $(p^k, (\omega_i^k)_{i=1}^m)_{k=0}^K$ is either not rationalizable, or it is rationalizable using tractable u_i for all agents: utilities such that the problems

$$\max \left\{ u_i(x) : x \in \mathbb{Z}_+^d,\ p \cdot x \leq p \cdot \omega_i \right\}$$

can be solved in strongly polynomial time. Further, from the discussion in Section 2 it is easy to see that a similar result holds for infinitely divisible goods (i.e., $\mathcal{X}_i^d = \mathbb{R}_+^d$) as a consequence of Afriat's Theorem. The key observation necessary to obtain these results is that the assumption that the market must clear (i.e., supply must match demand) does not impose any additional constraints on the problems solved by the agents.

However, it is important to realize that our results do not address the complexity of *finding* a Walrasian equilibria. We have limited the discussion to the individual consumer's problem, not the collective problem of finding an equilibrium. The later question is clearly important and interesting, and it is a focus of continuing work on this topic. The exact formulation of the revealed preference view for this extension is a special case of the general formulation that we introduce in Section 4.

4. A GENERAL FORMULATION

In this paper we focus on one particular theory, consumer choice theory; however it is clear that the revealed preference view of computational complexity can be studied much more broadly. In this section we present a general formulation of the revealed preference view which can be applied, for example, to test the impact of computational constraints on the empirical content of the theory of Nash equilibrium, the theory of stable matchings, and other economic theories.

To begin the general formulation, let $\mathcal{I}$ be a set of possible *inputs*, and $\mathcal{O}$ be a set of possible *outputs*. For example, in consumer theory, $\mathcal{I}$ is the set of all price-budget pairs (p, b), while $\mathcal{O}$ is the consumption space $(\mathcal{X}^d)$.

We represent a *theory* as a collection $\mathcal{G} = \{g_\tau : \tau \in \mathcal{T}\}$ of correspondences, $g_\tau \subseteq \mathcal{I} \times \mathcal{O}$, which we index by a set $\mathcal{T}$ for convenience. For example, consumer choice theory is the collection $\{\psi_u : u \in U\}$ where U is the set of all monotone increasing utility functions $u : \mathcal{X}^d \to \mathbb{R}$ and $\psi_u(p, b)$ is the demand function obtained from maximizing u over the budget set defined by (p, b).

Classical revealed preference theory

When taking a revealed preference perspective on a theory, the goal is to test the theory using data. We define a *data set* D as a finite collection $D = (i_k, o_k)_{k=1}^n$ of pairs of inputs and outputs. The set of all possible data sets is $\mathcal{D} = (\mathcal{I} \times \mathcal{O})^*$, i.e., all finite sequences of pairs in $\mathcal{I} \times \mathcal{O}$.

A data set $(i_k, o_k)_{k=1}^n$ is *rationalizable* by the theory $\mathcal{G} = \{g_\tau : \tau \in \mathcal{T}\}$ if there is $\tau \in \mathcal{T}$ such that $o_k \in g_\tau(i_k)$ for all $k = 1, \ldots, n$. In that case, we say that g_τ *rationalizes* the data.

Further, we define a *rationalization rule* $r : \mathcal{D} \to (\mathcal{I} \to \mathcal{O})$ such that for each rationalizable data set D, $r(D) = g_\tau$ for some $\tau \in \mathcal{T}$ such that g_τ rationalizes the data.

Finally, define the set of data sets rationalizable by theory $\mathcal{G}$ as

$$\mathcal{R}_\mathcal{G} = \{D \in \mathcal{D} : \exists \tau \in \mathcal{T} : g_\tau \text{ rationalizes } D\}.$$

Given this setup, some classic revealed preference questions are:

> *Is theory $\mathcal{G}$ refutable, i.e., Is $\mathcal{R}_\mathcal{G} \subsetneq \mathcal{D}$?*
> *Is data D rationalizable by theory $\mathcal{G}$, i.e., Is $D \in \mathcal{R}_\mathcal{G}$?*

However, these classic questions ignore computational constraints on the theory.

Adding computational constraints

Our revealed preference view of computational complexity can be fit into the above framework as follows.

Consider again the rationalization rule $r : \mathcal{D} \to (\mathcal{I} \to \mathcal{O})$. We now seek to understand the impact of imposing an additional constraint on $r(D) = g_\tau$ which rationalizes D — it must be "tractable." Formally, we say that $g_\tau(i) = [r(D)](i)$ is *tractable* if it is computable in time polynomial in the size of both D and i. We require it to be polynomial in the size of D for reasons discussed below (and in Section 2).

Define the set of data sets that are rationalizable using tractable instances of theory $\mathcal{G}$ as

$$\mathcal{E}_\mathcal{G} = \{D \in \mathcal{D} : \exists \tau \in \mathcal{T}.\ g_\tau \text{ rationalizes } D \textit{ and } g_\tau \text{ is tractable }\}.$$

Given this framework, the general version of the question posed by the revealed preference view of complexity is:

> *Do computational constraints have empirical consequences, i.e., Is $\mathcal{E}_\mathcal{G} \subsetneq \mathcal{R}_\mathcal{G}$?*

In general, the set $\mathcal{E}_\mathcal{G}$ constitutes a test for the joint hypotheses of assuming the economic theory $\mathcal{G}$, and requiring that the economic system not solve unrealistically hard problems. If $\mathcal{E}_\mathcal{G} \subsetneq \mathcal{R}_\mathcal{G}$ then one would seek to characterize $\mathcal{E}_\mathcal{G}$ so that actual tests of the joint hypotheses can be carried out.

[8]One can, instead, assume that only individual incomes are observable, and not individual endowments. The results are the same (see [6]).

One final remark about this formulation is that it may initially seem strange that the computational time of g_τ depends on size of D, but, as we saw in the case of consumer choice theory, this is necessary in order to ensure that g_τ rationalizes D.

In fact, we can generalize Propositions 6 and 7 for this general formulation as follows. For a theory $\mathcal{G}$, define

$$\mathcal{R}_\mathcal{G}\left(\{i_k\}_{k=1}^n\right) := \mathcal{R}_\mathcal{G} \cap \left\{\{(i_k, o_k)\}_{k=1}^n \;:\; \forall k,\; o_k \in \mathcal{O}\right\}$$

to be the set of rationalizable data sets on input sequence $\{i_k\}_{k=1}^n$. Then we have the following lower bounds on the running time of r and space required to represent $g_\tau \in \mathcal{G}$. The proofs are deferred to Appendix C.

PROPOSITION 8. *Fix a theory $\mathcal{G}$ and $n \in \mathbb{N}$. The running time required to compute $[r(D)](i)$ for D of size n is*

$$\Omega\left(\frac{\max_{(i_1,\ldots,i_n)} \log_2 \left|\mathcal{R}_\mathcal{G}\left(\{i_k\}_{k=1}^n\right)\right|}{\log n}\right)$$

in the worst case on a RAM with wordsize $\Theta(\log n)$, where the max is taken over all input sequences $\{i_k\}_{k=1}^n$ of length n.

PROPOSITION 9. *Fix a theory $\mathcal{G}$ and $n \in \mathbb{N}$. The space required to represent any $g_\tau \in \mathcal{G}$ rationalizing a rationalizable data set of size n is at least $\max_{(i_1,\ldots,i_n)} \log_2 \left|\mathcal{R}_\mathcal{G}\left(\{i_k\}_{k=1}^n\right)\right|$ bits in the worst case, where the max is taken over all input sequences $\{i_k\}_{k=1}^n$ of length n.*

These propositions highlight that there is an explicit tradeoff between the generality of the theory being tested and the running time of r and the space complexity of g_τ. The generality of the theory is measured by the quantity $\max_{(i_1,\ldots,i_n)} \left|\mathcal{R}_\mathcal{G}\left(\{i_k\}_{k=1}^n\right)\right|$, which captures the notation that a more general theory can explain (rationalize) a larger class of data sets.

5. CONCLUDING REMARKS

The core idea presented by this paper is that there is a philosophical difference in how many computer scientists and economists view economic models, and that the lack of broad acceptance of worst-case complexity results in economics stems partially from the difference between these viewpoints. We posit that while computer scientists tend to think 'algorithmically' about economic models, economists tend to think 'empirically' about the models.

In particular, an *algorithmic view* of the model assumes the model is fixed and literally true, and then proceeds to ask about the demands placed on the agents by the model. That is, it assumes that the agent is simply an implementation of the model and asks whether the agent can efficiently compute its decisions.

In contrast, an *empirical view* of the model takes the model as a tool for thinking about reality. One does not presume agents literally follow the model, only that the model provides a way to explain the observed behavior, i.e., the data. Thus, an empirical view of economic models is that they provide 'as-if' tools: one postulates a model and claims the observable variables behave as if the model is true.

Note that the empirical view does not deny that computational issues should be studied. To the contrary, a model still loses credibility if the agents must solve computationally hard problems; however, worst-case complexity is no longer the relevant concept. Instead, the question is whether data from an observed phenomenon can always be explained by the theory under the additional constraint that agents are not required to solve computationally hard problems.

This paper presents a formulation of how to incorporate computational information into the empirical view; however the algorithmic view continues to be very important. Many problems require the design of automated agents who participate in various economic interactions: in this case explicit utility functions are provided by the designer, and are obviously not theoretical unknowns. Using classical economic jargon, one could say that the algorithmic view is relevant for normative economics while the empirical view is relevant for positive economics.

Acknowledgments

The authors wish to thank Vincent Conitzer for helpful discussions and the anonymous reviewers for their valuable feedback. This work was supported in part by the Center for the Mathematics of Information at Caltech and by the NSF through grants SES-0751980 and CNS-0846025.

6. REFERENCES

[1] S. N. Afriat. The construction of utility functions from expenditure data. *International Economic Review*, 8(1):67–77, feb 1967.

[2] S. N. Afriat. Efficiency estimation of production functions. *International Economic Review*, 13(3):568–598, oct 1972.

[3] M.-F. Balcan and A. Blum. Approximation algorithms and online mechanisms for item pricing. *Theory of Computing*, 3(9):179–195, 2007.

[4] E. Beigman and R. Vohra. Learning from revealed preference. In *Proceedings of the 7th ACM conference on Electronic commerce*, EC '06, pages 36–42, New York, NY, USA, 2006. ACM.

[5] S. Boyd and L. Vandenberghe. *Convex Optimization*. Cambridge University Press, 2004.

[6] D. J. Brown and R. L. Matzkin. Testable restrictions on the equilibrium manifold. *Econometrica*, 64(6):1249–1262, November 1996.

[7] D. J. Brown and C. Shannon. Uniqueness, stability, and comparative statics in rationalizable Walrasian markets. *Econometrica*, 68(6):1529–1439, November 2000.

[8] C. P. Chambers and F. Echenique. Supermodularity and preferences. *Journal of Economic Theory*, 144(3):1004–1014, May 2009.

[9] C. P. Chambers, F. Echenique, and E. Shmaya. On behavioral complementarity and its implications. Forthcoming, *Journal of Economic Theory*, 2009.

[10] X. Chen, D. Dai, Y. Du, and S.-H. Teng. Settling the complexity of Arrow-Debreu equilibria in markets with additively separable utilities. In *FOCS '09: Proceedings of the 2009 50th Annual IEEE Symposium on Foundations of Computer Science*, pages 273–282, Washington, DC, USA, 2009. IEEE Computer Society.

[11] X. Chen, X. Deng, and S.-H. Teng. Settling the complexity of computing two-player Nash equilibria. *J. ACM*, 56(3):1–57, 2009.

[12] C. Daskalakis. Nash equilibria: Complexity, symmetries, and approximation. *Computer Science Review*, 3(2):87–100, 2009.

[13] C. Daskalakis, P. W. Goldberg, and C. H. Papadimitriou. The complexity of computing a Nash equilibrium. *SIAM J. Comput.*, 39(1):195–259, 2009.

[14] W. E. Diewert and C. Parkan. Linear progamming tests of regularity conditions for production functions. In W. Eichhorn, R. Henn, K. Neumann, and R. Shephard, editors, *Quantitative Studies on Production and Prices*, pages 131–158. Physica-Verlag, Vienna, 1983.

[15] K. Etessami and M. Yannakakis. On the complexity of Nash equilibria and other fixed points. *SIAM J. Comput.*, 39(6):2531–2597, 2010.

[16] U. Feige. A threshold of $\ln n$ for approximating set cover. *Journal of the ACM*, 45(4):634 – 652, July 1998.

[17] M. R. Garey and D. S. Johnson. *Computers and Intractability: A Guide to the Theory of NP-Completeness*. W. H. Freeman & Co., New York, NY, USA, 1979.

[18] I. Gilboa, A. Postlewaite, and D. Schmeidler. The complexity of the consumer problem and mental accounting. Mimeo: Tel-Aviv University, 2010.

[19] V. Guruswami, J. D. Hartline, A. R. Karlin, D. Kempe, C. Kenyon, and F. McSherry. On profit-maximizing envy-free pricing. In *SODA '05: Proceedings of the sixteenth annual ACM-SIAM symposium on Discrete algorithms*, pages 1164–1173, Philadelphia, PA, USA, 2005. Society for Industrial and Applied Mathematics.

[20] K. Jain. A polynomial time algorithm for computing an Arrow–Debreu market equilibrium for linear utilities. *SIAM J. Comput.*, 37(1):303–318, 2007.

[21] H. Kellerer, U. Pferschy, and D. Pisinger. *Knapsack problems*, chapter 12. Springer, 1 edition, 2004.

[22] S. Khot. Ruling out PTAS for graph min-bisection, dense k-subgraph, and bipartite clique. *SIAM J. Comput.*, 36(4):1025–1071, 2006.

[23] A. Mas-Colell. On revealed preference analysis. *The Review of Economic Studies*, 45(1):121–131, 1978.

[24] R. L. Matzkin. Axioms of revealed preference for nonlinear choice sets. *Econometrica*, 59(6):1779–1786, November 1991.

[25] N. Nisan, T. Roughgarden, E. Tardos, and V. V. Vazirani, editors. *Algorithmic Game Theory*. Cambridge University Press, New York, NY, USA, 2007.

[26] M. K. Richter. Revealed preference theory. *Econometrica*, 34(3):635–645, jul 1966.

[27] M. K. Richter. Rational choice. In J. S. Chipman, L. Hurwicz, M. K. Richter, and H. F. Sonnenschein, editors, *Preferences, Utility and Demand*, pages 29–58. Harcourt Brace Jovanivic Inc., 1971.

[28] T. Roughgarden. Computing equilibria: a computational complexity perspective. *Economic Theory*, 42(1):193–236, January 2010.

[29] P. Samuelson. A note on the pure theory of consumer's behaviour. *Economica*, 5(17):61–71, 1938.

[30] K. Shirai. On the existence of a submodular utility function. Mimeo: Waseda University, 2010.

[31] H. A. Simon. Rationality in psychology and economics. *The Journal of Business*, 59:209–224, 1986.

[32] H. R. Varian. The nonparametric approach to demand analysis. *Econometrica*, 50(4):945–974, jul 1982.

[33] H. R. Varian. Non-parametric tests of consumer behaviour. *Review of Economic Studies*, 50(1):99–110, jan 1983.

[34] H. R. Varian. Revealed preference. In M. Szenberg, L. Ramrattan, and A. Gottesman, editors, *Samuelsonian economics and the twenty-first century*, pages 99–115. Oxford University Press, USA, 2006.

[35] V. V. Vazirani and M. Yannakakis. Market equilibrium under separable, piecewise-linear, concave utilities. In *Proc. Innovations in Computer Science*, pages 156–165, Beijing, China, January 2010.

[36] Y. Ye. A path to the Arrow–Debreu competitive market equilibrium. *Mathematical Programming*, 111(1):315–348, 2008.

APPENDIX

A. PROOFS FOR THE CONSUMER CHOICE MODEL

In this section we prove Theorem 5 via a sequence of lemmas culminating in Theorem 14 and Corollary 15.

LEMMA 10. *If R_0 is acyclic, then $\preceq := (R_0 \cup \leq)^*$ is acyclic.*

PROOF. The proof follows from the definition of budget set. Here, we use the convention that $x\, R_0\, y$ is the same as $(x, y) \in R_0$, meaning x is revealed–preferred to y.

Now suppose by way of contradiction that R_0 is acyclic, but $\preceq$ contains a minimal cycle C. Since $\leq$ is transitive, any minimal cycle consists only of edges in X^2 (recall X is the set of consumption bundles observed in the data plus the zero lattice point). Otherwise C contains edges (x, y) and (y, z) for some $y \notin X$. Since these pairs cannot be in R_0, we have $x \leq y$ and $y \leq z$. Hence $x \leq z$ and we can replace (x, y) and (y, z) with (x, z), which violates the minimality of C.

Since R_0 is acyclic by assumption, C must contain an edge $(x, y) \notin R_0$. Because $(x, y) \in (R_0 \cup \leq)^*$ by assumption, this means $x \leq y$. However, since $x, y \in X$ from our earlier argument, and because the budget sets are downward–closed with respect to $\leq$, $x \leq y$ implies $(x, y) \in R_0$ by definition of R_0. This contradictions our earlier assumption that $(x, y) \notin R_0$. Hence no minimal cycle exists, and $\preceq$ is acyclic. □

LEMMA 11. *Algorithm $\mathcal{A}$ computes a choice function ψ such that $\psi(p, b) \in B(p, b)$ for all p and b.*

PROOF. For all valid p and b, $\mathbf{0} \in B(p, b) \cap X$, and all elements $x \in X$ have distinct ranks $r(x)$, so $z(p, b)$ and hence $x(p, b)$ are well defined, and by construction, the output $x(p, b) \in B(p, b)$. □

LEMMA 12. *Let r be the ranking computed during preproccessing. Let $\preceq := (R_0 \cup \leq)^*$ and assume R_0 is acyclic. Fix $x, y \in X$. Then ranks are distinct, i.e., $x \neq y$ implies $r(x) \neq r(y)$, and the ranks are monotone in $\preceq$, i.e., $x \preceq y$ implies $r(x) \leq r(y)$.*

PROOF. The first part, $x \neq y$ implies $r(x) \neq r(y)$, holds by construction since $r(\cdot)$ is the rank within a permutation π and no two elements have the same rank. Now suppose $x \preceq y$. Then by definition of $\preceq$ there is a path P in $(R_0 \cup \leq)^*$ from x to y. We claim there must be a path P' from x to y in the digraph $G = (X, E)$ constructed during preproccessing, since (i) all the edges in R_0 are present in E, and (ii) every maximal subpath of P starting and ending at lattice points in X and consisting only of edges in $\leq$ can be traversed by a single edge in E_0 by the transitivity of $\leq$, and $E_0 \subseteq E$, and (iii) P can be decomposed into edges in R_0 and maximal subpaths of P starting and ending at lattice points in X. Hence there is a path in G from x to y and so the topological sort must place x before y in π, which implies $r(x) \leq r(y)$. (Note that since R_0 is acyclic by assumption, $\preceq$ is acyclic by Lemma 10, which in turn implies G is acyclic, and thus there exists a topological ordering of its vertices.) □

LEMMA 13. *Assume that R_0 is acyclic. The choice function ψ computed by $\mathcal{A}$ explains the data, i.e., $\psi(p^i, b^i) = x^i$ for all $i \in [n]$.*

PROOF. Fix $i \in [n]$ arbitrarily. Recall B^i is the budget set faced by the consumer when x^i was chosen. Note $x^i \in B^i \cap X$, so it is considered in the arg max in the computation of $z(p^i, b^i)$. We consider two cases, namely $z(p^i, b^i) = x^i$ and $z(p^i, b^i) \neq x^i$.

In the first case, we have $\psi(p^i, b^i) = x^i$, as x^i is a maximal element of the budget set with respect to the lattice ordering $\leq$, and hence the evaluation of the lex max in the computation of $x(p^i, b^i)$ is over the singleton set $\{x^i\}$, and so the output of $\mathcal{A}$ is $x(p^i, b^i) = x^i$.

We next argue that the second case cannot occur. Suppose by way of contradiction that $z(p^i, b^i) \neq x^i$. Then there must be some $x^j \neq x^i$ such that $r(x^i) < r(x^j)$ and $x^j \in B^i$, by the definition of $z(p^i, b^i)$. However, the fact that $x^j \in B^i$ and x^i was chosen in the ith observation implies $(x^j, x^i) \in R_0$ and hence $x^j \preceq x^i$, where $\preceq := (R_0 \cup \leq)^*$ as before. Lemma 12 then implies $r(x^j) \leq r(x^i)$, contradicting our earlier deduction that $r(x^i) < r(x^j)$. □

We now introduce R_ψ, the preference relation revealed by $\psi(\cdot)$:

$$R_\psi := \{(x, y) \ : \ \exists p, b \,.\, x \in B(p, b) \setminus \{y\} \text{ and } y = \psi(p, b)\}. \tag{4}$$

Note $\psi(p^i, b^i) = x^i$ for all $i \in [n]$ implies $R_0 \subset R_\psi$.

THEOREM 14. *Algorithm $\mathcal{A}$ computes a choice function ψ such that if R_ψ is the preference relation revealed by ψ and R_0 is acyclic, then ψ explains the data and $(R_\psi \cup \leq)^*$ is acyclic.*

PROOF. We prove ψ explains the input in Lemma 13. Suppose, by way of contradiction, that R_0 is acyclic and yet there is a minimal cycle C in the induced binary relation $(R_\psi \cup \leq)^*$. Note that $\preceq$ is acyclic by Lemma 10.

Suppose that C consists of k edges $\{(y^i, y^{i+1}) : 1 \leq i \leq k\}$, where we define $y^{k+1} := y^1$ for convenience. We can suppose that each edge (y^i, y^{i+1}) is in R_ψ; the proof of this fact is similar to the proof of Lemma 10. Let $p(y^i)$ and $b(y^i)$ denote the prices and budget corresponding to the choice of y^i, so that $\psi(p(y^i), b(y^i)) = y^i$. Let $B(y^i) := B(p(y^i), b(y^i))$ denote the corresponding budget set. Let $z^i := z(p(y^i), b(y^i))$ be the intermediate lattice point computed when running $\mathcal{A}$ with input $(p(y^i), b(y^i))$ and the ranking $r(\cdot)$. We consider two cases, namely $z^i = z^j$ for all $i, j \in [k]$, or there exists i, j with $z^i \neq z^j$.

We start with the case that $z^i = z^j$ for all $i, j \in [k]$. By construction,

$$y^i \equiv x(p(y^i), b(y^i)) = \operatorname{lex\,max}\left\{x \ : \ x \in B(y^i), z^i \leq x\right\}$$

for all i. Since $(y^i, y^{i+1}) \in C$, we know $y^i \in B(y^{i+1})$, i.e., y^i is affordable for the budget set for which the consumer purchases y^{i+1}. Since $z^i = z^{i+1}$, this implies y^i is in the set over which the algorithm computes the lex max when running on input $(p(y^{i+1}), b(y^{i+1}))$, namely $\{x : x \in B(y^{i+1}), z^{i+1} \leq x\}$. Since y^{i+1} was selected, y^i is lexicographically less than or equal to y^{i+1}, which we denote by $y^i \leq_{\text{Lex}} y^{i+1}$. Since i was arbitrary,

$$y^1 \leq_{\text{Lex}} y^2 \leq_{\text{Lex}} \cdots \leq_{\text{Lex}} y^k \leq_{\text{Lex}} y^{k+1} = y^1.$$

Since lexicographic order is a partial order, we infer $y^1 = y^2 = \cdots = y^k$, contradicting the assumption that C is a cycle.

Moving on to the second case, suppose there exists i, j with $z^i \neq z^j$. Then there exists $i \in [k]$ with $z^i \neq z^{i+1}$. Recall that since $(y^i, y^{i+1}) \in C$, $y^i \in B(y^{i+1})$. Clearly, $y^{i+1} \in B(y^{i+1})$. Note for all x and y such that $x \leq y$, and for all prices p and budgets b, we have $y \in B(p, b)$ implies $x \in B(p, b)$. Since by construction $z^i \leq y^i$ and $z^{i+1} \leq y^{i+1}$, we infer $z^i, z^{i+1} \in B(y^{i+1})$. From this fact, the definitions of z^i and z^{i+1}, and the fact that distinct lattice points in X have distinct ranks (as stated in Lemma 12), we can infer $r(z^i) < r(z^{i+1})$.

Of course, for any j, if $z^j = z^{j+1}$ then $r(z^j) = r(z^{j+1})$. Hence for all $j \in [k]$, either $r(z^j) = r(z^{j+1})$ or $r(z^j) < r(z^{j+1})$, so that for all $j \in [k]$, $r(z^j) \leq r(z^{j+1})$, and moreover there is at least one strict inequality: $r(z^i) < r(z^{i+1})$. Altogether these facts yield

$$r(z^1) \leq \cdots \leq r(z^i) < r(z^{i+1}) \leq \cdots \leq r(z^{k+1}) = r(z^1)$$

contradicting the well-ordering of $\leq$ for $\mathbb{Z}_{++}$. □

COROLLARY 15. *A data $\{(x^i, p^i, b^i)\}_{i=0}^n$ is rationalizable if and only if algorithm $\mathcal{A}$ computes a demand function ψ such that ψ explains the data and is generated by a monotone utility function.*

PROOF. By Theorem 3, Lemma 10, and Theorem 14, a data $\{(x^i, p^i, b^i)\}_{i=0}^n$ is rationalizable if and only if the constructed ψ is such that $(R_\psi \cup \leq)^*$ is acyclic. Acyclicity implies (by a version of Szpilrajn's lemma) that $(R_\psi \cup \leq)^*$ has an extension to $\mathbb{Z}_+^d$. Since $\mathbb{Z}_+^d$ is countable, the extension trivially satisfies the standard order-denseness condition for a utility representation. The utility representation rationalizes ψ by definition of R_ψ; and it is monotone because it represents an extension of $\leq$. □

B. HARDNESS PROOFS

In this section we prove various hardness and inapproximability results cited in Section 2. These results show that the consumer is faced with solving an intractable problem according to a worst-case view of computational complexity in the consumer choice model. These results are not surprising or difficult but are included for completeness of presentation.

We start by proving the hardness of maximizing utility subject to a budget constraint under monotone utility functions.

LEMMA 16. *Maximizing utility subject to a budget constraint is NP-hard for monotone utility functions, both for divisible and indivisible goods.*

PROOF. For indivisible goods, the problem is NP-hard even for linear utility functions, since the problem

$$\arg\max\{u \cdot x \ : \ p \cdot x \leq b, \ x \in \mathbb{Z}_+\}$$

is precisely the UNBOUNDED KNAPSACK problem, a classic NP-hard problem [17].

For divisible goods, we may fix arbitrary nonnegative constants $v_1, \ldots, v_d$ and define the utility function as $u(x) = \sum_{i=1}^d v_i \mathbf{1}\{x_i \geq 1\}$, where $\mathbf{1}\{P\}$ is the indicator variable for predicate P, i.e., $\mathbf{1}\{P\} = 1$ if P is true, and $\mathbf{1}\{P\} = 0$ otherwise. Note u is monotone. The resulting problem,

$$\arg\max\{u(x) \ : \ p \cdot x \leq b, \ x \in \mathbb{R}_+\},$$

is again equivalent to UNBOUNDED KNAPSACK. The less-approximable DENSEST-k-SUBGRAPH problem can likewise be encoded: given $G = (V, E)$ set $u(x) = \sum_{(u,v) \in E} \mathbf{1}\{x_u \geq 1 \text{ and } x_v \geq 1\}$, $b = k$, and $p = \mathbf{1}$. □

Next, We provide an inapproximability result for maximizing a monotone supermodular function f subject to a cardinality constraint. A special case of this problem called QUADRATIC KNAPSACK has long been known to be NP-hard [21], via a simple reduction from DENSEST-k-SUBGRAPH.

Despite much effort, accurate bounds on the best approximation factor obtainable for DENSEST-k-SUBGRAPH by an efficient algorithm under reasonable complexity assumptions have eluded all attempts to date. We can, however, exploit a construction due to Khot to obtain the following result.

THEOREM 17. *Fix any constant $c \geq 1$, and let $\alpha(n) = 2^{n^c}$. There is no polynomial time $\alpha(n)$-approximation algorithm for maximizing a monotone supermodular function f subject to a cardinality constraint, unless NP has randomized subexponential time algorithms, i.e., unless NP $\subseteq \cap_{\epsilon>0}$BPTIME $\left(2^{n^\epsilon}\right)$, where $n = \log_2 |\operatorname{dom}(f)|$ is the size of the groundset V.*

PROOF. Fix a constant $d \geq 1$ and a DENSEST-k-SUBGRAPH input (G = (V,E), k), and define $f(S) := |E \cap \binom{S}{2}|$ for a subset of vertices S. Let $\tau(x) := 2^{x^d}$ and let $F(S) := \tau(f(S))$ where $\tau(x) := 2^{x^d}$. It may be easily verified that f is monotone supermodular, hence $g \circ f$ is as well for any monotone increasing and convex function g, such as τ. Thus F is monotone supermodular. For now, assume that there is a distribution $\mathcal{D}$ on DENSEST-k-SUBGRAPH instances such that no polynomial time algorithm can distinguish instances with $\max_{|S|\leq k} f(S) \leq x$ from those with $\max_{|S|\leq k} f(S) \geq \alpha x$, when they are drawn from $\mathcal{D}$. Then it must be hard to distinguish instances with $\max_{|S|\leq k} F(S) \leq 2^{x^d}$ and those with $\max_{|S|\leq k} F(S) \geq 2^{(\alpha x)^d}$, because they correspond to exactly the same distinction. Note also that all integers in the range of F can be written with polynomial in n bits, so the problem size (which we take to be $|V| + \log F(V)$, where V is the ground set) increases only by a polynomial factor when going from f to F. It follows that polynomial-time α-inapproximability for the first problem implies polynomial-time β-inapproximability for the latter, with $\beta := 2^{(\alpha x)^d}/2^{x^d}$. It remains to establish a lower bound on β.

To lower bound β, it is useful to understand possible values for x and α. Khot [22] (*c.f.* section C.2) proves the existence of a distribution $\mathcal{D}$ with $x = \Omega(n)$ and $\alpha = (1+\epsilon)$, under the complexity-theoretic assumption NP $\not\subseteq \cap_{\epsilon>0}$BPTIME $\left(2^{n^\epsilon}\right)$. Define constant $\delta > 0$ so that $x = \delta n$ in Khot's hard input distribution. Then $\log_2(\beta) = (\delta n)^d \left((1+\epsilon)^d - 1\right)$. Setting $d \geq \frac{1}{\log_2(1+\epsilon)}$ ensures $\log_2(\beta) \geq (\delta n)^d$. Hence we have an inapproximability factor of $2^{(\delta n)^d}$ for arbitrarily large constant d, which is equivalent to an inapproximability factor of 2^{n^c} for arbitrarily large constant c. □

C. PROOFS OF SPACE COMPLEXITY AND RUNNING TIME LOWER BOUNDS

We provide proofs for Propositions (6), (7), (8), and (9) in the reverse order of their appearance. We do so because we find it convenient to start with the proofs for general theories and then proceed to the proofs for the theory of the consumer.

PROOF OF PROPOSITION 9. Any g_τ that rationalizes data $D := \{(i_k, o_k)\}_{k=1}^n$ must encode a function $h : \{i_k : 1 \leq k \leq n\} \to \mathcal{O}$ that maps i_k to o_k for all k, since $g_\tau(i_k) = o_k$ by the assumption that g_τ rationalizes D. Fix an input sequence $\{i_k\}_{k=1}^n$. There are $N := |\mathcal{R}_\mathcal{G}\left(\{i_k\}_{k=1}^n\right)|$ possible functions h that map the elements of $\{i_k\}_{k=1}^n$ to outputs such that the resulting sequence $\{(i_k, h(i_k))\}_{k=1}^n$ is rationalizable. Hence g_τ encodes one of N states, which requires at least $\log_2 N$ bits in the worst-case. Since $\{i_k\}_{k=1}^n$ is an arbitrary input sequence of length n, we may maximize over such sequences to obtain the claimed worst-case bound. □

PROOF OF PROPOSITION 8. Fix theory $\mathcal{G}$, and let

$$N := \max_{(i_1,\ldots,i_n)} |\mathcal{R}_\mathcal{G}\left(\{i_k\}_{k=1}^n\right)|.$$

Let $\{i_k\}_{k=1}^n$ be an input sequence achieving $|\mathcal{R}_\mathcal{G}\left(\{i_k\}_{k=1}^n\right)| = N$. Without loss of generality, we assume the inputs i_k are distinct, otherwise we may remove duplicates to obtain a smaller input sequence $\{i'_k\}_{k=1}^{n'}$ with $|\mathcal{R}_\mathcal{G}\left(\{i'_k\}_{k=1}^{n'}\right)| = N$. Fix a RAM with wordsize $w = \Theta(\log n)$, and assume there is a deterministic algorithm $\mathcal{A}^*$ in this machine model which computes a function $f : \mathcal{D} \times \mathcal{I} \to \mathcal{O}$ in worst case time $t = t(|D|, |i|)$ such that $i \mapsto f(D,i)$ is a demand function rationalizing D. Fix a data set $D \in \mathcal{R}_\mathcal{G}\left(\{i_k\}_{k=1}^n\right)$, and define o_k for $k \in [n]$ such that $D = \{(i_k, o_k)\}_{k=1}^n$. Since we may permute the data points (i_k, o_k) in D arbitrary, this implies that for any $i \in \{i_k\}_{k=1}^n$ this algorithm $\mathcal{A}^*$ can infer the value of $f(D,i)$ after reading *any* $q := t\left\lceil \frac{w}{s} \right\rceil$ data points, where s is the number of bits to encode a data point. By the distinctness of the inputs, $s \geq \log_2(n)$, so that $q = \mathcal{O}(t)$. Since $\mathcal{A}^*$ can infer the value of $f(D,i)$ for all $i \in \{i_k\}_{k=1}^n$ using the same q data points, it can compute D given $\{i_k\}_{k=1}^n$. Hence, qw bits suffice to identify which element of $\mathcal{R}_\mathcal{G}\left(\{i_k\}_{k=1}^n\right)$ is the actual data set, which implies $qw \geq \log_2 N$. Therefore, we obtain $\log_2 N \leq qw = \mathcal{O}(tw)$, which may be rearranged to yield the claimed bound $t = \Omega\left(\frac{\log_2 N}{w}\right)$. □

PROOF OF PROPOSITION 7. By Proposition 9, it suffices to exhibit a sequence $\{i_k\}_{k=1}^n$ such that $\log|\mathcal{R}_\mathcal{G}\left(\{i_k\}_{k=1}^n\right)| = \Omega(n \log n)$, which we will now proceed to do.

Suppose we are in the indivisible goods case. Recall an input in this theory consists of a price vector p and a budget b, and an output is a consumption bundle. We suppose $p^k = \mathbf{1}$ and $b^k = k$ for all $k \in [n]$. Next, we count the number of rationalizable data sets whose inputs consist of such p^k and b^k, i.e., $N := |\mathcal{R}_\mathcal{G}\left(\{i_k\}_{k=1}^n\right)|$ where $i_k := (p^k, b^k)$ for all k.

We claim $N = (n+1)!$. To show this, we show that for all k with $1 \leq j < n$, for any choice of $x^1, \ldots, x^{j-1}$ such that $\{(x^k, p^k, b^k)\}_{k=0}^{j-1}$ is rationalizable, there are $j+1$ choices for x^j such that $\{(x^i, p^i, b^i)\}_{i=0}^{j}$ is also rationalizable. So, we proceed by induction on j. The base case, $j = 1$ is trivial, since the consumer can buy one unit of either of the two goods. For the induction case, we claim that any consumption bundle $(x_1, x_2) \in \mathbb{Z}_+^2$ such that $x_1 + x_2 = j$ yields a rationalizable extension of the data. By Theorem 3, it suffices to prove that the new data point $(x^j, p^j, b^j) := ((x_1, x_2), \mathbf{1}, j)$ does not introduce a cycle into the induced preference relation R_0. However this is clearly impossible since $(x^j, x^i) \notin R_0$ for all $i < j$. Since the number of solutions $(x_1, x_2) \in \mathbb{Z}_+^2$ to $x_1 + x_2 = j$ is $j+1$, this concludes the induction step. Hence we get the rather trivial recurrence $N(j) = (j+1)N(j-1)$ with $N(1) = 2$, which has solution $N := N(n) = (n+1)!$. Finally, we note that $\log_2(n+1)! = (1 - o(1))n \log_2 n$, which completes the proof. □

PROOF OF PROPOSITION 6. Proposition 6 claims that any function $f : \mathcal{D} \times \mathcal{I} \to \mathcal{O}$ such that $i \mapsto f(D,i)$ is a demand function rationalizing D implies f takes worst-case $\Omega(|D|)$ time, where $|D|$ is the number of data points (i.e., pairs (i_k, o_k)) in D. At a high level is this due to the simple observation that f must read all of D in the worst case. We can prove it by applying Proposition 8, using the construction of Proposition 7 which gives an input sequence with $\log|\mathcal{R}_\mathcal{G}\left(\{i_k\}_{k=1}^n\right)| = \Omega(n \log n)$. Combining the two immediately yields the claimed lower bound of $\Omega(n)$. □

Repeated Matching Pennies with Limited Randomness*

Michele Budinich†
IMT - Institute for Advanced Studies
Lucca, Italy
m.budinich@imtlucca.it

Lance Fortnow
Northwestern University
Evanston, Il
fortnow@eecs.northwestern.edu

ABSTRACT

We consider a repeated Matching Pennies game in which players have limited access to randomness. Playing the (unique) Nash equilibrium in this n-stage game requires n random bits. Can there be Nash equilibria (or ε-Nash equilibria) that use less than n random coins?

Our main results are as follows

- We give a full characterization of approximate equilibria, showing that, for any $\gamma \in [0,1]$, the game has a γ-Nash equilibrium if and only if both players have $(1-\gamma)n$ random coins.
- When players are bound to run in polynomial time with n^{δ} bits of randomness, approximate Nash equilibria can exist if and only if one-way functions exist.
- It is possible to trade-off randomness for running time. In particular, under reasonable assumptions, if we give one player only $O(\log n)$ random coins but allow him to run in arbitrary polynomial time with n^{δ} bits of randomness and we restrict his opponent to run in time n^k, for some fixed k, then we can sustain an ε-Nash equilibrium.
- When the game is played for an infinite amount of rounds with time discounted utilities, under reasonable assumptions, we can reduce the amount of randomness required to achieve a ε-Nash equilibrium to n^{δ}, where n is the number of random coins necessary to achieve an approximate Nash equilibrium in the general case.

Categories and Subject Descriptors

J.4 [**Social and Behavioral Sciences**]: Economics

*This research was partially supported by NSF grants CCF-0829754 and DMS-0652521.

†This work was done while the author was visiting Northwestern University, Department of Electrical Engineering and Computer Science.

EC'11, June 5–9, 2011, San Jose, California, USA.

General Terms

Theory, Economics

Keywords

Pseudo-random Number Generators, Repeated Games, Nash Equilibrium, Bounded Rationality.

1. INTRODUCTION

In the classical setting of Game Theory, one of the core assumptions is that all participating agents are "fully rational". This amounts not only to the fact that an agent must be able to make optimal decisions, given the other players' actions, but also to the fact that he must understand how these actions will affect the behavior of all other participants. If this is the case, a Nash equilibrium can be viewed as a set of strategies in which each agent is simply computing his best response given his opponents' actions. However, in real world strategic interactions, people often behave in manners that are not fully rational. There are many reasons behind non-rational behavior, we focus on two: limitations on computation and limitations on randomness.

Since the work of Herbert Simon [13], much research has focused on defining models that take computational issues into account. In recent years, the idea that the full rationality assumption is often unrealistic has been formalized using tools and ideas from computational complexity. It is in fact easy to come up with settings, as in Fortnow and Santhanam [4], in which simply computing a best response strategy involves solving a computationally hard problem. Furthermore there is strong evidence that, in general, the problem of finding a Nash equilibrium is computationally difficult for matrix games (Daskalakis, Goldberg and Papadimitriou [3], Chen and Deng [2]).

Traditionally bounded rationality has focused on two computational resources: time and space. In this paper we focus on another fundamental resource: randomness.

It is a basic fact that games in which agents are not allowed to randomize might have no Nash equilibrium. In this sense, randomness is essential in game theory. We focus on a simple two player zero-sum game that captures this: Matching Pennies (Figure 1). Specifically, we consider the repeated version of Matching Pennies, played for n rounds. In this game, the unique Nash equilibrium is the one in which, at every round, both players choose one of their two strategies uniformly at random. The algorithm that implements this strategy requires n random coins, one for each round. The main question we address in this paper is: can there

Player 1 (P1) \ Player 2 (P2)	H	T
H	1, −1	−1, 1
T	−1, 1	1, −1

Figure 1: The payoff bimatrix for the Matching Pennies game.

be Nash equilibria if the amount of randomness available to both players is less than n?

First we show that, in general, the game cannot have a Nash equilibrium in which both players have only a fraction of n random coins. In particular, when we give both players $n(1-\gamma)$ random coins, we can only achieve a γ-Nash equilibrium. This turns out to be tight, in the sense that we can show that any game with a γ-Nash equilibrium both players must have at least $n(1-\gamma)$ coins.

The proof of this fact, however, relies on the players' ability to implement a strategy that runs in exponential time. We then consider games in which the players' strategies are polynomially-bounded. Using ideas developed in cryptography and computational complexity we show that, in this setting, ε-Nash equilibria that use only n^δ coins exist if and only if one-way functions exist.

We also show that the amount of randomness can be "traded" for time. If we allow one of the players to run in arbitrary polynomial time, but use only $O(\log n)$ bits, we can still achieve a ε-Nash equilibrium if we restrict his opponent to run in time n^k for some fixed $k > 0$, while giving him n^δ random bits.

Finally we consider an infinitely repeated game with time discounted utilities. In this case, in general, for any discount factor δ and approximation ε, we can always achieve a ε-Nash equilibrium with only n random coins, if n is large enough. When we limit players' strategies to polynomial size circuits, we can reduce the amount of randomness to n^δ, for any $\delta > 0$.

Related Work

There are many recent approaches to bounded rationality using a computational complexity perspective. For instance Halpern and Pass [7] study games in which players' strategies are Turing machines. The idea of considering randomness as a costly resource in game theory has received only limited attention. Kalyanaraman and Umans [11] study zero-sum games, and give both an efficient deterministic algorithm for finding ε-Nash equilibria, as well as a weaker, but more general, result in the spirit of our Lemma 3.1, giving a randomness-efficient adaptive on-line algorithm for playing repeated zero-sum games. Hu [9] also considers a similar setting but he is concerned with computability rather than complexity. He considers infinitely repeated plays of 2 player zero-sum games that have no pure strategy Nash equilibrium, and in which players have a set of feasible actions, which represents both the strategies they can play and the strategies they can predict. In this setting Hu gives necessary and sufficient conditions for the existence of Nash equilibria. Finally Gossner and Tomala [6], give entropy bounds on Bayesian learning in a game theoretic setting, in a more general framework then this paper. Their results applied to Matching Pennies do not achieve the tight bounds we get in Lemma 3.1.

The rest of the paper is organized as follows. In Section 2 we introduce the notation and known results used. Section 3 presents an information theoretic impossibility result. Section 4 considers players whose strategies are limited to polynomial sized Boolean circuit families, while Sections 5 and 6 give extensions of the main results to complexity pseudorandom number generators and infinitely repeated versions of the game.

2. BACKGROUND AND DEFINITIONS

2.1 Game Theory Notation

Throughout the paper we consider a repeated game of Matching Pennies. We focus on this game because it captures one of the fundamental aspects of randomness in game theory. Studying such a simple game also allows us to get tight bounds. However, variations of our results extend to other similar 2 person zero-sum repeated games.

The payoffs at each round are shown in Figure 1. Let $h : \{\text{H,T}\} \times \{\text{H,T}\} \to \{-1, 1\}$, be the payoff to Player 1 (P1), and $-h$ the payoff for P2. When we allow the players to randomize, we denote as S_i a randomized strategy on $\Delta\{H, T\}$ for player i. P1's expected payoff in one round is

$$\mathbf{E}[h(S_1, S_2)] = \sum_{s_1, s_2 \in \{\text{H,T}\}} \Pr(S_1 = s_1) \Pr(S_2 = s_2)\, h(s_1, s_2).$$

Let $u : \{\text{H,T}\}^n \times \{\text{H,T}\}^n \to \{-n, \cdots, n\}$ be P1's cumulative payoff when the game is played for n rounds. In the repeated game, mixed strategies can be viewed as distribution over sequences of length n that are dependend on the opponent's strategy. Given the adversary's strategy, let $R_i = (r_i^1, \cdots, r_i^n) \in \Delta\{\text{H,T}\}^n$ denote a randomized strategies for player i. P1's expected cumulative payoff is

$$\mathbf{E}[u(R_1, R_2)] = \sum_{t=1}^{n} \mathbf{E}\left[h(r_1^t, r_2^t)\right].$$

Finally we define the expected average payoff to P1 for the n-round game as

$$\mathbf{E}[U(R_1, R_2)] = \frac{\mathbf{E}[u(R_1, R_2)]}{n},$$

and consequently P2's expected payoff is $-\mathbf{E}[U(R_1, R_2)]$. To denote player's i payoff we will sometimes use the standard notation $\mathbf{E}[U(R_i, R_{-i})]$, where R_i is player's i mixed strategy and R_{-i} is his opponent's mixed strategy.

Definition 2.1 (Nash equilibrium). *A pair of mixed strategies (R_1, R_2) is a Nash equilibrium for the n-stage Matching Pennies game if, for $i = 1, 2$:*

$$\mathbf{E}[U(R_i, R_{-i})] \geq \mathbf{E}\left[U(R_i', R_{-i})\right] \quad \textit{for all } R_i' \in \Delta\{H, T\}^n.$$

In some cases we will consider a relaxed notion of equilibrium, namely ε-Nash equilibrium.

DEFINITION 2.2 (ε-NASH EQUILIBRIUM). *A pair of mixed strategies* (R_1, R_2) *is a* ε*-Nash equilibrium for the n-stage Matching Pennies game if, for* $i = 1, 2$*:*

$$\mathbf{E}[U(R_i, R_{-i})] \geq \mathbf{E}[U(R_i', R_{-i})] - \varepsilon \quad \textit{for all } R_i' \in \Delta\{H, T\}^n.$$

2.2 Complexity and Pseudorandomness

We give a brief description of the pseudorandomness tools we need for this paper. For more details we recommend the textbooks of Arora and Barak [1] and Goldreich [5].

The model of computation used throughout most of the paper is based on Boolean Circuits. We consider circuits with AND, OR and NOT gates, and denote by C_n a circuit with n input nodes. A circuit family $\{C_i\}_{i\in\mathbb{N}}$ is an infinite collection of circuits, intuitively one for each input length.

The size of a circuit $|C_n|$ is the number of gates. A circuit family is polynomial sized if there is a $k > 0$ such that, for all n, $|C_n| \leq n^k$. The class of languages recognizable by families of polynomial sized circuits is called $\mathsf{P/Poly}$. Any language that can be decided in polynomial time by a deterministic or randomized Turing machine is also in $\mathsf{P/Poly}$. Formally $\mathsf{P} \subseteq \mathsf{BPP} \subseteq \mathsf{P/Poly}$.

A function is one-way if it is easy to compute and hard to invert.

DEFINITION 2.3 (ONE-WAY FUNCTION). *A one-way function is a polynomial-time computable function* $f : \{0,1\}^n \to \{0,1\}^n$ *such that, for all polynomial size circuits* D *and* $y = f(x)$ *(where* x *is chosen uniformly at random on* $\{0,1\}^n$*),* $\Pr(f(D(y)) = f(x)) < n^{-c}$ *for all* $c > 0$ *and sufficiently large* n.

Informally, two objects are indistinguishable if no polynomial sized circuit family can tell them apart with noticeable probability.

DEFINITION 2.4 (INDISTINGUISHABILITY). *Let* X, Y *be two random variables on* $\{0,1\}^n$*. We say that* X *and* Y *are computationally indistinguishable if for every family of polynomial size circuits* $\{C_i\}_{i\in\mathbb{N}}$*, every* $c > 0$ *and for sufficiently large* n

$$\left| Pr(C_n(X) = 1) - Pr(C_n(Y) = 1) \right| < \frac{1}{n^c}.$$

A cryptographic pseudorandom number generator (PRNG) is a deterministic algorithm whose output is computationally indistinguishable from the uniform distribution, provided that it's input is truly random. We will denote by U_k a random variable uniformly distributed on $\{0,1\}^k$.

DEFINITION 2.5 (CRYPTOGRAPHIC PRNG). *A cryptographic pseudorandom number generator is a deterministic polynomial time algorithm* $G : \{0,1\}^{l(n)} \to \{0,1\}^n$*, where* $l(n) < n$ *is a polynomial time computable function, such that* $G(U_{l(n)})$ *and* U_n *are computationally indistinguishable.*

There are two basic properties about pseudorandom number generators that we will use. One relates the notion of pseudorandomness to the notion of predictability.

DEFINITION 2.6 (UNPREDICTABLE). *Let* $G : \{0,1\}^{l(n)} \to \{0,1\}^n$ *be a polynomial time algorithm, and* $G(x) = (y_1, \cdots, y_n)$*. We call* G *unpredictable if for every family of polynomial size circuits* $\{D_i\}_{i\in\mathbb{N}}$*, all* $c > 0$ *and for sufficiently large* n

$$Pr(D_i(y_1, \ldots, y_{i-1}) = y_i) \leq \frac{1}{2} + \frac{1}{n^c}.$$

Intuitively a pseudorandom number generator must be unpredictable, otherwise we could easily build a test for it by using the predictor circuits. In 1982 Yao [14] proved the opposite implication, thus establishing the following theorem.

THEOREM 2.7 (YAO'S THEOREM). *A polynomial time algorithm* $G : \{0,1\}^{l(n)} \to \{0,1\}^n$ *is unpredictable if and only if* G *is a pseudorandom number generator.*

Håstad, Impagliazzo, Luby and Levin in 1999 [8] showed how to construct pseudorandom number generators with polynomial expansion based on one-way functions.

THEOREM 2.8 (PRNG'S FROM ONE-WAY FUNCTIONS). *One way functions exist if and only if for every* $\delta > 0$ *there is a pseudorandom number generator with* $l(n) = n^\delta$.

Cryptographic pseudorandom number generators' main power lies in the ability to fool any polynomial sized adversary, while running in polynomial time. However, in other areas of complexity, such as derandomization, the crucial issue is having a smaller seed.

DEFINITION 2.9 (COMPLEXITY PRNG). *A complexity pseudorandom number generator is a* $2^{l(n)}$ *time computable function* $G : \{0,1\}^{l(n)} \to \{0,1\}^n$*, such that for any circuit* C *of size* n

$$\left| Pr(C(U_{l(n)}) = 1) - Pr(C(G(U_n)) = 1) \right| < n^{-1}.$$

The essential difference with cryptographic pseudorandom number generators is the order of quantifiers. A cryptographic pseudorandom number generator fools circuits of an arbitrary polynomial size. The complexity pseudorandom number generator fools circuits only of a fixed polynomial size but under the right assumptions requires far fewer random bits.

Impagliazzo and Wigderson [10] building on a series of paper starting with Nisan and Wigderson [12] characterize when complexity pseudorandom number generators exist.

THEOREM 2.10. *There exists* $L \in \mathsf{DTIME}(2^{O(l(n))})$ *and* $\varepsilon > 0$ *such that no circuit of size at most* $2^{\varepsilon l(n)}$ *can compute* L *if and only if there exists a complexity pseudorandom number generator with* $l(n) = C \log n$ *for some* $C > 0$.

3. INFORMATION THEORETIC BOUNDS

In this section we make no computational assumptions on the players, and show that there can be no Nash equilibrium if we limit the amount of randomness available to both players.

LEMMA 3.1. *For any* $\gamma \in [0,1]$*, if P2 has less than* $n(1-\gamma)$ *random bits, then P1 has a deterministic strategy* A *that achieves an expected average payoff of at least* γ.

PROOF. We will give a strategy $A = (a^1, \cdots, a^n)$ for P1 that achieves a high payoff against any strategy $B = (b^1, \cdots, b^n)$ from P2.

Player 1 will enumerate all of P2's possible coin flips, and will obtain a set of $2^{n(1-\gamma)}$ possible strategies, one of which is the one being used by P2. After each play by P2, P1 can eliminate all the strategies that do not play that action at that round. Let S^t be the set of strategies that are consistent with P2's plays up to round t. Initially the set S^1 contains $2^{n(1-\gamma)}$ strategies, and, for all t, $|S^{t+1}| \leq |S^t|$.

The strategy A for P1 is straightforward: at round t, P1 will play based on the most likely event: he will consider all strategies in S^t and play H if the majority of strategies in S^t use H at round t and play T otherwise. Let p^t be the exact fraction of strategies that are the majority at round t,

$$p^t = \frac{\max\{|\{b^t \mid b^t = H\}|, |\{b^t \mid b^t = T\}|\}}{|S^t|}, \quad (1)$$

so that $p^t \in [1/2, 1]$. P1's expected payoff at round t is:

$$\mathbf{E}\left[h(a^t, b^t)\right] = p^t - (1 - p^t) = 2p^t - 1 \geq 0.$$

Thus P1's average expected payoff is at least 0. To show that P1 can actually achieve an average expected payoff of γ we need to consider the amount of information P1 gains at each round. We define the following potential function $\phi : \{1, \ldots, n\} \to \mathbb{R}$:

$$\phi(t) = \sum_{k=1}^{t-1} h(a^k, b^k) - \log |S^t|,$$

which considers both the accumulated payoff for P1 and the log-size of the set of consistent strategies. At time $t = 1$ there are $2^{n(1-\gamma)}$ possible strategies for P2, so $\phi(1) = -n(1-\gamma)$. We will now lower bound the expected increase in ϕ at each round. We can express this as

$$\begin{aligned}\mathbf{E}\left[\phi(t+1) - \phi(t)\right] &= \left(\mathbf{E}\left[\sum_{k=1}^{t} h(a^k, b^k)\right] - \mathbf{E}\left[\sum_{k=1}^{t-1} h(a^k, b^k)\right]\right) \\ &\quad - \left(\mathbf{E}\left[\log |S^{t+1}|\right] - \mathbf{E}\left[\log |S^t|\right]\right) \\ &= \mathbf{E}\left[h(a^t, b^t)\right] - \left(\mathbf{E}\left[\log |S^{t+1}| - \log |S^t|\right]\right) \\ &= 2p^t - 1 - \left(\mathbf{E}\left[\log |S^{t+1}| - \log |S^t|\right]\right).\end{aligned}$$

Now consider $\mathbf{E}\left[\log |S^{t+1}|\right]$. When P1 looses he can eliminate a p^t fraction of strategies, thus the new set S^{t+1} will contain a $(1 - p^t)$ fraction of the strategies in S^t. On the other hand, when P1 wins, $|S^{t+1}| = p^t |S^t|$. To complete the analysis we have to consider two cases, since if $p^t = 1$ then $\mathbf{E}\left[\log |S^{t+1}|\right]$ is not well defined.

First assume $p^t = 1$. This happens when all feasible strategies for P2 have the same action at round t. In this case P1 will win with probability 1, and the size of the set of feasible strategies will stay the same. So, overall, the increase in ϕ will be 1.

Now assume $p^t \in [1/2, 1)$. Then, the expected size of the set S^{t+1} is:

$$\mathbf{E}\left[\log |S^{t+1}|\right] = \left((1 - p^t) \log(1 - p^t)|S^t| + p^t \log p^t |S^t|\right). \quad (2)$$

The expected change in $\log |S^t|$ does not depend on S^t, but only on p^t, since

$$\begin{aligned}\mathbf{E}\left[\log |S^{t+1}| - \log |S^t|\right] &= \left[(1 - p^t) \log(1 - p^t)|S^t| \right. \\ &\quad \left. + p^t \log p^t |S^t|\right] - \log |S^t| \\ &= (1 - p^t) \log(1 - p^t) + p^t \log p^t.\end{aligned}$$

So that the overall change in potential when $p^t < 1$ is

$$\mathbf{E}\left[\phi(t+1) - \phi(t)\right] \geq 2p^t - 1 - (1 - p^t) \log(1 - p^t) - p^t \log p^t,$$

which is always at least 1 for $p^t \geq 1/2$.

So, for all $p^t \in [1/2, 1]$, at each step the potential function φ increases by at least 1. Thus, after n rounds we have that

$$\begin{aligned}\mathbf{E}\left[\phi(n)\right] &\geq \phi(1) + \min_t\{n\mathbf{E}\left[\phi(t+1) - \phi(t)\right]\} \\ &\geq -n(1 - \gamma) + n = n\gamma.\end{aligned}$$

Since P1's expected payoff is at least $\mathbf{E}\left[\phi(n)\right]$, this completes the proof. □

This result immediately implies that, without any computational assumption, there can be no equilibrium with less than n random coins.

COROLLARY 3.2. *For all $\gamma_1, \gamma_2 \in [0, 1]$ such that $\gamma_1 + \gamma_2 > 0$, if P1 and P2 have, respectively, $n(1 - \gamma_1)$ and $n(1 - \gamma_2)$ random coins, then there can be no Nash equilibrium in the n-stage Matching Pennies repeated game.*

PROOF. Assume, by contradiction, that (S_1, S_2) is such a Nash equilibrium. By Lemma 3.1, P1's expected payoff must be $\mathbf{E}\left[U(S_1, S_2)\right] \geq \gamma_2$ and P2's payoff $-\mathbf{E}\left[U(S_1, S_2)\right] \geq \gamma_1$, otherwise they would be better off by using the majority strategy in the proof of Lemma 3.1. Summing the two inequalities we get $\gamma_1 + \gamma_2 \leq 0$, a contradiction, since we assume $\gamma_1 + \gamma_2 > 0$. □

However, if we limit the amount of randomness available to both players, we are still able to achieve an ε-Nash equilibrium. Furthermore, if the game has a ε-Nash equilibrium, then both players must have at least $(1 - \varepsilon)n$ random coins.

THEOREM 3.3. *Let $\gamma \subset [0, 1]$. The game has a γ-Nash equilibrium if and only if both players have $n(1 - \gamma)$ random coins.*

For simplicity we assume γ is the same for both players, however a similar result holds even in the case where the two players have a different amount of random coins.

PROOF. To show the "only-if" implication, consider, by way of contradiction, a game that has a γ-Nash equilibrium (S_1, S_2) but in which both players have less than $n(1 - \gamma)$ random bits. Thus there must be a $\gamma' > \gamma$ such that they have exactly $n(1 - \gamma')$ random bits. Since (S_1, S_2) is a γ-Nash equilibrium, it must be the case that, for any strategy S'_1 for P1

$$\mathbf{E}\left[U(S_1, S_2)\right] \geq \mathbf{E}\left[U(S'_1, S_2)\right] - \gamma.$$

By Lemma 3.1 we know that both players have a strategy that achieves a payoff of at least $\gamma' > \gamma$, so that the above implies $\mathbf{E}\left[U(S_1, S_2)\right] > 0$. Applying the same argument to P2, we get $-\mathbf{E}\left[U(S_1, S_2)\right] > 0$, a contradiction.

The "if" part follows from Lemma 3.4 below. □

LEMMA 3.4. *Let $\gamma \in [0, 1]$. If both players have $n(1 - \gamma)$ random coins, then the game has a γ-Nash equilibrium.*

For simplicity we assume γn is even.

PROOF. Consider the following strategies: both player use their random coins to play uniformly at random for the first $n(1 - \gamma)$ rounds. Thereafter P1 will always play H, while P2 will alternate between H and T, playing $H, T, \ldots$. We claim that this is a γ-Nash equilibrium.

First notice that no player can improve his payoff in the first $n(1 - \gamma)$ rounds, given his opponent's strategy. Let's consider the remaining $n\gamma$ rounds. P1 could improve his payoff by playing $H, T, H, T \ldots$, however this only increases his payoff by γ. This holds also for P2, that could play $T, T, \ldots$, however gaining only γ. □

4. COMPUTATIONALLY EFFICIENT PLAYERS

The proof of Lemma 3.1 in the previous section relies heavily the fact that we make no computational assumptions. In particular, to implement the majority strategy and compute p^t in (1) requires solving #P hard problems, by reduction from #SAT. If we restrict the players to run in time polynomial in n this particular strategy likely becomes unfeasible. In this setting, under reasonable complexity assumptions, it is possible to greatly reduce the amount of randomness and, at the same time, achieve a ε-Nash equilibrium.

We consider players' whose actions are polynomial size Boolean circuits. A strategy is thus a circuit family $\{C_i\}_{i\in\mathbb{N}}$, such that circuit $C_{l(n)}$ takes as input $l(n)$ random coins and outputs the n actions to be played. Notice that this definition implies that each agent can simulate any of his opponent's strategies.

We consider equilibria that use n^δ random coins for any $\delta > 0$. Theorem 4.1 shows that such ε-Nash equilibria exist if and only if one-way functions exist.

THEOREM 4.1. *If players are bound to run in time polynomial in n, then, for all $\delta > 0$ and sufficiently large n, ε-Nash equilibria that use only n^δ random coins exist, where $\varepsilon = n^{-k}$ for all $k > 0$ and sufficiently large n's, if and only if one-way functions exist.*

PROOF. The if part is Lemma 4.3, while the only-if part is Lemma 4.4. □

As a preliminary result we show that, in our setting, the expected utility when at least one player uses a pseudorandom number generator can't be too far from the expected utility when playing uniformly at random.

LEMMA 4.2. *Assume one-way functions exist, and let G be the strategy corresponding to the output of a pseudorandom number generator. For any strategy S that runs in time polynomial in n, for all $k > 0$ and sufficiently large n,*

$$\Big|\mathbf{E}\left[U(G,S)\right]\Big| \le n^{-k} \text{ and } \Big|\mathbf{E}\left[U(S,G)\right]\Big| \le n^{-k}.$$

PROOF. We prove only the first inequality, the proof for the second one being symmetric.

Proof by contradiction. Assuming there is a $k > 0$ such that $\Big|\mathbf{E}\left[U(G,S)\right]\Big| > n^{-k}$ for infinitely many n's, we will construct a test T for G, and show that

$$\Big|\Pr\left(T\left(G\left(U_{l(n)}\right)\right) = 1\right) - \Pr\left(T\left(U_n\right) = 1\right)\Big| > n^{-c} \quad (3)$$

for some $c > 0$ and infinitely many n's, thus contradicting the assumption that G is a pseudorandom number generator.

First consider the n random variables $A_i(G,S)$, for $i = 1, \cdots, n$, where $A_i(G,S)$ is simply P1's payoff at round i. Since $\sum_{i=1}^{n} A_i(G,S) = nU(G,S)$,

$$\sum_{i=1}^{n} \mathbf{E}\left[A_i(G,S)\right] > n^{1-k}.$$

This implies that there must be an i such that $\mathbf{E}\left[A_i(G,S)\right] > n^{-k}$. Fix that i.

The test T takes as input an n-bit sequence x and generates a sequence of plays s according to strategy S. Now T simulates an n-stage repeated Matching Pennies game with strategies (x, s). If P1 wins the i-th round then it will output 1, otherwise the output will be 0. In other words, T outputs 1 if and only if $A_i(x,s) = 1$. Notice that T runs in time polynomial in n.

When x is drawn from the uniform distribution, P1 will win with probability 1/2, or $\Pr\left(T(U_n) = 1\right) = 1/2$.

Now notice, that since $A_i \in \{-1, 1\}$, $\Pr\left(A_i = 1\right) = \frac{\mathbf{E}[A_i]+1}{2}$. This implies that

$$\Pr\left(T(G(U_{l(n)})) = 1\right) = \frac{\mathbf{E}\left[A_i\right] + 1}{2} > \frac{1}{2n^k} + \frac{1}{2}.$$

Thus

$$\Big|\Pr\left(T\left(G_1\left(U_{l(n)}\right)\right) = 1\right) - \Pr\left(T\left(U_n\right) = 1\right)\Big| > \frac{1}{2n^k},$$

which proves the lemma. □

LEMMA 4.3. *If one-way functions exist and players are bound to run in time polynomial in n, then for every $\delta, k > 0$ and for sufficiently large n, the n-stage has an n^{-k}-Nash equilibrium in which each player uses at most n^δ random bits.*

PROOF. Assume, by contradiction, that one-way functions exist but there are values $\delta > 0$ and $k > 0$ such that the game has no n^{-k}-Nash equilibrium in which players use at most n^δ random coins.

Since we assume one-way functions exist, by Theorem 2.8 there exist pseudorandom number generators that use n^δ coins. Assume both players use the output of such pseudorandom number generators as their strategies (which we call, respectively, G_1 and G_2). Since we are assuming that this is not a n^{-k}-Nash equilibrium, one of the players, say Player 1, must have a strategy A such that

$$\mathbf{E}\left[U\left(A, G_2\right)\right] > \mathbf{E}\left[U\left(G_1, G_2\right)\right] + n^{-k}. \quad (4)$$

By Lemma 4.2 we can choose a $k' > 0$ such that

$$\mathbf{E}\left[U\left(A, G_2\right)\right] > -n^{-k'} + n^{-k}. \quad (5)$$

Pick $c = k' = k + 1$, so that $\mathbf{E}\left[U\left(A, G_2\right)\right] > n^{-c}$ for $n > 2$. This contradicts Lemma 4.2, proving the claim. □

We now prove the opposite direction, that is that the existence of Nash equilibria that use few random bits implies the existence of one-way functions.

LEMMA 4.4. *If for every $\delta > 0$ there is a Nash equilibrium in which each player uses n^δ random bits and runs in time polynomial in n, then one-way functions exist.*

PROOF. Let (A, B) be such a Nash equilibrium and assume, by contradiction, that one-way functions don't exist. This implies that pseudorandom number generators can't exist (Goldreich [5]), and so, A and B can't be sequences that are computationally indistinguishable from uniform.

Thus, by Yao's theorem (Theorem 2.7), we know that there are polynomial size circuit families $\{C_i\}_{i\in\mathbb{N}}$ and $\{D_i\}_{i\in\mathbb{N}}$ such that

$$\Pr\left(C_i(y_1, \ldots, y_i) = y_{i+1}\right) > 1/2 + \delta_1$$
$$\Pr\left(D_i(z_1, \ldots, z_i) = z_{i+1}\right) > 1/2 + \delta_2,$$

for some $\delta_1, \delta_2 > 0$, where $A(x_1, \ldots, x_{l_1(n)}) = (y_1, y_2, \ldots, y_n)$ and $B(x_1, \ldots, x_{l_2(n)}) = (z_1, z_2, \ldots, z_n)$.

To get a contradiction it is sufficient to show that players are better off by using the predictor circuits C and D.

Consider Player 1: using D, at each round he can guess, given the previous history, the opponent's next move with probability $\frac{1}{2} + \delta_1$. Thus his expected payoff at any round t is

$$\mathbf{E}\left[h(d^t, b^t)\right] > \frac{1}{2} + \delta_1 - \frac{1}{2} + \delta_1 = 2\delta_1,$$

where the expectation is over the internal coin tosses of the predictor circuit D. The overall expected payoff is

$$\mathbf{E}\left[U(D, B)\right] > \frac{1}{n}\sum_{t=1}^{n} 2\delta = 2\delta_1.$$

Now, let $w = \mathbf{E}\left[U(A, B)\right]$ be the value of the expected payoff when players play (A, B). Consider the following cases:

1. $w \leq 0$: this implies that Player 1 could gain $2\delta_1$ by using strategy D,
2. $w > 0$: by definition Player 2's expected payoff is $-\mathbf{E}\left[U(A, B)\right] < 0$, so Player 2 can achieve a higher payoff by using his predictor circuit C,

In both cases we see that (A, B) can't be a Nash equilibrium, a contradiction. □

5. EXCHANGING TIME FOR RANDOMNESS

In this section we determine conditions under which a ε-Nash equilibrium can arise, given that one of the players has only a logarithmic amount of randomness and his opponent must run in time n^k for some fixed k. This shows how we can trade off randomness for time; the player with $O(\log n)$ random bits runs in time polynomial in n, while the player with more random bits runs in fixed polynomial time.

THEOREM 5.1. *Assume there exists $f \in \mathsf{DTIME}(2^{O(l(n))})$ and $\varepsilon > 0$ such that no circuit of size at most $2^{\varepsilon l(n)}$ can compute f and that one-way functions exist. Let Player 1's strategies be circuits of size at most n^k that use at most n^δ random bits for some $k > 2 + c\delta$, where $c \geq 1$ is a constant related to the implementation of a cryptographic pseudorandom number generator. Assume Player 2 has access to only $M \log n$ random bits. As long as $M > Ck$, where C is the constant in Theorem 2.10, then for all $\varepsilon > 0$ and sufficiently large n there is a ε-Nash equilibrium.*

PROOF. Let G_1 be the cryptographic pseudorandom number generator available to Player 1 and G_2 be the complexity pseudorandom number generator used by player 2. Furthermore let $\mathcal{S}_1$ be the set of all possible strategies for P1 (for all $\delta > 0$ circuits of size at most n^k that use n^δ random bits), and $\mathcal{S}_2$ the set of strategies available to P2 (polynomial size circuit families and $M \log n$ random coins). We will show that for all $\varepsilon > 0$ and sufficiently large n, (G_1, G_2) is a ε-Nash equilibrium with the required properties.

First we argue that, for all $\gamma > 0$ and sufficiently large n, $|\mathbf{E}\left[U(G_1, G_2)\right]| < \gamma$. The proof of this fact is similar to the proof of Lemma 4.2, showing by way of contradiction, that if $|\mathbf{E}\left[U(G_1, G_2)\right]| \geq \gamma$ then we can build a test for the cryptographic pseudorandom number generator G_1.

Now we show that, for the appropriate setting of parameters, G_1 fools $\mathcal{S}_2$ and G_2 fools $\mathcal{S}_1$. For any k, Player 2 can fool circuits of size n^k by using $C \log n^k = Ck \log n$ random bits. So, for $M > Ck$, G_2 fools $\mathcal{S}_1$. Notice also that since Player 2 runs in time $O(n^{Ck})$, the cryptographic pseudorandom number generator G_1 fools $\mathcal{S}_2$. Let h be the one-way permutation used by the pseudorandom number generator G_1, and assume h us computable in time n^c for some $c > 0$. Given h, G_1 is defined as follows: let $x, y \in \{0,1\}^{\frac{n^\delta}{2}}$, and let (x, y) be G_1's seed (notice that $|(x, y)| = n^\delta$), then

$$G_1(x, y) = \left(f^n(x) \odot y, f^{n-1}(x) \odot y, \ldots, f(x) \odot y\right),$$

where $x \odot y = \sum_i x_i y_i \mod 2$. There are $O(n^2)$ applications of h, so G_1 runs in time $O(n^{2+c\delta})$. So, for $k \geq 2 + c\delta$, G_1 fools $\mathcal{S}_2$.

At this point we're almost done. As in Lemma 4.3 assume, by contradiction, that the assumptions in the theorem hold but (G_1, G_2) is not a ε-Nash equilibrium for some $\varepsilon > 0$. This implies that at least one of the two players can improve his expected payoff by more than ε by switching to some other strategy. First consider P2, and assume there is a strategy $S_2 \in \mathcal{S}_2$ such that

$$\mathbf{E}\left[U(G_1, S_2)\right] > \mathbf{E}\left[U(G_1, G_2)\right] + \varepsilon.$$

As in Lemma 4.3 this implies that S_2 would be a test for the cryptographic pseudorandom number generator G_1, contradicting the fact that G_1 fools $\mathcal{S}_2$. Similarly, assume P1 has a strategy $S_1 \in \mathcal{S}_1$ such that

$$\mathbf{E}\left[U(S_1, G_2)\right] > \mathbf{E}\left[U(G_1, G_2)\right] + \varepsilon.$$

Again, S_1 can easily be made into a test for G_2, contradicting the fact that G_2 fools $\mathcal{S}_1$. □

6. INFINITE PLAY

We now consider an infinitely repeated game of Matching Pennies, and show that, if utilities are time discounted, we can always achieve a ε-Nash equilibria using a large enough (but finite) amount of random coins. First we determine the least amount of randomness required to achieve a ε-Nash equilibrium in the general, i.e. computationally unbounded, case.

LEMMA 6.1. *For all discount factors $\delta \in (0,1)$ and all $\varepsilon > 0$, there is an ε-Nash equilibrium in which the players use only n random bits, for $n > \frac{\log \varepsilon(1-\delta)}{\log \delta}$.*

PROOF. Given $\delta, \varepsilon > 0$ consider the following strategies: both players play the Nash equilibrium strategy for the first n rounds. After this P1 will always play H, while P2 will play H and T alternatively. The overall expected payoff is 0. However, after round n, both players could switch to a strategy that always wins, achieving a total expected payoff of $0 + \sum_{t=n}^{\infty} \delta^t = \frac{\delta^n}{1-\delta}$. To ensure that our strategies are indeed a ε-Nash equilibrium we just need to make sure that

$$0 > \frac{\delta^n}{1-\delta} - \varepsilon.$$

Rearranging and taking logarithms we get $n > \frac{\log \varepsilon(1-\delta)}{\log \delta}$. □

Now we consider players' whose strategies are families of polynomial size Boolean circuits (as in Section 4), and assume one-way functions exist. We first give a version of Lemma 4.2 for time discounted utilities on a finite number of rounds.

LEMMA 6.2. *Assume one-way functions exist, and let $G = (g^1, \ldots, g^n)$ be the strategy corresponding to the output of* *a cryptographic pseudorandom number generator. Let $S = (s^1, \ldots, s^n)$ be any strategy. For all $\delta \in (0, 1)$, $k > 0$ and for sufficiently large n*

$$\left|\mathbf{E}\left[\sum_{t=1}^{n} \delta^t h(g^t, s^t)\right]\right| \le n^{-k} \text{ and } \left|\mathbf{E}\left[\sum_{t=1}^{n} \delta^t h(s^t, g^t)\right]\right| \le n^{-k}.$$

PROOF. Again we give the proof only for the first inequality. Assume, by contradiction, that $|\mathbf{E}[\sum_{t=1}^{n} \delta^t h(g^t, s^t)]| > n^{-k}$ for some δ, k and infinitely many n's. Consider the random variables $A_1(c_1^1, c_2^1), \ldots, A_n(c_1^n, c_2^n)$, defined as $A_t(c_1^t, c_2^t) = 1$ if P1 wins round t when playing according to (C_1, C_2) and 0 otherwise. Let $A(C_1, C_2) = \sum_t \delta^t A_t(c_1^t, c_2^t)$, so that $\mathbf{E}[A(G, S)] \ge |\mathbf{E}[\sum_{t=1}^{n} \delta^t h(g^t, s^t)]| > n^{-k}$. This implies that there is a t such that $\delta^t \mathbf{E}[A_t(g^t, s^t)] > n^{-k-1}$, which implies $\mathbf{E}[A_t(g^t, s^t)] > n^{-k-1}$. Fix that t. As in Lemma 4.2, consider the test T that, given a sequence of plays x, generates a play s from S and outputs 1 if P1 wins round t and outputs 0 otherwise.

When x is drawn uniformly at random, $\Pr(T(U_n) = 1) = 1/2$. On the other hand, when x is G's output,

$$\Pr(T(G(U_{l(n)})) = 1) = \mathbf{E}[A_t] > n^{-k-1}.$$

Now

$$\left|\Pr(T(G(U_{l(n)})) = 1) - \Pr(T(U_n) = 1)\right| > \frac{1}{2} - \frac{1}{n^{k+1}} = \frac{1}{n^c},$$

for $c > -\frac{\log(1/2 - n^{-1-k})}{\log n} \ge 0$, contradicting the assumption that G is a pseudorandom number generator. □

Using the above Lemma we can show that, for all discount factors, we can greatly reduce the amount of random coins needed to get an ε-Nash equilibrium.

LEMMA 6.3. *For all discount factors $\delta \in (0, 1)$, all $\varepsilon > 0$ and all $\xi > 0$, there is a n^{-k}-Nash equilibrium in which players use only n^{ξ} random coins, for sufficiently large n's.*

PROOF. As in the proof of Lemma 6.1 we consider the following strategy for both players: for the first n rounds play the output of a cryptographic pseudorandom number generator G, with seed length n^{ξ}. Thereafter P1 will always play H, while P2 will alternate between H and T. Pick any $k > 0$, we now show that this is a n^{-k}-Nash equilibrium. By Lemma 6.2 we can pick $k' = k/2$ such that the expected utility in the first n rounds lies in the interval $[-n^{-k'}, n^{-k'}]$. To ensure that this is a n^{-k}-Nash equilibrium we just need to show that

$$-n^{-k'} > n^{-k'} + \frac{\delta^n}{(1-\delta)} - n^{-k},$$

or

$$-2n^{-k'} + n^{-2k'} > \frac{\delta^n}{(1-\delta)}.$$

Now, for any $c > 0$, if we set $k' = \frac{\log((\sqrt{c+1}-1)/c)}{\log n}$, then the left hand side of the above inequality is c, so that it always holds for sufficiently large n's. □

Thus, given any n that satisfies the conditions in Lemma 6.1, there can be a n^{-k}-Nash equilibrium using n^{δ} coins, for any $\delta > 0$. To see this, consider an m sufficiently large so that Lemma 6.3 holds and pick $\xi = \delta \frac{\log n}{\log m}$.

7. CONCLUSIONS

We have shown how, in a simple setting, reducing the amount of randomness available to players affects Nash equilibria. In particular, if we make no computational assumptions on the players, there is a direct tradeoff between the amount of randomness and the approximation to a Nash equilibrium we can achieve. If, instead, players are bound to run in polynomial time, we can get very close to a Nash equilibrium with only n^{δ} random coins, for any $\delta > 0$.

Some directions for future research include:

- Is it possible to extend Lemma 3.1 to m player games, for $m > 2$? Notice that the strategy used in that proof does not generalize to this setting.
- Under what circumstances is it possible to further reduce the amount of randomness available (say to $O(\log n)$ for both players)?
- Is it possible to extend these results to general zero-sum games or even non zero-sum games?

Acknowledgments.

We wish to thank Tai-Wei Hu, Peter Bro Miltersen, Rahul Santhanam and Rakesh Vohra for fruitful discussions.

8. REFERENCES

[1] S. Arora and B. Barak. *Computational Complexity: A Modern Approach.* Cambridge University Press, 2009.
[2] X. Chen and X. Deng. Settling the Complexity of Two-player Nash Equilibrium. In *47th FOCS*, 2006.
[3] C. Daskalakis, P. W. Goldberg, and C. H. Papadimitriou. The complexity of computing a nash equilibrium. *SIAM J. Comput.*, 39(1):195–259, 2009.
[4] L. Fortnow and R. Santhanam. Bounding Rationality by Discounting Time. In *1st ICS*, 2010.
[5] O. Goldreich. *Foundations of Cryptography: Basic Applications.* Cambridge University Press, 2004.
[6] O. Gossner and T. Tomala. Entropy Bounds on Bayesian Learning. *Journal of Mathematical Economics*, 44(1):24–32, 2008.
[7] J. Y. Halpern and R. Pass. Game theory with costly computation: Formulation and application to protocol security. In *1st ICS*, pages 120–142, 2010.
[8] J. Hastad, R. Impagliazzo, L. Levin, and M. Luby. A Pseudorandom Generator from any One-way Function. *SIAM Journal on Computing*, 28(4):1364–1396, 1999.
[9] T.-W. Hu. Complexity and Mixed Strategy Equilibria. `http://bit.ly/e4N8cN`, 2010. Working Paper.
[10] R. Impagliazzo and A. Wigderson. Randomness vs time: Derandomization under a uniform assumption. *J. Comput. Syst. Sci.*, 63(4):672–688, 2001.
[11] S. Kalyanaraman and C. Umans. Algorithms for Playing Games with Limited Randomness. In *15th ESA*, 2007.
[12] N. Nisan and A. Wigderson. Hardness vs Randomness. *J. Comput. Syst. Sci.*, 49(2):149–167, 1994.
[13] H. Simon. A Behavioral Model of Rational Choice. *The Quarterly Journal of Economics*, 69(1):99–118, 1955.
[14] A. Yao. Theory and Application of Trapdoor Functions. In *23rd FOCS*, 1982.

Polynomial-time Computation of Exact Correlated Equilibrium in Compact Games

Albert Xin Jiang
Department of Computer Science
University of British Columbia
Vancouver, BC, Canada
jiang@cs.ubc.ca

Kevin Leyton-Brown
Department of Computer Science
University of British Columbia
Vancouver, BC, Canada
kevinlb@cs.ubc.ca

ABSTRACT

In a landmark paper, Papadimitriou and Roughgarden [2008] described a polynomial-time algorithm ("Ellipsoid Against Hope") for computing sample correlated equilibria of concisely-represented games. Recently, Stein, Parrilo and Ozdaglar [2010] showed that this algorithm can fail to find an exact correlated equilibrium, but can be easily modified to efficiently compute approximate correlated equilibria. Currently, it remains an open problem to determine whether the algorithm can be modified to compute an exact correlated equilibrium. We show that it can, presenting a variant of the Ellipsoid Against Hope algorithm that guarantees the polynomial-time identification of exact correlated equilibrium. Also, our algorithm is the first to tractably compute correlated equilibria with polynomial-sized supports; such correlated equilibria are more natural solutions than the mixtures of product distributions produced previously, and have several advantages including requiring fewer bits to represent, being easier to sample from, and being easier to verify. Our algorithm differs from the original primarily in its use of a separation oracle that produces cuts corresponding to pure-strategy profiles. As a result, we no longer face the numerical precision issues encountered by the original approach, and both the resulting algorithm and its analysis are considerably simplified. Our new separation oracle can be understood as a derandomization of Papadimitriou and Roughgarden's original separation oracle via the method of conditional probabilities.

Categories and Subject Descriptors

F.2.0 [**Analysis of Algorithms and Problem Complexity**]: General

General Terms

Algorithms, Economics, Theory

Keywords

correlated equilibrium, ellipsoid method, separation oracle, derandomization

1. INTRODUCTION

We consider the problem of computing a sample correlated equilibrium (CE) [Aumann, 1974; Aumann, 1987] given a finite, simultaneous-move game. It is known that correlated equilibria of a game can be formulated as probability distributions over pure strategy profiles satisfying certain linear constraints. The resulting linear feasibility program has size polynomial in the size of the normal form representation of the game. However, the size of the normal form representation grows exponentially in the number of players. This is problematic when games involve large numbers of players. Fortunately, most large games of practical interest have highly-structured payoff functions, and thus it is possible to represent them compactly. A line of research thus exists to look for *compact game representations* that are able to succinctly describe structured games, including work on graphical games [Kearns *et al.*, 2001] and action-graph games [Bhat & Leyton-Brown, 2004; Jiang *et al.*, 2011]. But now the size of the linear feasibility program for CE can be exponential in the size of compact representation; furthermore a CE can require exponential space to specify.

The "Ellipsoid Against Hope" algorithm [Papadimitriou, 2005; Papadimitriou & Roughgarden, 2008] is a polynomial-time method for identifying a (polynomial-size representation of a) CE, given a game representation satisfying two properties: *polynomial type*, which requires that the number of players and the number of actions for each player are bounded by polynomials in the size of the representation, and the *polynomial expectation property*, which requires access to a polynomial-time algorithm that computes the expected utility of any player under any product distribution. Many existing compact game representations (including graphical games, symmetric games, congestion games, polymatrix games and action-graph games) satisfy these properties. This important result extends CE's attractive computational properties to the case of compactly represented games; note in contrast that the problem of finding a Nash equilibrium is PPAD-hard for normal form games [Chen & Deng, 2006; Daskalakis & Papadimitriou, 2005] as well as for certain compact game representations [Goldberg & Papadimitriou, 2006; Jiang *et al.*, 2011].

At a high level, the Ellipsoid Against Hope algorithm works by solving an infeasible dual LP (D) using the ellipsoid method (exploiting the existence of a separation oracle), and arguing that the LP (D') formed by the generated cutting planes must also be infeasible. Solving the dual of this latter LP (which has polynomial size) yields a CE, which is represented as a mixture of the product distributions generated by the separation oracle.

1.1 Recent uncertainty about the complexity of exact CE

In a recent paper, Stein, Parrilo and Ozdaglar [2010] raised two interrelated concerns about the Ellipsoid Against Hope algorithm. First, they identified a symmetric 3-player, 2-action game with rational utilities on which the algorithm can fail to compute an exact CE. Indeed, they showed that the same problem arises on this game for a whole class of related algorithms. Specifically, if an algorithm (a) outputs a rational solution, (b) outputs a convex combination of product distributions, and (c) outputs a convex combination of symmetric product distributions when the game is symmetric, then that algorithm fails to find an exact CE on their game, because the only CE of their game that satisfies properties (b) and (c) has irrational probabilities. This implies that any algorithm for exact rational CE must violate (b) or (c).

Second, Stein, Parrilo and Ozdaglar also showed that the original analysis in [Papadimitriou & Roughgarden, 2008] incorrectly handles certain numerical precision issues, which we now briefly describe. Recall that a run of the ellipsoid method requires as inputs an initial bounding ball with radius R and a volume bound v such that the algorithm stops when the ellipsoid's volume is smaller than v. To correctly certify the (in)feasibility of an LP using the ellipsoid method, R and v need to be set to appropriate values, which depend on the maximum encoding size of a constraint in the LP. However (as pointed out by Papadimitriou and Roughgarden [2008]), each cut returned by the separation oracle is a convex combination of the constraints of the original dual LP (D) and thus may require more bits to represent than any of the constraints in (D); as a result, the infeasibility of the LP (D') formed by these cuts is not guaranteed. Papadimitriou and Roughgarden [2008] proposed a method to overcome this difficulty, but Stein *et al.* showed that this method is insufficient for finding an exact CE. For the related problem of finding an approximate correlated equilibrium (ϵ-CE), Stein *et al.* gave a slightly modified version of the Ellipsoid Against Hope algorithm that runs in time polynomial in $\log \frac{1}{\epsilon}$ and the game representation size.[1] For problems that can have necessarily irrational solutions, it is standard to consider such approximations as efficient; however, there always exists a rational CE in a game with rational utilities, since CE are defined by linear constraints. It remains an open problem to determine whether the Ellipsoid Against Hope algorithm can be modified to compute an exact, rational correlated equilibrium.[2]

[1]An ϵ-CE is defined to be a distribution that violates the CE incentive constraints by at most ϵ.

[2]In a recent addendum to their original paper, Papadimitriou and Roughgarden [2010] acknowledged the flaw in the original algorithm. We note also that Stein *et al.* have recently withdrawn their paper from arXiv. It is our impression that their results are nevertheless still believed to be correct; we discuss them here because they help to motivate our alternate approach.

1.2 Our results

In this paper, we use an alternate approach—completely sidestepping the issues just discussed—to derive a polynomial-time algorithm for computing an exact (and rational) correlated equilibrium given a game representation that has polynomial type and satisfies the polynomial expectation property. Specifically, our approach is based on the observation that if we use a separation oracle (for the same dual LP formulation as in [Papadimitriou & Roughgarden, 2008]) that generates cuts corresponding to pure-strategy profiles (instead of Papadimitriou and Roughgarden's separation oracle that generates nontrivial product distributions), then these cuts are actual constraints in the dual LP, as opposed to the convex combinations of constraints produced by Papadimitriou and Roughgarden's separation oracle. As a result we no longer encounter the numerical accuracy issues that prevented the previous approaches from finding exact correlated equilibria. Both the resulting algorithm and its analysis are also considerably simpler than the original: standard techniques from the theory of the ellipsoid method are sufficient to show that our algorithm computes an exact CE using a polynomial number of oracle queries.

The key issue is the identification of pure-strategy-profile cuts. It is relatively straightforward to show that such cuts always exist: since the product distribution generated by the Ellipsoid Against Hope algorithm ensures the nonnegativity of a certain expected value, then by a simple application of the probabilistic method there must exist a pure-strategy profile that also ensures the nonnegativity of that expected value. The key is to go beyond this nonconstructive proof of existence to also *compute* pure-strategy-profile cuts in polynomial time. We show how to do this by applying the method of conditional probabilities [Erdős & Selfridge, 1973; Spencer, 1994; Raghavan, 1988], an approach for derandomizing probabilistic proofs of existence. At a high level, our new separation oracle begins with the product distribution generated by Papadimitriou and Roughgarden's separation oracle, then sequentially fixes a pure strategy for each player in a way that guarantees that the corresponding conditional expectation given the choices so far remains nonnegative. Since our separation oracle goes though players sequentially, the cuts generated can be asymmetric even for symmetric games. Indeed, we can confirm (see Section 4.2) that it makes such asymmetric cuts on Stein, Parrilo and Ozdaglar's symmetric game—thus violating their condition (c)—because our algorithm always identifies a rational CE.

Another effect of our use of pure-strategy-profile cuts is that the correlated equilibria generated by our algorithm are guaranteed to have polynomial-sized supports; i.e., they are mixtures over a polynomial number of pure strategy profiles. Correlated equilibria with polynomial-sized supports are known to exist in every game (e.g., [Germano & Lugosi, 2007]); intuitively this is because CE are defined by a polynomial number of linear constraints, so a basic feasible solution of the linear feasibility program would have a polynomial number of non-zero entries. Such small-support correlated equilibria are more natural solutions than the mixtures of product distributions produced by the Ellipsoid Against Hope algorithm: because of their simpler form they require fewer bits to represent and fewer random bits to sample from; furthermore, verifying whether a given polynomial-support distribution is a CE only requires evaluating the utilities of a polynomial number of pure strategy profiles, whereas verifying whether a mixture of product distributions is a CE would require evaluating expected utilities under product distributions, which is generally more expensive. No tractable algorithm has previously been proposed for identifying such a CE, thus our algorithm is first algorithm that computes in polynomial time a CE with polynomial support given a compactly-represented game. In fact we show that any CE computed by our algorithm corresponds to a basic feasible solution of the linear feasibility program that defines CE, and is thus an extreme point of the set of CE of the game.

The rest of the paper is organized as follows. We start with basic definitions and notation in Section 2. In Section 3 we summarize Papadimitriou and Roughgarden's Ellipsoid Against Hope algorithm. In Section 4 we describe our algorithm and prove its correctness, and Section 5 concludes.

2. PRELIMINARIES

We largely follow the notation of Papadimitriou [2005] and Papadimitriou and Roughgarden [2008]. Consider a simultaneous-move game with n players. Denote a player p, and player p's set of pure strategies (i.e., actions) S_p. Let $m = \max_p |S_p|$. Denote a pure strategy profile $s = (s_1, \ldots, s_n) \in S$, with s_p being player p's pure strategy. Denote by S_{-p} the set of partial pure strategy profiles of the players other than p. Player p's utility under pure strategy profile s is u_s^p. We assume that utilities are nonnegative integers (but results in this paper can be straightforwardly adapted to the case of rational utilities). Denote the largest utility of the game as u.

A *correlated distribution* is a probability distribution over pure strategy profiles, represented by a vector $x \in \mathbb{R}^M$, where $M = \prod_p |S_p|$. Then x_s is the probability of pure strategy profile s under the distribution x. A correlated distribution x is a *product distribution* when it can be achieved by each player p randomizing independently over her actions according to some distribution x^p, i.e., $x_s = \prod_p x^p_{s_p}$. Such a product distribution is also known as a mixed-strategy profile, with each player p playing the mixed strategy x^p.

Throughout the paper we assume that a game is given in a representation satisfying two properties, following Papadimitriou and Roughgarden [2008]:

- *polynomial type*: the number of players and the number of actions for each player are bounded by polynomials in the size of the representation.
- *the polynomial expectation property*: We have access to an algorithm that computes the expected utility of any player p under any product distribution x, i.e., $\sum_{s \in S} u_s^p x_s$, in time polynomial in the size of the representation.

DEFINITION 2.1. *A correlated distribution x is a* correlated equilibrium *(CE) if it satisfies the following* incentive constraints*: for each player p and each pair of her actions $i, j \in S_p$,*

$$\sum_{s \in S_{-p}} [u^p_{is} - u^p_{js}] x_{is} \geq 0, \tag{1}$$

where the subscript "is" (respectively "js") denotes the pure strategy profile in which player p plays i (respectively j) and the other players play according to the partial profile $s \in S_{-p}$.

We write these incentive constraints in matrix form as $Ux \geq 0$. Thus U is an $N \times M$ matrix, where $N = \sum_p |S_p|^2$. The rows of U, corresponding to the left-hand sides of the constraints (1), are indexed by (p, i, j) where p is a player and $i, j \in S_p$ are a pair of p's actions. Denote by U_s the column of U corresponding to pure strategy profile s. These incentive constraints, together with the constraints

$$x \geq 0, \quad \sum_{s \in S} x_s = 1, \tag{2}$$

which ensure that x is a probability distribution, form a linear feasibility program that defines the set of CE. The largest value in U is at most u.

We define the *support* of a correlated equilibrium x as the set of pure strategy profiles assigned positive probability by x. Germano and Lugosi [2007] showed that for any n-player game, there always exists a correlated equilibrium with support size at most $1 + \sum_p |S_p|(|S_p| - 1) = N + 1 - \sum_p |S_p|$. Intuitively, such correlated equilibria are basic feasible solutions of the linear feasibility program for CE, i.e., they are vertices of the polyhedron defining the feasible region. Furthermore, these basic feasible solutions involve only rational numbers for games with rational payoffs (see e.g. Lemma 6.2.4 of [Grötschel *et al.*, 1988]).

3. THE ELLIPSOID AGAINST HOPE ALGORITHM

In this section, we summarize Papadimitriou and Roughgarden's Ellipsoid Against Hope algorithm for finding a sample CE [Papadimitriou, 2005; Papadimitriou & Roughgarden, 2008], which can be seen as an efficiently constructive version of earlier proofs [Hart & Schmeidler, 1989; Nau & McCardle, 1990; Myerson, 1997] of the existence of CE. We will concentrate on the main algorithm and only briefly point out the numerical issues discussed at length by both Papadimitriou and Roughgarden [2008] and Stein *et al.* [2010], as our analysis will ultimately sidestep these issues.

Papadimitriou and Roughgarden's approach considers the linear program

$$\max \sum_{s \in S} x_s \tag{P}$$
$$Ux \geq 0, \qquad x \geq 0,$$

which is modified from the linear feasibility program for CE by replacing the constraint $\sum_{s \in S} x_s = 1$ from (2) with the maximization objective. (P) either has $x = 0$ as its optimal solution or is unbounded; in the latter case, taking a feasible solution and scaling it to be a distribution yields a correlated equilibrium. Thus one way to prove the existence of CE is to show the infeasibility of the dual problem

$$U^T y \leq -1, \qquad y \geq 0. \tag{D}$$

The Ellipsoid Against Hope algorithm uses the following lemma, versions of which were also used by Nau and McCardle [1990] and Myerson [1997].

LEMMA 3.1 ([PAPADIMITRIOU & ROUGHGARDEN, 2008]). *For every dual vector $y \geq 0$, there exists a product distribution x such that $xU^T y = 0$. Furthermore there exists an algorithm that given any $y \geq 0$, computes the corresponding x (represented by $x^1, \ldots, x^n$) in time polynomial in n and m.*

We will not discuss the details of this algorithm; we will only need the facts that the resulting x is a product distribution and can be computed in polynomial time. Note also that the resulting x is symmetric if y is symmetric. Lemma 3.1 implies that the dual problem (D) is infeasible (and therefore a CE must exist): xU^Ty is a convex combination of the left hand sides of the rows of the dual, and for any feasible y the result must be less than or equal to -1.

The Ellipsoid Against Hope algorithm runs the ellipsoid algorithm on the dual (D), with the algorithm from Lemma 3.1 as separation oracle, which we call the the Product Separation Oracle. At each step of the ellipsoid algorithm, the separation oracle is given a dual vector $y^{(i)}$. The oracle then generates the corresponding product distribution $x^{(i)}$ and indicates to the ellipsoid algorithm that $(x^{(i)}U^T)y \leq -1$ is violated by $y^{(i)}$. The ellipsoid algorithm will stop after a polynomial number of steps and determine that the program is infeasible. Let X be the matrix whose rows are the generated product distributions $x^{(1)}, \ldots, x^{(L)}$.

Consider the linear program

$$[XU^T]y \leq -1, y \geq 0, \qquad (D')$$

and observe that the rows of $[XU^T]y \leq -1$ are the cuts generated by the ellipsoid method. If we apply the same ellipsoid method to (D') and use a separation oracle that returns the cut $x^{(i)}U^Ty \leq -1$ given query $y^{(i)}$, the ellipsoid algorithm would go through the same sequence of queries $y^{(i)}$ and cutting planes $x^{(i)}U^Ty \leq -1$ and return infeasible. Presuming that numerical problems do not arise,[3] we will find that (D') is infeasible. This implies that its dual $[UX^T]\alpha \geq 0$, $\alpha \geq 0$ is unbounded and has polynomial size, and thus can be solved for a nonzero feasible α. We can thus scale α to obtain a probability distribution. We then observe that $X^T\alpha$ satisfies the incentive constraints (1) and the probability distribution constraints (2) and is therefore a correlated equilibrium. The distribution $X^T\alpha$ is the mixture of product distributions $x^{(1)}, \ldots, x^{(L)}$ with weights α, and thus can be represented in polynomial space and can be efficiently sampled from.

One issue remains. Although the matrix XU^T is polynomial sized, computing it using matrix multiplication would involve an exponential number of operations. On the other hand, entries of XU^T are differences between expected utilities that arise under product distributions. Since we have assumed that the game representation admits a polynomial-time algorithm for computing such expected utilities, XU^T can be computed in polynomial time.

[3]Since each row of (D')'s constraint matrix XU^T may require more bits to represent than any row of the constraint matrix U^T for (D), running the ellipsoid algorithm on (D') with the original bounding ball and volume lower bound for (D) would not be sound, and as a result (D') is not guaranteed to be infeasible. Indeed, Stein *et al.* [2010] showed that when running the algorithm on their symmetric game example, (D') would remain feasible, and thus the output of the algorithm would not be an exact CE. Furthermore, since the only CE of that game that is a mixture of symmetric product distributions is irrational, there is no way to resolve this issue without breaking at least one of the symmetry and product distribution properties of the Ellipsoid Against Hope algorithm. For more on these issues and possible ways to address them, please see Papadimitriou and Roughgarden [2008]; Stein *et al.* [2010]; Papadimitriou and Roughgarden [2010].

LEMMA 3.2 ([PAPADIMITRIOU & ROUGHGARDEN, 2008]). *There exists an algorithm that given a game representation with polynomial type and satisfying the polynomial expectation property, and given an arbitrary product distribution x, computes xU^T in polynomial time. As a result, XU^T can be computed in polynomial time.*

4. OUR ALGORITHM

In this section we present our modification of the Ellipsoid Against Hope algorithm, and prove that it computes exact CE. There are two key differences between our approach and the original algorithm for computing approximate CE.

1. Our modified separation oracle produces pure-strategy-profile cuts;
2. The algorithm is simplified, no longer requiring a special mechanism to deal with numerical issues (because pure-strategy-profile cuts can be represented directly as rows of (D)'s constraint matrix).

4.1 The Purif ed Separation Oracle

We start with a "purified" version of Lemma 3.1.

LEMMA 4.1. *Given any dual vector $y \geq 0$, there exists a pure strategy profile s such that $(U_s)^Ty \geq 0$.*

PROOF. Recall that Lemma 3.1 states that given dual vector $y \geq 0$, a product distribution x can be computed in polynomial time such that $xU^Ty = 0$. Since $x[U^Ty]$ is a convex combination of the entries of the vector U^Ty, there must exist some nonnegative entry of U^Ty. In other words, there exists a pure strategy profile s such that $(U_s)^Ty \geq xU^Ty = 0$. □

The proof of Lemma 4.1 is a straightforward application of the probabilistic method: since xU^Ty is the expected value of $(U_s)^Ty$ under distribution x, which we denote $E_{s\sim x}[(U_s)^Ty]$, the nonnegativity of this expectation implies the existence of some s such that $(U_s)^Ty \geq 0$. Like many other probabilistic proofs, this proof is not efficiently constructive; note that there are an exponential number of possible pure strategy profiles.

It turns out that for game representations with polynomial type and satisfying the polynomial expectation property, an appropriate s can indeed be identified in polynomial time. Our approach can be seen as derandomizing the probabilistic proof using the method of conditional probabilities [Erdős & Selfridge, 1973; Spencer, 1994; Raghavan, 1988]. At a high level, for each player p our algorithm picks a pure strategy s_p, such that the conditional expectation of $(U_s)^Ty$ given the choices so far remains nonnegative. This requires us to compute the conditional expectations, but this can be done efficiently using the expected utility subroutine guaranteed by the polynomial expectation property.

LEMMA 4.2. *There exists a polynomial-time algorithm that given*

- *an instance of a game in a representation satisfying polynomial type and the polynomial expectation property,*
- *a polynomial-time subroutine for computing expected utility under any product distribution (as guaranteed by the polynomial expectation property), and*

Algorithm 1 Computes a pure strategy profile s such that $(U_s)^T y \geq 0$.

1. Given $y \geq 0$, identify a product distribution x satisfying $xU^T y = 0$, using the algorithm described in Lemma 3.1.
2. For each player p,
   (a) iterate through actions $s_p \in S_p$, and compute $x_{(p \to s_p)} U^T$ using the algorithm described in Lemma 3.2, until we find an action $s_p^* \in S_p$ such that $\left[x_{(p \to s_p^*)} U^T\right] y \geq 0$.
   (b) set x to be $x_{(p \to s_p^*)}$.
3. The resulting x corresponds to a pure strategy profile s. Output s.

- *a dual vector* $y \geq 0$,

finds a pure strategy profile $s \in S$ *such that* $(U_s)^T y \geq 0$.

PROOF. Given a product distribution x, let $x_{(p \to s_p)}$ be the product distribution in which player p plays s_p and all other players play according to x. Since x is a product distribution, $x_{(p \to s_p)} U^T y$ is the conditional expectation of $(U_s)^T y$ given that p plays s_p, and furthermore we have for any p,

$$xU^T y = \sum_{s_p} \left[x_{(p \to s_p)} U^T y\right] x^p_{s_p}. \qquad (3)$$

Since x^p is a distribution, the right hand side of (3) is a convex combination and thus there must exist an action $s_p \in S_p$ such that $x_{(p \to s_p)} U^T y \geq xU^T y \geq 0$. Since $x_{(p \to s_p)}$ is a product distribution, this process can be repeated for each player to yield a pure strategy profile s such that $(U_s)^T y \geq xU^T y \geq 0$. This is formalized in Algorithm 1.

We now consider the running time of Algorithm 1. Due to the polynomial expectation property, the algorithm described in Lemma 3.2 is polynomial, which implies that in Step 2a, for each $s_p \in S_p$, $x_{(p \to s_p)} U^T$ can be computed in polynomial time. Since Step 2a requires at most $|S_p|$ such computations, and since polynomial type implies that n and $|S_p|$ are polynomial in the input size, the algorithm runs in polynomial time. □

A straightforward corollary is the following:

COROLLARY 4.3. *Algorithm 1 can be used as a separation oracle for the dual LP (D) in the Ellipsoid Against Hope algorithm: for each query point y, the oracle computes the corresponding pure-strategy profile s according to Algorithm 1 and returns the half space* $(U_s)^T y \leq -1$. *We call this the Purified Separation Oracle. This separation oracle has the following properties:*

- *Each returned half space is one of the constraints of* (D).
- *Since Algorithm 1 iterates through the players sequentially, the generated pure-strategy profiles can be asymmetric even for symmetric games and symmetric y.*
- *Since a pure-strategy profile is a special case of a product distribution, the resulting pure-strategy profile s also satisfies Lemma 3.1, with x being the unit vector corresponding to s.*

4.2 The Simplif ed Ellipsoid Against Hope Algorithm

We now modify the Ellipsoid Against Hope Algorithm by replacing the Product Separation Oracle with our Purified Separation Oracle. The rows of X in (D') become unit vectors corresponding to the pure-strategy profiles generated by the oracle. Thus, we can write (D') as

$$(U')^T y \leq -1, y \geq 0, \qquad (D'')$$

where the matrix $U' \equiv UX^T$ consists of the columns $U_{s^{(i)}}$ that correspond to pure-strategy profiles $s^{(i)}$ generated by the separation oracle. Note that each constraint of (D'') is also one of the constraints of (D), and as a result neither the maximum value of the coefficients nor the right-hand sides of (D'') are greater than in (D). Therefore, a starting ball and volume lower bound that are valid for a run of the ellipsoid method on (D) would also be valid for (D''). We thus avoid the precision issues faced by the Ellipsoid Against Hope algorithm, and it is sufficient to use standard values for the initial radius and volume lower bound (and standard perturbation methods for dealing with non-full-dimensional solutions). The resulting CE is a mixture over a polynomial number of pure strategy profiles. We can make a further conceptual simplification of the algorithm: instead of using X as in the Ellipsoid Against Hope algorithm, we can directly treat the generated pure-strategy profiles as columns of U, and use U' in place of UX^T.

We now formally state and prove our result. Note that although we only briefly discussed the way numerical issues are addressed in the original Ellipsoid Against Hope algorithm in Section 3, we need to go into detail about how our algorithm ensures its own numerical accuracy. Nevertheless that task is comparatively easy, as it is sufficient for us to directly apply standard techniques from the theory of the ellipsoid method. Our analysis makes use of the following lemma from [Grötschel *et al.*, 1988].

LEMMA 4.4 (LEMMA 6.2.6, [GRÖTSCHEL *et al.*, 1988]). *Let* $P = \{y \in \mathbb{R}^N | Ay \leq b\}$ *be a full-dimensional polyhedron defined by the system of inequalities, with the encoding length of each inequality at most* φ. *Then P contains a ball with radius* $2^{-7N^3\varphi}$. *Moreover, this ball is contained in the ball with radius* $2^{5N^2\varphi}$ *centered at 0.*

We note that the only restriction on P is full dimensionality; we do not need to assume that P is bounded, or that A has full row rank.

THEOREM 4.5. *Given a game representation with polynomial type and satisfying the polynomial expectation property, Algorithm 2 computes an exact and rational CE with support size at most* $1 + \sum_p |S_p|(|S_p| - 1)$ *in polynomial time.*

PROOF. We begin by proving the correctness of the algorithm. First, we will show that the ellipsoid method in Step 1 is a valid run for (D), which certifies that the feasible set of (D) is either empty or not full dimensional.[4] Suppose the contrary, i.e., the feasible set of (D) is feasible and full

[4]Since the ellipsoid method relies on shrinking the volume of the candidate set, it is not able to distinguish between non-full-dimensional feasible sets and infeasibility. We overcome this by perturbing the LP after the ellipsoid method has been applied; another method perturbs the LP in advance to ensure the feasible set is either empty or full dimensional.

Algorithm 2 Computes an exact rational CE given a game representation satisfying polynomial type and the polynomial expectation property.

1. Apply the ellipsoid method to (D), using the Purified Separation Oracle, a starting ball with radius of $R = u^{5N^3}$ centered at 0, and stopping when the volume of the ellipsoid is below $v = \alpha_N u^{-7N^5}$, where α_N is the volume of the N-dimensional unit ball.

2. Form the matrix U' whose columns are $U_{s^{(1)}}, \ldots, U_{s^{(L)}}$ generated by the separation oracle during the run of the ellipsoid method.

3. Compute a basic feasible solution x' of the linear feasibility program

$$U'x' \geq 0, x' \geq 0, \mathbf{1}^T x' = 1, \qquad (P^*)$$

by applying the ellipsoid method on the explicitly represented (P^*) and recovering a basis using, e.g., Algorithm 4.2 of [Dantzig & Thapa, 2003].

4. Output x' and $s^{(1)}, \ldots, s^{(L)}$, interpreted as a distribution over pure-strategy profiles $s^{(1)}, \ldots, s^{(L)}$ with probabilities x'.

dimensional. Since the encoding length of each constraint of (D) is at most $N \log_2 u$, then by Lemma 4.4, the feasible set must contain a ball with radius u^{-7N^4}, and thus volume $\alpha_N u^{-7N^5}$, and furthermore this ball must be contained in the ball with radius u^{5N^3} centered at 0, which is the initial ball of our ellipsoid method in Step 1. Since at the end of Step 1 the ellipsoid method certifies that the intersection of the initial ball and the feasible set has volume less than $v = \alpha_N u^{-7N^5}$, we reach a contradiction and therefore either the LP (D) must be infeasible or the feasible set must not be full dimensional. Since the largest magnitude of the coefficients in (D'') is also u, Step 1 is also a valid run for (D'') and therefore either (D'') must be infeasible or the feasible set of (D'') must not be full dimensional.

Of course a non-full-dimensional feasible set is not sufficient for our purpose; we now perturb (D'') to get an infeasible LP. Fix $\rho > 1$. Perturbing the constraints $(U')^T y \leq -1$ of (D'') by multiplying the RHS by ρ, we get the following LP:

$$\begin{aligned} &\min 0 && (4)\\ &(U')^T y \leq -\rho \mathbf{1} \\ &y \geq 0. \end{aligned}$$

We claim that (4) is infeasible. Suppose otherwise: then there exists a $y \in \mathbb{R}^N$ such that $y \geq 0$ and $(U')^T y \leq -\rho\mathbf{1}$. Let $y' \in \mathbb{R}^N$ be a vector such that $0 \leq y'_j - y_j \leq \frac{\rho-1}{Nu}$ for all j. Then $y' \geq 0$, and each component s of $U'^T y'$ satisfies

$$\begin{aligned} (U'_s)^T y &\leq (U'_s)^T y + \frac{\rho-1}{Nu} \sum_j |U'^j_s| \\ &\leq -\rho + \rho - 1 \\ &\leq -1. \end{aligned}$$

Thus, any such y' is feasible for (D''). However, the set of all such vectors y' is a full-dimensional cube. This contradicts the fact that (D'') is either infeasible or not full dimensional, and therefore (4) is infeasible. This means that (4)'s dual

$$\begin{aligned} &\max \rho \mathbf{1}^T x' && (5)\\ &U'x' \geq 0 \\ &x' \geq 0 \end{aligned}$$

is unbounded (since it is feasible, e.g. $x' = 0$). Then a nonzero feasible vector x' is (after normalization) a distribution over the pure strategy profiles corresponding to columns of U'. Treating it as a sparse representation of a correlated distribution x, it satisfies the feasibility program for CE and is therefore an exact CE.

This CE is exact but its support could be greater than $1 + \sum_p |S_p|(|S_p| - 1)$ (although as we argue below it is still polynomial). To get a CE with the required support size, we notice that since (5) is unbounded, a feasible solution of the bounded linear feasibility program (P^*) is a CE. Note that (P^*) has the same set of rows constraints as the feasibility program for CE defined by (1) and (2), and that for each player p and action $i \in S_p$, the incentive constraint (p, i, i) corresponds to deviating from action i to itself and is therefore redundant. Thus the number of bounding constraints of (P^*) is at most $1 + \sum_p |S_p|(|S_p| - 1)$ and therefore a basic feasible solution x' of (P^*) will have the required support size. Since the coefficients and right-hand sides of (P^*) are rational, then (by e.g. Lemma 6.2.4 of [Grötschel *et al.*, 1988]) its basic feasible solution x' is also rational and can be represented using at most $4N^3 u$ bits.

We now consider the running time of the algorithm. Since Step 1 is a standard run of the ellipsoid method, it terminates in a polynomial number of iterations. For example if we use the ellipsoid algorithm presented in Theorem 3.2.1 of [Grötschel *et al.*, 1988], then by Lemma 3.2.10 of [Grötschel *et al.*, 1988] the ratio between volumes of successive ellipsoids $\text{vol}(E_{k+1})/\text{vol}(E_k) \leq e^{-1/(5N)}$. With the volume of the initial ellipsoid at most $\alpha_N R^N$ and stopping when volume is below v, the number of iterations L is at most

$$\begin{aligned} &5N \left[\ln(\alpha_N R^N) - \ln v\right] \\ &= 5N \left[5N^4 \ln u + 7N^5 \ln u\right] \\ &= O(N^6 \ln u), \end{aligned}$$

which is polynomial in the input size since N is polynomial. Since each call to the separation oracle takes polynomial time by Lemma 4.2, Step 1 takes polynomial time. L being polynomial also ensures that (P^*) has polynomial size, and thus a basic feasible solution can be found in polynomial time. □

We note that the estimates on R and v (and thus L) can be improved, but our main goal here is to prove that the running time of our algorithm is polynomial.

The reader may wonder how our algorithm would deal with Stein *et al.* [2010]'s counterexample, a symmetric game in which the only CE that is a convex combination of symmetric product distributions has irrational probabilities. Since we have proved that our algorithm computes a rational CE as a convex combination of product distributions, it must violate the symmetry property. Indeed as we discussed in Section 4.1, our Purified Separation Oracle can return asymmetric cuts for symmetric games and symmetric queries, and thus for this game it must return at least one asymmetric cut during the algorithm.

5. CONCLUSION

We have proposed a polynomial-time algorithm, a variant of Papadimitriou and Roughgarden's Ellipsoid Against Hope approach, for computing an exact CE given a game representation with polynomial type and satisfying the polynomial expectation property. A key component of our approach is a derandomization of Papadimitriou and Roughgarden's separation oracle using the method of conditional probabilities, yielding a polynomial-time separation oracle that outputs cuts corresponding to pure-strategy profiles. Our approach is then spared from dealing with the numerical precision issues that were a major focus of previous approaches, and the algorithm is considerably simplified as a result. Furthermore, the correlated equilibria returned by our algorithm have polynomial-sized supports. We expect these properties of our algorithm to be independently interesting, beyond its usefulness in resolving the recent uncertainty about the computational complexity of identifying exact CE. For example, our techniques can be applied to existing algorithms that are based on the Ellipsoid Against Hope approach, such as Hart and Mansour's [2010] CE procedure with polynomial communication complexity and Huang and Von Stengel's [2008] polynomial-time algorithm for extensive-form correlated equilibria, yielding in both cases exact solutions with polynomial-sized supports.

Our algorithm has additional practical benefits: the resulting cutting planes are deeper cuts than those produced by the original oracle, resulting in a smaller number of iterations required to reach convergence, albeit at the cost of more work per iteration. It is also possible to return cuts corresponding to pure strategy profiles with (e.g.) good social welfare, yielding a heuristic method for generating correlated equilibria with good social welfare; we do note, however, that finding a CE with optimal social welfare is generally NP-hard for many game representations [Papadimitriou & Roughgarden, 2005].

References

Aumann, R. (1974). Subjectivity and correlation in randomized strategies. *Journal of Mathematical Economics, 1*(1), 67–96.

Aumann, R. (1987). Correlated equilibrium as an expression of Bayesian rationality. *Econometrica: Journal of the Econometric Society*, 1–18.

Bhat, N., & Leyton-Brown, K. (2004). Computing Nash equilibria of action-graph games. *UAI: Proceedings of the Conference on Uncertainty in Artificial Intelligence* (pp. 35–42).

Chen, X., & Deng, X. (2006). Settling the complexity of 2-player Nash-equilibrium. *FOCS: Proceedings of the Annual IEEE Symposium on Foundations of Computer Science* (pp. 261–272).

Dantzig, G., & Thapa, M. (2003). *Linear programming 2: Theory and extensions.* Springer.

Daskalakis, C., & Papadimitriou, C. (2005). Three-player games are hard. *ECCC, TR05-139.*

Erdős, P., & Selfridge, J. L. (1973). On a combinatorial game. *Journal of Combinatorial Theory, Series A, 14*(3), 298 – 301.

Germano, F., & Lugosi, G. (2007). Existence of sparsely supported correlated equilibria. *Economic Theory, 32*(3), 575–578.

Goldberg, P. W., & Papadimitriou, C. H. (2006). Reducibility among equilibrium problems. *STOC: Proceedings of the Annual ACM Symposium on Theory of Computing* (pp. 61–70).

Grötschel, M., Lovász, L., & Schrijver, A. (1988). *Geometric algorithms and combinatorial optimization.* Springer-Verlag, New York, NY.

Hart, S., & Mansour, Y. (2010). How long to equilibrium? the communication complexity of uncoupled equilibrium procedures. *Games and Economic Behavior, 69*(1), 107–126.

Hart, S., & Schmeidler, D. (1989). Existence of correlated equilibria. *Mathematics of Operations Research, 14*(1), 18–25.

Huang, W., & Von Stengel, B. (2008). Computing an extensive-form correlated equilibrium in polynomial time. *WINE: Proceedings of the Workshop on Internet and Network Economics* (pp. 506–513).

Jiang, A. X., Leyton-Brown, K., & Bhat, N. (2011). Action-graph games. *Games and Economic Behavior, 71*(1), 141–173.

Kearns, M., Littman, M., & Singh, S. (2001). Graphical models for game theory. *UAI: Proceedings of the Conference on Uncertainty in Artificial Intelligence* (pp. 253–260).

Myerson, R. (1997). Dual reduction and elementary games. *Games and Economic Behavior, 21*(1-2), 183–202.

Nau, R., & McCardle, K. (1990). Coherent behavior in noncooperative games. *Journal of Economic Theory, 50*(2), 424–444.

Papadimitriou, C. (2005). Computing correlated equilibria in multiplayer games. *STOC: Proceedings of the Annual ACM Symposium on Theory of Computing* (pp. 49–56).

Papadimitriou, C., & Roughgarden, T. (2005). Computing equilibria in multi-player games. *SODA: Proceedings of the ACM-SIAM Symposium on Discrete Algorithms* (pp. 82–91).

Papadimitriou, C., & Roughgarden, T. (2008). Computing correlated equilibria in multi-player games. *Journal of the ACM, 55*(3), 14.

Papadimitriou, C., & Roughgarden, T. (2010). Comment on "computing correlated equilibria in multi-player games". `http://theory.stanford.edu/~tim/papers/comment.pdf`, accessed Jan. 10, 2011.

Raghavan, P. (1988). Probabilistic construction of deterministic algorithms: Approximating packing integer programs. *Journal of Computer and System Sciences, 37*(2), 130 – 143.

Spencer, J. (1994). *Ten lectures on the probabilistic method.* CBMS-NSF regional conference series in applied mathematics. Society for Industrial and Applied Mathematics.

Stein, N. D., Parrilo, P. A., & Ozdaglar, A. (2010). Exchangeable equilibria contradict exactness of the Papadimitriou-Roughgarden algorithm. `http://arxiv.org/abs/1010.2871v1`.

Distributed Algorithms via Gradient Descent for Fisher Markets

Benjamin Birnbaum*
University of Washington
birnbaum@cs.washington.edu

Nikhil R. Devanur
Microsoft Research, Redmond
nikdev@microsoft.com

Lin Xiao
Microsoft Research, Redmond
lin.xiao@microsoft.com

ABSTRACT

Designing distributed algorithms that converge quickly to an equilibrium is one of the foremost research goals in algorithmic game theory, and convex programs have played a crucial role in the design of algorithms for Fisher markets. In this paper we shed new light on both aspects for Fisher markets with linear and spending constraint utilities. We show fast convergence of the *Proportional Response* dynamics recently introduced by Wu and Zhang [WZ07]. The convergence is obtained from a new perspective: we show that the Proportional Response dynamics is equivalent to a gradient descent algorithm (with respect to a Bregman divergence instead of euclidean distance) on a convex program that captures the equilibria for linear utilities. We further show that the convex program program easily extends to the case of spending constraint utilities, thus resolving an open question raised by [Vaz10]. This also gives a way to extend the Proportional Response dynamics to spending constraint utilties. We also prove a technical result that is interesting in its own right: that the gradient descent algorithm based on a Bregman divergence converges with rate $O(1/t)$ under a condition that is weaker than having Lipschitz continuous gradient (which is the usual assumption in the optimization literature for obtaining the same rate).

Categories and Subject Descriptors

J.4 [**Social and Behavioral Sciences**]: Economics; F.2.0 [**Analysis of Algorithms and Problem Complexity**]: General

General Terms

Algorithms, Economics, Theory

Keywords

Market equilibrium, Proportional Response, Gradient descent, Distributed algorithm

*Part of this work was done while at Microsoft Research, Redmond.

EC'11, June 5–9, 2011, San Jose, California, USA.

1. INTRODUCTION

The computational complexity of equilibria has been the focus of much research in Algorithmic Game Theory over the last decade, not to mention the considerable amount of work in the economics literature. Although most papers consider algorithms in the centralized model of computation, what are more relevant in practice are *distributed algorithms* that converge to an equilibrium. Such algorithms are especially important in the context of automated markets that have emerged due to the Internet, such as the market for online advertising. In such markets trading is often done by automated agents. Distributed algorithms can be thought of as protocols that these agents are programmed to follow. The design and analysis of distributed algorithms converging to equilibria in the context of games has also recieved considerable attention, most commonly convergence of best response dynamics [AGM$^+$08, CS07, Ros73, AAE$^+$08].

For markets, essentially the only distributed algorithms that have been studied are variants of the tatonnement process. Wu and Zhang [WZ07] proposed a new distributed algorithm, called the *Proportional Response* (PR) dynamics, as a protocol for trading bandwidth on a peer-to-peer network.[1] The PR dynamics involves a sequence of bids by the buyers and prices by the sellers that respond to each other. The seller prices are simply set to be the sum of all the bids they receive. The buyers set their bids proportional to the utility they would obtain with the bids and the prices in the previous round.

PR seems to converge really fast to equilibrium in practice, and yet the reason for this remained a mystery. Zhang [Zha09] analyzed PR dynamics for Fisher markets and showed the following: "if τ is large enough, then there exists a $t < \tau$ such that the bids and prices in round t are close to the equilibrium." This does not quite show *convergence* of the dynamics to an equilibrium. Moreover the proof uses a potential function that gives little insight into why this happens.

In this paper we *demystify* the PR dynamics: we show that the PR dynamics are equivalent to a generalized gradient descent algorithm with Bregman divergences (instead of Euclidean distance) on a convex program introduced by Shmyrev [Shm09] that captures the equilibria of Fisher markets with linear utilities. This insight gives an intuitive understanding of why such dynamics work. PR dynamics fit so well with this perspective that we can confidently say this is the "right" way of thinking about them. Moreover, we get true convergence, of the form, "if t is large enough, then the bids and prices in round t are close to an equilibrium."

Further we show that the convex program and the PR dynam-

[1]It has since been shown to be an effective solution for BitTorrent [LLSB08].

ics generalize to the *spending constraint* utilities, thus resolving an open question of Vazirani [Vaz10].

1.1 Fisher's Market Model with Linear and Spending Constraint Utilities

In the Fisher market model with linear utilities, there are n buyers and m perfectly divisible goods. There is a unit[2] supply of each good. Each buyer i has a budget B_i, and for each item j, a number u_{ij}, which represents the utility of that buyer for one unit of item j. Given an allocation vector $x \in \mathbb{R}_+^{n\times m}$, the utility of buyer i is $\sum_j u_{ij}x_{ij}$.

An allocation $x \in \mathbb{R}_+^{n\times m}$ and price vector $p \in \mathbb{R}_+^m$ are an *equilibrium* if two conditions are satisfied. The first, *buyer optimality*, is that given p, each player maximizes his utility subject to his budget constraint. In other words, for all i, the allocation x optimizes the following program (where p is a constant):

$$\begin{array}{ll} \text{maximize} & \sum_j u_{ij}x_{ij} \\ \text{subject to} & \sum_j p_j x_{ij} \le B_i. \\ & x_{ij} \ge 0,\ \forall j. \end{array}$$

The second equilibrium condition, *market clearance*, is

$$\sum_i x_{ij} = 1, \quad \forall j.$$

In the *spending constraints* model, the utility of a buyer also depends on the prices, as follows. The utility is still additive across goods, that is, the total utility for a bundle of goods is the sum of utilities for each good separately. For a given good, the utility function is divided into segments; each segment l has a constant rate of utility u_{ij}^l, and a budget B_{ij}^l. The utility of the buyer for x_{ij}^l amount of good j under segment l is $u_{ij}^l x_{ij}^l$, but is subject to the constraint that $p_j x_{ij}^l \le B_{ij}^l$. Hence the utility maximizing program for a given buyer i is now as follows.

$$\begin{array}{ll} \text{maximize} & \sum_{j,l} u_{ij}^l x_{ij}^l \\ \text{subject to} & \sum_{j,l} p_j x_{ij}^l \le B_i. \\ & 0 \le x_{ij}^l \text{ and } p_j x_{ij}^l \le B_{ij}^l\ \forall j,l. \end{array}$$

1.2 Proportional Response Dynamics

The *Proportional Response (PR) Dynamics* is a distributed algorithm for computing market equilibrium and was introduced by Wu and Zhang [WZ07] in the context of a bandwidth trading market model for peer-to-peer networks and by Zhang [Zha09] in the current context of the Fisher markets. The algorithm proceeds in discrete time steps, and for each time $t = 0, 1, 2, \ldots$, buyer i submits a bid $b_{ij}(t)$ for each good j. Given the bids, a price vector $p(t)$ is computed by summing the bids for each item: $p_j(t) = \sum_i b_{ij}(t)$. Each buyer i is allocated an amount $x_{ij}(t) = b_{ij}(t)/p_j(t)$ of item j. The buyers then update their bids for the next time step so that their new bid for a good is proportional to the *utility obtained* from this good in the current round, that is $b_{ij}(t) \propto u_{ij}x_{ij}(t)$. In summary, the new bid vector is computed according to the following recursion:

$$b_{ij}(t+1) = B_i \frac{u_{ij}x_{ij}(t)}{\sum_{j'} u_{ij'}x_{ij'}(t)} . \tag{1}$$

The PR dynamics has many desirable properties that are also unique.

- The PR dynamics are simple, distributed and require no global communication.[3] In every step, a buyer only has to know the prices of the goods he is interested in, and a good only has to know the bids placed on it.
- PR dynamics is also *stateless*: the bids at any time step depend only on the bids of the previous step, and there is no special starting point.
- Unlike all other dynamics, which depend on choosing the right step size, PR dynamics does not need a step size to choose and adapt.

In this paper, we analyze the PR dynamics from the perspective of general convex optimization algorithms. Along the way, we establish a new convergence condition for generalized gradient descent methods based on Bregman divergences and extend both Shmyrev's convex program and the PR dynamics to markets with spending constraint utilities.

2. MAIN RESULTS

2.1 The Convex Program

A well-known convex program called the Eisenberg-Gale [EG59] convex program captures equilibrium allocations of a linear Fisher market. Here we consider an alternate convex program discovered recently by Shmyrev [Shm09] that also does the same. As we shall see this convex program is closely related to the Proportional Response (PR) dynamics. The convex program is as follows.

$$\begin{array}{ll} \text{maximize} & \sum_{i,j} b_{ij}\log u_{ij} - \sum_j p_j \log p_j \\ \text{subject to} & \forall\, j, \sum_i b_{ij} = p_j, \\ & \forall\, i, \sum_j b_{ij} = B_i, \\ & \forall\, i,j,\ 0 \le b_{ij}. \end{array} \tag{2}$$

The variable p_j corresponds to the price of good j. The variable b_{ij} represents the amount of money spent on good j by buyer i. Hence given a solution to the above program, the allocation x_{ij} is given by b_{ij}/p_j. It is easy to see that for any feasible solution to the program, the corresponding prices and allocations are such that the market always clears, and the buyers always exhaust their budgets. The only other condition required for equilibrium is that each buyer be allocated his optimal bundle of goods.

THEOREM 1 ([SHM09]). *Let $b^\star$ and $p^\star$ be an optimum solution to Convex Program (2). Then $p^\star$ and allocation $x_{ij}^\star = b_{ij}^\star/p_j^\star$ is an equilibrium for the Fisher market with linear utilities given by the u_{ij}'s and the B_i's.*

This convex program can be generalized to markets with spending constraint utilities. This resolves an important open problem raised by Vazirani [Vaz10].

$$\begin{array}{ll} \text{maximize} & \sum_{i,j,l} b_{ij}^l \log u_{ij}^l - \sum_j p_j \log p_j \\ \text{subject to} & \forall\, j, \sum_{i,l} b_{ij}^l = p_j, \\ & \forall\, i, \sum_{j,l} b_{ij}^l = B_i, \\ & \forall\, i,j,l,\ 0 \le b_{ij}^l \le B_{ij}^l. \end{array} \tag{3}$$

As before, the allocation is given by $x_{ij}^l = b_{ij}^l/p_j$, and the only condition that needs verifying is buyer optimality.

THEOREM 2. *An optimum solution to Convex Program (3) corresponds to an equilibrium for the Fisher market with spending constraint utilities given by the u_{ij}^l's, B_{ij}^l's and the B_i's.*

[2]This is without loss of generality, by the choice of unit, since the goods are divisible.

[3]Except for the fact that they need to be synchronized, in the sense that the dynamics happen in rounds and in every round, every bidder updates his bids.

2.2 Generalized Gradient Descent with Bregman Divergence

Both of the convex programs (2) and (3) are special cases of the constrained optimization problem

$$\begin{array}{ll}\text{minimize} & f(x)\\ \text{subject to} & x \in C\end{array} \tag{4}$$

where C is a compact convex set, and $f(x)$ is a differentiable convex function with $\operatorname{dom} f \supseteq C$ (i.e., f is finite on C). The conventional *projected gradient descent* method (e.g., [Ber99]) for solving (4) is

$$x(t+1) = \pi_C\big(x(t) - \mu_t \nabla f(x(t))\big) \tag{5}$$

where μ_t is an appropriate stepsize, and $\pi_C(\cdot)$ denotes Euclidean projection on the set C. Let

$$\ell_f(x; y) := f(y) + \langle \nabla f(y), x - y\rangle$$

be the linear approximation of f using the gradient at y. The method (5) is equivalent to

$$x(t+1) = \arg\min_{x\in C}\left\{\ell_f(x; x(t)) + \frac{1}{2\mu_t}\|x - x(t)\|_2^2\right\}, \tag{6}$$

where the *proximal* term $(1/2)\|x - x(t)\|_2^2$ is the squared Euclidean distance between two points. In the *generalized gradient descent* method the squared Euclidean distance in (6) is replaced by a generalized distance function $d(x, x(t))$, i.e.,

$$x(t+1) = \arg\min_{x\in C}\left\{\ell_f(x; x(t)) + \gamma_t\, d(x, x(t))\right\}, \tag{7}$$

where the parameter $\gamma_t > 0$, and its reciprocal $1/\gamma_t$ play the role of stepsize μ_t in the Euclidean case. In particular, we let $d(x, y)$ be the *Bregman divergence* [Bre67] of a differentiable convex function $h(x)$ (assuming $\operatorname{dom} h \supseteq C$), defined as

$$d_h(x, y) = h(x) - \ell_h(x; y), \quad \forall x \in C,\ y \in \operatorname{rint} C,$$

where $\operatorname{rint} C$ denotes the *relative interior* of C [Roc70, Section 6]. As an example, $d_h(x, y) = (1/2)\|x - y\|_2^2$ if $h(x) = (1/2)\|x\|_2^2$. We often drop the subscript h whenever there is no confusion from context. We say h is the *kernel* of d, and d is generated by h. We assume that both f and h are differentiable and they satisfy

$$f(x) \le \ell_f(x; y) + \gamma d_h(x, y), \quad \forall x \in C,\ y \in \operatorname{rint} C, \tag{8}$$

for some constant $\gamma > 0$. We show convergence of the generalized gradient descent method under the assumption of (8), which is weaker than the typical assumption of Lipshitz continuity of the gradient of f.

THEOREM 3. *Suppose that the sequence $x(t)$ is defined by Equation (7), that f and h are convex and differentiable functions, and that f and h satisfy Condition (8). Then for all t,*

$$f(x(t)) - f(x^\star) \le \frac{\gamma d(x^\star, x(0))}{t}.$$

In particular we show the following two lemmas from which the above theorem follows immediately.

LEMMA 4. *The total deviation of f from the optimum throughout the run of the algorithm is bounded by a value that is independent of how long the algorithm is run.*

$$\sum_t \big(f(x(t)) - f(x^\star)\big) \le \gamma d(x^\star, x(0)).$$

LEMMA 5. *For all t, $f(x(t+1)) \le f(x(t))$.*

2.3 PR as Gradient Descent

One can easily see the similarities between the PR dynamics (1) and Convex Program (2) in the way the prices and allocations are defined. In particular, the market clears automatically in the PR dynamics and the only condition we need to worry about is buyer optimality. In fact as detailed below, we show that the PR dynamics is exactly the gradient descent algorithm given by (7) on Convex Program (2).

First of all, we can eliminate the p_j variables from the program (2); in fact, p_j can be thought of as a function of the b_{ij}'s, defined as $p_j(b) = \sum_i b_{ij}$. We stick to the notation p_j without the argument when there is no confusion[4] from the context. Let the objective function[5] of the convex program be denoted by

$$\varphi(b) = -\sum_{i,j} b_{ij} \log u_{ij} + \sum_j p_j(b)\log(p_j(b)),$$

and the feasible region by

$$S = \left\{b \in \mathbb{R}^{n\times m} : \sum_j b_{ij} = B_i\ \forall\, i, b_{ij} \ge 0\ \forall\, i, j\right\}.$$

Without loss of generality assume that $\sum_i B_i = 1$. Also define the Bregman divergence d with the kernel function being the unnormalized negative entropy,

$$h(b) = \sum_{i,j}(b_{ij}\log b_{ij} - b_{ij}) = \sum_{i,j} b_{ij}\log b_{ij} - \sum_i B_i$$

for $b \in S$. A straightforward calculation shows that

$$d(a, b) = \sum_{i,j} a_{ij} \log\frac{a_{ij}}{b_{ij}} = D\,(a\,||\,b)\,,$$

where $D\,(\cdot\,||\,\cdot)$ is the *KL-divergence* between two probability distributions.

THEOREM 6. *The proportional response dynamics (1) is equivalent to the gradient descent algorithm (7) with $d(a, b) = D\,(a\,||\,b)$ as above, $f = \varphi$, $C = S$ and $\gamma = 1$.*

In order to use our results about convergence of the above algorithm (Theorem 3), we need to show that Condition (8) is satisfied, which we do in the following lemma.

LEMMA 7. *For all $a, b \in S$,*

$$\varphi(b) \le \ell_\varphi(b; a) + D\,(b\,||\,a)\,.$$

Thus, PR dynamics satisfies the convergence properties as specified in Theorem 3 with $f = \varphi$ and $\gamma = 1$. If the initial bids are $b_{ij}(0) = B_i/m$ for all i and j, then $D\,(b^\star\,||\,b(0)) \le \log(mn)$ (see Lemma 13). A more detailed analysis of the convergence is given in Section 5.

For markets with spending constraints, the algorithm (7) leads to an *iterative PR and capping* algorithm, which has the same convergence properties as the PR dynamics (see Section 4.1).

---

[4]Similarly, we use $p_j(t)$ to denote $p_j(b(t))$ and $p_j^\star$ to denote $p_j(b^\star)$.

[5]To maintain consistency with our notation in the previous subsection, we rephrase the convex program as minimizing a convex function instead of maximizing a concave function.

2.4 Related Work and Motivation

The algorithmic study of equilibrium concepts in general, and of market equilibria in particular, are motivated by the question of whether markets can feasibly operate at equilibrium. After almost a decade since this line of research started, the computational complexity of equilibrium concepts is fairly well understood. The hardness results [CT09, CDDT09, CD06, DGP06, CSVY06] point towards the unlikeliness that markets in general operate at equilibria, with recent results [CT09, CDDT09, VY10] showing that even for the simple class of separable piecewise linear functions, it is PPAD-hard to compute an equilibrium. The algorithmic results [DPS02, DPSV08, Jai07, DV04, CPV05, CMV05, JV10, DK08, Ye08] provide hope for certain special classes of markets. A good survey of algorithms for market equilibria can be found in [Vaz07] and [CV07], with the summary being that we can find equilibria for markets with weak gross substitutes property, for certain resource allocation markets [JV10], and when there are a bounded number of goods [DK08].

Algorithmic results in a centralized model of computation do not directly address the question of market *dynamics*: how might agents interacting in a market arrive at an equilibrium? Here, the quest is for simple and distributed algorithms that are guaranteed to converge fast. Such distributed algorithms are especially applicable when the agents involved are automated, and one has to prescribe a particular *protocol* for them to follow. This is true in many networking applications, and also in markets such as search advertising where often the bids are updated automatically. There is also a huge amount of work in the networking community on designing such distributed algorithms that achieve *proportional fairness* (e.g., [Kel97, KMT98]). It is known that proportional fairness is equivalent to market equilibrium in many settings (including linear utilities), via an Eisenberg-Gale type convex program [KV]. Our results could potentially be useful for these applications as well, and is a direction for future work.

Almost all dynamics considered in the literature are variants of the *tatonnement* process first defined by Leon Walras [Wal74]. The most general version of tatonnement just says that prices are increased when demand exceeds supply and are decreased when supply exceeds demand. Many versions of this [ABH59, Uza60, CMV05, FGK+08, GK06] have been analyzed over the years, but none of these until recently gave simple, fast and distributed algorithms. Some of the early work in economics [ABH59, Uza60] ignored the convergence rate entirely. [CMV05] showed polynomial time convergence of a version of tatonnement for markets with weak gross substitutes, but had to transform the market *a priori* which then translates to passing around global information in every round. The auction algorithm of Garg and Kapoor [GK06] requires that it be started from a particular state. The algorithm of [FGK+08] suffers from disadvantages such as having to take the average of all the prices and the average of all the allocations to get an equilibrium. The exception is the algorithm given by [CF08] which is distributed and asynchronous and converges fast for markets with weak gross substitutes property. The convergence time however depends on certain market parameters which tend to infinity for linear Fisher markets. One reason for the difficulty in designing tatonnement style processes for linear Fisher markets is that the demand of a buyer is not always uniquely determined. Thus at equilibrium one needs to specify the allocation in addition to the prices. The PR dynamics elegantly takes care of the problem of non-uniqueness of demand, since the bids uniquely determine the prices and the allocations.

PR was first proposed as a protocol for trading bandwidth on a peer-to-peer network by Wu and Zhang [WZ07] and has been shown to be an effective solution for BitTorrent [LLSB08]. Zhang [Zha09] shows the following about PR dynamics in Fisher markets: "if τ is large enough, then there exists a $t < \tau$ such that $b(t)$ is close to optimal." We get true convergence, of the form, "if t is large enough, then $b(t)$ is close to optimal." In fact, we rephrase Zhang's proof and give a detailed comparison with ours in Section 5.2. We extend the results to spending constraint utilities as well. Clearly the extension was only possible because of our insights into the connection between PR dynamics and the Convex Program (2). Moreover, Zhang [Zha09] also considers Constant Elasticity of Substitution (CES) utilities, $U_i = \sum_j (u_{ij}x_{ij})^{\rho_i}$ with $0 < \rho_i \leq 1$. He gets a better bound on the convergence rate for these utilities: PR converges to an ϵ-approximate equilibrium in

$$O\left(\frac{L + \log(1/\epsilon)}{1 - (\max_i \rho_i)^2}\right)$$

rounds, where L is the bit-complexity of the input. Our techniques extend to CES utilities as well, and we strengthen Zhang's results as before, by obtaining the stronger form of convergence. The details of this will be presented in the full version.

The convex program (2) was recently discovered by Shmyrev [Shm09], and was actually rediscovered by us. The convex program (2) is in fact related to the EG convex program as follows: take the dual of the EG program, perform a change of variables, and if you take the dual of this program again, you get the convex program (2). See [Dev09] for details on this connection.

The spending constraint model is an interesting special class of markets that is amenable to efficient algorithms. The spending constraint utilities for the Fisher was introduced by Vazirani [Vaz10] and extended to the more general Arrow-Debreu model by Devanur and Vazirani [DV04]. Vazirani [Vaz10] extended the primal-dual algorithm for linear utilities of Devanur et. al. [DPSV08] to the spending constraint utilities. The primal-dual interpretation of the algorithm of Devanur et. al. was based on the Eisenberg-Gale convex program, but no such program is known for spending constraints. Based on this, Vazirani [Vaz10] conjectured that there must exist a convex program that captures the spending constraint model as well. We finally resolve this conjecture positively in this paper.

The generalized gradient descent method, also known as *mirror-descent* has been well studied in the optimization community, see, e.g., [NY83, BT03]. In the optimization literature however, the kernel function h is usually assumed to be strongly convex. Then with a diminishing stepsize $1/\gamma_t = O(1/\sqrt{t})$, the generalized gradient method (7) converges with rate $O(1/\sqrt{t})$, even if f is non-differentiable (e.g, [BT03, Nem05]). If f is further differentiable and ∇f is Lipschitz-continuous, then (7) converges with rate $O(1/t)$ using a constant γ that is no smaller than the Lipschitz constant. (e.g., [Ber99, Nes04]). In this case, more sophisticated variations of (7) can achieve a convergence rate $O(1/t^2)$; see, e.g., [Nes83, Nes04, Nes05, Tse08]. In this paper, we show that the method (7) can have convergence rate $O(1/t)$ with Condition (8). Condition (8) is implied by the assumptions that ∇f is Lipschitz continuous and h is strongly convex (e.g., [Nes04]) and is hence a weaker assumption. Without these stronger assumptions, Condition (8) often requires a close connection between the functions f and h, which is the case for our analysis of the PR dynamics in Section 4.

Organization: In Section 3 we prove Theorem 3. Theorem 6 is proved in Section 4. In Section 5, we define various measures of distance to equilibrium and show convergence of PR dynamics with respect to these measures. We also compare these in detail with

Zhang's results in Section 5.2. We conclude with directions for future research in Section 6.

3. GRADIENT DESCENT

In this section, we prove convergence properties of the generalized gradient method (7) based on the assumption (8) as stated in Theorem 3. We start by noting some key properties of Bregman divergences:

- $d(x, y) \geq 0$ for all $x, y \in \operatorname{dom} h$. If h is strictly convex, then $d(x, y) = 0$ if and only if $x = y$.
- In general $d(x, y) \neq d(y, x)$, and it does not satisfy the triangle inequality.
- The following *three-point identity* follows directly from definition:

$$d(x, z) = d(x, y) + d(y, z) + \langle \nabla h(y) - \nabla h(z),\, x - y \rangle. \quad (9)$$

If h is not strictly convex, then the solution to the minimization problem in (7) may not be unique. However, a solution always exists because we assume C is compact.

Recall that in order to prove Theorem 3, it is sufficient to prove Lemmas 5 and 4. We first prove Lemma 5.

PROOF OF LEMMA 5. We have

$$\begin{aligned} f(x(t+1)) &\leq \ell_f(x(t+1); x(t)) + \gamma d(x(t+1), x(t)) \\ &\leq \ell_f(x(t); x(t)) + \gamma d(x(t), x(t)) \\ &= f(x(t)). \end{aligned}$$

The first inequality follows from (8). The second inequality is by definition of $x(t+1)$. The last equality is also by definition, since $d(x, x) = 0$. □

The key step in the proof of Lemma 4 is the following lemma. Let $x^\star := \arg\min_{x \in C}\{f(x)\}$ be an optimum solution to (4).

LEMMA 8. *For all t,*

$$f(x(t+1)) - f(x^\star) \leq \gamma d(x^\star, x(t)) - \gamma d(x^\star, x(t+1)).$$

Before we prove Lemma 8, we show how Lemma 4 follows from it.

PROOF OF LEMMA 4. The lemma follows by simply summing over all t the conclusion of Lemma 8 and using the fact that $d(x, y)$ is always greater than 0. □

In order to prove Lemma 8, we need a result on optimization with Bregman divergence. Consider the following optimization problem:

$$\begin{array}{ll} \text{minimize} & g(x) + d(x, y) \\ \text{subject to} & x \in C \end{array} \quad (10)$$

where $g(x)$ is a convex function and C is a compact convex set. The following lemma can be found in, e.g., [CT93].

LEMMA 9. *If x^+ is the optimal solution to the optimization problem (10), then*

$$g(x) + d(x, y) \geq g(x^+) + d(x^+, y) + d(x, x^+). \quad (11)$$

We apply Lemma 9 with $g(x) = (1/\gamma)\ell_f(x; x(t))$ to obtain the following corollary.

COROLLARY 10. *For all $z \in C$,*

$$\begin{aligned} &\ell_f(x(t+1); x(t)) + \gamma d(x(t+1), x(t)) \\ &\quad \leq \ell_f(z; x(t)) + \gamma d(z, x(t)) - \gamma d(z, x(t+1)). \end{aligned}$$

Lemma 8 follows as a consequence of this corollary.

PROOF OF LEMMA 8. We have

$$\begin{aligned} f(x(t+1)) &\leq \ell_f(x(t+1); x(t)) + \gamma d(x(t+1), x(t)) \\ &\leq \ell_f(x^\star; x(t)) + \gamma d(x^\star, x(t)) \\ &\quad - \gamma d(x^\star, x(t+1)) \\ &\leq f(x^\star) + \gamma d(x^\star, x(t)) - \gamma d(x^\star, x(t+1)). \end{aligned}$$

The first and third inequalities follow from (8), and the second inequality follows from Corollary 10. □

4. PR AS GRADIENT DESCENT

In this section, we show the equivalence of the PR dynamics and the gradient descent algorithm on the new convex program, that is, we prove Theorem 6 and Lemma 7.

Recall the function $\varphi(b) = -\sum_{i,j} b_{ij} \log(u_{ij}/p_j)$ and feasible region S defined in the introduction. The components of the gradient of φ are given as

$$(\nabla \varphi(b))_{ij} = 1 - \log\left(\frac{u_{ij}}{p_j}\right).$$

It is clear that $\nabla\varphi$ is not Lipschitz continuous on S. Therefore we need the weaker assumption (8) to show $O(1/t)$ convergence.

The gradient descent algorithm (7) when applied to φ, S, with d being the KL-divergence and with $\gamma = 1$ is

$$b(t+1) := \arg\min_{a \in S}\{\ell_\varphi(b(t); a) + D(a \,||\, b(t))\}. \quad (12)$$

It is well known[6] that this update rule takes the following form:

$$\begin{aligned} b_{ij}(t) &= \frac{1}{Z_i'(t)} b_{ij}(t) \exp\left(\left(\nabla\varphi(b(t))\right)_{ij}\right) \\ &= \frac{1}{Z_i(t)} b_{ij}(t)\left(\frac{u_{ij}}{p_j(t)}\right), \end{aligned}$$

where $Z_i(t)$ is chosen such that $\sum_{j=1}^n b_{ij}(t) = B_i$. This shows Theorem 6.

We now prove Lemma 7. The proof mainly relies on the following characterization of φ.

LEMMA 11. *For all $a, b \in S$,*

$$\varphi(b) = \ell_\varphi(b; a) + D(p(b) \,||\, p(a)).$$

PROOF. We have

$$\begin{aligned} \varphi(b) - \ell_\varphi(b; a) &= \varphi(b) - \varphi(a) - \langle \nabla\varphi(a), b - a \rangle \\ &= -\sum_{i,j} b_{ij} \log\frac{u_{ij}}{p_j(b)} + \sum_{i,j} a_{ij} \log\frac{u_{ij}}{p_j(a)} \\ &\quad - \sum_{i,j}\left(1 - \log\frac{u_{ij}}{p_j(a)}\right)(b_{ij} - a_{ij}) \\ &= \sum_{i,j} b_{ij} \log\frac{p_j(b)}{p_j(a)} = D(p(b) \,||\, p(a)), \end{aligned}$$

where in the third equality we used $\sum_{i,j} b_{ij} = \sum_{i,j} a_{ij} = 1$. □

PROOF OF LEMMA 7. The lemma follows from Lemma 11 and the fact that $D(p(b) \,||\, p(a)) \leq D(b \,||\, a)$, which we can prove us-

[6]Theorem 12 shows a more general statement.

ing the convexity of the function $q(x,y) = x\log(x/y)$:

$$D(p(b)\,||\,p(a)) = n\sum_j \left(\frac{1}{n}q(p_j(b), p_j(a))\right)$$
$$= n\sum_j q\left(\frac{1}{n}\sum_i b_{ij}, \frac{1}{n}\sum_i a_{ij}\right)$$
$$\leq n\sum_j \frac{1}{n}\sum_i q(b_{ij}, a_{ij}) = D(b\,||\,a).$$

This finishes the proof. □

4.1 Extension to Spending Constraint Utilities

For Fisher markets with spending constraint utilities, let φ be the negative objective function of the convex program (3):

$$\varphi(b) = -\sum_{i,j,l} b^l_{ij}\log(u^l_{ij}) + \sum_j p_j \log(p_j).$$

The components of its gradient is

$$(\nabla\varphi(b))_{i,j,l} = 1 - \log\left(\frac{u^l_{ij}}{p_j}\right).$$

We use the same gradient descent method (12), but with the constraint set

$$S = \left\{a : \sum_{j,l} a^l_{ij} \leq B_i,\ \forall i, \text{ and } 0 \leq a^l_{ij} \leq B^l_{ij},\ \forall i,j,l\right\}.$$

THEOREM 12. *Each bidding vector $b_i(t+1)$ can be computed separately by using the following iterative PR and capping algorithm.*

Algorithm: Iterative PR and Capping
input: B_i and B^l_{ij}, u^l_{ij}, and $b^l_{ij}(t)$ for all j and l.
initialize: let A_i be set of all pairs (j,l), and $C_i = \emptyset$.
repeat:

1. Let $A_i = A_i \setminus C_i$, $\bar{B}_i = B_i - \sum_{(j,l)\in C_i} B^l_{ij}$, and $Q_i = \sum_{(j,l)\in A_i} (u^l_{ij}/p_j(t))b^l_{ij}(t)$.
2. Let
$$b^l_{ij}(t+1) = \begin{cases} \dfrac{(u^l_{ij}/p_j(t))b^l_{ij}(t)}{Q_i}\bar{B}_i & \text{if } (j,l)\in A_i, \\ B^l_{ij} & \text{otherwise.}\end{cases}$$
3. Let $C_i = \{(j,l)\in A_i : b^l_{ij}(t+1) > B^l_{ij}\}$. If $C_i = \emptyset$, stop and return $b_i(t+1)$; otherwise continue.

PROOF. The minimization problem (12) can be solved separately for each agent i,

$$b_i(t+1) = \operatorname*{arg\,min}_{\substack{\sum_{j,l} a^l_{ij}\leq B_i,\\ 0\leq a^l_{ij}\leq B^l_{ij},\ \forall j,l}} \left\{\sum_{j,l} a^l_{ij}(\nabla\varphi(b(t)))_{i,j,l} + \sum_{j,l} a^l_{ij}\log\left(\frac{a^l_{ij}}{b^l_{ij}(t)}\right)\right\}.$$

To solve this problem, we introduce Lagrange multipliers λ_i and μ^l_{ij}. The Lagrangian is

$$L_i(a_i, \lambda_i, \mu_i)$$
$$= \sum_{j,l} a^l_{ij}(\nabla\varphi(b(t)))_{i,j,l} + \sum_{j,l} a^l_{ij}\log\left(\frac{a^l_{ij}}{b^l_{ij}(t)}\right)$$
$$+ \lambda_i\left(\sum_{j,l} a^l_{ij} - B_i\right) + \sum_{j,l}\mu^l_{ij}\left(a^l_{ij} - B^l_{ij}\right)$$
$$= \sum_{j,l} a^l_{ij}\left((\nabla\varphi(b(t)))_{i,j,l} + \lambda_i + \mu^l_{ij}\right)$$
$$+ \sum_{j,l} a^l_{ij}\log\left(\frac{a^l_{ij}}{b^l_{ij}(t)}\right) - \lambda_i B_i - \sum_{j,l}\mu^l_{ij}B^l_{ij}.$$

Taking derivatives with respect to a^l_{ij} and setting them to be zero, i.e., let $(\nabla L_i(a_i,\lambda_i,\mu_i))_{jl} = 0$, we have

$$(\nabla\varphi(b(t)))_{i,j,l} + \lambda_i + \mu^l_{ij} + \log\left(\frac{a^l_{ij}}{b^l_{ij}(t)}\right) + 1 = 0.$$

The solution is

$$a^l_{ij} = \frac{1}{\exp(2+\lambda_i+\mu^l_{ij})}\,\frac{u^l_{ij}b^l_{ij}(t)}{p_j(t)}.$$

Using the optimality conditions (KKT conditions),

$$\mu^l_{ij}\left(a^l_{ij} - B^l_{ij}\right) = 0, \quad \forall i,j,l,$$

we can find the optimal solution $b_i(t+1)$ using an iterative PR and capping algorithm. □

5. CONVERGENCE PROPERTIES

The PR dynamics may never get to an exact equilibrium. Therefore we consider approximate equilibria, based on a measure of how close a given solution is to equilibrium. There are different ways to measure the "distance" from equilibria. We show that all of these can be related to $\varphi(b(t)) - \varphi(b^\star)$, the difference in the objective function between the current point and the optimum. (The additive difference is a reasonable measure since we normalized the sum of all budgets to 1.) Thus, any convergence bound we show with respect to the objective function can easily be translated to one for the particular measure of approximation.

The PR dynamics is defined for any initial bid vector b^0, and the convergence time is proportional to $D(b^\star\,||\,b(0))$ (Theorem 3). For the sake of concreteness, we state our bounds assuming that $b_{ij}(0) = B^i/m$, that is each buyer initially divides his budget equally between all the items. With this, we have the following bound on $D(b^\star\,||\,b(0))$.

LEMMA 13. *If $b_{ij}(0) = B_i/m$ for all i and j, then*

$$D(b^\star\,||\,b(0)) \leq \log(mn)\ .$$

PROOF. We have

$$\begin{aligned} D(b^\star \,||\, b(0)) &= \sum_{i,j} b^\star_{ij} \log \frac{b^\star_{ij}}{b(0)_{ij}} = \sum_{i,j} b^\star_{ij} \log \frac{m b^\star_{ij}}{B_i} \\ &= \log m + \sum_{i,j} b^\star_{ij} \log b^\star_{ij} - \sum_{i,j} b^\star_{ij} \log B_i \\ &= \log m - \sum_i B_i \log B_i + \sum_{i,j} b^\star_{ij} \log b^\star_{ij} \\ &\le \log m - \sum_i B_i \log B_i \\ &\le \log m + \log n. \end{aligned}$$

□

We now have the following convergence results.

$$\varphi(b(t)) - \varphi(b^\star) \le \frac{\log(mn)}{t}. \tag{13}$$

$$\sum_t (\varphi(b(t)) - \varphi(b^\star)) \le \log(mn). \tag{14}$$

$$\varphi(b(t+1)) \le \varphi(b(t)). \tag{15}$$

In other words, if $t \ge \frac{\log(mn)}{\epsilon}$ then $\varphi(b(t)) - \varphi(b^\star) \le \epsilon$.

5.1 Measures of Approximation

As mentioned before, we now show how to translate the convergence results mentioned above to other ways of measuring the distance from an equilibrium. Recall that we assumed without loss of generality, that the input has been scaled so that there is exactly one unit of each item and $\sum_i B_i = 1$. We may further assume that $\sum_j u_{ij} = 1$ for all i. Let $u_{\min} = \min_{i,j:u_{ij}>0} u_{ij}$ and $B_{\min} = \min_i B_i$.

- The KL-divergence is a well known (asymmetric) measure of dissimilarity between probability distributions, defined as $D(x \,||\, y) := \sum_i x_i \log(x_i/y_i)$. Since we normalized the total budget to be 1, the sum of the prices is also 1. In other words, one can think of the price vectors as probability distributions and use KL-divergence to measure the distance between them. Also it is well known that $\frac{1}{2}\|x-y\|_1^2 \le D(x \,||\, y)$. We show that

$$D(p(t) \,||\, p^\star) \le \varphi(b(t)) - \varphi(b^\star) \;. \tag{16}$$

- Let ψ be the objective function of the Eisenberg-Gale convex program for $x_{ij} = b_{ij}/p_j$. We can measure

$$\psi(b(t)) - \psi(b^\star) = \sum_i B_i \log(u_i^\star / u(t)_i),$$

  where $u_i^\star$ is the utility of buyer i at equilibrium. We show that

$$\psi(b(t)) - \psi(b^\star) \le \varphi(b(t)) - \varphi(b^\star) \;. \tag{17}$$

- We can measure a relative notion of distance from the equilibrium price vector: $\eta := \max_j \left|\frac{p_j(t)-p_j^\star}{p_j^\star}\right|$. We show that

$$\eta^2 \le O\left(\frac{n}{u_{\min}}\right)(\varphi(b(t)) - \varphi(b^\star)) \;. \tag{18}$$

- We can measure the maximum sub-optimality of the allocations. Let $u_i(t)$ be the utility of buyer i given his current allocation and $\tilde{u}_i^t$ be the maximum utility buyer i could have obtained if the prices were set to $p(t)$. We show that there exists a ζ such that $u_i(t) \ge (1-\zeta)\tilde{u}_i(t)$ for all i, and

$$\zeta^2 \le O\left(\frac{n}{u_{\min} B_{\min}^2}\right)(\varphi(b(t)) - \varphi(b^\star)) \;. \tag{19}$$

- We can also measure an aggregate notion of suboptimality. To this end, let the vector δ be such that $u_i(t) = (1-\delta_i)\tilde{u}_i(t)$ for all i. Then we measure $\xi := \sum_i \delta_i B_i$. We show that

$$\xi^2 \le O\left(\frac{n}{u_{\min}}\right)(\varphi(b(t)) - \varphi(b^\star)). \tag{20}$$

5.2 Comparison with Zhang's results

We now rephrase the main result in [Zha09] for ease of comparison. They follow the same framework as outlined earlier, first show convergence of a potential function and then relate that potential function to other measures of approximation. Whereas we show convergence of $\varphi(b(t)) - \varphi(b^\star)$, Zhang does the same for the quantity $\psi(b(t+1)) - \psi(b^\star) + D(p^\star \,||\, p(t))$, where $\psi(b)$ is the value of the objective function of the Eisenberg-Gale convex program with $x_{ij} = b_{ij}/p_j$:

$$\psi(b) = -\sum_i B_i \log\left(\sum_j \frac{u_{ij} b_{ij}}{p_j}\right).$$

Zhang's main result can be summarized by the following lemmas. Let $p^\star_{\min} = \min_j p^\star_j$.

LEMMA 14 ([ZHA09]).

$$\sum_t \left(\psi(b(t+1)) - \psi(b^\star) + D(p^\star \,||\, p(t))\right) \le D(b^\star \,||\, b(0)) \,.$$

PROOF IN OUR FRAMEWORK. First by using Corollary 10, we have

$$\begin{aligned} \varphi(b(t+1)) &\le \ell_\varphi(b(t+1); b(t)) + D(b(t+1) \,||\, b(t)) \\ &\le \ell_\varphi(b^\star; b(t)) + D(b^\star \,||\, b(t)) - D(b^\star \,||\, b(t+1)) \,. \end{aligned}$$

Next using Lemma 11, i.e., $\varphi(b^\star) = \ell_\varphi(b^\star; b(t)) + D(p^\star \,||\, p(t))$, we get

$$\begin{aligned} &\varphi(b(t+1)) - \varphi(b^\star) + D(p^\star \,||\, p(t)) \\ &\quad\le D(b^\star \,||\, b(t)) - D(b^\star \,||\, b(t+1)) \,. \end{aligned}$$

Summing the above inequality over all t and noticing

$$D(b^\star || b(t+1)) \ge 0,$$

lead to

$$\sum_t \left(\varphi(b(t+1)) - \varphi(b^\star) + D(p^\star \,||\, p(t))\right) \le D(b^\star \,||\, b(0)) \,.$$

Further using Lemma 19 finishes the proof. □

LEMMA 15 ([ZHA09]). *Let* $\eta := \max_j \left|\frac{p_j(t)-p_j^\star}{p_j^\star}\right|$ *and assume* $\eta \le 1$. *Then* $\eta^2 \le 16\frac{D(p(t) \,||\, p^\star)}{p^\star_{\min}}$.

LEMMA 16 ([ZHA09]). *For all i, let $u_i(t)$ be buyer i's utility at time t, and let $\tilde{u}_i(t)$ be the maximum utility he can achieve given the prices p(t). Then there exists a ζ such that $u_i(t) \ge (1-\zeta)\tilde{u}_i(t)$ for all i and*

$$\zeta^2 \le \frac{256}{p^\star_{\min} B^2_{\min}}\left(\psi(b(t)) - \psi(b^\star) + D(p(t) \,||\, p^\star)\right) \,.$$

LEMMA 17 ([ZHA09]). $p^\star_{\min} \ge u_{\min} B_{\min}/m$.

However, it is not known if $\psi(b(t+1)) - \psi(b^\star) + D(p^\star \,||\, p(t))$ is monotonically decreasing. So you simply obtain that for all τ, *there exists* a $t \le \tau$ such that

$$\psi(b(t)) - \psi(b^\star) + D(p^\star \,||\, p(t)) \le \frac{D(b^\star \,||\, b(0))}{\tau}. \qquad (21)$$

instead of obtaining that for all t

$$\psi(b(t)) - \psi(b^\star) + D(p^\star \,||\, p(t)) \le \frac{D(b^\star \,||\, b(0))}{t}.$$

In fact, we can derive all of Zhang's results in the stronger form by bounding each of $\psi(b(t)) - \psi(b^\star)$ and $D(p(t) \,||\, p^\star)$ separately by $\varphi(b(t)) - \varphi(b^\star)$ (and the fact that φ is monotonically decreasing).

LEMMA 18. *For all t, $D(p(t) \,||\, p^\star) \le \varphi(b(t)) - \varphi(b^\star)$.*

PROOF. By Lemma 11,

$$\begin{aligned}\varphi(b(t)) &= \ell_\varphi(b(t); b^\star) + D(p(t) \,||\, p^\star) \\ &= \varphi(b^\star) + \langle \nabla\varphi(b^\star),\, b(t) - b^\star \rangle + D(p(t) \,||\, p^\star)\end{aligned}$$

By optimality, $\langle \nabla\varphi(b^\star),\, b(t) - b^\star \rangle \ge 0$, so the lemma follows. □

LEMMA 19. *For all $b \in S$, $\psi(b) - \psi(b^\star) \le \varphi(b) - \varphi(b^\star)$.*

PROOF. It suffices to show

$$\psi(b) \le \varphi(b) - \sum_i B_i \log B_i$$

and

$$\psi(b^\star) = \varphi(b^\star) - \sum_i B_i \log B_i.$$

For the inequality above, we use convexity of $-\log$:

$$\begin{aligned}\psi(b) &= -\sum_i B_i \log\left(\sum_j u_{ij}\frac{b_{ij}}{p_j}\right) \\ &= -\sum_i B_i \log\left(\sum_j \frac{u_{ij}}{p_j}\frac{b_{ij}}{B_i}\right) - \sum_i B_i \log B_i \\ &\le -\sum_i B_i \sum_j \frac{b_{ij}}{B_i}\log\frac{u_{ij}}{p_j} - \sum_i B_i \log B_i \\ &= -\sum_{i,j} b_{ij}\log\frac{u_{ij}}{p_j} - \sum_i B_i \log B_i.\end{aligned}$$

For the equality at $b^\star$, we use the optimality conditions:

$$\begin{aligned}\psi(b^\star) &= -\sum_i B_i \log\left(\sum_j \frac{u_{ij}}{p_j^\star}\frac{b_{ij}^\star}{B_i}\right) - \sum_i B_i \log B_i \\ &= -\sum_i B_i \log\left(\max_j \frac{u_{ij}}{p_j^\star}\right) - \sum_i B_i \log B_i \\ &= -\sum_{i,j} b_{ij}^\star \log\frac{u_{ij}}{p_{ij}^\star} - \sum_i B_i \log B_i.\end{aligned}$$

□

We also have the following bound on the total deviation of the *symmetric* KL-divergence between $p^\star$ and $p(t)$.

LEMMA 20.

$$\begin{aligned}&\sum_t \Big(D(p^\star \,||\, p(t)) + D(p(t) \,||\, p^\star)\Big) \\ &\qquad \le D(b^\star \,||\, b(0)) + \big(\varphi(b(0)) - \varphi(b^\star)\big).\end{aligned}$$

PROOF. First using Corollary 10, we have

$$\begin{aligned}\varphi(b(t+1)) &\le \ell_\varphi(b(t+1); b(t)) + D(b(t+1) \,||\, b(t)) \\ &\le \ell_\varphi(b^\star; b(t)) + D(b^\star \,||\, b(t)) - D(b^\star \,||\, b(t+1)).\end{aligned}$$

Plugging in $\ell_\varphi(b^\star; b(t)) = \varphi(b(t)) + \langle \nabla\varphi(b(t)), b^\star - b(t)\rangle$ gives

$$\begin{aligned}\langle \nabla\varphi(b(t)), b(t) - b^\star \rangle &\le D(b^\star \,||\, b(t)) - D(b^\star \,||\, b(t+1)) \\ &\quad + \varphi(b(t)) - \varphi(b(t+1)).\end{aligned}$$

The optimality of $b^\star$ implies $\langle \nabla\varphi(b^\star), b(t) - b^\star \rangle \ge 0$. Subtracting $\langle \nabla\varphi(b^\star), b(t) - b^\star \rangle$ from the left hand gives

$$\begin{aligned}&\langle \nabla\varphi(b(t)) - \nabla\varphi(b^\star), b(t) - b^\star \rangle \\ &\le D(b^\star \,||\, b(t)) - D(b^\star \,||\, b(t+1)) + \varphi(b(t)) - \varphi(b(t+1)).\end{aligned}$$

Using $\nabla\varphi(b) = 1 - \log(u_{ij}/p_j)$, we have

$$\begin{aligned}&\langle \nabla\varphi(b(t)) - \nabla\varphi(b^\star), b(t) - b^\star \rangle \\ &= \sum_{i,j}(b_{ij}(t) - b_{ij}^\star)\log\frac{p_j(t)}{p_j^\star} \\ &= \sum_j (p_j(t) - p_j^\star)\log\frac{p_j(t)}{p_j^\star} \\ &= D(p(t) \,||\, p^\star) + D(p^\star \,||\, p(t)).\end{aligned}$$

Therefore,

$$\begin{aligned}&D(p(t) \,||\, p^\star) + D(p^\star \,||\, p(t)) \\ &\le D(b^\star \,||\, b(t)) - D(b^\star \,||\, b(t+1)) + \varphi(b(t)) - \varphi(b(t+1)).\end{aligned}$$

Summing over all t gives the desired result. □

5.3 Improved bounds

The bounds mentioned in Section 5.1 (in particular, (18) and (19)) are stronger than the corresponding ones in [Zha09]. These are obtained by using Lemmas 15 and 16 with a better bound for $p^\star_{\min}$, which is as in the following lemma.

LEMMA 21. *$p^\star_{\min} \ge u_{\min}/n$.*

PROOF. Let $b^\star$ be an equilibrium bid vector, and let

$$\beta_i^\star = \max_j u_{ij}/p_j^\star \ .$$

Suppose for contradiction that there exists an item $\tilde{j}$ such that $p_{\tilde{j}}^\star < u_{\min}/n$. Then for all bidders i,

$$\beta_i^\star \ge \frac{u_{i\tilde{j}}}{p_{\tilde{j}}^\star} \ge \frac{u_{\min}}{p_{\tilde{j}}^\star} > n \ .$$

By the buyer optimality condition, $b_{ij}^\star > 0$ implies $u_{ij}/p_j^\star = \beta_i^\star$. Combining this with the above yields the condition

$$b_{ij}^\star > 0 \implies p_j^\star < \frac{u_{ij}}{n} \ .$$

We now obtain the contradiction

$$\begin{aligned}1 = \sum_{i,j \,:\, b_{ij}^\star > 0} b_{ij}^\star &\le \sum_{i,j \,:\, b_{ij}^\star > 0} p_j^\star \\ &< \sum_{i,j \,:\, b_{ij}^\star > 0} \frac{u_{ij}}{n} \le \frac{1}{n}\sum_{i,j} u_{i,j} = 1.\end{aligned}$$

Hence, we conclude that there can be no such item $\tilde{j}$, and therefore $p^\star_{\min} \ge u_{\min}/n$. □

Finally, we also give a bound on the aggregate notion of suboptimality of allocations (20) that is new.

LEMMA 22. *Suppose $\varphi(b(t)) - \varphi(b^\star) \leq u_{\min}^2/(8n^2)$. Let the vector δ be such that*

$$u_i(t) = (1-\delta_i)\tilde{u}_i(t),$$

where $u_i(t) = \sum_j u_{ij} b_{ij}(t)/p_j(t)$ is the utility of buyer i at time t and $\tilde{u}_i(t) = B_i \max_j(u_{ij}/p_j(t)) = B_i\beta_i(t)$ is the maximum utility that buyer i could obtain given the prices $p(t)$. Then

$$\left(\sum_i B_i\delta_i\right)^2 = O\left(\frac{n}{u_{\min}}\right)(\varphi(b(t)) - \varphi(b^\star)) \; .$$

PROOF. To ease notation, we drop the argument t. For all i,j, let $\alpha_i = \log\beta_i = \max_j \log(u_{ij}/p_j)$, $\varepsilon_{ij} = \alpha_i - \log(u_{ij}/p_j)$, and $\varepsilon_i = \sum_j b_{ij}\varepsilon_{ij}/B_i$. Observe

$$\begin{aligned} u_i &= \sum_j b_{ij}\frac{u_{ij}}{p_j} = \sum_j b_{ij}\beta_i \exp(-\varepsilon_{ij}) \\ &\geq \sum_j b_{ij}\beta_i(1-\varepsilon_{ij}) \\ &= B_i\beta_i - \beta_i \sum_j b_{ij}\varepsilon_{ij} \\ &= B_i\beta_i - B_i\beta_i\varepsilon_i = (1-\varepsilon_i)\tilde{u}_i', \end{aligned}$$

and hence $\delta_i \leq \varepsilon_i$ for all i. Therefore,

$$\sum_i B_i\delta_i \leq \sum_i B_i\varepsilon_i = \sum_{i,j} b_{ij}\varepsilon_{ij} \; ,$$

and it suffices to bound $\sum_{i,j} b_{ij}\varepsilon_{ij}$. In particular, we show that $\sum_{i,j} b_{ij}\varepsilon_{ij} \leq O(\eta) + \varepsilon$. The proof then follows immediately from (18). To do this, we start by rewriting the objective function $\varphi(b)$ as

$$\begin{aligned} \varphi(b) &= -\sum_{i,j} b_{ij}\left(\log\frac{u_{ij}}{p_j} - \alpha_i + \alpha_i\right) \\ &= \sum_{i,j} b_{ij}\varepsilon_{ij} - \sum_{i,j} b_{ij}\alpha_i \\ &= \sum_{i,j} b_{ij}\varepsilon_{ij} - \sum_i B_i\alpha_i. \end{aligned}$$

Let $\alpha_i^\star = \max_j \log(u_{ij}/p_j^\star)$. The optimality condition states that $\varphi(b^\star) = -\sum_i B_i\alpha_i^\star$. Let $\varepsilon = \varphi(b) - \varphi(b^\star)$. Then

$$\sum_{i,j} b_{ij}\varepsilon_{ij} = \sum_i B_i(\alpha_i - \alpha_i^\star) + \varepsilon \; .$$

Since $\sum_i B_i = 1$, we have

$$\sum_i B_i(\alpha_i - \alpha_i^\star) \leq \max_i(\alpha_i - \alpha_i^\star).$$

Furthermore, for all i,

$$\begin{aligned} \alpha_i - \alpha_i^\star &= \max_j \log\frac{u_{ij}}{p_j} - \max_j \log\frac{u_{ij}}{p_j^\star} \\ &= \max_j\left(\log\frac{u_{ij}}{p_j^\star} + \log\frac{p_j^\star}{p_j}\right) - \max_j \log\frac{u_{ij}}{p_j^\star} \\ &\leq \max_j \log\frac{u_{ij}}{p_j^\star} + \max_j \log\frac{p_j^\star}{p_j} - \max_j \log\frac{u_{ij}}{p_j^\star} \\ &= \max_j \log\frac{p_j^\star}{p_j} \leq O(\eta). \end{aligned}$$

□

6. CONCLUSION AND FUTURE WORK

Our work opens up many interesting directions for future research.

- Eisenberg-Gale-type convex programs also capture equilibria for other classes of markets, especially for many resource allocation markets [JV10] and markets with Leontief utilities. It is not clear if there are analogs of convex program (2) for these markets. Convex program (2) seems to capture a different class of markets since it generalizes to the spending constraint utilities, for which the EG program does not generalize to. Such programs might lead to interesting algorithms and dynamics for these other markets as well. Also such programs have been used to design distributed algorithms to achieve proportional fairness. It is conceivable that our new convex program and/or the PR dynamics could get better results for the same.

- Can we get a better convergence bound for PR dynamics? While it seems difficult to get a convergence rate better than $O(1/\epsilon)$ w.r.t φ, it is possible one could get faster rates w.r.t other notions of approximate equilibria that we discuss.

- Can we design other similar dynamics that converge faster? We note that under the stronger condition of Lipschitz continuity of gradients, there are gradient algorithms [Nes83, Nes05, Tse08] that converge in time $O(1/\sqrt{\epsilon})$ (as opposed to the one we use which converges in time $O(1/\epsilon)$). However, these algorithms do not seem to work with the weaker assumption that we have. It would be very interesting (from a more general convex programming point of view) to get an $O(1/\sqrt{\epsilon})$ time algorithm with our weaker assumption.

- There is a natural asynchronous version of the PR dynamics: in each iteration, the bids of a single buyer and the corresponding prices are updated, with some non-saturation condition saying that every buyer updates his bids frequently enough. There are also randomized versions where a buyer wakes up with a Poisson clock and updates his bids and the corresponding prices. We believe our techniques (perhaps combined with some of the techniques from the book by Bertsekas and Tsitsiklis [BT97]) could be extended to handle these cases as well.

7. REFERENCES

[AAE+08] Baruch Awerbuch, Yossi Azar, Amir Epstein, Vahab S. Mirrokni, and Alexander Skopalik. Fast convergence to nearly optimal solutions in potential games. In *ACM Conference on Electronic Commerce*, pages 264–273, 2008.

[ABH59] K. Arrow, H. Block, and L. Hurwicz. On the stability of the competitive equilibrium: II. *Econometrica*, 27(1):82–109, 1959.

[AGM+08] Heiner Ackermann, Paul W. Goldberg, Vahab S. Mirrokni, Heiko Röglin, and Berthold Vöcking. Uncoordinated two-sided matching markets. In *ACM Conference on Electronic Commerce*, pages 256–263, 2008.

[Ber99] D. P. Bertsekas. *Nonlinear Programming*. Athena Scientific, 2nd edition, 1999.

[Bre67] L. Bregman. The relaxation method of finding the common points of convex sets and its application to the solution of problems in convex programming. *U.S.S.R. Comput. Math. and Math. Phys.*, 7:200–217, 1967.

[BT97] Dimitri P. Bertsekas and John N. Tsitsiklis. *Parallel and Distributed Computation: Numerical Methods*. Athena Scientific, 1997.

[BT03] A. Beck and M. Teboulle. Mirror descent and nonlinear projected subgradient methods for convex optimization. *Operations Research Letters*, 31:167–175, 2003.

[CD06] Xi Chen and Xiaotie Deng. Settling the complexity of two-player Nash equilibrium. In *FOCS*, pages 261–272, 2006.

[CDDT09] Xi Chen, Decheng Dai, Ye Du, and Shang-Hua Teng. Settling the complexity of Arrow-Debreu equilibria in markets with additively separable utilities. In *FOCS*, 2009.

[CF08] Richard Cole and Lisa Fleischer. Fast-converging tatonnement algorithms for one-time and ongoing market problems. In *STOC*, pages 315–324, 2008.

[CMV05] Bruno Codenotti, Benton McCune, and Kasturi R. Varadarajan. Market equilibrium via the excess demand function. In *STOC*, pages 74–83, 2005.

[CPV05] Bruno Codenotti, Sriram V. Pemmaraju, and Kasturi R. Varadarajan. On the polynomial time computation of equilibria for certain exchange economies. In *SODA*, pages 72–81, 2005.

[CS07] Steve Chien and Alistair Sinclair. Convergence to approximate Nash equilibria in congestion games. In *SODA*, pages 169–178, 2007.

[CSVY06] Bruno Codenotti, Amin Saberi, Kasturi R. Varadarajan, and Yinyu Ye. Leontief economies encode nonzero sum two-player games. In *SODA*, pages 659–667, 2006.

[CT93] G. Chen and M. Teboulle. Convergence analysis of a proximal-like minimization algorithm using Bregman functions. *SIAM Journal on Optimization*, 3(3):538–543, August 1993.

[CT09] Xi Chen and Shang-Hua Teng. Spending is not easier than trading: On the computational equivalence of Fisher and Arrow-Debreu equilibria. *CoRR*, abs/0907.4130, 2009.

[CV07] Bruno Codenotti and Kasturi Varadarajan. *Algorithmic Game Theory*, chapter Computation of Market Equilibria by Convex Programming. Cambridge University Press, 2007.

[Dev09] Nikhil R Devanur. Fisher markets and convex programs. Working paper available from http://research.microsoft.com/en-us/um/people/nikdev/, 2009.

[DGP06] Constantinos Daskalakis, Paul W. Goldberg, and Christos H. Papadimitriou. The complexity of computing a Nash equilibrium. In *STOC*, pages 71–78, 2006.

[DK08] Nikhil R. Devanur and Ravi Kannan. Market equilibria in polynomial time for fixed number of goods or agents. In *FOCS*, pages 45–53, 2008.

[DPS02] Xiaotie Deng, Christos H. Papadimitriou, and Shmuel Safra. On the complexity of equilibria. In *STOC*, pages 67–71, 2002.

[DPSV08] Nikhil R. Devanur, Christos H. Papadimitriou, Amin Saberi, and Vijay V. Vazirani. Market equilibrium via a primal–dual algorithm for a convex program. *J. ACM*, 55(5), 2008.

[DV04] Nikhil R. Devanur and Vijay V. Vazirani. The spending constraint model for market equilibrium: algorithmic, existence and uniqueness results. In *STOC*, pages 519–528, 2004.

[EG59] Edmund Eisenberg and David Gale. Consensus of subjective probabilities: The pari-mutuel method. *Ann. Math. Statist.*, 30(1):165–168, 1959.

[FGK+08] Lisa Fleischer, Rahul Garg, Sanjiv Kapoor, Rohit Khandekar, and Amin Saberi. A fast and simple algorithm for computing market equilibria. In *WINE*, pages 19–30, 2008.

[GK06] Rahul Garg and Sanjiv Kapoor. Auction algorithms for market equilibrium. *Math. Oper. Res.*, 31(4):714–729, 2006.

[Jai07] Kamal Jain. A polynomial time algorithm for computing an Arrow-Debreu market equilibrium for linear utilities. *SIAM J. Comput.*, 37(1):303–318, 2007.

[JV10] Kamal Jain and Vijay V. Vazirani. Eisenberg-Gale markets: algorithms and game-theoretic properties. *Games and Economic Behavior*, 70(1), 2010.

[Kel97] F. P. Kelly. Charging and rate control for elastic traffic. *European Transactions on Telecommunications*, 8:33–37, 1997.

[KMT98] F. P. Kelly, A. K. Maulloo, and D. K. H. Tan. Rate control in communication networks: shadow prices, proportional fairness and stability. *Journal of the Operational Research Society*, 49:237–252, 1998.

[KV] F. P. Kelly and V. V. Vazirani. Rate control as a market equilibrium. Manuscript, 2002.

[LLSB08] Dave Levin, Katrina LaCurts, Neil Spring, and Bobby Bhattacharjee. Bittorrent is an auction: analyzing and improving bittorrent's incentives. In *SIGCOMM '08: Proceedings of the ACM SIGCOMM 2008 conference on Data communication*, pages 243–254, New York, NY, USA, 2008. ACM.

[Nem05] A. Nemirovski. Lectures on modern convex optimization. Lecture notes, Georgia Institute of Technology, 2005.

[Nes83] Yu. Nesterov. A method for unconstrained convex minimization problem with the rate of convergence $o(1/k^2)$. *Soviet Math. Docl. (Doklady AN SSSR)*, 269:543–547, 1983.

[Nes04] Yu. Nesterov. *Introductory Lectures on Convex Optimization: A Basic Course*. Kluwer, Boston, 2004.

[Nes05] Yu. Nesterov. Smooth minimization of nonsmooth functions. *Mathematical Programming*, 103(1):127–152, 2005.

[NY83] A. Nemirovsky and D. Yudin. *Problem Complexity and Method Efficiency in Optimization*. J. Wiley & Sons, New York, 1983.

[Roc70] R. T. Rockafellar. *Convex Analysis*. Princeton University Press, 1970.

[Ros73] R.W. Rosenthal. A class of games possessing pure-strategy Nash equilibria. *International Journal of Game Theory*, 2:65–67, 1973.

[Shm09] V. Shmyrev. An algorithm for finding equilibrium in the linear exchange model with fixed budgets. *Journal of Applied and Industrial Mathematics*, 3:505–518, 2009.

[Tse08] P. Tseng. On accelerated proximal gradient methods for convex-concave optimization. Submitted to *SIAM Journal on Optimization*, 2008.

[Uza60] H. Uzawa. Walras' tatonnement in the theory of exchange. *Review of Economic Studies*, 27:182–94, 1960.

[Vaz07] Vijay V. Vazirani. *Algorithmic Game Theory*, chapter Combinatorial Algorithms for Market Equilibria. Cambridge University Press, 2007.

[Vaz10] Vijay V. Vazirani. Spending constriant utilities, with applications to the adwords market. *Math. of Operations Research*, 35(2), 2010. A manuscript has been publicly available since 2003.

[VY10] Vijay V. Vazirani and Mihalis Yannakakis. Market equilibrium under separable, piecewise-linear, concave utilities. In *ICS*, 2010.

[Wal74] L. Walras. *Éléments d'économie politique pure ou théorie de la richesse sociale (Elements of Pure Economics, or the theory of social wealth)*. Lausanne, Paris, 1874. (1899, 4th ed.; 1926, rev ed., 1954, Engl. transl.).

[WZ07] Fang Wu and Li Zhang. Proportional response dynamics leads to market equilibrium. In *STOC '07: Proceedings of the thirty-ninth annual ACM symposium on Theory of computing*, pages 354–363, New York, NY, USA, 2007. ACM.

[Ye08] Y. Ye. A path to the Arrow-Debreu competitive market equilibrium. *Mathematical Programming*, 111:315–348, 2008.

[Zha09] Li Zhang. Proportional response dynamics in the Fisher market. In *ICALP '09: Proceedings of the 36th Internatilonal Collogquium on Automata, Languages and Programming*, pages 583–594, Berlin, Heidelberg, 2009. Springer-Verlag.

Economies with Non-Convex Production and Complexity Equilibria

Christos H. Papadimitriou*
Computer Science Division
University of California at Berkeley
Berkeley, CA 94720
christos@cs.berkeley.edu

Christopher A. Wilkens*
Computer Science Division
University of California at Berkeley
Berkeley, CA 94720
cwilkens@cs.berkeley.edu

ABSTRACT

The convexity assumptions required for the Arrow-Debreu theorem are reasonable and realistic for preferences; however, they are highly problematic for production because they rule out economies of scale. We take a complexity-theoretic look at economies with non-convex production. It is known that in such markets equilibrium prices may not exist; we show that it is an intractable problem to achieve Pareto efficiency, the fundamental objective achieved by equilibrium prices. The same is true for core efficiency or any one of an array of concepts of stability, with the degree of intractability ranging from $F\Delta_2^P$-completeness to PSPACE-hardness. We also identify a novel phenomenon that we call *complexity equilibrium* in which agents quiesce, not because there is no way for any one of group of them to improve their situation, but because discovering the changes necessary for (individual or group) improvement is intractable. In fact, we exhibit a somewhat natural distribution of economies that has an average-case hard complexity equilibrium.

Categories and Subject Descriptors

F.2.2 [**Analysis of Algorithms and Problem Complexity**]: Nonnumerical Algorithms and Problems; J.4 [**Social and Behavioral Sciences**]: Economics

General Terms

Theory, Economics

Keywords

Market Equilibrium, Computation of Market Equilibrium, Non-Convex Production

*Supported by NSF Award CCF-0635319.

1. INTRODUCTION

General Equilibrium Theory studies stable outcomes in markets — outcomes where each agent is doing as well as he can given the actions of others [18]. In the standard model, a market consists of consumers with initial endowments (vectors of goods) and preferences (utility functions), and firms with production sets (specifying what vector(s) of goods can be produced with each combination of raw materials); consumers own shares in firms.

By far the most studied kind of stable market outcome is the price equilibrium: Each firm optimizes its profit at market prices, and each consumer optimizes her utility at the same prices, selling her endowment and purchasing her preferred bundle of goods. Magically, this uncoordinated activity *clears the market:* no goods are left unsold, and all demand is satisfied. Most importantly, the resulting allocation of goods is *efficient* in the sense of Pareto: there is no allocation that is better in the sense that it dominates, in terms of utility, the allocation achieved via the price mechanism (this is known as the First Theorem of Welfare Economics).

Price equilibria had been studied by economists since the mid 19th century, but it was not until 1954 that Arrow and Debreu [3] made the idea irresistibly powerful and attractive by proving that (under assumptions) an equilibrium price vector is guaranteed to always exist. This result promises a kind of *Arrow-Debreu paradise*, where equilibrium is both beneficient (it achieves Pareto efficiency) and universally guaranteed[1]. The theory has spawned an entire area of Economics, and of course more recently a variety of results in Algorithmic Game Theory, including many algorithms for special cases (see [19], Chapters 5 and 6 for a survey, as well as [14, 12, 13] for production-specific algorithms).

There are of course wrinkles in General Equilibrium Theory. The existence proof in [3] is non-constructive, and this has been shown to imply some form of intractability, weaker than NP-completeness [21, 7]. The basic theorem holds for a very simplified model; in more realistic models parameters may be stochastic, time-varying, and generation-specific, among many other complications, and much work has been done addressing such difficulties. The model also hides tricky externalities (for example, production, or con-

[1]In an excellent Microeconomics textbook [17] one reads after the statement of the First Theorem: "You should now be hearing choirs of angels and choruses of trumpets. The invisible hand of the price mechanism produces equilibria that cannot be improved upon." The author goes on to expose and discuss the many problems of the theory.

sumption, by one can harm the environment for all). Many other objections (e.g., that goods are available at different places and times) can be absorbed in the model by enlarging it. The focus of this paper is one of the most fundamentally objectionable assumptions of the theory, namely *the convexity assumption for production.*[2]

Convexity in utilities is quite natural: it states that you may draw less pleasure from your tenth evening dress than you did from your first. In contrast, convexity in production is very questionable because it *rules out economies of scale.* In other words, producing the hundredth airplane cannot, in any way, be easier than producing the first one. In the absence of this utterly unrealistic assumption — that is to say, in realistic economies — a price equilibrium may not exist, and thus the First Theorem cannot guarantee Pareto efficiency: Paradise lost.

Market Equilibrium Theory without Convexity of Production.

Since price equilibria may not exist in the absence of convexity in production, economists have studied the set of Pareto optima (which do generally exist). The first work in this line was by Guesnerie [9], whose stated goal was "to characterize precisely Pareto-optimal states and to examine the possibility of achieving them in a decentralized economy" (a task which is, as we point out, unattainable for reasons of complexity). Since then, a vast literature has developed; for two excellent surveys, see [6, 1] — the first one actually contains a discussion of computation.

A standard approach is to assume that firms price goods at marginal cost, in other words, postulate that prices depend on production decisions; this assumption is quite strong and rather artificial and unrealistic, but it often yields an allocation that is Pareto efficient — not always, of course. The state of the art in this direction (e.g. the marginal pricing rule of [5]) still seeks a decentralized model of agent behavior that is guaranteed to achieve Pareto efficiency. Our results, outlined next, suggest that there are huge computational impediments in the way of this ambition.

Our Results: Computational Complexity in Markets with Non-Convex Production.

We study markets with non-convex production from the perspective of computational complexity. To the best of our knowledge, the only other work with a computational flavor is [24], which employs dimensional communication complexity to differentiate this case from the convex one: it is shown in [24] that $\approx m{\cdot}n$ real numbers are needed to achieve Pareto efficiency in this case, where m is the number of goods and n the number of agents and firms, as opposed to only m in the convex case.

We show that the theory of markets with non-convex production is plagued with very bleak negative complexity results, as many natural concepts of rationality are hard for various levels of the polynomial hierarchy. We start by showing that computing a Pareto efficient outcome in a market with non-convex production is $\mathrm{F}\Delta_2^P$-complete. Economists regard Pareto efficiency as a sine qua non for any concept of stability or rationality in markets. Hence, our negative result for the complexity of finding Pareto efficient outcomes is a lower-bound for any "reasonable" equilibrium concept. Finally, in sections 4 and 5, we give similar results for two concepts of stability more sophisticated than Pareto efficiency: It is $\mathrm{F}\Sigma_2^P$-complete to tell if an allocation is in the core (no coalition of agents has an incentive to defect and create its own economy). And for a natural models of sequential production, we show that computing equilibria is $\mathrm{F}\Delta_3^P$-complete and PSPACE-hard, respectively.

Perhaps most significantly, we show in the process that such economies can have a novel kind of "equilibrium," from which deviation may yield tremendous improvement for any and all agents, but the agents are stuck at a suboptimal solution of a particular instance of an NP-hard optimization problem. We call such a situation a *complexity equilibrium* (Definition 6.2). When agents are at such an equilibrium, standard complexity-theoretic assumptions imply that no computationally efficient procedure would generally allow them to improve – indeed, it is even intractable to recognize that improvement is possible. We also present a somewhat natural *average-case* NP-hard construction of a complexity equilibrium.

Apart from deliberate complexity-theoretic studies in game theory (e.g. [23]), the only other natural economic setting we know where computational complexity begets stability is voting, where outcome manipulation may be computationally intractable (e.g. [22, 11]).

2. FOUNDATIONS AND MODELS

In this section we introduce the standard economic model and relevant complexity classes.

2.1 The Economic Model

We will employ a slightly simplified version of the standard private ownership economy used in general equilibrium theory [18]. We define an economy E as follows:

Agents: An economy has n agents.

Goods: An economy has m divisible, tradable goods.

Utilities: Each agent i has a utility function $u_i : \mathbb{R}^m \to \mathbb{R}$ mapping bundles of goods to amounts of utility. An agent's consumption in an economy is specified by a vector of goods $x_i \in \mathbb{R}^m$, and her utility is $u_i(x)i$. In general, we assume that $u_i(x)$ satisfies standard assumptions and is efficiently computable. Our hardness results use *Leontief* utilities:

$$u(x) = \min_j \frac{x_j}{\alpha_j} \ ,$$

i.e. goods are demanded in constant proportions specified by the parameters $\{\alpha_j\}$ (possibly 0).

Endowments: Each agent i is endowed with a quantity of each good, i.e. a vector $e_i \in \mathbb{R}^m$.

Production: Each firm in the economy is specified by a production function $f_k : \mathbb{R}_+^m \to \mathbb{R}_+^m$ where f_k maps a bundle of input goods to a bundle of output goods[3]. The

[2]Convexity in production refers to convexity of the set of net production vectors. For example, if a firm can produce according to net production (input/output) vectors y_1 and y_2, then it can also produce according to any production vector $\alpha y_1 + (1-\alpha)y_2$ for $\alpha \in [0,1]$.

[3]Standard General Equilibrium Theory specifies a production firm by a set of possible net production vectors Y_k instead of a function f_k. However, when modeling economies

behavior of a production firm may be specified by either the vector of inputs consumed by the firm x_k (in which case the output produced is $f_k(x_k)$), or by a net production vector $y_k = f_k(x_k) - x_k$. Note that the vector x_i denotes consumption by agent i and x_k denotes consumption by firm k.

Each agent in an economy owns[4] a set of production firms F_i, meaning that agent i provides the inputs and receives the outputs of production. This is a slight restriction of the natural extension of the private ownership economy to this domain.

Our reductions use one very simple form of non-convex production function, namely *Leontief production functions with fixed costs.* Such a function f takes the form

$$f(x) = z \cdot \max\left(\min_j \left(\frac{x_j - \beta_j}{\alpha_j}\right), 0\right)$$

where z is a bundle of goods and β_j is a fixed cost of each good required to have positive production. Interestingly, the addition of fixed costs is sufficient to force the agent to solve a discretized problem. This will be a key technique in our reductions.

We make the following assumptions about production in the economy:

1. The production function $f(x)$ is efficiently computable for all x.
2. The total set of production possibilities is closed and bounded. The total set of production possibilities contains any net production vector that may achieved by the economy. I.e. it contains a vector $y \geq 0$ if and only if there is a set of vectors $\{y_k \in Y_k\}$ such that $\sum_i e_i + \sum_k y_k = y$.
3. There is no x such that $f(x) - x \geq 0$ other than $x = 0$ (no free lunch).
4. For all $f(x)$, a bounded input x implies a bounded output $f(x)$.

With the exception of the computability assumption, these are standard or weakened versions of standard assumptions in the economic literature. The efficient computability assumption is nonstandard insofar as the issue has not been considered.

Finally, we recognize that smoothness is a common assumption in economics. While the functional forms we use for f (and u) are not smooth, they may be made smooth without affecting the results in this paper.

We also use the following standard economic vocabulary (see [18]):

it is common to use a production function instead of a production set. While there are scenarios that differentiate the two representations, e.g. where firms would like to have free disposal, we will not encounter them here.

[4]In the standard private ownership economy, agents are said to own *shares* in production firms and receive the appropriate fraction of the profit. Since we avoid discussion of prices, the total ownership restriction avoids the issue of cooperative production for which there is already a literature, e.g. [8].

DEFINITION 2.1. *An* economic allocation *(hereafter an allocation) is an assignment (x, y) such that x_i is the vector of goods consumed by agent i and y_k is the vector of net outputs for firm k.*

An allocation is feasible *if the amount consumed is less than the amount available in the economy, i.e.*

$$\sum_i x_i \leq \sum_i e_i + \sum_k y_k$$

where $y_k = f_k(x_k) - x_k$ for the vector of goods x_k used as input to f_k.

DEFINITION 2.2. *An economic allocation (x_1, y_1) is said to be* strictly Pareto preferred *to another allocation (x_2, y_2) if some agent receives more utility in allocation 1 than in allocation 2 and no agent receives less utility.*

An allocation (x^*, y^*) is Pareto efficient *or* Pareto optimal *if no feasible allocation is strictly Pareto preferred to it.*

DEFINITION 2.3. *The* social welfare *W of an allocation (x, y) is the sum of the utilities obtained by consumers in the economy, i.e.*

$$W = \sum_i u_i(x_i).$$

The particular form of Leontief utilities gives the following:

PROPOSITION 2.4. *(Free disposal under Leontief utilities.) When utility functions are Leontief, then $x' \geq x$ implies $u_i(x') \geq u_i(x)$.*

This allows us to make a key assumption: when an agent has a good $\hat{s}$ and only one possible use for that good, no agent may be harmed by assuming that $\hat{s}$ is applied to that use.

2.2 The Polynomial Hierarchy

Our computational complexity results will locate variations on the General Equilibrium problem in different classes of the polynomial hierarchy. The relevant portions of the polynomial hierarchy, Σ_k^P and Δ_k^P, are defined recursively as

$$\Sigma_0^P = \Delta_0^P = \mathrm{P}$$

$$\Sigma_k^P = \mathrm{NP}^{\Sigma_{k-1}^P}$$

$$\Delta_k^P = \mathrm{P}^{\Sigma_{k-1}^P}$$

in other words, Σ_k^P is equal to NP with an oracle for Σ_{k-1}^P. A prefixed "F" denotes the corresponding class of functional problems, e.g. $\mathrm{F}\Sigma_k^P$.

Krentel [15] defines the related complexity class OptP as the class of problems that may be expressed as the maximum (or minimum) value along any branch of a nondeterministic Turing machine. Relevant to our work, he shows that any OptP-complete problem is complete for the class $\mathrm{F}\Delta_2^P$ and shows a similar generalization to $\mathrm{F}\Delta_k^P$ [16]. For our purposes, we use the fact that any OptP problem is in $\mathrm{F}\Delta_2^P$.

3. COMPUTING PARETO OPTIMA

In Economics, Pareto efficiency (the requirement that no allocation is preferred to the current one by all) is essentially a prerequisite for any reasonable solution concept or prediction. By showing negative complexity results for finding a Pareto efficient allocation, we lower bound the complexity of any equilibrium concept that achieves Pareto efficiency. Our first result classifies the hardness of computing a Pareto efficient allocation:

THEOREM 3.1. *Computing a Pareto efficient allocation in an economy with non-convex production functions and polynomial-time computable utilities is* $F\Delta_2^P$*-complete.*

We prove this theorem after introducing two gadgets.

3.1 Gadgets

The proof for Theorem 3.1 constructs an economy out of the following gadgets:

The Choice Gadget.

The choice gadget $Choice(\alpha_1 \cdot \hat{\jmath}_1, \ldots \alpha_c \cdot \hat{\jmath}_c)$ enforces indivisibility: given a set of production options, agent i must choose to produce α_k units of good $\hat{\jmath}_k$ for some $k \in \{1, \ldots, c\}$ (she cannot produce a convex combination). Specifically, when agent i has a choice gadget $Choice(\cdots)$, the economy includes the following:

Goods: $\hat{s}$, $\hat{\jmath}_1, \ldots \hat{\jmath}_c$.

Production: agent i owns firms with the following production functions:

$$\forall \hat{\jmath}_k : \; x_{\hat{\jmath}_k} = f_{j_k}(x_{\hat{s}}) = \alpha_k \cdot \max(x_{\hat{s}} - 1, 0)$$

In words, for each good $\hat{\jmath}_k$, agent i has a production function to turn $x_{\hat{s}}$ units of good $\hat{s}$ into $\alpha_k \cdot (x_{\hat{s}} - 1)$ units of good $\hat{\jmath}_k$. where the values α_k are scalar parameters specified by $Choice(\alpha_1 \cdot \hat{\jmath}_1, \ldots \alpha_c \cdot \hat{\jmath}_c)$.

Endowment: $e_{i,\hat{s}} = 2$, i.e. agent i is endowed with 2 units of $\hat{s}$.

This construction ensures that only one good $\hat{\jmath}_k$ may be produced in positive quantities. If $x_{\hat{s}}^{\hat{\jmath}_k}$ is the amount of $\hat{s}$ used to produce $\hat{\jmath}_k$, then because of fixed costs $x_{\hat{\jmath}_k} > 0$ implies $x_{\hat{s}}^{\hat{\jmath}_k} > 1$. Thus, if two or more goods $\hat{\jmath}_k$ is present in positive quantities, $x_{\hat{s}} \geq \sum_k x_{\hat{s}}^{\hat{\jmath}_k} > 2$. However, agent i has only 2 units of good $\hat{s}$, so only one good may be present.

In order to ensure that all of good $\hat{s}$ is consumed, we stipulate that no agent has any other use for good $\hat{s}$, either as a source of utility in consumption or as an input to production. Thus, by Proposition 2.4 (free disposal), we may assume that agent i will use all 2 units of good $\hat{s}$ and, therefore, produce exactly α_k units of the chosen good $\hat{\jmath}_k$.

The Limit Gadget.

The limit gadget enables the economy to limit the production of a specific good $\hat{\jmath}$ to α units. An instance of $Limit(\hat{\jmath}, \alpha)$ consists of

Goods: $\hat{\hat{\jmath}}$, $\hat{r}$, and $\hat{\jmath}$.

Production: (owned by agent i):

$$x_{\hat{\jmath}} = f(x_{\hat{\hat{\jmath}}}, x_{\hat{r}}) = \min(x_{\hat{\hat{\jmath}}}, x_{\hat{r}}) \; .$$

Endowment: $e_{i,\hat{r}} = \alpha$.

The good $\hat{r}$ acts as a limiting reagent in the production function $f(x_{\hat{\hat{\jmath}}}, x_{\hat{r}})$ — since the endowment of $\hat{r}$ is fixed at α, agent i may produce as much $\hat{\jmath}$ as desired up to α units.

To enforce this limit, all production functions that produce $\hat{\jmath}$ are modified to produce $\hat{\hat{\jmath}}$, thereby forcing all of good $\hat{\jmath}$ to come from $f(x_{\hat{\hat{\jmath}}}, x_{\hat{r}})$ or an endowment.

3.2 Proof

First, we must note that Pareto optima always exist in our economies:

PROPOSITION 3.2. *Under the general assumptions of Section 2.1, a Pareto efficient allocation always exists.*

PROOF. Observe that if an allocation (x', y') is strictly Pareto preferred to (x, y), then (x', y') must have a higher social welfare than (x, y). Since the set of net production possibilities are closed and bounded and utilities are continuous (a standard assumption), it follows that the maximum social welfare W^* is well defined, and any allocation that achieves W^* is a Pareto optimum. □

We now prove Theorem 3.1.

PROOF. (Proof of Theorem 3.1.) First, we show that an efficient allocation may be computed in $F\Delta_2^P$.

Consider the following problem: *compute a feasible allocation* (x, y) *with social welfare at least* W. It may be solved in NP by guessing the goods x_i consumed by each agent and the goods x_k used as inputs by each firm. (The assumptions of computability imply that we may efficiently compute (x, y) and W from the x_i and x_k vectors.) As in Proposition 3.2, an allocation with optimal social welfare W^* must be Pareto efficient. Thus, a Pareto efficient allocation may be expressed as the optimum of an NP problem, so it is in OptP and therefore $F\Delta_2^P$.

To show that computing a Pareto efficient allocation is $F\Delta_2^P$-hard, we reduce the $F\Delta_2^P$-complete problem Weighted MAX-SAT [15] an economy. Let $(\Phi = \bigwedge_j \phi_j, \{\alpha_j\})$ be a Weighted MAX-SAT instance with n_Φ variables and m_Φ clauses, i.e. we desire a boolean assignment χ to the CNF formula Φ that maximizes $\sum_j \alpha_j \phi_j(\chi)$. The economy is:

Agents: One agent i for each variable χ_i and one agent j for each clause ϕ_j.

Goods: A utility good $\hat{\gamma}$.

For each SAT variable χ_i: two goods $\hat{\chi}_i$ and $\hat{\bar{\chi}}_i$.

For each clause ϕ_j: one good $\hat{\phi}_j$.

Utilities: All agents have $u(x) = x_{\hat{\gamma}}$, i.e. they only want $\hat{\gamma}$.

Production: Each variable agent i owns:

$$Choice(\hat{\chi}_i, \hat{\bar{\chi}}_i) \; ,$$

and each clause agent j owns:

$$\forall \chi_i \in \phi_j : \; x_{\hat{\phi}_j} = f_{\phi_j, \chi_i}(x_{\hat{\chi}_i}) = m_\Phi \cdot x_{\hat{\chi}_i}$$

$$\forall \bar{\chi}_i \in \phi_j : \; x_{\hat{\phi}_j} = f_{\phi_j, \bar{\chi}_i}(x_{\hat{\bar{\chi}}_i}) = m_\Phi \cdot x_{\hat{\bar{\chi}}_i}$$

$$Limit\left(\hat{\phi}_j, 1\right)$$

$$x_{\hat{\gamma}} = f_{\gamma, \phi_j}(x_{\hat{\phi}_j}) = \alpha_j \cdot x_{\hat{\phi}_j} - \frac{1}{2} \; .$$

In this economy, a the goods $\hat{\chi}_i$ and $\hat{\hat{\chi}}_i$ represent an assignment to the variables χ_i. As argued previously, the choice gadget ensures that the economy will either produce precisely 1 unit of $\hat{\chi}_i$ or 1 unit of $\hat{\hat{\chi}}_i$. Thus, we say that $\chi_i = 1$ if $\hat{\chi}_i$ is present and $\chi_i = 0$ if $\hat{\hat{\chi}}_i$ is present.

Given the goods $\hat{\chi}_i$ and $\hat{\hat{\chi}}_i$, the clause agents will use them to produce clause goods $\hat{\phi}_j$. By construction the only way to use $\hat{\chi}_i$ (resp. $\hat{\hat{\chi}}_i$) is to create the clause good $\hat{\phi}_j$ for a clause j which is satisfied by $\chi_i = 1$ (resp. $\chi_i = 0$). Conversely, if ϕ_j is not satisfied by the assignment, there is no way to produce $\hat{\phi}_j$. Thus, the economy can produce $\hat{\phi}_j$ if and only if ϕ_j is satisfied by the assignment χ.

The limit gadgets ensure that exactly 1 unit of $\hat{\phi}_j$ is created for each satisfied clause. Consider the following production plan: $\frac{1}{m_\Phi}$ units of each χ_i good are "allotted" to each clause ϕ_j, and if the assignment to χ_i satisfies ϕ_j, then $m_\Phi \cdot \frac{1}{m_\Phi} = 1$ units of $\hat{\phi}_j$ are produced (otherwise the $\frac{1}{m_\Phi}$ units of the χ_i good are not used). This produces ≥ 1 units of $\hat{\phi}_j$ for each satisfied clause ϕ_j and, since each clause good $\hat{\phi}_j$ is limited to 1 unit, it therefore yields the maximum production of clause goods possible given the assignment χ. Since the variable goods $\hat{\chi}_i$ and $\hat{\hat{\chi}}_i$ have no use apart from creating clause goods, we may assume that 1 unit of $\hat{\phi}_j$ is present in the economy if and only if ϕ_j is satisfied by χ.

Finally, the clause goods are turned into the utility good $\hat{\gamma}$. Given that 1 unit of a clause good will be present if and only if ϕ is satisfied, the form of $f_{\gamma,\phi_j}(x_{\hat{\phi}_j})$ ensures that the amount of $\hat{\gamma}$ is precisely the weight of the assignment.

Since agents only desire $\hat{\gamma}$, it follows that any Pareto efficient allocation must create the maximum amount of $\hat{\gamma}$, i.e. solve the weighted MAX-SAT instance. Thus, computing a Pareto efficient allocation is $F\Delta_2^P$-complete. □

Of course some non-convex economies may have price equilibria, or, more generally, have equilibria in marginal prices; is the previous complexity result irrelevant in such favorable special cases? Alas, it is hard to recognize economies with equilibria:

THEOREM 3.3. *It is NP-hard to distinguish an economy that has no efficient marginal price equilibria from one that has a price equilibrium.*

A sketch is in the Appendix.

4. COMPUTING CORE ALLOCATIONS

Pareto efficient allocations are stable in a cooperative sense, that is, with respect to a concept of deviation that requires all agents to cooperate and change their production and consumption. In this section, we consider allocations that are also stable with respect to certain selfish defections. A standard concept of rationality in economics is the *core*. An allocation is said to be in the core if no coalition would prefer to defect, i.e. no subset of agents can achieve strictly higher utility among themselves by creating a separate economy in which they are the only agents [18]. Price equilibria are always in the core; however, since price equilibria do not exist as such, we potentially lose this property when we lose convexity. A complexity equilibrium therefore is an allocation from which it is intractable to find another allocation where some agents do strictly better using only their own endowment and production technologies.

We find that computing core allocations is harder than computing Pareto optima:

THEOREM 4.1. *Computing an allocation in the core is $F\Sigma_2^P$-complete (and such an allocation may not exist).*

Additionally, if we relax our rationality requirements to include only single-agent deviations, then rational allocations are guaranteed to exist and are as easy to find as Pareto optima:

THEOREM 4.2. *Computing an allocations that is rational with respect to single-agent deviations and Pareto improvement is $F\Delta_2^P$-complete.*

The remainder of Section 4 contains proof sketches for Theorems 4.1 and 4.2. Certain full proofs may be found in Appendix A.

4.1 Proof Sketches

The Circle-of-Death Gadget.

The circle-of-death $COD(\hat{d})$ constructs a group of three agents for which it is impossible to achieve a core allocation unless they may consume $\geq \frac{1}{2}$ units of good $\hat{d}$. (The construction is given in Appendix A.)

PROOF. *(Proof sketch for Theorem 4.1.)* To show $F\Sigma_2^P$-completeness, the difficult direction is to show that it is $F\Sigma_2^P$-hard to find a core allocation (x^c, y^c). We reduce from the $F\Sigma_2^P$-complete problem Σ_2SAT [2]:

$$\exists \chi_1 \forall \chi_2 \Phi(\chi_1, \chi_2) \ .$$

(The full reduction is given in Appendix B.) As shown earlier, we can construct an economy that attempts to satisfy Φ. The trick is to engineer the payoffs such that a coalition defects if there is a χ_2 that falsifies Φ given χ_1. We encode χ_1 in the identities of the agents who defect so the defecting coalition can only produce one value for χ_1, and we use a circle of death gadget to ensure that no allocation intentionally falsifying Φ can ever be in the core. As a result, any allocation in the core must make Φ true for any setting of χ_2, i.e. χ_1 is as desired. □

PROOF. *(Proof sketch for Theorem 4.2.)* To show $F\Delta_2^P$-hardness, first, assume a single agent i to leaves the economy. The defecting agent will maximize his utility using only his endowment e_i and his own production functions F_i. We will call his resulting utility his batna,[5] b_i. Note that we can compute b_i in $F\Delta_2^P$, and, given the b_i's, optimizing production subject to individual rationality is also in $F\Delta_2^P$. □

5. COMPUTING EQUILIBRIA IN A SEQUENTIAL MODEL

Thus far, we have considered the most common models of rationality in markets — individual defection and core rationality. However, since production often involves intermediate goods, it seems natural to consider a model that makes this sequential property explicit.

For example, consider a production sequence in which $\hat{a}$ is transformed into $\hat{b}$, $\hat{b}$ is traded and transformed into $\hat{c}$,

[5]The acronym BATNA, meaning "Best Alternative To a Negotiated Agreement," is commonly used in negotiation theory.

and $\hat{c}$ is again traded. Moreover, imagine that the agent who transforms $\hat{b}$ into $\hat{c}$ would rather just keep the $\hat{b}$ that he gets. It seems natural that this agent should be able to wait to defect until she receives $\hat{b}$, but core rationality ignores this possibility.

Since we are not aware of a standard, general model of sequential production, we adopt what we believe is a natural model. Specifically, we augment the production model to specify time:

DEFINITION 5.1. *A* sequential production plan *is a specification* $(\{x_i\}, \{x_{k,t}\})$ *including the vector of goods* x_i *consumed by agent* i *and the vector of production inputs* $x_{k,t}$ *used by firm* k *at time* t. *A feasible production plan is one in which all production inputs required at time* t *exist in the economy, i.e.*

$$\sum_k x_{k,t} \leq \sum_{\tau=0}^{t-1} \sum_k (f_k(x_{k,\tau}) - x_{k,t}) + \sum_i e_i \ .$$

To ensure that all sequential production plans have polynomial size, we require that each function f_k may be used at most once and that some production function f_k is used at each timestep.

First, we assume that defectors are isolated for the remainder of the production plan, i.e. an agent will participate until time t_d and then choose to deviate, after which he cannot trade and can only use his own production technologies F_i. In this setting, we classify the complexity and show that complexity equilibria exist under the natural generalization:

THEOREM 5.2. *In a model in which defecting individuals will face subsequent isolation, it is* $\mathrm{F}\Delta_3^P$*-complete to find the optimal sequential production plan in which no individual wishes to defect.*

Second, we observe that isolation is not always a credible threat. We would like a "subgame perfect" allocation; however, a subgame perfect equilibrium may require an exponentially large specification. Thus, we ask for a production plan that is consistent with the realization of some subgame perfect equilibrium. We show that this problem is computationally harder:

THEOREM 5.3. *In a model in which defectors are not isolated, it is PSPACE-hard to find a sequential production plan that is consistent with a subgame perfect equilibrium.*

The proofs for Theorems 5.2 and 5.3 are omitted.

6. COMPLEXITY EQUILIBRIA

Perhaps the most interesting complexity-theoretic phenomenon in non-convex economies is the existence of allocations that are stable because profitable deviation is computationally intractable. To formalize complexity equilibria, one must recognize that stable outcomes in Economics are defined in terms of an appropriate concept of *deviation.*

DEFINITION 6.1. *A deviation scheme is a mapping* $\mathcal{D}$ *assigning each feasible allocation and subset of agents a set of feasible allocations. Intuitively, if* (x, y) *is a feasible allocation and* $S \subseteq [n]$, *then* $\mathcal{D}((x, y), S)$ *is the set of all allocations to which the agents in* S *can drive the economy in one step called* a deviation by S. *Deviation* $(x', y') \in \mathcal{D}((x, y), S)$ *is a profitable deviation by* S *if each* $i \in S$ *has at least as good utility in* (x', y') *than in* (x, y), *and at least one agent* $i \in S$ *has strictly better utility. A* $\mathcal{D}$*-equilibrium is an allocation* (x, y) *such that for all* S $\mathcal{D}((x, y), S)$ *contains no profitable deviations.*

Suppose that, for all allocations (x, y) $\mathcal{D}((x, y), S)$ is the set of all feasible allocations whenever $S = [n]$, and is the empty set otherwise; then $\mathcal{D}$-equilibria are precisely the Pareto optimal allocations. To define the core, $\mathcal{D}((x, y), S)$ contains all feasible allocations that are also feasible if the endowments, consumption, and production by agents not in S is set to zero. And for the sequential production model, $\mathcal{D}((x, y), \{i\})$ contains all allocations that can be achieved by having agent i unilaterally change her production decisions; all other values of $\mathcal{D}$ are empty.

We can now define complexity equilibria:

DEFINITION 6.2. *We say that a family of economies* $\mathcal{E}$ *has* complexity equilibria *with respect to deviation scheme* $\mathcal{D}$ *if the following propblem is NP-complete: Given an allocation* $(x^+, y^+)_E$ *in an economy* $E \in \mathcal{E}$, *find a profitable* $\mathcal{D}$*-deviation.*

THEOREM 6.3. *Economies with non-convex production possibilities have complexity equilibria with respect to Pareto improvement, core rationality, and sequential rationality. Moreover, the inefficiency of the complexity equilibrium is unbounded.*

The proof of this theorem follows later in this section.

Through standard complexity theory arguments involving so-called *complexity cores*, this result implies that, unless P = NP, there are families of allocations on which any group of polynomial-time agents would almost always be stuck. Specifically, a result of Orponen and Schöning [20] implies the following corollary:

COROLLARY 6.4. *Unless P = NP, there exists an infinite set of economies* $\mathcal{E}$ *with the following properties:*

1. *Any set of polynomial-time agents will be stuck at complexity equilibria in almost all economies* $E \in \mathcal{E}$ *(in all but a finite number of economies).*
2. *The set* $\mathcal{E}$ *is not too small — if* $f(n)$ *is the number of economies* $E \in \mathcal{E}$ *with size* $|E| = n$, *then* $f(n)$ *is superpolynomial in* n.

Moreover, we show families of economies exist with complexity equilibria relative to average-case NP-hardness. We refer the reader to Bogdanov and Trevisan's survey [4] for background on average-case complexity.

THEOREM 6.5. *There exists a distribution of economies* $(\mathcal{D}, \mathcal{E})$ *with complexity equilibria from which Pareto improvement is average-case NP-hard.*

Significantly, the family of economies exhibiting average-case hardness is a somewhat natural model — certainly quite natural compared to many of the other distributional problems for which one can prove average-case results. We sketch the proof in Appendix C.

Finally, we return to the proof that complexity equilibria exist:

PROOF. *(Theorem 6.3)* A nonconstructive existence proof follows from the economy of Theorem 3.1 and the fact that it is NP-hard to satisfy $k+1$ clauses of a CNF SAT formula given given an assignment satisfying k clauses. To give a constructive example and demonstrate unbounded inefficiency, we modify the economy to satisfy a standard CNF SAT instance.

Let $\Phi = \bigwedge \phi_j$ be a CNF SAT instance with n_Φ variables χ_i and m_Φ clauses ϕ_j. We use the economy of Theorem 3.1 with the following modified production functions:

Production: The functions for producing $\hat{\gamma}$ are replaced by

$$\begin{aligned} x_{\hat{\gamma}} = f_{\gamma,\Phi}(x_{\hat{\phi}_1}, \ldots x_{\hat{\phi}_{m_\Phi}}) &= \min_j x_{\hat{\phi}_j} \\ x_{\hat{\gamma}} = f_{\gamma,\hat{s}}(x_{\hat{s}_1}, \ldots x_{\hat{s}_{n_\Phi}}) &= \frac{1}{4} \min_i x_{\hat{s}_i} \end{aligned}$$

where $\hat{s}_i$ is the source good from i's choice gadget.

As in Theorem 3.1, the agents may pick an assignment ϕ and produce 1 unit of the clause good for each satisfied clause. The welfare W will be the amount of $\hat{\gamma}$ produced. The production function $f_{\gamma,\Phi}$ only produces $\hat{\gamma}$ if all clause goods are present, so agents want to satisfy Φ. When Φ is satisfied, the maximum amount of $\hat{\gamma}$ is 1.

The function $f_{\gamma,\hat{s}}$ provides a back door to generate $\hat{\gamma}$. However, since there are only 2 units of each $\hat{s}_i$ good, at most $\frac{1}{2}$ unit of $\hat{\gamma}$ will be produced. Since $f_{\gamma,\hat{s}}$ is the only way to produce $\hat{\gamma}$ apart from $f_{\gamma,\Phi}$, no allocation can achieve welfare higher than $W = \frac{1}{2}$ without satisfying Φ.

Thus, an allocation in which the agents achieve a social welfare of $\frac{1}{2}$ by using all their $\hat{s}_i$ in $f_{\gamma,\hat{s}}$ is a complexity equilibrium — it is certainly not Pareto efficient if Φ has a solution; however, finding an allocation that is Pareto preferred requires achieving $W > \frac{1}{2}$ and therefore satisfying Φ, which is NP-hard. Moreover, if we eliminate $f_{\gamma,\hat{s}}$, the relative inefficiency (relative social welfare of the complexity equilibrium compared to a true Pareto optimum) is unbounded because the social welfare at the complexity equilibrium is 0 and the social welfare at a Pareto optimum is 1. □

7. DISCUSSION AND OPEN PROBLEMS

We showed that economies with nonconvexities — in other words, real economies — can be theaters of extreme complexity phenomena, including a novel kind of equilibrium in which agents quiesce because of the intractability of the task of finding a better allocation. One remark here is in order: economists often respond to complexity results such as the PPAD-completeness of Nash equilibria by questioning the relevance, and plausibility in real life, of the complex games with specialized structure that arise in those reductions. In the present situation, however, the intractability is, intuitively, more "generic." Nonconvex optimization is a hard problem, and in hard optimization problems "gaps" between optima and defaults are common. As a result, the present complexity results may be a little more compelling to economists.

One could hope for a proof that, in a well-defined sense to be determined, nonconvex economies are "often," or even "almost always," computationally hard. Our average-case hard construction takes a step in this direction, and, we believe, gives hope that stronger results are possible.

8. REFERENCES

[1] C. D. Aliprantis, B. Cornet, and R. Tourky. Economic equilibrium: Optimality and price decentralization. *Positivity*, 6(3):205–241, 2002.

[2] Sanjeev Arora and Boaz Barak. *Computational Complexity: A Modern Approach.* Cambridge University Press, New York, NY, USA, 2009.

[3] Kenneth J. Arrow and Gerard Debreu. Existence of an equilibrium for a competitive economy. *Econometrica*, 22(3):265–290, 1954.

[4] Andrej Bogdanov and Luca Trevisan. Average-case complexity. *CoRR*, abs/cs/0606037, 2008.

[5] J.-M. Bonnisseau and B. Cornet. Existence of equilibria with a tight marginal pricing rule. *Journal of Mathematical Economics*, 44(7-8):613 – 624, 2008. Special Issue in Economic Theory in honor of Charalambos D. Aliprantis.

[6] Donald J. Brown. Chapter 36 equilibrium analysis with non-convex technologies. volume 4 of *Handbook of Mathematical Economics*, pages 1963 – 1995. Elsevier, 1991.

[7] Bruno Codenotti, Amin Saberi, Kasturi Varadarajan, and Yinyu Ye. Leontief economies encode nonzero sum two-player games. In *SODA '06: Proceedings of the seventeenth annual ACM-SIAM symposium on Discrete algorithm*, pages 659–667, New York, NY, USA, 2006. ACM.

[8] Luis C. Corchon and M. Socorro Puy. Individual rationality and voting in cooperative production. *Economics Letters*, 59(1):83 – 90, 1998.

[9] Roger Guesnerie. Pareto optimality in non-convex economies. *Econometrica*, 43(1):1–29, 1975.

[10] Yuri Gurevich. Average case completeness. *JOURNAL OF COMPUTER AND SYSTEM SCIENCES*, 42:346–398, 1991.

[11] Glenn W. Harrison and Tanga McDaniel. Voting games and computational complexity. *Oxford Economic Papers*, 60(3):546–565, 2008.

[12] Kamal Jain and Kasturi Varadarajan. Equilibria for economies with production: constant-returns technologies and production planning constraints. In *SODA '06: Proceedings of the seventeenth annual ACM-SIAM symposium on Discrete algorithm*, pages 688–697, New York, NY, USA, 2006. ACM.

[13] Kamal Jain, Vijay V. Vazirani, and Yinyu Ye. Market equilibria for homothetic, quasi-concave utilities and economies of scale in production. In *SODA '05: Proceedings of the sixteenth annual ACM-SIAM symposium on Discrete algorithms*, pages 63–71, Philadelphia, PA, USA, 2005. Society for Industrial and Applied Mathematics.

[14] Sanjiv Kapoor, Aranyak Mehta, and Vijay Vazirani. An auction-based market equilibrium algorithm for a production model. *Theor. Comput. Sci.*, 378(2):153–164, 2007.

[15] M W Krentel. The complexity of optimization problems. In *STOC '86: Proceedings of the eighteenth annual ACM symposium on Theory of computing*, pages 69–76, New York, NY, USA, 1986. ACM.

[16] Mark W. Krentel. Generalizations of opt p to the polynomial hierarchy. *Theor. Comput. Sci.*, 97(2):183–198, 1992.

[17] David M. Kreps. *A Course in Microeconomic Theory.* Princeton University Press, February 1990.

[18] Andreu Mas-Colell, Michael D. Whinston, and Jerry R. Green. *Microeconomic Theory.* Oxford University Press, June 1995.

[19] Noam Nisan, Tim Roughgarden, Eva Tardos, and Vijay V. Vazirani. *Algorithmic Game Theory.* Cambridge University Press, New York, NY, USA, 2007.

[20] Pekka Orponen and Uwe Schoning. The density and complexity of polynomial cores for intractable sets. *Information and Control*, 70(1):54 – 68, 1986.

[21] Christos H. Papadimitriou. On the complexity of the parity argument and other inefficient proofs of existence. *J. Comput. Syst. Sci.*, 48(3):498–532, 1994.

[22] Ariel D. Procaccia and Jeffrey S. Rosenschein. Junta distributions and the average-case complexity of manipulating elections. In *Proceedings of the fifth international joint conference on Autonomous agents and multiagent systems*, AAMAS '06, pages 497–504, New York, NY, USA, 2006. ACM.

[23] Grant Schoenebeck and Salil Vadhan. The computational complexity of nash equilibria in concisely represented games. In *EC '06: Proceedings of the 7th ACM conference on Electronic commerce*, pages 270–279, New York, NY, USA, 2006. ACM.

[24] Guoqiang Tian. On the informational requirements of decentralized pareto-satisfactory mechanisms in economies with increasing returns. October 2006.

APPENDIX

A. GADGETS

The SAT Gadget.

The $SAT_\Phi(\{\hat{\chi}_i\}, \{\hat{\hat{\chi}}_i\}, \hat{\Phi}_{TRUE}, \hat{\Phi}_{FALSE})$ gadget allows an agent i to evaluate an arbitrary boolean formula Φ to produce exactly one unit of either $\hat{\Phi}_{TRUE}$ or $\hat{\Phi}_{FALSE}$. Let Φ be expressed as a tree T on which each literal in Φ is a leaf and each internal node represents the AND or OR of its children. Then the SAT gadget is described by the following subset of an economy:

Goods: For all variables χ_i in Φ: goods $\hat{\chi}_i$ and $\hat{\hat{\chi}}_i$.

For each internal node t in tree T: goods $\hat{t}$ and $\hat{\hat{t}}$.

Let r refer to the root of the tree. Then $\hat{r}$ and $\hat{\hat{r}}$ are synonyms for $\hat{\Phi}_{TRUE}$ and $\hat{\Phi}_{FALSE}$.

Production: For all AND nodes t in T with children c_j: the functions

$$x_{\hat{t}} = f_t(x) = \min_j x_{\hat{c}_j}$$

$$\forall \bar{c}_j : \; x_{\hat{\hat{t}}} = f_{\bar{t}}(x) = x_{\hat{\hat{c}}_j}$$

and for all OR nodes t with children $c_1, \ldots$: two functions

$$\forall c_j : \; x_{\hat{t}} = f_t(x) = x_{\hat{c}_j}$$

$$x_{\hat{\hat{t}}} = f_{\bar{t}}(x) = \min_j x_{\hat{\hat{c}}_j}$$

Finally, we ensure that at most one unit of the true and false good exists with the following limit gadgets: $Limit(\hat{\Phi}_{TRUE}, 1)$ and $Limit(\hat{\Phi}_{FALSE}, 1)$. (When necessary, constant scalars may be added to ensure that at least one unit of $\hat{\Phi}_{TRUE}$ or $\hat{\Phi}_{FALSE}$ is created.)

In the manner of previous SAT reductions, this gadget allows direct evaluation of Φ given sufficient quantities of the goods setting each variable χ_i. The main differences from our previous reductions are that this gadget evaluates arbitrary formulas and that it explicitly signals false as well as true.

The Circle-of-Death Gadget.

The circle-of-death constructs a group of three agents who will continually defect unless they are given a particular good. The gadget $COD(\hat{d})$ includes the following:

Agents: Three agents 1, 2, and 3.

Goods: For each agent i, there is one source good $\hat{s}_i$ and one product good $\hat{p}_i$. There is also a deactivator good $\hat{d}$.

Endowments: Agent i is endowed with 2 units of $\hat{s}_i$ and nothing else.

Utilities: Agent i has utility function $u_i(x) = x_{\hat{p}_i}$.

Production: Agent i has a production function for producing the *bundle*

$$[x_{\hat{p}_{i-1}}, x_{\hat{p}_i}] = f_i(x)$$
$$= [2, 1] \cdot \max(\min(x_{\hat{s}_{i-1}} - 1, x_{\hat{s}_i} - 1), 0)$$

and a "deactivated" production function

$$x_{\hat{p}_i} = f_{\hat{d},i}(x_{\hat{s}_i}, x_{\hat{d}}) = \min(x_{\hat{s}_i}, 6x_{\hat{d}})$$

The f_i are designed with three properties:

1. Because of fixed costs, only one function f_i may be used at a time. Thus, if f_i is used, agent $i+1$ will get 0 units of utility, agent i will get 1 unit, and agent $i-1$ will get 2.
2. For any choice of f_i to use, the function f_{i+1} gives 2 units of utility to agent i, 1 unit to agent $i+1$ and 0 units to agent $i-1$. Moreover, agents i and $i+1$, both of whom strictly prefer using f_{i+1}, have both the endowment and production technology to achieve this result in isolation. Thus, in the absence of $\hat{d}$, there is always a defecting coalition.
3. Agents may opt out of the circle-of-death and use the deactivator good to produce utility if present, but the "losing" agent in the cycle must be able to generate at least 1 unit of utility if the cycle is to be broken, requiring $\geq \frac{1}{2}$ units of $\hat{d}$.

Consequently, if $< \frac{1}{2}$ units of $\hat{d}$ are available in the economy, then the core is empty, i.e. some pair of agents would always benefit from defecting.

Binary Counting Gadget.

The gadget $BCG(\hat{\gamma}, \hat{j}_0, \ldots \hat{j}_c)$ treats $x_{\hat{j}_0}, \ldots x_{\hat{j}_c}$ as the binary representation of a c-bit number x and produces x units of $\hat{\gamma}$. It includes the following:

Goods: The "counting" good $\hat{\gamma}$ and the c input bit goods $\hat{j}_k$.

Production: For each good $\hat{j}_k$:

$$x_{\hat{\gamma}} = f_k(x_{\hat{j}_k}) = 2^k \cdot x_{\hat{j}_k} \quad .$$

Generalized Choice Gadget.

The gadget $GChoice(\hat{s}, x_1, \ldots x_c)$ is identical to the choice gadget (see Section 3) except that the input good $\hat{s}$ is provided by the economy and the choice is over bundles x_k instead of individual goods $\hat{j}_k$:

Goods: A source good $\hat{s}$ and bundles $x_1, \ldots x_k$ over the space of all other goods $\mathbb{R}^{m-1}$.

Production: Agent i owns firms with the following production functions: $Limit(\hat{s}, 2)$ and

$$\forall j_k : \quad z = f_{j_k}(x_{\hat{s}}) = x_k \max(x_{\hat{s}} - 1, 0) \ .$$

B. RATIONAL REDUCTIONS

PROOF. *(of Theorem 4.1.)* It is easy to certify that an allocation (x, y) is not in the core (i.e. testing core membership is in coNP): demonstrate a coalition and an allocation (x', y') such that the coalition strictly prefers (x', y') to (x, y). Thus, a core allocation (x^c, y^c) may be found in $F\Sigma_2^P = FNP^{NP}$ as follows: guess the core allocation and use an oracle call to check that it is in the core.

Next, we give the reduction from the $F\Sigma_2^P$-complete problem Σ_2SAT [2]: find x_1 such that $\forall x_2 \Phi(x_1, x_2) = 1$. Let n_Φ be the number of variables in Φ.

We will describe the economy in stages. The globally relevant parts of the economy include:

Agents: Two directors A and B.

For each variable χ in x_1: two agents χ and $\bar{\chi}$.

Goods: One utility good $\hat{\gamma}_i$ for each agent i.

One deactivator good for a circle-of-death, $\hat{d}$.

Utilities: Agent i desires his utility good, i.e. $u_i(x) = x_{\hat{\gamma}_i}$.

Production: A circle of death $COD(\hat{d})$.

Director A wants Φ to be true and director B wants it to be false. The circle of death will ensure that Φ can never actually be falsified in a core allocation. (Note that the χ agents are defined only for the variables in x_1.)

In the first stage, director B decides whether to pick x_1 himself or defer to director A:

Goods: Authorization goods $\hat{a}_A$ and $\hat{a}_B$.

A choice source good $\hat{s}_{D,\chi}$ for each director D and variable χ in Φ.

Production: Director B has

$$Choice((2n_\Phi + 2)\hat{a}_A, (2n_\Phi + 1)\hat{a}_B)$$

Director A has $Limit(\hat{d}, 1)$ and

$$x_{\hat{d}} = f_{\hat{d}}(x) = x_{a_A} \ .$$

For each variable χ, each director D has $Limit(\hat{s}_{D,\chi}, 2)$ and

$$x_{s_{D,\chi}} = f_{s_{D,\chi}}(x) = x_{a_D} \ .$$

The director D whose good $\hat{a}_D$ is chosen will produce exactly two units of $\hat{s}_{D,\chi}$ for each variable χ. If A is chosen, he will also produce one unit of $\hat{d}$. (Because of the limit gadgets, the directors have no other way to consume all the authorization goods, so, following Proposition 2.4, we may assume that they do. This logic carries through the remainder of the construction.)

Next, the chosen director picks x_1. Both directors D have the following infrastructure (note that we use generalized choice gadgets as defined in Appendix A):

Goods: For each variable χ in x_1, two choice authorization goods $\hat{a}_{D,\chi}$ and $\hat{a}_{D,\bar{\chi}}$, and two assignment goods $\hat{\chi}$ and $\hat{\bar{\chi}}$.

For each variable χ in x_2, a choice source good $\hat{s}_{D,\chi}$ and two assignment goods $\hat{\chi}$ and $\hat{\bar{\chi}}$.

Production: Each director D owns, for each variable $\chi \in x_1$:

$$GChoice(\hat{s}_{D,\chi}, 3\hat{a}_{D,\chi}, 3\hat{a}_{D,\bar{\chi}})$$

and for each variable $\chi \in x_2$:

$$GChoice(\hat{s}_{D,\chi}, \hat{\chi}, \hat{\bar{\chi}}) \ .$$

Each χ agent has (for both directors): $Limit(x_{\hat{\chi}}, 1)$ and

$$x_{\hat{\chi}} = f_{\hat{\chi}}(x) = x_{\hat{a}_{D,\chi}}$$

(the $\bar{\chi}$ agents have similar functions).

In essence, the director produces x_2 himself; however, though he chooses x_1, he must delegate the production of the $\hat{\chi}$ goods for x_1 to the χ and $\bar{\chi}$ agents. The extra authorization good $\hat{a}$ will later be used to generate utility.

Next Φ is evaluated:

Goods: True and false goods $\hat{\Phi}_{TRUE}$ and $\hat{\Phi}_{FALSE}$ to represent the value of Φ.

Production: Director B has a

$$SAT_\Phi(\{\hat{\chi}_i\}, \{\hat{\bar{\chi}}_i\}, \hat{\Phi}_{TRUE}, \hat{\Phi}_{FALSE})$$

gadget to evaluate Φ given the $\hat{\chi}$ and $\hat{\bar{\chi}}$ goods.

Note that a coalition of B and the χ agents may evaluate Φ without the help of any other agents. Moreover, those same agents are required to compute Φ even if A is involved. This will restrict the possible defecting coalitions.

Finally, agents receive their payoffs:

Goods: For each χ (resp. $\bar{\chi}$) agent and each director D, an intermediate utility good $\hat{\alpha}_{D,\chi}$ (resp. $\hat{\alpha}_{D,\bar{\chi}}$).

Production: Director A has $Limit(\hat{\gamma}_A, 1)$ and

$$x_{D,\hat{\gamma}_A} = f_{\gamma_A}(x) = \min((2n+2)x_{\Phi_{TRUE}}, x_{\hat{a}_A}) \ .$$

Similarly, director B has $Limit(\hat{\gamma}_A, 1)$ and

$$x_{\hat{\gamma}_A} = f_{\gamma_A}(x) = \min((2n+2)x_{\Phi_{FALSE}}, x_{\hat{a}_B}) \ .$$

Each χ agent has, for each director D: $Limit(\hat{\alpha}_{D,\chi}, 1)$ and

$$x_{\hat{\alpha}_{D,\chi}} = f_{D,\alpha_\chi}(x) = x_{\hat{a}_{D,\chi}} \ ,$$

(and $\bar{\chi}$ have similar functions).

Finally, each χ agent has

$$\begin{aligned}
x_{\hat{\gamma}_\chi} = f_{A,\gamma_\chi,\chi}(x) &= \min(x_{\hat{\alpha}_{A,\chi}}, (2n+2)x_{\Phi_{TRUE}}) \\
x_{\hat{\gamma}_\chi} = f_{A,\gamma_\chi,\bar{\chi}}(x) &= 2\min(x_{\hat{\alpha}_{A,\bar{\chi}}}, (2n+2)x_{\Phi_{TRUE}}) \\
x_{\hat{\gamma}_\chi} = f_{B,\gamma_\chi,\chi}(x) &= \frac{3}{2}\min(x_{\hat{\alpha}_{B,\chi}}, (2n+2)x_{\Phi_{FALSE}}) \\
x_{\hat{\gamma}_\chi} = f_{B,\gamma_\chi,\bar{\chi}}(x) &= \frac{3}{2}\min(x_{\hat{\alpha}_{B,\bar{\chi}}}, (2n+2)x_{\Phi_{FALSE}})
\end{aligned}$$

(similar for the $\bar{\chi}$ agents).

Payoffs are summarized in the following table (D represents the chosen director):

Agent	$\Phi = 1$, $D = A$	$\Phi = 0$, $D = A$	$\Phi = 1$, $D = B$	$\Phi = 0$, $D = B$
A	1	0	0	0
B	0	0	0	1
χ produces x_1	1	0	0	$\frac{3}{2}$
χ does not produce x_1	2	0	0	$\frac{3}{2}$

Agents A and B fight over whether Φ is true or false. In allocations where A makes Φ true, the χ agents who don't participate in producing x_1 will get 2 units of utility and be happy, but the agents who do produce x_1 will only get 1 unit. Thus, if they can falsify Φ with B, the coalition would rather defect and get $\frac{3}{2}$. Note that if they defect, the only setting of x_1 that they can produce is the one originally chosen by A (because any other setting requires the production firms of the χ agents who got 2 and, therefore, would not want to join the coalition).

Since nobody gets any utility if Φ is not evaluated, we may assume that it is evaluated in any core allocation. Moreover, for the same reason, A must be the director if Φ is evaluated to true, and B must be the director if Φ is false. (A coalition of agents would clearly like to defect from an allocation in which nobody receives any utility.)

For the moment, let us assume that the Σ_2SAT instance is true, i.e. a "solution" x_1 exists. In this case, a core allocation is the one in which A picks an x_1 that solves the Σ_2SAT problem. In this case, the only agents who could reasonably defect are B and the χ agents who produce x_1. However, as noted, they are bound by A's choice of x_1, therefore they will not be able to falsify Φ and would receive no utility if they defect. Thus, the allocation is in the core. In contrast, if A picks the wrong x_1 and still tries to satisfy Φ, that same coalition will defect and falsify Φ on its own. Finally, any allocation in which A is not in charge is precluded by the circle-of-death. The case that no solution x_1 exists is merely a subset of the cases mentioned above.

Thus, any core allocation must correspond to an x_1 that "solves" the Σ_2SAT instance. It follows that core allocations are $F\Sigma_2^P$-complete to compute. $\square$

PROOF. (of Theorem 3.3) Given a SAT formula Φ, we construct an economy with the following properties: if Φ is unsatisfiable, the economy has a trivial price equilibrium. If Φ is satisfiable, then we get the economy in Section 4 of [6] that has no efficient price equilibrium (marginal or regular). The main trick is to manipulate the set of production possibilities for the two goods $\hat{a}$ and $\hat{b}$: when Φ is satisfiable, we want it to be $T = \{x_{\hat{a}}, x_{\hat{b}} | x_{\hat{a}} \leq 2 \text{ and } x_{\hat{b}} \leq 2 \text{ and } (x_{\hat{a}} \leq 1 \text{ or } x_{\hat{b}} \leq 1)\}$ (see the picture in [6]), and when it is unsatisfiable, we want it to be $F = \{x_{\hat{a}}, x_{\hat{b}} | x_{\hat{a}} \leq 1 \text{ and } x_{\hat{b}} \leq 1\}$ (this is a convex set, so there will be a price equilibrium).

To accomplish this, we construct a SAT gadget, as above. When Φ is false, we have a false good. We give agents the technology to turn this good into any quantity of goods $\hat{a}$ and $\hat{b}$ from set F. Since this set is convex (and the other goods, i.e. those used in the SAT formula are not traded), the economy has a price equilibrium. Now, when Φ is true, we allow the economy to produce from T as follows: a choice gadget produces one of two intermediate goods. The first can be used in production of any vector of goods up to $\hat{a} = 1$ and $\hat{b} = 2$, while the other can be used in production of any vector of goods up to $\hat{a} = 2$ and $\hat{b} = 1$. It is straightforward to integrate the utilities and endowments to make the example work. $\square$

C. AVERAGE-CASE COMPLEXITY EQUILIBRIUM

PROOF. (Rough sketch for Theorem 6.5.) Consider modeling an economy as an undirected graph $G = (V, E)$. Each vertex $v \in V$ corresponds to a location, and each edge corresponds to a route along which goods may be transfered. This is repeated for each time $t \in \{1, \dots T\}$, and a vertex (location) may choose to save goods or borrow against the future (like an edge from v_t to v_{t+1} in a product graph).

A feasible configuration of the economy is a specification of the net production at each location v, the net transfer along each edge, and the net savings at v from time t to $t + 1$. The production choices at v will dictate how goods are exchanged, i.e. a production process will inherently require that goods be saved or that they be exchanged with a particular neighbor u. Using non-convexity as in the choice gadget, a location is forced to make a discrete choice among possible sets of net-transfer vectors.

In the Arrow-Debreu framework, we model this economy by creating separate copies of the goods and production functions for each time t and location and edge. (Note that Arrow and Debreu [3] suggest modeling an economy over time and space by copying goods, so this is not unprecedented.) Arbitrarily, we assume one agent per vertex v.

Hardness will follow because this economic model is a superset of an edge tiling problem defined by Gurevich [10]. An edge tiling problem consists of a set of tiles T, an $n \times n$ square, and some initial conditions. The goal is to place one tile at each location in the square such that adjacent labels match and all initial constraints are satisfied.

Gurevich [10] shows that when the first row is randomly filled according to a certain "uniform" distribution (the initial conditions) and all possible sets of tiles T occur with positive probability, it is average-case NP-complete to decide if the $n \times n$ square may be tiled.

The edge tiling problem corresponds to an economy where agents are organized on a line. A production task (a tile) is chosen for each vertex at each time such that the net transfers to neighbors (the left and right labels) and the net savings (the top and bottom labels) match accordingly. Similar to the construction in Theorem 6.3, players only receive a payoff if the square is completely tiled.

Reducing from Gurevich shows that when production at time $t = 0$ (i.e. filling the first row) is done according to the proper distribution, *improving from payoff 0 in such an economy is average-case NP-hard for any distribution over possible production tasks such that every set of tiles occurs with positive probability.* $\square$

The economy in this proof is somewhat reasonable. It is powerful because the precise distribution does not matter, provided it satisfies the very general (though questionable) condition that all sets of tiles are possible. The linear topology is an artifact of this particular proof rather than a fundamental requirement.

The main drawback of this construction is that it requires randomization over discrete production tasks. In contrast, a more natural reduction would fix the discrete choices and randomize over continuous parameters of those choices. We do not know of a natural construction that does this.

Liquidity in Credit Networks: A Little Trust Goes a Long Way

Pranav Dandekar
Stanford University
ppd@stanford.edu

Ashish Goel
Stanford University
ashishg@stanford.edu

Ramesh Govindan
University of Southern California
ramesh@usc.edu

Ian Post
Stanford University
itp@stanford.edu

ABSTRACT

Credit networks represent a way of modeling trust between entities in a network. Nodes in the network print their own currency and trust each other for a certain amount of each other's currency. This allows the network to serve as a decentralized payment infrastructure—arbitrary payments can be routed through the network by passing IOUs between trusting nodes in their respective currencies—and obviates the need for a common currency. Nodes can repeatedly transact with each other and pay for the transaction using trusted currency. A natural question to ask in this setting is: how long can the network sustain liquidity, i.e. how long can the network support the routing of payments before credit dries up? We answer this question in terms of the long term failure probability of transactions for various network topologies and credit values.

We prove that the transaction failure probability is independent of the path along which transactions are routed. We show that under symmetric transaction rates, the transaction failure probability in a number of well-known graph families goes to zero as the size, density or credit capacity of the network increases. We also show via simulations that even networks of small size and credit capacity can route transactions with high probability if they are well-connected. Further, we characterize a centralized currency system as a special type of a star network (one where edges to the root have infinite credit capacity, and transactions occur only between leaf nodes) and compute the steady-state transaction failure probability in a centralized system. We show that liquidity in star networks, complete graphs and Erdös-Rényi networks is comparable to that in equivalent centralized currency systems; thus we do not lose much liquidity in return for their robustness and decentralized properties.

Categories and Subject Descriptors

K.4.4 [**Computing Milieux**]: Electronic Commerce

General Terms

Theory, Economics

Keywords

liquidity, trust, reputation, currency, credit networks

1. INTRODUCTION

One of the primary functions of money is as a medium of exchange. This function is facilitated by governments and central banks that issue currency and declare it to be legal tender, i.e. the state promises to accept that currency back as payment for goods and services. Thus currency represents an obligation issued by the state, and when used to make a payment, results in a transfer of the state's obligation from the payer to the payee. A decision to accept payment in a currency is therefore a decision to trust the issuer of the currency to fulfill its obligations.

The modern banking system is a centralized currency infrastructure. The central bank sits at the root of the tree. It issues currency, government notes, etc. Retail banks, individuals and businesses form the leaves of this tree. Since they cannot print their own currency, they trust the central bank for an infinite amount of money (in theory, at least). Many non-governmental organizations also issue their own currencies, known as *scrip*. Examples of such scrip systems in the online world include Facebook credits, Yootles [16], P2P systems where such currency is used to solve the free-rider problem [18, 1], and virtual worlds such as Everquest and Second Life that have their own currencies. A challenge with scrip systems is to determine how much currency to issue in order to ensure liquidity without devaluing the currency [10].

We study an alternate model of credit, credit networks, introduced independently by DeFigueiredo and Barr [3], by Ghosh et al. [4], and by Karlan et. al. [9]. We generalize the model based on the insight that payments can be made in any currency as long as it is trusted by the payee. So nodes in our model act as banks and print their own currency and trust each other for certain amounts of each other's currency. This allows them to transact with each other without the need for a common currency: as long as there is a chain of sufficient credit from the payee to the payer, arbitrary payments can be made by passing obligations between trusting agents in their respective currencies. We study the question of long-term liquidity (i.e. capacity to route payments) in credit networks when nodes repeatedly transact with each other.

Illustrative Example. Consider a credit network with three nodes u, v and w with edge (u, v) having credit limit c_1 (i.e. u trusts v for up to c_1 units of v's currency) and edge (v, w) having a credit limit c_2. If w wants to purchase a product or service from u worth p units of w's currency, where $p \leq \min\{c_1, c_2\}$, the transaction proceeds by w issuing an IOU to v worth p units of w's currency and v issuing an IOU to u worth p units of v's currency. However, if $p > \min\{c_1, c_2\}$ the transaction fails. As a result of a successful transaction, the edges (u, v) and (v, w) now have capacities $c_1 - p$ and $c_2 - p$ respectively (since v and w have depleted part of their credit line). But this transaction also results in the creation of edges (v, u) and (w, v) each having capacity p, since now v can trust u for up to p units of its own currency, and w can trust v for up to p units of its own currency. Thus routing payments in credit networks is identical to routing residual flows in general flow networks.

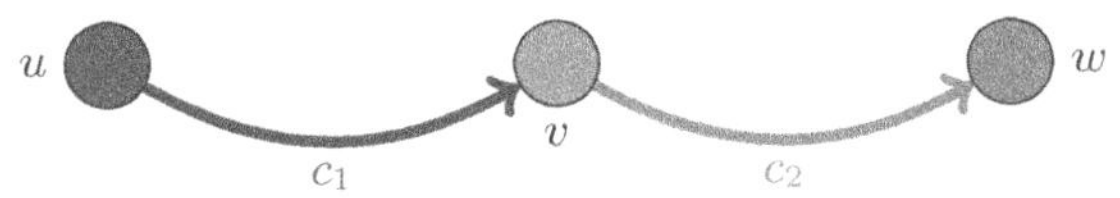

(a) Before the transaction

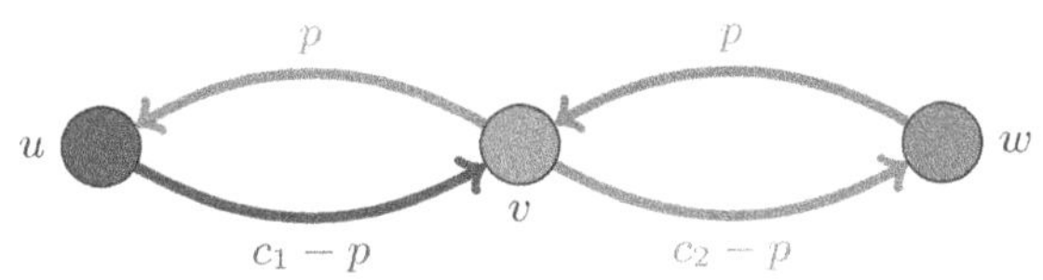

(b) After the transaction

Figure 1: Illustrative Example

The papers that introduced this model used it as a generalization of budget constraints in auctions [4] and as a mechanism for providing social collateral/insurance for transactions between untrusting agents in a network [3, 9]. In addition to these papers, Resnick and Sami [17] study how to update credit values along edges over time while ensuring robustness to Sybil attacks. They show that there is a social cost to allowing transactions via intermediaries—any protocol for updating credit values that is Sybil-proof in a certain sense can lead to a reduction in overall credit balances in expectation. Previous work on this model used the term "trust network" for it; we prefer the term "credit network" to distinguish this model from all the previous ones that also model trust/reputation in networks in settings unrelated to ours such as web search [15, 7] and studying people's opinions of each other [6, 12].

Credit networks have a number of interesting and useful properties. First, the loss incurred by nodes in the network is *bounded*. Consider a scenario where a potential attacker, say node x, injects nodes into this network. The attacker's nodes can extend each other credit lines worth arbitrary amount of money, but in order to transact with one of the honest players the attacker x must dupe one of them, say u, into extending him a line of credit. If u extends x a credit line for c units, x can transact with honest nodes in the network for up to c units by giving u IOUs worth c units in its currency. Once the transaction is complete, x can then disappear leaving u with unredeemable IOUs worth c units, and u incurs a loss equal to c units in x's currency. This demonstrates that the total loss incurred by the nodes in the network is bounded by the total credit extended by honest nodes to the attacker's nodes. In particular, the loss incurred by the nodes in the network does not depend on the number of nodes the attacker injects. Second, since a node in the network only accepts IOUs from other nodes to whom it has extended a line of credit, the loss incurred by honest players in the network is *localized*. In other words, the only nodes that incur a loss are the ones that extended credit to the attacker nodes. In this sense, the system is fair; it protects a node from losses resulting from another node's lack of judgement. Finally, routing payments in credit networks is efficient since it only requires a max-flow computation [3, 4, 9].

These properties make this model useful not only for monetary transactions, but also in any setting where there is a need to model trust between nodes in a network. It is particularly well-suited for transactions in exchange economies such as P2P networks where it can be used to improve inefficiencies resulting from asynchronous demand and bilateral trading [13]. It has been used as part of a system called Ostra [14] designed to thwart spam in email. Ostra is similar in spirit to Gmail's Priority Inbox. This model can also be used in settings such as combating spam in viral marketing over social networks and packet routing in mobile ad-hoc networks. There is a large body of work in economics and sociology on social capital and favor exchanges in networks [8]. This model provides a rigorous way of not only keeping track of favors owed to and by each individual in a network, but also a way to exchange favors, via trusted intermediaries, between individuals that do not know each other directly.

However, in order for the model to be of practical use it should be able to support repeated transactions between nodes over a long period of time. This motivates the following question, which we formulate and study in this paper: if the network is sufficiently well-connected and has sufficient credit to begin with, can we sustain transactions in perpetuity without additional injection of credit? How does liquidity depend upon network topology and transaction rates between nodes, and how does it compare with the centralized model described above?

We show positive results for all of the above questions. We show that the failure probability of transactions is independent of the path used to route flow between nodes. For symmetric transaction rates, we show analytically and via simulations that the failure probability for complete graphs, Erdös-Rényi graphs, and preferential attachment graphs goes to zero as the size, the density or the credit capacity of the network increases. Further, we characterize a centralized currency system as a special type of a star network (one where edges to the root have infinite credit capacity, and transactions occur only between leaf nodes) and compute its steady-state failure probability. We show how to construct a centralized system that is equivalent to a given credit network and that the steady-state failure probability in star networks and complete graphs is within a constant-factor of that in equivalent centralized currency systems. We show that the node bankruptcy probability in credit networks is $\Theta(1/h_G)$ whereas that in an equivalent centralized system is $\Theta(1/\bar{c}_G)$, where h_G is the harmonic mean of the total credit capacities on edges incident upon nodes in G and $\bar{c}_G$ is the corresponding arithmetic mean. These results are similar in spirit to price of anarchy bounds—in return for all the benefits resulting from the decentralized nature of the system, we do not lose much liquidity compared to a centralized model with a common currency.

We would like to qualify our results by stating that nodes in our model are not endowed with any rationality. We treat credit values on edges and transaction rates between nodes as being exogenously defined. We also ignore currency exchange ratios, i.e. we assume them to be unity for clarity of exposition; this does not qualitatively affect our results. These questions represent promising directions for further study of this model and we discuss them at the end of the paper along with other open problems.

The rest of the paper is organized as follows: Section 2 defines our model and describes our main results, Section 3 contains steady-state analysis of the transaction failure probability in our model and its comparison with a centralized model of credit, Section 4 discusses results of simulating repeated transactions on two random graph families, Erdös-Rényi graphs and power-law graphs constructed using the Barabási-Albert preferential attachment model [2], and finally Section 5 has concluding remarks along with a discussion of some interesting directions for further study of this model.

2. OUR MODEL & RESULTS

A credit network $G = (V, E)$ is a directed graph with n nodes and m edges. Nodes represent entities or agents. Edges represent pairwise credit limits between agents. An edge $(u, v) \in E$ has capacity $c_{uv} > 0$, which implies that u has extended a credit line of c_{uv} units to v in v's currency. If a node s needs to pay p units in her currency to node t (for example, to buy a good that t is selling), the payment can go through if the maximum credit flow from t to s is at least p units. The payment will get routed through a chain of trusted nodes from s to t. Note that payment flows in the opposite direction of credit, so a payment merely results in a redistribution of credit; the total credit in the network remains unchanged.

We study liquidity under the following simple model of repeated transactions: we assume that each edge (u, v) in G has total credit capacity $c_{uv}+c_{vu} = c$ where c_{uv}, c_{vu} are integers. The transaction rate between nodes is given by the $n \times n$ matrix $\Lambda = \{\lambda_{uv} : u, v \in V; \lambda_{uu} = 0\}$ such that $\sum_{u,v} \lambda_{uv} = 1$. At each time step, we pick a pair of nodes (s, t) with probability λ_{st} and try to route a unit payment along the shortest feasible path from s to t. If such a path exists, we route the flow along that path and modify edge capacities along the path as described previously (i.e. for each edge (u, v) on the path, increment c_{uv} by 1 and decrement c_{vu} by 1). The transaction fails if there is no path between s and t.

We begin by noting that at any time step an edge between nodes u and v can be in one of $(c+1)$ states, having capacity c from u to v and 0 from v to u, having capacity $c - 1$ from u to v and 1 from v to u and so on down to having 0 capacity from u to v and c from v to u. Each successful transaction results in a change of state for all edges along the shortest path from the source to the destination. Therefore, these repeated transactions between nodes in G induce the following Markov chain $\mathcal{M}(G, \Lambda)$: each state of the Markov chain encapsulates the state of all the edges in the network. Since there are m edges, each of which can be in one of $(c + 1)$ states, the Markov chain has $(c + 1)^m$ states. A successful transaction results in a transition between two states. Let P be the transition matrix. The transition probability, $P(\mathcal{S}_1, \mathcal{S}_2)$ from state $\mathcal{S}_1$ to $\mathcal{S}_2$ is equal to λ_{st} where routing a unit payment from s to t in state $\mathcal{S}_1$ along the shortest feasible path results in the network being in state $\mathcal{S}_2$. The probability $P(\mathcal{S}, \mathcal{S})$ is the probability that the transaction is infeasible when the network is in state $\mathcal{S}$. This is equal to the sum of all probabilities λ_{st} such that the network in state $\mathcal{S}$ has no path from s to t.

A note on terminology: we will sometimes refer to an edge (u, v) as being "bidirectional" if both c_{uv} and c_{vu} are non-zero, and as "unidirectional" if exactly one of c_{uv} and c_{vu} is zero.

We describe our main results below. Our first result obviates the need to route payments along the shortest feasible path.

THEOREM. Let $(s_1, t_1), (s_2, t_2), \dots, (s_T, t_T)$ be the set of transactions of value $v_1, v_2, \dots, v_T$ respectively that succeed when the payment from s_i to t_i is routed along a path $\mathcal{P}_i$. Then the same set of transactions succeed when the payment from s_i to t_i is routed along any other feasible path $\mathcal{P}'_i$.

In order to prove this, we observe that routing flow along a directed cycle changes the state of the network but does not affect the total credit available to any node. This motivates the following definition:

Definition 1. Given a credit network G, let $\mathcal{S}$ and $\mathcal{S}'$ be two states of G. We say that $\mathcal{S}'$ is *cycle-reachable* from $\mathcal{S}$ if the network can be transformed from state $\mathcal{S}$ to state $\mathcal{S}'$ by routing a sequence of payments along feasible cycles (i.e. from a node to itself along a feasible path).

Cycle-reachability defines a partition $\mathcal{C}$ over the set of possible states of the network; each equivalence class in $\mathcal{C}$ is the set of states that are cycle-reachable from each other. We show the following result about the steady-state distribution of $\mathcal{M}$ over equivalence classes in $\mathcal{C}$:

THEOREM. Consider a Markov chain $\mathcal{M}_{\mathcal{S}_0}(G, \Lambda)$ starting in state $\mathcal{S}_0$ induced by a symmetric transaction rate matrix Λ over nodes in G. Let $\mathcal{C}_{\mathcal{S}_0} \subseteq \mathcal{C}$ be the set of equivalence classes accessible from $\mathcal{S}_0$ under the regime defined by Λ. Then $\mathcal{M}_{\mathcal{S}_0}$ has a uniform steady-state distribution over $\mathcal{C}_{\mathcal{S}_0}$.

We use this result to bound the steady-state node bankruptcy probability in general graphs and transaction failure probability for trees, cycles and complete graphs. A node being bankrupt is a sufficient but not necessary condition for a transaction with that node as the payer to fail; the necessary and sufficient condition for a transaction to fail is that the network has a directed cut of zero capacity between the payer and the payee. Let d_v be the total credit capacity of all edges incident upon node v in a graph G. Let h_G be the harmonic mean of the d_vs and $\bar{d}_G$ be the arithmetic mean. We show that if $\mathcal{M}(G, \Lambda)$ is ergodic and Λ is symmetric, the average steady-state bankruptcy probability of a node in a credit network is $\Theta(1/h_G)$ whereas that in an equivalent centralized system is $\Theta(1/\bar{d}_G)$. We show that if Λ is uniform, the steady-state transaction failure probability in star networks is $\Theta(1/c)$, the steady-state success probability for line graphs is $\Theta(c/n^2)$ and that for cycles is $\Theta(c/n)$. We also show that if Λ is symmetric, the steady-state transaction failure probability for complete graphs is $\Theta(1/nc)$. Our results imply that for "thin" graphs such as lines and cycles, the steady-state failure probability goes to one with the size of the network, whereas for well-connected graphs such as star networks, complete graphs and Erdös-Rényi networks[1], the steady-state failure probability goes to zero with the size, the average node degree or the credit capacity in the network.

Further, we characterize a centralized currency system as a special type of a tree network (one where edges to the root have infinite credit capacity, and transactions occur only between leaf nodes) and compute its steady-state failure probability. We show how to construct a centralized system that is equivalent to a given credit network and that the steady-state failure probability in star networks and complete graphs is within a constant-factor of that in equivalent centralized currency systems.

Table 1 shows our main analytical results on liquidity for a number of network topologies and their comparison with equivalent centralized currency systems.

In addition to these analytical results, we simulated repeated transactions on two random graph families: Erdös-Rényi graphs and power-law graphs generated using the Barabási-Albert preferential attachment (BA) model [2]. The simulations showed that relatively small values of density and credit capacity were sufficient to attain a transaction success probability in excess of 0.9. We also demonstrate that for both topologies, if we hold the average node degree and credit capacity on edges constant, the size of the net-

[1]For a connected Erdös-Rényi network, $G_c(n, p)$, the node bankruptcy probability is $\Theta(1/(npc))$.

[2]We conjecture based on simulations and heuristic calculations that the transaction failure probability is $\Theta(1/(npc))$.

[3]We conjecture based on simulations that the failure probability is $\Theta(1/(dc))$.

Network Topology	Transaction Regime	Credit Network	Centralized System
Star	uniform	$\Theta(1/c)$	$\Theta(1/c)$
Line	uniform	1 - $\Theta(c/n^2)$	$\Theta(1/c)$
Cycle	uniform	1 - $\Theta(c/n)$	$\Theta(1/c)$
Complete	symmetric	$\Theta(1/nc)$	$\Theta(1/nc)$
Erdös-Rényi[2]: $G_c(n,p)$	symmetric	$\Theta(1/npc)$	$\Theta(1/npc)$
Barabási-Albert[3]: $G_c^{BA}(n,d)$	symmetric	$\Theta(1/dc)$	$\Theta(1/dc)$

Table 1: Failure probability comparison between credit networks and equivalent centralized currency systems

work (i.e. number of nodes) had no effect on the steady-state success probability.

3. ANALYSIS

We first analyze the combinatorial structure induced by this model of making payments through passing IOUs. An understanding of this combinatorial structure allows us to characterize the steady-state behavior of the Markov chain induced by repeated transactions for a number of network topologies. Finally, we compare the steady-state success probability in credit networks with various topologies to that in an equivalent centralized currency infrastructure.

3.1 Combinatorial Structure

A state of the network can be associated with a *generalized score vector*, which characterizes the credit available to each node in that state.

Definition 2. Given a labeled, directed graph D over n nodes with edges having associated capacities, a vector $V = \langle v_1, \ldots, v_n \rangle \in \mathbb{R}_+^n$ is the *generalized score vector* of D if the total capacity on outgoing edges from i in D is v_i for $i = 1, \ldots, n$.

This is a generalization of the score vector defined by the outdegree of nodes in an orientation of a labeled multigraph [11]. Note that two cycle-reachable states have the same generalized score vector, and in fact, generalized score vectors characterize classes of cycle-reachable states:

LEMMA 1 (GENERALIZATION OF PROPOSITION 4.10 IN [5]). *Given a credit network G, two states $\mathcal{S}$ and $\mathcal{S}'$ of G are cycle-reachable if and only if they have the same generalized score vector.*

Moreover, two cycle-reachable states have exactly the same set of feasible transactions:

LEMMA 2. *For any equivalence class $C \in \mathcal{C}$ of a given network, if a transaction (s, t, v) (i.e. routing a payment of v units from node s to node t) is feasible in some state $S \in C$, it is feasible in all states $S' \in C$.*

Using the definition of cycle-reachability and the above observations, we show the following:

THEOREM 1. *Let $(s_1, t_1), (s_2, t_2), \ldots, (s_T, t_T)$ be the set of transactions of value $v_1, v_2, \ldots, v_T$ respectively that succeed when the payment from s_i to t_i is routed along a path $\mathcal{P}_i$. Then the same set of transactions succeed when the payment from s_i to t_i is routed along any other feasible path $\mathcal{P}_i'$.*

PROOF. Note that a failed transaction does not change the state of the network, so without loss of generality, we assume that the set of successful transactions (s_i, t_i) occurred in successive timesteps $i = 1$ to T. We prove the result by induction on T. The statement clearly holds for $T = 1$.

Assume that the statement holds for $T = k$. Let the initial state of the network be $\mathcal{S}_0$. Let $\mathcal{S}_k$ be the state of the network when, starting from $\mathcal{S}_0$, transactions (s_i, t_i) for $i = 1, \ldots, k$ were routed along path $\mathcal{P}_i$. Let $\mathcal{S}_k'$ be the corresponding state of the network after, again starting from $\mathcal{S}_0$, the same set of transactions were routed along paths $\mathcal{P}_i', i = 1, \ldots, k$. We will show that $\mathcal{S}_k$ is cycle-reachable from $\mathcal{S}_k'$.

A successful transaction (s, t) only changes the credit extended to s and t; the credit extended to any of the intermediate nodes remains unchanged. Since $\mathcal{S}_k$ and $\mathcal{S}_k'$ are the resulting states of the network after the same sequence of payments were successfully routed starting at the same state, the credit distribution (or equivalently, the generalized score vectors) in $\mathcal{S}_k$ and $\mathcal{S}_k'$ must be identical. Therefore, $\mathcal{S}_k$ and $\mathcal{S}_k'$ are cycle-reachable. Thus, from Lemma 2 if the transaction (s_{k+1}, t_{k+1}) is feasible in $\mathcal{S}_k$ then it is also feasible in $\mathcal{S}_k'$. This proves the result. ☐

This result shows that routing in credit networks has a *path-independence property*: the choice of paths along which a sequence of payments are routed does not affect their feasibility. Lemma 1 and Lemma 2 immediately implies the following corollary:

COROLLARY 1. *If a transaction (s, t, v) in some state in equivalence class C_i results in a transition to a state in equivalence class C_j, then the reverse transaction (t, s, v) from any state in C_j will result in a transition to a state in C_i.*

Note that the above observations do not require the edge capacities or payment flows to be integral. However, when restricted to a setting where edge capacities are integers and we route unit flows between nodes, the states of the credit network become equivalent to orientations of a labeled multigraph (since an edge of capacity c can be viewed as c labeled edges of unit capacity each). It is known that there is a bijection between score vectors of a labeled multigraph and forests of a labeled multigraph [11]. In the rest of the paper, we assume that edge capacities are integers and we route unit flows between nodes. This allows us to use the equivalence between forests, score vectors and cycle-reachable equivalence classes to characterize the steady-state of the Markov chain induced by repeated transactions.

3.2 Steady-state Analysis

Using observations about the combinatorial structure of the model, we next prove that the Markov chain induced by a symmetric transaction rate matrix Λ has a uniform steady-state distribution over $\mathcal{C}$.

THEOREM 2. *Consider a Markov chain $\mathcal{M}_{\mathcal{S}_0}(G, \Lambda)$ starting in state $\mathcal{S}_0$ induced by a symmetric transaction rate matrix Λ over nodes in G. Let $\mathcal{C}_{\mathcal{S}_0} \subseteq \mathcal{C}$ be the set of equivalence classes accessible from $\mathcal{S}_0$ under the regime defined by Λ. Then $\mathcal{M}_{\mathcal{S}_0}$ has a uniform steady-state distribution over $\mathcal{C}_{\mathcal{S}_0}$.*

PROOF. As a consequence of the above facts, we can represent transactions as resulting in transitions between equivalence classes in $\mathcal{C}$ instead of transitions between states of $\mathcal{M}(G,\Lambda)$. Let $\mathcal{T}_{ij}$ be the set of transactions (s,t) that result in a transition from some state in C_i to some state in C_j. Then, (overloading the symbol P) we define the transition matrix over equivalence classes in $\mathcal{C}_{\mathcal{S}_0}$ as

$$P(C_i, C_j) = \sum_{(s,t)\in\mathcal{T}_{ij}} \lambda_{st}$$

Note that Corollary 1 implies that $(s,t) \in \mathcal{T}_{ij}$ if and only if $(t,s) \in \mathcal{T}_{ji}$. Further since Λ is symmetric, for any equivalence classes $C_i, C_j \in \mathcal{C}_{\mathcal{S}_0}, P(C_i,C_j) = P(C_j,C_i)$. Since P is a symmetric stochastic matrix, the uniform distribution is stationary with respect to P. □

This immediately gives the following corollary:

COROLLARY 2. *If $\mathcal{M}(G,\Lambda)$ is an ergodic Markov chain induced by a symmetric transaction rate matrix Λ, it has a uniform steady state distribution over $\mathcal{C}$.*

Next we show a sufficient condition for $\mathcal{M}$ to be ergodic.

LEMMA 3. *If for all $u \neq v, \lambda_{uv} > 0$, then $\mathcal{M}$ is ergodic.*

PROOF. $\mathcal{M}$ has a finite number of states. Since $\forall u,v,u \neq v, \lambda_{uv} > 0$, for all states $\mathcal{S}$ of $\mathcal{M}$, $P(\mathcal{S},\mathcal{S}) < 1$. Therefore, $\mathcal{M}$ does not have a sink state. It is irreducible since for any states $\mathcal{S}$ and $\mathcal{S}'$ such that the "edit distance" between $\mathcal{S}$ and $\mathcal{S}'$ is k, the k-step transition probability from $\mathcal{S}$ to $\mathcal{S}'$, $P^k(\mathcal{S},\mathcal{S}') > 0$. Finally, to see that $\mathcal{M}$ is aperiodic, consider a state $\mathcal{S}$ such that $P(\mathcal{S},\mathcal{S}) > 0$. For this state, both $P^2(\mathcal{S},\mathcal{S})$ and $P^3(\mathcal{S},\mathcal{S})$ are non-zero. Therefore, state i is aperiodic. Since $\mathcal{M}$ is finite-state, irreducible and aperiodic, it is ergodic. □

Theorem 2 and Corollary 2 reduce the problem of computing the steady-state transaction failure probability to a counting problem. We instantiate this theorem for various network topologies to characterize their steady-state distribution and infer from it the steady-state failure probability in those topologies. For general graphs, we can use this theorem to bound the bankruptcy probability of a node.

THEOREM 3. *Let $\mathcal{M}(G,\Lambda)$ be an ergodic Markov chain induced by a symmetric transaction matrix Λ over nodes in G. Fix a vertex v. The steady-state probability that v goes bankrupt is at most $1/(d_v+1)$, where $d_v = \sum_{(v,u)\in E}(c_{uv}+c_{vu})$ is total credit capacity of all edges incident upon node v.*

PROOF. From Corollary 2, we know that $\mathcal{M}(G,\Lambda)$ has a uniform steady-state distribution over the cycle-reachable equivalence classes of G. So the steady-state probability that v goes bankrupt is simply the fraction of equivalence classes in which v is bankrupt.

We know that the total number of cycle-reachable equivalence classes of G is the number of subforests over all n nodes, whereas the number of equivalence classes in which v is bankrupt is equal to the number of subforests on the remaining $n-1$ nodes [11]. Let $F(G)$ be the total number of subforests of G and $F(G_{-v})$ be the number of subforests on nodes other than v. An edge $e = (u,v)$ having total credit capacity c_e can be viewed as c_e labeled edges each of unit capacity. So, each subforest on the remaining $n-1$ nodes can be extended to a subforest on all n nodes by adding one of the d_v edges incident on v or adding v without adding any edges. Therefore $F(G) \geq (d_v+1)F(G_{-v})$. Thus, the steady-state probability that v goes bankrupt, $F(G_{-v})/F(G)$, is at most $1/(d_v+1)$. □

Therefore, if h_G is the harmonic mean of the d_vs in G, then the average node bankruptcy probability in G is $\Theta(1/h_G)$.

3.2.1 Trees

The above results allow us to make the following observations about the steady-state distribution over trees. We denote by $T_{n;c}$ a tree with n nodes whose each edge has total credit capacity c.

THEOREM 4. *If $\mathcal{M}(T_{n;c},\Lambda)$ is an ergodic Markov chain induced by a symmetric transaction rate matrix Λ on a tree $T_{n;c}$, then $\mathcal{M}(T_{n;c},\Lambda)$ has a uniform steady-state distribution over its states.*

PROOF. The result follows directly from Corollary 2 and the fact that, since trees have no cycles, each equivalence class in $\mathcal{C}$ is a singleton. □

Since $\mathcal{M}(T_{n;c},\Lambda)$ has a uniform steady-state distribution over its states, the steady-state probability that a transaction over a path of length l will succeed is $[c/(c+1)]^l$; this follows from the fact that each edge along the path should have non-zero capacity in the direction of the transaction. Therefore, the steady-state success probability, $\mathbb{P}_s$, for $T_{n;c}$ is given by

$$\mathbb{P}_s(T_{n;c}) = \mathbb{E}_l\left(\frac{c}{c+1}\right)^l$$

Using this expression for the steady-state success probability, we can show that if Λ is uniform (i.e. $\lambda_{st} = 1/n(n-1)$ for all s,t), the steady-state success probability for tree networks has a lower bound of $\Theta(c/n^2)$ and an upper bound of $\Theta(c/(c+1))$. The lower bound is attained for line networks and the upper bound for star networks.

3.2.2 Cycles

Next we derive the steady-state success probability for cycle graphs. Let $G^\circ_{n;c}$ be a cycle graph of $n > 2$ nodes where each edge has a total credit capacity of c. Let $\mathcal{M}(G^\circ_{n;c},\Lambda)$ be an ergodic Markov chain induced by a symmetric transaction matrix Λ. Then $\mathcal{M}(G^\circ_{n;c},\Lambda)$ will have a uniform steady-state distribution over the cycle-reachable equivalence classes of $G^\circ_{n;c}$. We use this fact to show the following result:

THEOREM 5. *If $\mathcal{M}(G^\circ_{n;c},\Lambda)$ is an ergodic Markov chain induced by a symmetric transaction matrix Λ over nodes in $G^\circ_{n;c}$, then the steady-state transaction success probability, $\mathbb{P}_s(G^\circ_{n;c})$, is given by*

$$\mathbb{P}_s(G^\circ_{n;c}) = \mathbb{E}_l\frac{r^l + r^{n-l} - 2r^n}{1-r^n}$$

where $r = c/(c+1)$ and l is the number of edges between a pair of transacting nodes.

The proof involves counting the total number of equivalence classes of $G^\circ_{n;c}$ and the number of classes which allow a transaction between a pair of nodes that have l edges between them. See Appendix A for the proof.

3.2.3 Complete Graphs

Let $K_{n;c}$ be a complete graph over n nodes such that each edge has total capacity c. From Theorem 3, we know that the bankruptcy probability of a node in $K_{n;c}$ is $\Theta(1/nc)$. Next we will show that the steady-state transaction failure probability between two nodes in $K_{n;c}$ is also $\Theta(1/nc)$. Note that a node being bankrupt is a sufficient but not necessary condition for a transaction with that node as the payer to fail.

THEOREM 6. *Let $\mathcal{M}(K_{n;c},\Lambda)$ be an ergodic Markov chain induced by a symmetric transaction matrix Λ over nodes in $K_{n;c}$. Then the steady-state transaction failure probability in $K_{n;c}$ is $\Theta(1/nc)$.*

See Appendix B for the proof. We will compare this probability with that in an equivalent centralized model to show that liquidity in credit networks with this topology is comparable to the centralized system.

3.2.4 Erdös-Rényi Networks

Here we prove that under a symmetric transaction regime, the steady-state probability that a node in a Erdös-Rényi network, $G_c(n,p)$, will go bankrupt is $\Theta(1/(npc))$. Note that $G_c(n,p)$ is a random graph over n nodes where every edge is present with probability p and has capacity c if present.

THEOREM 7. *Consider a $G_c(n,p)$ graph where $p > 8(\ln cn)/n$ (just slightly more than the connectivity threshold of $2\ln n/n$). Let $\mathcal{M}(G_c(n,p),\Lambda)$ be an ergodic Markov chain induced by a symmetric transaction matrix Λ over nodes in $G_c(n,p)$. Fix a vertex v. The steady-state probability that v goes bankrupt is $\Theta(1/(npc))$.*

PROOF. From Theorem 3, we know that the bankruptcy probability of v is at most $1/(d_v+1)$. We need to show that in expectation this term is $\Theta(1/(npc))$. By Chernoff bounds, $\mathbb{P}[d_v \leq npc/2] \leq e^{-np/8} \leq e^{-\ln cn} = 1/(cn)$, which bounds $\mathbb{E}_G[1/(d_v+1)]$ as follows:

$$\mathbb{E}_G[1/(d_v+1)] \leq \mathbb{P}[d_v < npc/2]\cdot 1 + \mathbb{P}[d_v \geq npc/2]\frac{1}{npc/2}$$
$$\leq \frac{1}{cn} + \frac{2}{npc} = \Theta\left(\frac{1}{npc}\right)$$

□

We conjecture that the steady-state failure probability of transactions between nodes in a $G_c(n,p)$ network under a symmetric transaction regime is also $\Theta(1/(npc))$. This is based on heuristic calculations using the generating functions for complete graphs with pc instead of c, as well as on simulation results (see Section 4.2).

CONJECTURE 1. *Let $G_c(n,p)$ be a connected credit network (i.e. $p > \ln n/n$) and let $\mathcal{M}(G_c(n,p),\Lambda)$ be an ergodic Markov chain induced by a symmetric transaction matrix Λ over nodes in $G_c(n,p)$. Then, the steady-state transaction failure probability in $G_c(n,p)$ is $\Theta(1/npc)$.*

As with complete graphs, we will also compute this probability in an equivalent centralized model and argue that this conjecture, if true, would imply that the failure probability in $G_c(n,p)$ credit networks is within a constant factor of the equivalent centralized model.

3.2.5 Barabási-Albert Preferential Attachment Networks

We state a conjecture regarding the steady-state transaction failure probability in power-law graphs constructed using the Barabási-Albert preferential attachment model. The Barabási-Albert model is a evolving random graph model where each arriving node creates edges to existing nodes with probability proportional to their degrees. It is parameterized by the number of nodes in the network, n, and the number of edges d that each new node creates.

CONJECTURE 2. *Let $G_c^{BA}(n,d)$ be a random graph over n nodes created using the Barabási-Albert preferential attachment model where each arriving node creates d edges and each edge has total credit capacity c. Let $\mathcal{M}(G_c^{BA}(n,d),\Lambda)$ be an ergodic Markov chain induced by a symmetric transaction matrix Λ over nodes in $G_c^{BA}(n,d)$. Then, the steady-state transaction failure probability in $G_c^{BA}(n,d)$ is $\Theta(1/dc)$.*

Note that we conjecture the transaction failure probability to be independent of network size n. This conjecture is supported by simulation results (see Section 4).

3.3 Centralized Currency Infrastructure

Since we introduced credit networks as an alternative to a centralized currency infrastructure, a natural question arises: how does the steady-state failure probability in a credit network compare with that in a centralized infrastructure? Next we address this question.

As described previously, a centralized currency infrastructure can be modeled as a tree with a bank at its root and individuals as leaves. However, this setup is different from a star network in that the root does not participate in any transactions; all transactions occur between leaf nodes, i.e. along paths of length two. Let the centralized infrastructure be represented by a network $\mathcal{G}^*$ with a root node r representing the bank, and n leaf nodes representing individuals. Let $c_{ru} < \infty$ be the credit extended by bank r to node u. Note that since the bank issues a common currency a leaf node trusts the bank for an infinite sum of money, i.e. $c_{ur} = \infty$. A successful transaction of unit value leads to an increase by one of the payee's credit and a decrease by one of the payer's credit; the total credit extended to leaf nodes in the system stays constant. We can prove that if the total credit extended to leaf nodes is C, then the steady-state transaction failure probability in a centralized currency system is $(n-1)/(C+n-1)$.

THEOREM 8. *Let $\mathcal{M}(\mathcal{G}^*,\Lambda)$ be an ergodic Markov chain induced by a symmetric transaction matrix Λ over a centralized payment network $\mathcal{G}^*$ with n leaf nodes. Let C be the total credit extended to the leaf nodes. Then the steady-state transaction failure probability in $\mathcal{M}$ is $(n-1)/(C+n-1)$.*

PROOF. Since the number of leaf nodes is n and the total credit extended to leaf nodes is C, the Markov chain has $\binom{C+n-1}{n-1}$ states: this is the number of ways of distributing C objects among n people. In the centralized system, unlike credit networks, a transaction fails if and only if the payer in the transaction, say node u, is bankrupt, i.e. $c_{ru}=0$. Therefore, the transaction failure probability is equal to the probability that a node is bankrupt. The number of states in which a given node is bankrupt is given by $\binom{C+n-2}{n-2}$: this is the number of ways of distributing the total credit among the remaining $n-1$ leaf nodes. From Corollary 2, we know that $\mathcal{M}$ has a uniform steady-state distribution over its states. Therefore, the steady-state probability that a node is bankrupt is given by

$$\frac{\binom{C+n-2}{n-2}}{\binom{C+n-1}{n-1}} = \frac{n-1}{C+n-1}$$

□

So if $\bar{c}=C/n$ is the average credit extended to a node in $\mathcal{G}^*$, then the node bankruptcy probability of a node (as well as the transaction failure probability) is $\Theta(1/\bar{c})$. Note that since the Markov chain has a uniform distribution over states of the network, the steady-state transaction failure probability is independent of the initial state (i.e. the initial credit of each node in the network).

3.3.1 Equivalence between Credit Networks and Centralized Currency Infrastructure

In order to be able to compare liquidity in the two models, we need to define the notion of equivalence between the two models. Given a credit network $G=(V,E)$ with n nodes, we construct an equivalent centralized currency infrastructure $\mathcal{G}(G)$ as follows: $\mathcal{G}$ has nodes $V\cup\{r\}$ (where r is the root node) and a bidirectional edge between each node u and the root r. For each node u in G, the total credit extended to it by the bank in the centralized model, c_{ru}, is given by $c_{ru} = \sum_{v \in V} c_{vu}$ where c_{vu} is the initial credit extended by v to u before the nodes start transacting. And finally, for all nodes u, we set $c_{ur} = \infty$. This ensures that each node has access to the same amount of credit in both models.

3.3.2 Liquidity Comparison

The procedure to convert a credit network in to an equivalent centralized currency system allows us to compare liquidity in credit networks with that in an equivalent currency system. For the credit network topologies that we analyzed in Section 3.2, we state the steady-state failure probability for their equivalent centralized systems under a symmetric, ergodic transaction regime by invoking Theorem 8.

Cycle Graph.

For a cycle graph with n nodes where each edge has capacity c, the total capacity is nc. So, the steady-state failure probability in the equivalent centralized system is $(n-1)/(nc+n-1) = \Theta(1/c)$. On the other hand, in a uniform transaction regime, credit networks on cycle graphs have a steady-state failure probability of $1 - \Theta(c/n)$ (see Appendix A). However, for graphs with high expansion, the failure probability in credit networks is within a constant factor of that in equivalent centralized systems (see below).

Complete Graph.

For a complete graph on n nodes where the total credit capacity between any pair of nodes is c, the total credit capacity in the system is Nc, where $N = \binom{n}{2}$. So, the steady-state failure probability in the equivalent centralized system is $(n-1)/(Nc+n-1) = \Theta(1/nc)$, the same as that in the original credit network (Theorem 6).

Erdös-Rényi Graph.

For an Erdös-Rényi network, $G_c(n,p)$, the expected total credit capacity in the network is Npc, where $N = \binom{n}{2}$. Therefore, the steady-state failure probability in the equivalent centralized system is $(n-1)/(Npc+n-1) = \Theta(1/npc)$. Thus, if Conjecture 1 is true, the failure probability in $G_c(n,p)$ credit networks would be within a constant factor of that in the equivalent centralized system.

Barabási-Albert Graph.

For a Barabási-Albert preferential attachment network, $G_c^{BA}(n,d)$, the total credit capacity in the network is ndc (i.e. nd edges each having total credit c). Therefore, the steady-state failure probability in the equivalent centralized system is $(n-1)/(ndc+n-1) = \Theta(1/dc)$. Like Erdös-Rényi networks, if the conjecture about steady-state failure probability for $G_c^{BA}(n,d)$ credit networks (Conjecture 2) is true, then, credit networks with this topology too will have a steady-state failure probability within a constant factor of that in an equivalent centralized system.

4. SIMULATIONS

Next we present the results of simulating repeated transactions on credit networks from two well-studied families of random graphs: $G_c(n,p)$ (this is a Erdös-Rényi random graph with edge orientation chosen randomly and each edge assigned capacity c) and power-law graphs generated using the Barabási-Albert preferential attachment (BA) model [2]. The Barabási-Albert model is a evolving random graph model where each new node creates d edges to existing nodes with probability proportional to their degrees. After constructing the graph, we assigned edge orientations randomly and set the capacity of each edge to c. The goal of the simulations was to understand how the steady-state success probability in these networks depends on key network parameters and to determine what values of network parameters yield a "high enough" success probability. In this sense, the qualitative results obtained from running simulations complement the asymptotic analysis described in the previous section. For $G_c(n,p)$ the parameters of interest are n, p and c. However, since varying either n or p changes the density of the graph (i.e. average node degree), we also ran simulations where we changed both n and p such that np was held constant. For BA graphs, the parameters of interest are the number of nodes (n), the number of edges each node creates (d), and credit capacity (c) of each edge.

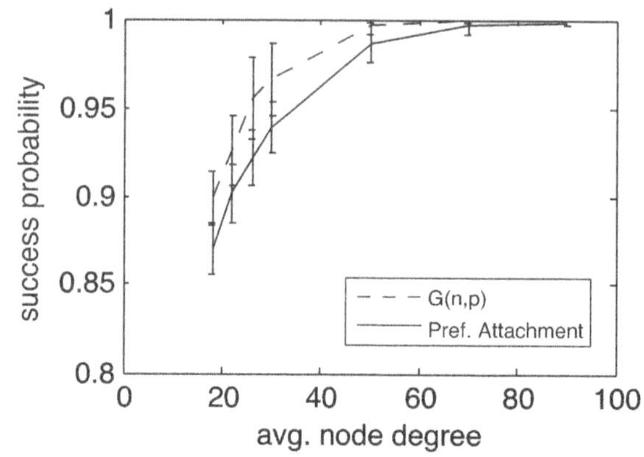

Figure 2: Effect of varying graph density (average node degree) on the steady-state success probability in $G_c(n,p)$ and $G_c^{BA}(n,d)$ graphs with n = 200 and c = 1.

A simulation run consisted of constructing a network with a given set of parameters and doing repeated transactions on it. At each time step, we chose a node pair (s,t) with uniform probability and tried to route a unit payment from s to t via the shortest feasible path. If there was a path from s to t, we routed the payment and modified edge capacities along the path. Otherwise, we counted the transaction as a failure. We repeated this until the success-rate (i.e fraction of transactions that succeed) in two consecutive time windows was within ε of each other. We used a window size of 1000 time steps and $\varepsilon = 0.002$. When the process converged, we measured the success rate at convergence, i.e. the total number of successful transactions divided by the total number of time steps. We called this the steady-state success probability for that set of network parameters. For each combination of network parameter values, we ran simulations on 100 graphs constructed from the same distribution and computed the average and the standard deviation in success-rate over the 100 runs. In order to understand how the success probability depends upon various network parameters, we repeated the set of 100 runs for different values of one of the parameters, keeping the rest constant.

4.1 Effect of Variation in Network Density

In order to study the effect of density, we fixed $n = 200$ and $c = 1$ for both graph families. For $G_c(n,p)$ we varied p from 0.18 to 0.45 and for BA graphs we varied d from 18 to 45. The average node degree of PA graphs is equal to $2d$ whereas for $G_c(n,p)$ the expected node degree is given by $(n-1)p$. We picked d corresponding to each p such that $2d \approx (n-1)p$ so that we can compare the plots for the two graph families.

Figure 2 shows the success probability as a function of average node degree for $G_c(n,p)$ and BA graphs when np is sufficiently

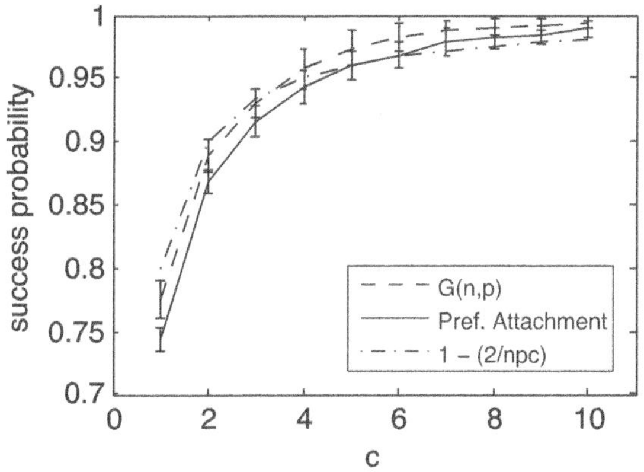

Figure 3: Effect of varying credit capacity on the steady-state success probability in $G_c(n,p)$ and $G_c^{BA}(n,d)$ graphs with n = 100 and avg. node degree = 10.

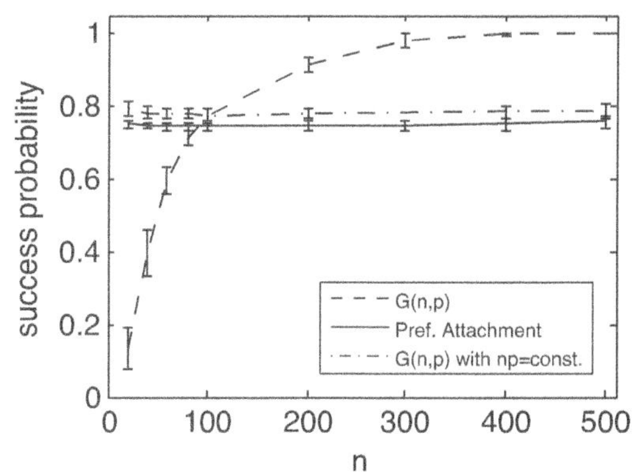

Figure 4: Effect of varying network size (number of nodes) on the steady-state success probability in $G_c(n,p)$ and $G_c^{BA}(n,d)$ graphs with c = 1 and avg. node degree = 10.

larger than $\ln n$ so that the $G_c(n,p)$ graph is connected. The success rate for both graph families is concave, non-decreasing in p. Note that for networks of 200 nodes with edge capacity of 1 and an average node degree as low as 25, the success probability for both topologies is in excess of 0.9. Moreover, the success probability quickly reaches a point of diminishing returns where making the network denser does not help significantly. This is useful since it means that, in practice, the network does not need to be very dense in order to route payments with a sufficiently high probability.

4.2 Effect of Variation in Credit Capacity

In order to study the effect of varying credit capacity in the network, we fixed $n = 100$ for both graphs. We set $p = 0.10$ for $G_c(n,p)$ and $d = 5$ for BA graphs, thereby ensuring that their densities were equal. This choice of p and d also ensured that all the graphs we constructed were connected. We varied c from 1 to 10. Figure 3 shows the mean and standard deviation in the steady-state success-rate for both graph families as we vary c. In addition to the two plots, we also plot $1 - (2/npc)$ as a function of c. That plot tracks those for $G_c(n,p)$ as well as for BA fairly closely and is further evidence in support of our conjecture that the steady-state failure probability in $G_c(n,p)$ graphs is $\Theta(1/npc)$ and in $G_c^{BA}(n,d)$ is $\Theta(1/dc)$ and consequently, credit networks with these topologies are within a constant-factor of the equivalent centralized currency system in terms of liquidity.

4.3 Effect of Variation in Network Size

In order to study the effect of varying network size for BA graphs, we fixed $d = 5$ and $c = 1$ and varied n from 20 to 500. However, the same approach does not work for $G_c(n,p)$ graphs since if we fix p and c and varied n, it would also vary the average node degree. So, we ran two sets of simulations for $G_c(n,p)$ graphs: one where we varied n keeping $p = 0.10$ and $c = 1$ and the other where we fixed $c = 1$ and varied both n and p such that np was kept constant at 10.

Figure 4 shows the effect of varying network size on the success probability of both graph families. The noteworthy observation is that if the density of the network is kept constant, then network size has no effect on the success rate for either graph family; the success rate remains nearly constant at about 0.75 for BA graphs and about 0.78 for $G_c(n,p)$ graphs. The same pattern is also observed if np is held constant at 20 instead of 10 (so it is not an artifact of that specific value of np). This is another observation in support of our conjecture about the steady-state failure probability in $G_c(n,p)$ and BA graphs. If, however, np is not held constant, then success probability is again a concave non-decreasing function of n (much the same way as it is of p).

5. CONCLUSION & OPEN PROBLEMS

In this paper we generalized the credit network model by allowing every node to print its own currency, and formulated and studied the question of long-term liquidity in this network under a simple model of repeated transactions. Using the notion of cycle-reachability, we showed that routing payments in credit networks has a *path-independence* property. We also showed that the Markov chain induced by a symmetric transaction regime has a uniform steady-state distribution over the cycle-reachable equivalence classes. We used this fact to derive the node bankruptcy probability in general graphs and the transaction failure probability in a number of network topologies and show that liquidity in those credit networks is comparable to that in equivalent centralized currency systems.

Our results can be extended in a number of ways. One question that arises from our analysis is whether credit network topologies with a high expansion have liquidity that is comparable with equivalent centralized systems. We also leave unanswered the question of mixing times of the Markov chain: our simulations on $G_c(n,p)$ and BA graphs converged relatively quickly but we do not have analytical results on the mixing time of the Markov chain and how it depends on credit capacity and network topology. In this work, we assume that nodes in the network are not strategic. Can we endow the nodes with a model of rationality that will govern how much credit they extend each other and how that changes over time, as a function of transaction rates, success probabilities, network topology, etc.? Another broad direction is the application of this model in various practical settings, some of which we mention in the introduction. Of particular interest are analytical results as well as empirical or simulation-based studies that evaluate the effectiveness of this model in settings such as IP routing, peer-to-peer systems, viral marketing, etc. compared to existing models.

6. REFERENCES

[1] C. Aperjis and R. Johari. A Peer-to-Peer System as an Exchange Economy. In *Proceedings of the 2006 Workshop on Game theory for Communications and Networks*, GameNets '06, New York, NY, USA, 2006. ACM.

[2] A. L. Barabasi and R. Albert. Emergence of Scaling in Random Networks. *Science*, 286(5439):509–512, 1999.

[3] D. B. DeFigueiredo and E. T. Barr. Trustdavis: A non-exploitable online reputation system. In *CEC '05: Proceedings of the 7th IEEE International Conference on E-Commerce Technology*, pages 274–283, Washington, DC, USA, 2005.

[4] A. Ghosh, M. Mahdian, D. M. Reeves, D. M. Pennock, and R. Fugger. Mechanism Design on Trust Networks. In *WINE '07: Proceedings of the 3rd international workshop on Internet and Network Economics*, pages 257–268, 2007.

[5] E. Gioan. Enumerating Degree Sequences in Digraphs and a Cycle-cocycle Reversing System. *European Journal of Combinatorics*, 28(4):1351–1366, 2007.

[6] R. Guha, R. Kumar, P. Raghavan, and A. Tomkins. Propagation of Trust and Distrust. In *WWW '04: Proceedings of the 13th International Conference on World Wide Web*, pages 403–412, New York, NY, USA, 2004. ACM.

[7] Z. Gyöngyi, H. Garcia-Molina, and J. Pedersen. Combating web spam with trustrank. In *VLDB '04: Proceedings of the 30th International Conference on Very Large Databases*, pages 576–587. ACM, 2004.

[8] M. O. Jackson, T. Rodríguez Barraquer, and X. Tan. Social Capital and Social Quilts: Network Patterns of Favor Exchange. *SSRN eLibrary*, 2010.

[9] D. Karlan, M. Mobius, T. Rosenblat, and A. Szeidl. Trust and Social Collateral. *Quarterly Journal of Economics*, 124(3):1307–1361, August 2009.

[10] I. A. Kash, E. J. Friedman, and J. Y. Halpern. Optimizing Scrip Systems: Efficiency, Crashes, Hoarders, and Altruists. In *EC '07: Proceedings of the 8th ACM Conference on Electronic Commerce*, pages 305–315, 2007.

[11] D. J. Kleitman and K. J. Winston. Forests and Score Vectors. *Combinatorica*, 1(1):49–54, 1981.

[12] J. Leskovec, D. P. Huttenlocher, and J. M. Kleinberg. Signed Networks in Social Media. In *CHI '10: Proceedings of the 28th International Conference on Human Factors in Computing Systems*, pages 1361–1370. ACM, 2010.

[13] Z. Liu, H. Hu, Y. Liu, K. W. Ross, Y. Wang, and M. Mobius. P2P Trading in Social Networks: The Value of Staying Connected. In *IEEE INFOCOMM '10: Proceedings of the 29th IEEE International Conference on Computer Communications*, pages 1–9, March 2010.

[14] A. Mislove, A. Post, K. P. Gummadi, and P. Druschel. Ostra: Leverging Trust to Thwart Unwanted Communication. In *Proceedings of the 5th Symposium on Networked Systems Design and Implementation (NSDI'08)*, April 2008.

[15] L. Page, S. Brin, R. Motwani, and T. Winograd. The PageRank Citation Ranking: Bringing Order to the Web. Technical report, Stanford InfoLab, 1999.

[16] D. M. Reeves, B. M. Soule, and T. Kasturi. Yootopia! Technical report, Yahoo! Research, 2007.

[17] P. Resnick and R. Sami. Sybilproof Transitive Trust Protocols. In *EC '09: Proceedings of the 10th ACM Conference on Electronic Commerce*, pages 345–354, 2009.

[18] V. Vishnumurthy, S. Chandrakumar, and E. Sirer. KARMA: A Secure Economic Framework for Peer-to-Peer Resource Sharing. In *Workshop on the Economics of Peer-to-Peer Systems*, 2003.

7. ACKNOWLEDGEMENTS

This research was supported in part by NSF award IIS-0904325. Part of the research was sponsored by the Army Research Laboratory and was accomplished under Cooperative Agreement Number W911NF-09-2-0053. The views and conclusions contained in this document are those of the authors and should not be interpreted as representing the official policies, either expressed or implied, of the Army Research Laboratory or the U.S. Government. The U.S. Government is authorized to reproduce and distribute reprints for Government purposes notwithstanding any copyright notation here on.

APPENDIX

A. SUCCESS PROBABILITY IN CYCLES

PROOF OF THEOREM 5. Since $\mathcal{M}$ has a uniform steady-state distribution over the cycle-reachable equivalence classes, the steady-state success probability between a pair of nodes separated by l edges in $G^{\circ}_{m;c}$ is simply the fraction equivalence classes which allow a transaction between that pair of nodes.

Note that each equivalence class can be characterized by a state in which at least one edge in $G^{\circ}_{c,m}$ has zero capacity in the counterclockwise direction (any state where all edges are bidirectional is cycle-reachable from one where at least one edge is unidirectional). Assume that the nodes are numbered $1, \ldots, m$ and the edge between nodes j and $j+1$ is numbered j. Let the jth edge be the first edge that has zero capacity in the counterclockwise direction. Then the first $j-1$ edges can each be in one of c states, and the remaining $m-j$ edges can each be in one of $c+1$ states. Thus, the total number of states where one or more edges have zero capacity in the counterclockwise direction is given by:

$$\sum_{j=1}^{m} c^{j-1}(c+1)^{m-j} = (c+1)^{m-1}\sum_{j=1}^{m}\left(\frac{c}{c+1}\right)^{j-1} = (c+1)^{m-1}\frac{1-r^m}{1-r}$$

where $r = c/(c+1)$. Now fix nodes s and t that are a distance l apart in the clockwise direction from s to t. Lets call the path of length l between s and t, $\mathcal{P}_1$, and that of length $m-l$, $\mathcal{P}_2$. A successful transaction between s and t along $\mathcal{P}_1$ requires edges in $\mathcal{P}_1$ to have capacity in the counterclockwise direction, whereas that along $\mathcal{P}_2$ requires edges in $\mathcal{P}_2$ to have capacity in the clockwise direction. If the jth edge lies in $\mathcal{P}_1$ then there is no path of length l between s and t. On the other hand, a path of length $m-l$ between s and t requires each of the $m-l$ edges to be in one of c states. Thus, the number of equivalence classes that only have a path of length $m-l$ between s and t is

$$\sum_{j=1}^{l} c^{j-1}(c+1)^{l-j}c^{m-l} = (c+1)^{l-1}c^{m-l}\sum_{j=1}^{l}\left(\frac{c}{c+1}\right)^{j-1} = c^{m-l}(c+1)^{l-1}\frac{1-r^l}{1-r}$$

where $r = c/(c+1)$. However, if the jth edge is in $\mathcal{P}_2$, it implies that all edges in $\mathcal{P}_1$ have positive capacity in the counterclockwise direction. Thus, the number of equivalence classes that have a path of length l between s and t is

$$\sum_{j=l+1}^{m} c^{j-1}(c+1)^{m-j} = c^l(c+1)^{m-l-1}\sum_{j=1}^{m-l}\left(\frac{c}{c+1}\right)^{j-1} = c^l(c+1)^{m-l-1}\frac{1-r^{m-l}}{1-r}$$

Note that the above equation includes equivalence classes that have capacity along both $\mathcal{P}_1$ and $\mathcal{P}_2$ as well as those that have capacity along only $\mathcal{P}_1$.

Thus, the probability that a transaction between nodes separated by l edges will succeed is given by

$$\frac{c^l(c+1)^{m-l-1}(1-r^{m-l})+c^{m-l}(c+1)^{l-1}(1-r^l)}{(c+1)^{m-1}(1-r^m)}$$
$$=\frac{r^l(1-r^{m-l})+r^{m-l}(1-r^l)}{1-r^m}=\frac{r^l+r^{m-l}-2r^m}{1-r^m}$$

Taking expectation over the length l of the transaction path gives the result. □

As a corollary, we can show that the steady-state success probability in cycle graphs under a uniform transaction regime is $\Theta(c/n)$.

COROLLARY 3. *Let $G^\circ_{n;c}$ be a cycle graph of $n > 2$ nodes where each edge has a total credit capacity of c. If $\mathcal{M}(G^\circ_{n;c}, \Lambda)$ is an ergodic Markov chain induced by a uniform transaction matrix Λ over nodes in $G^\circ_{n;c}$, then the steady-state transaction success probability, $\mathbb{P}_s(G^\circ_{n;c})$, is $\Theta(c/n)$.*

PROOF. $\mathbb{P}_s(G^\circ_{n;c})$ under a symmetric transaction regime is given by

$$\mathbb{P}_s(G^\circ)=\mathbb{E}_l\frac{r^l+r^{n-l}-2r^n}{1-r^n}\ (\text{where } r=c/(c+1))$$

Therefore, under a uniform transaction regime, as $n\to\infty$

$$\lim_{n\to\infty}\mathbb{P}_s(G^\circ)\le\lim_{n\to\infty}\sum_{l=1}^{n/2}\frac{2n}{n(n-1)}\frac{r^l+r^{n-l}-2r^n}{1-r^n}$$
$$\le\lim_{n\to\infty}\frac{2}{(n-1)(1-r^n)}\sum_{l=1}^{n/2}\left(r^l+r^{n-l}\right)$$
$$=\lim_{n\to\infty}\frac{2}{(n-1)(1-r^n)}\left(\frac{r(1-r^{n/2})+r^{n/2}(1-r^{n/2})}{1-r}\right)$$
$$=\frac{2r}{(n-1)(1-r)}=\Theta(c/n)$$

□

B. FAILURE PROBABILITY IN COMPLETE GRAPHS

PROOF OF THEOREM 6. We know that there is a bijection between equivalence classes of a graph and labeled forests [5, 11], and the number of forests, $a_{n,c}$, in $K_{n;c}$ converges to [11]

$$a_{n,c}\sim e^{1/2c}c^{n-1}n^{n-2} \tag{1}$$

where $f_n\sim g_n$ means $\lim_{n\to\infty}f_n/g_n=1$. By Cayley's formula there are n^{n-2} trees on n labeled nodes, so $a_{n,1}\ge n^{n-2}$. Any forest has at most $n-1$ edges, so with c labeled copies of each edge $c^{n-1}n^{n-2}\le a_{n,c}\le c^{n-1}a_{n,1}$. Equation (1) implies that there exists a constant n_0 such that for all $n\ge n_0$, $a_{n,1}\le 2e^{1/2}n^{n-2}$. Combining these equations, for all $n\ge n_0$,

$$c^{n-1}n^{n-2}\le a_{n,c}\le 2e^{1/2}c^{n-1}n^{n-2}$$

Fix two nodes u and v in $K_{n;c}$, and consider a cut between u and v such that the partition containing u has k nodes and that containing v has $n-k$ nodes. Assume that no payment can be made from u's partition to v's partition. Then, the number of equivalence classes containing this cut is at most $a_{k,c}a_{n-k,c}$. Summing over all cuts separating u and v in $K_{n;c}$, we upper bound the transaction failure probability between nodes u and v as

$$\frac{1}{a_{n,c}}\sum_{k=1}^{n-1}\binom{n-2}{k-1}a_{k,c}a_{n-k,c}=$$
$$2\sum_{k=1}^{n_0-1}\binom{n-2}{k-1}\frac{a_{k,c}a_{n-k,c}}{a_{n,c}}+\sum_{k=n_0}^{n-n_0}\binom{n-2}{k-1}\frac{a_{k,c}a_{n-k,c}}{a_{n,c}}$$

Bounding the first term,

$$\sum_{k=1}^{n_0-1}\binom{n-2}{k-1}\frac{a_{k,c}a_{n-k,c}}{a_{n,c}}$$
$$=O\left(\sum_{k=1}^{n_0-1}\frac{n^{k-1}}{(k-1)!}\frac{(c^{k-1}a_{k,1})(c^{n-k-1}(n-k)^{n-k-2})}{c^{n-1}n^{n-2}}\right)$$
$$=O\left(\frac{1}{nc}\sum_{k=1}^{n_0-1}\frac{a_{k,1}}{(k-1)!}\left(\frac{n-k}{n}\right)^{n-k-2}\right)=O\left(\frac{1}{nc}\right)$$

using that $a_{k,1}=O(1)$ when $k\le n_0$. For the second term,

$$\sum_{k=n_0}^{n-n_0}\binom{n-2}{k-1}\frac{a_{k,c}a_{n-k,c}}{a_{n,c}}$$
$$=O\left(\sum_{k=n_0}^{n-n_0}\binom{n-2}{k-1}\frac{(c^{k-1}k^{k-2})(c^{n-k-1}(n-k)^{n-k-2})}{c^{n-1}n^{n-2}}\right)$$
$$=O\left(\frac{1}{nc}\sum_{k=n_0}^{n-n_0}\binom{n-2}{k-1}\frac{k^{k-2}(n-k)^{n-k-2}}{n^{n-3}}\right)$$
$$=O\left(\frac{1}{nc}\sum_{k=1}^{n-1}\frac{n!}{n(n-1)}\frac{k(n-k)}{k!(n-k)!}\frac{k^k(n-k)^{n-k}}{n^n}\frac{n^3}{k^2(n-k)^2}\right)$$
$$=O\left(\frac{1}{nc}\sum_{k=1}^{n-1}\frac{n}{(n-k)k}\frac{n!}{n^n}\frac{k^k}{k!}\frac{(n-k)^{n-k}}{(n-k)!}\right) \tag{2}$$

Instead of using the standard Stirling's approximation, we will use the more precise *Stirling Series*:

$$n!=\sqrt{2\pi n}\left(\frac{n}{e}\right)^n\left(1+\frac{1}{12n}+\frac{1}{288n^2}-\frac{139}{51840n^3}\pm\cdots\right)$$

Therefore, $n!$ can be written as

$$n!=\sqrt{2\pi n}\left(\frac{n}{e}\right)^n c_n,\ \text{where } 1\le c_n\le 2 \text{ when } n\ge 1$$

Substituting this into (2) and simplifying, we get

$$\frac{1}{nc}\sum_{k=1}^{n-1}\frac{n}{(n-k)k}\frac{n!}{n^n}\frac{k^k}{k!}\frac{(n-k)^{n-k}}{(n-k)!}=O\left(\frac{1}{nc}\sum_{k=1}^{n-1}\left(\frac{n}{(n-k)k}\right)^{3/2}\right)$$

Either k or $n-k$ is at least $n/2$, so

$$\sum_{k=1}^{n-1}\left(\frac{n}{(n-k)k}\right)^{3/2}\le 2\sum_{k=1}^{(n-1)/2}\left(\frac{2}{k}\right)^{3/2}=O(1)$$

Summarizing,

$$\frac{1}{a_{n,c}}\sum_{k=1}^{n-1}\binom{n-2}{k-1}a_{k,c}a_{n-k,c}=O\left(\frac{1}{nc}\right)$$

Also, since the node bankruptcy probability in $K_{n;c}$ is $\Theta(1/nc)$, the transaction failure probability is $\Omega(1/nc)$. This completes the proof. □

The Role of Social Networks in Online Shopping: Information Passing, Price of Trust, and Consumer Choice

Stephen Guo
Stanford University
Stanford, CA, USA
sdguo@cs.stanford.edu

Mengqiu Wang
Stanford University
Stanford, CA, USA
mengqiu@cs.stanford.edu

Jure Leskovec
Stanford University
Stanford, CA, USA
jure@cs.stanford.edu

ABSTRACT

While social interactions are critical to understanding consumer behavior, the relationship between social and commerce networks has not been explored on a large scale. We analyze Taobao, a Chinese consumer marketplace that is the world's largest e-commerce website. What sets Taobao apart from its competitors is its integrated instant messaging tool, which buyers can use to ask sellers about products or ask other buyers for advice. In our study, we focus on how an individual's commercial transactions are embedded in their social graphs. By studying triads and the directed closure process, we quantify the presence of information passing and gain insights into when different types of links form in the network.

Using seller ratings and review information, we then quantify a price of trust. How much will a consumer pay for transaction with a trusted seller? We conclude by modeling this consumer choice problem: if a buyer wishes to purchase a particular product, how does (s)he decide which store to purchase it from? By analyzing the performance of various feature sets in an information retrieval setting, we demonstrate how the social graph factors into understanding consumer behavior.

Categories and Subject Descriptors: H.2.8 Database Management: Database Applications – Data mining

General Terms: Measurement; Experimentation.

Keywords: E-Commerce, Viral Marketing, Recommender Systems, Triadic Closure, Price of Trust.

1. INTRODUCTION

Use of personal social networks to gather information is fundamental to purchasing behavior [6]. It is something so common in our daily routine that we usually do not even make a note of it. When we make a purchase from a retail store, we often speak beforehand to the shopkeeper about suitable products. When we need to purchase something we are unfamiliar with, we consult our friends and family for advice. When we purchase a popular new product, we have an urge to tell everyone we know about it.

Although personal social networks are implicit in the offline shopping experience, their introduction to the online world is a relatively new phenomenon. E-commerce websites, such as Amazon, eBay and Epinions, have successfully integrated product reviews, recommendations, search and product comparison, but they have been much slower at adopting social networking features as a part of customer experience. Recommendation engines and product comparison sites help consumers discover new products and receive more accurate evaluations, however they cannot completely substitute for the personalized recommendations and information that one receives from a friend or relative. Basic behavioral psychology drives consumers to value and trust their friends' purchasing decisions more than anonymous opinions. For example, a Lucid Marketing survey found that 68% of individuals consulted friends and relatives before purchasing home electronics [3].

Understanding how social networks are used and how they shape purchasing decisions is one of the fundamental interests of e-commerce. Only recently have social networks been used in e-commerce applications to some success. For example, group purchasing companies such as Groupon and LivingSocial allow consumers to come together to buy products in bulk and save money, while social shopping sites such as Kaboodle provide consumers the ability to share shopping lists with each other. The use of social networks in online shopping provides marketers and businesses with new revenue opportunities, while providing consumers with product information and both economic and social rewards for sharing [11].

Present work. When discussing the relationship between electronic commerce and social networks, various questions come to mind. How do friends influence consumer purchasing decisions and product adoption? What factors influence the success of word-of-mouth product recommendations? How does social influence and reputation affect commercial activity? In this paper, we will address these questions through a detailed study of the world's largest e-commerce website Taobao.

The fundamental process we focus upon throughout this study is what we term *information passing*: an individual purchases a product, then messages a friend, what is the likelihood that the friend will then purchase the product? Where will he purchase it from? Understanding the flow of social influence in commerce networks is an important question. For example, information passing provides insight into how companies can structure online viral marketing campaigns to target consumers. It can also be used to optimize algorithms within product recommendation engines. However important information passing is to electronic commerce, it still has not been well studied on a large scale due to the inaccessibility of suitable data.

To facilitate our research, we obtained a dataset describing the behavior of one million users in the world's largest e-commerce network Taobao. Taobao connects buyers and sellers, and provides an integrated instant messaging platform for communication

EC'11, June 5-9, 2011, San Jose, California, USA.

among all its users. By modeling Taobao as a network of three types of edges (trades, messages, contacts), we are able to directly study how social communication and commercial transactions are interrelated in an online setting. Our study provides insights into three main aspects of the social-commercial relationship: information passing, the price of trust, and consumer choice prediction.

We begin our study of social commerce by quantifying the presence of information passing through analysis of triadic closure processes. We show that the influence of information passing is directly proportional to message strength, and is inversely proportional to product price, as well as the time between the purchase and the recommendation. Additionally, we explain how information passing varies greatly between different product categories. We then investigate the general edge formation process in the context of directed triadic closure, and demonstrate that the formation of triad-closing message and trade edges is highly dependent upon user roles (buyer or seller). Our results indicate that information passing via buyer-buyer communication is one of the primary drivers of purchasing.

A subtle point regarding information passing is that the spread of product recommendations, through word-of-mouth, inherently relies upon a notion of buyer-buyer *trust*. Trust, from the perspective of social psychology, can be defined as perceived credibility or benevolence to the target [7]. In the context of electronic marketplaces, buyer-seller trust, most directly encapsulated by seller reputations and ratings, are the natural concept to study. A fundamental idea behind the nature of trust is its price. How much extra will a buyer pay for transaction security with a highly-rated seller? Although an intuitive idea, initial studies did not find evidence for a price of trust [25], and only recently has a price of trust been established in small, controlled, and single product settings [26, 13, 23]. In our study, we analyze transaction information across over 10,000 products. Using the overall customer satisfaction (i.e., average rating) of the seller, we observe a small but super-linear effect of the seller rating upon the price premium they can charge and still engage in transactions.

To further study the relationship between social networks and consumer behavior, we then consider the question, "How does an online consumer decide upon a seller to purchase from when there are many sellers offering the same product?" We model this question of *consumer choice* through a machine learning task and predict which particular seller a buyer will purchase from, given that the sellers all offer the same relevant product. Utilizing primarily social networking features, we construct a model that can predict, for the case of a buyer choosing from among 10 possible sellers, the correct seller 42% of the time, approximately 4 times better than baseline. We also contrast a variety of feature sets (both graph-based and product/seller metadata), and demonstrate that the social graph is the most important feature in predicting consumer choice. In particular, the social graph is a far better determinant of consumer behavior than metadata features such as seller reputation or product price. Our results nicely connect to Granovetter's work, which argues that economic transactions are embedded in dynamic social networks, and that an individual's social graph dictates how they choose sellers to transact with [10].

Further Related Work. For all of the importance of social networks in consumer shopping, though, their use in electronic commerce still is not well understood. Previous research examined the use of social networks in e-commerce, but has mostly focused upon one aspect of the use of social networks, such as product recommendations [12, 17, 2], product recommendation engines [29, 28], or have been based upon a limited set of data [4, 15].

Network	Nodes	Edges	Avg Deg	Avg CCF
Contact	663,346	3,208,043	9.67	0.0135
Message	750,158	3,908,339	5.21	0.0194
Trade	1,000,000	1,337,497	1.34	0.0086

Table 1: Dataset statistics.

The electronic marketplace eBay is perhaps the most well studied e-commerce website. Various aspects of eBay including auction efficiency [14], product recommendations [31], seller strategies [8], and summarization [22], have been studied. Closely related to our work on consumer choice prediction, Wu and Bolivar created a model to predict item purchase probability [30]. The primary difference here is that we utilize the social networks of the buyers and sellers, along with product and user metadata, to perform consumer choice prediction, whereas they consider only seller and product information.

Our study of information passing and triadic closure builds upon classical works by Rapoport [24] and Granovetter [9]. Triadic closure has been explored in various settings: community growth [1], link prediction [21], signed networks [19], and social [18] and information [27] network evolution. In contrast, we demonstrate the existence of implicit recommendation behavior in a network not specifically designed for information passing.

The paper proceeds as follows. In section 2, we describe the Taobao dataset. In section 3, we analyze dyadic relationships in the network. In section 4, we provide a detailed analysis of information passing and directed triadic closure processes. In section 5, we quantify a price for trust. And last, in section 6, we model the consumer choice prediction problem.

2. TAOBAO NETWORK

The data we use in this study comes from the Chinese website Taobao, one of the world's largest electronic marketplaces, with over 370 million registered users at the end of 2010. Although transactions on Taobao can be either business-to-consumer, business-to-business, or consumer-to-consumer, the bulk of the products are sold by online storefronts operated by small businesses or individuals. Perhaps the most unique aspect of Taobao is its integrated in-browser instant messaging platform, which allows us to correlate users' communication patterns and purchasing behavior. Any user can purchase goods from other users, add other users onto their contact list, and message other users. Note that non-contacts can message each other as well.

Our data is composed of all activities of the set of the first one million users that engaged in at least one commercial transaction during September 1 through October 28, 2009. For each of these users, we have all information regarding their transactions with other users in the set, where a transaction is specified by a product identifier, price, quantity, and timestamp. We also obtained the contact lists and timestamps of messages exchanged between these users during the two month observation period. Note that we do not have the contents of the messages exchanged.

We model the Taobao network as a multigraph composed of directed trade edges, directed message edges, and undirected contact/friendship edges.[1] Table 1 shows the basic statistics of the Taobao network when each edge type is viewed as a separate network. The 3,908,339 directed message edges are equivalent to

[1]The multigraph is modeled such that if there are multiple trades or messages from one user to another, we aggregate it all into a single directed edge, with supplementary message and trade information being associated with that edge. There can be up to 5 edges between a pair of users (2 directed trades, 2 directed messages, 1 undirected contact).

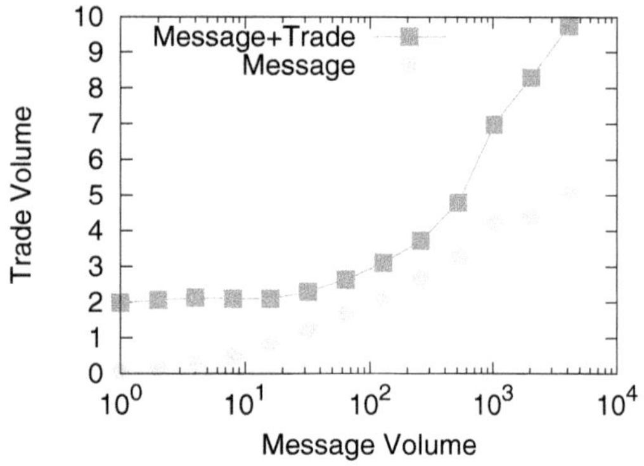

Figure 1: Trade Volume versus Message Volume. ***Message*** **is computed over all pairs of users that exchange at least one message.** ***Message+Trade*** **is computed over all pairs of users that exchange at least one message and one trade.**

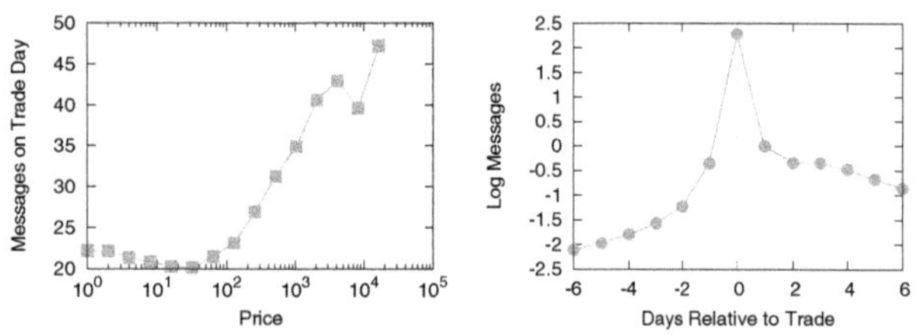

Figure 2: Buyer-Seller Messages vs. Transaction Price (left), relative to Trade Date (right).

2,241,729 undirected message edges, as messages are often reciprocated during discourse between a pair of users. In contrast, the 1,337,497 directed trade edges are equivalent to 1,336,502 undirected trade edges, as purchases are almost never reciprocated.

Throughout the rest of this paper, when we refer to a node as a "buyer" or "seller," we are speaking about its role in a particular transaction. Thus, we do not a priori label the nodes as buyers or sellers, but we use these terms to aid explanation. As a point of reference, 968,149 users make at least one purchase, 69,494 users make at least one sale, and 37,643 users make both a purchase and sale during the observation period. The products purchased and sold by these users are classified by Taobao into 82 categories.

3. DYADIC RELATIONSHIPS

To facilitate our goal of understanding how commercial transactions are embedded in the social networks of buyers and sellers, we first examine dyadic relationships in Taobao. In particular, we are interested in determining if messaging activity is correlated with trading activity. We graph trade volume versus message volume across pairs of users in Figure 1, and find that there is a positive increasing relationship between message volume and trade volume. Ignoring all pairs of users that only message and do not trade, we see an even more pronounced increasing relationship, displayed in the *Message+Trade* curve. The positive correlation between messaging and trading activity across dyads is supportive of our hypothesis that commercial activity is embedded in social networks. We will investigate the relationship between communication and commerce in much greater detail in our study of triadic structures.

Focusing upon the subset of dyads between pairs of users who have historically transacted, our question of interest is, "Do buyers talk to sellers more about expensive products?" We expect that expensive products are talked about more, but how much more are they talked about? To answer this question, we count the number of messages sent from buyer to seller on transaction date, assuming that at least one message is exchanged, and plot it versus product price (in Chinese Yuan, CNY), displayed in Figure 2(left). We find that the number of messages sent is relatively constant for products of price below 100 CNY, then increases logarithmically for products of higher price. This relationship can be explained by messaging being one of the primary tools in Taobao through which a buyer can minimize transaction risk.

In order to minimize transaction risk, one would expect that buyers speak to sellers often before transaction to inquire about product details. How often do buyers speak to sellers before and after trades? We graph the number of buyer-seller messages versus trade date in Figure 2(right). As expected, most messages occur on the day of transaction, likely being product negotiation. What we find particularly interesting is that post-trade messages are significantly more common than pre-trade messages. In the Taobao system, buyers have an option of using an escrow service, where the seller first ships the product, and payment is exchanged after the buyer examines the product. The observed post-trade messages are likely discussion regarding product satisfaction and payment confirmation.

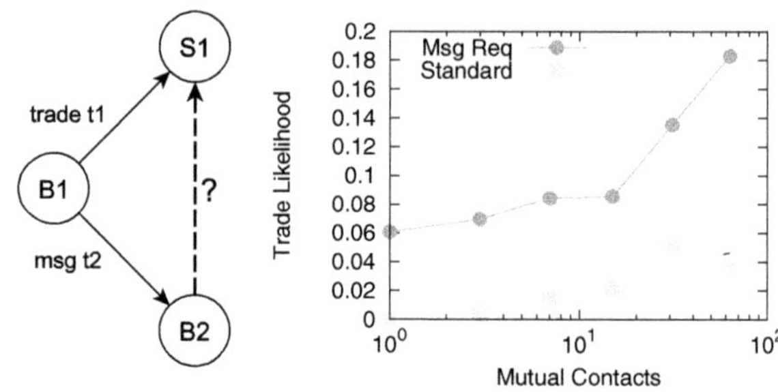

Figure 3: Given that B1 first purchased from S1 and then talked to B2, will B2 purchase from S1? (left) and Mutual Contacts (right).

4. INFORMATION PASSING

From our study of dyadic buyer-seller relationships, we learn that messaging activity is correlated with trading activity across pairs of users. However, dyadic relationships are only the tip of the iceberg when thinking about the interplay between communication and purchasing decisions in a social commerce network. Imagine the following situation: a buyer notices a deal offered at an electronic store, makes a purchase, then messages his friend about the deal. Will the friend also make a purchase from the same store? How large is the influence of the buyer?

We quantify and investigate this economic diffusion behavior which we term *information passing*, illustrated in Figure 3(left). More formally, if buyer B_1 purchases from seller S_1 and then talks to user B_2, will user B_2 then purchase from seller S_1 as well?[2] In the subsequent sections, we analyze information passing through the study of (1) local mutual neighborhoods in static networks, (2) information passing in dynamic networks, (3) influences upon information passing, and (4) directed triadic closure.

Information Passing and Triadic Closure. We begin our study of information passing by examining local neighborhoods in each edge type network (trade, message, contact) of a static endtime snapshot of Taobao. We are interested in understanding how the mutual relationships in one static network are correlated with the edge likelihood in another static network. Of particular interest is

[2]Again, we assign buyer and seller roles with respect to particular transactions. So user B_2 can be a seller and user S_1 can be a buyer in some other transactions.

the question of how *social proximity* is correlated with trade likelihood between a pair of users, where social proximity is measured by the number of mutual contacts between the pair. If we demonstrate that there is correlation between social proximity and trade likelihood, then information passing processes, as shown in Figure 3(left), are likely present in Taobao.

We find that the more mutual contacts a pair of users has, the greater the likelihood that they engaged in a commercial transaction, labeled as *Standard* in Figure 3(right). If we restrict our attention to only users who have exchanged at least one message (*Msg Req*), then for a given number of mutual contacts, the transaction probability is noticeably greater than before.[3] From these results, we can infer that trades are more likely to be embedded in the dense subgraphs of communication networks. This implies that social proximity and trade likelihood are correlated, and are a signal that information passing and product recommendation may be present in the Taobao network. In general, a direct relationship in one network is not only embedded in the local neighborhood of that relationship, but is also positioned in the context of networks with other edge types. This suggests that edges in one network can be used to help understand the link formation process in another. Building on this idea, we next perform a similar experiment in a dynamic triadic closure setting.

Information Passing. Following our examination of the static network, we study network relationships in the dynamic network. In particular, we look at how the message and contact networks influence the trade network by checking for the presence of information passing, as displayed in Figure 3(left).

To quantify information passing in the Taobao network, we measure the *information passing success rate* of the network, which we define as Prob(B_2 buys from S_1 at $t_2 + \Delta \mid B_1$ buys from S_1 at t_1 and B_1 messages B_2 at t_2, $t_2 > t_1$).[4]

Before computing the information passing success rate for the Taobao network, we require a random baseline for comparison. For our baseline, we compute the information passing success rate of an edge-rewired version of the Taobao network, where the edge-rewired network is constructed by randomly rewiring all 3 types of edges in the original network, while leaving node degrees and edge creation times unchanged.

We compute the information passing success rate over 3,906,354 node pair instances in the original network and observe a probability of 0.00203. In contrast, the information passing success rate of the rewired network is computed to be 0.00006. The observed probability of recommendation success is two orders of magnitude more likely than the random baseline, implying that information passing in Taobao is statistically significant and non-random.

Having verified the presence of information passing by checking for edge formation in the forward direction, we confirm the presence of information passing in the reverse direction. Suppose that B_1 buys from S_1 at time t_1 and B_2 buys from the same S_1 at time $t_1+\delta$, we measure the number of messages exchanged between B_1 and B_2 in the time intervals *Before* $[t_1-\delta, t_1]$, *Between* $[t_1, t_1+\delta]$, and *After* $[t_1+\delta,\ t_1+2\delta]$ the purchases of B_1 and B_2. One expects that if information passing is present, then most messages exchanged betweeen the two buyers occur after B_1 purchases, but before B_2 purchases. Table 2 shows the messages for the 3 time periods versus δ, averaged over all instances. We see that the largest proportion of messages exchanged between the buyers occur between their corresponding trade dates. For example, when the buyers transact two days apart, twice as many messages are exchanged *Between* the purchase dates, as compared to *Before* or *After*. Since messages exchanged *Between* are more likely to be recommendations, this is additional evidence that information passing is present in the Taobao network.

Days between purchases	Before	Between	After
1	4.16	5.29	4.76
2	7.78	14.29	7.76
3	8.60	10.52	7.44
4	7.34	15.90	10.79
5	21.87	30.70	21.18

Table 2: Messages between two buyers relative to their trade dates with the same seller.

Through examination of both forward and backward processes, we demonstrate that information passing is present in the Taobao network. In particular, we show that the observed information passing success rate is two orders of magnitude more likely than a random baseline. Prior studies providing evidence of information passing have been primarily conducted in product recommendation networks [17]. Our work shows that information passing, involving both buyer-buyer and buyer-seller relationships, occurs implicitly in Taobao, where the communication tool is primarily intended for buyer-seller communication. This result is significant because it illustrates how offline consumer behavior, asking or informing a personal social network about products, is also manifested implicitly in online social commerce networks.

Influences upon Information Passing. Having demonstrated the existence of information passing in the Taobao network, the next question is, "What factors influence the success rate of information passing?" In the following experiments, we examine how information passing success varies with respect to 4 variables: communication strength, time difference, product price, and product category.

Perhaps the primary influence upon the success of information passing is the amount of communication between the initial buyer, B_1, and his messaging partner, B_2. One can hypothesize that the stronger the communication between the two users, the more likely that B_2 will also purchase the product from the seller that sold to B_1. Counting the number of messages exchanged within time window $[t_1-\delta,\ t_1+\delta]$, the *Standard* curve of Figure 4(left) shows the probability of closure with δ = 3 days. As expected, the stronger the communication between the two users, the more likely that B_2 will be influenced by B_1. Adding a requirement to consider only users B_2 who have never purchased from S_1 historically (*FirstBuy Req*), we get a slightly lower, but still similar likelihood curve.

Note that an alternative possible explanation for these findings is that both B_1 and B_2 are active users in Taobao who communicate with other users frequently, make more purchases, and are thus more likely to purchase from the same sellers. However, we demonstrate this hypothesis is incorrect by performing an experiment where we keep the communication network and the number of purchases of a buyer unchanged, but randomize the sellers (*i.e.*, buyers buy from random sellers). We find that the increased communication between the two users does not correlate with the information passing success rate (*Random* curve of Figure 4(left)), meaning that the stronger the communication, the stronger the effect of information passing.

The results from this experiment lead to several observations. First, messaging generally increases purchasing behavior in the Taobao network. Second, information passing is present in the net-

[3]To compare, the likelihood that a pair of direct contacts have transacted historically is 0.089.

[4]We only consider the time t_2 corresponding to the first message from B_1 to B_2 after t_1. We also add a requirement of $\Delta \leq 2$ days, i.e., B_2 makes a purchase soon after talking to B_1, to dampen the effects of regular purchases that occur irrelevant to messaging behavior.

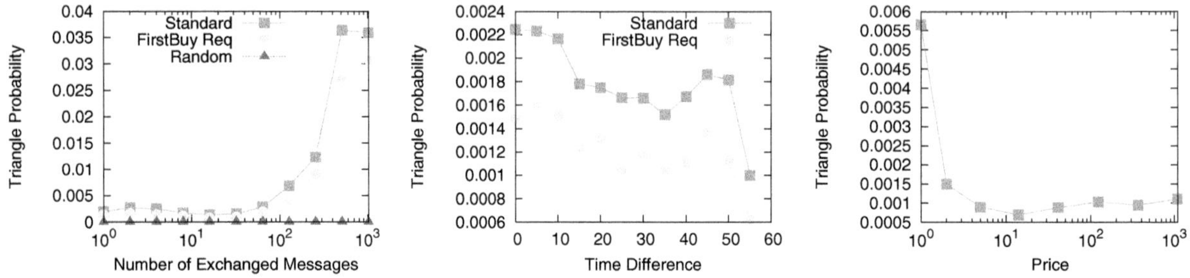

Figure 4: Triadic Closure Probability given Message Strength (left), Time Difference in Days (middle), and Price in CNY (right).

work. Additionally, communication leads to purchases, and social network structure provides a surprisingly strong signal indicating which seller a buyer will purchase from. This latter result will be quite useful later when we study consumer choice prediction.

In addition to counting the number of messages exchanged between buyers, one should also consider the time difference, $t_2 - t_1$, between the initial trade and message from B_1 to B_2. We expect that the larger the time difference between the initial purchase and message, the lower the influence of the message upon the purchasing behavior of B_2. As shown in Figure 4(middle), the probability of information passing success steadily decreases with time. We observe the same effect regardless of whether we require the trade (B_2, S_1) to be a first time trade (*FirstBuy Req*) or any trade (*Standard*). This implies that social product recommendation and influence spreading is most effective when utilized immediately after initial product adoption or purchase.

Although communication between B_1 and B_2 is a significant influence upon information passing, the characteristics of the product itself also affect the success of information passing. We can imagine that the most important product attribute to consider is the price (in Chinese Yuan, CNY) of the initial purchase. As displayed in Figure 4(right), we find that the information passing success rate decreases with product price for the price range from 1 CNY to 15 CNY, then increases slightly for products priced above 15 CNY. The large closure probability at a price of 1 CNY is due to the popularity and virality of virtual goods, such as game credits.

In addition to product price, we also consider the category of the product itself when measuring the information passing success rate. We find that a few categories exhibit recommendation success rates much higher than other categories, while many categories exhibit nearly no information passing at all. For example, the category *women's clothing* exhibits a success rate of over 20%, while the category *home decorations* exhibits a success rate of 1.47%. A major possible influence for the variability of these numbers are the regular group-purchasing deals offered by large stores on Taobao, which provide financial incentives for consumers to convince their friends to join them in purchases.

In summary, our experiments demonstrate that the success of information passing is directly proportional to the communication strength between the initial buyer and their message partner, inversely proportional to the time difference between the purchase and initial recommendation, inversely proportional to product price, and highly category specific. It is clear that influencing an individual to purchase a product is a complex affair. We believe these results are informative and can provide guidance to viral marketing campaigns when trying to promote product recommendation and adoption among online users.

Directed Triadic Closure. Our previous study of local information passing processes can be seen as a special case of the more general directed triadic closure problem. We next investigate the process of directed triadic closure on a global scale. In the following study, we answer various questions regarding triadic closure including: What types of triads are more likely to be formed? What types of edges are more likely to close triads?

For our task, we focus upon the link formation process in the context of triadic closure for the message and trade networks. In particular, consider a triple of nodes U, X, V, where first pairs U, X and V, X interact via messaging or trading, and then a triangle closing edge $U \rightarrow V$ or $V \rightarrow U$ forms. We are interested in how the type of interaction (message vs. trade) and the direction of interaction (i.e., $U \rightarrow X$ vs. $X \rightarrow U$) affects the formation of the triad-closing edge between U and V.

Let us define a Directed Configuration Set (U; X; V) as a situation where an edge forms between U and X at time t_1, then an edge forms between V and X at time t_2 ($t_2 > t_1$). We are interested in the probability that a triad-closing edge forms between nodes U and V at a time t_3 ($t_3 > t_2$). There are 16 possible Directed Configuration Sets, displayed in the first column of Table 3: the left node represents U, middle node X and right node V. For the triad-closing edge, we use the following shorthand notation: m_i is the message edge (V,U), while m_o is the message edge in the opposite direction (U,V). Similarly, t_i is the trade edge (V,U), while t_o denotes the trade edge in the opposite direction (U,V). We use the term *instance* to refer to a particular example of a configuration set.

Now in Table 3, we examine various properties of configuration sets. In particular, we are interested in knowing, "How many times does a particular configuration set get closed with a third edge? And what is the type of that edge?" For easier reasoning about various configuration sets, we denote hypothetical buyer/seller designations for the middle node X in the last column of Table 3. For example, if the configuration contains a purchase by X and no sale, then we say that X has a "buyer" role. Similarly, if the configuration contains a sale by X and no purchase, then we say that X has a "seller" role. In all other cases, the role of X is ambiguous.

To begin our study of directed triadic closure, first observe that there is little brokerage or reselling in the network, as the two configurations where X both "buys" and "sells" have the lowest unique node X as well as instance counts (Columns *# Uniq. X*, *# Instances*). This is indicative of the general bipartite structure of Taobao, where users primarily take on either buyer or seller roles.

Another important observation is that configurations where X has a "seller" role are represented approximately 100 times more often than configurations where X has a "buyer" role. The number of unique buyers exceeds the number of unique sellers in these configurations, as shown in Column *# Uniq. X*, implying that activity levels for sellers are much higher than those for buyers. The large difference in activity levels is likely due to how individuals actually use Taobao. Buyers browse Taobao casually and interact with others primarily when interested, whereas sellers spend their day speaking with potential clients. Given the bipartiteness of Taobao and the general activity level of sellers, we can imagine that seller nodes are local "star" structures in the Taobao graph.

Dir. Config Set	# Instances	# Uniq. X	P(close)	P(t|close)	P(m|close)	s(t_o)	s(t_i)	X "role"
○←t—○—t→○	590,635	235,088	0.4146	0.4027	0.5973	69.19	63.39	B
○←t—○←t—○	469,755	28,046	0.3925	0.3295	0.6705	3.09	16.87	
○—t→○—t→○	410,951	27,302	0.3319	0.3636	0.6364	18.75	6.13	
○—t→○←t—○	516,941,038	45,741	0.0018	0.1242	0.8758	-18.11	-18.30	S
○←t—○—m→○	2,661,874	382,690	0.5034	0.3191	0.6809	41.26	101.61	B
○←t—○←m—○	2,738,167	428,334	0.5470	0.3220	0.6780	41.94	118.83	B
○—t→○—m→○	253,840,924	45,318	0.0048	0.1308	0.8692	-9.28	-5.40	S
○—t→○←m—○	252,983,480	45,931	0.0050	0.1299	0.8701	-9.26	-5.03	S
○←m—○—t→○	3,106,078	421,888	0.5103	0.3309	0.6691	126.17	61.89	B
○←m—○←t—○	276,047,807	46,475	0.0070	0.1595	0.8405	-0.59	2.09	S
○—m→○—t→○	3,174,237	475,074	0.5019	0.3324	0.6676	141.02	65.23	B
○—m→○←t—○	272,424,037	47,524	0.0070	0.1598	0.8402	-0.04	2.63	S
○←m—○—m→○	420,018,116	403,220	0.0289	0.1386	0.8614	52.92	63.96	
○←m—○←m—○	280,943,201	436,865	0.0458	0.1369	0.8631	56.03	75.16	
○—m→○—m→○	276,848,803	442,548	0.0438	0.1409	0.8591	67.61	70.19	
○—m→○←m—○	272,535,699	469,549	0.0467	0.1398	0.8602	68.69	80.00	

Table 3: Directed Configuration Set (*U*; *X*; *V*), where *X* is the middle node, *U* is the left node, *V* is the right node. # Instances = number of instances. # Uniq. X = number of unique *X* nodes over all instances. P(close) = 100 * probability of a triad-closing third edge. P(t|close) = proportion of triads closed by a trade. P(m|close) = proportion of triads closed by a message. s(t_o) = surprise for directed trade edge (*U*, *V*). s(t_i) = surprise for directed trade edge (*V*, *U*). X "role" = hypothesized role of *X*.

Following our comparison of configuration instance counts, we consider the question, "When will an instance of a Directed Configuration Set be closed by a third edge?" We compute the probability of the configuration (*U*; *X*; *V*) being closed by an edge (*U*,*V*). Observe that configurations where *X* is a buyer have much higher closure probabilities (average 0.0051) than configurations where *X* is a seller (average 0.000046). The large difference in closure probabilities is due to the fact that triads with middle buyers primarily consist of two buyers and one seller, with the required third edge being a buyer-seller edge. In contrast, triads with middle sellers likely contain one seller and two buyers, with the required third edge being a buyer-buyer edge. Since the Taobao network is essentially a bipartite network of buyers and sellers, buyer-seller edges occur much more often than buyer-buyer edges, leading to triadic closure for buyers being over 100 times more likely than for sellers.

Triad-Closing Edge Type Distribution. After computing the instance counts and triad-closing probabilities of each Directed Configuration Set, we next examine the distribution of edge types closing each type of configuration. For each of the 16 configurations c_i, we count the number of instances that are closed by messages and trades in each direction. Column *P(m|close)* of Table 3 shows that messages close most of the triads in the network. However, messages are also approximately 3 times as common as trade edges in the data. Therefore, we need to compute expectations for each of the 4 possible triad-closing edge types (m_i, m_o, t_i, and t_o).

We define a node's *generative baseline* as the proportion of its out-edges that are trades. We assume that when a node A creates an edge, it generates a trade edge with a probability equal to its generative baseline, denoted by $p_t(A)$. For the configuration c_i, the expected number of triads that are closed by a trade from U to V is equal to $\sum_{U \in c_i} p_t(U)$, where the summation is over all instances of the configuration c_i. Similarly, the expected number of triads that are closed by a trade from V to U is $\sum_{V \in c_i} p_t(V)$. Viewing each instance of edge generation as a separate Bernoulli trial, we derive an expression for *surprise* [20] to indicate the number of signed standard deviations by which an observed edge type count differs from expected. For the configuration c_i, the surprise of the triad-closing edge (*U*,*V*) being a trade is $s_{t_o} = \frac{\#observed - \sum_{U \in c_i} p_t(U)}{\sqrt{\sum_{U \in c_i} [p_t(U) * (1 - p_t(U))]}}$, where #observed is the number of instances of c_i that are closed by a trade edge (*U*,*V*). Similarly, we compute the surprise s_{t_i} of the triad-closing edge (*V*,*U*) being a trade. These trade surprise values are listed in Columns *s(t_o)*, *s(t_i)* of Table 3.[5]

After computing these edge type surprises, we can compare observed triad-closing edge counts with expected edge counts from our generative baseline. Our first observation regarding directed edge surprises is that for configurations where X is a buyer, the triad-closing edge being a trade edge is observed significantly more than expected, as shown in Table 3. An explanation for this is that configurations with middle buyers primarily consist of two buyers and one seller, with the required third edge being a buyer-seller edge. Since Taobao is essentially a bipartite network, trade surprises for such configurations vary from 40 to 140 standard deviations more than expected.

For configurations where X is a buyer and only one of U and V is a seller, s(t_o) and s(t_i) differ by a factor of 2. In particular, the trade surprise of the edge directed toward the seller is twice as large as the other direction. This is an example of how the role of each of the nodes in a configuration influence both the edge type and edge direction probabilities of the triad-closing third edge.

In contrast, for configurations where X is a seller, both trade surprises, s(t_o) and s(t_i), are negative. As previously mentioned, when X is a seller, U and V are likely to be both buyers. Since buyers rarely purchase from each other on Taobao, this leads to messages being observed more than expected between U and V.

Our analysis of edge type surprises indicates the significance of user roles in dictating edge formation in the Taobao network. Message edges close the majority of the triads in Taobao due to their relative proportion among all network edges. However, the relative proportion of triad-closing edges being a message edge is primarily dictated by the user role of the middle node X.

[5]We do not explicitly compute the surprises for directed message edges since $p_m(X) = 1 - p_t(X)$, implying that s(m_o) = -s(t_o) and s(m_i) = -s(t_i).

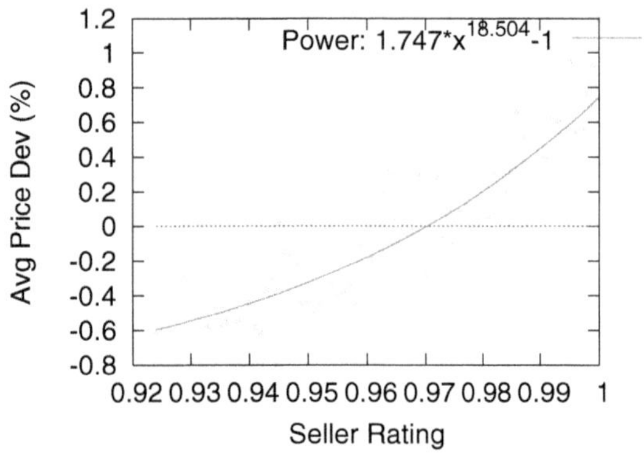

Figure 5: Per Item: Average price deviation from median (%) vs seller rating(%).

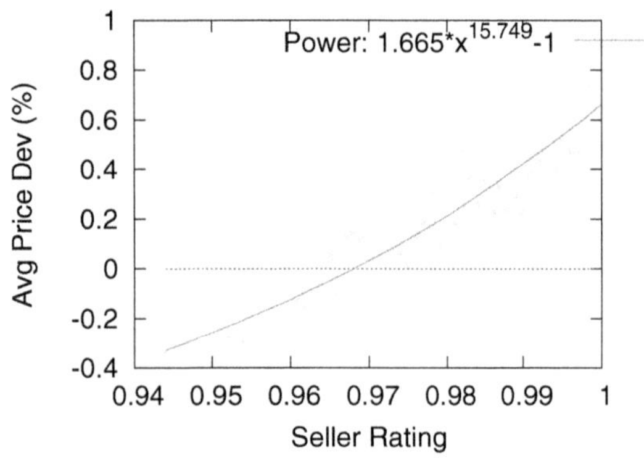

Figure 6: Aggregated Per Seller: Average price deviation from median (%) vs seller rating(%).

5. PRICE OF TRUST

The prior study of information passing relies upon the spread of influence through buyer-buyer communication, which can be seen as an implicit form of buyer-buyer trust. We next examine a more explicit form of buyer-seller trust encapsulated by seller ratings. In the context of electronic marketplaces, buyers are unsure about seller trustworthiness, so buyers put their trust into seller ratings and reviews, and are willing to pay a premium to sellers with good reputations [26]. How much extra will a buyer pay for transaction with a highly rated seller?

Data Preparation. To answer this question, we use the large Taobao transaction dataset to study how good seller reputations are rewarded on Taobao and quantify a price for trust. To facilitate our experiments, we perform a web crawl of the Taobao website to obtain product and seller metadata associated with the transactions in our original dataset. Each transaction in Taobao is rated by the buyer, so we use the percentage of positive reviews that each seller has received in the past as a proxy for seller reputation and trustworthiness. Henceforth, we shall refer to that ratio as seller *rating*.

With this rating information, we compare sellers of the same product and determine how their sale prices differ. The difficult step of the experimental setup is identification of all product listings in our dataset which correspond to the same products. We develop a high precision method targeted toward specific types of products and use our method to identify and group together product listings referring to the same product into *product clusters*. The resulting dataset for our study of trust consists of 382,980 items, 11,293 product clusters (corresponding to unique product types), and 6,199 unique sellers. Each of these product clusters contains a set of items which correspond to the same exact product.

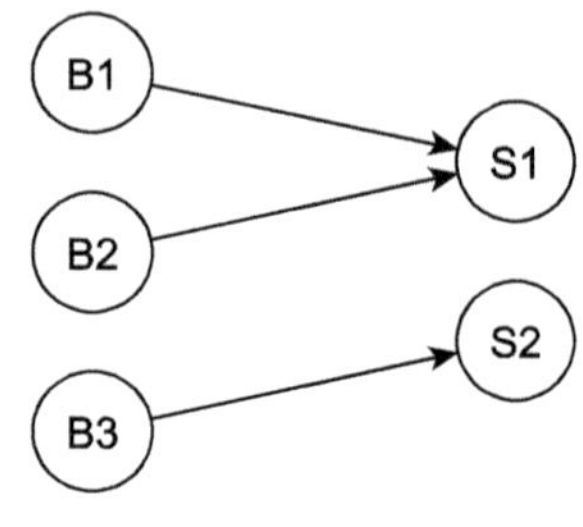

Figure 7: Buyer-Seller Cluster. Given that S1 and S2 both sell exactly the same product that the buyers buy, predict the correct seller for each buyer B1, B2, B3.

Quantifying Trust. With our product cluster dataset, we study the relationship between seller rating and the price at which a seller can transact. For each product cluster, for each listing within a cluster, we compute % deviation from median cluster price. We plot the average price deviation from the median per listing versus seller rating in Figure 5, and fit the data with a power function (R^2 of 0.80). From the super-linear fit, we see that a higher rating is associated with a seller selling his products at a premium compared to most of his peers. Another interesting observation is that a seller rating of 97.1% corresponds to transaction at the median cluster price. The lack of negative reviews in such data has been observed in other e-commerce data such as eBay [25], and has been hypothesized to be the result of a "high-courtesy" social norm.

Next, we aggregate the average price difference of all items sold by a seller and plot that against seller rating, shown in Figure 6. The primary difference between this plot and the previous one is that we now aggregate all the different instances of a seller's transactions within the same cluster, and compare the sellers in a cluster against each other.[6] We find that a power function fits our data particularly well (R^2 of 0.87). Looking across all sellers, the elasticity of product price with respect to seller rating is a small, positive quantity, indicating that there is a direct relationship between seller rating and increased sales price.

One possible explanation for our findings is that highly rated sellers incur higher costs associated with their products, hence they can sell their products at a price premium. For example, highly rated sellers may provide better services, such as replying to messages from customers in a timely fashion, or shipping products more frequently. An alternative explanation is that buyers are willing to pay more to highly rated sellers to minimize transaction risk, thus sellers who maintain good reputations are financially rewarded. Although higher seller ratings are correlated with higher sales prices, the small magnitude of the elasticity indicates that buyer purchasing decisions are likely influenced by other variables, such as the social network in which the purchases are embedded. This leads us to consider the scenario of consumer choice prediction.

6. CONSUMER CHOICE PREDICTION

In order to demonstrate the power of network structure, we now consider the problem of *consumer choice prediction*. Imagine the following situation: a user comes to Taobao and issues an exact query for the product (s)he aims to buy. There is a list of k sellers selling the exact product the buyer is going to buy. Which seller will the buyer purchase the item from? The seller with the lowest price? The most trusted seller? The seller who interacted with the buyer's friends in the past?

[6]There is large variation between activity levels among different sellers, so we only display those who have sold at least 15 items.

Given that our prior experiments have demonstrated the importance of the social network and the strong presence of information passing, we aim to investigate the role that social and communication networks play in consumer decision making [5]. If the social network has no influence upon buyer behavior, then we expect that buyers will purchase from sellers that offer the lowest price. However, as we will see, it is exactly the social network information that gives the strongest signal in predicting which seller a buyer will make a purchase from.

For this consumer choice prediction task, we use the product cluster data described previously in our study of trust. Each product cluster consists of a set of transactions between different pairs of people, but corresponding to the exact same product. We convert each product cluster into a bipartite subgraph composed of buyer and seller nodes, as shown in Figure 7, where the buyers and sellers have all either bought or sold the same particular product. We will term these bipartite subgraphs *buyer-seller clusters*, and henceforth shall perform prediction with these clusters.

Typically a seller will transact with multiple buyers in the same cluster, while a buyer purchases the product from a single seller in the cluster. Both buyers and sellers can be included in more than one buyer-seller cluster if they buy or sell multiple types of products. We restrict our focus to buyer-seller clusters with at least 2 and no more than 10 sellers. Overall, our prediction data is composed of 9,950 clusters, with a per-cluster average of 5.91 buyers and 3.13 sellers. It is important to understand that, by construction, all sellers offer a product for sale that is exactly relevant to the buyer's interests. The task now is, within a cluster, given a particular buyer, rank the sellers such that the seller the buyer is going to buy from is ranked as high as possible.

Problem Statement: For each buyer-seller cluster C_i, there is an associated set B_i of buyers and set S_i of sellers. For each cluster C_i, for each buyer B_{ij} in B_i, predict which seller(s) from S_i the buyer B_{ij} will purchase their product(s) from.

We model this prediction problem as a ranking problem, where for each buyer B_{ij} in cluster C_i, we wish to generate a ranking of the sellers S_{ik}, such that the true seller from whom B_{ij} actually purchased the product has the highest rank (i.e., score). Since the positive and negative examples for our problem come in sets, it is natural to use a ranking based machine learning approach. In particular, we use the Support Vector Machine SVM-rank [16].

For consumer choice prediction, we use a base set of 23 features that describe product, buyer and seller metadata. We also use features that describe the buyer-seller interactions and network structure. Table 4 lists the features we use in our experiments, along with the networks they are computed on.[7]

Experimental Setup and Evaluation. Our data consists of 58,812 sets of training examples (i..e, buyer-seller pairs where a buyer can buy the same product from multiple sellers). We split the data into 75% train and 25% test sets. The SVMs were trained with linear kernels and loss functions were chosen to minimize the number of incorrect constraints. Since we typically have one positive example per buyer decision, this is equivalent to optimizing Precision@1.

As a point of comparison for our models, we construct three simple rule-based baselines:

- **Random** baseline - rank the sellers randomly
- **MinPrice** baseline - rank the sellers by increasing price.
- **MostMsg** baseline - rank the sellers by decreasing buyer-seller message volume. Defaults to Random if no message edge is present.

[7]For each buyer decision, network features are computed from the snapshot of the network which existed the day prior to the true purchase date. This is necessary to properly model buyer decisions.

Feature Set	P@1	MRR	MR
All Features	0.56	0.72	2.00
Only Network	0.55	0.72	2.02
Only Meta	0.33	0.57	2.62
Meta + Msgs	0.50	0.69	2.13
Meta + Trades	0.43	0.64	2.34
Meta + Contacts	0.42	0.63	2.40
Meta + Direct	0.56	0.72	2.00
Meta + Indirect	0.34	0.58	2.58
MostMsg	0.50	0.69	2.11
Random	0.31	0.53	2.90
MinPrice	0.29	0.54	2.77

Table 5: Customer choice prediction results.

We evaluate the models and baselines using the following three metrics:[8]

- **Precision at Top 1** (P@1) - Fraction of times that the top ranked seller is actually the true seller. (Higher is better)
- **Mean Rank** (MR)- Average *Rank* of the true seller. (Lower is better)
- **Mean Reciprocal Rank** (MRR) - Average *Reciprocal Rank* ($\frac{1}{Rank}$) of the true seller. (Higher is better)

Experimental Results. Table 5 gives an overview of our experimental results where we compare the models using various feature sets and the baselines. First, we note that the model trained on all 23 features gives a 79% improvement over the P@1 of the Random baseline and a 38% improvement over Random's MRR. The model also gives a 13% improvement over the MostMsg baseline and a 93% improvement over the MinPrice baseline. For all our evaluation metrics, the model displays significantly better performance than the 3 baselines. It is interesting to note the poor performance of MinPrice compared to MostMsg. This suggests that communication links and the social graph are essential to understanding how consumers make purchasing decisions in social commerce networks. Note that a natural explanation for the importance of the social graph can be that a buyer first messages a seller, then immediately trades with him. However, we control for this by discarding all communication on and after the trade date.

To evaluate prediction performance in more detail, we graph the P@1 and MRR of the Full model (labeled as *SVM*) and the 3 baselines versus the number of sellers in the buyer-seller cluster (i.e., how many different sellers a buyer can choose from) in Figures 8(a),(e). As expected, the performance of all models and baselines decreases as the number of sellers in the cluster increases. Observe that the performance gap between the Full model and MostMsg, the strongest baseline, widens as the number of sellers to choose from increases and prediction becomes more difficult. If we look at the proportional P@1 improvement of the Full model over MostMsg, we see only a 4.5% improvement when there are 2 sellers, but a 39.5% improvement when there are 10 sellers. In particular, we would like to highlight the Full model's strong P@1 of 42.1% for the challenging prediction task with 10 sellers. In general, the full power of the model is not realized until the prediction problem becomes difficult for simple rule-based heuristics.

Different Feature Sets. Having constructed a successful predictive model, we now ask, "What features are most valuable when modeling consumer choice?" In the following set of experiments, we contrast the performance of SVM models trained on different sets of graph and metadata features in order to better understand how consumers make purchasing decisions.

[8]Performance was also evaluated with several other standard ranking metrics. Results are similar, so hence not displayed.

Feature Type	Feature Name	Feature Description	T	M	C
Product Metadata Features	Fractional Price Rank	Seller ranking using their median product price			
	Fractional Rating Rank	Seller ranking using their rating percentage			
	Historical Sold	Num. of all products sold by seller. 1) fractional rank 2) log of value			
	Inventory Sold	Quantity already sold in the particular product listing.			
	Insurance	If the product is insured by the seller			
Direct Network Features	Buyer-Seller Interactions	1) Trade volume 2) Message volume 3) Are they contacts?	X	X	X
	Time Since Last Transaction	Computed for both message and trade networks	X	X	
	Fractional Message Rank	Seller ranking using number of buyer-seller messages		X	
	Nodal Trade Volumes	Number of trades for buyer and seller in the 2 month observation period	X		
Indirect Network Features	Number of mutual partners	Number of nodes who have messaged or transacted with both buyer and seller		X	X
	Seller Clustering Coefficients	Computed for both message and contact networks		X	X
	Mutual Densities	Frac. of edges between the set of nodes mutual with both buyer and seller		X	X
	Seller PageRanks	Computed for static endtime networks	X	X	X

Table 4: Feature Set. T, M, C denote if the feature is computed on the trade, message, and contact networks, respectively.

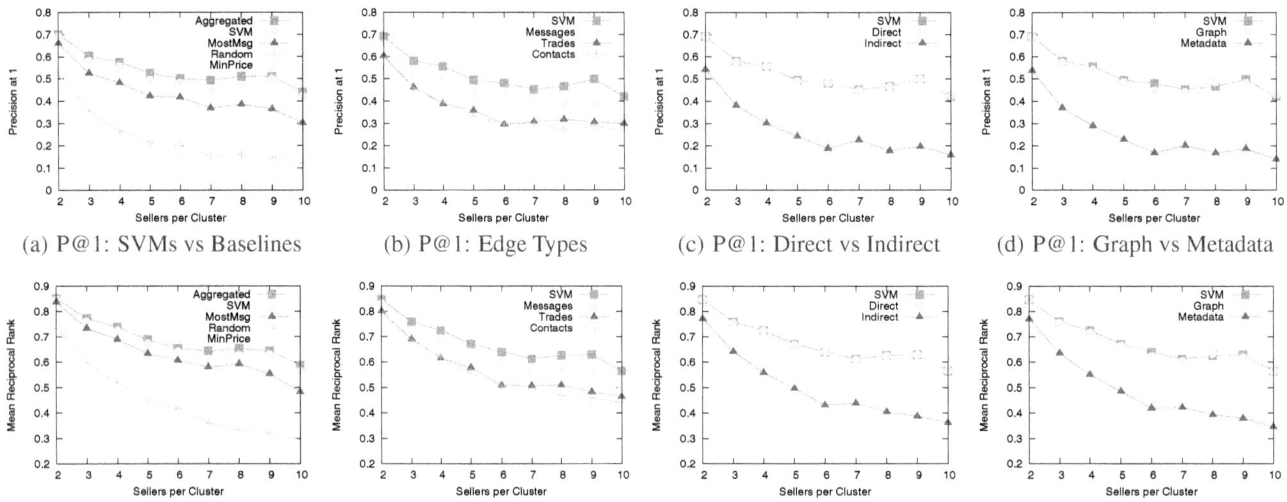

(a) P@1: SVMs vs Baselines (b) P@1: Edge Types (c) P@1: Direct vs Indirect (d) P@1: Graph vs Metadata

(e) MRR: SVMs vs Baselines (f) MRR: Edge Types (g) MRR: Direct vs Indirect (h) MRR: Graph vs Metadata

Figure 8: Consumer choice prediction performance. The social graph is the most important feature in predicting which seller a buyer will purchase from.

When doing prediction, are network features as valuable as metadata features such as product price and seller rating? We first compare the performance of a SVM trained on network (graph) features versus a SVM trained on metadata (seller profile and product description) features. We find that the P@1 of the graph features SVM is only slightly worse than the Full model, whereas the metadata features SVM is not much better than Random, as displayed in Table 5. Most notably, there is a large performance gap between the graph features SVM compared to the metadata features SVM, as illustrated in Figures 8(d),(h). This implies that prediction using only seller and product information is inadequate, the social and trade networks in the neighborhood of the buyer and seller must be taken into account. Buyers likely do not just use seller profile and product information when making purchasing decisions.

Given that network features are essential when predicting consumer choice, what type of network features are more valuable for prediction: direct features or indirect features (i.e., clustering coefficients, PageRanks)? For this experiment, we train SVM models on direct and indirect network features, the different graph feature classes we use are listed in Table 4. Note that when comparing direct and indirect network features, we include all metadata features in both sets. Figures 8(c),(g) illustrate the large performance gap between the *Meta + Direct* SVM vs the *Meta + Indirect* SVM, labeled as *Direct* and *Indirect* respectively in the figures. We observe that direct graph information provided by buyer-seller edges is significantly more valuable than the collective information provided by other edges in the local neighborhoods. This is not surprising because powerful information content is present in direct edges. Historical buyer-seller message volume can be indicative of an existing social relationship or historical product queries, while historical buyer-seller trade volume can be indicative of customer loyalty and trust with the seller.

Which network (contact, message, trade) is most useful for predicting consumer choice? In this section, we contrast SVM models trained on each of the separate Taobao networks. We include all metadata features with each set of network features in this experiment as well, prediction results are displayed in Table 5. The performance of the 3 network feature sets versus the number of sellers in the cluster are displayed in Figures 8(b),(f). Our experiment demonstrates that the message network is the most valuable network to utilize when predicting consumer choice. One possible explanation for this finding is that historical message volume is an indicator of familiarity between buyer and seller, i.e., an existing trust relationship between buyer and seller. Historical message volume can also indicate previous potential purchase interest.

We also observe that prediction with the trade network is slightly better than that with the contact network. This suggests that customer loyalty, the primary trade network feature we use, is a more important indicator of consumer choice than the network of contacts. Our explanation for this is that, inherently, contact links are less valuable than trade or message links in such social networks. It takes little effort to add someone to a friends list, as it is a one-time operation. In contrast, maintaining a conversation requires an investment of time and mutual interest on the part of both parties.

Forming a trade link is arguably the most costly as it requires currency and an actual transaction to make the connection.

Per-Category Performance. After performing prediction with a single SVM ranking model, the next question to ask is, "Can we perform better prediction through the use of multiple models?" To answer this question, we segment all historical transactions in our dataset into their respective product categories, and train separate SVM ranking models for each category. The results of our model testing are displayed as *Aggregated* in Figure 8(a),(e). As expected, the aggregated performance of the category SVMs is slightly better than the single Full SVM, with a P@1 of 0.58 compared to 0.56.

Our study of consumer choice prediction demonstrates that in social commerce sites such as Taobao, user communication and social activity is the primary influence upon consumer choice. Utilizing primarily social networking features, we are able to construct an SVM model that can predict, for the case of a buyer choosing from among 10 possible sellers, the correct seller 42% of the time, approximately 4 times better than random. When faced with a selection of substitute goods offered by different sellers, buyers will not just choose their preferred seller through simple heuristics regarding price or rating. We can imagine that buyers utilize many sources of information (seller history, advice of friends, seller's messages), and each buyer processes the information in their own way in order to make a personal purchasing decision. Although we cannot say with certainty what buyers are thinking, we can definitively state that the social graph in which the buyer and seller are embedded is the best feature to look at when predicting consumer choice.

7. CONCLUSION

Our work analyzes the activities of one million users of the Chinese social commerce site Taobao. Through the study of directed closure rules, we empirically verify that implicit information passing is present in the Taobao network, and show that communication between buyers is a fundamental driver of purchasing activity. We then investigate the directed triadic closure process and explain how link formation is highly dependent upon the distribution of buyer/seller roles for the nodes of a social commerce network. Third, we use Taobao review data to demonstrate how high seller ratings are associated with product price premiums, and thus quantify a price for trust. Finally, we develop a machine learning model to accurately predict consumer choice, and demonstrate that the social network is the most important feature in predicting how consumers choose their transaction partners.

We hope that our study will motivate future research into social shopping, as well as give impetus to established e-commerce companies to add more social networking features. Future areas of related study include: analysis of user browsing data to develop refined consumer choice models for social commerce, study of information passing while factoring in both buyer-buyer and buyer-seller trust relationships, and viral marketing to influence consumer choice in social commerce.

Acknowledgements. Research was in-part supported by NSF CNS-1010921, NSF IIS-1016909, Albert Yu & Mary Bechmann Foundation, IBM, Lightspeed, Microsoft and Yahoo.

8. REFERENCES

[1] L. Backstrom, D. Huttenlocher, J. Kleinberg, and X. Lan. Group formation in large social networks: membership, growth, and evolution. In *KDD*, 2006.
[2] R. Bhatt, V. Chaoji, and R. Parekh. Predicting product adoption in large-scale social networks. In *CIKM*, 2010.
[3] K. Burke. As consumer attitudes shift, so must marketing strategies. 2003.
[4] J. Chevalier and D. Mayzlin. The effect of word of mouth on sales: Online book reviews. *J. of Marketing Research*, 2006.
[5] A. Degeratu, A. Rangaswamy, and J. Wu. Consumer choice behavior in online and traditional supermarkets: The effects of brand name, price, and other search attributes. *Intl. J. of Res. in Marketing*, 2000.
[6] P. DiMaggio and H. Louch. Socially embedded consumer transactions: for what kinds of purchases do people most often use networks? *Amer. Soc. Rev.*, 63(5):619–637, 1998.
[7] P. Doney and J. Cannon. An examination of the nature of trust in buyer-seller relationships. *J. of Marketing*, 1997.
[8] Q. Duong, N. Sundaresan, N. Parikh, and Z. Shen. Modeling Seller Listing Strategies. *Agent-Mediated El. Comm.*, 2010.
[9] M. Granovetter. The strength of weak ties. *American Journal of Sociology*, 78(6):1360–1380, 1973.
[10] M. Granovetter. Economic Action and Social Structure: The Problem of Embeddedness. *Amer. J. of Sociology*, 1985.
[11] T. Hennig-Thurau, K. Gwinner, G. Walsh, and D. Gremler. Electronic word-of-mouth via consumer-opinion platforms: What motivates consumers to articulate themselves on the Internet? *J. of Interactive Marketing*, 18(1):38–52, 2004.
[12] S. Hill, F. Provost, and C. Volinsky. Network-based marketing: Identifying likely adopters via consumer networks. *Statistical Science*, 21(2):256–276, 2006.
[13] D. Houser and J. Wooders. Reputation in auctions: Theory, and evidence from eBay. *J. of Econ. & Man. Strat.*, 2006.
[14] W. Hu and A. Bolivar. Online auctions efficiency: a survey of ebay auctions. In *WWW*, 2008.
[15] R. Iyer, S. Han, and S. Gupta. Do Friends Influence Purchases in a Social Network? *Harvard Business School Working Paper*, 2009.
[16] T. Joachims. Training linear SVMs in linear time. In *KDD*, 2006.
[17] J. Leskovec, L. Adamic, and B. Huberman. The dynamics of viral marketing. *ACM TWEB*, 1(1):5, 2007.
[18] J. Leskovec, L. Backstrom, R. Kumar, and A. Tomkins. Microscopic evolution of social networks. In *KDD*, 2008.
[19] J. Leskovec, D. Huttenlocher, and J. Kleinberg. Predicting positive and negative links in online social networks. In *WWW*, 2010.
[20] J. Leskovec, D. Huttenlocher, and J. Kleinberg. Signed networks in social media. In *CHI*, 2010.
[21] D. Liben-Nowell and J. Kleinberg. The link-prediction problem for social networks. In *CIKM*, 2003.
[22] Y. Lu, C. Zhai, and N. Sundaresan. Rated aspect summarization of short comments. In *WWW*, 2009.
[23] D. Lucking-Reiley, D. Bryan, N. Prasad, and D. Reeves. Pennies from ebay: the determinants of price in online auctions. *The J. of Industrial Economics*, 2007.
[24] A. Rapoport. Spread of information through a population with socio-structural bias: I. Assumption of transitivity. *Bulletin of Mathematical Biology*, 15(4):523–533, 1953.
[25] P. Resnick and R. Zeckhauser. Trust among strangers in Internet transactions: Empirical analysis of eBay's reputation system. *Adv. in Appl. Microecon.: A Research Ann.*, 2002.
[26] P. Resnick, R. Zeckhauser, J. Swanson, and K. Lockwood. The value of reputation on eBay: A controlled experiment. *Experimental Economics*, 9(2):79–101, 2006.
[27] D. Romero and J. Kleinberg. The directed closure process in information networks with an analysis of link formation on twitter. In *ICWSM*, 2010.
[28] B. Sarwar, G. Karypis, J. Konstan, and J. Riedl. Analysis of recommendation algorithms for e-commerce. In *EC*, 2000.
[29] J. Schafer, J. Konstan, and J. Riedi. Recommender systems in e-commerce. In *EC*, 1999.
[30] X. Wu and A. Bolivar. Predicting the conversion probability for items on C2C ecommerce sites. In *CIKM*, 2009.
[31] J. Zheng, X. Wu, J. Niu, and A. Bolivar. Substitutes or complements: another step forward in recommendations. In *EC*, 2009.

Who Moderates the Moderators? Crowdsourcing Abuse Detection in User-Generated Content

Arpita Ghosh
Yahoo! Research
Santa Clara, CA, USA
arpita@yahoo-inc.com

Satyen Kale
Yahoo! Research
Santa Clara, CA, USA
skale@yahoo-inc.com

Preston McAfee
Yahoo! Research
Burbank, CA, USA
mcafee@yahoo-inc.com

ABSTRACT

A large fraction of user-generated content on the Web, such as posts or comments on popular online forums, consists of abuse or spam. Due to the volume of contributions on popular sites, a few trusted moderators cannot identify all such abusive content, so viewer ratings of contributions must be used for moderation. But not all viewers who rate content are trustworthy and accurate. What is a principled approach to assigning trust and aggregating user ratings, in order to accurately identify abusive content?

In this paper, we introduce a framework to address the problem of moderating online content using crowdsourced ratings. Our framework encompasses users who are untrustworthy or inaccurate to an unknown extent — that is, both the content and the raters are of unknown quality. With no knowledge whatsoever about the raters, it is impossible to do better than a random estimate. We present efficient algorithms to accurately detect abuse that only require knowledge about the *identity* of a *single* 'good' agent, who rates contributions accurately more than half the time. We prove that our algorithm can infer the quality of contributions with error that rapidly converges to zero as the number of observations increases; we also numerically demonstrate that the algorithm has very high accuracy for much fewer observations. Finally, we analyze the robustness of our algorithms to manipulation by adversarial or strategic raters, an important issue in moderating online content, and quantify how the performance of the algorithm degrades with the number of manipulating agents.

Categories and Subject Descriptors

H.1.2 [**Information Systems**]: Models and Principles User/Machine Systems

General Terms

Algorithms

EC'11, June 5–9, 2011, San Jose, California, USA.

Keywords

User-generated content, Moderation, Crowdsourcing

1. INTRODUCTION

The Web is growing, and the extent of active user participation on the Web is growing with it as well. Most websites that display content now also allow user comments and discussions, and attract a huge volume of user posts— for instance, the popular website Slashdot receives over thousands of comments on its posts each day, while the more popular articles on Yahoo! News might receive thousands of comments *each.* Many of these posts are insightful or informative, or otherwise add value to the reader's experience, but there is a large quantity of abuse as well: according to a recently released study, as much as 95% of user-generated posts on Web sites are spam or malicious[1].

As the volume of user-generated content (UGC) increases, a solitary trusted moderator cannot single-handedly deal with the problem of identifying bad content. Even a small group of hand-picked moderators is grossly inadequate— quoting from Slashdot, "The (moderation) system worked well, but as Slashdot continued to grow, it was obvious that these 25 (trusted) people wouldn't be enough to keep up with the thousands of posts we were getting each day". The only solution to dealing with the problem of moderating the huge volume of user-generated content is to crowdsource the job of moderating content as well. Indeed, most websites now allow users the option to rate individual pieces of content as good or bad, usually using thumbs-up/thumbs-down style buttons, with a view to using this feedback to infer quality.

The problem of moderating user-generated content using viewer ratings, though, is not an easy one — *if* users were all reliable, these ratings would be adequate to determine whether a particular contribution is inappropriate. But *not all users who rate content rate it 'right'*: even the most evidently undesirable posts receive a non-zero number, and sometimes a significant fraction, of thumbs-up votes, and conversely perfectly good content is voted down by trolls as well. To make matters worse, raters are not simply 'good' or 'bad', consistently rating content right or consistently rating it wrong— the same user might rate some contributions accurately but some others inaccurately, either deliberately or due to random error from misjudging the threshold of acceptability. So we have a situation where in addition to content itself being good or bad, the *ratings* themselves may

[1]http://www.daniweb.com/news/story258407.html

be questionable, leading to the following dilemma: when a user votes down a piece of content, how do we know whether the *rating or the content is bad*?

If we only observe users' ratings for a single contribution, the best we can do in the absence of any other information is to treat all ratings as equally likely to be correct, and use simple aggregation by majority vote. But there is typically more information available, since most systems that allow users to rate content also require them to be logged in to do so— this allows us to observe users' ratings over many contributions. Now suppose we have some way to estimate the appropriateness of some contributions, perhaps using ratings from some 'good' users whose identities are known to the system. Can these extra observations be used to do better, and under what conditions— what and how much prior information do we need about raters, and how reliable do we need our good raters to be, to be able to effectively use this information?

Most moderation schemes used by websites hosting user-generated content indeed use information about a user's past behavior to decide whether she is reliable or trustworthy enough to moderate, and how much moderation power to assign to her[2]. But what is a measure of reliability or trust anyway? We emphasize that the primary goal of a moderation system is *not* deciding which raters are trustworthy or to what extent, but rather only to accurately infer the quality of each contribution — any estimate of a rater's quality is merely a means towards this end. The question of deciding what a suitable measure of trust is and how to estimate it, is therefore closely related to the question of how to *aggregate* ratings to accurately estimate the appropriateness of each contribution. What is a principled approach to assigning 'moderation power' and aggregating ratings, and how do we quantify susceptibility to manipulation?

Our Contributions. In this paper, we introduce a framework within which to address the problem of *moderating* user-generated content, when the viewers who rate content are not perfectly accurate or trustworthy, *and* have unknown accuracy. Our model allows us to quantify the robustness of the moderation scheme in the presence of manipulation by adversarial raters of different kinds: this is an important factor in the UGC moderation context where trolling, either to promote a particular agenda or to generally attack the moderation system, is a common occurrence.

While we phrase our discussion in terms of abuse on online forums, e.g., spam or malicious content in comments on Slashdot or YouTube, our framework also applies to other instances of UGC where some kinds of contributions are clearly undesirable, and recognizable (albeit with error) as such. One particular example is *biased* reviews of products or services, such as when a user trying to promote a particular product or service (or bring down a competing product or service) posts an evidently biased review; this is not uncommon, for example, on Amazon. We also note that while in this paper we only address the problem of moderation, or identifying inappropriate content, this model could provide a first step for addressing further questions like accurately inferring more fine-grained ratings or accurately ranking content as well; see §7.

In our model, contributions are either 'good' or 'bad', and each rater, or agent, i rates contributions correctly with some *unknown* probability ψ_i: ψ_i can be thought of as a continuous version of the measure of a rater's trustworthiness that is used for assigning moderation privileges by various online moderation schemes. Clearly, with no knowledge at all about agents' rating abilities ψ_i, it is impossible to predict contributions' qualities more accurately than random guessing. We show that all we need to know is the *identity of a single agent* with $\psi_i > 1/2$, *i.e.*, an agent who rates accurately more than half the time, to achieve good performance— we emphasize that we do not need to know the exact value of ψ for this agent, nor do we need her to rate well almost all the time, or rate all items. We present efficient algorithms based on spectral decomposition that, armed with the identity of this one 'good' agent, infer the quality of contributions with error rate that rapidly falls to zero as we observe more and more contributions; we also numerically verify that the algorithm identifies inappropriate content with high accuracy even for much fewer observations.

Organization. We begin with presenting our model in §2. In §3, we give an algorithm for estimating the quality of contributions based on relating the top eigenvector of the matrix $\mathbb{E}[UU^\top]$, where U is the matrix of observations, to the vector of actual contribution qualities, and analyze its performance (§3.1). In §4, we present and analyze an online version of this algorithm which estimates the rating abilities of the agents, ψ_i, using the same eigenvalue decomposition, and then infers the quality of each additional contribution as it arrives based on these estimates of ψ_i and its ratings. (We note that these algorithms have almost indistinguishable performance in numerical simulations, see §6.) Finally, in §5, we analyze the robustness of our algorithms to manipulation designed to attack the entire moderation system, *i.e.*, affect all ratings, as well as to manipulations targeted at a single contribution, such as by a group of agents with an agenda. All missing proofs can be found in the appendix of the full version of the paper.

Related Work. The problem of moderating user-generated content is a major issue that is widely discussed on online forums, and there are even companies[3] consulting on best practices for addressing UGC abuse. These focus on solutions like content filtering based on the text of contributions, and ad hoc solutions for the problem of aggregating viewer ratings. While there has recently been work [12, 14, 8, 13] on inferring labels obtained from crowdsourcing image-annotation tasks, the specifics of the problem and consequently the model and approaches differ from ours, and to the best of our knowledge there is no work on formal models or algorithmic approaches to the problem of crowdsourcing the moderation of UGC.

There is a growing body of work on user-generated content. The recent work [6] addresses quality in UGC from the perspective of incentivizing users to contribute high-quality content. While [6] assumes *nonstrategic accurate ratings* by viewers and uses these to incentivize contributors, we do not

[2]A number of these (e.g., StackOverflow) assign points based on behavior, and assign moderation privileges to different extents based on the number of accumulated points.

[3]www.eModeration.com

address the issue of disincentivizing spammers — we merely take their presence as given and ask how to accurately identify spam content in the presence of inaccurate ratings. We also note that while we address robustness to manipulation, we do not address the issue of actually incentivizing users to rate accurately. [3] proposes an algorithm to incentivize users to rate honestly in *revenue-generating* ranking and reputation systems like search engines or online retailers such as Amazon that is based on sharing revenue with raters; whether these incentives and models apply to UGC is an open question.

The problem of moderating online content is reminiscent of the literature on voting [4], as well as recommender [1] and reputation systems [5]. The important distinction with the voting and recommender systems literature arises because items, or candidates, have an *underlying quality* in our problem: a contribution is either abuse or not[4].In contrast, agents have different preferences over items in voting problems, *i.e.*, items have no underlying common quality. This distinction also applies to recommender systems, where different users might have different opinions about the same item; again, ratings for items are subjective and there is no notion of underlying item quality. Thus the goal of a recommender system is to decide whether a *user* might like a particular item given his and other users' ratings, whereas our problem is to identify whether the *item* is good or bad.

The distinction with the reputation system literature is the following: the goal of a moderation system is to judge content, and *not* the raters— any estimate of raters' abilities is useful only to the extent that it helps accurately rate content. Specifically, if a user is producing bad and good comments, we would like to identify the bad comments as bad and the good ones as good, rather than infer that the user produces good content half the time. While one could imagine estimating the 'reputation' of each contribution via user ratings, the nature of the problems addressed by the reputation system literature, such as building up a high reputation to cash in on it or starting afresh with a new identity after earning a bad reputation, do not quite apply to this mapping since contributions are not active agents in the sense used in reputation systems. We note that there is also work on inferring reputation in the presence of Sybil attacks, *i.e.*, the creation of numerous fake identities; see for instance [15]. Our algorithms can tolerate a small constant fraction of Sybil nodes.

Technically, the analysis of our algorithm is based on concentration bounds for random matrices. Similar analysis has been applied for data mining previously [2], where the main technical tool used is a high probability bound on the spectrum of random matrices. However, such techniques yield very weak bounds in our application. We resort to a different technique, a recently developed Chernoff-type concentration inequality [10] for sums of random rank one matrices, which give us much tighter performance guarantees. To our knowledge, this is the first application of such Chernoff bounds to the analysis of data mining algorithms.

2. MODEL

The main components of our model are the *contributions*, which are of unknown quality, and the *raters*, who rate these contributions with unknown accuracy: we would like to aggregate these ratings in such a way as to accurately identify the quality of contributions. While quality in UGC spans the whole spectrum from excellent contributions to mediocre-poor content which is neither harmful nor valuable, all the way down to abuse, we focus here on abuse, or unambiguously bad content such as spam, malicious links, posts on entirely unrelated topics, and explicit comments. We next formally describe the model.

There are n users, or agents, $i = 1, \dots, n$, who rate content. There are T contributions, or items, $t = 1, \dots, T$. Each item is either *good*, corresponding to having quality $q_t = 1$, or *bad*, corresponding to having quality $q_t = -1$. The 'bad' items correspond to spam or abusive contributions that are unambiguously undesirable to the website. The remaining 'good' contributions, while not necessarily all of equal quality, are the non-spam contributions.

The system does not know the values of q_t, and would like to infer the qualities of items using agents' ratings.

Agents rate items as ± 1, corresponding to voting using the thumbs-up/thumbs-down button which is very widely used online to obtain viewer feedback on content. Different agents have different *probabilities* of rating items correctly: ψ_i is the probability that agent i rates items correctly, *i.e.*, that her rating agrees with the true quality of the item. That is, suppose $u_{ti} \in \{-1, 1\}$ is agent i's rating for item t. Then,

$$u_{ti} = \begin{cases} q_t & \text{w.p. } \psi_i \\ -q_t & \text{w.p. } 1 - \psi_i. \end{cases}$$

We emphasize that the values of ψ_i are *unknown* to the system, *i.e.*, the ψ_i are latent variables and the system does not know in advance how well each agent rates contributions.

In general, agents might not rate all items. We will use p_i to denote the probability that agent i rates an item. For simplicity, we will present most of our analysis for $p_i = 1$, the case where all agents rate all items, and indicate how to extend the analysis to incomplete ratings.

With no knowledge whatsoever about the ψ_i values, it is easy to see that there is no hope of correctly inferring the quality of a contribution even if we have ratings from all agents on a very large number of items. We therefore make the following very weak assumption about the information the system has about the ψ_i. We assume that the agent knows the identity of *one* 'good' or trustworthy rater, where our requirement of goodness is also very weak— suppose agents are numbered so that this good agent is agent 1. We will assume that agent 1 rates items correctly strictly more than half the time: $\psi_1 > 1/2$.

We emphasize that we do not assume that the exact *value* of ψ_1 is known to the system, nor that ψ_1 is very close to 1— we simply need to know the *identity* of a single user with $\psi > 1/2$. We will sometimes use γ to denote how much better than random agent 1 rates, *i.e.*, $\gamma = \psi_1 - 1/2$; by assumption, $\gamma > 0$.

DEFINITION 2.1 (COMPETENCE: $\kappa, \bar{\kappa}$). *Define the* competence *of an agent i to be $\kappa_i = (2\psi_i - 1)^2 = 4(\psi_i - \frac{1}{2})^2$: κ_i is a number in $[0,1]$ which indicates how informative i's rating is in determining the quality of an item, with 0 being the least informative corresponding to $\psi_i = 1/2$, and 1 being fully informative corresponding to $\psi_i = 1$ or $\psi_i = 0$. Define the total competence $\kappa = \sum_i \kappa_i$, and the average*

[4]We do not attempt here to rank, or distinguish between good and mediocre, content, but only to identify abuse.

competence

$$\bar{\kappa} = \frac{\kappa}{n} = \frac{4}{n}\sum_{i=1}^{n}(\psi_i - \tfrac{1}{2})^2.$$

The average competence will show up repeatedly in the analysis of our algorithm, with the error being inversely proportional to the average competence.

Given a set of observed ratings U and knowing that agent 1 has $\psi_1 > 1/2$, our goal is to infer the qualities of items, *i.e.*, the vector $q = [q_t]$, as well as possible.

Notation. q is the $T \times 1$ column vector of item qualities, and ψ is the $n \times 1$ vector of probabilities of agents voting correctly. For a vector v, we will use $\hat{v}$ to denote the unit vector in the direction of v, *i.e.*, $\hat{v} = \frac{1}{\|v\|}v$, where $\|v\|$ denotes the ℓ_2 norm of v.

We use $A^\top$ to denote the transpose of a matrix A. We use $\|A\|_2$ to denote the spectral norm of a matrix A, *i.e.*, its largest singular value.

3. ESTIMATING q

In this section, we will present our first algorithm for estimating the qualities q using the observations U. The algorithm is based on a spectral decomposition of the matrix $UU^\top$, and also forms the basis of an online algorithm which we describe in the next section. We begin with some preliminaries that motivate the algorithm, and then analyze and bound the error rate as a function of the number of observations n, T and the average competence $\bar{\kappa}$ in Theorem 3.1. We discuss the efficiency of the eigenvector computation required by the algorithm in §3.3.

Let $U = [u_{ti}]$ represent the matrix of observed ratings, where the ith column u_i is the vector of agent i's ratings on the items $1, \ldots, T$. The expected value of u_{ti} is

$$\mathbb{E}[u_{ti}] = q_t\psi_i - q_t(1-\psi_i) = q_t(2\psi_i - 1).$$

Therefore, we have

$$\mathbb{E}[U] = q(2\psi - \mathbf{1})^\top,$$

where recall that q is the $T \times 1$ column vector of item qualities, ψ is the $n \times 1$ vector of probabilities of agents voting correctly, and $\mathbf{1}$ denotes the $n \times 1$ column vector with all coordinates equal to 1. Note that $\mathbb{E}[U]$ is a rank-one matrix, with left singular vector proportional to q, and right singular vector proportional to $(2\psi - \mathbf{1})$. This singular value decomposition of $\mathbb{E}[U]$ suggests an algorithm for estimating q from the singular value decomposition of U. To analyze this algorithm, though, we will use the fact that the top left singular vector of U is identical to the top eigenvector of $UU^\top$, and relate the top eigenvector of $UU^\top$ to the top eigenvector of its expected value $\mathbb{E}[UU^\top]$. Next, we write $\mathbb{E}[UU^\top]$ in terms of q and ψ (note that $\mathbb{E}[UU^\top]$ is not the same as $\mathbb{E}[U]\mathbb{E}[U^\top]$).

Let $\phi_{ti} \in \{-1, 1\}$ be a random variable taking the value 1 if agent i rates item t correctly (which happens with probability ψ_i), and -1 otherwise (which happens with probability $1 - \psi_i$). Then, $u_{ti} = \phi_{ti}q_t$. (While ϕ_{ti} has the same distribution for each t, the realization of course might be distinct and thus the random variables need separates names.)

If $t \neq s$, then

$$\phi_{ti}\phi_{si} = \begin{cases} 1 & \text{w.p. } \psi_i^2 + (1-\psi_i)^2 \\ -1 & \text{w.p. } 1 - \psi_i^2 - (1-\psi_i)^2. \end{cases}$$

so

$$\begin{aligned}\mathbb{E}[\phi_{ti}\phi_{si}] &= \psi_i^2 + (1-\psi_i)^2 - (1 - \psi_i^2 - (1-\psi_i)^2) \\ &= (2\psi_i - 1)^2.\end{aligned}$$

If $t = s$, then $\phi_{ti}\phi_{si} = 1$, so $\mathbb{E}[\phi_{ti}\phi_{si}] = 1$ also.

The (s,t) element in $UU^\top$ is $\sum_{i=1}^n u_{si}u_{ti} = q_sq_t\sum_{i=1}^n \phi_{si}\phi_{ti}$, with expected value

$$\begin{aligned}\mathbb{E}[\textstyle\sum_{i=1}^n u_{si}u_{ti}] &= q_sq_t\mathbb{E}\left[\textstyle\sum_{i=1}^n \phi_{si}\phi_{ti}\right] \\ &= \begin{cases} \sum_{i=1}^n (2\psi_i - 1)^2 & \text{if } t \neq s \\ n & \text{if } t = s. \end{cases}\end{aligned}$$

Therefore, given the latent model ψ_i of agents' probabilities of rating items correctly, we can write the matrix $\mathbb{E}[UU^\top]$ as

$$\begin{aligned}\mathbb{E}[UU^\top] &= \left(\textstyle\sum_{i=1}^n (2\psi_i - 1)^2\right)qq^\top + \left(n - \textstyle\sum_{i=1}^n (2\psi_i - 1)^2\right)I \\ &= \kappa qq^\top + (n - \kappa)I, \qquad (1)\end{aligned}$$

where κ is the total competence (Definition 2.1), and I is the $T \times T$ identity matrix.

This matrix $\mathbb{E}[UU^\top]$ therefore has a very simple spectral decomposition: it has top eigenvalue

$$\lambda_1 = \kappa\|q\|^2 + (n - \kappa) = \kappa T + (n - \kappa)$$

with corresponding eigenvector q. The remaining eigenvalues λ_i, for $i \geq 2$, are all equal, with value $n - \kappa$, and the corresponding eigenvectors lie in the orthogonal complement of the space spanned by q. This inspires the following algorithm for estimating q from the observations U.

Algorithm Spectral-Rating.

1. Compute the top eigenvector v of the matrix $UU^\top$ (scaled so $\|v\| = 1$), and let $s = sgn(v)$ (component-wise sign).
2. If $u_1 \cdot s \geq 0$, set $\sigma = 1$, else set $\sigma = -1$.
3. Output $q' = \sigma s$ as the estimated quality vector.

The first step computes the top eigenvector v of $UU^\top$, inspired by the fact that the top eigenvector of $\mathbb{E}[UU^\top]$ is q. Now note that if v is an eigenvector of $UU^\top$, then so is $-v$, but these correspond to exactly opposite estimates of the items' qualities. How do we decide which sign to choose for the eigenvector? The second step uses the fact that agent 1 rates items correctly more than half the time to choose the sign for the eigenvector based on correlation with agent 1's ratings. The third step simply estimates the quality of item i as the sign of the corresponding entry in σs.

Now, *if* we had access to the matrix $\mathbb{E}[UU^\top]$, extracting its top eigenvector would give us exactly the vector of actual qualities q. But of course, we only have access to U, and therefore $UU^\top$. How closely does the top eigenvector of $UU^\top$, which is a random matrix with mean $\mathbb{E}[UU^\top]$, resemble the top eigenvector q of $\mathbb{E}[UU^\top]$? The difference between these two eigenvectors will tell us how close q', our estimate of the quality derived from the top eigenvector of $UU^\top$, is to the actual quality vector q. We next analyze this difference.

3.1 Analysis

Our main result is Theorem 3.1, the proof of which is structured as follows. First, we adapt a matrix version of a Chernoff bound which tells us that the random matrix $UU^\top$

and its expectation $\mathbb{E}[UU^\top]$ are not very different, as measured by the spectral norm, with some probability. We use this bound to say that with the same probability, every pair of corresponding eigenvalues of $UU^\top$ and $\mathbb{E}[UU^\top]$ are close. We use both these results to bound the angle between the top eigenvector v of the observed matrix $UU^\top$, and q, which is the top eigenvector of the expectation $\mathbb{E}[UU^\top]$. Finally, we translate this bound on the angle between the two eigenvectors to the error in the algorithm, which is the number of coordinates in which q and v differ in sign. The probability with which this bound on the error holds is given by a union bound over the probability with which the Chernoff bound holds, and the probability that we choose the correct sign for v based on the correlation with the ratings of the known good agent.

We begin with the following bound, from [10], on the difference between a random matrix and its expectation (measured by the spectral norm)[5]:

LEMMA 3.1 ([10]). *If vectors $y_1, y_2, \ldots, y_n \in \mathbb{R}^d$ are drawn from independent distributions such that for some parameter M we have $\|y_i\| \leq M$, then there is an absolute constant c (independent of M and the dimension d) such that for any $\delta > 0$ we have*

$$Pr\left[\left\|\frac{1}{n}\sum_{i=1}^{n} y_i y_i^\top - \mathbb{E}\left[\frac{1}{n}\sum_{i=1}^{n} y_i y_i^\top\right]\right\|_2 > \delta\right] \leq 2\exp\left[\frac{-cn\delta^2}{\log(n)M^2}\right].$$

Now, $UU^\top = \sum_i u_i u_i^\top$, where u_i is the $T \times 1$ column vector of ratings by agent i. Since each entry in u_i is either 1 or -1, $\|u_i\|^2 = T$. Therefore, for our problem, setting $y_i = u_i$ and $M = \sqrt{T}$ we get

$$Pr\left[\left\|\frac{1}{n}UU^\top - \frac{1}{n}\mathbb{E}[UU^\top]\right\|_2 > \delta\right] \leq 2\exp\left[\frac{-cn\delta^2}{\log(n)T}\right]. \quad (2)$$

So for $\delta = \sqrt{\frac{\log(n)T\log(4/\eta)}{cn}}$, the RHS above becomes smaller than $\eta/2$. Thus, w.p. at least $1-\eta/2$, we have

$$\|UU^\top - \mathbb{E}[UU^\top]\|_2 \leq n\delta. \quad (3)$$

We assume this is the case from here on.

The following lemma says that if the difference of two positive semidefinite matrices (here, $UU^\top$ and $\mathbb{E}[UU^\top]$) has a small spectral norm, then the top eigenvectors of the two matrices cannot be too far away from each other if (one of) the matrices have an adequate spectral gap, *i.e.*, difference between the first and second eigenvalue.

LEMMA 3.2. *Let A and B be symmetric, positive semidefinite matrices such that $\|A-B\|_2 \leq \delta$. Let v_1 and w_1 be the unit eigenvectors corresponding to the top eigenvalues of A and B respectively. Let λ_1 and λ_2 be the top two eigenvalues of B. Then*

$$(v_1 \cdot w_1)^2 \geq 1 - \frac{\lambda_2 + 3\delta}{\lambda_1}.$$

This is indeed the case with the matrix $\mathbb{E}[UU^\top]$, where the difference between the top two eigenvalues is large when the number of items T is large, which is the regime of interest, corresponding to moderating a large number of contributions. Applying Lemma 3.2 (with $A = UU^\top$ and $B = \mathbb{E}[UU^\top]$), we get that

$$(\hat{q} \cdot v)^2 \geq 1 - \frac{\lambda_2 + 3n\delta}{\lambda_1},$$

where $\hat{q} = \frac{q}{\sqrt{T}}$ is the unit vector in the direction of q, and v is the unit eigenvector of $UU^\top$ computed in Step 1 of the algorithm.

Using the values $\lambda_1 = \kappa T + (n-\kappa)$ and $\lambda_2 = (n-\kappa)$, we get that

$$(\hat{q} \cdot v)^2 \geq 1 - \frac{n - \kappa + 3n\delta}{\kappa T + (n-\kappa)}.$$

For our choice of $\delta = \sqrt{\frac{\log(n)T\log(4/\eta)}{cn}}$, we get that with probability at least $1-\eta/2$, we have

$$(\hat{q} \cdot v)^2 \geq 1 - \epsilon/2, \quad (4)$$

where, assuming $T > n$,

$$\epsilon = 2 \cdot \frac{n - \kappa + 3n\sqrt{\frac{\log(n)T\log(4/\eta)}{cn}}}{\kappa T + (n-\kappa)} < \frac{8}{\bar{\kappa}}\sqrt{\frac{\log(n)\log(4/\eta)}{cnT}}. \quad (5)$$

So far we have shown that $(\hat{q} \cdot v)^2$ must be small with high probability. In Lemma 3.3 below, we show that when T (and n) are large enough, we choose the right sign for v: specifically, if $T > \frac{2}{\gamma^2}\log(\frac{4}{\eta})$, then with probability at least $1-\eta/2$, we have $\hat{q}\cdot(\sigma v) \geq 0$ (recall that $\gamma = \psi_1 - 1/2$). In this case, we can we conclude that $\hat{q}\cdot(\sigma v) \geq \sqrt{1-\epsilon/2} > 1-\epsilon/2$, *i.e.*, the angle between the vectors $\hat{q}$ and v is small with high probability.

Next we will translate this to a bound on the actual number of errors made by the algorithm in its estimate. Let $M = \{i : q_t = -q'_t\}$ denote the set of items on which our estimate is wrong. Since $\hat{q}$ and σv both have unit norm, we have

$$\|\hat{q} - \sigma v\|^2 = 1 + 1 - 2(\hat{q} \cdot \sigma v) < \epsilon. \quad (6)$$

But,

$$\|\hat{q} - \sigma v\|^2 \geq \sum_{t \in M}\left(\frac{q_t}{\sqrt{T}} - \sigma v_t\right)^2 \geq \sum_{i \in M}\frac{1}{T} = \frac{|M|}{T}. \quad (7)$$

The second inequality follows because for $t \in M$, $q_t \neq q'_t$, and $q'_t = sgn(\sigma v_t)$ so that $|\frac{q_t}{\sqrt{T}} - \sigma v_t| \geq \frac{1}{\sqrt{T}}$. This implies that the fraction of errors is bounded by ϵ.

The following lemma shows that we choose the right sign for the estimated ratings vector when T and n are large enough.

LEMMA 3.3. *If $T > \frac{2}{\gamma^2}\log(4/\eta)$ and $\frac{n}{\log(n)} > \frac{128}{c\bar{\kappa}^2}$, then with probability at least $1-\eta/2$, we have $\hat{q}\cdot(\sigma v) \geq 0$.*

PROOF. Assume without loss of generality that the vector v obtained at the end of step 1 of the algorithm satisfies $\hat{q}\cdot v \geq 0$. Then we want to show that with high probability, $u_1 \cdot s \geq 0$, and thus we choose $\sigma = 1$ and $\hat{q}\cdot(\sigma v) \geq 0$.

For this, we make use of the fact that we know that user 1 is good with $\psi_1 > 0.5$. We have $\psi_1 = 0.5 + \gamma$, where $\gamma > 0$ is a constant. Then for any item t, $\mathbb{E}[u_{t1}q_t] = \psi_1 - (1-\psi_1) = 2\gamma$. Thus, $\mathbb{E}[u_1 \cdot q] = 2\gamma T$. Hoeffding bounds say that for

[5]Note that the statement of the bound in [10] assumes that the vectors y_i are drawn independently from identical distributions. It is easy to check that their analysis carries through to give the stated bound even if the distributions of the y_i vectors are different, as long as the vectors are drawn independently.

T independent random variables $X_1, X_2, \ldots, X_T \in \{-1, 1\}$, for any $\delta > 0$, we have

$$\Pr\left[\mathbb{E}\left[\sum_{t=1}^{T} X_t\right] - \sum_{t=1}^{T} X_t \geq \delta\right] \leq \exp\left(\frac{-\delta^2}{2T}\right).$$

Applying this bound to our setting with $X_t = u_{t1}q_t$ and $\delta = \gamma T$, we get

$$\Pr[u_1 \cdot q < \gamma T] < \exp(-\gamma^2 T/2).$$

So if $T > \frac{2}{\gamma^2}\log(4/\eta)$, then the probability that $u_1 \cdot q < T\gamma$ is at most $\eta/2$. Thus, with probability at least $1 - \eta/2$, we have $u_1 \cdot q \geq \gamma T$, which implies that

$$|\{t : u_{1t} = q_t\}| \geq (1/2 + \gamma/2)T.$$

Now, because we assumed that $\hat{q} \cdot v \geq 0$, the same calculations as in inequalities (6) and (7) applied to the vectors $\hat{q}$ and v (instead of σv) imply that

$$|\{t : q_t \neq s_t\}| < \epsilon T.$$

Thus, we have

$$|\{t : u_{1t} = s_t\}| > (1/2 + \gamma/2 - \epsilon)T \geq T/2,$$

which is equivalent to $u_1 \cdot s \geq 0$. The inequality above holds if $\epsilon \leq \gamma/2$. This is indeed true for $T > \frac{2}{\gamma^2}\log(4/\eta)$, equation (5) implies that $\epsilon < \frac{1}{\bar{\kappa}}\sqrt{\frac{32\log(n)}{cn}} \cdot \gamma < \gamma/2$ for the specified range of n. □

This finally gives us the following high probability bound on the fraction of errors made.

THEOREM 3.1. *There is a constant c such that if $T > \frac{2}{\gamma^2}\log(4/\eta)$ and $\frac{n}{\log(n)} > \frac{128}{c\bar{\kappa}^2}$, then for any $\eta \in (0,1)$, with probability at least $1 - \eta$, we have*

$$\frac{1}{T}|\{t : q'_t \neq q_t\}| \leq \frac{8}{\bar{\kappa}}\sqrt{\frac{\log(n)}{cnT}}\log(\frac{4}{\eta}).$$

The theorem essentially says that when T and n are large enough, the fraction of errors is bounded with high probability by $O(\sqrt{\frac{\log(n)}{nT}})$. This is a vanishing fraction of errors as n and T become large. Note also the inverse dependence of ϵ on the average competence, $\bar{\kappa}$: the larger the $\bar{\kappa}$, the smaller the error. This precisely quantifies how the agents' ability to rate accurately, *i.e.*, the ψ_i, affect performance. We discuss this in greater detail in §5.

We note that the algorithm actually delivers high accuracy even for much smaller values of n, T than predicted by this bound; we include numerical simulations demonstrating this in §6 (these simulations involve incomplete ratings, which are analyzed next.)

3.2 Accounting for Incomplete Ratings

In reality, not all agents rate all items, and a number of entries in the matrix U may be missing: the (i, j) entry in U is missing if agent j does not rate item i. The algorithm and analysis above can be extended to deal with this case as well, as follows. Suppose that agent i rates items independently with probability p_i. Set $u_{ti} = 0$ if agent i does not rate item t. Then,

$$u_{ti} = \begin{cases} q_t & \text{w.p. } p_i\psi_i \\ -q_t & \text{w.p. } p_i(1-\psi_i) \\ 0 & \text{w.p. } 1-p_i. \end{cases}$$

Using similar calculations as those for obtaining (1), it is easy to check the following:

$$\mathbb{E}[UU^\top] = (\textstyle\sum_i p_i^2(2\psi_i - 1)^2)qq^\top + (\sum_i p_i - p_i^2(2\psi_i - 1)^2)I.$$

This expression reduces to (1) in the case that all $p_i = 1$.

We can now analyze the same algorithm as before. Repeating the same calculations as in the previous section, we immediately obtain the following bound on the error rate.

THEOREM 3.2. *There is a constant c such that if $T > \frac{3}{p_1\gamma^2}\log(4/\eta)$ and $\frac{n}{\log(n)} > \frac{88p_1}{c\delta^2}$, then for any $\eta \in (0,1)$, with probability at least $1 - \eta$, we have*

$$\frac{1}{T}|\{t : q_t \neq q'_t\}| \leq \frac{8}{\bar{\kappa}_p}\sqrt{\frac{\log n}{cnT}}\log(4/\eta). \tag{8}$$

Structurally, the bound is similar to that of Theorem 3.1. The only difference is that the dependence on $\bar{\kappa}$ is replaced by the same dependence on $\bar{\kappa}_p = \frac{\sum_i p_i^2(2\psi_i - 1)^2}{\sum_i p_i}$. If all the p_i's are equal to some value r, then the $\bar{\kappa}_p = r\bar{\kappa}$; so the bound below says that the fraction of errors increases by a factor of $\frac{1}{r}$.

3.3 Computing Eigenvectors Efficiently

Our algorithm for estimating the qualities of contributions relies on computing the eigenvector of a $T \times T$ matrix. T is likely to be rather large in practice, since crowdsourcing moderation is necessary only when the number of contributions are large; also, the algorithm's performance improves with increasing T, so we would like to use as many observations as possible as input. Here we discuss the feasibility of this computation.

Eigenvector computations are extremely efficient in practice [11]. In particular, computing the top eigenvector of a positive semidefinite matrix can be done very efficiently using iterative methods such as the power method or the Lanczos iteration. The benefit of these iterative methods is that they only rely on matrix-vector products and thus can take advantage of sparsity in the matrix. In our case, even though the matrix $UU^\top$ can be dense, computing its product with a vector can be done in linear time in the number of non-zero entries of U: simply multiply by $U^\top$ first, and then multiply the result by U.

In our application, we actually do not even need to compute the top eigenvector exactly: rather, it suffices to approximate v, the top eigenvector of $UU^\top$, in the following sense. Find a vector y such that $(v \cdot \hat{y})^2 \geq (1 - \epsilon')$, where ϵ' is an error parameter. Then $\hat{y}$ can be used in place of v in Algorithm Spectral-Rating, and it can be shown easily that the fraction of errors only increases by $O(\epsilon')$. Thus, choosing $\epsilon' = \Theta(\epsilon^c)$ for some constant c, the performance of the algorithm remains essentially unchanged.

Now, because the difference between the top eigenvalues of $UU^\top$ is large, the power method converges extremely fast: in a constant number of iterations, *i.e.*, independent of T! This implies that a good approximation to the top eigenvector can be computed in linear time in the number of non-zero entries of U. The following lemma makes this precise; the probability of success can be boosted to any desired level by repeating the power iteration with different random starting vectors and finally taking the one with the largest Rayleigh quotient with $UU^\top$.

LEMMA 3.4. *Let $\epsilon' = \Theta(\epsilon^c)$ for some constant c. Let x be a randomly chosen vector in $\{-1,1\}^n$. Let $y = (UU^\top)^k x$, Then for a large enough constant k, with probability at least $1/8$, we have $(v \cdot \hat{y}) \geq 1 - \epsilon'$.*

4. AN ONLINE ALGORITHM

In this section, we design an online version of the algorithm in the previous section for estimating the quality of each item, and provide bounds on its performance.

Algorithm Spectral-Rating can be thought of as a batch algorithm: it generates estimated ratings given a batch of data. Such a batch algorithm is not efficient enough to scale to large data sets, where a lightweight algorithm that uses some statistics computed from a reasonable batch of data to predict ratings of new items as they arrive, in an online fashion, is much preferable. We now present an online algorithm based on Algorithm Spectral-Rating, which first estimates the raters' competencies ψ_i using the ratings on some large number T of items, and then uses these estimated ψ_i and the observed ratings u_{ti} to estimate q_t for items $t \geq T+1$. This algorithm is more efficient when an item's quality must be estimated immediately upon arrival, since we can simply use the precomputed ψ vector to output an estimate q_t, rather than re-computing an eigenvector of $UU^\top$ each time a new item arrives (*i.e.*, a new row is added to U).

It is well known that the optimal decision rule for estimating q_t, given the votes u_{ti}, is to use a weighted majority rule with logarithmic weights:

LEMMA 4.1 ([9, 7]). *Given agents with probabilities ψ_i of voting correctly, the decision rule that maximizes the probability of returning the correct outcome is weighted majority with weights*

$$w_i = \frac{1}{2}\log\left(\frac{\psi_i}{1-\psi_i}\right).$$

Of course, we do not know the ψ_i exactly but only have an estimate of the ψ_i from Spectral-Rating; we will use this approximate estimate of the ψ_i's as input to the weighted majority calculation.

The algorithm for estimating the ψ_i's is as follows:

Algorithm Estimate-ψ.

1. Run Algorithm Spectral-Rating to get the vector q'.
2. For each user i, output the estimate

$$\psi'_i = \frac{1}{2}\left(\frac{1}{T}(q' \cdot u_i) + 1\right).$$

The prediction algorithm is essentially weighted majority with the estimated ψ_i. A small twist is a clipping of estimated ψ_i to the range $[\alpha, 1-\alpha]$ for some $\alpha = O(1/\sqrt{T})$ to make the algorithm stable (note that the logarithmic weights tend to infinity at 0 or 1) and allow an error analysis.

Algorithm Predict

1. Run Algorithm Estimate-ψ to obtain ψ'_i and set $\psi''_i = \min\{\max\{\psi'_i, \alpha\}, 1-\alpha\}$, where $\alpha = 2\sqrt{\frac{1}{T}\log(\frac{4n}{\eta})}$.
2. Compute $w_i = \frac{1}{2}\log(\frac{\psi''_i}{1-\psi''_i})$.
3. When item $t \geq T+1$ arrives, output the estimate of its quality $q'_t = sgn\left(\sum_i w_i u_{t,i}\right)$.

4.1 Analysis

Since the algorithms are based on Algorithm Spectral-Rating, we assume throughout this section that the conditions for Theorem 3.1 hold, *i.e.*, $T > \frac{2}{\gamma^2}\log(4/\eta)$ and $\frac{n}{\log(n)} > \frac{128}{c\bar{\kappa}^2}$, so that with probability at least $1-\eta$, the error rate of Algorithm Spectral-Rating is bounded by $\epsilon = \frac{8}{\bar{\kappa}}\sqrt{\frac{\log(n)\log(8/\eta)}{cnT}}$.

We first analyze the quality of approximation to the ψ_i's achieved by Algorithm Estimate-ψ:

THEOREM 4.1. *With probability at least $1-\eta$, we have for all i,*

$$|\psi''_i - \psi_i| \leq \alpha.$$

PROOF. First, note that $\mathbb{E}[q_i u_{ti}] = 2\psi_i - 1$. By the Hoeffding bounds, we have

$$\Pr\left[\left|\frac{1}{T}\sum_{t=1}^{T} q_t u_{ti} - (2\psi_i - 1)\right| > \epsilon'\right] < \eta/2n,$$

where $\epsilon' = \sqrt{\frac{1}{T}\log(4n/\eta)}$. Next, by Theorem 3.1, we have

$$\Pr[|\{t:\ q_t \neq q'_t\}| > \epsilon T] < \eta/2,$$

where $\epsilon = \frac{8}{\bar{\kappa}}\sqrt{\frac{\log(n)\log(8/\eta)}{cnT}}$. This implies that with probability at least $1-\eta/2$,

$$\left|\frac{2}{T}\sum_{t=1}^{T} q_t u_{ti} - \frac{1}{T}\sum_{t=1}^{T} q'_t u_{ti}\right| < 2\epsilon,$$

since $|u_{ti}| = 1$. Applying a union bound over all i, we get that with probability at least $1-\eta$, for all i, we have

$$\left|\frac{1}{T}\sum_{t=1}^{T} q_t u_{ti} - (2\psi_i - 1)\right| < 2\epsilon + \epsilon' < 4\epsilon',$$

using $\epsilon \leq 2\epsilon'$ since we assumed that $\frac{n}{\log(n)} \geq \frac{128}{c\bar{\kappa}^2}$. This implies that

$$|\psi'_i - \psi_i| < 2\epsilon' = \alpha.$$

The clipping of ψ'_i to the range $[\alpha, 1-\alpha]$ to produce ψ''_i maintains $|\psi''_i - \psi_i| \leq \alpha$. □

We can now give bounds on the error rate of Algorithm Predict. This is expressed as a bound on the probability that an error is made on item q_{T+1}. Naturally, this bound also holds for any subsequent item $t > T+1$. The bound shows that as long as T is large enough so that $\alpha \ll \bar{\kappa}$ (note that $\alpha = O(\sqrt{\log(n)/T})$), the probability of making an error drops *exponentially* with n.

THEOREM 4.2. *Assume that the assertion of Theorem 4.1 holds, i.e. for all i, we have $|\psi''_i - \psi| \leq \alpha$. Assume further that T is large enough so that $\alpha \leq 0.05$. Then*

$$\Pr[q'_{T+1} \neq q_{T+1}] < \exp(-0.5(\bar{\kappa} - 24\alpha)n).$$

PROOF. Without loss of generality, assume that $q_{T+1} = 1$. Algorithm Predict makes an error if $\sum_i w_i u_{T+1,i} < 0$. Consider the function $\exp(-\sum_i w_i u_{T+1,i})$. This is always non-negative, and at least 1 whenever Algorithm Predict makes an error. Hence, we have

$$\Pr[q'_{T+1} \neq q_{T+1}] = \mathbb{E}[1_{\sum_i w_i u_{T+1,i} < 0}]$$
$$\leq \mathbb{E}[\exp(-\sum_i w_i u_{T+1,i})]$$
$$= \prod_i \mathbb{E}[\exp(-w_i u_{T+1,i})] \text{ (by independence of } u_{T+1,i})$$
$$= \prod_i (\psi_i \exp(-w_i) + (1-\psi_i)\exp(w_i))$$
$$= \prod_i \left(\psi_i \cdot \sqrt{\frac{1-\psi_i''}{\psi_i''}} + (1-\psi_i) \cdot \sqrt{\frac{\psi''}{1-\psi_i''}}\right).$$

In Lemma 4.2 below, we bound the term in the product above by $\exp(-0.5(2\psi_i - 1)^2 + 12\alpha)$. Plugging in this bound, we get that

$$\Pr[q'_{T+1} \neq q_{T+1}] \leq \exp(-0.5(\bar{\kappa} - 24\alpha)n).$$

□

LEMMA 4.2. *If $\alpha \leq 0.05$, the following bound holds:*

$$\left(\psi_i \cdot \sqrt{\frac{1-\psi_i''}{\psi_i''}} + (1-\psi_i) \cdot \sqrt{\frac{\psi''}{1-\psi_i''}}\right) \leq \exp(-0.5(2\psi_i - 1)^2 + 12\alpha).$$

5. MANIPULATION

Finally, we address the issue of manipulation. We consider three kinds of agents: (i) agents who choose their value of ψ_i strategically to most degrade the performance of the algorithm; (ii) agents who deviate from the model and rate *each contribution adversarially* to most degrade the performance of the algorithm, *i.e.*, such agents' ratings need not be drawn according to a distribution given by ψ for any value of ψ, and (iii) agents who only want to influence the system's estimate of the quality of a *single* item — for instance, a group of agents might want to influence the outcome for a particular contribution either positively or negatively, but still rate other contributions accurately to the extent given by their ψ_i (either out of benevolence, or to maximize their 'trust' prior to manipulation). For all three cases, we analyze the robustness of the algorithm to manipulation, and quantify how the performance of the algorithm degrades with the number of manipulating agents.

Stochastic Manipulation. This first case, where agents continue to rate according to the model, but choose ψ to degrade the algorithm's performance, is easy. Recall that the performance of the algorithm depends on the competence of each agent in a simple way: the error rate ϵ is inversely proportional to the average competence $\bar{\kappa}$, *i.e.*, the smaller $\bar{\kappa}$, the larger the error. In fact, since this is the only term containing ψ_i in the expression for ϵ, a malicious agent who wants to attack the system by adversarially choosing ψ_i will do the most harm by choosing $\psi_i = 1/2$, *i.e.*, by simply randomly voting items good or bad. In particular, this algorithm is robust to agents who intentionally rate every (or most) items the opposite of its actual quality, which corresponds to ψ_i close to zero: such agents in fact are quite useful to the algorithm since the algorithm can essentially invert their judgment. The performance bound follows by simply setting $\psi = 1/2$ for each manipulator in Theorem 3.1.

Adversarially choosing u_j. We now consider a different kind of malicious attack, where a malicious agent does not behave according to a probability distribution as postulated in the model at all, but chooses all her ratings adversarially to most degrade the performance of the algorithm. If there is more than one such agent, we will allow for the fact that these agents might collude, *i.e.*, the set of ratings from all these agents could be adversarially chosen.

Suppose there are b such bad agents, and the remaining $n_g = n - b$ agents rate stochastically. That is, the $n - b$ columns in U corresponding to these 'good' (though possibly not very competent) agents are stochastically generated, but the b columns corresponding to the bad agents are arbitrary vectors in $\{-1, 1\}^T$. In the following, all probability and expectation calculations are over the randomness of the good agents.

The bound below shows that the fraction of errors is essentially what can be obtained by applying Theorem 3.1 to the n_g good agents, plus an additional $\frac{b}{\bar{\kappa}_g n_g}$ term. Thus, if $b \ll n$, and $\bar{\kappa}_g = \frac{\kappa_g}{n_g} > 0$, then this additional term becomes negligible. This means that Algorithm Spectral-Rating can tolerate a small constant fraction of malicious agents, even if these agents are colluding.

LEMMA 5.1. *Under the assumptions of Theorem 3.1, we have that with probability $1 - \eta$,*

$$\frac{1}{T}|\{t : q_t \neq q'_t\}| \leq \frac{8}{\bar{\kappa}_g}\sqrt{\frac{\log(n_g)\log(2/\eta)}{cn_g T}} + \frac{b}{\bar{\kappa}_g n_g}.$$

PROOF. Let $\kappa_g = \sum_{i \notin B}(2\psi_i - 1)^2$ be the total competence of the good agents. Then, a calculation similar to the previous one shows that

$$\mathbb{E}[UU^\top] = \kappa_g qq^\top + (n_g - \kappa_g)I + \sum_{j \in B} u_j u_j^\top.$$

Next, the matrix Chernoff-bound calculations as in (2) lead to the following bound:

$$Pr\left[\|UU^\top - \mathbb{E}[UU^\top]\|_2 > n_g\delta\right] \leq 2\exp\left(\frac{-cn_g\delta^2}{\log(n_g)T}\right). \quad (9)$$

Note that this uses the fact that $\sum_{j \in B} u_j u_j^\top$ term cancels out in $UU^\top - \mathbb{E}[UU^\top]$. For $\delta = \sqrt{\frac{\log(n_g)T\log(2/\eta)}{cn_g}}$, the RHS becomes smaller than η.

Now note that

$$\|\mathbb{E}[UU^\top] - (\kappa_g qq^\top + (n_g - \kappa_g)I)\|_2 = \|\sum_{j \in B} u_j u_j^\top\|_2 \leq bT.$$

Hence, with probability at least $1 - \eta$, we have

$$\|UU^\top - (\kappa_g qq^\top + (n_g - \kappa_g)I)\|_2 \leq n_g\delta + bT.$$

Again as before, by Lemma 3.2, we get that

$$(\hat{q} \cdot v)^2 \geq 1 - \frac{\lambda'_2 + 3n_g\delta + 3bT}{\lambda'_1},$$

where $\lambda'_1 = \kappa_g T + (n_g - \kappa_g)$, and $\lambda'_2 = (n_g - \kappa_g)$. For our choice of parameters, we get that $(\hat{q} \cdot v)^2 \geq 1 - \epsilon/2$, where

$$\epsilon < \frac{8}{\bar{\kappa}_g}\sqrt{\frac{\log(n_g)\log(2/\eta)}{cn_g T}} + \frac{b}{\bar{\kappa}_g n_g},$$

where $\bar{\kappa}_g = \frac{\kappa_g}{n_g}$. Reasoning as before, ϵ gives a bound on the fraction of errors. □

Choosing u_{tj} to influence outcome for a particular item t. Now we consider what happens if some set B of b agents are interested in manipulating the outcome for a single item, although not necessarily in bringing down the entire moderation system as a whole. This is quite a realistic possibility, since a spammer with a particular agenda might be interested only in making sure that a post on that agenda is not accurately identified as spam[6]: in fact, it is to these agents' benefit to rate other items accurately to acquire as much of the system's trust as possible before attempting to manipulate the outcome for their chosen item.

To analyze this kind of manipulation, we will use the online version of our algorithm from §4, which allows us to address the error for a specific contribution rather than an average error over contributions. We will show that as long as b is small compared to κ_g, the total competence of the good agents, the probability of making an error still remains exponentially small. In the following theorem, $n_g = n - b$ denotes the number of good agents, and $\beta = \frac{1}{2}\log(\frac{1-\gamma}{\gamma})$ is an upper bound on the magnitude of the weights w_i produced by algorithm Estimate-ψ, where $\gamma = \max\{\alpha, \min_i\{1-\psi_i\}, \min_i\{\psi_i\}\}$. If every ψ_i is bounded away from 0 or 1, a reasonable assumption, β will be a moderately sized constant, because of the logarithm.

The bound below is similar in spirit to the bound of Lemma 5.1. It says that the error rate is what one might expect by applying Theorem 4.2, times an additional factor of $\exp(\beta b)$. Thus, if $b \ll n$, and $\bar{\kappa}_g > 0$, then the additional factor becomes negligible. The implication is that Algorithm Predict is resistant to manipulation by a small constant fraction of malicious agents, even if they are colluding.

LEMMA 5.2. *Under the assumptions of Theorem 4.2, we have*

$$\Pr[q'_{T+1} \neq q_{T+1}] < \exp(-0.5(\bar{\kappa}_g - 24\alpha - \beta\tfrac{b}{n_g})n_g).$$

PROOF. Assume as before that $q_{T+1} = 1$. The bad agents can do the most damage by choosing all their own ratings to be -1. We now want to bound the probability that the weighted majority rule makes an error, i.e. $\sum_i w_i u_{i,T+1} < 0$. This is equivalent to

$$\sum_{i \notin B} w_i u_{i,T+1} < \sum_{i \in B} w_i.$$

The RHS above is bounded by βb. We now bound the probability that $\sum_{i \notin B} w_i u_{i,T+1} < \beta b$. For this, we use the same technique as before:

$$\begin{aligned}\Pr[\sum_{i\notin B} w_i u_{i,T+1} < \beta b] &= \mathbb{E}[1_{\sum_{i\notin B} w_i u_{i,T+1} < \beta b}] \\ &\leq \mathbb{E}[\exp(\beta b - \textstyle\sum_{i\notin B} w_i u_{i,T+1})] \\ &= \exp(\beta b) \prod_{i\notin B} \mathbb{E}[\exp(-w_i u_{i,T+1})].\end{aligned}$$

The rest of the analysis is the same as before, and results in specified bound on the error rate.
□

[6]This comment on a YouTube video clearly falls in this category: "hey everyone we have a group on facebook but now we have a youtube channel so? go to our channel and subscribe to us!"; it actually had 10 thumbs-up votes.

6. SIMULATIONS

The performance bounds proved in the previous sections guarantee that the fraction of errors goes to 0 as n and T grow. However, the bounds given are worst-case and might yield needlessly pessimistic requirements on how large n and T need to be to obtain small error. In this section, we numerically evaluate the performance of our algorithms for small values of n and T, and show that the accuracy of the algorithm is high even for these regimes. Note that there are no computational difficulties associated with handling larger numbers of observations[7]; here, we only want to demonstrate that a very large amount of data is not essential for accuracy.

We imagine two scenarios, and plot how the error rate of the algorithm changes with increasing $\bar{\kappa}$, the average competence of the raters.:

1. A modestly sized website with a relatively small number of users and a modest number of contributions, with modest rating probabilities p_i. Specifically, we set $n = 100$ users, $T = 1000$ contributions, and the p_i's are randomly drawn uniformly from $[0, 0.3]$. This corresponds to collecting an average of 150 thumbs-up/down ratings by users, a reasonable number.

2. A large website with a large number of users and contributions, but smaller p_i. Here we set $n = 1000$ users, $T = 5000$ contributions, and the p_i's are randomly drawn uniformly from $[0, 0.1]$.

Competencies for the raters are randomly drawn from the normal distribution with mean $0.5 + t$ and variance 0.01 clipped to the $[0, 1]$ interval. Here t is a parameter that is changed to obtain different values of $\bar{\kappa}$.

While we ran both Algorithm Spectral-Rating and Algorithms Estimate+Predict, for clarity we only show results for Algorithm Spectral-Rating since the performance of Algorithms Estimate+Predict was nearly identical. The error rate depicted in the graph is the 90% quantile obtained from 100 runs of the algorithm. We use the 90% quantile instead of the mean because there are sometimes a few outliers with large error causing small spikes in the mean (note that our bounds also only hold with probability $1-\eta$); the 90% quantile curve is smoother and shows the trend of the error rate quite clearly, while still being a reasonable indicator of the performance.

The plots clearly demonstrate the effectiveness of the algorithm for much smaller values of T than required by the theoretical bounds. The performance improves rapidly as $\bar{\kappa}$ increases: when $\bar{\kappa}$ is zero, essentially all agents are rating randomly, and so the algorithm cannot do very much better than random guessing. However the error rates fall very rapidly to values in the range of a few percent even for very small values of $\bar{\kappa}$, and in the case of Scenario 2, the error rate improves even faster, falling to 0 for $\bar{\kappa} = 0.3$.

7. DISCUSSION

In this paper, we introduced a model for the problem of moderating user-generated content using crowdsourced ratings of unknown reliability, and presented efficient algorithms to accurately identify abusive content. There are

[7]The online algorithm's performance is almost identical to that of the batch algorithm for the same parameters, so even larger amounts of data can be used to improve accuracy without sacrificing speed.

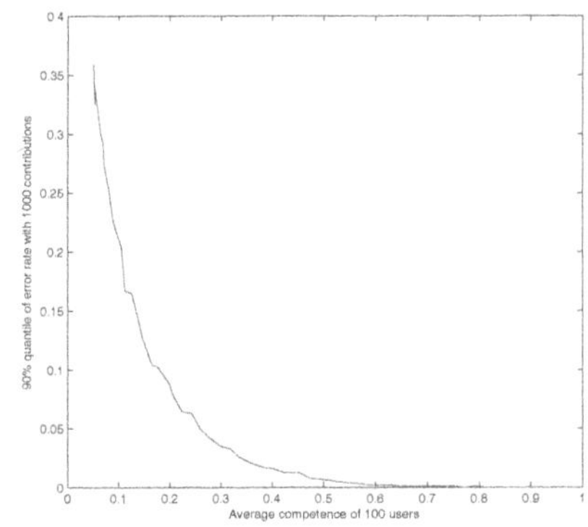

Figure 1: Average comptence v.s. 90% quantile of error rate, in Scenario 1: 100 users, 1000 contributions, p_i's drawn uniformly from $[0, 0.3]$.

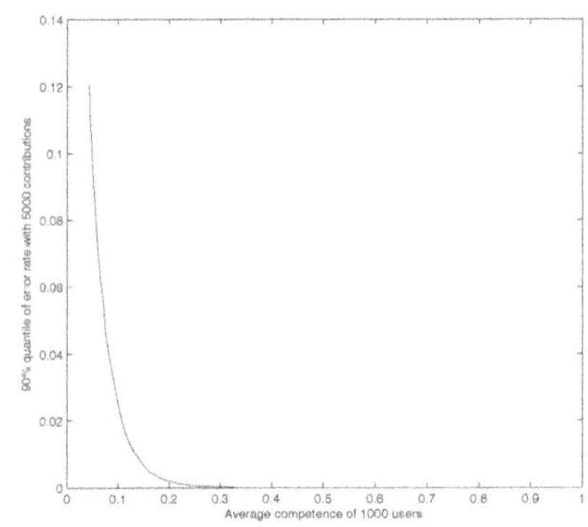

Figure 2: Average comptence v.s. 90% quantile of error rate, in scenario 2: 1000 users, 5000 contributions, p_i's drawn uniformly from $[0, 0.1]$.

a number of interesting directions for further work. First, while we focused on identifying unambiguously bad content, user ratings can also be used to infer the relative qualities of non-abusive contributions: not all non-spam UGC is of the same quality, and displaying better quality contributions more prominently improves user experience. How accurately can an algorithm infer the true rankings of the items according to their qualities in the presence of inaccurate ratings, and how sensitive is it to manipulation? For example, the order in which restaurants appear in the Yelp rankings likely strongly influences whether a user notices them or not; the ranking is generated precisely on the basis of user ratings that may not be accurate or honest. The model presented in this paper might provide a first step towards addressing this question.

Another interesting direction is robustness against manipulation: how can we design algorithms that are optimized against manipulation, to tolerate a larger number of malicious agents, and what are the trade-offs? Finally, we note that the most general model for UGC would involve both strategic contributors and strategic raters. The question of how to design a mechanism for this setting that both incentivizes contributors to produce high quality and raters to rate honestly is a promising direction for future work, potentially requiring insights from other fields to accurately model incentives for all agents.

8. REFERENCES

[1] G. Adomavicius and A. Tuzhilin. Toward the next generation of recommender systems: A survey of the state-of-the-art and possible extensions. *IEEE Transactions on Knowledge and Data Engineering*, 17(6):734–749, June 2005.

[2] Y. Azar, A. Fiat, A. R. Karlin, F. McSherry, and J. Saia. Spectral analysis of data. In *STOC*, pages 619–626, 2001.

[3] R. Bhattacharjee and A. Goel. Algorithms and incentives for robust ranking. In *SODA*, pages 425–433, 2007.

[4] V. Conitzer. Making decisions based on the preferences of multiple agents. *Commun. ACM*, 53(3):84–94, 2010.

[5] E. Friedman, P. Resnick, and R. Sami. Manipulation-resistant reputation systems. *Algorithmic Game Theory*, 2007.

[6] A. Ghosh and R. P. McAfee. Incentivizing high-quality user generated content. In *Proc. WWW*, 2011.

[7] B. Grofman and L. Shapley. Optimizing group judgmental accuracy in the presence of interdependencies. *Public Choice*, 43:329–343, 1984.

[8] P. G. Ipeirotis, F. Provost, and J. Wang. Quality management on amazon mechanical turk. In *Proc. Workshop on Human Computation*, 2010.

[9] S. Nitzan and J. Paroush. Optimal Decision Rules in Uncertain Dichotomous Choice Situations. *International Economic Review*, 23(2):289–297, June 1982.

[10] M. Rudelson and R. Vershynin. Sampling from large matrices: An approach through geometric functional analysis. *J. ACM*, 54(4), 2007.

[11] L. N. Trefethen and D. Bau. *Numerical Linear Algebra*. SIAM, 1997.

[12] P. Welinder, S. Branson, S. Belongie, and P. Perona. The multidimensional wisdom of crowds. In *NIPS*, 2010.

[13] P. Welinder and P. Perona. Online crowdsourcing: Rating annotators and obtaining cost-effective labels. In *Computer Vision and Pattern Recognition Workshop*, 2010.

[14] J. Whitehill, P. Ruvolo, J. Bergsma, T. Wu, and J. Movellan. Whose vote should count more: Optimal integration of labels from labelers of unknown expertise. In *Advances in Neural Information Processing Systems*, 2009.

[15] H. Yu, M. Kaminsky, P. B. Gibbons, and A. D. Flaxman. Sybilguard: Defending against sybil attacks via social networks. *IEEE/ACM Trans. Netw.*, 16(3):576–589, 2008.

Axiomatic Attribution for Multilinear Functions

[Extended Abstract]*

Yi Sun†
Google, Inc. / MIT
Cambridge, MA 02139 USA
yisun@mit.edu

Mukund Sundararajan
Google, Inc.
Mountain View, CA 94043 USA
mukunds@google.com

ABSTRACT

We study the *attribution* problem. That is, given a real-valued characteristic function f of n variables and initial and final values r and s for its independent variables, our objective is to divide the responsibility for the change $f(s) - f(r)$ in the characteristic function among each of its independent variables. We call these assigned responsibilities *attributions*, and we would like the attributions to form a complete partition of the total change.[1] When $r = 0$, the attribution problem coincides with a standard cost sharing model from the social choice literature (cf. Moulin [2]), where the characteristic function is the cost function, the independent variables are the demands of the agents, and the attributions are cost shares for the agents.[2]

We follow the cost sharing literature in identifying good attribution methods axiomatically (for a classical example, see Friedman and Moulin [1]). We consider:

- `Additivity` – attributions are additive in the characteristic function,
- `Dummy` – if the characteristic function does not depend on a variable, then its attribution is zero, and
- `Affine Scale Invariance` – attributions are invariant under simultaneous affine transformation of the characteristic function and the variables.

First, we show that when the characteristic function is the sum of a multilinear function and an additively separable one, every attribution method satisfying these axioms is a random order method. Intuitively, a multilinear function is determined by its values on the vertices of a hypercube, so its attributions should depend on these values alone, leading to the space of random order methods. The proof proceeds by using this idea to count dimensions.

Second, in our main result, we show that there is a unique attribution method satisfying these axioms and `Anonymity` (which requires attributions to be invariant under relabeling of the variables) if and only if the characteristic function is the sum of a multilinear function and an additively separable one.[3] The main technical tool is the use of Stokes' Theorem to compare attribution methods. The resulting method coincides with the classical Aumann-Shapley and Shapley-Shubik methods, and thus we term it the *Aumann-Shapley-Shubik* method. When the characteristic function is multilinear, our result prescribes this method for use; to this end, we provide a computationally efficient implementation.

Together, our results single out the class of multilinear characteristic functions as a particularly nice one for attribution problems. We give several examples of natural attribution problems where such functions arise, including pay-per-click advertising, website traffic analysis, portfolio analysis, and performance analysis of sports teams.

*Full version: `http://arxiv.org/abs/1102.0989`.

†Work was done while author was at Google Research.

[1]Here the characteristic function may be nonlinear and the changes in the variables large, ruling out a naive approach based on linear approximation of the characteristic function.

[2]A significant difference is that cost sharing assumes monotone cost functions, while attribution relaxes this requirement. Therefore, while negative cost shares do not make sense, negative attributions are possible in some contexts.

Categories and Subject Descriptors

H.1.m [**Information Systems**]: Models and Principles—*Miscellaneous*; J.4 [**Computer Applications**]: Social and Behavioral Sciences—*Economics*

General Terms

Economics, Theory

Keywords

Cost sharing, Axioms, Attribution, Causality

REFERENCES

[1] Friedman, E., and Moulin, H. Three methods to share joint costs or surplus. *J. Econ. Theory 87*, 2 (August 1999), 275–312.

[2] Moulin, H. Axiomatic cost and surplus sharing. In *Handbook of Social Choice and Welfare*, K. J. Arrow, A. K. Sen, and K. Suzumura, Eds., vol. 1 of *Handbook of Social Choice and Welfare*. Elsevier, April 2002, ch. 6, pp. 289–357.

[3] Redekop, J. Increasing marginal cost and the monotonicity of Aumann-Shapley pricing. mimeo, University of Waterloo, 1996.

[3]Unlike this result, most axiomatic results in cost sharing quantify over all cost functions and may not apply to a smaller class (see Redekop [3] for an example for the axiomatization of the Aumann-Shapley method in [1]).

Strategic Sequential Voting in Multi-Issue Domains and Multiple-Election Paradoxes

Lirong Xia
Dept. of Computer Science
Duke University
Durham, NC 27708, USA
lxia@cs.duke.edu

Vincent Conitzer
Dept. of Computer Science
Duke University
Durham, NC 27708, USA
conitzer@cs.duke.edu

Jérôme Lang
LAMSADE
Université Paris-Dauphine
75775 Paris Cedex, France
lang@lamsade.dauphine.fr

ABSTRACT

In many settings, a group of voters must come to a joint decision on multiple issues. In practice, this is often done by voting on the issues in sequence. We model sequential voting in multi-issue domains as a complete-information extensive-form game, in which the voters are perfectly rational and their preferences are common knowledge. In each step, the voters simultaneously vote on one issue, and the order of the issues is given exogenously before the process. We call this model *strategic sequential voting*.

We focus on domains characterized by multiple binary issues, so that strategic sequential voting leads to a unique outcome under a natural solution concept. We show that under some conditions on the preferences, this leads to the same outcome as truthful sequential voting, but in general it can result in very different outcomes. In particular, sometimes the order of the issues has a strong influence on the winner. We also analyze the communication complexity of the corresponding social choice rule.

Most significantly, we illustrate several *multiple-election paradoxes* in strategic sequential voting: there exists a profile for which the winner under strategic sequential voting is ranked nearly at the bottom in all voters' true preferences, and the winner is Pareto-dominated by almost every other alternative. We show that changing the order of the issues cannot completely prevent such paradoxes. We also study the possibility of avoiding the paradoxes for strategic sequential voting by imposing some constraints on the profile, such as separability, lexicographicity or $\mathcal{O}$-legality.

Categories and Subject Descriptors

I.2.11 [**Distributed Artificial Intelligence**]: Multiagent Systems; J.4 [**Computer Applications**]: Social and Behavioral Sciences—*Economics*

General Terms

Economics, Theory

Keywords

Social choice, strategic voting, multi-issue domains, multiple-election paradoxes

1. INTRODUCTION

In a traditional voting system, each voter is asked to report a linear order over the alternatives to represent her preferences. Then, a *voting rule* is applied to the resulting profile of reported preferences to select a winning alternative. In practice, the set of alternatives often has a *multi-issue* structure. That is, there are p issues $\mathcal{I} = \{\mathbf{x}_1, \ldots, \mathbf{x}_p\}$, and each issue can take a value in a *local domain*. In other words, the set of alternatives is the Cartesian product of the local domains. For example, in *multiple referenda*, the inhabitants of a local district are asked to vote on multiple inter-related issues [5]. Another example is *voting by committees*, in which the voters select a subset of objects [1], where each object can be seen as a binary issue.

Voting in multi-issue domains has been extensively studied by economists, and more recently has attracted the attention of computer scientists. Previous work has focused on proposing a natural and compact *voting language* for the voters to represent their preferences, as well as designing a sensible voting rule to make decisions based on the reported preferences using such a language. A natural approach is to let voters vote on the issues separately, in the following way. For each issue (simultaneously, not sequentially), each voter reports her preferences for that issue, and then, a *local rule* is used to select the winning value that the issue will take. This voting process is called *issue-by-issue* or *seat-by-seat* voting.

Computing the winner for issue-by-issue voting rules is easy, and it only requires a modest amount of communication from the voters to the mechanism. Nevertheless, issue-by-issue voting has some drawbacks. First, a voter may feel uncomfortable expressing her preferences over one issue independently of the values that the other issues take [15]. It has been pointed out that issue-by-issue voting avoids this problem if the voters' preferences are *separable* (that is, for any issue i, regardless of the values for the other issues, the voter's preferences over issue i are always the same) [14]. Second, *multiple-election paradoxes* arise in issue-by-issue voting [5, 14, 21, 23]. In models that do not consider strategic (game-theoretic) voting, previous works have shown several types of paradoxes: sometimes the winner is a Condorcet loser; sometimes the winner is Pareto-dominated by another alternative (that is, that alternative is preferred to the winner in all votes); and sometimes the winner is ranked in a very low position by all voters.

One way to partly escape these paradoxes consists in organizing the multiple elections *sequentially*: given an order $\mathcal{O}$ over all issues (without loss of generality, we take $\mathcal{O}$ to be $\mathbf{x}_1 > \cdots > \mathbf{x}_n$), the voters first vote on issue $\mathbf{x}_1$; then, the value collectively chosen for $\mathbf{x}_1$ is determined using some voting rule and broadcast to the voters, who then vote on issue $\mathbf{x}_2$, and so on. When the issues are all binary, it is natural to choose the majority rule at each stage (plus, in the case of an even number of voters, some tie-breaking mechanism). Such processes are conducted in many real-life situations. For instance, suppose there is a full professor position and an assistant professor position to be filled. Then, it is realistic to expect that the committee will first decide who gets the full professor position. Another example is that at the executive meeting of the co-owners of a building, important decisions like whether a lift should be installed or not, how much money should be spent to repair the roof are usually taken before minor decisions. In each of these cases, it is clear that the decision made on one issue influences the votes on later issues, thus the order in which the issues are decided potentially has a strong influence on the final outcome.

Now, if voters are assumed to know the preferences of other voters well enough, then we can expect them to vote strategically at each step, forecasting the outcome at later steps conditional on the outcomes at earlier steps. Let us consider the following motivating example.

Example 1 Three residents want to vote to decide whether they should build a swimming pool and/or a tennis court. There are two issue $\mathbf{S}$ and $\mathbf{T}$. $\mathbf{S}$ can take the value of s (meaning "to build the swimming pool") or $\bar{s}$ (meaning "not to build the swimming pool"). Similarly, $\mathbf{T}$ takes a value in $\{t, \bar{t}\}$. Suppose the preferences of the three voters are, respectively, $st \succ \bar{s}t \succ s\bar{t} \succ \bar{s}\bar{t}$, $s\bar{t} \succ st \succ \bar{s}t \succ \bar{s}\bar{t}$ and $\bar{s}t \succ \bar{s}\bar{t} \succ s\bar{t} \succ st$. Voter 2 and 3 took the budget constraint into consideration so that they do not rank st as their first choices. Suppose the voters first vote on issue $\mathbf{S}$ then on $\mathbf{T}$. Moreover, since both issues are binary, the local rule used at each step is majority (there will be no ties, because the number of voters is odd). Voter 1 is likely to reason in the following way: *if the outcome of the first step is s, then voters 2 and 3 will vote for $\bar{t}$, since they both prefer $s\bar{t}$ to st, and the final outcome will be $s\bar{t}$; but if the outcome of the first step is $\bar{s}$, then voters 2 and 3 will vote for t, and the final outcome will be $\bar{s}t$; because I prefer $\bar{s}t$ to $s\bar{t}$, I am better off voting for $\bar{s}$, since either it will not make any difference, or it will lead to a final outcome of $\bar{s}t$ instead of $s\bar{t}$.* If voters 2 and 3 reason in the same way, then 2 will vote for s and 3 for $\bar{s}$; hence, the result of the first step is $\bar{s}$, and then, since two voters out of three prefer $\bar{s}t$ to $\bar{s}\bar{t}$, the final outcome will be $\bar{s}t$. Note that the result is fully determined, provided that (1) it is common knowledge that voters behave strategically according to the principle we have stated informally, (2) the order in which the issues are decided, as well as the local voting rules used in all steps, are also common knowledge, and (3) voters' preferences are common knowledge. Therefore, these three assumptions allow the voters and the modeler (provided he knows as much as the voters) to predict the final outcome.

Let us take a closer look at voter 1 in Example 1. Her preferences are *separable*: she prefers s to $\bar{s}$ whatever the value of $\mathbf{T}$ is, and t to $\bar{t}$ whatever the value of $\mathbf{S}$ is. *And yet she strategically votes for* $\bar{s}$, because the outcome for $\mathbf{S}$ affects the outcome for $\mathbf{T}$. Moreover, while voters 2 and 3 have nonseparable preferences, still, all three voters' preferences enjoy the following property: their preferences over the value of $\mathbf{S}$ are independent of the value of $\mathbf{T}$. Such a profile is called a *legal* profile with respect to the order $\mathbf{S} > \mathbf{T}$, meaning that the voters vote on $\mathbf{S}$ first, then on $\mathbf{T}$. Lang and Xia [15] defined a family of sequential voting rules on multi-issue domains, restricted to $\mathcal{O}$-legal profiles for some order $\mathcal{O}$ over the issues, where at each step, each voter is expected to vote for her preferred value for the issue $\mathbf{x}_i$ under consideration given the values of all issues decided so far [1]; then, the value of $\mathbf{x}_i$ is chosen according to a local voting rule, and this local outcome is broadcast to the voters. For example, suppose the local rule used to decide an issue is always majority. For the profile given in Example 1, the outcome of the first step under the sequential voting rule will be s (since two voters out of three prefer s to $\bar{s}$, unconditionally), and the final outcome will be $s\bar{t}$. This outcome is different from the outcome we obtain if voters behave strategically. The reason for this discrepancy is that in [15], voters are not assumed to know the others' preferences and are assumed to vote truthfully.

We have seen that even if the voters' preferences are $\mathcal{O}$-legal, voters may in fact have no incentive to vote truthfully. Consequently, existing results on multiple-election paradoxes are not directly applicable to situations where voters vote strategically.

[1]The $\mathcal{O}$-legality condition ensures that this notion of "preferred value of $\mathbf{x}_i$" is meaningful.

Our contributions

In this paper, we analyze the complete-information game-theoretic model of sequential voting that we illustrated in Example 1. This model applies to any preferences that the voters may have (not just $\mathcal{O}$-legal ones), though they must be strict orders on the set of all alternatives.

We focus on voting in multi-binary-issue domains, that is, for any $i \leq p$, $\mathbf{x}_i$ must take a value in $\{0_i, 1_i\}$. This has the advantage that for each issue, we can use the majority rule as the local rule for that issue. We use a game-theoretic model to analyze outcomes that result from sequential voting. Specifically, we model the sequential voting process as a p-stage complete-information game as follows. There is an order $\mathcal{O}$ over all issues (without loss of generality, let $\mathcal{O} = \mathbf{x}_1 > \mathbf{x}_2 > \cdots > \mathbf{x}_p$), which indicates the order in which these issues will be voted on. For any $1 \leq i \leq p$, in stage i, the voters vote on issue $\mathbf{x}_i$ simultaneously, and the majority rule is used to choose the winning value for $\mathbf{x}_i$. We make the following game-theoretic assumptions: it is common knowledge that all voters are perfectly rational; the order $\mathcal{O}$ and the fact that in each step, the majority rule is used to determine the winner are common knowledge; all voters' preferences are common knowledge.

We can solve this game by a type of backward induction already illustrated in Example 1: in the last (pth) stage, only two alternatives remain (corresponding to the two possible settings of the last issue), so at this point it is a weakly dominant strategy for each voter to vote for her more preferred alternative of the two. Then, in the second-to-last ($(p-1)$th) stage, there are two possible local outcomes for the $(p-1)$th issue; for each of them, the voters can predict which alternative will finally be chosen, because they can predict what will happen in the pth stage. Thus, the $(p-1)$th stage is effectively a majority election between two alternatives, and each voter will vote for her more preferred alternative; etc. We call such a procedure the *strategic sequential voting procedure (SSP)*.

Given exogenously the order $\mathcal{O}$ over the issues, this game-theoretic analysis maps every profile of strict ordinal preferences to a unique outcome. Since any function from profiles of preferences to alternatives can be interpreted as a voting rule, the voting rule that corresponds to SSP is denoted by $SSP_{\mathcal{O}}$.

After the introduction of SSP, we show that, unfortunately, multiple-election paradoxes also arise under SSP. To better present our results, we introduce a parameter which we call the *minimax satisfaction index (MSI)*. For an election with m alternatives and n voters, it is defined in the following way. For each profile, consider the highest position that the winner obtains across all input rankings of the alternatives (the ranking where this position is obtained corresponds to the most-satisfied voter); this is the *maximum satisfaction index* for this profile. Then, the minimax satisfaction index is obtained by taking the minimum over all profiles of the maximum satisfaction index. A low minimax satisfaction index means that there exists a profile in which the winner is ranked in low positions in all votes, thus indicating a multiple-election paradox. Our main theorem is the following.

Theorem 2 *For any $p \in \mathbb{N}$ and any $n \geq 2p^2 + 1$, the minimax satisfaction index of SSP when there are $m = 2^p$ alternatives and n voters is $\lfloor p/2 + 2 \rfloor$. Moreover, in the profile P that we use to prove the upper bound, the winner $SSP_{\mathcal{O}}(P)$ is Pareto-dominated by $2^p - (p+1)p/2$ alternatives.*

We note that an alternative c Pareto-dominates another alternative c' implies that c beats c' in their pairwise election. Therefore, Theorem 2 implies that the winner for SSP is an almost Condorcet loser. It follows from this theorem that SSP exhibits all three types of multiple-election paradoxes: the winner is ranked almost in the bottom in every vote, the winner is an almost Condorcet loser, and the winner is Pareto-dominated by almost every other alternative. We further show a paradox (Theorem 3) that states that there exists a profile such that for *any* order $\mathcal{O}$ over the issues, for every voter, the SSP winner w.r.t. $\mathcal{O}$ is ranked almost in the bottom position. We also show that even when the voters' preferences can be represented by CP-nets that are compatible with a common order, multiple-election paradoxes still arise.

Related work and discussion

Our setting is closely related to the *multi-stage sophisticated voting*, studied by McKelvey and Niemi [17], Moulin [18], and Gretlein [13]. They investigated the model where the backward induction outcomes correspond to the truthful outcomes of voting trees. Therefore, our SSP is a special case of multi-stage sophisticated voting. However, their work focused on the characterization of the outcomes as the outcomes in the *sophisticated voting* [10], and therefore did not shed much light on the quality of the equilibrium outcome. We, on the other hand, are primarily interested in the strategic outcome of the natural procedure of voting sequentially over multiple issues. Also, the relationship between sequential voting and voting trees takes a particularly natural form in the context of domains with multiple binary issues, as we will show. More importantly, we illustrate several multiple-election paradoxes for SSP, indicating that the equilibrium outcome could be extremely undesirable.

Another paper that is closely related to part of this work was written by Dutta and Sen [9]. They showed that social choice rules corresponding to binary voting trees can be implemented via backward induction via a sequential voting mechanism. This is closely related to the relationship revealed for multi-stage sophisticated voting and will also be mentioned later in this paper, that is, an equivalence between the outcome of strategic behavior in sequential voting over multiple binary issues, and a particular type of voting tree. It should be pointed out that the sequential mechanism that Dutta and Sen consider is somewhat different from sequential voting as we consider it—in particular, in the Dutta-Sen mechanism, one voter moves at a time, and a move consists not of a vote, but rather of choosing the next player to move (or in some states, choosing the winner).

Nevertheless, the approach by Dutta and Sen and our approach are related at a high level, though they are motivated quite differently: Dutta and Sen are interested in social choice rules corresponding to voting trees, and are trying to create sequential mechanisms that implement them via backward induction. We, on the other hand again, are primarily interested in the strategic outcome of the natural mechanism for voting sequentially over multiple issues, and use voting trees merely as a useful tool for analyzing the outcome of this process.

Less closely related, implementation by voting trees has previously been studied at EC: Fischer et al. [11] consider the known result that the Copeland rule cannot be implemented by a voting tree [20], and set out to *approximate* the the Copeland score using voting trees.

It has been pointed out that typical multiple-election paradoxes partly come from the incompleteness of information about the preferences of the voters [14]. However, the paradoxes in this paper show that assuming that voters' preferences are common knowledge does not allow to get rid of multiple election paradoxes. Another interpretation of these results is that we may need to move beyond sequential voting to properly address voting in multi-issue domains. However, note that other approaches than sequential voting may be extremely costly in terms of communication and computation, which comes down to saying, one more time, that voting on multiple related issues is an extremely challenging problem for which probably no perfect solution exists.

Lastly, in a recent paper [25], Xia and Conitzer studied a voting game with a different type of sequential nature: in it, the voters cast their votes one after another (strategically), and after all the voters have cast their votes, a common voting rule (not necessarily the plurality rule) is used to select the winner. This type of voting games has been studied in the literature [24, 7, 2, 8]. In [25], a strong general paradox was shown for these voting games, implying that for most common voting rules, there exists a profile such that the unique winner in subgame-perfect equilibrium is ranked within the bottom two positions in almost all the voters' true preferences. Desmedt and Elkind [8] showed similar paradoxes for such voting games with the plurality rule, where random tie-breaking is used and the voters seek to maximize their expected utility. We note that the voting games studied in [25] are quite different from the voting games studied in this paper: there, the voters move in sequence, the set of alternatives does not need to have a combinatorial structure, and a voter casts her complete vote all at once; here in this paper, the voters move simultaneously, the set of alternatives has a combinatorial structure, and the voters vote on one issue at a time.

2. PRELIMINARIES

2.1 Basics of voting

Let $\mathcal{X}$ be the set of *alternatives*, $|\mathcal{X}| = m$. A vote is a linear order (that is, a transitive, antisymmetric, and total relation) over $\mathcal{X}$. The set of all linear orders over $\mathcal{X}$ is denoted by $L(\mathcal{X})$. For any $c \in \mathcal{X}$ and $V \in L(\mathcal{X})$, we let $rank_V(c)$ denote the position of c in V from the top. For any $n \in \mathbb{N}$, an *n-profile* P is a collection of n votes, that is, $P \in L(\mathcal{X})^n$. For any $c, d \in \mathcal{X}$ and any profile P, we say c *Pareto-dominates* d, if for every $V \in P$, c is ranked higher than d in V, that is, $c \succ_V d$. A *voting rule* r is a mapping that assigns to each profile a unique winning alternative. That is, $r : L(\mathcal{X}) \cup L(\mathcal{X})^2 \cup \ldots \to \mathcal{X}$. For example, when there are two alternatives, the *majority* rule selects the alternative that is preferred by the majority of voters.

2.2 Multi-issue domains

In this paper, the set of all alternatives $\mathcal{X}$ is a *multi-binary-issue domain.* That is, let $\mathcal{I} = \{\mathbf{x}_1, \ldots, \mathbf{x}_p\}$ $(p \geq 2)$ be a set of *issues*, where each issue $\mathbf{x}_i$ takes a value in a binary *local domain* $D_i = \{0_i, 1_i\}$. The set of alternatives is $\mathcal{X} = D_1 \times \cdots \times D_p$, that is, an alternative is uniquely identified by its values on all issues. For any $Y \subseteq \mathcal{I}$ we denote $D_Y = \prod_{\mathbf{x}_i \in Y} D_i$.

Given a preference relation $\succ$ in $L(\mathcal{X})$, an issue $\mathbf{x}_i$, and a subset of issues $W \subseteq \mathcal{I}$, let $U = \mathcal{I} \backslash (W \cup \{\mathbf{x}_i\})$; then, $\mathbf{x}_i$ is *preferentially independent of W given U (with respect to $\succ$)* if for any $\vec{u} \in D_U$, any $a_i, b_i \in D_i$, and any $\vec{w}, \vec{w}' \in D_W$, $(\vec{u}, a_i, \vec{w}) \succ (\vec{u}, b_i, \vec{w})$ if and only if $(\vec{u}, a_i, \vec{w}') \succ (\vec{u}, b_i, \vec{w}')$. Informally, if we wish to find out whether changing the value of $\mathbf{x}_i$ from a_i to b_i (while keeping everything else fixed) will make the voter better or worse off, we only need to know the values of the issues in U.

Let $\mathcal{O} = \mathbf{x}_1 > \cdots > \mathbf{x}_p$. A preference relation $\succ$ is *$\mathcal{O}$-legal* if for any $i \leq p$, $\mathbf{x}_i$ is preferentially independent of $\{\mathbf{x}_{i+1}, \ldots, \mathbf{x}_p\}$ given $\{\mathbf{x}_1, \ldots, \mathbf{x}_{i-1}\}$. In words, to find out whether a particular change in the value of an issue will make the voter better or worse off, we only need to know the values of earlier issues. A preference relation $\succ$ is *separable* if for any $i \leq p$, $\mathbf{x}_i$ is preferentially independent of $\mathcal{X} \setminus \{\mathbf{x}_i\}$. That is, we do not need to know the value of any other issue to find out whether a particular change in the value of an issue will make the voter better or worse off. It follows directly that a separable preference relation is $\mathcal{O}$-legal for any $\mathcal{O}$.

A preference relation $\succ$ is *$\mathcal{O}$-lexicographic* if for any $i \leq p$, any $\vec{u} \in D_1 \times \cdots \times D_{i-1}$, any $a_i, b_i \in D_i$, and any $\vec{d_1}, \vec{d_2}, \vec{e_1}, \vec{e_2} \in D_{i+1} \times \cdots \times D_p$, $(\vec{u}, a_i, \vec{d_1}) \succ (\vec{u}, b_i, \vec{e_1})$ if and only if she prefers $(\vec{u}, a_i, \vec{d_2}) \succ (\vec{u}, b_i, \vec{e_2})$. In words, if a profile is $\mathcal{O}$-lexicographic, then it is $\mathcal{O}$-legal, and moreover, earlier issues are more important—that is, to compare two alternatives, it suffices to know the values of the issues up to and including the first issue $\mathbf{x}_i$ on which they differ. (While the values of $\mathbf{x}_1, \ldots, \mathbf{x}_{i-1}$ will be the same, they still matter in that they affect the voter's preferences on $\mathbf{x}_i$.) We note that $\mathcal{O}$-lexicographicity and separability are incomparable notions. For example, $0_1 0_2 \succ 1_1 0_2 \succ 0_1 1_2 \succ 1_1 1_2$ is separable (flipping 1_1 or 1_2 always makes the alternative rank higher) but not ($\mathbf{x}_1 > \mathbf{x}_2$)-lexicographic ($0_1 0_2 \succ 1_1 1_2$ but $1_1 0_2 \succ 0_1 1_2$). On the other hand, $0_1 0_2 \succ 0_1 1_2 \succ 1_1 1_2 \succ 1_1 0_2$ is ($\mathbf{x}_1 > \mathbf{x}_2$)-lexicographic but not separable. A profile is separable/$\mathcal{O}$-lexicographic/$\mathcal{O}$-legal if it is composed of preference relations that are all separable/$\mathcal{O}$-lexicographic/$\mathcal{O}$-legal.

We can now define sequential composition of local voting rules. Given a vector of *local rules* $(r_1, \ldots, r_p)$ (where for any $i \leq p$, r_i is a voting rule for preferences over D_i), the *sequential composition* of $r_1, \ldots, r_p$ with respect to $\mathcal{O}$, denoted by $Seq_{\mathcal{O}}(r_1, \ldots, r_p)$, is defined for all $\mathcal{O}$-legal profiles as follows: $Seq_{\mathcal{O}}(r_1, \ldots, r_p)(P) = (d_1, \ldots, d_p) \in \mathcal{X}$, where for any $i \leq p$, $d_i = r_i(P|_{\mathbf{x}_i : d_1 \cdots d_{i-1}})$, where $P|_{\mathbf{x}_i : d_1 \cdots d_{i-1}}$ is composed of the voters' local preferences over $\mathbf{x}_i$, given that the issues preceding it take values $d_1, \ldots, d_{i-1}$. Thus, the winner is selected in p steps, one for each issue, in the following way: in step i, d_i is selected by applying the local rule r_i to the preferences of voters over D_i, conditioned on the values $d_1, \ldots, d_{i-1}$ that have already been determined for the issues that precede $\mathbf{x}_i$. In this paper, we focus on the case where every r_i is the majority rule, because it is the most natural voting rule for two alternatives.

3. STRATEGIC SEQUENTIAL VOTING

3.1 Formal definition

Sequential voting on multi-issue domains can be seen as a game where in each step, the voters decide whether to vote for or against the issue under consideration after reasoning about what will happen next. We make the following assumptions.

1. All voters act strategically (in an optimal manner that will be explained later), and this is common knowledge.
2. The order in which the issues will be voted upon, as well as the local voting rules used at the different steps (namely, majority rules), are common knowledge.
3. All voters' preferences on the set of alternatives are common knowledge.

Assumption 1 is standard in game theory. Assumption 2 merely means that the rule has been announced. Assumption 3 (complete information) is the most significant assumption. It may be interesting to consider more general settings with incomplete information, resulting in a Bayesian game. Nevertheless, because the complete-information setting is a special case of the incomplete-information setting (where the prior distribution is degenerate), in that sense, *all negative results obtained for the complete-information setting also apply to the incomplete-information setting*. That is, the restriction to complete information only strengthens negative results. Of course, for incomplete information setting in general, we need a more elaborate model to reason about voters' strategic behavior.

Given these assumptions, the voting process can be modeled as a game that is composed of p stages where in each stage, the voters vote simultaneously on one issue. Let $\mathcal{O}$ be the order over the set of issues, which without loss of generality we assume to be $\mathbf{x}_1 > \cdots > \mathbf{x}_p$. Let P be the profile of preferences over $\mathcal{X}$. The game is defined as follows: for each $i \leq p$, in stage i the voters vote simultaneously on issue i; then, the value of $\mathbf{x}_i$ is determined by the majority rule (plus, in the case of an even number of voters, some tie-breaking mechanism), and this local outcome is broadcast to all voters.

We now show how to solve the game. Because of assumptions 1 to 3, at step i the voters vote strategically, by recursively figuring out what the final outcome will be if the local outcome for $\mathbf{x}_i$ is 0_i, and what it will be if it is 1_i. More concretely, suppose that steps 1 to $i-1$ resulted in issues $\mathbf{x}_1, \ldots, \mathbf{x}_{i-1}$ taking the values $d_1, \ldots, d_{i-1}$, and let $\vec{d} = (d_1, \ldots, d_{i-1})$. Suppose also that if $\mathbf{x}_i$ takes the value 0_i (respectively, 1_i), then, recursively, the remaining issues will take the tuple of values $\vec{a}$ (respectively, $\vec{b}$). Then, $\mathbf{x}_i$ is determined by a pairwise comparison between $(\vec{d}, 0_i, \vec{a})$ and $(\vec{d}, 1_i, \vec{b})$ in the following way: if the majority of voters prefer $(\vec{d}, 0_i, \vec{a})$ over $(\vec{d}, 1_i, \vec{b})$, then $\mathbf{x}_i$ takes the value 0_i; in the opposite case, $\mathbf{x}_i$ takes the value 1_i. This process, which corresponds to the strategic behavior in the sequential election, is what we call the *strategic sequential voting (SSP)* procedure, and for any profile P, the winner with respect to the order $\mathcal{O}$ is denoted by $SSP_{\mathcal{O}}(P)$.

As we shall see later, SSP can not only be thought of as the strategic outcome of sequential voting, but also as a voting rule in its own right. The following definition and two propositions merely serve to make the game-theoretic solution concept that we use precise; a reader who is not interested in this may safely skip them.

Definition 1 *Consider a finite extensive-form game which transitions among* states. *In each nonterminal state s, all players simultaneously take an action; this joint local action profile $(a_1^s, \ldots, a_n^s)$ determines the next state s'.*[2] *Terminal states t are associated with payoffs for the players (alternatively, players have ordinal preferences over the terminal states). The current state is always common knowledge among the players.*[3]

Suppose that in every final nonterminal state s (that is, every state that has only terminal states as successors), every player i has a (weakly) dominant action a_i^s. At each final nonterminal state, its local profile of dominant actions $(a_1^s, \ldots, a_n^s)$ results in a terminal state $t(s)$ and associated payoffs. We then replace each final nonterminal state s with the terminal state $t(s)$ that its dominant-strategy profile leads to. Furthermore suppose that in the resulting smaller tree, again, in every final nonterminal state, every player

[2]In the extensive-form representation of the game, each state is associated with multiple nodes, because in the extensive form only one player can move at a node.

[3]Hence, the only imperfect information in the extensive form of the game is due to simultaneous moves within states.

has a (weakly) dominant strategy. Then, we can repeat this procedure, etc. *If we can repeat this all the way to the root of the tree, then we say that the game is solvable by* within-state dominant-strategy backward induction (WSDSBI).

We note that the backward induction in perfect-information extensive-form games is just the special case of WSDSBI where in each state only one player acts.

Proposition 1 *If a game is solvable by WSDSBI, then the solution is unique.*

Proposition 2 *The complete-information sequential voting game with binary issues (with majority as the local rule everywhere) is solvable by WSDSBI when voters have strict preferences over the alternatives.*

Proposition 1 is obviously true. Due to the space constraints, most proofs are omitted.

We note that SSP corresponds to a particular balanced voting tree, as illustrated in Figure 1 for the case $p = 3$. In this voting tree, in the first round, each alternative is paired up against the alternative that differs only on the pth issue; each alternative that wins the first round is then paired up with the unique other remaining alternative that differs only on the $(p-1)$th and possibly the pth issue; etc. This bottom-up procedure corresponds exactly to the backward induction (WSDSBI) process.

Of course, there are many voting trees that do *not* correspond to an SSP election; this is easily seen by observing that there are only $p!$ different SSP elections (corresponding to the different orders of the issues), but many more voting trees. The voting tree corresponding to the order $\mathcal{O} = \mathbf{x}_1 > \cdots > \mathbf{x}_p$ is defined by the property that for any node v whose depth is i (where the root has depth 1), the alternative associated with any leaf in the left (respectively, right) subtree of v gives the value 0_i (respectively, 1_i) to $\mathbf{x}_i$.

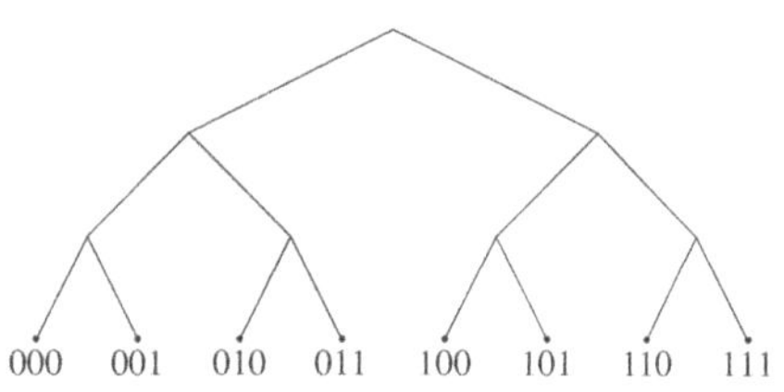

Figure 1: A voting tree that is equivalent to the strategic sequential voting procedure ($p = 3$). 000 is the abbreviation for $0_1 0_2 0_3$, etc.

3.2 Strategic sequential voting vs. truthful sequential voting

We have seen on Example 1 that even when the profile P is $\mathcal{O}$-legal, $SSP_{\mathcal{O}}(P)$ can be different from $Seq_{\mathcal{O}}(maj, \ldots, maj)(P)$. This means that even if the profile is $\mathcal{O}$-legal, voters may be better off voting strategically than truthfully. However, $SSP_{\mathcal{O}}(P)$ and $Seq_{\mathcal{O}}(maj, \ldots, maj)(P)$ are guaranteed to coincide under the further restriction that P is $\mathcal{O}$-lexicographic.

Proposition 3 *For any $\mathcal{O}$-lexicographic profile P, $SSP_{\mathcal{O}}(P) = Seq_{\mathcal{O}}(maj, \ldots, maj)(P)$.*

The intuition for Proposition 3 is as follows: if P is $\mathcal{O}$-lexicographic, then, as is shown in the proof of the proposition, when voters vote strategically under sequential voting (the *Seq* process), they are best off voting according to their true preferences in each round (their preferences in each round are well-defined because voters have $\mathcal{O}$-legal preferences in this case). When voters with $\mathcal{O}$-legal preferences vote truthfully in each round under sequential voting, the outcome is $Seq_{\mathcal{O}}(maj, \ldots, maj)(P)$; when they vote strategically, the outcome is $SSP_{\mathcal{O}}(P)$; and so, these must be the same when preferences are $\mathcal{O}$-lexicographic.

Now, there is another interesting domain restriction under which $SSP_{\mathcal{O}}(P)$ and $Seq(maj, \ldots, maj)(P)$ coincide, namely when P is $inv(\mathcal{O})$- legal, where $inv(\mathcal{O}) = (\mathbf{x}_p > \ldots > \mathbf{x}_1)$.

Proposition 4 *Let $inv(\mathcal{O}) = \mathbf{x}_p > \ldots > \mathbf{x}_1$. For any $inv(\mathcal{O})$-legal profile P, $SSP_{\mathcal{O}}(P) = Seq_{inv(\mathcal{O})}(maj, \ldots, maj)(P)$.*

As a consequence, when P is separable, it is *a fortiori* $inv(\mathcal{O})$-legal, and therefore, $SSP_{\mathcal{O}}(P) = Seq_{inv(\mathcal{O})}(maj, \ldots, maj)(P)$, which in turn is equal to $Seq_{\mathcal{O}}(maj, \ldots, maj)(P)$ and coincides with seat-by-seat voting [3].

Corollary 1
If P is separable, then $SSP_{\mathcal{O}}(P) = Seq_{\mathcal{O}}(maj, \ldots, maj)(P)$.

3.3 A second interpretation of SSP

The first interpretation of SSP (that we follow in this paper) is the one we have discussed so far, namely, SSP consists in modeling sequential voting as a complete-information game, which allows us to analyze sequential voting on multi-issue domains from a game-theoretic point of view. For this, assumptions 1, 2, and 3 above are crucial. Under this interpretation, $SSP_{\mathcal{O}}(P)$ is a (specific kind of) equilibrium for sequential voting.

However, there is a second interpretation of SSP. It consists in seeing $SSP_{\mathcal{O}}$ as a new voting rule on multi-issue domains (which is implementable in complete-information contexts by using sequential voting).[4] This defines a family of voting rules (one for each order over issues), which can be applied to any profile. The family of voting rules thus defined is a distinguished subset of the family of voting trees. This interpretation does not say anything about how preferences are to be elicited; unlike in the game-theoretic interpretation, the p-step protocol does not apply here. The communication complexity of finding the outcome of $SSP_{\mathcal{O}}$ (without any complete-information assumption, of course)[5] is given as follows.

Proposition 5 *When the voters' preferences over alternatives are unrestricted, the communication complexity of $SSP_{\mathcal{O}}$ is $\Theta(2^p \cdot n)$.*

Proof of Proposition 5: This now follows immediately from a result in [6], where it is established that the communication complexity for balanced voting trees is $\Theta(m \cdot n)$ for m alternatives and n voters. Since we do not place any restrictions on the preferences in the multi-issue domain in the statement of the proposition, the communication complexity is identical, and $m = 2^p$. □

The upper bound in this proposition is obtained simply by eliciting the voters preferences for every pair of alternatives that face each other in the voting tree.

Now, Propositions 3 and 4 immediately give us conditions under which this communication complexity can be reduced. Indeed, these Propositions say that when P is $\mathcal{O}$-lexicographic or $inv(\mathcal{O})$-legal, then the SSP winner coincides with the sequential election winner in the sense of [15]. Now, the sequential election winner in the sense of [15]. can be found with $O(pn)$ communication, simply by having each agent vote for a value for the issue at each round. This leads immediately to the following two corollaries (to Propositions 3 and 4, respectively).

[4] Of course, by Gibbard-Satterthwaite [12, 22], SSP is not strategy-proof.

[5] The communication complexity of a voting rule is the smallest number of bits that must be transmitted to compute the winner of that rule (i.e., taking the minimum across all correct protocols). See [6].

Corollary 2 *When the voters' preferences over alternatives are $\mathcal{O}$-lexicographic, the communication complexity of $SSP_{\mathcal{O}}$ is $O(pn)$.*

Corollary 3 *When the voters' preferences over alternatives are $inv(\mathcal{O})$-legal, the communication complexity of $SSP_{\mathcal{O}}$ is $O(pn)$.*

3.4 The winner is sensitive to the order over the issues

In the definition of SSP, we simply fixed the order $\mathcal{O}$ to be $\mathbf{x}_1 > \mathbf{x}_2 > \cdots > \mathbf{x}_p$. A question worth addressing is, to what extent is the outcome of SSP sensitive to the variation of the order $\mathcal{O}$? More precisely, given a profile P, let $\text{PW}(P) = |\{\vec{d} \in \mathcal{X} \mid \vec{d} = SSP_{\mathcal{O}'}(P)$ for some order $\mathcal{O}'\}|$. $\text{PW}(P)$ is the number of different alternatives that can be made SSP winners by choosing a particular order $\mathcal{O}'$. Then, for a given number of binary issues p, we look for the maximal value of $\text{PW}(P)$, for all profiles P on $\mathcal{X} = D_1 \times \ldots \times D_p$; we denote this number by $\text{MW}(p)$.

A first observation is that there are $p!$ different choices for $\mathcal{O}'$. Therefore, a trivial upper bound on $\text{MW}(p)$ is $p!$. Since there are 2^p alternatives, the $p!$ upper bound is only interesting when $p! < 2^p$, that is, $p \leq 3$. Example 2 shows that when $p = 2$ or $p = 3$, this trivial upper bound is actually tight, i.e. $\text{MW}(2) = 2!$ and $\text{MW}(3) = 3!$: there exists a profile such that by changing the order over the issues, all $p!$ different alternatives can be made winners. Due to McGarvey's theorem [16], any complete and asymmetric directed graph G over the alternatives corresponds to the majority graph of some profile (we recall that the majority graph of a profile P is the directed graph whose vertices are the alternatives and containing an edge from c to c' if and only if a majority of voters in P prefer c to c'). Therefore, in the example, we only show the majority graph instead of explicitly constructing the whole profile.

Example 2 *The majority graphs for $p = 2$ and $p = 3$ are shown in Figure 2. Let P (respectively, P') denote an arbitrary profile whose majority graph is the same as Figure 2(a) (respectively, Figure 2(b)). It is not hard to verify that $SSP_{\mathbf{x}_1 > \mathbf{x}_2}(P) = 00$ and $SSP_{\mathbf{x}_2 > \mathbf{x}_1}(P) = 01$. For P', the value of $SSP_{\mathcal{O}'}(P')$ for the six possible orders is shown on Table 1. Note that $2! = 2$ and $3! = 6$. It follows that when $p = 2$ or $p = 3$, there exists a profile for which the SSP winners w.r.t. different orders over the issues are all different from each other.*

The order	$\mathbf{x}_1 > \mathbf{x}_2 > \mathbf{x}_3$	$\mathbf{x}_1 > \mathbf{x}_3 > \mathbf{x}_2$	$\mathbf{x}_2 > \mathbf{x}_1 > \mathbf{x}_3$
SSP winner	010	011	001
The order	$\mathbf{x}_2 > \mathbf{x}_3 > \mathbf{x}_1$	$\mathbf{x}_3 > \mathbf{x}_1 > \mathbf{x}_2$	$\mathbf{x}_3 > \mathbf{x}_2 > \mathbf{x}_1$
SSP winner	100	110	101

Table 1: The SSP winners for P' w.r.t. different orders over the issues.

When $p \geq 4$, $p! > 2^p$. However, it is not immediately clear whether $\text{MW}(p) = 2^p$ or not, *i.e*, whether each of the 2^p alternatives can be made a winner by changing the order over the issues. The next theorem shows that this can actually be done, that is, $\text{MW}(p) = 2^p$.

Theorem 1 *For any $p \geq 4$ and any $n \geq 142 + 4p$, there exists an n-profile P such that for every alternative $\vec{d}$, there exists an order $\mathcal{O}'$ over $\mathcal{I}$ such that $SSP_{\mathcal{O}'}(P) = \vec{d}$.*

The proof of the theorem is by induction on p. Surprisingly, the hardest part in the inductive proof is the base case: when $p = 4$, we need to construct a profile P such that each of the 16 alternatives can be made a $SSP_{\mathcal{O}'}$ winner for at least one $\mathcal{O}'$ out of the 24 orders over four issues. We prove directly that it satisfies the desired property, and we also wrote a computer program to verify its correctness. The code (implemented in Java) can be found via the following link.

`http://www.cs.duke.edu/~lxia/Files/SSP.zip`

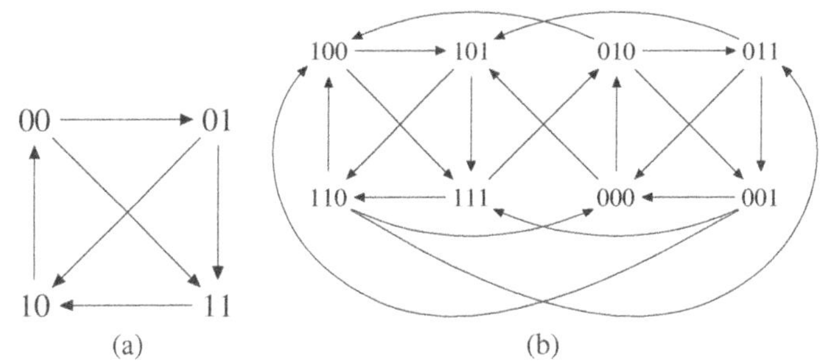

Figure 2: (a) The majority graph for $p = 2$. (b) The majority graph for $p = 3$, where four edges are not shown in the graph: $100 \to 000$, $101 \to 001$, $110 \to 010$, and $111 \to 011$. The directions of the other edges are defined arbitrarily. 000 is the abbreviation for $0_1 0_2 0_3$, etc.

4. MINIMAX SATISFACTION INDEX

In the rest of this paper, we will show that strategic sequential voting on multi-issue domains is prone to paradoxes that are almost as severe as previously studied multiple-election paradoxes under models that are not game-theoretic [5, 14]. To facilitate the presentation of these results, we define an index that is intended to measure one aspect of the quality of a voting rule, called *minimax satisfaction index*.

Definition 2 *For any voting rule r, the* minimax satisfaction index (MSI) *of r is defined by*

$$MSI_r(m, n) = \min_{P \in L(\mathcal{X})^n} \max_{V \in P} \left(m + 1 - rank_V(r(P))\right)$$

where m is the number of alternatives, n is the number of voters, and $rank_V(r(P))$ is the position of $r(P)$ in vote V.

We note that in this paper $m = 2^p$, where p is the number of issues. The MSI of a voting rule is not the final word on it. For example, the MSI for dictatorships is m, the maximum possible value, which is not to say that dictatorships are desirable. However, if the MSI of a voting rule is low, then this implies the existence of a paradox for it, namely, a profile that results in a winner that makes all voters unhappy.

Many of the multiple-election paradoxes known so far implicitly refer to such an index. For example, Lacy and Niou [14] and Benoit and Kornhauser [3] showed that for multiple referenda, if voters vote on issues separately (under some assumptions on how voters vote), then there exists a profile such that in each vote, the winner is ranked near the bottom–therefore the rule has a very low MSI.

5. MULTIPLE-ELECTION PARADOXES FOR STRATEGIC SEQUENTIAL VOTING

In this section, we show that over multi-binary-issue domains, for any natural number n that is sufficiently large (we will specify the number in our theorems), there exists an n-profile P such that $SSP_{\mathcal{O}}(P)$ is ranked almost in the bottom position in each vote in P. That is, the minimax satisfaction index is extremely low for the strategic sequential voting procedure.

We first calculate the MSI for $SSP_{\mathcal{O}}$ when the winner does not depend on the tie-breaking mechanism. That is, either n is odd, or n is even and there is never a tie in any stage of running the election sequentially. This is our main multiple-election paradox result.

Theorem 2 *For any $p \in \mathbb{N}$ ($p \geq 2$) and any $n \geq 2p^2 + 1$, $MSI_{SSP_{\mathcal{O}}}(m,n) = \lfloor p/2 + 2 \rfloor$.*[6] *Moreover, in the profile P that we use to prove the upper bound, the winner $SSP_{\mathcal{O}}(P)$ is Pareto-dominated by $2^p - (p+1)p/2$ alternatives.*

Proof of Theorem 2: The upper bound on $MSI_{SSP_{\mathcal{O}}}(m,n)$ is constructive, that is, we explicitly construct a paradox.

For any n-profile $P = (V_1, \ldots, V_n)$, we define the mapping $f_P : \mathcal{X} \to \mathbb{N}^n$ as follows: for any $c \in \mathcal{X}$, $f_P(c) = (h_1, \ldots, h_n)$ such that for any $i \leq n$, h_i is the number of alternatives that are ranked below c in V_i. For any $l \leq p$, we denote $\mathcal{X}_l = D_l \times \cdots \times D_p$ and $\mathcal{O}_l = \mathbf{x}_l > \mathbf{x}_{l+1} > \cdots > \mathbf{x}_p$. For any vector $\vec{h} = (h_1, \ldots, h_n)$ and any $l \leq p$, we say that $\vec{h}$ is *realizable* over $\mathcal{X}_l$ (through a balanced binary tree) if there exists a profile $P_l = (V_1, \ldots, V_n)$ over $\mathcal{X}_l$ such that $f_{P_l}(SSP_{\mathcal{O}_l}(P_l)) = \vec{h}$. We first prove the following lemma.

Lemma 1 *For any l such that $1 \leq l < p$,*

$$\vec{h}_* = (\underbrace{0, \ldots, 0}_{\lfloor n/2 \rfloor - p + l}, \underbrace{1, \ldots, 1}_{p-l+1}, \underbrace{2^{p-l+1} - 1, \ldots, 2^{p-l+1} - 1}_{\lceil n/2 \rceil - 1})$$

is realizable over $\mathcal{X}_l$.

Proof of Lemma 1: We prove that there exists an n-profile P_l over $\mathcal{X}_l$ such that $SSP_{\mathcal{O}_l}(P_l) = 1_l \cdots 1_p$ and $\vec{h}_*$ is realized by P_l. For any $1 \leq i \leq p-l+1$, we let $\vec{b}_i = 1_l \cdots 1_{p-i} 0_{p+1-i} 1_{p+2-i} \cdots 1_p$. That is, $\vec{b}_i$ is obtained from $1_l \cdots 1_p$ by flipping the value of $\mathbf{x}_{p+1-i}$. We obtain $P_l = (V_1, \ldots, V_n)$ in the following steps.

1. Let $W_1, \ldots, W_n$ be null partial orders over $\mathcal{X}_l$. That is, for any $i \leq n$, the preference relation W_i is empty.
2. For any $j \leq \lfloor n/2 \rfloor - p + l$, we put $1_l \cdots 1_p$ in the bottom position in W_j; we put $\{\vec{b}_1, \ldots, \vec{b}_{p-l+1}\}$ in the top positions in W_j.
3. For any j with $\lfloor n/2 \rfloor + 2 \leq j \leq n$, we put $1_l \cdots 1_p$ in the top position of W_j, and we put $\{\vec{b}_1, \ldots, \vec{b}_{p-l+1}\}$ in the positions directly below the top.
4. For j with $\lfloor n/2 \rfloor - p + l + 1 \leq j \leq \lfloor n/2 \rfloor + 1$, we define preferences as follows. For any $i \leq p-l+1$, in $W_{\lfloor n/2 \rfloor - p + l + i}$, we put $\vec{b}_i$ in the bottom position, $1_l \cdots 1_p$ in the second position from the bottom, and all the remaining b_j (with $j \neq i$) at the very top.
5. Finally, we complete the profile arbitrarily: for any $j \leq n$, we let V_j be an arbitrary extension of W_j.

Let $P_l = (V_1, \ldots, V_n)$. We note that for any $i \leq p - l + 1$, $\vec{b}_i$ beats any alternative in $\mathcal{X}_l \setminus \{1_l \cdots 1_p, \vec{b}_1, \ldots, \vec{b}_{p-l+1}\}$ in pairwise elections. Therefore, for any $i \leq p - l + 1$, the ith alternative that meets $1_l \cdots 1_p$ is $\vec{b}_i$, which loses to $1_l \cdots 1_p$ (just barely). It follows that $1_l \cdots 1_p$ is the winner, and it is easy to check that $f_{P_l}(1_l \cdots 1_p) = \vec{h}_*$. This completes the proof of the lemma. □

Because the majority rule is anonymous, for any permutation π over $1, \ldots, n$ and any $l < p$, if $(h_1, \ldots, h_n)$ is realizable over $\mathcal{X}_l$, then $(h_{\pi(1)}, \ldots, h_{\pi(n)})$ is also realizable over $\mathcal{X}_l$. For any $k \in \mathbb{N}$, we define $H_k = \{\vec{h} \in \{0,1\}^n : \sum_{j \leq n} h_j \geq k\}$. That is, H_k is composed of all n-dimensional binary vectors in each of which at least k components are 1. We next show a lemma to derive a realizable vector over $\mathcal{X}_{l-1}$ from two realizable vectors over $\mathcal{X}_l$.

Lemma 2 *Let $l < p$, and let $\vec{h}_1$, $\vec{h}_2$ be vectors that are realizable over $\mathcal{X}_l$. For any $\vec{h} \in H_{\lfloor n/2 \rfloor + 1}$, $\vec{h}_1 + (\vec{h}_2 + \vec{1}) \cdot \vec{h}$ is realizable over $\mathcal{X}_{l-1}$, where $\vec{1} = (1, \ldots, 1)$, and for any $\vec{a} = (a_1, \ldots, a_n)$ and any $\vec{b} = (b_1, \ldots, b_n)$, we have $\vec{a} \cdot \vec{b} = (a_1 b_1, \ldots, a_n b_n)$.*

[6] If n is even, then to prove $MSI_{SSP_{\mathcal{O}}}(m,n) \geq \lfloor p/2 + 2 \rfloor$, we restrict attention to profiles without ties.

Proof of Lemma 2: Without loss of generality, we prove the lemma for $\vec{h} = (\underbrace{0, \ldots, 0}_{\lceil n/2 \rceil - 1}, \underbrace{1, \ldots, 1}_{\lfloor n/2 \rfloor + 1})$. Let P_1, P_2 be two profiles over $\mathcal{X}_l$, each of which is composed of n votes, such that $f(P_1) = \vec{h}_1$ and $f(P_2) = \vec{h}_2$. Let $P_1 = (V_1^1, \ldots, V_n^1)$, $P_2 = (V_1^2, \ldots, V_n^2)$, $\vec{a} = SSP_{\mathcal{O}_l}(P_1)$, $\vec{b} = SSP_{\mathcal{O}_l}(P_2)$. We define a profile $P = (V_1, \ldots, V_n)$ over $\mathcal{X}_{l-1}$ as follows.

1. Let $W_1, \ldots, W_n$ be n null partial orders over $\mathcal{X}_{l-1}$.
2. For any $j \leq n$ and any $\vec{e}_1, \vec{e}_2 \in \mathcal{X}_l$, we let $(1_{l-1}, \vec{e}_1) \succ_{W_j} (1_{l-1}, \vec{e}_2)$ if $\vec{e}_1 \succ_{V_j^1} \vec{e}_2$; and we let $(0_{l-1}, \vec{e}_1) \succ_{W_j} (0_{l-1}, \vec{e}_2)$ if $\vec{e}_1 \succ_{V_j^2} \vec{e}_2$.
3. For any $\lceil n/2 \rceil \leq j \leq n$, we let $(1_{l-1}, \vec{a}) \succ_{W_j} (0_{l-1}, \vec{b})$.
4. Finally, we complete the profile arbitrarily: for any $j \leq n$, we let V_j be an (arbitrary) extension of W_j such that $(1_{l-1}, \vec{a})$ is ranked as low as possible.

We note that $(1_{l-1}, \vec{a})$ is the winner of the subtree in which $\mathbf{x}_{l-1} = 1_{l-1}$, $(0_{l-1}, \vec{b})$ is the winner of the subtree in which $\mathbf{x}_{l-1} = 0_{l_1}$, and $(1_{l-1}, \vec{a})$ beats $(0_{l-1}, \vec{b})$ in their pairwise election (because the votes from $\lceil n/2 \rceil$ to n rank $(1_{l-1}, \vec{a})$ above $(0_{l-1}, \vec{b})$). Therefore, $SSP_{\mathcal{O}_{l-1}}(P) = (1_{l-1}, \vec{a})$.

Finally, we have that $f_P((1_{l-1}, \vec{a})) = \vec{h}_1 + (\vec{h}_2 + \vec{1}) \cdot \vec{h}$. This is because $(1_{l-1}, \vec{a})$ is ranked just as low as in the profile P_1 for voters 1 through $\lceil n/2 \rceil - 1$; for any voter j with $\lceil n/2 \rceil \leq j \leq n$, additionally, $(0_{l-1}, \vec{b})$ needs to be placed below $(1_{l-1}, \vec{a})$, which implies that also, all the alternatives $(0_{l-1}, \vec{b}')$ for which j ranked $\vec{b}'$ below $\vec{b}$ in P_2 must be below $(1_{l-1}, \vec{a})$ in j's new vote in P. This completes the proof of the lemma. □

Now we are ready to prove the main part of the theorem. It suffices to prove that for any $n \geq 2p^2 + 1$, there exists a vector $\vec{h}_p \in \mathbb{N}^n$ such that each component of $\vec{h}_p$ is no more than $\lfloor p/2 + 1 \rfloor$, and $\vec{h}_p$ is realizable over $\mathcal{X}$. We first prove the theorem for the case in which n is odd. We show the construction by induction in the proof of the following lemma.

Lemma 3 *Let n be odd. For any $l' < p$ (such that l' is odd),*

$$\vec{h}_{l'} = (\underbrace{\lfloor l'/2 \rfloor, \ldots, \lfloor l'/2 \rfloor}_{\lceil n/2 \rceil - (l'^2+1)/2}, \underbrace{\lceil l'/2 \rceil, \ldots, \lceil l'/2 \rceil}_{\lfloor n/2 \rfloor + (l'^2+1)/2})$$

is realizable over $\mathcal{X}_{p-l'+1}$, and if $l' < p$, then

$$\vec{h}_{l'+1} = (\underbrace{\lfloor l'/2 \rfloor, \ldots, \lfloor l'/2 \rfloor}_{l'+1}, \underbrace{\lceil l'/2 \rceil, \ldots, \lceil l'/2 \rceil}_{n-(l'+5)(l'+1)/2}, \underbrace{\lceil l'/2 \rceil + 1, \ldots, \lceil l'/2 \rceil + 1}_{(l'+3)(l'+1)/2})$$

is realizable over $\mathcal{X}_{p-l'}$.

Proof of Lemma 3: The base case in which $l' = 1$ corresponds to a single-issue majority election over two alternatives, where $\lceil n/2 \rceil - 1$ voters vote for one alternative, and $\lfloor n/2 \rfloor + 1$ vote for the other, so that only the latter get their preferred alternative.

Now, suppose the claim holds for some $l' \leq p - 2$; we next show that the claim also holds for $l' + 2$. To this end, we apply Lemma 2 twice. Let $l = p - l' + 1$.

First, let $\vec{h}_* = (\underbrace{1, \ldots, 1}_{l'}, \underbrace{2^{l'} - 1, \ldots, 2^{l'} - 1}_{l'+1}, \underbrace{0, \ldots, 0}_{\lfloor n/2 \rfloor - l' + 1}, \underbrace{2^{l'} - 1, \ldots, 2^{l'} - 1}_{\lceil n/2 \rceil - l' - 2})$

By Lemma 1, $\vec{h}_*$ is realizable over $\mathcal{X}_l$ (via a permutation of the voters). Let $\vec{h} = (\underbrace{1,\ldots,1}_{l'}, \underbrace{0,\ldots,0}_{l'+1}, \underbrace{1,\ldots,1}_{\lfloor n/2\rfloor - l'+1}, \underbrace{0,\ldots,0}_{\lceil n/2\rceil - l'-2})$.

Then, by Lemma 2, $\vec{h}_{l'} + (\vec{h}_* + \vec{1}) \cdot \vec{h}$ is realizable over $\mathcal{X}_{l-1}$. We have the following calculation.

$$\begin{aligned}
&\vec{h}_{l'} + (\vec{h}_* + \vec{1}) \cdot \vec{h} \\
=&(\underbrace{\lceil l'/2\rceil + 1,\ldots,\lceil l'/2\rceil + 1}_{l'}, \\
&\underbrace{\lfloor l'/2\rfloor,\ldots,\lfloor l'/2\rfloor}_{l'+1}, \underbrace{\lceil l'/2\rceil,\ldots,\lceil l'/2\rceil}_{\lceil n/2\rceil-(l'+3)(l'+1)/2}, \\
&\underbrace{\lceil l'/2\rceil + 1,\ldots,\lceil l'/2\rceil + 1}_{(l'+1)^2/2+1}, \underbrace{\lceil l'/2\rceil,\ldots,\lceil l'/2\rceil}_{\lfloor n/2\rfloor - l'-1})
\end{aligned}$$

The partition of the set of voters into these five groups uses the fact that $n \geq 2p^2+1$ implies $\lceil n/2\rceil - (l'+3)(l'+1)/2 \geq 0$. After permuting the voters in this vector, we obtain the following vector which is realizable over $\mathcal{X}_{l-1}$:

$$\begin{aligned}
\vec{h}_{l'+1} =&(\underbrace{\lfloor l'/2\rfloor,\ldots,\lfloor l'/2\rfloor}_{l'+1}, \underbrace{\lceil l'/2\rceil,\ldots,\lceil l'/2\rceil}_{n-(l'+5)(l'+1)/2}, \\
&\underbrace{\lceil l'/2\rceil + 1,\ldots,\lceil l'/2\rceil + 1}_{(l'+3)(l'+1)/2})
\end{aligned}$$

We next let $\vec{h}' = (\underbrace{1,\ldots,1}_{\lfloor n/2\rfloor+1}, \underbrace{0,\ldots,0}_{\lceil n/2\rceil-1})$ and

$$\vec{h}'_* = (\underbrace{1,\ldots,1}_{l'+1}, \underbrace{0,\ldots,0}_{\lfloor n/2\rfloor - l'}, \underbrace{2^{l'+1}-1,\ldots,2^{l'+1}-1}_{\lceil n/2\rceil-1})$$

By Lemma 1, the latter is realizable over $\mathcal{X}_{l-1}$. Thus, by Lemma 2, $\vec{h}_{l'+1} + (\vec{h}'_* + \vec{1}) \cdot \vec{h}'$ is realizable over $\mathcal{X}_{l-2}$. Through a permutation over the voters, we obtain the desired vector:

$$\vec{h}_{l'+2} = (\underbrace{\lfloor l'/2\rfloor + 1,\ldots,\lfloor l'/2\rfloor + 1}_{\lceil n/2\rceil-(l'+2)(l'+1)/2-1}, \underbrace{\lceil l'/2\rceil + 1,\ldots,\lceil l'/2\rceil + 1}_{\lfloor n/2\rfloor+(l'+2)(l'+1)/2+1})$$

which is realizable over $\mathcal{X}_{l-2}$. Therefore, the claim holds for $l'+2$. This completes the proof of the lemma. □

If p is odd, from Lemma 3 we know that the theorem is true, by setting $l' = p$. If p is even, then we first set $l' = p-1$; then, the maximum component of $\vec{h}_{l'+1}$ is $\lceil l'/2\rceil + 1 = \lceil (p-1)/2\rceil + 1 = p/2+1$. Thus we have proved the upper bound in the theorem when n is odd.

When n is even, we have the following lemma (the proof is similar to the proof of Lemma 3, so we omitted its proof).

Lemma 4 *Let n be even. For any $l' < p$ (such that l' is odd),*

$$\vec{h}_{l'} = (\underbrace{\lfloor l'/2\rfloor,\ldots,\lfloor l'/2\rfloor}_{n/2-(l'^2-l'+1)/2}, \underbrace{\lceil l'/2\rceil,\ldots,\lceil l'/2\rceil}_{n/2+(l'^2-l'+1)/2})$$

is realizable over $\mathcal{X}_{p-l'+1}$, and if $l'+1 \leq p$, then

$$\begin{aligned}
\vec{h}_{l'+1} =&(\underbrace{\lfloor l'/2\rfloor,\ldots,\lfloor l'/2\rfloor}_{l'+1}, \underbrace{\lceil l'/2\rceil,\ldots,\lceil l'/2\rceil}_{n-1-(l'+4)(l'+1)/2}, \\
&\underbrace{\lceil l'/2\rceil + 1,\ldots,\lceil l'/2\rceil + 1}_{(l'+2)(l'+1)/2+1})
\end{aligned}$$

is realizable over $\mathcal{X}_{p-l'}$.

The upper bound in the theorem when n is even follows from Lemma 4. Moreover, we note that in the step from l' to $l'+1$ (respectively, from $l'+1$ to $l'+2$), no more than l' new alternatives are ranked lower than the winner in the profile that realizes $\vec{h}_{l'+1}$ (respectively, $\vec{h}_{l'+2}$). It follows that in the profile that realizes $\vec{h}_{l'+1}$ (respectively, $\vec{h}_{l'+2}$) in Lemma 3 or Lemma 4, the number of alternatives that are ranked lower than the winner by at least one voter is no more than $(l'+1)l'/2 + l' + 1 = (l'+1)(l'+2)/2$ (respectively, $(l'+2)(l'+3)/2$), which equals $(p+1)p/2$ if $l'+1 = p$ (respectively, $(p+1)p/2$ if $l'+2 = p$). Therefore, in the profile that we use to obtain the upper bound, the winner under $SSP_{\mathcal{O}}$ is Pareto-dominated by $2^p - (p+1)p/2$ alternatives.

Finally, we show that $\lfloor p/2+2\rfloor$ is a lower bound on $MSI_{SSP_{\mathcal{O}}}(m,n)$. Let P be an n-profile; let $SSP_{\mathcal{O}}(P) = \vec{a}$, and let $\vec{b}_1,\ldots,\vec{b}_p$ be the alternatives that $\vec{a}$ defeats in pairwise elections in rounds $1,\ldots,p$. It follows that in round j, more than half of the voters prefer $\vec{a}$ to $\vec{b}_j$, because we assume that there are no ties in the election. Therefore, summing over all votes, there are at least $p \times (\lfloor n/2\rfloor + 1)$ occasions where $\vec{a}$ is preferred to one of $\vec{b}_1,\ldots,\vec{b}_p$. It follows that there exists some $V \in P$ in which $\vec{a}$ is ranked higher than at least $\lceil p \times (\lfloor n/2\rfloor + 1)/n\rceil \geq \lfloor p/2 + 1\rfloor$ of the alternatives $\vec{b}_1,\ldots,\vec{b}_p$. Thus $MSI_{SSP_{\mathcal{O}}}(m,n) \geq \lfloor p/2+2\rfloor$.

(End of proof for Theorem 2.) □

We note that the number of alternatives is $m = 2^p$. Therefore, $\lfloor p/2+2\rfloor$ is exponentially smaller than the number of alternatives, which means that there exists a profile for which every voter ranks the winner very close to the bottom. Moreover, $(p+1)p/2$ is still exponentially smaller than 2^p, which means that the winner is Pareto-dominated by almost every other alternative.

Naturally, we wish to avoid such paradoxes. One may wonder whether the paradox occurs only if the ordering of the issues is particularly unfortunate with respect to the preferences of the voters. If not, then, for example, perhaps a good approach is to randomly choose the ordering of the issues.[7] Unfortunately, our next result shows that we can construct a single profile that results in a paradox for *all* orderings of the issues. While it works for all orders, the result is otherwise somewhat weaker than Theorem 2: it does not show a Pareto-dominance result, it requires a number of voters that is at least twice the number of alternatives, the upper bound shown on the MSI is slightly higher than in Theorem 2, and unlike Theorem 2, no matching lower bound is shown.

Theorem 3 *For any $p, n \in \mathbb{N}$ (with $p \geq 2$ and $n \geq 2^{p+1}$), there exists an n-profile P such that for any order $\mathcal{O}$ over $\{\mathbf{x}_1,\ldots,\mathbf{x}_p\}$, $SSP_{\mathcal{O}}(P) = 1_1 \cdots 1_p$, and any $V \in P$ ranks $1_1 \cdots 1_p$ somewhere in the bottom $p+2$ positions.*

Proof of Theorem 3: We first prove a lemma.

Lemma 5 *For any $c \in \mathcal{X}$, $\mathcal{C} \subset \mathcal{X}$ such that $c \notin \mathcal{C}$, and any $n \in \mathbb{N}$ ($n \geq 2m = 2^{p+1}$), there exists an n-profile that satisfies the following conditions. Let $F = \mathcal{X} \setminus (\mathcal{C} \cup \{c\})$.*

- *For any $c' \in \mathcal{C}$, c defeats c' in their pairwise election.*
- *For any $c' \in \mathcal{C}$ and $d \in F$, c' defeats d in their pairwise election.*
- *For any $V \in P$, c is ranked somewhere in the bottom $|\mathcal{C}|+2$ positions.*

Proof of Lemma 5: We let $P = (V_1,\ldots,V_n)$ be the profile defined as follows. Let $F_1,\ldots,F_{\lfloor n/2\rfloor+1}$ be a partition of F such

[7] Of course, for any ordering of the issues, there exists a profile that results in the paradoxes in Theorem 2; but this does not directly imply that there exists a single profile that works for all orderings over the issues.

that for any $j \leq \lfloor n/2 \rfloor + 1$, $|F_j| \leq \lceil 2m/n \rceil = 1$. For any $j \leq \lfloor n/2 \rfloor + 1$, we let $V_j = [(F \setminus F_j) \succ c \succ \mathcal{C} \succ F_j]$. For any $\lfloor n/2 \rfloor + 2 \leq j \leq n$, we let $V_j = [\mathcal{C} \succ F \succ c]$. It is easy to check that P satisfies all conditions in the lemma. □

Now, let $c = 1_1 \cdots 1_p$ and $\mathcal{C} = \{0_1 1_2 \cdots 1_p, 1_1 0_2 1_3 \cdots 1_p, \ldots, 1_1 \cdots 1_{p-1} 0_p\}$. By Lemma 5, there exists a profile P such that c beats any alternative in $\mathcal{C}$ in pairwise elections, any alternative in $\mathcal{C}$ beats any alternative in $\mathcal{X} \setminus (\mathcal{C} \cup \{c\})$ in pairwise elections, and c is ranked somewhere in the bottom $p + 2$ positions. This is the profile that we will use to prove the paradox.

Without loss of generality , we assume that $\mathcal{O} = \mathbf{x}_1 > \mathbf{x}_2 \cdots > \mathbf{x}_p$. (This is without loss of generality because all issues have been treated symmetrically so far.) c beats $1_1 \cdots 1_{p-1} 0_p$ in the first round; c will meet $1_1 \cdots 1_{p-2} 0_{p-1} 1_p$ in the next pairwise election, because $1_1 \cdots 1_{p-2} 0_{p-1} 1_p$ beats every other alternative in that branch (they are all in F), and c will win; and so on. It follows that $c = SSP_{\mathcal{O}}(P)$. Moreover, all voters rank c in the bottom $p + 2$ positions.
(End of proof for Theorem 3.) □

6. MULTIPLE-ELECTION PARADOXES FOR SSP WITH RESTRICTIONS ON PREFERENCES

The paradoxes exhibited so far placed no restriction on the voters' preferences. While SSP is perfectly well defined for any preferences that the voters may have over the alternatives, we may yet wonder what happens if the voters' preferences over alternatives are restricted in a way that is natural with respect to the multi-issue structure of the setting. In particular, we may wonder if paradoxes are avoided by such restrictions. It is well known that natural restrictions on preferences sometimes lead to much more positive results in social choice and mechanism design—for example, single-peaked preferences allow for good strategy-proof mechanisms [4, 19].

In this section, we study the MSI for $SSP_{\mathcal{O}}$ for the following three cases: (1) voters' preferences are separable; (2) voters' preferences are $\mathcal{O}$-lexicographic; and (3) voters' preferences are $\mathcal{O}$-legal. For case (1), we show a mild paradox (and that this is effectively the strongest paradox that can be obtained); for case (2), we show a positive result; for case (3), we show a paradox that is nearly as bad as the unrestricted case.

Theorem 4 *For any $n \geq 2p$, when the profile is separable, the MSI for $SSP_{\mathcal{O}}$ is between $2^{\lceil p/2 \rceil}$ and $2^{\lfloor p/2 \rfloor + 1}$.*

That is, the MSI of $SSP_{\mathcal{O}}$ when votes are separable is $\Theta(\sqrt{m})$. We still have that $\lim_{m \to \infty} \Theta(\sqrt{m})/m = 0$, so in that sense this is still a paradox. However, its convergence rate to 0 is much slower than for $\Theta(\log m)/m$, which corresponds to the convergence rate for the earlier paradoxes.

Theorem 5 *For any $p \in \mathbb{N}$ ($p \geq 2$) and any $n \geq 5$, when the profile is $\mathcal{O}$-lexicographic, $MSI(SSP_{\mathcal{O}}) = 3 \cdot 2^{p-2} + 1$. Moreover, $SSP_{\mathcal{O}}(P)$ is ranked somewhere in the top 2^{p-1} positions in at least $n/2$ votes.*

Naturally $\lim_{m \to \infty}(3m/4 + 1)/m = 3/4$, so in that sense there is no paradox when votes are $\mathcal{O}$-lexicographic.

Under the previous two restrictions (separability and $\mathcal{O}$-lexicographicity), $SSP_{\mathcal{O}}$ coincides with $Seq(maj, \ldots, maj)$ (by Corollary 1 and Proposition 3, respectively). Therefore, Theorems 4 and 5 also apply to sequential voting rules as defined in [15]; furthermore, Theorem 4 also applies to seat-by-seat voting [3].

Finally, we study the MSI for $SSP_{\mathcal{O}}$ when the profile is $\mathcal{O}$-legal. Theorem 6 shows that it is nearly as bad as the unrestricted case (Theorem 2). The proof of Theorem 6 is the most involved proof in the paper and is omitted due to the space constraint. The idea of the proof is similar to that of the proof for Theorem 2, but now we cannot apply Lemma 2, because $\mathcal{O}$-legality must be preserved. We start with a simpler result that shows the idea of the construction.

Claim 1 *There exists a way to break ties in $SSP_{\mathcal{O}}$ such that the following is true. Let $SSP'_{\mathcal{O}}$ be the rule corresponding to $SSP_{\mathcal{O}}$ plus the tiebreaking mechanism. For any $p \in \mathbb{N}$, there exists an $\mathcal{O}$-legal profile that consists of two votes, such that in one of the two votes, no more than $\lceil p/2 \rceil$ alternatives are ranked lower than the winner $SSP'_{\mathcal{O}}(P)$; and in the other vote, no more than $\lfloor p/2 \rfloor$ alternatives are ranked lower than $SSP'_{\mathcal{O}}(P)$.*

We emphasize that, unlike any of our other results, Claim 1 is based on a specific tie-breaking mechanism. The next theorem studies the more general and complicated case in which n can be either odd or even, and the winner does not depend on the tie-breaking mechanism. That is, there are no ties in the election. The situation is almost the same as in Theorem 2.

Theorem 6 *For any $p, n \in \mathbb{N}$ with $n \geq 2p^2 + 2p + 1$, there exists an $\mathcal{O}$-legal profile such that in each vote, no more than $\lceil p/2 \rceil + 4$ alternatives are ranked lower than $SSP_{\mathcal{O}}(P)$. Moreover, $SSP_{\mathcal{O}}(P)$ is Pareto-dominated by at least $2^p - 4p^2$ alternatives.*

Of course, the lower bound on the MSI from Theorem 2 still applies when the profile is $\mathcal{O}$-legal, so together with Theorem 6 this proves that the MSI for $SSP_{\mathcal{O}}$ when the profile is $\mathcal{O}$-legal is $\Theta(\log m)$, just as in the unrestricted case.

7. CONCLUSION AND FUTURE WORK

Combinatorial voting settings, in which the space of all alternatives is exponential in size, constitute an important area in which techniques from computer science can be fruitfully applied. Perhaps the simplest and most natural combinatorial voting setting is that of multi-issue domains, where the space of alternatives is the Cartesian product of the local domains. In practice, common decisions on multiple issues are often reached by voting on the issues sequentially. In this paper, we considered a complete-information game-theoretic analysis of sequential voting on binary issues, which we called strategic sequential voting. Specifically, given that voters have complete information about each other's preferences and their preferences are strict, the game can be solved by a natural backward induction process (WSDSBI), which leads to a unique solution. We showed that under some conditions on the preferences, this process leads to the same outcome as the truthful sequential voting, but in general it can result in very different outcomes. We analyzed the effect of changing the order over the issues that voters vote on and showed that, in some elections, every alternative can be made a winner by voting according to an appropriate order over the issues.

Most significantly, we showed that strategic sequential voting is prone to multiple-election paradoxes; to do so, we introduced a concept called minimax satisfaction index, which measures the degree to which at least one voter is made happy by the outcome of the election. We showed that the minimax satisfaction index for strategic sequential voting is exponentially small, which means that there exists a profile for which the winner is ranked almost in the bottom positions in all votes; even worse, the winner is Pareto-dominated by almost every other alternative. We showed that changing the order of the issues in sequential voting cannot completely avoid the paradoxes. These negative results indicate that the solution of the sequential game can be extremely undesirable for every voter. We also showed that multiple-election paradoxes can be avoided to some extent by restricting voters' preferences to be separable or lexicographic, but the paradoxes still exist when the voters' preferences are $\mathcal{O}$-legal.

There are many topics for future research. For example, is there any criterion on the selection of the order over the issues? Perhaps more importantly, how can we get around the multiple-election paradoxes in sequential voting games? For example, Theorem 5 shows that if the voters' preferences are lexicographic, then we can avoid the paradoxes. It is not clear if there are other ways to avoid the paradoxes (paradoxes occur even if we restrict voters' preferences to be separable or $\mathcal{O}$-legal, as shown in Theorem 4 and Theorem 6). Another approach is to consider other, non-sequential voting procedures for multi-issue domains. What are good examples of such procedures? Will these avoid paradoxes? What is the effect of strategic behavior for such procedures? How should we even define "strategic behavior" for such procedures, or for sequential voting with non-binary issues, or for voting rules in general?[8] How can we extend these results to incomplete-information settings?[9] Also, beyond proving paradoxes for individual rules, is it possible to show a general impossibility result that shows that under certain minimal conditions, paradoxes cannot be avoided?[10]

Acknowledgements

Lirong Xia is supported by a James B. Duke Fellowship. Lirong Xia and Vincent Conitzer acknowledge NSF CAREER 0953756 and IIS-0812113, and an Alfred P. Sloan fellowship for support. Jérôme Lang thanks the ANR project ComSoc (ANR-09-BLAN-0305). We thank Michel Le Breton, all EC-10, LOFT-10, and EC-11 reviewers, as well as the participants of the Dagstuhl Seminar 10101 "Computational Foundations of Social Choice", the 2010 Bertinoro Workshop on Frontiers in Mechanism Design, LOFT-10, and University of Amsterdam ILLC Computational Social Choice Seminar, for their helpful comments.

8. REFERENCES

[1] Salvador Barbera, Hugo Sonnenschein, and Lin Zhou. Voting by committees. *Econometrica*, 59(3):595–609, 1991.

[2] Marco Battaglini. Sequential voting with abstention. *Games and Economic Behavior*, 51:445–463, 2005.

[3] Jean-Pierre Benoit and Lewis A. Kornhauser. Only a dictatorship is efficient or neutral. Technical report, 2006.

[4] Duncan Black. On the rationale of group decision-making. *Journal of Political Economy*, 56(1):23–34, 1948.

[5] Steven J. Brams, D. Marc Kilgour, and William S. Zwicker. The paradox of multiple elections. *Social Choice and Welfare*, 15(2):211–236, 1998.

[6] Vincent Conitzer and Tuomas Sandholm. Communication complexity of common voting rules. In *Proceedings of the ACM Conference on Electronic Commerce (EC)*, pages 78–87, Vancouver, BC, Canada, 2005.

[7] Eddie Dekel and Michele Piccione. Sequential voting procedures in symmetric binary elections. *Journal of Political Economy*, 108:34–55, 2000.

[8] Yvo Desmedt and Edith Elkind. Equilibria of plurality voting with abstentions. In *Proceedings of the ACM Conference on Electronic Commerce (EC)*, pages 347–356, Cambridge, MA, USA, 2010.

[9] Bhaskar Dutta and Arunava Sen. Implementing generalized Condorcet social choice functions via backward induction. *Social Choice and Welfare*, 10(2):149–160, 1993.

[10] Robin Farquharson. *Theory of Voting*. Yale University Press, 1969.

[11] Felix Fischer, Ariel D. Procaccia, and Alex Samorodnitsky. A new perspective on implementation by voting trees. In *Random Structures and Algorithms*, forthcoming, 2011. Early version appeared in *EC-10*.

[12] Allan Gibbard. Manipulation of voting schemes: a general result. *Econometrica*, 41:587–601, 1973.

[13] Rodney J. Gretlei. Dominance elimination procedures on finite alternative games. *International Journal of Game Theory*, 12(2):107–113, 1983.

[14] Dean Lacy and Emerson M.S. Niou. A problem with referendums. *Journal of Theoretical Politics*, 12(1):5–31, 2000.

[15] Jérôme Lang and Lirong Xia. Sequential composition of voting rules in multi-issue domains. *Mathematical Social Sciences*, 57(3):304–324, 2009.

[16] David C. McGarvey. A theorem on the construction of voting paradoxes. *Econometrica*, 21(4):608–610, 1953.

[17] Richard D. McKelvey and Richard G. Niemi. A multistage game representation of sophisticated voting for binary procedures. *Journal of Economic Theory*, 18(1):1 – 22, 1978.

[18] Hervé Moulin. Dominance solvable voting schemes. *Econometrica*, 47(6):1137–51, 1979.

[19] Hervé Moulin. On strategy-proofness and single peakedness. *Public Choice*, 35(4):437–455, 1980.

[20] Hervé Moulin. Choosing from a tournament. *Social Choice and Welfare*, 3:271–291, 1986.

[21] Donald G. Saari and Katri K. Sieberg. The sum of the parts can violate the whole. *The American Political Science Review*, 95(2):415–433, 2001.

[22] Mark Satterthwaite. Strategy-proofness and Arrow's conditions: Existence and correspondence theorems for voting procedures and social welfare functions. *Journal of Economic Theory*, 10:187–217, 1975.

[23] Marco Scarsini. A strong paradox of multiple elections. *Social Choice and Welfare*, 15(2):237–238, 1998.

[24] Birgitte Sloth. The theory of voting and equilibria in noncooperative games. *Games and Economic Behavior*, 5:152–169, 1993.

[25] Lirong Xia and Vincent Conitzer. Stackelberg voting games: Computational aspects and paradoxes. In *Proceedings of the National Conference on Artificial Intelligence (AAAI)*, pages 921–926, Atlanta, GA, USA, 2010.

[26] Lirong Xia and Vincent Conitzer. Strategy-proof voting rules over multi-issue domains with restricted preferences. In *Proceedings of the Sixth Workshop on Internet and Network Economics (WINE)*, pages 402–414, Stanford, CA, USA, 2010.

[8]In [26], Xia and Conitzer studied strategy-proof voting rules over multi-issue domains composed of not-necessarily-binary issues. Among other contributions, Xia and Conitzer characterized all strategy-proof voting rules when the votersąŕ preferences are lexicographic and their possible local preferences over each issue are restricted.

[9]Because the complete-information setting is a special case of incomplete-information-settings, our results, which are worst-case results, still hold in the latter.

[10]This may require quite restrictive conditions or a different notion of a paradox.

A Game-Theoretic Analysis of Rank-Order Mechanisms for User-Generated Content

Arpita Ghosh
Yahoo! Research
Santa Clara, CA, USA
arpita@yahoo-inc.com

Patrick Hummel
Yahoo! Research
Berkeley, CA, USA
phummel@yahoo-inc.com

ABSTRACT

Many websites rank user-generated content (UGC) using viewer votes, displaying higher quality contributions more prominently and suppressing lower quality ones. Such an allocation of attention constitutes a *mechanism*, which can influence the quality of content elicited from attention-motivated contributors. In this paper, we analyze equilibrium behavior in the widely used *rank-order* mechanism, where contributions are allocated positions on the page in decreasing order of their ratings, and the *proportional* mechanism which distributes attention in proportion to the number of positive ratings, in a game-theoretic model where agents are motivated by attention and the cost of making a contribution is increasing in its quality.

The rank-order mechanism always possesses a symmetric mixed strategy equilibrium in which all agents decide whether to contribute with the same probability, and randomly draw a quality from a common distribution conditional on participating. We investigate equilibrium behavior in the limit of diverging attention, and show that the *lowest* quality that can arise in a mixed strategy equilibrium of the rank-order mechanism becomes optimal as the amount of available attention diverges. We then compare equilibrium qualities in the proportional and the rank-order mechanism and show that the probability an agent chooses a higher quality in the rank-order mechanism than in the proportional mechanism goes to one as the amount of available attention diverges. Thus the rank-order mechanism almost always incentivizes higher quality contributions in equilibrium than the proportional mechanism.

Categories and Subject Descriptors

J.4 [**Computer Applications**]: Social & Behavioral Sciences

General Terms

Economics

Keywords

User-generated content (UGC), Attention economics, Quality of online content, Game theory

1. INTRODUCTION

There is a proliferation of user contributed content on the Web, and a multitude of instances where user contributed content adds significant value to websites. The product reviews written by users on Amazon, for instance, are a very valuable component of the service that Amazon provides, while question-and-answer sites such as Yahoo! Answers and StackOverflow or sites aggregating service reviews such as Yelp owe almost all their utility to contributions from users. But while there is a large amount of user contributed content online, not all of it is of the same *quality*— some content is excellent, while some is mediocre and some is outright bad.

Many websites attempt to *rank* content according to its quality, using thumbs-up/thumbs-down style ratings by viewers— this is the case, for example, with comments on Yahoo! News, reviews on Amazon, and posts on Reddit. These websites display higher quality contributions more prominently by placing them near the top of the page and pushing lower quality ones to the bottom. Since content displayed near the top of the page is more likely to be viewed by a user, ranking good content higher leads to a better user experience. But there is also another aspect to displaying better content more prominently: it potentially provides an *incentive* to produce high quality content that might appeal to a contributor's desire for attention. In other words, how contributions are displayed as a function of their estimated quality constitutes a *mechanism* for allocating attention, which might affect the incentives of contributors and influence the quality of their contributions.

What can we understand, using a game-theoretic approach, about how the mechanism used to display content influences the quality of the contributions? In particular, how does the choice of mechanism influence quality when the number of potential viewers, and therefore the potential available attention, grows very large? The diverging attention regime is arguably the most important from the perspective of user-generated content. First, these are the situations where delivering high quality content matters the most from the perspective of viewer welfare. Second, the popular sites are the ones that draw the most attention-motivated contributors, as well as the ones that tend to attract contributions of varying quality[1]. Indeed, tremendously large amounts of attention are not uncommon for popular content on the web; for instance, the most popular YouTube videos have been viewed over a hundred million times and even days-old 'trending' videos have hundred of thousands of views, numbers that clearly belongs to the diverging attention regime.

In this paper, we analyze two mechanisms that use viewer ratings to allocate attention to content— the widely used rank-order mechanism, where contributions are allocated positions on the page in decreasing order of their ratings, and a *proportional* mechanism [2, 3], which distributes attention in proportion to the number of positive ratings. The rank-order mechanism is ubiquitous on UGC sites all over the Web, while the proportional mechanism is a natural and more 'fair' alternative: if two contributions receive very similar numbers of votes, it only seems fair that they receive similar amounts of attention as well, but this does not necessarily hold in the rank-order mechanism. What happens to equilibrium quality and participation in the rank-order mechanism as the amount of available attention diverges, and how does it compare against the more fair proportional mechanism?

Our Contributions. We analyze equilibrium behavior in the rank-order mechanism in a game-theoretic model where contributors are motivated by attention and have a cost of participation that increases with the quality of their content, as in [3]. Contributors in our model are strategic agents who choose *both* whether to contribute, modeled by their probability of participation, *and* the quality of their contribution conditional on participating, to maximize their payoff. This ensures that participation is *endogenously* determined as a strategic choice by potential contributors, as in [3]: capturing endogenous participation is important in the UGC setting since users have the option of not contributing should they prefer not to do so.

Analyzing the rank-order mechanism is nontrivial because an agent's payoff depends on her choice of quality and other agents' choices of quality in a complicated way— the number of votes m_i an agent i receives is a *random variable* in her quality q_i. The final payoff to i depends on the *rank* of the instantiation of this random variable amongst the m_{-i}, the number of votes received by other agents, which are *also* random variables in the other agents' quality choices.

We first show that symmetric mixed strategy equilibria, where all agents participate with probability β and randomly choose a quality from a common distribution $F(q)$ if contributing, always exist for the rank-order mechanism. We then investigate equilibrium behavior as the amount of attention increases, and show that the *lowest* quality that can arise in a mixed strategy equilibrium tends to the highest possible quality (*i.e.*, the optimal quality) as the available attention diverges. We also show that if there are not too many potential contributors, it is possible to choose the number of votes used by the mechanism to rank contributions in such a way as to guarantee full participation (*i.e.*, $\beta = 1$) in the limit of diverging attention.

[1]For example, Slashdot notes in its comments moderation FAQ that when Slashdot was small, it received a small number of good quality posts— the need for rating comments arose only after it grew larger and more popular, which led to posts of varying quality.

Finally, we compare the rank-order mechanism to the more equitable proportional mechanism. We show that the proportional mechanism always has an equilibrium in which all agents participate with probability β and choose a fixed quality q_p upon participating. However, unlike the rank-order mechanism, whether this equilibrium quality converges asymptotically to the optimal quality *depends* on how the number of potential contributors grows with the number of viewers. We then compare the random equilibrium quality choices in the rank-order mechanism with the deterministic quality choices in the proportional mechanism and show that the probability an agent chooses higher quality in the rank-order mechanism than in the proportional mechanism tends to 1 as the amount of available attention diverges. Thus the rank-order mechanism elicits higher quality contributions in equilibrium than the proportional mechanism.

Related Work. There is a growing body of research on human computing systems and user contributed content, but relatively little of this work addresses the analysis and design of these systems from a game-theoretic perspective [2, 7, 8]. [2] studies the question of designing incentives for online question-and-answer forums, and focuses on incentives for participants to contribute their answers *quickly* instead of delaying their contribution, but does not address the issue of incentivizing high quality contributions. The most relevant paper to our work is [3], which introduces a model to address the quality of user-generated content. This paper shows that a simple mechanism which eliminates contributions that are not uniformly rated highly by all voters achieves optimal quality in the limit as the amount of available attention diverges. Our model has a few technical differences from that in [3], and is also used to instead address the problem of incentives in the widely used rank-order mechanism and compare those to incentives in the proportional mechanism.

There is a large literature in economics on using rank-order tournaments as incentive schemes (e.g. [4], [5], [10], [12]). This literature analyzes the consequences of employee compensation schemes which reward employees based on how their output compares to that of other employees in the organization. While agents in our model are also ranked based on how the number of positive votes they receive compares to that of other agents, there are several important differences between our paper and this work. In our paper, an individual's observable output is the random number of users who vote positively on her contribution, but this type of framework is not captured by the assumptions made in existing work on rank-order tournaments. Also, not all agents need participate in equilibria in our model, but all employees must work in the economics literature. In addition, most existing work on rank-order tournaments focuses on equilibria in which all agents exert a deterministic level of effort in equilibrium,[2] whereas we extensively analyze mixed strategy equilibria. The focus on the limiting case we consider as well as the comparison between the rank-order and proportional mechanisms is also missing in this literature.

There is also a literature in political economy that compares how allocating political power in proportion to the number of votes received rather than in order of which can-

[2]One very rare exception is [12], which briefly mentions that agents may have an incentive to exert random levels of effort, but does not conduct an extensive analysis of such equilibria.

didates receive the most votes affects elections (e.g. [6], [11], [13], [14]). However, these papers do not focus on how these differences would affect incentives for individuals to produce high quality actions.

2. MODEL

Content. Each unit of content, or contribution, has a *quality* q, where $q \in [0, 1]$ is the probability that a viewer will like the contribution, *i.e.*, rate it as 'good' or 'useful'. The quality q of a contribution is not directly observable in our model, but it influences the number of positive votes the content receives.

Each contribution is rated by T viewers, where we later allow T to be a parameter that can be chosen by the mechanism. We assume that viewers are not strategic, and simply provide this binary feedback non-strategically by truthfully answering the question of whether they found the contribution to be good or useful.

Given a contribution i with quality q_i, the number of positive votes it receives is a random variable. We let m_i denote the number of positive votes received this contribution, and note that the distribution of m_i is binomial with parameters (T, q_i). We also let m_{-i} denote the vector of the numbers of positive votes received by other contributions.

Contributors. There is a pool of potential contributors, or agents, of size K. Each agent can choose the *probability* with which she will contribute, as well as the *quality* of her contribution should she decide to participate. We denote the probability that agent i decides to contribute by β_i and the quality she chooses when she contributes by q_i. Since each potential contributor decides whether to participate or not probabilistically, the number of actual contributors is a random variable. We denote the instantiation of this random variable by k, and note that the distribution of k depends on K as well as $\beta_1, \dots, \beta_K$.

Contributors are *strategic*: they choose both β and q strategically to maximize their expected payoffs given the potential costs and benefits from contributing. We describe these payoffs next.

If an agent chooses not to contribute, then she incurs no cost but also receives no benefit, so her net payoff is 0. Otherwise, the agent must pay a cost reflecting the effort she expended to produce content, and obtains a benefit reflecting the attention she was able to get as a result of producing that content.

The *cost* incurred by a contributor depends on the quality of the content she chooses to produce: the cost of producing content of quality q is $c(q)$, which is an increasing function of q (*i.e.*, producing higher quality content is more costly). We make the following assumptions:

1. The cost function c is continuously differentiable in q for all $q < 1$.
2. $c(0) > 0$ and $\lim_{q \to 1} c(q) = \infty$.
3. c is convex and $c'(0) = 0$.

The condition $c(0) > 0$ indicates that making a contribution, even a very poor one, takes more effort than not participating at all. The assumption that $\lim_{q \to 1} c(q) = \infty$, as in [3], indicates that producing perfect content, which corresponds to making every viewer happy, is nearly impossible. The final assumption is a standard assumption for cost functions in the economics literature and indicates that it is more difficult to improve higher-quality content, while improving awful content takes almost no effort at all.

The *benefit* derived by a contributor, as in [3], depends on the amount of attention she receives, which can depend in general both on the rating of her contribution and the number and ratings of other contributions. Let A denote the total amount of attention that is available to distribute amongst contributions[3]. We assume that an agent's benefit is exactly equal to the attention that she receives. If contributor i is allocated a fraction $\alpha_i(m_i, m_{-i}) \geq 0$ of the attention A, then her benefit from receiving this attention is $V(m_i, m_{-i}) = \alpha_i(m_i, m_{-i})A$. A *mechanism* in this setting determines how to partition the available attention amongst the various contributions; thus the value of $V(m_i, m_{-i})$ is decided by the mechanism.

A contributor i's *payoff* from generating content of quality q_i is the difference between her expected benefit and cost,

$$\pi(q_i, q_{-i}, \beta_{-i}) = E[V(m_i, m_{-i})|(q_i, q_{-i}, \beta_{-i})] - c(q_i),$$

where $q_{-i} = (q_1, \dots, q_{i-1}, q_{i+1}, \dots, q_k)$ denotes the quality choices of the other contributors, and β_{-i} denotes the participation probabilities of the remaining contributors. (Here we assume that i has already decided to contribute, so her participation probability does not affect this payoff.) Note that the expectation in this payoff is taken over the random number of contributors k as well as the random variables m_i that are determined in part by the parameters q_i.

We assume that every viewer who visits a page or site brings at least one unit of attention, but possibly more, corresponding to the fact that each viewer will read at least one contribution but some read more. Thus A is at least as large as the number of viewers. We will also assume throughout that the number of potential contributors K is no larger than the number of potential viewers and therefore the total amount of attention, *i.e.*, $K \leq A$.

Solution Concept. Since agents' payoff functions are symmetric in the parameters of the game, we focus throughout on symmetric equilibria. In a symmetric equilibrium, each contributor participates with the same probability and follows the same strategy of quality choices conditional on participating. Formally, a *symmetric mixed strategy equilibrium* is a probability β and a distribution F over qualities q such that when every agent contributes with probability β, and chooses a quality drawn from the CDF $F(q)$ conditional on contributing, no agent can increase her expected payoff by deviating from this strategy, *i.e.*, by changing either the probability of participation or the distribution over qualities with which to contribute.

Asymptotics. We will be particularly interested in the qualities and participation levels in equilibrium in the limiting case as the amount of attention A goes to infinity. We will assume that this diverging amount of attention comes from a diverging number of viewers; therefore, the number of potential contributors, K, as well as the number of viewers available to vote on contributions, T, can increase with A as well.

We will sometimes write $K(A)$ and $T(A)$ to make explicit the possible dependence of K and T on A, and assume that as A diverges, $K(A)$ diverges and $T(A)$ can be chosen to di-

[3]If the agents did not know the exact value of A, but instead only knew its distribution, then the equilibrium analysis would stay the same except that A would be replaced with $E[A]$.

verge as well. This corresponds to the observation in practice that as sites grow more popular in terms of viewership (A increases), they attract more users who are interested in contributing ($K(A)$), and more viewers are available to rate the generated content ($T(A)$). For instance, the growing popularity of YouTube has led to an increasing number of videos posted to YouTube, as well as an increasing number of ratings on these videos. We emphasize, though, that $T = T(A)$ is a parameter chosen by the mechanism, and specifically can be chosen to be small compared to A, since the mechanism can choose to use only a subset of the available ratings (for instance, the first T votes) to rank contributions. Thus, the actual number of ratings is only an upper bound on T, and not necessarily the value of T chosen by the mechanism.

3. PRELIMINARIES

First note that if $A \leq c(0)$, *i.e.*, the total available attention is smaller than the cost of producing even zero quality content, then no agents would want to participate since an agent's payoff from participating is nonpositive even if there is no other agent with whom attention must be shared. The case where no agents participate is not interesting, so we will assume that

$$A > c(0)$$

for the remainder of this paper. This assumption guarantees that $\beta > 0$ in any symmetric equilibrium[4].

A pair $(\beta, F(q))$ with $\beta \in (0, 1]$ constitutes a symmetric mixed strategy equilibrium if the following two conditions are satisfied:

1. No agent wants to choose a different β: For this to hold when $\beta = 1$, the expected payoff to an agent from participating must be nonnegative when she chooses a quality from $F(q)$ and the remaining agents participate with probability $\beta = 1$ and choose quality from $F(q)$. For this to hold for $\beta \in (0, 1)$, an agent's expected payoff from participating must be exactly zero since otherwise she would want to either always participate or never participate.

2. For any q in the support of F, no agent can obtain a strictly larger payoff by choosing some other quality $q' \in [0, 1)$ instead of q upon participating, given that remaining agents use the strategy $(\beta, F(q))$.

We next elaborate on the conditions that must hold for $\beta \in (0, 1]$ to be an equilibrium participation probability in a symmetric equilibrium.

If all agents participate with probability $\beta = 1$ and draw their qualities from the same distribution $F(q)$ upon participating, then by symmetry, each agent receives the same amount of attention as every other agent in expectation. Therefore, each agent's expected benefit is $\frac{A}{K}$ ($\beta = 1$ so $k = K$, *i.e.*, all agents contribute) and each agent's expected cost is $E[c(q)|q \sim F(q)]$. In order for an agent to not be able to profitably deviate by changing her participation probability, we must thus have $\frac{A}{K} \geq E[c(q)|q \sim F(q)]$.

Now suppose all other agents participate with probability $\beta \in (0, 1)$ and agent i decides that she will participate and use the same quality distribution $F(q)$ as the other agents. Then agent i obtains an expected benefit of $E[\frac{A}{k}|$ i enters; other agents enter with probability $\beta]$, where the expectation is over the random decisions of other agents to contribute. This holds because each agent draws qualities from the same distribution, so by symmetry each agent's expected benefit from participating is $\frac{A}{k}$ when $k - 1$ of the $K - 1$ remaining contributors participate. The expected cost of using strategy $F(q)$, conditional on participating, is $E[c(q)|q \sim F(q)]$. Thus in order for agent i to be indifferent between participating and not participating, we must have that $E[\frac{A}{k}|$ i enters; other agents enter with probability $\beta] = E[c(q)|q \sim F(q)]$.

To summarize, the necessary conditions to have an equilibrium in which each agent participates with probability $\beta \in (0, 1]$ and chooses quality drawn from the distribution $F(q)$ upon participating are the following:

1. If $\beta \in (0, 1)$, the expected benefit from participating must equal the expected cost:
$$E[\frac{A}{k}\ |i \text{ enters; other agents enter with probability } \beta] = E[c(q)|q \sim F(q)].$$

2. If $\beta = 1$, the expected benefit from participating is not smaller than the expected cost:
$$\frac{A}{K} \geq E[c(q)|q \sim F(q)].$$

3. For any q in the support of F, no agent can obtain a strictly larger payoff by choosing some other quality $q' \in [0, 1)$ instead of q upon participating, given that remaining agents use the strategy $(\beta, F(q))$.

4. RANKING MECHANISM

We first consider *ranking* mechanisms. A ranking mechanism arranges contributions in decreasing order of the number of positive votes they receive and allocates more attention to contributions which are ranked higher. The common practice of displaying comments or answers on a webpage in decreasing order of the number of positive votes received, used by most sites hosting UGC, corresponds to such a ranking mechanism since more users view content near the top of the page than the bottom. In this section, we analyze the mixed strategy equilibria of ranking mechanisms, and then prove results about how equilibrium quality and participation probability behave as the amount of available attention becomes large. We first formally define ranking mechanisms.

DEFINITION 4.1 (RANKING MECHANISM $M_r(T, \alpha)$). *Let $\alpha_j(k) \geq 0$ be a sequence of numbers that is nonincreasing in j for all k and satisfies $\sum_{j=1}^{k} \alpha_j(k) = 1$, where the values of α_j* do not depend *on the qualities q for any j, although they can depend on the* number *of contributors k.*

Suppose there are k contributors and each contribution is voted on by T viewers. The ranking mechanism ranks contributions in decreasing order of the number of positive votes received (with ties broken randomly) and awards the jth ranked contribution attention $\alpha_j A$.

Note that both α, which specifies the distribution of attention amongst the ranks, as well as T, the number of votes used to determine the rankings, are *parameters* of the mechanism that can be chosen to achieve desirable properties.

We first state the following simple proposition.

[4] $\beta = 0$ cannot be an equilibrium participation probability since then an agent can improve her current payoff of 0 by entering and producing zero quality content.

PROPOSITION 4.1. *Suppose $q_i > q_j$, and let the number of votes received by i and j be m_i and m_j respectively. Then* $\lim_{T\to\infty} Pr(m_i > m_j) = 1$.

Thus a higher quality contribution receives a larger number of positive votes, and is therefore ranked higher, than a lower quality contribution in the limit as the number of votes T goes to infinity.

We first show that the ranking mechanism always has a symmetric mixed strategy equilibrium in which all agents choose the same probability of entry, and choose a quality from the same distribution if they decide to contribute.

THEOREM 4.1. *For any values of A, K, T, and α, there exists a symmetric mixed strategy equilibrium in which all contributors enter with probability β and choose a quality drawn from the same cumulative distribution function $F(q)$ conditional on contributing.*

PROOF. First note that no player in this game would ever choose a quality $q > c^{-1}(A)$, as a player could always obtain a strictly greater expected payoff by not participating than by participating and choosing a quality $q > c^{-1}(A)$. Thus any mixed strategy equilibrium to the game in which players are restricted to choosing $q \in [0, c^{-1}(A)]$ is also a mixed strategy equilibrium of the original game.

Now note that this modified game in which players are restricted to choosing $q \in [0, c^{-1}(A)]$ is a symmetric game in which each player has a pure strategy space that is compact and Hausdorff. Also note that each player's expected payoff in this modified game is continuous in the actions of the players. It thus follows from Theorem 1 of [1] that there exists a symmetric mixed strategy equilibrium of this modified game. This in turn implies that there is a symmetric mixed strategy equilibrium of the original game. □

Thus it always makes sense to analyze symmetric mixed strategy equilibria of the form discussed in §2. While mixed strategies are more difficult to analyze than pure strategies, the use of mixed strategies as a solution concept is particularly reasonable in this setting as it allows for the possibility that different contributors produce different quality content. This correlates well with observation in practice, where not all contributions, for example answers to a question on StackOverflow or comments on a news article, are of the same quality.

In general, a mechanism can have multiple mixed strategy equilibria. A natural question to ask is whether any of these equilibria is '*bad*', in the sense of inducing low-quality equilibrium contributions. Our first result illustrates that as long as there is at least a small difference between the amount of attention allocated to contributions that are ranked differently, such bad Nash equilibria cannot exist. Specifically, we show that if T, the number of votes used to rank the contributions, becomes large as the amount of attention grows, contributors will choose quality arbitrarily close to 1 in the limit as the amount of attention diverges.

THEOREM 4.2. *Suppose that $\alpha_j(k) - \alpha_{j+1}(k) = \Theta(k^{-2})$ for all $j \le k-1$, $\alpha_k(k) = 0$ for sufficiently large k, and $\lim_{A\to\infty} T(A) = \infty$. Then, for any $q^* < 1$, the probability an agent who contributes chooses quality $q > q^*$ goes to 1 as A goes to infinity.*

In a mixed strategy equilibrium, a contributor can draw any quality in the support of the equilibrium distribution: the theorem says that the *lowest* quality in this equilibrium distribution tends to the optimal quality as the amount of attention diverges.

Since the precise equilibrium strategies that agents use may vary with A, we will henceforth use $\beta(A)$ to denote the dependence of the equilibrium participation probability, and $F_A(q)$ to denote the dependence of the equilibrium distribution from which contributors choose their quality, on the available attention A. We now prove the result.

PROOF OF THEOREM 4.2. Suppose by means of contradiction that there exists some $q^* < 1$ and some $\gamma > 0$ such that the probability a contributor chooses quality $q \le q^*$ is at least γ for an infinite number of A. If q_A denotes the minimum value of the set of all q in the support of $F_A(q)$, then $q_A \le q^*$ holds for all such A. For small $\epsilon > 0$, let $p_A(\epsilon) = F_A(q_A + \epsilon)$ denote the probability that a contributor chooses some quality $q \le q_A + \epsilon$ for a given A.

Our proof breaks down into three steps. We first show that if we restrict attention to a subsequence of A for which the probability a contributor chooses quality $q \le q^*$ is at least γ, it must be the case that $\lim_{A\to\infty} p_A(\epsilon) \le C\epsilon$ for some constant C and small $\epsilon > 0$, where the limit is taken along this subsequence. We then show that if $\lim_{A\to\infty} p_A(\epsilon) \le C\epsilon$, then it must be the case that $\lim_{A\to\infty} \frac{\beta(A)K(A)}{A} = 0$ along this subsequence. Finally, we show that if $\lim_{A\to\infty} p_A(\epsilon) \le C\epsilon$ and $\lim_{A\to\infty} \frac{\beta(A)K(A)}{A} = 0$ along this subsequence, then it cannot be the case that q_A is in the support of $F_A(q)$.

Step 1: We first show that if we restrict attention to a subsequence of A for which the probability a contributor chooses quality $q \le q^*$ is at least γ, it must be the case that $\lim_{A\to\infty} p_A(\epsilon) \le C\epsilon$ for some constant C and small $\epsilon > 0$, where the limit is taken along this subsequence.

To see this, suppose by means of contradiction that there is no constant C such that $\lim_{A\to\infty} p_A(\epsilon) \le C\epsilon$ for small $\epsilon > 0$ along this subsequence. Note that if a contributor chooses quality $q = q_A$, then the probability she receives a higher ranking than a particular other contributor who chooses quality $q \le q_A + \epsilon$ is no greater than $\frac{1}{2}$. So if $\eta_A(\epsilon)$ denotes the expected fraction of contributors who choose quality $q > q_A + \epsilon$ and receive a lower ranking than this contributor for a given A, then the expected total fraction of contributors who receive a lower ranking than her is no greater than $\frac{p_A(\epsilon)}{2} + \eta_A(\epsilon)$.

Now note that if this contributor instead uses quality $q = q_A + 2\epsilon$ for some $\epsilon > 0$, then the probability she receives a higher ranking than a particular other contributor who chooses quality $q \le q_A + \epsilon$ goes to 1 in the limit as T goes to infinity. The expected fraction of contributors who choose quality $q > q_A + \epsilon$ and receive a lower ranking than a contributor who uses quality $q = q_A + 2\epsilon$ is at least as large as the expected fraction of contributors who choose quality $q > q_A + \epsilon$ and receive a lower ranking than a contributor who uses quality $q = q_A$. Thus if she instead uses quality $q = q_A + 2\epsilon$ for some $\epsilon > 0$, then the expected fraction of contributors who choose quality $q > q_A + \epsilon$ and receive a lower ranking than her is at least $\eta_A(\epsilon)$. From this it follows that the expected total fraction of contributors who receive a lower ranking than this contributor when she chooses quality $q = q_A + 2\epsilon$ is at least $p_A(\epsilon) + \eta_A(\epsilon)$ in the limit as T goes to infinity.

Thus, choosing quality $q = q_A + 2\epsilon$ instead of $q = q_A$ results in this contributor receiving a higher ranking than an expected fraction of at least $\frac{p_A(\epsilon)}{2}$ more contributors. Therefore, if there are k participating contributors, the expected number of contributors that she beats increases by at least $\frac{p_A(\epsilon)k}{2}$ as a result of this change. Moving up in the rankings by one spot increases a contributor's payoff by $\Theta(\frac{A}{k^2})$ since $\alpha_j(k) - \alpha_{j+1}(k) = \Theta(k^{-2})$ for all $j \leq k-1$. Thus choosing quality $q = q_A + 2\epsilon$ instead of $q = q_A$ increases her expected benefits by $\Theta(\frac{p_A(\epsilon)k}{2}(\frac{A}{k^2})) = \Theta(\frac{p_A(\epsilon)A}{k})$. So if $b_A(\epsilon)$ denotes the change in expected benefits from choosing quality $q = q_A + 2\epsilon$ instead of choosing quality $q = q_A$, there is no constant C such that $\lim_{A\to\infty} b_A(\epsilon) \leq C\epsilon$ for small $\epsilon > 0$.

Now let $c_A(\epsilon)$ denote the added cost a contributor incurs by choosing quality $q = q_A + 2\epsilon$ instead of choosing quality $q = q_A$. Note that there exists some constant C such that $c_A(\epsilon) \leq C\epsilon$ for small $\epsilon > 0$ since $q_A \leq q^* < 1$ implies $c'(q_A) \leq c'(q^*)$, which is finite. Combining this with the result in the previous paragraph shows that there exists some large A and some small $\epsilon > 0$ such that a contributor obtains a strictly larger expected payoff from choosing the quality $q = q_A + 2\epsilon$ instead of choosing quality $q = q_A$. This contradicts the fact that q_A is in the support of $F_A(q)$ and proves that there exists some constant C such that $\lim_{A\to\infty} p_A(\epsilon) \leq C\epsilon$ for small $\epsilon > 0$ along this subsequence.

Step 2: Now we show that if there exists some constant $C > 0$ such that $\lim_{A\to\infty} p_A(\epsilon) \leq C\epsilon$ for small $\epsilon > 0$ along this subsequence, then it must be the case that $\lim_{A\to\infty} \frac{\beta(A)K(A)}{A} = 0$ along this subsequence.

To see this, note that if there exists some constant $C > 0$ such that $\lim_{A\to\infty} p_A(\epsilon) \leq C\epsilon$ for small $\epsilon > 0$ along this subsequence, then as T becomes large, the expected fraction of contributors who receive a lower ranking than a contributor who participates with quality $q = q_A$ goes to zero, for the following reason. Let $\epsilon(T)$ denote the largest value of $\epsilon > 0$ such that the probability of an agent with quality q_A receiving a higher ranking than one with quality $q_A + \epsilon(T)$ is at least $\frac{1}{T}$; then, $\lim_{T\to\infty} \epsilon(T) = 0$. Thus the expected fraction of contributors who receive a lower ranking than a contributor who participates with quality q_A is no greater than $p_A(\epsilon(T)) + \frac{1}{T}$ for any T. This tends to zero as T goes to infinity.

Thus if $g(A)$ denotes the expected fraction of contributors who receive a lower ranking than a contributor who participates with quality q_A, then $\lim_{A\to\infty} g(A) = 0$. Now if there are k contributors, then the expected number of contributors who receive a lower ranking than one who participates with quality q_A is $g(A)k$. Combining this with the facts that $\alpha_j(k) - \alpha_{j+1}(k) = \Theta(k^{-2})$ for all $j \leq k-1$ and $\alpha_k(k) = 0$ for sufficiently large k shows that a contributor who participates with quality q_A obtains an expected amount of attention $\Theta(g(A)k\frac{A}{k^2}) = \Theta(g(A)\frac{A}{k})$.

Now $\frac{k}{\beta(A)K(A)}$ converges in probability to 1 as $A \to \infty$, so $\Theta(g(A)\frac{A}{k}) = \Theta(g(A)\frac{A}{\beta(A)K(A)})$. Thus if $\lim_{A\to\infty} \frac{\beta(A)K(A)}{A} = 0$ does not hold along this subsequence, then $\lim_{A\to\infty} g(A) = 0$ implies it must be the case that a contributor who contributes with quality q_A receives an expected amount of attention that approaches zero as A goes to infinity. But this means that an agent could obtain a strictly higher payoff by not contributing than by contributing with quality q_A for some large A, contradicting the fact that q_A is in the support of $F_A(q)$. This contradiction shows that $\lim_{A\to\infty} \frac{\beta(A)K(A)}{A} = 0$ must hold along this subsequence.

Step 3: Finally we show that if $\lim_{A\to\infty} \frac{\beta(A)K(A)}{A} = 0$ holds along this subsequence, then it cannot be the case that q_A is in the support of $F_A(q)$.

To see this, let $\gamma_A = F_A(q^*)$ denote the probability that a contributor chooses a quality $q \leq q^*$ for a given A, and note that $\gamma_A \geq \gamma$ for all A in the subsequence. Also note that if a contributor uses quality $q = q^* + \epsilon$ instead of using quality $q = q_A$, then this costs her no more than $c(q^* + \epsilon) - c(q_A) \leq c(q^* + \epsilon)$.

Now if this contributor uses quality $q = q_A$, then the probability she receives a higher ranking than a particular other contributor who chooses quality $q \leq q^*$ is no greater than $\frac{1}{2}$. Thus if δ_A denotes the expected fraction of contributors who choose quality $q > q^*$ and receive a lower ranking than this contributor using quality q_A, then the expected total fraction of contributors that receive a lower ranking than her is no greater than $\frac{\gamma_A}{2} + \delta_A$.

Now, if she instead uses quality $q = q^* + \epsilon$ for some $\epsilon > 0$, then the probability she receives a higher ranking than a particular other contributor who chooses quality $q \leq q^*$ goes to 1 in the limit as T goes to infinity. The expected fraction of contributors who choose quality $q > q^*$ and receive a lower ranking than a contributor who uses quality $q = q^* + \epsilon$ is at least as large as the expected fraction of contributors who choose quality $q > q^*$ and receive a lower ranking than a contributor who uses quality $q = q_A$. Thus if the contributor instead uses quality $q = q^* + \epsilon$ for some $\epsilon > 0$, then the expected fraction of contributors who choose quality $q > q^*$ and receive a lower ranking than the contributor is at least δ_A. From this it follows that the expected fraction of contributors who receive a lower ranking than this contributor when she chooses quality $q = q^* + \epsilon$ is at least $\gamma_A + \delta_A$ in the limit as T goes to infinity.

Thus choosing quality $q = q^* + \epsilon$ instead of $q = q_A$ results in receiving a higher ranking than an expected fraction of at least $\frac{\gamma_A}{2}$ additional contributors. Thus if there are k participating contributors, this contributor increases the expected number of agents she beats by at least $\frac{\gamma_A k}{2}$ as a result of this change. As before, moving up in the rankings by one spot increases the payoff by $\Theta(\frac{A}{k^2})$ since $\alpha_j(k) - \alpha_{j+1}(k) = \Theta(k^{-2})$ for all $j \leq k-1$. Thus if a contributor chooses quality $q = q^* + \epsilon$ instead of choosing quality $q = q_A$, then she increases her expected benefits by $\Theta(\frac{\gamma_A k}{2}(\frac{A}{k^2})) = \Theta(\frac{A}{k}) = \Theta(\frac{A}{\beta(A)K(A)})$.

But for sufficiently large A in the subsequence, it follows that this increase in expected benefits is greater than $c(q^* + \epsilon)$ since $\lim_{A\to\infty} \frac{A}{\beta(A)K(A)} = \infty$ in the subsequence but $c(q^* + \epsilon)$ is a constant independent of A. Thus from this it follows that a contributor obtains a strictly greater expected payoff from choosing quality $q = q^* + \epsilon$ instead of choosing quality $q = q_A$ for sufficiently large A in the subsequence. This contradicts the existence of some such q^* and proves the desired result. □

This theorem uses the condition that $\alpha_j(k) - \alpha_{j+1}(k) = \Theta(k^{-2})$. It is worth noting that the result that contributors produce arbitrarily high quality content does not depend crucially on this assumption. If we instead replace the assumption that $\alpha_j(k) - \alpha_{j+1}(k) = \Theta(k^{-2})$ for all $j \leq k-1$ in Theorem 4.2 with the weaker assumption that $\alpha_j(k) - \alpha_{j+1}(k) = \Omega(k^{-2})$ for all $j \leq k-1$, then the result would go through with a very similar proof. That is, there is no problem inducing high quality content as long there is at least some minimum difference between the attention allocated to content ranked differently.

To understand the intuition behind this result, first note that in any equilibrium it must be the case that a large fraction of participating contributors produce content with quality close to q_A, where q_A is the minimum quality in the support of $F_A(q)$: if only a small fraction of agents produce content with quality close to q_A, then a contributor who produces quality q_A will achieve a lower ranking than almost all other contributors, and will obtain almost no attention. Thus such an agent could achieve a higher expected payoff by not contributing, and it would not be possible for q_A to be in the support of $F_A(q)$.

But if a large fraction of participating contributors are producing content with quality close to q_A, then for large T, an agent can ensure that she will achieve a higher ranking than a significant number of additional contributors by producing content with quality $q = q_A + \epsilon$ for some small $\epsilon > 0$ (in contrast with choosing quality $q = q_A$). Thus if q_A is bounded away from 1, an agent could profitably deviate by producing content with quality $q = q_A + \epsilon$ instead of content with quality $q = q_A$ for some small $\epsilon > 0$. From this it follows that q_A must be close to 1 for large A.

Next we show that one can choose the number of individuals who vote on the content, T, in such a way to induce all contributors to participate in the limit, as long as the pool of potential contributors does not grow too quickly with the number of viewers.

THEOREM 4.3. *Suppose that* $\lim_{A\to\infty} \frac{K(A)}{A} = 0$ *and* $\alpha_j(k) - \alpha_{j+1}(k) = \Theta(k^{-2})$ *for all* $j \leq k-1$. *Then there exists a sequence* $\{T(A)\}_{A=1}^{\infty}$ *such that* $\lim_{A\to\infty} T(A) = \infty$ *and* $\beta = 1$ *in equilibrium for sufficiently large* A.

We prove this theorem in the appendix in the full version of the paper. This result indicates that if $T(A)$ does not grow too quickly with A, then all contributors will participate for sufficiently large A (note that $T(A)$ still diverges so that quality still becomes optimal, albeit at a slower rate). While this result makes use of a technical assumption that $\lim_{A\to\infty} \frac{K(A)}{A} = 0$, we believe this is the most critical case to ensure large participation, as this is the case where there is only a relatively small number of agents who may contribute.

To understand the intuition behind this result, note that if $T(A)$ does not increase too quickly with A, then contributors will have a relatively lower incentive to choose high quality because producing higher quality content does not result in an especially large increase in one's probability of being ranked highly. But when contributors are not producing exceedingly high quality content, the cost to participating with a quality that will be competitive in the mechanism is relatively small, and agents find it worthwhile to participate. Thus if $T(A)$ does not increase too quickly with A, then all agents will participate for sufficiently large A.

Implementing Ranking Mechanisms. Theorem 4.2 requires a mechanism designer to choose the values of α to satisfy $\alpha_j(k) - \alpha_{j+1}(k) = \Theta(k^{-2})$ and $\alpha_k(k) = 0$ to induce high quality. The needed difference in attention between two contributions can be achieved as follows: To increase the difference in attention between two contributions, one can show one contribution prominently more often than the other, and to decrease the difference one can show the two contributions in prominent positions roughly equally often. One can also easily ensure that $\alpha_k(k) = 0$ by simply never showing a contribution that is ranked last by the initial voting.

The analysis in Theorem 4.3 suggests that a mechanism designer will want to choose T so that $T(A)$ does not grow too quickly with A in order to induce full participation. This can also be achieved in practice by simply ignoring votes beyond the first T votes. Thus the type of restrictions on T and α used in these results should be easily implementable in practice.

5. PROPORTIONAL MECHANISM

Since all agents produce similar qualities in equilibrium in the rank-order mechanism, it might seem unfair to give significantly greater amounts of attention to agents who receive higher numbers of positive votes, even though the difference between the numbers of positive votes the contributors receive is likely to be very small. A natural and more equitable alternative is to reward contributors in proportion to the number of positive votes they receive— in such a proportional mechanism, two agents who both receive very similar numbers of positive votes also receive similar amounts of attention[5]. However, while the proportional system might allocate attention in a more equitable manner, the mechanism also significantly changes incentives for agents to produce high quality content in equilibrium. In this section, we analyze the equilibria of the proportional mechanism.

First we formally define the proportional mechanism.

DEFINITION 5.1 (PROPORTIONAL MECHANISM $M_p(T)$). *Suppose k agents contribute, each contribution is voted on by T viewers, and each participating contributor i receives m_i positive votes. Then the proportional mechanism gives the ith contributor a share* $\frac{m_i}{\sum_{j=1}^{k} m_j}$ *of the available attention if $m_i > 0$ for some i. If $m_i = 0$ for all i, every contributor receives a share $\frac{1}{k}$ of the available attention.*

Note that in the proportional mechanism, only the number of votes used by the mechanism, T, is available as a parameter of the mechanism that can be varied to achieve desirable incentives. We first prove a result on the nature of the equilibrium in the proportional mechanism.

THEOREM 5.1. *For any values of A, K, and T, there exists a symmetric equilibrium to the proportional mechanism in which all contributors participate with probability β and choose the same quality q conditional on contributing.*

PROOF. Define $\beta(q)$ to be the unique value of $\beta \in [0,1]$ that satisfies either

$$c(q) = E[\frac{A}{k} | \, i \text{ enters; other agents enter with probability } \beta]$$

if this holds for some $\beta \in (0,1)$, $\beta(q) = 0$ if $c(q) \geq A$, and $\beta(q) = 1$ if $c(q) \leq \frac{A}{K}$. Note that $\beta(q)$ is unique and well-defined for all $q \in [0,1)$ and that $\beta(q)$ is continuous in q.

[5]Lazear [9] notes that fairness can lead to desirable equilibrium outcomes in certain settings where malicious sabotage is a concern.

Define $b(q_i, q_{-i}, \beta)$ to be the expected amount of attention that a contributor i obtains if contributor i contributes with quality q_i, all other agents who participate contribute with quality q_{-i}, and all other agents participate with probability β. Thus $b(q_i, q_{-i}, \beta) = E[\frac{m_i}{m_i+\sum_{j\neq i} m_j}|\beta, q_i, q_{-i}]$. Note that $b(q^*, q^*, \beta(q^*))$ is continuously differentiable in q^* for all $q^* \in [0, 1)$ since the probability that a particular realization of positive votes (m_i, m_{-i}) takes place is a continuously differentiable function of (q_i, q_{-i}, β).

Now note that $c'(0) < \frac{\partial b}{\partial q_i}(0, 0, \beta(0))$ since $c'(0) = 0$ and $\frac{\partial b}{\partial q_i}(0, 0, \beta(0)) > 0$ since the proportional mechanism assigns equal attention to all participants if all participants obtain zero positive votes. Also note that $\lim_{q^*\to 1} c'(q^*) > \lim_{q^*\to 1} \frac{\partial b}{\partial q_i}(q^*, q^*, \beta(q^*))$ because $\lim_{q^*\to 1} c'(q^*) = \infty$ but $\frac{\partial b}{\partial q_i}(q^*, q^*, \beta(q^*))$ is finite for all $q^* \in [0, 1]$. Since $c'(q^*)$ and $\frac{\partial b}{\partial q_i}(q^*, q^*, \beta(q^*))$ are continuous in q^* for all $q^* \in [0, 1)$, it follows from the intermediate value theorem that there exists some $q^* \in (0, 1)$ such that $c'(q^*) = \frac{\partial b}{\partial q_i}(q^*, q^*, \beta(q^*))$. This shows that there is a quality q^* at which the *local* conditions for not deviating from the quality choice are satisfied, if all participants enter with probability $\beta(q^*)$. To show that this pair of values indeed constitutes an equilibrium, we need to show that (i) no agent wants to choose a different participation probability β', and (ii) there are no *non-local* profitable deviations of quality.

First note that it must be the case that $\beta(q^*) > 0$ for this q^*. If $\beta = 0$, then we know that $\frac{\partial b}{\partial q_i}(q^*, q^*, \beta) = 0$, so $c'(q^*) \neq \frac{\partial b}{\partial q_i}(q^*, q^*, \beta(q^*))$ since the fact that $c(q)$ is increasing and convex in q implies $c'(q^*) > 0$ for $q^* > 0$. Thus $\beta(q^*) = 0$ cannot hold for this q^* and we have $\beta(q^*) > 0$.

Now if $\beta(q^*) \in (0, 1)$, then by definition of $\beta(q)$, it must be the case that

$$c(q^*) = E[\frac{A}{k} | \, i \text{ enters; other agents enter with probability } \beta]$$

and agents are indifferent between participating with quality q^* and not participating. And if $\beta(q^*) = 1$, then $c(q^*) \leq \frac{A}{K}$ and all agents prefer to participate with quality q^* than to not participate. Thus if all agents contribute with probability $\beta(q^*)$ and produce quality q^*, no agent can profitably deviate by participating with a different probability from $\beta(q^*)$.

Now we show that no agent can profitably deviate by contributing with a quality $q_i \neq q^*$ conditional on participating. Note that if an agent participates with quality q_i and all other agents participate with quality q^* and contribute with probability $\beta(q^*)$, then the marginal change in an agent's payoff from contributing with a slightly larger quality is $\frac{\partial b}{\partial q_i}(q_i, q^*, \beta(q^*)) - c'(q_i)$. Since $c(q_i)$ is convex, it follows that $-c'(q_i)$ is decreasing in q_i for all $q_i \in [0, 1)$.

Now we show that $\frac{\partial b}{\partial q_i}(q_i, q^*, \beta(q^*))$ is decreasing in q_i. Note that the marginal benefit from receiving an additional positive vote is smaller when m_i is larger for any fixed values of m_{-i} since the difference between $\frac{m_i+1}{m_i+1+\sum_{j\neq i} m_j}$ and $\frac{m_i}{m_i+\sum_{j\neq i} m_j}$ is decreasing in m_i. Now if $G(m_i|q_i)$ denotes the distribution of the values of m_i given that agent i is producing quality q_i, then $q_i' > q_i$ implies that $G(m_i|q_i')$ first order stochastically dominates $G(m_i|q_i)$. Thus if $q_i' > q_i$, then the expected benefit from receiving an additional positive vote is smaller when an agent is producing with quality q_i' than it is when an agent is producing with quality q_i. From this it follows that $\frac{\partial b}{\partial q_i}(q_i, q^*, \beta(q^*))$ is decreasing in q_i.

Putting this all together shows that $\frac{\partial b}{\partial q_i}(q_i, q^*, \beta(q^*)) - c'(q_i)$ is decreasing in q_i. Thus since $\frac{\partial b}{\partial q_i}(q^*, q^*, \beta(q^*)) - c'(q^*) = 0$, it follows that $\frac{\partial b}{\partial q_i}(q_i, q^*, \beta(q^*)) - c'(q_i) > 0$ when $q_i < q^*$ and $\frac{\partial b}{\partial q_i}(q_i, q^*, \beta(q^*)) - c'(q_i) < 0$ when $q_i > q^*$. But this means that an agent prefers to contribute with quality q^* than with any quality q_i satisfying either $q_i < q^*$ or $q_i > q^*$. From this it follows that an agent cannot profitably deviate by choosing some quality different from q^* and there is an equilibrium in which all agents participate with probability $\beta(q^*)$ and contribute with quality q^* conditional on participating. □

Next we investigate asymptotic equilibrium quality choices in the proportional mechanism. In contrast to the ranking mechanism, whether equilibrium quality choices converge to the optimal quality in the proportional mechanism *depends* on how quickly the number of potential contributors grows with the number of viewers. If this number grows slowly enough that $\frac{K(A)}{A}$ goes to 0 as A goes to infinity, then equilibrium quality converges 1. But if not, equilibrium quality remains strictly less than one in the limit.

Before proving this, we first state a lemma regarding the derivative of the cost function at the equilibrium quality, which we will use for both our remaining results.

LEMMA 5.1. *Let $\beta(A)$ and $q_p(A)$ denote equilibrium participation probabilities and quality choices in the proportional mechanism for a given A. Then $c'(q_p(A)) = \Theta(\frac{A}{\beta(A)K(A)})$.*

This lemma is proven in the appendix in the full version of the paper. Now we use this lemma to illustrate how equilibrium quality choices vary in the proportional mechanism as the amount of available attention diverges.

THEOREM 5.2. *If $\lim_{A\to\infty} \frac{K(A)}{A} = 0$, then $\lim_{A\to\infty} q_p(A) = 1$ and $\beta = 1$ for sufficiently large A. If $\liminf_{A\to\infty} \frac{K(A)}{A} > 0$, then $\limsup_{A\to\infty} q_p(A) < 1$.*

PROOF. Note that if $\lim_{A\to\infty} \frac{K(A)}{A} = 0$, then the fact that $c'(q_p(A)) = \Theta(\frac{A}{\beta(A)K(A)}) = \Omega(\frac{A}{K(A)})$ implies $\lim_{A\to\infty} c'(q_p(A)) = \infty$ and $\lim_{A\to\infty} q_p(A) = 1$. Also note that if $\beta(A) < 1$ for some large A, then the equilibrium conditions for indifference between contributing and not contributing indicate that $c(q_p(A)) = \Theta(\frac{A}{\beta(A)K(A)})$. Combining this with the fact that $c'(q_p(A)) = \Theta(\frac{A}{\beta(A)K(A)})$ shows that $\frac{c'(q_p(A))}{c(q_p(A))} = \Theta(1)$. But since $\lim_{q\to 1} c(q) = \infty$, $\lim_{q\to 1} \log c(q) = \infty$ as well, $\lim_{q\to 1} \frac{d}{dq} \log c(q) = \infty$, and $\lim_{q\to 1} \frac{c'(q)}{c(q)} = \infty$. Thus the fact that $\lim_{A\to\infty} q_p(A) = 1$ implies that $\lim_{A\to\infty} \frac{c'(q_p(A))}{c(q_p(A))} = \infty$, meaning $\frac{c'(q_p(A))}{c(q_p(A))} = \Theta(1)$ cannot hold. Thus for sufficiently large A, it is not possible to have $\beta(A) < 1$, and it must be the case that $\beta = 1$ for sufficiently large A.

Now suppose that $\liminf_{A\to\infty} \frac{K(A)}{A} > 0$. In this case, if $\beta = 1$ for sufficiently large A, then the fact that $c'(q_p(A)) = \Theta(\frac{A}{\beta(A)K(A)})$ implies that $c'(q_p(A)) = \Theta(1)$ and $\limsup_{A\to\infty} q_p(A) < 1$. And if $\beta(A) < 1$ for some infinite subsequence of A, then an identical argument to that given in the previous paragraph shows that $\frac{c'(q_p(A))}{c(q_p(A))} = \Theta(1)$ and $\limsup_{A\to\infty} q_p(A) < 1$ along this subsequence. From this it follows that $\liminf_{A\to\infty} \frac{K(A)}{A} > 0$ implies $\limsup_{A\to\infty} q_p(A) < 1$. □

We note that both regimes in this theorem, $\frac{K(A)}{A} \to 0$ and $\frac{K(A)}{A} \to r > 0$, are of interest in the context of user-generated content. In question-and-answer sites such as Yahoo! Answers or StackOverflow, the number of users $K(A)$ who can answer a question is often significantly smaller than the number of users who consume the answer, possibly via a search engine, and $\frac{K(A)}{A} \to 0$ is likely. On the other hand, in settings like posts on discussion forums or comments on blogs where many consumers are also producers, the number of contributors may not be negligible compared to the number of viewers who consume the content, *i.e.*, $\frac{K(A)}{A}$ is not vanishingly small. The theorem says that the proportional mechanism elicits the optimal quality in the first kind of setting, but not in the second.

6. COMPARING MECHANISMS

In this section, we compare equilibrium qualities in the ranking mechanism and the proportional mechanism. We already know from Theorems 4.2 and 5.2 that when $\lim_{A\to\infty} \frac{K(A)}{A} > 0$, the lowest quality in the support of the equilibrium distribution in the ranking mechanism converges to 1, but not in the proportional mechanism. For this case, therefore, the ranking mechanism leads to higher quality contributions than the proportional mechanism in the limit of diverging attention. We now complete this comparison by investigating the case where $\lim_{A\to\infty} \frac{K(A)}{A} = 0$. We show that in this case also, the ranking mechanism elicits higher quality contributions than the proportional mechanism in equilibrium.

First we prove a simple technical lemma.

LEMMA 6.1. *The minimum value of* $\sum_{i=1}^n x_i^2$ *subject to the constraints* $x_i \geq 0$ *and* $\sum_{i=1}^n x_i = 1$ *is* $\frac{1}{n}$.

PROOF. Note that subject to the constraints $x_i \geq 0$ and $\sum_{i=1}^n x_i = 1$, the expression $\sum_{i=1}^n x_i^2$ is minimized when $x_i = \frac{1}{n}$ for all i. To see this, note that if $x_i = \frac{1}{n} + \delta_i$ for some $\{\delta_i\}_{i=1}^n$ satisfying $\sum_{i=1}^n \delta_i = 0$, then $\sum_{i=1}^n x_i^2 = \sum_{i=1}^n (\frac{1}{n} + \delta_i)^2 = \sum_{i=1}^n (\frac{1}{n^2} + \frac{2}{n}\delta_i + \delta_i^2) = \frac{1}{n} + \sum_{i=1}^n \delta_i^2$. But $\frac{1}{n} + \sum_{i=1}^n \delta_i^2$ is minimized when $\delta_i = 0$ for all i. From this it follows that the expression $\sum_{i=1}^n x_i^2$ is minimized when $x_i = \frac{1}{n}$ for all i, and the minimum value of $\sum_{i=1}^n x_i^2$ subject to the constraints $x_i \geq 0$ and $\sum_{i=1}^n x_i = 1$ is $\frac{1}{n}$. □

Now we use this to show that agents almost always choose higher quality in the ranking mechanism than in the proportional mechanism when the amount of attention available becomes large.

THEOREM 6.1. *Suppose* $\lim_{A\to\infty} \frac{K(A)}{A} = 0$, $\lim_{A\to\infty} T(A) = \infty$, *and* α *in the ranking mechanism satisfies* $\alpha_j(k) - \alpha_{j+1}(k) = \Theta(k^{-2})$ *for all* $j \leq k-1$. *Let* $q_r(A)$ *denote the (possibly random) quality chosen by the contributors in some equilibrium of the ranking mechanism, and let* $q_p(A)$ *be an equilibrium quality in the proportional mechanism. Then* $\lim_{A\to\infty} Pr(q_r(A) > q_p(A)) = 1$.

PROOF. Suppose by means of contradiction that $Pr(q_r(A) \leq q_p(A)) \geq \gamma > 0$ for an infinite number of A. Restrict attention to values of A satisfying $Pr(q_r(A) \leq q_p(A)) \geq \gamma$, and define $q^*(A)$ to be the largest quality such that $Pr(q_r(A) < q^*(A)) \leq \frac{\gamma}{2}$ for any such A. From this it follows that $Pr(q^*(A) \leq q_r(A) \leq q_p(A)) \geq \frac{\gamma}{2}$ for all A in this subsequence. We also know from Theorem 4.2 that $\lim_{A\to\infty} q^*(A) = 1$.

Now suppose that a contributor deviates from $F_A(q)$ by making the following change: if she draws a quality $q \in [q^*(A), q_p(A)]$, then she instead chooses a quality $q + \epsilon$ for some infinitesimal amount $\epsilon > 0$; if she draws a quality $q \notin [q^*(A), q_p(A)]$, then she makes no change to her quality. We seek to show that this is a profitable deviation for a contributor for sufficiently large A in the subsequence. To do this, we first show that the additional expected cost from this deviation is bounded above by the marginal costs of producing higher quality content in the proportional mechanism, and then show that the expected benefit in the ranking mechanism from this deviation exceeds these marginal costs.

First note that this change in quality costs a contributor an additional amount no greater than $E[c(q+\epsilon) - c(q) | q \in [q^*(A), q_p(A)]]$ which, in the limit as $\epsilon \to 0$, converges to $\epsilon E[c'(q) | q \in [q^*(A), q_p(A)]] \leq \epsilon c'(q_p(A)) = \Theta(\epsilon \frac{A}{K(A)})$ (since $\beta(A) = 1$ for large A in the proportional mechanism when $\lim_{A\to\infty} \frac{K(A)}{A} = 0$). Next we calculate the expected benefits from this increase in quality.

Suppose a contributor i chooses a quality $q \in [q^*(A), q_p(A)]$. (This happens with probability at least $\gamma/2 > 0$ by assumption). Then there exists an infinite sequence $\hat{q}(A)$ such that $\lim_{A\to\infty} \hat{q}(A) = 1$ and $Pr(\frac{m_i}{T} \geq \hat{q}(A)) \geq \frac{1}{2}$ for all A. Thus if two contributors both choose qualities in $[q^*(A), q_p(A)]$, then the probability that they both receive at least $\hat{q}(A)T$ positive votes is at least $\frac{1}{4}$. Moreover, conditional on both receiving at least $\hat{q}(A)T$ positive votes, the probability a contributor receives any particular number of votes is the same for both contributors.

From Lemma 6.1, we know that if two contributors both receive at least $\hat{q}(A)T$ positive votes and they both receive any particular number of votes with the same probability, then the probability that both contributors receive an equal number of votes is at least $\frac{1}{(1-\hat{q}(A))T}$. Thus if one contributor receives an additional vote when both receive at least $\hat{q}(A)T$ positive votes, then this additional vote increases her probability of being ranked ahead of the other contributor by at least $\frac{1}{2(1-\hat{q}(A))T}$. (An agent is ranked ahead of another agent with probability $\frac{1}{2}$ when both receive the same number of votes and with probability 1 when one receives a strictly larger number of votes, so the additional vote increases the agents's probability of being ranked ahead of the other agent by a factor of $\frac{1}{2}$.)

Now the probability both contributor i and some other contributor choose qualities $q \in [q^*(A), q_p(A)]$ is at least $(\frac{\gamma}{2})^2$. And we have seen that the probability that both contributors receive at least $\hat{q}(A)T$ positive votes if they choose qualities $q \in [q^*(A), q_p(A)]$ is at least $\frac{1}{4}$. Combining this with the results in the previous paragraph shows that an additional vote for contributor i increases the probability of her being ranked ahead of a particular other contributor by at least $(\frac{\gamma}{2})^2 \frac{1}{4} \frac{1}{2(1-\hat{q}(A))T(A)} = \frac{\gamma^2}{32(1-\hat{q}(A))T(A)}$.

Now increasing quality by an infinitesimal amount

$\epsilon(A) = o(\frac{1}{T(A)})$ leads to an additional positive vote with probability $\Theta(\epsilon(A)T(A))$. Therefore, increasing quality by $\epsilon(A)$ increases the probability of being ranked ahead of a particular other contributor by an amount $\Omega(\epsilon(A)T(A)\frac{\gamma^2}{32(1-\hat{q}(A))T(A)}) = \Omega(\frac{\epsilon(A)}{1-\hat{q}(A)})$.

This implies that a contributor's change in expected ranking from increasing quality by $\epsilon(A)$ when $q \in [q^*(A), q_p(A)]$ is $\Omega(\frac{\epsilon(A)k}{1-\hat{q}(A)})$. And moving up in the rankings by one spot increases one's payoff by $\Theta(\frac{A}{k^2})$ since $\alpha_j(k) - \alpha_{j+1}(k) = \Theta(k^{-2})$ for all $j \leq k-1$. Thus if an agent increases her quality by $\epsilon(A)$ when $q \in [q^*(A), q_p(A)]$, then her expected benefit increases by an amount $\Omega(\frac{\epsilon(A)k}{1-\hat{q}(A)}\frac{A}{k^2}) = \Omega(\frac{\epsilon(A)A}{(1-\hat{q}(A))\beta(A)K(A)})$.

Thus, increasing quality by $\epsilon(A)$ when $q \in [q^*(A), q_p(A)]$ leads to an additional benefit of $\Omega(\frac{\epsilon(A)A}{(1-\hat{q}(A))\beta(A)K(A)})$, at an additional cost of $\Theta(\frac{\epsilon(A)A}{K(A)})$. Since $\lim_{A\to\infty} q(A) = 1$, it follows that this is a profitable deviation for sufficiently large A. This contradicts the assumption that there is a sequence of equilibria for which $Pr(q_r(A) \leq q_p(A)) \geq \gamma > 0$ for an infinite number of A and proves the desired result. □

To understand the intuition behind this result, suppose for the time being that agents chose quality in the ranking mechanism according to a symmetric pure strategy, $q_r(A)$. Then if an agent makes a small change in quality from $q = q_r(A)$ to $q = q_r(A)+\epsilon$ for some $\epsilon > 0$, the agent goes from obtaining an average ranking in expectation to almost certainly being ranked near the very top. Thus such a change dramatically increases an agent's expected payoff. By contrast, in the proportional mechanism, increasing one's quality by $\epsilon > 0$ does relatively little to improve the expected attention that an agent receives. Thus incentives to produce higher quality content are greater in the ranking mechanism than in the proportional mechanism. The proof of the theorem illustrates how this intuition can be extended when the agents choose quality according to a mixed strategy.

7. DISCUSSION

In this paper, we have analyzed the widely used rank-order mechanism for displaying user contributed content in a model with strategic attention-driven contributors, and shown that the rank-order mechanism elicits contributions of optimal quality in the limit as the amount of available attention diverges. By contrast, whether equilibrium quality in the proportional mechanism becomes optimal depends on the relative rates of growth of the number of potential contributors and the number of viewers. Even when equilibrium quality in the proportional mechanism tends to the optimal quality, quality is almost always lower in the proportional mechanism than in the ranking mechanism. Thus, despite being more equitable, the proportional system creates inferior incentives for eliciting high quality contributions than the ranking mechanism.

We note that the ranking mechanism is a relatively robust mechanism, in the sense that the presence of even a large number of voters who are error prone or vote 'good' or 'bad' on all content uniformly does not affect the limiting equilibrium quality, as long as the number of voters voting according to quality continues to diverge. This is in contrast to the mechanism analyzed in [3], where even a small fraction of raters who vote thumbs down on content can lead to no content being displayed on the site.

There are a number of interesting directions for further work; we discuss two specific directions. On most sites, there are almost always some contributors who produce consistently low quality contributions, despite receiving little or no attention for it. This indicates that some subset of contributors have zero cost for producing low-quality content. An ideal mechanism in this setting would continue to elicit high quality contributions and high participation from the remaining contributors: an interesting question is how effective the ranking mechanism is when such contributors are present, and whether other mechanisms might be more effective. A second interesting direction regards questions related to malicious voters. The ranking mechanism is robust to voters who do not vote according to the model as long as they do this uniformly for all content. However, it is less clear how robust the results are in a model in which some malicious voters try to bring up specific contributions or put down others. Addressing this is an open question.

Acknowledgements

We thank Preston McAfee, David Reiley, and Michael Schwarz for helpful discussions and the anonymous reviewers for comments.

8. REFERENCES

[1] J.G. Becker, D.S. Damianov, *On the Existence of Symmetric Mixed Strategy Equilibria*, Economics Letters, 90(1), 84-87, 2006.

[2] Y. Chen, S. Jain, D. Parkes, *Designing Incentives for Online Question and Answer Forums*, ACM EC, 2009.

[3] A. Ghosh, R.P. McAfee, *Incentivizing High-Quality User Generated Content*, 20th International World Wide Web Conference (WWW), 2011.

[4] J.R. Green, N.L. Stokey, *A Comparison of Tournaments and Contracts*, Journal of Political Economy, 91(3), 349-364, 1983.

[5] B. Holmstrom, *Moral Hazard in Teams*, Bell Journal of Economics, 13(2), 324-340, 1982.

[6] P. Hummel, *Proportional Versus Winner-Take-All Electoral Vote Allocations*, Public Choice, forthcoming.

[7] S. Jain, D. Parkes, *The Role of Game Theory in Human Computation Systems* (Position Paper), HCOMP 2009.

[8] S. Jain, D. Parkes, *A Game-Theoretic Analysis of the ESP Game*, Working Paper.

[9] E.P. Lazear, *Pay Equality and Industrial Politics*, Journal of Political Economy, 97(3), 561-580, 1989.

[10] E.P. Lazear, S. Rosen, *Rank-Order Tournaments as Optimum Labor Contracts*, Journal of Political Economy, 89(5), 841-864, 1981.

[11] A. Lizzeri, N. Persico, *The Provision of Public Goods under Alternative Electoral Systems*, American Economic Review, 91(1), 225-239, 2001.

[12] B.J. Nalebuff, J.E. Stiglitz, *Prizes and Incentives: Towards a General Theory of Compensation and Competition*, Bell Journal of Economics, 14(1), 21-43, 1983.

[13] T. Persson, G. Tabellini, *The Size and Scope of Government: Comparative Politics with Rational Politicians*, European Economic Review, 43(4), 699-735, 1999.

[14] J.M. Snyder, *Election Goals and the Allocation of Campaign Resources*, Econometrica, 57(3), 637-660, 1989.

Selling Privacy at Auction

Arpita Ghosh
Yahoo Research
Santa Clara, CA
arpita@yahoo-inc.com

Aaron Roth
Microsoft Research
New England Campus
Cambridge, MA
aaroth@cis.upenn.edu

ABSTRACT

We initiate the study of markets for private data, through the lens of differential privacy. Although the purchase and sale of private data has already begun on a large scale, a theory of privacy as a commodity is missing. In this paper, we propose to build such a theory. Specifically, we consider a setting in which a data analyst wishes to buy information from a population from which he can estimate some statistic. The analyst wishes to obtain an *accurate* estimate *cheaply*, while the owners of the private data experience some cost for their loss of privacy, and must be compensated for this loss. Agents are selfish, and wish to maximize their profit, so our goal is to design *truthful mechanisms*.

Our main result is that such problems can naturally be viewed and optimally solved as variants of multi-unit procurement auctions. Based on this result, we derive auctions which are optimal up to small constant factors for two natural settings:

1. When the data analyst has a fixed accuracy goal, we show that an application of the classic Vickrey auction achieves the analyst's accuracy goal while minimizing his total payment.

2. When the data analyst has a fixed budget, we give a mechanism which maximizes the accuracy of the resulting estimate while guaranteeing that the resulting sum payments do not exceed the analyst's budget.

In both cases, our comparison class is the set of envy-free mechanisms, which correspond to the natural class of fixed-price mechanisms in our setting.

In both of these results, we ignore the privacy cost due to possible correlations between an individual's private data and his valuation for privacy itself. We then show that generically, no individually rational mechanism can compensate individuals for the privacy loss incurred due to their reported valuations for privacy. This is nevertheless an important issue, and modeling it correctly is one of the many exciting directions for future work.

Categories and Subject Descriptors

F.0 [**Theory of Computation**]: General

General Terms

Economics, Theory

Keywords

Differential privacy, Auctions

1. INTRODUCTION

Organizations such as the Census Bureau and hospitals have long maintained databases of personal information. However, with the advent of the Internet, many corporations are now able to aggregate enormous quantities of sensitive information, and use, buy, and sell it for financial gain. Up until recently, the purchase and sale of private information was the exclusive domain of aggregators – it was obtained for free from the actual owners of the data, for whom it was sensitive. However, recently, companies such as "mint.com" and "Bynamite" have started acting as brokers for private information at the consumer end, paying users for access to their sensitive information [Loh10, Cli10]. Many others, such as Yahoo, Microsoft, Google, and Facebook are also implicitly engaging in the purchase of private information in exchange for non-monetary compensation. In short, "privacy" has become a commodity that has already begun to be bought and sold, in a variety of ad-hoc ways.

Despite the commoditization of privacy in practice, markets for privacy lack a theoretical foundation. In this paper, we initiate the rigorous study of markets *for* private data. Our goal is not to provide a complete solution for the myriad problems involved in the sale of private data, but rather to introduce a crisp model with which to investigate some of the many questions unique to the sale of private data. The study of privacy as a commodity is of immediate relevance, and also a source of many interesting theoretical problems: we hope that this paper elicits more new questions than it answers.

First, let us briefly consider some of the issues that make *privacy* distinct from other commodities that we often deal with, and why this may complicate its sale:

1. First and foremost, in order sell *privacy*, it is important to be able to define and quantify what we mean by privacy. In this regard, the commoditization of privacy has dovetailed nicely with the development of the theoretical underpinnings of privacy: recent work on *differential privacy* [DMNS06] (Definition 2.1) provides a compelling definition and a precise way in which to quantify its sale. Importantly, as we will discuss, the guarantee of differential privacy has a natural utility-theoretic interpretation that makes it a natural quantity to buy and sell.

2. Private data is a good that exhibits intrinsic complementarities: a data analyst will typically not be interested in the private data of any particular individual, but rather in a representative sample from a large population. Nevertheless, he must purchase the data from particular individuals! Clearly, if there may be unknown correlations between individuals values for privacy and their private data, then the typical strategy of "buying from the cheapest sellers" is doomed to fail in this regard. How should an auction be structured by an analyst who wishes to calculate some value which is representative of an entire population?

3. An individual's cost for privacy may itself be private information. Suppose that Alice visits an oncologist, and subsequently is observed to significantly increase her value for privacy: this is of course disclosive! Is it possible to run an auction for private data that compensates individuals for the privacy loss they incur, simply due to the effect that their bids have on the behavior of the mechanism?

1.1 Differential Privacy as a Commodity

Differential privacy, formally defined in Section 2, was introduced by Dwork et al. [DMNS06] as a technical definition for database privacy. Informally, an algorithm is ϵ-differentially private if changing the data of a single individual does not change the probability of any outcome of the mechanism by more than an $\exp(\epsilon) \approx (1+\epsilon)$ multiplicative factor. Differential privacy also has a natural utility-theoretic interpretation that makes it a compelling measure with which to quantify privacy when buying or selling it[1].

An important property of an ϵ-differentially private algorithm A is that its composition with any other database-independent function f has the property that $f(A)$ remains ϵ-differentially private. This allows us to reason about events that might seem quite far removed from the actual output of the algorithm. Quite literally, a guarantee of ϵ-differential privacy is a guarantee that the probability of receiving phone calls during dinner, or of being denied health insurance will not increase by more than an $\exp(\epsilon)$ factor. This allows us to interpret differential privacy as a strong utility theoretic guarantee that holds simultaneously for arbitrary, unknown utility functions: for any individual, with any utility function u over (arbitrary) future events, an ϵ-differentially private computation will decrease his future expected utility by at most an $\exp(-\epsilon) \approx (1-\epsilon)$ multiplicative factor, or equivalently, by an $\epsilon \mathrm{E}[u(x)]$ additive factor, where the expectation is taken over all future events that the individual has preferences over. Therefore, there is a natural way for an individual to assign a cost to the use of his data in an ϵ-differentially private manner: it should be worth to him an ϵ-fraction of his expected future utility. We expand on this in Appendix A.

1.2 Results

Our main contribution is to show that any differentially private mechanism that guarantees a certain accuracy *must* purchase a certain minimum amount of privacy from a certain minimum number of agents (both of which depend on the desired accuracy), which reduces the problem of privately providing an accurate answer to a relatively simple form of procurement problem. Specifically, we study the following stylized model. There are n individuals $[n]$, each of whom possesses a private bit b_i, which is already known by the administrator of the private database (for example, a hospital). Each individual also has a certain *cost* function $c_i : \mathbb{R}_+ \to \mathbb{R}_+$, which determines what her cost $c_i(\epsilon)$ is for her private bit b_i to be used in an ϵ-differentially private manner. Any feasible mechanism must pay each individual enough to compensate him for the use of his private data. Moreover, individuals may mis-report their cost functions in an attempt to maximize their payment, and so we are interested in mechanisms which properly incentivize individuals to report their true cost for privacy. On the other side of the market, the *data analyst* wishes to estimate the quantity $s = \sum_{i=1}^{n} b_i$, and must compensate each individual through the mechanism's payments for this estimate. The data analyst may either have a fixed accuracy objective and wish to minimize his payments subject to obtaining the desired accuracy, or alternately have a fixed budget and wish to maximize the accuracy of his estimate within this budget.

We first consider the simpler model, in which individuals must be compensated for loss of privacy to their bits b_i, but not for any privacy-leakage due to implicit correlations between b_i and their cost function c_i (*i.e.*, if the mechanism does not use an individual's bit b_i at all in computing an estimate for the data analyst, the mechanism does not have to compensate individual i, even if changing her cost function would result in a different outcome for the mechanism). In trying to design an auction that guarantees the data analyst an accurate estimate of s, one might consider any number of complicated mechanisms that (for example) randomly sample individuals, and then attempt to buy from entire random samples – there are many variations therein, and indeed, this was the direction from which we first explored the problem. Our main result is that it is not necessary to consider such mechanisms. We show that we may abstract away the structure of the mechanism, and without loss of generality consider multi-unit procurement auctions. This has some immediate consequences: if we are interested in the setting for which the data analyst has a fixed accuracy goal, subject to which he wishes to minimize his payment, then we show that the standard VCG mechanism is optimal among the set of envy-free mechanisms. If we are instead interested in the setting for which the data analyst has a fixed budget subject to which he wishes to maximize his accuracy, then we are in a more unusual procurement-auction setting: the buyer wishes to maximize the number of sellers he can buy from, and the cost to the sellers is a function of who else sells their data! In this setting, we give a truthful mechanism that is instance-by-instance optimal among the set of all fixed-price (envy free) mechanisms. We remark that our choice of fixed-price mechanisms as a benchmark has become standard in prior-free mechanism design (see, e.g. [HK07, HR08]), but stands on firmer ground in auction settings for which Bayesian-optimal mechanisms are known also to charge fixed prices. We operate in a setting in which Bayesian-optimal mechanisms are not known, and so justifying (or improving) this choice of benchmark in our setting is an interesting open problem.

We then show a generic impossibility result: it is not, in general, possible for any mechanism to compensate individuals for their privacy loss due to unknown correlations between their private bits b_i and their cost functions c_i. If their costs are known to lie in some fixed range initially, it is possible to offer them some non-trivial privacy guarantee, but finding the correct model in which to study the issue of unknown correlations between data and valuation for privacy is another important direction in which to take this research agenda.

[1] This utility theoretic interpretation has been used in another context: the work of McSherry and Talwar, and Nissim, Smorodinsky and Tennenholtz [MT07, NST10] using differential privacy as a tool for traditional mechanism design.

1.3 Related Work

1.3.1 *Differential Privacy as a Tool in Mechanism Design*

McSherry and Talwar proposed that differential privacy could itself be used as a *solution concept* in mechanism design [MT07]. They observed that a differentially private mechanism is approximately truthful, while simultaneously having some resilience to collusion. Using differential privacy as a solution concept as opposed to dominant strategy truthfulness, they gave some improved results in a variety of auction settings. Gupta et al. also used differential privacy as a solution concept in auction design [GLM$^+$10].

In a beautiful follow-up paper, Nissim, Smorodinsky, and Tennenholtz [NST10] made the point that differential privacy may not be a compelling solution concept when beneficial deviations are easy to find (as indeed they are in the mechanism of [MT07]). Nevertheless, they demonstrated a generic methodology for using differentially private mechanisms as tools for designing exactly truthful mechanisms *that do not require payments*, and demonstrate the utility of this framework by designing new mechanisms for several problems.

In this paper, we consider an orthogonal problem: we do not try to use differential privacy as a tool in traditional mechanism design, but instead try to use the tools of traditional mechanism design to *sell* differential privacy as a commodity. Nevertheless, we also use the utility theoretic properties of differential privacy that allow McSherry and Talwar to prove that it implies approximate truthfulness to motivate why it is natural for individuals to have linear cost functions for differential privacy.

1.3.2 *Auctions Which Preserve Privacy*

Recently, Feigenbaum, Jaggard, and Schapira considered (using a different notion of privacy) how the implementation of an auction can affect how many bits of information are leaked about individuals bids [FJS10]. Specifically, they study to what extent information must be leaked in second price auctions and in the millionaires problem. Protecting the privacy of bids is an important problem, and although it is not the main focus of this paper, we consider it in the context of differential privacy in Section 5. We consider somewhat orthogonal notions of privacy and implementation that make our results incomparable to those of [FJS10].

1.3.3 *Privacy in the Economics Literature*

Privacy and its relation to mechanism design has also been studied in the economics literature, although primarily in the context of how preferences for privacy by agents may affect mechanisms, rather than in the context of markets *for* privacy. For example, Calzolari and Pavan study the optimal disclosure policy when designing contracts for buyers who are in the position of repeatedly choosing between multiple sellers [CP06], and the recent work of Taylor, Conitzer, and Wagman [TCW10] studies the relationship between the ability of consumers to keep their identity private, and the ability of a monopolist to engage in price discrimination.

An exception is the essay of Laudon [Lau96], which proposes the idea of a market for personal information— a 'National Information Market'— where individuals can choose to sell or lease their information (possibly to be used in aggregation with other individuals' information) in exchange for a share of the revenue generated from its use; he argues that only individuals whose cost from the 'annoyance' caused by releasing their information is lower than the payment they receive will participate in this market. In the same spirit, the work of Kleinberg, Papadimitrou and Raghavan [KPR01] quantifies the value of private information in some specific settings, and proposes that individuals should be compensated for the use of their information to the extent of this value. Our individually rational auctions for privacy are conceptually similar to this, but are investigated within the formal framework of differential privacy, and from the perspective of auction design.

1.3.4 *Relationship to the Privacy Literature*

The now large literature on differential privacy (see [Dwo08] for an excellent overview) has almost exclusively focused on techniques for guaranteeing ϵ-differential privacy for various tasks, where ϵ has been taken as a given parameter. What has been almost entirely missing is any normative guidance for how to pick ϵ. There is a natural tradeoff between the privacy parameter ϵ and the accuracy of privacy-preserving estimates (which is well-understood in the case of single statistics, see [GRS09, BN10]). Therefore, this paper proposes to answer the question of how ϵ should be chosen: it should be the smallest value that the data analyst is able to afford, given the individuals' valuations for privacy (or equivalently, the smallest value that the owners of the data are willing to accept in exchange for their payment).

We also highlight in this work the explicit tradeoff between compensating individuals for the use of their private information, and the accuracy of our resulting estimates. Implicit in previous works on privacy has been the idea that for fixed values of ϵ, individuals should be willing to participate in private databases given only some small positive incentive. However, this incentive may be different for different individuals, and without running an auction, a data collector is engaging in selection bias: he is only collecting data from those individuals who value their privacy at a low enough level to make participation in a given database worth while. Such individuals might not be representative of the general population, and resulting estimates may therefore be inaccurate. This source of inaccuracy is hidden in previous works, but we point out that it should be a real concern, and we explicitly address it in this paper.

2. PRELIMINARIES

We consider a database consisting of the data of n individuals $\{1, \ldots, n\}$ whom we denote by $[n]$. Each individual i is associated with a private bit $b_i \in \{0, 1\}$. (We may think of this bit as representing the answer to some arbitrary yes or no question). Each bit b_i is already known to a trusted database administrator (for example, a hospital), and so throughout our discussion, we will not endow individuals with the ability to lie about their private bit.

2.1 Differential Privacy

We say that the collection of all individuals' private bits is a *database* $D \in \{0,1\}^n$. Two databases $D, D^{(i)} \in \{0,1\}^n$ are *neighbors* if they differ only in the private bit of a single individual, *i.e.*, if $D_j = D_j^{(i)}$ for all $j \neq i$. The quantification of privacy we employ is that of *differential privacy*, due to Dwork et al. [DMNS06]:

DEFINITION 2.1. *An algorithm $A : \{0,1\}^n \to \mathbb{R}$ satisfies ϵ_i-differential privacy with respect to individual i if for any pair of neighboring databases $D, D^{(i)} \in \{0,1\}^n$ differing only in their i'th bit, and for any $S \subset \mathbb{R}$:*

$$\frac{\Pr[A(D) \in S]}{\Pr[A(D^{(i)}) \in S]} \leq e^{\epsilon_i}$$

*An algorithm A is ϵ_i-*minimally private *with respect to individual i if $\epsilon_i = \inf \epsilon$ such that A is ϵ-differentially private with respect to individual i. Throughout this paper, whenever we say that an al-*

gorithm is ϵ_i-differentially private, we mean that it is ϵ_i-minimally differentially private.

REMARK 2.2. *ϵ-differential privacy becomes less meaningful for large values of ϵ. In this paper, we will restrict our attention to values of $\epsilon < 1$. Note that in this case, $\exp(\epsilon) \approx 1 + \epsilon$.*

The following easy fact follows immediately [DMNS06]:

FACT 1. *Consider an algorithm $A : \{0,1\}^n \to \mathbb{R}$ that satisfies ϵ_i-differential privacy with respect to each individual i, and let $T \subset [n]$ denote a set of indices. Consider two databases $D, D^T \in \{0,1\}^n$ at Hamming distance $|T|$ that differ exactly on the indices in T. Then:*

$$\frac{\Pr[A(D) \in S]}{\Pr[A(D^T) \in S]} \leq e^{\sum_{i \in T} \epsilon_i}$$

A useful primitive for differential privacy is the Laplacian distribution, adding random noise from which produces differentially private output [DMNS06]:

DEFINITION 2.3. *Denote by Lap(σ) the symmetric Laplacian distribution with mean 0 and scaling σ. This distribution has probability density function:*

$$f(x) = \frac{1}{2\sigma} \exp\left(-\frac{|x|}{\sigma}\right)$$

We will sometimes abuse notation and write Lap(σ) to denote the realization of a random variable drawn from the Laplacian distribution with parameter σ.

2.2 Mechanism Design

Every individual has some (unknown to the mechanism) cost function $c_i : \mathbb{R}_+ \to \mathbb{R}_+$, where $c_i(\epsilon)$ represents player i's cost for having his bit b_i used in an ϵ-differentially private manner. Because we consider small values of ϵ for which $\exp(\epsilon) \approx (1+\epsilon)$, it will be most natural to consider *linear* cost functions for which $c_i(\epsilon) = v_i\epsilon$ for some unknown $v_i \in \mathbb{R}_+$. For clarity, we will assume throughout that individuals have linear cost functions, but our results will hold for any single-parameter family of cost functions that admit a total ordering independent of ϵ. That is, the property that our results will require is that for any $i \neq j$, and for any $\epsilon, \epsilon' \in \mathbb{R}_+$, it should hold that $c_i(\epsilon) = c_i(\epsilon, v_i) \leq c_j(\epsilon, v_j)$ if and only if $v_i \leq v_j$. Linear cost functions of course obey this property, but so do many other natural choices, such as exponential cost functions of the form $c_i(\epsilon) = \exp(\epsilon v_i)$.

A mechanism $M : \mathbb{R}_+^n \times \{0,1\}^n \to \mathbb{R} \times \mathbb{R}_+^n$ takes as input a vector of cost functions $v = (v_1, \ldots, v_n) \in \mathbb{R}_+^n$ and a database $D \in \{0,1\}^n$, and outputs the evaluation of some algorithm $A(D)$ that is $\epsilon_i(v)$-differentially private with respect to D to the data analyst, as well as a vector of payments $p(v) \in \mathbb{R}_+^n$ to each individual in D. For any $v_i' \in \mathbb{R}_+$ we let (v_{-i}, v_i') denote the vector that results from changing entry v_i in v to v_i'. A player i derives utility $u_i = p_i(v) - v_i\epsilon_i(v)$ from such an outcome. Since any individual may opt against participating in our mechanism, we require first that our mechanisms be *individually rational*:

DEFINITION 2.4. *A mechanism $M : \mathbb{R}_+^n \times \{0,1\}^n \to \mathbb{R} \times \mathbb{R}_+^n$ is* individually rational *if for all $v \in \mathbb{R}_+^n$:*

$$p_i(v) \geq v_i\epsilon_i(v)$$

That is, each player must be guaranteed non-negative utility by participating and truthfully reporting his value to the mechanism.

Since individuals may misreport their costs so as to maximize their gain, we also require our mechanisms to be *truthful*:

DEFINITION 2.5. *A mechanism $M : \mathbb{R}_+^n \times \{0,1\}^n \to \mathbb{R} \times \mathbb{R}_+^n$ is* dominant-strategy truthful *if for all $v \in \mathbb{R}_+^n$, for all $i \in [n]$, and for all $v_i' \in \mathbb{R}_+$:*

$$p_i(v) - v_i\epsilon_i(v) \geq p_i(v_{-i}, v_i') - v_i\epsilon_i(v_{-i}, v_i'),$$

that is, no player can ever increase his utility by misreporting his value for privacy.

The mechanism is run on behalf of some data analyst, who wishes to know an estimate of the statistic $s \equiv \sum_{i=1}^n b_i$. The mechanism outputs some randomized estimate of this quantity $\hat{s} = A(D)$, where the randomization is to ensure differential privacy, and the analyst prefers more accurate answers. We choose to focus on statistics which can be represented as sums of boolean variables because of the central role that they play in the privacy literature (in which they are known as *counting queries* or *predicate queries*). In particular, the ability to accurately answer queries of this sort is sufficient to be able to implement a wide range of machine learning algorithms over the data (see [BDMN05]).

DEFINITION 2.6. *A mechanism M satisfies k-accuracy if for any $D \in \{0,1\}^n$, it outputs an estimate $\hat{s} = A(D)$ such that:*

$$\Pr[|\hat{s} - s| \geq k] \leq \frac{1}{3}$$

where the probability is taken over the internal coins of the mechanism.

The constant $1/3$ is of course inconsequential: it can be changed to any desired constant without qualitatively affecting the results.

We may consider two dual objectives for our mechanism. Our data analyst may have a fixed goal of k-accuracy for some k in which case we want to design mechanisms which deliver k-accurate estimates of s so as to minimize the sum of the payments. Alternately, our data analyst may have a fixed budget $B \in \mathbb{R}_+$ (say an NSF grant that can be used for data procurement). In this case, our goal is to design a mechanism which is k-accurate for the smallest possible value of k, while under the constraint that the sum of the payments never exceeds B.

3. CHARACTERIZING ACCURATE MECHANISMS

In this section, we show necessary and sufficient conditions on the amount of privacy that a mechanism must purchase from each player in order to guarantee a fixed level of accuracy— to obtain a given level of accuracy, we show that a mechanism must purchase *at least* ϵ–privacy, from *at least* $|H|$ people, where the values of ϵ and $|H|$ depend on the desired accuracy. We emphasize that these necessary conditions are independent of any truthfulness requirements on the mechanism, and arise purely because of the need to achieve accuracy. This greatly simplifies the mechanism-design process for auctions for private data, because it allows us to restrict our attention to multi-unit procurement auctions without loss of generality. We remark that ϵ-differential privacy is inherently a property of randomized mechanisms, so our lower bounds of course hold even for mechanisms with randomized allocation and payment rules.

THEOREM 3.1. *Let $0 < \alpha < 1$. Any differentially private mechanism that is $\alpha \cdot n/4$-accurate must select a set of users $H \subseteq [n]$ such that:*

1. *$\epsilon_i \geq \frac{1}{\alpha n}$ for all $i \in H$.*
2. *$|H| \geq (1-\alpha)n$.*

PROOF. Let M be a mechanism that is $\alpha \cdot n/4$-accurate, and let $H \subset [n]$ be the set of individuals i such that $\epsilon_i \geq 1/\alpha n$. For point of contradiction, suppose that $|H| < (1-\alpha)n$. Let $\bar{H} = [n] \setminus H$. We have that $|\bar{H}| > \alpha n$. Let $S = \{x \in \mathbb{R} : |x - s| < \frac{\alpha n}{4}\}$, where $s = \sum_{i=1}^n b_i$. By the accuracy of the mechanism, we have that the estimate $\hat{s}$ output by the mechanism $M(v, D)$ satisfies:

$$\Pr[\hat{s} \in S] \geq \frac{2}{3}.$$

Let $\bar{H}^1 = \{i \in \bar{H} : b_i = 1\}$ and let $\bar{H}^0 = \{i \in \bar{H} : b_i = 0\}$. Since $\bar{H}^0$ and $\bar{H}^1$ form a partition of $\bar{H}$, it must be that

$$\max(|\bar{H}^0|, |\bar{H}^1|) > \alpha n/2.$$

Without loss of generality, assume that $|\bar{H}^0| > \alpha n/2$ (the other case is identical). Let $T \subset \bar{H}^0$ such that $|T| = \alpha n/2$. Let D' be the database that results in setting each bit $b'_i = b_i$ if $i \notin T$, and $b'_i = 1$ otherwise. Note that D' and D have hamming distance $|T| = \alpha n/2$, and differ exactly on the indices of T. Let $\hat{s}'$ be the estimate generated by $M(v, D')$. By differential privacy of M, we have, using Fact 1:

$$\begin{aligned}\Pr[\hat{s}' \in S] &\geq \exp(-\sum_{i \in T} \epsilon_i) \cdot \Pr[\hat{s} \in S] \\ &\geq \exp(-\frac{\alpha n}{2} \cdot \frac{1}{\alpha n}) \cdot \frac{2}{3} \\ &= \frac{2}{3\sqrt{e}} \\ &> \frac{1}{3}.\end{aligned}$$

Let $s' = \sum_{i=1}^n b'_i$. Note that $s' = s + \alpha n/2$. If $\hat{s}' \in S$, then by definition: $|\hat{s}' - s| < \alpha n/4$. By the triangle inequality, we must therefore have that $|\hat{s}' - s'| > \alpha n/4$ with probability strictly greater than $1/3$, contradicting the assumption that M is $\alpha \cdot n/4$ accurate. □

This theorem can be thought of as our main result, quantifying the necessary trade-off between accuracy and privacy: to guarantee $\alpha n/4$-accuracy, at least $(1-\alpha)$ fraction of the population *must* incur at least a $\frac{1}{\alpha n}$ privacy loss. The corollary below follows immediately, translating this into a lower bound on payment.

COROLLARY 3.2. *Any αn-accurate individually rational mechanism must pay out a total payment of at least:*

$$\sum_{i=1}^n p_i \geq \sum_{i=1}^{(1-4\alpha)n} c_i\left(\frac{1}{4\alpha n}\right)$$

where bidders are ordered such that $c_1(\cdot) \leq c_2(\cdot) \leq \cdots c_n(\cdot)$.

We remark that this corollary assumes only individual rationality, and is in general achievable only by an omniscient mechanism that knows all players' cost functions. No *truthful* αn-accurate mechanism is able to pay as little as this benchmark in general.

Theorem 3.1 gave necessary conditions on the privacy costs of an accurate mechanism. Next, we show that up to small constant factors, they are also *sufficient* conditions for an accurate mechanism:

THEOREM 3.3. *Let $0 < \alpha < 1$. There exists a differentially private mechanism that is $(\frac{1}{2} + \ln 3)\alpha \cdot n$-accurate and selects a set of individuals $H \subseteq [n]$ such that:*

1. $\epsilon_i = \begin{cases} \frac{1}{\alpha n}, & \text{for } i \in H; \\ 0, & \text{for } i \notin H. \end{cases}$
2. $|H| = (1-\alpha)n$.

PROOF. Let $H \subset [n]$ be any collection of individuals of size $|H| = (1-\alpha)n$, selected independently of their private bits b_i, and let $t = \sum_{i \in H} b_i + \alpha n/2$. Observe that for any database D, $|t - s| \leq \alpha n/2$. Consider the mechanism that outputs $\hat{s} = t + \text{Lap}(\alpha n)$. First, we claim that this mechanism is $(1/2 + \ln 3)\alpha n$-accurate. This follows by the triangle inequality conditioned on the event that $\text{Lap}(\alpha n) \leq (\ln 3)\alpha n$. It remains to verify that this holds with probability at least $2/3$. This is in fact the case:

$$\begin{aligned}\Pr[|\text{Lap}(\alpha n)| \geq (\ln 3)\alpha n] &= \frac{1}{2\alpha n}\int_{-\infty}^{-(\ln 3)\alpha n} \exp\left(-\frac{|x|}{\alpha n}\right) dx \\ &+ \frac{1}{2\alpha n}\int_{(\ln 3)\alpha n}^{\infty} \exp\left(-\frac{|x|}{\alpha n}\right) dx \\ &= \frac{1}{3}.\end{aligned}$$

We now verify the differential privacy guarantee, which follows from the analysis given in [DMNS06] of the Laplace mechanism. Let $\hat{s}$ be the estimate calculated on database D (via sum t) and let $\hat{s}'$ be the estimate calculated on neighboring database $D^{(i)}$ (via sum t'). Clearly, for any $i \notin H$ and for any $S \subset \mathbb{R}$, $\Pr[\hat{s} \in S] = \Pr[\hat{s}' \in S]$ and so $\epsilon_i = 0$. Now consider some $i \in H$ and $S \subset \mathbb{R}$. For any $S \subset \mathbb{R}$ and $r \in \mathbb{R}$, let $S - r$ denote $\{x - r : x \in S\}$.

$$\begin{aligned}\Pr[\hat{s} \in S] &= \Pr[\text{Lap}(\alpha n) \in S - t] \\ &= \int_{x \in S-t} \frac{1}{2\alpha n}\exp\left(-\frac{|x|}{\alpha n}\right) dx \\ &\leq \exp\left(\frac{1}{\alpha n}\right) \cdot \int_{x \in S-t'} \frac{1}{2\alpha n}\exp\left(-\frac{|x|}{\alpha n}\right) dx \\ &= \exp\left(\frac{1}{\alpha n}\right) \cdot \Pr[\hat{s}' \in S]\end{aligned}$$

where the inequality follows from the fact that $|t - t'| \leq 1$. □

Theorems 3.3 and 3.1 taken together have the effect of greatly simplifying the space of possible mechanisms for private data that we need to consider. They imply that without loss of generality (up to small constant factors in their error term), when searching for αn-accurate mechanisms, we may restrict our attention to a special class of multi-unit procurement auctions, where we seek to purchase exactly $1/\alpha n$ units of some good (in this case, differential privacy) from exactly $(1-\alpha)n$ individuals. Once we do this, we have purchased a sufficient quantity of privacy to run the Laplace mechanism employed in Theorem 3.3, which guarantees the desired accuracy! In the next section, we consider such mechanisms.

4. DERIVING TRUTHFUL MECHANISMS

4.1 Maximizing Accuracy Subject to a Budget Constraint

In this section, following the characterization of accurate mechanisms in Section 3, we restrict our attention to algorithms that guarantee $O(\alpha n)$-accuracy by purchasing $1/\alpha n$ units of privacy from exactly $(1-\alpha)n$ individuals. We consider the problem of obtaining an estimate $\hat{s}$ of maximum accuracy, subject to a hard budget constraint[2]: $\sum_{i=1}^n p_i \leq B$. This is a natural objective, for example, in the case of a data analyst who has B dollars of grant

[2]This question is related to the problem of designing budget feasible mechanisms in [Sin10, CGL11], but differs in that our privacy auction has *externalities*: a seller's cost for her good is a function of how many other sellers are chosen as winners by the mechanism.

money with which to buy data for a study, and wishes to buy the most accurate data that he can afford. We give a truthful and individually rational mechanism for this problem, and show that it is instance-by-instance optimal among the class of envy-free mechanisms. For clarity of exposition, we assume in this section that all cost functions are linear, *i.e.*, $c_i(\epsilon) = v_i\epsilon$.

FairQuery(v, D, B) :

Sort v such that $v_1 \leq v_2 \leq \ldots \leq v_n$.
Let k be the largest integer such that $\frac{v_k}{n-k} \leq \frac{B}{k}$.
Output $\hat{s} = \sum_{i=1}^{k} b_i + \frac{n-k}{2} + \text{Lap}(n-k)$
Pay each $i > k$ $p_i = 0$ and each $i \leq k$ $p_i = \min(\frac{B}{k}, \frac{v_{k+1}}{n-k})$.

We first prove that FairQuery is truthful and individually rational.

THEOREM 4.1. *FairQuery is truthful and individually rational, and never exceeds the data analyst's budget B.*

PROOF. First note that by the analysis from Theorem 3.3, for any $i \leq k$, $\epsilon_i = \frac{1}{n-k}$, and for any $i > k$, $\epsilon_i = 0$. For $i > k$ therefore, $p_i = v_i \cdot 0 = 0$. For $i \leq k$, $p_i = \min(\frac{B}{k}, \frac{v_{k+1}}{n-k}) \geq v_i/(n-k)$ because $v_i/(n-k) \leq B/k$ by construction and $v_i \leq v_{i+1}$ by definition. Hence, individual rationality is satisfied. Note also that $\sum_{i=1}^{n} p_i = k \cdot \min(\frac{B}{k}, \frac{v_{k+1}}{n-k}) \leq B$, and so the budget constraint is also satisfied. It remains to verify truthfulness:

Fix any v, i, v'_i and consider $k = k(v)$, $k' = k(v_{-i}, v'_i)$, $p_i = p_i(v)$, $p'_i = p'_i(v_{-i}, v'_i)$, $\epsilon_i = \epsilon_i(v)$, and $\epsilon'_i = \epsilon'_i(v_{-i}, v'_i)$. There are four cases:

1. Case 1: $v'_i < v_i$ and $p_i > 0$. In this case, v'_i moves earlier in the ordering and $\epsilon_i = \epsilon'_i$, and $p_i = p'_i$.
2. Case 2: $v'_i > v_i$ and $p_i = 0$. In this case, v'_i moves later in the ordering and $\epsilon_i = \epsilon'_i = p_i = p'_i = 0$.
3. Case 3: $v'_i < v_i$ and $p_i = 0$. In this case, v'_i moves earlier in the ordering, but if $p'_i > 0$ then by construction $p'_i = \min(\frac{B}{k'}, \frac{v_{k'+1}}{n-k'}) \leq v_i/(n-k')$. This follows because k' is such that $v_{k'+1} \leq v_i$ for all $i > k$ such that $p'_i > 0$.
4. Case 4: $v'_i > v_i$ and $p_i > 0$. In this case, v'_i moves later in the ordering, and either $p'_i = p_i$ and $\epsilon'_i = \epsilon_i$, or $p'_i = 0$ and $\epsilon_i = 0$. In the second case, by individual rationality, $p_i - v_i\epsilon_i \geq 0 = p'_i - v_i\epsilon'_i$.

Thus in all four cases, deviations are not beneficial, and the mechanism is truthful. □

The next natural question to ask is: does FairQuery guarantee the data analyst a good level of accuracy, given his budget? As is always the case in prior-free mechanism design, it is important to specify what our benchmark is – good compared to what? Because mechanisms of the kind that we are considering always buy the same amount of privacy from an individual from whom they buy any privacy at all, a natural benchmark to consider is the set of all "envy-free" mechanisms which guarantee that no individual would prefer the outcome granted to any other.

DEFINITION 4.2. *A mechanism for private data is* envy-free *if for all possible valuation vectors v, and for all individuals i, j, $p_i - \epsilon_i v_i \geq p_j - \epsilon_j v_i$. That is, after the mechanism has determined the privacy costs and payments to each individual, there are no individuals who would prefer to have the payment and privacy cost granted to any other individual.*

OBSERVATION 4.3. *Any truthful envy-free mechanism which buys either no privacy or ϵ-privacy from each individual (i.e., if $\epsilon_i > 0, \epsilon_j > 0$ then $\epsilon_i = \epsilon_j$) must have the property that for all i, j with $\epsilon_i > \epsilon_j > 0$, $p_i = p_j$. Call such mechanisms* fixed purchase mechanisms. *That is, envy free fixed purchase mechanisms must pay each individual from whom privacy is purchased the same fixed price.*

Note that by the characterization in Section 3, we may restrict ourselves to considering fixed purchase mechanisms essentially without loss of generality (we may lose only a small constant factor). Therefore we can compare our mechanism to the envy free benchmark:

PROPOSITION 4.4. *For any set of valuations $v \in \mathbb{R}_+^n$ (i.e., on an instance-by-instance basis) FairQuery achieves the optimal accuracy given budget B, among the set of all truthful, individually rational envy-free fixed purchase mechanisms.*

PROOF. First, observe the easy fact that FairQuery is indeed an envy free fixed purchase mechanism. We then merely observe that for any vector of valuations v, if FairQuery sets $\epsilon_i > 0$ for k individuals, then by the definition of k, it must be that $\frac{v_{k+1}}{(n-k-1)} > \frac{B}{k+1}$, and so any mechanism that set $\epsilon_i > 0$ for k' individuals for $k' > k$ must have $p_{k+1} > \frac{B}{(k+1)}$ by individual rationality. But by envy-freeness, it must have $p_i = p_{k+1} > \frac{B}{(k+1)}$ for all $i \leq k$. But in this case, we would have

$$\sum_{i=1}^{n} p_i \geq k' \cdot p_{k+1} > (k+1) \cdot \frac{B}{k+1} = B$$

which would violate the budget constraint. □

4.2 Minimizing Payment Subject to an Accuracy Constraint

In this section, we consider mechanisms for the dual goal of truthfully obtaining a k-accurate estimate for some fixed accuracy constraint k while minimizing the payment required. Again, we restrict ourselves to the model of multi-unit procurement auctions justified in Section 3. In this setting, we show that the VCG mechanism is in fact optimal.

Recall that for a fixed accuracy goal αn, by Theorem 3.3, it is sufficient to buy $\frac{(1/2+\ln 3)}{\alpha n}$ units of privacy from $(1 - \frac{\alpha}{(1/2+\ln 3)})n$ people. We may therefore view our setting as a multi-unit procurement auction in which every individual is selling a single good ($\frac{(1/2+\ln 3)}{\alpha n}$ units of privacy), for which they have valuation $v_i = c_i(\frac{(1/2+\ln 3)}{\alpha n})$ (note that v_i is now the *total* cost for the $\frac{(1/2+\ln 3)}{\alpha n}$ units of privacy). The constraint on accuracy simply states that we must buy $(1 - \frac{\alpha}{(1/2+\ln 3)})n)$ units of the good. In this case, we can analyze a simple application of the standard VCG mechanism:

MinCostAuction(v, D, α):

Let $\alpha' = \frac{\alpha}{1/2+\ln 3}$ and $k = \lceil (1-\alpha')n \rceil$.
Sort $v = c_i(\frac{1}{n-k})$ such that $v_1 \leq v_2 \leq \ldots \leq v_n$.
Output $\hat{s} = \sum_{i=1}^{k} b_i + \frac{n-k}{2} + \text{Lap}(\alpha' n)$
Pay each $i > k$ $p_i = 0$ and each $i \leq k$ $p_i = v_{k+1}$.

We first show that MinCostAuction does indeed satisfy the constraints of truthfulness and individual rationality, while obtaining sufficient accuracy.

PROPOSITION 4.5. *MinCostAuction is truthful, individually rational and αn-accurate.*

PROOF. That MinCostAuction is αn-accurate follows immediately from Theorem 3.3. Moreover, by Theorem 3.3, for each $i \leq k$, $\epsilon_i = 1/(\alpha' n)$ and for $i > k$, $\epsilon_i = 0$. Truthfulness and individual rationality then follow immediately from the fact that each $v_i = c_i(1/(\alpha' n))$ and MinCostAuction is an instantiation of the classical VCG mechanism. □

MinCostAuction achieves its target utility at a cost of $\sum_{i=1}^{n} p_i = k \cdot v_{k+1}$. We now show that no other envy-free multi-unit procurement auction with the same accuracy guarantees (i.e. one that guarantees buying k units) makes smaller payments than MinCostAuction.

THEOREM 4.6. *No truthful, individually rational, envy-free multi-unit procurement auction that guarantees purchasing k units can have total payment less than $k \cdot v_{k+1}$.*

PROOF. For the sake of contradiction, suppose we have such a mechanism M. Fix some vector of valuations v that yields payments $p(v)$ such that $\sum_{i=1}^{n} p_i(v) < k \cdot v_{k+1}$ (again, note that v_i now denotes the total cost for purchasing data, not the per-unit privacy cost). First, if it is not already the case, we will construct a bid profile such that an item is purchased from some seller who is not among the k lowest sellers. It must be that there exists some i such that an item is purchased from i at a price of p_i, such that $v_i \leq p_i < v_{k+1}$ (otherwise $\sum_{i=1}^{n} p_i(v) \geq k \cdot v_{k+1}$). Let $v' = (v_{-i}, (p_i + v_{k+1})/2)$ be a bid profile in which bidder i raises his bid to be above p_i while remaining below v_{k+1}. Let $p' = p'(v)$ be the new payment vector. By individual rationality and truthfulness, it must be that in this new bid profile v', player i is no longer allocated an item: by individual rationality, he would have to be paid $p'_i > p_i$ if he were allocated an item, but if his true valuation were v_i, then this would be a beneficial deviation, contradicting truthfulness. Because the mechanism is constrained to always buy at least k items, it must be that in v', an item is now purchased from some seller j such that $j \geq k + 1$. By individual rationality, $p'_j \geq v_j \geq v_{k+1}$. But by envy-freeness, it must be that for every seller i from whom an item was purchased, $p'_i = p'_j \geq v_{k+1}$. Because at least k items are purchased, we therefore have $\sum_{i=1}^{n} p'_i \geq k \cdot v_{k+1}$, which contradicts the purported payment guarantee of mechanism M. □

5. PRESERVING THE PRIVACY OF THE BID

In Section 4, we considered truthful, individually rational mechanisms that compensated users for the privacy loss due to the mechanisms' use of the individual's private bits b_i, but *not* due to the mechanisms' use of their valuations for privacy, v_i. Nevertheless, as we observed in the introduction, it is quite reasonable to assume that individual's valuations for privacy are correlated with their private bits. Can we design mechanisms that treat individuals' valuations for privacy as private data as well, and compensate individuals for the privacy loss due to the use of their valuations v_i? In this section, we show that the answer is generically 'no' if we allow individuals to have arbitrarily high valuations for privacy. Moreover, we note that if we try to impose an a-priori bound on individual's valuations for privacy, then we re-introduce the same source of sampling bias that we had hoped to solve by running an auction.

A mechanism has two outputs: the estimate $\hat{s}$, and the payment P that the data analyst must make. Note that if the bids are private data as well, then a mechanism which is ϵ_i-differentially private with respect to bidder i must satisfy, for every set of estimate/payment tuples $S \subset \mathbb{R}_+^2$ and for each $(v, D) \in \mathbb{R}_+^n \times \{0,1\}^n$, $\Pr[M(v, D) \in S] \leq \exp(\epsilon_i)\Pr[M(v^{(i)}, D^{(i)}) \in S]$, where $v^{(i)}$ and $D^{(i)}$ are arbitrary vectors that are identical to v and D everywhere except possibly on their ith index.

THEOREM 5.1. *If bidder valuations for privacy may be arbitrarily large (i.e., $v \in \mathbb{R}_+^n$) then no individually rational mechanism M can protect the privacy of the bidder valuations and promise k-accuracy for any $k < n/2$ (i.e., any nontrivial value).*

PROOF. Assume that M is k-accurate for some $k < n/2$. Run the mechanism $M(v, D)$ and obtain an estimate $\hat{s}$ and privacy costs ϵ_i for each $i \in [n]$. Let $P = \sum_{i=1}^{n} p_i$ be the payment that the data analyst makes. By individual rationality, $P \geq \sum_{i=1}^{n} \epsilon_i v_i \geq \min_i v_i \cdot \sum_{i=1}^{n} \epsilon_i$. We trivially have that either $\Pr[\hat{s} \in [0, n/2)] \geq 1/2$ or $\Pr[\hat{s} \in [n/2, n]] \geq 1/2$. Without loss of generality, assume $\Pr[\hat{s} \in [0, n/2)] \geq 1/2$. Let $D' = 1^n$, and let $\hat{s}'$ be the estimate obtained by running $M(v, D')$. By accuracy, we have that: $\Pr[\hat{s}' \in (n/2, n]] \geq \frac{2}{3}$. However, by differential privacy, together with Fact 1 we have:

$$\frac{2}{3} \leq \Pr[\hat{s}' \in (n/2, n]] \leq \exp(\sum_{i=1}^{n} \epsilon_i) \Pr[\hat{s} \in (n/2, n]]$$

$$\leq \frac{\exp(\sum_{i=1}^{n} \epsilon_i)}{2}$$

Solving, we find that $\sum_{i=1}^{n} \epsilon_i \geq \ln(4/3)$, independent of v. We therefore have by individual rationality that $\Pr[P \in [0, \ln(4/3)\min_i v_i)] = 0$. By differential privacy, this must hold simultaneously for all inputs to the mechanism (v, D): that is, such a mechanism can not charge a finite price P for *any* input, which completes the proof. □

REMARK 5.2. *A natural (partial) way around the impossibility result of Theorem 5.1 is to restrict bidder valuations to lie in a bounded range (e.g. $[0, 1]$). This is unsatisfying, however, because it re-introduces the very source of sampling bias that we wanted to solve by running an auction. That is, bidders who happen to value their privacy at a higher rate than allowed by the mechanism will simply not participate in the auction, which might systematically skew the resulting estimate in a way that we cannot measure.*

6. FUTURE DIRECTIONS

The main contribution of this paper is to formalize the notion of auctions *for* private data, and to show that the design space of such auctions can without loss of generality be taken to be the simple setting of multi-unit procurement auctions. This initiates an intriguing new area of study that raises many questions. Among these are:

1. What is the proper benchmark for auctions in our setting? In this paper, we used the class of fixed-price (or envy free) mechanisms, which has become standard in the field of prior-free mechanism design [HR08, HK07]. However, this approach is better motivated in settings in which Bayesian optimal mechanisms are well understood and indeed charge fixed prices to winners. Bayesian optimal mechanisms are not known for our settings (e.g. budget constrained auctions with the objective function of buying as many units as possible). Studying Bayesian optimal mechanism design for these auctions, which correspond to natural markets for privacy would help identify and justify appropriate benchmarks.

2. We have shown that generically, no mechanism can compensate individuals for the loss of privacy which results from correlations between their private data and their reported costs for privacy. Nevertheless, such correlations exist! It is unsatisfying to restrict individual valuations for privacy to lie in a bounded range, because this reintroduces the very source of bias that we hoped to overcome by designing auctions. However, is there some restricted sense in which we can protect (and compensate users for) the privacy of their *valuations for privacy*? This requires the development of new models.

3. We have assumed throughout this paper that the private bits of the users, b_i are already known to some database administrator, such as a hospital. Although this is a natural assumption in some settings, what if it does not hold? Is there any way to mediate the purchase of private data directly from individuals who have the power to lie about their private data?

4. In this paper we considered an extremely simple market, in which there was a single data analyst wanting to buy data from a population. How about a two sided market, in which there are multiple data analysts, competing for access to the private data from multiple populations? Can we privately compute the market clearing prices for access to data in this way?

5. In this paper we considered a one-shot mechanism. In reality, the administrator of a private database will face multiple requests for access to his data as time goes on. How should the data analyst reason about these online requests and his value for the marginal privacy loss that he will incur after answering each request?

7. ACKNOWLEDGEMENTS

This paper has benefitted from discussions with many people. In particular, we would like to thank Frank McSherry for suggesting the problem of treating differential privacy as a currency to be bought and sold at the 2010 IPAM workshop on differential privacy, Tim Roughgarden for helpful early discussions on benchmarks for prior-free mechanisms for private data, and Sham Kakade, Ian Kash, Michael Kearns, Katrina Ligett, Mallesh Pai, Ariel Procaccia, David Parkes, Kunal Talwar, Salil Vadhan, Jon Ullman, and Bumin Yenmez for helpful comments and discussions. We would also like to thank Yu-Han Lyu for pointing out several typos in an earlier version of the paper.

8. REFERENCES

[BN10] H. Brenner and K. Nissim. Impossibility of Differentially Private Universally Optimal Mechanisms. In *Proceedings of the 51st Annual IEEE Symposium on Foundations of Computer Science (FOCS)*, 2010.

[BDMN05] A. Blum, C. Dwork, F. McSherry and K. Nissim. Practical privacy: The SuLQ framework. In *Proceedings of the twenty-fourth ACM SIGMOD-SIGACT-SIGART Symposium on Principles of Database Systems*, 2005.

[CGL11] N. Chen, N. Gravin, and P. Lu. On the Approximability of Budget Feasible Mechanisms. In *Proceedings of the ACM-SIAM Symposium on Discrete Algorithms (SODA)*, 2011.

[Cli10] Stephanie Clifford. Web startups offer bargains for users data. *The New York Times*, May 2010.

[CP06] G. Calzolari and A. Pavan. On the optimality of privacy in sequential contracting. *Journal of Economic Theory*, 130(1):168–204, 2006.

[DMNS06] C. Dwork, F. McSherry, K. Nissim, and A. Smith. Calibrating noise to sensitivity in private data analysis. In *Proceedings of the Third Theory of Cryptography Conference TCC*, volume 3876 of *Lecture Notes in Computer Science*, page 265. Springer, 2006.

[Dwo08] C. Dwork. Differential privacy: A survey of results. In *Proceedings of Theory and Applications of Models of Computation, 5th International Conference, TAMC 2008*, volume 4978 of *Lecture Notes in Computer Science*, page 1. Springer, 2008.

[FJS10] J. Feigenbaum, A.D. Jaggard, and M. Schapira. Approximate privacy: foundations and quantification (extended abstract). In *Proceedings of the 11th ACM conference on Electronic commerce*, pages 167–178. ACM, 2010.

[GLM+10] A. Gupta, K. Ligett, F. McSherry, A. Roth, and K. Talwar. Differentially Private Approximation Algorithms. In *Proceedings of the ACM-SIAM Symposium on Discrete Algorithms*, 2010.

[GRS09] A. Ghosh, T. Roughgarden, and M. Sundararajan. Universally utility-maximizing privacy mechanisms. In *Proceedings of the 41st annual ACM symposium on Symposium on Theory of Computing*, pages 351–360. ACM New York, NY, USA, 2009.

[HK07] J. Hartline and A. Karlin. Profit maximization in mechanism design. *Algorithmic Game Theory*, page 331, 2007.

[HR08] J.D. Hartline and T. Roughgarden. Optimal mechanism design and money burning. In *Proceedings of the Annual Symposium on Theory of Computing (STOC)*. Citeseer, 2008.

[Lau96] K. Laudon. Markets and privacy. *Communications of the ACM*, 39(9):-104, 1996.

[KPR01] J. Kleinberg and C. Papadimitriou and P. Raghavan. On the Value of Private Information *Proc. 8th Conf. on Theoretical Aspects of Rationality and Knowledge*, 2001.

[Loh10] Steve Lohr. You want my personal data? reward me for it. *The New York Times*, July 2010.

[MT07] F. McSherry and K. Talwar. Mechanism design via differential privacy. In *Proceedings of the 48th Annual Symposium on Foundations of Computer Science*, 2007.

[NST10] K. Nissim, R. Smorodinsky, and M. Tennenholtz. Approximately Optimal Mechanism Design via Differential Privacy. *Arxiv preprint arXiv:1004.2888*, 2010.

[Sin10] Y. Singer. Budget Feasible Mechanisms. In *Proceedings of the 51st Annual IEEE Symposium on Foundations of Computer Science (FOCS)*, 2010.

[TCW10] C.R. Taylor, V. Conitzer, and L. Wagman. Online Privacy and Price Discrimination. *Economic Research*, 2010.

APPENDIX

A. A UTILITY THEORETIC VIEW OF VALUING DIFFERENTIAL PRIVACY

In this section, we provide a brief justification for why individuals should be able to quantify their cost for experiencing an ϵ-differentially private use of their private data. Say that $\mathcal{A}$ denotes the set of all future events for which an individual i has preferences over outcomes, and $u_i : \mathcal{A} \to \mathbb{R}$ is a function mapping events to i's utility for that event. Suppose that $D \in \mathcal{D}$ is a data-set containing individual i's private data, and that $M : \mathcal{D} \to T$ is a mechanism operating on D promising ϵ_i-differential privacy to individual i. Let D' be a data-set that is identical to D except that it does not include the data of individual i (equivalently, it includes the data of individual i, but it is used in a 0-differentially private manner), and let $f : T \to \Delta\mathcal{A}$ be the (arbitrary) function that determines the distribution over all future events, conditioned on the output of mechanism M.

A basic consequence of differential privacy is the following:

FACT 2. *If $M : \mathcal{D} \to T$ is ϵ_i-differentially private with respect to individual i, and $f : T \to U$ is any arbitrary (randomized) function independent of D, then the composition $f \circ M : \mathcal{D} \to U$ is also ϵ_i-differentially private with respect to individual i.*

By the guarantee of differential privacy together with Fact 2, we have:

$$\begin{aligned}
\mathrm{E}_{x\sim f(M(D))}[u_i(x)] &= \sum_{x\in\mathcal{A}} u_i(x) \cdot \Pr_{f(M(D))}[x] \\
&\leq \sum_{x\in\mathcal{A}} u_i(x) \cdot \exp(\epsilon_i) \Pr_{f(M(D'))}[x] \\
&= \exp(\epsilon_i)\mathrm{E}_{x\sim f(M(D'))}[u_i(x)]
\end{aligned}$$

Similarly,

$$\mathrm{E}_{x\sim f(M(D))}[u_i(x)] \geq \exp(-\epsilon_i)\mathrm{E}_{x\sim f(M(D'))}[u_i(x)]$$

Therefore, when individual i is deciding whether or not to allow his data to be used in an ϵ_i-differentially private way, he is facing the decision about whether he would like his data to be used in such a way that could change his future utility by at most an additive factor of

$$\Delta u_i \equiv (\exp(\epsilon_i) - 1)\mathrm{E}_{x\sim f(M(D'))}[u_i(x)]$$

and so this is a natural quantity for i to value his privacy at. Note that for small values of ϵ_i, this is approximately $\epsilon_i \cdot \mathrm{E}_{x\sim f(M(D'))}[u_i(x)]$, which (by setting $v_i = \mathrm{E}_{x\sim f(M(D'))}[u_i(x)]$) conveniently leads to the form of linear utility functions that we explore in this paper.

Mechanisms for Multi-Level Marketing

Yuval Emek
Computer Engineering and Networks Laboratory
ETH Zurich
Zurich, Switzerland
yuval.emek@tik.ee.ethz.ch

Ron Karidi
Microsoft Israel Innovation Lab
Herzeliya, Israel
ronkar@microsoft.com

Moshe Tennenholtz
Microsoft Israel R&D Center
and
Technion–Israel Institute of Technology
Herzeliya, Israel
moshet@microsoft.com

Aviv Zohar
Microsoft Research
Silicon Valley Lab
Mountain View, CA, USA
avivz@microsoft.com

ABSTRACT

Multi-level marketing is a marketing approach that motivates its participants to promote a certain product among their friends. The popularity of this approach increases due to the accessibility of modern social networks, however, it existed in one form or the other long before the Internet age began (the infamous Pyramid scheme that dates back at least a century is in fact a special case of multi-level marketing). This paper lays foundations for the study of reward mechanisms in multi-level marketing within social networks. We provide a set of desired properties for such mechanisms and show that they are uniquely satisfied by geometric reward mechanisms. The resilience of mechanisms to false-name manipulations is also considered; while geometric reward mechanisms fail against such manipulations, we exhibit other mechanisms which are false-name-proof.

Categories and Subject Descriptors

J.4 [**Social and Behavioral Sciences**]: Economics

General Terms

Economics, Theory

Keywords

multi-level marketing, pyramid scheme, reward mechanisms

1. INTRODUCTION

Social networks are everywhere: our e-mail and phone address books, our family relatives, and our business connections, all define either explicit or implicit social networks.

Social networks have existed long before the Internet, but their recent web-based form, as exhibited by companies like Facebook, Twitter, or LinkedIn, made them more tangible. In their new manifestation, social networks have become an attractive playground for viral marketing: the dream of any marketer is that her products will be promoted via "word of mouth" (which relies on social networks). In order to make that dream a reality, various forms of marketing have been advocated. The so-called affiliate marketing, direct marketing, and multi-level marketing all refer to (overlapping) approaches that facilitate viral marketing. In this paper, we shall adhere to the term multi-level marketing, as it seems to be the least restrictive one.

The fundamental idea behind multi-level marketing is that Alice, who already purchased the product, is rewarded for *referrals*, i.e., for purchases made by Bob as a result of Alice's promotion. The *reward mechanism* associated with multi-level marketing may take various forms. In particular, Alice may be rewarded for both purchases made by Bob and for Bob's own referrals in a recursive manner.

The potential to accumulate small rewards from each person to a sizable sum is important as it allows advertisers to attract early adopters and trendsetters that are of great value to them. On the downside, the possibility of gathering a large sum has also inspired more illicit versions of multi-level marketing, namely *pyramid schemes*. These illegal[1] mechanisms, essentially based on the notion of indirect referrals, are not intended to promote a real product, but rather to collect money from the social network, although sometimes a product is used in an attempt to cover the nature of the pyramid scheme and bypass legal restrictions. In these cases, customers seldom enjoy the actual product being promoted (when a product is being promoted), but are only participating in the (usually false) hope of getting rewards from recruiting others.

Needless to say that selecting an appropriate reward mechanism is inherent to the design of a successful multi-level marketing scheme. Interestingly, despite the popularity of

[1]The current paper does not take legal issues into consideration. In particular, our analysis will not make the distinction between legitimate multi-level marketing and pyramid schemes.

work on information spreading and influence in social networks (see, e.g., the survey in [11]) the study of reward mechanism design in that context has been almost completely neglected. Such study is the main subject of the current paper.

Consider for example the following basic *coupon driven* scheme. Upon purchase of the product, Alice is given coupons that she can distribute among her friends. Then, for any purchase made by Bob in which Alice's coupon is used, Alice is rewarded with appropriate rebates on future purchases. This scheme and similar ones, are easy to implement and have become quite standard in our daily life. Note that the coupon driven scheme does not exploit indirect referrals: Alice is not rewarded by purchases made with Bob's coupons or with the coupons of Bob's referrals.

Reward mechanisms that exploit indirect referrals used to be difficult to implement as they require some central authority that keeps track of the referral structure. Information technology has made this task much easier. Consider for example the setting in which Alice promotes a product by publishing a link to the seller's web-site in her blog or Facebook page. Bob can buy the product by clicking on that link; together with the actual product, Bob receives a link to the seller's web-site that he can also publish in his blog or Facebook page. The seller's web-site can easily identify Bob as a buyer that followed Alice's link.[2] This way a complete record of direct and indirect referrals can clearly be maintained. This ease of implementation makes reward mechanisms that take indirect referrals into account even more appealing than they have been before.

Are indirect referrals really that important? We believe so. To demonstrate their significance, suppose that Bob is a rock music authority and that following Alice's promotion, he downloads a new rock song. If Bob recommends this song in his blog, and consequently many other users download this song, then Alice certainly played a major role in the promotion process, even if she only had a few direct referrals. A reward mechanism that depends only on direct referrals is therefore bound to miss the bigger picture.

The referrals tree model.

There are many possible ways to take the social network that forms the basis of the referral process into account. In principle, one may wish to consider the times at which promoting messages were sent from one user to another, to consider referrals that were not followed up by a purchase of the product being promoted, or even to consider the social links along which a referral was *not* made. However, all of this information may not be available to the original seller.[3] We therefore take the straightforward approach of looking only at the structure of successful referrals. For each buyer, we mark only a single referrer for introducing the product to her (in reality, this would typically be specified at the time of purchase). The induced structure of referrals forms a collection of directed trees, each rooted at a node that corresponds to some buyer that has purchased the product directly from the seller. We shall refer to this tree collection as the *referrals forest*, denoted $\mathcal{T}$, and to the rooted trees in $\mathcal{T}$ as the *referrals trees*. We find the assumption that $\mathcal{T}$ can be maintained by the seller sufficiently weak.

It should be clarified that the referrals forest corresponds to a single multi-level marketing campaign (typically associated with a single product). Moreover, social network users that did not purchase the product are not represented in $\mathcal{T}$ even if some of their friends attempted at promoting the product to them. For ease of presentation, we assume that $\mathcal{T}$ is fully known when the rewards are to be distributed, although all the mechanisms explored in this paper are also suited for incremental payments performed online. It will also be convenient to identify the buyers with their corresponding nodes in $\mathcal{T}$, denoting the reward of (the buyer corresponding to) node u under the referrals forest $\mathcal{T}$ by $\mathrm{R}_{\mathcal{T}}(u)$.

Constraints on the reward mechanism.

The reward mechanism is essentially a function that maps the referrals forest $\mathcal{T}$ to the non-negative real rewards of its nodes. However, not every such function should be considered; specifically, we impose three constraints on the reward mechanisms. The first one is the *subtree constraint*: $\mathrm{R}_{\mathcal{T}}(u)$ is uniquely determined by $\mathcal{T}_u$, namely, by the subtree of $\mathcal{T}$ rooted at u. This is sensible, as each user u can really be credited only for bringing in users she promoted the product to, either directly (the children of u in $\mathcal{T}$) or indirectly (lower level descendants of u). Moreover, a dependence of $\mathrm{R}_{\mathcal{T}}(u)$ on the position of u within $\mathcal{T}$ (rather than on $\mathcal{T}_u$ only) may result in an undesirable behavior on behalf of u: in some cases u is better off delaying the purchase of the product after receiving a referral in hope for a "better" offer, i.e., for a referral that would place u in a better position within $\mathcal{T}$.

One of the consequences of the subtree constraint is that there is no point in dealing with the referrals forest $\mathcal{T}$ in full, but rather focus on trees which are rooted at the nodes whose reward we are trying to calculate. In other words, the reward mechanism is completely specified by the function $\mathrm{R}(T)$ that maps the rooted tree T to the non-negative real reward of its root (which may be an internal node within the whole referrals forest).

The second constraint that we impose on the reward mechanism is the *budget constraint*: the seller is willing to spend at most a certain fraction $\phi \leq 1$ of her total income on rewarding her buyers for referrals. Given that the price of the product is π, this means that the total sum of rewards given to all nodes is at most $\phi \cdot \pi|\mathcal{T}|$. We assume without loss of generality that π and ϕ are scaled so that $\phi \cdot \pi = 1$. Thus,

$$\sum_{u \in \mathcal{T}} \mathrm{R}(\mathcal{T}_u) \leq |\mathcal{T}| .$$

The third constraint is the *unbounded reward constraint*: there is no limit to the rewards one can potentially receive even under the assumption that each user has a limited circle of friends in the underlying social network (imposing a limited number of direct referrals). Formally, the unbounded reward constraint dictates that there exists some positive integer d (a property of the reward mechanism) such that for every real R, there exists some tree T of maximum degree d (i.e., every node has at most d children) such that $\mathrm{R}(T) \geq R$. In particular, this constraint implies that the

[2]This can be implemented by associating Alice's link with a unique identifier. In the current paper we abstract away this technical issue.

[3]In some social networks such as Facebook there is often more explicit knowledge of social connections, but general referral systems do not necessarily have all the information about the underlying social structure and may not be able to track messages in the network.

reward mechanisms we consider must take indirect referrals into account.

Our results.

We begin our exploration of reward mechanisms with a well known family of mechanisms, namely, *geometric reward mechanisms*. Under these mechanisms, the contribution of a node to the rewards of its ancestors in the referrals tree decreases exponentially (by a fixed factor) with the distance from these ancestors. Three desired properties of geometric reward mechanisms are listed: additivity, child-dependence, and depth-level-dependence. We show that these three properties fully characterize the family of geometric mechanisms in the sense that any mechanism that satisfies all three properties must be a geometric mechanism. (This may explain why pyramid schemes typically rely on geometric reward mechanisms or some close variant of them.) We go on to show that none of the properties is redundant: if any one of the three is left out, alternative reward mechanisms can be found that possess the remaining three.

We then look at one more important property of reward mechanisms, namely, resilience to false-name manipulations (a.k.a. Sybil attacks). The geometric mechanism family turns out to be susceptible to manipulations by users that can create false identities. In fact, we show that mechanisms that are resilient to false-name manipulations cannot guarantee a user some constant fraction of the reward of even its least influential child. Moreover, it turns out that even if one replaces the child-dependence and depth-level-dependence properties with the much weaker monotonicity property, resilience to false-name manipulations is still impossible. On the positive side, we present and analyze two reward mechanisms that maintain resilience to false-name manipulations; the two mechanisms differ in their level of resilience and ease of implementation.

Related work.

The general idea of diffusion of opinions and conventions in societies has for long been a topic of study in the social sciences [15, 9] and got attention by game theorists (e.g., [20]) and AI researchers (e.g., [16]) among others, quite a while ago. The effects of the social structure on emergent behavior and norms has also been studied, e.g., in [14, 17].

The more explicit algorithmic questions that arise when one considers an endeavor such as viral marketing have been posed more recently. The original question of how to select a good set of influential users has appeared in a seminal paper by Domingo & Richardson [8], and has later been explored (with various related models) in a series of papers, e.g. [7] and many other following works [10, 3, 5]. These generally assume that the spread of information in the social network occurs through some contagion model (i.e., that a user is more likely to be "infected" with an idea if more of her neighbors are) in which users do not explicitly exert effort. The rigorous study of incentive design for facilitating diffusion or product adoption was typically left without proper explicit treatment, and all works we are aware of in the context of viral marketing do not try to influence the amount of effort exerted to spread the information further.

The issue of incentives in social networks has however received attention in other particular contexts. For example, fair distribution of costs/gains of members in a network, using standard power indices from cooperative game theory, such as the Shapley and Banzhaf values has been a subject of study (see e.g., [13, 4, 2]). However, these do not provide a general rigorous study of reward mechanisms for social distribution. Kleinberg & Raghavan [12] consider a setting that is perhaps the most similar in spirit to our own, in which they elicit effort from agents that forward queries in a social network. Unlike our setting, they allow each agent that receives the query and forwards it to offer its own reward for a successful answer. The final rewards are only allocated along the path to the agent that gave the answer as each agent along the way receives the reward for passing the answer back along the path. A similar reward mechanism (that was more structured) was used by the team from MIT that won the DARPA network challenge [1].

Finally, our work also deals with the issue of Sybil attacks that have appeared in many other contexts such as reputation mechanisms [6], combinatorial auctions [18], and social choice [19].

2. PRELIMINARIES

Unless stated otherwise, all trees addressed in this paper are assumed to be finite and directed from the (unique) root towards the leaves. A typical tree will be denoted by T; its root is denoted by r. We use the standard (directed) tree notions of *parent*, *child*, *leaf*, *descendant*, and *ancestor* in their natural sense; the parent of a (non-root) node u in T is denoted $p_T(u)$. The *degree* of node $u \in T$, denoted $\deg_T(u)$, is just the number of children u has in T. Given two nodes $u, v \in T$ such that u is an ancestor of v, we define the *distance* from u to v, denoted $\delta_T(u, v)$, as the number of hops (i.e., edges) along the unique path in T leading from u to v; the distance from u to itself is defined to be $\delta_T(u, u) = 0$. If $\delta_T(u, v) = k > 0$, then we refer to u as the kth *ancestor* of v. We denote the subtree of T rooted at u by T_u. The *height* of T, denoted $\mathrm{h}(T)$, is defined to be the maximum distance from r to any leaf in T; the *height* of u in T, denoted $\mathrm{h}_T(u)$, is simply $\mathrm{h}(T_u)$. The *depth* of u in T, denoted $\mathrm{dep}_T(u)$, is the distance $\delta_T(r, u)$ from the root of T to u. When the tree T is clear from the context, we may omit the subscripts and simply write $p(u)$, $\deg(u)$, $\delta(u, v)$, $\mathrm{h}(u)$, and $\mathrm{dep}(u)$.

A reward mechanism is a function that maps a non-negative real reward $\mathrm{R}(T)$ to every finite rooted tree T. We think of T as a (subtree of a) referrals tree and of $\mathrm{R}(T)$ as the reward of the root r of T. (Recall that defining the reward in that manner is made possible due to the subtree constraint requiring that the reward of a node in the referrals forest depends only on its subtree.) The *profit* of r is actually $\mathrm{R}(T) - \pi$ as r paid $\pi \geq 1$ for purchasing the product when she joined the referrals forest. By the budget constraint, it is assumed that $\sum_{u \in T} \mathrm{R}(T_u) \leq |T|$. The unbounded reward constraint guarantees the existence of some positive integer d such that for every real R, there exists some tree T of maximum degree d such that $\mathrm{R}(T) \geq R$. The notation $\mathrm{R}_{\mathcal{M}}(\cdot)$ is used when it is important to emphasize that the function $\mathrm{R}(\cdot)$ is associated with the reward mechanism $\mathcal{M}$.

3. THE GEOMETRIC MECHANISM

In this section we focus on the following family of reward mechanisms, referred to as *geometric mechanisms*. Given two constants $0 < a < 1$ and $b > 0$ such that $b + 1 \leq 1/a$, the reward from a referral tree T under the (a, b)-*geometric mechanism* is defined to be

$$\mathrm{R}(T) = \sum_{u \in T} a^{\mathrm{dep}(u)} \cdot b .$$

The constraints on a and b ensure that the amount contributed by each node to the reward of its ancestors will not exceed 1. This simple mechanism is very popular with pyramid schemes; as we will show soon, this is no coincidence. Let us begin by defining and discussing three basic properties of reward mechanisms:

Additivity (ADD): We define the operation $\cup$ on trees such that if T_1, T_2 are trees, then $T_1 \cup T_2$ is the tree formed by contracting (or merging) the roots of T_1 and T_2. ADD is then stated as follows: $\mathrm{R}(T) + \mathrm{R}(T') = \mathrm{R}(T \cup T')$.

This property suggests that if two disjoint trees are merged at the root, then the reward of the root is exactly the sum of the rewards of the two original trees. Generally speaking this property implies that the reward to each node can be independently attributed to the subtrees rooted at its children.

Child Dependence (CD): The reward of the root is uniquely determined by the rewards of its children. This property ensures that the actual computation of the rewards can be performed locally. In fact, we shall consider a weaker condition for this property: If the root of T has a single child u, then $\mathrm{R}(T)$ is uniquely determined by $\mathrm{R}(T_u)$. This is captured by a function $\chi : \mathbb{R}_{>0} \to \mathbb{R}_{>0}$ (a property of the mechanism) so that $\mathrm{R}(T) = \chi(\mathrm{R}(T_u))$.

Depth Level Dependence (DLD): $\mathrm{R}(T)$ is uniquely determined by the number of nodes on each depth level in T. We denote by d_k the number of nodes of T at depth level $k > 0$, and the infinite vector containing these numbers for all depth levels by $d = (d_1, \ldots, d_h, 0, 0, \ldots)$, where h is the height of the tree. Let $\mathcal{D}$ be the set of all such vectors, i.e., the set of all infinite vectors over $\mathbb{Z}_{\geq 0}$ with a strictly positive prefix followed by a countably infinite suffix of zeros. Then DLD implies that there exists some function $f : \mathcal{D} \to \mathbb{R}_{\geq 0}$ (a property of the mechanism) such that $\mathrm{R}(T) = f(d)$.

This property essentially means that the credit for a referral depends solely on how direct (or better said, indirect) this referral is.

THEOREM 1. *A reward mechanism satisfies DLD, ADD, and CD if and only if it is a geometric mechanism.*

To prove the theorem, we will need the definition of the following additional property:

Summing Contributions (SC): There exists a sequence $\{c_k\}_{k \geq 1}$ of non-negative reals such that

$$\mathrm{R}(T) = \sum_{u \in T} c_{\mathrm{dep}(u)} = \sum_{k=1}^{\infty} \#\text{nodes at depth level } k \cdot c_k .$$

That is, SC implies that each node in the tree T contributes some independent amount to the root, and that amount depends only on its depth. The following lemma reveals the connection between this property and the ones we have already defined.

LEMMA 2. *A reward mechanism satisfies SC if and only if it satisfies DLD and ADD.*

PROOF. We start with some useful notation. Let $d^{>k}$ denotes the infinite vector d after the first k elements have been removed, i.e., $d^{>k} = (d_{k+1}, d_{k+2}, \ldots)$. We denote by $m \circ d$ the infinite vector that starts with the element m and continues with the elements of the infinite vector d, i.e., $m \circ d = (m, d_1, d_2, \ldots)$. Finally, we denote the all-zeros infinite vector by $\vec{0} = (0, 0, \ldots)$.

The direction in which SC implies DLD and ADD is trivial. We shall establish the converse direction using an inductive argument. Specifically, we prove by induction on k that for every $k \geq 0$, there exist non-negative reals $c_1, \ldots, c_k$ and an additive function[4] $g_k : \mathcal{D} \to \mathbb{R}_{\geq 0}$ such that

$$\mathrm{R}(T) = \sum_{i=1}^{k} c_i \cdot d_i + g_k(d^{>k}) .$$

The base of the induction, for $k = 0$, is satisfied by setting $g_0(d) = f(d)$, where f is the function promised by DLD. The additivity of g_0 is then guaranteed by ADD.

For the inductive step, we assume that there exist some non-negative reals $c_1, \ldots, c_{k-1}$ and an additive function $g_{k-1} : \mathcal{D} \to \mathbb{R}_{\geq 0}$ such that

$$\mathrm{R}(T) = \sum_{i=1}^{k-1} c_i \cdot d_i + g_{k-1}(d^{>k-1}) .$$

The assertion for k is established by setting

$$c_k = g_{k-1}(1 \circ \vec{0}) \; ; \textit{and}$$
$$g_k(d) = g_{k-1}(1 \circ d) - c_k .$$

To verify that the function g_k is indeed additive, we employ the additivity of g_{k-1}, observing that

$$\begin{aligned} g_k(d+e) &= g_{k-1}(1 \circ (d+e)) - c_k \\ &= g_{k-1}(2 \circ (d+e)) - g_{k-1}(1 \circ \vec{0}) - c_k \\ &= g_{k-1}(1 \circ d) + g_{k-1}(1 \circ e) - 2 \cdot c_k \\ &= g_k(d) + g_k(e) . \end{aligned}$$

The proof of the inductive step can now be completed due to the inductive hypothesis since

$$\begin{aligned} & f(d) \\ &= \sum_{i=1}^{k-1} c_i \cdot d_i + g_{k-1}(d^{>k-1}) \\ &= \sum_{i=1}^{k-1} c_i \cdot d_i + g_{k-1}(d_k \circ d^{>k}) \\ &= \sum_{i=1}^{k-1} c_i \cdot d_i + g_{k-1}(1 \circ d^{>k}) + g_{k-1}((d_k - 1) \circ \vec{0}) \\ &= \sum_{i=1}^{k-1} c_i \cdot d_i + g_k(d^{>k}) + c_k + (d_k - 1) \cdot c_k \\ &= \sum_{i=1}^{k} c_i \cdot d_i + g_k(d^{>k}) . \end{aligned}$$

The lemma follows by taking $k = \mathrm{h}(T)$ as every additive function g must satisfy $g(\vec{0}) = 0$ (by definition, $g(\vec{0}) = g(\vec{0} + \vec{0}) = 2 \cdot g(\vec{0})$). $\square$

Theorem 1 is established by showing that the contribution values c_k form a geometric progression.

[4]In this context a function $g : \mathcal{D} \to \mathbb{R}_{\geq 0}$ is said to be additive if $g(d + d') = g(d) + g(d')$, where the summation in $d + d'$ is coordinate-wise.

LEMMA 3. *A reward mechanism satisfies* SC *and* CD *if and only if it is a geometric mechanism.*

PROOF. It is trivial to show that a geometric mechanism satisfies both properties, so we focus on the converse direction. Let us restrict our attention to a specific class of trees: For $n > 1$ and $m > 0$, we denote by $T(n,m)$ the tree consisting of $n+m$ nodes organized as a path of length $n-1$ emerging from the root with the last node in this path having m children, all of which are leaves. Refer to Figure 1 for illustration.

Recall that SC implies the existence of constants $c_1, c_2, \ldots$ that determine the contribution of nodes at each depth level to the reward of the root. We first argue that c_k must be strictly positive for every $k \geq 1$. To that end, suppose that $c_{k^*} = 0$ for some $k^* \geq 1$ and consider the trees $T(k^*, m)$ and $T(k^*, m')$ for some $m, m' > 0$, $m \neq m'$. SC implies that $\mathrm{R}(T(k^*, m)) = \mathrm{R}(T(k^*, m'))$ since $c_{k^*} = 0$. By CD, we conclude that the same holds for $T(k^*+1, m)$ and $T(k^*+1, m')$, namely, $\mathrm{R}(T(k^*+1, m)) = \mathrm{R}(T(k^*+1, m'))$, because both the root of $T(k^*+1, m)$ and that of $T(k^*+1, m')$ have a single child whose reward is $\mathrm{R}(T(k^*, m)) = \mathrm{R}(T(k^*, m'))$. This implies that c_{k^*+1} must also be 0 and by induction, that $c_k = 0$ for every $k \geq k^*$. But this contradicts the unbounded reward constraint: if $c_k = 0$ for every $k \geq k^*$, then no tree T of maximum degree d can provide a reward greater than $2 \cdot d^{k^*}$.

So, assume hereafter that $c_k > 0$ for every $k \geq 1$. In attempt to simplify the analysis, we shall impose another assumption on the contribution values c_k. Specifically, we assume that each c_k is rational, so that $c_k = x_k / y_k$ for some positive integers x_k and y_k. We later on outline how this assumption can be lifted.

Let us compare the reward that is given to the root node in two specific $T(n,m)$ trees (recall that a $T(n,m)$ tree has one node at each level 0 to $n-1$, and m nodes at level n):

$$\begin{aligned} & \mathrm{R}(T(k-1, x_k \cdot y_{k-1} + 1)) \\ &= \sum_{i=1}^{k-2} c_i + (x_k \cdot y_{k-1} + 1) \cdot c_{k-1} \\ &= \sum_{i=1}^{k-1} c_i + x_{k-1} \cdot x_k \\ &= \sum_{i=1}^{k-1} c_i + x_{k-1} \cdot y_k \cdot c_k \\ &= \mathrm{R}(T(k, x_{k-1} \cdot y_k)) \ . \end{aligned} \tag{1}$$

Now, observe that CD implies that if $\mathrm{R}(T(n,m)) = \mathrm{R}(T(n',m'))$, then $\mathrm{R}(T(n+1,m)) = \mathrm{R}(T(n'+1,m'))$. By applying this observation to Equation 1, we conclude that

$$\mathrm{R}(T(k, x_k \cdot y_{k-1} + 1)) = \mathrm{R}(T(k+1, x_{k-1} \cdot y_k)) \ .$$

SC then implies that

$$\sum_{i=1}^{k-1} c_i + (x_k \cdot y_{k-1} + 1) \cdot c_k \ = \ \sum_{i=1}^{k} c_i + (x_{k-1} \cdot y_k) \cdot c_{k+1} \ ,$$

hence $x_k \cdot y_{k-1} \cdot c_k = (x_{k-1} \cdot y_k) \cdot c_{k+1}$. It follows that

$$(c_k)^2 = c_{k-1} \cdot c_{k+1} \ , \tag{2}$$

which implies a geometric progression (c_k is the geometric mean of c_{k-1} and c_{k+1}).

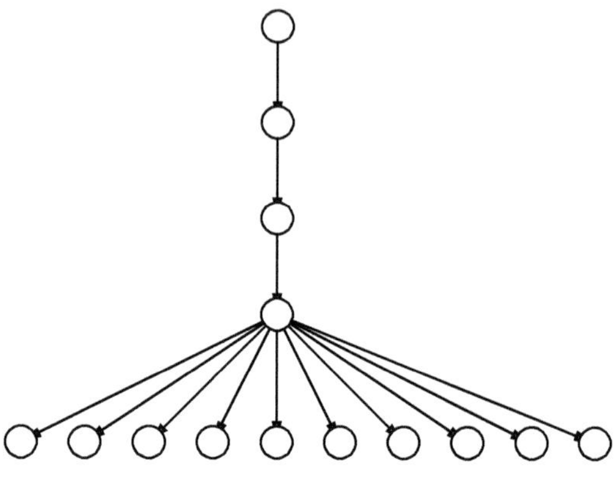

Figure 1: $T(n,m)$ **for** $n = 4$ **and** $m = 10$**.**

Recall that our proof thus far only works if all c_k's are rational numbers. We can extend the proof to irrational numbers if we add a requirement on the continuity of the function that determines the rewards of a parent from the reward of its children. If the c_k's are not rational, it is possible to approximate them as closely as one wishes with rational numbers x_k / y_k and with the extra assumption, the derivation above results in an equation similar to Equation 2 which is modified with terms that represent the error in the approximation of c_k. As this error can be made arbitrarily small, Equation 2 holds even for irrational values. □

Another appealing property of geometric mechanisms is that the contribution of descendants to their ancestor decreases with distance. This reflects the fact that the ancestor gets less credit for more distant indirect referrals.

It is important to point out that each of the three properties we used to characterize the family of geometric mechanisms is needed, i.e., if we remove one of the three properties then there exists another mechanism (outside the geometric family) for which the remaining three hold. This is established in the full version of this paper.

4. SYBIL ATTACKS

Our goal in this section is to develop reward mechanisms which are not vulnerable to forging identities on behalf of the users. Let us begin by introducing the notions of a *split* and a *local split*. Consider some tree T and some node $v \in T$ and let $u_1, \ldots, u_k$ be the children of v in T. Intuitively speaking, a split of v refers to a scenario in which v presents itself as *several* nodes — a.k.a. *replicas* — thus modifying the (sub)tree T_v that determines its reward (possibly turning it into several trees), while keeping $T_{u_1}, \ldots, T_{u_k}$ intact. A local split refers to the special case of a split in which $u_1, \ldots, u_k$ are forced to share the same parent in the resulting tree.

Formally, we say that the tree collection $\{\widetilde{T}^1, \ldots, \widetilde{T}^m\}$ can be obtained from T_v by a *split* of v if
(1) for every $1 \leq i \leq k$, there exists a single $1 \leq j(i) \leq m$ such that $u_i \in \widetilde{T}^{j(i)}$; and
(2) $\widetilde{T}^{j(i)}_{u_i} = T_{u_i}$ for every $1 \leq i \leq k$.
The nodes in

$$\left(\widetilde{T}^1 \cup \cdots \cup \widetilde{T}^m\right) - \left(\widetilde{T}^{j(1)}_{u_1} \cup \cdots \cup \widetilde{T}^{j(k)}_{u_k}\right)$$

are referred to as the *replicas* of v under that split. By definition, u_i must be a (direct) child of some replica of v for every $1 \leq i \leq k$ as otherwise, at least one of the subtrees rooted at $u_1, \ldots, u_k$ must have been changed, thus violating condition (2). Refer to Figure 2 for an illustration of a split. The split is called *local* if $u_1, \ldots, u_k$ are all children of the same replica of v.

The semantic of the aforementioned split is as follows. The user corresponding to v forges some new identities that correspond to its replicas in $\widetilde{T}^1, \ldots, \widetilde{T}^m$. Some of these replicas purchase the product via referrals from $p_T(v)$ — they form the roots of the trees $\widetilde{T}^1, \ldots, \widetilde{T}^m$; the rest of the replicas purchase the product via the referrals of other replicas that already purchased it. The referrals to $u_1, \ldots, u_k$ are then made from the appropriate replicas, so that eventually T_v is replaced by the trees $\widetilde{T}^1, \ldots, \widetilde{T}^m$, the roots of which are all children of $p_T(v)$.

It is assumed that u_i does not distinguish between the original v and its new replicas. Therefore the new referral (made from a replica of v rather than from v itself) looks to u_i like a referral from v and she relies on it to purchase the product just like she did with the referral from v in the original scenario. Under local splits, this assumption is lifted as all children of v purchase the product from the same replica that may have the identity of v herself.

What's in it for v? Clearly, v has to invest $\pi \times \#\text{replicas}$ in introducing the new replicas (purchasing new copies of the product). However, she now collects the rewards from all her replicas, which sums up to

$$\sum_{i=1}^{m} \sum_{\text{replica } u \text{ of } v \text{ in } \widetilde{T}^i} \mathrm{R}(\widetilde{T}^i_u) .$$

Thus, the profit[5] of v changes from $\mathrm{R}(T_v) - \pi$ to

$$\sum_{i=1}^{m} \sum_{\text{replica } u \text{ of } v \text{ in } \widetilde{T}^i} \mathrm{R}(\widetilde{T}^i_u) - \pi \times \#\text{replicas} ;$$

the split is called *profitable* for v if this change is positive. This leads to the definition of the following two properties of reward mechanisms.

Split Proof (SP): A reward mechanism satisfies SP if it does not admit a profitable split for any node v in any tree T.

Local Split Proof (LSP): A reward mechanism satisfies LSP if it does not admit a profitable local split for any node v in any tree T.

The geometric mechanisms presented in Section 3 do not satisfy SP. In fact, they do not even satisfy LSP (see Section 4.1). A simple mechanism that do satisfy SP is the *single level* mechanism defined by fixing $\mathrm{R}_{\mathcal{M}_{\text{sl}}}(T) = \alpha \cdot \deg(r)$ for some constant $\alpha \leq 1$, however, this mechanism does not adhere to the unbounded reward constraint.

In Section 4.1 we establish two negative results regarding the design of split-proof mechanisms. On the positive side, we devise two mechanisms which are resilient to false-name manipulations. The first one, presented in Section 4, satisfies the stronger property SP, however, it is complicated to implement and not very appealing. The second one, presented in Section 4.3, satisfies only LSP, but it is more natural and much easier to implement.

[5]Here, we assume that a user has no usage in more than one copy of the product. This is a valid assumption, e.g., in the context of information goods.

4.1 Negative Results

Let us now exhibit two negative results (proofs are deferred to the full version of the paper) regarding the design of split-proof mechanisms. The first result shows that the reward guaranteed to a node in a split-proof mechanism cannot be a constant fraction of even its least influential child.

LEMMA 4. *A reward mechanism that satisfies* LSP *cannot guarantee a node some fraction* $0 < \alpha \leq 1$ *of the reward of its least rewarded child.*

Next, we show that even a family of reward mechanisms much wider than geometric mechanisms is still not split-proof. This requires the introduction of another property which is clearly satisfied by every geometric mechanism, yet, cannot replace any of the characterizing properties listed in Theorem 1.

Monotonicity (MONO): If the tree T can be obtained from the tree T' by removing some leaf, then $\mathrm{R}(T) < \mathrm{R}(T')$.

LEMMA 5. *A reward mechanism that satisfies* MONO *and* ADD *cannot satisfy* SP.

4.2 A Split-Proof Mechanism

In this section we present a split-proof reward mechanism, denoted $\mathcal{M}_{\text{split}}$. Informally, the mechanism $\mathcal{M}_{\text{split}}$ is defined in two stages: in the first stage, we define a simple *base* mechanism, denoted $\mathcal{M}_{\text{base}}$; $\mathcal{M}_{\text{split}}$ is then defined with respect to the maximum profit a node can make under $\mathcal{M}_{\text{base}}$ from splits.

Mechanism $\mathcal{M}_{\text{base}}$.

The base mechanism $\mathcal{M}_{\text{base}}$ is defined by setting $\mathrm{R}_{\mathcal{M}_{\text{base}}}(T)$ to be the maximum $h \in \mathbb{Z}_{\geq 0}$ such that T exhibits as a subtree, a perfect binary tree[6] B rooted at r whose height is h. In that case we say that B *realizes* $\mathrm{R}_{\mathcal{M}_{\text{base}}}(T)$ (see Figure 3). If there are several perfect binary trees that can realize $\mathrm{R}_{\mathcal{M}_{\text{base}}}(T)$, then it will be convenient to take the first one in a lexicographic order based on a breadth-first-search traversal and consider it as *the* perfect binary tree that realizes $\mathrm{R}_{\mathcal{M}_{\text{base}}}(T)$.

A node $u \in T$ is said to be *visible* in T if it belongs to the perfect binary tree that realizes $\mathrm{R}_{\mathcal{M}_{\text{base}}}(T)$; otherwise, u is said to be *invisible* in T. This definition is extended as follows: given some ancestor v of u in T, u is said to be *visible* (respectively, *invisible*) to v if u is visible (resp., invisible) in T_v. Note that if u is invisible to v, then it is also invisible to $p_T(v)$ (assuming of course that $v \neq r$). The contrary is not necessarily true: u may be visible to v but invisible to $p_T(v)$. By definition, for every node $u \in T$ and for every $j \in \mathbb{Z}_{\geq 1}$, it holds that u admits either 2^j or 0 visible depth-j descendants.

The mechanism $\mathcal{M}_{\text{base}}$ can be redefined by setting

$$\mathrm{R}_{\mathcal{M}_{\text{base}}}(T) = \sum_{\text{visible } u \in T} 2^{-\delta_T(u,r)} .$$

This alternative view of mechanism $\mathcal{M}_{\text{base}}$ calls for the definition of *contributions*: a node $u \in T$ *contributes* 2^{-k} to the reward of its kth ancestor v, $k \geq 1$, if u is visible to v; otherwise, u does not contribute anything to the reward of v.

[6]A perfect binary tree is a rooted tree in which all leaves are at the same distance from the root and all non-leaves have exactly two children.

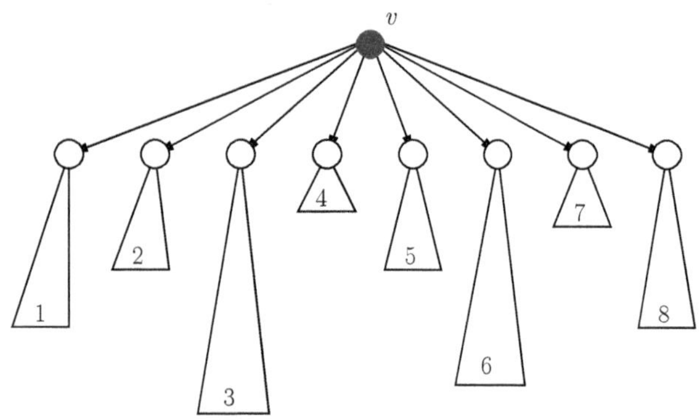

(a) T_v

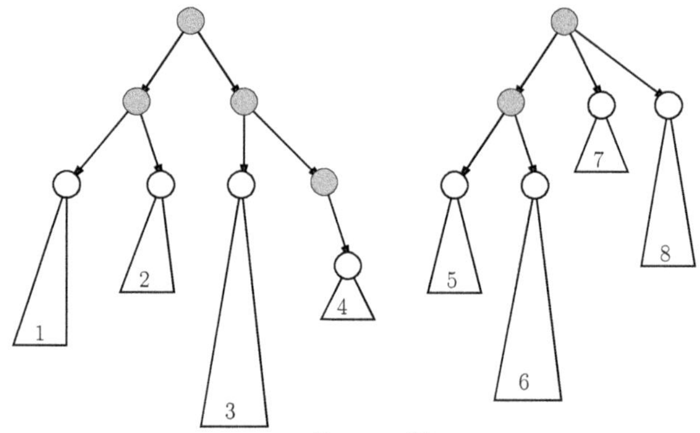

(b) $\widetilde{T}^1$ and $\widetilde{T}^2$

Figure 2: The tree collection $\{\widetilde{T}^1, \widetilde{T}^2\}$ can be obtained from T_v by a split of v. The white circles depict the children of v in T (2(a)) and their positions in $\widetilde{T}^1$ and $\widetilde{T}^2$ after the split (2(b)). The gray circles in 2(b) depict the replicas of v under that split.

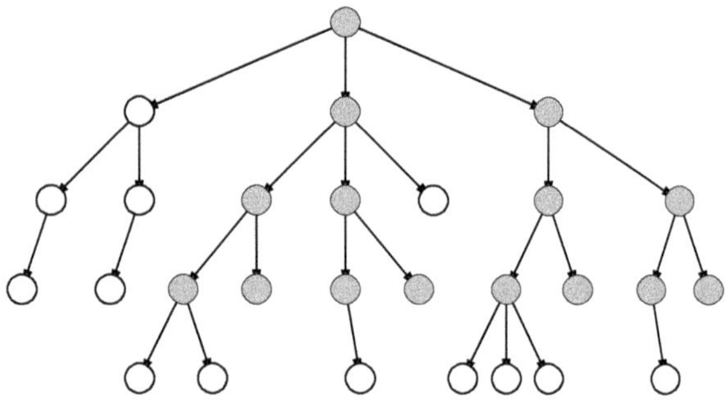

Figure 3: The tree T and the perfect binary tree that realizes $\mathrm{R}_{\mathcal{M}_{\mathbf{base}}}(T)$ (nodes depicted by gray circles).

Let $\mathrm{C}_{\mathcal{M}_{\mathrm{base}}}(u, v)$ denote the contribution of u to the reward of v under $\mathcal{M}_{\mathrm{base}}$. The reward of a node can now be calculated by summing the contributions that its descendants make to it. This implies that $\mathcal{M}_{\mathrm{base}}$ satisfies the budget constraint: the total contribution made by a node $u \in T$ to all its ancestors is bounded from above by the geometric sum $\sum_{j=1}^{\delta(u,r)} 2^{-j} < 1$, hence, by changing the summation, we conclude that $\sum_{v \in T} \mathrm{R}_{\mathcal{M}_{\mathrm{base}}}(T_v) < |T|$.

Mechanism $\mathcal{M}_{\mathrm{split}}$.

The mechanism $\mathcal{M}_{\mathrm{split}}$ is defined by setting $\mathrm{R}_{\mathcal{M}_{\mathrm{split}}}(T)$ so that it reflects the maximum profit that r can get under $\mathcal{M}_{\mathrm{base}}$ from splits. More formally, let $\mathcal{S}$ be the collection of all tree collections that can be obtained from T by a split of r. Then $\mathcal{M}_{\mathrm{split}}$ is defined by setting

$$\mathrm{R}_{\mathcal{M}_{\mathrm{split}}}(T) = \sup_{\widetilde{\mathcal{T}}=\{\widetilde{T}^1 \dots, \widetilde{T}^m\} \in \mathcal{S}} \left\{ \left(\sum_{i=1}^{m} \sum_{\text{repl. } v \text{ of } r \text{ in } \widetilde{T}^i} \mathrm{R}_{\mathcal{M}_{\mathrm{base}}}(\widetilde{T}^i_v) \right) - \pi \cdot \left(\left| \widetilde{T}^1 \cup \cdots \cup \widetilde{T}^m \right| - |T| \right) \right\} .$$

To avoid cumbersome notation, we shall denote $\rho(\widetilde{\mathcal{T}}) \equiv \sum_{i=1}^{m} \sum_{\text{replica } v \text{ of } r \text{ in } \widetilde{T}^i} \mathrm{R}_{\mathcal{M}_{\mathrm{base}}}(\widetilde{T}^i_v)$ and $\bigcup \widetilde{\mathcal{T}} \equiv \widetilde{T}^1 \cup \cdots \cup \widetilde{T}^m$ so that $\mathrm{R}_{\mathcal{M}_{\mathrm{split}}}(T) = \sup_{\widetilde{\mathcal{T}} \in \mathcal{S}} \{\rho(\widetilde{\mathcal{T}}) - \pi \cdot (|\bigcup \widetilde{\mathcal{T}}| - |T|)\}$. Refer to Figure 4 for illustration.

We first observe that $\mathrm{R}_{\mathcal{M}_{\mathrm{split}}}(\cdot)$ is well defined by showing that we may assume without loss of generality that $\mathcal{S}$ is finite. To that end, we argue that it is sufficient to consider $\widetilde{\mathcal{T}} \in \mathcal{S}$ such that every replica of r in $\widetilde{\mathcal{T}}$ is of degree at least 2, which means that there are less than $\deg_T(r)$ replicas in total, and hence there are finitely many different options for $\widetilde{\mathcal{T}}$. Indeed, assume that v is a replica of r in some tree $\widetilde{T} \in \widetilde{\mathcal{T}}$ so that $\deg_{\widetilde{T}}(v) < 2$ and let $\widetilde{T}'$ be the tree obtained from $\widetilde{T}$ by removing v and turning its sole child (in case that $\deg_{\widetilde{T}}(v) = 1$) into a child of $p_{\widetilde{T}}(v)$ or into the new root if v is the root of $\widetilde{T}$. Note that by the definition of splits, $\widetilde{\mathcal{T}} \cup \{\widetilde{T}'\} - \{\widetilde{T}\}$ can also be obtained from T by a split of r. Since $\deg_{\widetilde{T}}(v) < 2$, we know that $\mathrm{R}_{\mathcal{M}_{\mathrm{base}}}(\widetilde{T}_v) = 0$. Moreover, every descendant u of v in $\widetilde{T}$ must be invisible to the ancestors of v in $\widetilde{T}$ (which are also replicas of r), hence u does not contribute anything to the rewards of these ancestors under $\mathcal{M}_{\mathrm{base}}$. The argument is established by recalling that the total contribution of v to the rewards of its ancestors in $\widetilde{T}$ is smaller than $1 \leq \pi$, which means that it was not worthwhile for r to generate the replica v.

We say that the tree collection $\widetilde{\mathcal{T}} \in \mathcal{S}$ *realizes* $\mathrm{R}_{\mathcal{M}_{\mathrm{split}}}(T)$ if $\mathrm{R}_{\mathcal{M}_{\mathrm{split}}}(T) = \rho(\widetilde{\mathcal{T}}) - \pi \cdot (|\bigcup \widetilde{\mathcal{T}}| - |T|)$. If there are several tree collections that can realize $\mathrm{R}_{\mathcal{M}_{\mathrm{split}}}(T)$, then it will be convenient to choose one (arbitrarily) and consider it as *the* tree collection that realizes $\mathrm{R}_{\mathcal{M}_{\mathrm{split}}}(T)$.

Excessive contributions.

It is easy to see that $\mathcal{M}_{\mathrm{split}}$ satisfies the subtree constraint and the unbounded reward constraint ($\mathcal{M}_{\mathrm{base}}$ already satisfies the unbounded reward constraint and the rewards under $\mathcal{M}_{\mathrm{split}}$ dominates those of $\mathcal{M}_{\mathrm{base}}$). Moreover, by definition, $\mathcal{M}_{\mathrm{split}}$ satisfies SP, i.e., a node cannot increase its profit by splitting (recall that the mechanism takes every possible split into account). The difficult part is

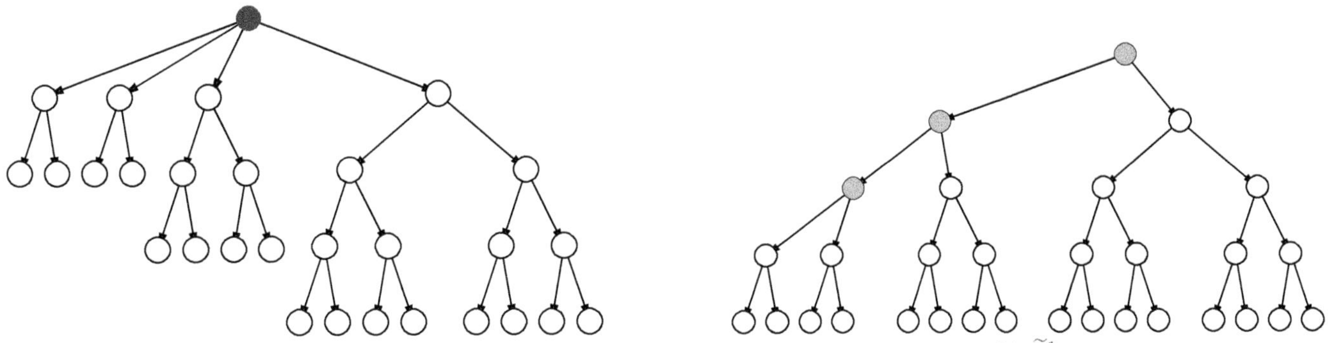

(a) T (b) $\widetilde{T}^1$

Figure 4: The tree T and a possible split of its root r (into a single tree $\widetilde{T}^1$). The gray circles in 4(b) depict the replicas of r under that split. If $\pi = 1$, then this split realizes $\mathrm{R}_{\mathcal{M}_{\text{split}}}(T) = 2 + 3 + 4 - 2 \cdot \pi = 7$.

to show that $\mathcal{M}_{\text{split}}$ satisfies the budget constraint, that is, $\sum_{v \in T} \mathrm{R}_{\mathcal{M}_{\text{split}}}(T_v) \leq |T|$.

The first step towards fulfilling this task is to extend the notion of contribution to the reward mechanism $\mathcal{M}_{\text{split}}$. Consider some node $u \in T$ and some ancestor v of u. Let $\widetilde{\mathcal{T}}$ be the tree collection obtained from T_v by a split of v that realizes $\mathrm{R}_{\mathcal{M}_{\text{split}}}(T_v)$ and let $\widetilde{T}$ be the tree in $\widetilde{\mathcal{T}}$ that contains u. By definition, several replicas of v in $\widetilde{T}$ may be ancestors of u (in $\widetilde{T}$); denote these replicas by $v_1, \ldots, v_\ell$. The *contribution* of u to v under $\mathcal{M}_{\text{split}}$, denoted $\mathrm{C}_{\mathcal{M}_{\text{split}}}(u, v)$, is then defined to be

$$\mathrm{C}_{\mathcal{M}_{\text{split}}}(u, v) = \sum_{j=1}^{\ell} \mathrm{C}_{\mathcal{M}_{\text{base}}}(u, v_j) . \quad (3)$$

We argue that

$$\sum_{v \in T} \mathrm{R}_{\mathcal{M}_{\text{split}}}(T_v) \leq \sum_{u \in T} \sum_{\text{ancestors } v \text{ of } u} \mathrm{C}_{\mathcal{M}_{\text{split}}}(u, v) . \quad (4)$$

At first glance, inequality (4) may be surprising as its right hand side does not take into account contributions made by replicas that do not exist in T. However, $\mathcal{M}_{\text{split}}$ is defined with respect to the profit (rather than reward) that a node can get under $\mathcal{M}_{\text{base}}$ from splits. The total contribution of a node to all its ancestors under $\mathcal{M}_{\text{base}}$ is smaller than 1, hence each replica of node u contributes less than 1 to the rewards of the other replicas of u (it does not contribute anything to any other node in T). Inequality (4) follows since π is assumed to be larger than 1. Our goal in what follows is to show that

$$\sum_{u \in T} \sum_{\text{ancestors } v \text{ of } u} \mathrm{C}_{\mathcal{M}_{\text{split}}}(u, v) \leq |T| . \quad (5)$$

In attempt to establish inequality (5), it may seem natural to bound the total contribution that each node makes to its ancestors, showing that this is at most 1, as we did with $\mathcal{M}_{\text{base}}$. Unfortunately, this does not work: If the contribution $\mathrm{C}_{\mathcal{M}_{\text{split}}}(u, v)$ of node u to its ancestor v under $\mathcal{M}_{\text{split}}$, as defined in equation (3), is composed from $\mathcal{M}_{\text{base}}$-contributions to several (more than one) replicas of v, then $\mathrm{C}_{\mathcal{M}_{\text{split}}}(u, v) > \mathrm{C}_{\mathcal{M}_{\text{base}}}(u, v)$. Consequently, the total contribution that u makes to the rewards of all its ancestors under $\mathcal{M}_{\text{split}}$ may exceed 1. This obstacle requires a careful accounting argument that we now turn to describe.

Consider some node $u \in T$. Let $\Gamma(u)$ denote the set of all ancestors v of u in T such that $\mathrm{C}_{\mathcal{M}_{\text{split}}}(u, v) > 0$. Assuming that $\Gamma(u) \neq \emptyset$, let $\varphi(u)$ be the node $v \in \Gamma(u)$ that maximizes $\delta_T(v, u)$. Now, consider some node $v \in \Gamma(u)$. Let $\widetilde{\mathcal{T}}$ be the tree collection obtained from T_v by a split of v that realizes $\mathrm{R}_{\mathcal{M}_{\text{split}}}(T_v)$, let $\widetilde{T}$ be the tree in $\widetilde{\mathcal{T}}$ that contains u, and let $\tilde{v}$ be the highest ancestor of u in $\widetilde{T}$ such that u is visible to $\tilde{v}$. Note that $\tilde{v}$ must be a replica of v in $\widetilde{T}$ since $v \in \Gamma(u)$. Moreover, $\delta_{\widetilde{T}}(\tilde{v}, u) \geq \delta_T(v, u)$ and the contribution of u to v's reward under $\mathcal{M}_{\text{split}}$ is $\mathrm{C}_{\mathcal{M}_{\text{split}}}(u, v) = \sum_{j=\delta_T(v,u)}^{\delta_{\widetilde{T}}(\tilde{v},u)} 2^{-j}$. Thus, the parameter $\delta_{\widetilde{T}}(\tilde{v}, u)$ plays an important role in the calculation of $\mathrm{C}_{\mathcal{M}_{\text{split}}}(u, v)$ — denote it by $\Delta(u, v)$, so that $\mathrm{C}_{\mathcal{M}_{\text{split}}}(u, v) = 2^{1-\delta_T(v,u)} - 2^{-\Delta(u,v)}$.

Deficits and surpluses.

Recall that $\mathrm{C}_{\mathcal{M}_{\text{base}}}(u, v) = 2^{-\delta_T(v,u)}$ and that such a contribution would have resulted in the desired bound of 1 on the total contribution of node u to all its ancestors. Informally speaking, if $\Delta(u, v) > \delta_T(v, u)$, then u exhibits a *deficit*. On the other hand, if $\varphi(u) = v$, then u does not contribute anything to the rewards of the ancestors of v, which leaves us with a small *surplus*. Our argument will rely on covering the total deficits with the total surpluses.

Formally, given some nodes $u \in T$ and $v \in \Gamma(u)$, define

$$\begin{aligned} \text{deficit}(u, v) &= \mathrm{C}_{\mathcal{M}_{\text{split}}}(u, v) - \mathrm{C}_{\mathcal{M}_{\text{base}}}(u, v) \\ &= 2^{-\delta_T(v,u)} - 2^{-\Delta(u,v)} \end{aligned}$$

and

$$\text{surplus}(u) = 2^{-\Delta(u,\varphi(u))} .$$

Using these notions, we have

$$\begin{aligned}
&\sum_{v \in \Gamma(u)} \mathrm{C}_{\mathcal{M}_{\mathrm{split}}}(u, v) \\
&= \sum_{v \in \Gamma(u)} 2^{1-\delta_T(u,v)} - 2^{-\Delta(u,v)} \\
&\le \sum_{k=1}^{\delta_T(\varphi(u),u)} 2^{-k} + \sum_{v \in \Gamma(u)} 2^{-\delta_T(v,u)} - 2^{-\Delta(u,v)} \\
&= 1 - 2^{-\delta_T(\varphi(u),u)} + \sum_{v \in \Gamma(u)} \mathrm{deficit}(u, v) \\
&= 1 - \mathrm{deficit}(u, \varphi(u)) - \mathrm{surplus}(u) \\
&\quad + \sum_{v \in \Gamma(u)} \mathrm{deficit}(u, v) \\
&= 1 - \mathrm{surplus}(u) + \sum_{v \in \Gamma(u) - \{\varphi(u)\}} \mathrm{deficit}(u, v) .
\end{aligned}$$

We establish the fact that $\mathcal{M}_{\mathrm{split}}$ satisfies the budget constraint by showing that

$$\sum_{u \in T} \sum_{v \in \Gamma(u) - \{\varphi(u)\}} \mathrm{deficit}(u, v) \le \sum_{u \in T} \mathrm{surplus}(u) , \qquad (6)$$

thus "covering" the deficits with the surpluses. This is done in the following manner.

Consider some node $v \in T$ and let $\widetilde{\mathcal{T}}$ be the tree collection obtained from T_v by a split of v that realizes $\mathrm{R}_{\mathcal{M}_{\mathrm{split}}}(T_v)$; consider some tree $\widetilde{T} \in \widetilde{\mathcal{T}}$. Fix some replica $\tilde{v}$ of v in $\widetilde{T}$ and let h be the height of the perfect binary tree that realizes $\mathrm{R}_{\mathcal{M}_{\mathrm{base}}}(\widetilde{T}_{\tilde{v}})$. Given some $1 \le \ell \le h$, let $D_{\tilde{v},\ell}$ be the set of descendants u of $\tilde{v}$ in $\widetilde{T}$ that satisfy: (1) $\tilde{v}$ is the highest ancestor of u in $\widetilde{T}$ to which u is visible; and (2) $\Delta(u, v) = \delta_{\widetilde{T}}(\tilde{v}, u) = \ell$. It is interesting to point out that different nodes u in $D_{\tilde{v},\ell}$ may have different values of $\delta_T(v, u)$, although they all have the same value of $\delta_{\widetilde{T}}(\tilde{v}, u) = \ell$.

A crucial observation is that for every two nodes $u \in T$ and $v \in \Gamma(u)$, there exists a unique choice of $\tilde{v}$ and ℓ such that $u \in D_{\tilde{v},\ell}$. Let $D^+_{\tilde{v},\ell}$ be the set of all nodes $u \in D_{\tilde{v},\ell}$ such that $v = \varphi(u)$, i.e., those nodes that do not contribute to the reward of any ancestor of v. Let $D^-_{\tilde{v},\ell} = D_{\tilde{v},\ell} - D^+_{\tilde{v},\ell}$. Inequality (6) is established by proving the following lemma.

LEMMA 6. *The nodes in* $D_{\tilde{v},\ell}$ *satisfy* $\sum_{u \in D^-_{\tilde{v},\ell}} \mathrm{deficit}(u, v) \le \sum_{u \in D^+_{\tilde{v},\ell}} \mathrm{surplus}(u)$.

PROOF. Denote $D^- = D^-_{\tilde{v},\ell}$ and $D^+ = D^+_{\tilde{v},\ell}$. Recall that v has either 2 or 0 children which are visible to $p_T(v)$; the latter implies that $D^- = \emptyset$, so assume in what follows that the former holds and let v_1, v_2 be the children of v in T which are visible to $p_T(v)$. Let $D^-_i = D^- \cap T_{v_i}$ for $i = 1, 2$. By definition, $D^- = D^-_1 \cup D^-_2$ and $D^-_1 \cap D^-_2 = \emptyset$. Moreover, all nodes u in D^-_i have the same value of $\delta_T(v_i, u)$ — denote it by k_i.

Recall that $\mathrm{deficit}(u_i, v) = 2^{-k_i-1} - 2^{-\ell}$ for every node $u_i \in D^-_i$. Since $|D^-_i| = 2^{k_i}$, we conclude that

$$\begin{aligned}
\sum_{u_i \in D^-_i} \mathrm{deficit}(u_i, v) &= 2^{k_i} \left(2^{-k_i-1} - 2^{-\ell}\right) \\
&= \frac{1}{2} - 2^{k_i-\ell}
\end{aligned}$$

and

$$\sum_{u \in D^-} \mathrm{deficit}(u, v) = 1 - 2^{k_1-\ell} - 2^{k_2-\ell} .$$

On the other hand, $\mathrm{surplus}(u) = 2^{-\ell}$ for every node $u \in D^+$. Since $|D^+| = 2^\ell - |D^-_1| - |D^-_2| = 2^\ell - 2^{k_1} - 2^{k_2}$, it follows that

$$\begin{aligned}
\sum_{u \in D^+} \mathrm{surplus}(u) &= 2^{-\ell}\left(2^\ell - 2^{k_1} - 2^{k_2}\right) \\
&= 1 - 2^{k_1-\ell} - 2^{k_2-\ell}
\end{aligned}$$

which establishes the assertion. □

4.3 Resilience to Local Splits

The mechanism presented in Section 4.2 is resilient to splits, but it is far from being intuitive. Moreover, users who recruit a large number of buyers may find that they are not rewarded for many of them (due to limited visibility). We therefore briefly describe another mechanism (in fact, a family of mechanisms) — this time with resilience only to local splits — that is much simpler than the one we have previously shown.

The mechanism $\mathcal{M}_{\mathrm{local}}$ is similar to the geometric mechanism (with some choice of parameters $0 < a < 1$ and $b > 0$ such that $b + 1 \le 1/a$), only that here, we ignore the contributions coming from one of the subtrees rooted at r's children, say, the largest subtree. More formally, let $v_1, \ldots, v_k$ be the children of r in T and assume without loss of generality that $|T_{v_1}| \ge \cdots \ge |T_{v_k}|$. Then,

$$\mathrm{R}_{\mathcal{M}_{\mathrm{local}}}(T) = \sum_{u \in T_{v_2} \cup \cdots \cup T_{v_k}} a^{\mathrm{dep}_T(u)} \cdot b .$$

Note that a node with one child obtains no reward.

It is easy to see that $\mathcal{M}_{\mathrm{local}}$ satisfies the subtree constraint and the unbounded reward constraint. Moreover, since the rewards under $\mathcal{M}_{\mathrm{local}}$ are dominated by those of a geometric mechanism, it also satisfies the budget constraint. The following lemma establishes the resilience of $\mathcal{M}_{\mathrm{local}}$ to local splits.

THEOREM 7. *The reward mechanism* $\mathcal{M}_{\mathrm{local}}$ *satisfies LSP.*

PROOF PROOF SKETCH. Let r be the root of T and let $v_1, \ldots, v_k$ be its children. By definition, in any local split of r, the nodes $v_1, \ldots, v_k$ are children of the same replica of r. A straightforward calculation shows that r does not gain anything from replicas that do not have $v_1, \ldots, v_k$ as descendants, hence it suffices to consider local splits that replace T with a tree T' obtained by identifying the root of T with the (sole) leaf of some directed path P. (In that case, the replicas of r are the nodes of P.) The design of $\mathcal{M}_{\mathrm{local}}$ implies that the total reward of r from such a local split remains $\mathrm{R}_{\mathcal{M}_{\mathrm{local}}}(T)$ which obviously turns the split into a non-profitable move. □

5. CONCLUSIONS

We have presented a theoretical framework for multi-level marketing mechanisms. Our framework gives host to many possible reward mechanisms, with varying properties. A full characterization of the geometric mechanism family, which is recognized in particular with Pyramid schemes, is established. While we find that geometric mechanisms are not resilient to false-name manipulations, we have instead shown two different mechanisms that can withstand such manipulations.

There are many open avenues for future work. First, many different characterizations can be found for the mechanisms that we presented. It is possible to think of other intuitive properties and attempt to substitute them for the ones we have defined. In addition, the split-proof mechanisms that we have shown may be hard to implement (they are hard to explain to users and deny rewards for some of the referrals that are made). It will be nice to find mechanisms that improve these aspects as well. It will also be interesting to explore other models for marketing in the context of social networks, including models that take the underlying structure of the network into account, and perhaps other details such as the percentage of successful referrals and the timing of messages. Finally, we believe that much can be learned from experimental evaluation, or even deployment of mechanisms that we have suggested. User trials can reveal defects in these reward schemes, and show how readily human users are willing to accept them.

6. REFERENCES

[1] DARPA network challenge. http://balloon.media.mit.edu/mit/rules/.

[2] T. Ågotnes, W. van der Hoek, M. Tennenholtz, and M. Wooldridge. Power in normative systems. In *AAMAS*, pages 145–152, 2009.

[3] D. Arthur, R. Motwani, A. Sharma, and Y. Xu. Pricing strategies for viral marketing on social networks. In *Proceedings of the 5th International Workshop on Internet and Network Economics*, WINE '09, pages 101–112, Berlin, Heidelberg, 2009. Springer-Verlag.

[4] Y. Bachrach and J. S. Rosenschein. Computing the banzhaf power index in network flow games. In *AAMAS*, 2007.

[5] N. Chen. On the approximability of influence in social networks. *SIAM J. Discret. Math.*, 23:1400–1415, September 2009.

[6] A. Cheng and E. Friedman. Sybilproof reputation mechanisms. In *Proceedings of the 2005 ACM SIGCOMM workshop on Economics of peer-to-peer systems*, P2PECON '05, pages 128–132, New York, NY, USA, 2005. ACM.

[7] J. K. David Kempe and E. Tardos. Maximizing the spread of influence in a social network. In *9th ACM SIGKDD International Conference on Knowledge Discovery and Data Mining*, pages 137–146, 2003.

[8] P. Domingos and M. Richardson. Mining the network value of customers. In *Proceedings of the seventh ACM SIGKDD international conference on Knowledge discovery and data mining*, KDD '01, pages 57–66, New York, NY, USA, 2001. ACM.

[9] M. Granovetter. Threshold models of collective behavior. *American Journal of Sociology*, 83:1420–1443, 1978.

[10] J. Hartline, V. Mirrokni, and M. Sundararajan. Optimal marketing strategies over social networks. In *Proceeding of the 17th international conference on World Wide Web*, WWW '08, pages 189–198, New York, NY, USA, 2008. ACM.

[11] J. Kleinberg. Cascading behavior in networks: Algorithmic and economic issues. In E. T. V. V. N. Nisan, T. Roughgarden, editor, *Algorithmic Game Theory*. Cambridge University Press, 2007.

[12] J. M. Kleinberg and P. Raghavan. Query incentive networks. In *FOCS*, pages 132–141, 2005.

[13] N. Megiddo. Computational complexity of the game theory approach to cost allocation for a tree. *Mathematics of Operations Research*, 3(3):189–196, 1978.

[14] S. Morris. Contagion. *Review of Economic Studies*, 67:137–146, 2003.

[15] T. Schelling. *Micromotives and Macrobehavior.* Norton, London: Penguin, 1978.

[16] Y. Shoham and M. Tennenholtz. On the emergence of social conventions: Modeling, analysis, and simulations. *Artif. Intell.*, 94(1-2):139–166, 1997.

[17] M. Tennenholtz. Convention Evolution in Organizations and Markets. *Computational and Mathematical Organization Thoery*, 2(4):259–283, 1996.

[18] T. Todo, A. Iwasaki, M. Yokoo, and Y. Sakurai. Characterizing false-name-proof allocation rules in combinatorial auctions. In *Proceedings of The 8th International Conference on Autonomous Agents and Multiagent Systems - Volume 1*, AAMAS '09, pages 265–272, Richland, SC, 2009. International Foundation for Autonomous Agents and Multiagent Systems.

[19] L. Wagman and V. Conitzer. Optimal false-name-proof voting rules with costly voting. In *Proceedings of the 23rd national conference on Artificial intelligence - Volume 1*, pages 190–195. AAAI Press, 2008.

[20] P. Young. *Individual Strategy and Social Structure: An Evolutionary Theory of Institutions.* Princeton University Press, 1998.

Concordance among Holdouts*

[Extended Abstract]†

Scott Duke Kominers
Department of Economics, Harvard University
& Harvard Business School
Cambridge, MA 02138 USA
skominers@hbs.edu

E. Glen Weyl
Harvard Society of Fellows
Cambridge, MA 02138 USA
weyl@fas.harvard.edu

ABSTRACT

When no agent has substantial influence on a public good outcome, he or she can demand the full surplus. Thus, in rich environments, private (voluntary and self-financing) provision of public goods—or bads such as land assembly—to a large number of self-interested citizens is impossible. This *holdout* problem is well-known and ubiquitous throughout economics: Holdout was first formalized by Cournot [2], and takes its precise modern form in the work of Mailath and Postelwaite [4]. Unlike in classical auction settings, where increasing competition may offset imperfections in market design ([1, 3]), there is no easy way around the necessity of social engineering to solve holdout. Consequently, holdout concerns have informed wide-ranging policy decisions, including eminent domain and corporate takeover laws.

In this paper, we study holdout in settings where a good owned by a disparate community of sellers is desired by a buyer only in its entirety; for concreteness, we focus on the particularly salient application of land assembly. In these settings, no mechanism can simultaneously achieve full efficiency and complete individual rationality ([4]). However, as we show, it is possible to strike an attractive balance between these two goals.

We propose two desiderata for holdout-alleviating market mechanism design:

1. *bilateral efficiency* – outcomes should always be as efficient as a bilateral bargain between the prospective buyer and a single agent representing the community of sellers in its entirety – and
2. *approximate individual rationality* – each individual should be assured of receiving as compensation at least an approximation to her value based on all but her own information.

As we show, these two properties are mutually consistent. Moreover, they are satisfied by any mechanism in a simple and intuitive *Concordance mechanism* class that we introduce and characterize.[1]

Concordance mechanisms are asymptotically efficient under truthful reporting by sellers, and exhibit tradeoffs between incentive-compatibility and budget-balance familiar from auction design. To implement Concordance mechanisms, market organizers do not need to know sellers' subjective valuations; rather, they need only an approximation of each seller's share of the total community value.[2]

Extensions of our approach yield mechanisms for classical collaboration and public goods problems.

Categories and Subject Descriptors: J.4 Computer Applications: Social and Behavioral Sciences – Economics; K.4.4 Computers and Society: Electronic Commerce

General Terms: Economics, Theory

Keywords: Holdout, Public goods, Mechanism design with complementarities, Land assembly, Patent pool formation, Concordance

REFERENCES

[1] Bulow, J. I., and Klemperer, P. D. Auctions versus negotiations. *American Economic Review 86* (1996), 180–194.

[2] Cournot, A. A. *Recherches sur les Principes Mathematiques de la Theorie des Richess.* Paris, 1838.

[3] Klemperer, P. D. What really matters in auction design. *Journal of Economic Perspectives 16* (2002), 169–189.

[4] Mailath, G. J., and Postelwaite, A. Asymmetric information bargaining problems with many agents. *Review of Economic Studies 57* (1990), 351–367.

*Kominers gratefully acknowledges the support of a National Science Foundation Graduate Research Fellowship, a Yahoo! Key Scientific Challenges Program Fellowship, the Danielan Fund, and a Terence M. Considine Fellowship in Law and Economics funded by the John M. Olin Center. Weyl is grateful to the Harvard Milton Fund for support, and to the Centro de Investigación Económica at the Instituto Tecnológico Autónomo de México (CIE-ITAM), which hosted him on a visit while he conducted parts of this research. Both authors additionally acknowledge the Harvard Real Estate Academic Initiative's support of the excellent research assistance of Stephanie Lo, Balaji Narain and Will Weingarten, and appreciate numerous useful comments supplied on this research by their colleagues—especially those of Ted Bergstrom, Jeremy Bulow, Eric Budish, Andy Eggers, Ben Golub, Sonia Jaffe, and Alexandru Nichifor.

†A full version of this paper is available online at `http://www.scottkom.com/articles/Kominers_Weyl_Holdout.pdf`.

[1] Our Concordance mechanisms are inspired Cournot's theory of collaboration—*concours*—among producers, hence we use the term "Concordance" directly derived from *concours*.

[2] The quality of this share approximation determines the degree to which approximate individual rationality resembles full individual rationality. If sellers' relative shares are perfectly assessed, then all Concordance mechanisms are fully individually rational.

EC'11, June 5–9, 2011, San Jose, California, USA.
ACM 978-1-4503-0261-6/11/06.

Only Valuable Experts Can Be Valued (Extended Abstract*)

Moshe Babaioff
Microsoft Research
Mountain View, CA 94043
moshe@microsoft.com

Liad Blumrosen†
Department of Economics
The Hebrew University
Jerusalem, Israel
blumrosen@huji.ac.il

Nicolas S. Lambert‡
Graduate School of Business
Stanford University
Stanford, CA 94305
nlambert@gsb.stanford.edu

Omer Reingold
Microsoft Research
Mountain View, CA 94043
omer.reingold@microsoft.com

ABSTRACT

Suppose a principal Alice wishes to reduce her uncertainty regarding some future payoff. Consider a self-proclaimed expert Bob that may either be an informed expert knowing an exact (or approximate) distribution of a future random outcome that may affect Alice's utility, or an uninformed expert who knows nothing more than Alice does. Alice would like to hire Bob and solicit his signal. Her goal is to incentivize an informed expert to accept the contract and reveal his knowledge while deterring an uninformed expert from accepting the contract altogether. The starting point of this work is a powerful negative result by Olszewski and Sandroni [1], which tells us that in the general case for any contract which guarantees an informed expert some positive payoff an uninformed expert (with no extra knowledge) has a strategy which guarantees him a positive payoff as well.

At the face of this negative result, we reexamine the notion of an expert and conclude that knowing some hidden variable (i.e., the description of the aforementioned distribution) does not make Bob an expert, or at least not a "valuable expert". The premise of our paper is that if Alice only tries to incentivize experts which are valuable to her decision making then she *can* indeed screen them from uninformed experts.

On a more technical level, we consider the case where the distribution of a future event cannot be an arbitrary distribution but rather comes from some closed subset $\mathcal{P}$ of all possible distributions. Bob gets a signal about this distribution (in this abstract we consider a perfectly accurate signal, in the paper we also discuss imperfect signals).

We first consider situations where Alice has some prior over $\mathcal{P}$, and this prior is also known to Bob (even if Bob is uninformed). It turns out that the ability to screen agents crucially depends on the convexity of $\mathcal{P}$, or more concretely, on whether the average distribution $\bar{p}$ is in $\mathcal{P}$ or not. In the spirit of the result of [1] we observe that when $\bar{p}$ is in $\mathcal{P}$ then a contract accepted by all informed agents will also be accepted by an uninformed agent that actually reports $\bar{p}$, thus screening is impossible. We complement this result by showing that screening is *possible* when $\mathcal{P}$ does not contain $\bar{p}$. Moreover, when $\mathcal{P}$ *does* contain $\bar{p}$ we show how Alice can define a contract that is rejected by uninformed experts and accepted by informed experts that are sufficiently valuable. We discuss several natural applications where $\bar{p} \notin \mathcal{P}$. One such example is when Alice wishes to discover the probability $p \in [0, 1]$ of a binary event, and Alice observes *two* independent samples from this distribution; Screening in this scenario is possible since for every non-trivial prior on the possible distributions, the average distribution of the outcome of the two samples does not correspond to any valid distribution.

We also study cases where neither an uninformed expert nor Alice knows a prior over $\mathcal{P}$. We present an impossibility results which is analogous to the known-prior case, saying that if $\mathcal{P}$ is convex then some informed expert is not valuable as it would not help increase the utility of Alice, regardless of her utility function and strategy. We also show that if $\mathcal{P}$ is non-convex (that is, missing one of its convex combination and some neighborhood around it), then there exists a contract that screens informed experts from uninformed experts.

*The full version of the paper is available at the authors' web pages.

†Part of this research was performed while at Microsoft Research - Silicon Valley. This research was also supported by a grant from the Israel Science Foundation number 032-1782.

‡Part of this research was performed while visiting Microsoft Research - Silicon Valley.

Categories and Subject Descriptors

J.4 [**Social and behavioral sciences**]: Economics

General Terms

Economics, Theory

Keywords

Experts, Scoring Rules, Elicitation, Screening

1. REFERENCES

[1] Olszewski, W., and Sandroni, A. Contracts and Uncertainty. *Theoretical Economics 2*, 1 (2007), 1–13.

Single Valued Combinatorial Auctions with Budgets

Amos Fiat
Tel-Aviv University
Tel Aviv, Israel
fiat@math.tau.ac.il

Stefano Leonardi
Sapienza University of Rome
Rome, Italy
leon@dis.uniroma1.it

Jared Saia
University of New Mexico
Albuquerque, USA
saia@cs.unm.edu

Piotr Sankowski*
University of Warsaw
Warsaw, Poland
sank@mimuw.edu.pl

"... any color that he [the customer] wants so long as it is black."

— Henry Ford, My Life and Work (1922)

"... Illogical approach to advertising budgets ..."

— Michael Schudson, Advertising, The Uneasy Persuasion: Its Dubious Impact on American Society (1984)

ABSTRACT

We consider budget constrained combinatorial auctions where bidder i has a private value v_i for each of the items in some set S_i, and a budget constraint b_i on his total payment. The value to agent i of a set of items R is $|R \cap S_i| \cdot v_i$ when his payment does not exceed his budget. Such auctions capture adword auctions, where advertisers offer a bid for those adwords that (hopefully) reach their target audience, and advertisers have budgets as well. It is known that even if all items are identical and all budgets are public it is not possible to be truthful and maximize social welfare. Our main result is a novel auction that runs in polynomial time, is incentive compatible, and ensures efficiency by Pareto-optimality. The auction is incentive compatible with respect to the private valuations, v_i, whereas the budgets, b_i, and the sets of interest, S_i, are assumed to be public knowledge. This extends the result of Dobzinski et al. [7, 8] for auctions of multiple *identical* items and public budgets to single-valued *combinatorial* auctions with public budgets.

Categories and Subject Descriptors

F.2.m [**ANALYSIS OF ALGORITHMS AND PROBLEM COMPLEXITY**]: Miscellaneous

*Work partially supported by the Polish Ministry of Science, Grant N N206 355636 and by the ERC StG Project PAAl no. 259515.

General Terms

Algorithms, Economics, Theory

Keywords

Multi-Unit Auctions, Combinatorial auctions, Truthfulness, Pareto-optimality

1. INTRODUCTION

In recent years ad auctions have attracted considerable attention from computer scientists. In ad auctions advertisers bid on given set of keywords. Their valuation for keywords depends on the click-through-rate and can be included into a generalized second price auction, which is used by firms such as Google, Yahoo, and Microsoft [9]. Such an auction can be used if keywords are linearly ordered by their valuations.

In contrast, we consider every potential advertising slot as an different "item". We assume that advertisers have the same valuation for each item they are interested to get. We consider the problem of agents with additive valuations that have single (private) value for any of an agent-specific set of items. E.g., adwords "Corn" or "Gold" are worth 75 cents per impression to agent A, adwords "Gold" or "Silver" or, sometimes, "Lead", ("Lead only if between 5-9PM EST), are each worth 60 cents to agent B, and so forth. *I.e.*, the sets of items the two agents are interested in are potentially different, and may overlap. Each agent has a private value, the same value for each of the items in the agent's set of interest. In addition, every agent has an agent-specific budget, e.g., agent A has a budget of \$55, agent B has a budget of \$7.

The Vickrey multiunit auction [15] was designed to deal with a setting where all items are different and agents can have arbitrary valuation functions. However, it cannot be used when agents have budgets. In a seminal paper on multiunit auctions with budgets by Dobzinski, Lavi and Nisan [7, 8], they consider the case when all units are identical, i.e., all agents are interested in getting all items.

Dobzinski *et al.* give an incentive-compatible auction (with respect to valuation) that produces a Pareto-optimal allocation. This result holds if one assumes that the budgets are public information. They also show that this assumption cannot be dropped, i.e., there is no incentive-compatible auction with respect to both valuation and budgets that produces a Pareto-optimal allocation.

This paper is an extension of [7, 8] to a single valued combinatorial auction. This shows that even in the single-valued combinatorial setting achieving some notion of efficiency is possible. Pareto-optimality is a basic notion for efficiency of allocation, *i.e.*, it seems to be the least one should aim for. If an allocation were not Pareto-optimal then agents could trade amongst themselves and improve their lot, thus increasing efficiency. However, in many settings we would like to achieve something stronger. We would like to produce an allocation such that no trades are possible because such allocations are less prone to speculations [11]. The main technical part of our approach is to show that in our setting both "no trade" and Pareto-optimality conditions are equivalent. This result is of independent interest.

For a comparison between the different settings see Table 1.

Our work seeks to map out the frontier of the possible. We give an incentive compatible combinatorial auction that produces Pareto-optimal allocation in the case when agents have budgets and their valuations are private. This setting is not entirely general but also gives a non-trivial class of auctions that contains some existing auctions, e.g., Google's auctions for TV ads [13]. Furthermore, we show that these restrictions are unavoidable.

The Setting

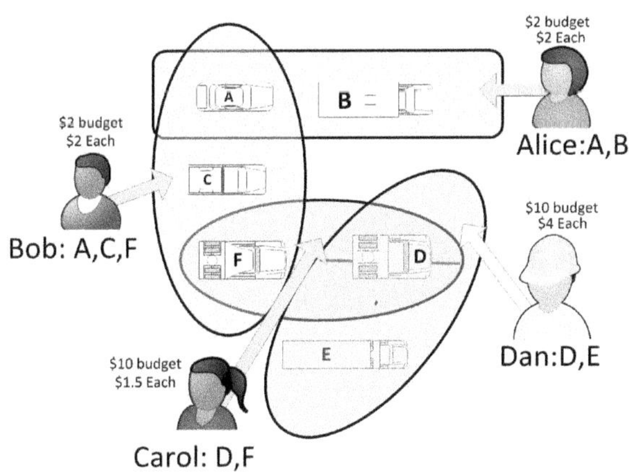

Figure 1: Example with four bidders, each interested in a subset of items, with a value per item and an overall budget.

In this paper we study combinatorial auctions of the following **general form**:

- Every agent (bidder) $1 \le a \le n$ has a *publicly known* budget, $b_a \ge 0$, and an unknown (private) valuation $v_a > 0$;
- Every agent a is "interested" in some *publicly known* set of items, S_a. We assume that there is at least one agent interested in every item. Agent a is allocated some (possibly empty) subset of S_a. An example is given in Figure 1.
- The auction produces an allocation (M, P).
  1. $M \subseteq \{1, \ldots, n\} \times \{1, \ldots, m\}$ is a (partial) assignment of agents to items: items are assigned to some agent, there may be agents that have no items assigned to them.
  2. $P \in \Re^n$ is a vectors of payments made by the agents.
- For agent $1 \le a \le n$, let M_a be the number of items sold to agent a over the course of the auction and P_a be the total payment made by agent a during the course of the auction. The allocation (M, P) must obey the following conditions:
  1. The payment by agent a, P_a, cannot exceed the budget b_a.
  2. The utility for agent $1 \le a \le n$ is $u_a = M_a v_a - P_a$.
  3. The utility for the auctioneer is $\sum_{j=1}^{n} P_j$.
  4. Bidder-rationality: for all agents $1 \le a \le n$, $u_a \ge 0$.
  5. Auctioneer-rationality: the utility of the auctioneer, $\sum_{j=1}^{n} P_j \ge 0$.

Note[1] that auctioneer-rationality is implied by *no positive transfers*: $P_a \ge 0$ for all $1 \le a \le n$.

Given valuations, v_a, budgets, b_a, and sets of interest, S_a, we define (M, P) to be *Pareto-optimal* if there is no other allocation (M', P') such that[2]

1. The utility of a bidder in (M, P) is no less than her utility in (M', P'); and
2. The utility of the auctioneer in (M, P) is no less than the utility in (M', P'); and
3. At least one bidder or the auctioneer is better off in (M', P') compared with (M, P).

An auction is said to be incentive compatible if it is a dominant strategy for all bidders to reveal their true valuation. An auction is said to be Pareto-optimal if the allocation it produces is Pareto-optimal. An auction is said to make no positive transfers if the allocation it produces has no positive transfers.

Related work.

The Dobzinski et al. [7, 8] multi-unit auction with budgets is based on the clinching auction by Ausubel [3]. Our setting is an extension of their work to single valued combinatorial auctions with budgets.

One possible justification for such auctions is the paper of Nisan et al. [13] describing Google's auction for TV Ads. Google's auction allows bidders to select shows, times, and days they wish to advertise on; and then give a per-ad impression bid and a total budget. The auction is not incentive compatible (even if budgets are assumed to be public). The Google TV ad interface allows agents to describe a set of interest, S_i, and a (single) per-impression bid. *I.e.*, if all slots have the same number of impressions then this fits our setting.

Ascending clinching auctions are used in the FCC spectrum auctions [12, 4, 3]. We believe that studying properties of such auctions, is not only of theoretical interest, but could help to design better auctions in practice.

[1]In [8] the authors refer to what we call auctioneer rationality by the term "weakly no positive transfers".

[2]Note that no restrictions are placed on the matching M' or on the payments P'.

Setting	Valuation	Auction	Private Data	Public Data	Properties
Multiunit Value function (f_a) No Budgets	f_a(# items)	Vickrey [15] Multiunit	f_a	—	Maximizes Social Welfare
Multiunit Additive Value v_a Finite Budgets (b_a)	$v_a \cdot$ #items	DLN [7]	v_a	b_a	Pareto Optimal
Combinatorial (S_a) Additive Value (v_a) Finite Budgets (b_a)	$v_a \cdot \#(\text{items} \in S_a)$	This Paper	v_a	b_a, S_a	Pareto Optimal

Table 1: Incentive compatible Multi unit and Single Valued Auctions

Bhattacharya et al. [5] showed that for one infinitely divisible good, a bidder cannot improve her utility by under reporting her budget. This leads to a randomized truthful in expectation algorithm (of one infinitely divisible good) with private budgets and private valuations. In [6] Bhattacharya et al. also consider revenue optimal Bayesian incentive compatible auctions with budgets.

Aggarwal et al. [1] (and independently Ashlagi et al. [2]) considered the case where bidders seek at most one item — not quite relevant for ad auctions. In this setting they give an incentive compatible auction, with respect to both valuation and budgets.

Our auction is simultaneously a specialization and a generalization of the Ausubel-Milgrom ascending package auction [4]. The Ausubel-Milgrom ascending package auction is a non-transferable utility core allocation, even when budgets are present. *I.e.*, no coalition can perform a "trade", preserving budgets, where the coalition members are better off. However, the combinatorial complexity of the set of possible packages makes this a non-polynomial time algorithm, and the incentive compatibility (with respect to valuation) was only known if all items are identical (the multi-unit case) and the budgets are public. Hatfield and Milgrom [10] present a unified way of viewing the Ausubel-Milgrom auction as well as various other matching problems (not quasi-linear) .

Our Results.

In this paper we give a combinatorial auction with the properties described above ("The Setting"). *I.e.*, our auction is incentive compatible with respect to private valuations, individually rational, and the auctioneer makes no positive transfers. We describe the auction as an ascending clinching auction. Alternately, agents may supply the mechanism with their valuation, (the budget and set of interest is assumed to be public), and the mechanism will simulate the ascending clinching auction described herein.

Our combinatorial auction is polynomial time and deterministic. This would not be possible if we were to consider the full generality of combinatorial auctions.

Our result is an extension of [7] from the case of multiple *identical* items to a new combinatorial setting where items are distinct and different agents may be interested in different items. In particular, for the non-combinatorial multi-unit setting of [7, 8], our auction and their auction produce the same allocation.

In light of the impossibility results of Dobzinski et al. [7] we cannot hope to achieve this result when budgets are private knowledge. We further show that the requirement that budgets are public knowledge is insufficient for Pareto-optimality and incentive compatibility. We show that one cannot avoid the following restrictions:

- If budgets are public but the sets of interest and the valuations are private then no truthful Pareto-optimal auction is possible.
- if budgets are public and private arbitrary valuations are allowed, no truthful and Pareto-optimal auction is possible. This follows by simple reduction to the previous claim on private sets of interest.

In Section 3 we present our mechanism. It is straightforward to show that the mechanism is truthful with respect to valuations. However, it is more involved to prove that the mechanism is Pareto-optimal — we show that the allocation produced by the mechanism is in fact Pareto-optimal in Section 4. In Section 5 we complement our positive result by showing that with public budgets, private valuations, and private sets of interest, there can be no truthful Pareto-optimal auction.

2. PARETO-OPTIMALITY AND TRADE PATHS

The main aim of this section is to introduce the main definitions: trading paths and Pareto-optimality, and to show the equivalence between allocations with no trading paths and Pareto optimal allocations. At the end of the section we will attempt to give some intuition as to why these two notions are related. First, let us define formally the notion of Pareto-optimality.

Definition 2.1 *An allocation (M, P) is Pareto-optimal if for no other allocation (M', P') are all players at least as well off, $M_i' v_i - P_i' \geq M_i v_i - P_i$, including the auctioneer, $\sum_i P_i' \geq \sum_i P_i$, with at least one of these inequalities being strict.*

We now define alternating paths.

Definition 2.2 *Consider a path*

$$\pi = (a_1, t_1, a_2, t_2, \ldots, a_{j-1}, t_{j-1}, a_j),$$

in a bipartite graph G. We say that the path π is an alternating path with respect to an allocation M if $(a_i, t_i) \in M$ and $t_i \in S_{i+1}$ for all $1 \leq i < j$. We say that an alternating path is simple if no agent appears more than once along the path. Note that all alternating paths are of even length (even number of edges).

An example of an alternating path from agent i to agent j that includes three items is shown on Figure 2. The solid edge indicates the allocation of an item to an agent whereas a dotted edge indicates that the item belongs to the preference set of the agent.

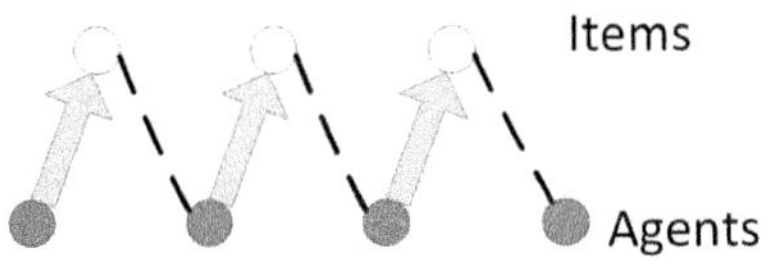

Figure 2: An alternating path

Definition 2.3 *A path* $\pi = (a_1, t_1, a_2, t_2, \ldots, a_{j-1}, t_{j-1}, a_j)$ *is called a* trading path *with respect to the allocation* (M, P) *if the following hold:*

1. *π is a simple alternating path with respect to M, (which implies that agent a_i, $i < j$, was allocated item t_i during the course of the auction).*
2. *The valuation of agent a_j, v_{a_j} is strictly greater than the valuation of agent a_1, v_{a_1}.*
3. *The remaining (unused) budget of agent a_j at the conclusion of the auction, $b^*_{a_j}$, is $\geq$ the valuation of agent a_1, v_{a_1}.*

Intuitively, trading paths, as their name suggests, represent possible trades amongst agents. A trading path describes a possible trade, i.e., item t_i is given to agent a_{i+1} for each $i = 1, \ldots, j-1$. After this trade the endpoints of the path are better off and the interior agents are not worse off. (In fact, they can all be made better off by paying a "commission" along the path).

We now move to the following equivalence:

Theorem 2.4 *Any allocation (M, P) is Pareto-optimal*[3] *if and only if*

1. *All items are sold in (M, P), and*
2. *There are no trading paths in G with respect to (M, P).*

Proof. Let $\mathcal{Q}$ be the predicate that (M, P) is Pareto-optimal, $\mathcal{R}_1$ be the predicate that all items are sold in (M, P), and $\mathcal{R}_2$ the predicate that there are no trading paths in G with respect to (M, P). We seek to show that $\mathcal{Q} \Leftrightarrow \mathcal{R}_1 \cap \mathcal{R}_2$.

$\mathcal{Q} \Rightarrow (\mathcal{R}_1 \cap \mathcal{R}_2)$: to prove this we show that $(\neg\mathcal{R}_1 \cup \neg\mathcal{R}_2) \Rightarrow \neg\mathcal{Q}$.

If both $\mathcal{R}_1$ and $\mathcal{R}_2$ are true then this becomes False $\Rightarrow \mathcal{Q}$ which is trivially true.

If the allocation (M, P) does not assign all items $(\neg\mathcal{R}_1)$ then it is clearly not Pareto-optimal $(\neg\mathcal{Q})$. We can get a better allocation by assigning all unsold items to any agent i with such items in S_i. This increases the utility of agent i.

If $\neg\mathcal{R}_2$ then there exists a trading path π in G with respect to (M, P), let $\pi = (a_1, t_1, a_2, t_2, \ldots, a_{j-1}, t_{j-1}, a_j)$, as $v_{a_j} > v_{a_1}$ and $b^*_{a_j} \geq v_{a_1}$ then we can decrease the payment of agent a_1 by v_{a_1}, increase the payment of agent a_j by the same v_{a_1}, and move item t_i from agent a_i to agent a_{i+1} for all $i = 1, \ldots, j-1$. In this case, the utility of agents $a_1, a_2, \ldots, a_{j-1}$ is unchanged, the utility of agent a_j increases by $v_{a_j} - v_{a_i} > 0$, and the utility of the auctioneer is unchanged. The sum of payments by the agents is likewise unchanged. This contradicts the assumption that (M, P) is Pareto-optimal.

We now prove that $(\mathcal{R}_1 \cap \mathcal{R}_2) \Rightarrow \mathcal{Q}$. Again we show the contrapositive: $\neg\mathcal{Q} \Rightarrow (\neg\mathcal{R}_1 \cup \neg\mathcal{R}_2)$. Assume $\neg\mathcal{Q}$, i.e., assume that (M, P) is not Pareto-optimal. Further assume $\mathcal{R}_1$, that M assigns all items. We will show $\neg\mathcal{R}_2$, i.e. that there is a trading path with respect to (M, P). Since (M, P) is not Pareto-optimal, there must be some other allocation (M', P') that is not worse for all players (including the auctioneer) and strictly better for at least one player. We can assume that (M', P') assigns all items as well, as otherwise we can take an even better allocation that would assign all items.

By Lemma 2.5 (see below) we know that M and M' are related by a set of simple paths and cycles. On a path, the first agent gives up one item, whereas the last agent receives one item more, after items are exchanged along the path. Cycles represent giving up one item in return for another by passing items around along it. Cycles don't change the number of items assigned to the bidders along the cycles so we will ignore them. Let $x_1, \ldots, x_z$ and $y_1, \ldots, y_z$ denote the start and end agents along these z alternating paths. Note that the same agent may appear multiple times amongst x_i's or multiple times amongst y_i's, but cannot appear both as an x_i and as a y_i (we can concatenate two such paths into one). Such an alternating path represents a shuffle of items between agents where agent x_j looses an item, and agent y_j gains an item when moving from M to M'. In general, these two items may be entirely different.

Assume there are no trading paths with respect to (M, P). Then it must be the case that for every one of these z alternating paths either

α. $v_{y_j} \leq v_{x_j}$ holds. Define $I = \{j | v_{y_j} \leq v_{x_j}\}$.

β. $b^*_{y_j} < v_{x_j}$ holds (where $b^*_{y_j}$ is the budget left over for agent y_j at the end of the mechanism). Define $J = \{j | b^*_{y_j} < v_{x_j}\}$.

Now, no bidder is worse off in (M', P') (in comparison to (M, P)), and the auctioneer is not worse off, and, by assumption, either

A. Some bidder is strictly better off. Or,

B. The auctioneer is strictly better off.

First, we rule out case B above: Consider the process of changing (M, P) into (M', P') as a two stage process: at first, the agents $x_1, \ldots, x_z$ give up items. During this first stage, the payments made by these agents must decrease (in sum) by at least $Z^- = \sum_{i=1}^{z} v_{x_i}$. The 2nd stage is that agents $y_1, \ldots, y_z$ receive their extra items. In the 2nd stage, the maximum extra payment that can be received from agents $y_1, \ldots, y_z$ is no more than

$$Z^+ = \sum_{j \in I} v_{y_j} + \sum_{j \in J} b^*_{y_j} \leq \sum_{j \in I} v_{x_j} + \sum_{j \in J} v_{x_j} = Z^-, \quad (1)$$

by definition of sets I and J above. Thus, the total increase in revenue to the auctioneer is $Z^+ - Z^- \leq 0$. This rules

[3] We remark that an analogous (but simpler) claim made in the proceedings version of the multi unit auction with budget paper [7] was incorrect but was corrected in [8].

out case B. Moreover, as the auctioneer cannot be worse off, $Z^+ = Z^-$ and from Equation (1) we conclude that

$$\sum_{j \in I} v_{y_j} + \sum_{j \in J} b^*_{y_j} = \sum_{j \in I} v_{x_j} + \sum_{j \in J} v_{x_j}. \quad (2)$$

By definition, we have for $j \in I$, that $v_{y_j} \leq v_{x_j}$; and for $j \in J$, we have that $b^*_{y_j} < v_{x_j}$. Thus, if $J \neq \emptyset$ then the lefthand side of Equation (2) is strictly less than the righthand side, a contradiction.

Therefore, case A must hold and it must be that $J = \emptyset$, we will conclude the proof of the theorem by showing that these two are inconsistent. So, we have that

$$\begin{aligned} M'_a v_a - P'_a &= M_a v_a - P_a && \text{for agents } a \text{ whose utility is unchanged} \\ M'_{\hat{a}} v_{\hat{a}} - P'_{\hat{a}} &> M_{\hat{a}} v_{\hat{a}} - P_{\hat{a}} && \text{for some agent } \hat{a} \\ \sum_a P'_a &= \sum_a P_a. \end{aligned}$$

We can now derive that

$$\begin{aligned} \sum_a M'_a v_a &> \sum_a M_a v_a - \left(\sum_a P'_a - \sum_a P_a\right) \\ &= \sum_a M_a v_a. \\ \Rightarrow \sum_a (M'_a - M_a) v_a &> 0. \end{aligned} \quad (3)$$

Now, whenever $a = x_j$ we decrease $M'_a - M_a$ by one, whenever $a = y_j$ we increase $M'_a - M_a$ by one. Thus, rewriting Equation (3) we get that

$$\begin{aligned} \sum_a (|\{j|a = y_j\}| - |\{j|a = x_j\}|) v_a &> 0 \\ \Rightarrow \sum_{j=1}^{z} v_{y_j} - \sum_{j=1}^{z} v_{x_j} &> 0 \\ \Rightarrow \sum_{j=1}^{z} v_{y_j} &> \sum_{j=1}^{z} v_{x_j}. \end{aligned} \quad (4)$$

But, Equation (4) is inconsistent with Equation (2) as $J = \emptyset$ implies that $I = \{1, \ldots, z\}$. □

The following technical lemma was required in the proof of Theorem 2.4 above; its proof is deferred to the full version of this paper.

Lemma 2.5 *Let M and M' be two allocations that allocate all items, then, the symmetric difference between these two allocations, $M \oplus M'$, can be decomposed into a set of simple alternating paths (with respect to M) and alternating cycles (also with respect to M) that are edge disjoint. Moreover, there are no two simple alternating paths such that one ends and the other begins at the same agent.*

The following comments will hopefully help in clarifying the notion of Pareto-optimality we use.

1. Pareto-optimality as given in Definition 2.1, allows any alternative allocation and pricing, even allowing positive transfers to the bidders. If Pareto-optimality was defined only with respect to any other allocation with no positive transfers, i.e., "*such that $P'_i \geq 0$ for all i*", then "Pareto-optimal" assignments could in fact contain trading paths.

2. Pareto-optimality as given in Definition 2.1 is a more desirable social goal than "Pareto-optimal" with no positive transfers. If we only insisted on "Pareto-optimal" assignments that forbid positive transfers then we could get assignments that are inefficient in the sense that, after the auction, bidders could trade amongst themselves and improve their utilities.

3. However, it may also be desirable that no agent actually get paid from the mechanism. Thus, it may be desirable that the actual allocation has no positive transfers ($P_i \geq 0$ for all i), yet at the same time is Pareto-optimal in the strong sense of Definition 2.1. By Theorem 2.4 after such allocation is presented, no agents will desire to trade amongst themselves. The existence of such allocation is the claim of Theorem 4.1 that applies to the auction we present in the next section.

3. DYNAMIC CLINCHING

In this section we describe our auction in detail. It can be viewed as an incentive compatible ascending auction (where incentive compatible means ex-post Nash) in the spirit of the mechanism proposed by [7] for the simpler case of multiunit auction. The ascending auction raises the price of unsold items until all items are clinched, i.e., allocated to the bidders. We describe the mechanism as a direct revelation mechanism and assume that the private value $\tilde{v}_a$ is equal to the bid v_a.

We make extensive use of maximal B-matchings (on bipartite graphs) in the course of our auction. A B-matching [14] in a graph G is a subgraph of G where vertices have degree constraints, i.e. $B_v \geq 0$ is an upper bound on the degree of v in the B-matching. Given the vector B, and a graph $G = (V, E)$ one can compute a maximal weight B-matching in polynomial time. Often in the paper we denote such B-matchings simply by *matchings*.

The main details of the auction are described by Algorithms 1, 2 and 3.

Throughout the algorithm there is always some current price p (initially zero); a set of unsold items U; current number of unsold items, m (initally equal to to total number of items); and current remaining budgets $b = (b_1, b_2, \ldots, b_n)$, where b_a is the remaining budget for agent $1 \leq a \leq n$. We also denote by d_i the current demand of agent i. The auction repeatedly computes a B-matching of unsold items, i.e., a maximal matching that assigns to agent i at most d_i items from $U \cap S_i$.

A key tool used in our auction is that of S-avoid matchings. These are maximal matchings that try to avoid, if at all possible, assigning any items to bidders in some set S. Finding such a matching requires a min-cost max-flow computation, where there is high cost to direct flow through a vertex of S. The mechanism will sell items only when the S-avoid matching will still assign items to agents of S. All items assigned to agents of S will actually be sold to agents of S.

The algorithm also keeps a set of active agents A — those with current demand greater than zero. Not all active agents are in the same position with respect to the auction. The auction will distinguish a set of *value limited agents* V —

those with valuation equal to the current price:

$$A = \{1 \le a \le n | d_a > 0\}, \quad (5)$$

$$V = \{1 \le a \le n | d_a > 0, v_a = p\}. \quad (6)$$

For every agent $1 \le i \le n$, the algorithm makes use of values D_i, D_i^+, and d_i, these values are functions of the current values of p, m, b. D_i is equal to the number of items that agent i is interested in purchasing at current p, m, and b (Equation 7). Later on, we omit these arguments in the description of the algorithm. In Equation 8 we define D_i^+, which is equal to the number of items that agent a_i would be interested in purchasing if the price were increased by an infinitesimally small amount, thus $D_i^+ \le D_i$. In addition, the algorithm maintains a vector of variables $d = (d_1, d_2, \ldots, d_n)$. The current demand d_i of agent i will either be equal to D_i or to D_i^+ depending on the state of the execution.

Formally:

$$D_i[p, m, b] = \begin{cases} \min\{m, |S_i|, \lfloor b_i/p \rfloor\} & \text{if } p \le v_i \\ 0 & \text{if } p > v_i \end{cases} \quad (7)$$

$$D_i^+[p, m, b] = \lim_{\epsilon \to 0^+} D_i[p + \epsilon, m, b]; \quad (8)$$

Observe that the algorithm repeatedly tries to sell items at the current level of demand for all the players. When no items can be sold then the demand of some active bidder a is reduced from D_a to D_a^+, for . This will reflect in the decrease by 1 of the demand of bidder a. When neither action can be done, the price increases. A step through execution of this mechanism, at the critical points, for the instance described in Figure 1, appears in Figure 3.

In general, the auction prefers to sell items only at the last possible moment (alternately phrased, the highest possible price) at which this item can still be sold while still preserving incentive compatibility. We will prove that the auction will in fact sell all items (Lemma 4.2).

Once a price has been updated, the auction checks to see if it must sell items to value limited bidders. Such bidders will receive no real benefit from the item (their valuation is equal to their payment), but this is important so as to increase the utility of the auctioneer. Our definition of Pareto-optimality includes all bidders and the auctioneer. To check if this is necessary, the auction computes a V-avoid matching, trying to avoid the bidders in V. If this cannot be done, then items are sold to these V bidders. After items are sold to value limited bidders, these bidders effectively disappear and we are only left to consider selling to active bidders. The main loop of the mechanism checks whether any items must be sold to any of the currently active bidders. This is where incentive compatibility comes into play. The auction sells an item to some bidder, a, at the lowest price where the remaining bidders total demand is such that an item can be assigned to a without creating a shortage. Again, this makes use of the $\{a\}$-avoid matching, if in the $\{a\}$-avoid matching some item is matched to a then a must be sold that item. If no item can be sold than the demand d_i of a bidder with $d_i > D^+(i)$ is reduced by setting $d_i = D^+(i)$. When neither action can be done, the price increases.

4. PARETO-OPTIMALITY

The goal of this section is to show that the final allocation produced by Algorithm 1 sells all items and contains no trading paths, thus proving the following theorem:

Algorithm 1 Combinatorial Auction with Budgets

procedure COMBINATORIAL AUCTION WITH BUDGETS($v, b, \{S_i\}$) Implicitly defined D_a, D_a^+, A, and V — see Equations (7), (8), (5) and (6).
$B(\neg\{a\})$ - number of items assigned to agents in $A \setminus \{a\}$ in $\{a\}$-avoid matching
  $p \leftarrow 0$
  while ($A \neq \emptyset$) **do**
    Sell(V)
    $A \leftarrow A - V$
    repeat
      if $\exists i | B(\neg\{i\}) < m$ **then** Sell(i)
      else
        For arbitrarily agent i with $d_i > D_i^+(p)$:
          $d_i \leftarrow D_i^+(p)$
      end if
    until $\forall i$: ($d_i = D^+(i)$) and $B(\neg\{i\}) \ge m$)
    Increase p until for some i, $D_i(p) \neq D_i^+(p)$)
  end while
end procedure

Algorithm 2 Computing an avoid matching, can be done via min cost max flow

procedure S-AVOID MATCHING
  Construct interest graph G:
  - Active agents, A, on left, capacity constraint of agent $a \in A = d_a$
  - Unsold items, U, on right, capacity constraint 1.
  - Edge (a, t) from agent $a \in A$ to unsold item $t \in U$ iff $t \in S_a$.

  Return maximal B-matching with minimal number of items assigned to agents in S, amongst all maximal B-matchings.
end procedure

Algorithm 3 Selling to a set S

procedure SELL(S)
  repeat
    Compute $Y = S$-AVOID MATCHING
    For arbitrary (a, t) in Y, $a \in S$, sell item t to agent a.
  until $B(\neg S) \ge m$
end procedure

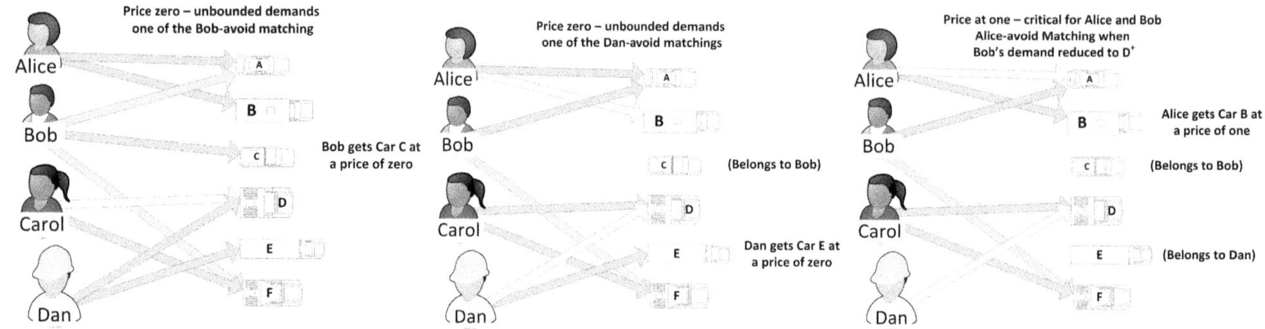

Figure 3: Significant points during mechanism execution, input from Figure 1. Example continues in Figure 4.

Theorem 4.1 *The allocation (M^*, P^*) produced by Algorithm 1 is Pareto-optimal. Moreover, the mechanism makes no positive transfers.*

We first show that the auction sells all items.

Lemma 4.2 *If every item appears in $\cup_{i=1}^{n} S_i$ then the auction will sell all items.*

PROOF. We prove that throughout the auction, there is always a matching that can sell all remaining items at the current price without exceeding the budget of any agent. As prices only increase, eventually all items must be sold. The lines below refer to Algorithm 1 unless stated otherwise.

Initially, all items can be sold at price zero. The d_a capacity constraints are all equal to $|S_a|$.

Furthermore, we argue that it is always true that all unsold items can be sold to active agents at the current price without violating the capacity constraints. We prove this invariant by case analysis of the following events:

- Increase in price followed by setting $d_a = D_a$ for each active bidder $a \in A$: The repeat loop in lines 6 – 12 ends with all the d_a's set to D_a^+ and $B(\neg\{a\}) \geq m$ for all agents a.

  Any increment in price in line 13 will set D_a equal to the previous D_a^+, which means that the new d_a's are equal to the old ones. Thus, any matching valid at the old price is valid at the new price.

- The Sell(V) operation (line 4 of Algorithm 1, Algorithm 3) sells items to agents in V only if all other unsold items can be matched to agents not in V.

- Setting $A \leftarrow A - V$ (line 5 of Algorithm 1)is OK because nothing be sold to $a \in V$ at any higher price.

- The Sell(a) operation (line 7 of Algorithm 1, Algorithm 3) sells items to agent a only if all other unsold items can be matched to other agents.

- Setting $d_i \leftarrow D_i^+(p)$ (line 10) is done only if $B(\neg\{a\}) \geq m$, i.e., all unsold items can be matched to the other agents (not including a).

Thus, the mechanism will sell all items. □

As a warm up for the proof for the single-valued combinatorial auction case we show a short proof of the theorem in the multiunit case, i.e., identical preference sets for all players.

Theorem 4.3 *The allocation (M^*, P^*) produced by Algorithm 1 is Pareto-optimal for Multi-unit auction with budgets. Moreover, the mechanism makes no positive transfers.*

PROOF. The proof is by contradiction. Assume a final allocation with any two bidders i, j, such that $v_j > v_i$, $b_j \geq v_i$, and bidder i allocated with at least one item. Denote by p the price paid for the last item allocated to bidder i from a call to Sell(V) ($i \in V$) or Sell($i|d(A/i) < m$) ($i \notin V$). Denote by M_k the number of items allocated to agent k at any time after the last item was allocated to i.

We distinguish two cases:

1. Agent $i \in V$ when it receives the item. Observe $j \notin V$. We derive a contradiction to the allocation of the item to i from the following:

$$\begin{aligned} m &= \#\text{ items to be sold to } V + \sum_{k \in A/\{V \cup j\}} M_k + M_j \\ &< \#\text{ items to be sold to } V + \sum_{k \in A/\{V \cup j\}} D_k + D_j. \end{aligned}$$

   The inequality stems from $D_j \geq M_j + 1$, since $b_j \geq v_i = p$ at the end of the auction and all M_j items have been sold to bidder j at price p or higher, and of course $\forall k, D_k \geq M_k$.

2. Agent $i \notin V$ when it receives the item. We derive a similar contradiction from the following:

$$\begin{aligned} m &= \#\text{ items to be sold to } i + \sum_{k \in A/\{i \cup j\}} M_k + M_j \\ &< \#\text{ items to be sold to } i + \sum_{k \in A/\{i \cup j\}} d_k + d_j. \end{aligned}$$

   The inequality follows from $d_j \geq M_j + 1$, since from $i \notin V$ and from the fact that all M_j items have been allocated to bidder j at price p or higher we derive $b_j \geq v_i > p$, and of course $\forall k, d_k \geq M_k$.

□

We next give the proof of the Theorem 4.1 for agents with different preference sets. We need to show that there are no trading paths in the final allocation (M^*, P^*) produced by Algorithm 1.

Consider the set of all trading paths Π in the final allocation M^*.

Definition 4.4 *We define the following for every $\pi \in \Pi$:*

- *Let Y^π be the S-avoid matching used the first time some item t is sold to some agent a where (a,t) is an edge along π. Y^π is either a V-avoid matching (line 4 of Algorithm 1) or an a-avoid matching for some agent-item edge (a,t) along π (line 7 of Algorithm 1).*
- *If Y^π is a V-avoid matching, let V^π be this set of value limited agents.*
- *If Y^π is an a-avoid matching, let a^π be this agent.*
- *Let $F^\pi \subset M^*$ be the set of edges (a,t) such that item t was sold to agent a at or subsequent to the first time that some item t' was sold to some agent a' for some edge $(a',t') \in \pi$ ((a',t') is itself in F^π).*
- *Let m^π be the number of unsold items just before the first time some edge along π was sold. I.e., m^π is equal to the number of items matched in F^π.*
- *Let p^π be the price at which item[s] were sold from Y^π.*
- *Let b_a^π be the remaining budget for agent a before any items are sold in Sell(V^π) or Sell(a^π).*

We partition Π into two classes of trading paths:

1. Π_V is the set of trading paths such that $\pi \in \Pi_V$ iff Y^π is some V^π-avoid matching used in Sell(V^π) (line 4 of Algorithm 1).
2. $\Pi_{\neg V}$ is the set set of trading paths such that $\pi \in \Pi_{\neg V}$ iff Y^π is some a^π-avoid matching used in Sell(a^π) (line 7 of Algorithm 1).

Lemma 4.5 $\Pi_V = \emptyset$.

PROOF. We need the following Claim:

Claim 4.6 *Let $\pi = (a_1, t_2, \ldots, a_{j-1}, t_{j-1}, a_j) \in \Pi_V$ be a trading path, and let (a_i, t_i) be the last edge belonging to Y^π along π. Then the suffix of π starting at a_i, $(a_i, t_i, \ldots, a_j)$, is itself a trading path.*

PROOF. This trivially follows as the valuation of a_i is equal to current price when Sell(V^π) was done (p^π), and the valuation of a_1 is $\geq p^\pi$ as edge (a_1, t_1) was unsold prior to this Sell(V^π) and does belong to the final F^π. □

From the Claim above we may assume, without loss of generality, that if $\Pi_V \neq \emptyset$ then $\exists \pi \in \Pi_V$ such that the first edge along π was also the first edge sold amongst all edges of π, furthermore, all subsequent edges do not belong to Y^π.

As agents $a \in V^\pi$ will not be sold any further items after this Sell(V^π), the items assigned to a_1 in Y^π are the same items assigned to a_1 in F^π.

We seek a contradiction to the assumption that Y^π was a V^π-avoid matching. Note that the matching F^π is a V^π-avoid matching by itself, because exactly the items assigned to V-type agents in Y^π are sold. We now show how to construct from F^π another matching that assigns less items to V-type agents.

We show that the number of items assigned to agent a_1 in F^π (which is the same as in Y^π) can be reduced by one by giving agent a_{k+1} item t_k for $k = 1, \ldots, j-1$. This is also a full matching but it remains to show that this does not exceed the capacity constraints for agent a_j, d_{a_j}.

As $d_{a_j} = D_{a_j}$ for all $a \in A$ when Sell(V^π) is done, agent a_j has remaining budget $\geq v_1$ at the conclusion of the auction, and all items assigned to agent a_j in F^π are at price $\geq p^\pi = v_1$. This implies that at the time of Sell(V^π) we have $D_{a_j} >$ the number of items assigned to a_j in F^π. Thus, we can increase the number of items allocated to a_j by one without exceeding the demand constraint $d_{a_j} = D_{a_j}$.

Now, note that a_j is not V-type agent, so the new matching constructed assigns less items to V type agents then the matching F^π. Hence, F^π is not an V^π-avoid matching, and in turn neither Y^π is V^π-avoid matching.

We've shown that $\Pi_V = \emptyset$. It remains to show that $\Pi_{\neg V} = \emptyset$.

Assume $\Pi_{\neg V} \neq \emptyset$. Order $\pi \in \Pi_{\neg V}$ by the first time at which some edge along π was sold. We know that this occurs within some Sell(a^π) for some a^π and that $a^\pi \notin V$. Let us define $\pi = (a_1, t_1, a_2, t_2, \ldots, a_{j-1}, t_{j-1}, a_j)$ be the last path in this order, and let $e = (a^\pi, t^\pi) = (a_i, t_i)$.

Recall that Y^π is the a^π-avoid matching used when item t^π was sold to agent a^π. Also, $F^\pi \subset M^*$ is the set of edges added to M^* in the course of the auction from this point on (including the current Sell(a_i)).

Lemma 4.7 *Let π, $a^\pi = a_i$, $t^\pi = t_i$, be as above, we argue that when Y^π was computed as an a^π-avoid matching there was another full matching X with the following properties:*

1. *The suffix of π from a_i to a_j:*

   $$\pi[a_i, \ldots, a_j] = (a_i, t_i, a_{i+1}, t_{i+1}, \ldots, a_{j-1}, t_{j-1}, a_j),$$

   is an alternating path with respect to X. (I.e., edges (a_k, t_k), $i \leq k \leq j-1$, belong to X).
2. *The number of items assigned to a_i in X is equal to the number of items assigned to a_i in Y^π.*
3. *The number of items assigned to a_j in X is equal to the number of items assigned to a_j in F^π.*

The proof will be given in the full version of this paper.

Corollary 4.8 $\Pi_{\neg V} = \emptyset$.

PROOF. Assume $\pi \in \Pi_{\neg V} \neq \emptyset$ and let $a^\pi = a_i$, $t^\pi = t_i$, we now seek to derive a contradiction as follows:

- When Y^π was computed there was also an an alternate full matching Y' with fewer items assigned to agent a_i, contradicting the assumption that Y^π is an a_i avoid matching. Or,
- We show that the remaining budget of agent a_j at the end of the auction, $b^*_{a_j}$, has $b^*_{a_j} < v_1$, contradicting the assumption that π is a trading path.

Let X be a matching as in Lemma 4.7 and F^π be as defined in Definition 4.4. Also, let $X(a)$, $F^\pi(a)$, be the number of items assigned to agent a in full matchings X, F^π, respectively.

We consider the following cases regarding d_{a_j} when Y^π, the a_i-avoid matching, was computed:

1. $d_{a_j} > X(a_j)$: then, like in Lemma 4.5, we can decrease the number of items sold to a_i by assigning item t_k to agent a_{k+1} for $k = i, \ldots, j-1$, without exceeding the d_{a_j} demand constraint.

2. $d_{a_j} = X(a_j)$, by subcase analysis we show that $b^\pi_{a_j} \leq (X(a_j)+1)p^\pi$:

   (a) $D_{a_j} = D^+_{a_j}$: Observe that $X(a_j) < m$, the current number of unsold items. This follows because $X(a_i) = Y^\pi(a_i) \geq 1$ by assumption that t_i was assigned to a_i in Y^π. This means that $d_{a_j} = X(a_j) < m$ so

   $$\begin{aligned} X(a_j) &= d_{a_j} = \left\lfloor b^\pi_{a_j}/p^\pi \right\rfloor > b^\pi_{a_j}/p^\pi - 1 \\ \Rightarrow b^\pi_{a_j} &< (X(a_j)+1)p^\pi. \end{aligned}$$

   (b) $D_{a_j} \neq D^+_{a_j}$: Observe that $a_j \notin V$ as $v_{a_j} > v_{a_i}$ and $a_i \notin V$. As $a_j \notin V$, the only reason that $D_{a_j} \neq D^+_{a_j}$ is because the remaining budget of agent a_j, $b^\pi_{a_j}$, is an integer multiple of the current price p^π. Then, $D^+_{a_j} = D_{a_j} - 1$ and $D_{a_j} = \lfloor b^\pi_{a_j}/p^\pi \rfloor = b^\pi_{a_j}/p^\pi$, it follows that

   $$\begin{aligned} X(a_j) &= d_{a_j} \geq D^+_{a_j} = D_{a_j} - 1 = b^\pi_{a_j}/p^\pi - 1 \\ \Rightarrow b^\pi_{a_j} &\leq (X(a_j)+1)p^\pi. \end{aligned}$$

   Note that the current price $p^\pi < v_{a_i}$ because we assume that a_i was sold t_i as a result of Sell(a_i) and not Sell(V). It is also true that $v_{a_i} \leq v_{a_1}$ as (a_i, t_i) was the first edge that was sold along π. By condition 3 of Lemma 4.7 we can deduce that

   $$b^\pi_{a_j} \leq (X(a_j)+1)p^\pi = (F^\pi(a_j)+1)p^\pi.$$

   Agent a_j is sold exactly $F^\pi(a_j)$ items at a price not lower that p^π, to at the end of the auction the remaining budget for agent a_j, $b^*_{a_j}$, is $\leq p^\pi$. This contradicts the assumption that π is a trading path since

   $$b^*_{a_j} \leq p^\pi < v_{a_i} \leq v_{a_1}.$$

□

5. MAPPING THE FRONTIER

In this paper we gave a mechanism that is incentive compatible with respect to valuation, and produces a Pareto-optimal allocation, but with various restrictions and assumptions:

- public budgets;
- public sets of interest;
- moreover, agents are restricted to have a step function valuation for items, if the item is in S_i then it's valuation is v_i, otherwise zero.

This poses the question: can we remove these assumptions/restrictions? Just how far can we go?

As for private budgets, it was shown by [7] that even for the multi unit case, one cannot achieve incentive compatibility with respect to valuation along with bidder rationality, auctioneer rationality, and obtain a Pareto-optimal allocation.

We argue that even if one assumes public budgets, the other restrictions are also necessary. This is summarized in the following theorems:

Theorem 5.1 *There is no truthful, bidder rational, auctioneer rational and Pareto-optimal auction with public budgets, b_a, private valuations, v_a, and private sets of interest, S_a.*

PROOF. We assume the step function valuations (as done throughout this paper). We also say that an agent wins an item if the item is assigned to the agent.

For the proof of the theorem consider two agents, 1 and 2, and two items t_1, t_2. Let $S_1 = \{t_1\}$ and $S_2 = \{t_1, t_2\}$.

Recall the uniqueness result of [7]:

Theorem 5.2 (Theorem 5.1 of [7]) *Let A be a truthful, bidder-rational, auctioneer rational, and Pareto-optimal multi unit auction (identical items) with 2 players with known (public) budgets b_1, b_2 that are generic[4] then if $v_1 \neq v_2$ the allocation produced by A is identical to that produced by the Dynamic clinching auction of [7] (and, in particular, with our auction when applied to these inputs).*

For all the details of the proof please see [8], as the original publication [7] includes only a sketch.

The next two lemmas allows us to argue about the payments of the auction. The proofs will be given in the fill version of this paper.

Lemma 5.3 *Consider any Pareto-optimal, incentive compatible, bidder rational and auctioneer rational combinatorial auction that produces an allocation (M, P): if agent 2 wins both items than the payment P_1 by agent 1 is zero.*

Lemma 5.4 *Consider any Pareto-optimal, incentive compatible, bidder rational and auctioneer rational combinatorial auction that produces an allocation (M, P): if agent 2 does not win item t_1 then $P_2 = 0$.*

The next lemma will tell us which matching is chosen. The proof will be given in the full version of this paper.

Lemma 5.5 *If $b_1 < b_2$, $b_1 < v_2$, and $v_1 < v_2$, then any incentive compatible, Pareto-optimal, bidder rational and auctioneer rational combinatorial auction has to assign both items to agent 2.*

We are now ready to prove the main result of this section.

Consider the case of two agents, 1 and 2, and two items t_1, t_2. Let $S_1 = \{t_1, t_2\}$ and $S_2 = \{t_1, t_2\}$. Additionally, Fix $v_1 = 10$, $v_2 = 11$, $b_1 = 4$ and $b_2 = 5$. In this case, by Theorem 5.2, the allocation must coincide with the result of the dynamic clinching auction of [7].

I.e., both agents get one of the two items, $p_1 = 3$, and $p_2 = 2$. Without loss of generality assume that item t_1

[4]Not all pairs of values are generic, but for our purposes assume that this holds for every such pair.

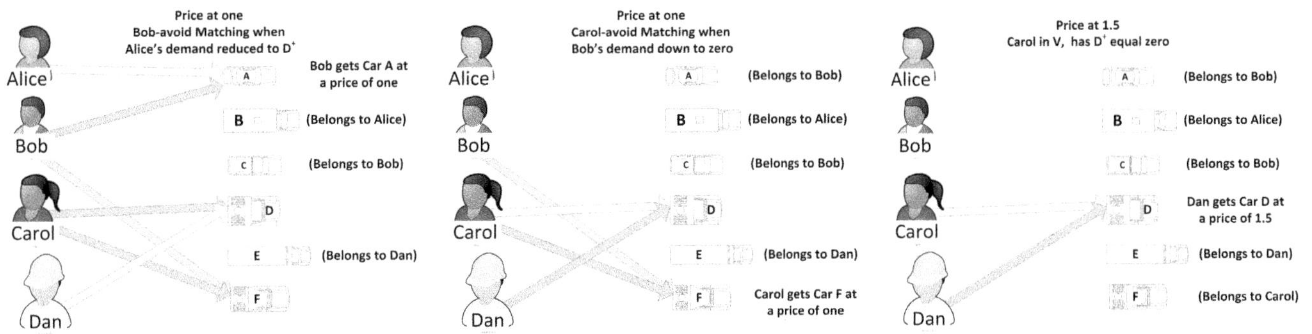

Figure 4: Significant points during mechanism execution, input from Figure 1. Sales at cost > 0.

is assigned to agent 1 with probability at least $\frac{1}{2}$ (if the mechanism is randomized).

Now, assume that the true set of interest for agent 1 was in fact $S_1 = \{t_1\}$. We argue that agent 1 now has incentive to lie about S_1:

- if agent 1 reports her true set of interest – then by Lemma 5.5 both items end up assigned to agent 2, and by Lemma 5.3 $P_1 = 0$, so her utility is zero as well;
- if agent 1 lies and reports $\{t_1, t_2\}$ as her set of interest – then with probability $\leq \frac{1}{2}$ her utility is equal to $0 - 3$, and with probability at least $\frac{1}{2}$ her utility is equal to $10 - 3 = 7$, so on average his utility is at least $-3 \cdot \frac{1}{2} + 7 \cdot \frac{1}{2} = 2$.

This concludes the proof as agent 1 has incentive to lie in any incentive compatible, Pareto-optimal, bidder rational and auctioneer rational combinatorial auction. □

Corollary 5.6 *There is no truthful, bidder rational, auctioneer rational and Pareto-optimal auction with public budgets, b_a, and private item-dependent valuations v_{at}.*

Proof. This follows immediately from Theorem 5.1. Consider the case where the private valuations v_{at} are zero for any $t \notin S_a$, and v_a for $t \in S_a$. □

6. REFERENCES

[1] G. Aggarwal, S. Muthukrishnan, D. Pál, and M. Pál. General auction mechanism for search advertising. In *WWW '09: Proceedings of the 18th international conference on World wide web*, pages 241–250, New York, NY, USA, 2009. ACM.

[2] I. Ashlagi, M. Braverman, A. Hassidim, R. Lavi, and M. Tennenholtz. Position auctions with budgets: Existence and uniqueness, 2009.

[3] L. M. Ausubel. An efficient ascending-bid auction for multiple objects. *American Economic Review*, 94(5):1452–1475, December 2004.

[4] L. M. Ausubel and P. R. Milgrom. Ascending auctions with package bidding. *Frontiers of Theoretical Economics*, 1:1019–1019, 2002.

[5] S. Bhattacharya, V. Conitzer, K. Munagala, and L. Xia. Incentive compatible budget elicitation in multi-unit auctions. *CoRR*, abs/0904.3501, 2009.

[6] S. Bhattacharya, G. Goel, S. Gollapudi, and K. Munagala. Budget constrained auctions with heterogeneous items. In *STOC '10: Proceedings of the 42nd ACM symposium on Theory of computing*, pages 379–388, New York, NY, USA, 2010. ACM.

[7] S. Dobzinski, R. Lavi, and N. Nisan. Multi-unit auctions with budget limits. In *FOCS*, pages 260–269. IEEE Computer Society, 2008.

[8] S. Dobzinski, R. Lavi, and N. Nisan. Multi-unit auctions with budget limits, 2010.

[9] B. Edelman, M. Ostrovsky, M. Schwarz. Internet advertising and the generalized second price auction: Selling billions of dollars worth of keywords. *American Economic Review*, 97, 2005.

[10] J. Hatfield and P. Milgrom. Matching with contracts. *The American Economic Review*, 95(4):913–935, 2005.

[11] P. Milgrom. *Putting auction theory to work.* Cambridge University Press, 2004.

[12] P. Milgrom. Putting auction theory to work: The simultaneous ascending auction. *Journal of Political Economy*, 108:245–272, 1998.

[13] N. Nisan, J. Bayer, D. Chandra, Tal Franji, Robert Gardner, Yossi Matias, Neil Rhodes, Misha Seltzer, Danny Tom, Hal R. Varian, and Dan Zigmond. Google's auction for tv ads. In S. Albers, A. Marchetti-Spaccamela, Y. Matias, S. E. Nikoletseas, and W. Thomas, editors, *ICALP (2)*, volume 5556 of *Lecture Notes in Computer Science*, pages 309–327. Springer, 2009.

[14] W. Pulleyblank. Dual integrality in b -matching problems. In R. W. et. al. Cottle, editor, *Combinatorial Optimization*, volume 12 of *Mathematical Programming Studies*, pages 176–196. Springer Berlin Heidelberg, 1980.

[15] W. Vickrey. Counterspeculation, auctions, and competitive sealed tenders. *The Journal of Finance*, 16(1):8–37, 1961.

Multi-Unit Auctions: Beyond Roberts

Shahar Dobzinski*
Department of Computer Science
Cornell University, Ithaca NY 14853
shahar@cs.cornell.edu

Noam Nisan†
School of Computer Science and Engineering
Hebrew University
noam@cs.huji.ac.il

ABSTRACT

We exhibit incentive compatible multi-unit auctions that are not affine maximizers (i.e., are not of the VCG family) and yet approximate the social welfare to within a factor of $1+\epsilon$. For the case of two-item two-bidder auctions we show that these auctions, termed Triage auctions, are the only scalable ones that give an approximation factor better than 2. "Scalable" means that the allocation does not depend on the units in which the valuations are measured. We deduce from this that any scalable computationally-efficient incentive-compatible auction for m items and $n \geq 2$ bidders cannot approximate the social welfare to within a factor better than 2. This is in contrast to arbitrarily good approximations that can be reached under computational constraints alone, and in contrast to the existence of incentive-compatible mechanisms that achieve the optimal allocation.

Categories and Subject Descriptors

F.2.8 [**Analysis of Algorithms and Problem complexity**]: Miscellaneous

General Terms

Theory

Keywords

Multi-Unit Auctions, Incentive Compatibility

*Supported by an Alfred P. Sloan Foundation Fellowship and a Microsoft Research New Faculty Fellowship.

†Supported by a grant from the Israeli Science Foundation, and by the Google Inter-university center for Electronic Markets and Auctions.

EC'11, June 5–9, 2011, San Jose, California, USA.

1. INTRODUCTION

Background

The field of *Algorithmic Mechanism Design* [27] designs mechanisms for achieving various computational goals, under the assumption of rational selfishness of the involved parties. The notions used are taken from the economic field of Mechanism Design, and a basic notion is that of *incentive compatibility* – where rational players are motivated to act *truthfully*. For background and survey see part II of [28]. This paper will consider only the simplest and most robust notion of incentive compatibility, that of dominant strategies in quasi-linear settings with independent private values. The typical question in the field asks for a computationally-efficient incentive compatible mechanism that implements a certain type of outcome, usually the approximate optimization of some target "social" goal. There are two variants of this challenge, the first considers situations where incentive compatibility itself is hard to achieve and the computational efficiency is just an additional burden, with the prime example being approximate minimization of the makespan in scheduling problems [27]. The second variant focuses on cases where each of the two constraints of incentive compatibility and computational efficiency can be achieved separately, and the challenge is to get them simultaneously, with the prime example being approximate welfare maximization in various types of combinatorial auctions [24].

While there has been much work and some progress on these types of challenges, with particular emphasis on the problems mentioned above of combinatorial auctions (e.g., [22, 20, 3, 15, 23, 16, 13, 6]) and scheduling (e.g., [7, 21, 2]), the basic challenge remains mostly unanswered. As noted in [22], the main issue turns out to be the richness of the domain of player's valuations, i.e., of their private information. On one extreme are single-dimensional domains where the private information of each participant is captured by a scalar (or domains very close to it, e.g., [24]). For these types of problems, incentive-compatible mechanisms are well characterized by a certain monotonicity condition and, in most cases, the challenge of reconciling incentives with computational efficiency has been met [24, 1, 5, 9, 8]. On the other extreme are problems which are "fully dimensional" (or close to fully dimensional, e.g., [29, 17]) where there is no structure on valuations, in which case a key theorem of Roberts [30] characterizes incentive compatible mechanisms as "affine maximizers" "on a sub-range" – simple generalizations of the VCG mechanism. While such affine maximizers on a sub-range are not completely powerless in polynomial time, in most cases this characterization implies impossibility of good computationally efficient truthful mechanisms. Most interesting problems, including those mentioned above, lie in an intermediate range where the valuation spaces are neither single dimensional nor fully dimensional, a range for which very little is known. The main problem seems to be the lack of a good characterization of incentive compatibility in these intermediate ranges[1]. In particular, the key unknown is whether any useful truthful non-VCG mechanisms exist in the intermediate range[2].

Multi-unit Auctions

As mentioned, the paradigmatic problems for the reconciliation of computational constraints with incentive constraints are the various subclasses of combinatorial auctions. In this paper we consider the simplest variant which exhibits this tension: multi-unit auctions. In this problem there are m identical items for sale among n bidders, where each bidder i has a valuation function $v_i : \{0...m\} \to \Re$, where $v_i(k)$ denotes player i's value for receiving k items. The valuations v_i are assumed to be monotone non-decreasing (free disposal) with $v_i(0) = 0$ (normalization). Key and implicit here is that there are no externalities: the value of bidder i depends only on what he gets rather than also on the allocation to the others. The optimization goal is to find an allocation of items to the bidders, where bidder i gets s_i items, with $\sum_i s_i \le m$, that maximizes social welfare $\sum_i v_i(s_i)$.

The problem becomes computationally challenging when the number of items m is "large", i.e., when the running time of the mechanism is not allowed to be polynomial in m but rather just in $\log m$. There are two variant models in this case, the first assumes that the valuation functions are given as "black boxes" that the algorithm may query[3], and the second assumes that the valuation functions are given in some succinct bidding language. Finding the optimal allocation is essentially a knapsack problem and is computationally hard in both models: in the black-box model it requires exponentially many queries, and in the succinct representation model, it is NP-hard. Just like Knapsack, the optimal social welfare can be approximated arbitrarily well (in both models) and has an FPTAS: approximation ratio of $1+\epsilon$ obtained in time that is polynomial in n, $\log m$, and ϵ^{-1}. This FPTAS does not imply any incentive compatible approximation though, and the question boils down to what degree of approximation can be obtained in an incentive compatible way in polynomial time.

Already in Vickrey's seminal paper [32] multi-unit auctions were considered, restricted to the case of downward sloping valuations, i.e., $v_i(k+1) - v_i(k) \le v_i(k) - v_i(k-1)$ for all $0 < k < m$. For this case the optimal allocation can be found efficiently, as an "equilibrium price" exists, which can be found by binary search (together with the optimal allocation it implies), and attaching the Vickrey payments – the point of his paper – gives incentive compatibility. For general valuations the exact optimum is computationally hard to achieve, so further work considered approximations. The single-dimensional "single minded" case was shown to have a truthful FPTAS [5], improving an earlier 2-approximation [25]. In addition, a PTAS exists for somewhat richer valuations that can be described using certain "bidding languages" (e.g., k-minded bidders for a fixed k) [14]. The general case was studied in [14] where a truthful 2-approximation was obtained using a maximal-in-range VCG mechanism[4]. It was also shown there that no computationally-efficient maximal in range VCG mechanism can achieve a better approximation ratio.

The main open problem was whether there exist *non-VCG* truthful mechanisms with a better approximation ratio. Some evidence [22, 17] supported the conjecture that that there are no such mechanisms: truthful mechanisms *for two players that always allocate all items* must be affine maximizers[5]. It should be emphasized that the question regards deterministic mechanisms, as a randomized FPTAS was obtained by [12][6].

Our Results

Given the evidences and our own intuition, we were surprised to find that there are non-VCG mechanisms that provide arbitrarily good approximation ratios:

Theorem: For every $\epsilon > 0$, there exists a truthful $(1+\epsilon)$-approximation mechanism for multi-unit auctions of m items between two players which is not an affine maximizer.

We call these mechanisms *Triage mechanisms* as they split the valuation domain into three sub-domains, depending on the ratios $v(1)/v(m)$ and $v(m-1)/v(m)$. Their payment structure mimics VCG prices with two exceptions: in the "low sub-domain", the price for a single item is decreased to a specific fraction of the value of all items, and in the "high sub-domain", the payments of all non-empty bundles are increased, by the same amount, in a specific linear way. This family of mechanisms is parameterized by three parameters (specifying a weight and the "high thresholds" for both players), with all other parameters uniquely determined by them. We also exhibit two other families of finitely approximating incentive compatible mechanisms, but their approximation factor is worse.

Our next, and main, result shows that these Triage mechanisms are the only *scalable* incentive compatible mechanisms with a good approximation ratio for the case of two items and two players. Scalability means that the auction's allocation rule does not depend on the "units" in which the valuations are given: multiplying all valuations by the same

[1]The "weak monotonicity" [4, 31] characterization is from the point of view of a single player and is not specific enough to be useful in this regard.

[2]With a single positive exception for certain multi-unit combinatorial auctions [3].

[3]The usual query assumed is a "value query", asking for $v_i(k)$ for some k, but most lower bounds hold for any queries, as they apply in the communication complexity model.

[4]The situation in multi-unit auctions mirrors, with different parameters, that of other types of combinatorial auctions where there is a gap between the computationally achievable approximation ratio and the best known computationally efficient truthful mechanism known for the multi-parameter case, which is a maximal-in-range VCG mechanism (see, e.g., [15, 18, 14]).

[5]The driving force of these and similar characterization results is the annulment of the no-externalities condition as everything not won by one player must be given to the other player.

[6]This again mirrors the situation in other types of combinatorial auctions where randomized mechanisms obtain better approximation ratios than those obtained by the known deterministic ones [11, 12].

positive constant does not change the allocation[7]. Triage mechanisms and the other mechanisms mentioned above are all scalable.

Theorem: A scalable truthful c-approximation mechanism, for $c < 2$, in a multi-unit auction of two items among two bidders must be a Triage mechanism for some choice of parameters.

This is the first characterization of truthfulness in an auction domain or, more generally, in a domain with no externalities. Our novel approach is radically different than previous characterization results (e.g., [30]): we analyze the *payment functions* of the players, rather than the allocation rule directly. The proof is quite involved and reveals the properties of the payment functions (monotonicity, continuity, invertibility, linearity, etc.) gradually, one property after the other. The proof also makes repeated use of the *approximation guarantee* of the mechanism, in contrast to previous results that characterized *all* mechanisms in a certain domain, and were not conditioned on the approximation ratio.

Triage mechanisms are affine maximizers on the "middle sub-domain" and we show that this extends to auctions of an arbitrary number of items among two players.

Theorem: A scalable truthful c-approximation mechanism, for $c < 2$, in a multi-unit auction of $m > 2$ items among two bidders, must be identical to an affine maximizer with VCG payments on the sub-domain where $v_i(1) = 0$ and $v_i(m-1) = v_i(m-2)$ for every player i.

Adopting the point of view of economics, our theorem can be interpreted as follows: Green and Laffont [19] characterize efficient (read: welfare-maximizing) mechanisms and show that VCG is the unique efficient mechanism. We relax the efficiency requirement to "approximate efficiency" and (almost completely) characterize all truthful (scalable) mechanisms in the multi-unit auction domain.

Interestingly, the theorem is not proved by direct characterization, but rather by reducing the characterization problem to the two-item case. We achieve this by introducing a new technical tool that enables us to use our two-item characterization as a black box: *induced mechanisms*. The technique might be of independent interest: it hints that in general characterizing truthful mechanisms may require only the characterization of small instances. The theorem immediately implies computational hardness, a first-of-a-kind result for an auction domain:

Theorem: Fix a model of computation in which finding the exact social-welfare maximizing allocation of m items between two players is computationally hard, even with valuations restricted to $v_i(1) = 0$ and $v_i(m-1) = v_i(m-2)$. Then, getting a scalable truthful c-approximation, for $c < 2$, of the social welfare in a multi-unit auction of m items among any $n \geq 2$ bidders, is also computationally hard.

This implies an exponential lower bound on communication in the black-box model [14] and implies NP-hardness in the succinct representation model, with, e.g., the bidding language allowing valuations to be specified by boolean circuits [22][8].

Very recently a different approach was introduced for proving the impossibility of polynomial-time truthful mechanisms for combinatorial auctions with submodular bidders that use only value queries [10]. However, we do not know how to apply the technique of [10] to multi-unit auctions. Also note that, unlike [10], the results in this paper are not restricted to a specific type of query. Furthermore, we believe that obtaining characterizations of truthful mechanisms, whenever possible, is of interest regardless of computational considerations.

The main open problem is to get rid of the scalability assumption which we believe is not really necessary for all our theorems. We note that our reduction to the two-item case from an arbitrary number of items does not require scalability, so the hurdle is really just in characterizing the two-item two-bidder case. The fixed small size would perhaps suggest a direct attack, perhaps even a computer-assisted one, but obviously we were not able to do so.

Organization

In Section 2 the setting and basic definitions are given. Triage auctions (and two additional families of auctions) are discussed in Section 3. Section 4 characterizes two-item two-bidder truthful and scalable mechanisms. Finally, Section 5 provides a characterization of mechanisms for any number of items.

2. PRELIMINARIES

The Setting

In a multi-unit auction there is a set of m identical items, and a set $N = \{1, 2, \ldots, n\}$ of bidders. Each bidder i has a valuation function $v_i : [m] \to \mathbb{R}^+$, which is normalized ($v_i(0) = 0$) and non-decreasing. Denote by V the set of all normalized an non-decreasing valuations. An allocation of the items $\vec{s} = (s_1, \ldots, s_n)$ is a vector of non-negative integers such that $\Sigma_i s_i \leq m$ (we say that an allocation $(s_1, \ldots, s_n)$ is *infeasible* if $\Sigma_i s_i > m$). Denote the set of allocations by S. The goal is to find an allocation that maximizes the welfare: $\Sigma_i v_i(s_i)$.

In most of this paper we concentrate in the case where $n = 2$. For convenience, we name the bidders Alice and Bob. We usually denote Alice's valuation by v, and Bob's by u. When $m = 2$ we sometimes use the notation $(v(1), v(2))$ to denote Alice's valuation and $(u(1), u(2))$ to denote's Bob.

Truthfulness

The reader is referred to [26] for the (standard) proofs missing in this subsection. An n-bidder mechanism for multi-unit auctions is a pair (A, p) where $A : V^n \to S$ and $p = (p^{(1)}, \cdots, p^{(n)})$, where for each i, $p^{(i)} : V^n \to \mathbb{R}$.

DEFINITION 2.1. *Let (A, p) be a mechanism. (A, p) is* truthful *if for all i, all v_i, v_i' and all v_{-i} we have that:*

$$v_i(A(v_i, v_{-i})_i) - p^{(i)}(v_i, v_{-i}) \geq v_i(A(v_i', v_{-i})_i) - p^{(i)}(v_i', v_{-i})$$

[7]In terms of pure computation, scalability comes for free as one can always scale all inputs by the largest value. We also note that the truthful randomized FPTAS of [12] is scalable.

[8]As expected, the theorem does not imply hardness for, say, single minded bidders, since finding the welfare-maximizing allocation among two single-minded bidders is computationally easy.

It is well known that an algorithm (for multi-unit auctions) is truthful if and only if each bidder is presented with a payment for each bundle t that does not depend on bidder i's valuation (i.e., $p^{(i)} : V^{n-1} \to \mathbb{R}$). Denote this payment by $p_t^{(i)}(v_{-i})$. Each bidder is allocated a bundle that maximizes his profit: $v_i(t) - p_t^{(i)}(v_{-i})$ (this is called the "taxation principle" – we will sometimes say that these payments are *induced* by v_{-i}). We note that we may assume without loss of generality that for $t > t'$, $p_t^{(1)}(v) \geq p_{t'}^{(1)}(v)$ ("payment monotonicity"): otherwise, we have a mechanism with the same allocation rule by using $p_t^{(1)}(v) = p_{t'}^{(1)}(v)$ and the appropriate tie-breaking between bundles t and t' when $u(t) = u(t')$.

We assume that the mechanisms are *individually rational*: the payment of a bidder with an identically zero valuation is 0. Every mechanism can be made individually rational as follows: let x be the number of items a bidder receives when his valuation is identically zero and subtract $p_x^{(i)}(v_{-i})$ from all prices induced by v_{-i}. Notice that the relative preference of bundles by i has not changed (since we subtract the same constant from all prices), thus the allocation rule of the mechanism may remain the same. This normalization implies, together with the price uniqueness theorem (e.g., [26]) that in our setting there is exactly one set of prices that implement each truthful mechanism.

The following definition and proposition are standard:

DEFINITION 2.2. *An is an* affine maximizer *if there exist a set of allocations $\mathcal{R}$, a constant $\alpha_i \geq 0$ for each $i \in N$, and a constant $\beta_{\vec{s}} \in \Re$ for each $\vec{s} \in S$, such that $A(v_1, ..., v_n) \in \arg\max_{\vec{s}=(s_1,...,s_n) \in \mathcal{R}} (\Sigma_i(\alpha_i v_i(s_i)) + \beta_s)$. A is called* welfare maximizer[9] *if $\beta_{\vec{s}} = 0$ for each $\vec{s} \in S$.*

PROPOSITION 2.3. *Let A be an affine maximizer (in particular, welfare maximizer). There are payments p such that (A, p) is a truthful mechanism.*

Notice that when A is a two-bidder welfare maximizer, the payments are as follows: there is a constant $w > 0$ such that for each t, a valuation v of Alice and a valuation u of Bob, $p_t^{(2)}(v) = w(v(m) - v(m - t))$ and $p_t^{(1)}(u) = (u(m) - u(m - t))/w$. We sometimes use a table notation to denote a 2-item instance. This notation is illustrated below for the 2-bidder welfare maximizer case (notice that each bidder's pavements depend only on the valuation of the other bidder):

Number of items	Alice's value	Alice's payment
One	$v(1)$	$(u(2) - u(1))/w$
Two	$v(2)$	$u(2)/w$

Number of items	Bob's value	Bob's payment
One	$u(1)$	$w(v(2) - v(1))$
Two	$u(2)$	$w \cdot v(2)$

Scalability

This paper considers two definitions of scalability.

[9]Some papers reserve the term "welfare maximizer" for affine maximizers in which all α_i's are equal, and use the term "weighted welfare maximizer" if they are not. For simplicity, we use a slightly different terminology in this paper.

DEFINITION 2.4. *An auction is* allocation scalable *if multiplying the valuations of all bidders by the same positive factor does not change the allocation.*

DEFINITION 2.5. *An auction is* payment scalable *if for each bidder i, valuations of the other bidders v_{-i}, and $\alpha > 0$, $\alpha \cdot p^{(i)}(v_{-i}) = p^{(i)}(\alpha \cdot v_{-i})$.*

We now show that every allocation scalable mechanism is also payment scalable, and thus in this paper we use the term *scalable* to denote the less restrictive notion of scalability – payment scalability.

PROPOSITION 2.6. *Let A be an allocation scalable mechanism. Then, A is also payment scalable.*

PROOF. We prove the proposition for the case of $n = 2$ but the proof easily extends to $n > 2$ bidders. Fix a valuation u of Bob. Let $B_t(u)$ be the set of all valuations v that assign Alice t items in input (v, u). Formally, $B_t(u) = \{v | A_1(v, u) = t\}$. We say that t is *in the range* of u if $B_t \neq \emptyset$.

We claim that t is in the range of u if and only if t is in the range of $\alpha \cdot u$. To see that, consider t that is in the range of u. We have that t is also in the range of $\alpha \cdot u$ since $A(v, u) = A(\alpha \cdot v, \alpha \cdot u)$. The 'only if' direction is symmetric.

We now show that for every t, t' in the range of u and $\alpha > 0$, $\alpha(p_t^{(i)}(u) - p_{t'}^{(i)}(u)) = p_t^{(i)}(\alpha \cdot u) - p_{t'}^{(i)}(\alpha \cdot u)$ (for bundles not in the range we set the payment to be equal to the payment of the next bigger bundle that is in the range, and use the appropriate tie-breaking rule). Fix some t in the range of u such that there exists $v \in B_t(u)$ that is on the border of $B_t(u)$ (in the usual topological sense). If there is no such point, Alice is always assigned t and we are done by letting $p_i^{(i)}(\alpha \cdot u) = 0$ for every $\alpha \neq 0$. Assume otherwise. There exists at least one $t' \neq t$ which is in every ϵ-neighborhood of v and in $B_{t'}$, since v is on the border. Thus we have $p_t^{(i)}(u) - p_{t'}^{(i)}(u) = v(t) - v(t')$. From scalability, we have that $\alpha \cdot v$ is on the border of $B_t(u)$ with t' playing the same role. We have that $p_t^{(i)}(\alpha \cdot u) - p_{\alpha \cdot t'}^{(i)}(u) = \alpha(v(t) - v(t')) = \alpha(p_t^{(i)}(u) - p_{t'}^{(i)}(u))$.

We continue similarly. Fix $t'' \neq t, t''$ where there exists $v \in B_{t''}(u)$, and v is on the border of $B_t \cup B_{t'}$. Thus, in every ϵ-neighborhood of v there exists a valuation v' for which $v' \in B_t$ or $v' \in B_{t''}$. Without loss of generality assume that $u' \in B_t$ (otherwise, switch the roles of t and t'). By using scalability similarly to the arguments above, we get that $v(t) - v(t'') = p_t^{(i)}(u) - p_{t''}^{(i)}(u)$, and consequently we also have $\alpha(v(t) - v(t'')) = p_t^{(i)}(\alpha \cdot u) - p_{t''}^{(i)}(\alpha \cdot u) = \alpha(p_t^{(i)}(u) - p_{t'}^{(i)}(u))$. The proof continues similarly until all bundles in the range are considered. □

3. THE TRIAGE AUCTION

We present three families of truthful mechanisms for multi-unit auctions that provide a bounded approximation ratio for multi-unit auctions with two bidders. Each of the families contain mechanisms that are not affine maximizers. The first family, the Triage auction, includes mechanism that guarantee an approximation ratio of $1 + \epsilon$, and the next sections show that triage auctions are the only two-item truthful and scalable mechanisms that provide an approximation ratio better than 2. The other two families – shifted welfare maximizers and fractions auctions – provide an approximation of almost 2. We postpone their description to the full version. To the best of our knowledge all previously known finitely-approximating mechanisms are either affine maximizers or are essentially single-parameter mechanisms (i.e., each bidder either receives all items, or no items at all).

We describe the mechanisms by specifying the payment functions of the bidders (recall that each function depends only on the other bidder's valuation). Truthfulness is obvious since each bidder is allocated a bundle that maximizes his profit, and we are left only with proving feasibility and analyzing the approximation ratio.

DEFINITION 3.1. *The Triage auction is parameterized by three parameters, w, θ_A, θ_B, for $w > 0$, $0 \leq \theta_A, \theta_B \leq 1$, and $\theta_A \geq 1 - \theta_B$. The payment functions are:*

- $p_m^{(2)}(v) = wv(m)$ *if* $v(1) < \theta_A v(m)$, *and* $p_m^{(2)}(v) = \frac{wv(1)}{\theta_A}$ *otherwise.*
- *For* $2 \leq k \leq m-1$, $p_k^{(2)}(v) = p_m^{(2)}(v) - w \cdot v(m-k)$.
- $p_1^{(2)}(v) = p_m^{(2)}(v) - wv(m-1)$ *if* $v(m-1) > (1-\theta_B)v(m)$, *and* $p_1^{(2)}(v) = p_m^{(2)}(v) - w(1-\theta_B)v(m)$ *otherwise (notice that in the latter case we have in fact* $p_m^{(2)}(v) = wv(m)$*).*

and

- $p_m^{(1)}(u) = w^{-1}u(m)$ *if* $u(1) < \theta_B u(m)$, *and* $p_m^{(1)}(u) = \frac{w^{-1}u(1)}{\theta_B}$ *otherwise.*
- *For* $2 \leq k \leq m-1$, $p_k^{(1)}(u) = p_m^{(1)}(u) - w^{-1} \cdot u(m-k)$.
- $p_1^{(1)}(u) = p_m^{(1)}(u) - w^{-1}u(m-1)$ *if* $u(m-1) > (1-\theta_A)u(m)$, *and* $p_1^{(1)}(u) = p_m^{(1)}(u) - w^{-1}(1-\theta_A)u(m)$ *otherwise (again, in the latter case* $p_m^{(1)}(u) = w^{-1}u(m)$*).*

THEOREM 3.2. *The* (w, θ_A, θ_B)*-Triage auction is feasible. The* $(1, \theta_A, \theta_B)$*-Triage auction provides an approximation ratio of* $\max(\frac{1}{\theta_A}, \frac{1}{\theta_B})$.

We remark that when $w = \theta_A = \theta_B = 1$ we get the VCG mechanism. We also note that Section 5 gives a proof that that Triage auctions require exponential time to run.

Before proving the theorem we introduce an important definition:

DEFINITION 3.3. *Fixing the other bidder's valuation, we say that a bundle of s items is in the* winning set *of a bidder, if this bundle maximizes his profit.*

For the algorithms we present in this paper, we assume that the algorithm chooses an allocation (s,t) with the maximal value such that s is in the winning set of Alice and t is in the winning set of Bob.

PROOF. We will use the following claim several times:

CLAIM 3.4. *For triage auctions with $w = 1$, for each optimal allocation $(k, m-k)$, Alice's winning set contains at least one of the following bundles: k items, one item, or no items. Similarly, Bob's winning set contains at least one of the following bundles: $m-k$ items, one item, or no items.*

PROOF. We will show that the equation $v(k) - p_k^{(1)}(u) \geq v(t) - p_t^{(1)}(u)$ holds for $t \neq 0, 1$. The equation implies that Alice prefers k items over t items, thus if t is in the winning set so does k, as needed. To see that the equation holds, observe that for each $t \neq 1, 0$ we have that $p_k^{(1)}(u) - p_t^{(1)}(u) \geq u(m-k) - u(m-t)$. Since $(k, m-k)$ is an optimal allocation, we also have that $v(k) + u(m-k) \geq v(t) + u(m-t)$. Together we have that $v(k) - p_k^{(1)}(u) \geq v(t) - p_t^{(1)}(u)$, for $t \neq 0, 1$. □

LEMMA 3.5. *The* (w, θ_A, θ_B)*-Triage auction is feasible.*

PROOF. We first note that without loss of generality we may assume that $w = 1$ (since multiplying one bidder's payments by w and dividing the other's by the same w maintains feasibility).

Consider first an optimal allocation $(k, m-k)$ where $k \neq 0, m$. We claim that in this case the mechanism is feasible: by Claim 3.4, Alice's winning set contains at least one of the following bundles: 0, 1, or k items. Similarly, Bob's winning set contains at least one of the following bundles: 0, 1, $m-k$. Thus there is a feasible allocation (s,t) such that s is in the winning set of Alice and t is in the winning set of Bob.

Thus from now on it suffices to assume that in all optimal allocations at least one bidder is assigned the empty bundle. We therefore assume that $(m, 0)$ is an optimal allocation (the case where $(0, m)$ is an optimal allocation is symmetric). By Claim 3.4 Bob's winning set contains at least one of the following: the empty bundle or the bundle of one item (the optimality of $(m, 0)$ implies that $v(m) \geq u(m)$, therefore if the bundle of m items is in the winning set, so is the empty bundle). Thus, we only have to show that if Bob's winning set contains only the bundle of 1 item, then Alice's winning set contains bundles that have less than m items.

If Bob's winning set contains only the bundle of one item, this implies that $u(1) > p_1^{(2)}(v)$. The definition of triage auction implies that $u(1) > v(m) - v(m-1)$ or $u(1) > v(m)\theta_B$, depending on the ratio between $v(m-1)$ and $v(m)$. The first case cannot happen since it implies that $u(1) + v(m-1) > v(m)$, which is false since we assumed that $(m, 0)$ is an optimal allocation. In the second case we have that $p_m^{(1)} = \frac{u(1)}{\theta_B}$, since $u(1) > v(m)\theta_B \geq u(m)\theta_B$. Therefore, the bundle of m items is not in Alice's winning set since $v(m) < \frac{u(1)}{\theta_B}$. □

LEMMA 3.6. *The* $(1, \theta_A, \theta_B)$*-Triage auction provides an approximation ratio of* $\max(\frac{1}{\theta_A}, \frac{1}{\theta_B})$.

PROOF. Let $(k, m-k)$ be an optimal allocation. In case Alice has the bundle of k items in her winning set and Bob has the bundle of $m-k$ items in his winning set then the approximation ratio is 1. By Claim 3.4, the only other cases to consider are when at least one of the bidders (without loss of generality Alice) does not have these bundles in his winning set.

The first case we consider is when Alice's winning set does not contain the bundle of k items, but contains the empty bundle (in particular, we have that $k \neq 0$). Since the empty bundle has a zero profit, it means that the profit from the bundle of k items is negative: $v(k) < p_k^1(u)$. By the definition of the payment function we either have that $p_k^1(u) \geq u(m) - u(m-k)$ or that $p_k^1(u) = \frac{u(1)}{\theta_B} - u(m-k)$.

The first option does not occur since otherwise $v(k) < u(m) - u(m-k)$. In other words, the social welfare of the allocation $(0, m)$ is bigger than the social welfare of the allocation $(k, m-k)$, a contradiction to the optimality of the latter. Thus, the second option occurs and in particular:

$$v(m) < \frac{u(1)}{\theta_B} \quad (1)$$

Since Alice's profit for the bundle of k items is negative, (i.e., $v(k) < \frac{u(1)}{\theta_B} - u(m-k)$), we have, in particular, that $v(m) < \frac{u(1)}{\theta_B}$. Therefore, to prove an approximation ratio of $\frac{1}{\theta_B}$, it suffices to show that that Bob has at least one non-empty bundle in his winning set. Suppose not, i.e.: $u(1) < p_1^{(2)}(v) \leq \theta_B v(m)$ (the last inequality is from the definition of the payment function – the payment for one item is always at most $\theta_B v(m)$). But then, $\frac{u(1)}{\theta_B} \leq v(m)$, a contradiction to (1).

We are left with considering the case where the only bundle in Alice's winning set is the bundle of one item. We start by showing that $u(m-1) \leq (1-\theta_A)u(m)$. Suppose for contradiction that $u(m-1) > (1-\theta_A)u(m)$. Since the bundle of one item maximizes the profit: $v(1) - p_1^{(1)}(u) > v(k) - p_k^{(1)}(u)$. Using the definition of the payment function: $v(1) + u(m-1) > v(k) + u(m-k)$. In other words, the allocation $(k, m-k)$ is not optimal, a contradiction. Thus we have established that

$$u(m-1) \leq (1-\theta_A)u(m) \quad (2)$$

Recall that the bundle of one item is profitable for Alice. Using (2) and the definition of the payment function, we claim that:

$$v(1) \geq \theta_A u(m) \quad (3)$$

Since the bundle of one item maximizes the profit, using the definition of the payment function: $v(1) + u(m-1) > v(k) + u(m-k)$. Using (2) we have that:

$$v(1) + (1-\theta_A)(m) > v(k) + u(m-k) \quad (4)$$

Thus, the approximation ratio is no worse than $\frac{v(k)+u(m-k)}{v(1)} \leq \frac{v(1)+(1-\theta_A)u(m)}{v(1)} \leq 1 + \frac{(1-\theta_A)u(m)}{\theta_A u(m)} \leq \frac{1}{\theta_A}$ (where the leftmost inequality is due to (4), and the middle one is due to (3)). □

4. CHARACTERIZATION OF SCALABLE TWO-ITEM AUCTIONS

This section is devoted to proving the following characterization result:

THEOREM 4.1 (TWO-ITEM CHARACTERIZATION). *The only feasible, scalable and truthful auctions with an approximation ratio strictly better than 2 for two identical goods and two bidders are triage auctions for some (w, θ_A, θ_B).*

We now provide a brief road map to the proof of the theorem. Very differently from Roberts' theorem proof, we analyze the *payment functions* of the bidders (rather then the allocation rule) and show that the payment functions are identical to the payment functions of some triage auction. Notice that in the two-item case, the payment functions of a triage auction are defined using three different regions that correspond to the ratio between the value for two items and the value for one item: high, mid, and low. The proof of the theorem is quite involved and for readability we divide it into subsections that roughly correspond to these regions. Subsection 4.1 gives an alternative definition of the triage auction, for the special case where $m = 2$, that is easier for us to work with. Subsection 4.2 characterizes the payment function for two items. The results of subsection 4.2 hold for any scalable mechanism with a bounded approximation ratio, not just ones with an approximation ratio better than 2. The next subsections are devoted to characterizing the payment functions for one item. Subsection 4.3 defines and "separates" the high-range from the mid and low ranges: it shows that, roughly speaking, a valuation that is not in the high range induces payment (for one item) that is also not in the high range. Due to lack of space we defer the next sections of the proof to the full version, and keep here only the first simpler parts: the next subsection (in the full version) proves some basic properties, like continuity, of the payment function in the low and mid range. The central part of the proof shows that the payment functions in the mid range are equivalent to the payment functions of weighted VCG. We conclude the proof with analyzing the value of the transition points between the high and mid range, and with characterizing the high range.

4.1 An Alternative Description of the Triage Auction with Two Items

DEFINITION 4.2. *Let $p, q : [0,1] \to \Re^+$ and $f, g : [0,1] \to [0,1]$ be real valued functions and r, s be two variables that take values in $[0,1]$. The scalable mechanism based on p and q is given by the following table.*

Number of items	*Alice's value*	*Alice's payment*
One	rv	$g(s) \cdot q(s) \cdot u$
Two	v	$q(s) \cdot u$

Number of items	*Bob's value*	*Bob's payment*
One	su	$f(r) \cdot p(r) \cdot v$
Two	u	$p(r) \cdot v$

PROPOSITION 4.3. *For any $p, q : [0,1] \to \Re^+$ and $f, g : [0,1] \to [0,1]$, the scalable mechanism based on them is scalable and truthful (but may be infeasible and allocate more than 2 items). Any truthful scalable mechanism (even a non-feasible one as long as it allocates at most two items to any bidder) is equivalent to one based on some functions.*

The proof of the proposition can be found in the full version. We now give an alternative (equivalent) definition of the triage auction, for the $m = 2$ case.

DEFINITION 4.4. *The (w, θ_A, θ_B)-triage auction for $w > 0$ and $0 \leq \theta_A, \theta_B \leq 1$, $\theta_A \geq 1 - \theta_B$, is the scalable mechanism based on:*

- *For $r \leq 1 - \theta_B$: $f(r) = \theta_B$, and $p(r) = w$.*
- *For $1 - \theta_B \leq r \leq \theta_A$: $f(r) = 1 - r$, and $p(r) = w$.*
- *For $r \geq \theta_A$: $f(r) = 1 - \theta_A$, and $p(r) = wr/\theta_A$.*

and

- *For $s \leq 1-\theta_A$: $g(s)=\theta_A$, and $q(s)=w^{-1}$.*
- *For $1-\theta_A \leq s \leq \theta_B$: $g(s)=1-s$, and $q(s)=w^{-1}$.*
- *For $s \geq \theta_B$: $g(s)=1-\theta_B$, and $q(s)=w^{-1}s/\theta_B$.*

4.2 Characterizing the Payment for Two Items

The results in this section hold for any scalable and truthful mechanism with a bounded approximation ratio. We usually prove the theorem only for the function p. The proof for q is symmetric.

LEMMA 4.5. *The function p is monotone non-decreasing.*

PROOF. Assume towards contradiction that for some $r' > r$ we have $p(r') < u < u' < p(r)$. Since $u > p(r')$, on inputs $(r', 1)$ and $(0, u)$ Bob must win both items, so Alice cannot win anything. Notice that $(r, 1)$ wins nothing against $(0, u'(1+\epsilon))$ (by payment scalability, $(0, u'(1+\epsilon))$ induces bigger payments than $(0, u')$, and Alice did not win any items with the bigger valuation $(r, 1)$), but also Bob does not win both items since $u'(1+\epsilon) < p(r)$ for small enough $\epsilon > 0$, so the total welfare achieved is 0 contradicting finite approximation. □

LEMMA 4.6 (WEIGHTING). $p(0)\cdot q(0) = 1$.

PROOF. Consider the following input:

Number of items	Alice's value	Alice's payment
One	0	?
Two	v	$uq(0)$

Number of items	Bob's value	Bob's payment
One	0	?
Two	u	$vp(0)$

The only allocations that give finite approximation ratio on inputs of the form $(0, v)$ and $(0, u)$ are those that give both items to one of the bidders. If $u < vp(0)$ then Bob does not win two items; whereas if $u > vp(0)$ then he wins both items, and dually for Alice. So we get a contradiction to feasibility if $u > vp(0)$ and $v > uq(0)$, i.e., if $p(0)q(0) < 1$. On the other hand, if $u < vp(0)$ and $v < uq(0)$, i.e., if $p(0)q(0) > 1$, then we get a total welfare of 0, contradicting finite approximation ratio. □

At this point we are ready to give a more precise definition of the payment function. We start with the low range, i.e., when $r < g(0)$. In particular we show that the function is constant in this range.

LEMMA 4.7 (LOW RANGE). *If $r < g(0)$ then $p(r) = p(0)$.*

PROOF. Assume that $p(r) \neq p(0)$ then, using monotonicity, let $p(r) > u' > u > p(0)$. On input $(0, 1)$ and $(0, u)$ Bob gets both items (since $u > p(0)$) and so Alice must get none. On inputs $(r, 1)$ and $(0, u')$ Alice gets at most 1 item (since, by the scalability of the payments, the payment induced by Bob for two items has increased), but since $u' < p(r)$ Bob does not get two items, and so for finite approximation, Alice must get an item, so $r \geq u'g(0)q(0) \geq p(0)q(0)g(0) = g(0)$. □

The following claim will be helpful in analyzing the payment function in the high range:

CLAIM 4.8. $p(r) \geq r/(g(0)q(0))$.

PROOF. Let $u > p(r)$, then on input $(r, 1)$ and $(0, u)$ Bob gets both items. Alice's payment for a single item is $ug(0)q(0)$ which for feasibility must be at least r. Since this holds for all $u > p(r)$ we get that $r \leq p(r)g(0)q(0)$ as required. □

For the high range ($r > g(0)$) we show that the payment grows in a specific linear way:

LEMMA 4.9 (HIGH RANGE). *If $r > g(0)$ then $p(r) = r/(g(0)q(0))$.*

PROOF. We will prove the contra-positive which by the previous claim assumes $p(r) > u > r/(g(0)q(0))$. Consider the following input:

Number of items	Alice's value	Alice's payment
One	r	$uq(0)g(0)$
Two	1	$uq(0)$

Number of items	Bob's value	Bob's payment
One	0	?
Two	u	$p(r)$

In this case Bob cannot win both items so he gets a value of 0. By the choice of u, Alice's payment for two items is $uq(0) > r/g(0)$ is greater than 1, thus she cannot win two items. Thus for finite approximation she must win one item and thus $r \geq uq(0)g(0)$ and since this is true for every $u < p(r)$, we have $r \geq p(r)g(0)q(0)$, contradiction. □

At this point we have completed the required characterization of p and q.

DEFINITION 4.10. *Let $w = p(0)$, $\theta_A = g(0)$, and $\theta_B = f(0)$.*

LEMMA 4.11 (SUMMARY OF SUBSECTION). *For $r \leq \theta_A$ we have that $p(r) = w$ and for $r \geq \theta_A$ we have $p(r) = wr/\theta_A$. Similarly, for $s \leq \theta_B$ we have that $q(s) = w^{-1}$ and for $s \geq \theta_B$ we have $q(s) = w^{-1}s/\theta_B$.*

PROOF. The low range lemma states the required fact for $r < \theta_A$. The high range lemma states the required fact for $r > \theta_A$, taking into account the inverse lemma, $p(0)q(0) = 1$, the same holds for q, replacing w with w^{-1}, again relying on $p(0)q(0) = 1$. For $r = \theta_A$ we observe that $p(r) = w$ since p is a monotone function and approaches w above and below w. □

4.3 Separating the high range

In this section we show that for $r \leq \theta_A$ we have that $f(r) \leq \theta_B$. Similarly it follows that for $s \leq \theta_B$ we have that $g(s) \leq \theta_A$. Note that by the previous section $r > \theta_A$ if and only if $p(r) > w$, and this last condition is what drives this section.

At this point we separate into two cases, according to whether $r > wf(r)$. We start with the easy case: we show that if the payment for one item is "too high" then we do not get the required approximation ratio.

LEMMA 4.12 (CASE I). *If* $r \le \theta_A$ *and* $r \le wf(r)$ *then* $f(r) \le \theta_B$.

PROOF. Assume by way of contradiction that $f(r) > \theta_B$ and so $q(f(r)) > w^{-1}$, and for ϵ small enough consider the input:

Number of items	Alice's value	Alice's payment
One	r	?
Two	1	$w(1-\epsilon)q(f(r)) > 1$

Number of items	Bob's value	Bob's payment
One	$f(r)(1-\epsilon)w$	$f(r)w$
Two	$(1-\epsilon)w$	w

Notice that Bob gets negative utility from taking an item or two items and thus takes nothing. Alice gets negative utility from taking two items so can take at most a single item. The total welfare is thus at most r, whereas the social optimum is at least $r + f(r)(1-\epsilon)w$. Since $r \le wf(r)$ this is a contradiction to better than 2-approximation. □

For the second case we first need to prepare two lemmas and a corollary.

LEMMA 4.13 (WEAK ONE-SIDE INVERSE). *If* $r \le \theta_A$ *then for any* $\delta > 0$, $wg(f(r)-\delta)q(f(r)-\delta) \ge r$.

PROOF. Assume to the contrary $wg(f(r)-\delta)q(f(r)-\delta) < r$ and consider the following input:

Number of items	Alice's value	Alice's payment
One	r	$wg(f(r)-\delta)q(f(r)-\delta)(1+\epsilon) < r$
Two	1	?

Number of items	Bob's value	Bob's payment
One	$(f(r)-\delta)w(1+\epsilon)$	$wf(r)$
Two	$w(1+\epsilon)$	w

Bob takes two items. However, when ϵ is small enough, Alice gets positive utility from one item so she will take (at least) a single item, contradicting feasibility. □

LEMMA 4.14. *For* $r > \theta_A$ *we have that* $r > f(r)p(r)$.

PROOF. Consider the input:

Number of items	Alice's value	Alice's payment
One	r	?
Two	1	$q(f(r))p(r)(1-\epsilon)$

Number of items	Bob's value	Bob's payment
One	$f(r)p(r)(1-\epsilon)$	$f(r)p(r)$
Two	$p(r)(1-\epsilon)$	$p(r)$

Bob has negative utility for either one item or two items. Since $p(r) > w$ and $q(f(r)) \ge w^{-1}$, Alice has negative utility for two items, as long as ϵ is small enough. Thus the total welfare is at most r, whereas the social optimum is at least $r + f(r)p(r)(1-\epsilon)$, so for better than 2-approximation we must have $r > f(r)p(r)$. □

COROLLARY 4.15. *If* $f(r) > \theta_B$ *then* $f(r) > g(f(r))q(f(r))$.

PROOF. This is the previous lemma with the roles of the players switched and with $s = f(r)$. □

We are now ready to handle the second case:

LEMMA 4.16 (CASE II). *If* $r \le \theta_A$ *and* $r > wf(r)$ *then* $f(r) \le \theta_B$.

PROOF. Assume towards contradiction that there exists $\delta > 0$ such that $f(r) - \delta > \theta_B$. Combining the weak one-sided inverse lemma and the previous corollary we have that $f(r) - \delta > g(f(r)-\delta)q(f(r)-\delta) \ge r/w$; Contradiction. □

Which concludes this subsection:

LEMMA 4.17. *For* $r \le \theta_A$ *we have* $f(r) \le \theta_B$. *For* $s \le \theta_B$ *we have* $g(s) \le \theta_B$.

PROOF. The Case I and Case II lemmas cover all possibilities for f; for g the situation is symmetric. □

5. CHARACTERIZING MECHANISMS FOR ANY NUMBER OF ITEMS

We showed that every two-item scalable mechanism that provides an approximation ratio better than 2 is a triage auction. This section gives an almost complete characterization for truthful and scalable mechanisms that guarantee an approximation ratio better than 2 for any number of items. In particular this section's characterization implies that truthful and scalable mechanisms for multi-unit auctions cannot guarantee an approximation ratio better than 2 in polynomial-time.

The two-item characterization is used as a black box to characterize mechanisms for more items. Importantly, the scalability assumption is not used in this section. In other words, proving that triage auctions are the only truthful mechanisms (scalable or not) that provide an approximation ratio better than 2 in multi-unit auctions with only two items, would immediately imply our characterization result for any number of items, and in particular would imply an unconditional lower bound on the power of all polynomial time truthful mechanisms. All missing proofs appear in the full version.

5.1 Induced Mechanisms: Definition and Basic Properties

Our main working horses will be induced mechanisms. Induced mechanisms allow us to define a two-item mechanism given an m-item mechanism. By leveraging our two-item characterization, we show that the induced two-item mechanisms are triage auctions. We then study the relationship between all induced mechanisms and prove that many of them must be welfare maximizers. We show that this implies that the m-item mechanism we started with must have a very specific form, as needed.

DEFINITION 5.1. *Let* l_1, h_1 *be such that* $1 \le l_1 < h_1 \le m$. *The* (l_1, h_1)-extension *of a two-item valuation* v, *denoted* v^{l_1,h_1}, *is defined as follows: for every* $k < l_1$, $v^{l_1,h_1}(k) = 0$. *For every* $h_1 > k \ge l_1$, $v^{l_1,h_1}(k) = v(1)$. *For every* $k \ge h_1$, $v^{l_1,h_1}(k) = v(2)$.

Definition 5.2 (Induced Mechanism). *Let A be a mechanism for multi-unit auctions with m items and 2 bidders. Let l_1, h_1, l_2, h_2 be positive integers with the following constraints: $l_1 < h_1 \leq m$, $l_2 < h_2 \leq m$, $l_1+l_2 \leq m$, $l_1+h_2 > m$ and $l_2+h_1 > m$. Define the* induced mechanism A^{l_1,h_1,l_2,h_2} *for 2 items as follows: given two valuations v and u run A with the (l_1,h_1)-extended valuation v^{l_1,h_1} and the (l_2,h_2)-extended valuation $u^{(l_2,h_2)}$. Let (a_1,a_2) be the output allocation of A and (p_1,p_2) be the payments the bidders are charged in A. If $a_1 < l_1$ then let $a_1' = 0$, if $l_1 \leq a_1 < h_1$ then let $a_1' = 1$, otherwise let $a_1 = 2$. If $a_2 < l_2$ then let $a_2' = 0$, if $l_2 \leq a_2 < h_2$ then let $a_2' = 1$, otherwise let $a_2 = 2$. The output of A^{l_1,h_1,l_2,h_2} on v and u is (a_1', a_2'). Alice's payment is p_1 and Bob's payment is p_2.*

Proposition 5.3. *Let A be a truthful and scalable mechanism for multi-unit auctions with m items and 2 bidders that provides an approximation ratio of α. Let A^{l_1,h_1,l_2,h_2} be an induced mechanism. A^{l_1,h_1,l_2,h_2} is feasible, truthful, scalable, and provides an approximation ratio of α.*

In this section we denote the $p^{(2)}$ function of A (the payments induced by Alice) by f and by f^{l_1,h_1,l_2,h_2} the $p^{(2)}$ function of the induced mechanism A^{l_1,h_1,l_2,h_2}. We denote by g the $p^{(1)}$ function of A (the payments induced by Bob) and by g^{l_1,h_1,l_2,h_2} the $p^{(1)}$ function of the induced mechanism A^{l_1,h_1,l_2,h_2}. As a corollary of Proposition 5.4 we get the following relationship between the payment functions of A and its induced mechanisms.

Corollary 5.4. *Let v be a two-item valuation and let $v^{(l_1,h_1)}$ be its (l_1,h_1)-extension. Let l_2, h_2 be such that A^{l_1,h_1,l_2,h_2} is an induced mechanism. $f_{l_2}(v^{h_1,l_1}) = f_1^{l_1,h_1,l_2,h_2}(v)$ and $f_{h_2}(v^{h_1,l_1}) = f_2^{l_1,h_1,l_2,h_2}(v)$.*

Symmetrically, let u be a two-item valuation and let $u^{(l_2,h_2)}$ be its (l_2,h_2)-extension. Let l_1, h_1 be such that A^{l_1,h_1,l_2,h_2} is an induced mechanism. $g_{l_1}(u^{h_2,l_2}) = g_1^{l_1,h_1,l_2,h_2}(u)$ and $g_{h_1}(u^{h_2,l_2}) = g_2^{l_1,h_1,l_2,h_2}(u)$.

5.2 Relations between Induced Mechanisms

Let A be a scalable and truthful mechanism for multi-unit auctions for m items with an approximation ratio better than 2. By our characterization and the discussion above above we have that all induced mechanisms of A are triage auctions. Denote the parameters of the triage mechanism A^{l_1,h_1,l_2,h_2} by $\theta_A^{l_1,h_1,l_2,h_2}, \theta_B^{l_1,h_1,l_2,h_2}, w^{l_1,h_1,l_2,h_2}$. The point of this subsection is to study the relations between the parameters of the induced triage mechanisms of A.

Claim 5.5. *Let A be a truthful and scalable mechanism for multi unit auctions with m items that provides an approximation ratio better than 2. Let A^{l_1,h_1,l_2,h_2} and $A^{l_1,h_1,l_2,h_2'}$ be two induced mechanisms of A. Then, $w^{l_1,h_1,l_2,h_2} = w^{l_1,h_1,l_2,h_2'}$, $\theta_A^{l_1,h_1,l_2,h_2} = \theta_A^{l_1,h_1,l_2,h_2'}$, and $\theta_B^{l_1,h_1,l_2,h_2} = \theta_B^{l_1,h_1,l_2,h_2'}$. Symmetrically, let A^{l_1,h_1,l_2,h_2} and A^{l_1,h_1',l_2,h_2} be two induced mechanisms of A. Then, $w^{l_1,h_1,l_2,h_2} = w^{l_1,h_1',l_2,h_2}$, $\theta_A^{l_1,h_1,l_2,h_2} = \theta_A^{l_1,h_1',l_2,h_2}$, and $\theta_B^{l_1,h_1,l_2,h_2} = \theta_B^{l_1,h_1',l_2,h_2}$.*

Claim 5.6. *Let A be a truthful and scalable mechanism for multi unit auctions with m items that provides an approximation ratio better than 2. Let A^{l_1,h_1,l_2,h_2} and A^{l_1,h_1,l_2',h_2} be two induced mechanisms of A. Then, $\theta_A^{l_1,h_1,l_2,h_2} = \theta_A^{l_1,h_1,l_2',h_2}$ and $w^{l_1,h_1,l_2,h_2} = w^{l_1,h_1,l_2',h_2}$. Symmetrically, let A^{l_1,h_1,l_2,h_2} and A^{l_1',h_1,l_2,h_2} be two induced mechanisms of A. Then, $\theta_B^{l_1,h_1,l_2,h_2} = \theta_B^{l_1',h_1,l_2,h_2}$ and $w^{l_1,h_1,l_2,h_2} = w^{l_1',h_1,l_2,h_2}$.*

We now use the claims to prove that all induced mechanisms share the same w. Thus, after proving it we may denote the w^{l_1,h_1,l_2,h_2} parameter of every induced mechanism A^{l_1,h_1,l_2,h_2} by (the same) w.

Lemma 5.7. *Let A be a truthful and scalable mechanism for multi unit auctions with m items that provides an approximation ratio better than 2. Let A^{l_1,h_1,l_2,h_2} and $A^{l_1',h_1',l_2',h_2'}$ be two induced mechanisms of A. Then, the following equality holds: $w^{l_1,h_1,l_2,h_2} = w^{l_1',h_1',l_2',h_2'}$.*

5.3 Some Induced Mechanisms are Welfare Maximizers

The heart of this section is here. We show that "many" of the induced triage auctions take the simple form of welfare maximizers. The crux is that the payment function for some items is simultaneously the payment function of one item for one induced mechanism, and the payment function for two items for another. Simple algebra then gives us that some θ's must equal to 1. We are then able to specify the payment functions of "simple" valuations.

Lemma 5.8. *Let A be a truthful and scalable mechanism for multi unit auctions with m items with an approximation ratio better than 2. Let $A^{l_1,m,l_2,m}$ where $l_1, l_2 \geq 2$. Then, $\theta_A^{l_1,m,l_2,m} = \theta_B^{l_1,m,l_2,m} = 1$.*

Definition 5.9. *A valuation v is l-*simple *if there exists some $0 < l < m$ such that for every $k < l$, $v(k) = 0$, and for every $l \leq k < m$ we have that $v(k) = v(l)$.*

Corollary 5.10. *Let $l \geq 2$. For every l-simple valuation v we have that $f_m(v) = wv(m)$ and for all $1 < t < m-1$ such that $l+t \leq m$ we have that $f_t(v) = w(v(m) - v(m-t))$. Similarly, for every l-simple valuation u we have that $f_m(u) = u(m)/w$ and for all $1 < t < m-1$ such that $l+t \leq m$ we have that $g_t(u) = (u(m) - u(m-t))/w$.*

Proof. For the first part, observe that $A^{l,m,t,m}$ is an induced mechanism for every t such that $l+t \leq m$ and apply Lemma 5.8. The proof of the second part is similar. □

5.4 Concluding the Characterization

We are now ready to obtain our final characterization. We give an almost complete description of the payment functions for valuations where the value of one item is 0. Lemma 5.11 provides the payment function for m items, and Lemma 5.12 provides the payment functions for smaller bundles.

Lemma 5.11. *For each v where $v(1) = 0$, $f_m(v) = wv(m)$. Symmetrically, for each u where $u(1) = 0$, $g_m(u) = \frac{u(m)}{w}$.*

Lemma 5.12. *Let v be a valuation with $v(1) = 0$. For every $k \neq 1, m-1$ we have that $f_k(v) = w(v(m) - v(m-k))$. Similarly, for every valuation u with $u(1) = 0$ we have, for every $k \neq 1, m-1$ that $g_k(u) = w^{-1}(u(m) - u(m-k))$.*

Our final characterization result is:

Definition 5.13. *A valuation v is* degenerate *if $v(1) = 0$ and $v(m-1) = v(m-2)$.*

THEOREM 5.14. **(Characterization of mechanisms for any number of items)** *Let A be a truthful and scalable two-bidder mechanism for $m > 2$ items that provides an approximation ratio better than 2. There exists a constant $w > 0$ such that for all degenerate v and u and on all inputs (v, u) A outputs a solution with value* $\max_k(v(k) + wu(m - k))$.

Acknowledgements

The first author wishes to thank Itai Ashlagi and Ron Lavi for several stimulating early discussions. The fractions auction of Section 3 was obtained during these discussions. We thank Bobby Kleinberg for helpful discussions. We thank Sigal Oren for numerous very helpful comments and ideas throughout the work on this paper.

6. REFERENCES

[1] Aaron Archer and Éva Tardos. Truthful mechanisms for one-parameter agents. In FOCS'01.

[2] Itai Ashlagi, Shahar Dobzinski, and Ron Lavi. An optimal lower bound for anonymous scheduling mechanisms. In EC'09.

[3] Yair Bartal, Rica Gonen, and Noam Nisan. Incentive compatible multi unit combinatorial auctions. In TARK'03.

[4] Sushil Bikhchandani, Shurojit Chatterji, Ron Lavi, Ahuva Mu'alem, Noam Nisan, and Arunava Sen. Weak monotonicity characterizes deterministic dominant-strategy implementation. *Econometrica*, 74(4):1109–1132, July 2006.

[5] Patrick Briest, Piotr Krysta, and Berthold Vöcking. Approximation techniques for utilitarian mechanism design. In STOC'05.

[6] Dave Buchfuhrer, Shaddin Dughmi, Hu Fu, Robert Kleinberg, Elchanan Mossel, Christos Papadimitriou, Michael Schapira, Yaron Singer, and Chris Umans. Inapproximability for vcg-based combinatorial auctions. In SODA'10.

[7] George Christodoulou, Elias Koutsoupias, and Angelina Vidali. A lower bound for scheduling mechanisms. In SODA'07.

[8] George Christodoulou and Annamária Kovács. A deterministic truthful PTAS for scheduling related machines. In SODA'10.

[9] Peerapong Dhangwatnotai, Shahar Dobzinski, Shaddin Dughmi, and Tim Roughgarden. Truthful approximation schemes for single-parameter agents. In FOCS'08.

[10] Shahar Dobzinski. An impossibility result for truthful combinatorial auctions with submodular valuations. In STOC'11.

[11] Shahar Dobzinski. Two randomized mechanisms for combinatorial auctions. In APPROX'07.

[12] Shahar Dobzinski and Shaddin Dughmi. On the power of randomization in algorithmic mechanism design. In FOCS'09.

[13] Shahar Dobzinski and Noam Nisan. Limitations of vcg-based mechanisms. Preliminary version in STOC'07.

[14] Shahar Dobzinski and Noam Nisan. Mechanisms for multi-unit auctions. In EC'07.

[15] Shahar Dobzinski, Noam Nisan, and Michael Schapira. Approximation algorithms for combinatorial auctions with complement-free bidders. In STOC'05.

[16] Shahar Dobzinski, Noam Nisan, and Michael Schapira. Truthful randomized mechanisms for combinatorial auctions. In STOC'06.

[17] Shahar Dobzinski and Mukund Sundararajan. On characterizations of truthful mechanisms for combinatorial auctions and scheduling. In EC'08.

[18] Uriel Feige. On maximizing welfare where the utility functions are subadditive. In STOC'06.

[19] J. Green and J.J. Laffont. Characterization of satisfactory mechanism for the revelation of preferences for public goods. *Econometrica*, pages 427–438, 1977.

[20] Ron Holzman, Noa Kfir-Dahav, Dov Monderer, and Moshe Tennenholtz. Bundling equilibrium in combinatrial auctions. *Games and Economic Behavior*, 47:104–123, 2004.

[21] Elias Koutsoupias and Angelina Vidali. A lower bound of 1+phi for truthful scheduling mechanisms. In MFCS'07.

[22] Ron Lavi, Ahuva Mu'alem, and Noam Nisan. Towards a characterization of truthful combinatorial auctions. In FOCS'03.

[23] Ron Lavi and Chaitanya Swamy. Truthful and near-optimal mechanism design via linear programming. In FOCS'05.

[24] Daniel Lehmann, Liadan Ita O'Callaghan, and Yoav Shoham. Truth revelation in approximately efficient combinatorial auctions. In *JACM 49(5)*, pages 577–602, Sept. 2002.

[25] Ahuva Mu'alem and Noam Nisan. Truthful approximation mechanisms for restricted combinatorial auctions. In AAAI'02.

[26] Noam Nisan. 2007. Introduction to Mechanism Design (for Computer Scientists). In "Algorithmic Game Theory", N. Nisan, T. Roughgarden, E. Tardos and V. Vazirani, editors.

[27] Noam Nisan and Amir Ronen. Algorithmic mechanism design. In STOC'99.

[28] Noam Nisan, Tim Roughgarden, Eva Tardos, and Vijay V. Vazirani. *Algorithmic Game Theory*. Cambridge University Press, New York, NY, USA, 2007.

[29] Christos Papadimitriou, Michael Schapira, and Yaron Singer. On the hardness of being truthful. In FOCS'08.

[30] Kevin Roberts. The characterization of implementable choice rules. In Jean-Jacques Laffont, editor, *Aggregation and Revelation of Preferences. Papers presented at the first European Summer Workshop of the Economic Society*, pages 321–349. North-Holland, 1979.

[31] Michael E. Saks and Lan Yu. Weak monotonicity suffices for truthfulness on convex domains. In EC'05.

[32] W. Vickrey. Counterspeculation, auctions and competitive sealed tenders. *Journal of Finance*, pages 8–37, 1961.

Envy, Truth, and Profit

Jason D. Hartline*
Electrical Engineering and Computer Science
Northwestern University
Evanston, IL, USA
hartline@eecs.northwestern.edu

Qiqi Yan†
Department of Computer Science
Stanford University
Stanford, CA, USA
qiqiyan@cs.stanford.edu

ABSTRACT

We consider profit maximizing (incentive compatible) mechanism design in general environments that include, e.g., position auctions (for selling advertisements on Internet search engines) and single-minded combinatorial auctions. We analyze optimal envy-free pricings in these settings, and give economic justification for using the optimal revenue of envy-free pricings as a benchmark for prior-free mechanism design and analysis. Moreover, we show that envy-free pricing has a simple nice structure and a strong connection to incentive compatible mechanism design, and we exploit this connection to design prior-free mechanisms with strong approximation guarantees.

Categories and Subject Descriptors

F.0 [**Theory of Computation**]: General

General Terms

Economics, Theory, Algorithms

Keywords

envy-free pricing, truthful mechanisms, revenue maximization, optimal auction, prior-free

1. INTRODUCTION

Mechanism design theory provides guidelines for the design of economic systems that obtain good performance in the presence of selfish behavior on the part of the participants. A standard approach is to restrict attention to mechanisms where each participant has a dominant strategy of truthfully reporting her preference over possible outcomes. This restriction imposes a constraint, known as *incentive compatibility*, on the mechanism that binds across all possible misreports of the agents. Reasoning about mechanisms, therefore, requires reasoning about the outcomes of the mechanism on all possible preferences, not just the true ones. A mechanism, therefore, may face a performance tradeoff across different possible preferences. For instance, there is such a performance tradeoff for the objective of profit maximization. Consequently, no mechanism obtains the maximum profit for all possible participant preferences.

In contrast to incentive compatibility, consider the "fairness" constraint of *envy-freedom*. The envy-free constraint requires that each participant prefers her own outcome to that of any other participant. Unlike incentive compatibility, envy-freedom is a constraint that binds point-wise on the true preferences. Consequently, for any performance metric, there is an envy-free outcome with the best performance.

As an example, suppose there are two identical units of an item for sale. Each agent wants one unit of the item, and her utility for the unit is her value for the unit minus the price she pays. There is one high-value agent with value 6 for a unit, and two low-value agents with value 4. It is envy-free to price each unit at 5, the high-value agent would opt to buy a unit, while others would not. It is not envy-free to price each unit at 2, as all three agents would want a unit, exceeding the supply.

Our goal is to design incentive compatible mechanisms that obtain good revenue point-wise, i.e., for any preferences of the participants. This contrasts from the standard *Bayesian* approach for optimal mechanism design in economics in which it is assumed that participant preferences are drawn from a known *prior* distribution. The knowledge about the distribution allows the designer to optimally trade-off revenue between different possible preferences of the participants. In contrast to the economics approach, our goal is to design good mechanisms without distributional assumptions, i.e., to be *prior free*.

Our approach to design good prior-free mechanisms is the following. We view envy-freedom (EF) as a relaxation of incentive compatibility (IC), characterize revenue-optimal envy-free pricings, relate the revenue of an IC mechanism to that of a corresponding EF pricing, and then use this connection between EF and IC revenues to design and analyze IC mechanisms.

We consider general single-parameter environments where each participant (a.k.a., agent) has a single value for receiving an abstract service and the designer has a feasibility constraint on which agents can be served simultaneously. In the previously mentioned multi-unit example, the abstract

*Supported in part by NSF CAREER Award CCF-0846113.
†Supported by a Stanford Graduate Fellowship.

service is a unit of the item and the feasibility constraint requires we serve sets of cardinality at most two.

An environment is *downward-closed* if any subset of a feasible set is also feasible. The following special cases are of interest. In a *digital good environment* all allocations are feasible. In a *multi-unit environment* there is a fixed number k of identical units available and each agent desires one unit, i.e., the feasible sets are those with cardinality at most k. In a *matroid environments* the feasible allocations correspond to the independent sets of a matroid. Matroid environments include multi-unit and constrained matching environments as special cases.[1]

We allow convex combinations of our basic feasibility environments. For instance, one can express *position auction environments*, as popularized by the auctioning advertising slots on Internet search engines, as a convex combination of multi-unit auctions. Position auction environments are specified by a decreasing sequence of probabilities for each position and a feasible outcome is a partial assignment of agents to positions. An agent assigned to a position receives a service with probability equal to the position's associated probability.

For many interesting single-parameter environments, e.g., position auctions, the feasibility constraint is inherently symmetric. Given a feasible allocation, for any permutation of the names of the agents, the permuted assignment is still feasible. As an example of an asymmetric environment, consider single-minded combinatorial auctions, i.e., where each agent has a single value for receiving a particular bundle of goods (and no value for any other bundle). In such an environment, an agent is considered "served" if she receives her desired bundle. Therefore, the feasible subsets of agents are the ones for which the desired bundles are disjoint. For such asymmetric feasibility constraints, the notion of envy-freeness as a fairness condition is ill-defined. However, we can symmetrize any asymmetric environment by assuming that the agents' roles with respect to the feasibility constraint are assigned by a random permutation. In the combinatorial auction example, this means that we start with a set of agent values and a set of desired bundles and the values are associated with the desired bundle via a random permutation. We refer to these environments as *permutation environments* and observe that the random permutation assumption on values is a natural prior-free analog of the i.i.d. assumption that is common in Bayesian mechanism design.

The first result of this paper is a characterization of revenue-optimal envy-free pricings. Importantly, this characterization mirrors the characterization of Bayesian revenue-optimal incentive compatible mechanisms of Myerson (for i.i.d. distributions). Optimal envy-free pricings are *ironed virtual surplus optimizers* in the sense that they are specified by a monotone non-decreasing function (known as the *ironed virtual valuation function*) and the agents served are the feasible set for which the total ironed virtual value is the highest. Furthermore, the ironed virtual valuation function that obtains this optimal revenue is the one that corresponds to the *empirical distribution* of the given agents' values.

The above description of ironed virtual surplus optimizers specifies how to decide which agents should receive services. It does not explicitly specify the payments. In fact, incentive compatibility and envy-freedom generally require different payments. This is because incentive compatible payments are counteracting agents' incentive to misreport while envy-free payments are counteracting agents' envy (or desire to swap). As these are different constraints, they lead to different payments. Our second result shows that for any ironed virtual surplus optimizer these payments are, in settings of interest,[2] not too far apart, specifically: $\mathrm{EF} \geq \mathrm{IC} \geq \mathrm{EF}/2$.

The first inequality above motivates the selection of the envy-free optimal revenue as a benchmark to which to compare prior-free mechanisms. Bayesian optimal IC mechanisms are ironed virtual surplus maximizers and their IC revenue is point-wise at most their EF revenue. Therefore, a prior-free mechanism that always approximates the optimal EF revenue is guaranteed to also approximate the revenue of any Bayesian optimal mechanism. Of course, the Bayesian optimal mechanism is the one that a designer would select if a prior were known, and so approximating it without any knowledge is a strong guarantee.

As a first example to illustrate the relevance of envy-freedom for prior-free mechanism design, we reduce the problem of approximating the optimal EF revenue for matroid permutation and position auction environments to multi-unit environments. This reduction is enabled by the fact that incentive compatibility is closed under convex combination and a structural equivalence between (1) the convex combinations of multi-unit auction environments, (2) position auction environments, and (3) matroid permutation environments. This implies that for any IC mechanism that is a β-approximation to the optimal EF revenue for multi-unit environments, there is an IC β-approximation mechanism for position auction environments and matroid permutation environments. In particular, results of [14, 8] imply a 6.5-approximation for these settings.

The second example we give considers general downward-closed environments such as single-minded combinatorial auctions. In such an environment we show that a prior-free incentive compatible mechanism based on random sampling approximates the optimal EF revenue (in permutation environments). The random sampling auction we consider works as follows. It first partitions the agents into a market set and a sample set. Then it calculates the ironed virtual value function for the empirical distribution of the sample and simulates ironed virtual value maximization with this function on the full set of agents. Finally, agents in the sample are rejected and agents in the market receive the allocation from the simulation and are charged the corresponding payments. To analyze this mechanism, we show that its EF revenue (as an ironed virtual surplus maximizer) approximates the optimal EF revenue, and consequently its IC revenue also approximates the optimal EF revenue.

Related work. Bayesian optimal mechanisms for single-parameter environments were characterized as ironed virtual surplus optimizers by Myerson [18]. The relationship between revenue curves and virtual valuations, a.k.a., marginal revenue, was identified by Bulow and Roberts [5]. We make heavy use of this machinery.

[1]A constrained matching environment is one where each agent has a value for "good" items and a set of items that are considered good. The agent wants at most one item, and each item can be allocated to at most one agent.

[2]The first inequality is known to hold for position auction and matroid permutation environments. The second inequality is known to hold under a technical condition.

This paper follows from a line of work that studies prior-free revenue properties of the random sampling auction of [12]. The tightest analysis of the random sampling auction for digital good environments is given by Alaei et al. [1]. For multi-unit environments, Hartline and Roughgarden [15] proposed a benchmark for prior-free analysis that is derived from Bayesian optimal auctions and discuss the desirability of a prior-free benchmark that implies approximation in the Bayesian setting. With this benchmark, Devanur and Hartline [8] extended the analysis from [1] to limited supply settings. In this context, the present paper further extends the benchmark of [15] and the analysis of [8] to general downward-closed environments.

It has been observed that position auctions are structurally equivalent to a convex combination of multi-unit auctions. For instance in Dughmi et al. [10], this equivalence was leveraged to show that the VCG mechanism with reserve gives the same revenue in these two environments. We extend this connection by doing the same thing for less well-behaved approximation mechanisms. We also make a similar connection between position auction and matroid permutation environments.

The prior-free mechanisms we discuss perform well even when there is no prior distribution; agent values can be adversarially chosen. If there is a prior distribution that is unknown it is possible to design good *prior-independent* mechanisms. Dhangwatnotai et al. [9] show that a mechanism based on a "single-sample" approach gives an 8-approximation for downward-closed environments with distributions that satisfy a standard *monotone hazard rate* condition, and a 2-approximation for structurally nicer matroid environments with distributions that satisfy a standard *regularity* condition. However, as we show, a single-sample cannot give better than a logarithmic approximation for the fully general distributional setting. In this context, we give a constant approximation for matroid environments with nearly general i.i.d. valuation distributions. This is important as many distributions, e.g., bimodal, do not satisfy the regularity condition required by [9].

Connections between envy-free pricings and prior-free mechanism design have been made before (e.g. in [13, 3]). Much of the work on envy-free pricing has been focused on multi-dimensional agent preferences. Part of our characterization of envy-free pricings in single-parameter environments is a special case of Mu'alem's "local efficiency" condition [17].

This paper uses envy-free pricings as a benchmark for gauging the performance of a prior-free mechanism. While it might be nice to have mechanisms that are both incentive compatible and envy-free, achieving both conditions together while obtaining a reasonable performance is impossible. This is discussed for profit maximization in digital good environments by Goldberg and Hartline [11], unrelated machine scheduling problems by Cohen et al. [6], and for welfare maximization in general combinatorial auctions by Ausubel and Milgrom [2]. In fact, Day and Milgrom [7] suggest that envy-freedom and related conditions (specifically the cooperative game theory condition of the *core*) are more important than incentive compatibility and when they are impossible to achieve together envy freedom should be chosen instead of incentive compatibility.

2. OPTIMAL ENVY-FREE PRICING

In this section we derive a theory of optimal envy-free pricings in single-dimensional environments that mirrors that of Bayesian optimal (incentive compatible) mechanisms for i.i.d. prior distributions [18, 5].

There are $n \geq 2$ agents. Each agent i has a valuation v_i for receiving an abstract service. The *valuation profile* is $\mathbf{v} = (v_1, \ldots, v_n)$. We assume that the agents are indexed in order of decreasing values, i.e., $v_i \geq v_{i+1}$. An agent i who is served with probability x_i and charged price p_i obtains utility $u_i = v_i x_i - p_i$. *Individual rationality* requires that u_i be non-negative.

We are allowed to serve certain feasible sets of agents as given by a set system. The set system is *downward-closed* in the sense if a set of agents is feasible, so is any of its subsets. The empty set is always feasible. We allow randomization in two senses (1) the set system constraint may be randomized (i.e., by convex combination over set systems) and (2) the set of agents served may be random (by convex combination over feasible sets). Notably, randomization in (1) is given by the environment and randomization in (2) is by our choice of outcome. We define an *allocation* as a vector $\mathbf{x} = (x_1, \ldots, x_n) \in [0, 1]^n$ where x_i is the probability that agent i is served. An allocation is feasible if it is the characteristic vector induced by the process above. The environments permitted include digital good auctions, multi-unit auctions, position auction environments, matroid environments, and single-minded combinatorial auctions.

We further assume in this section that feasibility constraint imposed by the environment is symmetric, i.e., the set of feasible allocations is closed under permutation. Digital good, multi-unit auction, and position auction environments are all symmetric. Given any asymmetric environment its corresponding *permutation environment* is obtained by randomly permuting the agents with respect to the feasibility constraint. Of special interest for us will be downward closed permutation environments and matroid permutation environments. By definition these environments are symmetric.

Definition 2.1 (Envy freedom). *An allocation* $\mathbf{x}$ *with payments* $\mathbf{p}$ *is* envy free *for valuation profile* $\mathbf{v}$ *if no agent prefers the outcome of another agent to her own. Formally,*

$$\forall i, j,\ v_i x_i - p_i \geq v_i x_j - p_j.$$

We first characterize envy-free pricings in terms of the allocation. For a given allocation $\mathbf{x}$ there may be several pricings $\mathbf{p}$ for which the allocation is envy-free. Since our objective is profit maximization we will characterize the $\mathbf{p}$ corresponding to $\mathbf{x}$ that gives the highest total revenue. We omit the proof of this characterization as it is nearly identical to that of the analogous (and standard) characterization of incentive compatible mechanisms.

Definition 2.2. *An allocation is* swap monotone *if the allocation probabilities have the same order as the valuations of the agents, i.e.,* $x_i \geq x_{i+1}$ *for all* i.

Lemma 2.1. *In symmetric environments, an allocation* $\mathbf{x}$ *admits a non-negative and individual rational payment* $\mathbf{p}$ *such that* $(\mathbf{x}, \mathbf{p})$ *is envy-free if and only if* $\mathbf{x}$ *is swap monotone. If* $\mathbf{x}$ *is swap monotone, then the maximum payments for which* $(\mathbf{x}, \mathbf{p})$ *is envy-free satisfy, for all* i*, (Figure 1)*

$$\begin{aligned} p_i &= \sum\nolimits_{j=i}^{n} (v_j - v_{j+1}) \cdot (x_i - x_{j+1}) \\ &= \sum\nolimits_{j=i}^{n} v_j \cdot (x_j - x_{j+1}). \end{aligned}$$

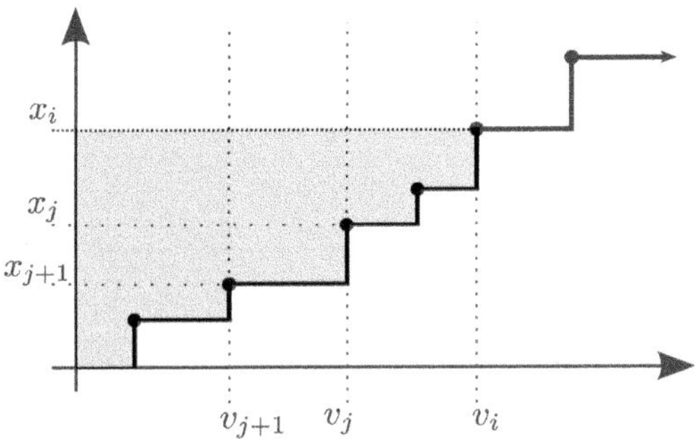

Figure 1: The solid curve depicts a swap monotone allocation as a function of the values (points). The shaded area corresponds to payment from Lemma 2.1 for agent i.

Importantly, the above characterization leaves us free to speak of the (maximum) envy-free revenue of any swap monotone allocation $\mathbf{x}$ on values $\mathbf{v}$, which we denote by $\mathrm{EF}^{\mathbf{x}}(\mathbf{v})$. For any $\mathbf{v}$ and any symmetric environment we now solve for the envy-free optimal revenue, denoted by $\mathrm{EFO}(\mathbf{v})$.

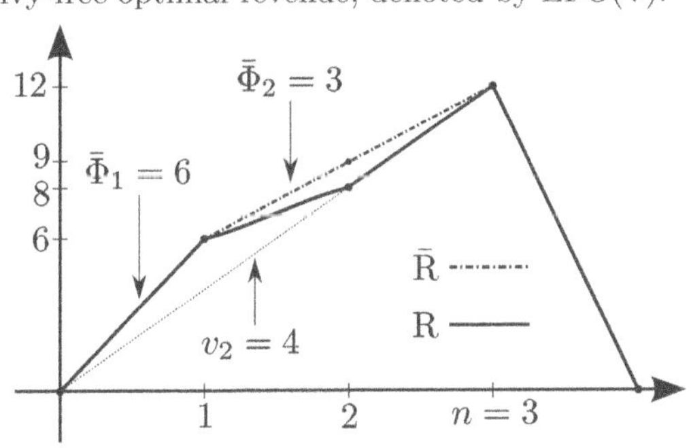

Figure 2: R and $\bar{\mathrm{R}}$ are the revenue curve and ironed revenue curve of the valuation profile $(6, 4, 4)$. The ironed virtual value of the high-value agent is 6, and the ironed virtual value of the two low-value agents are both $(12-6)/2 = 3$. E.g., the optimal EF revenue in the $k = 2$ unit environment is $\bar{\mathrm{R}}(2) = 9$.

We will characterize the envy-free optimal revenue in terms of properties of the valuation profile $\mathbf{v}$. Given a valuation profile $\mathbf{v}$ we denote the *revenue curve* by $\mathrm{R}^{\mathbf{v}}(i) = i \cdot v_i$ for $i = \{1, \ldots, n\}$ (recall v_i's are indexed in decreasing order). For convenience we also let $\mathrm{R}^{\mathbf{v}}(0) = \mathrm{R}^{\mathbf{v}}(n+1) = 0$. The *ironed revenue curve*, denoted $\bar{\mathrm{R}}^{\mathbf{v}}(i)$, is the minimum concave function that upper-bounds R. Likewise, define the *virtual valuation function* $\Phi^{\mathbf{v}}(v) = \mathrm{R}^{\mathbf{v}}(i) - \mathrm{R}^{\mathbf{v}}(i-1)$ and the *ironed virtual valuation function* $\bar{\Phi}^{\mathbf{v}}(v) = \bar{\mathrm{R}}^{\mathbf{v}}(i) - \bar{\mathrm{R}}^{\mathbf{v}}(i-1)$, where $i \in \{1, \ldots, n+1\}$ is such that $v \in [v_i, v_{i-1})$. (We set $v_0 = \infty$ for notational convenience.) See Figure 2.

$\mathrm{R}^{\mathbf{v}}(i)$ is the best envy-free revenue one can get from serving exactly i agents at the same price deterministically. Again consider the multi-unit auction example with two units of an item, one high-value agent with value 6, and two low-value agents with value 4. It is envy-free to serve one high-value agent and one low-value agent at price 4, achieving revenue $\mathrm{R}(2) = 8$. Interestingly, this is not optimal. The following allocation and payments are also envy-free: serve the high-value agent with probability 1 at price 5, and serve a low-value agent chosen at random at price 4. Both units are always sold and the total revenue is $\bar{\mathrm{R}}(2) = 9$. In what follows we will derive that this revenue is optimal among all envy-free allocations.

Lemma 2.2. *The (maximum) envy-free revenue of a swap monotone allocation* $\mathbf{x}$ *satisfies:*

$$\mathrm{EF}^{\mathbf{x}}(\mathbf{v}) = \sum_{i=1}^{n} \mathrm{R}^{\mathbf{v}}(i) \cdot (x_i - x_{i+1}) = \sum_{i=1}^{n} \Phi^{\mathbf{v}}(v_i) \cdot x_i.$$

Proof. The proof is by the following equalities:

$$\begin{aligned}\mathrm{EF}^{\mathbf{x}}(\mathbf{v}) &= \sum_{i=1}^{n} p_i = \sum_{i=1}^{n} \sum_{j=i}^{n} v_j \cdot (x_j - x_{j+1}) \\ &= \sum_{i=1}^{n} i v_i \cdot (x_i - x_{i+1}) = \sum_{i=1}^{n} \mathrm{R}(i) \cdot (x_i - x_{i+1}) \\ &= \sum_{i=1}^{n} (\mathrm{R}(i) - \mathrm{R}(i-1)) \cdot x_i = \sum_{i=1}^{n} \Phi^{\mathbf{v}}(v_i) \cdot x_i.\end{aligned}$$

□

An implication of the characterization of the envy-free revenue of a pricing as its *virtual surplus*, i.e., $\sum_i \Phi(v_i) x_i$, suggests that to maximize revenue, the allocation should maximize virtual surplus subject to swap monotonicity. In symmetric environments with monotone virtual valuation functions, the maximization of virtual surplus results in a swap monotone allocation. In general symmetric environments, the allocation that maximizes *ironed* virtual surplus is both swap monotone and revenue optimal among all swap monotone allocations.

Lemma 2.3. *In a symmetric environments, the allocation that maximizes ironed virtual surplus with ties broken randomly is swap monotone.*

Proof. Suppose $\bar{\Phi}(v_i) > \bar{\Phi}(v_j)$ then $x_i > x_j$; otherwise, swapping x_i for x_j would have higher ironed virtual surplus. Suppose $\bar{\Phi}(v_i) = \bar{\Phi}(v_j)$, then $x_i = x_j$ because of random-tie-breaking and the symmetry of the environment. □

Theorem 2.4. *In any symmetric environment with any valuation profile* $\mathbf{v}$*, the allocation* $\mathbf{x}$ *that maximizes ironed virtual surplus w.r.t.* $\bar{\Phi}^{\mathbf{v}}$ *maximizes envy-free revenue among all swap-monotone allocations. I.e.,* $\mathrm{EFO}(\mathbf{v}) = \mathrm{EF}^{\mathbf{x}}(\mathbf{v})$.

This theorem is proved by a useful lemma that relates revenue to ironed virtual surplus.

Lemma 2.5. *For any swap-monotone allocation* $\mathbf{x}$ *on valuation profile* $\mathbf{v}$,

$$\mathrm{EF}^{\mathbf{x}}(\mathbf{v}) \le \sum_{i=1}^{n} \bar{\Phi}^{\mathbf{v}}(i) \cdot x_i = \sum_{i=1}^{n} \bar{\mathrm{R}}^{\mathbf{v}}(i) \cdot (x_i - x_{i+1}),$$

with equality holding if and only if $x_i = x_{i+1}$ *whenever* $\bar{\mathrm{R}}^{\mathbf{v}}(i) > \mathrm{R}^{\mathbf{v}}(i)$.

Proof. To show the inequality, we have:

$$\begin{aligned}\mathrm{EF}^{\mathbf{x}}(\mathbf{v}) &= \sum_{i=1}^{n} \mathrm{R}(i) \cdot (x_i - x_{i+1}) \\ &= \sum_{i=1}^{n} \bar{\mathrm{R}}(i) \cdot (x_i - x_{i+1}) \\ &\quad - \sum_{i=1}^{n} (\bar{\mathrm{R}}(i) - \mathrm{R}(i)) \cdot (x_i - x_{i+1}) \\ &\le \sum_{i=1}^{n} \bar{\mathrm{R}}(i) \cdot (x_i - x_{i+1}),\end{aligned}$$

where we use the fact that $\bar{\mathrm{R}}(i) \ge \mathrm{R}(i)$ and $x_i \ge x_{i+1}$. Clearly the equality holds if and only if $x_i = x_{i+1}$ whenever $\bar{\mathrm{R}}(i) > \mathrm{R}(i)$. □

Proof of Theorem 2.4. Consider $\mathbf{x}$ that optimizes ironed virtual surplus with random tie breaking and also consider any other swap monotone $\mathbf{x}'$. Note that whenever $\bar{R}(i) > R(i)$, we have $\bar{\Phi}^{\mathbf{v}}(v_i) = \bar{\Phi}^{\mathbf{v}}(v_{i+1})$ for which random tie-breaking implies $x_i = x_{i+1}$. Therefore $\mathbf{x}$ satisfies Lemma 2.5 with equality, whereas $\mathbf{x}'$ satisfies it with inequality. Thus $EF^{\mathbf{x}}(\mathbf{v}) \geq EF^{\mathbf{x}'}(\mathbf{v})$ and $\mathbf{x}$ is optimal. □

As an example of this theorem, consider position auction environments with click probabilities $w_1 \geq w_2 \geq \ldots \geq w_n$. An ironed virtual surplus maximizer assigns agents with higher ironed virtual values to slots with larger click probabilities, breaking ties randomly, ignoring agents with negative ironed virtual values. The ironed virtual surplus, and thus revenue, is $\sum_{i\,:\,\bar{\Phi}(v_i)\geq 0} \bar{\Phi}(v_i)\cdot w_i$, which can be read off the revenue curve, e.g., Figure 2.

3. MATROIDS, POSITION AUCTIONS, AND MULTI-UNIT AUCTIONS

In this section we consider matroid permutation, position auction, and multi-unit environments. We show that for both incentive compatible mechanism design and envy-free pricing, these environments are closely related. In fact, for either IC or EF, respectively, the optimal mechanisms across these environments are the same and approximation mechanisms give the same approximation factor. As an example, we will focus on approximating the optimal EF revenue with a prior-free mechanism. For reasons we motivate in Section 5, the EF revenue benchmark that we will approximate is $EFO^{(2)}(\mathbf{v}) = EFO(\mathbf{v}^{(2)})$ where $\mathbf{v}^{(2)} = (v_2, v_2, v_3, \ldots, v_n)$. Our solution will be via a two-step reduction: we reduce matroid permutation to position auction environments, which we then reduce to multi-unit environments.

Recall that in a multi-unit environment it is feasible to serve any set of agents of cardinality at most some given k. In position auction environments there are weights $w_1 \geq w_2 \geq \cdots \geq w_n$ for positions and feasible outcomes are partial assignments of agents to positions. In matroid permutation environments there is a feasibility constraint given by independent sets of a matroid, but the roles of the agents are assigned by random permutation.

The property of these three settings that enables this reduction is that in each environment the greedy algorithm on ironed virtual values (with ties broken randomly) obtains the maximum ironed virtual surplus. The greedy algorithm works as follows: order the agents by ironed virtual value and serve each agent in this order if her ironed virtual value is positive and if doing so is feasible given the set of agents previously served. Notice that the only information needed to perform the surplus maximization is the ordering on the agents' ironed virtual values (but not their magnitudes).

Definition 3.1. *The* characteristic weights $w_1 \geq w_2 \geq \cdots \geq w_n$ *of a matroid environment are as follows: choose any valuation profile* $\mathbf{v}$ *with all distinct values, assign the agents to elements in the matroid via a random permutation, run the greedy algorithm w.r.t.* $\mathbf{v}$*, and define* w_i *to be the probability that agent* i *is served.*

3.1 Reduction for Ironed Virtual Surplus Maximizers

We first show ironed virtual surplus optimization in the three environments is equivalent.

Lemma 3.1. *The ironed virtual surplus maximizing assignment (and its virtual surplus) is equal in expectation in the following environments:*

1. *a matroid permutation environment with characteristic weights* $\mathbf{w}$*,*
2. *a position auction environment with weights* $\mathbf{w}$*,*
3. *a convex combination of multi-unit environments where* k *units are available with probability* $w_k - w_{k+1}$ *for* $k \in \{1, \ldots, n\}$ *and* $w_{n+1} = 0$*.*

Proof. Fix a tie-breaking rule, which induces an ordering on the agents. Consider the greedy algorithm on the agents with non-negative $\bar{\Phi}$ values according to this ordering. The j-th agent with non-negative $\bar{\Phi}$ value in this ordering (1) gets allocated with probability w_j in the matroid permutation setting by definition of characteristic weights, (2) gets assigned to position j in the position auction and hence gets allocated with probability w_j, and, (3) gets allocated in k-unit auction for each $k \geq j$, and hence has probability $\sum_{k\geq j}(w_k - w_{k+1}) = w_j$ of being served in the convex combination setting. Taking expectation over all tie-breaking orders, agent i has the same probability of being served in the three settings. □

The following corollary is immediate.

Corollary 3.2. *For any valuation profile* $\mathbf{v}$ *and any weights* $\mathbf{w}$*, the envy-free optimal revenue is the same in each of the environments of Lemma 3.1.*

A basic fact about incentive compatibility is that it is closed under convex combination, i.e., a randomization over two incentive compatible mechanisms is incentive compatible: truthtelling is an optimal strategy in each, and so it remains an optimal strategy in the combination.

We now illustrate how to use Lemma 3.1 to show that an incentive compatible prior-free approximation mechanisms for multi-unit environments can be adapted to give the same approximation factor in position auction and matroid permutation environments. Consider the following incentive compatible mechanism.

Definition 3.2. *The* Random Sampling Empirical Myerson (RSEM) *mechanism: (discussion of payments omitted)*

1. *randomly partitions the population of agents* $N = \{1, \ldots, n\}$ *into a market* M *and a sample* S*,*
2. *calculates the ironed virtual surplus function* $\bar{\Phi}^S$ *for the sample* S*, and,*
3. *serves a feasible subset of* M *to maximize surplus with respect to* $\bar{\Phi}^S$ *and rejects all other agents.*

Lemma 3.3. *[8] In multi-unit auction environments, RSEM is a prior-free incentive compatible 50-approximation to the envy-free benchmark* $EFO^{(2)}(\mathbf{v})$.

Notice that this mechanism can easily be generalized to other downward-closed environments. It remains incentive compatible for these settings because it is essentially an ironed virtual surplus optimizer on the set M, and furthermore, it is incentive compatible even if the permutation that assigns agents to the set system is fixed. As a final corollary of Lemma 3.1, we can view its revenue in the matroid permutation or position auction environment as the analogous convex combination of its revenue in multi-unit auction environments.

COROLLARY 3.4. *In matroid permutation and position auction environments, RSEM is a prior-free incentive compatible 50-approximation to the envy-free revenue* $\mathrm{EFO}^{(2)}(\mathbf{v})$.

3.2 General Reduction

The following prior-free approximations are essentially the best known for digital good and multi-unit environments. Notably, the mechanism from Corollary 3.7 below, is not based on ironed virtual surplus maximization and therefore Lemma 3.1 cannot be applied to a construct matroid permutation or position auction mechanism from it.

LEMMA 3.5. *[14] In the digital good environment, there is a prior-free incentive compatible 3.25-approximation to* $\mathrm{EFO}^{(2)}(\mathbf{v})$.

LEMMA 3.6. *[8] If there is a prior-free incentive compatible mechanism for the digital good environment that* β*-approximates* $\mathrm{EFO}^{(2)}(\mathbf{v})$, *then there is such a mechanism for multi-unit environments that* 2β*-approximates* $\mathrm{EFO}^{(2)}(\mathbf{v})$.

COROLLARY 3.7. *In multi-unit environments, there is an incentive compatible prior-free 6.5-approximation to* $\mathrm{EFO}^{(2)}(\mathbf{v})$.

We now show how to construct, from any multi-unit auction, a position auction and matroid permutation mechanism that has the exact same outcome (in expectation) as a convex combination of multi-unit auctions (as in Lemma 3.1). The challenge here is the distinct interfaces to the environment: in multi-unit auctions we are given a supply constraint k and we need to specify a set of at most k winners, whereas in position auctions, we are given weights and need to output a partial assignment of agents to positions.

DEFINITION 3.3 (POSITION AUCTION REDUCTION). *Given k-unit auction mechanisms for $k \in \{1, \ldots, n\}$, we construct the following mechanism for the position auction environment with weights* $\mathbf{w}$:

1. *Introduce n dummy agents and n dummy positions into the system, indexed by $\{n+1, \ldots, 2n\}$. Correspondingly, we pad weights $\mathbf{w}$ and valuation profile $\mathbf{v}$ with zeros such that they have dimension $2n$.*
2. *For each $k \in \{1, \ldots, n\}$, simulate the k-unit auction on valuation profile $\mathbf{v}$, and give the unallocated leftover units to the dummy agents arbitrarily for free. Let the resulting allocation of all $2n$ agents be $\mathbf{x}^{(k)}$.*
3. *Calculate the probability that each agent is served in the convex combination: $x_i = \sum_{k=1}^{n} x_i^{(k)}(w_k - w_{k+1})$, for $i \in \{1, \ldots, 2n\}$.*
4. *Solve for a set of permutation matrices $P_t \in \{0,1\}^{2n \times 2n}$ and nonnegative weights r_t with $\sum_t r_t = 1$ such that $\sum_t r_t \cdot P_t \cdot \mathbf{w} = \mathbf{x}$.*
5. *With probability r_t, assign agents to positions according to the permutation specified by P_t.*
6. *Discard dummy agents and dummy position assignments.*

To justify step 4, one can verify that $\mathbf{w}$ majorizes $\mathbf{x}$ in the sense that $\sum_{i=1}^{k} w_i \geq \sum_{i=1}^{k} x_i$ for $k \in \{1, \ldots, 2n\}$, with equality holding for $k = 2n$. Therefore by a theorem of Rado [19], the desired permutation matrices and weights exist. The following consequences are immediate.

LEMMA 3.8. *The resulting mechanism for position auction with weights $\mathbf{w}$ obtained from the above reduction has the same allocation as the convex combination of k-unit auctions with $(w_k - w_{k+1})$'s as probabilities.*

LEMMA 3.9. *Given an incentive compatible multi-unit auction, the mechanism from the position auction reduction is also incentive compatible.*

DEFINITION 3.4 (MATROID PERMUTATION REDUCTION). *Given a position auction mechanism for weights $\mathbf{w}$, we construct the following mechanism for matroid permutation environment with characteristic weights* $\mathbf{w}$:

1. *We run the position auction and for $i = 1, \ldots, n$, let j_i be the position assigned to agent i, or $j_i = \perp$ if i is not assigned a position.*
2. *Reject all agents i with $j_i = \perp$.*
3. *Run the greedy algorithm in the matroid permutation setting with agent i's value reset to j_i.*

The following conclusions are immediate.

LEMMA 3.10. *The resulting mechanism for matroid permutation environment obtained from the above reduction has the same allocation as the position auction.*

LEMMA 3.11. *Given an incentive compatible position auction, the mechanism from the matroid permutation reduction is incentive compatible (in matroid permutation environments).*

THEOREM 3.12. *The factor β to which there is a prior-free incentive compatible approximation of* $\mathrm{EFO}^{(2)}(\mathbf{v})$ *is the same for multi-unit, position auction, and matroid permutation environments.*

COROLLARY 3.13. *There is a prior-free incentive compatible 6.5-approximation to* $\mathrm{EFO}^{(2)}(\mathbf{v})$ *in position auction and matroid permutation environments.*

There are two weakness in the reductions implied by Theorem 3.12 in comparison to those implied by Lemma 3.1. Recall that for the latter, ironed virtual surplus maximizations are via the greedy algorithm, and so the reductions were algorithmically trivial. In contrast, Theorem 3.12 requires knowledge of the characteristic weights to run the construction, which may be hard to compute. In addition the mechanism that results from the matroid permutation reduction is only incentive compatible if the agents are assigned to roles in the matroid via a random permutation as suggested in the model. In contrast, RSEM in matroid environments is incentive compatible without any random permutation (Corollary 3.4).

4. INCENTIVE COMPATIBILITY VERSUS ENVY FREEDOM

The major challenge in designing and analyzing incentive compatible mechanisms is that the incentive constraint binds across all possible misreports of the agents. We therefore view a mechanism as an allocation rule and payment rule pair where $\mathbf{x}(\mathbf{v})$ and $\mathbf{p}(\mathbf{v})$ denote the allocation and payments as a function of the agent values.

DEFINITION 4.1 (INCENTIVE COMPATIBILITY). *A mechanism is* incentive compatible *if no agent prefers the outcome when misreporting her value to the outcome when reporting the truth. Formally,*

$$\forall i, z, \mathbf{v}, \quad v_i x_i(\mathbf{v}) - p_i(\mathbf{v}) \geq v_i x_i(z, \mathbf{v}_{-i}) - p_i(z, \mathbf{v}_{-i}),$$

where $(z, \mathbf{v}_{-i})$ *is obtained frmo* $\mathbf{v}$ *with* v_i *replaced by* z.

DEFINITION 4.2 (VALUE MONOTONICITY). *An allocation rule is* value monotone *if the probability that an agent is served is monotone non-decreasing in her value, i.e.,* $x_i(z, \mathbf{v}_{-i})$ *is non-decreasing in* z *for all agents* i.

The following well-known theorem characterizes ex post IC mechanisms.

THEOREM 4.1. *[18] An allocation rule* $\mathbf{x}(\cdot)$ *admits a non-negative and individually rational payment rule* $\mathbf{p}(\cdot)$ *such that* $(\mathbf{x}, \mathbf{p})$ *is incentive compatible if and only if* $\mathbf{x}(\cdot)$ *is value monotone, and the uniquely determined payment rule is:*

$$p_i(\mathbf{v}) = v_i x_i(\mathbf{v}) - \int_0^{v_i} x_i(z, \mathbf{v}_{-i}) dz.$$

Because the payments are uniquely determined by the allocation rule, for any allocation rule $\mathbf{x}(\cdot)$, we let $\text{IC}^{\mathbf{x}}(\mathbf{v})$ denote the IC revenue from running $\mathbf{x}(\cdot)$ over $\mathbf{v}$.

We now compare envy-free revenue to incentive compatible revenue for ironed virtual surplus optimizers in permutation environments, i.e., where agents are assigned to roles in the set system via a random permutation. We show that these quantities are often within a factor of two of each other.

First we lower bound IC revenue by half of the maximum envy-free revenue under a technical condition. In the following we use $\text{IC}_i^{\bar{\Phi}}(\mathbf{v})$ and $\text{EF}_i^{\bar{\Phi}}(\mathbf{v})$ to denote the IC and EF revenue from agent i by applying the ironed virtual surplus maximizer $\bar{\Phi}$, respectively.

LEMMA 4.2. *For downward-closed permutation environments, all valuations* $\mathbf{v}$*, and* $\bar{\Phi}$*, the ironed virtual valuation function corresponding to some* $\mathbf{v}'$ *obtained from* $\mathbf{v}$ *by setting a subset of agents' values to be 0, we have that* $\text{IC}_i^{\bar{\Phi}}(\mathbf{v}) \geq \frac{1}{2}\text{EF}_i^{\bar{\Phi}}(\mathbf{v})$ *for all* i.

PROOF. Let $\mathbf{x}(\cdot)$ denote the allocation rule of the ironed virtual surplus optimizer $\bar{\Phi}$. By the assumption of the lemma, for all j, $\bar{\Phi}(z)$ is constant for all $z \in [v_{j+1}, v_j)$, and hence the IC allocation rule in fact maps each $z \in [v_{j+1}, v_j)$ to $x_i(v_{j+1}, \mathbf{v}_{-i})$.

By Lemma 4.1, $\text{IC}_i^{\bar{\Phi}}(\mathbf{v})$ is equal to $\sum_{j=i}^{n}(v_j - v_{j+1}) \cdot (x_i(\mathbf{v}) - x_i(v_{j+1}, \mathbf{v}_{-i}))$ which, referring to Figure 3, equals the area above the IC curve and below the horizontal dotted line. On the other hand, $\text{EF}_i^{\bar{\Phi}}(\mathbf{v})$ is equal to $\sum_{j=i}^{n}(v_j - v_{j+1}) \cdot (x_i(\mathbf{v}) - x_{j+1}(\mathbf{v}))$, which similarly corresponds to the area above the EF curve and below the horizontal dotted line. It suffices to prove that: $x_i(\mathbf{v}) - x_i(v_{j+1}, \mathbf{v}_{-i}) \geq \frac{1}{2} \cdot (x_i(\mathbf{v}) - x_{j+1}(\mathbf{v}))$. Note that $x_i(v_{j+1}, \mathbf{v}_{-i}) = x_{j+1}(v_{j+1}, \mathbf{v}_{-i})$ as now agents i and $j+1$ have the same value, this is equivalent to $x_i(\mathbf{v}) + x_{j+1}(\mathbf{v}) \geq x_i(v_{j+1}, \mathbf{v}_{-i}) + x_{j+1}(v_{j+1}, \mathbf{v}_{-i})$.

The last inequality says that the total winning probability of agent i and $j+1$ can only decrease if agent i lowers her bid to v_{j+1}. To prove this, we fix the permutation that maps agents to roles of the set system, and show that the number of winning agents from i and $j+1$ can only be lower after agent i decreases her value. There are two cases to verify: (1) Agent i wins after the decrease. Then before the decrease, agent i had higher value, and the optimal feasible set would be the same. (2) Agent $j+1$ wins and agent i loses after the decrease. Then before the decrease, at least one of agents i and $j+1$ would win. □

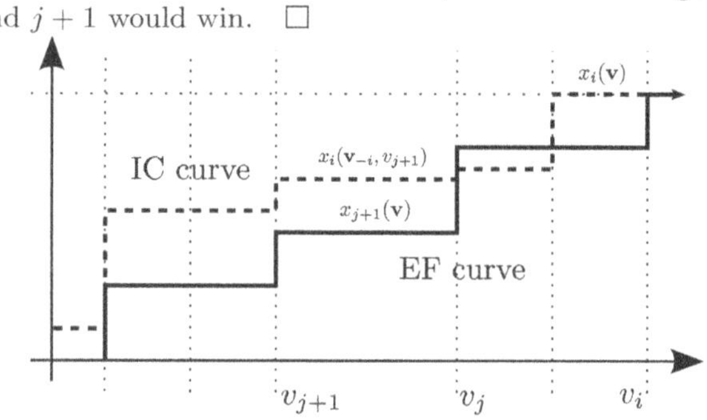

Figure 3: Depiction of EF allocation and IC allocation rule from which the payments for agent i are computed. The EF allocation curve maps each value in $[v_{j+1}, v_j)$ to $x_{j+1}(\mathbf{v})$, and the IC allocation curve maps each z to $x_i(z, \mathbf{v}_{-i})$.

In matroid permutation environments, envy-free revenue upper-bounds incentive compatible revenue.

LEMMA 4.3. *For matroid permutation environments, all valuations* $\mathbf{v}$*, and all ironed virtual valuation functions* $\bar{\Phi}$*, for all agent* i*,* $\text{EF}_i^{\bar{\Phi}}(\mathbf{v}) \geq \text{IC}_i^{\bar{\Phi}}(\mathbf{v})$.

PROOF. Recall that $\text{EF}_i^{\bar{\Phi}}(\mathbf{v}) = \sum_{j=i}^{n}(v_j - v_{j+1}) \cdot (x_i(\mathbf{v}) - x_{j+1}(\mathbf{v}))$ and $\text{IC}_i^{\bar{\Phi}}(\mathbf{v}) = \int_0^{v_i}(x_i(\mathbf{v}) - x_i(z, \mathbf{v}_{-i}))dz$. By the monotonicity of $x_i(z, \mathbf{v}_{-i})$ in z, $\text{IC}_i^{\bar{\Phi}}(\mathbf{v})$ is upper-bounded by $\sum_{j=i}^{n}(v_j - v_{j+1}) \cdot (x_i(\mathbf{v}) - x_i(v_{j+1}, \mathbf{v}_{-i}))$. Recall that $x_i(v_{j+1}, \mathbf{v}_{-i}) = x_{j+1}(v_{j+1}, \mathbf{v}_{-i})$. It suffices to prove that $x_{j+1}(\mathbf{v}) \leq x_{j+1}(v_{j+1}, \mathbf{v}_{-i})$. To see this, ironed virtual surplus maximizers are greedy algorithms in matroid permutation settings, and if agent i decreases her bid to v_{j+1}, agent $j+1$ is less likely to be blocked by i who was earlier in the greedy order, and is hence more likely to be allocated. □

5. PRIOR-FREE MECHANISM DESIGN AND BENCHMARKS

As discussed previously, no incentive compatible mechanism obtains an optimal profit point-wise on all possible valuation profiles. Therefore, to obtain point-wise guarantees, the literature on prior-free mechanism design looks for the incentive compatible mechanism that minimizes, over valuation profiles, its worst-case ratio to a given performance benchmark. It is important to identify a good benchmark for such an analysis to be meaningful.

If the designer had a prior distribution over the agent valuations then she could design the mechanism that maximizes revenue in expectation over this distribution. This is the approach of Bayesian optimal mechanism design as characterized by Myerson [18] and refined by Bulow and Roberts [5]. Given a distribution F, virtual values and revenue curves can be derived. The optimal mechanism is the one that maximizes ironed virtual surplus.

THEOREM 5.1. *[18] When values are i.i.d. from distribution* F *the optimal mechanism,* ICO^F*, is the ironed virtual surplus optimizer for* $\bar{\Phi}$ *corresponding to* F.

If the agent values are indeed drawn from a prior distribution, but the designer is unaware of the distribution, then a reasonable objective might be to design a mechanism that is a good approximation to the optimal mechanism for any unknown distribution. This *prior-independent* objective is a relaxation of our prior-free objective.

One important criterion for a prior-free benchmark is that its approximation should imply prior-independent approximation: if a mechanism is a constant approximation to the benchmark, then for a relevant class of distributions, it should be a constant approximation to the Bayesian optimal mechanism under any distribution from the class.

For matroid permutation environments, Lemma 4.3 implies that for any values $\mathbf{v}$ the optimal envy-free revenue $\mathrm{EFO}(\mathbf{v})$ (which is at least the envy-free revenue of any ironed virtual surplus optimizer) is at least the incentive compatible revenue of any ironed virtual surplus optimizer. By Theorem 5.1, the Bayesian optimal mechanism is an ironed virtual surplus optimizer so $\mathrm{EFO}(\mathbf{v})$ upper-bounds its revenue. Consequently, a prior-free β-approximation to EFO is also a prior-independent β-approximation for all distributions.

Unfortunately, even for simple the digital good environment it is not possible to obtain a prior-free constant approximation to EFO (see [12]). This impossibility arises because it is not possible to approximate the highest value v_1. For essentially the same reason, it is not possible to design a prior-independent constant approximation for all distributions. We therefore restrict attention to the large family of distributions with tails that are not too irregular.

DEFINITION 5.1 (TAIL REGULARITY). *A distribution F is n-tail regular if in n-agent 1-unit environments, the expected revenue of the Vickrey auction is a 2-approximation to that of the Bayesian optimal mechanism.*

The definition of tail regularity is implied by Myerson's regularity assumption via the Bulow-Klemperer Theorem [4]. The intuition for the definition is the following. For n-agent 1-unit environments, all the action happens in the tail of the distribution, i.e, values v for which $F(v) \approx 1 - 1/n$; therefore, irregularity of the rest of the distribution does not have much consequence on revenue. Tail regularity, then, restates the Bulow-Klemperer consequence, as a constraint on the tail of the distribution and leaves the rest unconstrained.

We now define the benchmark for prior-free mechanism design. Approximation of this benchmark guarantees prior-independent approximation of all n-tail-regular distributions.

DEFINITION 5.2. *The* envy-free benchmark *is* $\mathrm{EFO}^{(2)}(\mathbf{v}) = \mathrm{EFO}(\mathbf{v}^{(2)})$ *where* $\mathbf{v}^{(2)} = (v_2, v_2, v_3, \ldots, v_n)$.

THEOREM 5.2. *With any n-agent matroid permutation environment, any n-tail-regular distribution F, and any β-approximation mechanism to $\mathrm{EFO}^{(2)}$, the expected revenue of the mechanism with valuations $\mathbf{v}$ drawn i.i.d. from F is a 3β-approximation to the optimal mechanism for F.*

PROOF SKETCH. By the reduction from matroid permutation environments to multi-unit environments, we focus on showing the result for k-unit auctions. We use tail regularity to get a bound on the payment from the highest agent in terms of the Vickrey auction revenue, v_2. Of course, $\mathrm{EFO}^{(2)}(\mathbf{v})$ is at least v_2, and so the payment from the highest agent is at most $2\,\mathrm{EFO}^{(2)}(\mathbf{v})$ (in expectation over i.i.d. draws of $\mathbf{v}$ from F). The second part of the argument involves bounding the total payments of agents $\{2, \ldots, n\}$, point-wise from above, by $\mathrm{EFO}^{(2)}(\mathbf{v})$. This is possible by Lemma 4.3 and detailed analysis of k-unit auction payments. □

It is useful to compare the EFO benchmark to ones proposed in the literature that are based on the Vickrey-Clarke-Groves (VCG) mechanism with the best (for the particular valuation profile $\mathbf{v}$) reserve price (e.g., [16]). The VCG mechanism with a reserve price first rejects all agents whose values to not meet the reserve, then it serves the remaining agents to maximize the surplus (sum of values).

The VCG-with-reserve benchmark can be expressed as an ironed virtual surplus optimizer, and so by Lemma 4.3, in matroid permutation environments, EFO is no smaller. For a digital good, EFO and VCG-with-reserve are identical. For multi-unit auctions EFO is at most twice VCG-with-reserve [8]. For matroid permutation environments EFO can be (almost) a logarithmic factor larger than VCG-with-reserve. Therefore, the EFO-based benchmark results in stronger approximation guarantees.

LEMMA 5.3. *There exists a distribution F and n-agent matroid environment for which VCG with any reserve price is an $\Omega(\log n/ \log\log n)$-approximation to ICO^F.*

PROOF SKETCH. We construct a set system and an irregular distribution with a jagged revenue curve that has $m = \Omega(\frac{\log n}{\log \log n})$ deep "trenches", such that the following are true. (1) Myerson's mechanism gets about $1/m$ fraction of its revenue from each trench via ironing. (2) The VCG mechanism with reserve gets similar amount of good revenue from at most one of the trenches by setting an appropriate price, but only gets low revenue from the other trenches due to the lack of ironing. In total, VCG with reserve only gets about $1/m$ fraction of Myerson's revenue. □

6. DOWNWARD-CLOSED PERMUTATION ENVIRONMENTS

For downward-closed permutation settings, there are certain bizarre settings where the maximum envy-free revenue may not upper-bound the incentive compatible revenue, which means that approximating the EFO benchmark does not necessarily imply prior-independent approximation for i.i.d. distributions. (See full paper for proof.)

LEMMA 6.1. *There exists a downward-closed set system, and valuation profile $\mathbf{v}$, such that if $\bar{\Phi} = \bar{\Phi}^{\mathbf{v}}$ is the ironed virtual valuation function of $\mathbf{v}$, then $\mathrm{IC}^{\bar{\Phi}}(\mathbf{v}) > \mathrm{EF}^{\bar{\Phi}}(\mathbf{v})$.*

These settings seem pathological, and even in these settings the EF revenue seems to be not too far below the IC revenue of any ironed virtual surplus optimizer. Therefore we believe EFO remains an interesting benchmark for approximation in downward closed settings.

In this section, we will show that a variant of RSEM (recall Definition 3.2) approximates the envy-free benchmark by a constant factor.

DEFINITION 6.1 (RSEM′). *The variant RSEM′ is identical to RSEM except Step 3 where instead it:*

3′ finds the feasible subset W of N (the full set of agents) to maximize surplus with respect to $\bar{\Phi}^S$ and serves agents in $M \cap W$ (the winners from the market M) only, rejecting all others.

In the rest of this section we prove our main theorem.

THEOREM 6.2. *For downward-closed permutation environments,* $\mathrm{IC}^{\mathrm{RSEM}'}(\mathbf{v}) \geq \frac{1}{2560}\,\mathrm{EFO}^{(2)}(\mathbf{v})$ *for all* $\mathbf{v}$.

Consider $\mathrm{EF}^{\bar{\Phi}^S}(\mathbf{v})$, the envy-free revenue of Step 3′ of RSEM′. Notice that $\bar{\Phi}^S$, the ironed virtual valuation function for S, is not the right ironed virtual valuation function for optimizing envy-free revenue on $\mathbf{v}$. The goal of this section is to understand the envy-free revenue that results from optimizing using the wrong ironed virtual valuation function. To do this we introduce two auxiliary revenue curves $\widetilde{\mathrm{R}}$ and $\widehat{\mathrm{R}}$ (and their corresponding valuation profiles). Intuitively, $\widehat{\mathrm{R}}$ corresponds to the revenue we think we get when optimizing $\bar{\Phi}^S$ on $\mathbf{v}$, and $\widetilde{\mathrm{R}}$ corresponds to the revenue curve we actually end up with.

DEFINITION 6.2 (EFFECTIVE REVENUE CURVE $\widetilde{\mathrm{R}}$). *For values* $\mathbf{v}$ *and ironed virtual valuations* $\bar{\Phi}^S$ *for* S*: group agents with equal nonnegative* $\bar{\Phi}^S$ *values into consecutive classes* $\{1,\ldots,n_1\},\{n_1+1,\ldots,n_2\},\ldots,\{n_{t-1}+1,\ldots,n_t\}$ *and define the* effective revenue curve $\widetilde{\mathrm{R}}$ *from* $\mathrm{R}=\mathrm{R}^{\mathbf{v}}$ *by connecting the points* $(0,0),(n_1,\mathrm{R}(n_1)),\ldots,(n_t,R(n_t))$ *and then extending horizontally to* $(n,R(n_t))$*, i.e., ironing the values in each class.*

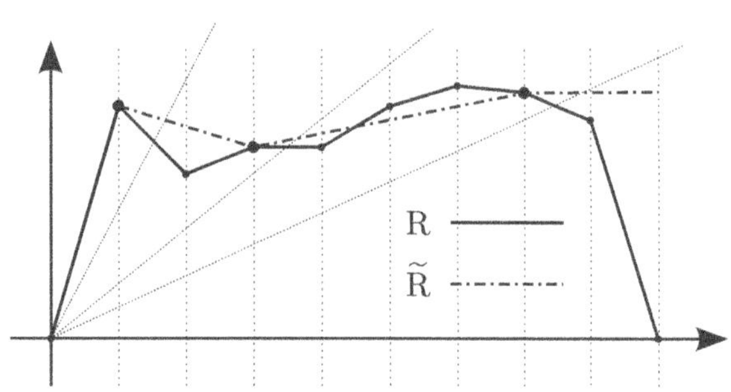

Figure 4: Effective Ironing

Figure 4 depicts an example of the effective revenue curve. The three rays from the origin, which correspond to values at which $\bar{\Phi}^S$ makes a piece-wise jump, divide the first orthant into four regions. For every region, every point $(i,\mathrm{R}(i))$ in the region (which corresponds to value v_i) has the same $\bar{\Phi}^S$ value. In each region these points get "ironed", and hence the line segment in $\widetilde{\mathrm{R}}$.

LEMMA 6.3. $\mathrm{EF}^{\bar{\Phi}^S}(\mathbf{v})=\sum_{i=1}^n \widetilde{\mathrm{R}}(i)\cdot(x_i^S(\mathbf{v})-x_{i+1}^S(\mathbf{v}))$.

PROOF.

$$\begin{aligned}\mathrm{EF}^{\bar{\Phi}^S}(\mathbf{v}) &= \sum\nolimits_{i=1}^n \mathrm{R}(i)\cdot(x_i^S(\mathbf{v})-x_{i+1}^S(\mathbf{v}))\\ &= \sum\nolimits_{i=1}^n \widetilde{\mathrm{R}}(i)\cdot(x_i^S(\mathbf{v})-x_{i+1}^S(\mathbf{v}))\end{aligned}$$

Here the first equality is by Lemma 2.5. To justify the second equality, note that whenever $\widetilde{\mathrm{R}}(i)\neq\mathrm{R}(i)$, there are two cases: (1) i is in $\{n_{j-1}+1,\ldots,n_j-1\}$ for some j, and so v_i and v_{i+1} have the same $\bar{\Phi}^S$ value, and hence $x_i^S(\mathbf{v})=x_{i+1}^S(\mathbf{v})$. (2) i is bigger than n_t, and so v_i and v_{i+1} both have negative $\bar{\Phi}^S$ value, and hence $x_i^S(\mathbf{v})=x_{i+1}^S(\mathbf{v})=0$. □

For a set of agents S, let $\mathbf{v}_S$ denote $(\mathbf{v}_S,\mathbf{0}_{N-S})$, i.e., the valuation profile (of n agents) obtained from $\mathbf{v}$ by decreasing the values of agents outside S to 0. Note that $\mathbf{v}=\mathbf{v}_N$. Let R^S and $\bar{\mathrm{R}}^S$ be the revenue curve and ironed revenue curve of the valuation profile $\mathbf{v}_S$ respectively.

LEMMA 6.4. *For all* $1\leq i\leq n$, $\widetilde{\mathrm{R}}(i)\geq\bar{\mathrm{R}}^S(i)$.

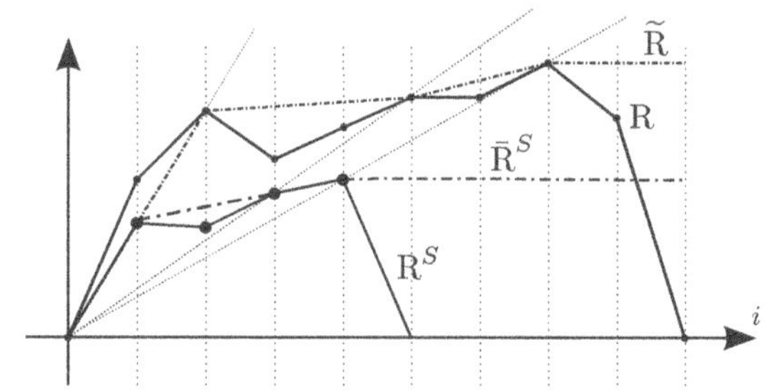

Figure 5: Revenue dominance

PROOF SKETCH. Figure 5 depicts the relationship between the revenue curves. Observe that revenue curve R dominates R^S in the sense that for every slope t, the intersection of the ray $y=tx$ with R is farther away from the origin than its intersection with R^S. Transforming R and R^S to the effective revenue curves using the same ironed virtual valuation function $\bar{\Phi}^S$ do not change such dominance relationship, and moreover, because $\bar{\mathrm{R}}^S$ is non-decreasing and concave, it follows that vertical dominance also holds, i.e., $\widetilde{\mathrm{R}}(i)\geq\bar{\mathrm{R}}^S(i)$ for all i. □

DEFINITION 6.3 (PERCEIVED REVENUE CURVE $\widehat{\mathrm{R}}$). *The* perceived revenue curve *for* $\bar{\Phi}^S$ *on* $\mathbf{v}$ *is given by* $\widehat{\mathrm{R}}(i)=\sum_{j=1}^i\bar{\Phi}^S(v_i)$ *for* $i\in N$.

Let $\hat{\mathbf{v}}$ be the valuation profile corresponding to $\widehat{\mathrm{R}}$, i.e., $\hat{v}_i=\widehat{\mathrm{R}}(i)/i$, and let $\mathbf{x}^{\hat{\mathbf{v}}}$ be the ironed virtual surplus maximizer for $\bar{\Phi}^{\hat{\mathbf{v}}}$.

LEMMA 6.5. $x_i^S(\mathbf{v})=x_i^{\hat{\mathbf{v}}}(\hat{\mathbf{v}})$.

PROOF. Compare running the ironed virtual surplus maximizer $\mathbf{x}^S$ for $\bar{\Phi}^S$ on $\mathbf{v}$ with running $\mathbf{x}^{\hat{\mathbf{v}}}$ for $\bar{\Phi}^{\hat{\mathbf{v}}}$ on $\hat{\mathbf{v}}$, the ironed virtual valuation of agent i in either case is equal to ϕ_i. Therefore these two ironed virtual surplus optimizers will choose the same allocation, and the lemma follows. □

Recall that there are at least two agents. We will focus on the case that agent 1 is in M, and agent 2 is in S.

DEFINITION 6.4. *We say that the partitioning* (S,M) *of agents* $N=\{1,\ldots,n\}$ *is* balanced *if* $Y_i\leq 3i/4$ *and* double-side balanced *if* $i/4\leq Y_i\leq 3i/4$ *for all* $i\in\{3,\ldots,n\}$ *and* $Y_i=|\{1,2,\ldots,i\}\cap S|$.

LEMMA 6.6. *Conditioning on* $1\in M, 2\in S$*, a random partitioning* (S,M) *of* N *is balanced with probability at least* 0.8*, and is double-side balanced with probability at least* 0.6.

LEMMA 6.7. *Given a balanced partitioning* (S,M)*, for every non-increasing sequence* $a_1,\ldots,a_n$ *of nonnegative reals and all* $i\in N$, $\sum_{j\in M\cap\{1,\ldots,i\}}a_j\geq\frac{1}{4}\sum_{j\in\{1,\ldots,i\}}a_j$.

LEMMA 6.8. *If* (S,M) *is a double-side balanced partitioning with* $1\in M, 2\in S$*, then* $\bar{\mathrm{R}}^S(i)\geq\frac{1}{4}\widehat{\mathrm{R}}(i)\geq\frac{1}{4}\bar{\mathrm{R}}^S(i)$ *for all* $1\leq i\leq n$.

PROOF. For each i, $\widehat{\mathrm{R}}(i) = \sum_{j=1}^{i} \phi_j$ and $\bar{\mathrm{R}}^S(i)$ is the sum of the i largest ϕ_j values with $j \in S$. Therefore $\widehat{\mathrm{R}} \geq \bar{\mathrm{R}}^S(i)$. Since (S, M) is double-side balanced, applying Lemma 6.7, we also have that for all i, $\bar{\mathrm{R}}^S(i) \geq \frac{1}{4}\widehat{\mathrm{R}}(i)$. □

Now we are ready prove the following key lemma:

LEMMA 6.9. *For any downward-closed permutation environments, any valuation profile* $\mathbf{v}$, *and double-side balanced partitioning* (S, M), $\mathrm{EF}^{\bar{\Phi}^S}(\mathbf{v}_N) \geq \frac{1}{4}\,\mathrm{EF}^{\bar{\Phi}^S}(\mathbf{v}_S) = \frac{1}{4}\,\mathrm{EFO}(\mathbf{v}_S)$.

PROOF. Let $\mathbf{x}^{\hat{\mathbf{v}}}$ be short-hands for the ironed virtual surplus optimizers with ironed virtual valuation functions defined for $\mathbf{v}_S$ and $\hat{\mathbf{v}}$, respectively. The proof is by the following inequalities:

$$\begin{aligned}
\mathrm{EF}^{\bar{\Phi}^S}(\mathbf{v}_N) &= \sum\nolimits_i \widetilde{\mathrm{R}}(i) \cdot (x_i^S(\mathbf{v}_N) - x_{i+1}^S(\mathbf{v}_N)) \\
&= \sum\nolimits_i \widetilde{\mathrm{R}}(i) \cdot (x_i^{\hat{\mathbf{v}}}(\hat{\mathbf{v}}) - x_{i+1}^{\hat{\mathbf{v}}}(\hat{\mathbf{v}})) \\
&\geq \tfrac{1}{4} \cdot \sum\nolimits_i \widehat{\mathrm{R}}(i) \cdot (x_i^{\hat{\mathbf{v}}}(\hat{\mathbf{v}}) - x_{i+1}^{\hat{\mathbf{v}}}(\hat{\mathbf{v}})) \\
&\geq \tfrac{1}{4} \cdot \sum\nolimits_i \widehat{\mathrm{R}}(i) \cdot (x_i^S(\mathbf{v}_S) - x_{i+1}^S(\mathbf{v}_S)) \\
&\geq \tfrac{1}{4} \cdot \sum\nolimits_i \bar{\mathrm{R}}^S(i) \cdot (x_i^S(\mathbf{v}_S) - x_{i+1}^S(\mathbf{v}_S)).
\end{aligned}$$

Here the first two equalities are guaranteed by our definitions of $\widetilde{\mathrm{R}}$ and $\widehat{\mathrm{R}}$. The first inequality is by Lemma 6.4 and Lemma 6.8, the second inequality is by the optimality of $\mathbf{x}^{\hat{\mathbf{v}}}$ for $\hat{\mathbf{v}}$, and the third inequality is by Lemma 6.8 again. □

The following lemma, together with symmetry, will help us relate $\mathrm{EFO}(\mathbf{v}_S)$ to $\mathrm{EFO}(\mathbf{v}_N)$.

LEMMA 6.10. *For a partitioning* (S, M) *of* N, *we have that* $\mathrm{EFO}(\mathbf{v}_S) + \mathrm{EFO}(\mathbf{v}_M) \geq \mathrm{EFO}(\mathbf{v}_N)$.

PROOF. $\mathrm{EFO}(\mathbf{v}_N) = \mathrm{EFO}(\mathbf{v}_{S \cup M})$ is the maximum revenue we can get from $S \cup M$ subject to the envy free constraints. Let agents in M contribute total revenue R to $\mathrm{EFO}(\mathbf{v}_N)$. By setting the agents in S to have zero valuations to obtain valuation profile $\mathbf{v}_S$, we basically removed envy-free constraints between agents in S and agents in M. With less envy free constraints, the maximum envy-free revenue we can get from M, i.e., $\mathrm{EFO}(\mathbf{v}_M)$, can only be larger. Similarly, the total revenue that S contributes to $\mathrm{EFO}(\mathbf{v}_N)$ is at most $\mathrm{EFO}(\mathbf{v}_S)$, and our lemma follows. □

Now we can establish the performance guarantee for RSEM′.

PROOF OF THEOREM 6.2. We condition our analysis on that agent 1 is in M, and agent 2 is in S, which happens with probability $1/4$. Conditioning on this, by Lemma 6.6, the partitioning (S, M) is double-side balanced with probability 0.6, and by Lemma 6.10 and symmetry, $\mathrm{EFO}(\mathbf{v}_S) \geq \frac{1}{2}\,\mathrm{EFO}(\mathbf{v}_N)$ with probability 0.5. Both of these events happen with probability at least $1 - (1 - 0.6) - (1 - 0.5) = 0.1$.

We assume both events happen. For each i, by Lemma 4.2, we have $\mathrm{IC}_i^{\mathbf{x}^S}(\mathbf{v}_N) \geq \frac{1}{2}\,\mathrm{EF}_i^{\bar{\Phi}^S}(\mathbf{v}_N)$. Note that $\mathrm{EF}_i^{\bar{\Phi}^S}(\mathbf{v}_N)$ is non-increasing in i. Because (S, M) is balanced, applying Lemma 6.7, we have $\sum_{i \in M} \mathrm{EF}_i^{\bar{\Phi}^S}(\mathbf{v}_N) \geq \sum_{i \in N} \frac{1}{4} \cdot \mathrm{EF}_i^{\bar{\Phi}^S}(\mathbf{v}_N)$ and therefore by Lemma 4.2, $\sum_{i \in M} \mathrm{IC}_i^{\mathbf{x}^S}(\mathbf{v}_N) \geq \frac{1}{8}\,\mathrm{EF}^{\bar{\Phi}^S}(\mathbf{v}_N)$. Together with that $\mathrm{EF}^{\bar{\Phi}^S}(\mathbf{v}_N) \geq \frac{1}{4}\,\mathrm{EF}^{\bar{\Phi}^S}(\mathbf{v}_S) \geq \frac{1}{8}\,\mathrm{EFO}(\mathbf{v}^{(2)})$ by Lemma 6.9 and Lemma 6.10, we have $\sum_{i \in M} \mathrm{IC}_i^{\mathbf{x}^S}(\mathbf{v}_N) \geq \frac{1}{64}\,\mathrm{EFO}(\mathbf{v}^{(2)})$, and our theorem follows by multiplying the ratio with the probabilities. □

7. REFERENCES

[1] S. Alaei, A. Malekian, and A. Srinivasan. On random sampling auctions for digital goods. In *Proc. 11th ACM Conf. on Electronic Commerce (EC)*, pages 187–196, 2009.

[2] L. Ausubel and P. Milgrom. Ascending auctions with package bidding. In *Frontiers of Theoretical Economics*, volume 1, 2002.

[3] M.-F. Balcan, A. Blum, J. Hartline, and Y. Mansour. Mechanism Design via Machine Learning. In *Proc. 46th IEEE Symp. on Foundations of Computer Science (FOCS)*, pages 605–614, 2005.

[4] J. Bulow and P. Klemperer. Auctions versus negotiations. *American Economic Review*, 86(1):180–194, 1996.

[5] J. Bulow and J. Roberts. The simple economics of optimal auctions. *The Journal of Political Economy*, 97:1060–90, 1989.

[6] E. Cohen, M. Feldman, A. Fiat, H. Kaplan, and S. Olonetsky. On the interplay between incentive compatibility and envy freeness. 2010.

[7] R. Day and P. Milgrom. Core-selecting auctions. *International Journal of Game Theory*, 36(3-4):393–407, 2008.

[8] N. Devanur and J. Hartline. Limited and online supply and the bayesian foundations of prior-free mechanism design. In *Proc. 11th ACM Conf. on Electronic Commerce (EC)*, 2009.

[9] P. Dhangwatnotai, T. Roughgarden, and Q. Yan. Revenue maximization with a single sample. In *Proc. 12th ACM Conf. on Electronic Commerce (EC)*, 2010.

[10] S. Dughmi, T. Roughgarden, and M. Sundararajan. Revenue submodularity. In *EC '09: Proceedings of the tenth ACM conference on Electronic commerce*, pages 243–252, 2009.

[11] A. Goldberg and J. Hartline. Envy-free auctions for digital goods. In *Proc. 5th ACM Conf. on Electronic Commerce (EC)*. ACM Press, 2003.

[12] A. Goldberg, J. Hartline, A. Karlin, M. Saks, and A. Wright. Competitive auctions. *Games and Economic Behavior*, 55(2):242–269, 2006.

[13] V. Guruswami, J. Hartline, A. Karlin, D. Kempe, C. Kenyon, and F. McSherry. On profit-maximizing envy-free pricing. In *Proc. 16th ACM Symp. on Discrete Algorithms (SODA)*, 2005.

[14] J. Hartline and R. McGrew. From optimal limited to unlimited supply auctions. In *Proc. 7th ACM Conf. on Electronic Commerce (EC)*, pages 175–182, 2005.

[15] J. Hartline and T. Roughgarden. Optimal mechanism design and money burning. In *Proc. 39th ACM Symp. on Theory of Computing (STOC)*, pages 75–84, 2008.

[16] J. Hartline and T. Roughgarden. Simple versus optimal mechanisms. In *Proc. 11th ACM Conf. on Electronic Commerce (EC)*, 2009.

[17] A. Mu'alem. On multi-dimensional envy-free mechanisms. In *Conference on Algorithmic Decision Theory*, pages 120–131, 2009.

[18] R. Myerson. Optimal auction design. *Mathematics of Operations Research*, 6(1):58–73, 1981.

[19] R. Rado. An equality. *J. London Math. Soc.*, 27:1–6, 1952.

Bayesian Mechanism Design for Budget-Constrained Agents *

Shuchi Chawla
Univ. of Wisconsin-Madison
Madison, WI, USA
shuchi@cs.wisc.edu

David L. Malec
Univ. of Wisconsin-Madison
Madison, WI, USA
dmalec@cs.wisc.edu

Azarakhsh Malekian
Northwestern University
Evanston, IL, USA
a-malekian@northwestern.edu

ABSTRACT

We study Bayesian mechanism design problems in settings where agents have budgets. Specifically, an agent's utility for an outcome is given by his value for the outcome minus any payment he makes to the mechanism, as long as the payment is below his budget, and is negative infinity otherwise. This discontinuity in the utility function presents a significant challenge in the design of good mechanisms, and classical "unconstrained" mechanisms fail to work in settings with budgets. The goal of this paper is to develop general reductions from budget-constrained Bayesian MD to unconstrained Bayesian MD with small loss in performance. We consider this question in the context of the two most well-studied objectives in mechanism design—social welfare and revenue—and present constant factor approximations in a number of settings. Some of our results extend to settings where budgets are private and agents need to be incentivized to reveal them truthfully.

Categories and Subject Descriptors

J.4 [**Social and Behavioral Sciences**]: Economics

General Terms

Algorithms, Economics, Theory

Keywords

Bayesian mechanism design, budgets, revenue, welfare

1. INTRODUCTION

Auction and mechanism design have for the most part focused on agents with quasilinear utility functions: each agent is described by a function that assigns values to possible outcomes, and the agent's utility from an outcome is her value minus any payment that she makes to the mechanism. This implies, for example, that an agent offered an outcome at a price below her value for the outcome should in the absence of better alternatives immediately accept that outcome. This simple model fails to capture a basic practical issue—agents may not necessarily be able to afford outcomes that they value highly. For example, most people would value a large precious stone such as the Kohinoor diamond at several millions of dollars (for its resale value, if not for personal reasons), but few can afford to pay even a fraction of that amount. Many real-world mechanism design scenarios involve financially constrained agents and values alone fail to capture agents' preferences. Budget constraints have frequently been observed in FCC spectrum auctions [5, 8], Google's auction for TV ads [18], and sponsored search auctions, to take a few examples.

From a theoretical viewpoint, the introduction of budget constraints presents a challenge in mechanism design because they make the utility of an agent nonlinear and discontinuous as a function of the agent's payment—the utility decreases linearly with payment while payment stays below the budget, but drops to negative infinity when the payment crosses the budget. The assumption of linearity in payments (i.e. quasilinearity of utility) underlies much of the theoretical framework for mechanism design. Consequently, standard mechanisms such as the VCG mechanism can no longer be employed in settings involving budgets.

The goal of this paper is to develop connections between budget-constrained mechanism design and the well-developed theory of unconstrained mechanism design. Specifically we ask "when can budget-constrained mechanism design be reduced to unconstrained mechanism design with some small loss in performance?" We consider this question in the context of the two most well-studied objectives in mechanism design—social welfare and revenue. Some of our results assume that the mechanism knows the budgets of the agents, but others hold even when budgets are private and agents need to be incentivized to reveal them truthfully.

Recent work in computer science has begun exploring a theory of mechanism design for budget-constrained agents (see, for example, [1, 4, 11, 10, 2]). Most of this work has focused on *prior-free* or worst-case settings, where the mechanism designer has no information about agents' preferences. Unsurprisingly, the mechanism designer has very little power in such settings, and numerous impossibility results hold. For example, in the worst-case setting no truthful mechanism can obtain a non-trivial approximation to social welfare [4]. The goal of achieving good social welfare has therefore been abandoned in favor of weaker notions such as Pareto optimality [11]. For the revenue objective while approximations can be achieved in simple enough settings, e.g. multi-unit auctions [4], hardness results hold for more general feasibility constraints even in the absence of budgets. In this paper, we sidestep these impossibility results by considering Bayesian settings where the mech-

*This work was supported in part by NSF awards no. CCF-0830494 and CCF-0643763, and a Sloan Foundation fellowship.

EC'11, June 5–9, 2011, San Jose, California, USA.

anism designer has prior information about the distributions from which agents' private values and private budgets are drawn.

We restrict our attention to direct revelation truthful mechanisms. Our mechanisms are allowed to randomize, and agents' utilities are computed in expectation over the randomness used by the mechanism. As is standard, we assume that both the mechanism and the agents possess a common prior from which values are drawn. While we optimize over the class of Bayesian incentive compatible (BIC) mechanisms, all of the mechanisms we develop are dominant strategy incentive compatible (DSIC) (see, for example, [17] for definitions of these solution concepts).

In addition, we require that our mechanisms satisfy the ex-post individual rationality (EPIR) constraint, namely that the payment of any agent never exceeds her value for the mechanism's outcome. This implies, in particular, that the mechanism cannot charge any agent to whom no item or service is allocated. In contrast, most previous work has enforced the individual rationality constraint only in expectation over the mechanism's randomness as well as the randomness in other agents' values (i.e. interim IR).

It is worth noting here that the EPIR constraint is not without loss in performance. Consider the following example: suppose we are selling a single item to one of n agents, each with a value of v with probability 1 (that is publicly known) and a public budget of v/n with probability 1. Now, under the IIR constraint, the optimal auction asks agents to pay what they bid and offers each agent that pays at least v/n a fair chance at winning the item. Each agent pays v/n, the item is allocated to a random agent, and the mechanism's revenue is v. Under the EPIR constraint, however, a mechanism can only charge the agent that wins the item and can charge this agent no more than v/n. As we can see, the revenue gap between the optimal IIR and the optimal EPIR mechanism gets larger and larger as n grows.

It is well known that over the class of BIC IIR mechanisms, the revenue-optimal as well as welfare-optimal mechanisms are both so-called "all-pay" auctions [15, 19]. In all-pay auctions agents pay the mechanism a certain (distribution dependent) function of their value regardless of the allocation that the mechanism makes. The optimality of all-pay auctions follows by noting that any allocation rule that admits some BIC budget-feasible payment function can be implemented with an all-pay payment rule with worst-case payments that are no larger than those in any other truthful payment rule and are therefore budget-feasible. Unfortunately all-pay auctions have many undesirable properties. In many settings it is simply not feasible to force the agents to pay upfront without knowing the outcome of the mechanism. Moreover all-pay auctions may admit many Bayes-Nash equilibria (BNE), truthtelling being merely one of them. Then the fact that a certain objective is achieved when all the agents report their true types does not necessarily imply that the objective will be achieved in practice if a different BNE gets played out. Therefore, in a departure from previous work, we choose to enforce ex-post individual rationality.

Our results and techniques.

We begin our investigation with the revenue objective and give an exact characterization of the optimal mechanism for a single agent with a public budget. While in the absence of budgets the optimal mechanism is a fixed sale price and therefore deterministic, with budgets the optimal mechanism may need to randomize and offer multiple buying options to the agent. This complicates the design of optimal mechanisms in more general settings involving multiple agents or private budgets. We therefore consider approximations. When budgets are known publicly, we obtain constant factor approximations in nearly all settings where constant factor approximations are known for unconstrained mechanism design. This includes, for example, all single-parameter settings with a downwards closed feasibility constraint, but also multi-parameter settings with "unit-demand" agents and a matroid feasibility constraint (see, e.g., [6]). Our mechanisms are for the most part direct reductions to unconstrained settings, and are extremely simple.

For private budgets, the problem becomes much harder and we focus on settings with single-dimensional values. We design a novel mechanism based on "lotteries" that obtains a good approximation whenever each agent's value distribution satisfies the monotone hazard rate (MHR) condition (see Section 2 for a definition). Our mechanism's novelty lies in offering each agent a carefully constructed set of different buying options such that the best option for the agent is to either spend his entire budget or a fraction of the monopoly price for that agent. The MHR assumption is a frequently used assumption in mechanism design literature and many natural distributions satisfy it. In fact the mechanism obtains a good approximation more generally under mild technical conditions on the values and budgets. We believe that our techniques should extend to provide good approximations for arbitrary distributions.

Next we examine the welfare objective. While for revenue, the budget of an agent is a natural upper bound on the contribution of that agent to the revenue and allows us to "cap" values at the budget, for welfare this doesn't work. In fact, a mechanism can generate a non-trivial guarantee on welfare even when budgets are 0. Consider a setting with two unit demand buyers and two items. Consider the following mechanism: the mechanism asks each agent to give a preference list of the items. If the top choices of the buyers are different, then each buyer gets allocated his top choice and welfare is maximized. Otherwise, the mechanism ignores the preferences of the buyers and computes the allocation that maximizes the social welfare ex-ante. Note that this mechanism is truthful. When agents' values for the items are i.i.d., the obtained social welfare from this example is at least $3/4$ of the maximum social welfare we can obtain with no budget constraint. On the other hand, a mechanism that "ignores" values above the budget (i.e. does not distinguish between them in the allocation function) cannot obtain an approximation better than $1/2$. The gap between the two mechanisms increases as the number of agents grows.

We again focus on single-parameter settings and public budgets, but with arbitrary downwards closed feasibility constraints. For these settings, we show a tradeoff between an approximation on budget and an approximation on welfare: for any ϵ, we can get a $1/\epsilon$ approximation to welfare with respect to the welfare that an optimal mechanism can get when budgets are scaled down by a factor of $1-\epsilon$. This mechanism has an extremely simple form: it replaces every value larger than its budget by its expectation conditioned on being larger than the budget, and runs the VCG mechanism on these modified values. Moreover, if we are willing to sacrifice EPIR in favor of the less restrictive IIR, we can convert this mechanism into a 4-approximate IIR mechanism (with no approximation on budgets).

Finally, if the value distributions satisfy the MHR condition, we achieve a $2(1+e)$-approximation to welfare via an EPIR mechanism by reducing budget-feasible welfare maximization to budget-feasible revenue maximization.

One nice property of our reductions from budget feasible mechanism design to unconstrained mechanism design is that they are for the most part oblivious to the feasibility constraint imposed on the mechanism. They therefore work for a broad range of feasibility constraints and add minimal complexity to the mechanism design problem.

Related work.

Several works in economics have studied characterizations of optimal BIC IIR budget-feasible mechanisms (e.g., [19, 14, 9, 15]). However, these works are generally weak in the kinds of settings they consider (typically just single-item auctions) and the kinds of value distributions they allow[1]. Laffont and Robert [14] considered single item settings where bidders have a private value and public common budget. Che and Gale [9] considered the setting with a single item and a single buyer, but allowed both the value and the budget to be private. Pai and Vohra [19] gave a more general result in which they designed an optimal auction for a single item and multiple buyers with private i.i.d. values and private budgets.

Bhattacharya et al. [3] were the first to study settings beyond single-item auctions and focused on revenue maximization. They considered a setting with heterogeneous items and additive values, and exhibited a (large) constant factor DSIC approximation mechanism as well as an all-pay auction which admits truthtelling as a BNE and in that BNE obtains a 4-approximation. However, these results required the value distributions to satisfy the MHR condition. The mechanisms are LP-based. In contrast most of our mechanisms are easy to compute, work for general distributions, enforce EPIR, and achieve small approximation factors.

In prior-free settings few results are known for revenue maximization. Borgs et al. [4] looked at multi unit auctions for homogeneous goods where agents have private values and budgets and considered worst case competitive ratio (see also [1]). They designed a mechanism based on random sampling that maximizes revenue when the number of bidders is large.

Social welfare maximization has also been considered under budget constraints. Maskin [15] considered the setting of a single item and multiple buyers with public budgets. He defined and showed how to compute the constrained efficient mechanism, the truthful feasible mechanism under budget constraints that maximizes the expected social welfare (however, the result holds only for some distribution functions [19]). In prior-free settings for multi unit homogeneous items, Nisan et al. [11] studied Pareto efficient DSIC mechanisms with budget constraints. They showed that if the budgets are private there is no Pareto optimal incentive compatible mechanism; for public budgets they showed that there exists a unique mechanism based on the *clinching auction*. Chen et al. [10] considered a setting with multiple goods and unit demand buyers and showed how to compute competitive prices that enforce truthfulness under budget constraints if such prices exist. Finally, the work of Alaei et al. [2] stands out in their study of "soft" budgets constraints, where buyers pay an increasing interest rate for payments made above their budgets. They showed how to exactly compute the smallest competitive prices in this setting that result in an incentive compatible mechanism with an outcome in the core.

2. NOTATION AND DEFINITIONS

In this work, we consider instances of the Bayesian mechanism design problem where agents have single- and multi-dimensional types; instances are of the form $\mathcal{I} = (\mathbf{F}, \mathcal{S}, \mathbf{B})$.

In the single-dimensional case, $\mathbf{F} = \prod_i F_i$ is a product distribution; each agent i has a single value $v_i \sim F_i$ for receiving service (and derives value 0 if not served), and an upper limit B_i on how much he or she can pay for service; and $\mathcal{S}$ is a feasibility constraint specifying which sets of agents may be simultaneously served.

In the multi-dimensional case, the seller offers a number of services indexed by j to agents, and $\mathbf{F} = \prod_{i,j} F_{ij}$ is again a product distribution; each agent i has a value for receiving service j of $v_{ij} \sim F_{ij}$ and is interested in receiving at most one service; and the agent has a budget limit of B_i. Here, $\mathcal{S}$ is a feasibility constraint over pairs (i, j).

We also consider settings with private budgets; in that case, we replace $\mathbf{B}$ with a distribution $\mathbf{G} = \prod_i G_i$ and agent i has a budget $B_i \sim G_i$.

We focus on incentive compatible (IC) and individually rational (IR) mechanisms, and further distinguish between Bayesian IC and dominant strategy IC, and interim IR and ex post IR. See [17] for definitions of these concepts.

Let M be a mechanism for the instance $\mathcal{I}$. We shall denote its expected allocation to each agent by the vector $\mathbf{x}(\mathbf{v}, \mathbf{B})$, and agents' expected payments by $\mathbf{p}(\mathbf{v}, \mathbf{B})$ (we omit the second parameter when $\mathbf{B}$ is fixed). Then the expected revenue of M is $\mathcal{R}^M = \mathrm{E}_{\mathbf{v},\mathbf{B}}[\mathbf{p}(\mathbf{v}, \mathbf{B}) \cdot \mathbf{x}(\mathbf{v}, \mathbf{B})]$, and its expected social welfare is $\mathrm{E}_{\mathbf{v},\mathbf{B}}[\mathbf{v} \cdot \mathbf{x}(\mathbf{v}, \mathbf{B})]$

Given that an agent i has a value v for receiving service, and a budget constraint B, his or her utility from receiving the service with probability x at a price p is $u(v, B) = x \cdot v - p$ if $p \leq B$, and $u(v, B) = -\infty$ otherwise. A mechanism is budget feasible if it never requests an agent to make a payment above his budget.

Virtual values and the monotone hazard rate condition.

In the absence of budget constraints, for revenue maximization Myerson in his seminal work [16] gives a characterization of the optimal mechanism as a "virtual value maximizer". Specifically, given any distribution function F with density f, Myerson defines a *virtual value* function as follows:

$$\phi(v) = v - \frac{1 - F(v)}{f(v)}$$

We use the following characterization by Myerson of the expected revenue of BIC mechanisms in terms of their virtual surplus.

LEMMA 1. *Consider any BIC mechanism with allocation function* $\mathbf{x}$ *for a single-parameter problem* $\mathcal{I} = (\mathbf{F}, \mathcal{S})$. *Then the expected revenue of the mechanism is exactly* $\mathrm{E}_{\mathbf{v} \sim \mathbf{F}}[\sum_i x_i(\mathbf{v})\phi_i(\mathbf{v})]$.

A distribution is said to be *regular* if $\phi(v)$ is a non-decreasing function of v. When value distributions are regular, a mechanism that allocates to the feasible set that maximizes the total virtual value is BIC and optimal. For a single agent, this mechanism allocates to the agent as long as his value is above the threshold $\phi^{-1}(0)$; we call this threshold the *monopoly price* corresponding to the value distribution.

When value distributions are not regular, Myerson gives an "ironing" procedure that converts a virtual value function into an ironed virtual value function, $\bar{\phi}$, such that maximizing ironed virtual surplus results in a BIC optimal mechanism. We omit the details of the ironing.

Some of our results require a stronger condition on distributions called the monotone hazard rate condition, a common assumption in mechanism design literature. This condition is satisfied by many common distributions such as the uniform, Gaussian, exponential, and power law distributions.

DEFINITION 1. *A distribution* F *with density* f *is said to have a* **monotone hazard rate** *if the function* $h(v) = f(v)/(1 - F(v))$ *is non-decreasing in* v. *Distributions satisfying MHR are regular.*

[1] E.g., [19] and [15] make the assumption that value distributions have a monotone hazard rate as well as a nondecreasing density function, conditions that few distributions satisfy in combination.

3. MAXIMIZING REVENUE

We first consider the revenue objective, and begin by characterizing the optimal budget feasible mechanism for a single agent setting. The characterization relies on describing the mechanism as a collection of so-called lotteries or randomized pricings. We then consider settings with public budgets. Our general approach towards budget-constrained mechanism design in these settings is to approximate the optimal revenue in two parts: the contribution to optimal revenue by agents whose budget is binding (i.e. their budget is less than their value), and the contribution by agents whose budget is not binding (i.e. their budget is above their value). We present different mechanisms for approximating these two benchmarks. We demonstrate this approach first in the simple setting of single-parameter agents with public budgets and an arbitrary downwards closed feasibility constraint. Then in subsequent sections we extend the approach to settings involving more complicated incentive constraints—multi-dimensional values and private budgets. In private budget settings, instead of asking agents to reveal budgets directly, our mechanism once again relies on collections of lotteries to motivate agents to pay a good fraction of their budgets when their values are high enough.

Single agent settings with public budgets.

Before presenting our general approach, we first consider the most basic version of this problem—namely a setting with one single-parameter agent and a public budget constraint. Even this simple setting, however, reveals the challenges budget constraints introduce to the problem of mechanism design. Without the budget constraint, the optimal mechanism is to offer the item at a fixed price. With budgets, however, the following example shows that a single fixed price can be a factor of 2 from optimal. After the example we proceed to characterize the optimal mechanism.

EXAMPLE 1. *Fix $n > 1$. Consider an agent whose value for receiving an item is $v = 1$ with probability $1 - 1/n$, and is $v = n^2$ with probability $1/n$. Let the agent have a budget of $B = n$. Any single fixed price that respects the budget in this setting receives a revenue of at most 1.*

We now describe the optimal mechanism. The mechanism offers two options to the agent: either buy the item at price n, or receive the item with a probability of $n/(n+1)$ at a price of $n/(n+1)$. This generates an expected revenue of $2n/(n+1) = 2 - o(1)$.

The optimal mechanism in the above example is what we call a *lottery menu* mechanism. A lottery is a pair (x, p) and offers to the agent at a price p a probability x of winning. A lottery menu is a collection of lotteries that an agent is free to choose from in order to maximize his expected utility. We will now show that for any single agent setting with a public budget, the optimal mechanism is a lottery menu mechanism with at most two options.

Consider a setting $\mathcal{I}$ with a single agent with private value $v \sim F$ and a public budget B. Let ϕ be the virtual value function corresponding to F. For ease of exposition, throughout the following discussion we will assume that F is regular and ϕ is non-decreasing; when F is non-regular, we can merely replace ϕ by $\bar{\phi}$, the ironed virtual value, in the following discussion.

We first note that if $B \geq \phi^{-1}(0)$ then the unconstrained optimal mechanism is already budget feasible. Therefore, for the rest of this section we assume that $B < \phi^{-1}(0)$. Following Lemma 1, our goal is to solve the following optimization problem.

$$\max_x \int x(v)\phi(v)f(v)dv \qquad \text{subject to}$$
$$\int (x_{\max} - x(v))dv \leq B \cdot x_{\max}, \qquad \text{and,}$$
$$x(v) \text{ is a non-decreasing function.}$$

Here $x_{\max} \leq 1$ is the probability of allocation at the upper end of the support of the value distribution. The first constraint encodes the budget constraint. In particular, the left hand side of the inequality is the expected payment made by the agent at his highest value; the right side is an upper bound on the expected payment under EPIR because the agent can pay a maximum of B when he gets allocated, and 0 otherwise.

Let x^* be the optimal solution to the above optimization problem. We make the following observations (each follows by observing that a function x can be modified in a natural fashion to satisfy them, while maintaining the constraints and improving the objective value). In the following, we denote the inverse virtual value of 0 as $v^* = \phi^{-1}(0)$ to simplify notation.

CLAIM 1. *Without loss of generality, we may assume $x^*_{max} = 1$.*

CLAIM 2. *Without loss of generality, we may assume that for all $v \geq v^*$, $x^*(v) = 1$.*

Following these claims, our optimization problem changes to the following (the monotonicity constraint on x is implicit).

$$\max_x \int x(v)\phi(v)f(v)dv \qquad \text{subject to}$$
$$\int (1 - x(v))dv \leq B$$
$$x(v) = 1 \ \forall v \geq v^*$$

This can be simplified to:

$$\min_x \int_0^{v^*} x(v)(-\phi(v)f(v))dv \qquad \text{subject to}$$
$$\int_0^{v^*} (1 - x(v))dv = B$$

Note that we replace the inequality in the budget constraint with an equality. This is because if the constraint is not tight, we can feasibly reduce $x(v)$ and thereby reduce the objective function value. For the sake of brevity, we define $B' = v^* - B$, and $g(v) = -\phi(v)f(v)$. The budget constraint then changes to $\int_0^{v^*} x(v)dv = B'$. Note that $v^* \geq B' \geq 0$, and g is nonnegative on $[0, v^*]$. Finally, we define the set of allocations

$$\mathcal{A} = \left\{ \begin{array}{c} \text{increasing } x : [0, v^*] \to [0, 1] \\ \text{such that } \int_0^{v^*} x(v)dv = B' \end{array} \right\}$$

Then, we can express our objective as

$$\min_{x \in \mathcal{A}} \int_0^{v^*} x(v)g(v)dv.$$

If g is non-increasing on $[0, v^*]$, then we immediately have that the optimal solution is to set $x(v) = 1$ if $v \geq v^* - B'$ $(= B)$ and 0 otherwise.

If g is not non-increasing, we "iron" the function g to produce a non-increasing function $\hat{g}$ with the property that any non-decreasing function x that is constant over intervals where $\hat{g}$ is constant has the same integral with respect to $\hat{g}$ as with respect to g. Let $\widetilde{\mathcal{A}}$ be the subset of $\mathcal{A}$ containing all functions x that are constant over intervals where $\hat{g}$ is constant. We obtain the following lemma. (The details of the ironing procedure and the proof of the following lemma can be found in the full version of the paper [7].)

LEMMA 2. *For all $x \in \mathcal{A}$, there exists a $\tilde{x} \in \widetilde{\mathcal{A}}$, such that $\int_0^{v^*} x(v)g(v)dv \geq \int_0^{v^*} \tilde{x}(v)g(v)dv$.*

The lemma lets us confine our optimization to the set $\widetilde{\mathcal{A}}$:

$$\min_{x \in \mathcal{A}} \int_0^{v^*} x(v)g(v)dv = \min_{x \in \widetilde{\mathcal{A}}} \int_0^{v^*} x(v)g(v)dv$$

Finally, we define $\mathcal{A}^*$ to be a subset of $\widetilde{\mathcal{A}}$ in which functions x take on at most three different values – 0, 1, and an intermediate value. The final part of our proof is to show that the optimal solution lies in this set.

THEOREM 3. *For any single agent setting $\mathcal{I} = (F, B)$, there is an optimal mechanism with allocation rule in the set $\mathcal{A}^*$.*

PROOF. Recall that the optimal solution x^* lies in the set $\widetilde{\mathcal{A}}$. Suppose for contradiction that this function takes on two different intermediate values, $x^*(v_1) = y$ and $x^*(v_2) = z$, between 0 and 1 with $y < z$. Then, since $\hat{g}$ is non-increasing and x^* is non-decreasing, we must have $\hat{g}(v_1) > \hat{g}(v_2)$. Now we can improve our objective function value by increasing x^* between v_2 and the value at which it becomes 1, and decreasing x^* between the value at which it becomes strictly positive and v_1, while maintaining the budget constraint. This contradicts the optimality of x^*. □

Single parameter setting with public budgets.

We now consider single parameter settings with multiple agents. Let $\mathcal{I} = (\mathbf{F}, \mathcal{S}, \mathbf{B})$ be an instance of single-parameter budget-constrained revenue maximization. Define the truncated distributions $\widehat{F}_i$ as follows.

$$\widehat{F}_i(v) = \begin{cases} F_i(v) & \text{if } v < B_i\text{; and} \\ 1 & \text{if } v \geq B_i. \end{cases} \tag{1}$$

Let $\widehat{\mathcal{I}} = (\widehat{\mathbf{F}}, \mathcal{S})$ be the modified setting where we replace $\mathbf{F}$ with $\widehat{\mathbf{F}}$ — note that for each i, the support of $\widehat{F}_i$ ends at or before B_i, and so we may remove the budgets since they place no constraint on the instance $\widehat{\mathcal{I}}$.

A mechanism for $\widehat{\mathcal{I}}$ naturally extends to $\mathcal{I}$, while satisfying budget feasibility and obtaining the same revenue. Our general technique will be to relate the revenue of a mechanism for $\mathcal{I}$ to that of a mechanism for $\widehat{\mathcal{I}}$. In general, the latter can be quite small, and so we introduce the following quantity to bound this loss. Define the set $\mathcal{B}$ as

$$\mathcal{B} = \operatorname*{argmax}_{S \in \mathcal{S}} \left\{ \sum_{i \in S} B_i \middle| \forall i \in S, v_i \geq B_i \right\}. \tag{2}$$

Our basic approach is to design a BIC mechanism $\widehat{M}$ for the setting $\widehat{\mathcal{I}}$ based on the original mechanism M such that we have

$$\mathcal{R}^M \leq \mathcal{R}^{\widehat{M}} + \mathrm{E}\left[\sum_{i \in \mathcal{B}} B_i\right]. \tag{3}$$

Then, the first term on the right is bounded above by the revenue of the optimal mechanism for $\widehat{\mathcal{I}}$. We further demonstrate in each case that we can bound the expectation $\mathrm{E}\left[\sum_{i \in \mathcal{B}} B_i\right]$ by another mechanism for $\widehat{\mathcal{I}}$.

We define the mechanism $\widehat{M}$ in terms of its expected allocation and payment. Let $\mathbf{x}(\mathbf{v})$ and $\mathbf{p}(\mathbf{v})$ be the expected allocations and expected payments for M, respectively. Define the expected allocation and expected payment rules for $\widehat{M}$ as follows. For each agent i in the setting $\widehat{\mathcal{I}}$ with valuation $\hat{v}_i$, draw a corresponding v_i consistent with $\hat{v}_i = \min(v_i, B_i)$; in this case that simply means $v_i = \hat{v}_i$ if $\hat{v}_i < B_i$, and $v_i \sim F_i(v \mid v \geq B_i)$ otherwise. Then $\widehat{M}$'s expected allocation and payment are given by

$$\hat{x}_i(\hat{\mathbf{v}}) = x_i(\mathbf{v}_{-i}, \hat{v}_i)\text{; and}$$
$$\hat{p}_i(\hat{\mathbf{v}}) = p_i(\mathbf{v}_{-i}, \hat{v}_i),$$

respectively.

LEMMA 4. *$\widehat{M}$ is a feasible BIC mechanism for $\widehat{\mathcal{I}}$.*

PROOF. We first note that from the point of view of a single agent i, the expected allocation and price function of $\widehat{M}$ behave as though other agents' values are the same as before. Therefore, the expected allocation is still an increasing function of value and the payments satisfy BIC. We will now argue that the expected allocation function can be implemented in a way that the resulting outcome is a randomization over feasible outcomes. To do so, we first compute $x_i(\mathbf{v})$, as well as $\hat{x}_i(\hat{\mathbf{v}})$ for all i. Starting with the allocation returned by $\mathbf{x}(\mathbf{v})$, for every agent i in this allocation, with probability $\hat{x}_i(\hat{\mathbf{v}})/x_i(\mathbf{v})$, we serve this agent, and with the remaining probability we remove her from the allocated set. Since $\mathcal{S}$ is a downward closed feasibility constraint, feasibility is maintained, and we achieve the target allocation probabilities. We remark here that our goal is to merely exhibit that $\widehat{M}$ is feasible and not to actually compute it. □

We now prove the bound (3) on $\mathcal{R}^M$.

LEMMA 5. *Given any mechanism M for $\mathcal{I} = (\mathbf{F}, \mathcal{S}, \mathbf{B})$, where $\mathcal{S}$ is downward-closed, if we define the mechanism $\widehat{M}$ for $\widehat{\mathcal{I}}$ as above, then* (3) *holds.*

PROOF. In order to prove the statement, we couple the values $\mathbf{v}$ that $\widehat{M}$ draws for each $\hat{\mathbf{v}}$ with the $\mathbf{v}$ in the other expectations. So fix some corresponding pair of value vectors $\mathbf{v}$ and $\hat{\mathbf{v}}$; consider the contribution of each agent i to the revenue of M. Split the agents into two sets L and H, defined by

$$L = \{i | v_i \leq B_i\}\text{; and} \qquad H = \{i | v_i \geq B_i\}.$$

Recall that for all $i \in L$, we have that $v_i = \hat{v}_i$, and so $\hat{p}_i(\hat{\mathbf{v}}) = p_i(\mathbf{v}_{-i}, \hat{v}) = p_i(\mathbf{v})$. Furthermore, since M faces the downward-closed feasibility constraint $\mathcal{S}$, any subset of H that M serves is one of the sets $\mathcal{B}$ maximizes over. Since M can never charge any agent more than their budget, we can see that

$$\begin{aligned} \mathcal{R}^M(\mathbf{v}) &= \sum_{i \in L} \mathcal{R}_i^M(\mathbf{v}) + \sum_{i \in H} \mathcal{R}_i^M(\mathbf{v}) \\ &\leq \sum_{i \in L} \mathcal{R}_i^{\widehat{M}}(\hat{\mathbf{v}}) + \sum_{i \in \mathcal{B}} B_i \\ &\leq \mathcal{R}^{\widehat{M}}(\hat{\mathbf{v}}) + \sum_{i \in \mathcal{B}} B_i. \end{aligned}$$

Taking expectations on both sides (according to the previously mentioned coupling) proves the claim. □

Note that $\mathcal{R}^{\widehat{M}}$ can be easily achieved by simply running the (unconstrained) revenue-optimal mechanism over $\widehat{\mathcal{I}}$. It remains to be shown that we can, in fact, upper bound $\mathrm{E}[\sum_{i \in \mathcal{B}} B_i]$ also by the revenue of the same (unconstrained) revenue-optimal mechanism over $\widehat{\mathcal{I}}$.

LEMMA 6. *There exists a mechanism $M_{\mathcal{B}}$ for the setting $\widehat{\mathcal{I}}$ such that* $\mathrm{E}_{\mathbf{v}\sim\mathbf{F}}\left[\sum_{i\in\mathcal{B}} B_i\right] \leq \mathcal{R}^{M_{\mathcal{B}}}$.

PROOF. We define the mechanism $M_{\mathcal{B}}$ as implementing the allocation rule $\mathcal{B}$. Note that membership of i in $\mathcal{B}$ is monotone in v_i, and that the truthful payment for $i \in \mathcal{B}$ is precisely B_i, since this is the minimum value required for allocation. Thus, we can immediately see that

$$\mathcal{R}^{M_{\mathcal{B}}} = \mathop{\mathrm{E}}_{\hat{\mathbf{v}}\sim\widehat{\mathbf{F}}}\left[\sum_{i\in\mathcal{B}} B_i\right] = \mathop{\mathrm{E}}_{\mathbf{v}\sim\mathbf{F}}\left[\sum_{i\in\mathcal{B}} B_i\right],$$

as desired. □

By combining the results of Lemmas 5 and 6, we get the following theorem.

THEOREM 7. *Given a single parameter setting $\mathcal{I} = (\mathbf{F}, \mathcal{S}, \mathbf{B})$, the optimal mechanism $\mathcal{M}$ for the modified setting $\widehat{\mathcal{I}} = (\widehat{\mathbf{F}}, \mathcal{S})$ gives a 2-approximation to the optimal revenue for $\mathcal{I}$.*

Multi-parameter setting with public budgets.

We next consider settings where a seller offers multiple kinds of service and agents have different preferences over them. Agents are unit-demand and want any one of the services; the seller faces a general downward closed feasibility constraint. As before, we use the tuple $\mathcal{I} = (\mathbf{F}, \mathcal{S}, \mathbf{B})$ to denote an instance of this problem; throughout, i indexes agents and j indexes services. Let $\mathcal{S}$ be a downward-closed feasibility constraint over (i, j) pairs, and furthermore assume each agent i has a budget B_i.

Ideally, we would like to follow the same approach as in the previous section. We use the same basic benchmark, defining $\widehat{\mathbf{F}}$ and $\mathcal{B}$ analogously to (1) and (2) for the instance $\mathcal{I}$. We can't apply the same reduction from M to $\widehat{M}$ directly, however, because truncating each of a multi-parameter agent's values to their budget affects the agents' preferences across different items, a concern we did not have before.

Instead, we make use of a reduction of Chawla et al. [6] from multi-parameter Bayesian MD to single-parameter Bayesian MD to first bring the problem into a single parameter domain and then apply the approach from the previous section. We describe the reduction and our mechanism in the full version of the paper [7], obtaining the following theorem.

THEOREM 8. *Let $\mathcal{I} = (\mathbf{F}, \mathcal{S}, \mathbf{B})$ be an instance with multi-parameter, unit-demand agents and $\mathcal{S}$ being a matroid or simpler feasibility constraint. Then, there exists a polynomial time computable mechanism for $\widehat{\mathcal{I}}$ that is budget feasible and DSIC for $\mathcal{I}$ and obtains a constant fraction of the revenue of the optimal budget-feasible mechanism for $\mathcal{I}$.*

Private budgets.

We next consider settings where budgets are part of agents' private types, but where the mechanism designer knows the distributions from which budgets are drawn. We assume that values and budgets are drawn from independent distributions. We focus on settings where agents' values are single-dimensional.

Let $\mathcal{I} = (\mathbf{F}, \mathcal{S}, \mathbf{G})$ denote an instance of this setting. We follow a similar approach as for public budgets. Switching from public to private budgets, however, adds new complexity; in particular it becomes tricky to achieve our benchmark $\mathrm{E}[\sum_{i\in\mathcal{B}} B_i]$. In this section, we present an approximately optimal mechanism for the case when each distribution in $\mathbf{F}$ satisfies the MHR condition (see Definition 1 in Section 2). Our analysis uses the MHR condition in a very mild way and in fact holds for any setting where for every agent the probability that his value exceeds his monopoly price is lower bounded by a constant. Even when this condition is not satisfied, we can obtain a good approximation through a slight modification of our mechanism under a technical condition on values and budgets. These details are discussed in the full version of the paper [7]. We believe that the general idea behind our mechanism can be extended to obtain good approximations for arbitrary distributions.

We focus on settings $\mathcal{I} = (\mathbf{F}, \mathcal{S}, \mathbf{G})$ where $\mathcal{S}$ is a matroid set system, and each distribution in $\mathbf{F}$ satisfies the MHR condition. We begin with some definitions. Given a pair of value and budget vectors, we consider the "extractable value" of an agent i to be $\min(v_i, B_i)$; we modify our definition of $\mathcal{B}$ to reflect this:

$$\mathcal{B} = \mathrm{argmax}_{S\in\mathcal{S}} \sum_{i\in S} \min(v_i, B_i).$$

Similarly to the public budgets case, our approach is to split the revenue of an arbitrary mechanism into two terms, which (loosely speaking) look like revenue in a truncated value setting, and the sum of the budgets in $\mathcal{B}$; we then demonstrate a lottery menu mechanism whose revenue upper bounds both of these terms.

Our proposed mechanism (which we denote $M^{\mathcal{L}}$) is based on lottery menus $\mathcal{L}(\underline{p}, \bar{p})$ parameterized by a minimum price $\underline{p}$ and a maximum price $\bar{p}$. (Recall the discussion of lotteries at the beginning of this section.) There are two cases. If $\underline{p} > \bar{p}/3$, then $\mathcal{L}(\underline{p}, \bar{p})$ contains the single fixed price of $\underline{p}$; otherwise, it contains, for all $2\underline{p}/\bar{p} \leq \alpha \leq 2/3$, a lottery that with probability $(1/3 + \alpha)$ allows the agent to purchase service at a price of $\alpha\bar{p}/2$.

Note that the probability of allocation in the above lottery system rises faster as a function of α than the price of the lottery. Effectively this ensures that the agent is willing to buy the most expensive lottery that he can afford. So, in particular, if all lotteries bring positive utility then the agent spends his entire budget, the maximum amount that any mechanism can hope to achieve from the agent. This powerful idea is what enables our approximation.

Note the following properties of the lottery menu $\mathcal{L}(\underline{p}, \bar{p})$.

LEMMA 9. *When an agent with $\min(v, B) \geq \underline{p}$ is offered the menu $\mathcal{L}(\underline{p}, \bar{p})$, he purchases an option yielding expected revenue at least $\underline{p}/3$.*

PROOF. Note that in either case, the lottery system $\mathcal{L}(\underline{p}, \bar{p})$ always contains an option with price exactly $\underline{p}$, and that this is the lowest priced option. Furthermore, for $\min(v, B) \geq \underline{p}$, this option always gives non-negative utility. Thus our claim follows immediately from the fact that every lottery assigns the item with probability at least $1/3$. □

LEMMA 10. *When an agent with $v \geq \bar{p}$ is offered the menu $\mathcal{L}(\underline{p}, \bar{p})$, he purchases an option yielding expected revenue at least $min(\bar{p}, B)/3$.*

PROOF. In the first case (when $\mathcal{L}(\underline{p}, \bar{p})$ contains the single price of $\underline{p}$), this follows trivially; in the other case, consider the utility of an agent with value v when purchasing the lottery with parameter α, which we denote $u_\alpha(v)$. We can see that

$$u_\alpha(v) = (1/3 + \alpha)(v - \alpha\bar{p}/2), \text{ and so}$$

$$\frac{\partial u_\alpha(v)}{\partial \alpha} = v - (\alpha + 1/6)\bar{p} \geq 0$$

by our assumption. So we can see that an agent will purchase the lottery with the highest α value they can afford; since the lottery for

$\alpha = 2/3$ assigns service with probability 1 at a price of $\bar{p}/3$, and every lottery provides service with probability at least one third, we can see that an agent will purchase a lottery yielding revenue at least $\min(\bar{p}, B)/3$. □

Our mechanism $M^{\mathcal{L}}$ serves the set $\mathcal{B}$. For each i, let T_i be the threshold corresponding to inclusion in $\mathcal{B}$, i.e. $T_i = \min\{v' : i \in \mathcal{B} \text{ for } ((\mathbf{v}_{-i}, v'), (\mathbf{B}_{-i}, v'))\}$. Our mechanism offers agent i the lottery system $\mathcal{L}(T_i, {\phi_i}^{-1}(0))$, where $\phi_i^{-1}(0)$ is the monopoly price for i.

In order to relate the revenue of a mechanism M for the setting $\mathcal{I}$ to that of our proposed mechanism $M^{\mathcal{L}}$, we break the revenue of M into two parts – that derived from agents in $\mathcal{B}$, and that derived from agents not in $\mathcal{B}$; we denote these quantities by $\mathcal{R}^{M\cap\mathcal{B}}$ and $\mathcal{R}^{M\setminus\mathcal{B}}$, respectively. We bound the two terms separately.

LEMMA 11. $\mathcal{R}^{M\setminus\mathcal{B}} \leq 3\mathcal{R}^{M^{\mathcal{L}}}$

PROOF. Let S denote the set of agents served by M. Note that by our definition of $\mathcal{B}$, it will always be a maximal independent set in $\mathcal{S}$; as such, for every pair of vectors $(\mathbf{v}, \mathbf{B})$, we can get a 1-1 function $g : S \setminus \mathcal{B} \to \mathcal{B}$ such that for all $i \in S \setminus \mathcal{B}$, $\mathcal{B} \setminus \{g(i)\} \cup \{i\} \in \mathcal{S}$. Note that by EPIR, we must have that the revenue M derives from each agent i is no more than $\min(v_i, B_i)$, and by the definition of T_i, we get that

$$\begin{aligned}\mathcal{R}^{M\setminus\mathcal{B}}(\mathbf{v}, \mathbf{B}) &\leq \sum_{i \in S\setminus\mathcal{B}} \min(v_i, B_i) \\ &\leq \sum_{i \in S\setminus\mathcal{B}} T_{g(i)} \leq \sum_{i\in\mathcal{B}} T_i \\ &\leq 3\mathcal{R}^{M^{\mathcal{L}}}(\mathbf{v}, \mathbf{B})\end{aligned}$$

Here the second inequality follows from noting that in order to be in the set $\mathcal{B}$, the agent $g(i)$ must have an extractable value no smaller than that of i. The last inequality follows from applying Lemma 9 to $\mathcal{L}(T_i, {\phi_i}^{-1}(0))$. Taking expectation over $(\mathbf{v}, \mathbf{B})$ completes the proof. □

In order to prove our next revenue bound, we need the following property of MHR variables (Lemma 4.1 in [12]):

LEMMA 12. *For v distributed according to some F satisfying the MHR, the probability that the value v exceeds the monopoly price $\phi^{-1}(0)$ is at least $1/e$.*

LEMMA 13. $\mathcal{R}^{M\cap\mathcal{B}} \leq 3e\mathcal{R}^{M^{\mathcal{L}}}$

PROOF. Consider some agent i, and fix $(\mathbf{v}_{-i}, \mathbf{B}_{-i})$; note that this fixes T_i as well. Fix B_i. Recall that an agent i contributes to $\mathcal{R}_i^{M\cap\mathcal{B}}$ only when $\min(v_i, B_i) \geq T_i$. We split the analysis into two cases; in each case we consider the optimal revenue a mechanism could derive from agents with $v_i \geq T_i$ if allowed to ignore the budgets constraints.

- Case 1: $T_i \geq {\phi_i}^{-1}(0)$. In this case, the maximum revenue that can be obtained from agent i conditioned on $v_i \geq T_i$ and ignoring feasibility constraints is T_i and can be obtained by offering a fixed price of T_i. Our mechanism on the other hand offers a single option of buying service at a fixed price of T_i. Therefore,

$$\begin{aligned}&\operatorname*{E}_{v_i}\left[\mathcal{R}_i^{M\cap\mathcal{B}}(\mathbf{v}, \mathbf{B}) \mid v_i \geq T_i\right] \\ &\qquad\leq \operatorname*{E}_{v_i}\left[\mathcal{R}^{M^{\mathcal{L}}}(\mathbf{v}, \mathbf{B}) \mid v_i \geq T_i\right]\end{aligned}$$

- Case 2: $T_i < {\phi_i}^{-1}(0)$. The maximum revenue that can be obtained from agent i conditioned on $v_i \geq T_i$ and ignoring feasibility constraints is at most ${\phi_i}^{-1}(0)$ and can be obtained by offering a fixed price of ${\phi_i}^{-1}(0)$. Considering the budget constraint we conclude that $\operatorname{E}_{v_i}[\mathcal{R}_i^{M\cap\mathcal{B}}(\mathbf{v}, \mathbf{B}) \mid v_i \geq T_i] \leq \min({\phi_i}^{-1}(0), B_i)$. On the other hand, applying Lemma 10 to $\mathcal{L}(T_i, {\phi_i}^{-1}(0))$, we get that for $v_i \geq {\phi_i}^{-1}(0)$, $\mathcal{R}_i^{M^{\mathcal{L}}} \geq \min({\phi_i}^{-1}(0), B_i)/3$. Lemma 12 implies that the event $v_i \geq {\phi_i}^{-1}(0)$ happens with probability at least $1/e$. So we get

$$\begin{aligned}&\operatorname*{E}_{v_i}[\mathcal{R}_i^{M\cap\mathcal{B}}(\mathbf{v}, \mathbf{B}) | \, v_i \geq T_i] \\ &\qquad\leq (1/3e) \operatorname*{E}_{v_i}[\mathcal{R}^{M^{\mathcal{L}}}(\mathbf{v}, \mathbf{B}) \mid v_i \geq T_i]\end{aligned}$$

We have $\operatorname{E}_{v_i}[\mathcal{R}_i^{M\cap\mathcal{B}}(\mathbf{v}, \mathbf{B})] \leq 3e\operatorname{E}_{v_i}[\mathcal{R}^{M^{\mathcal{L}}}(\mathbf{v}, \mathbf{B})]$ in either case; taking expectations over $(\mathbf{v}_{-i}, \mathbf{B})$, and summing over i yields our claim. □

Combining the above two lemmas immediately gives the following theorem.

THEOREM 14. *For any setting $\mathcal{I} = (\mathbf{F}, \mathcal{S}, \mathbf{G})$ where $\mathcal{S}$ is a matroid constraint and each distribution in $\mathbf{F}$ satisfies MHR, the mechanism $M^{\mathcal{L}}$ is a $3(1+e)$ approximation to the optimal revenue.*

In fact, we can use a similar lottery pricing technique to get a constant approximation even in the absence of the MHR assumption; however, we still need a technical assumption relating the distributions of agents' values and budgets. This once again ensures that there is a good probability that agents' values are high enough for the lottery system to extract a constant fraction of their budget. We state the theorem here, but defer the proof of this result to the full version of the paper [7].

THEOREM 15. *Suppose that every agent's median value is no smaller than a constant fraction of her maximum budget. Then we can construct a budget-feasible mechanism that is DSIC with respect to both values and budgets, and obtains a constant fraction of the revenue of the optimal such mechanism.*

4. MAXIMIZING WELFARE

In this section we focus on the welfare objective. In particular, the seller's goal is to maximize the total value of the allocation in expectation. Once again we assume that budgets are known publicly.

We first note that we cannot use the approach of the previous section as a roadmap. Even with public budgets, truncating values to the corresponding budgets does not work for the social welfare objective. In particular, the following example shows it is possible for a budget feasible mechanism to distinguish between values above the budget without exceeding the budget in payments.

EXAMPLE 2. *Consider an n agent single-item auction, where agents have i. i. d. values for the item. Each agent has a budget of 1. Each agent's value is 1 with probability $1 - 1/n$ and n with probability $1/n$. Then a mechanism that simply truncates values to budgets cannot distinguish between the agents and gets a social welfare of at most 2. On the other hand, consider a mechanism that orders agents in an arbitrary order and offers two options to each agent in turn while the item is unallocated: getting the item for free with probability $1/n$ and nothing otherwise, or purchasing the item at a price of 1. Then, an agent picks the first option if and only if her value is below $n/(n-1)$, and otherwise picks the second option.*

In particular, an agent with value n always picks the second option, and an agent with value 1 always picks the first option. For large n, with probability approaching $1 - 1/e$ at least one agent has value n, and with probability at least $1/e$ the item is unsold before the first agent with value n is made an offer. The mechanism's expected welfare is therefore at least $1/e(1 - 1/e)n = \Omega(n)$.

Note that the precise choice of budgets in the above example was critical: if budgets were any lower, the proposed mechanism would have been infeasible; and if they were any higher, truncation would have still allowed for distinguishing between agents with low and high values. This suggests considering bicriteria approximations where we compete against an optimal mechanism that faces smaller budgets. We first demonstrate a mechanism achieving an approximation of this sort; we then show that our mechanism also gives a good approximation if we relax the EPIR constraint to an IIR constraint, instead of relaxing budgets. Of course, our ultimate goal is to provide a good approximation for the social welfare objective via an EPIR budget feasible mechanism. While we are unable to do so in general, the final section presents a constant factor approximation for settings where the distributions F_i for every agent i satisfy the MHR condition (Definition 1 in Section 2).

A bicriteria approximation.

Consider a setting $\mathcal{I}$ with budgets $\mathbf{B}$. Let OPT′ denote the EPIR mechanism that is welfare-maximizing and feasible for budgets $(1 - \epsilon)\mathbf{B}$ (i.e. where each budget is scaled down by a factor of $1-\epsilon$). We claim that we can approximate the welfare of this mechanism while maintaining budget feasibility with respect to the original budgets $\mathbf{B}$.

THEOREM 16. *For a given instance $\mathcal{I} = (\mathbf{F}, \mathcal{S}, \mathbf{B})$, let $\mathcal{I}'$ be the instance $(\mathbf{F}, \mathcal{S}, (1 - \epsilon)\mathbf{B})$ where each agent's budget is scaled down by a factor of $1 - \epsilon$. Let OPT′ denote the welfare optimal budget feasible mechanism for $\mathcal{I}'$. Then, there exists an easy to compute ex post IR mechanism (namely, the VCG mechanism over a modified instance) that is budget feasible for $\mathcal{I}$ and obtains at least an ϵ fraction of the social welfare of OPT′.*

PROOF. We first use OPT′ to construct a new mechanism M. M proceeds as follows. It elicits values from agents. For all agents i with $v_i \geq B_i$, it resamples agent i's value from the distribution F_i restricted to the set $[B_i, \infty)$. Other values are left unchanged. It then runs the mechanism OPT′ on the resampled values. It is easy to see that M is budget feasible for $\mathcal{I}'$.

We claim that the social welfare of M is at least ϵ times the social welfare of OPT′. To prove the claim, consider a single agent i, and let ${x_i}^1$ denote the probability of allocation for this agent in OPT′ when her value is B_i, and ${x_i}^2$ denote the probability of allocation for this agent in OPT′ when her value is ${v_i}^{\max}$ (the agent's maximum possible value). Note that the expected payment that the agent makes at ${v_i}^{\max}$ is at least $({x_i}^2 - {x_i}^1)B_i$ plus the payment she makes at B_i. Then, EPIR implies that $({x_i}^2 - {x_i}^1)B_i$ is at most the budget $(1-\epsilon)B_i$ times ${x_i}^2$. This implies ${x_i}^2 < {x_i}^1/\epsilon$. Now, noting that the value distributions for agents are unaltered by resampling, it holds that for $v_i \geq B_i$, the probability of allocation for agent i at v_i under M is equal to the expected probability of allocation for the agent under OPT′ conditioned on the agent's value being in the range $[B_i, \infty)$. Since the probability of allocation under OPT′ for this range is always between ${x_i}^1$ and ${x_i}^2$, the expected probability of allocation is at least ${x_i}^1 \geq \epsilon {x_i}^2$. So compared to those under OPT', the probabilities of allocation under M are at most a factor of ϵ smaller. Therefore, the expected social welfare of M is also at most a factor of ϵ smaller than that of OPT′.

Our goal will then be to approximate the social welfare of M. Note that for every agent i, M treats values above B_i identically. We can therefore consider the following optimization problem: for an instance $\mathcal{I}$, construct a DSIC EPIR mechanism that maximizes social welfare subject to the additional constraint that for every agent i the mechanism's (distribution over) allocation should be identical across value vectors that differ only in agent i's value and where agent i's value is $\geq B_i$. For any such mechanism, agent i's expected contribution to social welfare from value vectors with $v_i \geq B_i$ conditioned on being allocated is $\overline{v}_i$, where $\overline{v}_i = E[v_i|v_i \geq B_i]$. Therefore, the following mechanism maximizes welfare over the above class of mechanisms: for every agent i with $v_i \geq B_i$, replace v_i by $\overline{v}_i$; other values remain unmodified; run the VCG mechanism over the modified value vector; charge every agent the minimum of the payment returned by the VCG mechanism and their budget. It is easy to verify that this mechanism is DSIC, ex post IR, budget feasible for the original budgets B_i, and obtains expected social welfare at least that of M. Therefore, it satisfies the claim in the theorem. □

An interim IR mechanism.

Next we note that it is in fact easy to remove the approximation on budget in the above theorem if we are willing to give up on EPIR. In particular, consider an optimal mechanism OPT on the instance $\mathcal{I} = (\mathbf{F}, \mathcal{S}, \mathbf{B})$. Then the above theorem implies the existence of a mechanism V that is budget feasible for $\mathcal{I}' = (\mathbf{F}, \mathcal{S}, 2\mathbf{B})$ and obtains half the welfare of OPT (taking $\epsilon = 1/2$). Now consider the mechanism V' described as follows. V' simulates V on the given value vector. Then for every agent i it charges i half the payment charged by V and with probability $1/2$ makes an allocation to i if V makes an allocation to i. Agent i's expected utility from any strategy under V' is exactly half her expected utility from the same strategy under V. Therefore, V' is DSIC. Moreover, it is budget feasible for the original budgets $\mathbf{B}$ since it always charges half the payments in V. Its expected social welfare is exactly half that of V. We therefore get the following theorem.

THEOREM 17. *For a given instance $\mathcal{I} = (\mathbf{F}, \mathcal{S}, \mathbf{B})$, let OPT denote the welfare optimal EPIR budget feasible mechanism for $\mathcal{I}$. Then, there exists an easy to compute IIR mechanism that is budget feasible for $\mathcal{I}$ and obtains at least a quarter of the social welfare of OPT.*

An ex-post IR mechanism for MHR distributions.

As previously remarked, our ultimate goal is to provide a good approximation for the social welfare objective via an EPIR budget feasible mechanism. We now show that under an MHR condition on distributions, we can achieve precisely this goal. In particular, we present a constant factor approximation for settings where the distributions F_i for every agent i satisfy the MHR condition (Definition 1 in Section 2).

Under the MHR condition, we can exhibit a close relationship between the welfare and revenue of any mechanism. Using this relationship along with results from the previous section, we can come up with a budget feasible approximately-revenue-maximizing mechanism that also provides an approximation to social welfare. The MHR condition is quite crucial to our approach. In fact our solution consists of two mechanisms, one of which charges no payments, and the other of which truncates values to their corresponding budgets – approaches that don't work for the example we considered above.

Let $v_i^* = {\phi_i}^{-1}(0)$ denote the monopoly price for the distribution F_i. We then get the following bound on social welfare, which we are able to approximate.

LEMMA 18. *For any instance $\mathcal{I} = (\mathbf{F}, \mathcal{S}, \mathbf{B})$, if all the distributions F_i satisfy the MHR condition, then for any non-decreasing allocation function $x(v)$, we have that*

$$\int_{\mathbf{v}} \left(\sum_i v_i x_i(\mathbf{v}) \right) d\mathbf{F}(\mathbf{v})$$
$$\leq \int_{\mathbf{v}} \left(\sum_i (\phi_i(v_i) + 2v_i^*) x_i(\mathbf{v}) \right) d\mathbf{F}(\mathbf{v}).$$

In order to prove the Lemma, we require some new definitions and claims. Consider a single agent with MHR distribution F, virtual value function ϕ, and monopoly price v^*. Let ϕ^+ and ϕ^- be the positive and negative portions of ϕ respectively; i.e. for all v, $\phi^+(v), \phi^-(v) \geq 0$ and $\phi(v) = \phi^+(v) - \phi^-(v)$. We can then claim the following (the first is a restatement of Lemma 3.1 in [13]).

LEMMA 19. *For a distribution F satisfying the MHR, all values v satisfy $v \leq v^* + \phi^+(v) = v^* + \phi(v) + \phi^-(v)$.*

LEMMA 20. *For any monotone allocation function $x(\cdot)$,*

$$\int \phi^-(v)x(v)dF(v) \leq \int v^* x(v)dF(v).$$

PROOF. We begin by recalling that by Lemma 1, the expected revenue of any BIC mechanism is equal to its expected virtual surplus. Now consider a mechanism for a single agent with value distribution F that always serves the agent. Clearly the revenue of this mechanism is 0. So we get

$$\int_v (\phi^+(v) - \phi^-(v))dF(v) = 0,$$

which implies that

$$\int_v \phi^+(v)dF(v) = \int_v \phi^-(v)dF(v).$$

Second, the revenue from offering the agent the monopoly price v^* is precisely $v^*(1 - F(v^*))$. Therefore,

$$\int_{v^*}^{\infty} (\phi^+(v) - \phi^-(v))dF(v) = \int \phi^+(v)dF(v)$$
$$= v^* \int_{v^*}^{\infty} dF(v),$$

where the first equality follows from regularity of F.

Note that the regularity of F implies that ϕ^+ and ϕ^- are identically 0 below and above v^*, respectively. Now, from the above two equalities, we can see that if x is monotone non-decreasing, then,

$$\int \phi^-(v)x(v)dF(v) \leq \int \phi^-(v)x(v^*)dF(v)$$
$$= x(v^*) \int \phi^+(v)dF(v) = x(v^*)v^* \int_{v^*}^{\infty} dF(v)$$
$$\leq \int v^* x(v)dF(v);$$

the claim follows. □

The proof of Lemma 18 follows immediately by combining Lemmas 19 and 20. The Lemma gives us the following approximation.

THEOREM 21. *Let $\mathcal{I} = (\mathbf{F}, \mathcal{S}, \mathbf{B})$ be an instance where all distributions F_i satisfy the MHR condition. Then, one of the following mechanisms obtains a $2(1 + e)$-approximation to the social welfare of a welfare-optimal budget-feasible mechanism for $\mathcal{I}$. Both of these mechanisms are DSIC, EPIR and budget feasible.*

- Mechanism 1: *Always allocate to the set S_1^* and charge zero payments, where $S_1^* = \text{argmax}_{S \in \mathcal{S}} \sum_{i \in S} v_i^*$.*
- Mechanism 2: *Elicit values from agents; for all i with $v_i > B_i$, replace v_i by B_i; run Myerson's mechanism on the resulting instance.*

PROOF. We begin by noting that an immediate consequence of Lemma 12 is that for a distribution F satisfying the MHR, $E_F[v] \geq v^*/e$.

Now, consider some budget feasible mechanism M for the instance $\mathcal{I}$. Then by Theorem 7, the optimal mechanism for the truncated distributions (1) obtains revenue, and therefore also social welfare, no less than a $1/2$ fraction of the expected revenue $\int \sum_i \phi_i(v_i)x_i(\mathbf{v})d\mathbf{F}(\mathbf{v})$.

Moreover, $\int_{\mathbf{v}} \sum_i v_i^* x(\mathbf{v})d\mathbf{F}(\mathbf{v})$ is upper bounded by $\sum_{i \in S^*} v_i^*$, where $S^* = \text{argmax}_{S \in \mathcal{S}} \sum_{i \in S} v_i^*$. Then a mechanism which always allocates to the set S^* and charges no payments is budget feasible, DSIC, and obtains welfare $\sum_{i \in S^*} E_{F_i}[v_i] \geq 1/e \sum_{i \in S^*} v_i^*$, where the inequality follows from Lemma 12. The original claim follows. □

Acknowledgments

We thank Saeed Alaei for many helpful discussions.

5. REFERENCES

[1] Z. Abrams. Revenue maximization when bidders have budgets. In *Proceedings of the seventeenth annual ACM-SIAM Symposium on Discrete Algorithms*, SODA '06, pages 1074–1082, New York, NY, USA, 2006. ACM.

[2] S. Alaei, K. Jain, and A. Malekian. Competitive equilibrium for unit-demand buyers with non quasi-linear utilities. In *CORR*, 2010.

[3] S. Bhattacharya, G. Goel, S. Gollapudi, and K. Munagala. Budget constrained auctions with heterogeneous items. In *STOC*, pages 379–388, 2010.

[4] C. Borgs, J. T. Chayes, N. Immorlica, M. Mahdian, and A. Saberi. Multi-unit auctions with budget-constrained bidders. In *ACM Conference on Electronic Commerce*, pages 44–51, 2005.

[5] S. Brusco and G. Lopomo. Simultaneous ascending auctions with complementarities and known budget constraints. *Economic Theory*, 38(1):105–124, January 2009.

[6] S. Chawla, J. D. Hartline, D. L. Malec, and B. Sivan. Multi-parameter mechanism design and sequential posted pricing. In *STOC*, pages 311–320, 2010.

[7] S. Chawla, D. L. Malec, and A. Malekian. Bayesian mechanism design for budget-constrained agents. *CoRR*, abs/1103.6280, 2011.

[8] Y.-K. Che and I. Gale. Standard auctions with financially constrained bidders. *Review of Economic Studies*, 65(1):1–21, January 1998.

[9] Y.-K. Che and I. Gale. The optimal mechanism for selling to a budget-constrained buyer. *Journal of Economic Theory*, 92(2):198–233, June 2000.

[10] N. Chen, X. Deng, and A. Ghosh. Competitive equilibria in matching markets with budgets. *CoRR*, 2010.

[11] S. Dobzinski, N. Nisan, and R. Lavi. Multi-unit auctions with budget limits. In *Proc. of the 49th Annual Symposium on Foundations of Computer Science (FOCS)*, 2008.

[12] J. Hartline, V. Mirrokni, and M. Sundararajan. Optimal marketing strategies over social networks. In *Proceeding of the 17th international conference on World Wide Web*, WWW '08, pages 189–198, New York, NY, USA, 2008. ACM.

[13] J. Hartline and T. Roughgarden. Simple versus optimal mechanisms. In *Proc. 11th ACM Conf. on Electronic Commerce*, 2009.

[14] J.-J. Laffont and J. Robert. Optimal auction with financially constrained buyers. *Economics Letters*, 52(2):181–186, 1996.

[15] E. S. Maskin. Auctions, development, and privatization: Efficient auctions with liquidity-constrained buyers. *European Economic Review*, 44(4-6):667–681, 2000.

[16] R. Myerson. Optimal auction design. *Mathematics of Operations Research*, 6:58–73, 1981.

[17] N. Nisan. Introduction to mechanism design. In N. Nisan, T. Roughgarden, E. Tardos, and V. V. Vazirani, editors, *Algorithmic Game Theory*, chapter 9, pages 209–242. Cambridge Press, 2007.

[18] N. Nisan, J. Bayer, D. Chandra, T. Franji, R. Gardner, Y. Matias, N. Rhodes, M. Seltzer, D. Tom, H. Varian, and D. Zigmond. Google's auction for tv ads. In *Proceedings of the 36th International Colloquium on Automata, Languages and Programming: Part II*, ICALP '09, pages 309–327, Berlin, Heidelberg, 2009. Springer-Verlag.

[19] M. M. Pai and R. Vohra. Optimal auctions with financially constrained bidders. Discussion papers, Northwestern University, Aug. 2008.

A Truthful Randomized Mechanism for Combinatorial Public Projects via Convex Optimization

[Extended Abstract] *

Shaddin Dughmi†
Department of Computer Science
Stanford University
Stanford, CA 94305
shaddin@cs.stanford.edu

ABSTRACT

In *Combinatorial Public Projects*, there is a set of projects that may be undertaken, and a set of self-interested players with a stake in the set of projects chosen. A public planner must choose a subset of these projects, subject to a resource constraint, with the goal of maximizing social welfare. Combinatorial Public Projects has emerged as one of the paradigmatic problems in *Algorithmic Mechanism Design*, a field concerned with solving fundamental resource allocation problems in the presence of both selfish behavior and the computational constraint of polynomial time.

We design a polynomial-time, truthful-in-expectation, $(1-1/e)$-approximation mechanism for welfare maximization in a fundamental variant of combinatorial public projects. Our results apply to combinatorial public projects when players have valuations that are *matroid rank sums (MRS)*, which encompass most concrete examples of submodular functions studied in this context, including coverage functions and matroid weighted-rank functions. Our approximation factor is the best possible, assuming $P \neq NP$. Ours is the first mechanism that achieves a constant factor approximation for a natural NP-hard variant of combinatorial public projects.

Categories and Subject Descriptors

F.0 [**Theory of Computation**]: General

General Terms

Algorithms, Economics, Theory

*A full version of this paper is available at `http://arxiv.org/abs/1103.0041`

†Supported by NSF Grant CCF-0448664.

EC'11, June 5–9, 2011, San Jose, California, USA.

1. INTRODUCTION

The overarching goal of *algorithmic mechanism design* is to design computationally efficient algorithms that solve or approximate fundamental resource allocation problems in which the underlying data is a priori unknown to the algorithm. A problem that has received much attention in this context – albeit mostly in the form of negative results – is *Combinatorial Public Projects* (CPP). Here, there are m *projects* being considered by a public planner, n *players*, and a bound $k \leq m$ on the number of projects that may be chosen. Each player i has a private *valuation* $v_i(S)$ for each subset S of the projects. We consider the *flexible* variant of CPP, where a feasible solution is a set of at most k projects[1]. The goal is to choose a feasible set of projects S maximizing *social welfare*: $\sum_i v_i(S)$. The valuations are initially unknown to the public planner, and must be elicited from the (self-interested) players. A "mechanism" for CPP extracts this information, and decides on a set of projects to undertake. The mechanisms we consider can charge the players payments in order to incentivize truthful reporting of their valuations. Moreover, we seek mechanisms that run in polynomial time.

Since CPP is highly inapproximable for general valuations – even by non-truthful algorithms – it is most interesting to study CPP for restricted classes of valuations. Most notable among these are submodular valuations, as they naturally model the pervasive notion of "diminishing marginal returns". In this paper, we study CPP for a fundamental and large subset of submodular valuations: *Matroid Rank Sum Valuations*. This class includes most concrete examples of submodular functions studied in this context. Most notably, it includes the canonical and arguably most natural example of submodularity: coverage functions.

Combinatorial public projects and its variants are examples of *welfare maximization problems*. There are many other examples, most notable among them are *combinatorial auctions*, with their many variants (see e.g. [25]). Welfare maximization problems occupy a central position in mechanism design, not only because of the fundamental nature of the utilitarian objective, but also due to the rich

[1]This is in contrast to the *exact* variant, where each feasible solution consists of *exactly* k projects – a difference that is uninteresting in an approximation algorithms context, yet has major implications when incentives are in the picture. For more on the distinction between the two variants, we refer the reader to [7].

economic theory surrounding them. Most notably, the celebrated Vickrey-Clarke-Groves (VCG) mechanism (see e.g. [25]) is a general solution for all these problems, at least from an economic perspective. The VCG mechanism is *truthful*, in that it is in a player's best interest to report his true valuations regardless of the reports of the other players. Moreover, VCG finds the welfare maximizing solution.

Unfortunately, however, most interesting welfare maximization problems, such as combinatorial public projects, are NP-hard. Therefore, implementing VCG efficiently – i.e. in polynomial time – is impossible unless $P = NP$. Moreover, as first argued in [24], most existing approximation algorithms – unlike exact algorithms – cannot be converted to truthful mechanisms by the imposition of a suitable payment scheme. This necessitates the design of carefully crafted approximation algorithms, tailored specifically for truthfulness. Understanding the power of these truthful approximation mechanisms is the central goal of algorithmic mechanism design. This research agenda was first advocated by Nisan and Ronen [23]. Since then, combinatorial auctions and combinatorial public projects have emerged as the paradigmatic "challenge-problems" of the field, with much work in recent years establishing upper and lower-bounds on truthful polynomial-time mechanisms for these problems, for example: [20, 11, 13, 12, 10, 6, 14, 27, 3, 4, 7, 17].

The "holy grail" of algorithmic mechanism design is to design polynomial-time truthful approximation mechanisms that match the approximation guarantee of the best (non-truthful) polynomial-time approximation algorithm. Unfortunately, several recent impossibility results have shed serious doubt on the possibility of this goal [10, 27, 3, 4, 7]. Combinatorial public projects, in particular, bore the brunt of the most brutal of these negative results [27, 4, 7]. Fortunately, all but one of these lower bounds apply exclusively to deterministic mechanisms, and none apply to randomized mechanisms for the – arguably more natural – flexible variant of combinatorial public projects.

As the limitations of deterministic mechanisms became apparent, a recent research direction has focused on designing randomized approximation mechanisms for the fundamental problems of algorithmic mechanism design [20, 8, 15, 9, 17]. These mechanisms are instances of the only general approach[2] known for designing (randomized) truthful mechanisms: via *maximal-in-distributional range (MIDR) algorithms* [8]. An MIDR algorithm fixes a set of distributions over feasible solutions – the *distributional range* – independently of the valuations reported by the self-interested participants, and outputs a random sample from the distribution that maximizes expected (reported) welfare. The "Vickrey-Clarke-Groves (VCG)" payment scheme renders an MIDR algorithm *truthful in expectation* – that is, a player unaware of the coin flips of the mechanism maximizes his expected utility by reporting truthfully.

Recently Dughmi, Roughgarden and Yan [17] presented the most general framework to date for the design of maximal-in-distributional-range algorithms. Their approach is based on convex optimization, and generalizes the celebrated linear-programming based approach of Lavi and Swamy [20]. Given a mathematical relaxation to a welfare maximization problem, [17] advocates designing randomized rounding schemes that are *convex*. Given a convex rounding scheme, the problem of finding the best *output* of the rounding scheme is a convex optimization problem solvable in polynomial time, and implements an MIDR allocation rule. They then show how to design a convex rounding scheme for combinatorial auctions with matroid rank sum valuations, yielding an optimal $(1 - 1/e)$ approximation mechanism. We elaborate on the framework of [17] in Section 2.5.

By reducing the problem of designing a truthful mechanism to that of designing a convex rounding scheme, the approach of [17] yielded the first optimal truthful mechanism for a variant of combinatorial auctions with restricted valuations. It is now natural to wonder if their approach is applicable to other welfare maximization problems. In particular, can the convex rounding framework be used to obtain optimal approximation mechanisms for interesting variants of Combinatorial Public Projects?

We answer this question in the affirmative, and elaborate on our contributions below.

1.1 Contributions

We design a $(1-1/e)$-approximate convex rounding scheme for combinatorial public projects with matroid rank sum valuations. This yields a $(1 - 1/e)$-approximate truthful-in-expectation mechanism for CPP, running in expected polynomial time. This is the best approximation possible for this problem, even without truthfulness, unless $P = NP$. Therefore, ours is the first truthful mechanism for an NP-hard variant of CPP that matches the approximation ratio of the best non-truthful algorithm. Our results works with "black-box" valuations, provided that players can answer a randomized analogue of value oracles.

To prove our results, we follow the general outline of [17]. However, our task is more challenging: whereas in combinatorial auctions, randomized rounding may allocate each item independently (the approach taken in [17]), this is not possible in CPP. We must respect the cardinality constraint of k on the set of chosen items, and therefore our rounding scheme must by fiat be *dependent*. This presents a major challenge in analyzing our rounding scheme. Whereas the expected value of a submodular function on a product distribution (i.e. independent rounding) has been studied extensively, and is closely related to the now well-understood multi-linear (see e.g. [5, 30]), analyzing the expected value of a dependent distribution – in particular proving it to be a concave function of underlying parameters – is a technical challenge that we overcome by combining techniques from combinatorics, convex analysis, and matroid theory.

1.2 Additional Related Work

Combinatorial Public Projects, in particular its *exact* variant, was first introduced by Papadimitriou, Schapira and Singer [27]. They show that no deterministic truthful mechanism for exact CPP with submodular valuations can guarantee better than a $O(\sqrt{m})$ approximation to the optimal social welfare. The non-strategic version of the problem, on the other hand, is equivalent to maximizing a submodular function subject to a cardinality constraint, and admits a $(1-1/e)$-approximation algorithm due to Nemhauser, Wolsey and Fisher [21], and this is optimal [28] assuming $P \neq NP$.

Buchfuhrer, Schapira and Singer [4] explored approxima-

[2]The random sampling approach used in [6], while arguably general, does not seem applicable beyond auction settings – in particular, it is not applicable to combinatorial public projects.

tion algorithms and truthful mechanisms for CPP with various classes of valuations in the submodular hierarchy. The most relevant result of [4] to our paper is a lower-bound of $O(\sqrt{m})$ on *deterministic* truthful mechanisms for the exact variant of CPP with coverage valuations – a class of valuations for which our *randomized* mechanism for flexible CPP obtains a $(1 - 1/e)$ approximation.

Most recently, Dobzinski [7] showed two lower bounds for CPP in the value oracle model: A lower bound of $O(\sqrt{m})$ on universally truthful mechanisms for flexible CPP with submodular valuations, and a lower bound of $O(\sqrt{m})$ on truthful-in-expectation mechanisms for *exact* CPP with submodular valuations. We note that the latter was the first unconditional lower bound on truthful-in-expectation mechanisms.

2. PRELIMINARIES

2.1 Combinatorial Public Projects

In *Combinatorial Public Projects* there is a set $[m] = \{1, \ldots, m\}$ of *projects*, a cardinality bound k such that $0 \leq k \leq m$, and a set $[n] = \{1, \ldots, n\}$ of *players*. Each player i has a valuation function $v_i : 2^{[m]} \to \mathbb{R}_+$ that is normalized ($v_i(\emptyset) = 0$) and monotone ($v_i(A) \leq v_i(B)$ whenever $A \subseteq B$). In this paper, we consider the *flexible* variant of combinatorial public projects: a feasible solution is a set $S \subseteq [m]$ of projects with $|S| \leq k$. Player i's value for outcome S is equal to $v_i(S)$. The goal is to choose the feasible set S maximizing *social welfare*: $\sum_i v_i(S)$.

We consider Combinatorial Public Projects where each player's valuation v_i is know to lie in some set $\mathcal{V}$ of valuation functions. We abbreviate the set of instances of CPP constrained to valuations $\mathcal{V}$ as CPP($\mathcal{V}$). As first defined in [27], CPP was considered with $\mathcal{V}$ equal to the set of monotone submodular functions. In this paper, we focus on CPP with matroid-rank-sum (MRS) valuations – a large subset of monotone submodular functions.

2.2 Mechanism Design Basics

We consider direct-revelation mechanisms for combinatorial public projects. Fix m,n, and k, and let $\mathcal{S} = \{S \subseteq [m] : |S| \leq k\}$ denote the set of feasible solutions. A mechanism comprises an *allocation rule*, which is a function from (hopefully truthfully) reported valuation functions $v_1, \ldots, v_n : 2^{[m]} \to \mathbb{R}$ to a feasible outcome $S \in \mathcal{S}$, and a *payment rule*, which is a function from reported valuation functions to a required payment from each player. We allow the allocation and payment rules to be randomized.

A mechanism with allocation and payment rules $\mathcal{A}$ and p is *truthful in expectation* if every player always maximizes its expected payoff by truthfully reporting its valuation function, meaning that

$$\mathbf{E}[v_i(\mathcal{A}(v)) - p_i(v)] \geq \mathbf{E}[v_i(\mathcal{A}(v_i', v_{-i})) - p_i(v_i', v_{-i})] \quad (1)$$

for every player i, (true) valuation function v_i, (reported) valuation function v_i', and (reported) valuation functions v_{-i} of the other players. The expectation in (1) is over the coin flips of the mechanism.

The mechanisms that we design can be thought of as randomized variations on the classical VCG mechanism, as we explain next. Recall that the *VCG mechanism* is defined by the (generally intractable) allocation rule that selects the welfare-maximizing outcome with respect to the reported valuation functions, and the payment rule that charges each player i a bid-independent "pivot term" minus the reported welfare earned by other players in the selected outcome. This (deterministic) mechanism is truthful; see e.g. [22].

Now let $dist(\mathcal{S})$ denote the probability distributions over the feasible set $\mathcal{S}$, and let $\mathcal{D} \subseteq dist(\mathcal{S})$ be a compact subset of them. The corresponding *Maximal in Distribution Range (MIDR)* allocation rule is defined as follows: given reported valuation functions $v_1, \ldots, v_n$, return an outcome that is sampled randomly from a distribution $D^* \in \mathcal{D}$ that maximizes the expected welfare $\mathbf{E}_{S \sim D}[\sum_i v_i(S)]$ over all distributions $D \in \mathcal{D}$. Analogous to the VCG mechanism, there is a (randomized) payment rule that can be coupled with this allocation rule to yield a truthful-in-expectation mechanism (see [8]).

2.3 Matroid Rank Sum Valuations

We now define matroid rank sum valuations. Relevant concepts from matroid theory are reviewed in Appendix B.1.

Definition 2.1. *A set function $v : 2^{[m]} \to \mathbb{R}$ is a* matroid rank sum (MRS) *function if there exists a family of matroid rank functions $u_1, \ldots, u_\kappa : 2^{[m]} \to \mathbb{R}$, and associated non-negative weights $w_1, \ldots, w_\kappa \in \mathbb{R}^+$, such that $v(S) = \sum_{\ell=1}^{\kappa} w_\ell u_\ell(S)$ for all $S \subseteq [m]$.*

We do not assume any particular representation of MRS functions, and require only oracle access to their (expected) values on certain distributions (see Section 2.4).

MRS valuations include most concrete examples of monotone submodular functions that appear in the literature – this includes coverage functions[3], matroid weighted-rank functions[4], and all convex combinations thereof. Moreover, as shown in [28], $1 - 1/e$ is the best approximation possible for CPP with coverage valuations – and hence also for MRS valuations – in polynomial time, even ignoring strategic considerations.

2.4 Lotteries and Oracles

A *value oracle* for a valuation $v : 2^{[m]} \to \mathbb{R}$ takes as input a set $S \subseteq [m]$, and returns $v(S)$. We define an analogous oracle that takes in a description of a simple lottery over sets $S \subseteq [m]$, and outputs the expectation of v over this lottery. The lotteries we consider will be of a very simple form, which we describe next.

Let $k \in [m]$, let $R \subseteq [m]$, and let $x \in [0, 1]^m$ be a vector such that $\sum_j x_j \leq 1$. We interpret x as a probability distribution over $[m] \cup \{*\}$, where $*$ represents not choosing a project. Specifically, project $j \in [m]$ is chosen with probability x_j, and $*$ is chosen with probability $1 - \sum_j x_j$. We define a distribution $D_k^R(x)$ over $2^{[m]}$, and call this distribution the *k-bounded lottery with marginals x and promise*

[3]A coverage function f on ground set $[m]$ designates some set $\mathcal{Y}$, and m subsets $A_1, \ldots, A_m \subseteq \mathcal{Y}$, such that $f(S) = |\cup_{\ell \in S} A_\ell|$. We note that $\mathcal{Y}$ may be an infinite, yet measurable, space. Coverage functions are arguably *the* canonical example of a submodular function.

[4]This is a generalization of matroid rank functions, where weights are placed on elements of the matroid. It is true, though not immediately obvious, that a matroid weighted-rank function can be expressed as a weighted combination of matroid (unweighted) rank functions – see e.g. [16].

R. We sample $S \sim D_k^R(x)$ as follows: Let $j_1, \ldots, j_k$ be independent draws from x, and let $S = R \cup \{j_1, \ldots, j_k\} \setminus \{*\}$. Essentially, this lottery commits to choosing projects R, and adds an additional k projects chosen randomly with replacement from distribution x. When $R = \emptyset$, as will be the case through most of this paper, we omit mention of the promised set. We can now define a randomized analogue of a value oracle that returns the expected value of a bounded-lottery.

DEFINITION 2.2. *A* bounded-lottery-value oracle *for set function $v : 2^{[m]} \to \mathbb{R}$ takes as input a vector $x \in [0,1]^m$ with $\sum_j x_j \leq 1$, a bound $k \in [m]$, and a set $R \subseteq [m]$, and outputs $\mathbf{E}_{S \sim D_k^R(x)}[v(S)]$.*

In our model for CPP, we assume that a player with valuation function v_i can answer bounded-lottery-value oracle queries for v_i. A bounded-lottery-value oracle is a generalization of value oracles. Nevertheless, it is the case that a bounded-lottery-value oracle can be implemented using a value oracle for some succinctly represented examples of MRS valuations, such as explicit coverage functions (In similar fashion to [17, Appendix A]).

More generally we note that bounded-lottery-value oracles can be approximated arbitrarily well, with high probability, using value oracles; this is done by random sampling, and we omit the technical details. Unfortunately, we are not able to reconcile the incurred sampling errors with the need for exactness characteristic of truthful mechanism design. However, we suspect that relaxing our solution concept to approximate truthfulness – also known as ϵ-truthfulness – would remove this difficulty, and allow us to relax our oracle model to the more traditional value-oracles.

2.5 Convex Rounding

In this section, we review *convex rounding*, a framework for the design of truthful mechanisms introduced by Dughmi, Roughgarden and Yan [17]. We present the main definitions and lemmas as they pertain to combinatorial public projects. For a more thorough and general treatment of convex rounding, we refer the reader to [17, Section 3].

We consider the standard integer programming formulation of CPP. There is a variable $x_j \in \{0,1\}$ for each project $j \in [m]$, and the goal is to set at most k of the variables to 1 so that the welfare $v(x) = \sum_i v_i(\{j : x_j = 1\})$ is maximized. We *relax* this integer program in the obvious way to the polytope $\mathcal{P} = \left\{x \in \mathbb{R}^m : \sum_j x_j \leq k, x \succeq 0\right\}$. We postulate a *rounding scheme* r that maps points of $\mathcal{P}$ to the feasible solutions $\mathcal{S} = \{S \subseteq [m] : |S| \leq k\}$ of CPP. We allow r to be randomized, so that $r(x)$ is a distribution over $\mathcal{S}$ for each $x \in \mathcal{P}$.

Traditionally, approximation algorithms optimize an objective $\widetilde{v}(x)$ – often a simple extension of v to $\mathcal{P}$ – over the set $\mathcal{P}$ of fractional solutions, and then round the optimal fractional point x^* to a solution $r(x^*)$ in the original feasible set $\mathcal{S}$. Many of the best approximation algorithms for various problems are based on this relax-solve-round framework. Unfortunately, however, this approach is almost always incompatible with the design of truthful mechanisms, due to the fact that the rounding step is often unpredictable. Truthful mechanism design, on the other hand, is intimately tied to *exact optimization*, as evidenced by the fact that the vast majority truthful mechanisms for multi-parameter problems are based on the VCG paradigm (see Section 2.2).

In an effort to reconcile the techniques of approximation algorithms and truthful mechanism design, Dughmi, Roughgarden and Yan proposed *optimizing directly on the output of the rounding scheme, rather than on its input.* This defines an optimization problem induced by relaxation $\mathcal{P}$ and rounding scheme r. Stated for CPP with the relaxation as described above, the problem is as follows.

$$\begin{array}{lll} \text{maximize} & \mathbf{E}_{S \sim r(x)}[\sum_i v_i(S)] & \\ \text{subject to} & \sum_{j=1}^m x_j \leq k & \\ & 0 \leq x_j \leq 1, & \text{for } j = 1, \ldots, m. \end{array} \quad (2)$$

They consider a simple allocation rule, which we state for CPP in Algorithm 1, that solves (2) optimally. They observe that this allocation rule is maximal in distributional range.

Algorithm 1 MIDR Allocation Rule for CPP

Parameter: n,m,k
Parameter: (Randomized) rounding scheme r
Input: Valuation functions $\{v_i\}_{i=1}^n$
Output: A set $S \subseteq [m]$ with $|S| \leq k$
1: Let x^* be an optimal solution to (2)
2: Let $S \sim r(x^*)$

LEMMA 2.3 ([17]). *Algorithm 1 is an MIDR allocation rule.*

For $\alpha \leq 1$, we say that the rounding scheme r for CPP($\mathcal{V}$) is *α-approximate* if, whenever x is an integer point of $\mathcal{P}$ corresponding to a set $S \in \mathcal{S}$, and $v_i \in \mathcal{V}$ for each i, we have that $\mathbf{E}_{T \sim r(x)}[\sum_i v_i(T)] \geq \alpha \sum_i v_i(S)$. In other words, rounding does not degrade the quality of an integer solution by more than α. Given the definition of Algorithm 1, it is easy to conclude the following lemma.

LEMMA 2.4 ([17]). *If r is an α-approximate rounding scheme for CPP($\mathcal{V}$), then Algorithm 1 is an α-approximation algorithm for CPP($\mathcal{V}$).*

For reasons outlined in [17], implementing Algorithm 1 efficiently is impossible for most rounding schemes r in the literature. To get around this difficulty, they advocate designing rounding schemes that render (2) a convex optimization problem.

DEFINITION 2.5. *Consider a randomized rounding scheme $r : \mathcal{P} \to dist(\mathcal{S})$. We say r is a* convex rounding scheme *for CPP($\mathcal{V}$) if, whenever $v_i \in \mathcal{V}$ for all i, the objective $\mathbf{E}_{S \sim r(x)}[\sum_i v_i(S)]$ is a concave function of x.*

LEMMA 2.6. *When r is a convex rounding scheme for CPP($\mathcal{V}$) , (2) is a convex optimization problem for each instance of CPP($\mathcal{V}$).*

Under additional technical conditions, discussed in the context of combinatorial public projects in Appendix A, convex program (2) can be solved efficiently (e.g., using the ellipsoid method). This reduces the design of a polynomial-time α-approximate MIDR algorithm to designing a polynomial time α-approximate convex rounding scheme.

Summarizing, Lemmas 2.3, 2.4, and 2.6 give the following informal theorem.

THEOREM 2.7 (Informal). *If there exists an α-approximate convex rounding scheme for CPP($\mathcal{V}$), then there exists a truthful-in-expectation, polynomial-time, α-approximate mechanism for CPP($\mathcal{V}$).*

3. THE MECHANISM

In this section, we prove the main result.

THEOREM 3.1. *There is a* $(1-1/e)$*-approximate, truthful-in-expectation mechanism for combinatorial public projects with matroid rank sum valuations in the bounded-lottery-value oracle model, running in expected* $\text{poly}(n, m)$ *time.*

We structure the proof of Theorem 3.1 as follows. We define the *k-bounded-lottery rounding scheme*, which we denote by r_k, in Section 3.1. We prove that r_k is $(1-1/e)$-approximate (Lemma 3.2), and convex (Lemma 3.3). Lemmas 2.3, 2.4 and 3.2, taken together, imply that Algorithm 1 when instantiated with $r = r_k$, is a $(1-1/e)$-approximate MIDR allocation rule. Lemma 3.3 reduces implementing this allocation rule to solving a convex program.

In Appendix A, we handle the technical and numerical issues related to solving convex programs. First, we prove that our instantiation of Algorithm 1 can be implemented in expected polynomial-time using the ellipsoid method under a simplifying assumption on the numerical conditioning of our convex program (Lemma A.2). Then we show in Section A.3 that the previous assumption can be removed by slightly modifying our algorithm.

Finally, we prove that truth-telling VCG payments can be computed efficiently in Lemma B.4. Taken together, these lemmas complete the proof of Theorem 3.1.

3.1 The k-Bounded-Lottery Rounding Scheme

We devise a rounding scheme r_k that we term the *k-bounded-lottery rounding scheme.* Given a feasible solution x to linear program (2), we let distribution $r_k(x)$ be the k-bounded-lottery with marginals x/k (and promise $\emptyset$), as defined in Section 2.4. We make this more explicit in Algorithm 2.

Algorithm 2 The k-Bounded-Lottery Rounding Scheme r_k

Input: Fractional solution $x \in \mathbb{R}^m$ with $\sum_j x_j \leq k$, and $0 \leq x_j \leq 1$ for all j.

Output: $S \subseteq [m]$ with $|S| \leq k$

1: For each $j \in [m]$ designate the interval $I_j = [\frac{1}{k}\sum_{j'<j} x_{j'}, \frac{1}{k}\sum_{j' \leq j} x_{j'}]$ of length $\frac{x_j}{k}$

2: Draw $p_1, \ldots, p_k$ independently and uniformly from $[0, 1]$

3: Let $S = \{j \in [m] : \{p_1, \ldots, p_k\} \cap I_j \neq \emptyset\}$

The k-bounded-lottery rounding scheme is $(1-1/e)$ approximate and convex. We prove the approximation lemma below. As for convexity, we present a simplified proof for the special case of coverage valuations in Section 3.2, and present the proof for MRS valuations in Section 3.3.

LEMMA 3.2. *The* k*-bounded-lottery rounding scheme is* $(1-1/e)$*-approximate when valuations are submodular.*

PROOF. Fix n, m, k and $\{v_i\}_{i=1}^n$. Let $S \subseteq [m]$ be a feasible solution to CPP – i.e. $|S| \leq k$. Let 1_S be the vector with 1 in indices corresponding to S, and 0 otherwise. Let $T \sim r_k(1_S)$. We will first show that each element of $j \in S$ is included in T with probability at least $1-1/e$. Observe that T is the union of k independent draws from a distribution on $[m] \cup \{*\}$, where each time the probability of $j \in S$ is $1/k$. Therefore, the probability that j is included in T is $1-(1-1/k)^k \geq 1-1/e$.

Submodularity now implies that $\mathbf{E}[v_i(T)] \geq (1-1/e) \cdot v_i(S)$ for each player i — this was proved in many contexts: see for example [19, Lemma 2.2], and the earlier related result in [18, Proposition 2.3]. This completes the proof. □

LEMMA 3.3. *The* k*–bounded-lottery rounding scheme is convex for CPP with MRS valuations.*

3.2 Warm-up: Convexity for Coverage Valuations

In this section, we prove a special case of Lemma 3.3 for coverage valuations. Recall that a coverage function f on ground set $[m]$ designates some set $\mathcal{Y}$, and m subsets $A_1, \ldots, A_m \subseteq \mathcal{Y}$, such that $f(S) = |\cup_{j \in S} A_j|$.

Fix n, m, k and $\{v_i\}_{i=1}^n$. Assume that, for each player i, the valuation function $v_i : 2^{[m]} \rightarrow \mathbb{R}$ is a coverage function. We let $v(S) = \sum_i v_i(S)$ be the welfare of a solution S to CPP. It is an easy observation that the sum of coverage functions is also a coverage function. Therefore $v(S)$ is a coverage function. We let $\mathcal{Y}$ be a set, and $A_1, \ldots, A_m \subseteq \mathcal{Y}$, such that $v(S) = |\cup_{j \in S} A_j|$. While our proof extends easily to the case where $\mathcal{Y}$ is an arbitrary measure space, we assume in this section that $\mathcal{Y}$ is a finite set for simplicity.

Let $\mathcal{P}$ denote the polytope of fractional solutions to CPP as given in (2). We now show that $\mathbf{E}_{S \sim r_k(x)}[v(S)]$ is a concave function of x for $x \in \mathcal{P}$, completing the proof of Lemma 3.3 for the special case of coverage valuations. Take an arbitrary $x \in \mathcal{P}$, and let $S \sim r_k(x)$ be a random variable. Using linearity of expectations, we can rewrite the expected welfare as follows.

$$\mathbf{E}[v(S)] = \mathbf{E}[|\cup_{j \in S} A_j|] = \sum_{\ell \in \mathcal{Y}} \mathbf{Pr}[\ell \in \cup_{j \in S} A_j]$$

Since the sum of concave functions is concave, showing that $\mathbf{Pr}[\ell \in \cup_{j \in S} A_j]$ is concave in x for each $\ell \in \mathcal{Y}$ suffices to complete the proof. For $\ell \in \mathcal{Y}$, let $T_\ell = \{j \in [m] : \ell \in A_j\}$ be the set of projects that "cover" ℓ. Let $p_1, \ldots, p_k$ and $I_1, \ldots, I_k$ be as in Algorithm 2. Note that $\{I_j\}_{j=1}^m$ are disjoint sub-intervals of $[0, 1]$, and $|I_j| = \frac{x_j}{k}$. We can rewrite the probability of covering ℓ as follows.

$$\begin{aligned}
\mathbf{Pr}[\ell \in \cup_{j \in S} A_j] &= \mathbf{Pr}[S \cap T_\ell \neq \emptyset] \\
&= \mathbf{Pr}[\{p_1, \ldots, p_k\} \cap \cup_{j \in T_\ell} I_j \neq \emptyset] \\
&= 1 - \mathbf{Pr}[\{p_1, \ldots, p_k\} \cap \cup_{j \in T_\ell} I_j = \emptyset] \\
&= 1 - \prod_{t=1}^{k} \mathbf{Pr}[p_t \notin \cup_{j \in T_\ell} I_j] \\
&= 1 - \prod_{t=1}^{k} (1 - |\cup_{j \in T_\ell} I_j|) \\
&= 1 - \left(1 - \frac{\sum_{j \in T_\ell} x_j}{k}\right)^k.
\end{aligned}$$

The final form is simply the composition of the concave function $g(y) = 1 - (1 - y/k)^k$ with the affine function $y \rightarrow \sum_{j \in T_\ell} x_j$. It is well known that composing a concave function with an affine function yields another concave function (see e.g. [2]). This completes the proof.

3.3 Convexity for MRS Valuations

In this section, we will prove Lemma 3.3 in its full generality. First, we recall the *discrete hessian matrix*, as defined in [17].

DEFINITION 3.4 ([17]). *Let $v : 2^{[m]} \to \mathbb{R}$ be a set function. For $S \subseteq [m]$, we define the discrete Hessian matrix $\mathcal{H}_S^v \in \mathbb{R}^{m\times m}$ of v at S as follows:*

$$\mathcal{H}_S^v(i,j) = v(S \cup \{i,j\}) - v(S\cup\{i\}) - v(S\cup\{j\}) + v(S) \quad (3)$$

for $i, j \in [m]$.

It was shown in [17] that the discrete hessian matrices are negative semi-definite for matroid rank sum functions.

CLAIM 3.5 ([17]). *If $v : 2^{[m]} \to \mathbb{R}^+$ is a matroid rank sum function, then $\mathcal{H}_S^v$ is negative semi-definite for each $S \subseteq [m]$.*

We now return to Lemma 3.3. Fix n and m. For each cardinality bound $k \in [m]$, let $\mathcal{P}_k$ denote the polytope of fractional solutions to CPP as given in (2). For a set of MRS valuations $v_1, \dots, v_n$, we observe that the social welfare $v(S) = \sum_{i=1}^n v_i(S)$ is – by the (obvious) fact that the sum of MRS functions is an MRS function – also an MRS function. Therefore, we will prove Lemma 3.3 by showing that, for each $k \in [m]$ and MRS function $v : 2^{[m]} \to \mathbb{R}$, the following function of $x \in \mathcal{P}_k$ is concave in x.

$$\begin{aligned} G_k^v(x) &= \mathop{\mathbf{E}}_{S\sim r_k(x)}[v(S)] \\ &= \sum_{S\subseteq[m]} v(S)\,\mathbf{Pr}[r_k(x) = S] \end{aligned} \quad (4)$$

We use techniques from combinatorics to write $\mathbf{Pr}[r_k(x) = S]$ in a form that will be easier to work with. For $T \subseteq [m]$, we use x_T as short-hand for $\sum_{j\in T} x_j$, and $\overline{T}$ as short-hand for $[m] \setminus T$.

CLAIM 3.6. *For each $k \in [m]$, $x \in \mathcal{P}_k$, and $S \subseteq [m]$*

$$\mathbf{Pr}[r_k(x) = S] = -1^{|S|} \sum_{R\subseteq S} -1^{|R|}\left(1 - \frac{x_{\overline{R}}}{k}\right)^k \quad (5)$$

PROOF. It is easy to see that $\mathbf{Pr}[r_k(x) = S]$ is equal to:

$$\mathbf{Pr}[r_k(x) \subseteq S] - \mathbf{Pr}[\bigvee_{j\in S} r_k(x) \subseteq S \setminus \{j\}] \quad (6)$$

Using the inclusion-exclusion principle, we can rewrite (6) as follows:

$$\mathbf{Pr}[r_k(x) \subseteq S] - \sum_{\emptyset\neq T\subseteq S} -1^{|T|-1}\,\mathbf{Pr}[r_k(x) \subseteq S \setminus T] \quad (7)$$

Letting $R = S \setminus T$ in (7), we get

$$\mathbf{Pr}[r_k(x) \subseteq S] - \sum_{R\subsetneq S} -1^{|S|-|R|-1}\,\mathbf{Pr}[r_k(x) \subseteq R] \quad (8)$$

We can easily simplify (8) to conclude that

$$\mathbf{Pr}[r_k(x) = S] = \sum_{R\subseteq S} -1^{|S|-|R|}\,\mathbf{Pr}[r_k(x) \subseteq R] \quad (9)$$

Next, we observe that the expression $\mathbf{Pr}[r_k(x) \subseteq R]$ can be expressed as a simple closed form in x. Let $p_1, \dots, p_k$ and $I_1, \dots, I_m$ be as in Algorithm 2. The event $r_k(x) \subseteq R$ occurs exactly when none of $p_1, \dots, p_k$ land in the intervals corresponding to projects $\overline{R}$. Recalling that the interval I_j of project j has length x_j/k, we get that the probability of any particular p_t falling in $\cup_{j\in\overline{R}} I_j$ is exactly $x_{\overline{R}}/k$. Therefore, by the independence of the variables $p_1, \dots, p_k$, we get that

$$\mathbf{Pr}[r_k(x) \subseteq R] = \left(1 - \frac{x_{\overline{R}}}{k}\right)^k \quad (10)$$

Combining (9) and (10) completes the proof. □

Building on Claim 3.6, we now express the Hessian matrix of G_k^v as a non-negative weighted sum of discrete Hessian matrices of v. We note that when $x \in \mathcal{P}_k$, it is easy to verify that $\frac{k-2}{k} \cdot x \in \mathcal{P}_{k-2}$, and therefore (11) is well defined.

CLAIM 3.7. *For each $k \in [m]$, $x \in \mathcal{P}_k$, and $v : 2^{[m]} \to \mathbb{R}$, we have*

$$\nabla^2 G_k^v(x) = \frac{k-1}{k} \sum_{S\subseteq[m]} \mathbf{Pr}\left[r_{k-2}\left(\frac{k-2}{k}\cdot x\right) = S\right] \mathcal{H}_S^v \quad (11)$$

PROOF. Fix $i, j \in [m]$, possibly with $i = j$. We work with G_k^v as defined in Equation (4), and plug in expression (5).

$$G_k^v(x) = \sum_{S\subseteq[m]} v(S)\cdot -1^{|S|} \sum_{R\subseteq S} -1^{|R|}\left(1 - \frac{x_{\overline{R}}}{k}\right)^k$$

Differentiating with respect to x_i and x_j gives:

$$\frac{\partial^2 G_k^v(x)}{\partial x_i \partial x_j} = \frac{k-1}{k} \sum_{S\subseteq[m]} v(S)\cdot -1^{|S|} \sum_{R\subseteq S\setminus\{i,j\}} -1^{|R|}\left(1 - \frac{x_{\overline{R}}}{k}\right)^{k-2}$$

We group the terms by projecting S onto $[m] \setminus \{i, j\}$, and then we simplify the resulting expression.

$$\begin{aligned} \frac{\partial^2 G_k^v(x)}{\partial x_i \partial x_j} =& \frac{k-1}{k} \sum_{S\subseteq[m]\setminus\{i,j\}} -1^{|S|} \sum_{R\subseteq S} -1^{|R|}\left(1 - \frac{x_{\overline{R}}}{k}\right)^{k-2} \\ &\cdot (v(S) - v(S\cup\{i\}) - v(S\cup\{j\}) + v(S\cup\{i,j\})) \\ =& \frac{k-1}{k} \sum_{S\subseteq[m]} -1^{|S|} \sum_{R\subseteq S} -1^{|R|}\left(1 - \frac{x_{\overline{R}}}{k}\right)^{k-2} \\ &\cdot (v(S) - v(S\cup\{i\}) - v(S\cup\{j\}) + v(S\cup\{i,j\})) \\ =& \frac{k-1}{k} \sum_{S\subseteq[m]} -1^{|S|} \sum_{R\subseteq S} -1^{|R|}\left(1 - \frac{x_{\overline{R}}}{k}\right)^{k-2} \mathcal{H}_S^v(i,j) \end{aligned} \quad (12)$$

The second equality follows from the fact that $v(S) - v(S \cup \{i\}) - v(S \cup \{j\}) + v(S \cup \{i,j\}) = 0$ when S includes either of i and j. The last equality follows by definition of $\mathcal{H}_S^v$.

Invoking Claim 3.6 with $k' = k - 2$ and $x' = \frac{k-2}{k} \cdot x$, and plugging the resulting expression into into (12), we conclude that

$$\frac{\partial^2 G_k^v(x)}{\partial x_i \partial x_j} = \frac{k-1}{k} \sum_{S\subseteq[m]} \mathbf{Pr}\left[r_{k-2}\left(\frac{k-2}{k}\cdot x\right) = S\right] \mathcal{H}_S^v(i,j).$$

□

Claims (3.5) and (3.7) establish that, when v is MRS and $k \in [m]$, $\nabla^2 G_k^v(x)$ is a non-negative weighted sum of negative semi-definite matrices for each $x \in \mathcal{P}_k$. A non-negative weighted sum of negative semi-definite matrices is negative semi-definite. Therefore, the Hessian matrix of G_k^v is negative semi-definite at each $x \in \mathcal{P}_k$, and we conclude that G_k^v is a concave function on $\mathcal{P}_k$. This completes the proof of Lemma 3.3.

4. REFERENCES

[1] A. Ben-Tal and A. Nemirovski. *Lectures on Modern Convex Optimization: Analysis, Algorithms, and Engineering Applications.* SIAM, 2001.

[2] S. Boyd and L. Vandenberghe. *Convex Optimization.* Cambridge University Press, 2004.

[3] D. Buchfuhrer, S. Dughmi, H. Fu, R. Kleinberg, E. Mossel, C. Papadimitriou, M. Schapira, Y. Singer, and C. Umans. Inapproximability for VCG-based combinatorial auctions. In *Proc. 21st ACM Symp. on Discrete Algorithms (SODA)*, 2010.

[4] D. Buchfuhrer, M. Schapira, and Y. Singer. Computation and incentives in combinatorial public projects. In *Proc. 12th ACM Conf. on Electronic Commerce (EC)*, 2010.

[5] G. Calinescu, C. Chekuri, M. Pál, and J. Vondrák. Maximizing a submodular set function subject to a matroid constraint. In *Proc. 12th Intl. Conference on Integer Programming and Combinatorial Optimization (IPCO)*, 2007.

[6] S. Dobzinski. Two randomized mechanisms for combinatorial auctions. In *Proc. 10th Intl. Workshop on Approximation Algorithms for Combinatorial Optimization Problems (APPROX)*, 2007.

[7] S. Dobzinski. An impossibility result for truthful combinatorial auctions with submodular valuations. In *Proceedings of the 43rd annual ACM Symposium on Theory of Computing (STOC)*, 2011.

[8] S. Dobzinski and S. Dughmi. On the power of randomization in algorithmic mechanism design. In *Proc. 50th IEEE Symp. on Foundations of Computer Science (FOCS)*, 2009.

[9] S. Dobzinski, H. Fu, and R. Kleinberg. Truthfulness via proxies. *CoRR*, abs/1011.3232, 2010.

[10] S. Dobzinski and N. Nisan. Limitations of VCG-based mechanisms. In *Proc. 38th ACM Symp. on Theory of Computing (STOC)*, 2007.

[11] S. Dobzinski, N. Nisan, and M. Schapira. Approximation algorithms for combinatorial auctions with complement-free bidders. In *Proc. 36th ACM Symp. on Theory of Computing (STOC)*, 2005.

[12] S. Dobzinski, N. Nisan, and M. Schapira. Truthful randomized mechanisms for combinatorial auctions. In *Proc. 37th ACM Symp. on Theory of Computing (STOC)*, 2006.

[13] S. Dobzinski and M. Schapira. An improved approximation algorithm for combinatorial auctions with submodular bidders. In *Proc. 17th ACM Symp. on Discrete Algorithms (SODA)*, 2006.

[14] S. Dobzinski and M. Sundararajan. On characterizations of truthful mechanisms for combinatorial auctions and scheduling. In *Proc. 10th ACM Conf. on Electronic Commerce (EC)*, 2008.

[15] S. Dughmi and T. Roughgarden. Black-box randomized reductions in algorithmic mechanism design. In *Proc. 51st IEEE Symp. on Foundations of Computer Science (FOCS)*, 2010.

[16] S. Dughmi, T. Roughgarden, and M. Sundararajan. Revenue submodularity. In *Proc. 11th ACM Conf. on Electronic Commerce (EC)*, 2009.

[17] S. Dughmi, T. Roughgarden, and Q. Yan. From convex optimization to randomized mechanisms: Toward optimal combinatorial auctions. In *Proceedings of the 43rd annual ACM Symposium on Theory of Computing (STOC)*, 2011.

[18] U. Feige. On maximizing welfare where the utility functions are subadditive. In *Proc. 37th ACM Symp. on Theory of Computing (STOC)*, 2006.

[19] U. Feige, V. S. Mirrokni, and J. Vondrák. Maximizing non-monotone submodular functions. In *Proc. 48th IEEE Symp. on Foundations of Computer Science (FOCS)*, 2007.

[20] R. Lavi and C. Swamy. Truthful and near-optimal mechanism design via linear programming. In *Proc. 46th IEEE Symp. on Foundations of Computer Science (FOCS)*, 2005.

[21] G. L. Nemhauser, L. A. Wolsey, and M. L. Fisher. An analysis of approximations for maximizing submodular set functions – I. *Mathematical Programming*, 14(3), 1978.

[22] N. Nisan. Introduction to mechanism design (for computer scientists). In N. Nisan, T. Roughgarden, E. Tardos, and V. Vazirani, editors, *Algorithmic Game Theory*. Cambridge University Press, 2007.

[23] N. Nisan and A. Ronen. Algorithmic mechanism design. In *Proc. 40th ACM Symp. on Theory of Computing (STOC)*, 1999.

[24] N. Nisan and A. Ronen. Computationally feasible VCG-based mechanisms. In *Proc. 2nd ACM Conf. on Electronic Commerce (EC)*, 2000.

[25] N. Nisan, T. Roughgarden, E. Tardos, and V. V. Vazirani. *Algorithmic Game Theory*. Cambridge University Press, New York, NY, USA, 2007.

[26] J. G. Oxley. *Matroid Theory*. Oxford University Press, 1992.

[27] C. Papadimitriou, M. Schapira, and Y. Singer. On the hardness of being truthful. In *Proc. 49th IEEE Symp. on Foundations of Computer Science (FOCS)*, 2008.

[28] R. Raz and S. Safra. A sub-constant error-probability low-degree test, and a sub-constant error-probability pcp characterization of np. In *Proc. 29th ACM Symp. on Theory of Computing (STOC)*, 1997.

[29] A. Schrijver. *Combinatorial Optimization*. Springer, 2003.

[30] J. Vondrák. Optimal approximation for the submodular welfare problem in the value oracle model. In *Proc. 39th ACM Symp. on Theory of Computing (STOC)*, 2008.

APPENDIX

A. SOLVING THE CONVEX PROGRAM

In this section, we overcome some technical difficulties related to the solvability of convex programs. We follow the general outline of [17, Appendix B], modifying the proofs throughout in order to handle the additional technical difficulties specific to CPP. We show in Section A.1 that, in the bounded-lottery-value oracle model, the four conditions for "solvability" of convex programs, as stated in Fact B.3, are easily satisfied for convex program (2) when $r = r_k$. However, an additional challenge remains: "solving" a convex program – as in Definition B.2 – returns an approximately optimal solution. Indeed the optimal solution of a convex program may be irrational in general, so this is unavoidable.

We show how to overcome this difficulty if we settle for polynomial runtime in expectation. While the optimal solution x^* of (2) cannot be computed explicitly, the random variable $r_k(x^*)$ can be sampled in expected polynomial-time. The key idea is the following: *sampling the random variable $r_k(x^*)$ rarely requires precise knowledge of x^**. Depending on the coin flips of r_k, we decide how accurately we need to solve convex program (2) in order compute $r_k(x^*)$. Roughly speaking, we show that the probability of requiring a $(1-\epsilon)$-approximation falls exponentially in $\frac{1}{\epsilon}$. As a result, we can sample $r_k(x^*)$ in expected polynomial-time. We implement this plan in Section A.2 under the simplifying assumption that convex program (2) is *well-conditioned* – i.e. is "sufficiently concave" everywhere. In Section A.3, we show how to remove that assumption by slightly modifying our algorithm.

A.1 Approximating the Convex Program

CLAIM A.1. *There is an algorithm for Combinatorial Public Projects with MRS valuations in the bounded-lottery-value oracle model that takes as input an instance of the problem and an approximation parameter $\epsilon > 0$, runs in $\text{poly}(n, m, \log(1/\epsilon))$ time, and returns a $(1-\epsilon)$-approximate solution to convex program (2) when $r = r_k$.*

It suffices to show that the four conditions of Fact B.3 are satisfied in our setting. The first three are immediate from elementary combinatorial optimization (see for example [29]). It remains to show that the first-order oracle, as defined in Fact B.3, can be implemented in polynomial-time in the bounded-lottery-value oracle model. We let $f(x)$ denote the objective function of convex program (2) when $r = r_k$. This objective can, by definition, be written as follows.

$$f(x) = \mathop{\mathbf{E}}_{S \sim r_k(x)} \left[\sum_i v_i(S) \right] = \sum_i G_k^{v_i}(x)$$

where v_i is the valuation function of player i and $G_k^{v_i}$ is as defined in (4). By definition, $G_k^{v_i}(x)$ is the outcome of querying the bounded-lottery-value oracle of v_i with bound k and marginals x/k. Therefore, we can evaluate $f(x)$ using n bounded-lottery-value queries, one for each player. It remains to show that we can also evaluate the (multi-variate) derivative $\bigtriangledown f(x)$ of $f(x)$. Using definition (4) and Claim 3.6, we take the partial derivative of $G_k^{v_i}$ with respect to x_j and simplify the resulting expression.

$$\begin{aligned}
\frac{\partial G_k^{v_i}}{\partial x_j}(x) =& \sum_{S \subseteq [m]} -1^{|S|} v_i(S) \sum_{R \subseteq S \setminus \{j\}} -1^{|R|+1} \left(1 - \frac{x_{\overline{R}}}{k}\right)^{k-1} \\
=& \sum_{S \subseteq [m] \setminus \{j\}} -1^{|S|} (v_i(S \cup \{j\}) - v_i(S)) \\
& \cdot \sum_{R \subseteq S} -1^{|R|} \left(1 - \frac{x_{\overline{R}}}{k}\right)^{k-1} \\
=& \sum_{S \subseteq [m]} -1^{|S|} (v_i(S \cup \{j\}) - v_i(S)) \\
& \cdot \sum_{R \subseteq S} -1^{|R|} \left(1 - \frac{x_{\overline{R}}}{k}\right)^{k-1} \\
=& \sum_{S \subseteq [m]} v_i(S \cup \{j\}) \,\mathbf{Pr}\left[r_{k-1}\left(\frac{k-1}{k} x\right) = S \right] \\
& - \sum_{S \subseteq [m]} v_i(S) \,\mathbf{Pr}\left[r_{k-1}\left(\frac{k-1}{k} x\right) = S \right]. \qquad (13)
\end{aligned}$$

The second equality follows by grouping the terms of the summation by the projection of S onto $[m] \setminus \{j\}$. The third equality follows from the observation that $v(S \cup \{j\}) - v(S) = 0$ when S includes j. The fourth equality follows by a simple re-arrangement and application of Claim 3.6.

Inspect the final form (13) in light of Definition 2.2 and the definition of r_k. Notice that the first term is the expected value of v_i over the $(k-1)$-bounded-lottery with marginals $\frac{k-1}{k}x$ and promise $\{j\}$. The second term is the expected value of v_i over the same lottery without the promise. Therefore, we can evaluate $\frac{\partial G_k^{v_i}}{\partial x_j}(x)$ using two queries to the bounded-lottery-value oracle of player i. This completes the proof of Claim A.1.

A.2 The Well-Conditioned Case

In this section, we make the following simplifying assumption: The objective function $f(x)$ of convex program (2) with $r = r_k$, when restricted to any line in the feasible set $\mathcal{P}$, has a second derivative of magnitude at least $\lambda = \frac{\sum_{i=1}^n v_i([m])}{2^{\text{poly}(n,m)}}$ everywhere, where the polynomial in the denominator may be arbitrary. This is equivalent to requiring that every eigenvalue of the Hessian matrix of $f(x)$ has magnitude at least λ when evaluated at any point in $\mathcal{P}$. Under this assumption, we prove Lemma A.2.

LEMMA A.2. *Assume the magnitude of the second derivative of $f(x)$ is at least $\lambda = \frac{\sum_{i=1}^n v_i([m])}{2^{\text{poly}(n,m)}}$ everywhere. Algorithm 1, instantiated with $r = r_k$, can be simulated in time polynomial in n and m in expectation.*

Let x^* be the optimal solution to convex program (2) with $r = r_k$. Algorithm 1 outputs a set of projects distributed as $r_k(x^*)$. The k-bounded-lottery rounding scheme, as described in Algorithm 2, requires making k independent decisions: for $\ell \in \{1, \ldots, k\}$, we draw p_ℓ uniformly from $[0, 1]$ and decide which interval I_j, if any, p_ℓ falls into. In other words, we find the minimum index j_ℓ (if any) such that $\sum_{j \le j_\ell} x_j^*/k \ge p_\ell$. Fix ℓ. For most realizations of p_ℓ, we can calculate j_ℓ using only coarse estimates $\widetilde{x}_j$ to x_j^*. Assume we have an *estimation oracle* for x^* that, on input δ, returns a δ-*estimate* $\widetilde{x}$ of x^*: Specifically, $\widetilde{x}_j - x_j^* \le \delta$ for each $j \in [m]$. If p_ℓ falls outside the "uncertainty zones" of $\widetilde{x}$, such as when $|p_\ell - \sum_{j' \le j} \widetilde{x}_{j'}/k| > \delta m/k$ for each $j \in [m]$, it is easy to see that we can correctly determine j_ℓ by using $\widetilde{x}$ in lieu of x. The total measure of the uncertainty zones of $\widetilde{x}$ is at most $2m^2\delta$, therefore p_ℓ lands outside the uncertainty zones with probability at least $1 - 2m^2\delta$. The following claim shows that if the estimation oracle for x^* can be implemented in time polynomial in $\log(1/\delta)$, then we can simulate the k-bounded-lottery rounding procedure in expected polynomial-time.

CLAIM A.3. *Let x^* be the optimal solution of convex program (2) with $r = r_k$. Assume access to a subroutine $B(\delta)$ that returns a δ-estimate of x^* in $\text{poly}(n, m, \log(1/\delta))$ time. Algorithm 1, instantiated with $r = r_k$, can be simulated in expected $\text{poly}(n, m)$ time.*

PROOF. Fix $\ell \in \{1, \ldots, k\}$. Draw $p_\ell \in [0, 1]$ uniformly at random as in the k-bounded-lottery rounding scheme in Algorithm 2. We will show how to find, in expected $\text{poly}(n, m)$ time, the minimum index j_ℓ (if any) such that $\sum_{j \le j_\ell} x_j^*/k \ge p_\ell$.

The algorithm proceeds as follows: Start with $\delta = \delta_0 = \frac{1}{2m^2}$. Let $\widetilde{x} = B(\delta)$. While $|p_\ell - \sum_{j' \le j} \widetilde{x}_{j'}/k| \le \delta m/k$ for some $j \in [m]$ (i.e. p_ℓ may fall inside an "uncertainty zone") do the following: let $\delta = \delta/2$, $\widetilde{x} = B(\delta)$ and repeat. After the loop terminates, we have a sufficiently accurate estimate of x^* to calculate j_ℓ.

It is easy to see that the above procedure is a faithful simulation of Algorithm (2) on x^*. It remains to bound its expected running time. Let $\delta_t = \frac{1}{2^{t+1}m^2}$ denote the value of δ at iteration t. By our initial assumption, iteration t takes $\text{poly}(n, m, \log(1/\delta_t)) = \text{poly}(n, m, \log(2^{t+1}m^2)) = \text{poly}(n, m, t)$ time. The probability this procedure does not terminate after t iterations is at most $2m^2\delta_t = 1/2^t$. Taken together, these two facts and a simple geometric summation imply that the expected runtime is polynomial in n and m. □

It remains to show that the estimation oracle $B(\delta)$ can be implemented in $\text{poly}(n, m, \log(1/\delta))$ time. At first blush, one may expect that the ellipsoid method can be used in the usual manner here. However, there is one complication: we require an estimate $\widetilde{x}$ that is close to x^* *in solution space* rather than in terms of objective value. Using our assumption on the curvature of $f(x)$, we will reduce finding a δ-estimate of x^* to finding an $1 - \epsilon(\delta)$ approximate solution to convex program (2) with $r = r_k$. The dependence of ϵ on δ will be such that $\epsilon \geq \text{poly}(\delta)/2^{\text{poly}(n,m)}$, thereby we can invoke Claim A.1 to deduce that $B(\delta)$ can be implemented in $\text{poly}(n, m, \log(1/\delta))$ time.

Let $\epsilon = \epsilon(\delta) = \frac{\delta^2 \lambda}{2\sum_i v_i([m])}$. Plugging in the definition of λ, we deduce that $\epsilon \geq \delta^2/2^{\text{poly}(n,m)}$, which is the desired dependence. It remains to show that if $\widetilde{x}$ is $(1-\epsilon)$-approximate solution to (2), then $\widetilde{x}$ is also a δ-estimate of x^*.

Using the fact that $f(x)$ is concave, and moreover its second derivative has magnitude at least λ, it a simple exercise to bound distance of any point x from the optimal point x^* in terms of its sub-optimality $f(x^*) - f(x)$, as follows:

$$f(x^*) - f(x) \geq \frac{\lambda}{2}||x - x^*||^2. \tag{14}$$

Assume $\widetilde{x}$ is a $(1-\epsilon)$-approximate solution to (2) with $r = r_k$. Equation (14) implies that

$$||\widetilde{x} - x^*||^2 \leq \frac{2}{\lambda}\epsilon f(x^*) = \frac{\delta^2}{\sum_i v_i([m])} f(x^*) \leq \delta^2,$$

where the last inequality follows from the fact that $\sum_i v_i([m])$ is an upper-bound on the optimal value $f(x^*)$. Therefore, $||x - x^*|| \leq \delta$, as needed. This completes the proof of Lemma A.2.

A.3 Guaranteeing Good Conditioning

In this section, we propose a modification r_k^+ of the k-bounded-lottery rounding scheme r_k. We will argue that r_k^+ satisfies all the properties of r_k established so far, with one exception: the approximation guarantee of Lemma 3.2 is reduced to $1 - 1/e - 2^{-2mn}$. Then we will show that r_k^+ satisfies the curvature assumption of Lemma A.2, demonstrating that said assumption may be removed. Therefore Algorithm 1, instantiated with $r = r_k^+$ for combinatorial public projects with MRS valuations in the bounded-lottery-value oracle model, is $(1 - 1/e - 2^{-2mn})$ approximate and can be implemented in expected $\text{poly}(n, m)$ time. Finally, we show in Remark A.4 how to recover the 2^{-2mn} term to get a clean $1 - 1/e$ approximation ratio, as claimed in Theorem 3.1.

Let $\mu = 2^{-2nm}$. We define r_k^+ in Algorithm 3. Intuitively, r_k^+ first chooses a tentative set $S \subseteq [m]$ of projects using r_k. Then it cancels its choice with small probability μ. Finally, with probability β it chooses a random project $j^* \in [m]$ and lets $S = \{j^*\}$. β is defined as the fraction of projects included in the original tentative choice of S. The motivation behind this seemingly bizarre definition of r_k^+ is purely technical: as we will see, it can be thought of as adding "concave noise" to r_k.

Algorithm 3 Modified k-bounded-lottery Rounding Scheme r_k^+

Input: Fractional solution $x \in \mathbb{R}^m$ with $\sum_j x_j \leq k$, and $0 \leq x_j \leq 1$ for all j.
Output: Feasible solution $S \subseteq [m]$ with $|S| \leq k$

Let $S = r_k(x)$
Let $\beta = \frac{|S|}{m}$
Draw $q_1 \in [0, 1]$ uniformly
if $q_1 \in [0, \mu]$ **then**
  Let $S = \emptyset$
  Draw $q_2 \in [0, 1]$ uniformly
  if $q_2 \in [0, \beta]$ **then**
    Choose project $j^* \in [m]$ uniformly at random.
    Let $S = \{j^*\}$
  end if
end if

We can write the expected welfare $\mathbf{E}_{S\sim r_k^+(x)}[\sum_i v_i(S)]$ as follows.

$$\mathop{\mathbf{E}}_{S\sim r_k(x)}\left[(1-\mu)\sum_i v_i(S) + \mu\beta\sum_i v_i(j^*)\right].$$

Using linearity of expectations and the fact that β is independent of the choice of j^* to simplify the expression, we get that $\mathbf{E}_{S\sim r_k^+(x)}[\sum_i v_i(S)]$ is equal to

$$(1-\mu)\mathop{\mathbf{E}}_{S\sim r_k(x)}[\sum_i v_i(S)] + \mu\,\mathbf{E}[\beta]\frac{\sum_{j=1}^m \sum_{i=1}^n v_i(\{j\})}{m}.$$

Observe that r_k chooses a project j with probability $1 - (1-x_j/k)^k$. Therefore, the expectation of β is $\frac{\sum_j 1-(1-x_j/k)^k}{m}$. This gives:

$$\mathop{\mathbf{E}}_{S\sim r_k^+(x)}[\sum_i v_i(S)] = (1-\mu)\mathop{\mathbf{E}}_{S\sim r_k(x)}[\sum_i v_i(S)] + \frac{\mu}{m^2}\left(\sum_{j=1}^m\sum_{i=1}^n v_i(\{j\})\right)\left(\sum_{j=1}^m 1 - (1-x_j/k)^k\right). \tag{15}$$

It is clear that the expected welfare when using $r = r_k^+$ is within $1 - \mu = 1 - 2^{-2nm}$ of the expected welfare when using $r = r_k$ in the instantiation of Algorithm 1. Using Lemma 3.2, we conclude that r_k^+ is a $(1 - 1/e - 2^{-2nm})$-approximate rounding scheme. Moreover, using Lemma 3.3, as well as the fact that $1 - (1 - x_j/k)^k$ is a concave function, we conclude that r_k^+ is a convex rounding scheme. Therefore, this establishes the analogues of Lemmas 3.2 and 3.3 for r_k^+. It is elementary to verify that our proof of Lemma A.2 can be adapted to r_k^+ as well.

It remains to show that r_k^+ is "sufficiently concave". This would establish that the conditioning assumption of Section A.2 is unnecessary for r_k^+. We will show that expression (15) is a concave function with curvature of magnitude at least $\lambda = \frac{\sum_{i=1}^n v_i([m])}{em^2 2^{2nm}}$ everywhere. Since the curvature of concave functions is always non-positive, and moreover the curvature of the sum of two functions is the sum of their curvatures, it suffices to show that the second term of the sum (15) has curvature of magnitude at least λ. We note that the curvature of $\sum_j \left(1-(1-x_j/k)^k\right)$ is at least e^{-1} over $x \in [0,1]^m$. Therefore, the curvature of the second term of (15) is at least

$$\frac{\mu}{m^2}\left(\sum_i v_i([m])\right)e^{-1} = \lambda$$

as needed.

REMARK A.4. *In this section, we sacrificed 2^{-2nm} in the approximation ratio in order to guarantee expected polynomial runtime of our algorithm even when convex program (2) is not well-conditioned. This loss can be recovered to get a clean $1-1/e$ approximation as follows. Given our $(1-1/e-2^{-2nm})$-approximate MIDR algorithm $\mathcal{A}$, construct the following algorithm $\mathcal{A}'$: Given an instance of combinatorial public projects, $\mathcal{A}'$ runs $\mathcal{A}$ on the instance with probability $1-e2^{-2nm}$, and with the remaining probability solves the instance optimally in exponential time $O(2^{2nm})$. It was shown in [15] that a random composition of MIDR mechanisms is MIDR, therefore $\mathcal{A}'$ is MIDR. The expected runtime of A' is bounded by the expected runtime of $\mathcal{A}$ plus $e2^{-2nm}\cdot O(2^{2nm}) = O(1)$. Finally, the expected approximation of A' is the weighted average of the approximation ratio of $\mathcal{A}$ and the optimal approximation ratio 1, and is at least $(1-e2^{-2nm})(1-1/e-2^{-2nm})+e2^{-2nm} \geq 1-1/e$.*

B. ADDITIONAL PRELIMINARIES

B.1 Matroid Theory

In this section, we review some basics of matroid theory. For a more comprehensive reference, see [26].

A *matroid* M is a pair $(\mathcal{X},\mathcal{I})$, where $\mathcal{X}$ is a finite *ground set*, and $\mathcal{I}$ is a non-empty family of subsets of $\mathcal{X}$ – often referred to as the *independent sets* of the matroid – satisfying the following two properties. (1) *Downward closure:* If S belongs to $\mathcal{I}$, then so do all subsets of S. (2) *The Exchange Property:* Whenever $T,S \in \mathcal{I}$ with $|T| < |S|$, there is some $x \in S \setminus T$ such that $T \cup \{x\} \in \mathcal{I}$.

We associate with matroid M a set function $rank_M : 2^{\mathcal{X}} \to \mathbb{N}$, known as the *rank function of* M, defined as follows: $rank_M(A) = \max_{S\in\mathcal{I}} |S \cap A|$. Equivalently, the rank of set A in matroid M is the maximum size of an independent set contained in A. A set function f on a ground set $\mathcal{X}$ is a *matroid rank function* if there exists a matroid M on the same ground set such that $f = rank_M$. It is well-known that matroid rank functions are monotone, normalized, and submodular.

B.2 Convex Optimization

In this section, we distill some basics of convex optimization. For more details, see [1].

DEFINITION B.1. *A maximization problem is given by a set Π of instances $(\mathcal{P},c)$, where $\mathcal{P}$ is a subset of some euclidean space, $c:\mathcal{P}\to\mathbb{R}$, and the goal is to maximize $c(x)$ over $x\in\mathcal{P}$. We say Π is a convex maximization problem if for every $(\mathcal{P},c)\in\Pi$, $\mathcal{P}$ is a compact convex set, and $c:\mathcal{P}\to\mathbb{R}$ is concave. If $c:\mathcal{P}\to\mathbb{R}^+$ for every instance of Π, we say Π is non-negative.*

DEFINITION B.2. *We say a non-negative maximization problem Π is R-solvable in polynomial time if there is an algorithm that takes as input the representation of an instance $\mathcal{I}=(\mathcal{P},c)\in\Pi$ — where we use $|\mathcal{I}|$ to denote the number of bits in the representation — and an approximation parameter ϵ, and in time $\mathrm{poly}(|\mathcal{I}|,\log(1/\epsilon))$ outputs $x\in\mathcal{P}$ such that $c(x)\geq(1-\epsilon)\max_{y\in\mathcal{P}} c(y)$.*

FACT B.3. *Consider a non-negative convex maximization problem Π. If the following are satisfied, then Π is R-solvable in polynomial time using the ellipsoid method. We let $\mathcal{I}=(\mathcal{P},c)$ denote an instance of Π, and let m denote the dimension of the ambient euclidean space.*

1. *Polynomial Dimension: m is polynomial in $|\mathcal{I}|$.*
2. *Starting ellipsoid: There is an algorithm that computes, in time $\mathrm{poly}(|\mathcal{I}|)$, a point $c\in\mathbb{R}^m$, a matrix $A\in\mathbb{R}^{m\times m}$, and a number $\mathcal{V}\in\mathbb{R}$ such that the following hold. We use $E(c,A)$ to denote the ellipsoid given by center c and linear transformation A.*
   (a) *$E(c,A)\supseteq\mathcal{P}$*
   (b) *$\mathcal{V}\leq volume(\mathcal{P})$*
   (c) *$\frac{volume(E(c,A))}{\mathcal{V}}\leq 2^{\mathrm{poly}(|\mathcal{I}|)}$*
3. *Separation oracle for $\mathcal{P}$: There is an algorithm that takes takes input $\mathcal{I}$ and $x\in\mathbb{R}^m$, and in time $\mathrm{poly}(|\mathcal{I}|,|x|)$ where $|x|$ denotes the size of the representation of x, outputs "yes" if $x\in\mathcal{P}$, otherwise outputs $h\in\mathbb{R}^m$ such that $h^Tx<h^Ty$ for every $y\in\mathcal{P}$.*
4. *First order oracle for c: There is an algorithm that takes input $\mathcal{I}$ and $x\in\mathbb{R}^m$, and in time $\mathrm{poly}(|\mathcal{I}|,|x|)$ outputs $c(x)\in\mathbb{R}$ and $\bigtriangledown c(x)\in\mathbb{R}^m$.*

B.3 Computing Payments

LEMMA B.4. *Let $\mathcal{A}$ be an MIDR allocation rule for combinatorial public projects, and let $v_1,\ldots,v_n$ be input valuations. Assume black-box access to $\mathcal{A}$, and value oracle access to $\{v_i\}_{i=1}^n$. We can compute, with $\mathrm{poly}(n)$ over-head in runtime, payments $p_1,\ldots,p_n$ such that $\mathbf{E}[p_i]$ equals the VCG payment of player i for MIDR allocation rule $\mathcal{A}$ on input $v_1,\ldots,v_n$.*

We note that an essentially identical lemma was proved in [17]. Nevertheless, we include a proof for completeness.

PROOF. Without loss of generality, it suffices to show how to compute p_1. Let $\mathbf{0}: 2^{[m]}\to\mathbb{R}$ be the valuation evaluating to 0 at each bundle. Recall (see e.g. [22]) that the VCG payment of player 1 is equal to

$$\mathop{\mathbf{E}}_{T\sim\mathcal{A}(\mathbf{0},v_2,\ldots,v_n)}\left[\sum_{i=2}^n v_i(T)\right] - \mathop{\mathbf{E}}_{S\sim\mathcal{A}(v_1,\ldots,v_n)}\left[\sum_{i=2}^n v_i(S)\right]. \quad (16)$$

Let S be a sample from $\mathcal{A}(v_1,\ldots,v_n)$, and let T be a sample from $\mathcal{A}(\mathbf{0},v_2,\ldots,v_n)$. Let $p_1=\sum_{i=2}^n v_i(T)-\sum_{i=2}^n v_i(S)$. Using linearity of expectations, it is easy to see that the expectation of p_1 is equal to the expression in (16). This completes the proof. □

REMARK B.5. *We note that the mechanism resulting from Lemma B.4 is individually rational in expectation, and each payment is non-negative in expectation. We leave open the question of whether it is possible to enforce individual rationality and non-negative payments ex-post.*

Mechanisms for Complement-Free Procurement

Shahar Dobzinski*
Department of Computer Science
Cornell University, Ithaca NY 14853
shahar@cs.cornell.edu

Christos Papadimitriou†
Computer Science Division
University of California at Berkeley, CA, 94720
christos@cs.berkeley.edu

Yaron Singer‡
Computer Science Division
University of California at Berkeley, CA, 94720
yaron@cs.berkeley.edu

ABSTRACT

We study procurement auctions when the buyer has complement-free (subadditive) objectives in the budget feasibility model [18]. For general subadditive functions we give a randomized universally truthful mechanism which is an $O(\log^2 n)$ approximation, and an $O(\log^3 n)$ deterministic truthful approximation mechanism; both mechanisms are in the demand oracle model. For cut functions, an interesting case of nonincreasing objectives, we give both randomized and deterministic truthful and budget feasible approximation mechanisms that achieve a constant approximation factor.

Categories and Subject Descriptors

F.2.8 [**Analysis of Algorithms and Problem complexity**]: Miscellaneous

General Terms

Theory

Keywords

Procurement Auctions, Incentive Compatibility, Truthfulness, Budget Feasibility

1. INTRODUCTION

When a principal wishes to buy items or services provided by strategic agents, her goal is to maximize an objective that assigns a valuation to any set of items. Since the agents may exaggerate their costs one is interested in designing *truthful mechanisms,* in which the allocation and prices are set in such a way so that it is provably in each agent's interest to reveal her true cost.

Such problems are extensively studied in the framework of *frugality* (see, for example, [1]), where the mechanism designer's aim is to minimize payments. The frugality approach deals with buyer objectives with 0-1 values (e.g., the buyer wants the set of edges to be a spanning tree of a graph, and all spanning trees are equally desirable).[1]

An alternative to frugality which encompasses much more general objectives, is the *budget feasibility* framework introduced in [18] and subsequently studied in [6, 13, 10]. In budget feasibility, our goal is to optimize the buyer's objective under a budget constraint.

A budget feasibility setting is fully defined by the buyer's objective, a function mapping subsets of items to the reals. The important question to ask here is, for which class objectives one can obtain truthful mechanisms with reasonable approximation guarantees? A first step in this direction was taken recently in [18], where truthful mechanisms with constant-factor approximation are developed for the important class of *submodular objective functions. In this paper we extend this result to much more general classes of objectives.*

What are the limits of our ambition here? One first observation is that even for very simple *superadditive* objectives (that is, objectives in which $V(S \cup T) > V(S) + V(T)$ for some sets S, T) mechanisms of the desired kind (truthful of bounded approximation ratio) do not exist. Consider for example the objective in which there is a crucial item a^* and the valuation $V(S)$ is 1 if $a^* \in S$ and 0 otherwise. Then it is easy to see that for this objective there can be no approximation guarantee, because the seller of the crucial item can always extract the whole budget (publicly known). In view of this, we consider objectives that are *complement-free,* or *subadditive,* valuations obeying $V(S \cup T) \leq V(S) + V(T)$. This is a class that is a substantial generalization of submodular valuation functions. We seek truthful mechanisms with reasonable approximation guarantees for complement-free objectives. As the example above shows, in procure-

*Supported by an Alfred P. Sloan Foundation Fellowship and a Microsoft Research New Faculty Fellowship.

†Supported in part by NSF grant ccf-0635319.

‡Supported in part by a Microsoft Research graduate fellowship.

EC'11, June 5–9, 2011, San Jose, California, USA.

[1]It is problematic to extend the frugality framework beyond 0-1 objectives, because that would bring us in the tricky realm of *multi-objective optimization.* This reduces the problem to budget feasibility: fixing the budget and maximizing the objective function.

ment auctions often desirable mechanisms are impossible *even with unbounded computational resources.* Therefore, we focus on the question of existence of a mechanism of the desired kind, with less attention on computational efficiency (even though, as it happens, our algorithms are polynomial time).

1.1 Our Results

For complement-free (subadditive) objectives we first give a randomized $O(\log^2 n)$ approximation mechanism that is universally truthful and budget feasible. We derandomize this mechanism and present a deterministic mechanism for this domain with an $O(\log^3 n)$ approximation guarantee. Since subadditive functions may require representation that is exponential in the number of agents, we assume we are given access to a *demand* oracle. Since the weaker value query oracles result in inapproximability as shown in [18], a stronger oracle model such as the one used here is required.

We also examine another class of objectives, namely *cut functions:* when agents represent vertices on a graph, a cut function is the cardinality of the cut procured. The optimization problem is a variant of the celebrated MAX-CUT problem, and the setting provides a nontrivial case valuation functions that can decrease in value as items are added. For such functions we give a randomized constant factor approximation mechanism that is universally truthful and budget feasible, as well as a deterministic constant factor approximation mechanism.

The deterministic mechanisms, for both classes of objectives, are based on their randomized analogues. In both cases derandomization in a manner that preserves truthfulness is nontrivial and requires constructing "monotone estimators" that are crucial for obtaining bounded approximation guarantees. Each construction uses a different technique, though their underlying principle is similar. We discuss these issues in the appropriate sections.

1.2 Related Work

In the past decade procurement auctions have been extensively studied in algorithmic game theory. The first line of work focused on minimizing total *cost*, not payments [17, 11, 12] using variants of the VCG mechanism. To address the issue of overpayments, the frugality framework was initiated in [1] where the problems typically studied assume there is some possible feasible set of solutions (e.g. all spanning trees in a graph) and that the mechanism designer's objective is to obtain a feasible set (without any preference among the sets) at minimal cost. The framework suggests designing truthful mechanisms with payment schemes that are guaranteed to be within a certain factor of a given benchmark (e.g. minimal payments at Nash equilibrium or a variant as suggested in [14]). In the past decade procurement has been studied in the frugality framework in various domains such as path auctions, spanning trees and vertex cover [19, 9, 14, 8, 4]. Recently, a general scheme has been independently suggested by [5] and [15], which uses spectral techniques to obtain desirable guarantees against the different benchmarks.

The budget feasibility framework has been recently initiated in [18], and this is the model we follow in this paper. The framework addresses the question of designing truthful mechanisms under budget constraint on payments that have provable guarantees in term of the buyer's objective function. The main result in [18] shows that for any increasing submodular function there is universally truthful constant factor approximation mechanism that is budget feasible. In [6] improved approximation ratios were achieved for the submodular case as well as various problems within the submodular class through use of sophisticated analysis. The framework has been adopted in the study of designing auctions for procuring private data [13] dynamic auctions [10] as well as other domains [6].

1.3 Open Questions

In this work we show that there exists an $O(\log^2 n)$ randomized mechanism that uses a polynomial number of demand queries. We conjecture that a constant approximation ratio requires using an exponential number of demand queries. A fundamental question is whether, regardless of computational constraints, a constant-factor budget feasible mechanism exists for subadditive function.

For cut functions, our goal in this work is in proving the existence of a mechanism with a constant factor approximation factor. It would be interesting to determine the best approximation factor achievable for this class. Another interesting open question is to determine the largest class for which there exist constant ratio approximation mechanisms. Can our mechanism be extended to handle all (not necessarily increasing) submodular functions?

Finally, we present techniques for derandomizing truthful mechanisms in a manner that preserves truthfulness. Extending our methods to derandomize mechanisms in other classes is an intriguing open question.

2. THE MODEL

We study procurement auctions where there are n items, each held by a single agent that associates a private cost $c_i \in \mathcal{R}_{\geq 0}$ with the item. The set of agents is denoted by $\mathcal{N}$ and we refer to agents and items interchangeably. The buyer has a public budget $B \in \mathcal{R}_{\geq 0}$ and a public valuation function $V : 2^{[n]} \to \mathcal{R}_{\geq 0}$ over the subsets of items.

The goal in this setting is to design mechanisms that approximate the optimal solution of the valuation function under the budget constraint. A mechanism $\mathcal{M} = (f, p)$ consists of an allocation function $f : \mathcal{R}^n_{\geq 0} \to 2^{[n]}$ and a payment function $p : \mathcal{R}^n_{\geq 0} \to \mathcal{R}^n_{\geq 0}$. The allocation function f maps a set of n bids to a selected subset of agents. The payment function p returns a vector $p_1, \ldots, p_n$ of payments to the agents. We seek normalized ($i \notin S$ implies $p_i = 0$), individually rational ($p_i \geq c_i$) mechanisms with no positive transfers ($p_i \geq 0$).

Truthfulness. In our model we assume the participating agents are strategic and may report false costs if it is in their benefit. We therefore seek truthful mechanisms so that reporting the true costs is a dominant strategy for agents. Formally, a mechanism $\mathcal{M} = (f, p)$ is *truthful* (*incentive compatible*) if for every $i \in \mathcal{N}$ with cost c_i and bid c'_i, and every set of bids by $\mathcal{N} \setminus \{i\}$ we have $p_i - s_i \cdot c_i \geq p'_i - s'_i \cdot c_i$, where (s_i, p_i) and (s'_i, p'_i) are allocation ($s_i, s'_i \in \{0, 1\}$) and payment pairs when the bidding is c_i and c'_i, respectively. A mechanism that is a randomization over truthful mechanisms is *universally truthful.*

As each bidder has a single private value, we shall rely on Myerson's well-known characterization for truthfulness in single parameter domains [16] that states that a mechanism $\mathcal{M} = (f, p)$ is truthful if and only if it is *monotone* and uses *threshold payments*. The mechanism is monotone if $\forall i \in [n]$, if $c'_i \leq c_i$ then $i \in f(c_i, c_{-i})$ implies $i \in f(c'_i, c_{-i})$ for every c_{-i}; winners are paid threshold payments if payment to each selected agent is $\inf\{c_i : i \notin f(c_i, c_{-i})\}$.

Budget Feasibility. We require that the mechanism is budget feasible: the mechanism's payments should not exceed the budget: $\sum_i p_i \leq B$.

The objective is to maximize the function under the budget, i.e. find the subset $S \in \{T | \sum_{i \in T} c_i \leq B\}$ for which $V(S)$ is maximized, under the constraint that the *payments* (not costs) are within the budget. We want the allocated subset to yield a high value for the buyer. When we are unable to output the optimal solution, we are interested in finding a set that has a value that is close to the optimal (when all costs are known) solution. Formally, for $\alpha \geq 1$ we say that a mechanism is α-approximate if in every instance the mechanism allocates to a set S such that $V(S^*) \leq \alpha V(S)$, where S^* is the optimal solution when all costs are known. As usual, when dealing with randomization we seek mechanisms that yield a good approximation in expectation over the internal random coins of the mechanism.

The mechanisms we construct have the additional property that the functions f and p can be computed in polynomial time. In cases where the valuation function requires exponential data to be represented, we take the common "black-box" approach and assume that V is represented by an oracle. We will define the exact model in the relevant sections, but as shown our mechanisms make polynomially many queries to the oracle.

3. SUBADDITIVE FUNCTIONS

A valuation function $V : 2^{[n]} \to R$ is subadditive if $V(S \cup T) \leq V(S) + V(T)$. A naive representation of subadditive functions requires exponential space in n, and thus we assume our mechanisms are given access to an oracle which enables evaluating the function V. A *value oracle* receives a subset S and returns $V(S)$. Since we know value oracles cannot obtain a reasonable approximation [18, 7], we investigate whether stronger types of queries enable us to do so. A *demand oracle* receives a vector of prices $p_1, \ldots, p_n$ and returns a subset S s.t. $S \in \text{argmax}_{T \in [n]} V(T) - \sum_{i \in T} p_i$ is maximal. Let $\mathcal{V} = \{1, 2, 4, \ldots 2^{\log(V(N))}\}$. A value query can be simulated by a polynomial number of demand queries [3] and we therefore allow our algorithms to use value queries. We assume, without loss of generality, that 1 is the smallest non-zero value of V. We note that in this section we assume that V is non-decreasing.

We start by describing a procedure for finding a bundle of size t with value close to the bundle of size t with the highest value. We show that polynomially many demand queries suffice to achieve a 4-approximation, even if the function is subadditive[2].

[2]In fact, our algorithm can be slightly modified to achieve a $(2 + \epsilon)$-approximation, but the improved approximation algorithm does not suffice for constructing truthful budget feasible mechanisms.

A Procedure for Finding an Approximate Bundle of Size t

For each v in $\mathcal{V}$:

a. Find the bundle S that maximizes the demand when the price per item is $\frac{v}{2t}$

b. If $V(S) - |S| \cdot t < \frac{v}{2}$ then set $S_v = \emptyset$ and continue to the next v

c. Else, if $|S| > t$, let S_v be some bundle of size t such that $S_v \subseteq S$. Else, let $S_v = S$

Output: (v, S_v) for the maximal $v \in \mathcal{V}$ such that S_v is not empty

The procedure clearly uses a polynomial number of demand queries. Before proving some properties of the procedure, including its correctness, we prepare a lemma.

CLAIM 3.1. *Let $S \in \arg\max_T V(T) - p \cdot |T|$. Then for each $S' \subseteq S$ we have that $V(S') \geq p \cdot |S'|$.*

PROOF. From subadditivity we have that

$$V(S) - |T| \cdot p \leq V(S \setminus S') - |S \setminus S'| \cdot p + V(S') - |S'| \cdot p$$

which implies that $V(S') - |S'| \cdot p \geq 0$ as otherwise S does not maximize the demand. We therefore have that:

$$V(S') \geq |S'| \cdot p$$

□

LEMMA 3.2. *Let $S^* \in \text{argmax}_{|S|=t} V(S)$. The procedure finds a subset S_v such that $V(S_v) > \frac{V(S^*)}{4}$. Furthermore, v is either the maximal $v \in \mathcal{V}$ such that $v \leq V(S^*)$ or v is the minimal $v \in \mathcal{V}$ such that $v > V(S^*)$.*

PROOF. First, consider an iteration for which $v \leq V(S^*)$. Setting a price $p = v/2t$ for all items, the demand query oracle finds a subset S that maximizes the demand, i.e. $S \in \text{argmax}_T V(T) - |T| \cdot p$. In particular:

$$\begin{aligned} V(S) &- |S| \cdot p \geq V(S^*) - |S^*| \cdot p \\ &= V(S^*) - t \cdot \frac{v}{2t} = V(S^*) - \frac{v}{2} \\ &\geq \frac{V(S^*)}{2} \end{aligned}$$

Clearly, $V(S) - |S| \cdot p \geq \frac{V(S^*)}{2}$ implies $V(S) \geq \frac{V(S^*)}{2}$.

If $|S| \leq t$ then $S_v| = S$ and we are already done. If $|S| > t$, by Claim 3.1: $V(S_v) \geq p \cdot t = t \cdot \frac{v}{2t} = \frac{v}{2}$.

Notice that for the maximal $v \in \mathcal{V}$ where $v \leq V(S^*)$, we have that $v \geq \frac{V(S^*)}{2}$, thus $V(S_v) > \frac{V(S^*)}{4}$. To finish the proof, consider $v > 2V(S^*)$. Observe that $V(S) - |S| \cdot \frac{v}{2t}$, thus any bundle of size less than t will have a negative profit in Step (b) and the iteration will fail. Thus, assume towards contradiction that the iteration passes Step (b). By our discussion, we have that $|S| > t$. In this case, Claim 3.1 gives us that $V(S_v) \geq t \cdot \frac{v}{2t} = \frac{v}{2} > V(S^*)$. A contradiction. □

3.1 A Randomized Mechanism

We first use the above procedure to construct a randomized mechanism. In the next subsection we will derandomize this construction to obtain a deterministic mechanism. For this section, let $\alpha = 2 \cdot \lceil \log n \rceil$ and $i^* \in \arg\max_k V(\{k\})$.

A Randomized Budget Feasible Approximation Mechanism

For each t in $\mathcal{T} = \{1, 2 \dots 2^{\lceil \log n \rceil}\}$ in decreasing order:

a. Let $\mathcal{N}'$ be the set of items with cost at most $B/(\alpha \cdot t)$ that are different than i^*

b. Using the procedure, find (v_t, S_t) among items in $\mathcal{N}'$

Output: Choose u.a.r between $\cup_t S_t$ and agent i^*

THEOREM 3.3. *The mechanism is universally truthful, budget feasible, and provides an expected approximation ratio of $O(\log^2 n)$.*

LEMMA 3.4. *The mechanism provides an approximation ratio of $O(\log^2 n)$.*

PROOF. Denote by S^* the set of agents participating in the optimal solution. Let $\overline{S^*} = \{i | i \in S^*, c_i > \frac{B}{\alpha}\}$, and $\underline{S^*} = S^* \setminus \overline{S^*}$.

Suppose that $V(\overline{S^*}) \geq \frac{V(S^*)}{2}$. Since the payment for each of the agents in $\overline{S^*}$ is at least $\frac{B}{\alpha}$, $|\overline{S^*}| \leq \alpha$. By subadditivity there must be one bidder $i \in \overline{S^*}$ such that $V\{i\} \geq \frac{V(\overline{S^*})}{\alpha}$. In particular we have that $V(\{i^*\}) \geq V(\{i\})$. Thus, if i^* is chosen this gives us an $O(\log n)$ approximation. Since i^* is chosen with probability $\frac{1}{2}$ the expected approximation guarantee is $O(\log n)$ in this case.

Assume now that $V(\underline{S^*}) \geq \frac{V(S^*)}{2}$ (this is the last case since by subadditivity $V(\overline{S^*}) + V(\underline{S^*}) \geq V(S^*)$). If $V(\{i^*\}) \geq \frac{V(\underline{S^*})}{2}$, then similarly to before we have a constant approximation if i^* is chosen (which happens with probability $\frac{1}{2}$). Let $\underline{S^*}' = \underline{S^*} \setminus \{i^*\}$. We have that $V(\underline{S^*}') \geq \frac{V(S^*)}{4}$. Now put agents in $\underline{S^*}$ in bins according to their cost s.t. agent $i \in \underline{S^*}$ is in bin j if and only if $B/(\alpha \cdot 2^{j+1}) \leq c_i < B/(\alpha \cdot 2^j)$ where $j \in \mathcal{T}$.

Since there are $O(\log n)$ bins, subadditivity implies that there is a single bin k with value that is at least $O(\log n)$-fraction of $V(\underline{S^*})$. It follows that the optimal solution of size $\alpha \cdot 2^k$ over all items with cost at most $B/(\alpha \cdot 2^k)$ has value at least $O(V(\underline{S^*})/\log n)$. Since one of the iterations of the procedure gives us a set S_k of size 2^k that is a 4-approximation to the solution of size 2^k, and by subadditivity the solution of size 2^k is an $O(\alpha)$-approximation to the solution of size $O(\alpha \cdot 2^k)$, we have that $V(\cup_t S_t) \geq V(\underline{S^*})/4 \log^2 n$. Therefore, with probability $\frac{1}{2}$ we have an $O(\log^2 n)$ approximation in this case. □

LEMMA 3.5. *The mechanism is universally truthful.*

PROOF. To prove the lemma we will show that the mechanism is monotone: an agent that is selected and reduces his cost is still selected.

Now fix the random coin and suppose that agent i^* wins. Notice that he will remain the winner regardless of his cost, and in particular will remain the winner if he reduces his cost.

Assume now that the selected set is $\cup_t S_t$, and consider some agent $i \neq i^*$ that wins and reduces his cost from c_i to c_i'. Let $t \in \mathcal{T}$ be the maximal such that $i \in S_t$. Notice that i will be selected to S_t also if he reduces his cost (since the procedure is oblivious to the actual cost of the agent and takes into account only that the cost is smaller than some threshold). Therefore we have that the mechanism is monotone. □

LEMMA 3.6. *The mechanism is budget feasible.*

PROOF. Recall that the payment for an agent is the maximal cost that he can declare and still win[3] (the *threshold cost*). It is not hard to see that if i^* is chosen then his payment is B. For each other agent i that is chosen we claim that the threshold cost is at most $\frac{B}{\alpha t_i}$ where t_i is the maximal index such that $i \in S_{t_i}$. This implies that the mechanism is budget feasible: observe that for each $t \in \mathcal{T}$, at most t agents may receive a payment of $B/(\alpha \cdot t)$. Thus the total payment in that case is $\sum_{t \in \mathcal{T}} t \cdot B/(\alpha \cdot t) \leq |\mathcal{T}| \frac{B}{\alpha} \leq B$.

We now show that for each other agent i that is chosen the threshold cost is at most $\frac{B}{\alpha t_i}$. Suppose agent i has cost bigger than $\frac{B}{\alpha t_i}$. In this case i will not be selected when the size of the bundle considered is t_i or smaller, because his cost is too high. Also i will not be selected in iterations in which the bundle size is larger than t_i: in these iterations either the procedure runs on the exact same set $\mathcal{N}'$ of items (if his cost is still small enough), and for this set of items we know that i is not selected, or i has a cost that is too high and thus is not considered for selection at all. □

3.2 A Deterministic Mechanism

Our next goal is to construct a *deterministic* mechanism with a good approximation ratio. The randomized mechanism uses only one random coin, so a first natural attempt is to select the highest-value outcome of the two possible ones. Unfortunately, this does not work: when an agent reduces his cost he might increase $V(\cup_t S_t)$[4]. Therefore, we use a "monotone estimator" for the value of the union that has the property that if the cost of an agent decreases the value of the monotone estimator increases. We make sure that the value of the monotone estimator is "close" to $V(\cup_t S_t)$. Comparing the value of the monotone estimator to the value of single agent with the best value gives us a monotone $O(\log^3 n)$ mechanism. We note that, ignoring computational constraints, one can use the optimal algorithm as a monotone estimator an obtain a deterministic $O(\log^2 n)$ approximation. Let $\alpha = 2 \cdot \lceil \log n \rceil$ and $i^* \in \arg\max_k V(\{k\})$.

[3]The mechanism is universally truthful so we fix the random coin and prove the budget feasibility of the mechanism for every outcome of the random coin.

[4]This may happen since we do not have exact mechanisms to find the best bundle of size t but rather use an approximation mechanism to do so.

A Deterministic Budget Feasible Approximation Mechanism
For each t in $\mathcal{T} = \{1, 2 \ldots 2^{\lceil \log n \rceil}\}$ in decreasing order: a. Let $\mathcal{N}'$ be the set of items with cost at most $B/(\alpha \cdot t)$ that are different than i^* b. Using the procedure, find (v, S_t), $\|S_t\| = t$, among items in $\mathcal{N}'$ c. Using the procedure, find (v_t, S), $\|S\| = \alpha t$, among items in $\mathcal{N}''$ **Output:** If $\sum_t v_t \geq V(\{i^*\})$ then output $\cup_t S_t$. Else choose only agent i^*

Notice that the mechanism uses only a polynomial number of demand queries.

LEMMA 3.7. *The mechanism provides an approximation ratio of* $O(\log^3 n)$.

PROOF. Denote by S^* the set of agents participating in the optimal solution. Let $\overline{S^*} = \{i | i \in S^*, c_i > \frac{B}{\alpha}\}$, and $\underline{S^*} = S^* \setminus \overline{S^*}$. We start by showing two useful facts. The first one is:

$$2 \cdot \Sigma_t v_t \geq V(\underline{S^*}) \qquad (1)$$

The first inequality follows since for every t, $2 \cdot v_t \geq V(S_t)$ and from the subadditivity of V. For each t, let S_t^* be the optimal solution of items of size at most $B/(\alpha \cdot t)$. The second inequality is:

$$\begin{aligned} \Sigma_t v_t &\leq 4\Sigma_t V(S_t^*) \\ &\leq 4 \log n \Sigma_t \cdot V(S_t) \\ &\leq 4 \log^2 n \cdot V(\cup_t S_t) \end{aligned} \qquad (2)$$

The first inequality follows since v_t is a 4 approximation to S_t^*. The second one follows since V is subadditive and since in S_t^* there are at most a multiplicative factor of $\log n$ more items than in S_t. The third inequality is because t can take at most $\log n$ values.

We now proceed to the proof itself. Suppose that $V(\overline{S^*}) \geq \frac{V(S^*)}{2}$. The payment of each of the agents in $\overline{S^*}$ is at least $\frac{B}{\alpha}$, hence $|\overline{S^*}| \leq \alpha$. Therefore, by subadditivity there must be one bidder $i \in \overline{S^*}$ such that $V\{i\} \geq \frac{V(\overline{S^*})}{\alpha}$. In particular we have that $V(\{i^*\}) \geq V(\{i\})$. Thus, if i^* is chosen this gives us an $O(\log n)$ approximation. Else, we have that:

$$\begin{aligned} 4 \log^2 n \cdot V(\cup_t S_t) &\geq \Sigma_t v_t \\ &\geq V(\{i^*\}) \\ &\geq \frac{V(\overline{S^*})}{\alpha} \\ &\geq \frac{V(S^*)}{2 \log n} \end{aligned}$$

The first inequality follows from (2). This proves that in the case that i^* is not chosen we have an $O(\log^3 n)$ approximation.

Assume now that $V(\underline{S^*}) \geq \frac{V(S^*)}{2}$ (this is the last case since by subadditivity $V(\overline{S^*}) + V(\underline{S^*}) \geq V(S^*)$). If $V(\{i^*\}) \geq \frac{V(\underline{S^*})}{2}$, then similarly to the previous case we have a constant approximation if i^* is chosen. If $\cup_t S_t$ is selected then arguments very similar to (3) prove that the approximation ratio is $O(\log^2 n)$ in this case.

Therefore, let $\underline{S^*}' = \underline{S^*} \setminus \{i^*\}$ and assume that $V(\underline{S^*}') \geq \frac{V(S^*)}{4}$. Using (1) and (2) together we have that $8 \log^2 n \cdot V(\cup_t S_t) \geq V(\underline{S^*})$, i.e., an $O(\log^2 n)$ approximation. If i^* is selected then, using (1), $V(i^*) \geq \Sigma_t v_t \geq \frac{V(\underline{S^*})}{4}$, i.e., a constant approximation in this case. □

LEMMA 3.8. *The mechanism is truthful.*

PROOF. To prove the lemma we will show that the mechanism is monotone: an agent that is selected and reduces his cost is still selected. Suppose that agent i^* wins. If he reduces his cost he clearly remains the winner, since the expression $\sum_t v_t$ remains the same. Therefore, assume that some agent $i \neq i^*$ wins and reduces his cost from c_i to c_i'. We will show that the expression $\sum_t v_t$ does not decrease in this case, and monotonicity will follow. Furthermore, we will show that for every t the value of v_t cannot decrease.

To see this, fix some t. The only case where the output of the procedure might change is when $c_i > \frac{B}{t}$ but $c_i' \leq \frac{B}{t}$. Notice that the difference is that the procedure considers one more item i. In this case it might happen that the value of the set $V(S_t)$ will go down, but we will show that the value v_t cannot decrease. This follows from the observation that the procedure succeeds for a certain value of $v \in \mathcal{V}$ if it succeeds in step b: i.e., if there exists a profit maximizing bundle with large enough value. However, if such bundle exists, it will still exist when considering more items. □

LEMMA 3.9. *The mechanism is budget feasible.*

The proof of this lemma is almost identical to the proof of Lemma 3.6. In conclusion:

THEOREM 3.10. *The mechanism uses a polynomial number of demand queries, is truthful, individually rational, and budget feasible. Its approximation ratio is* $O(\log^3 n)$.

4. CUT FUNCTIONS

An interesting class of objective functions within the complement-free domain are functions for which $S \subseteq T$ does not necessarily imply that $V(S) \leq V(T)$, a property we refer to as nonincreasing utilities[5]. Naturally, we are interested in investigating whether budget feasible mechanisms can be obtained for these classes as well. Here we take a first step in this direction by examining *cut functions*: valuation functions where the value of a subset of agents can be represented as a cut on a graph. This class of functions is a representative of the class of nonincreasing valuation functions, which, as we now show, has constant factor approximation mechanisms that are budget feasible. The results in this section lead us to conjecture that there are broader classes of nonincreasing valuation functions with desirable guarantees in the budget feasibility model.

4.1 Mechanisms for Cut Functions

A cut function $V : 2^{[n]} \rightarrow \mathcal{R}_{\geq 0}$ is a valuation function for which there exists a graph $G = (\mathcal{N}, E)$ s.t. $V(S) = |C(S)|$,

[5]In optimization literature this property is referred to as nonmonotnicity. To avoid confusion in discussion of monotonicity of the allocation function, we use the nonincreasing utilities term.

where C is the cut induced by S, i.e. $C(S) = \{(u,v) \in E : u \in S, v \in \mathcal{N} \setminus S\}$. We note that maximizing this function is a variant of the classic computationally intractable MAX CUT problem. We denote the degree of a vertex $v_i \in \mathcal{N}$ by d_i (when it will be clear from the context we will use i instead of v_i) and for any $T \subseteq \mathcal{N}$, we use $E(T) = \{(u,v) \in E : u \in T\}$ to denote the set of edges that have at least one vertex in T. In our setting each vertex is held by a single strategic agent with a private cost and our objective is to maximize $V(S) = |C(S)|$ under the budget constraint.

We first show a randomized mechanism that is budget feasible and obtains a constant factor approximation. We will then discuss its derandomization which also guarantees a constant factor approximation.

4.2 A Randomized Mechanism

THEOREM 4.1. *For cut functions there is a randomized $O(1)$-approximation mechanism that is universally truthful and budget feasible.*

In proof, consider the following mechanism:

A Randomized Budget Feasible Approx. Mechanism for Cut Functions

1. Set $\mathcal{N}' = \{i \in \mathcal{N} : c_i \leq B/2\}$, $i^* \in \text{argmax}_{i \in \mathcal{N}'} d_i$, $S = \{i^*\}$ and $i \in \text{argmax}_{i \in \mathcal{N}' \setminus \{i^*\}} \frac{d_i}{c_i}$
2. While $c_i \leq \frac{B}{24} \cdot \left(\frac{|C(S \cup \{v_i\})| - |C(S)|}{C(S \cup \{v_i\})|}\right)$:
   a. Add i to S
   b. Set $\bar{\mathcal{N}}$ to be all agents in $j \in \mathcal{N}' \setminus \{i^*\}$ for which $|C(S \cup \{j\})| - |C(S)| \geq \frac{2}{3} d_j$
   c. Set $i \in \text{argmax}_{j \in \bar{\mathcal{N}} \setminus \{i^*\}} \frac{|C(S \cup \{j\})| - |C(S)|}{c_j}$

Output: Choose u.a.r between S and $\text{argmax}_{i \in \mathcal{N} \setminus \mathcal{N}'} d_i$

It is easy to verify that the above mechanism is monotone in the agents' costs and thus truthful. We first prove its approximation guarantee before showing that it is indeed budget feasible. In the following proofs we will use S_i to denote the subset of agents selected by the mechanism after the ith stage.

LEMMA 4.2. *At each stage j we have $|C(S_j)| \geq \frac{1}{3}|E(S_j)|$.*

PROOF. We will show by induction on the stage of the mechanism that $|C(S_j)| \geq \frac{1}{3}\sum_{i \in S_j} d_i$ which suffices to prove the lemma since $\sum_{i \in S_j} d_i$ is an upper bound on $|E(S_j)|$.

In the first stage of the mechanism the inequality trivially holds. For a general step j, the vertex v_j that is selected must respect the condition $|C(S_{j-1} \cup \{v_j\})| - |C(S_{j-1})| \geq \frac{2}{3}d_j$. This condition implies that when adding v_j there are at most $\frac{1}{3}d_j$ edges between v_j and vertices in S_{j-1} and thus by adding v_j to S_{j-1} at most $\frac{1}{3}d_j$ edges will be removed from the cut and $\frac{2}{3}d_j$ edges will be added. Thus, together with the inductive hypothesis we have that:

$$\begin{aligned} |C(S_j)| &\geq \left(|C_{j-1}| - \frac{1}{3}d_j\right) + \frac{2}{3}d_j \\ &\geq \left(\frac{1}{3}\sum_{i \in S_{j-1}} d_i - \frac{1}{3}d_j\right) + \frac{2}{3}d_j \\ &= \frac{1}{3}\sum_{i \in S_j} d_i \end{aligned}$$

□

LEMMA 4.3. *Let S^* be the optimal solution over agents in $\mathcal{N}'$ with budget $B' = \frac{B}{24}$, then $|C(S)| \geq \frac{|C(S^*)|}{6}$.*

PROOF. Partition the set of edges in $C(S^*)$ to the following disjoint subsets of edges: $S_1^* = \{(u,v) \in C(S^*) : u, v \in S\}$, $S_2^* = \{(u,v) \in C(S^*) : u \in S, v \notin S\}$, $S_3^* = \{(u,v) \in C(S^*) : u, v \notin S\}$. First, as implied by Lemma 4.2, we have that $|E(S) \setminus C(S)| \leq 2|C(S)|$ and thus:

$$|C(S_1^*)| \leq |E(S) \setminus C(S)| \leq 2|C(S)| \quad (3)$$

In the case of S_2^*, since each vertex has an endpoint in S, it must be that $|C(S_2^*)| \leq |C(S)|$, and thus:

$$|C(S_2^*)| \leq |C(S)| \quad (4)$$

In the case where $S_3^* = \emptyset$ the above inequalities suffice to prove our lemma. Otherwise, to bound the ratio between $|C(S_3^*)|$ and $|C(S)|$, assume $S_3^* \neq \emptyset$ and w.l.o.g assume its vertices are labeled s.t. vertex v_i has the greatest ratio between marginal contribution to the cut and cost, given the cut induced by vertices $v_1, \ldots, v_{i-1}$. In such an ordering, for all $i < r = |S_3^*|$ we get:

$$\frac{|C(T_i)| - |C(T_{i-1})|}{c_i} \geq \frac{|C(T_{i+1})| - |C(T_i)|}{c_{i+1}}$$

where T_i is the subset that includes the first i vertices taken according to the ordering and $T_0 = \emptyset$.

Let v_k be the first vertex not selected by our mechanism to be in S. In this case we have that:

$$c_k > B' \cdot \left(\frac{|C(S \cup \{v_k\})| - |C(S)|}{|C(S \cup \{v_k\})|}\right) \quad (5)$$

Since we assume $S_3^* \neq \emptyset$ and $S \cap S_3^* = \emptyset$, all vertices in S_3^* respect the condition of having at least 2/3 of their edges not connected to vertices in S, and thus such a vertex must exist. Also, since $S_3^* \cap S = \emptyset$, it follows that v_k is either in S_3^*, or that every vertex in S_3^* has smaller marginal contribution ratio to cost than that of v_k. Thus, in either case for any $i \in [r]$ we have that:

$$\frac{c_k}{(|C(S \cup \{v_k\})| - |C(S)|)} \leq \frac{c_i}{d_i} \leq \frac{c_i}{(|C(T_i)| - |C(T_{i-1})|)} \quad (6)$$

where the first inequality is due to the fact that the vertices in S_3^* do not have endpoints in S and thus their marginal contribution equals their degree, and the second inequality is due to the decreasing marginal utilities property of the cut function.

Since S_3^* is feasible we have that $\sum_{i=1}^{r} c_i \leq B'$, which we can write as:

$$\sum_{i=1}^{r}\Big(\frac{c_i}{|C(T_i)|-|C(T_{i-1})|}\Big)\cdot\Big(|C(T_i)|-|C(T_{i-1})|\Big)\leq B'$$

Since $S_3^* = T_r$ we have that $|C(S_3^*)| = \sum_{i=1}^{r}\Big(|C(T_i)| - |C(T_{i-1})|\Big)$ and therefore together with (6) above we have:

$$c_k\cdot\Big(\frac{|C(S_3^*)|}{|C(S\cup\{v_k\})|-|C(S)|}\Big)\leq B'$$

The above inequality, together with (5) implies that $|C(S\cup\{v_k\})| > |C(S_3^*)|$. Since S includes the vertex with largest degree it follows that $|C(S)| \geq d_i$, for any $i \in \mathcal{N}'$, and thus:

$$2|C(S)| \geq |C(S)| + d_k \geq |C(S)\cup\{v_k\}| \geq C(S_3^*) \qquad (7)$$

To conclude, let $\alpha_i = \frac{|C(S_i^*)|}{|C(S^*)|}$ for $i \in \{1,2,3\}$. Since the sets are disjoint $\alpha_1+\alpha_2+\alpha_3 = 1$. Since there must exist an $\alpha_i \geq 1/3$, from (3),(4),and (7) it follows that $|C(S)| \geq \frac{|C(S^*)|}{6}$. □

The above lemma implies the desired constant factor approximation ratio. Let $OPT(c,\mathcal{N},B)$ denote the value of the optimal solution over the set of agents $\mathcal{N}$ with bid profile c and budget B. First, observe that since V is subadditive, for any natural $\alpha > 1$ when the agent i^* with largest value is selected is in $OPT(c,\mathcal{N}',B/\alpha)$, then we have that: $\alpha\cdot OPT(c,\mathcal{N},B/\alpha)+(\alpha-1)V(\{i^*\}) \geq OPT(c,\mathcal{N},B)$, and therefore $(2\alpha-1)OPT(c,\mathcal{N},B/\alpha) \geq OPT(c,\mathcal{N},B)$.

Since the vertex with largest degree in $\mathcal{N}'$ is included in S, we have that $47\cdot OPT(c,\mathcal{N}',B/24) \geq OPT(c,\mathcal{N}',B)$ and thus by Lemma 4.3 we have that $282|C(S)| \geq OPT(c,\mathcal{N}',B)$. Since we selected the optimal solution in $\mathcal{N}\setminus\mathcal{N}'$ with probability 1/2 and $OPT(c,\mathcal{N},B) \leq OPT(c,\mathcal{N}',B)+OPT(c,\mathcal{N}\setminus\mathcal{N}',B)$ the mechanism is a 564-approximation.

We will complete the proof of our theorem by showing the mechanism is indeed budget feasible. Unlike the approach taken in [18] where a characterization of payments was shown, we will prove budget feasibility by directly showing a bound on threshold payments.

LEMMA 4.4. *The mechanism is budget feasible.*

PROOF. It's easy to see that the threshold payment for i^* with largest degree in $\mathcal{N}'$ is $\frac{B}{2}$, as it is always selected by the mechanism. To bound the threshold payment of the other agents in S by the remaining budget $\frac{B}{2}$, for a given bidding profile $c = (c_1 \dots c_n)$, let v_j be a selected vertex with bid c_j, and let $c'_j > c_j$ be the maximum bid that v_j can declare and remain selected when all other agents declare the same cost, and let $c' = (c_1,\dots,c_{j-1},c'_j,c_{j+1}\dots,c_n)$. Let S' and S'_i denote the set of selected agents by the mechanism and agents selected at stage i, respectively, when the bid profile is c'.

First, observe that:

$$\begin{aligned}2\cdot OPT(c',\mathcal{N}',B') &\geq OPT(c,\mathcal{N}'\setminus\{j\},B')+d_j\\ &\geq OPT(c,\mathcal{N}',B')\\ &\geq |C(S)|\end{aligned}$$

From Lemma 4.3 it follows that $|C(S')| \geq \frac{OPT(c',\mathcal{N}',B')}{6}$ and thus we have that $|C(S')| \geq \frac{|C(S)|}{12}$.

W.l.o.g. assume v_j is selected at stage j when the bid profile is c. Notice that when running the mechanism with bid profile c', the same first $j-1$ agents are as when running the the mechanism with the profile c, and we have that $|C(S_{j-1})\cup\{v_j\}| - |C(S_{j-1})| \geq |C(S'_{r-1})\cup\{v_j\}| - |C(S'_{r-1})|$ where r is the stage in which v_j is selected when bidding c'_j. This implies:

$$\frac{c'_j}{(|C(S_j)|-C(S_{j-1})|)} \leq \frac{c'_j}{(|C(S_r\cup\{v_j\})|-C(S_r)|)} \leq \frac{B'}{|C(S')|}$$

.

where the second inequality is due to the fact that every agent $i \in S'$ respects the condition $c_i \leq B'\cdot\Big(\frac{|C(S'_i)|-|C(S'_{i-1})|}{|C(S')|}\Big)$. The above inequality implies:

$$\begin{aligned}c'_j &\leq B'\Big(\frac{|C(S_{j-1}\cup\{v_j\})|-|C(S_{j-1})|}{|C(S')|}\Big)\\ &\leq 12\cdot B'\Big(\frac{|C(S_{j-1}\cup\{v_j\})|-|C(S_{j-1})|}{|C(S)|}\Big)\end{aligned}$$

Since c'_j is the maximum bid an agent can declare, it follows that the threshold payments for any agent j are bounded from above by: $12\cdot B'\Big(\frac{|C(S_j|-|C(S_{j-1})|}{|C(S)|}\Big)$. Since $\sum_{j\in S'}(|C(S_j|-|C(S_{j-1})|) = |C(S)|$ and $B' = B/24$, the total payments to agents in $S\setminus\{i^*\}$ are bounded by $B/2$ which implies budget feasibility. □

4.3 A Deterministic Mechanism for Cut Functions

The approximation guarantee provided by our mechanism depends on randomizing between the subset S selected in steps (1) and (2) of the above mechanism and the vertex with largest degree in $\mathcal{N}\setminus\mathcal{N}'$. In order to derandomize the mechanism and provide a bounded approximation guarantee we need to select between the two solutions, based on the value of the cuts they produce. The problem with using a direct comparison between the values of two solutions is that it breaks monotonicity: when lowering her cost, an agent that is selected to S may change the order of the vertices that are selected and decrease the size of the cut so that it is smaller than the cut induced by the vertex with largest degree in $\mathcal{N}\setminus\mathcal{N}'$. If the mechanism would select based on a direct comparison between the two solutions an agent could loose her allocation by reducing her cost. We give a concrete example of such a case below.

EXAMPLE 1. *A direct comparison breaks monotonicity.*

PROOF. Consider a graph with the disjoint sets of vertices: $\{v_1,v_2,v_3,v_4\},\mathcal{N}_1,\mathcal{N}_2,\mathcal{N}_3,\mathcal{N}_4$, where $|\mathcal{N}_1| = n+2$, $|\mathcal{N}_2| = n, |\mathcal{N}_3| = n-1, |\mathcal{N}_4| = 3n$, v_2 is connected v_3 and each vertex $v \in \mathcal{N}_i$ is only connected to v_i, for all $i \leq 4$.

We would like to show that there is a cost profile s.t. the mechanism allocates to $\{v_1,v_2,v_3\}$, but as v_2 slightly decreases her cost declaration, v_3 is no longer allocated and since $d_4 = 3n \geq |C(\{v_1,v_2\})| = 2n+2$, a direct comparison between will result in v_2 not being selected, and thus breaking monotonicity.

For a budget $B = 2$ and costs $c_1 = \epsilon, c_2 = (\frac{n}{n+1})c_3+\epsilon, c_3 = \frac{n-1}{3n+2}+\epsilon, c_4 = B$, using a small ϵ and sufficiently large n (say $\epsilon = 2^{-n}, n > 100$) serves as such an example. In this instance, the mechanism runs procedure only on $\{v_1,v_2,v_3\}$

and compares its solution with d_4. Under these costs one can verify that the procedure selects $\{v_1, v_2, v_3\}$ which produce a cut with $3n+1 > d_4$. If v_2 reduces her cost to ϵ however, then v_1, v_2 are selected, v_3 is not selected as her marginal contribution now dropped, and since $C(\{v_1, v_2\}) = 2n+2 < d_4$, v_4 will be allocated instead. □

It is important to emphasize that such examples are not unique to our specific mechanism and not even to cut functions. This type of problem arises when applying greedy procedures in other setting like coverage, submodular, and subadditive valuation functions.

4.3.1 Derandomization via Relaxation

To derandomize the mechanism in a manner that preserves monotonicity and provides a constant factor approximation guarantee we suggest the following approach, which is inspired by [2]: rather than a direct comparison between the two solutions, we will compute a linear programming relaxation over $\mathcal{N}'$, compare between the value returned by this solution and the largest degree in $\mathcal{N} \setminus \mathcal{N}'$, and select S if and only if the solution returned by the relaxation is greater.

Since the solution returned by the relaxation will be an optimal *fractional* solution, such a scheme guarantees monotonicity: an agent in $\mathcal{N}'$ that reduces her cost can only increase the value of the optimal fractional solution, thus avoiding the problem discussed in the above example. As long as we can guarantee that the fractional solution returned by the relaxation is a constant factor away from the optimal integral solution over $\mathcal{N}'$, implementing such a scheme will guarantee a constant factor approximation.

More concretely, the optimization problem can be reformulated as the following integer program:

$$\max \sum_{i<j} z_{ij} \tag{8}$$

$$\text{s.t. } z_{ij} \leq x_i + x_j, \quad i<j, \tag{9}$$

$$z_{ij} \leq 2 - x_i - x_j \quad i<j, \tag{10}$$

$$\sum_{i \in \mathcal{N}} x_i c_i \leq B, \tag{11}$$

$$x_i, z_{ij} \in \{0,1\}, i \in \mathcal{N}, i<j \tag{12}$$

where x_i, c_i are variables representing the vertices and their costs, respectively and z_{ij} represent the edges. As discussed above, we would like to compute a fractional solution in polynomial time that will be a constant factor away from the optimal integral solution of the above program. We will do this by showing that the linear program relaxation has a constant integrality gap. To bound the integrality gap of the LP relaxation of the problem, we assume that $c_i \leq \frac{B}{2}$, for every i.

THEOREM 4.5. *The LP has a constant integrality gap.*

PROOF. To prove the theorem we consider the following randomized rounding algorithm:

Randomized Rounding for Cut Functions
1. Add each vertex v_i to the cut S with probability $\frac{x_i}{4}$
2. If $\sum_{i \in S} x_i \cdot c_i > B$ then set $S' = \emptyset$ else $S' = S$
Output: S'

We will show that $\Pr[(i,j) \in S'] \geq \frac{7z_{ij}}{64}$. Thus, if we let T_{ij} be the indicator variable that gets a value of 1 when $(i,j) \in S'$ and 0 otherwise, we have that $\mathbb{E}[T_{i,j}] \geq \frac{7z_{ij}}{64}$. By linearity of expectation, $\mathbb{E}[C(S')] = \sum_{(i,j)\in E} \mathbb{E}[T_{ij}] \geq \sum_{(i,j)\in E} \frac{7z_{ij}}{64}$. Therefore there must always be an integral solution that has a value of at least $\frac{7}{64}$ of the value of the optimal fractional solution.

We first calculate the probability that $(i,j) \in S$:

$$\begin{aligned}
\Pr[(i,j) \in S] &= (1-\frac{x_i}{4})\frac{x_j}{4} + (1-\frac{x_j}{4})\frac{x_i}{4} \\
&= \frac{x_i}{4} + \frac{x_j}{4} - 2 \cdot \frac{x_i}{4} \cdot \frac{x_j}{4} \\
&\geq \frac{z_{ij}}{4} - \frac{x_i \cdot x_j}{8} \\
&\geq \frac{z_{ij}}{4} - \frac{(\frac{z_{ij}}{2})^2}{8} \\
&\geq \frac{7z_{ij}}{32}
\end{aligned}$$

where the first equality is by the properties of the randomized rounding, the first inequality is by the LP constraints, and the second inequality by basic analysis and using $z_{ij} \leq x_i + x_j$. The last inequality uses the fact that $z_{ij} \in [0,1]$ and thus $z_{ij} > z_{ij}^2$.

Next we calculate $\Pr[S' = \emptyset | (i,j) \in S]$. If $(i,j) \in S$ this implies that exactly one of the vertices i and j is in S. Assume without loss of generality that $i \in S$. Now $S' = \emptyset$ only if the total budget exceeds B. Observe that $\mathbb{E}[\sum_{i' \in S, i' \neq j, i' \neq i} c_{i'} | i \in S, j \notin S] \leq \frac{B}{2}$ since each i' is selected into S with probability exactly $\frac{x_{i'}}{4}$ and that $\sum_{i \in \mathcal{N}} x_i c_i \leq B$ by the LP constraints. By Markov's inequality:

$$\Pr[\sum_{i' \in S, i' \neq j, i' \neq i} c_{i'} \geq \frac{B}{2} | i \in S, j \notin S] \leq \frac{1}{2}$$

Taking into account that $c_i \leq \frac{B}{2}$, by our assumption, we can now bound the probability that the budget used by S does not exceed B:

$$\Pr[S' \neq \emptyset | i \in S, j \notin S]$$

$$\geq \Pr[\sum_{i' \in S, i' \neq j, i' \neq i} c_{i'} \leq \frac{B}{2} | i \in S, j \notin S] \geq \frac{1}{2}$$

To conclude, $\Pr[(i,j) \in S] \geq \frac{7z_{ij}}{32}$ and also $\Pr[(i,j) \in S' | (i,j) \in S] \geq \frac{1}{2}$. Thus $\Pr[(i,j) \in S'] \geq \frac{7z_{ij}}{64}$, for every $(i,j) \in E$, as needed by the discussion above. □

We can now formally state the deterministic mechanism. We use A to denote the allocation rule in steps (1) and (2) of the randomized mechanism, f_{LP} to be the optimal fractional solution, and $LP(x)$ to be the value of the LP evaluated on x.

A Deterministic Mechanism for Cut Functions
1. Let $\mathcal{N}' = \{i :\in \mathcal{N} : c_i \leq B/2\}$, $i' = \text{argmax}_{i \in \mathcal{N} \setminus \mathcal{N}'} d_i$
2. Compute $S = A(\mathcal{N}')$ and $x^* = f_{LP}(\mathcal{N}')$
Output: if $LP(x^*) \geq d_{i'}$ return S o.w. return $\{i'\}$

THEOREM 4.6. *There is a $O(1)$-approximation polynomial time mechanism for cut functions which is truthful and budget feasible.*

PROOF. Truthfulness and budget feasibility follow from the arguments in the case of the randomized mechanism. For the approximation guarantee, note that $OPT(c, \mathcal{N}, B) \leq OPT(c, \mathcal{N}', B) + OPT(c, \mathcal{N} \setminus \mathcal{N}', B)$. Since i' is the optimal solution in $\mathcal{N} \setminus \mathcal{N}'$ if its value is larger than $LP(x^*)$ it must be larger than the optimal integral solution as well, and thus choosing i' guarantees a 2-approximation in this case. Otherwise we have:

$$|C(S)| \geq \frac{OPT(c, \mathcal{N}', B)}{282} \geq \frac{7 \cdot L(x^*)}{64 \cdot 282} \geq \frac{|C(\{a\})|}{2579}$$

Therefore in this case, we are guaranteed that $|C(S)| \geq \frac{OPT(c,\mathcal{N},B)}{5158}$. □

Acknowledgments

We thank Ashwinkumar B. V. for several helpful comments.

5. REFERENCES

[1] Aaron Archer and Éva Tardos. Frugal path mechanisms. In *SODA*, pages 991–999, 2002.

[2] Yossi Azar and Iftah Gamzu. Truthful unification framework for packing integer programs with choices. In *ICALP (1)*, pages 833–844, 2008.

[3] Liad Blumrosen and Noam Nisan. Combinatorial auctions. In Noam Nisan, Tim Roughgarden, Eva Tardos, and Vijay V. Vazirani, editors, *Algorithmic Game Theory*. Cambridge University Press, 2007.

[4] Matthew Cary, Abraham D. Flaxman, Jason D. Hartline, and Anna R. Karlin. Auctions for structured procurement. In *SODA*, pages 304–313, 2008.

[5] Ning Chen, Edith Elkind, Nick Gravin, and Fedor Petrov. Frugal mechanism design via spectral techniques. In *FOCS*, pages 755–764, 2010.

[6] Ning Chen, Nick Gravin, and Pinyan Lu. On the approximability of budget feasible mechanisms. 2011.

[7] Shahar Dobzinski, Noam Nisan, and Michael Schapira. Approximation algorithms for combinatorial auctions with complement-free bidders. *Math. Oper. Res.*, 35(1):1–13, 2010.

[8] Edith Elkind, Leslie Ann Goldberg, and Paul W. Goldberg. Frugality ratios and improved truthful mechanisms for vertex cover. In *ACM Conference on Electronic Commerce*, pages 336–345, 2007.

[9] Edith Elkind, Amit Sahai, and Kenneth Steiglitz. Frugality in path auctions. In *SODA*, pages 701–709, 2004.

[10] Ludwig Ensthaler and Thomas Giebe. A dynamic auction for multi-object procurement under a hard budget constraint. Discussion Papers 310, 2010.

[11] Joan Feigenbaum, Christos H. Papadimitriou, Rahul Sami, and Scott Shenker. A BGP-based mechanism for lowest-cost routing. In *PODC*, pages 173–182, 2002.

[12] Joan Feigenbaum, Rahul Sami, and Scott Shenker. Mechanism design for policy routing. In *PODC*, pages 11–20, 2004.

[13] Arpita Ghosh and Aaron Roth. Selling privacy at auction. In *ACM Conference on Electronic Commerce*, 2011.

[14] Anna R. Karlin, David Kempe, and Tami Tamir. Beyond VCG: Frugality of truthful mechanisms. In *FOCS*, pages 615–626, 2005.

[15] David Kempe, Mahyar Salek, and Cristopher Moore. Frugal and truthful auctions for vertex covers, flows and cuts. In *FOCS*, pages 745–754, 2010.

[16] R. Myerson. Optimal auction design. *Mathematics of Operations Research*, 6(1), 1981.

[17] Noam Nisan and Amir Ronen. Algorithmic mechanism design. *Games and Economic Behaviour*, 35:166 – 196, 2001. A preliminary version appeared in STOC 1999.

[18] Yaron Singer. Budget feasible mechanisms. In *FOCS*, pages 765–774, 2010.

[19] Kunal Talwar. The price of truth: Frugality in truthful mechanisms. In *STACS*, pages 608–619, 2003.

Implementing Efficient Graphs in Connection Networks

Ruben Juarez
University of Hawaii
Honolulu, HI, USA
rubenj@hawaii.edu

Rajnish Kumar
Louisiana State University
Baton Rouge, LA, USA
rajnishkumar@lsu.edu

Abstract

We consider the problem of sharing the cost of a network that meets the connection demands of a set of agents. The agents simultaneously choose paths in the network connecting their demand nodes. A mechanism splits the total cost of the network formed among the participants.

We introduce two new properties of implementation. The first property, *Pareto Nash Implementation (PNI)*, requires that the efficient outcome is always implemented in a Nash equilibrium, and that the efficient outcome Pareto dominates any other Nash equilibrium. The *average cost mechanism (AC)* and other asymmetric variations are the only rules that meet PNI. These mechanisms are also characterized under Strong Nash Implementation.

The second property, *Weakly Pareto Nash Implementation (WPNI)*, requires that the least inefficient equilibrium Pareto dominate any other equilibrium. The *egalitarian mechanism (EG)*, a variation of AC that meets individual rationality, and other asymmetric mechanisms are the only rules that meet WPNI and Individual Rationality.

PNI and WPNI provide the first economic justification of the Price of Stability (PoS), a seemingly natural measure in the computer science literature but not easily embraced in economics. EG minimizes the PoS across all individually rational mechanisms.

Categories & Subject Descriptors: B.4.4, C.4, J.4

General Terms: Algorithms, Design, Economics, Theory.

Authors Keywords: Cost-sharing, Implementation, Average Cost, Egalitarian Mechanism.

EC'11, June 5–9, 2011, San Jose, California, USA.
ACM 978-1-4503-0261-6/11/06.

Optimal Cost Sharing Protocols for Scheduling Games

Philipp von Falkenhausen
Berlin Institute of Technology
Institute of Mathematics
p.falkenhausen@gmail.com

Tobias Harks
Berlin Institute of Technology
Institute of Mathematics
harks@math.tu-berlin.de

ABSTRACT

We consider the problem of designing cost sharing protocols to minimize the price of anarchy and stability for a class of scheduling games. Here, we are given a set of players, each associated with a job of certain non-negative weight. Any job fits on any machine, and the cost of a machine is a non-decreasing function of the total load on the machine. We assume that the private cost of a player is determined by a cost sharing protocol. We consider four natural design restrictions for feasible protocols: stability, budget balance, separability, and uniformity. While budget balance is self-explanatory, the stability requirement asks for the existence of pure-strategy Nash equilibria. Separability requires that the resulting cost shares only depend on the set of players on a machine. Uniformity additionally requires that the cost shares on a machine are instance-independent, that is, they remain the same even if new machines are added to or removed from the instance. We call a cost sharing protocol basic, if it satisfies only stability and budget balance. Separable and uniform cost sharing protocols additionally satisfy separability and uniformity, respectively. For n-player games we show that among all basic and separable cost sharing protocols, there is an optimal protocol with price of anarchy and stability of precisely $\mathcal{H}_n = \sum_{i=1}^{n} 1/i$. For uniform protocols we present a strong lower bound showing that the price of anarchy is unbounded. Moreover, we obtain several results for special cases in which either the cost functions are restricted, or the job sizes are restricted. As a byproduct of our analysis, we obtain a complete characterization of outcomes that can be enforced as a pure-strategy Nash equilibrium by basic and separable cost sharing protocols.

Categories and Subject Descriptors

J.4 [**Computer Applications**]: Social and Behavioral Sciences—*Economics*; I.2.8 [**Artificial Intelligence**]: Problem Solving, Control Methods, and Search—*Scheduling*

EC'11, June 5–9, 2011, San Jose, California, USA.

General Terms

Theory

Keywords

Cost sharing, scheduling, congestion games

1. INTRODUCTION

Congestion games play a fundamental role for many applications, including traffic networks, telecommunication networks and economics. In a congestion game, there is a set of resources and a pure strategy of a player consists of a subset of resources. The cost of a resource depends only on the number of players choosing the resource, and the private cost of a player is the sum of the costs of the chosen resources. Under these assumptions, Rosenthal proved the existence of a pure Nash equilibrium (PNE for short) [20]. An important question in congestion games is the degree of suboptimality caused by selfish resource allocation. Koutsoupias and Papadimitriou [17] introduced a measure to quantify the inefficiency of Nash equilibria which they termed the *price of anarchy*. The price of anarchy is defined as the worst-case ratio of the cost of a Nash equilibrium over the cost of a system optimum. In the past decade, considerable progress has been made in exactly quantifying the price of anarchy for many interesting classes of games. In the context of nonatomic network routing games, the price of anarchy for specific classes of cost functions is well understood, see Roughgarden and Tardos [23], Roughgarden [21] and Correa, Schulz, and Stier-Moses [11]. (For an overview of these results, we refer to the book by Roughgarden [22].) Awerbuch et al. [4], Christodoulou and Koutsoupias [9], Aland et al. [2] and Bhawalkar et al. [5] derived several tight bounds on the price of anarchy for weighted and unweighted congestion games with specific classes of latency functions. Despite these bounds, it is known that the price of anarchy for general latency functions is unbounded even on simple *parallel-arc* networks [5, 23].

Motivated by the fact that pure Nash equilibria may be very inefficient even in parallel-arc networks, we focus in this paper on the design of *cost sharing methods* as a means to leverage the resulting price of anarchy. The concrete scenario that we consider is the problem of scheduling jobs on parallel machines. We are given a set of players, each associated with a job of certain non-negative weight. Any job fits on any machine, and the cost of a machine is a non-decreasing function of the total load on the machine. We assume that the private cost of a player is determined by a cost sharing method. For instance, a simple cost sharing method that has been analyzed in the aforementioned literature is *average cost sharing*, see [5, 11, 23]. In almost all settings in the theory and practice of mechanism or protocol design, a designer may only choose protocols out of a set of *feasible* protocols. Therefore, we have to precisely define the design space of feasible protocols. To this end, we define the following four properties listed below which are defined more formally in Section 2. These properties have been introduced first by Chen et al. [8] in the context of the design of cost sharing protocols for network design games (a formal definition of these games will be given in Section 1.2).

1. *Stability*: There is at least one pure strategy Nash equilibrium in each scheduling game induced by the cost sharing protocol.

2. *Budget-balance*: For every outcome of a scheduling game induced by the cost sharing protocol, the cost of each resource is exactly covered by the collected cost shares of the players using the resource.

3. *Separability*: In each scheduling game induced by the cost sharing protocol, the cost shares of each resource are completely determined by the set of players that use it.

4. *Uniformity*: Across all scheduling games induced by the cost sharing protocol, the cost shares of a resource (for each potential set of users) depend only on the resource cost, and not on the set of available resources.

A cost sharing method is called *basic* if it satisfies (1)-(2), *separable* if it satisfies (1)-(3), and *uniform* if it satisfies (1)-(4). We briefly discuss the above four properties and refer to [8] for a more detailed treatment. The condition (2) is the least controversial in the context of cost sharing protocols. The stability condition (1) requires the existence of at least one Nash equilibrium in pure strategies. While this requirement restricts the search space for cost sharing protocols, it is certainly the solution concept of choice when mixed or correlated strategies have no meaningful physical interpretation in the game played; see also the discussion in Osborne and Rubinstein [19, § 3.2] about critics of mixed Nash equilibria. While condition (3) seems restrictive, it is crucial for practical applications in which cost sharing methods have only local information about their own resource usage (see for instance the TCP/IP protocol design, where routers drop packets based on some function of the number of packets in the queue, see [24]). Uniformity (4) is the strongest and perhaps the most problematic design restriction. A uniform protocol is not only separable but also *strongly local* in the sense that the cost shares of a resource are independent of the set of resources available to the game designer. This property may be crucial for systems in which the resources can be added or removed over time and a reconfiguration of the system (changing the cost sharing protocol) is too costly.

The goal of this paper is twofold. On the one hand side, we want to systematically analyze the achievable worst-case efficiency of Nash equilibria by basic, separable and uniform cost sharing protocols in the context of scheduling games. Besides this worst-case perspective, we also ask a larger question: Which outcomes can actually be enforced as pure Nash equilibria? More precisely, we call an outcome of a scheduling game *weakly-enforceable* if there is a basic protocol that induces the outcome as a pure Nash equilibrium. We call an outcome of a scheduling game *strongly-enforceable* if there is a basic protocol that induces the outcome as the most expensive pure Nash equilibrium.

1.1 Our Results

We study protocol design problems in the context of scheduling games, where the goal is to minimize the induced price of anarchy and the price of stability. Our results for these problems can be summarized as follows.

Among all basic and separable protocols, we provide an *optimal* protocol minimizing the resulting price of anarchy and price of stability simultaneously. For n-player scheduling games, the optimal value of the price of anarchy and stability is precisely the n-th harmonic number $\mathcal{H}_n = \sum_{i=1}^{n} 1/i$. Moreover, we obtain a complete characterization of weakly-enforceable outcomes. This characterization can be used for designing cost sharing protocols minimizing the price of stability with respect to an arbitrary objective function. We also derive sufficient conditions for an outcome to be strongly-enforceable. Our proof of this result is constructive by providing a cost sharing protocol that strongly enforces an outcome satisfying the sufficient conditions. We then show that this protocol gives rise to an optimal cost sharing protocol minimizing the price of anarchy and stability as mentioned above. For scheduling games with cost functions that have non-decreasing per-unit costs, we derive an optimal cost sharing protocol with price of anarchy equal to 1. We remark that this assumption is quite weak insofar as non-decreasing and convex cost functions satisfy non-decreasing per-unit costs.

We also study the achievable price of anarchy of uniform cost sharing protocols. We show that there is no uniform cost sharing protocol with a bounded price of anarchy. This bound even holds for a family of instances with only 3 players, at most 3 machines and cost functions with non-decreasing costs per unit. Only for instances in which the demands are integer multiples of each other, we present a cost sharing protocol with a bounded price of anarchy of n.

1.2 Related Work

There is a large body of work on scheduling games (or singleton congestion games) with unweighted and weighted players [1, 12, 13, 14, 15, 18]. Most of these papers study the existence and price of anarchy of pure Nash equilibria for the uniform cost sharing protocol in which the private cost of every player is equal to the cost on the resource. These works, however, do not consider the design perspective of cost sharing protocols. Christodoulou et al. [10] and follow-up papers such as [6, 16] study *coordination mechanisms* and their price of anarchy in scheduling games in which n players assign a task to one of m machines. Rather than paying a share of the resulting cost of a machine as in our scenario, the players in these games consider the completion time of their respective job as private cost. This completion time depends on the sequence in which the jobs on a machine are processed which in turn is given by the *coordination mechanism*. The notion of private cost in these papers establishes an entirely different set of Nash equilibria compared to our work and hence their results concerning the price of anarchy are unrelated to ours.

Our work is motivated by the paper by Chen et al. [8].

In this paper, the authors study the design of cost sharing protocols for network design games, see also Anshelevich et al. [3] and Chen and Roughgarden [7] for earlier work on network design games. In a network design game, each player i has a unit demand that she wishes to send along a path in a (directed or undirected) network connecting her source node s_i to her terminal node t_i. Every edge has a constant non-negative cost and the problem is to design a separable or uniform cost sharing protocol so as to minimize the price of anarchy and stability in this setting. Our approach follows their lead in terms of the feasible protocol space, but we apply cost sharing protocols to the structural different class of scheduling models. On the one hand, such scheduling models are more general in the sense that we allow arbitrary non-decreasing cost functions instead of constant costs on the resources. Moreover, in contrast to [8], we allow players to have different non-negative weights. On the other hand, scheduling models are more restricted in the sense that we consider a relatively simple strategy space for the players, that is, a pure strategy for a player is simply a single resource. Moreover, in contrast to [8], our games are symmetric, that is, every player has access to every resource. These structural differences result in different approaches and also the results of [8] are different to ours. For example, while Chen et al. [8] proved bounds on the price of anarchy for uniform protocols of order $\Theta(\log(n)), \Theta(\text{polylog}(n))$, and n for undirected single-sink instances, undirected multicommodity instances, and directed single-sink instances, respectively, we show that for scheduling games such results are impossible. The price of anarchy for uniform protocols inducing scheduling games is unbounded. Finally, it is worth noting that, while [8] analyzed separable and uniform protocols, we additionally analyze the larger class of basic protocols.

2. MODEL AND PROBLEM STATEMENT

A *scheduling model* is represented by a tuple (N, M, d, c). Here, $N = \{1, \dots, n\}$ is a nonempty set of players and $M = \{a_1, \dots, a_m\}$ is a nonempty set of machines. Every player is associated with a task of weight d_i and $d = (d_1, \dots, d_n)$ is the combined weight vector. Every machine $a \in M$ has an associated non-negative and non-decreasing cost function $c_a : \mathbb{R}^+ \to \mathbb{R}^+$. We assume $c_a(0) = 0$ for all $a \in M$. The vector of cost functions is denoted by $c = (c_1, \dots, c_m)$. Given a scheduling model (N, M, d, c), we associate a strategic game represented by the tuple (N, X, ξ). Here, it is assumed that every task fits on every machine, thus, the set of pure strategies for player $i \in N$ is $X_i = M$ and the overall strategy space is $X = M^n$. The outcomes $x = (x_1, \dots, x_n) \in M^n$ are vectors of machines where the strategy played by player i is machine x_i. The private cost of player $i \in N$ in such an outcome x is determined by the *cost sharing method* $\xi_i : X \to \mathbb{R}^+$. A *cost sharing protocol* $\Xi : (N, M, d, c) \mapsto \xi$ provides every scheduling model with a vector $\xi = (\xi_i)_{i \in N}$ of such cost sharing methods. For $x \in M^n$, the set of players using some machine $a \in M$ is denoted by $S_a(x) := \{i \in N : x_i = a\}$ and for $a \in M$, the load on machine a is defined as $\ell_a(x) := \sum_{i \in S_a(x)} d_i$. The cost of an outcome is defined as $C(x) := \sum_{a \in M} c_a(\ell_a(x))$. Abusing notation, we will often write $c_a(x)$ instead of $c_a(\ell_a(x))$. We consider cost minimization games, thus, when choosing her strategy, each player strives to minimize her resulting private cost $\xi_i(x)$. We say that the game (N, X, ξ) on a scheduling model (N, M, d, c) is induced by the protocol Ξ.

An important solution concept in non-cooperative game theory for the analysis of strategic games are pure Nash equilibria. Using standard notation in game theory, for an outcome $x \in M^n$ we denote by

$$(a, x_{-i}) := (x_1, \dots, x_{i-1}, a, x_{i+1}, \dots, x_n) \in M^n$$

the outcome that arises if only player i deviates to strategy a.

Definition 2.1. (Pure Nash Equilibrium) Let (N, X, ξ) be a scheduling game. The outcome x is a pure Nash equilibrium if no player i can strictly reduce her private cost by unilaterally moving to a different machine, that is, for all $i \in N$

$$\xi_i(x) \leq \xi_i(a, x_{-i}) \quad \text{for all } a \in M. \tag{2.1}$$

Two well established concepts that quantify the efficiency of Nash equilibria are the *price of anarchy* and the *price of stability*. The price of anarchy measures the largest possible ratio of the cost of a Nash equilibrium and the cost of an optimal outcome. The price of stability measures the smallest ratio of the cost of a Nash equilibrium and the cost of an optimal outcome. For a cost sharing protocol Ξ, we define by $PoA(\Xi)$ and $PoS(\Xi)$ the corresponding worst case price of anarchy and price of stability across games induced by protocol Ξ. The main goal of this paper is to design cost sharing protocols that minimize the price of anarchy and price of stability, respectively. Of course, the attainable objective values crucially depend on the design space that we permit. The following properties have been first proposed by Chen et al. [8] in the context of designing cost sharing methods for network design games.

Definition 2.2. (Properties of cost sharing protocols) A cost sharing protocol Ξ is

1. *stable* if it induces only games that admit at least one pure Nash equilibrium.

2. *basic* if it is stable and additionally *budget balanced*, i.e. if it assigns all scheduling models (N, M, d, c) with cost sharing methods $(\xi_i)_{i \in N}$ such that

$$c_a(x) = \sum_{i \in S_a(x)} \xi_i(x) \text{ for all } a \in M, x \in M^n. \tag{2.2}$$

   This property requires $c_a(0) = 0$ for unused machines, which we will assume in the paper.

3. *separable* if it is basic and if it induces only games (N, M^n, ξ) for which in any two outcomes $x, x' \in M^n$

$$S_a(x) = S_a(x') \Rightarrow \xi_i(x) = \xi_i(x') \; \forall i \in S_a(x), a \in M.$$

4. *uniform* if it is separable and if it assigns any two models (N, M, d, c), (N, M', d, c') with cost sharing methods $(\xi_i)_{i \in N}$ and $(\xi'_i)_{i \in N}$ such that the following condition holds. For all $a \in M \cap M'$ with $c_a = c'_a$ and all outcomes $x \in M^n$, $x' \in M'^n$

$$S_a(x) = S_a(x') \Rightarrow \xi_i(x) = \xi'_i(x') \text{ for all } i \in S_a(x).$$

Informally, separability means that in an outcome x the value $\xi_i(x)$ depends only on the set $S_{x_i}(x)$ of players sharing machine x_i and disregards all other information contained in

x. Still, separable protocols can assign cost sharing methods that are specifically tailored to the given scheduling model, for example based on an optimal outcome. Uniform protocols are not allowed to do this, they even disregard the layout of the model and assign the same cost sharing methods when machines are added to or removed from the model.

We denote by $\mathcal{B}_n, \mathcal{S}_n$ and $\mathcal{U}_n$ the set of basic, separable and uniform cost sharing protocols for scheduling games with n players, respectively. We obtain the following optimization problems that we address in this paper.

$$\min_{\Xi \in \mathcal{B}_n} PoA(\Xi),\ \min_{\Xi \in \mathcal{B}_n} PoS(\Xi),\ \min_{\Xi \in \mathcal{S}_n} PoA(\Xi),\ \min_{\Xi \in \mathcal{S}_n} PoS(\Xi),$$

$$\min_{\Xi \in \mathcal{U}_n} PoA(\Xi),\ \min_{\Xi \in \mathcal{U}_n} PoS(\Xi)\ .$$

3. BASIC AND SEPARABLE PROTOCOLS

We start with studying basic and separable cost sharing protocols. While our goal is to find a cost sharing protocol minimizing the induced PoA and PoS, we first study the issue of enforceability of pure Nash equilibria by basic and separable cost sharing protocols. To be more precise, given a scheduling model (N, M, d, c), we first ask which outcomes $x \in M^n$ can be enforced as pure Nash equilibria by some basic or separable cost sharing protocol. We will differentiate between *weakly* enforceable outcomes and *strongly* enforceable outcomes, see the definition below.

Definition 3.1. (Enforceable outcomes) Consider a scheduling model (N, M, d, c) and an outcome $x \in M^n$.

i) x is *weakly-enforceable* if there exists a basic cost sharing protocol Ξ such that x is a Nash equilibrium in the game (N, M^n, ξ) induced by Ξ.

ii) x is *separable weakly-enforceable* if there exists a separable cost sharing protocol Ξ such that x is a Nash equilibrium in the game (N, M^n, ξ) induced by Ξ.

iii) x is *strongly-enforceable* if there exists a separable cost sharing protocol Ξ such that x is the most expensive Nash equilibrium in the game (N, M^n, ξ) induced by Ξ, i.e. $C(x') \leq C(x)$ for all Nash equilibria $x' \in M^n$.

In the following section, we will give an exact characterization of weakly-enforceable and separable weakly-enforceable outcomes. This characterization provides a structural property that can be used to design cost sharing protocols for minimizing the price of stability for *arbitrary* objective functions.

Throughout this section, the players are assumed to be ordered by non-decreasing weights: $d_1 \leq d_2 \leq \cdots \leq d_n$.

3.1 Weakly-Enforceable Outcomes

This section provides an exact characterization of weakly-enforceable outcomes. Our characterization relies on the notion of *decharged outcomes* defined below.

Definition 3.2. (Weakly decharged outcome) Consider a scheduling model (N, M, d, c). A machine $a \in M$ is *weakly decharged* in an outcome $x \in M^n$ if

$$c_a(x) \leq \sum_{i \in S_a(x)} \min_{b \in M} c_b(b, x_{-i}). \tag{3.1}$$

The outcome x itself is called *weakly decharged* if all machines are weakly decharged.

We further introduce the weak x-enforcing protocol.

Definition 3.3. (Weak x-enforcing protocol) The *weak x-enforcing protocol* takes as input a weakly decharged outcome x. We use x to define for any outcome z and machine a the sets $S_a^0(z) := \{i \in S_a(z) \cap S_a(x)\}$ *(home players on a)* and $S_a^1(z) := \{i \in S_a(z) \backslash S_a(x)\}$ *(foreign players on a)*. Then, the weak x-enforcing protocol assigns for all $i \in N, z \in M^n$ the following cost sharing methods

$$\xi_i(z) := \begin{cases} \dfrac{\min_{b \in M} c_b(b, x_{-i})}{\sum_{j \in S_{x_i}(x)} \min_{b \in M} c_b(b, x_{-j})} \cdot c_{x_i}(x), \\ \qquad \text{if } S_{z_i}(z) = S_{z_i}(x) \text{ and } c_{x_i}(x) > 0, \\ c_{z_i}(z), \text{ if } S_{z_i}^1(z) \neq \emptyset \text{ and } i = \min S_{z_i}^1(z), \\ c_{z_i}(z), \text{ if } S_{z_i}^1(z) = \emptyset,\ S_{z_i}(z) \subset S_{z_i}(x) \\ \qquad \text{and } i = \min S_{z_i}(z), \\ 0, \text{ else.} \end{cases}$$

Informally, if $S_a(z) = S_a(x)$, the players on machine a share the cost proportional to their opportunity cost (cost of change) in outcome x. Otherwise, the smallest foreign player (deviating from outcome x) or, if there are none, the smallest home player (not deviating) pays the entire cost of the machine. Observe that in weakly decharged outcomes x we have $\sum_{j \in S_a(x)} \min_{b \in M} c_b(b, x_{-j}) > 0$ for all $a \in M$ with $c_a(x) > 0$ and thus the protocol is well defined. We are now ready to state our first main result.

THEOREM 3.4. *For any scheduling model (N, M, d, c) and outcome x, the following statements are equivalent.*

(i) the outcome x is weakly decharged,

(ii) the outcome x is weakly-enforceable,

(iii) the outcome x is separable weakly-enforceable.

Observe that (iii) $\Rightarrow$ (ii) holds because by definition separable protocols are a subclass of basic protocols. We prove (i) $\Rightarrow$ (iii) and (ii) $\Rightarrow$ (i) by two lemmas.

LEMMA 3.5. *For every weakly decharged outcome x, the weak x-enforcing protocol is a separable cost sharing protocol and weakly enforces x.*

PROOF. Budget balance and separability of the cost sharing methods are clear from the definition of the protocol, thus, we prove only that x is a Nash equilibrium. For all machines $a \in M$ with $c_a(x) > 0$ we are in the first case of the definition of the protocol, thus, we obtain

$$\xi_i(x) = \frac{\min_{b \in M} c_b(b, x_{-i})}{\sum_{j \in S_a(x)} \min_{b \in M} c_b(b, x_{-j})} \cdot c_a(x)$$
$$\leq \min_{b \in M} c_b(b, x_{-i}) \leq \min_{b \in M \backslash \{a\}} \xi_i(b, x_{-i}) \text{ for all } i \in S_a(x),$$

where the first inequality holds because outcome x is weakly decharged. For all other machines $a \in M$, we have $\xi_i(x) = c_a(x) = 0$ for all $i \in S_a(x)$ and thus x is a pure Nash equilibrium. □

LEMMA 3.6. *Consider the scheduling model (N, M, d, c). Then, any weakly-enforceable outcome x is weakly decharged.*

PROOF. Say x is a Nash equilibrium under the basic protocol Ξ that assigns cost sharing methods ξ. Then $\xi_i(x) \leq \min_{b\in M} \xi_i(b, x_{-i})$ for all $i \in N$ and hence due to budget balance of Ξ,

$$c_a(x) = \sum_{i\in S_a(x)} \xi_i(x) \leq \sum_{i\in S_a(x)} \min_{b\in M} \xi_i(b, x_{-i})$$
$$\leq \sum_{i\in S_a(x)} \min_{b\in M} c_b(b, x_{-i})$$

for all machines $a \in M$. Thus, x is weakly decharged. □

The above characterization has a direct consequence for the design of cost sharing protocols so as to minimize the price of stability with respect to an arbitrary objective function over the strategy space. As formalized below, by Theorem 3.4 this problem reduces to solving a well-structured finite-dimensional optimization problem.

COROLLARY 3.7. *Let (N, M, d, c) be a scheduling model and let $F : M^n :\to \mathbb{R}$ be a social welfare function. Then, $\min_{\xi\in\mathcal{B}_n} PoS(\xi; F)$ and $\min_{\xi\in\mathcal{S}_n} PoS(\xi; F)$ can be reduced to solving the optimization problem*

$$\min_{x\in M^n} F(x) \;\; s.t. \;\; c_a(x) \leq \sum_{i\in S_a(x)} \min_{b\in M} c_b(b, x_{-i}) \, \forall\, a \in M.$$

3.2 Strongly-Enforceable Outcomes

In this section, we turn to strongly-enforceable outcomes. We present a slightly extended protocol that we term the the strong x-enforcing protocol. We will show that outcomes that are strongly decharged (a definition will follow shortly) are strongly-enforceable by this protocol.

Definition 3.8. (Strongly Decharged Outcome) Consider a scheduling model (N, M, d, c). A machine $a \in M$ is *strongly decharged* if it is weakly decharged and additionally

$$c_a(x) < \sum_{i\in S_a(x)} \min_{b\in M} c_b(b, x_{-i}), \text{ if } |S_a(x)| > 1 \text{ and } c_a(x) > 0. \tag{3.2}$$

Machines that are not strongly decharged are called *charged*. The outcome x is called *strongly decharged* if all machines are strongly decharged.

We now introduce the strong x-enforcing protocol.

Definition 3.9. (Strong x-enforcing protocol) The *strong x-enforcing protocol* takes as input a strongly decharged outcome x. As before, we use x to define for any outcome z and machine a the sets $S_a^0(z)$ and $S_a^1(z)$. Additionally, we define the set $S_a^2(z) := \{i \in S_a(z)\backslash S_a(x) : c_{x_i}(x) = 0\}$ that we term *strong foreign players on a*. Then, the strong x-enforcing protocol assigns for all $i \in N, z \in M^n$, the following cost sharing methods:

$$\xi_i(z) := \begin{cases} \dfrac{\min_{b\in M} c_b(b, x_{-i})}{\sum_{j\in S_{x_i}(x)} \min_{b\in M} c_b(b, x_{-j})} \cdot c_{x_i}(x), & \\ \qquad \text{if } S_{z_i}(z) = S_{z_i}(x) \text{ and } c_{x_i}(x) > 0, & \\ c_{z_i}(z), \text{ if } S^2_{z_i}(z) \neq \emptyset \text{ and } i = \min S^2_{z_i}(z), & \\ c_{z_i}(z), \text{ if } S^2_{z_i}(z) = \emptyset,\, S^1_{z_i}(z) \neq \emptyset,\, i = \min S^1_{z_i}(z), & \\ c_{z_i}(z), \text{ if } S^1_{z_i}(z) = \emptyset,\, S_{z_i}(z) \subset S_{z_i}(x), i = \min S_{z_i}(z) & \\ 0, \quad \text{else.} & \end{cases}$$

The protocol works almost the same as the weak x-enforcing protocol, it only accounts differently for strong foreign players.

THEOREM 3.10. *If an outcome x is strongly decharged, then the strong x-enforcing protocol is separable and strongly enforces x.*

PROOF. Separability follows from the definition of the strong x-enforcing protocol. We only show that for any Nash equilibrium $z \neq x$ we have $C(z) \leq C(x)$. To this end, fix such a z and let

$$i := \min\{j \in N : z_j \neq x_j\} \tag{3.3}$$

be the smallest player who deviates from x. First, note that for all $j > i$,

$$\xi_j(z) \leq \begin{cases} \xi_j(z_i, z_{-j}) = 0 \;, \text{ if } c_{x_j}(x) > 0 \\ \xi_j(x_j, z_{-j}) = 0 \;, \text{ if } c_{x_j}(x) = 0, \end{cases} \tag{3.4}$$

because z is a Nash equilibrium. Hence,

$$c_a(z) = 0 \text{ for all } a \neq z_i \text{ with foreign players } S^1_a(z) \neq \emptyset. \tag{3.5}$$

Also, $c_a(z) \leq c_a(x)$ for all machines $a \neq z_i$ that only have home players $S^0_a(z) = S_a(z)$, because for these machines $\ell_a(z) \leq \ell_a(x)$. Thus, we already have

$$c_a(z) \leq c_a(x) \quad \text{for all machines } a \neq z_i. \tag{3.6}$$

If there is a strong foreign player on z_i, then even $c_{z_i}(z) = 0$ and we are done. Thus, from now on we assume that there are no strong foreign players on z_i. We can bound $c_{z_i}(z)$ from above using the Nash inequality $c_{z_i}(z) = \xi_i(z) \leq \xi_i(x_i, z_{-i})$. The remaining proof focuses on bounding the value $\xi_i(x_i, z_{-i})$ from above.

The value of $\xi_i(x_i, z_{-i})$ assigned by the x-enforcing protocol depends on $S_{x_i}(x_i, z_{-i})$ and $c_{x_i}(x)$, for which there are three possibilities, according to the definition of the strong x-enforcing protocol.These cases are

1. $S_{x_i}(x_i, z_{-i}) = S_{x_i}(x)$ and $c_{x_i}(x) > 0$, where the protocol returns $\xi_i(x_i, z_{-i}) = \xi_i(x)$.

2. $S_{x_i}(x_i, z_{-i}) \subset S_{x_i}(x)$ and $i = \min S_{x_i}(x_i, z_{-i})$, where the protocol returns $\xi_i(x_i, z_{-i}) = c_{x_i}(x_i, z_{-i})$.

3. All cases in which the protocol returns $\xi_i(x_i, z_{-i}) = 0$.

In each case we will find $c_{x_i}(z) + c_{z_i}(z) \leq c_{x_i}(x) + c_{z_i}(x)$ and thus with (3.6) we have $C(z) \leq C(x)$, which proves the Theorem. Note that (3.6) already implies $c_{x_i}(z) \leq c_{x_i}(x)$.

We begin with Case 1. The condition $c_{x_i}(x) > 0$ implies that if there is some strong foreign player $j > i$ (with $z_j \neq x_j$ and $c_{x_j}(x) = 0$), then $c_{z_i}(z) = \xi_i(z) \leq \xi_i(z_j, z_{-i}) = 0$ and we are done. Thus, we will in the following assume that there are no strong foreign players at all. If $\xi_i(x) = 0$, we obtain $0 = \xi_i(x) = \xi_i(x_i, z_{-i}) \geq \xi_i(z) = c_{z_i}(z)$, because we are in Case 1. Thus, we will also assume

$$\xi_i(x) > 0. \tag{3.7}$$

We now compare the allocation of load in the outcomes z and x, respectively. First, we consider machines $a \neq z_i$, which host foreign players $j \in S_a(z) \setminus S_a(x)$. For these foreign players we obtain

$$\min_{b \in M} c_b(b, x_{-j}) \geq \min_{b \in M} c_b(b, x_{-i}) \quad (3.8a)$$
$$\geq \xi_i(x) \quad (3.8b)$$
$$> 0. \quad (3.8c)$$

Observe that (3.3) implies $j > i$ and hence (weights are ordered non-decreasingly) $d_j \geq d_i$. As the cost functions are non-decreasing, the first inequality (3.8a) follows. Inequality (3.8b) holds since x is decharged. The last inequality (3.8c) follows from (3.7). We conclude for machine a

$$c_a(a, x_{-j}) \geq \xi_j(a, x_{-j}) \geq \xi_j(x) \quad (3.9)$$
$$= \frac{c_{x_j}(x)}{\sum_{k \in S_{x_j}(x)} \min_{b \in M} c_b(b, x_{-k})} \cdot \min_{b \in M} c_b(b, x_{-j}) \quad (3.10)$$
$$> 0 = c_a(z), \quad (3.11)$$

where (3.9) holds because x is a Nash equilibrium and (3.10) stems from the definition of the protocol because there are no strong foreign players and hence $c_{x_j}(x) > 0$. The inequality (3.11) holds because of (3.8) and the equality holds because of (3.5). Hence, there must be a non-empty set of players $S_a(x) \setminus S_a(z)$. These players cannot be strong foreign players, thus $c_a(x) > 0$. With $c_a(z) = 0$ and $c_a(x) > 0$ we have $\ell_a(x) > \ell_a(z)$ for all machines $a \neq z_i$ with foreign players. For all machines a without foreign players we know $\ell_a(x) \geq \ell_a(z)$ and for machine x_i even $\ell_{x_i}(x) = \ell_{x_i}(z) + d_i$ because we are in Case 1. Since the total load is the same in x and z, we have for machine z_i

$$\ell_{z_i}(z_i, x_{-i}) = \ell_{z_i}(x) + d_i \leq \ell_{z_i}(z). \quad (3.12)$$

Consequently,

$$\xi_i(z) = c_{z_i}(z) \geq c_{z_i}(z_i, x_{-i}) \quad (3.13)$$
$$\geq \frac{c_{x_i}(x)}{\sum_{j \in S_{x_i}(x)} \min_{b \in M} c_b(b, x_{-j})} \cdot \min_{b \in M} c_b(b, x_{-i}) \quad (3.14)$$
$$= \xi_i(x) = \xi_i(x_i, z_{-i}), \quad (3.15)$$

where the first inequality (3.13) holds because of (3.12) and the second inequality (3.14) because x is decharged and $c_{z_i}(z_i, x_{-i}) \geq \min_{b \in M} c_b(b, x_{-i})$. Equality (3.15) holds by the definition of the strong x-enforcing protocol for Case 1 and the last equation holds because we assume Case 1. If $|S_{x_i}(x)| > 1$, then inequality (3.14) is strict, because x is strongly decharged (i.e., (3.2) holds) which implies $\xi_i(z) > \xi_i(x_i, z_{-i})$. This contradicts the fact that z is a Nash equilibrium. Thus, $S_{x_i}(x) = \{i\}$ and $c_{z_i}(z) = \xi_i(z) \leq \xi_i(x_i, z_{-i}) = c_{x_i}(x_i, z_{-i}) = c_{x_i}(x)$. Moreover, using $c_{x_i}(z) = 0$, because $\ell_{x_i}(z) = 0$, we obtain $c_{x_i}(z) + c_{z_i}(z) \leq c_{x_i}(x) + c_{z_i}(x)$ as desired.

Case 2 is $S_{x_i}(x_i, z_{-i}) \subset S_{x_i}(x)$ and $i = \min S_{x_i}(x_i, z_{-i})$. Here, we obtain

$$c_{z_i}(z) = \xi_i(z) \leq \xi_i(x_i, z_{-i}) = c_{x_i}(x_i, z_{-i}) \leq c_{x_i}(x),$$

where the first inequality holds because z is a Nash equilibrium. The second inequality holds because Case 2 implies $\ell_{x_i}(x_i, z_{-j}) \leq \ell_{x_i}(x)$. We also get

$$c_{x_i}(z) = \sum_{j \in S_{x_i}(z)} \xi_j(z) \leq \sum_{j \in S_{x_i}(z)} \xi_j(z_i, z_{-j}) = 0.$$

This inequality is a result of (3.4), because in this case all players $j \in S_{x_i}(z)$ have a higher index $j > i$. Consequently, we have again $c_{x_i}(z) + c_{z_i}(z) \leq c_{x_i}(x) + c_{z_i}(x)$.

Finally, we examine Case 3 where the protocol returns $\xi_i(x_i, z_{-i}) = 0$ and thus for the Nash equilibrium z we have $c_{z_i}(z) = \xi_i(z) \leq \xi_i(x_i, z_{-i}) = 0$. Again, $c_{x_i}(z) + c_{z_i}(z) \leq c_{x_i}(x) + c_{z_i}(x)$. $\square$

3.3 An Optimal Protocol

Using the insights gained in the previous sections, we show that among all basic and separable protocols, the strong x-enforcing protocol gives rise to an optimal protocol simultaneously minimizing the price of anarchy and stability. Our main result involves the n-th harmonic number $\mathcal{H}_n = \sum_{i=1}^{n} \frac{1}{i}$.

THEOREM 3.11.

$$\min_{\Xi \in \mathcal{B}_n} PoA(\Xi) = \min_{\Xi \in \mathcal{B}_n} PoS(\Xi) = \min_{\Xi \in \mathcal{S}_n} PoA(\Xi)$$
$$= \min_{\Xi \in \mathcal{S}_n} PoS(\Xi) = \mathcal{H}_n.$$

We will prove the theorem by two subsequent lemmas. In the first lemma, we prove that $\mathcal{H}_n$ is a lower bound on the price of stability for every basic cost sharing protocol. We then continue by presenting an algorithm that returns for any scheduling model a strongly decharged outcome of cost at most $\mathcal{H}_n$ times the cost of an optimal outcome. Together with the strong x-enforcing protocol we conclude that the price of anarchy of the thus defined protocol is precisely $\mathcal{H}_n$.

LEMMA 3.12. *For basic cost sharing protocols on scheduling models with n players and non-decreasing cost functions, the price of stability is at least $\mathcal{H}_n$. This lower bounds holds even for models with unit demands.*

PROOF. Consider the scheduling model (N, M, d, c) with n players that have unit demand $d_i = 1$ for all $i \in N$ and n machines with cost functions as in Table 1.

Table 1: Cost functions for machines used in the proof of Lemma 3.12

ℓ	$c_{a_1}(\ell)$	$c_{a_2}(\ell)$	...	$c_{a_i}(\ell)$	...	$c_{a_n}(\ell)$
0	0	0	...	0	...	0
1	$1+\epsilon$	$\frac{1}{2}$	...	$\frac{1}{i}$	...	$\frac{1}{n}$
>1	$1+\epsilon$	n	...	n	...	n

for some small $\epsilon > 0$.

The only optimal outcome is clearly $y = (a_1, \ldots, a_1)$ with $C(y) = 1+\epsilon$. An outcome z can only be a Nash equilibrium if it is weakly decharged (Lemma 3.6). We show that the cheapest weakly decharged outcomes are those in which each machine is used by exactly one player, which all have the same cost as $x = (a_1, \ldots, a_n)$. It is easy to see that outcome x is decharged and with $C(x) = \sum_{i=1}^{n} \frac{1}{i} = \mathcal{H}_n$ this proves the lemma.

If in an outcome z some machine other than a_1 is used by multiple players, then $C(z) \geq n$, thus such outcomes are more expensive than x. If in outcome z multiple players use machine a_1, say k players, then there are at least $k-1$ unused machines and for the cheapest of these, say machine $\hat{a}$, we have $c_{\hat{a}}(1) \leq \frac{1}{k}$. Thus, z is not weakly decharged as

$$c_{a_1}(z) = 1 + \epsilon > 1 = \sum_{i \in S_{a_1}(z)} \frac{1}{k} \geq \sum_{i \in S_{a_1}(z)} \min_{b \in M} c_b(b, z_{-i}).$$

Algorithm 1 Find strongly decharged outcome x

1: $k \leftarrow 1$ {stepnumber}
2: $x^1 \leftarrow y$ {starts with optimal outcome y}
3: $t_i \leftarrow 0$ for all $i \in N$ {stores when a player was last moved}
4: **while** there are charged machines **do**
5: $a^k \leftarrow \text{argmax}\,\{c_a(x^k) : a \in M \text{ is charged}\}$ {select the most expensive charged machine}
6: **if** $\min\{c_b(b, x^k_{-i}) : b \in M\} = 0$ for $i = \min S_{a^k}(x^k)$ **then**
7: {i can move to cost-free machine, called *Zero-move*}
8: $i^k \leftarrow \min S_{a^k}(x^k)$ {select smallest player}
9: **else if** $\max\{t_i : i \in S_{a^k}(x^k)\} > 0$ **then**
10: {a player on a^k was moved before, called *Shuffle*}
11: $i^k \leftarrow \text{argmax}\,\{t_i : i \in S_{a^k}(x^k)\}$ {select last moved player}
12: **else**
13: {no foreign players on a^k, called *Kick-off*}
14: $i^k \leftarrow \min S_{a^k}(x^k)$ {select smallest player}
15: **end if**
16: $b^k \leftarrow \text{argmin}\,\{c_b(b, x^k_{-i^k}) : b \in M\}$ {select cheapest available machine}
17: $x^{k+1} \leftarrow (b^k, x^k_{-i^k})$ {move player}
18: $t_{i^k} \leftarrow k$ {store stepnumber}
19: $k \leftarrow k + 1$ {iterate}
20: **end while**
21: **return** $x \leftarrow x^k$

Altogether, only such outcomes in which all machines are used by exactly one player are cheap weakly-enforceable outcomes. □

While the previous Lemma showed that there sometimes are no weakly-enforceable outcomes cheaper than $\mathcal{H}_n$ times the cost of an optimal outcome, the following lemma shows that we always find strongly decharged outcomes of at most $\mathcal{H}_n$ times the cost of an optimal outcome.

LEMMA 3.13. *Any scheduling model (N, M, d, c) with an optimal outcome y has a strongly decharged outcome x with $C(x) \leq \mathcal{H}_n \cdot C(y) = \sum_{k=1}^{n} \frac{1}{k} \cdot C(y)$.*

PROOF. The desired outcome x is found by Algorithm 1. The algorithm takes as input an optimal outcome y. In each cycle k of the algorithm's main loop (lines 4 - 20), a player i^k on the most expensive charged machine a^k is selected (line 5) and moved to the cheapest available machine b^k (lines 16, 17). If possible, the algorithm selects a player who can be moved to a cost-free machine, this is called *Zero-move* (line 6). Otherwise, it selects a player that has been moved before in a last-in/first-out scheme which is maintained through the variables t_i that store the cycle in which each player was last moved. Such moves are called *Shuffles* (line 9). If neither a Zero-move nor a Shuffle is possible, the smallest player on the machine is selected, which is called *Kick-off* (line 12). The algorithm terminates when no charged machines are left.

First, we show that the algorithm terminates. To this end, observe that Shuffles are only performed when Zero-moves are not possible. Hence, if in cycle k a Shuffle is performed, the following inequalities hold.

$$\min_{b \in M} c_b(b, x^k_{-j}) > 0 \quad \text{for all } j \in S_{a^k}(x^k). \tag{3.16}$$

We now consider two cases. For $|S_{a^k}(x^k)| = 1$, we obtain

$$c_{a^k}(x^k) > \min_{b \in M} c_b(b, x^k_{-i^k}) \tag{3.17}$$
$$= c_{b^k}(b^k, x^k_{-i^k}) = c_{b^k}(x^{k+1}), \tag{3.18}$$

where (3.17) follows because a^k is charged in x^k. Equality (3.18) follows since Algorithm 1 moves i^k to the cheapest available machine.

If $|S_{a^k}(x^k)| > 1$, then we obtain

$$c_{a^k}(x^k) \geq \sum_{j \in S_{a_k}(x^k)} \min_{b \in M} c_b(b, x^k_{-j}) \tag{3.19}$$
$$> \min_{b \in M} c_b(b, x^k_{-i^k}) \tag{3.20}$$
$$= c_{b^k}(b^k, x^k_{-i^k}) = c_{b^k}(x^{k+1}),$$

where (3.19) is valid because a^k is charged in x^k. The second inequality (3.20) holds because of (3.16) and the equalities follow as above. In both cases, a Shuffle moves the player to a strictly cheaper machine. To see that the algorithm terminates, we will now follow some player i over the course of the algorithm. Each Zero-move and each Shuffle take her to a strictly cheaper machine. If the player is moved in cycle k and is next moved by a Shuffle in cycle l, the cost of her machine $x_i^{k+1} = x_i^l$ may increase in the meantime as other players arrive on that machine. The algorithm assures by its last-in/first-out mechanism that these other players have been moved again before the Shuffle in cycle l and consequently the cost has decreased to the original level $c_{x_i^{k+1}}(x^{k+1}) \geq c_{x_i^l}(x^l)$. Since only machines with positive costs can be charged, this implies that after a Zero-move, the player will never again be considered for Shuffles. Hence, a player can be moved by at most one Kick-off, afterwards a sequence of Shuffles and thereafter only Zero-moves. The sequence of Shuffles is finite because each Shuffle takes the player to a strictly cheaper machine. Once the player has has been moved by a Zero-move, further Zero-moves are only possible if in between some other player arrives on the player's machine via a Kick-off or a Shuffle, but again this is only finitely often possible. Altogether, each player can only be moved finitely often and thus the algorithm terminates after a finite number of cycles.

To complete the proof, we show that the final outcome x has cost $C(x) \leq \mathcal{H}_n \cdot C(y)$. The concept of this final part of the proof is that in outcome x the cost of every used machine is determined by the player who has last moved there or, if there are no such players, the home players. For this, some new notation is needed. Let $p_i, i \in N$, correspond to the position (by index) of player i on her optimal machine y_i, i.e., on any machine a we have $p_j = 1$ for player $j = \max S_a(y)$, $p_{j'} = 2$ for $j' = \max(S_a(y) \backslash \{j\})$ and so on. Consequently, when some player i performs her Kick-off in cycle k, there are p_i players sharing her machine $a^k = y_i$ at that moment and she is the smallest of them. We obtain for machine b^k

that she is moved to

$$c_{b^k}(x^{k+1}) = c_{b^k}(b^k, x^k_{-i}) = \min_{b\in M} c_b(b, x^k_{-i})$$

$$\leq \frac{1}{p_i} \cdot \sum_{j\in S_{a^k}(x^k)} \min_{b\in M} c_b(b, x^k_{-j}) \tag{3.21}$$

$$\leq \frac{1}{p_i} \cdot c_{a^k}(x^k) \tag{3.22}$$

$$\leq \frac{1}{p_i} \cdot c_{y_i}(y), \tag{3.23}$$

where the first inequality (3.21) is valid because i is the smallest of the p_i players on machine a^k in step k, the second inequality (3.22) holds because a^k is charged in x^k and the last inequality (3.23) holds because there are no foreign players on $a^k = y_i$ and hence $\ell_{a^k}(x^k) \leq \ell_{a^k}(y) = \ell_{y_i}(y)$.

Since Shuffles and Zero-moves assign player i to cheaper machines, after her last move in cycle k', she is on machine $b^{k'}$ at cost $c_{b^{k'}}(x^{k'}) \leq \frac{1}{p_i} \cdot c_{y_i}(y)$. Altogether, in the final outcome x, the cost of a machine $a \in M$ to which players have been moved is determined by the last player who was moved there, that is, $i_a := \text{argmax}\,\{t_i : i \in S_a(x)\}$. We thus obtain $c_a(x) \leq \frac{1}{p_{i_a}} \cdot c_{y_{i_a}}(y)$. For machines $a \in M$ that are used in x but where no player has been moved, the player $i_a := \max S_a(y)$ with $p_{i_a} = 1$ is still on machine a. In this case, the cost is bounded from above by $c_a(x) \leq c_a(y) = \frac{1}{p_{i_a}} \cdot c_{y_{i_a}}(y)$. Unused machines $a \in M$ have cost $c_a(x) = 0$. Altogether, we obtain $c_a(x) = \frac{1}{p_{i_a}} \cdot c_{y_{i_a}}(y)$ for all $a \in M$ with $\ell_a(x) > 0$, and $c_a(x) = 0$ for all $a \in M$ with $\ell_a(x) = 0$. This yields the desired bound for the cost of outcome x, because now every used machine $a \in M$ has a unique player i_a that determines the machine's cost. We obtain

$$C(x) = \sum_{a\in M} c_a(x) \leq \sum_{\substack{a\in M\\ \ell_a(x)>0}} \frac{1}{p_{i_a}} \cdot c_{y_{i_a}}(y) \leq \sum_{i\in N} \frac{1}{p_i} \cdot c_{y_i}(y)$$

$$\leq \sum_{a\in M} \mathcal{H}_{p_{\max}} \cdot c_a(y) = \mathcal{H}_{p_{\max}} \cdot C(y) \leq \mathcal{H}_n \cdot C(y),$$

where $p_{\max} := \max\,\{|S_a(y)| : a \in M\}$.

Observe that the bound for the price of anarchy obtained here can be much lower than $\mathcal{H}_n$ for scheduling models that have optimal outcomes, where the players are scattered over the machines and where therefore $p_{\max}$ is smaller than n. ☐

Remark 3.14. While Lemma 3.13 shows that an optimal outcome can be turned into a strongly decharged outcome of cost at most $\mathcal{H}_n$ times the cost of an optimal outcome, this holds true more generally: Algorithm 1 turns every outcome into a strongly decharged outcome with a cost increase of a factor at most $\mathcal{H}_n$. This may be useful if the computation of an optimal outcome is not possible in polynomial time. Still, Algorithm 1 does not run in polynomial time and this issue deserves further attention.

3.4 Non-Decreasing Cost per Unit

In this section we require that the cost functions are non-negative, non-decreasing and the per-unit costs $\frac{c(x)}{\ell(x)}$ are non-decreasing with respect to the load $\ell(x)$. Such functions are still quite rich as they contain non-negative, non-decreasing and convex functions.

We introduce the *opt-enforcing protocol* for which we prove a price of anarchy of 1. The intuition behind this protocol is similar to the x-enforcing protocols: make all undesired outcomes unstable by charging some player a very high price.

Definition 3.15. (opt-enforcing protocol) Given a scheduling model (N, M, d, c) the *opt-enforcing protocol* takes as input an optimal outcome y. We again denote for any outcome z and machine a the set of foreign players on a by $S^1_a(z) = \{i \in S_a(z)\backslash S_a(y)\}$. Then, the opt-enforcing protocol assigns the cost sharing methods

$$\xi_i(z) := \begin{cases} d_i \cdot \dfrac{c_{z_i}(z)}{\ell_{z_i}(z)}, \text{ if } S^1_{z_i} = \emptyset & \text{(3.24a)}\\ c_{z_i}(z), \text{ if } S^1_{z_i} \neq \emptyset \text{ and } i = \min S^1_{z_i}(z) & \text{(3.24b)}\\ 0, \text{ else.} & \text{(3.24c)} \end{cases}$$

Under the opt-enforcing protocol, the players share the cost proportional to their job weights on all machines without foreign players. On machines with foreign players, the foreign player with the smallest index pays the entire cost of the machine.

THEOREM 3.16. *The opt-enforcing protocol is separable and has a price of anarchy of* 1.

PROOF. Budget balance and separability are clear from the definition of the private cost functions. For stability it can easily be verified that for an instance (N, M, d, c) the optimal outcome y is a Nash equilibrium. We only proof the bound on the price of anarchy, showing that all Nash equilibria x are optimal outcomes using the Nash inequalities $\xi_i(x) \leq \xi_i(y_i, x_{-i})$ for any $i \in N$. Two cases are to be considered for such a machine y_i: either it hosts foreign players $S^1_{y_i}(x)$ or $S^1_{y_i}(x) = \emptyset$. If there are foreign players on y_i, then one of them will pay for the entire cost there and hence (3.24c) gives $\xi_i(x) \leq \xi_i(y_i, x_{-i}) = 0$. If there are no foreign players on y_i, then $d_i \leq \ell_{y_i}(y_i, x_{-i}) \leq \ell_{y_i}(y)$ yields

$$\frac{c_{y_i}(y_i, x_{-i})}{\ell_{y_i}(y_i, x_{-i})} \leq \frac{c_{y_i}(y)}{\ell_{y_i}(y)},$$

because the cost per unit is non-decreasing. Plugging this into (3.24a) we have $\xi_i(x) \leq \xi_i(y_i, x_{-i}) \leq \xi_i(y)$. In both cases $\xi_i(x) \leq \xi_i(y)$ for all $i \in N$ and thus

$$C(x) = \sum_{i\in N} \xi_i(x) \leq \sum_{i\in N} \xi_i(y) = C(y)$$

which implies that every Nash equilibrium x is also an optimal outcome. ☐

4. UNIFORM PROTOCOLS

The separable protocols that we introduced so far were always tailored to some desirable outcome, either an enforceable outcome or even an optimal outcome. Since uniform protocols need to assign cost sharing methods independent of the set M, they cannot be based on specific outcomes. We show in this section that uniformity leads in general to an unbounded price of anarchy. Only for games in which the demands are integer multiples of each other we introduce the semi-ordered protocol that gives a price of anarchy of n. The question of $\min_{\xi\in\mathcal{U}_n} PoS(\xi)$ remains open.

4.1 Lower Bound

THEOREM 4.1. *There is no uniform protocol for which the price of anarchy has an upper bound. This holds even for models with at most* 3 *players,* 3 *machines and non-decreasing costs per unit.*

PROOF. The essence of uniform protocols is that adding machines to or removing them from the model does not change the cost shares of players using a certain machine, as long as the player set and the weight vector remain the same. This motivates the definition of cost share functions $\hat{\xi}_i$ that return the private cost ξ_i of player i as a function of the machine a that she uses and the set of players $S \subseteq N$ sharing the machine.

$$\hat{\xi}_i(a, S) := \xi_i(x) \, \forall \, a \in M, S \subseteq N, i \in S, x \in M^n : S_a(x) = S. \tag{4.1}$$

Nash equilibria can be expressed via cost share functions as follows. For all $i \in N, a \in M$ it holds that

$$\hat{\xi}_i(x_i, S_{x_i}(x)) \leq \hat{\xi}_i(a, S_a(x) \cup \{i\}). \tag{4.2}$$

For the proof of the theorem, we propose a number of scheduling models and show that for any uniform cost sharing protocol at least one of these models has a Nash equilibrium of more than q times the cost of an optimal outcome for arbitrary $q \geq 2$. Throughout the entire proof, the player set will always be $N = \{1, 2, 3\}$ with weights $d = (4, 3, 2)$. The machines will be a subset of $M = \{a_1, \dots, a_7\}$ with cost functions as outlined in Table 2.

Table 2: Cost functions used in proof of Theorem 4.1

ℓ	$c_{a_1}(\ell)$	$c_{a_2}(\ell)$	$c_{a_3}(\ell)$	$c_{a_4}(\ell)$	$c_{a_5}(\ell)$	$c_{a_6}(\ell)$	$c_{a_7}(\ell)$
0	0	0	0	0	0	0	0
2	0	0	0	0	0	q^2	0
3	0	0	0	q^3	0	q^4	0
4	1	q	1	$2q^3$	q^3	$2q^4$	q^4
5	2	q^3	q^5		$2q^3$		
6	q^3	q^5					
7	q^4						

First, consider the model with machines $M_1 = \{a_1, a_2\}$ and their respective cost functions. The optimal outcome $y_1 = (a_2, a_1, a_1)$ has cost $C(y_1) = q + 2$, while the outcome $x_1 = (a_1, a_2, a_2)$ has cost $C(x_1) = q^3 + 1$. Either x_1 is a Nash equilibrium and hence the protocol has a price of anarchy greater than q or or one of the three players can reduce her private cost by choosing a different machine, which results by (4.2) in the following three cases.

a) $\hat{\xi}_1(a_2, \{1, 2, 3\}) < \hat{\xi}_1(a_1, \{1\}) = 1$. In this case, consider the model with machines $M_2 = \{a_2, a_3\}$. The optimal outcome $y_2 = (a_3, a_2, a_2)$ with $C(y_2) = q^3 + 1$ is not a Nash equilibrium and due to stability some other outcome x with cost $C(x) \geq q^5$ has to be a Nash equilibrium.

b) $\hat{\xi}_2(a_1, \{1, 2\}) < \hat{\xi}_2(a_2, \{2, 3\}) \leq q^3$. In this case, consider $M_3 = \{a_1, a_2, a_4\}$. The optimal outcome $y_3 = (a_1, a_2, a_4)$ has cost $C(y_3) = 1$, while the outcome $x_3 = (a_2, a_1, a_4)$ has cost $C(x_3) = q$. Either x_3 is a Nash equilibrium or, again, one of the players can reduce her private cost by choosing a different machine, which leads to the following cases.

   b.1) $\hat{\xi}_1(a_1, \{1, 2\}) < \hat{\xi}_1(a_2, \{1\}) = q$. This contradicts b), that is $\hat{\xi}_1(a_1, \{1, 2\}) = c_1(d_1 + d_2) - \hat{\xi}_2(a_1, \{1, 2\}) > q^4 - q^3 > q$.

   b.2) $\hat{\xi}_1(a_4, \{1, 3\}) < \hat{\xi}_1(a_1, \{1\}) = q$. In this case, consider $M_4 = \{a_2, a_4, a_5\}$. The optimal outcome $y_4 = (a_2, a_5, a_4)$ with $C(y_4) = q$ is not a Nash equilibrium and due to stability some other outcome x with cost $C(x) \geq q^3$ has to be a Nash equilibrium.

   b.3) Players 2 and 3 cannot reduce their private cost as $\xi_2(x_3) = c_{a_1}(x_3) = 0$ and $\xi_3(x_3) = c_{a_4}(x_3) = 0$.

c) $\hat{\xi}_3(a_1, \{1, 3\}) < \hat{\xi}_3(a_2, \{2, 3\}) \leq q^3$. In this case, consider $M_5 = \{a_1, a_2, a_6\}$. The optimal outcome $y_5 = (a_2, a_1, a_1)$ has cost $C(y_5) = q + 1$, while the outcome $x_5 = (a_1, a_2, a_6)$ has cost $C(x_5) = q^2 + 1$. Either x_5 is a Nash equilibrium or, again, one of the players can reduce her private cost by choosing a different machine.

   c.1) $\hat{\xi}_1(a_2, \{1, 2\}) < \hat{\xi}_1(a_1, \{1\}) = 1$. In this case, consider again $M_3 = \{a_1, a_2, a_4\}$. The optimal outcome $y_3 = (a_1, a_2, a_4)$ with $C(y_3) = 1$ is not a Nash equilibrium and due to stability some other outcome x with cost $C(x) \geq q$ has to be a Nash equilibrium.

   c.2) $\hat{\xi}_1(a_6, \{1, 3\}) < \hat{\xi}_1(a_1, \{1\}) = 1$. In this case, consider $M_6 = \{a_3, a_5, a_6\}$. The optimal outcome $y_6 = (a_3, a_5, a_6)$ with $C(y_6) = q^2 + 1$ is not a Nash equilibrium and due to stability some other outcome x with cost $C(x) \geq q^3$ has to be a Nash equilibrium.

   c.3) Player 2 cannot reduce her private cost because $\xi_2(x_5) = c_{a_2}(x_5) = 0$.

   c.4) $\hat{\xi}_3(a_1, \{1, 3\}) < \hat{\xi}_3(a_6, \{3\}) = q^2$. In this case, consider $M_7 = \{a_1, a_6, a_7\}$. The optimal outcome $y_7 = (a_1, a_7, a_6)$ with $C(y_7) = q^2 + 1$ is not a Nash equilibrium and due to stability some other outcome x with cost $C(x) \geq q^3$ has to be a Nash equilibrium.

   c.5) $\hat{\xi}_3(a_2, \{2, 3\}) < \hat{\xi}_3(a_6, \{3\}) = q^2$. This extends the original assumption from c) $\hat{\xi}_3(a_1, \{1, 3\}) < \hat{\xi}_3(a_2, \{2, 3\}) < q^2$ and therefore implies c.4).

Altogether, every uniform cost sharing protocol allows in at least one of the analyzed cases a Nash equilibrium of at least q times the cost of an optimal outcome for an arbitrary $q \geq 2$. Consequently, the price of anarchy is not bounded. □

4.2 Models with Restricted Weights

Although uniform protocols in general do not allow a bound on the price of anarchy, the following class of games permits uniform cost sharing protocols with a bounded price of anarchy. We assume that the player's weights are either uniform, i.e. $d_1 = \ldots = d_n$, or they are multiples of each other. In the following, we propose a semi-ordered protocol that a has a price of anarchy of at most n for such games. In this section, we assume that the players are indexed with their weights in non-increasing order: $d_1 \geq d_2 \geq \ldots \geq d_n$. The semi-ordered protocol lets the players one after the other choose a machine and lets them pay only for the additional cost they cause on that machine, thus making the choice of a player i independent of the choices of all players $j > i$.

Definition 4.2. (Semi-ordered Protocol) The semi-ordered protocol assigns for all $i \in N$

$$\xi_i(x) := c_{x_i}\Bigg(\sum_{j \in S_{x_i}(x): j \leq i} d_j \Bigg) - c_{x_i}\Bigg(\sum_{j \in S_{x_i}(x): j < i} d_j \Bigg). \tag{4.3}$$

THEOREM 4.3. *The semi-ordered protocol is uniform and its price of anarchy is at most n for instances, where the players' weights are multiples of each other, i.e.* $d_i = q_i \cdot d_{i+i}$ *for all* $i < n$ *and some* $q_i \in \mathbb{N}$.

PROOF. Budget balance, separability and uniformity of the cost sharing methods are clear. A Nash equilibrium can be found by asking the players in the order of their index to choose a machine that minimizes their private cost considering the choice of all previous players. For proving the bound on the price of anarchy, consider a model (N, M, d, c) which fulfills the restriction on the players' weights. Suppose y is an optimal outcome and x a Nash equilibrium. First, we show that $\xi_i(x) \leq \max_{j \leq i} \xi_j(y)$ holds for all $i \in N$, which is motivated by the idea that a player can always choose a machine that she or one of the larger players had chosen in the optimal outcome. To this end, fix player $i \in N$. On some machine $a \in \{y_1, \ldots, y_{i-1}\}$ there is in outcome x less load from the first $i-1$ players than in the optimal outcome y from the first i players. Due to the restriction on the players' weights this difference in load on machine a has to be at least d_i yielding

$$\sum_{j \in S_a(x):j<i} d_j + d_i \leq \sum_{j \in S_a(y):j \leq i} d_j.$$

Also, there is a player $k \leq i$ (hence $d_k \geq d_i$), $k \in S_a(y)$ who in outcome y uses machine a and for whom due to the weight restrictions

$$\sum_{j \in S_a(y):j<k} d_j \leq \sum_{j \in S_a(x):j<i} d_j < \sum_{j \in S_a(x):j<i} d_j + d_i \leq \sum_{j \in S_a(y):j \leq k} d_j.$$

Combining the above inequalities with (4.3) yields

$$\begin{aligned}
\xi_i(x) &\leq \xi_i(a, x_{-i}) \\
&= c_a\Big(\sum_{j \in S_a(x):j<i} d_j + d_i\Big) - c_a\Big(\sum_{j \in S_a(x):j<i} d_j\Big) \\
&\leq c_a\Big(\sum_{j \in S_a(y):j \leq k} d_j\Big) - c_a\Big(\sum_{j \in S_a(y):j<k} d_j\Big) \\
&= \xi_k(y) \leq \max_{j \leq i} \xi_j(y).
\end{aligned}$$

This implies:

$$C(x) = \sum_{i \in N} \xi_i(x) \leq \sum_{i \in N} \max_{j \leq i} \xi_j(y) \leq n \cdot \max_{j \in N} \xi_j(y) \leq n \cdot C(y)$$

proving the claim. □

5. REFERENCES

[1] H. Ackermann, H. Röglin, and B. Vöcking. Pure Nash equilibria in player-specific and weighted congestion games. *Theor. Comput. Sci.*, 410(17):1552–1563, 2009.

[2] S. Aland, D. Dumrauf, M. Gairing, B. Monien, and F. Schoppmann. Exact price of anarchy for polynomial congestion games. In *Proc. of STACS*, pages 218–229, 2006.

[3] E. Anshelevich, A. Dasgupta, J. Kleinberg, É. Tardos, T. Wexler, and T. Roughgarden. The price of stability for network design with fair cost allocation. *SIAM J. Comput.*, 38(4):1602–1623, 2008.

[4] B. Awerbuch, Y. Azar, and A. Epstein. The price of routing unsplittable flow. In *Proc. of STOC*, pages 57–66. ACM, 2005.

[5] K. Bhawalkar, M. Gairing, and T. Roughgarden. Weighted congestion games: Price of anarchy, universal worst-case examples, and tightness. In *Proc. of ESA*, pages 17–28. Springer, 2010.

[6] I. Caragiannis. Efficient coordination mechanisms for unrelated machine scheduling. In *Proc. of SODA*, pages 815–824, 2009.

[7] H.-L. Chen and T. Roughgarden. Network design with weighted players. *Theor. Comput. Syst.*, 45(2):302–324, 2009.

[8] H.-L. Chen, T. Roughgarden, and G. Valiant. Designing network protocols for good equilibria. *SIAM J. Comput.*, 39(5):1799–1832, 2010.

[9] G. Christodoulou and E. Koutsoupias. The price of anarchy of finite congestion games. In *Proc. of STOC*, pages 67–73, 2005.

[10] G. Christodoulou, E. Koutsoupias, and A. Nanavati. Coordination mechanisms. In *Proc. of ICALP*, pages 45–56. Springer, 2004.

[11] J. R. Correa, A. S. Schulz, and N. E. Stier-Moses. Selfish routing in capacitated networks. *Math. of Oper. Res.*, 29:961–976, 2004.

[12] E. Even-Dar, A. Kesselman, and Y. Mansour. Convergence time to Nash equilibrium in load balancing. *ACM Trans. Algorithms*, 3(3):32, 2007.

[13] D. Fotakis, S. Kontogiannis, E. Koutsoupias, M. Mavronicolas, and P. Spirakis. The structure and complexity of Nash equilibria for a selfish routing game. In *Proc. of ICALP*, pages 123 – 134, 2002.

[14] M. Gairing, B. Monien, and K. Tiemann. Routing (un-) splittable flow in games with player-specific linear latency functions. In *Proc of ICALP*, pages 501–512, 2006.

[15] S. Ieong, R. McGrew, E. Nudelman, Y. Shoham, and Q. Sun. Fast and compact: A simple class of congestion games. In *Proc. AAAI*, pages 489–494, 2005.

[16] N. Immorlica, L. Li, V. Mirrokni, and A. Schulz. Coordination mechanisms for selfish scheduling. *Theor. Comput. Sci.*, 410(17):1589–1598, 2009.

[17] E. Koutsoupias and C. H. Papadimitriou. Worst-case equilibria. In *STACS*, pages 404–413, 1999.

[18] I. Milchtaich. Congestion games with player-specific payoff functions. *Games Econom. Behav.*, 13(1):111 – 124, 1996.

[19] M. Osborne and A. Rubinstein. *A Course in Game Theory*. MIT Press, 1994.

[20] R. Rosenthal. A class of games possessing pure-strategy Nash equilibria. *Inter. J. Game Theory*, 2(1):65–67, 1973.

[21] T. Roughgarden. The price of anarchy is independent of the network topology. *Journal of Computer and System Sciences*, 67:341–364, 2002.

[22] T. Roughgarden. *Selfish Routing and the Price of Anarchy*. The MIT Press, 2005.

[23] T. Roughgarden and É. Tardos. How bad is selfish routing? *J. ACM*, 49(2):236–259, 2002.

[24] R. Srikant. *The Mathematics of Internet Congestion Control*. Birkhäuser Boston, 2003.

Non-Price Equilibria in Markets of Discrete Goods

[Extended Abstract] *

Avinatan Hassidim
Google, Tel-Aviv

Haim Kaplan†
Google, Tel Aviv
and
School of Computer Science
Tel Aviv University

Yishay Mansour‡
School of Computer Science
Tel Aviv University

Noam Nisan§
School of Computer Science
and Engineering
Hebrew University of
Jerusalem

ABSTRACT

The basic question that Economics deals with is how to "best" allocate scarce resources. The basic answer is that trade can improve everyone's welfare, and will lead to a market equilibrium: a vector of resource prices that "clear the market" and lead to an efficient allocation. Indeed, Arrow and Debreu and much further work show that such market equilibria exist in general settings.

Or do they...? An underlying assumption for the existence of price-equilibria is always some notion of "convexity". However, markets of discrete items – arguably the main object of study in computerized markets and auctions – are only rarely "convex" and indeed in most cases do *not* have any price-based equilibria. What can we predict to happen in such markets? Will these outcomes be efficient in any sense? In this paper we approach these questions by viewing the market as a game, and studying its Nash-equilibria.

We study a very basic model of a market where a single seller is selling m heterogeneous indivisible items to n buyers, where buyers may have arbitrary valuations over bundles of items. The usual notion of price-based equilibrium in this model is called a Walrasian equilibrium, but these only rarely exist – exactly when the associated integer program has no integrality gap. We analyze this market situation as a *game* where each player announces a bid for each item and the high bidder on each item gets it and pays his bid. We present the following results in this setting:

- Walrasian equilibria of the associated market are in 1-1 correspondence with pure Nash equilibria of the associated game. In particular, pure equilibria always maximize social welfare (a "first welfare theorem").
- While existence of mixed Nash equilibria is not trivial since buyers have a continuum of strategies and discontinuous utilities, we show that they do exist (for some tie breaking rule). We consider several basic cases that do not have any price equilibrium and find mixed Nash equilibria for them.
- We analyze the social welfare achieved by mixed Nash equilibria. We exhibit examples with a loss ("price of anarchy") factor of $\Omega(\sqrt{m})$, bound the loss by $O(m)$ in general, and by a factor of 2 for the sub-modular case. This is also generalized to Bayesian settings.

Categories and Subject Descriptors

J.4 [**Computer Applications**]: Social and behavioral Sciences

General Terms

Theory

Keywords

Markets, Nash Equilibrium

*A full version of this paper is available at `http://arxiv.org/abs/1103.3950`

†This research was supported in part by a grant from the Israel Science Foundation (ISF) and by a grant from United States-Israel Binational Science Foundation (BSF).

‡This research was supported in part by a grant from the Israeli Science Foundation (ISF), by a grant from United States-Israel Binational Science Foundation (BSF), by a grant from the Israeli Ministry of Science (MoS), and by the Google Inter-university center for Electronic Markets and Auctions.

§This research was supported by a grant from the Israeli Science Foundation (ISF) and by the Google Inter-university center for Electronic Markets and Auctions.

EC'11, June 5–9, 2011, San Jose, California, USA.
ACM 978-1-4503-0261-6/11/06.

An Optimization-Based Framework for Automated Market-Making

Jacob Abernethy
EECS Department
UC Berkeley
jake@cs.berkeley.edu

Yiling Chen
School of Engineering and Applied Sciences
Harvard University
yiling@eecs.harvard.edu

Jennifer Wortman Vaughan
Computer Science Department
UCLA
jenn@cs.ucla.edu

ABSTRACT

We propose a general framework for the design of securities markets over combinatorial or infinite state or outcome spaces. The framework enables the design of computationally efficient markets tailored to an arbitrary, yet relatively small, space of securities with bounded payoff. We prove that any market satisfying a set of intuitive conditions must price securities via a convex cost function, which is constructed via conjugate duality. Rather than deal with an exponentially large or infinite outcome space directly, our framework only requires optimization over a convex hull. By reducing the problem of automated market making to convex optimization, where many efficient algorithms exist, we arrive at a range of new polynomial-time pricing mechanisms for various problems. We demonstrate the advantages of this framework with the design of some particular markets. We also show that by relaxing the convex hull we can gain computational tractability without compromising the market institution's bounded budget.

Categories and Subject Descriptors

J.4 [**Social and Behavioral Sciences**]: Economics; G.1.6 [**Numerical Analysis**]: Optimization

General Terms

Algorithms, Economics, Theory

1. INTRODUCTION

Securities markets play a fundamental role in economics and finance. A securities market offers a set of *contingent securities* whose payoffs depend on the future state of the world. For example, an Arrow-Debreu security pays \$1 if a particular state of the world is reached and \$0 otherwise [3, 4]. Consider an Arrow-Debreu security that will pay off in the event that a category 4 or higher hurricane passes through Florida in 2011. A Florida resident who worries about his home being damaged might buy this security as a form of insurance to hedge his risk; if there is a hurricane powerful enough to damage his home, he will be compensated. Additionally, a risk-neutral trader who has reason to believe that the probability of a category 4 or higher hurricane landing in Florida in 2011 is p should be willing to buy this security at any price below p or (short) sell it at any price above p to capitalize his information. For this reason, the market price of the security can be viewed as the traders' collective estimate of how likely it is that a powerful hurricane will occur. Securities markets thus have dual functions: *risk allocation* and *information aggregation*

Insurance contracts, options, futures, and many other financial derivatives are examples of contingent securities. A securities market primarily focused on information aggregation is often referred to as a *prediction market*. The forecasts of prediction markets have proved to be accurate in a variety of domains [5, 24, 32]. While our work builds on ideas from prediction market design [2, 10, 28], our framework can be applied to any contingent securities.

A securities market is said to be *complete* if it offers $|\mathcal{O}|-1$ independent securities over a set $\mathcal{O}$ of mutually exclusive and exhaustive states of the world, which we refer to as *outcomes* [3, 4, 25]. For example, a prediction market with n Arrow-Debreu securities for n outcomes is complete. In a complete securities market without transaction fees, a trader may bet on any combination of the securities, allowing him to hedge any possible risk he may have. It is generally assumed that the trader may *short sell* a contract, betting against the given outcome; in a market with short selling, the nth security is not strictly necessary, as a trader can substitute the purchase of this contract by short selling all others. Furthermore, traders can change the market prices to reflect any valid probability distribution over the outcome space, allowing them to reveal any belief. Completeness therefore provides expressiveness for both risk allocation and information aggregation.

Unfortunately, completeness is not always achievable. In many real-world settings, the outcome space is exponentially large or even infinite. For instance, a competition among n candidates results in an outcome space of $n!$ rank orders, while the future price of a stock has an infinite outcome space, namely $\mathbb{R}_+$. In such situations operating a complete securities market is not practical for two reasons: (a) humans are notoriously bad at estimating small probabilities and (b) it is computationally intractable to manage such a large set of contracts. Instead, it is natural to offer a smaller set of structured securities. For example, rather than offer a security corresponding to each rank ordering,

EC'11, June 5–9, 2011, San Jose, California, USA.

in *pair betting* a market maker offers securities of the form "\$1 if candidate A beats candidate B" [11]. There has been a surge of recent research examining the tractability of running standard prediction market mechanisms (such as the popular Logarithmic Market Scoring Rule (LMSR) market maker [20]) over combinatorial outcome spaces by limiting the space of available securities [29]. While this line of research has led to a few positive results [1, 13, 14, 19], it has led more often to hardness results [12, 14] or to markets with undesirable properties such as unbounded loss of the market institution [16].

In this paper, we propose a general framework to design *automated market makers* for securities markets. An automated market maker is a market institution that adaptively sets prices for each security and is always willing to accept trades at these prices. Unlike previous research aimed at finding a space of securities that can be efficiently priced using an existing market maker like LMSR, we start with an arbitrary space of securities and design a *new* market maker tailored to this space. Our framework is therefore extremely general and includes both the LMSR and Quad-SCPM [2] market makers.

We take an axiomatic approach. Given a relatively small space of securities with bounded payoff, we define a set of intuitive conditions that a reasonable market maker should satisfy. We prove that a market maker satisfying these conditions must price securities via a convex potential function (the *cost function*), and that the space of reachable security prices must be precisely the convex hull of the payoff vectors for each outcome (that is, the set of vectors, one per outcome, denoting the payoff for each security if that outcome occurs). We then incorporate ideas from online convex optimization [22, 31] to define a convex cost function in terms of an optimization over this convex hull; the vector of prices is chosen as the optimizer of this convex objective. With this framework, instead of dealing with the exponentially large or infinite outcome space, we only need to deal with the lower-dimensional convex hull. The problem of automated market making is reduced to the problem of convex optimization, for which we have many efficient techniques to leverage.

To demonstrate the advantages of our framework, we provide two new computationally efficient markets. The first market can efficiently price *subset bets* on permutations, which are known to be #P-hard to price using LMSR [12]. The second market can be used to price bets on the landing location of an object on a sphere.

Finally, for situations where the convex hull cannot be efficiently represented, we show that we can relax the convex hull to gain computational tractability without compromising the market maker's bounded budget. This allows us to provide a computationally efficient market maker for the aforementioned pair betting, which is also known to be #P-hard to price using LMSR [12]. In addition, this relaxation could potentially allow the market maker to charge transaction fees so that the depth of the market can be dynamically increased as the number of trades increases. This desirable property is discussed in Othman et al. [28] who proposed a corresponding market that extends the LMSR; utilizing our techniques for this purpose is left for future work.

This paper builds upon intuitions from earlier work [10] exploring the striking mathematical connections between complete, cost function based prediction markets and no-regret learning and online convex optimization. In this paper, we pursue a general convex optimization framework for pricing an arbitrary set of securities over a potentially very large outcome space. Agrawal et al. [2] and Peters et al. [30] also use convex optimization for automated market making. In addition to only considering complete markets, they formulate the convex optimization quite differently – their formulation is for limit orders and does not explicitly make the connection with conjugate duality as our framework does. To the best of our knowledge, this paper is the first work on designing markets that are tailored to the *incomplete* security spaces without explicitly reasoning over a large outcome space.

2. PRELIMINARIES

A simple cost function based market maker [9, 10, 20, 21] offers $|\mathcal{O}|$ Arrow-Debreu securities, each corresponding to a potential outcome. The market maker determines how much each security should cost using a differentiable *cost function*, $C : \mathbb{R}^{|\mathcal{O}|} \to \mathbb{R}$, which is simply a potential function specifying the amount of money currently wagered in the market as a function of the number of shares of each security that have been purchased. If $q_{\mathfrak{o}}$ is the number of shares of security $\mathfrak{o}$ currently held by traders, and a trader would like to purchase a bundle of $r_{\mathfrak{o}}$ shares for each security $\mathfrak{o} \in \mathcal{O}$ (where some $r_{\mathfrak{o}}$ could be zero or even negative, representing a sale), the trader must pay $C(\mathbf{q}+\mathbf{r}) - C(\mathbf{q})$ to the market maker. The instantaneous price of security $\mathfrak{o}$ (that is, the price per share of an infinitely small portion of a security) is then $\partial C(\mathbf{q})/\partial q_{\mathfrak{o}}$, and is denoted $p_{\mathfrak{o}}(\mathbf{q})$.

The market designer is free to choose any differentiable cost function C that satisfies a few basic properties. First, it must be the case that for every $\mathfrak{o} \in \mathcal{O}$ and every $\mathbf{q} \in \mathbb{R}^{|\mathcal{O}|}$, $p_{\mathfrak{o}}(\mathbf{q}) \geq 0$. This ensures that the price of a security is never negative. Second, assuming short sells are allowed, if the market designer wishes to prevent arbitrage, it must be the case that for every $\mathbf{q} \in \mathbb{R}^{|\mathcal{O}|}$, $\sum_{\mathfrak{o}\in\mathcal{O}} p_{\mathfrak{o}}(\mathbf{q}) = 1$. That is, the sum of the instantaneous prices of the securities must always be 1. If the prices summed to something less than (respectively, greater than) 1, then a trader could purchase (respectively, sell) small equal quantities of each security for a guaranteed profit.[1] These conditions ensure that the current prices can always be viewed as a probability distribution over the outcome space. One example of a cost function based market that has received considerable attention is Hanson's Logarithmic Market Scoring Rule (LMSR) [9, 20, 21]. The cost function of the LMSR is $C(\mathbf{q}) = b \log \sum_{\mathfrak{o}\in\mathcal{O}} e^{q_{\mathfrak{o}}/b}$, where $b > 0$ is a parameter of the market controlling the rate at which prices change. The corresponding price function for each security $\mathfrak{o}$ is $p_{\mathfrak{o}}(\mathbf{q}) = \partial C(\mathbf{q})/\partial q_{\mathfrak{o}} = e^{q_{\mathfrak{o}}/b} / \sum_{\mathfrak{o}'\in\mathcal{O}} e^{q_{\mathfrak{o}'}/b}$.

When $|\mathcal{O}|$ is large or infinite, calculating the cost of a purchase becomes intractable in general. Recent research has focused on restricting the allowable securities over a combinatorial outcome space and examining whether LMSR prices can be computed efficiently in the restricted space. If the outcome space contains $n!$ rank orders of n competing candidates, it is #P-hard to price pair bets (e.g., "\$1 if and only if candidate A beats candidate B") or subset bets (e.g., "\$1 if one of the candidates in subset C finishes at position

[1]This no-arbitrage condition, while sometimes desirable, is not necessary. Othman et al. [28] recently analyzed a variation of LMSR in which $\sum_{\mathfrak{o}\in\mathcal{O}} p_{\mathfrak{o}}(\mathbf{q}) \geq 1$. We also explore relaxations of the no-arbitrage condition in Section 5.

k") using LMSR on the full set of permutations [12]. If the outcome space contains 2^n Boolean values of n binary base events, it is #P-hard to price securities on conjunctions of any two base events (e.g., "\$1 if and only if a Democrat wins Florida and Ohio") using LMSR [12]. This line of research has led to some positive results when the uncertain event enforces particular structure on the outcome space. In particular, for a single-elimination tournament of n teams, securities such as "\$1 if and only if team A wins a kth round game" and "\$1 if and only if team A beats team B given they face off" can be priced efficiently using LMSR [13]. For a taxonomy tree on some statistic where the value of the statistic of a parent node is the sum of those of its children, securities such as "\$1 if and only if the value of the statistic at node A belongs to $[x, y]$" can be priced efficiently using LMSR [19].

The framework we will introduce next takes a drastically different approach. Instead of searching for supportable spaces of securities for existing market makers, we design new market makers tailored to any security space of interest. Additionally, rather than requiring that securities have a fixed \$1 payoff when the underlying event happens, we allow more general contingent securities with arbitrary, efficiently computable and bounded payoffs.

3. A FRAMEWORK FOR MARKET-MAKING FOR COMPLEX SECURITIES

In the complete cost function based markets described above, the market maker offers an Arrow-Debreu security corresponding to each potential outcome. We consider a market-design scenario where the outcome space $\mathcal{O}$ could potentially be quite large, or even infinite, making it infeasible to run such a market. Instead, we allow the market maker to offer a menu of K securities for some reasonably-sized K, with the (nonnegative) payoff of each security described by an arbitrary but efficiently-computable function $\boldsymbol{\rho} : \mathcal{O} \to \mathbb{R}_+^K$. Specifically, if a trader purchases a share of security i and the outcome is $\mathfrak{o}$, then the trader is paid $\rho_i(\mathfrak{o})$. We call such security spaces *complex*. A complex security space reduces to the complete security space if $K = |\mathcal{O}|$ and for each $i \in \{1, \cdots, K\}$, $\rho_i(\mathfrak{o}) = 1$ if $\mathfrak{o}$ is the ith outcome and 0 otherwise. We consider traders that purchase *security bundles* $\mathbf{r} \in \mathbb{R}^K$. Negative elements of $\mathbf{r}$ encode sales. The payoff for $\mathbf{r}$ upon outcome $\mathfrak{o}$ is exactly $\boldsymbol{\rho}(\mathfrak{o}) \cdot \mathbf{r}$, where $\boldsymbol{\rho}(\mathfrak{o})$ denotes the vector of payoffs for each security for outcome $\mathfrak{o}$. Let $\boldsymbol{\rho}(\mathcal{O}) := \{\boldsymbol{\rho}(\mathfrak{o}) | \mathfrak{o} \in \mathcal{O}\}$.

While it is easy to put intuitive constraints on market prices to ensure that a complete market is "well-behaved", determining the comparable constraints on market prices for an arbitrary set of complex securities is challenging. In particular, while the no-arbitrage condition easily leads to the restriction that the security prices in a complete market need to sum to 1, it is much less clear what space of security prices should be allowed in order to prevent arbitrage in markets over complex securities. This is because the events under which complex securities will pay out are no longer mutually exclusive. This challenge leads us to take an axiomatic approach to understand what constraints a "well-behaved" market maker for complex securities must satisfy.

We do not presuppose a cost function based market. However, in Section 3.1, we show that the use of a convex cost function is *necessary* given the assumption of path independence on the contract purchases. We then derive additional constraints on the form of this cost function. In Sections 3.2–3.4, we go on to show how to design an appropriate cost function by employing techniques from online convex optimization.

3.1 Imposing Some Natural Restrictions on the Market Maker

In this section we introduce a sequence of conditions or axioms that one might expect a market to satisfy, and show that these conditions lead to some natural mathematical restrictions on the costs of security bundles. (We consider relaxations of these conditions in Section 5.) Similar conditions were suggested for complete markets by Chen and Vaughan [10], who defined the notion of a *valid cost function*, and by Othman et al. [28], who discussed properties similar to our notions of path independence and expressiveness, among others. However, no similar conditions have been described for complex markets.

Imagine a sequence of traders entering the marketplace and purchasing security bundles. Let $\mathbf{r}_1, \mathbf{r}_2, \mathbf{r}_3, \ldots$ be the sequence of security bundles purchased. After $t-1$ such purchases, the tth trader should be able to enter the marketplace and query the market maker for the cost of arbitrary bundles. The market maker must be able to furnish a cost $\texttt{Cost}(\mathbf{r}|\mathbf{r}_1, \ldots, \mathbf{r}_{t-1})$ for any bundle $\mathbf{r}$ given a previous trade sequence $\mathbf{r}_1, \ldots, \mathbf{r}_{t-1}$. If the trader chooses to purchase $\mathbf{r}_t$ at a cost of $\texttt{Cost}(\mathbf{r}_t|\mathbf{r}_1, \ldots, \mathbf{r}_{t-1})$, the market maker may update the costs of each bundle accordingly. Our first condition requires that the cost of acquiring a bundle $\mathbf{r}$ must be the same regardless of how the trader splits up the purchase.

CONDITION 1 (PATH INDEPENDENCE). *For any* $\mathbf{r}$, $\mathbf{r}'$, *and* $\mathbf{r}''$ *such that* $\mathbf{r} = \mathbf{r}' + \mathbf{r}''$, *for any* $\mathbf{r}_1, \ldots, \mathbf{r}_t$,

$$\texttt{Cost}(\mathbf{r}|\mathbf{r}_1, \ldots, \mathbf{r}_t) = \texttt{Cost}(\mathbf{r}'|\mathbf{r}_1, \ldots, \mathbf{r}_t) + \texttt{Cost}(\mathbf{r}''|\mathbf{r}_1, \ldots, \mathbf{r}_t, \mathbf{r}').$$

Path independence helps to reduce both arbitrage opportunities and the strategic play of traders, as they no longer need to reason about the optimal path leading to some target position. However, it is worth pointing out that there are interesting markets not satisfying this condition, for example, the continuous double auction (CDA) and the market maker for CDA considered by Das [15], which in our opinion deserve separate treatment.

It turns out that the path independence *alone* implies that prices can be represented by a cost function C, as illustrated in the following theorem. The proof is by induction on t.[2]

THEOREM 1. *Under Condition 1, there exists a cost function* $C : \mathbb{R}^K \to \mathbb{R}$ *such that we may always write*

$$\begin{aligned}&\texttt{Cost}(\mathbf{r}_t|\mathbf{r}_1, \ldots, \mathbf{r}_{t-1}) \\ &\quad = C(\mathbf{r}_1 + \ldots + \mathbf{r}_{t-1} + \mathbf{r}_t) - C(\mathbf{r}_1 + \ldots + \mathbf{r}_{t-1}).\end{aligned}$$

With this in mind, we drop the cumbersome $\texttt{Cost}(\mathbf{r}|\mathbf{r}_1, \ldots, \mathbf{r}_t)$ notation from now on, and write the cost of a bundle $\mathbf{r}$ as $C(\mathbf{q}+\mathbf{r}) - C(\mathbf{q})$, where $\mathbf{q} = \mathbf{r}_1 + \ldots + \mathbf{r}_t$ is the vector of previous purchases.

[2]An appendix containing omitted proofs is available in the version of this paper posted on the authors' websites.

Now, recall that one of the functions of a securities market is to aggregate traders' beliefs into an accurate prediction. Each trader may have his own (potentially secret) information about the future, which we represent as a distribution $\mathbf{p} \in \Delta_{|\mathcal{O}|}$ over the outcome space, where $\Delta_n = \{\mathbf{x} \in \mathbb{R}^n_{\geq 0} : \sum_{i=1}^n x_i = 1\}$, the n-simplex. The pricing mechanism should therefore incentivize the traders to reveal $\mathbf{p}$, but simultaneously avoid providing arbitrage opportunities. Towards this goal, we introduce four additional conditions on our pricing mechanism.

The first condition ensures that the gradient of C is always well-defined. If we imagine that a trader can buy or sell an arbitrarily small bundle, we would like the cost of buying and selling an infinitesimally small quantity of any particular bundle to be the same. If $\nabla C(\mathbf{q})$ is well-defined, it can be interpreted as a vector of instantaneous prices for each security, with $\partial C(\mathbf{q})/\partial q_i$ representing the price per share of an infinitesimally small amount of security i. Additionally, we can interpret $\nabla C(\mathbf{q})$ as the traders' current estimates of the expected payoff of each security, in the same way that $\partial C(\mathbf{q})/\partial q_{\mathfrak{o}}$ was interpreted as the probability of outcome $\mathfrak{o}$ when considering the complete security space.

Condition 2 (Existence of Instantaneous Prices). *C is continuous and differentiable everywhere.*

The next condition encompasses the idea that the market should react to trades in a sensible way in order to incorporate the private information of the traders. In particular, it says that the purchase of a security bundle $\mathbf{r}$ should never cause the market to lower the price of $\mathbf{r}$. It turns out that this condition is closely related to incentive compatibility for a myopic trader. It is equivalent to requiring that a trader with a distribution $\mathbf{p} \in \Delta_{|\mathcal{O}|}$ can never find it simultaneously profitable (in expectation) to buy a bundle $\mathbf{r}$ or to buy the bundle $-\mathbf{r}$. In other words, there can not be more than one way to express one's information.

Condition 3 (Information Incorporation). *For any $\mathbf{q}$ and $\mathbf{r} \in \mathbb{R}^K$, $C(\mathbf{q}+2\mathbf{r}) - C(\mathbf{q}+\mathbf{r}) \geq C(\mathbf{q}+\mathbf{r}) - C(\mathbf{q})$.*

The no arbitrage condition states that it is never possible for a trader to purchase a security bundle $\mathbf{r}$ and receive a positive profit regardless of the outcome.

Condition 4 (No Arbitrage). *For all $\mathbf{q}, \mathbf{r} \in \mathbb{R}^K$, there exists an $\mathfrak{o} \in \mathcal{O}$ such that $C(\mathbf{q}+\mathbf{r}) - C(\mathbf{q}) \geq \mathbf{r} \cdot \boldsymbol{\rho}(\mathfrak{o})$.*

Finally, the expressiveness condition specifies that any trader can set the market prices to reflect his beliefs about the expected payoffs of each security if arbitrarily small portions of shares may be purchased. Here $\bar{\mathbb{R}}$ denotes the extended real numbers, $[-\infty, \infty]$.

Condition 5 (Expressiveness). *For any $\mathbf{p} \in \Delta_{|\mathcal{O}|}$, $\exists \mathbf{q} \in \bar{\mathbb{R}}^K$ for which $\nabla C(\mathbf{q}) = \mathbb{E}_{\mathfrak{o}\sim\mathbf{p}}[\boldsymbol{\rho}(\mathfrak{o})]$.*

For any subset S of $\mathbb{R}^d$, let $\mathcal{H}(S)$ denote the convex hull of S. Recall that $\boldsymbol{\rho}(\mathcal{O}) := \{\boldsymbol{\rho}(\mathfrak{o}) | \mathfrak{o} \in \mathcal{O}\}$. We characterize the form of the cost function under these conditions.

Theorem 2. *If $\mathcal{H}(\boldsymbol{\rho}(\mathcal{O}))$ is closed,[3] then under Conditions 2-5, C must be convex with $\{\nabla C(\mathbf{q}) : \mathbf{q} \in \mathbb{R}^K\} = \mathcal{H}(\boldsymbol{\rho}(\mathcal{O}))$.*

Proof. We first prove convexity. Assume C is non-convex somewhere. Then there must exist some $\mathbf{q}$ and $\mathbf{r}$ such that $C(\mathbf{q}) > (1/2)C(\mathbf{q}+\mathbf{r}) + (1/2)C(\mathbf{q}-\mathbf{r})$. This means $C(\mathbf{q}+\mathbf{r}) - C(\mathbf{q}) < C(\mathbf{q}) - C(\mathbf{q}-\mathbf{r})$, which contradicts Condition 3, so C must be convex.

Now, Condition 2 trivially guarantees that $\nabla C(\mathbf{q})$ is well-defined for any $\mathbf{q}$. To see that $\{\nabla C(\mathbf{q}) : \mathbf{q} \in \mathbb{R}^K\} \subseteq \mathcal{H}(\boldsymbol{\rho}(\mathcal{O}))$, let us assume there exists some $\mathbf{q}'$ for which $\nabla C(\mathbf{q}') \notin \mathcal{H}(\boldsymbol{\rho}(\mathcal{O}))$. This can be reformulated in the following way: There must exists some halfspace, defined by a normal vector $\mathbf{r}$, that separates $\nabla C(\mathbf{q}')$ from every member of $\boldsymbol{\rho}(\mathcal{O})$. More precisely

$$\nabla C(\mathbf{q}') \notin \mathcal{H}(\boldsymbol{\rho}(\mathcal{O})) \iff \exists \mathbf{r} \forall \mathfrak{o} \in \mathcal{O} : \quad \nabla C(\mathbf{q}') \cdot \mathbf{r} < \boldsymbol{\rho}(\mathfrak{o}) \cdot \mathbf{r},$$

where the strict inequality is because $\mathcal{H}(\boldsymbol{\rho}(\mathcal{O}))$ is closed. On the other hand, letting $\mathbf{q} := \mathbf{q}' - \mathbf{r}$, we see by convexity of C that $C(\mathbf{q}+\mathbf{r}) - C(\mathbf{q}) \leq \nabla C(\mathbf{q}') \cdot \mathbf{r}$. Combining these last two inequalities, we see that the price of bundle $\mathbf{r}$ purchased with history $\mathbf{q}$ is always smaller than the payoff for *any* outcome. This implies that there exists some arbitrage opportunity, contradicting Condition 4.

Finally, since $\mathcal{H}(\boldsymbol{\rho}(\mathcal{O}) = \{\mathbb{E}_{\mathfrak{o}\sim\mathbf{p}}[\boldsymbol{\rho}(o)] | \mathbf{p} \in \Delta_{|\mathcal{O}|}\}$, Condition 5 implies that $\mathcal{H}(\boldsymbol{\rho}(\mathcal{O})) \subseteq \{\nabla C(\mathbf{q}) : \mathbf{q} \in \mathbb{R}^K\}$. □

What we have arrived at from the set of proposed conditions is that (a) the pricing mechanism is always described precisely in terms of a convex cost function C and (b) the set of reachable prices, that is the set $\{\nabla C(\mathbf{q}) : \mathbf{q} \in \mathbb{R}^K\}$, must be *identically* the convex hull of the payoff vectors for each outcome $\mathcal{H}(\boldsymbol{\rho}(\mathcal{O}))$. For complete markets, those with a single security corresponding to each of the n distinct outcomes, this would imply that the set of reachable prices should be the convex hull of the n standard basis vectors. Indeed, this comports exactly with the natural assumption that the vector of security prices in complete markets should represent a probability distribution, or equivalently that it should lie in the n-simplex.

3.2 Designing the Cost Function via Conjugate Duality

The natural conditions we introduced above imply that to design a market for a set of K securities with payoffs specified by an arbitrary payoff function $\boldsymbol{\rho} : \mathcal{O} \to \mathbb{R}^K_+$, we should use a cost function based market with a convex, differentiable cost function such that $\{\nabla C(\mathbf{q}) : \mathbf{q} \in \mathbb{R}^K\} = \mathcal{H}(\boldsymbol{\rho}(\mathcal{O}))$. We now provide a general technique that can be used to design and compare properties of cost functions that satisfy these criteria. In order to accomplish this, we make use of tools from convex analysis.

It is well known[4] that any closed, convex, differentiable function $C : \mathbb{R}^K \to \mathbb{R}$ can be written in the form $C(\mathbf{q}) = \sup_{\mathbf{x}\in\mathrm{dom}(R)} \mathbf{x} \cdot \mathbf{q} - R(\mathbf{x})$ for a strictly convex function R called the *conjugate* of C, where $\mathrm{dom}(R)$ denotes the domain of R. (The strict convexity of R follows from the differentiability of C.) Furthermore, any function that can be written in this form is convex. As we will show in Section 3.3, the gradient of C can be expressed in terms of this conjugate: $\nabla C(\mathbf{q}) = \mathrm{argmax}_{\mathbf{x}\in\mathrm{dom}(R)} \mathbf{x} \cdot \mathbf{q} - R(\mathbf{x})$. To generate a convex cost function C such that $\nabla C(\mathbf{q}) \in \Pi$ for all $\mathbf{q}$ for some set

[3]The closure assumption is not strictly necessary, but is perfectly natural in typical settings. We include it for convenience. Without it, the conclusion can be modified to $\{\nabla C(\mathbf{q}) : \mathbf{q} \in \mathbb{R}^K\} = \mathrm{closure}(\mathcal{H}(\boldsymbol{\rho}(\mathcal{O})))$.

[4]For a detailed discussion of convex conjugates and their properties, refer to a good text on convex optimization such as Boyd and Vandenberghe [6] or Hiriart-Urruty and Lemaréchal [23].

Π, it is therefore sufficient to choose an appropriate conjugate function R, restrict the domain of R to Π, and define C as

$$C(\mathbf{q}) = \sup_{\mathbf{x}\in\Pi} \mathbf{x}\cdot\mathbf{q} - R(\mathbf{x}) \ . \tag{1}$$

We call such a market a *complex cost function based market.* To generate a cost function C satisfying our five conditions, we need only to set $\Pi = \mathcal{H}(\boldsymbol{\rho}(\mathcal{O}))$ and select a strictly convex function R to serve as the conjugate.

This method of defining C is convenient for several reasons. First, it leads to markets that are efficient to implement whenever Π can be described by a polynomial number of simple constraints. The difficulty with combinatorial outcome spaces is that actually enumerating the set of outcomes can be challenging or impossible. In our proposed framework we need only work with the convex hull of the payoff vectors for each outcome when represented by a low-dimensional payoff function $\boldsymbol{\rho}(\cdot)$. This has significant benefits, as one often encounters convex sets which contain exponentially many vertices yet can be described by polynomially many constraints. Moreover, as the construction of C is based entirely on convex programming, we reduce the problem of automated market making to the problem of optimization for which we have a wealth of efficient algorithms. Similar techniques have been applied to design learning algorithms in the online convex optimization framework [22, 31], where R plays the role of a regularizer, and have been shown to be efficient in a variety of combinatorial applications, including online shortest paths, online learning of perfect matchings, and online cut set [7].

Second, this method yields simple formulas for properties of markets that help us choose the best market to run. Two of these properties, worst-case monetary loss and worst-case information loss, are analyzed below.

Note that both the LMSR and Quad-SCPM [2] are examples of complex cost function based markets, though they are designed for the complete market setting only.

3.3 Bounding Market Maker Loss and Loss of Information

Before discussing market properties, it is useful to review some helpful properties of conjugates. The first is a convenient duality: For any convex, closed function C, the conjugate of the conjugate of C is C itself. This implies that if C is defined as in Equation 1, we may write

$$R(\mathbf{x}) = \sup_{\mathbf{q}\in\mathbb{R}^K} \mathbf{q}\cdot\mathbf{x} - C(\mathbf{q}).$$

Since this maximization is unconstrained, and we are assuming that our cost function C is differentiable, the maximum occurs when $\nabla C(\mathbf{q}) = \mathbf{x}$. (Note that this may hold for many different values of $\mathbf{q}$.) Suppose for a particular pair $(\mathbf{x}^*, \mathbf{q}^*)$ we have $\nabla C(\mathbf{q}^*) = \mathbf{x}^*$. We can then rewrite this equation as $R(\mathbf{x}^*) = \mathbf{q}^*\cdot\mathbf{x}^* - C(\mathbf{q}^*)$, which gives us that $C(\mathbf{q}^*) = \mathbf{q}^*\cdot\mathbf{x}^* - R(\mathbf{x}^*)$. From Equation 1, this tells us that $\mathbf{x}^*$ must be a maximizer of $\mathbf{x}\cdot\mathbf{q} - R(\mathbf{x})$. In fact, it is the unique maximizer due to strict convexity. This implies, as mentioned above, that $\nabla C(\mathbf{q}) = \mathrm{argmax}_{\mathbf{x}\in\Pi}\, \mathbf{x}\cdot\mathbf{q} - R(\mathbf{x})$.

By a similar argument we have that for any $\mathbf{q}$, if $\nabla R(\mathbf{x}) = \mathbf{q}$ then $\mathbf{x}$ maximizes $\mathbf{x}\cdot\mathbf{q} - R(\mathbf{x})$ and therefore, as we have just shown, $\mathbf{x} = \nabla C(\mathbf{q})$. However, the fact that $\mathbf{x} = \nabla C(\mathbf{q})$ *does not* imply that $\nabla R(\mathbf{x}) = \mathbf{q}$; in the markets we consider, it is generally the case that $\mathbf{x} = \nabla C(\mathbf{q})$ for multiple $\mathbf{q}$.

We will make use of the notion of Bregman divergence. The *Bregman divergence* with respect to a convex function f is given by

$$D_f(\mathbf{x}, \mathbf{y}) := f(\mathbf{x}) - f(\mathbf{y}) - \nabla f(\mathbf{y})(\mathbf{x} - \mathbf{y}).$$

It is clear by convexity that $D_f(\mathbf{x}, \mathbf{y}) \geq 0$ for all $\mathbf{x}$ and $\mathbf{y}$.

Additionally, we will require notions like the interior and boundary of a convex set, yet we must introduce more careful terminology in order to consider the case that our price space is not of full rank. Given a convex set $S \subset \mathbb{R}^d$ that occupies d'-dimensional linear subspace, where potentially $d' < d$, we define the *relative interior* of S, relint(S), which is the interior of S when restricted to the d'-dimensional space (typically known as the *affine hull* of S). In addition, we define the *relative boundary* of S, relbnd(S), as the set closure$(S) \setminus$ relint(S).

With these tools in hand, we are ready to examine some market properties, and see how they depend on R.

3.3.1 Bounding the Market Maker's Monetary Loss

When comparing market mechanisms, it is useful to consider the market maker's worst-case monetary loss,

$$\sup_{\mathbf{q}\in\mathbb{R}^K} \left(\sup_{\mathfrak{o}\in\mathcal{O}} (\boldsymbol{\rho}(\mathfrak{o})\cdot\mathbf{q}) - C(\mathbf{q}) + C(\mathbf{0}) \right).$$

This quantity is simply the worst-case difference between the maximum amount that the market maker might have to pay the traders ($\sup_{\mathfrak{o}\in\mathcal{O}} \boldsymbol{\rho}(\mathfrak{o})\cdot\mathbf{q}$) and the amount of money collected by the market maker ($C(\mathbf{q}) - C(\mathbf{0})$). The following theorem provides a bound on this loss in terms of the conjugate function.

THEOREM 3. *Consider any complex cost function based market with $\Pi = \mathcal{H}(\boldsymbol{\rho}(\mathcal{O}))$. The worst-case monetary loss of the market maker is no more than*

$$\sup_{\mathbf{x}\in\boldsymbol{\rho}(\mathcal{O})} R(\mathbf{x}) - \inf_{\mathbf{x}\in\mathcal{H}(\boldsymbol{\rho}(\mathcal{O}))} R(\mathbf{x}),$$

and when $\mathfrak{o}$ is such that $\boldsymbol{\rho}(\mathfrak{o}) = \arg\max_{\mathbf{x}\in\mathcal{H}(\boldsymbol{\rho}(\mathfrak{o}))} R(\mathbf{x})$ then this loss is realized in the limit for $\mathbf{q}$ as $\nabla C(\mathbf{q}) \rightarrow \boldsymbol{\rho}(\mathfrak{o})$.

This theorem tells us that as long as the conjugate function is bounded on $\mathcal{H}(\boldsymbol{\rho}(\mathcal{O}))$, the market maker's worst-case loss is also bounded[5]. It says further that this loss is actually realized, for a particular outcome $\mathfrak{o}$, at least when the price vector approaches $\mathfrak{o}$. This suggests that loss to the market maker is worst when the traders are the most certain about the outcome.

3.3.2 Bounding Information Loss

Information loss can occur when securities are sold in discrete quantities (for example, single units), as they are in most real-world markets. Without the ability to purchase arbitrarily small bundles, traders may not be able to change the market prices to reflect their true beliefs about the expected payoff of each security, even if expressiveness is satisfied. We will argue that the amount of information loss is captured by the market's bid-ask spread

[5]In Section 5, we will state a more general, stronger bound on market maker loss capturing the intuitive notion that the market maker's profits should be higher when the distance between the final vector of prices and the payoff vector $\boldsymbol{\rho}(\mathfrak{o})$ of the true outcome $\mathfrak{o}$ is large; see Theorem 6.

for the smallest trading unit. Given some $\mathbf{q}$, the current bid-ask spread of security bundle $\mathbf{r}$ is defined to be $(C(\mathbf{q}+\mathbf{r}) - C(\mathbf{q})) - (C(\mathbf{q}) - C(\mathbf{q}-\mathbf{r}))$. This is simply the difference between the current cost of buying the bundle $\mathbf{r}$ and the current price at which $\mathbf{r}$ could be sold.

To see how the bid-ask spread relates to information loss, suppose that the current vector of quantities sold is $\mathbf{q}$. If securities must be sold in unit chunks, a rational, risk-neutral trader will not buy security i unless she believes the expected payoff of this security is at least $C(\mathbf{q}+\mathbf{e}_i) - C(\mathbf{q})$, where $\mathbf{e}_i$ is the vector that has value 1 at its ith element and 0 everywhere else. Similarly, she will not sell security i unless she believes the expected payoff is at most $C(\mathbf{q}) - C(\mathbf{q}-\mathbf{e}_i)$. If her estimate of the expected payoff of the security is between these two values, she has no incentive to buy or sell the security. In this case, it is only possible to infer that the trader believes the true expected payoff lies somewhere in the range $[C(\mathbf{q}) - C(\mathbf{q}-\mathbf{e}_i), C(\mathbf{q}+\mathbf{e}_i) - C(\mathbf{q})]$. The bid-ask spread is precisely the size of this range.

The bid-ask spread depends on how fast instantaneous prices change as securities are bought or sold. Intuitively, the bid-ask spread relates to the depth of the market. When the bid-ask spread is large, new purchases or sales can change the prices of the securities dramatically; essentially, the market is shallow. When the bid-ask spread is small, purchases or sales may only move the prices slightly; the market is deep. Based on this intuition, for complete markets, Chen and Pennock [9] use the inverse of $\partial^2 C(\mathbf{q})/\partial q_i^2$ to capture the notion of market depth for each security i independently. In a similar spirit, we define a *market depth parameter*, β, for our complex securities markets with twice-differentiable C. Larger values of β correspond to deeper markets. We will bound the bid-ask spread in terms of this parameter, and use this parameter to show that there exists a clear tradeoff between worst-case monetary loss and information loss; this will be formalized in Theorem 4 below.

DEFINITION 1. *For any complex cost function based market, if C is twice-differentiable, the* market depth parameter *$\beta(\mathbf{q})$ for a quantity vector $\mathbf{q}$ is defined as $\beta(\mathbf{q}) = 1/V_c(\mathbf{q})$, where $V_c(\mathbf{q})$ is the largest eigenvalue of $\nabla^2 C(\mathbf{q})$, the Hessian of C at $\mathbf{q}$. The worst-case market depth is $\beta = \inf_{\mathbf{q}\in\mathbb{R}^K} \beta(\mathbf{q})$.*

Let relint(Π) be the relative interior of Π. If C is twice-differentiable, then for any $\mathbf{q}$ such that $\nabla C(\mathbf{q}) \in$ relint(Π), we have a correspondence between the Hessian of C at $\mathbf{q}$ and the Hessian of R at $\nabla C(\mathbf{q})$. More precisely, we have that $\mathbf{u}^\top \nabla^2 C(\mathbf{q})\mathbf{u} = \mathbf{u}^\top \nabla^{-2} R(\nabla C(\mathbf{q}))\mathbf{u}$ for any $\mathbf{u} = \mathbf{x} - \mathbf{x}'$ with $\mathbf{x}, \mathbf{x}' \in \Pi$. (See, for example, Gorni [17] for more.) This means that $\beta(\mathbf{q})$ is equivalently defined as the smallest eigenvalue of $\nabla^2 R(\nabla C(\mathbf{q}))|_\Pi$; that is, where we consider the second derivative only within the price region Π.

The definition of worst-case market depth implies that $1/\beta$ is an upper bound on the curvature of C, which implies that C is locally bounded by a quadratic with Hessian I/β. We can derive the following.

LEMMA 1. *Consider a complex cost function based market with worst-case market depth β. For any $\mathbf{q}$ and $\mathbf{r}$ we have*

$$D_C(\mathbf{q}+\mathbf{r}, \mathbf{q}) \leq \frac{\|\mathbf{r}\|^2}{2\beta}.$$

It is easy to verify that the bid-ask spread can be written in terms of Bregman divergences. In particular, $C(\mathbf{q}+\mathbf{r}) - C(\mathbf{q}) - (C(\mathbf{q}) - C(\mathbf{q}-\mathbf{r})) = D_C(\mathbf{q}+\mathbf{r}, \mathbf{q}) + D_C(\mathbf{q}-\mathbf{r}, \mathbf{q})$. This implies that the worst-case bid-ask spread of a market with market depth β can be upperbounded by a constant times $1/\beta$. That is, as the market depth parameter increases, the bid-ask spread must decrease. The following theorem shows that this leads to an inherent tension between worst-case monetary loss and information loss. Here diam($\mathcal{H}(\boldsymbol{\rho}(\mathcal{O}))$) denotes the diameter of the hull of the payoff vectors for each outcome.

THEOREM 4. *For any complex cost function based market with worst-case market depth β, for any $\mathbf{r}$, $\mathbf{q}$ meeting the conditions in Lemma 1, the bid-ask spread for bundle $\mathbf{r}$ with previous purchases $\mathbf{q}$ is no more than $\|\mathbf{r}\|^2/\beta$. The worst-case monetary loss of the market maker is at least $\beta \cdot \mathrm{diam}^2(\mathcal{H}(\boldsymbol{\rho}(\mathcal{O})))/8$.*

We can see that there is a direct tradeoff between the upper bound[6] of the bid-ask spread, which shrinks as β grows, and the lower bound of the worst-case loss of the market maker, which grows linearly in β. This tradeoff is very intuitive. When the market is shallow (small β), small trades have a large impact on market prices, and traders cannot purchase too many shares of the same security without paying a lot. When the market is deep (large β), prices change slowly, allowing the market maker to gain more precise information, but simultaneously forcing the market maker to take on more risk since many shares of a security can be purchased at prices that are potentially too low. This tradeoff can be adjusted by scaling R, which scales β. This is analogous to adjusting the "liquidity parameter" b of the LMSR.

3.4 Selecting a Conjugate Function

We have seen that the choice of the conjugate function R impacts market properties such as worst-case loss and information loss. We now explore this choice in more detail.

In many situations, the ideal choice of the conjugate is a function of the form

$$R(\mathbf{x}) := \frac{\lambda}{2}\|\mathbf{x} - \mathbf{x}_0\|^2. \tag{2}$$

Here $R(\mathbf{x})$ is simply the squared Euclidean distance between $\mathbf{x}$ and an initial price vector $\mathbf{x}_0 \in \Pi$, scaled by $\lambda/2$. By utilizing this quadratic conjugate function, we achieve a market depth that is uniformly λ over the entire security space. Furthermore, if $\mathbf{x}_0$ is chosen as the "center" of Π, namely $\mathbf{x}_0 = \arg\min_{\mathbf{x}\in\Pi} \max_{\mathbf{y}\in\Pi} \|\mathbf{x}-\mathbf{y}\|$, then the worst-case loss of the market maker is $\max_{\mathbf{x}\in\Pi} R(\mathbf{x}) = (\lambda/8)\mathrm{diam}^2(\Pi)$. While the market maker can tune λ appropriately according to the desired tradeoff between worst-case market depth and worst-case loss, the tradeoff is tightest when R has a Hessian that is uniformly a scaled identity matrix, or more precisely where R takes the form in Equation 2.

Unfortunately, by selecting a conjugate of this form, or any R with bounded derivative, the market maker does inherit one potentially undesirable property: security prices

[6]Strictly speaking, as we are emphasizing the necessary tradeoff between bid-ask spread and worst-case loss, we should have a *lower bound* on the bid-ask spread. On the other hand, if the worst-case market depth parameter is β then there is some $\mathbf{q}$ and $\mathbf{r}$ such that $D_C(\mathbf{q}+\mathbf{r}, \mathbf{q})/\|\mathbf{r}\|^2 \approx 1/(2\beta)$ and this approximation can be made arbitrarily tight for small enough $\mathbf{r}$ when C is twice differentiable.

may become constant when $\nabla C(\mathbf{q})$ reaches a point at relbnd(Π), the relative boundary of Π (see Section 3.3). That is, if we arrive at a total demand $\mathbf{q}$ where $\nabla C(\mathbf{q}) = \rho(\mathfrak{o})$ for some outcome $\mathfrak{o}$, our mechanism begins offering securities at a price *equal to the best-case payoff*, akin to asking someone to bet a dollar for the chance to possibly win a dollar. The Quad-SCPM for complete markets is known to exhibit this behavior [2].

To avoid these undesirable pricing scenarios, it is sufficient to require that our conjugate function satisfy one condition. We say that a convex function R defined on Π is a *pseudo-barrier*[7] for Π if $\|\nabla R(\mathbf{x}_t)\| \to \infty$ for any sequence of points $\mathbf{x}_1, \mathbf{x}_2, \ldots \in \Pi$ which tends towards relbnd(Π). If we require our conjugate function R to be a pseudo-barrier, we are guaranteed that the instantaneous price vector $\nabla C(\mathbf{q})$ always lies in relint(Π), and does not become constant near the boundary.

It is important to note that, while it is desirable that $\|\nabla R(\mathbf{x}_t)\| \to \infty$ as $\mathbf{x}_t$ approaches relbnd(Π), it is generally not desirable that $R(\mathbf{x}_t) \to \infty$. Recall that the market maker's worst-case loss grows with the maximum value of R on Π and thus we should hope for a conjugate function that is bounded on the domain. A perfect example of convex function that is simultaneously bounded and a pseudo-barrier is the *negative entropy function* $H(\mathbf{x}) = \sum_i x_i \log x_i$, defined on the n-simplex Δ_n. It is perhaps no surprise that LMSR, the most common market mechanism for complete security spaces, can be described by the choice $R(\mathbf{x}) := \lambda H(\mathbf{x})$ where the price space $\Pi = \Delta_n$ [2, 10].

4. EXAMPLES OF COMPUTATIONALLY EFFICIENT MARKETS

In the previous section, we provided a general framework for designing markets on combinatorial or infinite outcome spaces. We now provide some examples of markets that can be operated efficiently using this framework.

4.1 Subset Betting

Consider the scenario in which the outcome is some *ranking* of a set of n competitors, such as n horses in a race. The outcome of such a race is a permutation $\pi : [n] \to [n]$, where $\pi(i)$ is the final position of i, with $\pi(i) = 1$ being best, and $[n]$ denotes the set $\{1, \cdots, n\}$. A typical market for this setting might offer n Arrow-Debreu securities, with the ith security paying off if and only if $\pi(i) = 1$. Additionally, there might be separate, *independent* markets allowing bets on horses to place (come in first or second) or show (come in first, second, or third). However, running independent markets for sets of outcomes with clear correlations is wasteful in that information revealed in one market does not automatically propagate to the others.

Chen et al. [11] proposed a betting language, *subset betting* in which traders can place bets (i, j), for any candidate i and any slot j, that pay out \$1 in the event that $\pi(i) = j$ and \$0 otherwise.[8] Chen et al. [12] showed that pricing bets of this form using LMSR is #P-hard and provided an algorithm for approximating the prices by exploiting the structure of the market. Using our framework, it is simple to design a computationally efficient market for securities of this form.

In order to set up such a combinatorial market within our framework, we must be able to efficiently work with the convex hull of the payoff vectors for each outcome. Notice that, for an outcome π, the associated payoff can be described by a matrix M_π, with $M_\pi(i, j) = I[\pi(i) = j]$, where $I[\cdot]$ is the indicator function. Taking this one step further, it is easy to verify that the convex hull of the set of permutation matrices is precisely the set of *doubly stochastic matrices*, that is the set

$$\Pi = \left\{ X \in \mathbb{R}_{\geq 0}^{n \times n} : \sum_{i'=1}^{n} X(i', j) = \sum_{j'=1}^{n} X(i, j') = 1 \ \forall i, j \right\},$$

where $X(i, j)$ represents the element at the ith row and jth column of the matrix X. Notice, importantly, that this set is described by only n^2 variables and $O(n)$ constraints.

To fully specify the market maker, we must also select a conjugate function R for our price space. While the quadratic conjugate function is an option, there is a natural extension of the entropy function, whose desirable properties were discussed in the previous section, for the space of stochastic matrices. For any $X \in \Pi$, let us set

$$R(X) = \lambda \sum_{i,j} X(i, j) \log X(i, j).$$

The worst-case market depth is computed as the minimum of the smallest eigenvalue of the Hessian of R within the relint(Π). This occurs at the matrix with all values $1/n$, hence the worst-case depth is $n\lambda$. The worst-case loss, on the other hand, is easily computed as $\lambda n \log n$.

4.2 Sphere Betting

We now consider an example in which the outcome space is infinite. An object orbiting the planet, perhaps a satellite, is predicted to fall to earth in the near future and will land at an unknown location, which we would like to predict. We represent locations on the earth as unit vectors $\mathbf{u} \in \mathbb{R}^3$. The difficulty of this example arises from the fact that the outcome must be a unit vector, imposing constraints on the three coordinates. We will design a market with three securities, each corresponding to one coordinate of the final location of the object. In particular, security i will pay off $u_i + 1$ dollars if the object lands in location $\mathbf{u}$. (The addition of 1, while not strictly necessary, ensures that the payoffs, and therefore prices, remain positive, though it will be necessary for traders to sell securities to express certain beliefs.) This means that traders can purchase security bundles $\mathbf{r} \in \mathbb{R}^3$ and, when the object lands at a location $\mathbf{u}$, receive a payoff $(\mathbf{u} + \mathbf{1}) \cdot \mathbf{r}$. Note that in this example, the outcome space is infinite, but the security space is small.

The price space $\mathcal{H}(\rho(\mathcal{O}))$ for this market will be the 2-norm unit ball centered at $\mathbf{1}$. To construct a market for this scenario, let us make the simple choice of $R(\mathbf{x}) = \lambda \|\mathbf{x} - \mathbf{1}\|^2$ for some parameter $\lambda > 0$. When $\|\mathbf{q}\| \leq 2\lambda$, there exists an $\mathbf{x}$ such that $\nabla R(\mathbf{x}) = \mathbf{q}$. In particular, this is true for $\mathbf{x} = (1/2)\mathbf{q}/\lambda + \mathbf{1}$, and $\mathbf{q} \cdot \mathbf{x} - R(\mathbf{x})$ is minimized at this

[7] We use the term pseudo-barrier to distinguish this from the typical definition of a barrier function on a set Π, which is a function that grows without bound towards the boundary of Π. The term *Legendre* was introduced by Cesa-Bianchi and Lugosi [8] for a similar notion, yet their definition requires the stronger condition that Π contain a nonempty interior.

[8] The original definition of subset betting allowed bets of the form "any candidate in set S will end up in slot j" or "candidate i will end up in one of the slots in set S." A bet of this form can be constructed easily using our betting language by bundling multiple securities.

point. When $\|\mathbf{q}\| > 2\lambda$, $\mathbf{q} \cdot \mathbf{x} - R(\mathbf{x})$ is minimized at an $\mathbf{x}$ on the boundary of $\mathcal{H}(\boldsymbol{\rho}(\mathcal{O}))$. Specifically, it is minimized at $\mathbf{x} = \mathbf{q}/\|\mathbf{q}\| + \mathbf{1}$. From this, we can compute

$$C(\mathbf{q}) = \begin{cases} \frac{1}{4\lambda}\|\mathbf{q}\|^2 + \mathbf{q}\cdot\mathbf{1}, & \text{when } \|\mathbf{q}\| \leq 2\lambda, \\ \|\mathbf{q}\| + \mathbf{q}\cdot\mathbf{1} - \lambda, & \text{when } \|\mathbf{q}\| > 2\lambda. \end{cases}$$

The market depth parameter β is 2λ; in fact, $\beta(\mathbf{x}) = 2\lambda$ for any price vector $\mathbf{x}$ in the interior of $\mathcal{H}(\boldsymbol{\rho}(\mathcal{O}))$. By Theorem 3, the worst-case loss of the market maker is no more than λ, which is precisely the lower bound implied by Theorem 4. Finally, the divergence $D_C(\mathbf{q}+\mathbf{r},\mathbf{q}) \leq \|\mathbf{r}\|^2/(4\lambda)$ for all $\mathbf{q},\mathbf{r}$, with equality when $\|\mathbf{q}\|, \|\mathbf{q}+\mathbf{r}\| \leq 2\lambda$, implying that the bid-ask spread scales linearly with $\|\mathbf{r}\|^2/\lambda$.

5. COMPUTATIONAL COMPLEXITY AND RELAXATIONS

In Section 3, we argued that the space of feasible price vectors should be precisely $\mathcal{H}(\boldsymbol{\rho}(\mathcal{O}))$, the convex hull of the payoff vectors for each outcome. In each of our examples, we have discussed market scenarios for which this hull has a polynomial number of constraints, allowing us to efficiently set prices via convex optimization [9]. Unfortunately, one should not necessarily expect that a given payoff function and outcome space will lead to an efficiently describable convex hull. In this section, we explore a couple of approaches to overcome such complexity challenges. First, we discuss the case in which $\mathcal{H}(\boldsymbol{\rho}(\mathcal{O}))$ has exponentially (or infinitely) many constraints yet gives rise to a *separation oracle*. Second, we show that the price space Π can indeed be *relaxed* beyond $\mathcal{H}(\boldsymbol{\rho}(\mathcal{O}))$ without increasing the risk to the market maker. Finally, we show how this relaxation applies in practice.

5.1 Separation Oracles

If we encounter a convex hull $\mathcal{H}(\boldsymbol{\rho}(\mathcal{O}))$ with exponentially-many constraints, all may not be lost. Recall that, in order to set prices, we need to solve the optimization problem $\max_{\mathbf{x}\in\mathcal{H}(\boldsymbol{\rho}(\mathcal{O}))} \mathbf{q}\cdot\mathbf{x} - R(\mathbf{x})$. Under certain circumstances this can still be solved efficiently.

Consider a convex optimization problem with a concave objective function $f(\mathbf{x})$ and constraints $g_i(\mathbf{x}) \leq 0$ for all i in some index set I. That is, we want to solve:

$$\begin{aligned} \max \quad & f(\mathbf{x}) \\ \text{s.t.} \quad & \mathbf{x} \in \mathbb{R}^d \\ & g_i(\mathbf{x}) \leq 0 \; \forall i \in I \end{aligned}$$

This can be converted to a problem with a linear objective in the standard way:

$$\begin{aligned} \max \quad & c \\ \text{s.t.} \quad & \mathbf{x} \in \mathbb{R}^d, c \in \mathbb{R} \\ & f(\mathbf{x}) \geq c \\ & g_i(\mathbf{x}) \leq 0 \; \forall i \in I \end{aligned}$$

Of course, if I is an exponentially or infinitely large set we will have trouble solving this problem directly. On the other hand, the constraint set may admit an efficient *separation oracle*, defined as a function that takes as input a point $(\mathbf{x}, c)$ and returns `true` if all the necessary constraints are satisfied or, otherwise, returns `false` *and* specifies a violated constraint[10]. Given an efficient separation oracle one has access to alternative methods for optimization, the most famous being Khachiyan's *ellipsoid method*, that run in polynomial time. For more details see, for example, Grötschel et al [18].

This suggests that a fruitful direction for designing computationally efficient market makers is to examine the pricing problem on an instance-by-instance basis, and for a particular instance of interest, leverage the structure of the instance to develop an efficient algorithm for solving the specific separation problem. We leave this for future research.

5.2 Relaxation of the Price Space

When dealing with a convex hull $\mathcal{H}(\boldsymbol{\rho}(\mathcal{O}))$ that has a prohibitively large constraint set and does not admit an efficient separation oracle we still have one tool at our disposal: we can modify $\mathcal{H}(\boldsymbol{\rho}(\mathcal{O}))$ to get an alternate price space Π which we *can* work with efficiently. Recall that in Section 3, we arrived at the requirement that $\Pi = \mathcal{H}(\boldsymbol{\rho}(\mathcal{O}))$ as a necessary conclusion of the proposed conditions on our market maker. If we wish to violate this requirement, we need to consider which conditions must be weakened and revise the resulting guarantees from Section 3.

We will continue to construct our markets in the usual way, via the tuple $(\mathcal{O}, \boldsymbol{\rho}, \Pi, R)$ where $\mathcal{O}$ is the outcome space, $\boldsymbol{\rho}$ is the payoff function, $\Pi \subseteq \mathbb{R}^d$ is a convex compact set of feasible prices, and $R : \mathbb{R}^d \to \mathbb{R}$ is a strictly convex function with domain Π. The market's cost function C will be the conjugate of R with respect to the set Π, as in Equation 1. The only difference is that we now allow Π to be distinct from $\mathcal{H}(\boldsymbol{\rho}(\mathcal{O}))$. Not surprisingly, the choice of Π will affect the interest of the traders and the market maker. We prove several claims which will aid us in our market design. Theorem 5 tells us that the expressiveness condition should not be relaxed, while Theorem 6 tells us that the no-arbitrage condition can be. Together, these imply that we may safely choose Π to be a *superset* of $\mathcal{H}(\boldsymbol{\rho}(\mathcal{O}))$.

THEOREM 5. *For any complex cost function based market, the worst-case loss of the market maker is unbounded if* $\boldsymbol{\rho}(\mathcal{O}) \not\subseteq \Pi$.

This (perhaps surprising) theorem tells us that expressiveness is not only useful for information aggregation, it is actually *necessary* for the market maker to avoid unbounded loss. The proof involves showing that if $\mathfrak{o}$ is the final outcome and $\boldsymbol{\rho}(\mathfrak{o}) \notin \Pi$, then it is possible to make an infinite sequence of trades such that each trade causes a constant amount of loss to the market maker.

In the following theorem, which is a simple extension of Theorem 3, we see that including additional price vectors in Π does not adversely impact the market maker's worst-case loss, despite the fact that the no-arbitrage condition is violated.

THEOREM 6. *Consider any complex cost function based market with R and Π satisfying* $\sup_{\mathbf{x}\in\mathcal{H}(\boldsymbol{\rho}(\mathcal{O}))} R(\mathbf{x}) < \infty$ *and*

[9] A convex program can be solved with arbitrarily small error ϵ in time polynomial of $1/\epsilon$ and the size of the problem input using standard techniques such as the interior-point method. In this paper, we do not worry about finding the exact solution to the convex programs.

[10] More precisely, a separation oracle returns any *separating hyperplane* that divides the input from the feasible set.

$\mathcal{H}(\boldsymbol{\rho}(\mathcal{O})) \subseteq \Pi$. *Assume that the initial price vector satisfies* $\nabla C(\mathbf{0}) \in \mathcal{H}(\boldsymbol{\rho}(\mathcal{O}))$. *Let* $\mathbf{q}$ *denote the vector of quantities sold and* $\mathfrak{o}$ *denote the true outcome. The monetary loss of the market maker is no more than*

$$R(\boldsymbol{\rho}(\mathfrak{o})) - \min_{\mathbf{x} \in \mathcal{H}(\boldsymbol{\rho}(\mathcal{O}))} R(\mathbf{x}) - D_R(\boldsymbol{\rho}(\mathfrak{o}), \nabla C(\mathbf{q})).$$

This tells us that expanding Π can only help the market maker; increasing the range of $\nabla C(\mathbf{q})$ can only increase the divergence term. This may seem somewhat counterintuitive. We originally required that $\Pi \subseteq \mathcal{H}(\boldsymbol{\rho}(\mathcal{O}))$ as a consequence of the no-arbitrage condition, and by relaxing this condition, we are providing traders with potential arbitrage opportunities. However, these arbitrage opportunities do not hurt the market maker. As long as the initial price vector lies in $\mathcal{H}(\boldsymbol{\rho}(\mathcal{O}))$, any such situations where a trader can earn a guaranteed profit are effectively created (and paid for) by other traders! In fact, if the final price vector $\nabla C(\mathbf{q})$ falls outside the convex hull, the divergence term will be strictly positive, improving the bound.

To elaborate on this point, let's consider an example where Π is strictly larger than $\mathcal{H}(\boldsymbol{\rho}(\mathcal{O}))$. Let $\mathbf{q}$ be the current vector of purchases, and assume the associated price vector $\mathbf{x} = \nabla C(\mathbf{q})$ lies in the interior of $\mathcal{H}(\boldsymbol{\rho}(\mathcal{O}))$. Consider a trader who purchases a bundle $\mathbf{r}$ such that the new price vector leaves this set, i.e., $\mathbf{y} := \nabla C(\mathbf{q} + \mathbf{r}) \notin \mathcal{H}(\boldsymbol{\rho}(\mathcal{O}))$. We claim that this choice can be strictly improved in the sense that there is an alternative bundle $\mathbf{r}'$ whose associated profit, for any outcome $\mathfrak{o}$, is strictly greater than the profit for $\mathbf{r}$.

For simplicity, assume $\mathbf{y}$ is an interior point of $\Pi \setminus \mathcal{H}(\boldsymbol{\rho}(\mathcal{O}))$ so that $\mathbf{q} + \mathbf{r} = \nabla R(\mathbf{y})$. Define $\pi(\mathbf{y}) := \arg\min_{\mathbf{y}' \in \mathcal{H}(\boldsymbol{\rho}(\mathcal{O}))} D_R(\mathbf{y}', \mathbf{y})$, the minimum divergence projection of $\mathbf{y}$ into $\mathcal{H}(\boldsymbol{\rho}(\mathcal{O}))$. The alternative bundle we consider is $\mathbf{r}' = \nabla R(\pi(\mathbf{y})) - \mathbf{q}$. Our trader pays $C(\mathbf{q} + \mathbf{r}) - C(\mathbf{q} + \mathbf{r}')$ less to purchase $\mathbf{r}'$ than to purchase $\mathbf{r}$. Hence, for any outcome $\mathfrak{o}$, we see that the increased profit for $\mathbf{r}'$ over $\mathbf{r}$ is

$$\begin{aligned}
&\boldsymbol{\rho}(\mathfrak{o}) \cdot (\mathbf{r}' - \mathbf{r}) - C(\mathbf{q} + \mathbf{r}') + C(\mathbf{q} + \mathbf{r}) \\
&\quad > \boldsymbol{\rho}(\mathfrak{o}) \cdot (\mathbf{r}' - \mathbf{r}) + \nabla C(\mathbf{q} + \mathbf{r}') \cdot (\mathbf{r} - \mathbf{r}') \\
&\quad = (\boldsymbol{\rho}(\mathfrak{o}) - \pi(\mathbf{y})) \cdot (\mathbf{r}' - \mathbf{r}). \qquad (3)
\end{aligned}$$

Notice that we achieve strict inequality precisely because $\nabla C(\mathbf{q} + \mathbf{r}') \neq \nabla C(\mathbf{q} + \mathbf{r})$. Now use the optimality condition for $\pi(\mathbf{y})$ to see that, since $\boldsymbol{\rho}(\mathfrak{o}) \in \mathcal{H}(\boldsymbol{\rho}(\mathcal{O}))$, $\nabla_{\pi(\mathbf{y})}(D_R(\pi(\mathbf{y}), \mathbf{y})) \cdot (\boldsymbol{\rho}(\mathfrak{o}) - \pi(\mathbf{y})) \geq 0$. It is easy to check that $\nabla_{\pi(\mathbf{y})}(D_R(\pi(\mathbf{y}), \mathbf{y})) = \nabla R(\pi(\mathbf{y})) - \nabla R(\mathbf{y}) = \mathbf{r}' - \mathbf{r}$. Combining this last expression with the inequality above and (3) tells us that the profit increase is strictly greater than $(\boldsymbol{\rho}(\mathfrak{o}) - \pi(\mathbf{y})) \cdot (\mathbf{r}' - \mathbf{r}) \geq 0$. Simply put, the trader receives a guaranteed positive increase in profit for any outcome $\mathfrak{o}$.

The next theorem shows that any time the price vector lies outside of $\boldsymbol{\rho}(\mathfrak{o})$, traders could profit by moving it back inside. The proof uses a nice application of minimax duality for convex-concave functions.

THEOREM 7. *For any complex cost function based market, given a current quantity vector* $\mathbf{q}_0$ *with current price vector* $\nabla C(\mathbf{q}_0) = \mathbf{x}_0$, *a trader has the opportunity to earn a guaranteed profit of at least* $\min_{\mathbf{x} \in \mathcal{H}(\boldsymbol{\rho}(\mathcal{O}))} D_R(\mathbf{x}, \mathbf{x}_0)$.

When $\mathbf{x}_0 \in \mathcal{H}(\boldsymbol{\rho}(\mathcal{O}))$, $D_R(\mathbf{x}, \mathbf{x}_0)$ is minimized when $\mathbf{x} = \mathbf{x}_0$ and the bound is vacuous, as we would expect. The more interesting case occurs when the prices have fallen outside of $\mathcal{H}(\boldsymbol{\rho}(\mathcal{O}))$, in which case a trader is guaranteed a riskless profit by moving $\nabla C(\mathbf{q})$ to the closest point in $\mathcal{H}(\boldsymbol{\rho}(\mathcal{O}))$.

5.3 Pair Betting via Relaxation

We return our attention to the scenario where the outcome is a ranking of n competitors, as described in Section 4.1. Consider a complex market in which traders make arbitrary *pair bets*: for every i, j, a trader can purchase a security which pays out \$1 whenever $\pi(i) > \pi(j)$. Like subset bets, pricing pair bets using LMSR is known to be #P-hard [12].

We can represent the payoff structure of any such outcome π by a matrix M_π defined by

$$M_\pi(i,j) = \begin{cases} 1, & \text{if } \pi(i) > \pi(j) \\ \frac{1}{2}, & \text{if } i = j \\ 0, & \text{if } \pi(i) < \pi(j). \end{cases}$$

We would like to choose our feasible price region as the set $\mathcal{H}(\{M_\pi : \pi \in S_n\})$, where S_n is the set of permutations on $[n]$. Unfortunately, the computation of this convex hull is necessarily hard: if given only a separation oracle for the set $\mathcal{H}(\{M_\pi : \pi \in S_n\})$, we could construct a linear program to solve the "minimum feedback arc set" problem, which is known to be NP-hard.

On the positive side, we see from the previous section that the market maker can work in a larger feasible price space without risking a larger loss. We thus relax our feasible price region Π to the set of matrices $X \in \mathbb{R}^{n^2}$ satisfying

$$\begin{aligned}
X(i,j) &\geq 0 && \forall i,j \in [n] \\
X(i,j) &= 1 - X(j,i) && \forall i,j \in [n] \\
X(i,j) + X(j,k) + X(k,i) &\geq 1 && \forall i,j,k \in [n]
\end{aligned}$$

This relaxation was first discussed by Meggido [26], who referred to such matrices as *generalized order matrices*. He proved that, for $n \leq 4$, we do have $\Pi = \mathcal{H}(\{M_\pi : \pi \in S_n\})$, but gave a counterexample showing strict containment for $n = 13$. By using this relaxed price space, the market maker allows traders to bring the price vector outside of the convex hull, yet includes a set of basic (and natural) constraints on the prices. Such a market could be implemented with any strongly convex conjugate function (e.g., quadratic).

6. CONCLUSION

We conclude by mentioning one nice direction of work. As we discussed, there is an inherent tradeoff between the bid-ask spread and the worst-case loss of the market maker. But if the market maker chooses to sell securities with an additional *transaction cost* for each security sold, then this money can not only help to cover the worst-case loss, but can also lead to a profit. Furthermore, if a market becomes popular, the market-maker may wish to increase the market depth. This idea has been explored by Othman et al. [28] for the case of complete markets, introducing a *liquidity sensitive* market maker, and they provide a new model with profit guarantees. Othman and Sandholm [27] recently extend the work and characterize a family of market makers that are liquidity sensitive. Via our framework, we can define an alternative method for simultaneously including transaction costs and guaranteeing profit. In particular, this is achieved through relaxing the price space, as discussed in Section 5.2. We leave the details to future work.

7. ACKNOWLEDGEMENTS

This material is based upon work supported by NSF under CNS-0937060 to the CRA for the CIFellows Project, CCF-0953516, NSF grant DMS-070706, DARPA grant FA8750-05-2-0249, and a Yahoo! PhD Fellowship. Any opinions, findings, conclusions, or recommendations expressed in this material are those of the authors alone.

References

[1] S. Agrawal, Z. Wang, and Y. Ye. Parimutuel betting on permutations. In *Proceedings of the 4th International Workshop On Internet And Network Economics*, 2008.

[2] S. Agrawal, E. Delage, M. Peters, Z. Wang, and Y. Ye. A unified framework for dynamic prediction market design. *Operations Research*, to appear, 2010.

[3] K. J. Arrow. The role of securities in the optimal allocation of risk-bearing. *Review of Economic Studies*, 31(2):91–96, 1964.

[4] K. J. Arrow. *Essays in the Theory of Risk Bearing*. North Holland, Amsterdam, 1970.

[5] J. E. Berg, R. Forsythe, F. D. Nelson, and T. A. Rietz. Results from a dozen years of election futures markets research. In C. A. Plott and V. Smith, editors, *Handbook of Experimental Economic Results*. 2001.

[6] S. Boyd and L. Vandenberghe. *Convex Optimization*. Cambridge University Press, 2004.

[7] N. Cesa-Bianchi and G. Lugosi. Combinatorial bandits. In submission, January 2010.

[8] N. Cesa-Bianchi and G. Lugosi. *Prediction, Learning, and Games*. Cambridge University Press, 2006.

[9] Y. Chen and D. M. Pennock. A utility framework for bounded-loss market makers. In *Proceedings of the 23rd Conference on Uncertainty in Artificial Intelligence*, 2007.

[10] Y. Chen and J. Wortman Vaughan. A new understanding of prediction markets via no-regret learning. In *Proceedings of the 11th ACM Conference on Electronic Commerce*, 2010.

[11] Y. Chen, L. Fortnow, E. Nikolova, and D.M. Pennock. Betting on permutations. In *Proceedings of the 8th ACM Conference on Electronic Commerce*, pages 326–335. ACM, 2007.

[12] Y. Chen, L. Fortnow, N. Lambert, D. M. Pennock, and J. Wortman. Complexity of combinatorial market makers. In *Proceedings of the 9th ACM Conference on Electronic Commerce*, 2008.

[13] Y. Chen, S. Goel, and D. M. Pennock. Pricing combinatorial markets for tournaments. In *Proceedings of the 40th ACM Symposium on Theory of Computing*, 2008.

[14] Yiling Chen, Lance Fortnow, Evdokia Nikolova, and David M. Pennock. Betting on permutations. In *Proceedings of the 8th ACM conference on Electronic commerce*, pages 326–335, 2007.

[15] S. Das. The effects of market-making on price dynamics. In *Proceedings of the 7th International Joint Conference on Autonomous Agents and Multiagent Systems*, pages 887–894, 2008.

[16] X. Gao, Y. Chen, and D. M. Pennock. Betting on the real line. In *Proceedings of the 5th Workshop on Internet and Network Economics*, 2009.

[17] G. Gorni. Conjugation and second-order properties of convex functions. *Journal of Mathematical Analysis and Applications*, 158(2):293–315, 1991.

[18] M. Grötschel, L. Lovász, and A. Schrijver. The ellipsoid method and its consequences in combinatorial optimization. *Combinatorica*, 1(2):169–197, 1981. ISSN 0209-9683.

[19] M. Guo and D. M. Pennock. Combinatorial prediction markets for event hierarchies. In *Proceedings of The 8th International Conference on Autonomous Agents and Multiagent Systems*, 2009.

[20] R. Hanson. Combinatorial information market design. *Information Systems Frontiers*, 5(1):105–119, 2003.

[21] R. Hanson. Logarithmic market scoring rules for modular combinatorial information aggregation. *Journal of Prediction Markets*, 1(1):3–15, 2007.

[22] E. Hazan. A survey: The convex optimization approach to regret minimization. Draft, Sept. 2009.

[23] J.-B. Hiriart-Urruty and C. Lemaréchal. *Fundamentals of Convex Analysis*. Springer, 2001.

[24] J. Ledyard, R. Hanson, and T. Ishikida. An experimental test of combinatorial information markets. *Journal of Economic Behavior and Organization*, 69:182–189, 2009.

[25] A. Mas-Colell, M. D. Whinston, and J. R. Green. *Microeconomics Theory*. Oxford University Press, New York, NY, 1995.

[26] N. Megiddo. Mixtures of order matrices and generalized order matrices. *Discrete Mathematics*, 19(2):177–181, 1977. ISSN 0012-365X.

[27] A. Othman and T. Sandholm. Homogeneous risk measures and liquidity-sensitive automated market makers. Carnegie Mellon University working paper, March 2011.

[28] A. Othman, T. Sandholm, D. M. Pennock, and D. M. Reeves. A practical liquidity-sensitive automated market maker. In *Proceedings of the 11th ACM Conference on Electronic Commerce*, 2010.

[29] D. M. Pennock and R. Sami. Computational aspects of prediction markets. In N. Nisan, T. Roughgarden, É. Tardos, and V. Vazirani, editors, *Algorithmic Game Theory*. Cambridge University Press, 2007.

[30] M. Peters, A. Man-Cho So, and Y. Ye. Pari-mutuel markets: Mechanisms and performance. In *Proceedings of the 3rd International Workshop on Internet and Network Economics*, pages 82–95, 2007.

[31] A. Rakhlin. Lecture notes on online learning. Draft, April 2009.

[32] J. Wolfers and E. Zitzewitz. Prediction markets. *Journal of Economic Perspective*, 18(2):107–126, 2004.

Market Making and Mean Reversion

Tanmoy Chakraborty
University of Pennsylvania
tanmoy@seas.upenn.edu

Michael Kearns
University of Pennsylvania
mkearns@cis.upenn.edu

ABSTRACT

Market making refers broadly to trading strategies that seek to profit by providing liquidity to other traders, while avoiding accumulating a large net position in a stock. In this paper, we study the profitability of market making strategies in a variety of time series models for the evolution of a stock's price. We first provide a precise theoretical characterization of the profitability of a simple and natural market making algorithm in the absence of any stochastic assumptions on price evolution. This characterization exhibits a trade-off between the positive effect of local price fluctuations and the negative effect of net price change. We then use this general characterization to prove that market making is generally profitable on *mean reverting* time series — time series with a tendency to revert to a long-term average. Mean reversion has been empirically observed in many markets, especially foreign exchange and commodities. We show that the slightest mean reversion yields positive expected profit, and also obtain stronger profit guarantees for a canonical stochastic mean reverting process, known as the *Ornstein-Uhlenbeck (OU) process*, as well as other stochastic mean reverting series studied in the finance literature. We also show that market making remains profitable in expectation for the OU process even if some realistic restrictions on trading frequency are placed on the market maker.

Categories and Subject Descriptors

F.2.2 [**Theory of Computation**]: Analysis of Algorithms and Problem Complexity; J.4 [**Social and Behavioral Sciences**]: Economics

General Terms

Theory, Economics, Algorithms

Keywords

Computational Finance, Algorithmic Trading, Market Making, Mean Reversion

1. INTRODUCTION

A market maker is a firm, individual or trading strategy that always or often quotes both a buy and a sell price for a financial instrument or commodity, hoping to make a profit by exploiting the difference between the two prices, known as the *spread*. Intuitively, a market maker wishes to buy and sell equal volumes of the instrument (or commodity), and thus rarely or never accumulate a large net position, and profit from the difference between the selling and buying prices.

Historically, the chief purpose of market makers has been to provide liquidity to the market — the financial instrument can always be bought from, or sold to, the market maker at the quoted prices. Market makers are common in foreign exchange trading, where most trading firms offer both buying and selling rates for a currency. They also play a major role in stock exchanges, and historically exchanges have often appointed trading firms to act as official market makers for specific equities. NYSE designates a single market maker for each stock, known as the *specialist* for that stock. In contrast, NASDAQ allows several market makers for each stock. More recently, fast electronic trading systems have led trading firms to behave like market makers without formally being designated so. In other words, many trading firms attempt to buy and sell a stock simultaneously, and profit from the difference between buying and selling prices. We shall refer to such trading algorithms generally as *market making algorithms*.

In this paper, we analyze the profitability of market making algorithms. Market making has existed as a trading practice for a long time, and it has also inspired significant amount of empirical as well as theoretical research [9, 5, 10, 1, 2, 3]. Most of the theoretical models [5, 9, 2, 3] view market makers as dealers who single-handedly *create* the market by offering buying and selling prices, and there is no trading in their absence (that is, all trades must have the market marker as one of the parties). On the other hand, much of the empirical work has focused on analyzing the behavior of specialist market makers in NYSE, using historical trading data from NYSE [10, 1]. In contrast, our theoretical and empirical work studies the behavior of market making algorithms in both very general and certain specific price time series models, where trading occurs at varying prices even in the absence of the market maker. This view seems appropriate in modern electronic markets, where any trading party whatsoever is free to quote on both sides of the market, and officially designated market makers and specialists are of diminishing importance.

Market Making vs. Statistical Arbitrage.

Before describing our models and results, we first offer some clarifying comments on the technical and historical differences between market making and statistical arbitrage, the latter referring to the activity of using computation-intensive quantitative modeling to design profitable automated trading strategies. Such clarification is especially called for in light of the blurred distinction between traditional market-makers and other kinds of trading activity that electronic markets have made possible, and the fact that many quantitative hedge funds that engage in statistical arbitrage may indeed have strategies that have market making behaviors.

Perhaps the hallmark of market making is the willingness to always quote competitive buy and sell prices, but with the goal of *minimizing directional risk.* By this we mean that the market maker is averse to acquiring a large net long or short position in a stock, since in doing so there is the risk of large losses should the price move in the wrong direction. Thus if a market maker begins to acquire a large net long position, it would continue to quote a buy price, but perhaps a somewhat lower one which is less likely to get executed. Alternatively (or in addition), the strategy might choose to lower its sell quote in order to increase the chances of acquiring short trades to offset its net long inventory. In this sense, pure market making strategies have no "view" or "opinion" on which direction the price "should" move — indeed, as we shall show, the most profitable scenario for a market maker is one in which there is virtually no overall directional movement of the stock, but rather a large amount of non-directional volatility.

In contrast, many statistical arbitrage strategies are the opposite of market making in that they deliberately want to make directional bets — that is, they want to acquire large net positions because they have a prediction or model of future price movement. To give one classic example, in the simplest form of pairs trading, one follows the prices of two presumably related stocks, such as Microsoft and Apple. After normalizing the prices by their historical means and variances, one waits for there to be a significant gap in their current prices — for instance, Apple shares becoming quite expensive relative to Microsoft shares given the historical normalization. At this point, one takes a large short position in Apple and an offsetting large long position in Microsoft. This amounts to a bet that the prices of the two stocks will eventually return to their historical relationship: if Apple's share price falls and Microsoft's rises, both positions pay off. If the gap continues to grow, the strategy incurs a loss. If both rise or both fall without changing the gap between, there is neither gain nor loss. The important point here is that, in contrast to market making, the source of profitability (or loss) are directional bets rather than price volatility.

Theoretical Model and Results.

We first summarize our theoretical models and our three main theoretical results. We assume there is an exogenous market where a stock can be bought and sold at prices dictated by a given time series process. At any given point of time, there is a single *exogenous asset price* at which the stock can both be bought as well as sold. The price evolution in the market is captured by the time series. The market making algorithm is an online decision process that can place buy and sell *limit orders* with some quoted limit order prices at any time, and may also cancel these orders at any future time. For simplicity, we assume that each order requests only one share of the stock (a trader may place multiple orders at the same price). If at any time after placing the order and before its cancellation, the asset price of the stock equals or exceeds (respectively, falls below) the quoted price on a sell order (respectively, buy order), then the order gets *executed at the quoted price*, *i.e.* the trader pays (respectively, gains) one share and gains (respectively, pays) money equal to the price quoted on the order. We shall refer to the net volume of the stock held by a trader at a given point of time as *inventory.* Note that inventory may be positive (net long position) or negative (net short position). To evaluate the profit made by a market making algorithm, we shall fix a time horizon when the algorithm must liquidate its inventory at the current asset price.

Our first and most general theoretical result is a succinct and *exact* characterization of the profit obtained by a simple market-making algorithm, given *any* asset price time series, in the model above. If the sum of absolute values of all *local price movements* (defined below) is K, and the difference between opening and closing prices is z, we show that the profit obtained is exactly $(K - z^2)/2$. The positive term K can be viewed as the product of the average volatility of the price and the duration for which the algorithm is run. The negative term z^2 captures the *net change in price* during the entire trading period. Thus this characterization indicates that *market making is profitable when there is a large amount of local price movement, but only a small net change in the price.* This observation matches a common intuition among market makers, and provides a theoretical foundation for such a belief. An unbiased random walk (or Brownian motion) provides a *boundary* of profitability — the algorithm makes zero expected profit (as do all trading algorithms), while any stochastic price process whose closing price has comparatively less variance from the opening price makes positive expected profit. The last observation leads to our second result.

Mean Reversion.

We next exhibit the benefit of obtaining a succinct and exact expression for profit by applying it to some classes of stochastic time series that help in understanding the circumstances under which the algorithm is profitable. We identify a natural class of time series called *mean-reverting* processes whose properties make our market making algorithm profitable in expectation. A stochastic price series is considered to be *reverting* towards its *long-term mean* μ if the price shows a downward trend when greater than μ and upward trend when less than μ. Prices of commodities such as oil [11, 13] and foreign exchange rates [8] have been empirically observed to exhibit mean reversion. Mean-reverting stochastic processes are studied as a major class of price models, as a contrast to stochastic processes with directional drift, or with no drift, such as Brownian motion. One widely studied mean-reverting stochastic process is the *Ornstein-Uhlenbeck process* [7].

Formally, our second result states that out market making algorithm has expected positive profit on any random walk that reverts towards its opening price. This result is quite revealing — it holds if the random walk shows even the slightest mean reversion, regardless of how complex the process may be (for instance, its evolution may depend not only on the current price, but also on the historical prices in an arbitrary way, as well as the current time). It identifies mean reversion as the natural property which renders market making profitable.

Our third result shows that simple market making algorithms yield stronger profit guarantees for specific mean-reverting processes. As an example, we consider the Ornstein-Uhlenbeck (OU) process. If the price series follows this process, we show that a simple market making algorithm is profitable when run for a sufficiently long time. Moreover, the profit grows *linearly* with the duration for which the algorithm is run, and the profit guarantees hold not only in expectation, but with high probability. We prove this by showing that while $\mathbf{E}[K]$ grows linearly with time, $\mathbf{E}[z^2]$ is upper bounded by a constant. Unlike our second result, we do not need the assumption that the price series begins at the long-term mean — the initial price appears in the upper bound on $\mathbf{E}[z^2]$.

We also show an analogous result for another mean reverting process that has been studied in the finance literature, a model studied by Schwartz [14]. In this model, the local volatility is a linear function of price, while the OU process models volatility as a constant.

We remark that the results outlined above assume a model where the market maker can place and cancel orders as frequently as it likes, and in fact our algorithm does so after every change in the exogenous asset price. In practice, however, a market maker cannot react to every change, since the asset price may change with every trade in the market (which may or may not involve this particular market maker), and the market maker may not be able to place new limit orders after every trade of a rapidly traded stock. So we also analyze the profitability of our market making algorithm when it is allowed to change its orders only after every L steps, by simulating our algorithm on random samples from the OU process. If the price series is the OU process, we show that the expected profit continues to grow linearly with time.

Other Related Work.

To our knowledge, no previous work has studied market making in an exogenously specified price time series model. Most of the theoretical work, as mentioned before, considers a single dealer model where all trades occurred through the market maker at its quoted prices [5, 9, 2, 3]. This includes the well-known Glosten-Milgrom model for market making [9]. On the other hand, there has been a fair amount of work in algorithmic trading, especially statistical arbitrage, that assumes an exogenous price time series. The closest line of research to our work in this literature is the analysis of pair trading strategies under the assumption that the price difference between the two equities show mean reversion (e.g. [4, 12]). As discussed before, such strategies are qualitatively very different from market making strategies. Moreover, most algorithmic trading work, to our knowledge, either analyze price series given by very specific stochastic differential equations (similar to Sections 3.1 and 3.2 of our paper), or empirically analyze these algorithms against historical trading data (e.g. [6]). In contrast, we also give profit guarantees for the weakest of mean reversion processes without assuming a specific form (Theorem 3.1), and in fact derive an exact expression for arbitrary price series (Theorem 2.1), inspired from the notion of worst-case analysis in theoretical computer science.

2. A GENERAL CHARACTERIZATION

We first describe our theoretical model formally. We assume that all events occur at discrete time steps $0, 1, 2 \ldots T$, where T is the time horizon when the market making algorithm must terminate. There is an asset price P_t of the stock at every time step $0 \leq t \leq T$. Thus $P_0, P_1 \ldots P_T$ is the *asset price time series*. We assume that all prices are *integral* multiples of a basic unit of money (regulations in NYSE/NASDAQ currently require prices to be integral multiples of a penny).

A trading algorithm may place and cancel (possibly both) buy and sell orders at any of these time steps, and each order requests a single share at a quoted limit order price Y. A buy (respectively, sell) order at price Y placed at time t gets *executed* at the earliest time $t' > t$ such that $P_{t'} \leq Y$ (respectively, $P_{t'} \geq Y$), provided that the order is not canceled before t'. Any buy order placed by our algorithms will quote a price $Y < P_t$, and so cannot get executed at time t itself; the same applies to sell orders as well. If the buy (respectively, sell) order gets executed (at some time in the future), then the algorithm pays (respectively, earns) Y units of money due to the execution. We assume *no market impact* — the orders placed by the algorithm (which may get executed) do not affect the prices in the future. We leave to future work the important topic of incorporation of market impact into our results.

The *inventory* held by the algorithm at time t is the number of shares held by it at that time. The inventory is incremented upon every executed buy order, and decremented upon every executed sell order. The initial inventory is, naturally, assumed to be zero. At time T, the algorithm must liquidate its accumulated inventory at the current asset price (alternatively, one may view it as the evaluation of the portfolio at time T). If the algorithm has inventory x (x may be negative) at time T, then it earns or pays xP_T from the liquidation. The *profit* obtained by the algorithm is then its net cash position (positive or negative) after liquidation.

A trading algorithm is considered to be an online process — it makes its decisions (about placing and canceling orders) at time t after observing the price series up to (and including) time t. The algorithm may or may not have additional information about the price series. Note that we assume *no latency* and *arbitrary frequency* (we relax the frequency assumption in our simulations) — the algorithm can look at current prices and place buy and sell orders instantaneously, and it can do so as frequently as it wishes. Again, we leave the relaxation of these unrealistic assumptions for future work.

Market Making Algorithms.

The basic class of market making algorithms that we consider is the following: At time t, the algorithm cancels all unexecuted orders, and places new buy orders at prices $Y_t, Y_t - 1, Y_t - 2 \ldots Y_t - C_t$ and new sell orders at prices $X_t, X_t + 1, X_t + 2 \ldots X_t + C_t$, where $Y_t < X_t$ and C_t is a non-negative integer. Such *ladders* of prices are set up to ensure that large sudden fluctuations in price causes a proportionally large volume of executions. C_t is called the *depth* of the price ladder at time t, and intuitively, the algorithm believes that

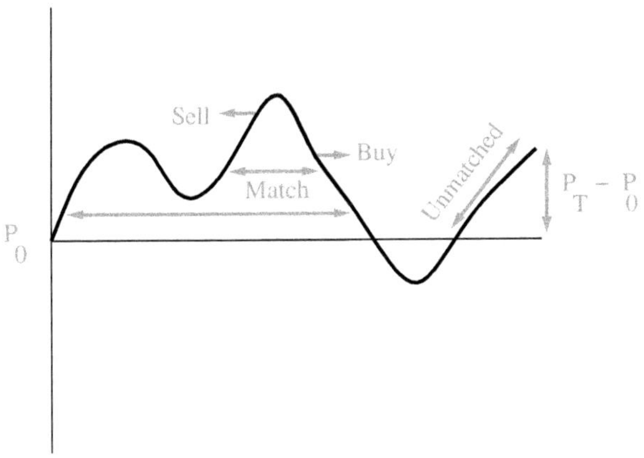

Figure 1: Matched and unmatched trades

the price fluctuation $|P_{t+1} - P_t|$ shall not exceed C_t. Unexecuted orders are canceled and fresh orders are placed at every time step (changes are necessary only if $X_{t+1} \neq X_t$ or $Y_{t+1} \neq Y_t$). Thus the algorithm is determined by the choices of X_t, Y_t and C_t for all t, and these choices may be made after observing the price movements up to time t.

We begin by presenting our basic result for a simple market making algorithm, that sets $X_t = P_t + 1$ and $Y_t = P_t - 1$.

THEOREM 2.1. *Let $P_0, P_1 \dots P_T$ be an asset price time series. Let $K = \sum_{t=1}^{T} |P_t - P_{t-1}|$, and let $z = P_T - P_0$. Suppose that $|P_{t+1} - P_t| \leq D_t \; \forall t$, where D_t is known to the algorithm at time t. If the market making algorithm, that sets $X_t = P_t + 1$, $Y_t = P_t - 1$ and ladder depth $C_t = D_t$, is run on this price series, then the inventory liquidated at time T is $-z$, and the profit is $(K - z^2)/2$.*

PROOF. Note that at any time step $t > 0$, at least one order gets executed if the price changes. Moreover, the number of orders executed at time $t \geq 1$ is $P_{t-1} - P_t$ (a negative value indicates that shares were sold). The statement holds as long as $|P_{t-1} - P_t| \leq C_{t-1}$, which is true by assumption. Thus K is equal to the total number of orders that gets executed. Moreover, the size of inventory held by the algorithm at time t is $P_0 - P_t$. We shall construct disjoint pairs of all but $|z|$ of the executed orders, such that each pair of executions comprises an executed buy and a sell execution, and the price of the buy order is 1 less than the price of the sell order, so that each such pair can be viewed as giving a profit of 1.

For $p > P_0$, we pair each sell order, priced at p, that gets executed when price increases to p or more, with the executed buy order, priced at $p - 1$, that gets executed at the earliest time in the future when the price falls back to $p - 1$ or less (if the price ever falls to $p - 1$ again). Note that these pairs are disjoint, since between every rise of the price from $p - 1$ to p, the price must obviously fall to $p - 1$. Similarly, for $p < P_0$, we pair each executed buy order when the price decreases to p or less, with the executed sell order at the earliest time in the future when the price increases to $p + 1$ or more (if it exists).

We claim that only $|z|$ executions remain unmatched (see Figure 2). If $z > 0$, then the only executions that remain unmatched are the sell orders executed when the price increases to p and never again falls below p: for each $P_0 + z \geq p > P_0$, there is one such executed order. During liquidation at time T, these unmatched sell orders are matched by buying z shares at price $P_T = P_0 + z$. The total loss during liquidation is $\sum_{p=P_0+1}^{P_0+z}((P_0 + z) - p) = z(z-1)/2$. Since there are $K - z$ paired executions, the profit obtained from them is $(K - z)/2$. Hence the net profit is $(K - z - z(z-1))/2 = (K - z^2)/2$. A symmetric argument holds for $z < 0$. □

Note that it is typically reasonable to assume that $|P_{t+1} - P_t| < C$ for some large enough C, since it is unlikely that the price of a stock would change by more than a few dollars within a few seconds. In that case, one may set $C_t = C \; \forall t$.

3. MEAN REVERSION MODELS

In this section, we use Theorem 2.1 to relate profitability to *mean reversion.*

DEFINITION 3.1. *A* unit-step walk *is a series $P_0, P_1 \dots P_T$ such that $|P_{t+1} - P_t| \leq 1 \; \forall T > t \geq 0$. A stochastic price series $P_0, P_1 \dots P_T$ is called a* random walk *if it is a unit-step walk almost surely. We say that a random walk is* unbiased *if $\mathbf{Pr}[P_{t+1} - P_t = 1 | P_t, P_{t-1} \dots P_0] = 1/2$, for all unit-step walks $P_t \dots P_0$, for all $T > t \geq 0$.*

We say a random walk is mean-reverting *towards μ if*

$$\mathbf{Pr}[P_{t+1} - P_t = 1 | P_t = x, P_{t-1} \dots P_0] \geq \mathbf{Pr}[P_{t+1} - P_t = -1 | P_t = x, P_{t-1} \dots P_0]$$

for all $x \leq \mu$, and

$$\mathbf{Pr}[P_{t+1} - P_t = 1 | P_t = y, P_{t-1} \dots P_0] \leq \mathbf{Pr}[P_{t+1} - P_t = -1 | P_t = x, P_{t-1} \dots P_0]$$

for all $y \geq \mu$, for all $t, P_{t-1}, P_{t-2} \dots P_0$ such that $P_0, \dots P_t$ is a unit-step walk, and at least one of these inequalities for $t < T$ is strict (i.e., it is not an unbiased random walk).

Note that all trading algorithms yield zero expected profit on an unbiased random walk. This is because the profit F_t of the algorithm, if its inventory were liquidated at time t, is a martingale, irrespective of the number of shares bought or sold at each time step, and so the expected profit is $\mathbf{E}[F_T] = \mathbf{E}[F_0] = 0$.

THEOREM 3.1. *For any random walk $P_0, P_1 \dots P_T$ that is mean-reverting towards $\mu = P_0$, the expected profit of the market making algorithm that sets $X_t = P_t + 1$ and $Y_t = P_t - 1$ (any $C_t \geq 0$ suffices) is positive.*

PROOF. Since the price does not change by more than 1 in a time step, the market making algorithm need not set a ladder of prices. By Theorem 2.1, the expected profit is $\mathbf{E}[(K - z^2)/2]$. Let $K_t = \sum_{i=1}^{t} |P_i - P_{i-1}|$, and let $z_t = P_t - P_0$. We show by induction on t that $\mathbf{E}[K_t] \geq \mathbf{E}[z_t^2]$ for all t. For $t = T$, this would imply positive expected profit for our algorithm. Without loss of generality, we assume that $P_0 = \mu = 0$.

For $t = 0$, the statement is trivially true, since $K_t = z_t = 0$. Suppose it is true for some $t \geq 0$, then we can show that it is true for $t + 1$. Let $\mathcal{F}_t$ denote the set of all unit-step walks such that $P_0 = \mu = 0$. For $s \in \mathcal{F}_t$, let $\alpha(s) = \mathbf{Pr}[P_{t+1} - P_t = 1 | P_t, P_{t-1} \dots P_0]$, and let $\beta(s) = \mathbf{Pr}[P_{t+1} - P_t = -1 | P_t, P_{t-1} \dots P_0]$. Also, let $\mathbf{Pr}[s]$ denote the probability that the first t steps of this random walk is s. Then we have

$$\mathbf{E}[K_{t+1}] = \mathbf{E}[K_t + |P_{t+1} - P_t|] = \mathbf{E}[K_t] + \sum_{s \in \mathcal{F}_t} \mathbf{Pr}[s](\alpha(s) + \beta(s)) \qquad (1)$$

$$
\begin{aligned}
\mathbf{E}[z_{t+1}^2] &= \mathbf{E}[P_{t+1}^2] \\
&= \sum_{s \in \mathcal{F}_t} \mathbf{Pr}[s]\left(\alpha(s)(P_t+1)^2 + \beta(s)(P_t-1)^2\right. \\
&\qquad\qquad \left. + (1-\alpha(s)-\beta(s))P_t^2\right) \\
&= \sum_{s \in \mathcal{F}_t} \mathbf{Pr}[s]\left(P_t^2 + \alpha(s) + \beta(s) + 2P_t(\alpha(s)-\beta(s))\right) \\
&= \mathbf{E}[P_t^2] + \sum_{s \in \mathcal{F}_t} \mathbf{Pr}[s](\alpha(s)+\beta(s)) \\
&\qquad + 2\sum_{s \in \mathcal{F}_t} \mathbf{Pr}[s] P_t(\alpha(s)-\beta(s)) \\
&\le \mathbf{E}[K_t] + \sum_{s \in \mathcal{F}_t} \mathbf{Pr}[s](\alpha(s)+\beta(s)) \\
&\qquad + 2\sum_{s \in \mathcal{F}_t} \mathbf{Pr}[s] P_t(\alpha(s)-\beta(s)) \\
&\qquad \text{(by induction hypothesis)} \\
&= \mathbf{E}[K_{t+1}] + 2\sum_{s \in \mathcal{F}_t} \mathbf{Pr}[s] P_t(\alpha(s)-\beta(s)) \\
&\qquad \text{(by Equation 1)}
\end{aligned}
$$

It suffices to show that that $P_t(\alpha(s) - \beta(s)) \le 0$ for all $s \in \mathcal{F}_t$. This follows immediately from the definition of a mean-reverting random walk: if $P_t > P_0 = 0$, then $\alpha(s) < \beta(s)$, and if $P_t < P_0 = 0$, then $\alpha(s) > \beta(s)$. Thus we have proved the induction hypothesis for $t+1$.

Finally, for the smallest t such that for some $s \in \mathcal{F}_t$ we have $\alpha(s) \ne \beta(s)$, the inequality in the induction hypothesis becomes strict at $t+1$, *i.e.* $\mathbf{E}[K_{t+1}] > \mathbf{E}[z_{t+1}^2]$, and so the expected profit for $T > t$ is strictly positive. □

3.1 Ornstein-Uhlenbeck Processes

One well-studied mean-reverting process is a continuous time, real-valued stochastic process known as the *Ornstein-Uhlenbeck (OU) process* [7]. We denote this process by Q_t. It is usually expressed by the following stochastic differential equation:

$$
\mathrm{d}Q_t = -\gamma(Q_t - \mu)\mathrm{d}t + \sigma \mathrm{d}W_t \ ,
$$

where W_t is a standard Brownian motion, and γ, σ are positive constants, and $\gamma < 1$. The value μ is a constant around which the price fluctuates — it is called the *long term mean* of the process. The coefficient of $\mathrm{d}t$ is called *drift*, while that of $\mathrm{d}W_t$ is called *volatility*. Observe that the drift is negative for $P_t > \mu$ and positive for $P_t < \mu$ — this is why the process tends to revert towards μ whenever it is far from it. γ is the rate of mean reversion. The OU process is memoryless (distribution of Q_t given Q_0 is the same as distribution of Q_{t+x} given Q_x), and given an opening value Q_0, the variable Q_t is known to be normally distributed, such that

$$
\begin{aligned}
\mathbf{E}[Q_t] &= \mu + (Q_0 - \mu)e^{-\gamma t}, \\
\mathbf{Var}[Q_t] &= \frac{\sigma^2}{2\gamma}(1 - e^{-2\gamma t})
\end{aligned}
\qquad (2)
$$

Now we consider the OU process Q_t as a price series in the unique model, and analyze profitability of our algorithm. However, since the OU process is a continuous time real-valued process, we need to define a natural restriction to a discrete integral time series that conforms to our theoretical model. We achieve this by letting P_t to be the nearest integer to Q_t, for all non-negative integers t. The rounding is practical since in reality prices are not allowed to be real-valued, and further, our algorithm reacts to only integral changes in price. We shall analyze our algorithm on P_t.

A significant hindrance in applying Theorem 2.1 to the OU process is that the jumps $|P_{t+1} - P_t|$ are not necessarily bounded by some constant C, so we have to put some effort into determining C_t. Since the OU process is memoryless, Equation 2 implies that given Q_t, Q_{t+1} is normally distributed with expectation $\mu + (Q_t - \mu)e^{-\gamma}$ and variance less than $\sigma^2/2\gamma$, so if we set $C >> \frac{\sigma^2}{2\gamma}\sqrt{\ln T}$ and then set $C_t = \mathbf{E}[|Q_{t+1} - Q_t| \; |Q_t] + C$, then the probability that the price jump at any time exceeds the depth of the ladder is vanishing, and such events do not contribute significantly to the expected profit if we simply stop the algorithm when such an event occurs.

THEOREM 3.2. *Let $P_0, P_1 \ldots P_T$ be a price series obtained from an OU process $\{Q_t\}$ with long-term mean μ. Then the market making algorithm that sets $X_t = P_t + 1$, $Y_t = P_t - 1$ and $C_t = \mathbf{E}[|Q_{t+1} - Q_t| \; |Q_t] + 10\frac{\sigma^2}{2\gamma}\sqrt{\ln T}$ yields long term expected profit $\Omega(\sigma T - \sigma^2/2\gamma - (\mu - Q_0)^2)$.*

PROOF. It is easy to show, as outlined above, that the contribution of events where a price jump larger than C_t occurs to the expected profit is negligible. We restrict our attention to the event when no such large jump occurs. By Theorem 2.1, the profit on a sample series is $(K - z^2)/2$, where $K = \sum_{t=1}^{T} |P_t - P_{t-1}|$, and $z = P_T - P_0$. The result follows by giving a lower bound on $\mathbf{E}[K]$ and an upper bound on $\mathbf{E}[z^2]$.

Let us derive a lower bound on $\mathbf{E}[|Q_{t+1} - Q_t|]$. Note that this quantity is equal to $\mathbf{E}[|Q_1' - Q_0'||Q_0' = Q_t]$, where Q_t' is an identical but independent OU process. This is because the OU process is Markov, and future prices depend only on the current price. Since $\gamma < 1$, so Equation 2 implies that given Q_t, Q_{t+1} is normally distributed with variance greater than $\sigma^2/4$, since $\frac{1-e^{-2\gamma}}{2\gamma} > 1/4$ when $\gamma < 1$. Hence $\mathbf{E}[|Q_{t+1} - Q_t|]$ is at least $\sigma/4$ (using properties of a folded normal distribution). Since P_t is obtained by rounding Q_t, we have $|P_{t+1} - P_t| > |Q_{t+1} - Q_t| - 2$. Thus for large enough σ (see comments at the end of the theorem), we get that $\mathbf{E}[K] = \Omega(\sigma T)$.

$\mathbf{E}[z^2]$ is approximated well enough by $\mathbf{E}[(Q_T - Q_0)^2]$, since $|z - (Q_T - Q_0)| < 2$ for all possible realizations. Again, Equation 2 implies that $Q_T - Q_0$ has mean $\mu + (Q_0 - \mu)e^{-\gamma T} - Q_0 = (\mu - Q_0)(1 - e^{-\gamma T})$ and variance $\sigma^2(1 - e^{-2\gamma T})/2\gamma$. Thus, we have

$$
\begin{aligned}
\mathbf{E}[(Q_T - Q_0)^2] &= \mathbf{Var}[Q_T - Q_0] + \mathbf{E}[Q_T - Q_0]^2 \\
&= \frac{\sigma^2(1 - e^{-2\gamma T})}{2\gamma} \\
&\qquad + (\mu - Q_0)^2(1 - e^{-\gamma T})^2 \\
&< \frac{\sigma^2}{2\gamma} + (\mu - Q_0)^2
\end{aligned}
$$

Thus, $\mathbf{E}[K]$ grows linearly with T, while $\mathbf{E}[z^2]$ is bounded by a constant. This completes the proof. □

A few points worth noting about Theorem 3.2: our lower bound on $\mathbf{E}[K]$ is actually $(\frac{\sigma}{4} - 2)T$ and σ must exceed 8 for this term to be positive and grow linearly with T. This is just an easy way to handle the arbitrary integral rounding of Q_t. Intuitively, the algorithm typically cannot place orders with prices separated by less than a penny. Thus the volatility needs to be sufficient for integral changes to occur in the price series. If the unit of money could be made smaller, the loss due to rounding should diminish. Then σ in terms of the new unit increases linearly, while γ remains constant (Q_t becomes cQ_t for some scaling factor c). Thus for any constant σ, a sufficiently small granularity of prices allows us to apply Theorem 3.2. In fact, it is not difficult to see from the above analysis that the profit will grow linearly with time as long as the limiting variance of the process $\sigma^2/2\gamma$ is larger than (or comparable to) the granularity of bidding (normalized to 1). If this does not hold, then the algorithm will rarely get its orders executed, and will neither profit nor lose any significant amount.

Moreover, in the proof of Theorem 3.2, one may note that z is a normal variable with variance bounded by a constant, while the lower bound on K grows linearly with T, and occurs with high probability. Thus the profit expression in Theorem 3.2 not only holds in expectation (as is the case in Theorem 3.1 for general mean-reverting walks), but with high probability. Furthermore, for even the smallest of γ, Theorem 3.2 says that the profit is positive if T is large enough. Thus, *even when mean reversion is weak, a sufficiently long time horizon can make market making profitable.*

Finally, the profit expression of the OU process has a term $(\mu - Q_0)^2$. While we can treat it as a constant independent of the time horizon, we can also apply another trick to reduce this constant loss if Q_0 is far from μ. This is because Equation 2 tells us that the process converges exponentially fast towards μ — in time $t = \gamma^{-1} \log|Q_0 - \mu|$, $|\mathbf{E}[Q_t - \mu]|$ is down to 1, and $\mathbf{Var}[Q_0 - \mu]$ is less than σ^2/γ. Thus if the horizon T is large enough, then the market maker would like to simply sit out until time t (if allowed by market regulations), and then start applying our market making strategy.

3.2 The Schwartz Model

We now analyze another stochastic mean reversion model that has been studied in the finance literature and was studied by Schwartz [14]. The OU process assumes that the volatility of the price curve is a constant. Schwartz proposed a model where the volatility is a linear function of the price:

$$\mathrm{d}Q_t = -\gamma Q_t(\ln Q_t - \ln\mu)\mathrm{d}t + \sigma Q_t \mathrm{d}W_t,$$

where μ is the long term mean price of the process, $\gamma < 1$, and $\sigma < 1$. Also assume that $Q_0 > 0$.

We shall show that the profitability of our market making algorithm for the Schwartz model is analogous to Theorem 3.2: $\mathbf{E}[K]$ grows linearly in T, while the expected loss due to liquidation $\mathbf{E}[z^2]$ is bounded by a constant, and hence the expected profit grows linearly in T . Applying Ito's lemma, Schwartz showed that $\log Q_t$ is an OU process, and so Q_t has a lognormal distribution, such that

$$\alpha_t = \mathbf{E}[\log Q_t] = (\ln\mu - \frac{\sigma^2}{2\gamma})(1 - e^{-\gamma t}) + Q_0 e^{-\gamma t},$$

$$\beta_t^2 = \mathbf{Var}[\log Q_t] = \frac{\sigma^2}{2\gamma}(1 - e^{-2\gamma t})$$

Then, by properties of lognormal distributions, we have

$$\mathbf{E}[Q_t] = e^{\alpha_t + \beta_t^2/2}, \qquad \mathbf{Var}[Q_t] = (e^{\beta_t^2} - 1)e^{2\alpha_t + \beta_t^2}$$

Suppose the unit of price is small enough so that $\ln\mu > \frac{\sigma^2}{2\gamma}$ (again, this is essentially equivalent to choosing a finer granularity of placing orders). Note that shrinking the size of a unit step by a factor c leaves both σ and γ unchanged, but inflates μ by c. Since α_t and β_t are upper bounded by constants, so are $\mathbf{E}[Q_t]$ and $\mathbf{Var}[Q_t]$, and hence $\mathbf{E}[z^2]$ is bounded by a constant.

It remains to show that $\mathbf{E}[K] = \Omega(T)$. It suffices to show that $\mathbf{E}[|Q_{t+1} - Q_t|]$ is at least some constant. Note that Q_t is always positive, since it has a lognormal distribution. We shall show that $\mathbf{E}[|Q_{t+1} - Q_t||Q_t]$ is at least some constant, for any positive Q_t. Since Q_t is a Markov process, this is equal to $\mathbf{E}[|Q_1' - Q_0'||Q_0' = Q_t]$ for an identical but independent process Q_t'. Observe that $\alpha_1 \geq (\ln\mu - \frac{\sigma^2}{2\gamma})(1-e^{-\gamma}) > 0$, if $Q_0 > 0$. Also, we have $\beta_1^2 > \sigma^2/4$. Thus

$$\mathbf{Var}[Q_1'] > e^{\sigma^2/4}(e^{\sigma^2/4} - 1) > \sigma^2 e^{\sigma^2/4}/4 \ .$$

This shows that $\mathbf{Var}[Q_1']$, given Q_0, is lower bounded by a constant (that depends on σ). Since Q_1' has a lognormal distribution, it follows that $\mathbf{E}[|Q_1' - Q_0'|]$ is also lower bounded by a constant. This completes the proof for $\mathbf{E}[K] = \Omega(T)$.

4. TRADING FREQUENCY

Our price series model makes the assumption that the market maker can place fresh orders after every change in price. In practice, however, there are many traders, and each trade causes some change in price, and an individual trader cannot react immediately to every change. We thus consider a more general model where the market maker places fresh orders after every L steps. Let us consider the same market making algorithm as before, in this infrequent order model. Thus, for every i, at time iL the algorithm places orders around P_{iL} in a ladder fashion as before. These orders remain unchanged (or get executed if the requisite price is reached) until time $(i+1)L$, and then the algorithm cancels the unexecuted orders and places fresh orders. We say that L is the *trading frequency* of the algorithm.

The profit of the algorithm can no longer be captured succinctly as before. In particular, the profit is not exclusively determined by (nor can it be lower bounded by a function of) the prices $P_0, P_L, P_{2L} \ldots P_{iL} \ldots$ at which the algorithm refreshes its orders — it depends on the path taken within every interval of L steps and not just the net change within this interval. Still, some of our profit guarantees continue to hold qualitatively in this model. In particular, we simulate the OU process and run our algorithm on this process, to analyze how trading frequency affects the profit of the algorithm. We simulate an OU process with $\gamma = 0.1$, $\sigma = 1$ and the initial price equal to the long term mean.

First, we find that the profit still shows a trend of growing linearly with time, for different trading frequencies L that are still significantly smaller than the time horizon T. We simulate the algorithm with different time horizons T and different trading frequencies, and all of them show a strong linear growth (see Figure 2).

Also, the profit is expected to fall as the trading frequency increases (keeping time horizon fixed), since the number of trades executed will clearly decrease. We find that for a

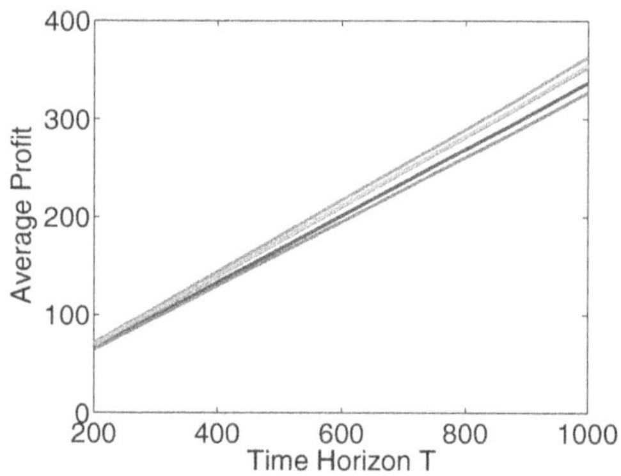

Figure 2: Profit increases linearly with the time horizon, for different trading frequencies $1, 2, 5, 10, 20$.

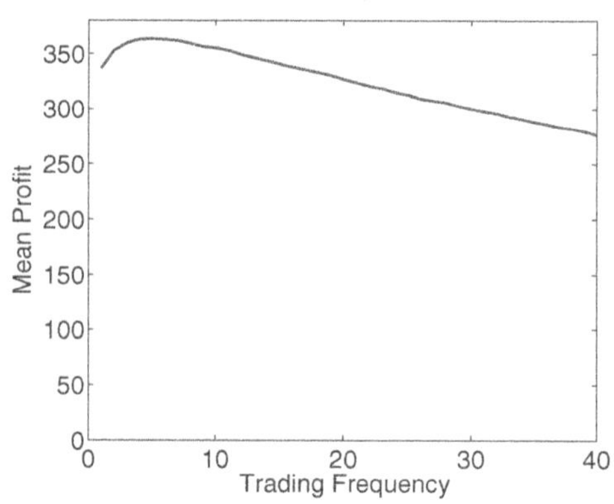

Figure 3: Mean profit decreases slowly with trading frequency (Horizon $T = 1000$).

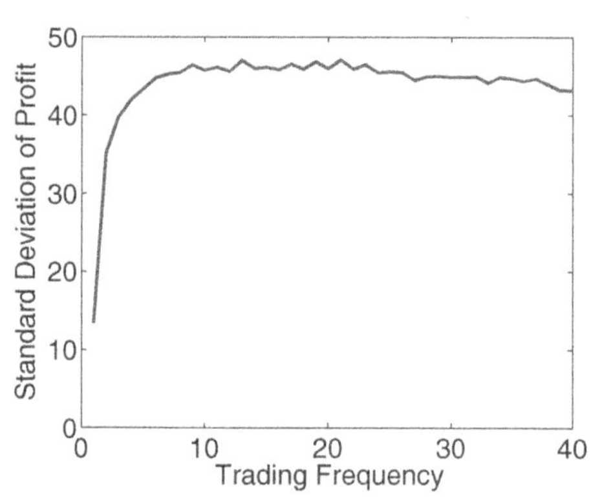

Figure 4: Standard deviation of profit increases quickly with trading frequency, then stabilizes (Horizon $T = 1000$).

large enough horizon ($T = 1000$), this is indeed the case, but the decrease in profit is quite slow, and even with trading frequency as high as 40, the expected profit is more than 80% of the expected profit with unit trading frequency (see Figure 3).

We computed average profit by simulating each setting 10000 times, to get a very narrow confidence interval. In fact, the standard deviation of the profit never exceeds 50 for any of our simulations, so the confidence interval (taken as 2σ divided by the square root of sample size) is less than 1, while the expected profit is much higher in all the cases.

The standard deviation in the profit itself goes up sharply as the trading frequency is increased from 1, but then quickly stabilizes (see Figure 4).The increase in variance of profit can perhaps be explained by the increase in variance of the number of shares that are liquidated at the end.

5. CONCLUSIONS

In this paper, we analyze the profitability of simple market making algorithms. Market making algorithms are a restricted class of trading algorithms, though there is no formal specification of the restrictions. Intuitively, the restriction is that a market maker has to always be present in the market, and offer prices that are close to the asset price. A future direction would be to put such a formal restriction, and try to design an optimal trading algorithm that satisfies the formal restrictions.

Acknowledgments

We give warm thanks to Yuriy Nevmyvaka for helpful comments and suggestions.

6. REFERENCES

[1] C. Comerton-Forde, T. Hendershott, C. M. Jones, P. C. Moulton, and M. S. Seasholes. Time variation in liquidity: The role of market maker inventories and revenues. *Journal of Finance*, 65:295–331, 2010.

[2] S. Das. A learning market-maker in the Glosten-Milgrom model. *Quantitative Finance*, 5(2):169–180, 2005.

[3] S. Das and M. Magdon-Ismail. Adapting to a market shock: Optimal sequential market-making. In *NIPS*, pages 361–368, 2008.

[4] R. J. Elliott, J. van der Hoek, and W. P. Malcolm. Pairs trading. *Quantitative Finance*, 5(3):271–276, 2005.

[5] M. B. Garman. Market microstructure. *Journal of Financial Economics*, 3(3):257–275, 1976.

[6] E. Gatev, W. N. Goetzmann, and K. G. Rouwenhorst. Pairs trading: Performance of a relative-value arbitrage rule. *Review of Financial Studies*, 19(3):797–827, 2006.

[7] G.E.Uhlenbeck and L.S.Ornstein. On the theory of Brownian motion. *Physical Review*, 36:823–841, 1930.

[8] L. A. Gil-Alana. Mean reversion in the real exchange rates. *Economics Letters*, 69(3):285–288, 2000.

[9] L. Glosten and P. Milgrom. Bid, ask and transaction prices in a specialist market with heterogeneously informed traders. *Journal of Financial Economics*, 14:71–100, 1985.

[10] T. Hendershott and M. S. Seasholes. Market maker inventories and stock prices. *American Economic Review*, 97:210–214, 2007.

[11] R. H. Litzenberger and N. Rabinowitz. Backwardation in oil futures markets: Theory and empirical evidence. *The Journal of Finance*, 50(5):1517–1545, 1995.

[12] S. Mudchanatongsuk, J. Primbs, and W. Wong. Optimal pairs trading: A stochastic control approach. *Proceedings of the American Control Conference*, pages 1035–1039, 2008.

[13] R. Pindyck. The dynamics of commodity spot and futures markets: A primer. *Energy Journal*, 22(3):1–29, 2001.

[14] E. S. Schwartz. The stochastic behavior of commodity prices: Implications for valuation and hedging. *The Journal of Finance*, 52(3):923–973, 1997.

Pseudorandom Financial Derivatives

[Extended Abstract]

David Zuckerman
Department of Computer Science
University of Texas at Austin
1616 Guadalupe, Suite 2.408
Austin, TX 78701
diz@cs.utexas.edu

ABSTRACT

Arora, Barak, Brunnermeier, and Ge [1] showed that taking computational complexity into account, a dishonest seller could dramatically increase the lemon costs of a family of financial derivatives. We show that if the seller is required to construct derivatives of a certain form, then this phenomenon disappears. In particular, we define and construct *pseudorandom derivative families*, for which lemon placement only slightly affects the values of the derivatives. Our constructions use expander graphs.

We study our derivatives in a more general setting than Arora et al. In particular, we analyze arbitrary tranches of the common collateralized debt obligations (CDOs) when the underlying assets can have significant dependencies.

Categories and Subject Descriptors

J.4 [**Social and Behavioral Sciences**]: Economics; F.m [**Theory of Computation**]: Miscellaneous

General Terms

Economics, Theory

Keywords

pseudorandom, finance, derivative, expander

1. INTRODUCTION

Financial derivatives play a major role in our financial system, as became all too apparent in the recent financial crisis. A derivative is a financial product whose value is a function of one or more underlying assets. They can be used to hedge risk, provide leverage, or simply to speculate. The major benefit of derivatives is that they facilitate the buying and selling of risk.

While a derivative may depend on only one asset, in this paper we study derivatives that depend on many assets. One supposed benefit of such derivatives is that they can mitigate the effects of asymmetric information. That is, a seller may be aware that certain underlying assets are lemons, and try to strategically place the lemons among the derivatives in order to minimize the derivatives' value. Nevertheless, an unknowledgeable buyer can buy less information-sensitive derivatives based on these assets without incurring significant risk. In other words, the *lemon cost* of these derivatives should be small. The lemon cost is the value without any lemons minus the value with lemons.

Arora, Barak, Brunnermeier, and Ge [1] introduced computational complexity into this discussion. They showed that contrary to the conventional wisdom, once computational complexity is accounted for, the lemon costs of derivatives could increase dramatically, at least under a plausible computational assumption. Indeed, in the recent financial crisis, it appears that sellers did pack lemons into their CDOs without buyers' knowledge; see for example Michael Lewis's *The Big Short* [7].

Before describing how we get around this problem, we first describe the setting of Arora et al. There are n assets and m derivatives, where each derivative is a function of r underlying assets. We will have $n \ll mr$, so that each asset underlies several derivatives. This is typically not the case if the underlying assets are, say, mortgages; however, in the common case that the underlying assets are credit default swaps, it is often the case that an asset can underlie several derivatives.

Arora et al. model the relationship between derivatives and underlying assets as a bipartite graph. The nodes are the derivatives and assets, and there is an edge between a derivative and an asset if the derivative depends on that asset. If the derivatives are for sale to the public, then the seller must make this graph public.

Now consider a seller who knows that certain underlying assets are lemons. For certain derivatives, it is advantageous for the seller to concentrate many of these lemons into a small number of derivatives. Thus, these lemons and the lemon-loaded derivatives will correspond to a dense subgraph of the original graph. Arora et al. observed that if it is computationally intractable to check whether an arbitrary graph (or even a somewhat random graph) contains a dense subgraph, then it is computationally intractable to catch such a dishonest seller. Therefore, the lemon cost could be quite high.

We circumvent this problem. Instead of allowing the seller to use an arbitrary bipartite graph to construct the CDO family, we mandate that the seller use a specific bipartite graph. Of course, the buyer can easily check that the seller did use the specified graph. While the seller will still be able to assign assets to nodes arbitrarily, we can choose the graph judiciously to avoid the dense subgraph problem, for the following reason. Although it may be computationally intractable to test whether an arbitrary graph, or even a somewhat-random graph, contains a dense subgraph, it is nevertheless possible to explicitly construct a graph with no dense subgraphs. We choose such a graph for the seller.

Graphs with no dense subgraphs are related to certain fundamen-

EC'11, June 5–9, 2011, San Jose, California, USA.

tal objects in the theory of pseudorandomness: randomness extractors and expander graphs. For a survey of these objects and other aspects of pseudorandomness, see [10].

Our constructions motivate the notion of a *pseudorandom derivative family*. This is a set of derivatives such that no matter how the lemons are placed by an adversary, the sum of the value changes of the derivatives will be small. In other words, adversarial placement of lemons behaves similarly to random placement.

Alternatively, we may decompose the lemon cost into the unavoidable lemon cost plus the cost of dishonesty. The unavoidable lemon cost is the lemon cost for an honest seller who randomly places the lemons. The cost of dishonesty is the additional cost from a dishonest seller who strategically places the lemons. A pseudorandom derivative family is one where the cost of dishonesty is small.

In our main result, we show how to construct good pseudorandom derivative families, using expander graphs with expansion close to the degree.

Of course, in order to analyze values we need a model for the underlying assets. Arora et al. assume the underlying assets are independent fair coin flips, taking the value 1 with probability 1/2, whereas the lemons always take value 0.

We analyze a more realistic model with dependencies. In particular, we only require that the probability distribution on any r assets depends only on how many of the assets are lemons. We also don't need to assume lemons have value 0. We do obtain our strongest results when we assume good assets "dominate" lemons, as explained below.

One model satisfying our requirements allows dependencies among assets to occur through some global random variable Z. This Z could represent the state of the economy and housing market, and other relevant information. We make no assumptions about Z. For each fixing of Z, to say z, there are two probability distributions $D_g = D_g(z)$ and $D_\ell = D_\ell(z)$. Conditioned on $Z = z$, our model assumes all assets are independent, with good assets chosen according to D_g, and lemons chosen according to D_ℓ. Moreover, we say good assets dominate lemons if for any z, if X is chosen according to $D_g(z)$ and Y is chosen according to $D_\ell(z)$, then for all a, $\Pr[X \geq a] \geq \Pr[Y \geq a]$.

We also need a model for the derivatives. One of the most common derivatives is the collateralized debt obligation, or CDO. The size of the CDO market was recently over a trillion dollars. Arora et al. analyze these CDOs, but only safe (senior) tranches, and they focus on an unrealistic binary variant of them. We focus on the realistic, tranched CDOs, and study arbitrary tranches. We obtain our strongest results for the entire CDO.

A CDO has a natural structure, packaging many underlying assets into *tranches*. For example, a CDO could have 100 underlying mortgages, each of which is supposed to pay \$1,000. The "senior" tranche, for instance, could collect the first \$85,000. Thus, if more than \$85,000 is paid from these 100 mortgages, this tranche receives \$85,000; if some amount $x \leq \$85,000$ is paid, the tranche receives x. The next tranche could range from \$85,000 to \$95,000. If more than \$95,000 is paid, this tranche receives the full \$10,000; if less than \$85,000 is paid, this tranche receives nothing. If the amount x paid is between \$85,000 and \$95,000, then the tranche receives $x-\$85,000$. In general, the $[a,b]$ tranche receives $\min(x,b) - \min(x,a)$.

We begin by explaining our model and defining key terms in Section 2. We then describe how expander graphs give pseudorandom CDOs in Section 3. We modify existing expander constructions to obtain our CDOs in Section 4. Finally, we analyze the case when good assets don't necessarily dominate lemons in Section 5.

2. THE MODEL AND KEY DEFINITIONS

First we give some notation. For a positive integer n, we let $[n]$ denote the set $\{1, 2, \ldots, n\}$. For a vector $v = (v_1, \ldots, v_s)$, we let $\|v\|_1 = \sum_i |v_i|$, the L_1 norm.

Our CDOs will be functions of underlying assets. We first describe our assumptions about the underlying assets, and then define pseudorandom CDOs.

2.1 Model for Underlying Assets

In our model, there are two types of assets, *lemons* and *good assets*. Good assets must dominate lemons in a sense below. This requirement will be satisfied if lemons always take value zero, but it allows more general distributions on lemons. Each CDO will depend on r assets. Our results hold as long as the probability distribution on any r assets depends only on how many of the assets are lemons.

We now elaborate on one natural model which satisfies the two requirements above. We model dependencies among assets as occurring through some global random variable Z. This Z could represent the state of the economy and housing market, and other relevant information. We make no assumptions about Z. For each fixing of Z, to say z, there are two probability distributions $D_g = D_g(z)$ and $D_\ell = D_\ell(z)$. Conditioned on $Z = z$, our model assumes all assets are independent, with good assets chosen according to D_g, and lemons chosen according to D_ℓ. Moreover, we say good assets dominate lemons if for any z and a,

$$\Pr_{X \sim D_g(z)}[X \geq a] \geq \Pr_{Y \sim D_\ell(z)}[Y \geq a].$$

We can relax the requirement that assets are conditionally independent. It suffices that the conditional distribution on assets is r-wise independent, i.e., any r of them are independent. (This does not imply that they are mutually independent.)

We normalize asset values so that each asset's maximum value is 1. We let μ and λ be the expected values of each good asset and lemon, respectively. The dominance requirement implies $\mu \geq \lambda$, and let $\delta = \mu - \lambda$ be the additional expected value of a good asset.

2.2 Pseudorandom CDOs

DEFINITION 2.1. *A collateralized debt obligation (CDO) is a derivative on an underlying portfolio of assets. For* $0 = a_0 < a_1 < \ldots < a_s$ *(called attachment points), the ith tranche is given by the interval* $[a_{i-1}, a_i]$. *If the underlying portfolio pays off* x, *then the value of the ith tranche is* $\text{value}_{[a_{i-1},a_i]}(x) = \min(x, a_i) - \min(x, a_{i-1})$. *If the tranche is understood, we often omit it as a subscript in* value.

Since assets are normalized to have maximum value 1, if the CDO depends on r assets, the last attachment point $a_s = r$.

We will be interested in families of CDOs.

DEFINITION 2.2. *An* (n, m, r)-CDO family *is a set of* m *CDOs on* n *assets identified with the set* $[n]$, *where each CDO depends on* r *assets.*

We will have $n \ll mr$, so that each asset underlies several derivatives.

The seller (creator of the CDOs) knows that some ℓ assets are lemons, and may identify the lemons with any subset $L \subseteq [n]$ of size ℓ. We will be interested in the total value of tranches in our CDO family.

DEFINITION 2.3. *For $L \subseteq [n]$, let $\mathrm{tv}_{[a,b]}(L)$ denote the total expected value of all $[a,b]$ tranches in the CDO family, if the assets corresponding to assets L are lemons. If the tranche is understood, we often omit it as a subscript. We define the vector $\vec{\mathrm{tv}}(L) = (\mathrm{tv}_{[a_0,a_1]}(L), \mathrm{tv}_{[a_1,a_2]}(L), \ldots, \mathrm{tv}_{[a_{s-1},a_s]}(L))$.*

A dishonest seller will try to choose the subset L to minimize $\mathrm{tv}(L)$. A CDO family is pseudorandom if the seller cannot gain significantly by this choice.

DEFINITION 2.4. *An (n,m,r)-CDO family is* pseudorandom *for ℓ lemons for $[a,b]$ tranches with error ϵ if for any two subsets $L, L' \subseteq [n]$ of size ℓ,*

$$|\,\mathrm{tv}_{[a,b]}(L') - \mathrm{tv}_{[a,b]}(L)| \leq \epsilon m(b-a).$$

Note that $m(b-a)$ is the maximum possible value of the $[a,b]$ tranches with no lemons. Thus, for any CDO family the error $\epsilon \leq 1$.

We further define pseudorandomness for the entire CDO family. We can't generalize the above definition naively, to say that the total value of the CDO doesn't change significantly if the lemons are moved. This is because the total value of the CDO equals the total value of the underlying assets; therefore moving lemons won't change the value at all. Instead, we strengthen the definition to ensure that not much value can be transferred among the different tranches. That is, we add up the value changes of each tranche; this gives the L_1-norm.

DEFINITION 2.5. *An (n,m,r)-CDO family is* pseudorandom *for ℓ lemons with error ϵ if for any two subsets $L, L' \subseteq [n]$ of size ℓ,*

$$\|\vec{\mathrm{tv}}(L') - \vec{\mathrm{tv}}(L)\|_1 \leq \epsilon m r.$$

Note that mr is the maximum possible value of the entire CDO family with no lemons. The error ϵ for the CDO family is at most the maximum error for a tranche, and hence at most 1.

We can compare our notion of pseudorandom error to the traditional notion of lemon cost. The lemon cost is the value without any lemons minus the value with lemons. In a sense, we are dividing the lemon cost into two components: the unavoidable lemon cost plus the cost of dishonesty. The unavoidable lemon cost is the lemon cost for an honest seller who randomly places the lemons. The cost of dishonesty is the additional cost from a dishonest seller who strategically places the lemons. Thus, the normalized cost of dishonesty is upper bounded by the pseudorandom error.

On the other hand, the pseudorandom error above is at most the normalized lemon cost, but it could be significantly less. For example, if all underlying assets are lemons, the lemon cost will be high, but the error in our definition will be 0, since the value doesn't change depending on the lemon placement. Indeed, the pseudorandom error is small if the lemon cost doesn't depend significantly on the lemon placement.

2.3 Bipartite Expander Graphs

Following Arora et al., we view the relationship between derivatives and underlying assets as a bipartite graph. We review the basic definitions.

DEFINITION 2.6. *A bipartite graph is a triple (A,B,E), with* left vertices A, right vertices B, *and* edges $E \subseteq A \times B$. *We usually view E as unordered pairs of vertices. Sometimes we refer to a bipartite graph on $A \cup B$ to mean some bipartite graph (A,B,E) with suitable choice of edges E. For a subset of vertices $S \subseteq A \cup B$, let $\Gamma(S) = \{v | (\exists w \in S)\{v,w\} \in E\}$ denote the set of* neighbors *of S. We often write $\Gamma(v)$ for $\Gamma(\{v\})$. The* degree *of a vertex v is $|\Gamma(v)|$. The graph is* d-left-regular *if all left vertices have degree d, and similarly for right-regular. The graph is (d,r)-biregular if it is d-left-regular and r-right-regular.*

The vertices A and B correspond to the assets and derivatives, respectively, with an edge between a derivative vertex and asset vertex if the derivative depends on the asset.

Since Arora et al. showed how dense subgraphs can be problematic, it is natural to try to choose a graph with no dense subgraphs. It is natural to use known constructions of suitable "randomness extractors," which can be shown to lack dense subgraphs. Indeed, this was our original approach. However, we obtain stronger results in a simpler manner by considering the related *expander graphs*, where we require expansion of asset vertices.

DEFINITION 2.7. *A bipartite graph on $[n] \cup [m]$ is an (ℓ_{max}, γ)-expander if for every subset $S \subseteq [n]$ of size at most ℓ_{max}, $|\Gamma(S)| \geq \gamma |S|$.*

Note that we only need expansion of left vertices; expansion of right vertices is not required. We will need a strong form of an expander, called a *unique-neighbor expander*.

DEFINITION 2.8. *Let $\Gamma_i(S)$ denote the set of vertices v with $|\Gamma(v) \cap S| = i$. $\Gamma_1(S)$ are called the* unique neighbors *of S.*

DEFINITION 2.9. *A bipartite graph on $[n] \cup [m]$ is an (ℓ_{max}, γ)-unique-neighbor expander if for every subset $S \subseteq [n]$ of size at most ℓ_{max}, $|\Gamma_1(S)| \geq \gamma |S|$.*

The following simple lemma is well known.

LEMMA 2.10. *A d-left-regular $(\ell_{max}, d-\Delta)$-expander is an $(\ell_{max}, d-2\Delta)$-unique neighbor expander.*

PROOF. Consider any subset S on the left of size $\ell \leq \ell_{max}$. It has at least $(d-\Delta)\ell$ neighbors, which leaves at most $\Delta\ell$ edges unaccounted for. Thus $|\Gamma_1(S)| \geq |\Gamma(S)| - \Delta\ell$, as required. □

It is not hard to show that random graphs are excellent expanders, using the probabilistic method. However, we need to be able to certify that a graph is an expander; otherwise Arora et al. showed how the seller can cheat. We therefore seek explicit constructions of expanders.

Explicit expander constructions are highly nontrivial. The classic constructions of Gabber and Galil [3] and Lubotzky-Phillips-Sarnak [8] do not give unique-neighbor expanders. Ta-Shma, Umans, and Zuckerman constructed the first unique-neighbor expanders of polylogarithmic left degree [9], and Capalbo et al. were the first to achieve constant left degree [2]. For our purposes, the best expanders were constructed by Guruswami, Umans, and Vadhan [5], although these have polylogarithmic degree. For more on expanders we refer the reader to the excellent survey [6].

3. EXPANDERS GIVE PSEUDORANDOM CDOS

Before discussing expander constructions, we first show how unique-neighbor expanders give pseudorandom CDOs. It is helpful to compare our bounds to a natural trivial bound. To this end, observe that any biregular (n,m,r)-CDO family is pseudorandom against ℓ lemons for $[a,b]$ tranches with error at most $d\ell\delta/(m(b-a))$. This is because converting ℓ good assets to lemons decreases the value of the entire CDO family by $d\ell\delta$, since each lemon is in d CDOs.

We show that a CDO family built from a (d,r)-biregular $(\ell, d-\Delta)$-unique neighbor expander has error at most $2\Delta\ell\delta/(m(b-a))$.

That is, we replace d from the trivial bound by 2Δ. Moreover, the naive bound on the error for the entire CDO is the maximum of the errors for each tranche. We are instead able to improve the error to $3\Delta\ell\delta/(mr)$.

The intuition for the proof is natural. We consider some placement of lemons. By the unique-neighbor expansion, we have fairly tight bounds on both the number of derivatives containing no lemons, and the number containing exactly one lemon. Thus, when we subtract values for two different lemon placements, there is a lot of cancellation.

THEOREM 3.1. *A CDO built from a (d, r)-biregular $(\ell, d-\Delta)$-unique neighbor expander is pseudorandom for ℓ lemons. For the tranche $[a, b]$, the error is at most $2\Delta\ell\delta/(m(b-a))$, and for the entire CDO the error is at most $3\Delta\ell\delta/(mr)$.*

Before beginning the proof, we define the following.

DEFINITION 3.2. *Let $\mathrm{val}_{[a,b]}(g) = \mathrm{E}[\mathrm{value}_{[a,b]}(X)]$, where the random variable X is the payoff of an underlying portfolio on r assets, g of which are good. If the tranche is understood, we often omit it as a subscript.*

Since good assets dominate lemons, we deduce that val is a non-decreasing function of g. This is obvious if lemons always take value zero, but requires a short proof in general.

LEMMA 3.3. *For any tranche $[a, b]$ and $g' \geq g$, $\mathrm{val}_{[a,b]}(g') \geq \mathrm{val}_{[a,b]}(g)$.*

PROOF. First fix $Z = z$. Now let F_D denote the cumulative distribution function of distribution D. We can choose random variables X and Y according to $D_g = D_g(z)$ and $D_\ell = D_\ell(z)$, respectively, by choosing $W \in [0, 1]$ uniformly and outputting $X = F_{D_g}^{-1}(W)$ and $Y = F_{D_\ell}^{-1}(W)$. This "coupling" and the domination condition imply that for every point in the probability space, $X \geq Y$. Thus, we may substitute good assets for lemons in such a way that for any point in the probability space, the value of every asset either increases or remains the same. The lemma follows. □

Since a CDO simply restructures payoffs, the sum of the expected payoffs of the CDO equals the sum of the payoffs of the underlying assets. This gives the following observation.

OBSERVATION 3.4. *For any g, $\sum_{i=1}^{s} \mathrm{val}_{[a_{i-1},a_i]}(g) = g\mu + (r-g)\lambda = r\lambda + g\delta$.*

Lemma 3.3 and Observation 3.4 imply the following corollary.

COROLLARY 3.5. *For any g, i, and tranche $[a, b]$, $0 \leq \mathrm{val}_{[a,b]}(g+i) - \mathrm{val}_{[a,b]}(g) \leq i\delta$.*

Let $t_i(L) = |\Gamma_i(L)|$, for $0 \leq i \leq r$. The following lemma is key to proving Theorem 3.1.

LEMMA 3.6. *For any tranche $[a, b]$ and any $L, L' \subseteq [n]$ with $|L| = |L'| = \ell$, we have:*

$$\mathrm{tv}_{[a,b]}(L') - \mathrm{tv}_{[a,b]}(L) \leq \Delta\ell(\mathrm{val}_{[a,b]}(r) - \mathrm{val}_{[a,b]}(r-1)) + \sum_{i=2}^{r} t_i(L)(\mathrm{val}_{[a,b]}(r) - \mathrm{val}_{[a,b]}(r-i)).$$

PROOF. Fix the tranche $[a, b]$. Since $\cup_{i=0}^{r}\Gamma_i(L) = [m]$, we have $\sum_{i=0}^{r} t_i(L) = m$.

We must study the quantity

$$\mathrm{tv}(L) = \sum_{i=0}^{r} t_i(L)\,\mathrm{val}(r-i).$$

By the unique neighbor expansion property, $t_1(L) \geq (d-\Delta)\ell$. Therefore, $|t_1(L) - t_1(L')| \leq \Delta\ell$. Assume without loss of generality that $\mathrm{tv}(L) \leq \mathrm{tv}(L')$. Using $\sum_{i=0}^{r} t_i(L) = \sum_{i=0}^{r} t_i(L')$, we can now bound:

$$\begin{aligned}
&\mathrm{tv}(L') - \mathrm{tv}(L) \\
=\ & \sum_{i=0}^{r}(t_i(L) - t_i(L'))(-\mathrm{val}(r-i)) \\
=\ & \sum_{i=0}^{r}(t_i(L) - t_i(L'))(\mathrm{val}(r) - \mathrm{val}(r-i)) \\
\leq\ & |t_1(L) - t_1(L')|(\mathrm{val}(r) - \mathrm{val}(r-1)) \\
&+ \sum_{i=2}^{r} t_i(L)(\mathrm{val}(r) - \mathrm{val}(r-i)) \\
\leq\ & \Delta\ell(\mathrm{val}(r) - \mathrm{val}(r-1)) + \sum_{i=2}^{r} t_i(L)(\mathrm{val}(r) - \mathrm{val}(r-i)).
\end{aligned}$$

□

We can now prove the theorem.

PROOF OF THEOREM 3.1. First note that

$$\sum_{i=1}^{r} i t_i(L) = d\ell,$$

since both sides count the number of edges incident to L. Since $t_1(L) \geq (d-\Delta)\ell$, we have

$$\sum_{i=2}^{r} i t_i(L) \leq \Delta\ell.$$

Now fix the tranche $[a, b]$, and we now bound its error. By Lemma 3.6, Corollary 3.5, and the above,

$$\begin{aligned}
&\mathrm{tv}(L') - \mathrm{tv}(L) \\
\leq\ & \Delta\ell(\mathrm{val}(r) - \mathrm{val}(r-1)) + \sum_{i=2}^{r} t_i(L)(\mathrm{val}(r) - \mathrm{val}(r-i)) \\
\leq\ & \Delta\ell\delta + \sum_{i=2}^{r} t_i(L) i\delta \\
\leq\ & 2\Delta\ell\delta.
\end{aligned}$$

Dividing by $m(b-a)$ gives the result for the $[a, b]$ tranche.

Now we analyze the error for the entire CDO. In a similar manner, we get:

$$\begin{aligned}
&\|\vec{\mathrm{tv}}(L') - \vec{\mathrm{tv}}(L)\|_1 \\
\leq\ & \Delta\ell \sum_{i=1}^{s}(\mathrm{val}_{[a_{i-1},a_i]}(r) - \mathrm{val}_{[a_{i-1},a_i]}(r-1)) + \\
&\sum_{i=1}^{s}\sum_{j=2}^{r}(t_j(L) + t_j(L'))(\mathrm{val}_{[a_{i-1},a_i]}(r) - \mathrm{val}_{[a_{i-1},a_i]}(r-j)) \\
=\ & \Delta\ell\delta + \sum_{j=2}^{r}(t_j(L) + t_j(L'))j\delta \\
\leq\ & 3\Delta\ell\delta.
\end{aligned}$$

Dividing by $mr = dn$ gives the required result. □

4. CONSTRUCTIVE EXPANDERS AND CDOS

In this section, we show how suitable explicit expanders yield pseudorandom CDOs. Roughly, if the number of lemons is small compared to the number of derivatives, we get a big gain over the trivial bound.

THEOREM 4.1. *For any $\alpha \in (0,1]$ and positive integers n, m, d, r such that $nd = mr$, the following holds for $\Delta = 2(2d)^{\alpha}(\log_d n)\log_d m$ and any positive integer $\ell_{max} \leq (\Delta m/(8d^3))^{\alpha}$. There is an explicit pseudorandom (n, m, r)-CDO family against ℓ lemons, for all $\ell \leq \ell_{max}$. For the tranche $[a,b]$, the error is at most $4\Delta\ell\delta/(m(b-a))$, and for the entire CDO the error is at most $6\Delta\ell\delta/(mr)$.*

To prove this, we use the strong and elegant expander construction of Guruswami, Umans, and Vadhan [5]. We will set parameters in a different order, so we use their Theorem 3.3, obtained before they set parameters.

THEOREM 4.2. *[5] For any positive integer h, a prime power q, and n and m powers of q, there is an explicit construction of a $(\ell_{max}, q-\Delta)$ expander on $[n] \cup [m]$ with left degree q, $\ell_{max} = h^{\log_q m - 1}$, and $\Delta = (h-1)(\log_q n - 1)(\log_q m - 1)$.*

Before setting parameters, we need the following simple observation.

OBSERVATION 4.3. *Suppose we are given a $(\ell_{max}, d-\Delta)$ expander with left-degree d. If we remove any left vertices, and add any right vertices, the graph remains a $(\ell_{max}, d-\Delta)$ expander. If for each left vertex, we remove an arbitrary $d - d'$ edges, then the graph becomes a $(\ell_{max}, d'-\Delta)$ expander with left degree d'.*

We now set parameters from Theorem 4.2 as follows.

COROLLARY 4.4. *For any $\alpha \in (0,1]$ and positive integers n, m, and d, there is an explicit construction of a $(\ell_{max}, d-\Delta)$ expander on $[n] \cup [m]$ with left degree d for $\ell_{max} = (m/(4d^2))^{\alpha}$ and $\Delta = (2d)^{\alpha}(\log_d n)\log_d m$.*

PROOF. Let q be the smallest power of 2 that is at least d. Let n' be the smallest power of q at least n, and let m' be the largest power of q at most m. By Observation 4.3, it suffices to construct a $(\ell_{max}, q-\Delta)$ expander on $[n'] \cup [m']$ with left-degree q. Set $h = \lceil q^{\alpha} \rceil$ and $\ell = \log_q m' = \lfloor \log_q m \rfloor$, so $q^{\ell} \leq m < q^{\ell+1}$. We use the expander constructed in Theorem 4.2. It suffices to lower bound ℓ_{max} and upper bound Δ. We get:

$$\ell_{max} \geq h^{\ell-1} \geq q^{\alpha(\ell-1)} > (m/q^2)^{\alpha} \geq (m/(4d^2))^{\alpha},$$

and

$$\begin{aligned}\Delta &\leq (h-1)(\log_q n' - 1)(\log_q m' - 1)\\ &< q^{\alpha}(\log_q n)\log_q m < (2d)^{\alpha}(\log_d n)\log_d m.\end{aligned}$$

This completes the proof. □

This and other known unique-neighbor expander constructions give left-regular graphs. However, we need the graph to be biregular. We show how to convert a left-regular graph to biregular while increasing the left-degree only slightly, at the expense of increasing the number of right vertices. The following extends a lemma from [4].

LEMMA 4.5. *Suppose we are given a d_0-left-regular (ℓ_{max}, γ) expander on $[n] \cup [m_0]$, and parameters m, d, r such that $nd = mr$, $d_0 < d \leq m_0$, and $m \geq m_0 d/(d-d_0)$. We can efficiently construct a (d,r)-biregular (ℓ_{max}, γ) expander on $[n] \cup [m]$.*

PROOF. Let $r_0 = nd_0/m_0$ denote the original average right degree. For any right node $v \in [m_0]$ of degree $r_v > r$, divide it into $\lceil r_v/r \rceil$ vertices, where $\lfloor r_v/r \rfloor$ have degree r and at most one has degree less than r. (Partition neighbors arbitrarily.)

The number of new nodes added is at most

$$\sum_{v\in[m_0]} \left(\left\lceil \frac{r_v}{r} \right\rceil - 1\right) < \sum_{v\in[m_0]} \frac{r_v}{r} = \frac{m_0 r_0}{r} = \frac{nd_0 m}{nd} = \frac{d_0 m}{d}.$$

Thus, the total number of right nodes is less than

$$m_0 + \frac{d_0}{d}m \leq \frac{d-d_0}{d}m + \frac{d_0}{d}m = m.$$

Add isolated nodes to the right to make the total number of right nodes exactly m. Now add edges arbitrarily to the right and left to make all left degree d and right degrees r, which is possible because $nd = mr$. Naively, this may allow multiple edges, but we can avoid this by filling edge slots in the following order. For left nodes, cycle over all nodes $d - d_0$ times, filling one edge slot each time. For right nodes, cycle over all nodes once, filling all edge slots for a node before proceeding to the next node. □

COROLLARY 4.6. *For any $\alpha \in (0,1]$ and positive integers n, m, d, and r such that $nd = mr$, there is an explicit construction of a (d,r)-biregular $(\ell_{max}, d-\Delta)$ expander on $[n] \cup [m]$ for $\Delta = 2(2d)^{\alpha}(\log_d n)\log_d m$ and $\ell_{max} = (\Delta m/(8d^3))^{\alpha}$.*

PROOF. Set $\Delta_0 = \Delta/2$, $d_0 = d - \Delta_0$, and $m_0 = \Delta_0 m/d$. By Corollary 4.4, there is an explicit construction of a $(\ell_{max}, d_0 - \Delta_0')$ expander on $[n] \cup [m_0]$ with left degree d_0 for $\ell_{max}' = (m_0/(4d_0^2))^{\alpha} \geq \ell_{max}$ and $\Delta_0' = (2d_0)^{\alpha}(\log_d n)\log_d m_0 \leq \Delta_0$. Now apply Lemma 4.5. □

Combining Corollary 4.6 and Lemma 2.10 with Theorem 3.1 yields Theorem 4.1.

If d is smaller, we could use the expanders of [2], but the degree is not as good a function in the error and our results are not as strong.

5. TWO GENERAL ASSETS

In this section we obtain bounds even if the probability distribution of lemons is not dominated by the probability distribution of good assets. We only assume that $\mu \geq \lambda$, where μ and λ are the expected values of each good asset and lemon, respectively. We don't need to think of the second asset as a lemon; instead consider two general assets with expected values $\mu \geq \lambda$. Now, even the "trivial" bounds change; such bounds can be deduced from our bounds below. We show that in the general case, the δ in Theorem 3.1 must be replaced by μ for the $[a,b]$ tranche. Moreover,we no longer get better bounds for the entire CDO than can be deduced from the bounds in the tranches.

THEOREM 5.1. *A CDO built from a (d,r)-biregular $(\ell, d-\Delta)$-unique neighbor expander is pseudorandom for ℓ lemons. For the tranche $[a,b]$, the error is at most $2\Delta\ell\mu/(m(b-a))$.*

In this case, Lemma 3.3 may no longer hold, and as a result, neither may Corollary 3.5. We instead obtain an analog of Corollary 3.5 with δ replaced by μ.

LEMMA 5.2. *For any g, i, and tranche $[a,b]$, $|\,\mathrm{val}_{[a,b]}(g+i) - \mathrm{val}_{[a,b]}(g)| \leq i\mu$.*

To prove this, it is helpful to use the following expression for the value of the $[a, b]$ tranche.

OBSERVATION 5.3. *Let X denote a random variable representing the payoff of a portfolio underlying a CDO. Then the value of the corresponding $[a, b]$ tranche is*

$$\int_a^b \Pr[X > x]dx.$$

PROOF OF LEMMA 5.2. It suffices to prove the lemma for $i = 1$. Let X be the payoff of a portfolio on $r - 1$ assets, g of which are good. Let Y be the payoff of a good asset, and Z the payoff of a lemon. We wish to show that

$$\left| \int_a^b \Pr[X + Y > w]dw - \int_a^b \Pr[X + Z > w]dw \right| \leq \mu.$$

To this end, first note that

$$\int_a^b \Pr[X + Y > w]dw \geq \int_a^b \Pr[X > w]dw,$$

and similarly for $X + Z$, since both Y and Z are nonnegative. It therefore suffices to show that

$$\int_a^b \Pr[X + Y > w]dw - \int_a^b \Pr[X > w]dw \leq \mu,$$

and hence the corresponding inequality for $X + Z$.

Condition on $X = x$; we show this inequality for any x. Observe that

$$\Pr[x + Y > w] - \Pr[x > w] = \begin{cases} \Pr[Y > w - x] & \text{if } x \leq w \\ 0 & \text{otherwise} \end{cases}$$

Letting $y = w - x$ gives:

$$\int_a^b (\Pr[x + Y > w] - \Pr[x > w])\, dw \leq \int_0^\infty \Pr[Y > y]dy = \mu.$$

This completes the proof. □

PROOF OF THEOREM 5.1. We now proceed as in our earlier proof, replacing Corollary 3.5 with Lemma 5.2. Everything else goes through as before. □

Acknowledgements

I thank Sanjeev Arora, Rafa Mendoza-Arriaga, Kumar Muthuraman, Ryan O'Donnell, and Stathis Tompaidis for useful comments and discussions. Thanks also to the anonymous referees for helpful comments.

6. REFERENCES

[1] S. Arora, B. Barak, M. Brunnermeier, and R. Ge. Computational complexity and information asymmetry in financial products. In *Innovations in Computer Science (ICS) conference*, 2010.

[2] M. Capalbo, O. Reingold, S. Vadhan, and A. Wigderson. Randomness conductors and constant-degree expansion beyond the degree/2 barrier. In *Proceedings of the 34th Annual ACM Symposium on Theory of Computing*, pages 659–668, 2002.

[3] O. Gabber and Z. Galil. Explicit construction of linear sized superconcentrators. *Journal of Computer and System Sciences*, 22:407–420, 1981.

[4] V. Guruswami, J. Lee, and A. Wigderson. Almost Euclidean subspaces of ℓ_1^n via expander codes. *Combinatorica*, 30:47–68, 2010.

[5] V. Guruswami, C. Umans, and S. Vadhan. Unbalanced expanders and randomness extractors from Parvaresh-Vardy codes. *Journal of the ACM*, 56:1–34, 2009.

[6] S. Hoory, N. Linial, and A. Wigderson. Expander graphs and their applications. *Bulletin of the American Mathematical Society*, 43:439–561, 2006.

[7] M. Lewis. *The Big Short*. W.W. Norton & Co., 2010.

[8] A. Lubotzky, R. Philips, and P. Sarnak. Ramanujan graphs. *Combinatorica*, 8:261–277, 1988.

[9] A. Ta-Shma, C. Umans, and D. Zuckerman. Lossless condensers, unbalanced expanders, and extractors. *Combinatorica*, 27:213–240, 2007.

[10] S. Vadhan. The unified theory of pseudorandomness. *SIGACT News*, 38, 2007.

Individual Rationality and Participation in Large Scale, Multi-hospital Kidney Exchange

[Extended Abstract]*

Itai Ashlagi
Massachusetts Institute of Technology
Cambridge, MA
iashlagi@mit.edu

Alvin E. Roth
Harvard University
Cambridge, MA
aroth@hbs.edu

ABSTRACT

As multi-hospital kidney exchange clearinghouses have grown, the set of players has grown from patients and surgeons to include hospitals. Hospitals have the option of enrolling only their hard-to-match patient-donor pairs, while conducting easily arranged exchanges internally. This behavior has already started to be observed.

We show that the cost of making it individually rational for hospitals to participate fully is low in almost every large exchange pool (although the worst-case cost is very high), while the cost of failing to guarantee individually rational allocations could be large, in terms of lost transplants. We also identify an incentive compatible mechanism.

Categories and Subject Descriptors: J.4 Computer Applications: Social and Behavioral Sciences – Economics.

General Terms: Algorithms, Economics, Theory.

Keywords: Matching, Market Design.

1. EXTENDED ABSTRACT

When kidney exchange was just beginning, most exchanges were conducted in single hospitals, or in closely connected networks of hospitals like the fourteen New England transplant centers organized by the New England Program for Kidney Exchange (Roth, Sönmez, and Ünver (2005)). But today exchanges often involve multiple hospitals that may have relatively little repeated interaction outside of kidney exchange. In this paper (Ashlagi and Roth(2011)) we study the problem of providing hospitals the incentive to participate fully, in order to achieve the gains that kidney exchange on a large scale makes possible.

Hospitals participate in a multi-center exchange by reporting a list of incompatible patient-donor pairs to a central clearinghouse, and a matching mechanism chooses which exchanges to carry out. Hospitals may report only a partial list of their incompatible pairs and conduct among their own patients internal exchanges. We assume that hospitals wish to maximize the number of their own patients that are matched.

As kidney exchange clearinghouses try to maximize the (weighted) number of transplants without attention to whether those transplants are internal to a hospital, it may not be even individually rational for a hospital to contribute those pairs it can match internally. For example, consider a hospital a with two pairs, $a1$ and $a2$, that it can match internally. Suppose it enters those two pairs in a centralized exchange. It may be that the weighted number of transplants is maximized by including $a1$ in an exchange but not $a2$, in which case only one of hospital a's patients will be transplanted, when it could have performed two transplants on its own.

In our model each hospital has a set of incompatible pairs (of constant size), and all incompatible pairs induce a "compatibility" graph. We first study the loss of transplants from requiring the allocation to be individually rational (guarantee each hospital the number of pairs it can internally match) rather than just efficient. We first show that the loss can be large in the deterministic case. Next we consider large random compatibility graphs and extend Erdos-Renyi results, to show both what efficient matches look like, and also construct an individual rational allocation (under some regularity condition on the size of the hospital) that is almost efficient.

We further use random compatibility graphs to show that there exists an incentive compatible mechanism that is almost efficient. Specifically we construct an almost efficient mechanism that (under a slightly stronger regularity condition on the hospital size) makes truth-telling an approximated Bayes-Nash equilibrium.[1]

REFERENCES

[1] I. Ashlagi and A. E. Roth. Individual rationality and participation in large scale, multi-hospital kidney exchange. Working paper, 2011.

[2] A. E. Roth, T. Sönmez, and M. U. Ünver. A kidney exchange clearinghouse in New England. *American Economic Review Papers and Proceedings*, 95(2): 376–380, 2005.

*A full version of this paper is available at `http://web.mit.edu/iashlagi/www/papers/LargeScaleKidneyExchange_1_13.pdf`.

EC'11, June 5–9, 2011, San Jose, California, USA.
ACM 978-1-4503-0261-6/11/06.

[1] An $\epsilon(n)$-Bayes-Nash equilibrium, where $\epsilon(n) = o(1)$ and n is the number of hospitals.

A Random Graph Model of Kidney Exchanges: Efficiency, Individual-Rationality and Incentives

Panos Toulis
Harvard University, SEAS
Cambridge, MA 02138, USA
ptoulis@fas.harvard.edu

David C. Parkes
Harvard University, SEAS
Cambridge, MA 02138, USA
parkes@eecs.harvard.edu

ABSTRACT

In kidney exchanges, hospitals share patient lists and receive transplantations. A kidney-paired donation (KPD) mechanism needs to promote full sharing of information about donor-patient pairs, and identify a Pareto efficient outcome that also satisfies participation constraints of hospitals. We introduce a random graph model of the KPD exchange and then fully characterize the structure of the efficient outcome and the expected number of transplantations that can be performed. Random graph theory allows early experimental results to be explained analytically, and enables the study of participation incentives in a methodological way. We derive a square-root law between the welfare gains from sharing patient-donor pairs in a central pool and the individual sizes of hospitals, illustrating the urgent need for the nationwide expansion of such programs. Finally, we establish through theoretical and computational analysis that enforcing simple individual rationality constraints on the outcome can mitigate the negative impact of strategic behavior by hospitals.

Categories and Subject Descriptors

J.4 [**Computer Applications**]: Social and Behavioral Sciences—*Economics*; G.2 [**Discrete Mathematics**]: Graph Theory—*Matchings in random graphs*

General Terms

Algorithms, Theory, Economics, Experimentation

Keywords

kidney exchange, random graph theory, maximum matching, individual rationality, mechanism design

1. INTRODUCTION

The scarcity of cadaver kidneys and significant medical benefits from live kidney donation has promoted the expansion of kidney-paired donation (KPD) in recent years. The idea is that kidney patients with one or more incompatible donors, might be able to receive compatible transplants through barter exchanges. It is typical for this to be performed as a two-way exchange, which involves four (typically simultaneous) operations.[1] Currently, there is a handful of such kidney-exchange programs in the USA and several others around the world [14]. Their expansion in large-scale has been hitherto hindered by the ethical, logistical and even incentive issues they entail.

Nevertheless, there are numerous reports favoring the benefit of kidney exchanges. From the medical literature, survival rates up to 100% are reported in a sample including 10 two-way, paired donations [8]. Further benefits in terms of total saved lives can be found where larger than two-way exchanges are considered [14]. Recent history has seen an increase in (KPD) through multi-regional KPD programs [11].

Naturally enough, if we would like to represent the patient-donor set as a graph, with each pair as a vertex, and focusing on two-way exchanges, then we could think of the compatibility relationships as being the edges. An edge indicates a two-way compatibility between the donor and patient of pair one and pair two, and vice-versa. If one considers utility to be achieved by a compatible transplant to a patient, then the Pareto-efficient solution with only two-way exchanges is a *maximum matching* [12]. In this paper, we make a clean start by defining a comprehensive *random graph* model of (two-way) KPD exchanges. The use of a random-graph model is appropriate here, because there are well defined probabilistic models of the blood and tissue type compatibility of donor-patient pairs entering KPD exchanges.

In addition to efficiency, an important consideration is in regard to the incentives of hospitals to participate, where a typical concern is that an individual hospital will hold back some pairs (to match locally, before or after the exchange clears) in order to increase the number of hospital-specific matches. This kind of strategic hiding of pairs can lead away from Pareto-efficient solutions. In Ashlagi et al. [3], this loss is shown to be 50% in the worst case for strategyproof

[1]Longer than 2-way exchanges are also possible. In 2007, a chain of 10 kidney transplantations was performed that lasted over 8 months [10] and that was triggered by a single altruistic donor with no designated recipient. Here, we will focus on 2-way exchanges that are easier to perform in practice and thus more prevalent

mechanisms, in short because one has to find the maximum matching individually for every hospital before looking at the global maximum. By adopting a random-graph model, we are able to complement the worst-case analysis in the literature with a meaningful average-case analysis. The main technical content of this paper involves developing a structural analysis of maximum matchings on domain-appropriate random graph models, and the main message is positive: our analytical and simulation results suggest that an appropriate exchange design can be very effective in mitigating incentives to hospitals for hiding patient-donor pairs.

We completely characterize the maximum matching properties of our model (i.e. Pareto-optimal outcomes). In stating our results, we work under two assumptions: the first is a *perfect matching (PM) assumption*, which is that any bipartite random graph, with the probability of an edge between two vertices defined in a way that is appropriate to the kidney domain, will assume a perfect matching. This is easily justified even for small-size patient lists of less than 10 pairs, and the resulting analytical model is very accurate, explaining early experimental results [1, 13, 15]. The second is a *regularity assumption* on the existence of optimal exchanges that possess a particular graph structure. We derive a square-root relationship between the welfare gains of sharing patient-donor pairs in a central pool and the individual sizes of hospitals. This serves as a formal proof for the necessity of collaborative, nationwide kidney exchange programs.

Based on our analysis of the structure of the matching problem, the strategic problem facing hospitals is reduced to a game of adding nodes on a bipartite graph, which enables us to show empirically that non-truthful sharing in a non-IR mechanism is hurtful in expectation to truthful hospitals. We also quantify this expected loss in a 2-hospital scenario. In the sequel, we consider two variants on individually-rational centralized mechanisms, both of which are efficient under the PM assumption when hospitals fully reveal their patient-donor pairs. Our preferred mechanism (`xCM`), computes a matching of a particular structure individually for each hospital, and completes with a random maximum matching of the remainder donor-patient pairs. We establish under an additional regularity assumption on the realized structure of maximum matchings in KPD graphs, that `xCM` is individually-rational, efficient and supports full sharing of donor/patient pairs in a Bayesian-Nash equilibrium.

In detailed simulations, we validate the incentive compatibility of the `xCM` mechanism. In comparison, a randomized, non-IR mechanism allows a strategic hospital to achieve $\sim 20\%$ more transplantations than the truthful ones. `xCM` eliminates this benefit and also keeps efficiency. Our model remains robust after the introduction of extra nuisance parameters (for example PRA sensitivity of patients) in which `xCM` is also able to restore fairness and retain almost 96% of efficiency.

Some proofs are omitted from this version of the paper in the interest of space and will be available in an extended version.

1.1 Related Work

Roth et al. [13] study priority mechanisms in which patients decide how to reveal the sets of their incompatible donors and the transplants they are willing to accept. Hospital incentives are analyzed in Ashlagi et al. [3], although in worst-case rather than random-graph framework.

Ashlagi and Roth [2], independently of our work, adopt a random-graph model with which to study individually-rational, multiple hospital mechanisms (including 3-way exchanges). While the themes and qualitative observations are quite similar, our results differ. First, we provide a detailed, quantified analysis of the welfare gains from a centralized pool (Theorem 2, Corollary 2 and 3.) Through this, we are also able to provide an almost perfect analytical explanation for existing numerical results in the literature. Second, our main equilibrium, IR and efficiency results are presented for the *xCM mechanism* and made under the PM and regularity assumptions. In comparison, Ashlagi and Roth [2] introduce a different mechanism, termed the *Bonus mechanism* and provide an equilibrium analysis under a different regularity assumption. In particular, we both focus on the set Ω of efficient outcomes, but Ashlagi and Roth [2] assume an expected property over the entire set, namely the *regular size assumption*, while we make a claim on the existence of an outcome $\alpha \in \Omega$ of a specific structure. Interestingly, we show (under our assumptions) that for 2-way exchanges, IR and efficiency can be achieved in a Bayes-Nash equilibrium of the xCM mechanism, while Ashlagi & Roth [2] establish (under their assumptions), and while allowing for 3-way exchanges, that IR can be achieved with a small efficiency loss that is about 1% of the individual hospital sizes in an epsilon Bayes-Nash equilibrium of the Bonus mechanism. In this sense, our works can be considered complementary. In addition, our positive results on xCM hold in both a truthful equilibrium and an equilibrium in which each hospital follows a canonical deviation and only hides pairs that form part of a maximum matching with a particular structure on its own, local graph.

2. MISE-EN-SCÈNE

Human blood has four different types, namely O, A, B and AB, depending on the presence or absence of the proteins A and B. Two people are blood-type compatible if the donor does not introduce new proteins to the recipient. For example, a donor with blood type A can donate to patients with type A or AB and a donor with type O can donate to any blood type since O denotes the absence of both proteins.

Blood-type compatibility is the first requirement for a kidney transplantation. In addition, the donor and the recipient should share as many common HLA antigens as possible to prevent a *positive crossmatch*, i.e. the transplant being rejected. The probability of a crossmatch between a donor and a patient selected at random has been calculated around 11% [17]. However, this number varies greatly among patients and we will adopt the analysis in [14] which identifies three distinct categories of tissue-type sensitivities, namely low, medium and high PRA, as shown in Table 1:

Sensitivity type	Distribution	p_c probability
Low-PRA	70.19%	0.05
Medium-PRA	20%	0.45
High-PRA	9.81%	0.9

Table 1: Positive crossmatch [14]

In this paper we will denote the positive crossmatch probability with p_c and we will fix its value to $p_c \approx 0.2$ to produce numerical results, i.e. the weighted average of the aforementioned distribution. In this case the probability that two pairs that are already blood-type compatible, are also tissue-type compatible is $(1-p_c)^2 = 0.64$, since every donor has to be compatible with the patient of the other pair. We therefore make the strong, simplifying assumption that tissue-type compatibilities are independent random events, ignoring blood and PRA sensitivity types for the moment. However, in Section 5.2 we show that our results remain robust even under these nuisance parameters.

Formally, a donor-patient pair is defined on $S \times S$, where $S = \{O, A, B, AB\}$ is the blood-type set. Following the terminology in Ünver [15], we break up the entire set into 4 distinct subsets as follows:

Definition 1. A donor-recipient pair is *under-demanded* (denoted U), if the donor is not ABO compatible with the patient. If in addition the pair contains only the types A and B, then it is called *reciprocal* (denoted by R).

Definition 2. A pair is *over-demanded* (denoted by O) if the donor and the patient are ABO compatible. If they also have the same type then the pair is called *self-demanded* (denoted by S).

The following table summarizes.

patient	O	A	B	AB
donor				
O	S	O	O	O
A	U	S	R	O
B	U	R	S	O
AB	U	U	U	S

Table 2: ABO subsets

The compatibilities of Lemma 1 are depicted graphically in Figure 1. It is now easy to establish the following:

LEMMA 1. *An under-demanded pair can only be matched to an over-demanded one. A reciprocal pair can be paired with an over-demanded or another reciprocal pair. A self-demanded pair can me matched to an over-demanded or another self-demanded pair.*

2.1 The random graph model

We model the donor-patient pairs of a hospital as a graph where a node represents one such pair and an edge represents the fact that two pairs can perform a paired donation. Obviously, an efficient two-way kidney exchange is a maximum matching on this graph. Our goal is then to study the expected properties of such a matching under two probabilistic assumptions: that blood types are drawn from some discrete blood-type distribution and that tissue-type compatibilities are independent Bernoulli trials with probability $1-p_c$ (robustness against these assumptions will be checked in subsequent sections). Random graph theory is therefore a natural way to study the expected properties of efficient outcomes and the Bayes-Nash equilibria of multi-hospital participation in KPD markets.

More formally, a *random donor-patient graph* that has n pairs is denoted by $\widetilde{G_n}$ and its vertex set is constructed by the following random process:

```
REPEAT until G_n has n pairs
        Draw 2 people  ~ Blood Type Frequencies
            IF not Blood Type Compatible
                Add to G_n
            ELSE
                Add to G_n with probability p_c
REPEAT ∀u,v ∈ V(G_n),
        IF u,v ABO compatible AND x ~ U(0,1), x > p_c
            ADD (u,v) to E(G_n)
```

In general, the O group is the most common, and A, B, AB follow in that order. For our analysis, we will consider a fixed distribution over the blood types. To produce arithmetical results we will consider a distribution of $O(50\%)$, $A(30\%)$, $B(15\%)$ and $AB(5\%)$ which is close to the world average (see [16]) but we will also check for robustness in the experimentation section of the paper.[2]

Unfortunately, the aforementioned process does not adhere to any well-known random graph model. Nevertheless, we will soon show how to combine known combinatorial results with the specific properties of $\widetilde{G_n}$, aiming to identify the structural properties that *most* of the model-generated graphs share with each other.

We start by identifying the vertex sets and the induced subgraphs in $\widetilde{G_n}$ that correspond to the pair types introduced in Definitions 1 and 2. In particular denote with O, U, S, R the vertex sets containing the over-demanded, under-demanded, self-demanded and reciprocal pairs respectively. The expected sizes of these sets are given by the following lemma.

LEMMA 2. *Denote with p_x the probability that a random pair in $\widetilde{G_n}$ belongs to the x vertex set, $x \in \{O, U, S, R\}$ and f_y the frequency of blood type y. Then it holds:*

$$p_O = \frac{w \cdot p_c}{V}, p_S = \frac{s \cdot p_c}{V}, p_U = \frac{w}{V}, p_R = \frac{r}{V} \quad (1)$$

Also (see Table 2),

$$V = w + w \cdot p_c + s \cdot p_c + r$$
$$w = f_O \cdot (f_A + f_B) + f_{AB} \cdot (f_O + f_A + f_B)$$
$$s = f_O^2 + f_A^2 + f_B^2 + f_{AB}^2$$
$$r = 2 \cdot f_A \cdot f_B$$

Furthermore, the expected sizes of the subgraphs of $\widetilde{G_n}$ are:

$$|O| = p_O \cdot n = \frac{w \cdot p_c}{V} \cdot n$$
$$|U| = p_U \cdot n = \frac{w}{V} \cdot n \quad (2)$$
$$|S| = p_S \cdot n = \frac{s \cdot p_c}{V} \cdot n$$
$$|R| = p_R \cdot n = \frac{r}{V} \cdot n$$

PROOF. By considering a fixed distribution of ABO bloodtypes, equations (1) and (2), follow immediately by the elementary properties of the uniform distribution. For the

[2]Blood-type distribution among human population varies a lot [16]. For example, Koreans are evenly distributed in types O, A and B while the Bororo people in Brazil are 100% of type O.

aforementioned distribution, the coefficients are $w = 0.2725$, $s = 0.365$, $r = 0.09$. □

By Lemma 2, the size of every vertex set is proportional to the total size n of a graph in $\widetilde{G_n}$. However, by inspection, the set O is much smaller than the set U since $\frac{|O|}{|U|} = p_c < 1$. A similar argument holds for the set S as well. In summary, Lemma 1 gives information about compatibilities among different pair types and Lemma 2 offers insight on their respective sizes. Figure 1 is a graphical depiction of the structure of a $\widetilde{G_n}$ graph. The edges in the figure correspond to compatibility relationships but the intra-type compatibilities (i.e. self-loops) have been omitted.

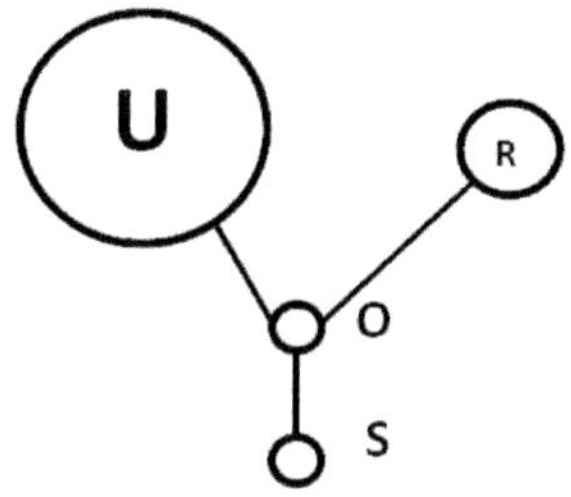

Figure 1: Vertex sets in $\widetilde{G_n}$

The sizes were calculated by considering the positive cross-match probability equal to $p_c = 0.2$. Obviously, the over-demanded pairs are more centrally placed within the graph and thus more likely to participate in a maximum matching. In addition, a large portion of the under-demanded pairs are left unmatched by any matching, due to the blood-type incompatibilities with each other, as shown in Lemma 1. These and similar remarks are summarized in the following lemma:

LEMMA 3. *The O subgraph (induced by the O vertex set) is connected to all other subgraphs. The U subgraph is isolated, i.e. it has no edges. The subgraph R is bipartite. The S subgraph is comprised by four disconnected components comprising the pairs $(O, O), (A, A), (B, B)$ and (AB, AB)*

PROOF. No under-demanded pair can be matched to an under-demanded pair by Lemma 1, thus the U subgraph is isolated. Pairs within the R subgraph are symmetric in Table 2 and hence R is bipartite with the vertex classes (A, B) and (B, A). Pairs in the S subgraph are on the main diagonal of Table 2 and hence S has 4 disconnected components, one for each blood type. □

As first shown in Roth et al. [13], the Pareto-optimal solution is essentially a maximum matching on the graph. It is therefore important to characterize the maximum matchings of $\widetilde{G_n}$, which in fact is a random graph as well. In the following section we will achieve approximate results which will form the basis for our subsequent analysis.

3. MAXIMUM MATCHING IN $\widetilde{G_N}$

In graph theory [4], the maximum matching of a graph is a subset of its edges with no common vertices and with the maximum cardinality possible. It has numerous applications as a combinatorial problem [9], and luckily it can be solved deterministically in polynomial time by Edmond's algorithm [6]. Random graph theory [5] on the other hand, studies distributions over graphs normally referred to as *random graph models*. For example, $G_{n,p}$ is often defined as a process producing graphs with n nodes such that each of the $\binom{n}{2}$ possible edges exists independently with a probability p. Combinatorial arguments are then used to explore graph invariants such as size, connectivity or chromatic number.

Despite the extensive research literature and to the best of our knowledge, no random graph model could be applied directly for the problem defined in this paper. However, it will suffice to prove a specific result regarding matchings in bipartite graphs and then make a few reasonable assumptions on how to proceed. In particular, let us denote with $G_{n \times n,p}$ the bipartite graph with n nodes in each class such that any node is connected to any node of the other class with probability p. It then holds:

THEOREM 1. *Graphs in model $G_{n \times n,p}$ with $p > \phi - 1$ (ϕ being the golden ratio) assume a perfect matching for sufficiently large n.*

Theorem 1 is sufficient in unveiling that a bipartite random graph always assumes a near-perfect matching. In order to facilitate our mathematical analysis for the rest of our technical results, we make the following assumption:

ASSUMPTION 1. **Perfect matching (PM)** *Every graph drawn from $G_{n \times n,p}$ assumes a perfect matching*

For example, under our kidney exchange model where $p = 1 - p_c = 0.8$ the probabilities of a perfect matching for $n = 4$ and $n = 6$ are 0.985 and 0.999 respectively. In addition, any graph in $G_{2n,p}$ can be reduced to a graph in $G_{n \times n,p}$ and thus inherit its matching properties. As a consequence of the PM assumption, we conclude that:

COROLLARY 1. *Under the PM assumption, every graph drawn from $G_{n,p}$ with n even, assumes a perfect matching*

We now proceed to characterize the maximum matching on $\widetilde{G_n}$. We make the PM assumption throughout the rest of the paper.

LEMMA 4. *The probability that the O subgraph cannot be completely matched to the U subgraph in random graph $\widetilde{G_n}$ decreases exponentially in n.*

PROOF. An O pair (x, y) is compatible with its symmetric (y, x) U pair. By Lemma 2, pairs (y, x) are expected to be $\frac{1}{p_c}$ times more than the pairs (x, y). Therefore, with n O pairs, $\frac{1-p_c}{p_c} \cdot n$ pairs in U will remain unmatched on average. This means that there will be $\alpha \cdot n$ pairs in U that will be unmatched, for some constant α. The probability that an over-demanded pair remains unmatched if subgraph O is matched only against the U subgraph is therefore equal to $p_c^{\alpha \cdot n}$. This tends to 0 for large n. □

The S subgraph is even more densely connected as shown in the following lemma:

LEMMA 5. *Consider the subgraph S with k pairs contained in some $\widetilde{G_n}$. Also denote with $s(k)$ the expected number of pairs that are matched in a maximum matching of S, and with β some value $O(1)$. Then:*

$$s(k) = k - \beta$$

For sufficiently large k it holds that $\beta = 2$.

We now turn our attention to the R subgraph. This is a bipartite graph (see Lemma 3) but it is unbalanced and therefore we cannot apply Assumption 1 directly.

LEMMA 6. *Consider the R subgraph with k pairs contained in some $\widetilde{G_n}$. Also denote with $r(k)$ the expected number of pairs that are matched in a maximum matching of R. It holds:*

$$r(k) = k - \Theta(\sqrt{k})$$

In particular,

$$k - r(k) \sim \sqrt{\frac{2}{\pi} \cdot k}$$

The unmatched pairs in the R subgraph actually follow the *folded binomial* distribution. Formally, if $X \sim Binom(n, p), p = 0.5$ then the variable defined by $Y = |2 \cdot X - n|$ follows a folded binomial. By Lemma 6 we have that $E[Y]$ approximates the value $\sqrt{\frac{2}{\pi} \cdot n}$. Now it is easy to prove the following:

LEMMA 7. *Consider m independent random variables X_i, such that $X_i \sim Binom(n, 0.5)$. Also define:*

$$Y_m = |(2X_1 - n) + \cdots + (2X_m - n)| = |2\sum_i X_i - m \cdot n|$$

Then it holds,

$$E[Y_m] \sim \sqrt{\frac{2}{\pi} \cdot n \cdot m} \tag{3}$$

PROOF. The sum of m random variables X_i defined as above follows $Binom(m \cdot n, 0.5)$. Applying Lemma 6 and a substitution of variables will get us the desired result. □

We can now put the pieces together and characterize maximum matchings globally on $\widetilde{G_n}$ by calculating the expected cardinality of a maximum matching.

THEOREM 2. *If $\mu(n)$ is the expected cardinality of a maximum matching in $\widetilde{G_n}$, then given the PM assumption, there exist positive constants $\gamma < 1$ and β such that:*

$$\mu(n) = \gamma \cdot n - \Theta(\sqrt{n}) - \beta$$

PROOF. Consider a matching in $\widetilde{G_n}$ where all O pairs are matched with pairs in U and subgraphs S and R assume maximum matchings internally. It is not possible to construct an alternating path for this matching since by Lemma 1 the U subgraph is isolated. Therefore, the matching is maximum (see also [9]). In expectation and in a population of n donor patient pairs and given equations (2), the unmatched pairs are equal to $|U| - |O| + \Theta(\sqrt{n}) + \beta = \lambda \cdot n + \Theta(\sqrt{n}) + \beta$. Therefore the expected number of matches is given by equation:

$$\mu(n) = n - (\lambda \cdot n + \Theta(\sqrt{n}) + \beta) \tag{4}$$

Setting $\gamma = 1 - \lambda$, we conclude that

$$\mu(n) = \gamma \cdot n - \Theta(\sqrt{n}) - \beta$$

□

In particular by equations (2) and $p_c = 0.2$ we have that $\lambda = (1 - p_c) \cdot \frac{w}{V} \approx 0.44$ and hence $\gamma = 1 - \lambda = 0.56$. We now make the following definition, which will be helpful when considering incentives.

Definition 3. Maximum matchings of $\widetilde{G_n}$ in which O is matched completely to U and the S and R subgraphs assume a maximum matching internally, are themselves random graphs denoted by $\widetilde{M_n}$. The remainder graph, $\widetilde{D_n} = \widetilde{G_n} - \widetilde{M_n}$ is also random and on expectation it contains:

- Pairs in the U subgraph, proportional to size n
- Pairs in R all of the *same* class (either A-B or B-A) proportional to $\sqrt{n}$
- A total of 2 pairs of the S type

Notice also that graphs from $\widetilde{D_n}$ are isolated, i.e. they contain no edges. The proof of Theorem 2 establishes that matchings of the form $\widetilde{M_n}$ exist with high probability for a given $\widetilde{G_n}$.

3.1 Interpretation of results

Using Theorem 2 and Lemma 6, and adopting $|R|$ as the size of the reciprocal subgraph, we can use the following approximation for the expected number of matched pairs in $\widetilde{G_n}$:

$$\mu(n) \approx 0.556 \cdot n - \sqrt{\frac{2}{\pi} \cdot |R|} - 2 \tag{5}$$

Using equation (2) we know that $|R| = \frac{r}{V} \cdot n = 0.18n$. Substituting in (5) we get:

$$\mu(n) \approx \gamma \cdot n - \delta \cdot \sqrt{n} - 2 \tag{6}$$
$$\gamma = 0.556, \ \delta = 0.342$$

We can now explain much of the assumptions and empirical observations of previous related work. The abundance of unmatched undemanded pairs is established in Lemma 2. The deviation from the *maximal-size* matching in Roth et al. [13] (See Propositions 1 & 2 and Table 2), are explained by virtue of Theorem 2. In particular, for the simulation with $n = 100$ the deviation from the expected ~ 56 exchanges is explained by equation (6) which yields $55.6 - 0.34 \cdot 10 - 2 = 50.2$. This result is very close to the value 49.7 that is reported in Roth et al. [13].

Similarly, simulation results in Table 1 of Abraham et al. [1], although they were based on few samples (100 trials), is also explained in light of Theorem 2. In particular, equation (6) almost always provides estimations between the reported mean and max values. Finally, Lemmas 4,5,6 prove analytically the assumptions behind kidney exchange models that focus on the reciprocal R subgraph, as in Ünver [15] which uses the number of (A, B) pairs as the representative state of a Markov chain model.

4. INCENTIVES IN KPD MARKETS

We now turn our attention to the case of multiple hospitals contributing their donor-patient graphs to a KPD market. We make this model more succinct through the following definitions:

Definition 4. The addition of two donor-patient graphs G_1, G_2 is defined by $G_1 \bigoplus G_2 = G_1 \bigcup G_2 \bigcup C$, where $C = \{(u, v)\}$, $u \in V(G_1)$, $v \in V(G_2)$, and pair u is blood-type compatible and tissue-type compatible with pair v, the latter independently with probability p_c. Let $V(G), E(G)$ and $M(G)$ denote the vertex set, the edges set and some maximum matching of graph G respectively.

Definition 5. A *hospital* h of size n has a donor-patient graph G_h as a type, which is a realization of random graph $\widetilde{G_n}$. A *strategy* s_h of a hospital h is a function such that $s_h(G_h) \subseteq G_h$. If $s_h(G_h) = G_h$ the strategy is *truthful.* If $s_h(G_h) \subset G_h$ it is *non-truthful.* A *selfish* strategy is defined by $s_h(G_h) = \oslash$

Definition 6. A *centralized mechanism* CM defined on m hospitals each of size n, and with graph type profile $G = (G_1, \cdots, G_m)$ and a strategy profile $s = (s_1, \cdots, s_m)$, computes a matching $CM(s, G)$ on graph $\hat{G} = \bigoplus_h s_h(G_h)$. The set of nodes on $CM(s, G)$ that belong to hospital h will be denoted by $CM_h(s, G)$.

The *utility* of a hospital from some outcome is given by $U_h(s, G) = |CM_h(s, G)| + |M(G_h - CM_h(s, G))|$. The implicit assumption is that hospitals will try to maximize the matches on the patients that were not matched by the mechanism. For a specific type G_h of h and a strategy profile s, the *expected utility* is $\overline{U_h}(s) = \mathbb{E}_{G_{-h}}[U_h(s, G_h \bigcup G_{-h})]$, where $G_{-h} = (G_1, \cdots, G_{h-1}, G_{h+1}, \cdots, G_m)$

The welfare $W(s, G)$ produced by the mechanism is thus equal to $W(s, G) = \sum_h U_h(s, G)$. For a strategy profile s, $\forall G$, an *efficient* CM allocates welfare $W(s, G) = |M(\bigoplus_h G_h)|$

An outcome $CM(s, G)$ is *individually rational* (IR) if $\forall h$ $CM_h(s, G) \geq |M(s_h(G_h))|$. Finally, a strategy profile $s = (s_h, s_{-h})$ is a Bayes-Nash equilibrium (BNE) if $\forall h$, $\forall s'_h$ it holds that $\overline{U_h}(s_h, s_{-h}) \geq \overline{U_h}(s'_h, s_{-h})$

4.1 Mechanisms

Definition 7. `rCM` is a CM which, given $\hat{G}$, outputs a uniformly sampled, maximum matching $M(\hat{G})$. A uniform sample from the maximum matchings of some graph G can be implemented through a relabeling of $V(G)$ and a generic maximum matching algorithm.

Definition 8. `irCM` is a CM which, given $\hat{G}$, repeatedly calls `rCM` until the outcome is also IR.

Definition 9. `xCM` is a CM which, operates in two stages: First, it clears internally the graphs $s_h(G_h), \forall h$, by enforcing the constraints of $\widetilde{M_n}$ (see Definition 3) and computing the most efficient matching possible, say L_h. Second, it runs `rCM` on the union of the individual remainder graphs, i.e. `rCM`(s, G).

It is straightforward to enforce the constraints of $\widetilde{M_n}$ in `xCM` through weighted matching (see [9]). Our implementation in Section 5 simply assigns larger weights to the edges between O and U pairs and then performs maximum weighted matching on the entire donor-patient graph.

Our first result, which stems directly from Theorem 2, quantifies the benefit of an institution as simple as `rCM`. Our baseline is the case when the mechanism is not used at all, or equivalently when all hospitals employ selfish strategies.

COROLLARY 2. *For mechanism* `rCM` *with m hospitals of size n and the parameters r, V defined in Lemma 2, and under the PM assumption, the welfare surplus $W(s, G)$ when hospitals employ truthful strategies compared to selfish ones is equal to:*

$$W(s, G) = (m - \sqrt{m}) \cdot \sqrt{\frac{2r}{\pi V}} \cdot n + (m - 1) \cdot \beta \qquad (7)$$

PROOF. Consider equation (6) of the average maximum matching in $\widetilde{G_n}$. When hospitals are selfish, total welfare is $m \cdot \mu(n)$ and when truthful welfare is $\mu(m \cdot n)$ since all hospitals draw independently from the same random graph model. Therefore, all we need to compute is:

$$W(s, G) = \mu(m \cdot n) - m \cdot \mu(n)$$

Substituting with Equation (6) for the value of $\mu(n)$ we get the desired result. □

By symmetry, the additional matches are distributed evenly among hospitals:

COROLLARY 3. *A hospital of size n that participates in* `rCM` *with m truthful participants, and under the PM assumption, will receive δU more transplantations on average, for which:*

$$\delta U = (1 - 1/\sqrt{m}) \cdot \sqrt{\frac{2r}{\pi V}} \cdot n + (1 - 1/m) \cdot \beta \qquad (8)$$

For large CMs where $m \to \infty$, it holds that,

$$\delta U = \sqrt{\frac{2r}{\pi V}} \cdot n + \beta \qquad (9)$$

A nationwide kidney exchange program can therefore yield individual benefits to participating hospitals that follow a square-root law to the size n of their patient lists, given that this sharing is truthful by all participants.

Continuing, we make the following key assumption:

ASSUMPTION 2. **(Regularity)** *For every $\widetilde{G_n}$, there exists a maximum matching drawn from some $\widetilde{M_n}$.*

In words, the regularity assumption claims the existence of a particular type of maximum matchings in $\widetilde{G_n}$. In such a matching all O pairs are completely matched to U pairs, and S and R pairs are self-matched. In the connectivity analysis of Section 3, we showed that this is a fair assumption to make, but simulation data is supportive as well. For example, in $\widetilde{G_n}$ with parameters $n = 40, p_c = 0.2$, the probabilities that there exists a matching of the form $\widetilde{M_n}$ that is either 0 or 1 exchange away from a maximum matching is 0.85 and 0.98 respectively. For a crossmatch probability $p_c = 0.11$ as reported in [17] these numbers are even higher, 0.94 and 0.998 respectively. If we include PRA sensitivity in our model (see Table 1) these numbers for $n = 40$ are 0.71 and 0.95. This hints at our model being robust even under this extra variability.

In order to emphasize the use of our two basic assumptions of perfect matching and regularity for studying incentives, we will make the following definition:

Definition 10. An *idealized* mechanism CM is a mechanism operating under the PM and Regularity assumptions.

By definition, the idealized `xCM` always computes matchings of the form $\widetilde{M_n}$ in the first stage of its operation. Lemma 8 establishes that individual rationality constraints do not affect the efficiency of our idealized mechanisms.

LEMMA 8. *Under truthful strategies, the idealized* irCM *and the idealized* xCM *are individually rational and efficient.*

However, mechanism irCM is not very computationally plausible since it searches blindly for IR and efficient matches, and in a straightforward implementation, takes a long time to finish. Our incentives analysis will thus focus on the xCM mechanism.

4.2 Incentives

We start with clarifying the concept of a hospital's deviating strategy.

Definition 11. Define a *proper subgraph* of G, a subgraph $P(G) \subseteq G$, $P(G) \neq \emptyset$, such that $\forall u \in V(P(G))$, if $(u,v) \in G$ then $v \in P(G)$.

Definition 12. Given hospital h with graph G_h, a *deviating* strategy d_h is defined by $d_h(G_h) = G_h - P(M_h)$, where $P(M_h)$ is a proper subgraph of some maximum matching M_h of G. If $P(M_h) = M_h$ the strategy is called *fully deviating.* If maximum matching M_h is of the form $\widetilde{M_n}$, then the strategy is called *canonically deviating.*

A strategy is both fully deviating and canonically deviating when a hospital is hiding completely an internal maximum matching of the form $\widetilde{M_n}$. We will soon show that canonical deviations are Bayes-Nash equilibria in kidney exchanges, however our equilibrium analysis will explore the entire space of possible strategies.

Let us first examine cases where hospitals fully deviate. The first natural question is whether this strategy is undesirable. For clarity, we focus on the simplest case of two hospitals, one being truthful and one (fully) deviating, denoted by h_t and h_d respectively. We will also use the following combinatorial definition:

Definition 13. Define $J(a,b,N)$ to be the number of white balls in a chain of N balls created by picking balls randomly from a jar with a white balls and b black balls without replacement.

It is easy to establish that the expected value $\overline{J}(a,b,N)$ is given by $\overline{J}(a,b,N) = \frac{a}{a+b} \cdot N$

We now seek to compute δU_t, the expected gain in utility of h_t being truthful compared to being selfish (i.e. reporting nothing). Also denote with δU_d the gains for hospital h_d. First, we will study rCM, as a typical non-IR mechanism and then xCM, which is IR by construction.

4.2.1 In mechanism rCM

We consider only pairs in the R subgraph since our analysis in Section 3 showed that all other pair types will not affect δU_t as much. In particular, say h_t reports s and w pairs in the two classes, such that $s \geq w$, and that h_d reports y pairs of the some specific kind. Then there are exactly three cases, as shown in Figure 2.

Mechanism rCM will allocate the following utilities:

$$\delta U_t = \begin{cases} J(s,y,w) - w & \text{case } (\alpha) \\ y & \text{case } (\beta) \\ s - 2w + J(w,y,s) & \text{case } (\gamma) \end{cases}$$

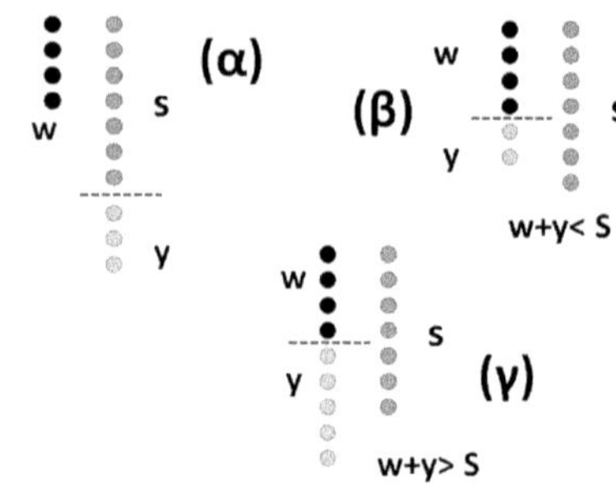

Figure 2: Deviating agent has y pairs of one kind (green). Truthful agent has s, w of both reciprocal pair types

For the fully deviating agent:

$$\delta U_d = \begin{cases} J(y,s,w) & \text{case } (\alpha) \\ y & \text{case } (\beta) \\ J(y,w,s) & \text{case } (\gamma) \end{cases}$$

It is hard to derive analytically the sign of δU_t, since $\delta U_t > 0$ for (α) and some (γ) and $\delta U_t < 0$ for (β) and some (γ). However, we can adopt simulations. Figure 3 depicts the average values of δU_t and δU_d in 1,000 test runs in rCM. Also notice from the equations, that $\delta U_d = \Theta(y)$ and since $y \propto \sqrt{|R|}$ by virtue of Lemma 6, it holds that $\delta U_d = \Theta(\sqrt{|R|})$. This is reflected in the shape of the red utility line for the strategic agent. A similar argument holds for the truthful agent as well.

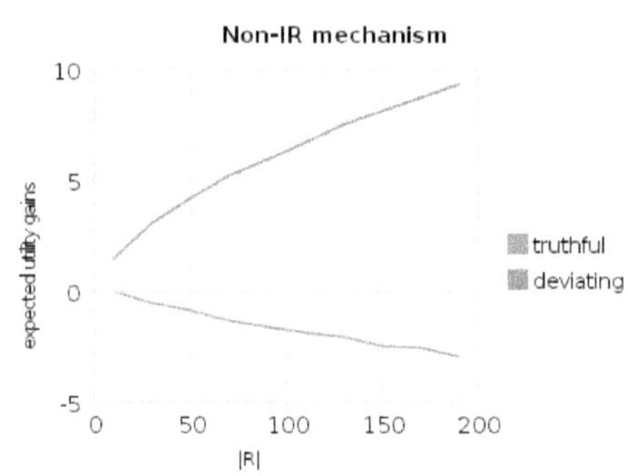

Figure 3: Truthful strategy has expected loss in a non-IR mechanism

It is straightforward to generalize to encompass multiple hospitals and show that, on average, deviating strategies not only yield benefits but also incur costs to truthful ones.

4.2.2 In mechanism xCM

We proceed to characterize the equilibrium strategies for mechanism xCM.

LEMMA 9. *Strategy profiles under idealized xCM in which, either hospitals are truthful or all hospitals are canonically deviating, are Bayes-Nash equilibria.*

Intuitively, given an edge (u,v) in a maximum matching, a hospital decides how to report u and v. If it reports both of them then xCM, by construction, will match them (or some other two of similar types). If it reports none, then they will be matched internally, otherwise If it reports only one, then there is some small probability that one pair will remain unmatched which is clearly undesirable. By induction, the first two cases can generate the truthful strategy and the canonical deviations and these are BNE.

Observe that the selfish strategy profile is also a BNE. However, we believe that the truthful equilibrium (or some form of canonical deviation) is much more likely in practice. A good reason is that the non-reporting BNE is not robust against pairwise deviations by hospitals and so would likely be unstable given the ability of hospitals to reach mutually advantageous agreements.

THEOREM 3. *The idealized mechanism xCM is individually rational and efficient in the truthful Bayes-Nash equilibrium, and also in every canonical deviation Bayes-Nash equilibrium.*

PROOF. We know that under truthful strategies the total welfare is $\mu(n \cdot m)$. By Lemma 9, in equilibrium, $\forall h \in H$, $\forall (w, M(w)) \in \widetilde{M_n}$ of that hospital, h will either report both w and $M(w)$ or none. In either case, these pairs will be matched before the second stage of xCM, which is equivalent in terms of efficiency to the case of all hospitals being truthful. However, by Lemma 8 the idealized xCM is efficient under truthful strategies and therefore it is efficient in all BNE with truthful or canonical deviation strategies. □

The average case analysis concluded with Theorem 3, proves that individual rationality enables efficiency under reasonable assumptions. Ashlagi & Roth [2] get a similar result for their "Bonus" mechanism. In fact, the first steps of their algorithm are similar to the first step of xCM, in the way that matches in the S and R subgraphs are implemented. From that point, their algorithm diverges since in 3-way kidney exchanges, matches between O, U and R pairs become available.

5. EXPERIMENTAL RESULTS

We used Perl to implement the $\widetilde{G_n}$ random graph model and test the theoretical results. In particular, maximum matchings were determined by an implementation of the Galil algorithm [7] that runs in $O(|V|^3)$ time, which proved faster than open-source LP libraries. Currently, on a dual-core PC with 2.4 Ghz/CPU, the donor-patient graph of 1,000 pairs is cleared in approximately 10 seconds.[3]

In our first experiments we generate random graphs $\widetilde{G_n}$ through the process defined in Section 2.1. The first two tables refer to the matching properties of the S and R subgraphs, in which we report the number of matched patients compared to the individual sizes of the subgraphs averaged over 1,000 samples.

The expected values for optimal matchings of the subgraph S (Table 3) are given by Lemma 5 and for the expected matchings in R by Lemma 6. The realized values are very close to what our analysis predicts. Notice also the increasing standard deviation for matchings in R, which stems from the properties of the folded binomial.

[3]The Perl source code is available for download from `http://www.eecs.harvard.edu/econcs/code/rgke.zip` Detailed instructions on how to reproduce the results of this section can be found in the package.

#pairs	#matches	$(\|S\| - \beta)$	sd
20	18.12	18.0	1.15
40	38.1	38.0	1.06
60	57.91	58.0	1.14
80	77.93	78.0	1.11
100	97.92	98.0	1.07

Table 3: Maximum matching in S

#pairs	#matches	$(\|R\| - \sqrt{\frac{2}{\pi} \cdot \|R\|})$	sd
20	16.64	16.43	2.64
40	34.94	34.95	3.73
60	54.16	53.82	4.79
80	72.97	72.86	5.67
100	91.76	92.02	6.12

Table 4: Maximum matching in R

For Theorem 2, which computes the expected cardinality of the maximum matchings of $\widetilde{G_n}$, we simply take 1,000 samples of $M(\widetilde{G_n})$ for various values of n. The results are shown in Table 5, and validate the analysis.

#pairs	#matches	$\mu(n)$	sd
20	7.83	7.57	3.16
40	18.12	18.04	4.46
60	28.56	28.66	5.66
80	39.2	39.35	6.69
100	49.51	50.09	7.33
200	104.75	104.18	11.22

Table 5: Maximum matching in $\widetilde{G_n}$

5.1 Experiments with incentives

We will put our theory to test on mechanism xCM, since irCM is not easy to implement efficiently and also lacks a thorough incentives analysis. We start by examining the welfare surplus of rCM with 3 truthful hospitals, each reporting some $\widetilde{G_n}$. Again, we take 1,000 samples for various sizes of n.

n	H-1	H-2	H-3	Total	Selfish	$W(s, G)$
20	9.63	9.36	9.45	28.44	22.77	5.94
40	20.26	20.05	20.31	60.62	54.24	6.74
60	31.05	31.22	31.23	93.49	86.14	7.36
80	41.99	41.97	42.31	126.26	118.27	7.88
100	52.97	52.37	52.59	157.93	150.55	8.33

Table 6: Surplus from rCM with truthful hospitals

The left part of Table 6 refers to the simulation results and the right one gives the theoretical predictions. The column titled *"Selfish"* gives the welfare when hospitals are not reporting anything to the centralized mechanism. Our theory predicts with high accuracy the expected welfare surplus. For example, for $n = 60$ we have that $W = 7.36$ using Corollary 2, when the real value is $93.49 - 86.14 = 7.35$. Last, notice that the surplus is distributed evenly among all hospitals with values that are very close to $\mu(n) + W/3$, as predicted in Corollary 2. For example, if $n = 60$, the predicted utility is $28.71 + 2.45 = 31.16$, which is very close to what all hospitals receive (see H-1,2,3 for $n = 60$)

Next, we proceed to study cases in which not all hospitals are truthful. Here we will consider only full deviations and for brevity we will refer to this as simply a deviation. Our analysis in Section 4 showed that deviating strategies are provably hurtful to the utility of truthful hospitals under a non-IR centralized mechanism. To validate the truthfulness of xCM, we modify our simulation so that H-1 deviates fully. We first run on the non-IR centralized mechanism we defined as rCM. See Table 7.

n	H-1_d	H-2	H-3	Total
20	10.67	8.60	8.65	27.92
40	23.08	18.39	18.52	59.99
60	35.45	28.68	28.81	92.93
80	47.71	38.62	38.55	124.88
100	60.68	49.18	48.94	158.8

Table 7: H-1 deviates in rCM

We again take 1,000 samples for each value of the hospital size n, and report the average values. First, notice that H-1 matches consistently more pairs any other truthful hospital. Second, it is interesting to see that total welfare is not hurt by the deviation (if we compare it to the one reported in Table 5). This should not come as a surprise, since Theorem 3 actually builds upon this property to deliver a mechanism that is IR and efficient on average. Next, we run xCM under the same setting to get the results in Table 8.

n	H-1_d	H-2	H-3	Total
20	9.28	9.46	9.27	28.01
40	19.74	19.79	20.03	59.57
60	30.65	30.51	30.54	91.69
80	41.66	41.91	41.13	124.7
100	52.02	52.39	52.36	156.76

Table 8: H-1 deviates under xCM

There are two important remarks. First, imposing IR is effective against incentives if one looks at the individual utilities received by each hospital (also compare with Table 6). Furthermore, the mechanism produces on average efficient outcomes if we compare with Table 6, as predicted by Theorem 3.

5.2 Robustness of results

The $\widetilde{G_n}$ model makes several simplifying assumptions, by using a specific blood type distribution and treating the tissue-type compatibilities as independent random events with probability $p_c = 0.2$. Here we test how relevant our model remains with the introduction of nuisance parameters.

In particular, we test two different blood-type distributions, one O(27%), A(32%), B(31%) and AB(10%) as in Korea and one set to O(44%), A(42%), B(10%) and AB(4%) as in the USA. Note that each distribution induces different parameters for the calculation of the $\mu(n)$ formula in Lemma 2. Let us denote with $\mu_K(n)$ and $\mu_U(n)$ the formulas for Korea and US respectively. Furthermore we endow p_c with a variability as in Table 1. In particular, every pair draws a PRA sensitivity from the distribution of Table 1 which defines its individual crossmatch probability. Two pairs i, j are then tissue-type compatible with probability $(1 - p_{c,i}) \cdot (1 - p_{c,j})$

We try to reproduce Table 5 in this more realistic scenario, since Theorem 2 is the core of our analysis. The results on 1,000 samples are shown in Table 9:

#pairs	#(Korea)	$\mu_K(n)$	#(USA)	$\mu_U(n)$
20	7.18	8.67	5.83	7.62
40	17.21	20.6	14.4	18.11
60	28.27	32.74	23.86	28.75
80	39.54	44.99	33.89	39.46
100	51.24	57.3	44.01	50.22
200	111.16	119.41	97.6	104.39

Table 9: Matches with different ABO distributions and with PRA sensitivity (see Table 1)

The theoretical predictions do become less accurate under these different assumptions due mostly to the introduction of PRA variability. However, our theoretical model remains robust, in that it shares the approximate behavior of the realized values. For example, one can observe that the ratios of simulation over theoretical values are decreasing and approaching 1 for large graph sizes.

Next, we would like to examine if xCM remains effective in mitigating the impact of strategic playing under PRA variability. To stress our analysis further, we will examine the US blood type distribution. Our baseline is again defined to be rCM. In the first scenario we wish to find out the best welfare that can be achieved and we assume this to happen when all hospitals are truthful. The results are shown in Table 10.

n	H-1	H-2	H-3	Total
20	8.05	7.88	7.75	23.67
40	18.37	18.08	18.04	54.49
60	29.15	29.13	28.99	87.27
80	39.82	39.85	39.4	119.06
100	50.99	50.71	51.21	152.92

Table 10: All truthful in rCM (PRA+US blood freqs.)

Next we let hospital H-1 deviate. The results shown in Table 11 reveal that H-1 is doing consistently better than truthful hospitals, but at the same time appears not to hurt much the overall efficiency ($\sim$ 1-2%).

n	H-1_d	H-2	H-3	Total
20	9.18	7.45	7.33	23.96
40	20.41	16.52	16.68	53.61
60	32.19	26.16	25.74	84.09
80	45.29	36.25	35.98	117.52
100	57.15	46.0	45.97	149.12

Table 11: H-1 deviating in rCM (PRA+US)

Next we run our simulation with H-1 deviating under mechanism xCM. The results are shown in Table 12.

n	H-1_d	H-2	H-3	Total
20	7.78	7.3	7.56	22.64
40	17.54	17.36	17.47	52.37
60	27.66	27.72	27.27	82.65
80	37.2	37.53	37.48	112.20
100	48.33	47.81	48.02	144.16

Table 12: H-1 deviating in xCM (PRA+US)

We conclude that xCM restores fairness since H-1_d receives approximately the same number of transplantations with truthful participants, while it consistently receives more than others under rCM. Furthermore, the cost in efficiency is small and stems mostly from the O and S subgraphs, which under the PRA model are more likely to contain highly sensitized patients. As a result, our connectivity assumptions are violated, thus leading to a noticeable loss in efficiency. For $n = 40$, that is for a *CM* with 120 total patients, this loss is $\sim 3.6\%$ of the total efficiency. Therefore, our analysis remains robust in dealing with parameters such as the PRA variability or different blood type distributions, that were not explicit parts of the model. Further improvements are expected by modeling PRA sensitivity within the $\widetilde{G_n}$ model and refactoring the analysis (Assumption 2).

6. CONCLUSIONS

We address efficiency and incentives in kidney exchanges through a quantified random graph analysis which is new on this domain. This perspective elucidates important aspects of centralized kidney exchanges which are currently in an experimental stage.

We started with the definition of a random graph model of kidney exchanges, namely the model $\widetilde{G_n}$. Subsequently, we exploited the skewed connectivity among its subgraphs to derive analytically $\mu(n)$, i.e. the expected number of patients matched in a maximum matching drawn from $\widetilde{G_n}$. This allowed us to explain much of early experimental results but more importantly to study multiple-hospital, centralized mechanisms (CM). In particular, we were able to quantify the expected individual benefit of a hospital as being $\propto \sqrt{n}$ in a CM with hospitals of size n. To the best of our knowledge, this is the first formal proof of the valuable network effect that comes from nationwide kidney exchanges.

Next, under a quantitatively and qualitatively reasonable argument (see Assumption 2), we leveraged our analysis to study the incentives problem. First, we showed that non-truthful strategies do have negative effects on individual and overall welfare. We then analyzed an archetypal IR mechanism, namely xCM and proved that it is efficient and IR in equilibrium. Extensive experimental results validated our theoretical predictions and the nice properties of xCM. Furthermore, we checked for robustness on an augmented model $\widetilde{G_n}(PRA, F)$ which takes into account a variable PRA sensitivity for patients (given in Table 1) and any ABO blood-type distribution F.

7. ACKNOWLEDGMENTS

We would like to thank Leslie Valiant, Itai Ashlagi, Ian Kash, Felix Fischer and the anonymous reviewers for their valuable feedback on earlier versions of this work.

8. REFERENCES

[1] D. Abraham, A. Blum, and T. Sandholm. Clearing algorithms for barter exchange markets: enabling nationwide kidney exchanges. In *Proceedings of the 8th ACM conference on Electronic commerce*, page 304. ACM, 2007.

[2] I. Ashlagi and A.E. Roth. Individual rationality and participation in large scale, multi-hospital kidney exchange. In *Proceedings of the 12th ACM Conference on Electronic Commerce*, (to appear) 2011.

[3] I. Ashlagi, F. Fischer, I. Kash, and A. Procaccia. Mix and match. In *Proceedings of the 11th ACM conference on Electronic Commerce*, pages 305–314. ACM, 2010.

[4] B. Bollobás. *Modern graph theory*. Springer Verlag, 1998.

[5] B. Bollobás. *Random graphs*. Cambridge Univ Pr, 2001.

[6] J. Edmonds. Paths, trees, and flowers. *Canadian Journal of Mathematics*, 17(3):449–467, 1965.

[7] Z. Galil. Efficient algorithms for finding maximum matching in graphs. *ACM Computing Surveys (CSUR)*, 18(1):23–38, 1986.

[8] R. Montgomery, A. Zachary, L. Ratner, D. Segev, J. Hiller, J. Houp, M. Cooper, L. Kavoussi, T. Jarrett, J. Burdick, et al. Clinical results from transplanting incompatible live kidney donor/recipient pairs using kidney paired donation. *Jama*, 294(13):1655, 2005.

[9] C. Papadimitriou and K. Steiglitz. *Combinatorial optimization: algorithms and complexity*. Dover Pubns, 1998.

[10] M. Rees, J. Kopke, R. Pelletier, D. Segev, M. Rutter, A. Fabrega, J. Rogers, O. Pankewycz, J. Hiller, A.E. Roth, et al. A nonsimultaneous, extended, altruistic-donor chain. *New England Journal of Medicine*, 360(11):1096, 2009.

[11] M. Rees, R. Pelletier, S. Mulgaonkar, D. Laskow, B. Nibhanupudy, J. Kopke, A.E. Roth, U. Unver, T. Sandholm, and J. Rogers. Report From A 60 Transplant Center Multiregional Kidney Paired Donation Program: 2. *Transplantation*, 86(2S):1, 2008.

[12] A.E. Roth, T. Sönmez, and M. Ünver. Kidney Exchange*. *Quarterly Journal of Economics*, 119(2):457–488, 2004.

[13] A.E. Roth, T. Sönmez, and M. Ünver. Efficient kidney exchange: Coincidence of wants in markets with compatibility-based preferences. *The American economic review*, 97(3):828–851, 2007.

[14] S. Saidman, A.E. Roth, T. Sönmez, M. Ünver, and F. Delmonico. Increasing the opportunity of live kidney donation by matching for two-and three-way exchanges. *Transplantation*, 81(5):773, 2006.

[15] M. Ünver. Dynamic kidney exchange. *Review of Economic Studies*, 77(1):372–414, 2010.

[16] Wikipedia. Blood type, 2010. [Online; accessed 22-December-2010].

[17] S. Zenios, E. Woodle, and L. Friedman Ross. Primum non nocere: Avoiding harm to vulnerable wait list candidates in an indirect kidney exchange. *Transplantation*, 72(4):648, 2001.

The College Admissions Problem With a Continuum of Students

[Extended Abstract]*

Eduardo M. Azevedo
Harvard University
Cambridge, MA
azevedo@fas.harvard.edu

Jacob D. Leshno
Harvard University & HBS
Cambridge, MA
jleshno@hbs.edu

ABSTRACT

In many two-sided matching markets, agents on one side are matched to a large number of agents on the other side (e.g. college admissions). Yet little is known about the structure of stable matchings when there are many agents on one side. We propose a variation of the Gale and Shapley [3] college admissions model where a finite number of colleges is matched to a continuum of students. It is shown that, generically (though not always) (i) there is a unique stable matching, (ii) this stable matching varies continuously with the underlying economy, and (iii) it is the limit of the set of stable matchings of approximating large discrete economies.

Categories and Subject Descriptors: J.4 Computer Applications: Social and Behavioral Sciences – Economics.

General Terms: Algorithms, Economics, Theory.

Keywords: Matching, Market Design.

1. EXTENDED ABSTRACT

Two-sided matching markets are markets where agents care about whom they interact with in the other side. This includes several real world examples, such as colleges and students, or Internet content providers and advertisers. In these, and several other prominent examples, each agent on one side is matched to a large number of agents on the other side. However, little is known about special properties of such markets. To investigate this, we propose a variation of the Gale and Shapley college admissions model, where a finite number of colleges is matched to a continuum of students. Colleges' preferences over students are represented by a score. A student's score at different colleges need not be the same.

A preliminary result is that, in both the continuum and the traditional discrete models, stable matchings have a very simple representation. Any stable matching can be described by a vector of threshold scores at each college, which we term a cutoff. We define a student's demand given cutoffs to be her favorite college out of the colleges for which her score is above the threshold. A set of cutoffs is said to clear the market if demand for colleges equals the supply of seats, or leaves empty seats in colleges with a cutoff equal to zero (the minimal score). The cutoff lemma guarantees that each stable matching corresponds to a market clearing cutoff, and vice versa. In the continuum case, this correspondence is a bijection. Cutoffs allow us to find the set of stable matchings by solving a set of simple market clearing equations.

We find that for almost every continuum matching market the following holds: (i) There is a unique stable matching. (ii) For any sequence of approximating discrete economies, the diameter of the set of stable matchings converges to 0. This complements previous findings that in large matching markets all stable matchings are very similar ([5], [4]).(iii) Moreover, the set of stable matchings converges to the stable matching of the continuum limit. (iv) Stable matchings of the continuum economy vary continuously with the parameters of the model. This theoretically supports using data and simulations to inform market design (as in [5]). (v) Stable matchings of discrete economies randomly generated from the distribution of agents in the limit converge almost surely to the limit economy's stable matching. This implies a simple characterization of the asymptotic behavior of several mechanisms, generalizing previous work on the random serial dictatorship mechanism.

We hope the continuum model will be useful not only to investigate general properties of large markets, but also as a tractable framework to study complex applied problems in market design and algorithmic game theory, where exact results in discrete models are hard to obtain. [1] uses the continuum model to investigate strategic interactions in matching markets where firms have market power. [2] apply it to study the Nash Equilibria of a non-strategyproof school choice mechanism. Both more applied problems and general asymptotic properties of matching markets are interesting avenues for future research.

*A full version of this paper is available at (`http://www.people.fas.harvard.edu/~jleshno/papers/College_continuum.pdf`).

EC'11, June 5–9, 2011, San Jose, California, USA.
ACM 978-1-4503-0261-6/11/06.

REFERENCES

[1] E. Azevedo. Imperfect competition in two-sided matching markets. Mimeo, 2010.

[2] E. Azevedo and J. Leshno. Can we make school choice more efficient? An example. Mimeo, 2010.

[3] D. Gale and L. Shapley. College admissions and the stability of marriage. *American Mathematical Monthly*, 69(1):9–15, 1962.

[4] N. Immorlica and M. Mahdian. Marriage, honesty, and stability. In *SODA* 2005.

[5] A. Roth and E. Peranson. The redesign of the matching market for american physicians: Some engineering aspects of economic design. *The American Economic Review*, 89(4):748–780, 1999.

Matching with Couples Revisited

[Extended Abstract]*

Itai Ashlagi
Massachusetts Institute of Technology
Cambridge, MA
iashlagi@mit.edu

Mark Braverman
University of Toronto
Toronto, Canada
mbraverm@cs.troronto.edu

Avinatan Hassidim
Google Israel
Israel
avinatanh@gmail.com

ABSTRACT

It is well known that a stable matching in a many-to-one matching market with couples need not exist. We introduce a new matching algorithm for such markets and show that for large random markets the algorithm will find a stable matching with high probability. In our model we allow the number of couples to grow at a near-linear rate. Furthermore, truth-telling is an approximated equilibrium in the game induced by the new matching algorithm. Our results are tight: for markets in which the number of couples grows at a linear rate, we show that with constant probability no stable matching exists.

Categories and Subject Descriptors: J.4 Computer Applications: Social and Behavioral Sciences – Economics.

General Terms: Algorithms, Economics, Theory.

Keywords: Matching, Market Design.

1. EXTENDED ABSTRACT

Two-sided matching markets are markets each player has preferences over being matched to players on the other side. In this paper (Ashlagi, Braverman and Hassidim (2010)) we study many-to-one matching markets, in which one side of the market contains couples. Examples for such markets are the National Resident Matching Program (NRMP) and the clearinghouse for psychology interns. In our model one side of the market consists of hospitals and the other consists of doctors, who can either be singles or part of a couple.

Naturally, when couples are present in the market, the preferences of the individuals within each couple depend on each other and often introduce complementarities, and a stable matching may not exist Roth (1984). Klaus and Klijn (2005) provided a maximal domain of preferences for which a stable matching exists. However, Kojima, Pathak, and Roth (2010) observe from real data that couples' preferences often do not belong to this domain. Adopting a random preferences approach, they use a simple algorithm to show that if there are n single doctors, and the number of couples is of order $\sqrt{n}$ a stable matching exists with probability converging to one as n approaches infinity. Real data, however, suggests that the number of couples is larger than $\sqrt{n}$.

We introduce a new matching algorithm, called Sorted Deferred Acceptance (SoDA). We first show that if the number of couples grows at a near-linear rate[1] , the probability that a stable matching exists and that the SoDA algorithm will find one approaches one as n grows. Furthermore, truth-telling is an approximated Bayes-Nash equilibrium in the game induced by SoDA. We then show that if the number of couples grows linearly there exist a constant probability that a stable matching does not exist.

We also show that the SoDA algorithm runs in polynomial time (in fact 'almost' linear), and provide simulations that test SoDA in various large random markets.

At the technical level, we aim to control the way in which complementarities introduced by couples may interfere with each other thus precluding a stable matching from being found. We introduce a notion of an "influence tree" that gives an upper bound on the range of the effect a particular couple may have. By analyzing the (typical) relationship between the influence trees of the couples, we are able to devise a way to produce a stable matching with high probability when the number of couples is sub-linear.

Our results add to a short list of positive results in setting with complementarities. We believe our techniques maybe useful in other such settings.

REFERENCES

[1] I. Ashlagi, M. Braverman, and A. Hassidim. Matching with Couples Revisited. Working paper, 2010.

[2] B. Klaus and F. Klijn. Stable Matchings and Preferences of Couples. *Journal of Economic Theory*, 121:75–106, 2005.

[3] F. Kojima, P. Pathak, and A. E. Roth. Matching with Couples: Stability and Incentives in Large Markets. Working paper, 2010.

[4] A. E. Roth. The Evolution of the Labor Market for Medical Interns and Residents: A Case Study in Game Theory. *Journal of Political Economy*, 92:991–1016, 1984.

*A full version of this paper is available at `http://web.mit.edu/iashlagi/www/papers/couplesFinal1.pdf`.

[1]For any $\epsilon > 0$, the number of couples is growing at a rate of $n^{1-\epsilon}$.

EC'11, June 5–9, 2011, San Jose, California, USA.
ACM 978-1-4503-0261-6/11/06.

Multilateral Matching*

[Extended Abstract]†

John William Hatfield
Graduate School of Business, Stanford University
Stanford, CA 94305 USA
hatfield_john@gsb.stanford.edu

Scott Duke Kominers
Department of Economics, Harvard University
& Harvard Business School
Cambridge, MA 02138 USA
skominers@hbs.edu

ABSTRACT

A natural equilibrium notion for multiparty contracting settings is matching-theoretic *stability*, the requirement that no set of agents can profitably recontract. Unfortunately, when contract participation is discrete, stable outcomes do not necessarily exist in the presence of complementarities across contracts. Consequently, standard matching theory rules out all forms of contractual complementarity, and thus can not be used to study multiparty enterprises.

This paper introduces a novel matching model with transferable utility in which sets of two or more agents may enter into multilateral contracts. Certain forms of complementarity can be expressed through such contracts; in particular, our model embeds a large class of economies with production complementarities. Our key insight is that stable multilateral contracting outcomes do exist when contract participation is continuous, so long as agents' utilities are concave in venture participation.[1] Furthermore, when agents' utilities are concave, stable outcomes directly correpsond to competitive equilibria. Conversely, competitive equilibria induce outcomes that are strongly group stable and in the core.[2] Analogues of the first and second welfare theorems hold as well, showing in particular that stable outcomes (and competitive equilibria) are efficient. While our basic model disallows contractual externalities, competitive equilibria continue to exist even when such externalities are introduced, although they may not be efficient.

Previous work in matching theory has required (either explicitly or implicitly) that agents interact via bilateral contractual relationships; in medical labor markets medical students "sell" their services to hospitals, and in school choice applications, schools "sell" their services to students. The restriction to bilateral contracts was material in the previous work as, in order to guarantee the existence of equilibria, agents were required to view contracts as substitutes (see [3] and references contained therein). Meanwhile, the difficulties of introducing multilateral contracting in matching models are well-known (see [1] and Chapter 2 of [4]); by allowing contracts to be continuously divisible, we avoid these difficulties.

The presence of continuously divisible contracts makes our underlying model similar to models of general equilibrium. However, unlike in general equilibrium theory, we consider production (and other) relationships that are agent-specific: in our framework, a set of agents may share a nonpublic production technology, and that technology may require inputs from specific agents, such as human capital. Notwithstanding, we do not strictly extend general equilibrium theory, as we impose the requirement that agents' utilities are quasilinear in a numeraire.

Categories and Subject Descriptors: J.4 Computer Applications: Social and Behavioral Sciences – Economics; K.4.4 Computers and Society: Electronic Commerce

General Terms: Economics, Theory

Keywords: Matching; Networks; Joint Ventures; Stability; Competitive Equilibrium; Core; Efficiency

REFERENCES

[1] ALKAN, A. Nonexistence of stable threesome matchings. *Mathematical Social Sciences 16* (1988), 207–209.

[2] ECHENIQUE, F., AND OVIEDO, J. A theory of stability in many-to-many matching markets. *Theoretical Economics 1* (2006), 233–273.

[3] HATFIELD, J. W., KOMINERS, S. D., NICHIFOR, A., OSTROVSKY, M., AND WESTKAMP, A. Stability and competitive equilibrium in trading networks. Mimeo, Stanford Graduate School of Business (2011).

[4] ROTH, A. E., AND SOTOMAYOR, M. A. O. *Two-sided matching: A study in game-theoretic modeling and analysis.* Econometric Society Monographs. Cambridge University Press, 1990.

---

*We are grateful to Susan Athey, Clayton Featherstone, Jeremy Fox, Drew Fudenberg, Ben Golub, Jerry Green, Yuichiro Kamada, Yair Livne, Preston McAfee, Michael Ostrovsky, Alvin E. Roth, Michael Schwarz, and workshop participants at Harvard for helpful comments. Hatfield appreciates the hospitality of Harvard Business School, which hosted him during parts of this research. Kominers gratefully acknowledges the support of a National Science Foundation Graduate Research Fellowship, a Yahoo! Key Scientific Challenges Program Fellowship, and a Terence M. Considine Fellowship in Law and Economics funded by the John M. Olin Center.

†A full version of this paper is available online at `http://scottkom.com/articles/Hatfield_Kominers_Multilateral_Matching.pdf`.

[1]The assumption of concavity is natural in settings with decreasing returns to scale and scope. However, it is violated in settings with fixed costs or increasing returns to scale.

[2]Hatfield et al. [3] obtain analogous results in a setting distinct from ours, in which agents trade via discrete, bilateral contracts. It is known that analogous results do not hold in matching settings without transfers ([2]).

EC'11, June 5–9, 2011, San Jose, California, USA.
ACM 978-1-4503-0261-6/11/06.

Mean Field Equilibria of Dynamic Auctions with Learning

Krishnamurthy Iyer
Department of Management Science and Engineering
Stanford University
kriyer@stanford.edu

Ramesh Johari
Department of Management Science and Engineering
Stanford University
ramesh.johari@stanford.edu

Mukund Sundararajan
Google Inc.
Mountain View, CA, USA
mukunds@google.com

Keywords

Dynamic auctions, learning, mean field equilibrium

General Terms

Economics, Theory

Categories and Subject Descriptors

J.4 [**Social and Behavioral Sciences**]: Economics

Abstract

Due to non-technical considerations, dynamic auctions in practice are rarely optimal dynamic mechanisms. Far more commonly, mechanisms used in practice are repetitions of *simple* one-shot mechanisms that may be far from being dynamically optimal (e.g., the repeated generalized second price auction in sponsored search). From an analytical standpoint, these simple mechanisms typically do not provide a dynamic truthtelling guarantee and can give rise to extremely *complex* bidder behavior.

In this paper, we consider a dynamic setting where identical copies of a good are sold through a sequence of second price auctions over time. Each agent in the market has an independent private valuation which determines the distribution of the reward she obtains from the good. However, the agents are unaware of their own private valuations. Every time an agent wins an auction and obtains a copy of the good, her realized reward from the good informs her about her valuation. Thus, each agent faces a trade-off between *exploration* (by bidding higher) and *exploitation* (by bidding close to her expected rewards).

There are two central problems with using standard equilibrium concepts (formally, perfect Bayesian equilibrium, or PBE) to analyze this model. First is that such equilibria are *intractable*: the state space complexity is enormous (since bidders must maintain beliefs over all that is unknown to them), and grows exponentially with the number of bidders. Second, and partly in consequence, is that such equilibria are *implausible*: PBE requires a bidder to accurately forecast and estimate *exactly* how her competitors will respond to any bid she makes today.

Here, we consider an approximation methodology that we refer to as a *mean field equilibrium* (MFE). In an MFE, individuals take a simpler view of the world: they postulate that fluctuations in the empirical distribution of other players' bids have "averaged out", and thus optimize holding the bid distribution of other players fixed. MFE requires a consistency check: the postulated bid distribution must arise from the optimal strategies agents compute. MFE is inspired by a *large market* approximation: with a large number of bidders, tracking and forecasting the exact behavior of individual bidders is impractical and implausible. The benefit of analyzing a large market using MFE is that for the agents to optimize their behavior, it is sufficient for them to just maintain beliefs about their *own* private valuation. This reduces the dimension of the system state that each agent needs to track, simplifying the analysis tremendously.

There are two main results in this paper. *First*, we show the existence of an MFE and explicitly characterize the optimal bidding strategy of an agent in a large market. We show a remarkable fact: in the large market model, the agent has an optimal strategy where she bids truthfully according to a *conjoint valuation*. The conjoint valuation is the sum of her current expected valuation, together with an overbid. The overbid amount is exactly the expected marginal benefit to one additional observation about her true private valuation. Thus the conjoint valuation characterizes explicitly how an agent balances the tradeoff between exploration and exploitation.

Second, we justify MFE as a good approximation to agent behavior as the number of agents increases. Formally, we show that if in a finite market, every agent except one follows the MFE strategy, then the remaining agent's loss on playing the MFE strategy converges to zero as the number of agents in the market increases. We emphasize, however, that MFE may be a useful approximation even when the number of agents is not large, simply because it more accurately captures the information available to bidders when they optimize (e.g., in sponsored search auctions, bidders are responding to *bid landscape*, i.e., the distribution of bids in a given category or keyword).

We conclude our paper by designing a heuristic to compute MFE; we show that this heuristic converges relatively fast, and use the heuristic to explore the impact of changes in market parameters on the equilibrium.

Acknowledgments. This work is supported by the NSF under grants CNS-0904609, CCF-0832820, CNS-0644114, and CMMI-0948434, and by DARPA under the ITMANET program.

Link to full paper: `http://ssrn.com/abstract=1799085`

EC'11, June 5–9, 2011, San Jose, California, USA.
ACM 978-1-4503-0261-6/11/06.

Simplicity-Expressiveness Tradeoffs in Mechanism Design

Paul Dütting*
Ecole Polytechnique Fédérale de Lausanne (EPFL)
CH-1015 Lausanne, Switzerland
paul.duetting@epfl.ch

Felix Fischer†
School of Engineering and Applied Sciences
Harvard University
Cambridge, MA 02138, USA
fischerf@seas.harvard.edu

David C. Parkes
School of Engineering and Applied Sciences
Harvard University
Cambridge, MA 02138, USA
parkes@eecs.harvard.edu

Everything should be made as simple as possible, but no simpler. – Albert Einstein

ABSTRACT

A fundamental result in mechanism design theory, the so-called revelation principle, asserts that for many questions concerning the existence of mechanisms with a given outcome one can restrict attention to truthful direct-revelation mechanisms. In practice, however, many mechanisms use a restricted message space. This motivates the study of the tradeoffs involved in choosing simplified mechanisms, which can sometimes bring benefits in precluding bad or promoting good equilibria, and other times impose costs on welfare and revenue. We study the simplicity-expressiveness tradeoff in two representative settings, sponsored search auctions and combinatorial auctions, each being a canonical example for complete information and incomplete information analysis, respectively. We observe that the amount of information available to the agents plays an important role for the tradeoff between simplicity and expressiveness.

Categories and Subject Descriptors

F.2 [**Theory of Computation**]: Analysis of Algorithms and Problem Complexity; J.4 [**Computer Applications**]: Social and Behavioral Sciences—*Economics*

General Terms

Algorithms, Economics, Theory

Keywords

Simplified Mechanisms, Expressiveness

*Research supported by a EURYI award.

†Research supported by DFG grant FI 1664/1-1.

1. INTRODUCTION

The revelation principle states that any equilibrium outcome of any mechanism can be obtained in a truthful equilibrium of a direct-revelation mechanism, i.e., an equilibrium in which agents truthfully reveal their types. In practice, however, the assumptions underlying the revelation principle often fail: other equilibria may exist besides the truthful one, or computational limitations may interfere. As a consequence, many practical mechanisms use a restricted message space. This motivates the study of the tradeoffs involved in choosing among mechanisms with different degrees of expressiveness. Despite their practical importance, these tradeoffs are currently only poorly understood.

In sponsored search auctions, and adopting a complete information analysis, allowing every agent i to submit a valuation v_{ij} for each slot j means that both the Vickrey-Clarke-Groves (VCG) mechanism and the Generalized Second Price (GSP) mechanism always admit a Nash equilibrium with zero revenue [22]. If agents face a small cost for submitting a non-zero bid, this becomes the unique equilibrium. If instead agent i is asked for a single bid b_i, and his bid for slot j is derived by multiplying b_i with a slot-specific click-through rate α_j, the zero-revenue equilibria are eliminated. More surprisingly, this simplification does not introduce new equilibria (even when α_j is not correct for every agent i), so minimum revenue over all Nash equilibria is strictly greater for the simplification than for the original mechanism. Moreover, if valuations can actually be decomposed into an agent-specific valuation v_i and click-through rates α_j, the simplification still has an efficient Nash equilibrium. Milgrom [22] concluded that simplification can be beneficial and need not come at a cost.

For combinatorial auctions, and adopting an incomplete information analysis, the maximum social welfare over all outcomes of a mechanism strictly increases with expressiveness, for a particular measure of expressiveness based on notions from computational learning theory [4]. Implicit in the result of Benisch et al. [4] is the conclusion that more expressiveness is generally desirable, as it allows a mechanism to achieve a more efficient outcome in more instances of the problem.

Each of these results tells only part of the story. While Milgrom's results on the benefits of simplicity are developed within an equilibrium framework and can be extended beyond sponsored search auctions, they critically require settings with complete information amongst agents in order to preclude bad equilibria while retaining good ones. In particular, Milgrom does not consider the potential loss in efficiency or revenue that can occur when agents are ignorant of each other's valuations when deciding how to bid within a simplified bidding language. Benisch et al., on the other hand, develop their results on the benefits of expressiveness (and thus the cost of simplicity) in an incomplete information context, but largely in the absence of equilibrium considerations.[1] In particular, these authors do not consider the potential problems that can occur due to the existence of bad equilibria in expressive mechanisms.

Our Contribution The contribution of this paper is twofold. On a conceptual level, we analyze how different properties of a simplification affect the set of equilibria of a mechanism in both complete and incomplete information settings and argue that well-chosen simplifications can have a positive impact on the set of equilibria as a whole; either by precluding undesirable equilibria or by promoting desirable equilibria. We thus extend Milgrom's emphasis on simplification as a tool that enables equilibrium selection. On a technical level, we analyze simplified mechanisms for sponsored search auctions with complete information and combinatorial auctions with incomplete information.

An important property when analyzing the impact of simplification on the set of equilibria is *tightness* [22], which requires that no additional equilibria are introduced. We observe that tightness can be achieved equally well in complete and incomplete information settings and give a sufficient condition.[2] Complementary to tightness is a property we call *totality*, which requires all equilibria of the original mechanism to be preserved. To the end of equilibrium selection, totality needs to be relaxed. Particular relaxations we consider in this paper are the preservation of the VCG outcome, i.e., the outcome obtained in the dominant strategy equilibrium of the fully expressive VCG mechanism, and the existence of an equilibrium with a certain amount of social welfare or revenue relative to the VCG outcome. In addition, one might require that the latter property holds for *every* equilibrium of the simplified mechanism.

In the context of sponsored search, one reason to prefer a simplification is to preclude the zero-revenue equilibria discussed above. Another interesting property of a simplified GSP mechanism is that it preserves the VCG outcome even when the assumed click-through rates α_j are inexact. Recognizing that this claim cannot be made for the VCG mechanism under the same simplification, Milgrom [22] uses this as an argument for the superiority of the GSP mechanism. But, this result that GSP is Vickrey-preserving requires an unnatural condition on the relationship between the assumed click-through rates and prices and thus agents' bids, and moreover does not preclude alternate simplifications of VCG that succeed in being Vickrey-preserving. In addition, we observe that the simplifications can still suffer arbitrarily low revenue in some equilibrium, in comparison with the VCG revenue.

In our analysis of sponsored search, we identify a simplified GSP mechanism that preserves the VCG outcome without requiring any knowledge of the actual click-through rates, precludes zero-revenue equilibria, and always recovers at least half of the VCG payments for all slots but the first. For simplified VCG mechanisms, we obtain a strong negative result: *every* simplification of VCG that supports the (efficient) VCG outcome in some equilibrium also has an equilibrium in which revenue is arbitrarily smaller than in the VCG outcome.

In the context of combinatorial auctions, paradigmatic of course of settings with incomplete information, we first recall the previous observations by Holzman et al. [15, 16] in regard to the existence of multiple, non-truthful, *ex-post* equilibria of the VCG mechanism, each of which offers different welfare and revenue properties. In particular, if one assumes that participants will select equilibria with a particular (maximum) number of bids, social welfare can differ greatly among the different equilibria, revenue can be zero for some of them, and the existence of multiple Pareto optimal equilibria can make equilibrium selection hard to impossible for participants.

Focusing again on *tight* simplifications, we connect the analysis of Holzman et al. [15, 16] with tightness, by establishing that a simplification is tight if and only if bids are restricted to a subset Σ of the bundles with a *quasi-field* structure [15, 16], with values for the other bundles derived as the maximum value of any contained bundle. Through insisting on a tight simplification, we ensure that the worst-case behavior is no worse than that of the fully expressive VCG mechanism, even when Σ (although simplified) contains too many bundles for agents to bid on all of them. Moreover, using a quasi-field simplification ensures that agents do not experience regret with respect to the bidding language, in the sense of wanting to send a message *ex post* that was precluded. Finally, as any restriction of the bids to a subset of the bundles, restricting the bids to a quasi-field Σ yields a mechanism that is maximal in range [23] and makes it a dominant strategy equilibrium for the agents to bid truthfully on these bundles. Simplification thus enables the mechanism designer to guide equilibrium selection, and our results suggest that the presence or absence of such guidance can have a significant impact on the economic properties of the mechanism.

The informational assumptions underlying our analysis are crucial, and the amount of information available to the agents plays an important role for the tradeoff between simplicity and expressiveness. In the sponsored search setting, both the existence of a zero-revenue equilibrium in the expressive mechanism, and the existence of the desirable equilibrium in the simplification, rely on the assumption of complete information. In other words, agents can on one hand use information about each others' types to coordinate and harm the auctioneer, but on the other hand, the same information guarantees that simplified mechanisms retain the desirable equilibria of the expressive mechanism. In combinatorial auctions the contrast is equally stark: while bids on every single package may be required to sustain an efficient equilibrium in the incomplete information setting, we show that such an equilibrium can be obtained with a number of bids that is quadratic in the number of agents, and potentially exponentially smaller than the number of bundles, given that agents have complete information.

Related Work Several authors have criticized the revelation principle because it does not take computational aspects of mechanisms into account. In this context, Conitzer and Sandholm [10] consider sequential mechanisms that reduce

[1]The equilibrium analysis that Benisch et al. provide is in regard to identifying a particular mechanism design in which the maximum social welfare achievable in any outcome can be achieved in a particular Bayes-Nash equilibrium.

[2]This condition was already considered by Milgrom, but only in the complete information case.

the amount of communication, and non-truthful mechanisms that shift the computational burden of executing the mechanism, and the potential loss when it is executed suboptimally, from the designer to the agents. Hyafil and Boutilier [17, 18] propose to circumvent computational problems associated with direct type revelation via the automated design of partial-revelation mechanisms, and in particular study approximately incentive compatible mechanisms that do not make any assumptions about agents' preferences. This approach is very general, but also hard to analyze theoretically, with complex, regret-based algorithms.

Blumrosen et al. [6] and Feldman and Blumrosen [12] consider settings with one-dimensional types and ask how much welfare and revenue can be achieved by mechanisms with a bounded message space. By contrast, we study mechanisms with message spaces that grow in some parameter of the problem and may even have infinite size, and obtain results both for one-dimensional and multi-dimensional types.

A different notion of simplicity of a mechanism was considered by Babaioff and Roughgarden [3]: the authors show that among all payment rules that guarantee an efficient equilibrium when ranking agents according to their bids, the GSP payment rule is optimally simple in the sense that prices depend on bids in a minimal way.

Shakkottai et al. [25] study the tradeoff between simplicity and revenue in the context of pricing rules for communication networks and define the "price of simplicity" as the ratio between the revenue of a very simple pricing rule and the maximum revenue that can be obtained.

2. PRELIMINARIES

A mechanism design problem is given by a set $N = \{1, 2, \ldots, n\}$ of *agents* that interact to select an element from a set Ω of *outcomes*. Agent $i \in N$ is associated with a *type* θ_i from a set Θ_i of possible types, representing private information held by this agent. We write $\theta = (\theta_1, \ldots, \theta_n)$ for a profile of types for the different agents, $\Theta = \prod_{i \in N} \Theta_i$ for the set of possible type profiles, and $\theta_{-i} \in \Theta_{-i}$ for a profile of types for all agents but i. Each agent $i \in N$ further employs preferences over Ω, represented by a *valuation function* $v_i : \Omega \times \Theta_i \to \mathbb{R}$. The quality of an outcome $o \in \Omega$ is typically measured in terms of its social welfare, which is defined as the sum $\sum_{i \in N} v_i(o, \theta_i)$ of agents' valuations. An outcome that maximizes social welfare is also called *efficient*.

A *mechanism* is given by a tuple (N, X, f, p), where $X = \prod_{i \in N} X_i$ is a set of *message profiles*, $f : X \to \Omega$ is an *outcome function*, and $p : X \to \mathbb{R}^n$ is a *payment function*. In this paper, we mostly restrict our attention to direct mechanisms, i.e., mechanisms where $X_i \subseteq \Theta_i$ for every $i \in N$. A direct mechanism (N, X, f, p) with $X = \Theta$ is called *efficient* if for every $\theta \in \Theta$, $f(\theta)$ is an efficient outcome. Just as for type profiles, we write $x_{-i} \in X_{-i}$ for a profile of messages by all agents but i. We assume quasi-linear preferences, i.e., the utility of agent i given a message profile $x \in X$ is $u_i(x, \theta_i) = v_i(f(x), \theta_i) - p_i(x)$. The *revenue* achieved by mechanism (N, X, f, p) for a message profile $x \in X$ is $\sum_{i \in N} p_i(x)$.

Game-theoretic reasoning is used to analyze how agents interact with a mechanism, a desirable criterion being stability according to some game-theoretic solution concept. We consider two different settings. In the *complete information* setting, agents are assumed to know the type of every other agent. A strategy of agent i in this setting is a function $s_i : \Theta \to X_i$. In the *(strict) incomplete information* setting, agents have no information, not even distributional, about the types of the other agents. A strategy of agent i in this setting thus becomes a function $s_i : \Theta_i \to X_i$.

The two most common solution concepts in the complete information setting are dominant strategy equilibrium and Nash equilibrium. A strategy $s_i : \Theta \to X_i$ is a *dominant strategy* if for every $\theta \in \Theta$, every $x_{-i} \in X_{-i}$, and every $x_i \in X_i$,

$$u_i((s_i(\theta), x_{-i}), \theta_i) \geq u_i((x_i, x_{-i}), \theta_i).$$

A profile $s \in \prod_{i \in N} s_i$ of strategies $s_i : \Theta \to X_i$ is a *Nash equilibrium* if for every $\theta \in \Theta$, every $i \in N$, and every $s_i' : \Theta \to X_i$,

$$u_i((s_i(\theta), s_{-i}(\theta)), \theta_i) \geq u_i((s_i'(\theta), s_{-i}(\theta)), \theta_i).$$

The existence of a dominant strategy $s_i : \Theta \to X_i$ always implies the existence of a dominant strategy $s_i' : \Theta_i \to X_i$ that does not depend on the types of other agents. The solution concept of dominant strategy equilibrium thus carries over directly to the incomplete information setting. Formally, a strategy $s_i : \Theta_i \to X_i$ is a *dominant strategy* in the incomplete information setting if for every $\theta_i \in \Theta_i$, every $x_{-i} \in X_{-i}$, and every $x_i \in X_i$,

$$u_i((s_i(\theta_i), x_{-i}), \theta_i) \geq u_i((x_i, x_{-i}), \theta_i).$$

The appropriate variant of the Nash equilibrium concept in that setting is that of an ex-post equilibrium. A profile $s \in \prod_{i \in N} s_i$ of strategies $s_i : \Theta_i \to X_i$ is an *ex-post equilibrium* if for every $\theta \in \Theta$, every $i \in N$, and every $s_i' : \Theta_i \to X_i$,

$$u_i((s_i(\theta_i), s_{-i}(\theta_{-i})), \theta_i) \geq u_i((s_i'(\theta_i), s_{-i}(\theta_{-i})), \theta_i).$$

We conclude this section with a direct mechanism due to Vickrey [27], Clarke [9], and Groves [14]. This mechanism starts from an efficient outcome function f and computes each agent's payment according to the total value of the other agents, thus aligning his interests with that of society. Formally, mechanism (N, X, f, p) is called Vickrey-Clarke-Groves (VCG) mechanism[3] if $X = \Theta$, f is efficient, and

$$p_i(\theta) = \max_{o \in \Omega} \sum_{j \neq i} v_j(o, \theta_j) - \sum_{j \neq i} v_j(f(\theta), \theta_j).$$

In the VCG mechanism, revealing types $\theta \in \Theta$ truthfully is a dominant strategy equilibrium [14]. We will refer to the resulting outcome as the VCG outcome for θ, and write $R^{VCG}(\theta)$ for the revenue obtained in this outcome.

3. SIMPLIFICATIONS

Our main object of study in this paper are simplifications of a mechanism obtained by restricting its message space. Consider a mechanism $M = (N, X, f, p)$. A mechanism $\hat{M} = (N, \hat{X}, \hat{f}, \hat{p})$ will be called a *simplification* of M if $\hat{X} \subseteq X$, $\hat{f}|_{\hat{X}} = f|_{\hat{X}}$, and $\hat{p}|_{\hat{X}} = p|_{\hat{X}}$.

We will naturally be interested in the set of outcomes that can be obtained in equilibrium, both in the original mechanism M and the simplified mechanism $\hat{M}$.[4] Milgrom [22]

[3]Actually, we consider a specific member of a whole family of VCG mechanisms, namely the one that uses the Clarke pivot rule.

[4]In the following, we will simply talk about equilibria without making a distinction between the different equilibrium

defines a property he calls tightness, which requires that the simplification does not introduce any additional equilibria. More formally, simplification $\hat{M}$ will be called *tight* if every equilibrium of $\hat{M}$ is an equilibrium of M.[5] Tightness ensures that the simplified mechanism is at least as good as the original one with respect to the worst outcome obtained in any equilibrium. It does not by itself protect good equilibrium outcomes, and we will in fact see examples of tight simplifications that eliminate *all* ex-post equilibria.

A property that will be useful in the following is a variant of Milgrom's outcome closure for exact equilibria. It requires that for every agent, and for every choice of messages from the restricted message spaces of the other agents, it is optimal for the agent to choose a message from his restricted message space. More formally, a simplification $(N, \hat{X}, \hat{f}, \hat{p})$ of a mechanism (N, X, f, p) satisfies *outcome closure* if for every $\theta \in \Theta$, every $i \in N$, every $\hat{x}_{-i} \in \hat{X}_{-i}$, and every $x_i \in X_i$ there exists $\hat{x}_i \in \hat{X}_i$ such that $u_i((\hat{x}_i, \hat{x}_{-i}), \theta_i) \geq u_i((x_i, \hat{x}_{-i}), \theta_i)$.

This turns out to be sufficient for tightness in both the complete and incomplete information case.[6]

PROPOSITION 1 (Milgrom [22]). *Every simplification that satisfies outcome closure is tight with respect to both Nash and ex-post equilibria.*

One way to guarantee good behavior in the *best case* is by requiring that a simplification $\hat{M}$ preserves all equilibria of the original mechanism M, in the sense that for every Nash equilibrium of M, there exists an equilibrium of $\hat{M}$ that yields the same outcome and payments. We will call a simplification satisfying this property *total*, and will return to total mechanisms in Section 6. To the end of equilibrium selection totality clearly needs to be relaxed, by requiring that only certain desirable outcomes are preserved. A typical desirable outcome in many settings is the VCG outcome. For example, although this outcome has some shortcomings in fully general combinatorial auction domains [2], it remains of significant interest in settings with unit-demand preferences, such as sponsored search. We will call simplification $\hat{M}$ *Vickrey-preserving* if for every $\theta \in \Theta$, it has an equilibrium that yields the VCG outcome for θ.

4. SPONSORED SEARCH AUCTIONS

In sponsored search (see, e.g., [20]), the agents compete for elements of a set $S = \{1, \ldots, k\}$ of slots, where $k \leq n$. Each outcome corresponds to a one-to-one assignment of agents to slots, i.e., $\Omega \subseteq \{1, \ldots, n\}^N$ such that $o_i \neq o_j$ for all $o \in \Omega$ and $i, j \in \{1, \ldots, n\}$ with $i \neq j$. We will assume that $v(o, \theta_i) = 0$ if $o_i > k$, and that there are no externalities, i.e., $v_i(o, \theta_i) = v_i(o', \theta_i)$ if $o_i = o'_i$. In slight abuse of notation, we will write $v_i(j, \theta_i)$ for the valuation of agent i for slot j.

We consider simplifications of two mechanisms, the Vickrey-Clarke-Groves (VCG) mechanism and the Generalized Second Price (GSP) mechanism, and analyze their behavior for different spaces of type profiles, which we denote by Θ, $\Theta^>$, and Θ^α. In Θ, valuations can be arbitrary non-negative numbers. $\Theta^>$ adds the restriction that valuations are strictly decreasing, i.e., $v_i(j, \theta_i) > v_i(j+1, \theta_i)$ for every $\theta \in \Theta^>$, $i \in N$, and $j \in \{1, \ldots, k-1\}$. Valuations in Θ^α are assumed to arise from "clicks" associated with each slot and a valuation per click. In other words, there exists a fixed click-through rate vector $\alpha \in \mathbb{R}^n_> = \{\alpha' \in \mathbb{R}^n : \alpha'_i > \alpha'_j \text{ if } i < j\}$, which may or may not be known to the mechanism, and $v_i(j, \theta_i) = \alpha_j \cdot v_i(\theta_i)$ for some $v_i(\theta_i) \in \mathbb{R}_{\geq 0}$. Thus, $\alpha_j = 0$ if $j > k$, and it will be convenient to assume that $\alpha_1 = 1$. We finally define $\Psi = \bigcup_{\alpha \in \mathbb{R}^n_>} \Theta^\alpha$, and observe that $\Psi \subset \Theta^> \subset \Theta$.

The message an agent $i \in N$ submits to the mechanisms thus corresponds to a vector of bids $x_{i,j} \in \mathbb{R}$ for slots $j \in S$. Given a message profile $x \in X$, the VCG mechanism assigns each agent i a slot $f_i(x) = o_i$ so as to maximize $\sum_i x_{i,o_i}$, and charges that agent $p_i(x) = \max_{o' \in \Omega} \sum_{j \neq i} x_{j,o'_j} - \sum_{j \neq i} x_{j,o_j}$. The GSP mechanism is defined via a sequence of second-price auctions for slots 1 through k: slot j is assigned to an agent i with a maximum bid for that slot at a price equal to the second highest bid, both with respect to the set of agents who have not yet been assigned a slot, i.e., $f_i(x) = o_i$ such that $x_{i,j} = \max_{i' \in N : o_{i'} \geq j} x_{i',j}$ and $p_i(x) = \max_{i' \in N : o_{i'} > j} x_{i,j}$.

4.1 Envy-Freeness and Efficiency

The original analysis of GSP due to Edelman et al. [11] and Varian [26] focuses on equilibria that are "locally envy-free."[7] Assume that $\theta \in \Theta^\alpha$, and consider an outcome in which agent i is assigned slot i, for all $i \in N$. Such an outcome is called locally envy-free if, in addition to being a Nash equilibrium, no agent could increase his utility by exchanging bids with the agent assigned the slot directly above him, i.e., if for every $i \in \{2, \ldots, n\}$, $\alpha_i \cdot v_i(\theta_i) - p_i \geq \alpha_{i-1} \cdot v_i(\theta_i) - p_{i-1}$. Restricting attention to envy-free equilibria immediately solves all revenue problems: as Edelman et al. point out, revenue in any locally envy-free equilibrium is at least as high as that in the dominant-strategy equilibrium of the VCG auction. Conversely, Milgrom's observation concerning zero-revenue equilibria contains an implicit critique of the assumptions underlying the restriction to equilibria that are envy-free. It will be instructive to make this critique explicit.

Edelman et al. argue that an equilibrium where some agent i envies some other agent j assigned the next higher slot is not a reasonable rest point of the bidding process, because agent i might increase the price paid by agent j without the danger of harming his own utility should j retaliate. There are two problems with this line of reasoning. First, it is not clear why agent j should retaliate, especially if he is worse off by doing so. Second, agent i might in fact have a very good reason *not* to increase the price paid by j, like a desire to keep prices low in the long run through tacit collusion.

We may instead ask under what conditions there exists a bid $x_{i,j}$ for agent i on slot j such that (i) agent j is forced out of slot j, in the sense that it becomes a better response for j to underbid i, and (ii) agent i is strictly better off after this response by j than at present. This is the case exactly

notions. Unless explicitly noted otherwise, our results concern Nash equilibria in the complete information case and ex-post equilibria in the incomplete information case.

[5]Milgrom [22] considers a slightly stronger notion of tightness defined with respect to (pure-strategy) ϵ-Nash equilibria.

[6]Milgrom stated the result only for complete information, but the proof goes through for incomplete information as well.

[7]Varian calls these equilibria "symmetric equilibria."

when

$$\alpha_i \cdot v_j(\theta_j) - p_i > \alpha_j \cdot v_j(\theta_j) - x_{i,j} \quad \text{and} \\ \alpha_j \cdot v_i(\theta_i) - x_{i,j} > \alpha_i \cdot v_i(\theta_i) - p_i, \tag{1}$$

where p_i is the price currently paid by agent i. The second inequality assumes that j will respond by bidding just below the bid $x_{i,j}$ of agent i, such that this becomes i's new price.

An equilibrium that does not allows deviations as above will be called *two-step stable*. It turns out that two-step stability exactly characterizes the set of efficient equilibria.

PROPOSITION 2. *Let $\alpha \in \mathbb{R}^n_>$, $\theta \in \Theta^\alpha$. Then, an equilibrium is two-step stable if and only it is efficient.*

Proof. Rewriting (1), it must hold that

$$x_{i,j} > (\alpha_j - \alpha_i) \cdot v_j(\theta_j) + p_i \quad \text{and} \\ x_{i,j} < (\alpha_j - \alpha_i) \cdot v_i(\theta_i) + p_i.$$

Clearly, a bid $x_{i,j}$ with this property exists if and only if $v_i(\theta_i) > v_j(\theta_j)$. In turn, agents i and j such that $v_i(\theta_i) > v_j(\theta_j)$ exist if and only if the current assignment is inefficient. □

This result provides a very strong argument against inefficient equilibria as rest points of the bidding process, much stronger than the argument against equilibria that are not envy-free. In the context of sponsored search auctions we will therefore restrict our attention to efficient equilibria. It is worth noting at this point that the set of efficient equilibria forms a strict superset of the set of locally envy-free equilibria, and in particular contains the zero-revenue equilibria identified by Milgrom and discussed next.

4.2 Comments on Milgrom's Analysis

Milgrom [22] observed that for every profile of agent types, both VCG and GSP have a Nash equilibrium that yields zero revenue, and that this equilibrium in fact becomes the unique equilibrium if there is a small cost associated with submitting a positive bid. To alleviate this fact, he proposed to restrict the message space of both VCG and GSP to $\hat{X} = \{(\alpha_1 \cdot b_i, \dots, \alpha_k \cdot b_i) : b_i \in \mathbb{R}_{\geq 0}\}$ for some $\alpha \in \mathbb{R}^n_>$.

The following proposition summarizes our knowledge about the resulting simplifications, which we will refer to as α-VCG and α-GSP. Most of these observations were already proved or at least claimed by Milgrom.

PROPOSITION 3. *Let $\alpha \in \mathbb{R}^n_>$. Then, α-GSP and α-VCG are tight on Θ, have positive revenue on $\Theta^>$ if $n, k \geq 2$, and are Vickrey-preserving on Θ^α.*

Assuming that the click-through rate vector α is known, both α-VCG and α-GSP look very appealing: they eliminate all zero-revenue equilibria, without affecting the truthful equilibrium and without introducing any new equilibria.

In practice, however, the relevant click-through rates may not be known. A somewhat more realistic model assumes a certain degree of heterogeneity among the population generating the clicks. More precisely, a certain fraction of this population is assumed to be "merely curious," such that clicks by this part of the population do not generate any value for the agents. This introduces an information asymmetry, where the mechanism observes the overall click-through rate vector α, while agents derive value from a different click-through rate vector β.[8] In the following we will assume that β is the same for all agents, and that β is again normalized such that $\beta_1 = 1$ and $\beta_j = 0$ if $j > k$.

For a slight variation of our model, in which there is a small dependence between α and β,[9] Milgrom established a separation between GSP and VCG: α-GSP retains the VCG outcome in situations where α-VCG fails to do so. We obtain an analogous observation in our model. The proof of the following result is given in the full version of the paper, where we also establish that α-VCG is usually not Vickrey-preserving.

PROPOSITION 4. *Let $\alpha, \beta \in \mathbb{R}^n_>$. Then, α-GSP is Vickrey-preserving on Θ^β if and only if the sequence $\{p_j(\theta)/\alpha_j\}_{j=1,\dots,k}$, where $p_j(\theta) = \sum_{i=j}^k (v_{i+1}(\theta_{i+1}) \cdot (\beta_i - \beta_{i+1}))$, is decreasing.*

But this line of reasoning seems a bit problematic for two reasons. First, there seems no reason to believe that the condition relating prices (and thus bids) and click-through rates in Proposition 4 would be satisfied in practice. Second, the above discussion only shows superiority of GSP over VCG with respect to a *particular* simplification, and it might well be the case that there exists a different simplification of VCG mechanism with comparable or even better properties.

An additional observation that we make, in regard to the ability of these simplifications to eliminate zero-revenue equilibria, is that there exist type profiles for which the minimum equilibrium revenue can be *arbitrarily small* compared to the revenue obtained in the VCG outcome.

THEOREM 1. *Let $\epsilon, r > 0$. Then there exist $\alpha \in \mathbb{R}^n_>$ and $\theta \in \Theta^\alpha$ such that $R^{VCG}(\theta) \geq r$ and α-VCG has an equilibrium with revenue at most ϵ. Similarly, there exist $\alpha \in \mathbb{R}^n_>$ and $\theta \in \Theta^\alpha$ such that $R^{VCG}(\theta) \geq r$ and α-GSP has an equilibrium with revenue at most ϵ.*

Proof. We consider a setting with three agents and three slots. The construction can easily be extended to an arbitrary number of agents and slots.

For α-VCG, let $v_i(\theta_i) = r + 1$ for all $i \in N$. Let $\alpha_1 = 1$, $\alpha_2 = 1/(r+1)$, and $\alpha_3 = 1/(2r+2)$. It is easily verified that the bids $b_1 = r + 1$ and $b_2 = b_3 = \epsilon$ form a Nash equilibrium of α-VCG. Given these bids, α-VCG assigns slot 1 to agent 1 at price $\epsilon - \epsilon/(2r+2)$, and slots 2 and 3 to agents 2 and 3 at prices $\epsilon/(r+1) - \epsilon/(2r+2)$ and zero. This yields revenue ϵ. In the truthful equilibrium of the VCG mechanism, on the other hand, the price is $r + \epsilon/(r+1) - \epsilon/(2r+2)$ for the first slot, $\epsilon/(r+1) - \epsilon/(2r+2)$ for the second slot, and zero for the third slot, for an overall revenue of $r + \epsilon/(r+2)$.

For α-GSP, again let $v_i(\theta_i) = r + 1$ for all $i \in N$. Let $\delta = \epsilon/(r+2)$, $\alpha_1 = 1$, $\alpha_2 = (1+\delta)/(r+1)$, and $\alpha_3 = 1/(r+1)$. It is easily verified that the bids $b_1 = r + 1$ and $b_2 = b_3 = \delta/(1+\delta) \cdot (r+1)$ form a Nash equilibrium of α-GSP. Given these bids, α-GSP assigns slot 1 to agent 1 at price $\delta/(1+\delta) \cdot (r+1)$, and slots 2 and 3 to agents 2 and 3 at prices δ and zero. This yields revenue $\delta/(1+\delta) \cdot (r+1) + \delta \leq \epsilon$. In the truthful equilibrium of the VCG mechanism, on the other hand, the price is r for the first slot, δ for the second

[8] As Milgrom [22] points out, "if the search company observes clicks but not sales or value for each position, its auction rule can entail adjusting bids in proportion to clicks but not in proportion to value" (p. 68).

[9] Milgrom assumes that there is a fraction λ of shoppers with click-through rate vector α and a fraction $(1 - \lambda)$ of curious searchers with click-through rate vector β. The click-through rate vector γ observed by the search provider is then given by $\gamma_j = \lambda \cdot \alpha_j + (1 - \lambda) \cdot \beta_j$.

slot, and zero for the third slot, for an overall revenue of $r + \delta$. □

4.3 A Sense in which GSP is Superior to VCG

The above observations raise the following prominent question: *does there exist a simplification that preserves the VCG outcome despite ignorance about the true click-through rates that affect bidders' values, and if so, can this simplification achieve improved revenue relative to the VCG outcome, in every equilibrium?*

For GSP the answer is surprisingly simple: a closer look at the proofs of Proposition 3 and Proposition 4 reveals that by ignoring the observed click-through rates α, and setting $\alpha = \mathbf{1} = (1, \dots, 1)$ instead, one obtains a simplification that is tight, guarantees positive revenue, and is Vickrey-preserving on *all* of Ψ. This strengthens Proposition 3 over the claims for α-GSP and α-VCG.

COROLLARY 1. *α-GSP is tight on Ψ, has positive revenue on Ψ if $n, k \geq 2$, and is Vickrey-preserving on Ψ, if and only if $\alpha = \mathbf{1} = (1, \dots, 1)$.*

The direction from left to right follows by observing that, for every $\alpha \neq \mathbf{1}$, we can find a β such that the condition of Proposition 4 is violated.

In light of Theorem 1, and given the arguments in favor of efficient equilibria, we may further ask for the minimum revenue obtained by **1**-GSP in any efficient equilibrium. It turns out that **1**-GSP always recovers at least half of the VCG revenue for all slots but the first.

THEOREM 2. *Let $\beta \in \mathbb{R}^n_>$, $\theta \in \Theta^\beta$, and assume that $v_1(\theta_1) \geq \cdots \geq v_n(\theta_n)$. Then, every efficient equilibrium of **1**-GSP for θ yields revenue at least*

$$\frac{1}{2}\left(R^{VCG}(\theta) - \sum_{j=1}^{k}(\beta_j - \beta_{j+1}) \cdot v_{j+1}(\theta_{j+1})\right).$$

Proof. Let $b(\theta)$ be a bid profile corresponding to an efficient equilibrium of **1**-GSP. It then holds that $b_1(\theta) \geq \cdots \geq b_n(\theta)$, and for all $i \in \{1, \dots, k\}$, **1**-GSP assigns slot i to agent i at price $p_i(\theta) = b_{i+1}(\theta)$. A necessary condition for $b(\theta)$ to be an equilibrium is that for every agent $j \in N$, $b_j(\theta)$ is large enough such that none of the agents $i > j$ would prefer being assigned slot j instead of i. In particular, for every $i \in N$,

$$\beta_{i+1} \cdot v_{i+1}(\theta_{i+1}) - p_{i+1}(\theta) \geq \beta_i \cdot v_{i+1}(\theta_{i+1}) - b_i(\theta) \quad \text{and}$$
$$\beta_{i+2} \cdot v_{i+2}(\theta_{i+2}) - p_{i+2}(\theta) \geq \beta_i \cdot v_{i+2}(\theta_{i+2}) - b_i(\theta).$$

Since $p_i(\theta) = b_{i+1}(\theta)$ and by rearranging,

$$\begin{aligned} b_i(\theta) &\geq (\beta_i - \beta_{i+1}) \cdot v_{i+1}(\theta_{i+1}) + p_{i+1}(\theta) \\ &= (\beta_i - \beta_{i+1}) \cdot v_{i+1}(\theta_{i+1}) + b_{i+2}(\theta) \quad \text{and} \\ b_i(\theta) &\geq (\beta_i - \beta_{i+2}) \cdot v_{i+2}(\theta_{i+2}) + p_{i+2}(\theta) \\ &\geq (\beta_{i+1} - \beta_{i+2}) \cdot v_{i+2}(\theta_{i+2}) + b_{i+3}(\theta). \end{aligned}$$

If we repeatedly substitute according to the first inequality, we obtain

$$b_i(\theta) \geq \sum_{j=1}^{\lfloor \frac{k-i}{2} \rfloor}(\beta_{i+2\cdot j-2} - \beta_{i+2\cdot j-1}) \cdot v_{i+2\cdot j-1}(\theta_{i+2\cdot j-1}) \quad \text{and}$$
$$b_i(\theta) \geq \sum_{j=1}^{\lfloor \frac{k-i}{2} \rfloor}(\beta_{i+2\cdot j-1} - \beta_{i+2\cdot j}) \cdot v_{i+2\cdot j}(\theta_{i+2\cdot j}).$$

By adding the two inequalities,

$$2 \cdot b_i(\theta) \geq \sum_{j=i}^{k}(\beta_j - \beta_{j+1}) \cdot v_{j+1}(\theta_{j+1}),$$

and, since $p_i(\theta) = b_{i+1}(\theta)$,

$$2 \cdot p_i(\theta) \geq \sum_{j=i+1}^{k}(\beta_j - \beta_{j+1}) \cdot v_{j+1}(\theta_{j+1}).$$

Now recall that $R^{VCG}(\theta) = \sum_{i \in N} r_i(\theta)$, where

$$r_i(\theta) = \sum_{j=i}^{k}(\beta_j - \beta_{j+1}) \cdot v_{j+1}(\theta_{j+1}).$$

Thus,

$$\sum_{i \in N} 2 \cdot p_i(\theta) \geq \sum_{i \in N} r_i(\theta) - \sum_{j=1}^{k}(\beta_j - \beta_{j+1}) \cdot v_{j+1}(\theta_{j+1}).$$

The revenue obtained in any efficient equilibrium of **1**-GSP is therefore at least

$$\sum_{i \in N} p_i(\theta) \geq \frac{1}{2}\left(R^{VCG}(\theta) - \sum_{j=1}^{k}(\beta_j - \beta_{j+1}) \cdot v_{j+1}(\theta_{j+1})\right).$$

□

Our analysis also leads to a satisfactory contrast between **1**-GSP and simplifications of VCG: *any* simplification of VCG that does not observe the value-generating click-through rates, and is Vickrey-preserving for all possible choices of these click-through rates, must admit an efficient equilibrium with arbitrarily low revenue.

THEOREM 3. *Let $\hat{M}$ be a simplification of the VCG mechanism that is Vickrey-preserving on Ψ. Then, for every $\theta \in \Psi$ and every $\epsilon > 0$, there exists an efficient equilibrium of $\hat{M}$ with revenue at most ϵ.*

Proof. Fix $\beta \in \mathbb{R}^n_>$ and consider an arbitrary type profile $\theta \in \Theta^\beta \subseteq \Psi$. Order the agents such that $v_1(\theta_1) \geq \cdots \geq v_n(\theta_n)$.

The proof proceeds in two steps. First we will argue that for some $c \geq 0$, every $\delta > 0$, and all $i \in N$, $\hat{X}_i$ must contain a message x_i^δ corresponding to bids b_{ij} such that $b_{ii} = \beta_i \cdot v_i(\theta_i) + c$, $b_{ij} \leq \beta_i \cdot v_i(\theta_i) + c + \delta$ for $1 \leq j < i$ and $b_{ij} \leq c + \delta$ for $i < j \leq k$. These messages will then be used to construct an equilibrium with low revenue.

To show that the restricted message spaces $\hat{X}_i$ must contain messages as described above, we show that these messages are required to reach the VCG outcome for a different type profile $\theta' \in \Theta^{\beta'} \subseteq \Psi$ for a particular $\beta' \in \mathbb{R}^n_>$. Denote by $p_i(\theta')$ the price of slot i for type profile θ'. We know that for $j \in \{2, \dots, k\}$, $\beta'_j \cdot v_j(\theta'_j) = \beta'_{j-1} \cdot v_j(\theta'_j) - p_{j-1}(\theta')$ (see, e.g., [22]). Consider an arbitrary $\delta > 0$. If we choose β' such that $\beta'_1 - \beta'_i$ and β'_{i+1} are small enough, we can choose θ' as above such that

$$\begin{aligned} &p_j(\theta') - p_i(\theta') \leq \delta && \text{for } j < i \text{ and} \\ &p_i(\theta') - p_j(\theta') \geq \beta_i \cdot v_i(\theta_i) - \delta && \text{for } j > i. \end{aligned}$$

A well-known property of the VCG outcome in the assignment problem is its envy-freeness (see, e.g., [21]): denoting by b_{ij} the bid of agent i on slot j and by p_j the price of slot j, it must hold for every agent i that

$$b_{ii} - p_i \geq b_{ij} - p_j \qquad \text{for all } j \in S.$$

For type profile θ', we thus obtain

$$\begin{aligned} b_{ij} - b_{ii} &\leq p_j(\theta') - p_i(\theta') \leq \delta & \text{for } j < i \text{ and} \\ b_{ii} - b_{ij} &\geq p_i(\theta') - p_j(\theta') \geq \beta_i \cdot v_i(\theta_i) - \delta & \text{for } j > i. \end{aligned}$$

Using messages x_i^δ, we now construct an efficient equilibrium with low revenue. Clearly, the allocation that assigns slot i to agent i is still efficient under message profile x^δ. Furthermore, for all $j \in \{1, \ldots, k\}$, the VCG price of slot j under x^δ goes to zero as δ goes to zero. In particular, we can choose δ such that the overall revenue is at most ϵ. We finally claim that there exists some $\delta' > 0$ such that x^δ is an equilibrium for every δ with $\delta' > \delta > 0$. To see this, recall that $\beta_i \cdot v_i(\theta_i) > \beta_j \cdot v_i(\theta_i)$ for $j > i$, so $u_i(x^\delta, \theta_i) > \beta_j \cdot v_i(\theta_i)$ for some small enough δ. If, on the other hand, agent i was assigned a slot $j < i$, his payment would be at least $\beta_j \cdot v_j(\theta_j) - \delta > \beta_j \cdot v_i(\theta_i) - \delta$. This would leave him with utility at most δ, which can be chosen to be smaller than $u_i(x^\delta, \theta_i)$. □

It is worth noting that despite having a reasonably good lower bound on revenue, **1**-GSP does not quite succeed in circumventing Theorem 1: there exists a type profile for which only the first slot generates a significant amount of VCG revenue, and an equilibrium of **1**-GSP for this type profile in which revenue is close to zero. On the other hand, for a wide range of click-through rates, there will be a large gap between the minimum revenue of **1**-GSP and simplifications of VCG in efficient equilibria.

Moreover, the revenue separation between simplifications of GSP and VCG only applies to simplifications of the latter that are Vickrey-preserving. Given how central the VCG outcome has been to the analysis of sponsored search auctions, this seems a reasonable property to impose. Nevertheless, it is an interesting question whether the result can be strengthened further.

5. COMBINATORIAL AUCTIONS

Mechanisms for combinatorial auctions allocate items from a set G to the agents, i.e., $\Omega = \prod_{i \in N} 2^G$ such that for every $o \in \Omega$ and $i, j \in N$ with $i \neq j$, $o_i \cap o_j = \emptyset$. We make the standard assumption that the empty set is valued at zero and that valuations satisfy free disposal, i.e., for all $i \in N$, $\theta_i \in \Theta_i$, and $o, o' \in \Omega$, $v_i(o, \theta_i) = 0$ when $o_i = \emptyset$ and $v_i(o, \theta_i) \leq v_i(o', \theta_i)$ when $o_i \subseteq o'_i$. The latter condition also implies that each agent is only interested in the package he receives, and we sometimes abuse notation and write $v_i(C, \theta_i)$ for the valuation of agent i for any $o \in \Omega$ with $o_i = C$. We further write $k = |G|$ for the number of items, $W(o, x) = \sum_{j \in N} v_j(o, x_j)$ for the social welfare of outcome $o \in \Omega$ under message profile $x \in X$, and $W_{max}(x) = \max_{o \in \Omega} W(o, x)$ for the maximum social welfare of any outcome. Finally, for every agent $i \in N$, message $x_i \in X$, and bundle of items $B \subseteq G$ we write $x_i(B)$ for agent i's bid on bundle B.

The VCG mechanism makes it a dominant strategy for every agent to bid his true valuation for every bundle of items. Since the number of such bundles is exponential in the number of items, however, computational constraints might prevent agents from playing this dominant strategy (even for a well-crafted bidding language [24, 19]). In light of these results, and in light of the observation that simplifications can help to isolate useful equilibria, it is interesting to ask which other (ex-post) equilibria the VCG auction can have. Holzman and Monderer [15] showed that these equilibria are precisely the projections of the true types to those subsets of the set of all bundles that form a quasi-field. Let $\Sigma \subseteq 2^G$ be a set of bundles of items such that $\emptyset \in \Sigma$. Σ is called a quasi-field if it is closed under complementation and union of disjoint subsets, i.e., if

- $B \in \Sigma$ implies $B^c \in \Sigma$, where $B^c = G \setminus B$ and
- $B, C \in \Sigma$ and $B \cap C$ implies $B \cup C \in \Sigma$.

For a message $x_i \in X_i$, write x_i^Σ for the projection of x_i to Σ, i.e., for the unique message such that for every bundle $B \subseteq G$ of items,

$$x_i^\Sigma(B) = \max_{B' \in \Sigma, B' \subseteq B} x_i(B').$$

The characterization given by Holzman and Monderer is subject to the additional constraint of *variable participation*: a strategy profile s for a set N of agents is an equilibrium of a VCG mechanism under variable participation if for every $N' \subseteq N$, the projection of s to N' is an equilibrium of every VCG mechanism for N'.

THEOREM 4 (Holzman and Monderer [15]). *Consider a VCG combinatorial auction with a set N of agents and a set G of items. Then, a strategy profile $s = (s_1, \ldots, s_n)$ is an ex-post equilibrium of this auction under variable participation if and only if there exists a quasi-field $\Sigma \subseteq 2^G$ such that for every type profile θ and every agent $i \in N$, $s_i(\theta_i) = \theta_i^\Sigma$.*

Intuitively, the social welfare obtained in these "bundling" equilibria decreases as the set of bundles becomes smaller. A simple argument shows, for example, that welfare in the bundling equilibrium for Σ, where $|\Sigma| = 2^m$ for some $m \leq k$, can be smaller by a factor of k/m than the maximum welfare. For this, consider a setting with k agents such that each agent desires exactly one of the items, i.e., values this item at 1, and each item is desired by exactly one of the agents. Clearly, maximum social welfare in this case is k. On the other hand, since Σ is a quasi-field, it cannot contain more than m bundles that are pairwise disjoint. Therefore, by assigning only bundles in Σ, one can obtain welfare at most m.

Welfare can also differ tremendously among quasi-fields of equal size, which suggests an opportunity for simplification.

PROPOSITION 5. *Let G be a set of items, $k = |G|$, and $m \leq k$. Then there exist quasi-fields $\Sigma, \Sigma' \subseteq 2^G$ with $|\Sigma| = |\Sigma'| = 2^m$ and a type profile θ such that*

$$\frac{W_{max}(\theta^\Sigma)}{W_{max}(\theta^{\Sigma'})} \geq \frac{m}{\lceil m^2/k \rceil}.$$

Proof. Consider a partition of G into sets $G_1, \ldots, G_m$ of size $\lceil \frac{k}{m} \rceil$ or $\lfloor \frac{k}{m} \rfloor$, and let Σ be the closure of $\{G_1, \ldots, G_m\}$ under complementation and union of disjoint sets. For every i, $1 \leq i \leq m$, choose an arbitrary $g_i \in G_i$, and define $\theta = (\theta_1, \ldots, \theta_m)$ such that for every i with $1 \leq i \leq m$, $v_i(X, \theta_i) = 1$ if $g_i \in X$ and $v_i(X, \theta_i) = 0$ otherwise. Clearly, $W_{max}(\theta^\Sigma) = m$. Now consider a second partition of G into sets $G'_1, \ldots, G'_m$ of size $\lceil \frac{k}{m} \rceil$ or $\lfloor \frac{k}{m} \rfloor$ such that $G'_j \supseteq \{g_i : (j-1)\lfloor k/m \rfloor + 1 \leq i \leq j\lfloor k/m \rfloor\}$, and let Σ' be the closure of $\{G_1, \ldots, G_m\}$ under complementation and union of disjoint sets. It is then easily verified that $W_{max}(\theta^{\Sigma'}) \leq \lceil m/(k/m) \rceil = \lceil m^2/k \rceil$, and the claim follows. □

Moreover, agents might disagree about the quality of the different bundling equilibria of a given maximum size. In particular, the set of these equilibria might contain several Pareto undominated equilibria, but no dominant strategy equilibrium. From the point of view of equilibrium selection, this is the worst possible scenario.

EXAMPLE 1. Let $N = \{1, 2, 3\}$, $G = \{A, B, C\}$, and consider a type profile $\theta = (\theta_1, \theta_2, \theta_3)$ such that

$$v_1(X, \theta_1) = \begin{cases} 4 & \text{if } \{A, C\} \subseteq X, \\ 3 & \text{if } A \in X \text{ and } C \notin X \\ 1 & \text{otherwise;} \end{cases}$$

$$v_2(X, \theta_2) = \begin{cases} 3 & \text{if } \{A, C\} \subseteq X \text{ or } \{B, C\} \subseteq X \text{ and} \\ 0 & \text{otherwise;} \end{cases}$$

$$v_3(X, \theta_3) = \begin{cases} 1 & \text{if } B \in X \\ 0 & \text{otherwise.} \end{cases}$$

Clearly, at least four bids are required to express θ_1. Since a quasi-field on G must contain both the empty set and G itself, there are four quasi-fields of size four or less:

$$\Sigma^1 = \{\emptyset, \{A\}, \{B, C\}, \{A, B, C\}\}$$
$$\Sigma^2 = \{\emptyset, \{B\}, \{A, C\}, \{A, B, C\}\}$$
$$\Sigma^3 = \{\emptyset, \{C\}, \{A, B\}, \{A, B, C\}\}$$
$$\Sigma^4 = \{\emptyset, \{A, B, C\}\}$$

For $i \in \{1, 2, 3, 4\}$, write $\theta^i = (\theta_1^{\Sigma^i}, \theta_2^{\Sigma^i}, \theta_3^{\Sigma^i})$ for the projection of θ to Σ^i. The following is now easily verified. In the VCG outcome for θ^1, agent 1 is assigned $\{A\}$ at price 0 for a utility of 3, and agent 2 is assigned $\{B, C\}$ at price 1 for a utility of 2. In the VCG outcome for θ^2, agent 1 is assigned $\{A, C\}$ at price 3 for a utility of 1, and agent 3 is assigned $\{B\}$ at price 0 for a utility of 1. Finally, in the VCG outcome for θ^3 and θ^4, agent 1 is assigned $\{A, B, C\}$ at price 3 for a utility of 1. The outcomes for θ^1 and θ^2 are both Pareto undominated. Also observe that social welfare is greater for θ^1, while θ^2 yields higher revenue.

Finally, the projection to a quasi-field can result in an equilibrium with revenue zero, even if revenue in the dominant strategy equilibrium is strictly positive. This is illustrated in the following example. It should be noted that this example, as well as the previous one, can easily be generalized to arbitrary numbers of agents and items and a large range of upper bounds on the size of the quasi-field.

EXAMPLE 2. Let $N = \{1, 2, 3\}$, $G = \{A, B, C, D\}$, and consider a type profile $\theta = (\theta_1, \theta_2, \theta_3)$ such that

$$v_1(X, \theta_1) = \begin{cases} 2 & \text{if } \{A, D\} \subseteq X \text{ and} \\ 0 & \text{otherwise;} \end{cases}$$

$$v_2(X, \theta_2) = \begin{cases} 2 & \text{if } \{A, B\} \subseteq X, \\ 1 & \text{if } B \in X \text{ and } A \notin X, \text{ and} \\ 0 & \text{otherwise;} \end{cases}$$

$$v_3(X, \theta_3) = \begin{cases} 2 & \text{if } C \in X, \text{ and} \\ 0 & \text{otherwise.} \end{cases}$$

In the VCG outcome for θ, agent 1 is assigned $\{A, D\}$ at price 1, agent 2 is assigned $\{B\}$ at price 0, and agent 3 is assigned $\{C\}$ at price 0, for an overall revenue of 1. In the VCG outcome for θ^{Σ}, on the other hand, where $\Sigma = \{\emptyset, AB, CD, ABCD\}$, agent 2 is assigned $\{A, B\}$ and agent 3 is assigned $\{C, D\}$, both at price 0. Revenue is 0 as well.

In theory, one way to solve these problems is to simplify the mechanism, and artificially restrict the set of bundles agents can bid on. Given a set $\Sigma \subseteq 2^G$ of bundles, call Σ-VCG the simplification of the VCG mechanism obtained by restricting the message spaces to $\hat{X}_i \subseteq X_i$ such that for every $\hat{x}_i \in \hat{X}_i$ and every bundle of items $B \subseteq G$,

$$\hat{x}_i(B) = \max_{B' \in \Sigma, B' \subseteq B} \hat{x}_i(B').$$

In other words, Σ-VCG allows agents to bid only on elements of Σ and derives bids for the other bundles as the maximum bid on a contained bundle. It is easy to see that Σ-VCG is *maximal in range* [23], i.e., that it maximizes social welfare over a subset of Ω. It follows that for each agent, truthful projection onto Σ is a dominant strategy in Σ-VCG.

This shows that simplification can focus attention on a focal (truthful) equilibrium and thus avoid equilibrium selection along a Pareto frontier. As Proposition 5 and the above examples suggest, this can have a significant positive impact on both social welfare and revenue. It does not tell us, of course, how Σ should be chosen in practice. One understood approach for maximizing social welfare without any knowledge about the quality of different outcomes, and without consideration to Σ being a quasi-field, is to partition G arbitrarily into m sets of roughly equal size, where m is the largest number of bundles agents can bid on. The welfare thus obtained is smaller than the maximum social welfare by a factor of at most $k/\sqrt{m}$ [16]. If additional knowledge is available, however, it may be possible to improve the result substantially, as the above results comparing the outcomes for different values of Σ show.

With that being said, there are (at least) two additional properties that are desirable for a simplification: that Σ-VCG is tight, and that Σ is a quasi-field. Tightness ensures that no additional equilibria are introduced as compared to the fully expressive VCG mechanism, such that the quality of the worst equilibrium outcome of the simplification is no worse than that of the original mechanism. This remains important when Σ may still be too large for agents to use its full projection, in which case agents would again have to select from a large set of possible ex-post equilibria. By requiring that Σ is a quasi-field, in addition to being a dominant strategy equilibrium of Σ-VCG, truthful projection to Σ is also an ex-post equilibrium of the fully expressive VCG mechanism, and thus stable against unrestricted unilateral deviations. This ensures that agents do not experience regret, in the sense of being prevented from sending a message they would want to send given the messages sent by the other agents.

It turns out that these two requirements are actually equivalent, i.e., that Σ-VCG is tight if and only if Σ is a quasi-field. The following result holds with respect to both Nash equilibria and ex-post equilibria.

THEOREM 5. *Let $\Sigma \subseteq 2^G$ such that $\emptyset \in \Sigma$. Then, Σ-VCG is a tight simplification if Σ is a quasi-field, and this condition is also necessary if $n \geq 3$.*

Proof. For the direction from right to left, assume that Σ is a quasi-field. By Proposition 1 it suffices to show that Σ-VCG satisfies outcome closure. Fix valuation functions v_j and types θ_j for all $j \in N$, and consider an arbitrary agent $i \in N$. We claim that for every $x_i \in X_i$ and every $\hat{x}_{-i} \in \hat{X}_{-i}$,

$$u_i((\theta_i^\Sigma, \hat{x}_{-i}), \theta_i) \geq u_i((x_i, \hat{x}_{-i}), \theta_i).$$

To see this, observe that there exists $\hat{\theta}_{-i} \in \Theta_{-i}$ such that $\hat{\theta}_{-i}^\Sigma = \hat{x}_{-i}$, and consider the type profile $(\theta_i, \hat{\theta}_{-i})$. Holzman et al. [16] have shown that the projection of the true types to a quasi-field Σ is an ex-post equilibrium of the (fully expressive) VCG mechanism. Thus, in particular, θ_i^Σ is a best response to $\hat{\theta}_{-i}^\Sigma = \hat{x}_{-i}$, which proves the claim.

For the direction from left to right, assume that Σ is not a quasi-field. Holzman et al. [16] have shown that in this case, θ^Σ is not an ex-post equilibrium of the VCG mechanism. On the other hand, θ^Σ is a dominant-strategy equilibrium of Σ-VCG, because Σ-VCG is maximal in range. This shows that Σ-VCG is not tight. □

Together with Theorem 4, this yields a characterization of the ex-post equilibria of Σ-VCG for the case when Σ is a quasi-field.

COROLLARY 2. *Let Σ be a quasi-field. Then, $\hat{x}$ is an ex-post equilibrium of Σ-VCG under variable participation if and only if $\hat{x} = \theta^{\Sigma'}$ for some quasi-field $\Sigma' \subseteq \Sigma$.*

Since a quasi-field of size m can contain at most $\log m$ bundles that are pairwise disjoint, insisting that a simplification be tight does come at a cost, decreasing the worst-case social welfare in the truthful projection by an additional factor of up to $\sqrt{m/\log m}$. Still, as discussed above, tightness brings other advantages to the simplified mechanism.

6. THE ROLE OF INFORMATION

Like most of the literature on sponsored search auctions, we have assumed that agents have complete information about each others' valuations for the different slots. It turns out that this assumption is crucial, and that the positive results for α-GSP do not extend to incomplete information settings.

In particular, α-GSP admits an ex-post equilibrium only in very degenerate cases. This complements a result of Gomes and Sweeney [13], who showed that α-GSP has an efficient Bayes-Nash equilibrium on type space Θ^α if and only if α decreases sufficiently quickly. Of course, ex-post equilibrium is stronger than Bayes-Nash equilibrium, but on the other hand our result precludes the existence of the former for a significantly larger type space. The proofs of all results in this section are given in the full version of the paper.

THEOREM 6. *Let $\alpha, \beta \in \mathbb{R}^n_>$. Then, α-GSP has an efficient ex-post equilibrium on type space Θ^β if and only if $n \leq 2$ or $k \leq 1$, even if $\alpha = \beta$.*

The α-VCG mechanism does only slightly better: it has an ex-post equilibrium only when it allows agents to bid truthfully (it is thus not a meaningful simplification, in that the language is in this sense exact).

THEOREM 7. *Let $\alpha, \beta \in \mathbb{R}^n_>$. Then, α-VCG has an efficient ex-post equilibrium on type space Θ^β if and only if $\alpha = \beta$, or $n \leq 2$, or $k \leq 1$.*

These results indicate that simplification is not very useful in sponsored search auctions without the assumption of complete information amongst bidders. Interestingly, simplification is also not necessary in this case to preclude equilibria with bad properties, at least in the special case of our model where the valuations are proportional to some (possibly unknown) vector of value-generating click-through rates. In particular, payments in *every* efficient ex-post equilibrium of the fully expressive VCG mechanism equal the VCG payments. Moreover, truthful reporting is the only efficient ex-post equilibrium when the number of agents is greater than the number of slots.

PROPOSITION 6. *Consider a VCG sponsored search auction with type profile $\theta \in \Theta^\alpha$, and assume that $s = (s_1, \dots, s_n)$ is an efficient ex-post equilibrium. Then, for all i with $1 \leq i \leq k$, the payment for slot i in the outcome for strategy profile s equals $p_i = \sum_{j=i}^{\min(k,n-1)}((\alpha_j - \alpha_{j+1}) \cdot v_{j+1}(\theta_{j+1}))$. Moreover, if $n > k$, then $s_i(k, \theta_i) = \alpha_k \cdot v_i(\theta_i)$ for all i with $1 \leq i \leq n$.*

In considering simplifications for combinatorial auctions, we have adopted the standard approach to assume incomplete information amongst agents, and in particular discussed a family of simplifications of the VCG mechanism that offers a tradeoff between social welfare and the amount of information agents have to communicate.

One may wonder why this tradeoff is necessary, and in how far it depends on the amount of information agents have about each others' types. It turns out that in the complete information case a much smaller number of bids is enough to preserve an efficient equilibrium, and in fact *all* equilibria, of the fully expressive VCG mechanism.

We show this using a simplification of the VCG mechanisms that we call n-VCG. The message space of n-VCG consists of all bid vectors with at most n non-zero entries, where n is the number of agents. This reduces the number of bids elicited from each agent from 2^k to at most n, which can be exponentially smaller. Surprisingly, this simplification is both tight and total, i.e., the set of Nash equilibria is completely unaffected by this restriction of the message space.

THEOREM 8. *The n-VCG mechanism is tight and total with respect to Nash equilibria.*

7. CONCLUSION AND FUTURE WORK

In this paper we have studied simplifications of mechanisms obtained by restricting their message space, and have found that they can be used to solve different kinds of equilibrium selection problems that occur in practice. Direct revelation mechanisms typically have several equilibria, which might be more or less desirable from the point of view of the designer. Computational constraints might also imply that only a subset of the equilibria of a mechanisms can actually be achieved, in which case agents might have to select among several Pareto optimal equilibria. On the other hand, restricting the message space of a mechanism often reduces the amount of social welfare that can be achieved theoretically, and this seems to pivot on whether or not agents have complete information about each others' types. The choice between mechanisms with different degrees of expressiveness therefore involves a tradeoff between a benefit of simplicity and a price of simplicity.

The *price* of simplicity can easily be quantified, for example, by the loss in social welfare potentially incurred by a simplification, and has been studied in the context of both sponsored search and combinatorial auctions. Abrams et al. [1] and Blumrosen et al. [7], among others, have given bounds on the loss of social welfare incurred by α-GSP for different classes of valuations that are not proportional to the click-through rates. Christodoulou et al. [8] and Bhawalkar and Roughgarden [5] have studied the potential loss in welfare when a set of items is sold through a simplification of the combinatorial auction in which only bids that are additive in items are allowed. This bidding language requires only a small number of bids, and welfare in equilibrium turns out to be smaller by at most a logarithmic factor in the number of agents than the optimum achieved by the fully expressive mechanism.

The *benefit* of simplicity is much harder to grasp as a concept. In this paper we have argued that simplification can improve the economic properties of a mechanism by precluding bad or promoting good equilibria. A remaining challenge is to understand the benefit of simplicity in the context of simplified mechanisms for which the computation of an equilibrium might be an intractable problem, like the ones of Christodoulou et al. and Bhawalkar and Roughgarden described above. In contrast to the simplifications considered in the present paper, these mechanisms may not be able to solve the computational or informational problem of enabling agents to bid in a straightforward way. More generally, it is far from obvious how "straightforwardness" of a mechanism should be measured, but it seems reasonable to require that agents' strategies can be computed in polynomial time.

REFERENCES

[1] Z. Abrams, A. Ghosh, and E. Vee. Cost of conciseness in sponsored search auctions. In *Proc. of 3rd WINE*, volume 4858 of *LNCS*, pages 326–334, 2007.

[2] L. M. Ausubel and P. Milgrom. The lovely but lonely Vickrey auction. In P. Cramton, Y. Shoham, and P. Steinberg, editors, *Combinatorial Auctions*, chapter 1, pages 17–40. MIT Press, 2006.

[3] M. Babaioff and T. Roughgarden. Equilibrium efficiency and price complexity in sponsored search auctions. In *Proc. of 6th Workshop on Ad Auctions*, 2010.

[4] M. Benisch, N. Sadeh, and T. Sandholm. A theory of expressiveness in mechanisms. In *Proc. of 23rd AAAI Conference*, pages 17–23, 2008.

[5] K. Bhawalkar and T. Roughgarden. Welfare guarantees for combinatorial auctions with item bidding. In *Proc. of 22nd SODA*, pages 700–709, 2011.

[6] L. Blumrosen, N. Nisan, and I. Segal. Auctions with severely bounded communication. *Journal of Artificial Intelligence Research*, 28:233–266, 2007.

[7] L. Blumrosen, J. Hartline, and S. Nong. Position auctions and non-uniform conversion rates. In *Proc. of 4th Workshop on Ad Auctions*, 2008.

[8] G. Christodoulou, A. Kovács, and M. Schapira. Bayesian combinatorial auctions. In *Proc. of 35th ICALP*, pages 820–832, 2008.

[9] E. H. Clarke. Multipart pricing of public goods. *Public Choice*, 11:17–33, 1971.

[10] V. Conitzer and T. Sandholm. Computational criticisms of the revelation principle. In *Proc. of 4th ACM-EC Conference*, pages 262–263, 2004.

[11] B. Edelman, M. Ostrovsky, and M. Schwartz. Internet advertising and the generalized second price auction: Selling billions of dollars worth of keywords. *American Economic Review*, 97(1):242–259, 2007.

[12] M. Feldman and L. Blumrosen. Implementation with a bounded action space. In *Proc. of 7th ACM-EC Conference*, pages 62–71, 2006.

[13] R. D. Gomes and K. S. Sweeney. Bayes-Nash equilibria of the generalized second price auction. In *Proc. of 10th ACM-EC Conference*, pages 107–108, 2009.

[14] T. Groves. Incentives in teams. *Econometrica*, 41:617–631, 1973.

[15] R. Holzman and D. Monderer. Characterization of ex post equilibrium in the VCG combinatorial auctions. *Games and Economic Behavior*, 47:87–103, 2004.

[16] R. Holzman, N. Kfir-Dahav, D. Monderer, and M. Tennenholtz. Bundling equilibrium in combinatorial auctions. *Games and Economic Behavior*, 47:104–123, 2004.

[17] N. Hyafil and C. Boutilier. Partial revelation automated mechanism design. In *Proc. of 22nd AAAI Conference*, pages 72–78, 2007.

[18] N. Hyafil and C. Boutilier. Mechanism design with partial revelation. In *Proc. of 20th IJCAI*, pages 1333–1340, 2007.

[19] S. Lahaie and D. C. Parkes. On the communication requirements of verifying the VCG outcome. In *Proc. of 9th ACM-EC Conference*, pages 108–113, 2008.

[20] S. Lahaie, D. M. Pennock, A. Saberi, and R. V. Vohra. Sponsored search auctions. In N. Nisan, T. Roughgarden, E. Tardos, and V. Vazirani, editors, *Algorithmic Game Theory*, chapter 28, pages 699–716. Cambridge University Press, 2007.

[21] H. B. Leonard. Elicitation of honest preferences for the assignment of individuals to positions. *Journal of Political Economy*, 91(3):461–479, 1983.

[22] P. Milgrom. Simplified mechanisms with an application to sponsored-search auctions. *Games and Economic Behavior*, 70(1):62–70, 2010.

[23] N. Nisan and A. Ronen. Computationally feasible VCG mechanisms. *Journal of Artificial Intelligence Research*, 29:19–47, 2007.

[24] N. Nisan and I. Segal. The communication requirements of efficient allocations and supporting prices. *Journal of Economic Theory*, 129(1):192–224, 2006.

[25] S. Shakkottai, R. Srikant, A. Ozdaglar, and D. Acemoglu. The price of simplicity. *IEEE Journal on Selected Areas in Communications*, 26(7):1269–1276, 2008.

[26] H. Varian. Position auctions. *International Journal of Industrial Organization*, 25:1163–1178, 2007.

[27] W. Vickrey. Counterspeculation, auctions, and competitive sealed tenders. *Journal of Finance*, 16(1):8–37, 1961.

Best-Response Auctions

Noam Nisan*
School of Engineering and Computer Science
The Hebrew University
Jerusalem, Israel
noam@cs.huji.ac.il

Michael Schapira
Department of Computer Science
Princeton University
Princeton, NJ USA
ms7@cs.princeton.edu

Gregory Valiant†
Department of Computer Science
UC Berkeley
Berkeley, CA USA
gregory.valiant@gmail.com

Aviv Zohar
Microsoft Research
Silicon Valley Lab
Mountain View, CA USA
avivz@microsoft.com

ABSTRACT

We present a new framework for auction design and analysis that we term "best-response auctions". We use this framework to show that the simple and myopic best-response dynamics converge to the VCG outcome and are incentive compatible in several well-studied auction environments (Generalized Second Price auctions, and auctions with unit-demand bidders). Thus, we establish that in these environments, given that all other bidders are repeatedly best-responding, the best course of action for a bidder is to also repeatedly best-respond. Our results generalize classical results in economics regarding convergence to equilibrium and incentive compatibility of ascending-price English auctions. In addition, our findings provide new game-theoretic justifications for some well-studied auction rules. Best-response auctions provide a way to bridge the gap between the full-information equilibrium concept and the usual private-information auction theory.

Categories and Subject Descriptors: K.4.4 [Computers and Society]: Electronic Commerce;
J.4 [Social and Behavioral Sciences]: Economics

General Terms: Algorithms, Economics, Theory

Keywords: Auctions, Best Response Dynamics

*Supported by a grant from the Israeli Science Foundation (ISF), and by the Google Inter-university center for Electronic Markets and Auctions.

†Supported by an NSF graduate research fellowship.

1. INTRODUCTION

1.1 Why Best-Respond?

Arguably, the most striking application of "electronic markets and auctions" are the billions of penny "ad-auctions" that bankroll much of the Internet as we know it. It is quite an embarrassment that the pricing rule used in these auctions, almost universally, is the "Generalized Second Price" (GSP), rather than the more theoretically-motivated "Vickrey-Clarke-Groves" (VCG) rule which basic mechanism design theory would suggest[1].

In the Generalized Second-Price (GSP) auction, there are k slots that are to be sold. Each slot j has a click-through-rate (CTR) α_j such that $\alpha_1 \geq \alpha_2 \geq \ldots \geq \alpha_k$ ("higher" slots are clicked more often that "lower" ones). There are n bidders (advertisers) and each bidder i has a private value $v_i \in \mathbf{R}^+$ per click (and thus his value for the j'th slot is $\alpha_j v_i$). GSP assigns the k slots to the k highest bidders (the highest bidder gets the highest slot, *etc.*) and charges each winning bidder a cost per-click that equals the bid of the bidder that was assigned the slot below his.

Two early landmark papers on ad auctions [4, 7] provide some explanation; they show that the theoretically motivated VCG pricing emerges as an equilibrium of the GSP rule. While at first sight this might lessen the embarrassment, at second sight it makes it even worse: the type of analysis under which this result is obtained is that of full-information, *i.e.*, this analysis is based on the implicit assumption that all bidders know each other's private values. That is, this explanation essentially reverts to classical economic theory without taking any information-economics considerations into account, disregarding the point of view that is at the foundation of mechanism design.

In particular, showing that VCG prices are an equilibrium of the GSP auction does not address the question of *how* the bidders may reach this equilibrium without having the required information. This issue was partially addressed by Cary et. al. [1], who show that if the bidders participate

[1]Of course there are various non-game-theoretic reasons why GSP was chosen, such as its simplicity relative to VCG, but still one would expect some game-theoretic/economic justification.

in a GSP auction repeatedly, and at each step best-respond to the others' previous bids, then the VCG equilibrium is indeed reached. The actual theorem is a bit more delicate as this only applies with high probability, when bidders' turns are chosen at random. This answer to the question "How?", begs the question "Why?": Why would we expect the bidders to repeatedly best-respond to the others?

While there is much intuitive appeal to the simple and myopic repeated best-response strategy, we seek a game-theoretic justification. Perhaps some other long-sighted strategy could improve a bidder's utility? Is the "repeated-best-response" strategy really a best response overall, in the extended (multiple round) game? We present a positive answer to this question. We show that if all bidders in the GSP auction are repeatedly best-responding, then so should you. This result allows us to resurrect some of the partial information assumptions: there is no need to know the exact values of bidders, only that they are best-responding according to *some* values.

We put this result in a wider context of auctions for which repeated-best-response converges to the full-information equilibrium and does so in an incentive-compatible manner. A companion paper [5] considers more general (non-auction) mechanisms with this property. Our model bridges the gap between the full-information equilibrium concept and the usual private-information auction theory.

1.2 Illustration: Iterative Single-Item Auction

It is instructive to informally demonstrate the types of results we get, via the first-price auction of a single item. It is well known, though still quite intriguing, we believe, that the full-information equilibrium of such a first-price auction is achieved at the second price, that is, at the VCG outcome.

Consider a discretized setting where bids must belong to some pre-defined discrete set $\{0, \delta, 2\delta, ...\}$ (that is, δ is the "minimal increment" for bids). In the full-information equilibrium of the first-price auction in this discretized setting, the highest bidder bids the lowest bid that exceeds the second highest valuation for the item v_2 and the second highest bidder bids the highest bid that does not exceed v_2. The ascending English auction, where bidders repeatedly increase their bids by the minimal increment, and drop from the auction once their values are exceeded, can be regarded as an effective mechanism for achieving exactly this outcome.

We suggest the following iterative auction mechanism. The auction allows bidders to repeatedly announce bids, based on the most recent bid announcements of the other bidders. The prescribed strategy for each bidder is to repeatedly best-respond to the most recent bid announcements of the others. Under the first-price auction base rule, this means that when a bidder's turn to act comes, if the bidder can outbid the current winner without exceeding his value for the item then he shall submit the minimal such bid (so as to minimize his payment). In the event that a bidder cannot outbid the current winner without exceeding his value, we prescribe that the bidder break ties between the multiple possible best-responses in favor of the highest bid that does not exceed his value.

The auction terminates after all bidders consecutively "pass", *i.e.*, repeat their last bid, in which case the outcome is according to the base auction rule on the final bids[2]. If the auction does not terminate within a pre-determined number of rounds then the item remains unallocated.

Observe that if the initial bids are all 0, then this best-response dynamics proceeds with the sequence of minimally-increasing prices, and thus mimicks the behavior of the ascending-price English auction. We show that in general, for any starting vector of bids and every order of bidders' best-responses, the second-price equilibrium of the full-information first-price auction is reached, provided that the tie-breaking rule is chosen carefully.

Our main result for this restricted environment is that repeated-best-response is indeed each bidder's global best-response to the others' repeated-best-response strategies. That is, given that all other bidders are following the prescribed behavior and repeatedly best-responding, a bidder cannot gain from not doing the same. Thus, the incentive compatibility of the English auction is but a special case of a more general result.

Theorem: (Informal) *Under the first-price auction base rule, repeated best-response strategies (with a specific tie-breaking rule) converge to the VCG outcome in an incentive compatible manner.*

1.3 GSP and Unit-Demand Auctions

As a generalization of the single item auction, we consider a framework for auction design that we term "*best-response auctions*". Given a base auction rule, a best-response auction allows bidders to repeatedly announce bids in response to the most recent bids of the others, and the prescribed strategy for each bidder is to repeatedly best-respond (under the base auction rule). A tie breaking rule specifies which bid to choose in cases where there are several different best-responses. This process goes on until (1) all bidders consecutively pass, in which case the outcome is according to the base auction rule on the final bids; or (2) the auction does not terminate within a pre-determined number of rounds, in which case all goods on sale remain unallocated.

Under this framework, we consider two well-studied auction environments: the GSP auction mentioned above and the auction of multiple heterogeneous items among unit-demand bidders, which has received much attention since the seminal paper of Demage, Gale, and Sotomayer (see [6]). In the unit-demand setting, each bidder i has a value $v_i(j)$ for each item j, and is interested in purchasing exactly one item. We consider a base auction rule where each item is sold individually in a first-price auction.

For both of these environments, we prove the general result that best-response dynamics converge to the optimal allocation of items, and are also in global equilibrium, *i.e.*, that each bidder is indeed best-off following the repeated-best-response strategy if the others are also doing so. In both cases, our best-response auction mechanism is *randomized*—in each round, a single bidder is selected uniformly at random to act. (Our results for GSP auctions actually also imply that deterministic repeated *better*-response dynamics studied in [1] also converge to the optimal allocation and are incentive compatible.)

[2]The fixed termination rule is important in our settings, and our results do not hold without it. This is in contrast to the results in our companion paper [5] that hold more generally.

Theorem: (Informal) *Under the GSP auction base rule, repeated best-response strategies (with a specific tie-breaking rule) converge to the VCG outcome in an incentive compatible manner.*

Theorem: (Informal) *Under our auction base rule for unit-demand bidders, repeated best-response strategies (with a specific tie-breaking rule) converge to the VCG outcome in an incentive compatible manner.*

We point out that generalized ascending-price English auction mechanisms that implement the VCG outcome in an incentive-compatible manner exist in both GSP auctions [4] and in auctions with unit-demand bidders [3]. As in the single-item first-price auction, these mechanisms can be regarded as specific executions of best-response dynamics and thus, as special cases of best-response auctions.

When designing best-response auctions we face two main challenges: (1) establishing convergence—showing that best-response dynamics reach a stable outcome (with probability 1); and (2) establishing incentive compatibility—showing that the stable outcome reached is such that no bidder has incentive to deviate from the prescribed behavior. The focus of our main effort in each of the two auction environments we consider is different: in the case of the GSP auction, convergence was known and our effort is concentrated on proving incentives; in the unit-demand auction most of our effort is focused on proving convergence. An independent and somewhat related study of convergence in the unit-demand case is carried out in [2], though the emphasis in that work is on revenue maximization.

1.4 Future Research

We view this work as a first step towards a more general research agenda. Our results establish that in several well-studied settings where the VCG outcome matches the full-information equilibrium, repeated best-response dynamics converge to the VCG outcome in an incentive compatible manner. We still lack a general understanding of when such results can be obtained (our results establish sufficient, but not necessary, conditions). What more general principle underlies our results? Specifically, under what conditions do repeated best-responses lead to optimal outcomes *and* do so in an incentive compatible manner?

Our results in this work pertain to convergence to *optimal* outcomes (that is, to an allocation of resources for which the overall social welfare is maximized). An interesting direction for future research is understanding in what environments repeated best-response provides reasonable *approximation* guarantees (again, in an incentive compatible manner). Answers to these questions could serve as the basis for the design of natural and simple to implement auction mechanisms.

In addition, our work focuses on a specific natural and myopic update rule—repeated best-response. We believe the examination of other dynamics (*e.g.*, fictitious play, regret minimization) from the perspective introduced here is also of interest.

1.5 Organization

We present our game-theoretic framework and illustrate our approach via single-item first-price auctions in Section 2. We present our convergence and incentive compatibility results for single-item first-price auctions, GSP auctions, and auctions with unit-demand bidders, in Section 3, Section 4, and Section 5, respectively.

2. OUR FRAMEWORK: BEST-RESPONSE AUCTIONS

A best-response auction can be regarded as a (finite time) execution of best-response dynamics in a game determined by the auction base rule. From this perspective, the outcome of a best-response auction corresponds to a pure Nash equilibrium of the game. We now present basic game theoretic terminology and explain the connection to best-response auctions.

2.1 Background: Games

We use standard game-theoretic notation. Let Γ be a *normal-form game* with n players $1,\ldots,n$. We denote by S_i the *strategy space* of the ith player. Let $S = S_1 \times \ldots \times S_n$, and let $S_{-i} = S_1 \times \ldots \times S_{i-1} \times S_{i+1} \times \ldots \times S_n$ be the cartesian product of all strategy spaces excluding S_i. Each player i has a *utility function* u_i that specifies i's *payoff* in every strategy-profile of the players. For each strategy $s_i \in S_i$, and every $(n-1)$-tuple of strategies $s_{-i} \in S_{-i}$, we denote by $u_i(s_i, s_{-i})$ the utility of the strategy profile in which player i plays s_i and all other players play their strategies in s_{-i}. We will make use of the following definitions.

DEFINITION 2.1 (BEST-RESPONSE STRATEGIES). *A strategy $s_i \in S_i$ is a* best response *of player i to a strategy profile $s_{-i} \in S_{-i}$ of the other players if*

$$s_i \in argmax_{s'_i \in S_i} u_i(s'_i, s_{-i}).$$

DEFINITION 2.2 (PURE NASH EQUILIBRIA). *A strategy profile s is a* pure Nash equilibrium *if, for every player i, s_i is a best response of i to s_{-i}*

Under best-response dynamics, players take turns in best-responding to other players' current strategies. The process proceeds as follows: Start from some arbitrary strategy profiles and allow players to best-respond, one by one in some order, to the current strategy profile. This goes on until a pure Nash equilibrium is reached. We refer to best-response dynamics in which the order of players' activations is cyclic as "*round-robin best-response dynamics*" and to best-response dynamics in which players are chosen uniformly at random to best-respond as "*randomized best-response dynamics*".

2.2 Best-Response Auctions and Games

Under a best-response auction, bidders repeatedly best-respond (given the auction base-rule) to the most recent bids of others. This goes on until a "stable state" is reached, or "sufficiently long" time has passed. Therefore, a best-response auction can be regarded as a finite-time execution of best-response dynamics in a game determined by the auction base-rule.

To illustrate this point, let us revisit the example of a single-item first-price auction discussed in the Introduction. We consider a discretized setting where there is a single item for sale and n bidders $1,\ldots,n$. Each bidder i has a private value $v_i \in [0, M\delta]$ (where $M > 0$ is fixed and δ is some small real number) for getting the item. The goal is to assign the object to the bidder that values it the most (breaking ties lexicographically if there are multiple such bidders).

Our best-response single-item auction can be regarded as round-robin best-response dynamics in the following game.

The 1st-price auction game: The bidders are the players. Each bidder's strategy space S_i is a predetermined discrete set $\{0, \delta, 2\delta, ..., M\delta\}$. The utility of player i from a strategy (bid) tuple $b = (b_1, \ldots, b_n)$ is $u_i(b) = v_i - b_i$ if i is the highest bidder (breaking ties lexicographically) and 0 otherwise.

Best-response single-item auctions: Under our best-response auction, players take part in round-robin best-response dynamics until a pure Nash equilibrium is reached, in which case the item is allocated to the highest bidder who is charged his bid, or until n^2M rounds have passed, in which case the item remains unallocated.

To fully specify the best-response single-item auction we must determine how bidders break ties between multiple best responses. Importantly, this tie-breaking rule must be "uncoupled", *i.e.*, depend solely on the player's private information (utility function) and not on information that is unavailable to him. Our tie-breaking rule in the 1st-price auction game context has the following simple form: fix, for each player i, an a-priori full order $\prec_i$ on S_i (that can depend on u_i), and instruct player i to break ties between multiple best-responses according to $\prec_i$, i.e., if both s_i and s'_i are best responses to s_{-i} and $s'_i \prec s_i$ then s_i will be played.

Tie-breaking rules for the 1st-price auction game: Each player i's tie breaking rule $\prec_i$ is as follows: $\forall s, t \in S_i$, if $s > v_i \vee t > v_i$ then $s \prec_i t$ iff $s > t$. Otherwise, $s \prec_i t$ iff $s < t$.

In Section 3, we prove that the best-response single-item auction converges to the (discretized) outcome of the second-price Vickrey auction in an incentive compatible manner.

3. WARMUP: BEST-RESPONSE SINGLE-ITEM AUCTION

We now present our results for the single item first-price auction rule. Specifically, we show that for any starting vector of bids, and every round-robin order of bidders' best-responses, the second-price equilibrium of the full-information first-price auction is reached, given our tie-breaking rule. Moreover, repeated-best-response is indeed each bidder's global best-response to the others' repeated-best-response strategies.

THEOREM 3.1. *The best-response single-item auction converges to the (discretized) outcome of the second-price Vickrey auction in an incentive compatible manner.*

PROOF. To prove the theorem we first establish convergence to the VCG outcome. We then prove the incentive properties of the auction.

Convergence: Assume all players are following the repeated best-response strategy with the prescribed tie breaking rules, and that the auction evolves from some arbitrary initial profile of bids. We will observe the dynamics in iterations of n rounds, during which every player is activated once. Notice that after the first such iteration, no bidder bids above his private value. This is because a bid above one's value is never a best response: Any winning bid above the value is strictly worse than bidding below it, and all losing bids above the value have the same utility, but our tie breaking rules prescribe a preference for bidding below the value in this case. For the same reasons, no player will ever bid above his value again. We say that a player is "out of the race" if from some point on, he bids his value exactly, and never changes his bid.

The proof continues by showing that as time progresses, players eliminate certain bids and will never bid them again: Let us look first at the weakest player, that has all ties broken against him. We argue that he will never bid 0 after the first iteration of activations, unless his value happens to be 0, in which case he will be out of the race. A bid of 0 by that player will always be a losing bid, and so, if it is under the player's value it will never be a best response to the bids of others (tie breaking rules prefer higher losing bids as long as they are under the valuation). If the weakest player is out of the race, then the second weakest player will, for similar reasons, never bid 0 after the following iteration or he will drop out of the race. This goes on either until we remain with only one player that is still in the race, or until the weakest player bids at least δ (and continue to bid at least that much during the rest of the process). In the latter case, after the next iteration, all other players will bid at least δ, and will do so during the rest of the process (as the weakest player in the race is never going to bid below that). Again, the weakest player still in the race will either drop out of the race or from this point on or never bid anything below 2δ. This line of reasoning goes on until we are left with only a single player in the race. At that point all other players bid their valuation and never change their bids. The remaining player will therefore bid the second price (or δ above that to break ties) and will never change his bid – this is his best response. All players will then pass, and we have converged.

Incentive Compatibility: Let us assume that some player i deviates from the repeated best-response strategy and gains by doing so. We argue that the player can only gain from the deviation if he wins the item because of it (otherwise his utility is 0, and before the deviation he did no worse). In particular, all players must have passed in the last iteration, as the mechanism would not allocate the item otherwise. If player i gains by deviating, then he must be getting the item at a price p that is lower than the price without the deviation. Since the price is lower, both the highest and second highest bidder (only one of whom might be player i) still wish to purchase the item at price p and so the final bidding profile cannot be stable, and at least one player would not pass. We therefore reach a contradiction. □

4. BEST-RESPONSE GSP AUCTIONS

The following "GSP game" was presented in [4, 7]. Our best-response GSP auction can be regarded as randomized best-response dynamics in this game.

The Game. There are k slots with click through rates $\alpha_1 > \alpha_2 > \ldots > \alpha_k$ that are being auctioned. The bidders are the players. Each bidder's strategy space S_i is some predetermined discrete set $\{0, \delta, 2\delta, \ldots, M\delta\}$ of possible bids, for some arbitrarily small δ. The bidders are awarded slots in decreasing order of their bids, so that the highest bidder is awarded the top most slot with click through rate α_1, and lower bidders get the slots with lower rates. For every bid-vector $b = (b_1, \ldots, b_n) \in S$, $\pi_j(b)$ denotes the bidder that is awarded the j'th slot. The utility of the bidder that gets slot j when the bid-vector is $b = (b_1, \ldots, b_n)$ is thus $u_{\pi_j(b)} = \alpha_j(v_{\pi_j(b)} - b_{\pi_{j+1}(b)})$, which reflects the fact the winner of slot j pays (for each click) the bid of the winner of slot $j+1$.

Tie-breaking rules: Consider the case that bidder i's best-response results in bidder i getting slot j. Then, i should select the bid b_i such that $\alpha_j \cdot (v_i - b_{\pi_{j+1}(b)}) = \alpha_{j-1} \cdot (v_i - b_i)$. Intuitively, i should choose a bid b_i such that i is indifferent between getting the j'th slot and paying the next highest bid, or getting the $(j-1)$'th slot and paying b_i. If none of bidder i's best-responses result in i getting a slot, then i should bid his highest feasible bid, *i.e*, the maximal bid b_i that does not exceed v_i.

Convergence: Cary et al. [1] study convergence of deterministic and randomized best- and better-response dynamics to the VCG outcome in GSP games and prove two positive results for convergence to the VCG outcome: (1) probabilistic convergence for best-response dynamics (with the above tie-breaking rules); and (2) deterministic convergence for specific better-response dynamics.

Incentive compatibility: We now show that the positive results in [1] are actually achieved in an incentive-compatible manner (no bidder is motivated to deviate from repeated best- and better-response). To establish this, we prove that there does not exist a "bad state" in GSP games, in the sense that there is no strategy profile from which all players but (possibly) a single player i do not wish to deviate, and that i strictly prefers to the pure Nash equilibrium that would be reached if all players follow the repeated best-response strategies. Observe that the nonexistence of such a bad state is indeed sufficient (and is clearly necessary) to establish the incentive compatibility of best-response auctions for this environment.

PROPOSITION 4.1. *Let N be the unique pure Nash equilibrium (under tie-breaking) in a GSP game (this is a VCG outcome). Then, there does not exist a state $b = (b_1, \ldots, b_n) \in S$, and player $i \in [n]$, such that $\forall j \neq i$, b_j is a best-response (under tie-breaking) to b and $u_i(b) > u_i(N)$.*

For ease of notation in our proof of the above proposition, let $b \in S$ denote the bad state; σ_j is the bidder that is allocated the j'th slot when the bid-vector is b; π_j is the bidder that gets slot j in the VCG outcome, and VCG_j is that bidder's bid in the VCG outcome. Observe that if the unstable bidder does not win a slot then his utility is 0 and so he is certainly not better off than in the unique pure Nash equilibrium outcome. Thus, the unstable bidder is awarded some slot $\bar{j}$. Our proof of Proposition 4.1 will follow easily from the following lemma.

LEMMA 4.2. *For each bidder i that wins a slot lower than $\bar{j}$ (that is, a slot $r > \bar{j}$) v_i is at least as high as that of the bidder that got the same slot in the VCG outcome, and b_i is at least as high as the bid of the bidder that got the same slot in the VCG outcome. That is,*

$$\forall r > \bar{j} \quad VCG_r \leq b_{\sigma_r} \quad \text{and} \quad v_{\pi_r} \leq v_{\sigma_r}.$$

PROOF. In the VCG outcome the $n-k$ losing bidders are the bidders with the lowest values and they bid these values. Observe that in b the losing bidders are the $n-k$ bidders with the lowest bids, and these bids are equal to their values, and thus for all $i \geq k+1$, we have that $v_{\sigma_i} \geq v_{\pi_i}$.

The lemma now follows easily by induction: assuming that for all $i \geq r \geq \bar{j}+2$, it holds that $v_{\sigma_i} \geq v_{\pi_i}$, and $b_{\sigma_i} \geq VCG_i$. Consider the bidder σ_{r-1}, since this bidder is following the prescribed best-responses, his value must be at least v_{σ_r}, and thus his value must be in the top $r-1$ valuations, and thus $v_{\sigma_{r-1}} \geq v_{\pi_{r-1}}$. Additionally, he will bid the prescribed "indifference price";

$$\begin{aligned} b_{\sigma_{r-1}} &= v_{\sigma_{r-1}} - \frac{\alpha_{r-1}}{\alpha_{r-2}}\left(v_{\sigma_{r-1}} - b_{\sigma_r}\right) \\ &\geq v_{\pi_{r-1}} - \frac{\alpha_{r-1}}{\alpha_{r-2}}\left(v_{\pi_{r-1}} - b_{\sigma_r}\right) \\ &\geq v_{\pi_{r-1}} - \frac{\alpha_{r-1}}{\alpha_{r-2}}\left(v_{\pi_{r-1}} - b_{\pi_r}\right) = VCG_{r-1}, \end{aligned}$$

where the second and third lines above follow from noting that the indifference price in the first line is an increasing function of both $v_{\sigma_{r-1}}$ and b_{σ_r}. $\square$

Proof of Proposition 4.1: The above lemma shows that the "unstable" bidder $\sigma_{\bar{j}}$ is forced to pay for the $\bar{j}$'th slot a price that is at least as high as the payment of the bidder who gets that slot in the VCG outcome, and thus the unstable bidder would prefer to be allocated the $\bar{j}$th slot in the VCG allocation. To conclude, since the VCG outcome ensures that each bidder gets at least as much utility from his allocation as he would get were he to receive the allocation allotted to another player, the unstable bidder gets at most the utility he would get were to to get item $\bar{j}$ in the VCG outcome, which gives at most as much utility as he would get in the actual VCG outcome. $\square$

5. BEST-RESPONSE UNIT-DEMAND AUCTIONS

Our best-response auction for unit-demand bidders can be regarded as best-response dynamics in the following class of games.

The 1st-price unit-demand auction game: The bidders are the players. Each bidder's strategy is a vector of non-negative bids $b = (b_1, \ldots, b_m)$, where each b_j represents the bid for item j and belongs to some predetermined discrete set $\{0, \delta, 2\delta, \ldots, M\delta\}$ for some arbitrarily small δ, which we refer to as the *discretization parameter.* Given an n-tuple of bid vectors (*i.e.*, players' strategies) $(b^1, \ldots, b^n)$, the induced price-vector $\overrightarrow{p} = (\mathbf{p}_1, \ldots, \mathbf{p}_m)$ is such that $\forall j \in [m]$, $p_j = \max_{i \in [n]} b^i_j$, where b^i_j is bidder i's bid for item j. To complete the specification of the game we need the following:

DEFINITION 5.1 (OVERDEMANDED SETS). *Given an n-tuple of bid vectors $\mathbf{b} = (b^1, \ldots, b^n)$, and the induced price vector $\mathbf{p}$, $\forall j \in [m]$, $B(j) := \{i \in [n] | \, b^i_j = p_j\}$ (that is, the set of highest bidders for j); $\forall i \in [n]$, $T(i) := \{j \in [m] | \, b^i_j = p_j\}$ (that is, the set of items bidder i is a highest bidder for). $X \subseteq [m]$ is overdemanded if $|\{i| \, T(i) \subset X\}| > |X|$. We say that such a set of items X is a* minimal *overdemanded set if no subset of X is overdemanded.*

Given an n-tuple of bid vectors $\mathbf{b} = (b^1, \ldots, b^n)$, the allocation of items $\Gamma(\mathbf{b})$ is defined as follows: (1) all items that are in minimal overdemanded sets remain unallocated; (2)

allocate bidder i the item with the lowest index for which i is the single highest bidder, if such an item exists; and (3) allocate all remaining items so that item j be given to a bidder i such that $i \in B(j)$, breaking ties among such allocations lexicographically, and allocating at most one item to each bidder. We are now ready to describe the utility function u_i of each bidder, i. Given an n-tuple of bid vectors $\mathbf{b} = (b^1, \ldots, b^n)$, let $\Gamma_i(\mathbf{b})$ be the set of items allocated to i in $\Gamma(\mathbf{b})$, and note that $|\Gamma_i(\mathbf{b})| \in \{0,1\}$. Then if $|\Gamma_i(\mathbf{b})| = 1$, $u_i(\mathbf{b}) = v_{i\Gamma_i(\mathbf{b})} - p_{\Gamma_i(\mathbf{b})}$, and $u_i = 0$ otherwise, where $\overrightarrow{p} = (p_1, \ldots, p_m)$ is the price vector associated with bids $\mathbf{b}$.

Our main theorem is that there exist tie-breaking rules under which the randomized best-response auction converges and is approximately incentive-compatible, in that by unilaterally deviating from the prescribed best-responses, one can increase one's utility by at most a factor proportional to the discretization parameter δ.

THEOREM 5.2. *there exist tie-breaking rules under which the randomized best-response auction converges and is approximately incentive-compatible. Specifically, in an instance of the unit-demand auction game with n players, m items, with player valuations v_{ij}, for $i \in [n], j \in [m]$, and discretization parameter δ, given any initial configuration of bids,*

- *After at least $k \leq n + m + (m^2+mn) \cdot \max_{i\in[n],j\in[m]} v_{ij}/\delta$, turns, with probability at least $1/n^k$, the unit-demand auction game is at a strategy profile for which no player has a prescribed best-response that deviates from his current bid.*

- *Given any strategy profile of the unit-demand auction game for which no player has a prescribed best-response that deviates from his current bid, the utility that each player receives is within $\delta(m+2)$ of the utility they receive in the VCG allocation of the corresponding unit-demand auction.*

Our proof of the above theorem consists of three main components. In Proposition 5.3, we show that all the pure Nash equilibria of the unit-demand auction game (under the prescribed tie-breaking rules) are similar to the VCG outcome, in that the final prices are close to the VCG payments from which it follows that the utility each player receives is similar to the utility that the player would receive under the VCG outcome. In Proposition 5.10, we show that given any configuration, there exists a prescribed sequence of at most $k \leq n + m + (m^2 + mn) \cdot \max_{i\in[n],j\in[m]} v_{ij}/\delta$ players such that after such a sequence of players best-responding, the game will be at a pure equilibrium, and no player will henceforth wish to deviate from his current strategy. The final component of our proof of Theorem 5.2 is Proposition 5.11, which shows that the above convergence occurs in an incentive-compatible manner, in that by unilaterally deviating from the prescribed best responses, no player can increase his utility by more than $\delta(m+2)$.

Before proceeding further, we shall motivate the prescribed tie-breaking rules, and rigorously state them. In short, a player first chooses the/an item that he desires most at the lowest price he would need to bid for that item in order to receive it, given everyone else's bids. His bid for that most-desired item, say item i, is then the lowest bid he would need to make for that item so as to receive it; his bid for all other items is such that he would receive δ *more* utility if he is allocated any of these other items at the prices he bids, than he would receive for his "most-desired", namely his bids b_j for all items $j \neq i$ satisfy $v_j - b_j = v_i - b_i + \delta$, where v_j denotes that player's valuation for item j.

Motivated by the Hungarian method, and similar approaches to computing efficient allocations (optimal weighted matchings), it is intuitively clear that players should roughly bid "level prices"—prices such that the player is indifferent to which item he receives at the prices he bids. Additionally, there must be some mechanism that allows the prices to fall in the case that, for example, an efficient matching has been found, yet the prices are all elevated (say the VCG allocation and the VCG prices increased by some constant); as we will see, by having each player bid δ less than his "level prices" for all but the most-desired item, we allow the prices to both rise, and fall, ultimately eventually finding a near-efficient allocation, with prices roughly the VCG prices. We note that finding tie-breaking that induce this behavior of best-responses is somewhat delicate; while many choices of tie-breaking rules will result in a competitive equilibrium, ensuring that the prices will fall to the VCG prices is more difficult. We now formally define the tie-breaking rules.

Tie-breaking rules. Given an n-tuple of bid vectors $\mathbf{b} = (b^1, \ldots, b^n)$, let $p_{\Gamma_i(\mathbf{b})}$ denote the price i pays for $\Gamma_i(\mathbf{b})$ (and $\Gamma_i(\mathbf{b}) = \emptyset$ if i is not allocated any items); $\forall j \in [m]$, p_j^* denotes the minimum bid i must place on item j (while bidding 0 on all other items) so as to receive j in the resulting allocation. Bidder i should break ties as follows.

- If $\max_{r\in[m]}(v_{ir} - p_r^*) < 0$, then bid $\max(0, v_{ir} - \delta)$ for all items.

- If $\max_{r\in[m]}(v_{ir} - p_r^*) \geq 0$, and either $\Gamma_i(\mathbf{b}) = \emptyset$ or $v_{i\Gamma_i(\mathbf{b})} - p_{\Gamma_i(\mathbf{b})} < \max_{r\in[m]}(v_{ir} - p_r^*)$, then do the following. Let $s := argmax_{r\in[m]}(v_{ir} - p_r^*)$. Bid p_s^* for item s, and $\max(0, v_{is} - v_{ir} + p_r^* - \delta)$ for all items $r \neq s$. Throughout, we shall call item s (the most desired item at the time of bidding) the "target item" for bidder i.

- If $v_{i\Gamma_i(\mathbf{b})} - p_{\Gamma_i(\mathbf{b})} = \max_{r\in[m]}(v_{ir} - p_r^*)$, bid $p_{\Gamma_i(\mathbf{b})}$ for item $\Gamma_i(\mathbf{b})$, and $\max(0, v_{ir} - v_{i\Gamma(\mathbf{b})} + p_{\Gamma_i(\mathbf{b})} - \delta)$ for all items $r \neq \Gamma_i(\mathbf{b})$.

5.1 Equilibria of Unit-Demand Auctions

In this section we prove that all pure Nash equilibria of the unit-demand auction game are "close" to the VCG outcome. The proof relies fundamentally on the well-known fact that the VCG outcome and prices are the minimal competitive equilibrium prices. In particular, to show that the prices at an equilibrium in the unit-demand auction game cannot be much lower than the VCG prices, we show that no δ-approximate competitive equilibrium can have prices too much lower than the VCG prices. Our proof that the equilibrium prices can not be too much higher than the VCG prices is slightly more involved, though at its core, leverages the fact that given any competitive equilibrium for which the prices are higher than the VCG prices, there exists some way of reallocating the items and decreasing some subset of the bids that only increases each player's utility.

PROPOSITION 5.3. *Let G be a unit-demand auction game, with discretization parameter δ. Then, all pure Nash equilibrium in G under the above tie-breaking rules are close to the VCG outcome.*

Specifically, letting $\overrightarrow{q} = (q_1, \ldots, q_m)$ denote the VCG prices, and $u_1^{VCG}, \ldots, u_n^{VCG}$ the associated utilities of each bidder in the VCG outcome, then if bid vectors $\mathbf{b} = b^1, \ldots, b^n$ are at equilibrium in the unit-demand auction game, then the associated allocation $\Gamma(\mathbf{b})$ and price vector $\overrightarrow{p} = (p_1, \ldots, p_m)$ satisfy:

- $\forall i \in [m], |p_i - q_i| \leq (m+1)\delta$.
- $\forall i \in [n], |u_i(\mathbf{b}) - u_i^{VCG}| \leq (m+2)\delta$.

We assume that $\forall i, j, v_{ij} \geq 0$. We begin by making two basic observations:

OBSERVATION 5.4. *At equilibrium $\mathbf{b}$, with associated prices $\overrightarrow{p} = (p_1, \ldots, p_m)$, for all bidders $i \in [n]$,*

$$u_i(\mathbf{b}) \geq \max_{j \in [m]} (v_{ij} - p_j) - \delta$$

OBSERVATION 5.5. *If bidder i's target item was item j, and in the current allocation $\Gamma_i(\mathbf{b}) \neq \{j\}$, then i has a best-response that deviates from his bid b^i.*

We now begin our proof of Proposition 5.3.

LEMMA 5.6. *If bid vectors $\mathbf{b} = b^1, \ldots, b^n$ with associated prices $\overrightarrow{p} = (p_1, \ldots, p_m)$ are at equilibrium in the unit-demand auction game, then every item i such that $p_i \geq \delta$ is allocated in $\Gamma(\mathbf{b})$.*

PROOF. Assume for the sake of contradiction that this is not the case, and some item $i \in [m]$ has $p_i \geq \delta$ but is unallocated. Let $B(i)$ be the set of bidders with the highest bid for item i. Since i is unallocated, every bidder in $B(i)$ that is not allocated an item must be bidding δ less than their value, but if there is such a player, then by bidding his value he would get the item; thus all bidders in $B(i)$ must already be allocated an item, which, because $\mathbf{b}$ is at equilibrium, must be each player's 'target' item (by Observation 5.5). But this is also a contradiction, since a player in $B(i)$ would value item i at price p_i δ more than the item he receives, and thus the best-response dynamics would prescribe him to change his target item to item i, and bid p_i for item i and drop his other bids accordingly. □

LEMMA 5.7. *Let $\overrightarrow{q} = (q_1, \ldots, q_m)$ denote the VCG prices. If bid vectors $\mathbf{b} = b^1, \ldots, b^n$ with associated prices $\overrightarrow{p} = (p_1, \ldots, p_m)$ are at equilibrium in the unit-demand auction game, then $p_i - q_i \leq (m+1)\delta$.*

PROOF. Assume for the point of contradiction that there is some item i such that $p_i - q_i \geq (m+2)\delta$. We split the argument into two cases: the case where there is some item j for which $p_j \leq q_j + \delta$, and the case where $p_j \geq q_j + 2\delta$ in every coordinate.

In the first case, by the pigeon-hole principle, there must exist some set $I \subset [m]$ such that $\forall i \in I$, $p_i - q_i \geq 2\delta$, and additionally, for all $j \notin I$, $p_i - q_i \geq 2\delta + p_j - q_j$. For example, if we sort the items in decreasing order according to $p_i - q_i$, there must be two items in consecutive order for which their respective values of $p - q$ differ by at least 2δ.

Now, consider the set of bidders $B(I)$ who have the highest bid for some item of I, and let $Q(I)$ denote the bidders who receive items in I in the VCG allocation. We claim that $B(I) = Q(I)$. First, note that $|B(I)| \geq |I|$, since all items in I have price at least 2δ, and thus by Lemma 5.6 are allocated. Since $|B(I)| \geq |I| \geq |Q(I)|$, it suffices to show that for each $i \in B(I)$, bidder i receives some item in I in allocation Q. First, note that bidder i must receive some item in allocation Q, since $\exists j \in [m]$ such that $v_{ij} - p_j \geq 0$, and thus $v_{ij} - q_j \geq p_j - q_j \geq 2\delta$, so bidder i would not be content without an item given prices $\overrightarrow{q}$. Let $j \in [m]$ denote an item such that $i \in B(j)$. From our definition of the set I, it follows that bidder i must receive some item that is also in set I, since for any item $k \notin I$, $p_j - q_j - 2\delta \geq p_k - q_k$, but because the procedure terminated, we know that $v_{ij} - p_j \geq v_{ik} - p_k - \delta$. Adding these two equations yields $v_{ij} - q_j \geq v_{ik} - q_k + \delta$, and thus bidder i must receive an item in I in allocation Q, and thus $B(I) = Q(I)$; that is, the highest bidders for items in the set I must be the set of bidders who are allocated items in I (in both allocation $\Gamma(\mathbf{b})$ and the VCG allocation Q).

To conclude this case, consider the directed graph (with no self-loops) whose vertex set is $B(I)$, and where there is a directed edge from i to i' if bidder i' has a highest bid for the item that i is allocated in $\Gamma(\mathbf{b})$. Because the protocol terminated, and the conclusion of the previous paragraph (that the highest bidders for items in the set I must be the set of bidders who are allocated items in I), each vertex must have out-degree at least one, and thus there must be some directed cycle C in the graph. The allocation Γ' induced by modifying the allocation $\Gamma(\mathbf{b})$ according to the cycle C would be a valid matching with fewer bidders receiving their target items than in $\Gamma(\mathbf{b})$, and thus at least one bidder would have a best response (which would get him the utility he would get in Γ').

We now consider the case that $\forall j \in [m], q_j \leq p_j - 2\delta$. The set of bidders having a highest bid in $\overrightarrow{p}$ must be the set of bidders receiving items in the allocation Q, because for such a bidder i, there is an item j such that $v_{ij} \geq p_j \geq q_j + 2\delta$. Now, the same argument as in the previous case (in which a directed graph as above with a cycle is constructed) yields the desired contradiction. □

We now prove the other direction—that the equilibrium prices can be at most $(m+1)\delta$ *less* than the corresponding VCG prices.

LEMMA 5.8. *Let $\overrightarrow{q} = (q_1, \ldots, q_m)$ denote the VCG prices. If bid vectors $\mathbf{b} = b^1, \ldots, b^n$ with associated prices $\overrightarrow{p} = (p_1, \ldots, p_m)$ are at equilibrium in the unit-demand auction game, then $q_i - p_i \leq (m+1)\delta$.*

PROOF. We first argue that there is some item $j \in [m]$ such that $p_j \geq q_j - \delta$. Assume otherwise, and note that any bidder $i \in [n]$ who does not receive an item in allocation $\Gamma(\mathbf{b})$ must have valuations $v_{ij} \leq p_j + \delta \leq q_j - \delta$, for all items j, and thus will not receive or desire an item in the VCG allocation Q. Additionally, since all bidders receiving items in allocation Q must also receive items in $\Gamma(\mathbf{b})$ (because otherwise, they would desire an item, and have a best-response), and all m items must be allocated in the VCG outcome since $q_i > 2\delta$ for all i, we conclude that the set of bidders receiving an item in allocation $\Gamma(\mathbf{b})$ must be the same as the set receiving an item in allocation Q. Decreasing every component of $\overrightarrow{q}$ by δ and keeping allocation

Q would yield a smaller competitive equilibrium, since every bidder receiving an item would still be at equilibrium given prices $\overrightarrow{q} - \delta$, and any bidder i who does not receive an item will still not desire an item, since, as noted above, it must be the case that $v_{ij} \le q_j - \delta$. This contradicts the minimality of the competitive equilibrium prices $\overrightarrow{q}$.

Given that there is some item $j \in [m]$ such that $p_j \ge q_j - \delta$, we now argue that $\max_{j\in[m]}(q_j - p_j) \le (m+1)\delta$. Assume otherwise, and consider the set of items I such that $\forall j \in I, k \notin I, q_j - p_j \ge 2\delta + q_k - p_k$, and $q_j - p_j \ge 2\delta$. Such a set exists and is nonempty by the pigeonhole principle, the fact that some item j satisfies $p_j \ge q_j - \delta$, and our assumption that some item k satisfies $q_k - p_k \ge (m+2)\delta$.

Note that $Q(I) = \Gamma_I(\mathbf{b})$, since bidders who get an item of I in allocation Q would not be at equilibrium at prices $\overrightarrow{p}$ unless they got an item of I. Next, for a bidder i who does not receive an item in allocation $\Gamma(\mathbf{b})$, it must be the case that $i \notin Q(I)$, and for item $j \in I$, $v_{ij} \le q_j - \delta$. For a bidder i who receives an item $j \notin I$ in allocation $\Gamma(\mathbf{b})$, for any item $k \in I$, we must have $(v_{ij} - p_j) - (v_{ik} - p_k) \ge -\delta$, which from the definition of the set I implies that $(v_{ij} - q_j) - (v_{ik} - q_k) \ge \delta$. Thus the price vector $\overrightarrow{q'}$ defined by decreasing every coordinate of $\overrightarrow{q}$ by δ will also be a competitive equilibrium, which is a contradiction, as desired. □

Proposition 5.3 now follows from the above two lemmas, and the observation that if the equilibrium price vector satisfies $|p_i - q_i| \le (m+1)\delta$, and for all bidders $i \in [n]$, $v_{i\Gamma_i(\mathbf{b})} - p_{\Gamma_i(\mathbf{b})} \ge \max_{j\in[m]}(v_{ij} - p_j) - \delta$, then the utility that bidder i derives from the outcome associated with $\mathbf{b}$ is at most $(m+2)\delta$ different than the utility he would receive in the VCG outcome.

5.2 Convergence of Repeated Best-Response

We first show that round-robin best-response dynamics can oscillate indefinitely in unit-demand auction games. We then consider randomized best-response dynamics; a single player is chosen to play uniformly at random at each turn. In this randomized setting, to show convergence, it suffices to show that given any initial conditions, there exists some finite *prescribed* sequence of players such that after the prescribed sequence of players best-response, an equilibrium will be reached. At a high-level, we prescribe such a list of players so that the dynamics of the prices have two general phases. In the first phase, the prices of all items only increase. This first phase resembles an "ascending-price auction" amongst some subset of the players. The second phase then closely resembles a "descending-price auction," in which the price of every item can only decrease.

Proposition 5.9. *There exists an initial configuration of the unit-demand auction game, such that if bidders perform best-responses in round-robin order, the dynamics cycle indefinitely.*

Proof. Consider the auction with bidder set $\{A, B, C\}$ and two items x, y. Let each bidder value each item for 2 units. Consider the initial values with bidder A bidding $1, 1+\epsilon$ for items x, y respectively, bidder B bidding $1+\epsilon, 1+2\epsilon$, for the two items, and bidder C bidding $1+\epsilon, 1$. Suppose the round-robin order has A responding first, then B, then C. We now consider the dynamics: let $(\cdot,\cdot)_A$ denote the vector of bids for player A response, and correspondingly for $(\cdot,\cdot)_B$ and $(\cdot,\cdot)_C$. It is easy to verify that the prescribed best-responses will be as follows:

$$(1+2\epsilon, 1+\epsilon)_A, (1, 1+\epsilon)_B, (1+\epsilon, 1+2\epsilon)_C, (1+\epsilon, 1)_A$$
$$(1+2\epsilon, 1+\epsilon)_B, (1, 1+\epsilon)_C, \ldots$$

We now see that after two full rounds of bidding, the configuration of bids is exactly as it was prior to the first best-response, except with the bids for items x switched with those for item y. Thus, by the symmetry of the bidders' valuations, and the fact that at every step, they have a unique most-desired item, after four complete rounds of bidding we will be in the exact same configuration as prior to the first best-response. □

Proposition 5.10. *Let n be the number bidders, and m the number of items. Given any initial configuration, after $k = n + m + (m^2 + mn) \cdot \max_{i\in[n],j\in[m]} v_{ij}/\delta$ best-responses, in which the player best-responding at each turn is chosen uniformly at random from $[n]$, the probability that an equilibrium has been reached is at least $1/n^k$.*

Proof. It suffices to show that that given any initial configuration, there exists at least one sequence of players of length at most k such that if the bidders are chosen according to that sequence, an equilibrium is reached. For any initial configuration, we will describe such a sequence of players; roughly, we will select the players such that dynamics will have two phases: the 'ascending phase', in which the vector of prices $\overrightarrow{p}$ associated with the bids $\mathbf{b}$ will only increase (as in an ascending auction with reserve prices), and the 'descending phase' that will resemble a descending-price auction. Let $\overrightarrow{p}^t = (p_1^t, \ldots, p_m^t)$ denote the vector of maximum prices at time t, and say $t = 0$ corresponds to the initial configuration.

We first let each player make a single best-response bid. Observe that after this initial set of n turns, each bid is at most $\max_{i\in[n],j\in[m]} v_{ij}$. We now begin the 'ascending phase' of the dynamics at time $t = n$. At each time step, we choose a player $i \in [n]$ to best-response who has the property that prior to his turn, he was not allocated an item, but after his turn, he will be allocated an item (and we say that the 'ascending phase' has ended when no such bidder can be chosen). Since no price can ever decrease, after at most m steps of the 'ascending phase', either the price for some item was increased by at least δ, or all items are allocated, in which case the next bidder must increase the price of some item. Thus by time $t = n + m^2 \cdot \max_{i\in[n],j\in[m]} v_{ij}/\delta$ turns the ascending phase will have terminated (since otherwise at least one of the m items would have a price above the maximum value of any item to any bidder, which is impossible). Finally, we let each player who is not allocated an item have a turn. Let time $t = t_1$ be at the completion of this extra set of turns. At this time, every bidder who could derive at least δ utility from receiving some item $j \in [m]$ and paying price $p_j^{t_1}$ is allocated an item. Additionally, for every item j, all players $i \in [n]$ who are not allocated an item at time t_1 are bidding $v_{ij} - \delta$.

We now begin the 'descending phase' of the dynamics. At each time step we choose a bidder $i \in [n]$ who has a best-response bid that differs from their current bid, provided that they are allocated an item in the timestep prior to their turn. Thus at each turn, no bid will ever be increased, and at least one bid will drop by at least δ, and thus this stage will terminate after at most $nm \cdot \max_{i\in[n],j\in[m]v_{ij}}/\delta$ turns. Next, we argue that a player i who is not allocated an item at time $t > t_1$ must be bidding $v_{ij} - \delta$ for all items. This is clearly true at time t_1. Now, note that if bidder i' best-responses at time $t+1$ and does not increase any of his bids, every bidder receiving an item at time t will also receive one at time $t+1$, and thus at every time $t \geq t_1$, it must be the case that the players who are not allocated an item must not have been allocated an item at time t_1.

Finally, any additional players whose best-responses differ from their current bids are given turns. We claim that the only players who have best-responses during this stage are players who are not allocated any item, but who share the highest bid for some item with at least one other such player. Consider the first player, i, to play in this stage; he must not be allocated an item prior to his turn (otherwise his turn would have been part of the 'descending phase'), and thus he must bid $v_{ij} - \delta$ for all items prior to his turn, and his best-response bid must be to increase his bid for some item j to v_{ij}, and he must be allocated item j as a result of his turn. Assume for the sake of contradiction that there is some other bidder i' with a bid of v_{ij} for item j. i' must not be allocated item j prior to the best response of bidder i (otherwise i would not have been able to get item j unless i' also had a highest bid for a non-overdemanded item j', in which case i' would have had a best-response that should have taken place as part of the 'descending phase'). But if i' was not allocated item j prior to the turn of i, but i is allocated j after his turn, then either j was not the target item of i', in which case i' would have had a best-response as part of the descending phase (in which he made j his target item and decreased his other bids), or item j was his target item, in which case he would also have a best-response as part of the descending phase. Thus after the best-response of i, he is the unique bidder to bid v_{ij} for item j, and all his other bids are unchanged; thus the above arguments hold for all additional players who best-response in this final stage.

To conclude, note that the final stage does not affect any bidder who was allocated an item prior to this final stage, and thus all bidders receiving an item after this stage still satisfy the property that they do not have a best-response deviation from their current bid. Additionally, all bidders i who do not receive an item are bidding $v_{ij} - \delta$ for all items, and additionally raising their bids to v_{ij} will not result in their getting an item. Thus an equilibrium has been reached. □

5.3 Incentive Compatibility

In this section we show that if any player unilaterally deviates from the prescribed best-responses in the unit-demand auction game, he can not significantly increase his utility, thus completing our proof of Theorem 5.2 to establish that the randomized best-response mechanism is incentive compatible.

Our proof approach is simple: we show that if, by deviating from the prescribed best-responses, player i induces the dynamics to converge to some outcome $\mathbf{b}$, it is the case that the outcome is, in fact, a pure Nash equilibrium of a related instance of the unit-demand auction game. Thus by Proposition 5.3 it follows that the outcome is close to the VCG outcome of this modified game. We then argue that player i can not prefer the VCG outcome of the modified game to the VCG outcome of the original game, and thus there is no incentive to deviate from the prescribed best-response dynamics.

PROPOSITION 5.11. *Let N be a pure Nash equilibrium (under tie-breaking) in a unit-demand auction game with discretization parameter δ. There does not exist a state $\boldsymbol{b} = (b_1, \dots, b_n) \in S$, and player $i \in [n]$, such that $\forall j \neq i$, b_j is a best-response (under tie-breaking) to $\boldsymbol{b}$ and $u_i(\boldsymbol{b}) > u_i(N) + 2(m+2)\delta$.*

PROOF. Let G denote the instance of the unit-demand auction game. Assume for the point of contradiction that there is some bidder $i \in [n]$, and some configuration $\mathbf{b}$ such that all bidders $j \neq i$ have no best-response deviation from their bids b_j, but for which $u_i(\mathbf{b}) > u_i(N) + 2(m+1)\delta$. Let $\overrightarrow{p}$ denote the corresponding vector of prices associated to $\mathbf{b}$. For ease of exposition, assume without loss of generality that $i = 1$.

First, note that $\Gamma_1(\mathbf{b}) \neq \emptyset$ We will now construct a related game G' whose set of bidders is $\{c^*, 2, \dots, n, c_1, \dots, c_m\}$, and whose set of items is $[m]$. The valuations are defined as follows: for all $i \in \{2, \dots, n\}$, the valuations are identical to those of the corresponding players in game G. Let $v_{c^*\Gamma_1(\mathbf{b})} = p_{\Gamma_1(\mathbf{b})}$, and for all items $j \neq \Gamma_1(\mathbf{b})$, $v_{c^*j} = p_j + \delta$. For the remaining bidders c_i, let $v_{c_i i} = p_i + \delta$, and $v_{c_i j} = 0$ for all $j \neq i$. Define bids $\mathbf{b}'$ for game G' as follows: each player $i \in \{2, \dots, m\}$ bids as in $\mathbf{b}$, bidder c_i bids p_i for item i and 0 for all other items, and bidder c^* bids $\overrightarrow{p}$. Note that bids $\mathbf{b}'$, induce the same price vector as $\mathbf{b}$ in game G. Additionally, bids $\mathbf{b}'$ are at equilibrium, and induce allocation Γ as in game G (except with bidder c^* replacing bidder 1. Thus by Proposition 5.3, the utility that bidder c^* gets is within $(m+2)\delta$ of the VCG outcome in auction G'.

The valuations in G' for bidders $2, \dots, n$ are as in game G, and since adding additional players can only increase the VCG prices, the VCG prices for game G' are at most the VCG prices in game G'' which is defined to be identical to game G but with player 1 replaced by player c^*. To conclude, since the VCG mechanism is truthful, bidder 1 would not prefer the VCG outcome of game G'' (item $\Gamma_1(\mathbf{b})$ at price $p_{\Gamma_1(\mathbf{b})}$) to the true VCG allocation of game G, which is at most $(m+2)\delta$ more profitable than the equilibrium that would be reached were he to best-respond. □

6. REFERENCES

[1] Matthew Cary, Aparna Das, Benjamin Edelman, Ioannis Giotis, Kurtis Heimerl, Anna R. Karlin, Claire Mathieu, and Michael Schwarz. Greedy bidding strategies for keyword auctions. In *EC*, pages 262–271, 2007.

[2] N. Chen and X. Deng. On Nash Dynamics of Matching Market Equilibria. *ArXiv e-prints*, March 2011. arXiv:1103.4196v1.

[3] Gabrielle Demange, David Gale, and Marilda Sotomayor. Multi-item auctions. *Journal of Political Economy*, 94(4):863–72, August 1986.

[4] Benjamin Edelman, Michael Ostrovsky, and Michael Schwarz. Internet advertising and the generalized second-price auction: Selling billions of dollars worth of keywords. *American Economic Review*, 97(1):242–259, March 2007.

[5] Noam Nisan, Michael Schapira, Gregory Valiant, and Aviv Zohar. Best-response mechanisms. In *ICS*, 2011.

[6] Alvin E. Roth and Marilda A. Oliveira Sotomayor. *Two-Sided Matching: A Study in Game-Theoretic Modeling and Analysis*. Cambridge University Press, 1990.

[7] Hal R. Varian. Position auctions. *International Journal of Industrial Organization*, 25(6):1163–1178, December 2007.

Money for Nothing: Exploiting Negative Externalities

Changrong Deng
The Fuqua School of Business
Duke University
Durham, NC 27708, USA
changrong.deng@duke.edu

Saša Pekeč
The Fuqua School of Business
Duke University
Durham, NC 27708, USA
pekec@duke.edu

ABSTRACT

We show that existence of negative externalities among market participants competing for a scarce resource, a setting typical for electronic commerce and internet advertising, allows for emergence of the no-allocation equilibrium with positive revenues for the seller. A monopolist selling K indivisible items to a large number of unit-demand buyers who face negative externalities whenever their rivals get the items, can exploit these negative externalities. If the number of buyers is large enough, the no-allocation equilibrium emerges: no items get allocated, yet buyers still pay the seller to avoid a potential exposure to negative externalities. We provide conditions on the magnitude of externalities and on the level of buyer competition that yield optimality of the no-allocation equilibrium.

In the context of internet advertising, the no-allocation equilibrium allows the monopolist seller of a limited number of ad slots to simultaneously (1) optimize revenues by collecting a small payment from each of the potential advertisers who are concerned with negative externality effects, and (2) ensure ad-free experience to its users. Therefore, our results describe settings in which ad-free user experience can be supported not just by charging users, but could be subsidized by potential advertisers whose ads will *not* be shown.

Categories and Subject Descriptors

J.4 [**Social and Behavioral Sciences**]: Economics

General Terms

Economics

Keywords

Mechanism Design, Internet Advertising, Negative Externalities

1. INTRODUCTION

When market participants compete for a scarce resource, they face a possibility of losses due to resource being allocated to competitors. This is the case in many electronic commerce situations. A typical situation is that of internet advertising. The number of impressions per webpage is limited and could be considered a scarce resource when demand is high. Many advertisers rely on their internet presence and ad placement as the main channel for attracting customers. If an advertiser cannot secure a webpage impression to reach a potential customer who will be shown that webpage, the advertiser might prefer that no competitor's ads are shown to the customer being exposed to competitors' ads.[1]

One should expect that design of optimal allocation and pricing mechanisms could be affected by the fact that market participants not only have private valuations for a scarce resource, but also face negative externalities when a competitor succeeds in obtaining the resource. One theoretical obstacle to finding an optimal mechanism is that information structure of market participants becomes two-dimensional. In addition, a potential usefulness of such optimal mechanism depends on whether such an optimal mechanism (a) allows for a manageable practical implementation, and (b) yields fundamentally different allocation and pricing decisions from those reached without exploiting negative externalities (e.g., if such externalities turn out to be negligible). In this paper we show that a monopolistic seller (or a social planner) could exploit existence of even minuscule negative externalities, provided sufficiently large demand for a scarce resource.

Intuitively, even if negative externalities are small, not allocating any resources might be optimal when the number of buyers is large; a small number of winners would trigger a large total value of negative externalities for all losers. A recent school naming-rights example illustrates this point: thirteen donors gave combined $85 million, with minimum single donor gift of $5 million, to the Wisconsin School of Business at the University of Wisconsin-Madison to *"preserve the Wisconsin name for at least 20 years. During that*

[1]This effect is not limited to e-commerce: a telecom company that does not obtain a frequency license might lose potential future customers who will be captured by a competitor who might have secured that license; a drug developer who does not obtain a regulatory approval is better off if all competitors also fail to obtain an approval, than if any of competitors succeed and are first to the market.

time, the school will not be named for a single donor or entity" [17]. Not only did the Wisconsin School of Business raise \$85 million for NOT naming the school (compared, e.g., with \$55 million naming gift for the Tepper School of Business at Carnegie Mellon University [16]), but they can also try to sell the name again in 2027.

This example indicates a potential for implementing such no-allocation equilibrium in the context of electronic commerce, and internet advertising specifically. A monopolist seller of limited ad space could attempt to collect a small amount of money from each of the potential advertisers who are concerned with negative externality effects, and by doing so optimize revenues and ensure ad-free experience to its users. Thus, our results show that ad-free user experience can be supported not just by a user-subscription fee model (used by several popular content providers), but could be subsidized by potential advertisers whose ads will *not* be shown.

In sponsored search, intense competition among internet advertisers for user attention and actions (measured by click-through rates and conversion rates), induces negative externalities whenever competing ads are displayed together. (This point has been argued in [7].) User attention and actions that an ad can attract in sponsored search depends on the total number of the ads shown simultaneously [12, 15], as well as on the relative position of the ad [5, 9]. The externalities due to user attention and click through rates, also labeled quantity effects [4], are analyzed in cascade models (e.g., [1, 11, 8]).

Since click through rates can be learned by a search engine as the data are observable, the quantity externalities are different from the value externalities, i.e., the value conditioned on receiving a click. These value externalities are private to advertisers [4]. The private information about value externalities may not be one dimensional, due to the dependence on the conversion probability [7]. Furthermore, only the ad owner has information on conversions, so the value of negative externality imposed onto a competitor might actually be private information of the ad owner. Such information structure has been studied in economics literature [10] in the limited context of a single unit resource. We will build on this model and extend it to an arbitrary but finite number of resources and study relationships involving externality valuations and intensity of competition.

A reasonable conjecture would be that incorporating externality valuations in the ad auction design ought to improve expressiveness, and could therefore improve both efficiency and the seller's revenue (for general discussion of expressiveness, see, e.g., [14]). Some recent papers explore mechanisms that use externality valuation information in different formats. In [7], extensions are designed and equilibria are analyzed for a Generalized Second Price auction in which an advertiser's private value depends on whether the ad is allocated exclusively or not. In their model advertiser places two bids: one for exclusive placement and one for being placed with multiple other ads. (The difference in the valuations correspond to negative externality of competitors' ads being placed.) The model in [6] assumes the value of an ad to an advertiser depends on the relative quality of the ad compared to the other ads that are shown simultaneously. In [4], a framework of the unit-bidder constraints for value externalities is considered: a bidder is allowed to specify a set of single competitor constraints, where each such constraint prohibits the bidder's ad being shown together with the ad of the competitor identified by the constraint. Clearly, the focus of such modeling approach is to deal with externalities by limiting possible allocations. Given somewhat complicated valuation structure that accounts for all externalities, even computing optimal allocation in the complete information setting could be unmanageable. In [3], a general representation of settings with externalities is provided and then the efficient computation of optimal outcomes are studied. (There is also a large body of literature on advertising, see [2].)

In this paper, we provide a theoretical analysis supporting the intuition behind optimality of the non-allocation. Our setting is that of a monopolistic seller of K identical indivisible items with n potential unit-demand buyers. The buyers have independent private values for the item, as well as independent private values for (negative) externality they would impose onto every rival if they get the item. This is the informational setting of the seminal work of Jehiel et al. [10]. They manage to provide the optimal mechanism for the single item case ($K = 1$), despite two-dimensional valuation structure. The optimal mechanism with $K > 1$ items (Theorem 1) is a straightforward generalization of the methodology in [10].

Our focus is on exploring properties of the optimal mechanism with multiple items and a large number of buyers. If there are sufficiently many buyers willing to pay a small amount in order to avoid negative externalities being imposed on them, the optimal mechanism will not allocate any items. We formalize this observation by specifying the joint effect of the number of buyers and the number of items to the emergence of an equilibrium with no allocation. Moreover, under the no-allocation equilibrium, the seller's expected profit increases in the number of buyers and the number of items.

Since negative externalities are the driving force behind possibility of the no-allocation equilibrium, our analysis includes a variety of externality valuation structures. Specifically, we show conditions for emergence of the no-allocation equilibrium under the assumption of externalities being independent of item valuations (independent externalities), as well as under the assumption of externalities depending on item valuations (dependent externalities). We also allow for scaling the magnitude of externality valuations relative to the magnitude of item valuations. This case is important for settings in which negative externality imposed onto rivals is much smaller than the value of the items (e.g., the value of the ad shown is much higher than the negative externality if rival's ad is shown.)

The multiple items setting of this paper also provides a way for understanding the relationship between exclusivity pricing and pricing negative externalities. In our model, the exclusivity premium is set to the payoff difference between an exclusive allocation and a sharing allocation, and is equal to the magnitude of aggregate externalities.

Our results establish emergence of the no-allocation equilibrium when negative externalities are present (possibly small) and when competition is intense. Therefore, auction mechanisms that exploit negative externalities could, in contrast to standard mechanisms that ignore negative externality information, yield optimal pricing and (no-)allocation, which in turn makes them relevant and desirable for use in practice.

The paper is organized as follows. In the next section, we describe our model. In section 3, we show the optimal mechanism. Section 4 illustrates our findings regarding conditions for the no-allocation equilibrium, for uniformly distributed valuations, with both independent and dependent externalities. The generalization of our results for general distributions is demonstrated in section 5. Brief concluding remarks close the paper.

2. MODEL

A risk-neutral seller is selling K identical indivisible items to n ($n > K$) potential risk-neutral buyers i, $i = 1, ..., n$. Each buyer has unit demand. We adopt the information structure of [10], and assume that buyer i's private information is given by a two-dimensional type: $t_i = (t_i^1, t_i^2) = (\pi_i, \alpha_i)$, where π_i is i's valuation of the item, and α_i is the externality imposed on buyer j ($j \neq i$) if buyer i obtains the item.[2] Note that $-\alpha_i$ can be viewed as a negative externality on buyer j when buyer i gets the item and buyer j does not, i.e., buyer i creates the negative (positive) externality on buyer j when $\alpha_i > 0$ ($\alpha_i < 0$). The seller's type is set to $t_0 = (0, 0)$. Buyer types are independent across buyers, so the type space is $T = T_1 \times T_2 \times ... \times T_n$ where types are drawn from $T_i = [\underline{\pi}, \overline{\pi}] \times [\underline{\alpha}, \overline{\alpha}]$, according to the joint probability density function (hereafter, PDF) f_i and joint cumulative density function (hereafter, CDF) F_i.

If valuations and externalities are independent, $f_i(t_i^1, t_i^2) = f_i^1(t_i^1) f_i^2(t_i^2)$.

We also make the following standard assumption:

Assumption 1. $\frac{1-F_i^1(\cdot)}{f_i^1(\cdot)}$ is a decreasing function for all i.

We next define the set of buyers with K highest valuations and the set of buyer i's rivals with K highest externalities imposed on i.

Definition 1. $K^1\left(\{t_j^1\}_{j=1}^n\right) \triangleq \{j(n), j(n-1), ..., j(n-K+1)\}$, where $t_{j(n)}^1 \geq t_{j(n-1)}^1 \geq ... \geq t_{j(n-K+1)}^1 \geq ... \geq t_{j(1)}^1$.

Definition 2. $K^2(\{t_j^2\}_{j=1}^n, i) \triangleq \{j(n), j(n-1), ..., j(n-K+1)\}$, where $t_{j(n)}^2 \geq t_{j(n-1)}^2 \geq ... \geq t_{j(n-K+1)}^2 \geq ... \geq t_{j(2)}^2$ and $t_{j(1)}^2 \triangleq t_i^2$.

[2]Our analysis and all results readily extend to the environment with different externalities on different buyers, i.e., where α_i is a length $n-1$ vector $(\alpha_{i1}, ..., \alpha_{i(i-1)}, \alpha_{i(i+1)}, ..., \alpha_{in})$. For simplicity of exposition, in this paper we present the model with identical externalities imposed on different buyers, i.e., $\alpha_{ij} = \alpha_i$ for all $j \neq i$.

A direct revelation mechanism is defined as (x, p, ρ). x is the payment vector from the buyer to the seller with $x_i : T \to R$. p is the allocation (probability) vector with $p : T \to \{z \in R_+^n \mid \sum z_i \leq K \text{ and } z_i \leq 1\}$. The probability $p_i(t_1, t_2, ..., t_n)$ is defined as the probability that buyer i obtains one of the K items, regardless of which one she occupies. ρ is the trigger strategy vector when buyer i refuses to participate with $\rho_i : T_{-i} \to \{z \in R_+^n \mid \sum z_i \leq K$ and $z_i \leq 1\}$. We also define the interim payment as

$$y_i(t_i) = \int_{T_{-i}} x_i(t_1, ..., t_n)\phi_{-i}(t_{-i})dt_{-i}, \tag{1}$$

and interim allocation rule as

$$q_i(t_i) = \int_{T_{-i}} p_i(t_1, ..., t_n)\phi_{-i}(t_{-i})dt_{-i}, \tag{2}$$

where $\phi = f_1 \times f_2 \times ... \times f_n$.

Note that when $K > 1$, externalities may be imposed on buyer i even when she obtains the item since buyer j could obtain the item as well. (Case $K = 1$ corresponds to the model in [10].)

In addition, we assume that each buyer's utility is additively separable. The interim utility of buyer i, when she reports s_i with true type t_i and her rivals truthfully report, is thus

$$\begin{aligned} &U_i(s_i, t_i) \\ &= q_i(s_i)t_i^1 - \textstyle\sum_{j\neq i}\int_{T_{-i}} p_j(s_i, t_{-i})t_j^2\phi_{-i}(t_{-i})dt_{-i} \\ &-y_i(s_i). \end{aligned}$$

Obviously, the seller's optimal trigger strategy for buyer i is to sell the K items to buyer i's opponents who have the K largest externalities. This strategy imposes the severest punishment on the buyer if she rejects to participate, i.e.,

$$\begin{aligned} \rho_{v(i,t_{-i})}^i(t_{-i}) &= 1, \\ \rho_j^i(t_{-i}) &= 0, \text{ for } j \neq v(i, t_{-i}) \\ &\text{and} \\ v(i, t_{-i}) &\in K^2(\{t_j^2\}_{j=1}^n, i). \end{aligned} \tag{3}$$

Under this optimal trigger strategy, the seller's problem is

$$\max_{\{x,p\}} \sum_{i=1}^n \int_{T_i} y_i(t_i)f_i(t_i)dt_i \tag{4}$$

subject to

$$U_i(t_i, t_i) \geq U_i(s_i, t_i) \quad \text{for all } i \text{ and all } s_i,\ t_i \in T_i \qquad \text{(ICC)}$$

$$U_i(t_i, t_i) \geq A_i \quad \text{for all } i \text{ and all } t_i \in T_i \qquad \text{(IRC)}$$

where

$$A_i \triangleq -\int_{T_{-i}} (\sum_{j\in K^2(\{t_h^2\}_{h=1}^n, i)} t_j^2)\phi_{-i}(t_{-i})dt_{-i}. \tag{5}$$

Inequality (ICC) is the Incentive Compatibility Constraint, which ensures that truthfully reporting is a Nash equilibrium. (IRC) is the Individual Rationality Constraint, under which there is no incentive for the buyers to reject participation.

In order to make analysis tractable, we will assume that distributions from which buyer types, $t_i = (\pi_i, \alpha_i)$, are drawn are i.i.d. across buyers. However, π_i and α_i may or may not be correlated.

3. OPTIMAL MECHANISM

We follow approach of [10] and their Proposition 2 that uses standard Myerson technique [13] to obtain expression for the seller's *ex ante* profit in the case $K = 1$, and thus we obtain

$$\begin{aligned} &EP \\ &= -\sum_{i=1}^n A_i \\ &+ \int (\sum_{i=1}^n [\pi_i - \tfrac{1-F_i^1(\pi_i)}{f_i^1(\pi_i)} - (n-1)E_i] p_i(\pi_1, \ ..., \pi_n)) \cdot \\ &\quad f_i^1(\pi_1) \cdots f_i^1(\pi_n) d\pi_1 \cdots d\pi_n \end{aligned}$$

where

$$E_i = \int_{\underline{\alpha}}^{\overline{\alpha}} \tau f_i^2(\tau) d\tau. \tag{6}$$

when externalities are independent of item valuations, and

$$\begin{aligned} &EP \\ &= -\sum_{i=1}^n A_i \\ &+ \int (\sum_{i=1}^n [\pi_i - \tfrac{1-F_i^1(\pi_i)}{f_i^1(\pi_i)} - (n-1)g_i(\pi_i)] p_i(\pi_1, \ ..., \pi_n)) \cdot \\ &\quad f_i^1(\pi_1) \cdots f_i^1(\pi_n) d\pi_1 \cdots d\pi_n \end{aligned}$$

for externalities perfectly correlated with item valuations, i.e., for $\alpha_i = g_i(\pi_i)$.

Therefore, we have the following theorem illustrating the optimal allocation rules and the optimal interim payment rules.

THEOREM 1. *1) If item valuations and externalities are independent, the optimal allocation rule is*

$$p_i^*(\pi_1, \ ..., \ \pi_n) = \begin{cases} 1 & \text{if } i \in K^1(\{\pi_j - \frac{1-F_j^1(\pi_j)}{f_j^1(\pi_j)} \\ & \quad -(n-1)E_j\}_{j=1}^n) \\ & \text{and} \\ & \pi_i - \frac{1-F_i^1(\pi_i)}{f_i^1(\pi_i)} - (n-1)E_i \geq 0, \\ 0 & \text{otherwise.} \end{cases}$$

2) If item valuations and externalities are perfectly correlated, i.e. $\alpha_i = g_i(\pi_i)$, the optimal allocation rule is

$$p_i^*(\pi_1, \ ..., \ \pi_n) = \begin{cases} 1 & \text{if } i \in K^1(\{\pi_j - \frac{1-F_j^1(\pi_j)}{f_j^1(\pi_j)} \\ & \quad -(n-1)g_j(\pi_j)\}_{j=1}^n) \\ & \text{and} \\ & \pi_i - \frac{1-F_i^1(\pi_i)}{f_i^1(\pi_i)} - (n-1)g_i(\pi_i) \geq 0, \\ 0 & \text{otherwise.} \end{cases}$$

3) The optimal interim payment is given by

$$\begin{aligned} y_i^*(t_i) &= -A_i + t_i^1 q_i^*(t_i) - \textstyle\int_{\underline{\pi}_i}^{t_i^1} q_i^*(v, t_i^2) dv \\ &- \textstyle\sum_{j \neq i} \int_{T_{-i}} p_j^*(t_i, t_{-i}) t_j^2 \phi_{-i}(t_{-i}) dt_{-i}, \end{aligned} \tag{7}$$

where $q_i^*(t_i)$ is obtained by substituting $p_i^*(\pi_1, \ ..., \ \pi_n)$ into the definition of the interim allocation rule (2).

4. UNIFORMLY DISTRIBUTED TYPES

Throughout this section we will assume that types are uniformly distributed. This will allow us to illustrate the conditions on the number of buyers n and the number of items K that yield the no-allocation equilibrium. We will also assume negative externalities, i.e. $\alpha > 0$.

We first consider the externality independence case with K items, i.e., $f_i(t_i^1, t_i^2) = f_i^1(t_i^1) f_i^2(t_i^2)$. The distribution of externalities can be scaled up or scaled down relative to valuations by some positive number c. We end this illustration by analyzing the externality dependence case.

4.1 Independent Externalities

We assume the valuation π_i is drawn from $[0, 1]$ uniform distribution, while the externalities α_i are drawn from a scaled down (up) $[0, c]$ uniform distribution, where $c < 1$ ($c > 1$). Then $F^1(\pi_i) = \pi_i$, $f^1(\pi_i) = 1$, $F^2(\alpha_i) = \alpha_i / c$, and $f^2(\alpha_i) = 1/c$. By the definition of E (6), the externality is

$$E = \int_0^c \tau \frac{1}{c} d\tau = \frac{c}{2}.$$

By Theorem 1, the items will be sold to those buyers whose valuations π_i are among the first K largest, i.e. $i \in K^1$, and, satisfy

$$\pi_i - \frac{1 - F^1(\pi_i)}{f^1(\pi_i)} - (n-1)E \geq 0.$$

With uniform distribution, the condition is

$$\pi_i \geq \frac{1}{2}[1 + \frac{c}{2}(n-1)]$$

Therefore, the items will not be allocated if

$$n > 1 + \frac{2}{c}.$$

Since, for $j = 0, ..., K-1$, the density of the $(n-1-j)^{\text{th}}$ largest out of $n-1$ i.i.d. random variables with CDF $F(x)$ and PDF $f(x)$, is

$$f_{x^{(n-1-j)}} = \frac{(n-1)!}{(n-j-2)!j!} F(x)^{n-j-2} (1 - F(x))^j f(x),$$

the threat A can be rewritten as

$$A = -\frac{n-1}{n}c\left[\left(\sum_{j=1}^{K-1}\frac{(n-2)!}{(n-j-2)!j!}\prod_{i=0}^{j-1}\frac{j-i}{n-(j-i)}\right)+1\right] \cdot \tag{8}$$

The calculation also involves two integrals,

$$\int_0^c (n-1)\left(\frac{x}{c}\right)^{n-1} dx = \frac{n-1}{n}c$$

and

$$\int_0^c \left(\frac{x}{c}\right)^{n-j-1}\left(1-\frac{x}{c}\right)^{j} dx$$
$$= \frac{j}{n-j}\int_0^c \left(\frac{x}{c}\right)^{n-j}\left(1-\frac{x}{c}\right)^{j-1} dx \text{ for } j \geq 1.$$

The seller's expected profit when the seller does not allocate any items is

$$EP = -nA$$
$$= (n-1)c\left[\left(\sum_{j=1}^{K-1}\frac{(n-2)!}{(n-j-2)!j!}\prod_{i=0}^{j-1}\frac{j-i}{n-(j-i)}\right)+1\right]$$
$$= (n-1)c\cdot \left[\left(\sum_{j=1}^{K-1}\frac{(n-2)!}{(n-j-2)!j!}\frac{j\cdot(j-1)\cdot\ldots\cdot 1}{(n-1)\cdot(n-2)\cdot\ldots\cdot(n-j)}\right)+1\right]$$
$$= (n-1)c\left[\left(\sum_{j=1}^{K-1}\frac{(n-2)!}{(n-j-2)!j!}\frac{j!(n-j-1)!}{(n-1)!}\right)+1\right] \tag{9}$$
$$= c\left[\sum_{j=1}^{K-1}(n-j-1)+(n-1)\right]$$
$$= nc\sum_{j=0}^{K-1}\frac{n-j-1}{n}$$
$$= c\left[(n-1)K - \frac{K(K-1)}{2}\right]$$

where $\sum_{j=0}^{K-1}\frac{n-j-1}{n}$ is the sum of expected values of the K largest order statistics for the uniform distribution.

In the next proposition we summarize the no-allocation result and describe how the number of buyers and the number of items affect the optimal expected profit.

PROPOSITION 1. *Suppose there are K items and n buyers with types (π_i, α_i) independently drawn from $U[0,1]\times U[0,c]$. If $n > 1+2/c$, the optimal mechanism will not allocate any of the items. Moreover, the seller's expected profit is increasing in the number of buyers n, and in the number of items K.*

Note that $n > 1+2/c$ is a sufficient condition to make the seller generate revenues without allocating any items. The result is intuitive: a small c means low externalities, and thus it requires a large number of buyers to make the no-allocation equilibrium feasible. On the other hand, c can be considered as a function of n. It follows from Proposition 1 that the no-allocation equilibrium emerges when $c(n) > 2/(n-1)$. From (9), we can observe that, when n is large enough, the seller can implement the no-allocation equilibrium and collect a small payment (close to c) from each buyer. This is achieved by threatening the buyers with allocating the items to other buyers, in particular, threatening to allocate to K buyers with the largest negative externality values.

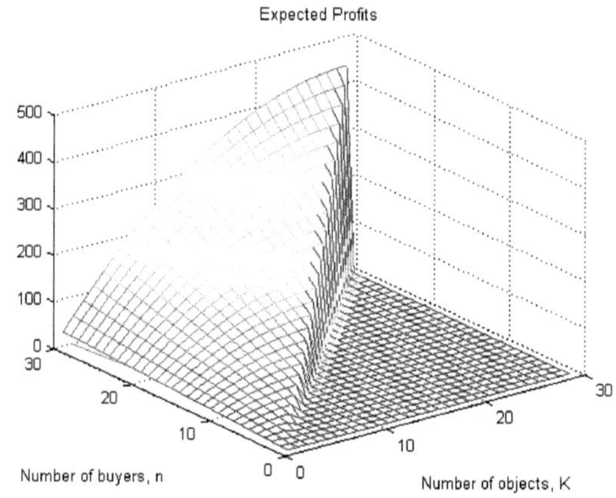

Figure 1: Figure 1 Expected Profit with n Buyers and K items. $(c = 1)$

Since the optimal expected profit is concave in K, the seller could achieve the largest expected profit when

$$K^* = n - 1/2.$$

Therefore, the expected profit increases in the number of items, K, because $K \leq n-1$.

Figure 1 shows how expected profits change with the number of buyers and the number of items, with $c = 1$, $1+\frac{2}{c} \leq n \leq 30$, and $1 \leq K \leq n-1$. The seller's expected profit increases linearly with the number of buyers n.

We further simplify the results above for a special case of the single item, $K = 1$, and for $c = 1$, which corresponds to the setting in [10].

By the definition of A_i (5), the expected utility of a non-participating buyer is given by

$$A = -(n-1)\int_0^1 \tau^{n-1} d\tau = -\frac{n-1}{n}.$$

By the definition of E (6), the externality is still

$$E = \int_0^1 \tau d\tau = \frac{1}{2}.$$

According to Theorem 1, the single item will be assigned to the buyer $i^* = \arg\max_i\{\pi_i - \frac{1-F^1(\pi_i)}{f^1(\pi_i)} - (n-1)E, 0\} = \arg\max_i\{2\pi_i - 1 - \frac{1}{2}(n-1), 0\}$. This requires $\pi_i \geq (n+1)/4$. Thus, the allocation rule is specified as

$$p_{i^*}(t_1, \ldots, t_n) = 1 \text{ and } p_{j\neq i^*}(t_1, \ldots, t_n) = 0.$$

There are two cases.

Case 1: $(n+1)/4 > 1$. Since $\pi_i \in [0,1]$, $p_i(t_1, \ldots, t_n) = 0$ for all i with the trigger strategy (3). Therefore, the interim payment for buyer i is $y_i^*(\pi_i) = -A + 0 - 0 - 0 = (n-1)/n$. The expected profit of the seller at this case is thus $EP = n - 1$.

Case 2: $(n+1)/4 \le 1$. If $\pi_i < (n+1)/4$, buyer i will not get the single item, and by (7) the interim payment is

$$y_i^*(\pi_i) = -A - 0 - 0$$
$$-(n-1)\int_{\frac{n+1}{4}}^{1} \pi_j^{n-2} dt_j^1 \int_0^1 t_j^2 dt_j^2$$
$$= \tfrac{n-1}{n} - \tfrac{1}{2}[1 - (\tfrac{n+1}{4})^{n-1}].$$

If $\pi_i \ge (n+1)/4$, buyer i may get the item. The optimal interim allocation rule is $q_i^*(t_i) = \int_{T_{-i}} p_i^*(t_i, t_{-i}) dt_{-i} = \pi_i^{n-1}$, and the optimal interim payment (7) is specified as

$$y_i^*(\pi_i)$$
$$= -A + t_i^1 q_i^*(t_i) - \int_0^{\pi_i} q_i^*(v, t_i^2) dv$$
$$-(n-1)\int_{\pi_i}^{1} \pi_j^{n-2} dt_j^1 \int_0^1 t_j^2 dt_j^2$$
$$= \tfrac{n-1}{n} + \pi_i^n - \tfrac{1}{n}\left[\pi_i^n - (\tfrac{n+1}{4})^n\right]$$
$$-\tfrac{1}{2}(1 - \pi_i^{n-1})$$
$$= \tfrac{n-1}{n} + \tfrac{n-1}{n}\pi_i^n + \tfrac{1}{n}\left(\tfrac{n+1}{4}\right)^n$$
$$-\tfrac{1}{2} + \tfrac{1}{2}\pi_i^{n-1}.$$

Therefore, the seller's expected profit in this case is

$$EP$$
$$= \sum_{i=1}^n \int_0^1 y_i^*(\pi_i) d\pi_i$$
$$= n\int_0^1 y_i^*(\pi_i) d\pi_i$$
$$= \tfrac{n(n+1)}{4}\left[\tfrac{n-1}{n} - \tfrac{1}{2}\left[1 - (\tfrac{n+1}{4})^{n-1}\right]\right]$$
$$+n\left(1 - \tfrac{n+1}{4}\right)\left[\tfrac{n-1}{n} - \tfrac{1}{2} + \tfrac{1}{n}\left(\tfrac{n+1}{4}\right)^n\right]$$
$$+n\int_{\frac{n+1}{4}}^{1}\left(\tfrac{n-1}{n}\pi_i^n + \tfrac{1}{2}\pi_i^{n-1}\right) d\pi_i.$$

Numerically, when $n = 1$, $EP = 0.25$; when $n = 2$, $EP = 1.115$ (consistent with the results in [10]); when $n = 3$, $EP = 2$; and when $n = 4$, $EP = 3$. For $n \le 3$, we are in Case 2. For $n \ge 4$, we are in Case 1. Therefore, for sufficiently large n, starting from $n = 4$ in this example, the single item will not be allocated to any buyer. However, the seller could raise revenues from the buyers by the trigger strategy. This is because each buyer would like to pay a small amount of money in order to avoid the impact of negative externalities. Moreover, the expected profit increases in the number of buyers since the expected profit increases in n when $n = 1, 2, 3$ and 4 and the expected profit is $n-1$ when $n \ge 4$.

4.2 Dependent Externalities

Here we assume valuation π_i is drawn from [0, 1] uniform distribution, and consider a perfectly linear correlation case, $\alpha_i = c_i \pi_i$, where c_i is publicly known, and $c_i > 0$. $c_i < 1$ means the externality is just a fraction of the valuation. Then, the allocation condition becomes

$$i \in K^1\left(\pi_i - \tfrac{1-F^1(\pi_i)}{f^1(\pi_i)} - (n-1)c_i\pi_i\right)$$
$$\text{and } \pi_i - \tfrac{1-F^1(\pi_i)}{f^1(\pi_i)} - (n-1)c_i\pi_i \ge 0.$$

With uniform distribution, it is

$$[2 - (n-1)c_i]\pi_i \ge 1.$$

Therefore, there will be no allocation if $2 - (n-1)c_i \le 0$ or $0 < 2 - (n-1)c_i < 1$.

Since π_i is drawn from $[0, 1]$ uniform distribution, α_i is uniform on $[0, c_i]$. By the definition of A_i (5), we get the same expression as in the previous subsection,i.e. (8)

$$A_i = -\tfrac{n-1}{n} c_i \cdot$$
$$\left[\left(\sum_{j=1}^{K-1} \tfrac{(n-2)!}{(n-j-2)!j!} \Pi_{i=0}^{j-1} \tfrac{j-i}{n-(j-i)}\right) + 1\right].$$

In particular, if $K = 1$,

$$\begin{aligned} A_i &= -(n-1)\int_0^1 c_i \tau^{n-1} d\tau \\ &= -\frac{n-1}{n} c_i. \end{aligned}$$

Consequently, the expected profit under the no-allocation equilibrium is the same as in the externality independence setting.

The following proposition summarizes these results.

Proposition 2. *Suppose there are K items and n buyers with types (π_i, α_i) where π_i is drawn from $U[0, 1]$ and $\alpha_i = c_i\pi_i$. If $n > \max_i\{1 + 1/c_i\}$, the optimal mechanism will not allocate any of the items. Moreover, the seller's expected profit is increasing in the number of buyers n, and in the number of items K.*

The condition from the proposition is only sufficient for the existence of the no-allocation equilibrium. In fact, when externality valuations are perfectly correlated with item valuations, buyers with highest item valuations are simultaneously the buyers who would impose highest negative externalities on rivals. Thus, with the same scales, a smaller number of buyers than in the independent externalities case will make negative externalities dominate item valuations and yield the no-allocation equilibrium. On the other hand, buyers with larger downward scales, i.e., a smaller c_i, impose smaller negative externalities on rivals. Thus, a larger number of buyers is required to yield the no-allocation equilibrium.

Corollary 1. *Under conditions of either Proposition 1 or Proposition 2, the expected profits under the no-allocation equilibrium are*

$$\begin{aligned} EP &= -\sum_{i=1}^n A_i \\ &= \sum_{i=1}^n \frac{c_i}{n}\left[(n-1)K - \frac{K(K-1)}{2}\right]. \end{aligned}$$

5. NO-ALLOCATION EQUILIBRIUM WITH INDEPENDENT EXTERNALITIES

We now show that the no-allocation equilibrium emerges for a large enough number of buyers, regardless of the distributional assumptions. We assume externality α_i to be independent from the item valuations π_i.

THEOREM 2. *Suppose there are K items for sale to n buyers with independent valuations and externalities. There exist N such that for $n > N$, it is optimal for the seller not to allocate any item. Moreover, the seller's expected profit is positive under the no-allocation equilibrium, and is increasing in both K and n.*

PROOF. See Appendix A. □

The independence assumption is not a critical one and the same proof strategy would go through even when externalities depend on the item valuations. The exact conditions for the no-allocation result would be determined by the dependence structure of externalities and valuations.

6. CONCLUDING REMARKS

In this paper we discuss an optimal mechanism that a monopolist seller could use to exploit possible (negative) externalities among large number of buyers interested in the limited number of items that are being sold. Specifically, we demonstrate that no allocation is an equilibrium even with modest negative externalities, provided sufficiently large demand. This provides an opportunity for the seller to generate revenues without having to sell any of the items. For example, a monopolistic seller of the ad space could generate revenues by charging potential advertisers for not showing any ads (thereby providing ads-free experience to the end users that are initial targets by the interested advertisers). For this strategy to be viable, (i) advertisers would have to be (ever so slightly) negatively impacted if rival's ad is shown, and (ii) the number of interested advertisers has to be large relative to the number of available ad slots.

Our formal analysis of the properties of the optimal mechanism is first illustrated in the case of uniformly distributed valuations. We show that it is optimal for the seller not to allocate any item to any buyer when there are many buyers. Moreover, under the no-allocation equilibrium, the seller's optimal expected profit is increasing in the number of buyers and the number of items. These results hold both in the case of independent externalities and in the case of dependent externalities. We then proceed to show the robustness of the results in a general distribution case.

A critical piece of our model is the two-dimensional valuation structure that we adopt from [10]. In addition to the private valuation of the item, externalities imposed to rivals are also private information of the buyer who creates these externalities by getting the item. For example, only the ad owner knows the conversion rates and can have an estimate of the negative externalities imposed on competitors whose ads are not shown. We discuss a slight modification of the negative externalities in the Appendix B and show that our main result holds regardless if negative externality is imposed on all competitors or on auction losers only.

It would be interesting to consider the case in which the externalities imposed on a buyer who does not get the item is privately known to that buyer, and not to a rival who got the item. However, the problem of analytically finding an optimal mechanism in such setting remains intractable, except in special cases. (For example, certain information structures could be transformed into setting of this paper.) This raises a question whether the emergence of the no-allocation equilibrium is a mere consequence of the valuation structure in our model or whether it holds for a variety of valuation structures. We conjecture that the intuitive reasoning (that we confirmed analytically within our model) ought to hold for any reasonable valuation structure: there should be no allocation when the sum of negative externalities imposed on a large number of buyers who do net get an item is larger than the total surplus of the small number of buyers who would get the items. In fact, special cases of our model such as commonly known value of negative externalities have direct special case analogues in other reasonable valuation structure models. Also, we can numerically confirm the results for a limited number of buyers with privately held values for the allocation in which negative externalities are imposed on them, but have to limit calculations to a small finite number of buyer types.

Our findings provide theoretical foundation for plausibility of existence of the no-allocation equilibrium. Thus, such option should not be ignored whenever negative externalities are present and competition is intense. Hence, design of computationally manageable and implementable direct mechanisms that exploit privately held information about negative externalities could have implications in practice.

We leave for future research an investigation of optimal mechanisms for valuation structures in which each buyer has private information on its valuation for any allocation. Furthermore, investigating optimal mechanisms in such valuation model would likely allow for important insights on the relationship between exclusivity and negative externalities that go beyond basic observations in this paper.

7. REFERENCES

[1] G. Aggarwal, J. Feldman, S. Muthukrishnan, and M. Pál. Sponsored search auctions with markovian users. In C. Papadimitriou and S. Zhang, editors, *Internet and Network Economics*, volume 5385 of *Lecture Notes in Computer Science*, pages 621–628. Springer Berlin / Heidelberg, 2008.

[2] K. Bagwell. The economic analysis of advertising. In M. Armstrong and R. Porter, editors, *Handbook of Industrial Organization*, volume 3, pages 1701–1844. Elsevier, 2007.

[3] V. Conitzer and T. Sandholm. Computing optimal outcomes under an expressive representation of settings with externalities. *To appear in Journal of Computer and System Sciences, Special Issue devoted to Knowledge Representation and Reasoning*, 2010.

[4] F. Constantin, M. Rao, C.-C. Huang, and D. C. Parkes. On expressing value externalities in position auctions. In *6th Workshop on Ad Auctions (at EC-10)*, 2010.

[5] N. Craswell, O. Zoeter, M. Taylor, and B. Ramsey. An experimental comparison of click position-bias models. In *Proceedings of the International Conference on Web Search and Web Data Mining*, WSDM '08, pages 87–94, New York, NY, USA, 2008. ACM.

[6] A. Ghosh and M. Mahdian. Externalities in online advertising. In *Proceeding of the 17th International Conference on World Wide Web*, WWW '08, pages 161–168, New York, NY, USA, 2008. ACM.

[7] A. Ghosh and A. Sayedi. Expressive auctions for externalities in online advertising. In *Proceedings of the 19th International Conference on World Wide Web*, WWW '10, pages 371–380, New York, NY, USA, 2010. ACM.

[8] I. Giotis and A. Karlin. On the equilibria and efficiency of the gsp mechanism in keyword auctions with externalities. In C. Papadimitriou and S. Zhang, editors, *Internet and Network Economics*, volume 5385 of *Lecture Notes in Computer Science*, pages 629–638. Springer Berlin / Heidelberg, 2008.

[9] R. Gomes, N. Immorlica, and E. Markakis. Externalities in keyword auctions: An empirical and theoretical assessment. In S. Leonardi, editor, *Internet and Network Economics*, volume 5929 of *Lecture Notes in Computer Science*, pages 172–183. Springer Berlin / Heidelberg, 2009.

[10] P. Jehiel, B. Moldovanu, and E. Stacchetti. How (not) to sell nuclear weapons. *The American Economic Review*, 86(4):814–829, 1996.

[11] D. Kempe and M. Mahdian. A cascade model for externalities in sponsored search. In C. Papadimitriou and S. Zhang, editors, *Internet and Network Economics*, volume 5385 of *Lecture Notes in Computer Science*, pages 585–596. Springer Berlin / Heidelberg, 2008.

[12] S. Muthukrishnan. Bidding on configurations in internet ad auctions. In H. Ngo, editor, *Computing and Combinatorics*, volume 5609 of *Lecture Notes in Computer Science*, pages 1–6. Springer Berlin / Heidelberg, 2009.

[13] R. B. Myerson. Optimal auction design. *Mathematics of Operations Research*, 6(1):58–73, 1981.

[14] D. C. Parkes and T. Sandholm. Optimize-and-dispatch architecture for expressive ad auctions. In *1st Workshop on Sponsored Search Auctions, at the ACM Conference on Electronic Commerce*, 2005.

[15] D. H. Reiley, S.-M. Li, and R. A. Lewis. Northern exposure: a field experiment measuring externalities between search advertisements. In *Proceedings of the 11th ACM Conference on Electronic Commerce*, EC '10, pages 297–304, New York, NY, USA, 2010. ACM.

[16] TSB. Meet the man behind the gift. *The Tepper School of Business, http://tepper.cmu.edu/news-multimedia/news/news-detail/index.aspx?nid=119*, 2004.

[17] WSB. Wisconsin naming partnership. *The Wisconsin School of Business, http://www.bus.wisc.edu/wng/about.asp*, 2007.

APPENDIX

A. PROOF OF THEOREM 2

PROOF. By the Assumption 1, the condition

$$\pi_i - \frac{1 - F^1(\pi_i)}{f^1(\pi_i)} - (n-1)E \geq 0$$

can be reduced to the condition

$$\pi_i \geq \widetilde{\pi}(n),$$

where $\widetilde{\pi}(n)$ increases with n. (Note that this argument may not hold in the externality dependence case for an arbitrary $f^1(\cdot)$ function and an arbitrary number c.)

As a result, we may have $\widetilde{\pi}(N_1) > \overline{\pi}$ for some large enough N_1. This is analogous to the no-allocation result from the uniform distribution case.

In order to study the expected profit under the no-allocation equilibrium, we consider $K = 1$ first. The interim payment is

$$\begin{aligned} & y_i(\pi_i) \\ &= (n-1)\int_{\underline{\alpha}}^{\overline{\alpha}} \tau (F^2(\tau))^{n-2} f^2(\tau) d\tau \\ &= \overline{\alpha} - \int_{\underline{\alpha}}^{\overline{\alpha}} (F^2(\tau))^{n-1} d\tau. \end{aligned}$$

Obviously,

$$\begin{aligned} & \tfrac{\partial y_i(\pi_i)}{\partial n} \\ &= -\int_{\underline{\alpha}}^{\overline{\alpha}} (F^2(\tau))^{n-1} \ln(F^2(\tau)) d\tau \geq 0 \end{aligned}$$

since $F^2(\tau) \in [0,1]$.

Since we are considering negative externalities, i.e. $\overline{\alpha} \geq \underline{\alpha} \geq 0$, we have $\tau(F^2(\tau))^{n-2} f^2(\tau) \geq 0$ for $\underline{\alpha} \leq \tau \leq \overline{\alpha}$. This indicates $y_i(\pi_i) > 0$ since $n > 1$.

Hence,

$$EP = n y_i(\pi_i)$$

is increasing in n for $n > N_1$.

Now we consider $K \geq 1$ under the no-allocation equilibrium. For $j = 0, ..., K-1$, the density of the $(n-1-j)^{\text{th}}$ largest out of $n-1$ i.i.d. random variables with CDF $F(x)$ and PDF $f(x)$, is

$$\begin{aligned} & f_{x^{(n-1-j)}} \\ &= \tfrac{(n-1)!}{(n-j-2)!j!} F(x)^{n-j-2} (1 - F(x))^j f(x). \end{aligned}$$

Therefore, the seller's expected profit is

$$\begin{aligned} & EP \\ &= n \textstyle\sum_{j=0}^{K-1} \int_{\underline{\alpha}}^{\overline{\alpha}} \tfrac{(n-1)!}{(n-j-2)!j!} F^2(\tau)^{n-j-2} \cdot \\ & \qquad (1 - F^2(\tau))^j f^2(\tau) \tau d\tau. \end{aligned}$$

With negative externalities, for each j,

$$\begin{aligned} & h(n,j) \\ & \triangleq \int_{\underline{\alpha}}^{\overline{\alpha}} \tfrac{(n-1)!}{(n-j-2)!j!} F^2(\tau)^{n-j-2} (1 - F^2(\tau))^j f^2(\tau) \tau d\tau \\ & \geq 0. \end{aligned}$$

This indicates EP is increasing in K by adding more non-negative terms.

For each $j > 0$, we do the integration by parts,

$\int_{\underline{\alpha}}^{\overline{\alpha}} F^2(\tau)^{n-j-2}(1-F^2(\tau))^j f^2(\tau)\tau d\tau$

$= \int_{\underline{\alpha}}^{\overline{\alpha}} \frac{1}{n-j-1}(1-F^2(\tau))^j \tau dF^2(\tau)^{n-j-1}$

$= \frac{1}{n-j-1}(1-F^2(\tau))^j F^2(\tau)^{n-j-1}\tau|_{\underline{\alpha}}^{\overline{\alpha}}$

$-\frac{1}{n-j-1}\int_{\underline{\alpha}}^{\overline{\alpha}} F^2(\tau)^{n-j-1}\cdot$

$\left((1-F^2(\tau))^j d\tau - j\left(1-F^2(\tau)\right)^{j-1}\tau dF^2(\tau)\right)$

$= \frac{1}{n-j-1}\int_{\underline{\alpha}}^{\overline{\alpha}} F^2(\tau)^{n-j-1} j\left(1-F^2(\tau)\right)^{j-1}\tau dF^2(\tau)$

$-\frac{1}{n-j-1}\int_{\underline{\alpha}}^{\overline{\alpha}}\left(F^2(\tau)\right)^{n-j-1}(1-F^2(\tau))^j d\tau$

$= \frac{1}{n-j-1}\frac{1}{n-j} j(1-F^2(\tau))^{j-1}F^2(\tau)^{n-j}\tau|_{\underline{\alpha}}^{\overline{\alpha}}$

$-\frac{1}{n-j-1}\frac{1}{n-j}\int_{\underline{\alpha}}^{\overline{\alpha}} jF^2(\tau)^{n-j}\cdot$

$[(1-F^2(\tau))^{j-1}d\tau - (j-1)\left(1-F^2(\tau)\right)^{j-2}\tau dF^2(\tau)]$

$-\frac{1}{n-j-1}\int_{\underline{\alpha}}^{\overline{\alpha}} F^2(\tau)^{n-j-1}(1-F^2(\tau))^j d\tau.$

If $j > 1$, the first term is zero and we can also continue the iteration of integration by parts,

$\int_{\underline{\alpha}}^{\overline{\alpha}} F^2(\tau)^{n-j-2}(1-F^2(\tau))^j f^2(\tau)\tau d\tau$

$= 0 + \frac{1}{n-j-1}\frac{1}{n-j} j\cdot$

$\int_{\underline{\alpha}}^{\overline{\alpha}}(j-1)\left(1-F^2(\tau)\right)^{j-2}F^2(\tau)^{n-j}\tau dF^2(\tau)$

$-\frac{1}{n-j-1}\frac{1}{n-j} j\int_{\underline{\alpha}}^{\overline{\alpha}} F^2(\tau)^{n-j}(1-F^2(\tau))^{j-1}d\tau$

$-\frac{1}{n-j-1}\int_{\underline{\alpha}}^{\overline{\alpha}} F^2(\tau)^{n-j-1}(1-F^2(\tau))^j d\tau.$

For $j > 0$, we thus have the general form

$\int_{\underline{\alpha}}^{\overline{\alpha}} F^2(\tau)^{n-j-2}(1-F^2(\tau))^j f^2(\tau)\tau d\tau$

$= \left(\frac{1}{n-j-1}\Pi_{l=0}^{j-1}\frac{1}{n-j+l}(j-l)\right)\overline{\alpha}$

$-\frac{1}{n-j-1}\sum_{l=0}^{j-1}\left(\Pi_{m=0}^{l}\frac{1}{n-j+m}(j-m)\right)\cdot$

$\int_{\underline{\alpha}}^{\overline{\alpha}} F^2(\tau)^{n-j+l}(1-F^2(\tau))^{j-l-1}d\tau$

$-\frac{1}{n-j-1}\int_{\underline{\alpha}}^{\overline{\alpha}} F^2(\tau)^{n-j-1}(1-F^2(\tau))^j d\tau$

$= \frac{(n-j-2)!}{(n-1)!} j!\overline{\alpha}$

$-\frac{1}{n-j-1}\sum_{l=0}^{j-1}\frac{j!(n-j-1)!}{(j-l-1)!(n-j+l)!}\cdot$

$\int_{\underline{\alpha}}^{\overline{\alpha}} F^2(\tau)^{n-j+l}(1-F^2(\tau))^{j-l-1}d\tau$

$-\frac{1}{n-j-1}\int_{\underline{\alpha}}^{\overline{\alpha}} F^2(\tau)^{n-j-1}(1-F^2(\tau))^j d\tau.$

Therefore, for each $j > 0$

$$\begin{aligned}
& h(n,j) \\
= & \int_{\underline{\alpha}}^{\overline{\alpha}} \frac{(n-1)!}{(n-j-2)!j!}F^2(\tau)^{n-j-2}(1-F^2(\tau))^j f^2(\tau)\tau d\tau \\
= & \overline{\alpha} \\
& -\frac{(n-1)!}{(n-j-1)!j!}\int_{\underline{\alpha}}^{\overline{\alpha}} F^2(\tau)^{n-j-1}(1-F^2(\tau))^j d\tau \\
& -\sum_{l=0}^{j-1}\frac{(n-1)!}{(j-l-1)!\,(n-j+l)!}\cdot \qquad (10) \\
& \int_{\underline{\alpha}}^{\overline{\alpha}} F^2(\tau)^{n-j+l}(1-F^2(\tau))^{j-l-1}d\tau. \qquad (11)
\end{aligned}$$

This formulation also yields the case $j = 0$.

Since for $j > 0$

$$(n-1)-(n-j-1) = j,$$

and for $0 \le l \le j-1$

$$(n-1)-(n-j+l) = j-l-1.$$

Hence,

$$\frac{(n-1)!}{(n-j-1)!j!}$$

has finite n terms in the numerator, and for each l

$$\frac{(n-1)!}{(j-l-1)!\,(n-j+l)!}$$

also has finite n terms in the numerator. Therefore,

$$-\frac{(n-1)!}{(n-j-1)!j!}\cdot \int_{\underline{\alpha}}^{\overline{\alpha}} F^2(\tau)^{n-j-1}(1-F^2(\tau))^j d\tau$$

and

$$-\sum_{l=0}^{j-1}\frac{(n-1)!}{(j-l-1)!\,(n-j+l)!}\cdot \int_{\underline{\alpha}}^{\overline{\alpha}} F^2(\tau)^{n-j+l}(1-F^2(\tau))^{j-l-1}d\tau$$

both increase in n for $n > N_2$, where N_2 is a sufficiently large number. To see this, take the first one for example. The derivative is

$$\frac{\partial}{\partial n}\left(-\frac{(n-1)!}{(n-j-1)!j!}\int_{\underline{\alpha}}^{\overline{\alpha}} F^2(\tau)^{n-j-1}(1-F^2(\tau))^j d\tau\right)$$

$$= -\int_{\underline{\alpha}}^{\overline{\alpha}} F^2(\tau)^{n-j-1}(1-F^2(\tau))^j d\tau \frac{\partial}{\partial n}\left(\frac{(n-1)!}{(n-j-1)!j!}\right)$$

$$-\frac{(n-1)!}{(n-j-1)!j!}\frac{\partial}{\partial n}\left(\int_{\underline{\alpha}}^{\overline{\alpha}} F^2(\tau)^{n-j-1}(1-F^2(\tau))^j d\tau\right).$$

By Leibniz's rule, we have

$$-\int_{\underline{\alpha}}^{\overline{\alpha}} F^2(\tau)^{n-j-1}(1-F^2(\tau))^j d\tau \frac{\partial}{\partial n}\left(\frac{(n-1)!}{(n-j-1)!j!}\right)$$

$$-\frac{(n-1)!}{(n-j-1)!j!}\int_{\underline{\alpha}}^{\overline{\alpha}} F^2(\tau)^{n-j-1}\cdot$$

$$(1-F^2(\tau))^j \ln\left(F^2(\tau)\right) d\tau$$

$$=\int_{\underline{\alpha}}^{\overline{\alpha}} F^2(\tau)^{n-j-1}(1-F^2(\tau))^j\cdot$$

$$\left(-\frac{(n-1)!}{(n-j-1)!j!}\ln\left(F^2(\tau)\right)-\frac{\partial}{\partial n}\left(\frac{(n-1)!}{(n-j-1)!j!}\right)\right)d\tau.$$

Since $F^2(\tau)\in[0,1]$, the derivative is positive for sufficiently large n.

As a result, for arbitrary K,

$$EP = n\sum_{j=0}^{K-1} h(n,j)$$

is increasing in n for $n > N \triangleq \max\{N_1, N_2\}$. □

B. AN ALTERNATIVE MODEL

We discuss the scenario where negative externalities are imposed only if the buyer does not obtain any of the item. Hence, the interim utility function is revised as

$$U(s_i,t_i)$$

$$= q_i(s_i)t_i^1 - y_i(s_i) - (1-q_i(s_i))\cdot$$

$$\sum_{j\neq i}\int_{T_{-i}} p_j(s_i,t_{-i})t_j^2\phi_{-i}(t_{-i})dt_{-i}$$

As a result, the envelope theorem gives potentials similar to the standard case, i.e.,

$$\frac{dU(t_i,t_i)}{dt_i^1} = q_i(t_i)$$

and

$$\frac{dU(t_i,t_i)}{dt_i^2} = 0.$$

The interim payment is thus

$$y_i(t_i) = -A_i + t_i^1 q_i(t_i) - \int_{\underline{\pi}_i}^{t_i^1} q_i(v,t_i^2)dv$$

$$-(1-q_i(t_i))\sum_{j\neq i}\int_{T_{-i}} p_j(t_i,t_{-i})t_j^2\phi_{-i}(t_{-i})dt_{-i}$$

where A_i has the same definition.

Hence, with independent externalities, the seller's expected profit is

$$EP = -\sum_{i=1}^n A + \int(\sum_{i=1}^n[\pi_i - \frac{1-F^1(\pi_i)}{f^1(\pi_i)} - (n-1)E_i]\cdot$$

$$p_i(\pi_1,\ \ldots,\pi_n))f^1(\pi_1)\ldots f^1(\pi_n)d\pi_1\ldots d\pi_n$$

$$+\sum_{i=1}^n\int q_i(t_i)(\sum_{j\neq i}\int_{T_{-i}} p_j(t_i,t_{-i})t_j^2\phi_{-i}(t_{-i})dt_{-i})\cdot$$

$$f^1(t_i^1)f^2(t_i^2)dt_i$$

where

$$E_i = \int_{\underline{\alpha}}^{\overline{\alpha}} \tau f_i^2(\tau)d\tau.$$

We focus on the last term, which is

$$Ext \triangleq \sum_{i=1}^n \int q_i(t_i)\cdot$$

$$(\sum_{j\neq i}\int_{T_{-i}} p_j(t_i,t_{-i})t_j^2\phi_{-i}(t_{-i})dt_{-i})f^1(t_i^1)f^2(t_i^2)dt_i$$

$$=\sum_{i=1}^n\int p_i(t_i,t_{-i})\cdot$$

$$(\sum_{j\neq i} E\int_{T_{-i}^1} p_j(t_i,t_{-i})\phi_{-i}^1(t_{-i}^1)dt_{-i}^1)f^1(t_i^1)\phi_{-i}^1(t_{-i}^1)dt_i^1$$

$$=\int(\sum_{i=1}^n\sum_{j\neq i} p_i(t_i,t_{-i})E\int_{T_{-i}^1} p_j(t_i,t_{-i})\phi_{-i}^1(t_{-i}^1)dt_{-i}^1)\cdot$$

$$f^1(\pi_1)\cdots f^1(\pi_n)d\pi_1\cdots d\pi_n \geq 0.$$

Since the allocation probabilities should satisfy

$$0 \leq \sum_{i=1}^n p_i(t_i,t_{-i}) \leq K,$$

the Ext must be bounded above by some finite positive number $\overline{Ext}$.

Moreover, with the i.i.d. assumption about the distributions and from (10), we obtain

$$-nA$$

$$= n\sum_{j=0}^{K-1} h(n,j)$$

$$= n\sum_{j=0}^{K-1}(\overline{\alpha} - \frac{(n-1)!}{(n-j-1)!j!}\cdot$$

$$\int_{\underline{\alpha}}^{\overline{\alpha}} F^2(\tau)^{n-j-1}(1-F^2(\tau))^j d\tau$$

$$-\sum_{l=0}^{j-1}\frac{(n-1)!}{(j-l-1)!(n-j+l)!}\cdot$$

$$\int_{\underline{\alpha}}^{\overline{\alpha}} F^2(\tau)^{n-j+l}(1-F^2(\tau))^{j-l-1}d\tau)$$

$$\to\infty \text{ as } n\to\infty$$

because the last two terms converge to zero as $n\to\infty$.

In addition, $-(n-1)E_i$ goes to $-\infty$ as $n\to\infty$. Therefore, when n is sufficiently large, it is still optimal to implement the no-allocation equilibrium and the seller's expected profit is

$$EP^* = -nA,$$

which is positive and increasing in n and K as illustrated in Theorem 2.

Menu Pricing Competition and a Common Agency with Informed Principals

Hamid Nazerzadeh
Microsoft Research
hamidnz@microsoft.com

Georgia Perakis
MIT Sloan School of Management
georgiap@mit.edu

Categories and Subject Descriptors

H.4 [**Information Systems Applications**]: Miscellaneous

General Terms

Economics,Theory, Management

Keywords

Horizontal Competition, Asymmetry of Information

Motivation

This work is motivated by a certain type of competition that is common in online marketplaces as well as traditional markets. For instance, websites such as *alibaba.com* provide a platform for matching retailers and suppliers in a wide range of industries such as apparel, energy, electronics, etc. In these online markets, costumers post a "buying lead", which describes a certain product and the quantity needed. Suppliers respond by sending quotes – these quotes are only observed by the costumers, not the other suppliers. The capacity each supplier can dedicate to each product is her private information. In the context of display advertising, advertisers (retailer) usually buy a large number of impressions from a publisher (supplier). Nevertheless, publishers can deliver a certain number of impressions and cannot always satisfy the large number of impressions demanded by a big advertising campaign. Hence, an advertiser sometimes works with more than one publisher. Another example comes from selling remnant inventories; hotels and airlines sell their (estimated) excess capacity to a secondary market via websites such as hotwire.com (which corresponds to the retailer in our setting).

Model

Motivated by the examples above, we study a setting that consists of two capacity-constrained suppliers who compete for a substitutable good that they are selling to a single retailer. The suppliers simultaneously offer menus of quantity-price contracts – i.e., inverse supply functions – to the retailer. Then the retailer chooses a set of contracts to maximize his own utility.

Our setting is in fact a (delegated) common agency model [1, 2], where the suppliers are the principals and the retailer is the agent. What distinguishes this paper from most of the previous work in the literature is that in the setting we consider the principals, not the agent, have private information. Namely, we assume that the capacity of each supplier is her *private information*. The goal of each supplier is to choose a menu of quantity-price contracts that maximizes her expected revenue at the equilibrium.

EC'11, June 5–9, 2011, San Jose, California, USA.
ACM 978-1-4503-0261-6/11/06.

Contributions

We study the effects of asymmetry of information in our setting. It is well-known that information structure can play a critical role in supply chain performance. We use the full information setting, (i.e., when capacities are public information), as a benchmark. We show that in both cases, the allocation is efficient; that is, either the market clears or the retailer receives all his demand. Moreover, the supplier with the larger capacity sells all her capacity. Nevertheless, the revenue is larger when the capacities are private information. Hence, even in the presence of a credible channel for information sharing, concealing information is a dominant strategy for the supplier.

We also investigate what happens if we restrict the form of contracts that can be offered by the suppliers. We consider linear pricing strategies (i.e., price-only or wholesale-price contracts) where essentially the contract offered by each supplier consists of a price-per-unit and a maximum allocation capacity. We provide examples that show this restriction would decrease the expected revenue of the suppliers.

The main technical contribution of this work is showing that there exists a pure strategy equilibrium for the suppliers, under certain natural conditions on the distributions of their private information. At the equilibrium, each supplier offers a menu of quantity-price contracts which uniquely maps to her private type (capacity). We stress that we impose no restrictions on the menu of contracts offered by each supplier which makes the problem of computing the best responses challenging. To address this, we reduce computing best-responses to a mechanism design problem and solve it using the techniques developed for designing optimal auctions.

1. REFERENCES

[1] D. Bernheim and M. Whinston. Common agency. *Econometrica*, 54(4):923–42, July 1986.

[2] D. Martimort and L. Stole. Market participation in delegated and intrinsic common-agency games. *RAND Journal of Economics*, 40(1):78–102, 2009.

Author Index

www.ingramcontent.com/pod-product-compliance
Ingram Content Group UK Ltd.
Pitfield, Milton Keynes, MK11 3LW, UK
UKHW051510290926
15471UKWH00008B/1543

9 781450 313841